Frommer's®

POSTCARDS

FROM

GERMANY

[handwritten notes:]
train & Courthouse bus office
for visitors & will spk English
say B & B. room w/breakfast
"Landgasthof"

D1114695

The cathedral in Cologne is one of the finest in the world. See chapter 13. © Bob Krist Photography.

In the midst of one of Berlin's most bustling and fashionable districts stands the bombed-out shell of the Kaiser Wilhelm Memorial Church, a poignant reminder of the destruction of World War II. See chapter 3. © Doug Armand/Tony Stone Images.

The Brandenburg Gate, Berlin's most famous landmark, once marked the boundary between East and West Berlin. See chapter 3. © Tony Stone Images.

The Pergamon Museum in Berlin contains reconstructions of some of antiquity's greatest monuments. This frieze lies at the base of the classical Pergamon Altar. See chapter 3. © Gian Berto Vanni/Art Resource.

Sausages and beer: among the staples of the German diet. © Dave Bartruff Photography.

A "Ratskeller" is a restaurant in the basement of the town's Rathaus (Town Hall). Come here for good, moderately priced German food in a traditional setting. © Kevin Galvin Photography.

The Thomaskirche (St. Thomas Church) in Leipzig, where Johann Sebastian Bach served as cantor, is the home of the St. Thomas Choir. You can attend the choir's performances here when it's not on tour. See chapter 4. © Dave Bartruff Photography.

Rothenburg is the most popular stop on the well-traveled Romantic Road. See chapter 6. © Bob Krist Photography.

Munich's Oktoberfest (which actually starts in late September) attracts millions of beer-lovers every year. See chapters 2 and 7. © Sylvain Grandadam/Tony Stone Images.

The towers of the Peterskirche (St. Peter's Church) and the Frauenkirche (Cathedral of Our Lady) loom dramatically over Munich at night. See chapter 7. © Bob Krist Photography.

The Marienplatz is the center of Munich's historic district. See chapter 7. © Kevin Galvin Photography.

The Karwendel Mountains, near Mittenwald, have some of Germany's best hiking trails. See chapter 8. © Werner Muller/Tony Stone Images.

Extravagantly painted façades, like this one in Mittenwald, are common sights in the towns of the Bavarian Alps. See chapter 8. © Kevin Galvin Photography.

Oberammergau's world-famous Passion Play, performed only one year out of ten, will next be shown in the summer of 2000. The actors are all members of the Oberammergau community. See chapter 8. © Kevin Galvin Photography.

A colorful cafe in the spa town of Baden-Baden. See chapter 10. © Bob Krist Photography.

The Black Forest has some of Germany's most scenic countryside. See chapter 9. © Paul Trummer/The Image Bank.

Imposing Sigmaringen Castle guards the Danube valley, south of Stuttgart. See chapter 5.
© Robert Everts/Tony Stone Images.

These half-timbered houses are in the Römerberg, the heart of old Frankfurt. See chapter 12. © Kevin Galvin Photography.

The best view of Heidelberg is from the Philosopher's Way, halfway up the hill on the north bank of the Neckar River. See chapter 11. © Bob Krist Photography.

Merchant homes along a canal in Hamburg. See chapter 16. © Lothar Reupert/The Image Bank.

Another side of Hamburg: the gaudy Reeperbahn, the city's red light district. See chapter 16. © Romilly Lockyer/The Image Bank.

Vineyards line the banks of the picturesque Mosel River. You can take a river cruise between the towns of Cochem and Trier. See chapter 14. © Kevin Galvin Photography.

The Rhine is another popular cruise-ship route. See chapter 13. © Hans Wolf/The Image Bank.

Esslingen is a stop on the Neckar Valley Cycle Path. See chapter 11. © Chad Ehlers/Tony Stone Images.

These vineyards are located in Bernkastel, the most colorful of the wine towns in the Mosel valley. See chapter 14. © Wolfgang Kaehler Photography.

A chapel nestled in the Bavarian Alps. See chapter 8. © *Rose Dietrich/Tony Stone Images.*

Frommer's® 2000

Germany

BIRGIT
09721/749361 private
09729/7690 parents
0172/3052431 cell phone

by Darwin Porter and Danforth Prince

with Online Directory by Michael Shapiro

MACMILLAN • USA

ABOUT THE AUTHORS

Darwin Porter and **Danforth Prince** are coauthors of a number of best-selling Frommer's guides, notably England, France, Italy, and Spain. Porter, a bureau chief for the *Miami Herald* at the age of 21, was the author of the first Frommer's guide to Germany and has traveled extensively throughout the country ever since. Prince is formerly of the Paris bureau of the *New York Times*.

MACMILLAN TRAVEL

Macmillan General Reference USA, Inc.
1633 Broadway
New York, NY 10019

Find us online at **www.frommers.com**

ISBN 0-02-863068-8
ISSN 1094-0227

Editor: Jeff Soloway, Margot Weiss
Production Editor: Jenaffer Brandt
Photo Editor: Richard Fox
Design by Michele Laseau
Staff Cartographers: John Decamillis, Roberta Stockwell
Page Creation by Ellen Considine, Sean Monkhouse, Carl Pierce, and Julie Trippetti
Front cover photo: Neuschwanstein castle

SPECIAL SALES

Bulk purchases (10+ copies) of Frommer's and selected Macmillan travel guides are available to corporations, organizations, mail-order catalogs, institutions, and charities at special discounts, and can be customized to suit individual needs. For more information write to Special Sales, Macmillan General Reference, 1633 Broadway, New York, NY 10019.

Manufactured in the United States of America

5   4   3   2

Contents

List of Maps

AN INVITATION TO THE READER

In researching this book, we discovered many wonderful places—hotels, restaurants, shops, and more. We're sure you'll find others. Please tell us about them, so we can share the information with your fellow travelers in upcoming editions. If you were disappointed with a recommendation, we'd love to know that, too. Please write to:

Darwin Porter and Danforth Prince
Frommer's Germany 2000
Macmillan Travel
1633 Broadway
New York, NY 10019

AN ADDITIONAL NOTE

Please be advised that travel information is subject to change at any time—and this is especially true of prices. We therefore suggest that you write or call ahead for confirmation when making your travel plans. The authors, editors, and publisher cannot be held responsible for the experiences of readers while traveling. Your safety is important to us, however, so we encourage you to stay alert and be aware of your surroundings. Keep a close eye on cameras, purses, and wallets, all favorite targets of thieves and pickpockets.

WHAT THE SYMBOLS MEAN

✪ Frommer's Favorites

Our favorite places and experiences—outstanding for quality, value, or both.

The following abbreviations are used for credit cards:

AE	American Express	EC	Eurocard
CB	Carte Blanche	JCB	Japan Credit Bank
DC	Diners Club	MC	MasterCard
DISC	Discover	V	Visa
ER	enRoute		

FIND FROMMER'S ONLINE

Arthur Frommer's Budget Travel Online (**www.frommers.com**) offers more than 6,000 pages of up-to-the-minute travel information—including the latest bargains and candid, personal articles updated daily by Arthur Frommer himself. No other Web site offers such comprehensive and timely coverage of the world of travel.

The Best of Germany

A unified, wealthy, industrial yet beautiful Germany awaits you, promising some of the most interesting travel experiences in Europe. Many of the country's historical and architectural treasures were lost in World War II, but much remains and much has been restored. In addition, German natural scenery, particularly in the Black Forest, the Mosel Valley, the Harz Mountains, and the Bavarian Alps, is a potent lure.

In the last 10 years, since East and West Germany were finally reunited in October 1990, the country has been growing and changing at an astonishing pace. The nation's capital has recently been relocated from Bonn to Berlin. Berlin's refurbished Reichstag, which in the spring of 1999 became the seat of German Parliament, in many ways represents the changing mood of the German nation. Its new glass dome glitters as a symbol of modernity. Berliners celebrated the Reichstag's rededication, not with patriotic glory and pomp, but with an oompah band, meatballs, and beer.

For those who want to see history in the making, we'd recommend visiting Potsdam, Leipzig, Dresden, Meissen, and Weimar, all centers of East Germany before German unification in October 1990. Keep in mind, however, that although political developments have been fast-paced, the infrastructure of the five new states cannot change overnight, and living standards here are still different from those in the former West Germany.

Finally, remember that though this guide is meant to help you decide where to go in Germany and how best to enjoy its charms, ultimately the most gratifying rewards will be your own serendipitous discoveries—drinking beer in a yard shaded by chestnut trees, picnicking in a Bavarian meadow, or spending time chatting with a wine maker in the Mosel Valley. The German people are among the world's most sophisticated and interesting. You will likely remember your experiences with them for years to come.

1 The Best Travel Experiences

- **Exploring the New Berlin:** Anyone who lived through the neuroses of the Cold War can't help but shudder at the memory of the Berlin Wall. Since reunification of the two Germanys in 1990, civic planners, with almost manic enthusiasm, have demolished large sections of what stood for 40 years as a scar across the face of a defeated nation. The architectural changes and urban

Germany

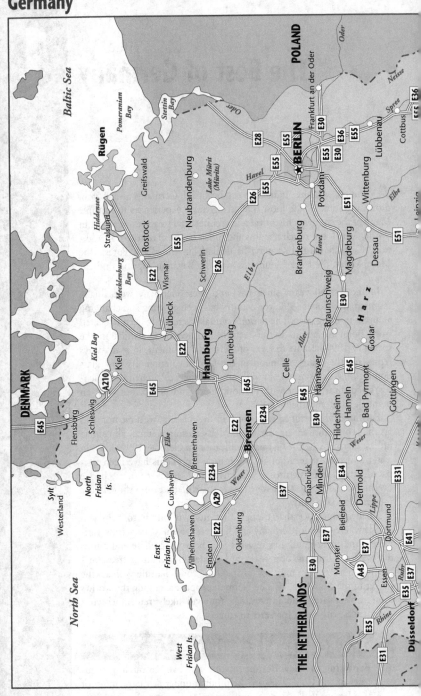

3

developments that are constantly updating the cityscape around Berlin's Friedrichstrasse and Potsdamer Platz can be very confusing. But regardless of which renewal program is churning up rubble at the time of your visit, a pilgrimage through what used to be the most bitterly contested urban turf in Europe can't help but provoke powerful emotions. See chapter 3.

- **A Midsummer Night's Dreaming in a Biergarten:** When the temperature rises, head immediately for the unpretentious cheer of the nearest biergarten. These watering holes, which often feature trellises, climbing vines, Chinese lanterns, and arbors, offer low-cost fun on soft summer nights. You can order platters of hearty food with your beer or bring your own picnic. Everybody in Germany seems to have his or her favorite, but some of the best are in Bamberg and Munich. See chapters 5 and 7.

- **Cruising the Elbe, the Danube, and the Rhine:** This trio of rivers, along with their tributaries, dominated German commerce for hundreds of years. Today, an armada of tugboats, barges, and cruise ships still ply the muddy waters beside riverbanks lined with the historic majesty (and sometimes the industrial might) of Central Europe. Cruises begin and end at large cities of historic interest and last anywhere from 6 hours to 7 days. **KD River Cruises of Europe** offers the most services; for more information, call ☎ **800/346-6525** or 0221/20881 in Cologne. See chapters 5 and 13.

- **A Boat Ride on the Königssee:** A romantic poet would praise the Königssee Lake, near Berchtesgaden in Bavaria, for the forest-covered mountains that surround its cold, deep, dark waters. The baroque chapels and fairy-tale hamlets on its shores supplement its natural grandeur. The boat you ride will be powered by very quiet electric motors, so that you can hear the extraordinary echoes that bounce off the rock faces. See chapter 8.

- **Hiking in the Bavarian Alps:** In summer, alpine hiking is a major attraction in Germany. Hikers are able to observe firsthand a variety of wildlife, often including endangered species. One of the best areas for hiking is the 4,060-foot Eckbauer, lying on the southern fringe of Partenkirchen. The tourism office in Garmisch-Partenkirchen will supply maps and details. Many visitors come in summer to hike through the Berchtesgaden National Park, bordering the Austrian province of Salzburg. See chapter 8.

- **Ascending the Zugspitze:** If the gentle inclines of the Harz Mountains or the Thuringian forests aren't dramatic enough for you, ride the cable car from Garmisch-Partenkirchen to the top of Germany's tallest mountain at 9,720 feet above sea level. The view from the top is suitably panoramic, and you'll find an appealing aura of German-ness that comes from the many hill climbers and trekkers who fan out across the hiking trails. See chapter 8.

- **A Motor Tour Along the Neckar:** The Neckar River meanders through about 50 miles of some of Germany's most famous vineyards. But the real appeal of the winding road along the water is in the medieval castles scattered along the way. Highlights en route include Heidelberg, Neckarsteinach, Hirschhorn, Eberbach, Zwingenberg, and Burg Hornberg. Don't forget to stop en route for samplings of the local wines. See chapter 11.

- **Taking the Waters at a Spa:** In Germany, the question isn't whether to visit a spa, but rather, which spa to visit? Each resort has its own virtues and historical associations and can supply a list of the health benefits associated with its awful-tasting waters. Regardless of your choice, you'll emerge from your treatment with a more relaxed attitude and a greater appreciation of German efficiency and German sensuality. The most famous spa is in Baden-Baden (see chapter 10).

- **Harvest Time in the German Vineyards:** Springtime in Germany brings the promise of bounty to the legendary vineyards of the Rhine and Mosel Valleys, but the autumn harvest is truly the time to visit. Between late August and mid-October, the banks of the rivers turn gold and russet, and armies of workers gather buckets of grapes from the rows of carefully pruned vines. Most of the medieval villages and historic castles scattered between Koblenz and Trier are associated with estates where the new wines can be sampled. See chapters 13 and 14.

- **Touring the Fairy-Tale Road (Märchenstrasse):** This is one of the newer marketing ideas of the German tourist authorities, but considering its appeal, you'll wonder why they didn't think of it earlier. From the town of Hanau (a 30-minute drive northeast of Frankfurt), the route zigzags northward along the Weser River for about 375 miles through some of Germany's most evocative folkloric architecture, terminating in Bremen. Scores of well-marked detours pepper the way. Required reading for the trip is a collection of the fairy tales of the Brothers Grimm and the Nibelungen legends. Don't overlook the psychological implications of Goldilocks, the Big Bad Wolf, and the Pied Piper of Hameln. See chapter 15.

- **Lounging on the Island of Sylt:** Don't expect a lush or verdant island—the climate is temperamental, the setting is savage, the winds blow cold from the north even in summer, and the grasses that manage to survive in the sandy dunes are as weathered and sturdy as the soldiers in a Prussian regiment. Why is it wonderful? Because here, the no-nonsense residents of north Germany can preen, flutter, and show off to each other, far from the strictures of their workplaces and the hard-working grind of their economic miracle. See chapter 17.

2 The Best Museums

Financial prosperity, artistic flair, and academic curiosity have helped the Germans develop some of the finest museums anywhere.

- **Gemäldegalerie** (Berlin): This is one of Europe's leading art museums, with a celebrated collection of works from the 13th to the 18th centuries. During the Cold War, the collection was divided between the eastern and western sectors of the city, but since mid-1998 the gallery has been reunited in one home. The lighting and the displays are better than ever. The cavalcade of major European masters ranges from Botticelli and Breughel to Vermeer and Velásquez. See chapter 3.

- **Dahlem Museums** (Berlin): This treasure trove is one of the three or four most impressive (and eclectic) museum complexes in Europe. It encompasses a half dozen museums whose collections focus on the arts of Europe, Asia, and the Middle East. One of these is the German Folk Museum (Museum für Völkerkunde), which celebrates the furniture, clothing, kitchenware, and household items of the German-speaking world since the 1500s. See chapter 3.

- **Pergamon Museum** (Berlin): Built in 1930 on an island in the Spree, this museum contains entirely reconstructed temples from ancient Assyria, Greece, Rome, and Sumer. And don't miss the sprawling exhibitions devoted to the ancient art of the Islamic world and the Far East. See chapter 3.

- **The Zwinger** (Dresden): This museum was designed for Augustus the Strong (Elector of Saxony and King of Poland) by his favorite architect, Pöppelmann (1662–1736). It's a vast rectangular esplanade flanked with pavilions, heroic statues, formal gardens, and galleries. Its firebombing by Allied warplanes in the final days of World War II brought about the poignant loss of one of the most beautiful buildings in what was once one of Germany's most beautiful cities. The Zwinger's postwar reconstruction was a triumph for the Communist East German government. Among the treasures amassed inside are paintings, antique porcelain from 18th-century Dresden, and an ornamental collection of antique weapons. See chapter 4.

- **Deutsches Museum** (Munich): Since 1925, this museum has been one of the most important showcases of science and technology in the world. Occupying an island in the Isar River, it features dozens of workable exhibits that go through their paces at the touch of a button. See chapter 7.

- **Old Pinakothek** (Alte Pinakothek, Munich): This massive and symmetrical building is one of the most visible in Munich, with a wraparound garden where urbanites like to walk during lunch hour. Inside is a staggering assortment of important paintings from every era, scattered over two sprawling floors of dignified splendor. See chapter 7.

- **Dachau Concentration Camp** (Dachau, near Munich): Heinrich Himmler first organized Dachau as a concentration camp for enemies of the Reich in 1933. An escaped inmate, Joseph Rovan, described it as "implacable, perverted, an organization that was totally murderous, a marvelous machine for the debasement and dehumanizing of man." Today, it's one of the most poignant museums in the world. See chapter 7.

- **Gutenberg Museum** (Mainz): This museum is one of the most comprehensive tributes to printing and publishing anywhere in the world. The bulky presses on which Johannes Gutenberg used movable type (42 lines per page) and two of the earliest Bibles ever printed are the primary displays here. There's also a historical rundown on the science and technologies that have dominated the printing industry ever since. See chapter 13.

- **Wallraf-Richartz Museum/Ludwig Museum** (Cologne): This museum, with two intertwining collections on three floors of an 1880s building, is the oldest in Germany. It showcases German art from 1300 to the present. It's best to approach the sprawling collection with a firm notion of your own artistic priorities. The building also contains a museum of photography. See chapter 13.

3 The Best Castles & Palaces

During the Middle Ages, Germany was divided into many intensely competitive feudal states and principalities. This unstable atmosphere encouraged the construction of fortified castles. As hostilities died down, architects began to design for comfort, style, and prestige, adding large windows and such grace notes as gilded stucco and plaster, frescoes, and formal gardens. As a result, Germany is full of all kinds and styles of castles *(burg)* and palaces *(schloss)*.

- **Sans-Souci** (Potsdam): Frederick the Great's retreat, where he came to read, to listen to music, and generally to renew his allegiance to the principles of the Enlightenment, is Germany's most successful blend of landscape and architecture. The more than 300 acres of intricately landscaped gardens have enough pavilions, fountains, orangeries, and heroic statues to keep a visitor intrigued for days. Its architectural highlight is the palace itself, approached by a terraced staircase of sublime beauty. See chapter 4.

- **Schloss Wartburg** (Eisenach): Built between 1067 and the 16th century, this was the headquarters of the Landgraves of Thuringia, a center of patronage for the troubadours *(minnesinger)* of Germany, and a place of refuge for Martin Luther, who completed his translation of the Bible within its massive walls. Wagner used it as inspiration for the setting of Tannhäuser, and Johann Sebastian Bach and Goethe both visited it. Today, from its position on a rocky hilltop, it functions as a regional museum. See chapter 4.

- **Residenz** (Würzburg Palace, Würzburg): Built between 1720 and 1744 as the official residence of the powerful bishops of Würzburg, this is one of the most massive baroque palaces in Germany. It combines a chapel (the Hofkirche) with gardens, a gallery of paintings, frescoes by Tiepolo, and enough decoration to satisfy the most demanding taste for ornamentation. Also within its showrooms are a worthy collection of ancient Greek and Roman artifacts and valuable paintings dating from the 14th to the 19th centuries. See chapter 6.

- **Neuschwanstein** (near Füssen): When the creators of California's Disneyland needed an inspiration for their fairy-tale castle, this is the model they picked. Neuschwanstein is the most lavishly romantic (and impractical) castle in the German-speaking world. A 19th-century theatrical set designer drew it up in a neofeudal style. The man who ordered its construction was (who else?) "Mad" King Ludwig of Bavaria. See chapter 6.

- **Hohenschwangau Castle** (near Füssen): It was completed in 1836, and built on the ruins of a feudal fortress from the 1100s. Its patron was the youthful prince regent, Maximilian II of Bavaria, who used it to indulge his taste for "troubadour romanticism" and the life of the English country manor. See chapter 6.

- **Schloss Nymphenburg** (Munich): It was originally conceived and constructed between 1664 and 1674 as an Italian-inspired summer home for the Bavarian monarchs. Subsequent Bavarian kings added on to its structure until around 1780, by which time the building and its lavish park bore a close resemblance to the French palace at Versailles. A highlight of the interior is the green, gold, and white banqueting hall, whose frescoes and ornate stucco are among the most memorable in Bavaria. See chapter 7.

- **Schloss Linderhof** (near Oberammergau): This palace was built in the 1870s as a teenage indulgence by Ludwig II. Its architects created a whimsically eclectic fantasy, inspired by Italian baroque architecture. In the surrounding park, Moorish pavilions and Mediterranean cascades appear against alpine vistas in combinations that are as startling as they are charming. See chapter 8.

- **Altes Schloss** (Meersburg): Legend has it that its cornerstone was laid by Dagobert, king of the Franks, in 628. The castle remained a Catholic stronghold even during the Protestant Reformation, housing bishops who appreciated its 10-foot-thick walls as a bulwark against the rising tempest around them. In the early 1800s, its owners threatened to tear the castle down, until a German Romantic, Baron Joseph von Lassberg, bought it and transformed it into a refuge for writers, poets, and painters. Although Altes Schloss remains a private residence, many parts of it can be visited. See chapter 9.

- **Heidelberg Castle** (Heidelberg): This castle originated as a Gothic-Renaissance masterpiece in the 1500s and was massively expanded as rival rulers competed for control of the Rhineland. After the French sacked and burned the town and the castle in 1689, it never regained its original glory. Today, from a position on a rocky hilltop high above the student revelry and the taverns of the folkloric city below, the ruins brood in dignified severity. See chapter 11.

- **Burg Eltz** (Moselkern, near Cochem): Its multiple turrets and towers, which rise amid a thick forest near the Mosel River, evoke the chivalry and poetry of the Middle Ages. This is one of the best-preserved medieval castles in Germany. See chapter 14.

4 The Best Cathedrals

- **Ulm Cathedral** (Ulm): The spire (528 feet) of this cathedral is the tallest in the world. Although its foundations were laid in 1377, this skyscraper wasn't completed vertically until 1890. See chapter 5.
- **Speyer Cathedral** (Speyer): Partly because of their age, Romanesque churches are the most impressive symbols of early medieval Germany. This massive church has a pedigree dating from 1030, four bell towers, a cornerstone laid by one of Germany's earliest kings, Konrad II, and an undeniable sense of the (anonymous) architect's aesthetic links with the traditions of ancient Rome. See chapter 13.
- **Worms Cathedral** (Worms): This cathedral's western chancel, completed in 1230, is the oldest Romanesque structure in Germany. The Diet of Worms, held here in 1521, condemned the beliefs of the young Martin Luther and banished him to the far boundaries of the Holy Roman Empire. See chapter 13.
- **Cologne Cathedral** (Cologne): Based on French Gothic models in Paris and Amiens, this cathedral was envisioned as one of the largest religious buildings in Christendom. It required 600 years to finish—work stopped for approximately 300 years (from 1560 to 1842), until the neo-Gothic fervor of the romantic age drove it to completion. In 1880 it was inaugurated with appropriate pomp and circumstance in the presence of the German kaiser. Today, its vast russet-colored bulk towers above the city, instantly recognizable from miles away. See chapter 13.
- **Imperial Cathedral** (Aachen): Its size and the stonework dating from 1414 are deeply impressive, but even more so is the cathedral's association with the earliest of the German emperors, Charlemagne. He was crowned in an older building on this site in A.D. 800. The cathedral's treasury contains gem-encrusted Christian artifacts from the 10th century whose heft and barbaric glitter evoke pre-Christian Germania. See chapter 13.

5 The Most Charming Small Villages

- **Dinkelsbühl:** This beautifully preserved medieval town lies along the Romantic Road. It's not as grand as the more celebrated Rothenburg, but it manages to retain more old-time charm. See chapter 6.
- **Rüdesheim:** The Rhine Valley's most justifiably popular wine town is set along the edge of the mighty river. Rüdesheim is known for its half-timbered buildings and its Drosselgasse, or "Thrush Lane," a narrow cobblestone lane stretching for 200 yards and lined with wine taverns and cozy restaurants. See chapter 13.
- **Mittenwald:** This town has long been celebrated as the most beautiful in the Bavarian Alps. Its magnificently decorated houses have painted facades and ornately carved gables. In the mid-17th century it was known as "The Village of a Thousand Violins," because of all the stringed instruments made here. See chapter 8.
- **Cochem:** The medieval riverside town of Cochem is famous for its huge castle, which dates from 1027. With its many country inns, all serving a regional cuisine along with plenty of Mosel wine, this is your best bet for a stopover along the Mosel River, which many visitors prefer to the more commercial Rhine. See chapter 14.
- **Lindau:** This beautiful lakeside town lies at the eastern end of Lake Constance. It once sheltered Roman ships of war and trade. One part of Lindau is known as the "Gartenstadt," because of its luxuriant flowers and shrubs. See chapter 9.

6 The Best Driving Tours

The appeal of the open road is a prominent part of German culture today, much as it is in America.

- **The Romantic Road:** This well-traveled route, which stretches between the Main River and the beginning of the Bavarian Alps, is dotted with lovely medieval towns. See chapter 6.
- **Alpine Road** (Deutsche Alpenstrasse): You can follow it for more than 300 miles, through the foothills of the Bavarian Alps and the Allgäu. Scenic majesty and architectural charm combine for an unforgettable experience. See chapter 8.
- **Upper Black Forest:** Fairy tales always seem to be more believable when you're in the Black Forest. The twisting secondary roads that connect Freiburg with Lake Titisee pass through lots of charming scenery and architecture. See chapter 10.
- **Mosel Valley:** The road along this Rhine tributary passes by some of the country's most famous vineyards. At least a half dozen of the cities en route are worth visiting. See chapter 14.

7 The Best Walks

- **Mainau Island:** A walk across the footbridge to the island of Mainau, in Lake Constance, is like a visit to a tropical country. Mainau Island is filled with exotic plants collected by the Baden princes and members of the Royal House of Sweden. Tropical brushwood and other botanical wonders still thrive in this mild climate. You'll hardly believe you're in Germany. See chapter 9.
- **Partnachklamm:** One of the most dramatic walks in all of the Bavarian Alps starts from the great winter sports resort of Garmisch-Partenkirchen. A sign-posted trail leads to the dramatic Partnachklamm Gorge. Carved from solid rock, the route passes two panoramic bottlenecks amid the thunder of falling water and clouds of spray. See chapter 8.
- **Cochem:** The Reichsburg castle, which towers over the little town of Cochem, can be reached on foot in about 45 minutes from the town's Markplatz, or market square. Although hardly an alpine climb, this walk is one of the most rewarding you'll find in Germany, with panoramas in all directions. See chapter 14.
- **The Royal Castle Walk:** After you've fought the crowds to get into the fabled royal castles of Bavaria, Hohenschwangau and Neuschwanstein, you can spend the remaining time hiking around the surrounding peaks and valleys. For one of the grandest panoramas in all of the Alps (in any country), hike up to the Marienbrücke, the bridge that spans the Pöllat Gorge behind Neuschwanstein Castle. From there, if you're up to it, you can continue uphill for about an hour for an amazing view of "Mad" King Ludwig's fantasy castle. See chapter 6.

8 The Best Biking

- **Lake Constance:** Rent a bike at the train station in the former imperial town of Lindau and set out in any direction to enjoy the views of this beautiful lake. The Lindau tourist office will provide you with a map and suggestions for the best routes to follow. See chapter 9.
- **Lüneburg Heath:** This wild heath in northern Germany is one of the country's major natural attractions. Rent a bike and pick up a map at the Lüneburg tourist

office and set out on your adventure. Some of Germany's greatest poets have waxed rhapsodic about this shrub-covered land. See chapter 15.

- **The Neckar Valley Cycle Path:** This signposted path allows you to follow the source of the Neckar, beginning in Villingen-Schwenningen and going all the way to the confluence of the Rhine at Mannheim. Instead of going the whole way, many visitors prefer to pick up a bicycle in Heidelberg and cycle along the river banks until they find a good spot for a picnic. See chapter 11.

- **Munich by Bike:** So many locals can be spotted riding bikes that Munich at first appears to be the biking capital of Germany. If you'd like to join in the fun, pick up a copy of the pamphlet *Radl-Touren für unsere Gäste* (available at the tourist office), which outlines various itineraries for touring Munich by bike. The city is full of bike paths and bike lanes. See chapter 7.

9 The Best Spas

- **Baden-Baden:** There is no better spa in all of Germany, and certainly none more fashionable or famous. Baden-Baden is also the site of the country's most celebrated casino. The spa's been going strong ever since the leisure class of the 19th century discovered its healing waters, although the Roman legions of the emperor Caracalla had discovered the springs here long before that. See chapter 10.

- **Wiesbaden:** One of Germany's oldest cities, Wiesbaden attracted Roman legions to its hot springs, and continues to lure today's fashionable traveler as well. It's not as chic as Baden-Baden, but Wiesbaden still has one of Germany's most elegant casinos and concert halls, along with two gourmet restaurants. In summer the beer garden at the Kurhaus is one of the most animated along the Rhine. See chapter 12.

- **Bad Reichenhall:** Many spa lovers head for this remote corner of Bavaria near the Austria border to "take the waters." Europe's largest saline source was first tapped here in pre-Christian times. There's a definite fin-de-siècle aura to the place. See chapter 8.

- **Bad Homburg:** Bad Homburg lies at the foot of the Taunus Hills in a setting of medieval castles and luxuriant forests. There are more than 31 fountains in the town's Kurpark. The Bad Homburg Palace was once the summer residence of Prussian kings. See chapter 12.

- **Bad Nauheim:** What do Elvis Presley and William Randolph Hearst have in common? Both stayed at Bad Neuheim—the newspaper czar by choice, along with his mistress Marion Davies, and Elvis by orders of the U.S. Army. The warm carbonic-acid springs of the spa are used in the treatment of heart and circulatory ailments along with rheumatic diseases. See chapter 12.

10 The Best Luxury Hotels

German efficiency and cleanliness are legendary around the world, so it's not surprising that you can choose from a staggering number of well-managed hotels.

- **Four Seasons** (Berlin; ☎ **800/332-3442** or 030/2-03-38): One of Germany's great new luxury hotels built after the Berlin Wall came tumbling down, this is all about opulence, superb service, and comfort. From its Austrian crystal chandeliers to its silk-covered chairs and antiques, this hotel is discreet, tasteful, reliable, and a brilliant addition to the roster of luxury leaders in Germany's capital. See chapter 3.

- **Kempinski Hotel Elephant** (Weimar; ☎ **03643/80-20**): This is one of Germany's most interesting hotels because of its age (over 300 years), its name (whose origins no one can remember), its 50-year survival in the Germany's eastern zone, and its associations with a range of the famous, such as Schiller, Franz Liszt, and Goethe. Today, it's a cost-conscious treasure chest of German history. See chapter 4.

- **Eisenhut** (Rothenburg ob der Tauber; ☎ 09861/70-50): This hotel's 16th-century walls and valuable collection of antiques enhance the appeal of the most authentic Renaissance town in Germany. See chapter 6.
- **Kempinski Hotel Vier Jahreszeiten München** (Munich; ☎ 800/426-3135 in the U.S., or 089/2-12-50): Munich's most prestigious choice on its premier shopping street offers elegance and luxury. The world's wealthy and titled have checked in here for more than a century, enjoying the ambience, the antiques, the style, and the grace. See chapter 7.
- **Der kleine Prinz** (Baden-Baden; ☎ 07221/34-64): This hotel's director once helped manage the New York Hilton and the Waldorf-Astoria. Today he and his wife (an interior decorator) run a century-old pair of neobaroque houses in the heart of Germany's most elegant resort, Baden-Baden. Der Kleine Prinz is among the most romantic of Germany's many Romantik Hotels. See chapter 10.
- **Krone Assmannshausen** (Rüdesheim-Assmannshausen; ☎ 06722/40-30): Sprawling along the banks of the Rhine in an oversized, grangelike, gingerbread-laden fantasy, this hotel has witnessed the arrival of many important Germans (including Goethe) in its 400-year history. On the second floor is a small but charming museum documenting the hotel's vivid history. The place also contains one of the best traditional restaurants in town. See chapter 13.
- **Park Hotel Bremen** (Bremen; ☎ 0421/340-86-02): Designed like an aristocratic manor house, this hotel lies within a 500-acre park (with its own lake) maintained by the city of Bremen. With plenty of infusions of grand bourgeois grace and impeccable service, it embodies the carefully maintained elegance of this North German trading port. See chapter 15.
- **Fürstenhof Celle** (Celle; ☎ 05141/20-10): This 17th-century manor, enlarged with a pair of half-timbered wings, stands out even in a town legendary for its medieval and Renaissance buildings. There's a cozy bar within the building's medieval cellar and one of the best dining rooms in Lower Saxony. See chapter 15.
- **Vier Jahreszeiten** (Hamburg; ☎ 800/223-6800 in the U.S. and Canada, or ☎ 040/3-49-40): Its dignified interior is as opulent as its 19th-century facade. This hotel's appeal is correctly aristocratic, but it still has a touch of the saltwater zestiness that has made Hamburg a great city. See chapter 16.

11 The Best Small Inns & Hotels

- **Sorat Art'otel** (Berlin; ☎ 030/88-44-70): This hotel in the heart of cosmopolitan Berlin is chic, discreet, and unique. The swirling action of the Ku'-damm lies right outside the door, but inside the decor is soothing and serene, the work of some of the continent's top designers, such as Philippe Starck and Arne Jacobsen. See chapter 3.
- **Das Kleine Stapelhäuschen** (Cologne; ☎ 0221/2-57-78-62): This inn, which stands on the site of Cologne's old fish market, was originally constructed in the 12th century by Scottish Benedictine monks. Today, it offers a slightly faded old-fashioned charm and much comfort—all at a reasonable price. See chapter 13.
- **Römischer Kaiser** (Trier; ☎ 0651/9-77-00): This small, turn-of-the-century building enjoys a prime location in Germany's oldest city. Formerly a patrician house, it has been skillfully converted to an attractive and well-kept hotel. See chapter 14.

- **Hanseatic Hotel** (Hamburg; ☎ **040/48-57-72**): This little hotel evokes a prim and proper English gentleman's club, with chintz upholstery, leather-bound books, and prints of horses. Bedrooms are one of a kind, often containing antiques. In summer, the owner can be spotted out front tending his flower garden, getting ready to welcome you. See chapter 16.
- **Parkhotel Atlantic** (Heidelberg; ☎ **06221/60-42-0**): Though the name sounds like that of a deluxe hotel, this place is actually a 23-room inn on the wooded outskirts of Heidelberg, near the famous castle. Comfort and convenience are found in every room, and in the afternoon you can go for long walks along the woodland trails surrounding the property. See chapter 11.
- **Admiral Hotel** (Wiesbaden; ☎ **0611/5-86-60**): A hotel of considerable charm, the Admiral offers the best value in this fashionable spa resort outside Frankfurt. The bedrooms are charmingly old-fashioned; some have antique brass beds. The owner is a retired U.S. army officer. See chapter 12.
- **Alstadt-Hotel Laubenwirt** (Passau; ☎ **0851/33-70**): This inexpensive hotel stands at the convergence of three rivers—the Danube, the Ilz, and the Inn. But the hotel offers more than river views. It's comfortably and traditionally furnished, and its regional cuisine and convivial pub attract the locals. See chapter 5.

12 The Best Restaurants

- **Rockendorf's** (Berlin; ☎ **030/4-02-30-99**): During the latter days of the Cold War, the interior of this art-nouveau villa was often photographed as a symbol of the "good life" available within Berlin's western zone. Since reunification, the restaurant has continued to serve ultramodern and creative cuisine to a clientele that includes the most important movers and shakers in Germany. See chapter 3.
- **Die Entenstub'n** (Nürnberg; ☎ **0911/5-98-04-13**): Its name (Duck Tavern) comes from its origin as the 18th-century hunting lodge of Bavarian king Ludwig III. The decor is lighthearted, but don't be fooled—this is the best restaurant in town. See chapter 5.
- **Weinhaus Zum Stachel** (Würzburg; ☎ **0931/5-27-70**): This is the oldest (ca. 1413) wine house in a town loaded with them. Portions are copious, the wine flows, and everyone has a wonderful time. It's old-time Deutschland at its most appealing. See chapter 6.
- **Tantris** (Munich; ☎ **089/361-95-90**): Savvy German food critics have honored Tantris's Hans Haas as the country's top chef. He serves some of the finest and most innovative food in Bavaria. See chapter 7.
- **Seehotel Siber** (Constance; ☎ **07531/6-30-44**): Bertold Siber remains one of the leading chefs of Germany, certainly without peer along the northern tier of Lake Constance. Both the service and the cuisine in his restaurant exhibit an amazing attention to detail. See chapter 9.
- **Goldener Pflug** (Merheim, near Cologne; ☎ **0221/89-55-09**): The gold-plated building was once a modest tavern, but now is a comfortable enclave of fine dining. The cuisine is sumptuous and sophisticated. See chapter 13.
- **Victorian Restaurant** (Düsseldorf; ☎ **0211/8-65-50-22**): Regulars know what a treasure they have in this restaurant. Market-fresh ingredients and a steady hand in the kitchen produce award-winning food, both traditional and modern. See chapter 13.
- **Fischereihafen** (Altona, near Hamburg; ☎ **040/38-18-16**): Everything about Fischereihafen celebrates the 19th-century mercantile prosperity that enriched

this rainy seaport. Patrons from Tina Turner to Helmut Kohl have pronounced the food here delightful. From a window seat, you can overlook the boats that might have hauled in your sole, eel, turbot, herring, or flounder from the seas that very day. See chapter 16.

13   The Best Beer Halls & Taverns

- **Hofbräuhaus am Platzl** (Munich; ☎ **089/22-16-76**): The Hofbräuhaus, owned by the state, is the world's most famous beer hall. It can accommodate some 4,500 beer drinkers on any given night. Music from live bands and huge mugs of beer served at wooden tables combine to produce the best of Bavarian nighttime fun. See chapter 7.
- **Zum Roten Ochsen** (Heidelberg; ☎ **06221/2-09-77**): Over the years, "The Red Ox" has drawn beer drinkers ranging from Mark Twain to Bismarck. Students have been getting plastered here since 1703, and the tradition continues just as strong as ever. See chapter 11.
- **Bayrisch Zell** (Hamburg; ☎ **040/31-42-81**): It doesn't quite have the charm of the fabled Hofbräuhaus in Munich, but after all, this is northern Germany. The bustling place seats 1,200, and on many nights there seems to be a lot more people here. It's one of the safe places in the notorious St. Pauli district. See chapter 16.
- **Ratskeller** (Göttingen; ☎ **0551/5-64-33**): The beer in the town of Göttingen flows freely in many taverns, but this place is the most reliable. This 600-year-old spot lies in the cellar of the historic town hall. See chapter 15.
- **Auerbachs Keller** (Leipzig; ☎ **0341/21-61-00**): The most famous tavern in eastern Germany, this is the place where Goethe staged the debate between Faust and Mephistopheles. The tavern dates from 1530 and has a series of murals evoking the Faust legend. See chapter 4.

14   The Best Shopping

Germany is neither a shopper's mecca nor the bargain basement of Europe, but it has some good buys. The best way to approach shopping here is to make it a part of your overall experience and not an end unto itself. Berlin and Munich are the major shopping centers.

- **Porcelain:** For centuries, Germany has been known for the quality of its porcelain. Names such as KPM, Rosenthal, and Meissen are household words. KPM, for example, has been a Berlin tradition for more than 2 centuries.
- **Timepieces:** Corny though they may be, carved Black Forest cuckoo clocks remain an enduring favorite. Also, Germany, like Switzerland, is known for its precision watches, which can be good buys. See chapter 10.
- **Cutlery:** WMF (Württembergische-Metalwaren-Fabrik) and J. A. Henckels are two of the country's premier producers of fine cutlery. Their knives are expensive, but longtime users say they last forever. WMF stores are found all over Germany.
- **Handcrafts:** In the Bavarian Alps, woodcarvers still carry on their time-honored tradition. The best place to purchase wood carvings is in the alpine village of Oberammergau. See chapter 8.
- **Optical Products:** German precision is best exemplified in its microscopes, binoculars, and other such precisely calibrated products.
- **Toys:** Nürnberg, the country's toy center, produces some of the most imaginative playthings in the world. See chapter 5.

2 Planning a Trip to Germany

This chapter covers everything you need to know to make trip-planning a snap, from when to go to how to shop for the best airfare. Browse through it to get started and make sure you've touched all the bases.

1 The Regions in Brief

Germany lies in the heart of Europe, bordered by Switzerland and Austria to the south; France, Luxembourg, Belgium, and the Netherlands to the west; Denmark to the north; and Poland and the Czech Republic to the east. The country encompasses 137,535 square miles and has a population of about 80 million. *Note:* For a map of Germany, see page 2.

Berlin & Potsdam   Berlin has once more taken its place as Germany's capital and cultural center. It beckons visitors with glorious museums, wonderful cultural offerings, and cutting-edge nightlife. Southwest of Berlin is Potsdam, with its famous palace and elegant gardens and parks, set in an idyllic landscape along the Havel River.

Thuringia   Long a tourist mecca for workers from the Eastern bloc countries, Thuringia, with its untouched villages, churches, and medieval fortress ruins, is now being discovered by Westerners. If your idea of East Germany was nothing but grim industrial cities and cheap housing projects, be prepared for a surprise. Here you can still see the small towns once known to Luther, Schiller, Bach, and Wagner. The region's densely forested mountains are prime hiking country. The cultural center, with many attractions, is the city of Weimar, once the bastion of such greats as Walter Gropius, Miës van der Rohe, Liszt, Goethe, and Schiller.

Saxony: Leipzig & Dresden   These were the two most important cities of East Germany; now they're taking their places as centers of the new Germany. Known for its annual trade fair that draws participants from around the world, Leipzig is the most important industrial center in the east, except for Berlin. But this city, once the home of Bach, is also a cultural treasure, with its museums, old churches, and Thomanerchor (the famous boys' choir). For those who find Berlin too overwhelming, Leipzig offers an excellent alternative.

But if it's a choice between Leipzig and Dresden, make it Dresden, still one of the most beautiful cities in Germany, though 80% of its center was destroyed in an infamous 1945 Allied air raid aimed more at German civilians and culture than military targets. In fact, the remaining ruins form one of its attractions. Kurt Vonnegut's *Slaughterhouse Five* told the story of Dresden's destruction and makes good reading before heading here. Today, Dresden is bouncing back—and fast.

Franconia & the German Danube   Some of Germany's greatest medieval and Renaissance treasures came from this region, which gave the world such artists as Albrecht Dürer and Lucas Cranach. Come here to visit some of the most beautiful and most historical towns in Germany, notably Regensburg, Bamberg, Nürnberg, and Bayreuth, the last where Wagner built his theater and created his *Festspiel,* the famous opera festival that's still so popular today. But if you can only visit one town here, head for Würzburg, Germany's baroque city. (Würzburg is also the ideal starting point of a tour of the Romantic Road; see below.) Located on the banks of the Main River, this glorious old city is overlooked by a fortified castle. Regensburg, 62 miles southeast of Nürnberg, is also worth a visit, though tourists often pass it by. It suffered no major bombings in World War II, and so remains one of the best preserved cities in Germany. Nürnberg, although it holds much of interest today with its many preserved art treasures, was heavily bombed and had to be virtually rebuilt. The Danube River, which flows through this region, isn't blue at all and doesn't have the allure, dramatic scenery, or castles of the Rhine, but it's also worth exploring for its own quiet charm.

The Romantic Road   One of the most scenically beautiful but also one of the most overrun attractions in Germany, the Romantic Road (or *Romantische Strasse)* winds its way south from the imperial city of Würzburg to the little town of Füssen at the foot of the Bavarian Alps. Along the way, Rothenburg ob der Tauber is one of the most splendidly preserved medieval towns in Europe, and as if that weren't enough, the road comes to an end at "Mad" King Ludwig's most fantastic creation: Neuschwanstein Castle. The idea of the "Romantic Road," originally a bit of PR hype to promote the area, was launched in 1950. It was such a success that the road is now clogged with traffic in summer, so the trip is best made in spring or autumn, before the tour buses arrive. (If you want an admittedly less scenic, but still charming, "romantic road," try the "Fairy-Tale Road" in Lower Saxony and North Hesse.) The region of the Romantic Road is known for its folk traditions, old-world charm, and unspoiled medieval towns still surrounded by their original walls. Despite its drawbacks, the road remains one of the most beautiful and interesting trails in all of Europe.

Munich & the Bavarian Alps   Rebuilt from the rubble of World War II, Munich is one of the most visited cities of Europe, and probably the best place in Germany for old-fashioned fun. It should be included even on the briefest of itineraries. Just as chic and cosmopolitan as Frankfurt or Berlin, Munich is also kitschy in the best sense of Bavarian tradition. A night at the Hofbräuhaus, Germany's most fabled beer hall, with its king-size liter mugs and oompah bands, will get you into the spirit of Munich life. After strolling through the Englischer Garten and having a glass of Bavarian wine in Schwabing (the legendary artists' district), you can tackle Munich's vast array of museums and palaces. Save time for the Deutsches Museum, the largest technological museum in the world. Munich also lies at the gateway to Germany's towering attraction, the Bavarian Alps. The best resorts here are Berchtesgaden and Garmisch-Partenkirchen. Shimmering alpine lakes, half-timbered houses frescoed with paintings, picture-postcard towns like Mittenwald and Oberammergau are all here, plus hiking, nature, wildlife, and alpine-ski trails in winter.

Lake Constance (Bodensee)   The 162-mile coastline of the Bodensee is shared with two other countries, Austria and Switzerland, but Germany got the best part, the lake's beautiful northern rim. A boat trip on the Bodensee, although not comparable to a Rhine cruise, is a major attraction. The tour takes in castles as well as towns built on islands near the shoreline. The best center is not Konstanz, the largest city on the lake, but Lindau at the southeastern part, only a mile or so from the Austrian frontier. Reached by a causeway, this island town has the most luxuriant growth of flowers and shrubs of any resort along the lake. But Konstanz also merits a visit, since it's one of the best preserved major medieval cities in Germany.

The Black Forest (Schwarzwald)   This dense fir forest, filled with beauty, charm, and myth, actually receives more sunshine than most other forests in Germany. The major center of the region is Freiburg, but the most visited city is the elegant resort Baden-Baden. Of course, Black Forest cake and smoked ham might be reason enough to visit the area, but there are many other allures as well, including casino gambling, great spa facilities, and plenty of hiking, bicycling, and cross-country skiing. Freiburg im Breisgau remains one of the most beautiful and historic towns in Germany and makes the best center for exploring the region. If you want a Black Forest cuckoo clock—just as good as the ones touted in Switzerland—head for Triberg and the *Haus der 1,000 Uhren* (House of 1,000 Clocks).

Heidelberg & the Neckar Valley   Except for the Bavarian Alps, there is no more tranquil and scenic part of Germany than the Neckar Valley. The area's *Burgenstrasse* (Castle Road) has more castles than any comparable stretch along the mighty Rhine, and the Neckar River Valley, in our view, is just as romantically charming as the more overrun Romantic Road. Allow time to take detours into hidden side valleys here, to see sleepy little Neckar towns, most often with a protective castle hovering over them. Heidelberg, the apotheosis of romantic Germany, needs no selling. This famous medieval university town with its historic castle perfectly captures the spirit of south Germany and has attracted poets and composers over the decades. Goethe and hard-to-impress Mark Twain both fell in love here—Goethe with a woman of striking beauty and the more cynical Twain with Heidelberg itself. Unfortunately, Heidelberg suffers from overcrowding, especially in July and August, when tourists descend by the busload.

Stuttgart & Tübingen   The capital of the state of Baden-Württemberg, Stuttgart is an industrial giant, the headquarters of both Mercedes and Porsche. It's also a city of high culture, home of the acclaimed Stuttgart Ballet and Stuttgart State Opera, with world-class museums. Its setting, surrounded by green hills with vineyards and orchards, is attractive, but the town isn't a serious contender for visitors when compared to Berlin or Munich. If you can give Stuttgart a day, fine. If not, head at once to nearby Tübingen, the ancient university city on the upper Neckar that has been compared favorably to Heidelberg. It doesn't have Heidelberg's grandeur (or its hordes of visitors), but we prefer its youthful air, its tranquility, and the quiet beauty of its half-timbered houses and alleyways. Don't worry about rushing around to see a lot of attractions—just soak up the place's old-time atmosphere.

The Rhineland   After beginning in the mountains of Switzerland as a narrow stream, this mighty river of legend and lore flows for some 850 miles through one of the most picturesque and also most industrialized regions of Europe. For 2,000 years it has been a major European trade route. Bonn, Cologne, Düsseldorf, and Koblenz all lie on its banks. For most visitors, the number-one attraction is a romantic cruise down the Rhine, through gorges and past ancient castles, vineyards, and the fabled Lorelei. The most panoramic stretch is between Rüdesheim and Koblenz. Start your Rhine cruise at Rüdesheim, Germany's favorite wine village, about 45 miles to the west of Frankfurt. If you have time for only one Rhineland city, make it Cologne rather than the more commercialized Düsseldorf. Cologne is dominated by its famous cathedral, the largest in Germany and one of the greatest on earth, but this ancient city is also filled with dozens of other attractions, including restored Romanesque churches, striking Roman ruins, and the best modern-art galleries in the country.

Mosel Valley   Known as *La Moselle* in nearby France, the Mosel River weaves a snake-like path through the mountains west of the Rhineland, and many of its vineyards— on both sides of the river—produce wines superior to those of the Rhine. The Mosel is the most famous tributary of the Rhine. Naturally, it doesn't have the Rhine's dramatic scenery, but we somehow prefer it, with its vineyards, castles, and fortresses that attract far fewer visitors. The swift-moving Rhine is filled with commercial traffic, but the Mosel is slow-moving, tranquil, and inviting, dotted with sleepy wine towns where you can sample some of the world's greatest vintages. Trains rumble all night along the Rhine, but not on the Mosel. (The inevitable tour buses do get through, however.) The best time to visit is during the annual fall grape harvests, centering in Cochem or Bernkastel-Kues. The very best for last: Near the Luxembourg border lies Trier, one of Europe's most fascinating antiques and the oldest city in Germany; it existed 1,300 years before Rome. Trier is a virtual theme park of Roman culture and architecture.

Lower Saxony & North Hesse: The Fairy-Tale Road   Hansel and Gretel, Rumpelstiltskin, the Pied Piper, and even Cinderella list their addresses as "The Fairy-Tale Road." Frankly, the Fairy-Tale Road isn't as architecturally splendid as the Romantic Road, but it's also not as crowded, and it does have a wealth of treasures for visitors interested in German lore and legend or lovers of the tales of the Brothers Grimm, who lived and worked here. The road begins at Hanau, just east of Frankfurt, and stretches for 370 miles north, coming to an end in Bremen. Along the way, the trail passes through colorful towns with half-timbered buildings and past plenty of castles for added measure. Naturally, it's haunted by witches and goblins and memories of the Pied Piper of Hameln.

Schleswig-Holstein & the Baltic Coast   You're never far from the roaring waves in Schleswig Holstein; the North Sea is to the west and the more peaceful Baltic Sea to the east. This is a special world rarely visited by most Americans. It's as close as Germany comes to duplicating the charms of Denmark, to the north. The province contains Germany's most sophisticated beachside resort, the long narrow island of Sylt, whose capital is Westerland, Germany's northernmost point. The main features of the climate here are iodine-rich air and lots of rain. Sylt doesn't exactly live up to its reputation as the St. Tropez of the north, but it's still a cosmopolitan playground, a favorite with celebrities. But if North Sea resorts aren't your dream, the ancient Hanseatic port of Lübeck, dating from the 12th century, is reason enough to visit. Surrounded by canals, the city was the home of the Mann family (both Heinrich and Thomas Mann) and the setting for Thomas's novel *Buddenbrooks*. Although heavily restored after World War II, Lübeck is loaded with attractions, and its Aldstadt (old town) has been labeled by UNESCO (United Nations Educational, Scientific, and Cultural Organization) as one of the world's greatest cultural and natural treasures. From Lübeck you can travel east along the Baltic Coast, all the way to the Polish border. The German beach towns still haven't thrown off their Communist aura yet, but the miles of sandy coastline and chalk cliffs give you a view of a world closed to most of the West for many years.

2 Visitor Information

Nearly all larger towns and all cities in Germany have tourist offices. The headquarters of the **German National Tourist Board** is at Beethovenstrasse 69, 60325 Frankfurt am Main (☎ **069/974-640; www.germany-tourism.de**).

You'll find a German National Tourist Board office in **New York** at 122 E. 42nd St., 52nd Floor, New York, NY 10168-0072 (☎ **212/661-7200**); in **Toronto** at 175 Bloor St. E., North Tower, 6th Floor, Toronto, ON M4W 3R8 (☎ **416/968-1570**); in **London** at Nightingale House, 65 Curzon St., London W1Y 8NE (☎ **0171/317-0908**); and in **Sydney** at Sydney South NSW 1235 (☎ **02/9267-8148**). There are also tourist offices in about 20 other international cities, including Hong Kong, Johannesburg, Milan, Paris, and Sydney.

3   Entry Requirements & Customs

PASSPORTS & VISAS

Every U.S., Canadian, and Australian traveler entering Germany must hold a valid passport. You won't need a visa unless you're staying longer than 3 months. Citizens of other European Union nations may travel to Germany and any other European Union country with only an identity card. A passport is not necessary.

Safeguard your passport in an inconspicuous, inaccessible place like a money belt. If you lose your passport, visit the nearest consulate of your native country as soon as possible for a replacement.

CUSTOMS

ENTERING GERMANY   In general, items required for personal and professional use or consumption may be brought in to Germany duty-free and without hassle. No duty is levied for a private car, provided that it is reported. You can also bring in gifts duty-free up to a total value of 780DM ($444.60); this includes a maximum of 115DM ($65.55) in items that are destined for non-European Union countries.

The following items are permitted into Germany duty-free from non-EU countries: 200 cigarettes; 1 liter of liquor above 44 proof, or 2 liters of liquor less than 44 proof, or 2 liters of wine; 50 grams of perfume and 0.25 liters of eau de cologne; 500 grams of coffee; 100 grams of tea. From EU countries the duty-free limits are higher: 300 cigarettes; 1.5 liters of liquor above 44 proof, or 3 liters of liquor less than 44 proof, or 4 liters of wine; 75 grams of perfume and 0.375 liters of eau de cologne; 750 grams of coffee; 150 grams of tea. Duty-free allowances are authorized only when the items are carried in the traveler's personal baggage.

RETURNING TO THE U.S.   Returning U.S. citizens who have been away for 48 hours or more are allowed to bring back, once every 30 days, $400 worth of merchandise duty-free. You'll be charged a flat rate of 10% duty on the next $1,000 worth of purchases. Be sure to have your receipts handy. You cannot bring fresh foodstuffs into the United States; tinned foods, however, are allowed. You can also mail gifts back to people in the U.S. duty-free if the value of the entire gift package does not exceed $100 (be sure to write on the package wrapping its dollar value and that it's a gift). For more information, contact the **U.S. Customs Service,** 1301 Constitution Ave. (P.O. Box 7407), Washington, DC 20044 (☎ **202/927-6724**), and request the free pamphlet "Know Before You Go," which is also available on the Web at www.customs. ustreas.gov/travel/kbygo.htm.

RETURNING TO CANADA   For a clear summary of Canadian rules, write for the booklet "I Declare," issued by **Revenue Canada,** 2265 St. Laurent Blvd., Ottawa K1G 4KE (☎ **613/993-0534**). Canada allows its citizens a Can$500 duty-free exemption, which includes 200 cigarettes, 2.2 pounds of tobacco, 40 imperial ounces of liquor, and 50 cigars. In addition, you're allowed to mail gifts to Canada from abroad at the rate of Can$60 a day, provided they're unsolicited and don't contain alcohol or tobacco (write on the package "Unsolicited gift, under $60 value"). *Note:* The Can$500 exemption can only be used once a year and only after an absence of 7 days.

RETURNING TO THE U.K., IRELAND & OTHER EU COUNTRIES   Citizens of the U.K. and Ireland who are returning from a European Union country will go through a separate Customs Exit (called the "Blue Exit") especially for EU travelers. In essence, there is no limit on what you can bring back from an EU country, as long as the items are for personal use (this includes gifts), and you have already paid the necessary duty and tax. However, Customs law sets out guidance levels. If you bring in more than these levels, you may be asked to prove that the goods are for your own use. Guidance levels on goods bought in the EU for your own use are 800 cigarettes, 200 cigars, 1 kilogram smoking tobacco, 10 liters of spirits, 90 liters of wine (of this not more than 60 liters can be sparkling wine), and 110 liters of beer. For more information, contact **HM Customs & Excise, Passenger Enquiry Point,** 2nd Floor Wayfarer House, Great South West Road, Feltham, Middlesex, TW14 8NP (☎ **0181/ 910-3744;** from outside the U.K. 44/181-910-3744), or consult its Web site at www.open.gov.uk.

RETURNING TO AUSTRALIA   The duty-free allowance in Australia is A$400 or, for those under 18, A$200. Citizens can bring in 250 cigarettes or 250 grams of loose tobacco, and 1.125 liters of alcohol. A helpful brochure, available from Australian consulates or Customs offices, is "Know Before You Go." For more information, contact **Australian Customs Services,** GPO Box 8, Sydney NSW 2001 (☎ **02/9213-2000**).

RETURNING TO NEW ZEALAND   The duty-free allowance for New Zealand is NZ$700. Citizens over 17 can bring in 200 cigarettes, or 50 cigars, or 250 grams of tobacco (or a mixture of all three if their combined weight doesn't exceed 250 grams); plus 4.5 liters of wine and beer, or 1.125 liters of liquor. Most questions are answered in a free pamphlet, available at New Zealand consulates and Customs offices, called "New Zealand Customs Guide for Travellers, Notice no. 4." For more information, contact **New Zealand Customs,** 50 Anzac Ave., P.O. Box 29, Auckland (☎ **09/ 359-6655**).

4 Money

The major cities of Germany are some of the world's most expensive. So if you want to see the country without breaking the bank, you may want to cut short your time in Frankfurt, Munich, or Berlin and concentrate on interesting regional capitals such as Freiburg in the Black Forest, where you can cut your travel cost by anywhere from 20 to 40%. Also, a moderately priced rail pass will allow you to see a lot of Germany in a short time.

But although prices in Germany are high, you generally get good value for your money. The inflation rate here has remained low. Hotels are usually clean and comfortable, and restaurants generally offer good cuisine and ample portions made with quality ingredients. Trains are fast and on time, and most service personnel treat you with respect.

Many people come to Germany just for winter sports. The most expensive resorts are places like Garmisch-Partenkirchen. However, if you avoid the chic places, you can enjoy winter fun at a moderate cost. Some of the winter spots in the Bavarian Alps that haven't been overrun by the beautiful people give you great value for your money. And prices in a village next to a resort are often 30% lower than at the resort itself.

In Germany, many prices for children (generally defined as ages 6 to 17) are considerably lower than for adults. And fees for children under 6 are often waived entirely.

The U.S. Dollar, the British Pound, the German Mark & the Euro

At this writing, one euro equals approximately 1.17 U.S. dollars and approximately 1.96 German marks.

For American Readers   At this writing, $1 equals approximately 1.75DM (or 1DM=57¢), and this is the rate of exchange used to calculate the dollar values given throughout this book.

For British Readers   At this writing, £1 equals approximately 2.86DM (or 1DM=35p), and this is the rate of exchange used to calculate the pound sterling values in the table below.

Note: The relative value of the deutschmark to other world currencies fluctuates from time to time and may not be the same when you travel to Germany. This table should be used only as an indication of approximate values.

DM	US$	UK	Euro	DM	US$	UK	Euro
1	0.57	0.35	0.51	75.00	42.75	26.25	38.25
2	1.14	0.70	1.02	100.00	57.00	35.00	51.00
3	1.71	1.05	1.53	125.00	71.25	43.75	63.75
4	2.28	1.40	2.04	150.00	85.50	52.50	76.50
5	2.85	1.75	2.55	175.00	99.75	61.25	89.25
6	3.42	2.10	3.06	200.00	114.00	70.00	102.00
7	3.99	2.45	3.57	225.00	128.25	78.75	114.75
8	4.56	2.80	4.08	250.00	142.50	87.50	127.50
9	5.13	3.15	4.59	275.00	156.75	96.25	140.25
10	5.70	3.50	5.10	300.00	171.00	105.00	153.00
15	8.55	5.25	7.65	350.00	199.50	122.50	178.50
20	11.40	7.00	10.20	400.00	228.00	140.00	204.00
25	14.25	8.75	12.75	500.00	285.00	175.00	255.00
50	28.50	17.50	25.50	1000.00	570.00	350.00	510.00

CASH/CURRENCY

The unit of German currency is the **deutschmark** (DM), which is subdivided into pfennig (pf). Bills are issued in denominations of 5, 10, 20, 50, 100, 200, 500, and 1,000 marks; coins come in 1, 2, 5, 10, and 50 pfennig.

THE EURO

The euro, the new European currency, became the official currency of Germany and 10 other countries on January 1, 1999, but not in the form of cash. There are still no euro banknotes or coins in circulation—payment in euros can only be made by check, credit card, or some other bank-related system. The German mark will remain the only currency in Germany for cash transactions until December 21, 2002. The symbol of the euro is €; its official abbreviation is EUR. Although at this time, very few, if any, German hotel and restaurant bills can actually be paid in euros, there will be an increasing emphasis on the new pan-European currency during the lifetime of this edition.

ATMS

ATMs worldwide are linked to a network that most likely includes your bank at home. **Cirrus** (☎ 800/424-7787; www.mastercard.com/atm/) and **PLUS** (☎ 800/843-7587; www.visa.com/atms) are the two most popular networks; check the back

What Things Cost in Berlin	U.S. $	U.K. £
Taxi from Tegel Airport to Europa-Center	$17.10	£10.25
Underground from Kurfürstendamm to Dahlem	$2.20	£1.30
Local telephone call	$5.70	£3.40
Double room at the Bristol Kempinski hotel	$148.20	£88.90
Double room at the Bogotà (inexpensive)	$79.80	£47.90
Lunch for one at Hardtke's (moderate)	$22.80	£13.70
Dinner for one, without wine, at Restaurant Marjellchen (moderate)	$22.80	£13.70
Dinner for one, without wine, at Alexanderkeller (inexpensive)	$17.10	£10.25
Half a liter of beer	$2.55	£1.55
Coca-Cola in a restaurant	$1.70	£1
Cup of Coffee	85¢–$2.30	50p–£1.40
Glass of wine	$4.55	£2.75
Roll of ASA 200 color film, 36 exposures	$2.85–$5.70	£1.70–£3.40
Admission to Pergamon Museum (adult)	$4.55	£2.75
Movie ticket	$6.85	£44.10
Ticket to Berlin Philharmonic Orchestra	$34.20–$102.60	£20.50–£61.55

of your ATM card to see which network your bank belongs to. Ask your bank for a list of overseas ATMs. Be sure to check the daily withdrawal limit before you depart, and ask whether you need a new PIN number for use in Germany.

CREDIT CARDS

Credit cards are invaluable when traveling. They are a safe way to carry money and provide a convenient record of all your expenses. Keep in mind that though credit cards are widely accepted throughout Germany, they're still not accepted quite as commonly as in the U.S., especially in smaller towns.

You can also withdraw cash advances from your credit cards. At many banks, you don't even need to go to a teller; you can get a cash advance at the ATM if you know your PIN number.

Almost every credit card company has an emergency 800-number that you can call if your wallet or purse is stolen. The company may be able to wire you a cash advance off your credit card immediately, and in many places, can deliver an emergency credit card in a day or two. **Citicorp Visa's** U.S. emergency number is ☎ **800/336-8472. American Express** cardholders and traveler's check holders should call ☎ **800/221-7282** for all money emergencies. **MasterCard** holders should call ☎ **800/307-7309.**

Note: As we went to press, there was talk from some major credit card companies, including Citibank, of adding on stiff fees, as high as 4%, for each foreign-currency transaction on top of the 1 to 2% already charged by Visa and MasterCard. Call your credit card company and make sure you understand what you'll be charged for each conversion.

TRAVELER'S CHECKS

Traveler's checks are something of an anachronism from the days before ATMs made cash accessible at any time around the world. But they still might be a good choice if you want to avoid the small fees charged whenever you use an ATM or if you value the added security they bring.

You can get traveler's checks at almost any bank. **American Express** offers denominations of $10, $20, $50, $100, $500, and $1,000. You'll pay a service charge ranging from 1 to 4%. You can also get American Express traveler's checks over the phone by calling ☎ 800/221-7282; by using this number, Amex gold and platinum cardholders are exempt from the 1% fee. **AAA** members can obtain traveler's checks without a fee at most AAA offices. **Visa** offers traveler's checks at Citibank locations nationwide, as well as several other banks, in denominations of $20, $50, $100, $500, and $1,000. The service charge ranges between 1.5 and 2%. **MasterCard** also offers traveler's checks. Call ☎ 800/223-9920 for a location near you.

Be sure to keep a record of the checks' serial numbers, separately from the checks of course, so you're ensured a refund in an emergency.

5 When to Go

CLIMATE

Germany's climate varies widely. In the north, winters tend to be cold and rainy; summers are most agreeable. In the south and in the Alps, it can be very cold in the winter, especially in January, and very warm in summer, but with cool, rainy days even in July and August. Spring and fall are often stretched out—in fact, we've enjoyed many a Bavarian-style "Indian summer" until late in October. The most popular tourist months are May through October, although winter travel to Germany is becoming increasingly popular, especially to the ski areas in the Bavarian Alps.

Berlin's Average Daytime Temperature & Rainfall (inches)

	Jan	Feb	Mar	Apr	May	June	July	Aug	Sept	Oct	Nov	Dec
°F	30	32	40	48	53	60	64	62	56	49	40	34
°C	–1	0	4	9	12	16	18	17	13	9	4	1.
Rainfall	2.2	1.6	1.2	1.6	2.3	2.9	3.2	2.7	2.2	1.6	2.4	1.9

Frankfurt's Average Daytime Temperature & Rainfall (inches)

	Jan	Feb	Mar	Apr	May	June	July	Aug	Sept	Oct	Nov	Dec
°F	34	36	42	49	57	63	66	66	58	50	41	35
°C		1	2	6	9	14	17	19	19	14	10	52
Rainfall	6.5	5.1	5.6	5.7	5.9	5.5	5.0	5.1	4.2	4.8	6.5	6.0

HOLIDAYS

Public holidays are January 1 (New Year's Day), Easter (Good Friday and Easter Monday), May 1 (Labor Day), Ascension Day (10 days before Pentecost/Whitsunday, the 7th Sunday after Easter), Whitmonday (day after Pentecost), October 3 (Day of German Unity), November 17 (Day of Prayer and Repentance), and December 25 to 26 (Christmas). In addition, the following holidays are observed in some German states: January 6 (Epiphany), Corpus Christi (10 days after Pentecost), August 15 (Assumption), and November 1 (All Saints' Day).

Germany Calendar of Events

Actual dates of events vary from year to year. Contact one of the branches of the German National Tourist Board (see "Visitor Information," above) for the exact dates or more information. The Board publishes a free calendar of forthcoming events three times a year, in April, October, and January; the first two are half-yearly calendars and

Don't Miss It

In the summer of the year 2000, Hannover will host **Expo 2000.** Officials expect as many as 20 million visitors for this major event.

the last is a yearly preview. They give the dates of trade fairs and exhibitions, theatrical and musical performances, local folk festivals, sporting events, conferences, and congresses throughout Germany.

January

- **New Year's Day International Ski Jumping,** Garmisch-Partenkirchen. One of Europe's major winter sporting events. For more information, contact the tourist bureau on Dr.-Richard-Strauss-Platz (☎ **08821/18-06**).

February

- ✪ **International Film Festival,** Berlin (at various theaters; announced in local newspapers). Stars, would-be stars, directors, and almost anyone with a film to peddle show up at this well-attended festival. It lasts for 1 week and is a showcase for the work of international film directors as well as the latest German films. Tickets can be purchased at any box office. Contact the **Full House Service** (☎ **030/25-48-92-54**) for more information. February 9 to 20.
- **Frankfurt International Spring Fair.** This is one of the principal consumer-goods trade fairs of Europe. Its origins go back centuries. For information, contact the **Messe Frankfurt Gubh** (☎ **069/7-57-50;** fax 069/75-75-64-33; 770/984-8023 in the U.S.). Late February.

March

- **Spring Fairs.** Highlights throughout Germany, especially in Augsburg, Münster, Nürnberg, Hamburg, and Stuttgart.
- **Fasching.** Carnival festivals take place throughout Germany, reaching their peak on the Tuesday (Mardi Gras) before Ash Wednesday (March 8). Particularly famous Carnivals take place in Bonn, Cologne, Düsseldorf, and especially Munich.

April

- **Walpurgis Festivals.** Celebrated in the Harz Mountains. Festivities occur on the night of April 30.

May

- ✪ **Passion Play,** Oberammergau. This legendary play, shown only 1 year out of 10, will be performed by the citizens of Oberammergau in the summer of 2000 between May 22 and October 8. See chapter 8 for more information.
- **Hamburg Summer.** A whole series of cultural events, including concerts, plays, festivals, and special exhibitions throughout May, June, and July. For information, contact the **Hamburg Tourist Bureau,** im Hauptbahnhof (☎ **040/30-05-13-00**).
- **International May Festival,** Wiesbaden. This city near Frankfurt hosts a premier cultural event—a series of artistic celebrations lasting 1 month. For information, contact the **Wiesbaden Tourist Office,** Rheinstrasse 15 (☎ **0611/1-72-97-80**).
- **Red Wine Festival,** Rüdesheim/Assmannshausen. This is held in Assmannshausen, the Rhine village most famous for red wines. For information, contact the **Rüdesheim Tourist Bureau,** Rheinstrasse 16 (☎ **06722/29-62**). Mid- to late May.
- **Mozart Festival,** Würzburg. Aficionados of the composer flock to this major cultural event in the baroque city of Würzburg. For more information, contact

Tourismus Zentrale im Würzburg-Palais, am Congress-Centrum (☎ 0931/37-33-35). May 31 to July 2.

June

✪ **Expo 2000,** Hannover. The first world exposition of the new millennium, and the first ever to take place in Germany, lasts from June 1 to October 31. See chapter 15 for more information.

• **Frankfurt Summertime Festival.** A series of cultural and artistic celebrations, plus outdoor events, staged throughout the city. For more information, contact the **Frankfurt Tourist Office** (☎ 069/21-23-87-08).

• **Floodlighting of the Castle,** Heidelberg. Fireworks enliven the display in this storied university city. For more information, contact the **Heidelberg Tourist Bureau,** Pavillon am Hauptbahnhof (☎ 06221/1-94-33). June 5, July 10, and September 4.

July

• **Freiburg Wine Tasting.** Local residents and visitors enjoy the first vintages from grapes grown in the Black Forest district. For more information, contact the **Freiburg Tourist Bureau,** Rotteckring 14 (☎ 0761/388-18-80). July 2 to July 7.

✪ **Richard Wagner Festival.** Bayreuth Festspielhaus. One of Europe's two or three major opera events, this festival takes place in the composer's Festspielhaus in Bayreuth, the capital of upper Franconia. Note that opera tickets often must be booked years in advance. For information, contact Festival Administration, **Bayreuther Festspiele,** Am Festspiele, 95445 Bayreuth (☎ 0921/7-87-80). Late July to late August.

September

✪ **Oktoberfest,** Munich. Germany's most famous festival happens mainly in September, not October. Millions show up, and hotels are packed. Most activities are at Theresienwiese, where local breweries sponsor gigantic tents that can hold up to 6,000 beer drinkers. Contact the **Munich Tourist Bureau** (☎ 089/2-33-03-00) for particulars, or just show up. Always reserve hotel rooms well in advance. Mid-September to the first Sunday in October.

• **Berliner Festwochen.** One of the high points on the cultural calendar of Germany, the Berlin Festival brings an international array of performing artists to Berlin. It features opera and symphony performances as well as major theatrical presentations. Contact the **Berlin Tourist Information Office** (☎ 030/25-00-25). September 1 to October 4.

October

• **Frankfurt Book Fair.** A major international event for publishers, book dealers, agents, and authors. Contact the **Frankfurt Tourist Office** (☎ 069/21-23-87-08). Usually mid-October.

November

• **Jazz-Fest Berlin.** This annual festival staged at the Philharmonie attracts some of the world's finest jazz artists, ranging from traditional to experimental. Contact the **Berlin Tourist Information Office** (☎ 030/25-00-25) for more information. November 5 to 8.

• **Winter Dom,** Hamburg. An annual amusement fair (sometimes called Hamburg Dom) at the Heiligengeistfeld. For more information, contact the **Hamburg Tourist Bureau,** Im Hauptbahnhof (☎ 040/30-05-13-00). November 5 to December 5.

December

- **Christmas Fair,** Mainz. Mainz stages its Christmas fair on the Rhine for 4 weeks preceding Christmas. For more information, contact the **Mainz Tourist Bureau,** Vruckenturm Am Raphaus (☎ **06131/28-62-10**). Other German towns hold Christmas fairs in November.

6 The Active Vacation Planner

Himalayan Travel has a variety of German adventure trips, including hiking, walking, trekking, and cycling tours of such areas as the Black Forest, Bavaria, and King Ludwig's Trail. The tours are self-guided, and luggage is transported by van from one hotel to the next. Rates include accommodations in two- and three-star hotels and some meals but not airfare. Contact the company at 110 Prospect St., Stamford, CT 06901 (☎ **800/225-2380**).

Uniquely Europe, 1940 116th Ave. NE, Bellevue, WA 98004 (☎ **800/426-3615**), offers a variety of self-guided walking and biking tours as well as cross-country skiing trips throughout Germany. It covers such areas as the Black Forest and King Ludwig's Trail, and will customize your trip if you wish.

Value Holidays will customize German walking tours for groups with special interests. Among its offerings are a Music Appreciation tour and a coach tour called "In the Footsteps of Luther." For information, write or call 10224 N. Port Washington Rd., Mequon, WI 53092 (☎ **800/558-6850**).

Abercromie & Kent, 15–20 Kensington Rd., Suite 212, Oak Brook, IL 60523-2141 (☎ **800/323-7308**), is well known for the exciting and extremely luxurious tours it offers around the globe. Its "Danube River Aboard the Magnificent M/S *River Cloud*" trip combines nostalgic, pre-war glamour with state-of-the-art engineering for a romantic 7-day voyage through Germany and then on to the former Austro-Hungarian Empire in the summer and fall.

BIKING   Pedaling through the Bavarian countryside is the way to go for many visitors. You can bike through green valleys and past rivers, such as the Danube, while enjoying rural landscapes and life in German villages. **Allgemeiner Deutscher Fahrrad-Club,** Hellerallee 23, 28209, Bremen (☎ **0421/34-62-90**), offers complete information on biking in Germany. For more information on touring Germany by bike, see "Getting Around," later in this chapter.

For the past 2 decades, **Classic Adventures** has offered bike tours of such areas as the Romantic Road; contact the company at P.O. Box 153, Hamlin, NY 14464 (☎ **800/777-8090**). **Euro-Bike Tours,** P.O. Box 990, DeKalb, IL 60115 (☎ **800/321-6060**), has a full range of bicycling and walking tours of Bavaria, as well as a 9-day biking tour of Germany, Switzerland, and France. The upscale outfitter **Butterfield & Robinson,** 70 Bond St., Toronto, Ontario, Canada M5B 1X3 (☎ **800/678-1147**), offers a new biking trip along the Romantic Road, past historic sites and along the banks of the Main, Tauber, and Neckar Rivers.

Dozens of companies in Britain offer guided cycling tours. One of the best is the **Cyclists Touring Club,** 69 Meadrow, Godalming, Surrey GU7 3HS (☎ **01483/417-217**). It charges £25 a year for membership.

CAMPING & CARAVANING   Germany boasts some 2,100 campsites, located in the most beautiful and popular resort districts and with all the necessary facilities. Blue signs bearing the international camping symbol—a black tent on a white background—make it easy to find campgrounds. Some 600 sites are kept open during the winter. You can obtain information on camping matters and campsites by writing to

"Taking the Waters"

More than any other country in Europe, Germany developed the spa process to a high art. The heyday of German spa construction coincided with the rise of the German bourgeoisie in the 19th century, when a lavish series of resorts was built around the dozens of mineral springs bubbling from the soil. Many of these springs had been known since the Middle Ages, or even Roman times, and to each was attributed specific cures for arthritis, gout, infertility, hypertension, and gynecological problems. (The German word *Kur—Kurort* means spa—is derived from the Latin *cura,* meaning care.) Going to a spa became an intensely ritualized social experience.

There are basically four types of spas.

1. **Mineral & Thermal Spas/Springs:** Springs with at least 1 gram of dissolved mineral substances per liter of natural water are designated "mineral springs." If the water emerges from the ground at a temperature of 68°F or more, it's called a "thermal spring." The treatment provided in mineral and thermal springs is as varied as the composition of the waters. Some of these waters are suitable for bathing.

2. **Climatic Health Resorts:** These health resorts lie in densely wooded areas permeated with fresh air. Climatic therapy consists of open-air kinesitherapy and constitutional walks along paths.

3. **Seaside Spas & Health Resorts:** Seawater and mud from coastal shallows are much used in therapeutic treatments. Seaside spa treatments are often used for treating circulatory disorders and cardiac defects, for rehabilitation after operations, and for skin diseases and other treatments.

4. **Kneipp (Hydropathic) Spas & Health Resorts:** This treatment was first developed by Sebastian Kneipp in 1849. It's based on a strengthening of the body's intrinsic immune system and on developing a proper macrobiotic rhythm. Warm water relaxes, cold water stimulates, and a natural way of life brings harmony—this is the basic Kneipp formula. Treatments consists of the following: (1) hydrotherapy for exercising the vascular and circulatory systems and for strengthening the immune system; (2) consumption of natural basic whole foods to ensure regular metabolism; (3) use of medicinal herbs to activate self-health powers; (4) physical training and kinesitherapy to improve cardiac activity and blood circulation; and (5) adjustment therapy to ensure a balanced way of life and a harmony of mind and body.

Don't expect frenzied nightlife or nonstop activities at a spa. Spas try to pad the emotional edges of life for their clientele and provide a soothing and unruffled

Allgemeiner Deutscher Automobil Club (ADAC) at Redaktion ADAC, Am Westpark 8, 81873 München (☎ **089/7-67-60**). You can also contact the **Deutscher Camping Club (DCC),** Mandlstrasse 28, 80802 München (☎ **089/380-14-20**).

FISHING   You can obtain information on fishing from any regional tourist office. In Germany, local catches include char, grayling, river and sea trout, carp, pike, perch, pike perch, rockfish, eel, and bream. An official license, called a *Fischereischein,* is required; it's available from local district or municipal authorities, and it is different in each area of Germany. Contact **Verband Deutscher Sportfischer,** Siemenstrasse 11–13 at 63071 Offerbach (☎ **069/85-50-06**).

environment that almost anyone can appreciate. The innards of the clinics often have a disturbing resemblance to hospitals, but you can avoid the interiors and still gain a fascinating insight into the ritualization of social life. Enjoy a leisurely meal in one of the resort's airy and elegantly formal restaurants, preferably one that overlooks a sprawling flower garden. Sit in a cafe, perhaps with a glass of wine, and watch the rituals of the prosperous bourgeoisie. And, if you choose, elect a spa treatment. Subject your travel-weary body to everything from mud baths to immersions in sulfur-rich water and endure the massages and skin treatments that will at least leave you more relaxed.

There are more than 300 health resorts in Germany today. The world *Bad* before the name in any town (for example, Bad Godesberg, Bad Orb) is a sure sign that the town has some sort of ritualized process for taking the waters. Most spa directors insist on a brief medical checkup—performed on site by resident doctors—before any treatment can begin.

In our view, no spa in Germany tops **Baden-Baden** in the Black Forest. It's where Elizabeth Taylor or Joan Collins might go to take a few years off—even men such as Plácido Domingo or José Carreras. Heads of state often slip in here. Baden-Baden has everything—not only the waters at its opulent Kurhaus, but also Germany's best casino. It also has more sightseeing attractions than any other spa in Germany, more deluxe hotels, and better food.

Another fabled spa, though somewhat less grand than Baden-Baden, is **Wiesbaden,** which is located outside Frankfurt, in the shelter of the Rhine and the Taunus Mountains. It has one of the finest open-air thermal pools in the country, and its thermal baths include both indoor and outdoor pools, along with endless massage rooms and solariums.

After Wiesbaden and Baden-Baden, the other leading spas fall off a bit, attracting mostly those interested in specific cures. For example, **Bad Reichenhall** in the Bavarian Alps is known for its saline waters, and also has a good reputation for the treatment of respiratory problems, skin ailments, and rheumatism. **Bad Kissingen** is known for its mud baths, seawater Jacuzzis, and saunas— but it's a bit dull when stacked up against its more glamorous siblings. **Bad Homburg,** in the foothills of the Taunus mountains, is long past its 19th-century heyday, but it still enjoys a reputation among spa devotees for the treatment of heart and circulatory diseases.

Regardless of the various medical claims made at the spas of Germany, the real reason to go, in our view, regardless of which spa you select, is to escape momentarily the stress of everyday life.

Franconia has some of the best fishing in Germany, especially along the Main River and in the vicinity of the ancient city of Coburg. The **Coburg Tourist Information, Herrngasse 4** (☎ **09561/7-41-80**), will supply complete information and hook you up with outfitters.

GOLF   Most German golf courses welcome visiting players who are members of courses at home. Weekday greens fees are usually around 30DM ($17.10), rising to as much as 60DM ($34.20) on Saturday and Sunday. For information about the various golf courses in Germany, write to the **Deutscher Golf/Verband,** Victoriastrasse 16, 65185 Wiesbaden (☎ **0611/99-02-00**).

Here are a few of the country's best places to golf. The Swabian region of Allgau has several good courses. The **Golf Club Obersaufen und Steibis** (☎ 08386/85-29), at Oberstaufen, is an 18-hole golf course close to a forest and nature park. Oftrerschwang, a small, charmingly peaceful resort on the scenically beautiful Tiefenberger Moor, has **Golf Club Sonnenalp** (☎ 08321/27-20). **Golf Baden Baden** (☎ 07221/23-57-9), in the spa city of Baden-Baden, offers a good 18-hole course, as does **Golf Bodensee** (☎ 08389/89191) on Lake Constance in southern Germany. Further north, the city of Augsburg has an 18-hole course at **Golf Augsburg** (☎ 08234/78-55).

HIKING & MOUNTAIN CLIMBING   These sports are popular in the German uplands. It's estimated that there are more than 80,000 marked hiking and mountain-walking tracks in the country. The **Verband Deutscher Gebirgs-und Wandervereine** services the trails and provides information from its address at Wilhelmshöher Alle 157-159, 34121 Kassel (☎ 0561/938-730). This outfit offers details not only about trails but also about shelters and huts and addresses of hiking associations in the various regions. The **Deutsche Alpenverein,** Von-Kahr-Strasse 2-4, 80997 München (☎ 089/14-00-30), owns and operates 50 huts in and around the Alps that are open to all mountaineers. This association also maintains a 9,500-mile network of alpine trails.

The best **alpine hiking** is in the Bavarian Alps, especially the 4,060-foot Eckbauer, lying on the southern fringe of Partenkirchen. The tourist office here will supply hiking maps and details (see chapter 8). Another great place for hiking is the Berchtesgaden National Park, bordering the Austrian province of Salzburg (see chapter 8). This park also offers the best organized hikes; for more information, or to hook up with various groups offering hikes, contact **Berchtesgaden National Park,** Kurgarten, Maximilianstrasse 1 (☎ 08652/22-07), in Berchtesgaden.

Waymark Holidays, 44 Windsor Rd., Slough, Berkshire SL1 2EJ England (☎ 01753/516-477), which is owned by avid naturalists and mountaineers, offers **walking tours** that focus on many of the particularly beautiful or folkloric regions of Germany. One popular trip is a 10-day walking tour through the Black Forest. The price of £575 ($948.75) includes 10 nights of lodging in a simple guest house, half board, round-trip transportation from Heathrow, and guided walking tours of around 5 hours a day. The tour is based in the alpine hamlet of Hinterzarten and includes trips to Lake Titisee and the Schlucksee (the largest lake in the Black Forest), as well as to the village of Breitnau and the nearby waterfall-filled gorges.

MOTORCYCLING   Guided motorcycle tours through Bavaria are the specialty of **Beach's Motorcycle Adventures,** 2763 W. River Pkwy., Grand Island, NY 14072 (☎ 716/773-4960). Two- to three-week tours on BMW bikes begin and end in Munich, with accommodations at small hotels and inns. Maps are provided, as well as information and suggestions for sightseeing and independent cruising along the way.

SAILING SCHOOLS   In the southern German region of the Allgäu there are more sailing schools than anywhere else in Germany. Sailing enthusiasts can take lessons at the recreational resort of Immenstadt on the region's largest natural lake, the Grosser Alpsee at the nearby **Segelschule** (Sailing School) in Bühl am Alpsee (☎ 08325/346). Lechbruck, on the upper Lech lake, has classes at **Segel und Windsurfschule** (☎ 08862/84-97). On the beautiful lake Constance, sailors can take advantage of the **Bodensee Yachtshule** (☎ 08382/94-45-88) in the delightful resort of Lindau.

WINTER SPORTS   More than 300 winter-sports resorts operate in the German Alps and wooded hill country such as the Harz Mountains and the Black Forest. In addition to outstanding ski slopes, trails, lifts, jumps, toboggan slides, and skating rinks, many larger resorts also offer ice hockey, ice boating, and bobsledding. Curling is very popular as well, especially in upper Bavaria. The Olympic sports facilities at

Germany for Jewish Visitors

In the last few years, Jews in Eastern Europe have decreased in population because of immigration; Jewish populations in some Western countries have also decreased because of intermarriage. Germany's Jewish population, on the other hand, is slowly increasing, mostly through immigration. It's estimated that there are between 40,000 and 80,000 Jews now living in the country, a figure that's nowhere near the pre-war high of 500,000, but that still represents significant growth. The most prominent of the new arrivals are from the ex-Soviet Union. Some 70% of Jews in such cities as Bremen and Hamburg are native Russian speakers.

The Jewish community in Berlin is the largest. Its 10,000 to 20,000 members are well served by several kosher restaurants, a Jewish high school, the new Mendelssohn Center at nearby Potsdam University, and both a weekly and monthly paper. Other important Jewish communities are located in Frankfurt (7,000), Munich (3,000), Düsseldorf (2,000), Stuttgart (1,600), Cologne (1,500), and Hamburg (1,500). Another 75 smaller communities are scattered throughout the country.

While anti-Semitism has not disappeared completely, in general, post-war Germany has worked hard to confront its past—far more so than Austria, for example. Some 30 museums today deal with Jewish issues, and former concentration camp sites display their grisly reminders to visitors. German high schools include Holocaust studies in their curriculum. In politics, there are about 80 extreme-right groups, 20 or so classified as neo-Nazi, with maybe 65,000 members, but this is in a country of more than 80 million people.

Berlin has the country's highest concentration of places of interest to Jewish visitors. The Jüdischer Friedhof at Weisensee, a suburb of Berlin, was Europe's largest Jewish cemetery, and today contains around 110,000 graves and a memorial to Jews murdered in the Nazi era. A darker sight is the chillingly elegant Wannsee Villa, overlooking the Wannsee Lake, where the "Final Solution" was formally proposed in January 1942. The most hopeful landmark is the newly renovated Orianburger Strasse Synagogue. Unlike the other five Berlin synagogues, this glorious and immense Moorish-style structure operates only as a memorial and museum. Berlin also has two museums dedicated to the city's Jews and many monuments, such as the Wives of Jewish Husbands Memorial, dedicated to the hundreds of non-Jewish women who demonstrated outside Gestapo headquarters in February 1943 after their husbands had been arrested.

Garmisch-Partenkirchen enjoy international renown, as do the ski jumps of Oberstdorf and the artificial-ice speed-skating rink at Inzell. More than 250 ski lifts are found in the German Alps, the Black Forest, and the Harz Mountains. Information on winter-sports facilities is available from local tourist bureaus and the offices of the German National Tourist Board (see "Visitor Information," above).

Garmisch-Partenkirchen (see chapter 8), is Germany's most famous winter sports center. Set in beautiful alpine scenery, this picturesque resort is close to Zugepitze, Germany's highest mountain. A mountain railway and a cable car can take you to the peak. In the town itself is the Olympic Ice Stadium, built in 1936, and the Ski Stadium, which has two jumps and a slalom course. Skiers of every level will be satisfied with the slopes on the mountain above the town. For information, contact the **Verkehrsamt** on Richard-Strauss-Platz (☎ **08821/18-06**).

7 Health & Insurance

STAYING HEALTHY

German medical facilities are among the best in the world. If a medical emergency arises, your hotel staff can usually put you in touch with a reliable doctor. If not, contact the American embassy or a consulate; each one maintains a list of English-speaking doctors. Medical and hospital services aren't free, so be sure that you have appropriate insurance coverage before you travel.

The water is safe to drink throughout Germany; however, do not drink the water in mountain streams, regardless of how clear and pure it looks.

If you suffer from a chronic illness, consult your doctor before your departure. For conditions like epilepsy, diabetes, or heart problems, wear a **Medic Alert Identification Tag** (☎ 800/825-3785; www.commedicalert.org), which will immediately alert doctors to your condition and give them access to your records through Medic Alert's 24-hour hot line. Membership is $35, plus a $15 annual fee.

Pack prescription medications in your carry-on luggage. Carry written prescriptions in generic, not brand-name form, and dispense all prescription medications from their original labeled vials. Also bring along copies of your prescriptions in case you lose your pills or run out.

Contact the **International Association for Medical Assistance to Travelers (IAMAT;** ☎ 716/754-4883 or 416/652-0137; www.sentex.net/~iamat). This organization offers tips on travel and health concerns in the countries you'll be visiting, and lists many local English-speaking doctors.

INSURANCE

There are three kinds of travel insurance: trip-cancellation, medical, and lost luggage coverage.

Trip-cancellation insurance is a good idea if you have paid a large portion of your vacation expenses up front, say, by purchasing a tour. Trip-cancellation insurance should cost approximately 6 to 8% of the total value of your vacation. (Don't buy it from your tour operator, though—talk about putting all your eggs in one basket!)

Your existing health insurance should cover you if you get sick while on vacation (though if you belong to an HMO, you should check to see whether you are fully covered when away from home). If you need hospital treatment, most health insurance plans and HMOs will cover out-of-country hospital visits and procedures, at least to some extent. However, most make you pay the bills up front at the time of care, and you'll get a refund after you've returned and filed all the paperwork. Members of **Blue Cross/Blue Shield** can now use their cards at select hospitals in most major cities worldwide (☎ 800/810-BLUE or www.bluecares.com/blue/bluecard/wwn for a list of hospitals). **Medicare** only covers U.S. citizens traveling in Mexico and Canada. For independent travel health-insurance providers, see below.

Your homeowner's insurance should cover stolen luggage. The airlines are responsible for $1,250 on domestic flights if they lose your luggage; if you plan to carry anything more valuable than that, keep it in your carry-on bag.

Check your existing policies before you buy additional insurance you might not need. But if you do require additional insurance, try one of the companies listed below: **Access America** (☎ 800/284-8300), **Travel Guard International** (☎ 800/826-1300), and **Travelex Insurance Services** (☎ 800/228-9792). In the U.K., there's **Columbus Travel Insurance** (☎ 0171/375-0011 in London; www2.columbusdirect.com/columbusdirect). Companies specializing in accident and medical care include: **MEDEX International** (☎ 888/MEDEX-00 or 410/453-6300; fax 410/ 453-6301;

www.medexassist.com); and **Travel Assistance International** (Worldwide Assistance Services, Inc.; ☎ **800/821-2828** or 202/828-5894; fax 202/828-5896).

8 Tips for Travelers with Special Needs

TIPS FOR TRAVELERS WITH DISABILITIES

Germany is one of the better countries for travelers with disabilities. In all the large cities, there are excellent facilities. The local tourist offices can issue permits for drivers, to allow them access to disabled parking areas. Older, smaller towns may pose more a problem, however, especially where the streets are cobblestone.

In any case, a disability shouldn't stop anyone from traveling. There are more resources out there than ever before. *A World of Options,* a 658-page book of resources for disabled travelers, covers everything from biking trips to scuba outfitters. It costs $35 ($30 for members) and is available from **Mobility International USA,** P.O. Box 10767, Eugene, OR 97440 (☎ **541/343-1284,** voice and TDD; www.miusa.org). Annual membership for Mobility International is $35, which includes their quarterly newsletter, *Over the Rainbow.*

The **Moss Rehab Hospital** (☎ **215/456-9600**) has been providing friendly and helpful phone advice and referrals to disabled travelers for years through its **Travel Information Service** (☎ **215/456-9603;** www.mossresourcenet.org).

You can join **The Society for the Advancement of Travel for the Handicapped (SATH),** 347 Fifth Ave. Suite 610, New York, NY 10016 (☎ **212/447-7284;** fax 212-725-8253; www.sath.org) for $45 annually, $30 for seniors and students, to gain access to a vast network of connections in the travel industry. The Society provides information sheets on travel destinations, and referrals to tour operators that specialize in traveling with disabilities. Its quarterly magazine, *Open World for Disability and Mature Travel,* is full of good information and resources. A year's subscription is $13 ($21 outside the U.S.).

Travelers with disabilities may also want to consider joining a tour that caters specifically to them. One of the best operators is **Flying Wheels Travel,** 143 West Bridge (P.O. Box 382), Owatonna, MN 55060 (☎ **800/535-6790**). It offers various escorted tours and cruises, as well as private tours in minivans with lifts. Other reputable specialized tour operators include **Access Adventures** (☎ **716/889-9096**), which offers sports-related vacations; **Accessible Journeys** (☎ **800/TINGLES** or 610/521-0339), for slow walkers and wheelchair travelers; **The Guided Tour,** Inc. (☎ **215/ 782-1370**); and **Directions Unlimited** (☎ **800/533-5343**).

Vision-impaired travelers should contact the **American Foundation for the Blind,** 11 Penn Plaza, Suite 300, New York, NY 10001 (☎ **800/232-5463**), for information on traveling with seeing-eye dogs.

British travelers with disabilities might contact **RADAR** (Royal Association for Disability and Rehabilitation), Unit 12, City Forum, 250 City Rd., London EC1V 8AF (☎ **0171/250-3222;** fax 0171/250-0212), which publishes vacation "fact packs," containing information on trip planning, travel insurance, specialized accommodations, and transportation abroad.

TIPS FOR GAY & LESBIAN TRAVELERS

Although Germany is one of the "gayest" countries of Europe, there is also prejudice and hostility here. Violence against gays and foreigners (especially nonwhite) is not unknown. On the other hand, homosexuality is widely accepted by a vast number of the country's millions, especially young people. All major cities, especially Berlin, have a wide and varied gay and lesbian nightlife. Keep in mind western Germany is far more gay-friendly than the more isolated outposts of the former East Germany. The legal minimum age for consensual homosexual sex is 18. Before you go, consider picking up a copy of *Frommer's Gay & Lesbian Europe.*

The **International Gay & Lesbian Travel Association (IGLTA; ☎ 800/ 448-8550** or 954/776-2626; fax 954/776-3303; www.iglta.org), with around 1,200 members, links travelers with appropriate gay-friendly service organizations or tour specialists. It offers quarterly newsletters, marketing mailings, and a membership directory. Most members are gay or lesbian businesses but individuals can join for $150 yearly, plus a $100 administration fee for new members. Members are kept informed of gay and gay-friendly hoteliers, tour operators, and airline and cruise-line representatives. Contact the IGLTA for a list of its member agencies, who will be tied into IGLTA's information resources.

General gay and lesbian travel agencies include **Family Abroad** (☎ **800/999-5500** or 212/459-1800; gay and lesbian); **Above and Beyond Tours** (☎ **800/397-2681;** mainly gay men); and **Yellowbrick Road** (☎ **800/642-2488;** gay and lesbian).

There are also two good, biannual English-language gay guidebooks, both focused on gay men but including information for lesbians as well. You can get the *Spartacus International Gay Guide* or *Odysseus* from most gay and lesbian book stores; or order them from Giovanni's Room (☎ **215/923-2960**) or from **A Different Light Bookstore** (☎ **800/343-4002** or 212/989-4850). Both lesbians and gays might want to pick up a copy of *Gay Travel A to Z* ($16). **The Ferrari Guides** (www.q-net.com) is yet another very good series of gay and lesbian guidebooks.

Out and About, 8 W. 19th St. no. 401, New York, NY 10011 (☎ **800/929-2268** or 212/645-6922), offers guidebooks and a monthly newsletter packed with good information on the global gay and lesbian scene. A year's subscription to the newsletter costs $49. *Our World,* 1104 North Nova Rd., Suite 251, Daytona Beach, FL 32117 (☎ **904/441-5367**), is a slicker monthly magazine promoting and highlighting travel bargains and opportunities. Annual subscription rates are $35 in the U.S., $45 outside the U.S.

TIPS FOR SENIORS

Don't be shy about asking for discounts, and always carry some kind of identification, such as a driver's license, that shows your date of birth. Many hotels and airlines offer special rates for seniors; ask when you make your reservations. In many cities, seniors qualify for reduced admission to theaters, museums, and other attractions, and discounted fares on public transportation.

Members of the **American Association of Retired Persons (AARP),** 601 E St. NW, Washington, DC 20049 (☎ **800/424-3410** or 202/434-2277), get discounts not only on hotels but on airfares and car rentals, too. AARP offers a wide range of special benefits, including *Modern Maturity* magazine and a monthly newsletter.

The National Council of Senior Citizens, 8403 Colesville Rd., Suite 1200, Silver Spring, MD 20910 (☎ **301/578-8800**), a nonprofit organization, offers a newsletter six times a year (partly devoted to travel tips) and discounts on hotel and auto rentals; annual dues are $13 per person or couple.

Mature Outlook, P.O. Box 9390, Des Moines, IA 50306 (☎ **800/336-6330**), began as a travel organization for people over 50, though it now caters to people of all ages. Members receive a bimonthly magazine and discounts on hotels (as well as free coupons for discounts from Sears). Annual membership is $19.95.

Golden Companions, P.O. Box 5249, Reno, NV 89513 (☎ **702/324-2227**), helps travelers 45-plus find compatible companions through a personal voice-mail service. Contact them for more information.

Another helpful publication is ***101 Tips for the Mature Traveler,*** available from **Grand Circle Travel,** 347 Congress St., Suite 3A, Boston, MA 02210 (☎ **800/ 221-2610** or 617/350-7500; fax 617/346-6700).

Grand Circle Travel is also one of the hundreds of travel agencies specializing in vacations for seniors, but many of these packages are of the tour-bus variety, with free trips thrown in for those who organize groups of 10 or more. Seniors seeking more independent travel should probably consult a regular travel agent. **SAGA International Holidays,** 222 Berkeley St., Boston, MA 02116 (☎ **800/343-0273**), offers inclusive tours and cruises for those 50 and older. SAGA also sponsors the more substantial "Road Scholar Tours" (☎ **800/621-2151**), which are fun-loving but with an educational bent.

If you want something more than the average vacation or guided tour, try **Elderhostel,** 75 Federal St., Boston, MA 02110-1941 (☎ **877/426-8056;** www. elderhostel.org), or the University of New Hampshire's **Interhostel** (☎ **800/733-9753**), both variations on the same theme: educational travel for senior citizens. On these escorted tours, the days are packed with seminars, lectures, and field trips, and all sightseeing is led by academic experts. Elderhostel arranges study programs around the world for those aged 55 and over (and a spouse or companion of any age). Most courses last about 3 weeks and many include airfare, accommodations in student dormitories or modest inns, meals, and tuition. Write or call for a free catalog, which lists upcoming courses and destinations. Interhostel takes travelers 50 and over (with companions over 40), and offers 2- and 3-week trips, mostly international.

9 Getting There

BY PLANE

Flying time to Frankfurt is about 7½ hours from New York, 10 hours from Chicago, and 12 hours from Los Angeles. There are also nonstop flights from the U.S. to Munich and Düsseldorf (though not to Berlin).

Lufthansa (☎ **800/645-3880;** www.lufthansa-usa.com) operates the most frequent service and flies to the greatest number of Germany's airports. From North America, Lufthansa serves 16 gateway cities, 12 of which are in the United States. In any season, there are more than 100 weekly flights from these cities to Germany. The largest of the gateways is the New York City area, where flights depart from both JFK and Newark airports. From JFK there are daily flights to Frankfurt and Düsseldorf; after a brief touchdown in Düsseldorf, the Lufthansa flight continues to Munich. From Newark, Lufthansa offers daily flights to Frankfurt and Munich. Lufthansa's other gateways include Atlanta, Boston, Chicago, Dallas/Fort Worth, Detroit, Houston, Los Angeles, Miami, Philadelphia, San Francisco, and Washington, D.C. Lufthansa also flies to Germany from Toronto, Vancouver, Calgary, and Mexico City. The airline has a 10% discount for seniors over 62; the reduction applies to a traveling companion as well.

Lufthansa recently entered into an alliance with **United Airlines** and **Air Canada** to provide seamless air service to Germany and other parts of the globe from North America. Dubbed "Star Alliance," the union allows cross-airline benefits, including travel on one or all of these airlines on one ticket and frequent-flyer credit to the participating airline of your choice. The Star Alliance also includes Scandinavian Airlines System, Thai Airways International, and Varig.

American Airlines (☎ **800/443-7300;** www.americanair.com) flies nonstop to Frankfurt daily from both Dallas/Fort Worth and Chicago. Nonstop daily service is also available between Miami and Frankfurt. From Frankfurt, Düsseldorf, and London, among others, American's flights connect easily with ongoing flights to many other German cities on Lufthansa or British Airways.

Continental Airlines (☎ 800/231-0856; www.flycontinental.com) offers daily nonstop service between Newark, New Jersey, and Frankfurt. The airline maintains excellent connections between Newark and its hubs in Cleveland and Houston. Continental also offers discounts and other benefits to seniors 62 and over and to their traveling companions, regardless of age.

From the Delta Flight Center at JFK airport in New York, **Delta Airlines** (☎ 800/241-4141; www.delta-air.com) offers daily service to both Frankfurt and (via Brussels) Hamburg. Delta is especially strong in service to Germany from its home base in Atlanta, with two nonstops a day to Frankfurt and daily nonstops to Munich, as well as Hamburg via Brussels, and Stuttgart via Amsterdam. Delta also offers frequent nonstops to Frankfurt from Cincinnati (one of its major midwestern hubs).

, If you fly one of **KLM**'s (☎ 800/374-7747; www.klm.nl) frequent nonstop flights into Amsterdam from New York's JFK and from Atlanta, you can include a stopover in Holland. From Amsterdam, many flights on both KLM and Lufthansa fly into all the major cities of Germany. Flights to Germany on **Northwest Airlines** (☎ 800/225-2525), KLM's partner, are available out of Boston and Washington, D.C.

United Airlines (☎ 800/538-2929; www.ual.com) offers daily nonstops from Washington, D.C., and Chicago to Frankfurt. Furthermore, because of the Star Alliance, discussed above, all German flights by Lufthansa or Air Canada will also be honored as a part of a United ticket. If you're interested in taking advantage of the Star Alliance, be sure to notify the United ticket agent when you are booking or inquiring about your flight.

From London, **British Airways** (☎ 0141/222-2345 in London, or 0345/ 222-111 inside the U.K.; www.british-airways.com) and **Lufthansa** (☎ 0345/737-747 inside the U.K.) are the most convenient carriers to the major German cities, including Düsseldorf, Cologne, Frankfurt, Munich, and Berlin. BA has seven flights a day to Cologne (flying time: 75 min.), five flights a day to Munich (1 hr. and 40 min.), and four nonstop and three one-stop flights to Berlin (1 hr. and 40 min.). It also services Bremen, Hannover, and Stuttgart as well. **British Midland** (☎ 0181/745-7321 in London, or 0345/554-554 inside the U.K.) has two daily flights to Cologne, four daily flights to Frankfurt, and one daily flight to Dresden.

From Ireland, **Aer Lingus** (☎ 01/886-8888) flies between Dublin and Frankfurt and Düsseldorf; **Lufthansa** (☎ 01/844-5544) flies from Frankfurt to Dublin. From Australia, **Qantas** (☎ 13-13-13 in Australia) flies from both Melbourne and Sydney to Frankfurt via Asia. Lufthansa no longer flies from Australia to Germany, but it does offer cheap fares in conjunction with Qantas.

FLYING FOR LESS: TIPS FOR GETTING THE BEST AIRFARES

1. **Keep your eyes peeled for sales.** Check your newspaper for advertised discounts or call the airlines directly and ask if any promotional rates or special fares are available. If you already hold a ticket when a sale breaks, it may even pay to exchange your ticket, which usually incurs a charge of $50 to $75. You'll never see sales in summer or around the Christmas holidays, but there have been amazing bargains in late winter, spring, and fall for the last few years.

   Note, however, that the lowest-priced fares are often nonrefundable, require advance purchase of 1 to 3 weeks and a certain length of stay, and carry penalties for changing dates of travel.

2. **Ask the reservations agent lots of questions.** If your schedule is flexible, ask if you can secure a cheaper fare by staying an extra day or by flying midweek. Many airlines won't volunteer this information, so you've got to be persistent on the phone.

3. **Consolidators,** also known as bucket shops, are a good place to find low fares. Consolidators buy seats in bulk from the airlines and then sell them back to the public at prices below even the airlines' discounted rates. Their small boxed ads usually run in the Sunday travel section at the bottom of the page. Before you pay a consolidator, however, ask for a record locator number and confirm your seat with the airline itself. Be prepared to book your ticket with a different consolidator—there are many to choose from—if the airline can't confirm your reservation. Also be aware that bucket shop tickets are usually nonrefundable or rigged with stiff cancellation penalties, often as high as 50% to 75% of the ticket price.

   Council Travel (☎ 800/226-8624; www.counciltravel.com) and **STA Travel** (☎ 800/781-4040; www.sta.travel.com) cater especially to young travelers, but their bargain basement prices are available to people of all ages. **Travel Bargains** (☎ 800/AIR-FARE; www.1800airfare.com) was formerly owned by TWA but now offers the deepest discounts on many other airlines, with a 4-day advance purchase. Other reliable consolidators include **1-800-FLY-CHEAP** (www. 1800flycheap.com); **TFI Tours International** (☎ 800-745-8000 or 212/ 736-1140), which serves as a clearinghouse for unused seats; or "rebators" such as **Travel Avenue** (☎ 800/333-3335 or 312/876-1116) and the **Smart Traveller** (☎ 800/448-3338 in the U.S. or 305/448-3338; www.smarttraveller@juno. com), which rebate part of their commissions to you.

4. **Surf the Web for bargains.** (But always check the lowest published fare before you shop for flights online, so you know if you're getting a deal.) See the Online Directory at the end of this book for lots of advice on how to use the Internet to your best advantage; it goes into much greater detail than we can here. However, just to mention a couple of sites briefly, good bets include **Arthur Frommer's Budget Travel** (www.frommers.com), **Microsoft Expedia** (www.expedia.com), **Yahoo**'s Travel Page (www.yahoo.com), **Travelocity** (www.travelocity.com), and **Trip.com** (www.trip.com). Several major airlines offer a free e-mail service known as **E-Savers,** via which they'll send you their best bargain airfares on a regular basis. It's really a service for the spontaneously inclined and travelers looking for a quick getaway. But the fares are cheap, so it's worth taking a look. See the Web addresses given above for each airline.

5. **Consider a charter flight.** Most charter operators advertise and sell their seats through travel agents, so they're your best source of information for available flights. Before deciding to take a charter flight, however, check the restrictions on the ticket: You may be asked to purchase a tour package, to pay in advance, to be amenable if the day of departure is changed, to pay a service charge, to fly on an airline you're not familiar with (this usually is not the case), and to pay harsh penalties if you cancel—but be understanding if the charter doesn't fill up and is canceled up to 10 days before departure. Summer charters fill up more quickly than others and are almost sure to fly, but if you decide on a charter flight, seriously consider cancellation and baggage insurance.

   Among charter-flight operators is **Council Charter,** a subsidiary of the Council on International Educational Exchange (CIEE), 205 E. 42nd St., New York, NY 10017 (☎ 212/822-2700). This outfit can arrange charter seats to most major European cities, including Madrid, on regularly scheduled aircrafts. Another big charter operator is **Travac,** 989 Sixth Ave., 16th Floor, New York, NY 10018 (☎ 800/TRAV-800 or 212/563-3303).

   Be warned: Some charter companies have proved unreliable in the past.

BY TRAIN

Many passengers, especially holders of the **Eurailpass,** travel to Germany by train from other European cities. (See "Getting Around," below, for information on purchasing the Eurailpass and other rail passes.)

British Rail runs four trains a day to Germany from Victoria Station in **London,** going by way of the Ramsgate-Ostend ferry or jetfoil. Two trains depart from London's Liverpool Street Station, via Harwich-Hook of Holland. Most trains change at Cologne for destinations elsewhere in Germany. Tickets can be purchased through British Rail travel centers in London (☎ 0990/484-950 in the U.K., or 01603/ 764-776). See "Under the Channel," below, for information about the Eurostar service running between London and Brussels via the Channel Tunnel.

Train journeys can be lengthy. If you go by jetfoil, Cologne is 9½ hours away from London; by Dover-Ostend ferry, it's 12½ hours; and via the Ramsgate-Ostend ferry, it's 13 hours. Berlin can be reached in about 20 hours. Travel from London to Munich, depending on the connection, can take from 18 to 22 hours. It's often cheaper to fly from London to Munich than to take the train.

From **Paris** several trains depart throughout the day for points east, fanning out across eastern France to virtually every part of Germany. The most glamorous of these is the **Orient Express,** which departs from the Gare de l'Est around 6pm, arriving in Munich around 3am. For railway information on the French rail lines anywhere in Europe, call ☎ 08-36-35-35-35. Likewise, trains depart from throughout Austria, Italy, Holland, Denmark, and the Czech Republic for all points in Germany, interconnecting into one of the most efficient, and densely routed, rail networks in the world. For information and timetables prior to your departure, call **RailEurope** at ☎ 800/438-7245.

The Bavaria (☎ 01-57-22-22) leaves Zurich at 7:30am daily, reaching Munich at 11:52am. The **Helvetia Express** (same phone number as The Bavaria) leaves Zurich daily at 11:57am, arriving in Hannover at 6:13pm and in Hamburg at 7:28pm.

BY CAR & FERRY

If you want to bring your car over from England, you face a choice of ports, from which you'll continue on driving to Germany. **P & O Stenna Lines** (☎ 800/ 677-8585 for North American reservations, or 0870/600-0600 in the U.K.) has 30 to 35 ferryboat crossings a day, depending on the season, between Dover in England and Calais in northeastern France. The crossing can take as little as 1 hour and 15 minutes. Other options involve passage through the Netherlands from Harwich, in the east of England, to the Hook of Holland, for a sea crossing of about 8 hours. Once in Calais, the drive to Cologne in Germany takes about 3 hours. You can also take your car via the Chunnel (see below).

BY BUS (COACH)

You can travel by bus to Germany's major cities from London, Paris, and many other cities in Europe. The continent's largest bus operator is **Eurolines,** 52 Grosvenor Gardens, London SW1W 0AU, which operates out of Victoria Coach Station in Central London. In Paris, the Eurolines office is within a 35-minute subway ride from Central Paris, at 28, avenue du Général-de-Gaulle, 93541 Bagnolet; Métro stop: Gallieni. For information about Eurolines in Britain, call ☎ 0990/143-219. For information about Eurolines in France, call ☎ 08/36-69-52-52. For information about Eurolines in Germany, contact **Deutsche Touring** (Eurolines Stadtböro), Am Römerhof 17, 60426 Frankfurt am Main (☎ 069/7-90-30). Eurolines does not maintain a U.S.-based sales agent, but many travel agents can arrange for a ticket on the bus lines that link Europe's major cities.

Buses on long-haul journeys are equipped with toilets and partially reclining seats. They stop for 60-minute breaks every 4 hours for rest and refreshment. At press time, the fare between Paris and Frankfurt was 88DM ($50.15) one-way, or 158DM ($90.05) round-trip; between Paris and Munich, it was 117DM ($66.70) one-way, or 211DM ($120.25) round-trip; between London and Frankfurt, it was 120DM ($68.40) one-way, or 194DM ($110.60) round-trip; between London and Munich, it was 142DM ($80.95) one-way, or 218DM ($124.25) round-trip. Note that the prices above are subject to change without notice, and often fluctuate from month to month. Discounts are sometimes available if you buy well in advance. In addition, discounts of around 20% are sometimes offered for bus passengers under age 26.

Buses from London to Frankfurt depart every evening; buses from London to Munich depart three times a week. The Frankfurt-bound itinerary from London leads through Ramsgate to the Belgian port of Ostend, then through Brussels and the historic German cities of Aachen, Cologne, Bonn, and Koblenz.

UNDER THE CHANNEL

The $15 billion **Channel Tunnel** (or "Chunnel"), one of the great engineering feats of all time, is the first link between Britain and the Continent since the Ice Age. The tunnel was built beneath the seabed through a layer of impermeable chalk marl and sealed with a reinforced concrete lining. The 31-mile journey between Great Britain and France takes 35 minutes, although actual time in the Chunnel is only 19 minutes. Once on the Continent, you can make a connection to Germany fairly easily.

Rail Europe sells tickets on the **Eurostar** direct train service between London and Paris or Brussels (☎ 800/94-CHUNNEL for information). A round-trip first-class fare between London and Paris costs $298, $278 in regular second class. In the United Kingdom, make reservations for **Eurostar** at ☎ 0345/303030; in Paris at ☎ 01-33-31-58-03; and in the United States at ☎ 800/677-8585. A journey from London to Paris via the Chunnel takes about the same amount of time as flying, if you calculate door-to-door travel time. Trains leave from London's Waterloo Station and arrive in Paris at the Gare du Nord.

The tunnel also accommodates passenger cars, charter buses, taxis, and motorcycles from Folkestone, England, to Calais, France. It operates 24 hours a day, 365 days a year, running every 15 minutes during peak travel times and at least once an hour at night. Tickets may be purchased at the toll booth. Contact **Le Shuttle** (☎ 800/4-EURAIL in the U.S. and Canada; 01304/288617 or 0990/353535 in England).

ESCORTED TOURS

Escorted tours may not be the option for you if you like to go your own way and be spontaneous. But some people love them. They let you relax and take in the sights while a bus driver fights traffic for you; they spell out your costs up front; and they take you to the maximum number of sights in the minimum amount of time with the least amount of hassle. If you do choose an escorted tour, you should ask a few simple questions before you buy:

1. What is the **cancellation policy**? Do they require a deposit? Can they cancel the trip if they don't get enough people? Do you get a refund if they cancel? If you cancel? How late can you cancel if you are unable to go? When do you pay in full?

2. How busy is the **schedule**? How much sightseeing do they plan each day? Do they allow ample time for relaxing by the pool, shopping, or wandering?

3. What is the **size** of the group? The smaller the group, the more flexible the itinerary, and the less time you'll spend waiting for people to get on and off the bus.

Tour operators may be evasive about this, but they should be able to give you a rough estimate. Some tours have a minimum group size and may cancel the tour if they don't book enough people.

4. What is included in the **price**? Don't assume anything. You may have to pay for transportation to and from the airport. A box lunch may be included in an excursion, but drinks might cost extra. Beer might be included, but wine might not. Can you opt out of certain activities, or does the bus leave once a day, with no exceptions? Are all your meals planned in advance? Can you choose your entree at dinner, or does everybody get the same chicken cutlet?

Note: If you choose an escorted tour, think strongly about purchasing travel insurance from an independent agency, especially if the tour operator asks you to pay up front. See the section on insurance earlier in this chapter. One final caveat: Since escorted tour prices are based on double occupancy, the single traveler is usually penalized.

American Express Vacations (☎ 800/446-6234 in the U.S. and Canada) is one of the biggest tour operators in the world. Its offerings are comprehensive, and unescorted customized package tours are available, too. **Brendan Tours** (☎ 800/421-8446) has a selection of 9- to 15-day tours. **Caravan Tours** (☎ 800/227-2826) offers tours of southern Germany and Austria, many of which begin and end in Berlin. Accommodations are at the better hotels, and rates include everything except airfare. **Collette Tours** (☎ 800/832-4656) has an Alpine Countries tour that covers southern Germany, Austria, and Switzerland. **Globus** (☎ 800/338-7092) offers 8- to 16-day tours of various parts of Germany. It also has a budget branch that offers tours at lower rates; all are escorted. **Maupintour** (☎ 800/255-4266) has a selection of upscale tours, such as a Rhine River tour of Berlin, Dresden, Meissen, Nürnberg, and Heidelberg, or an 18-day tour that goes from Vienna to Amsterdam. **Tauck Tours** (☎ 800/468-2825) has a wide selection of escorted tours, such as the 14-day Romantic Germany tour from Frankfurt to Berlin, with stops in Dresden, Heidelberg, and Oberammergau. Most meals are included in the rates, but airfare is extra.

Two companies offer superdeluxe tours (with prices to match). **Abercrombie & Kent** (☎ 630/954-2944) provides group tours to various areas of Germany and will customize to suit your needs. **Travcoa** (☎ 800/992-2003) offers top-of-the-line coach tours, such as a 16-day tour of Ludwig's castles and the Romantic Road, which begins in Munich and ends in Strasbourg, France.

Cruises

Germany's premier cruise carrier is **KD River Cruises of Europe.** For information, contact the carrier at 323 Geary St., Suite 603, San Francisco, CA 94102 (☎ 800/858-8587 or 415/392-8817), or 2500 Westchester Ave., Suite 113, Purchase, NY 10577 (☎ 800/346-6525).

Luxury 8- to 10-day cruises on the Rhine, Main, and Danube Rivers are also available through **Euro Cruises,** 303 W. 13th St., New York, NY 10014 (☎ 800/688-3876). These cruises feature optional shore excursions. All cabins have twin beds and windows. **Jody Lexow Yacht Charter** rents hotel barges (including crew, food, and beverages) and smaller self-drive craft for touring the canals and rivers of Germany. For additional information, contact 26 Coddington Wharf, Newport, RI 02840 (☎ 800/662-2628). **Etoile de Champagne,** 88 Broad St., Boston, MA 02110 (☎ 800/280-1492), can arrange a 6-night luxury barge cruise that runs from Trier to Koblenz, with daily excursion stops along the way.

Groups of 12 to 16 people can arrange 7- to 14-day tours of European breweries, both well-known and off the beaten track, through **MIR Corporation** (☎ **800/ 424-7289**). The tours begin in many European cities.

PACKAGE DEALS

See "By Plane," above; most airlines offer packages that may include car rentals and accommodations in addition to your airfare. For example, **Delta Vacations** (☎ **800/ 221-6666**) offers both fly/drive and fly/rail packages, plus 3-day "city sprees" in Berlin, Frankfurt, and Munich.

DER Tours (☎ **800/782-2424** or 847/692-4141) offers discounted airfares, car rentals, hotel packages, short regional tours, and GermanRail, Eurail, and other rail passes.

10 Getting Around

BY PLANE

From Frankfurt am Main, most **Lufthansa** (☎ **800/645-3880**) destinations in Germany can be reached in an average of 50 minutes, with at least four flights daily.

All German cities with commercial airports have an airport shuttle service, offering reduced fares and fast connections between the city proper and the airport. Departure points are usually the airlines' town offices and the city's main rail terminal. Luggage can be checked at the DB (GermanRail) baggage counter at the airport for delivery to the railroad station at your ultimate destination.

The **Lufthansa Airport Express** is a high-speed train that travels between the Frankfurt and Düsseldorf airports, with stops at Bonn, Stuttgart, Dortmund, and Cologne, incidentally giving the traveler an opportunity to view the Rhine Valley.

BY TRAIN

Whether you travel first or second class, you'll find that the trains of **GermanRail** (**DER Rail**) deserve their good reputation for comfort, cleanliness, and punctuality. All are modern and fast. Both first- and second-class trains carry smoker and non-smoker compartments. A snack bar or a dining car, serving German and international cuisine as well as good wine and beer, can usually be found on all trains except locals.

For city sightseeing, you can leave your baggage in a locker or check it at the station's baggage counter. In many cities, GermanRail provides door-to-door baggage service, allowing passengers to have luggage picked up at or delivered to their hotels. Accompanying baggage can be checked for a nominal fee. Suitcases, baby carriages, skis, bicycles, and steamer trunks are permitted as baggage. Insurance policies of various kinds, including a travel medical plan, are also available.

About 20,000 **InterCity (IC)** passenger trains offer express service every hour between most large and medium-size German cities. IC trains have adjustable cushioned seats and individual reading lights, and often offer telephone and secretarial services. Bars, lounges, and dining rooms are available too. A network of **EuroCity trains (EC)** connecting Germany with 13 other countries offers the same high standards of service as those of IC.

Germany's high-speed rail network, known as **InterCity Express (ICE)** trains, is among the fastest in Europe, reaching speeds of 165 miles per hour. One of these trains runs from Hamburg through Würzburg and Nürnberg to Munich; another goes from Frankfurt through Stuttgart to Munich; and yet another runs from Berlin to Munich via Frankfurt. Each train makes stops along the way. An ICE significantly reduces travel time from point to point, making transits north to south across the country easily possible in the course of a single day. Some 200 east-west connections have been added to the GermanRail timetable to link the Deutsche Bundesbahn (west) and the Deutsche Reichsbahn (east). Additional connections make Leipzig and Dresden more accessible.

The **InterCity Night (ICN)**—one of the most comfortable night trains in Europe—operates between Berlin and Bonn and Berlin and Munich. Even though the train doesn't depart until 10 or 11pm (depending on the city and station), you may board as early as 8 or 8:30pm. Arrival the next morning is between 6:55 and 7:55am, and you have the option of remaining aboard until 9 or 9:30am.

The ICN offers first and tourist class. Sleeping accommodations in first class include single or double sleeping compartments with shower and toilet. The compartments are equipped with key cards, phones for wake-up service, luggage storage, and other amenities. Tourist class offers open seating with sleeperettes (reclining seats). The ICN is equipped with a restaurant and bistro car, and breakfast buffet is included in the first-class fare. For an extra cost, a limited menu for dinner is offered. Advance reservations are mandatory for all sleeping accommodations.

DER Rail issues tickets for the ICN and also makes reservations. Eurail and GermanRail pass holders are accepted on this train but have to pay for the seat or sleeper reservation and also for meals. Youth-pass holders are only accepted in tourist class. Children under the age of 4 travel free, provided they do not require a separate seat; those between 4 and 12 are charged half fare.

Travelers wanting to avoid the fatigue of long-distance driving can reach their destination by taking themselves and their cars on car-sleeper **Auto Trains.** Some daytime automobile trains are also operated.

Before leaving for Germany, you can get complete details about the **German Federal Railroad** and the many plans it offers, as well as information about Eurailpasses, at 500 Mamaroneck Ave, suite 314, Harrison, NY 10528 (☎ **800-4-EURAIL** in the U.S., or 800/555-2748 in Canada).

If you plan to travel a great deal on German railroads, it's worth buying a copy of the *Thomas Cook European Timetable of European Passenger Railroads*. It's available exclusively in North America from **Forsyth Travel Library,** 226 Westchester Ave., White Plains, NY 10604 (☎ **800/FORSYTH**), at a cost of $27.95, plus $4.95 postage (priority airmail) in the United States or $6.95 U.S. to Canada.

GERMANRAIL TOURIST PASSES

You can buy a **GermanRail Pass** from a travel agent before you leave home. The pass allows 4 days of travel in 1 month, and costs $252 for first-class travel or $174 for second class. Additional days cost $32 in first class and $22 in second class.

A youth version of the same pass, valid only for persons under 26 years of age and available only in second class, costs $138 for 4 days in 1 month, $156 for 5 days in 1 month, $162 for 6 days in 1 month, $174 for 7 days in 1 month, $186 for 8 days in 1 month, $198 for 9 days in 1 month, and $210 for 10 days in 1 month. Another bargain is a **Twinpass,** for two adults traveling together. This pass costs $378 for 3 days in 1 month for first-class travel or $261 for second class. Additional days cost $48 for two in first class or $33 in second class.

The passes also entitle the bearer to additional benefits, such as free or discounted travel on selected bus routes operated by Deutsche Touring/Europabus, including destinations not serviced by trains, or excursions along particularly scenic highways such as the Romantic Road and the Castle Road. The pass also includes free travel on **KD German Line steamers** (day trips only) along the Rhine, Main, and Mosel Rivers.

These passes are most conveniently available from **Rail Europe** (☎ **800/ 4-EURAIL** in the U.S., or 800/361-RAIL in Canada). Rail Europe can also arrange cost-effective "Rail and Drive" packages that combine a certain number of days on the train with a certain number of days in a rental car. Here's an example of how it might work: Ride the train from Frankfurt to Munich, spend 3 days exploring the city, then rent a car for a 2-day excursion to Berchtesgaden and the Bavarian Alps. The GermanRail Flexipass is also sold by **DER Travel** (☎ **800/782-2424** in the U.S. and Canada) and by **CIT Travel** (☎ **800/248-7245** in the U.S. and Canada, or 847/318-7101 in Chicago).

EURAILPASSES

The Eurailpass is one of Europe's greatest bargains, permitting unlimited first-class rail travel through 17 countries in Europe, including Germany. Passes are for periods as short as 15 days or as long as 3 months and are strictly nontransferable.

The **Eurailpass** is sold only outside of Europe. It costs $554 for 15 days, $718 for 21 days, $890 for 1 month, $1,260 for 2 months, and $1,558 for 3 months. Children 3 and under travel free providing they don't occupy a seat (otherwise they're charged half fare); children 4 to 11 are charged half fare. If you're under 26, you can purchase a **Eurail Youthpass,** entitling you to unlimited second-class travel for $388 for 15 days, $499 for 21 days, $623 for 1 month, $882 for 2 months, and $1,089 for 3 months.

Seat reservations are required on some trains. Many of the trains have *couchettes* (sleeping cars), which cost extra. Obviously, the 2- or 3-month traveler gets the greatest economic advantages; the Eurailpass is ideal for such extensive trips. With the pass you can visit all of Germany's major sights, from Lake Constance to Saxony, then end your vacation in Norway, for example. Eurailpass holders are entitled to considerable reductions on certain buses and ferries as well.

If you'll be traveling for 2 weeks or a month, think carefully before you buy a pass. To get full advantage of a pass for 15 days or a month, you'll have to spend a great deal of time on the train.

The **Eurail Flexipass** allows you to travel through Europe with more flexibility. It's valid in first class and offers the same privileges as the Eurailpass. However, it provides a number of individual travel days that you can use over a much longer period of consecutive days. That makes it possible to stay in one city and yet not lose a single day of travel. There are two passes: 10 days of travel in 2 months for $654, and 15 days of travel in 2 months for $862. The **Eurail Youth Flexipass** is identical except that it's sold only to travelers under 26, and costs less: $458 for 10 days of travel within 2 months, and $599 for 15 days of travel within 2 months.

Another good option is the **Europass,** which is similar to the Eurailpass but covers fewer countries: Germany, France, Switzerland, Italy, and Spain (other countries may be added on at an additional cost). All passes are good for 2 months. Two adults can travel in first class for any 5 days during this period for $348; 6 days, $368; 8 days, $448; 10 days, $528; and 15 days, $728.

WHERE TO BUY RAIL PASSES

Travel agents in all towns and railway agents in major North American cities sell all these tickets, but the biggest supplier is **Rail Europe** (☎ **800/438-7245;** www.raileurope.com), which can also give you informational brochures.

For British travelers, an especially convenient outlet for buying railway tickets is opposite Platform 2 in Victoria Station, London. **Wasteels Ltd.** (☎ **0171/834-6744**) will provide railway-related services and discuss the various types of fares and rail passes and their drawbacks; its staff generally spends a bit more time with a client while planning an itinerary. Depending on circumstances, Wasteels sometimes charges a £5 fee for its services, but for the information available, the money is well spent.

Many different rail passes are available in the United Kingdom for travel in Britain and continental Europe. Stop in at the **International Rail Centre,** Victoria Station, London SWIV 1JY (☎ **0990/848848** in the U.K., or 0171/834-2345). Some of the most popular passes, including Inter-Rail and Euro Youth, are offered only to travelers under 26 years of age; these allow unlimited second-class travel through most European countries.

BY CAR

British travelers who want to bring their own cars over should see "Getting There," earlier in this chapter.

Competition in the European car-rental industry is fierce, so make sure you comparison shop. You can make reservations by calling these toll-free numbers: **Avis** (☎ **800/331-2112**), **Budget** (☎ **800/472-3325**), **Hertz** (☎ **800/654-3001**), **Kemwel Holiday Autos** (☎ **800/678-0678**), and **Auto Europe** (☎ **800/223-5555**). Cars can often be rented at one German city and returned at another for no additional charge.

There are some advantages to **prepaying rentals** in dollars before leaving the United States. You get an easy-to-understand net price (which you have to prepay at least 14 days before departure by credit card), the rental process is more streamlined, and you can avoid unpleasant surprises caused by sudden unfavorable changes in currency exchange rates. Remember, however, that if you opt to prepay and your plans change, you'll have to go through some rather complicated paperwork (and, in some cases, have to pay a penalty of around $25) for changing or canceling a prepaid contract.

A **collision-damage waiver (CDW)** is an optional insurance policy that can be purchased when you sign a rental agreement. For an extra fee, the rental agency agrees to eliminate all but a small percentage of your financial responsibility for collision damage in case of an accident. If you don't have a CDW and do have an accident, you'll usually pay for all damages, up to the cost of actually replacing the vehicle if the accident is serious enough. Some credit cards (especially gold cards) cover the CDW, so call your company to check on these benefits before you spend the extra money on additional insurance. However, note that credit card companies do *not* cover liability if you injure someone, so unless you have your own car insurance that will cover you abroad, you may want to take the extra liability coverage.

Some Driving Tips

GASOLINE Gasoline is readily available throughout Germany, and service stations appear frequently along the Autobahns. The cheapest gasoline is at stations marked SB-TANKEN or self-service, but remember that gas will always be much more expensive than in the U.S. A liter (about a fourth of a gallon) costs 1.30DM to 1.70DM (75¢ to 95¢). Gasoline pumps labeled BLEIFREI offer unleaded gas.

DRIVING RULES In Germany, you drive on the right side of the road. Both front-seat and back-seat passengers are required to wear safety belts. Children cannot ride in the front seat.

Easy-to-understand international road signs are posted, but U.S. travelers should remember that road signs are in kilometers, not miles. In congested areas, the speed limit is about 50 kilometers per hour (around 30 m.p.h.). On all other roads except the Autobahns, the speed limit is 100 kilometers per hour (about 60 m.p.h.).

In theory, there is no speed limit on the Autobahns (in the left, fast lane), but many drivers going too fast report that they have been stopped by the police and fined on the spot. So reasonable caution is recommended here, for safety if not other reasons. A German driver on the Autobahn can be a ferocious creature, and you may prefer the slow lane. The government recommends an Autobahn speed limit of 130 kilometers per hour (80 m.p.h.).

Note: Drinking while driving is a very serious offense in Germany. Be sure to keep any alcoholic beverages in the trunk or some other storage area.

BREAKDOWNS/ASSISTANCE   The major automobile club in Germany is **Automobilclub von Deutschland (AvD),** Lyoner Strasse 16, 60329 Frankfurt (☎ **069/6-60-60**). If you have a breakdown on the Autobahn, you can call from an emergency phone, each of which is spaced about a mile apart. On secondary roads, go to the nearest phone. If you don't belong to an auto club, call ☎ **01309/0-99-11.** In English, ask for "road service assistance." Emergency assistance is free, but you pay for parts or materials.

MAPS   The best maps, available at all major bookstores throughout Germany, are published by **Michelin,** which offers various regional maps. **Hallweg** also offers good maps.

DRIVER'S LICENSES   American drivers, and those from EU countries, need only a domestic license to drive. However, both in Germany and throughout the rest of Europe, you must also have an international insurance certificate, known as a green card *(carte verte).* Any car-rental agency will automatically provide one of these as a standard part of the rental contract, but it's a good idea to double-check all documents at the time of rental, just to be sure that you can identify the card if asked by border patrol or the police.

BY BUS

An excellent, efficient bus network services Germany. Many buses are operated by **Bahnbus,** which is owned by the railway. These are integrated to complement the rail service. Bus service in Germany is particularly convenient during slow periods of rail service, normally around midday and on Saturday and Sunday. German post offices often operate local bus services (contact local post offices for schedules and prices).

The most popular bus ride is along the Romantic Road (see chapter 6), where special green-and-white buses carry tourists regularly from town to town. For more information, ask a travel agent or call **Deutsche Touring GmbH** (☎ **069/79-03-50**), Amrömerhof 17, Frankfurt.

BY BOAT

Perhaps Germany's most beautiful features are its lakes and rivers. The mighty Rhine is the country's most traveled waterway. German cruise ships also run on the Main River between Mainz and Frankfurt; on the Danube from Nürnberg to Linz (Austria), going on to Vienna and Budapest; and on the Mosel between Cochem and Trier.

KD River Cruises of Europe operates the most services. Eurailpasses are valid for most KD excursions. The company also offers luxury cruises, the most popular being a 5-day cruise along the Rhine from Amsterdam to Basel or vice versa. For more information, contact KD River Cruises of Europe, 323 Geary St., Suite 603, San Francisco, CA 94102 (☎ **800/858-8587** or 415/392-8817), or 2500 Westchester Ave., Suite 113, Purchase, NY 10577 (☎ **800/346-6525**).

BY BICYCLE

For information about biking, write to the association of German cyclists, **Allgemeiner Deutscher Fahrrad-Club,** Hellerallee 23, 28209, Bremen 71 (☎ **0421/34-62-90**).

Bicycles can be rented at more than 300 rail depots throughout the country, for 8DM to 15DM ($4.55 to $8.55) per day or 30DM ($17.10) per week. If you have a valid rail ticket, the cost is often reduced by 50%. You can make arrangements to rent a bicycle at one rail depot and return it at another.

11 Tips on Accommodations

In general, Germany has one of the highest standards of innkeeping in the world. However, many of the hotels in the eastern section of Germany—once geared to tourism from the old Eastern bloc countries—are not of the same standard as those in the west.

Hotels range from five-star palaces of luxury and comfort to plain country inns and simple guest houses *(Gasthäuser)*, with a huge variation in rates. The cheapest accommodation is in pensions *(Fremdenheime)* or rooms in private homes (look for a sign saying ZIMMER FREI, meaning there's a room for rent). Hotels listed as *garni* provide no meals other than breakfast.

When you don't have time to make reservations on your own, you can call **Travel Interlink** at ☎ **800/888-5898.** Also, tourist offices will often book you into a room for a small charge. Obviously, the earlier you arrive in these offices, the more likely you are to get a good room at the price you want.

BUNGALOW, VILLA & APARTMENT RENTALS   Germans who own vacation homes or units often make them available for visitors when the homes are vacant. These villas, apartments, and bungalows—called *Ferienwohnungen* or *Ferienapartments*—shelter two to eight people in most cases. The longer you stay, the better the rate. Sometimes extra charges are imposed for utilities, but these matters have to be worked out, as does the arrangement for bed linens. Local tourist offices have details of rentals available in their areas.

EUROPEAN CASTLE HOTELS   A new breed of castle hotels has begun to pop up across what used to be Soviet-controlled territory of eastern and Central Europe. The Mannheim-based **Gastemschloss Group,** which is more of an affiliation than a chain, incorporates top-notch hotels with historic backgrounds, such as the Burg Hotel auf Schönburg in Oberwesel am Rhine, with newer contenders in Germany's eastern and Baltic zones. For information on these hotels contact **Euro-Connection,** 7500 212th St. SW, Suite 103, Edmonds, WA 98026 (☎ **800/645-3876**). This company also represents Romantik Hotels and Grandes étapes Françaises, a France-based affiliation of prestigious lodgings.

Fast Facts: Germany

Business Hours   Most **banks** are open Monday to Friday from 8:30am to 1pm and 2:30 to 4pm (on Thursday until 5:30pm). Money exchanges at airports and border-crossing points are generally open daily from 6am to 10pm. Exchanges at border railroad stations are kept open for arrivals of all international trains. Most **businesses** are open Monday to Friday from 9am to 5pm and on Saturday from 9am to 1pm. Store hours can vary from town to town, but **shops** are generally open Monday to Friday from 9 or 10am to 6 or 6:30pm (8:30pm on Thursday). Saturday hours are generally from 9am to 1 or 2pm, except on the first Saturday of a month, when stores may remain open until 4pm.

Drug Laws   Penalties for illegal drug possession in Germany are severe. You could go to jail or be deported immediately.

Drugstores   Pharmaceuticals are sold at an *Apotheke*. For cosmetics, go to a *Drogerie*. German pharmacies take turns staying open nights, on Sunday, and on holidays, and each *Apotheke* posts a list of those that are open off-hours.

Electricity   In most places the electricity is 220 volts AC (50 cycles). A transformer and a plug that fits the German socket will be needed for your U.S. appliances. Many leading hotels will supply these.

Embassies & Consulates   In the life of this edition, embassy and consulate addresses are likely to change, in the move from Bonn to Berlin. Call before you set out for a particular address. The embassy of the **United States** is at Deichmannsaue 29, 53170 Bonn (☎ **0228/33-91,** or 0228/3-39-20-53 for visa applications); there's also a U.S. embassy office at Neustaedtische Kirchstrasse 4-5, 10117 Berlin (☎ **030/2-38-51-74**). U.S. consulates are located at Clayallee 170, 14195 Berlin (☎ **030/8-32-92-33**); at Siesmayerstrasse 21, 60323 Frankfurt (☎ **069/7-53-50**); at Wilhelm-Seyfferth-Strasse 4, 04107 Leipzig (☎ **0341/ 21-38-40**); at Königinstrasse 5, 80539 München (☎ **089/2-88-80**); and at Alsterufer 27-28, 20354 Hamburg (☎ **040/41-17-10**). The consular information hot line is ☎ **0130/82-63-64.**

The embassy of the **United Kingdom** is at Unter den Linden 32–34, 10117 Berlin (☎ **030/20-18-40**). The British Consulate-General, handling passport and visa applications, is at Yorckstrasse 19, 40476 Düsseldorf (☎ **0211/ 9-44-80**); Harvestehuder Weg 8A, 20148 Hamburg (☎ **040/4-48-03-20**); Bockenheimer Landstrasse 42, 60323 Frankfurt (☎ **069/1-70-00-20**); Bürkleinstrasse 10, 80538 Munich (☎ **089/21-10-90**); and at Breite Strasse 2, 70173 Stuttgart (☎ **0711/16-26-90**).

The embassy of **Australia** is at Godesberger Allee 105–107, 53175 Bonn (☎ **0228/8-10-30**), with a Berlin office on Kempinski Plaza, at Uhlandstrasse 181–183, 10623 Berlin (☎ **030/8-80-08-80**), and a consulate at Gutleutstrasse 85, 60329 Frankfurt/Main (☎ **069/2-73-90-90**).

The embassy of **Canada** is at Friedrich-Wilhelm-Strasse 18, 53113 Bonn (☎ **0228/96-80**). Canada maintains a consulate at Friedrichstrasse 95, 23rd Floor, 10117 Berlin (☎ **030/2-61-11-61**); at Prinz-Georg-Strasse 126, 40479 Düsseldorf (☎ **0211/17-21-70**); at Tal 29, 80331 Munich (☎ **089/219-9570**); and at ABC Strasse 45, 20354 Hamburg (☎ **040/35-55-62-95**).

The embassy of **New Zealand** is at Bundeskanzlerplatz 2–10, 53113 Bonn (☎ **0228/22-80-70**). A consulate is at Heimhuderstrasse 56, 20148 Hamburg (☎ **040/4-42-55-50**).

Emergencies   Throughout Germany the emergency number for **police** is **110;** for fire or to call an ambulance, dial **112.**

Legal Aid   This may be hard to come by in Germany. The government advises foreigners to consult their embassy or consulate (see "Embassies & Consulates," above) in case of a dire emergency, such as an arrest. Even if a consulate or embassy declines to offer financial or legal help, officials can give advice as to how to get help locally, and will usually provide a list of attorneys who might represent you for a fee.

Liquor Laws   As in many European countries, drinking laws are flexible, enforced only if a problem develops. Officially, you must be 18 to consume any kind of alcoholic beverage. Bars and cafes rarely request proof of age. Drinking while driving, however, is treated as a very serious offense.

Mail   General delivery—mark it POSTE RESTANTE—can be used in any major town or city in Germany. You can pick up your mail upon presentation of a valid identity card or passport. Street mailboxes are painted yellow. It costs 3DM ($1.70) for the first 5 grams (about one-fifth ounce) to send an airmail letter to the United States or Canada, and 2DM ($1.15) for postcards. To mail a package, go to one of the larger post offices, preferably the main branch in the area (see the individual city listings). All letters to the United Kingdom cost 1.10DM (65¢) or 1DM (55¢) for postcards.

Medical Assistance   Most major hotels have a physician on staff or on call. If you can't get hold of a doctor, dial the emergency service, ☎ **112,** which is open day and night. Medical and hospital services aren't free, so be sure that you have appropriate insurance coverage before you travel.

Pets   Dogs and cats brought into Germany from abroad will require a veterinary certificate stating that the animal has been vaccinated against rabies not less than 30 days and not more than 1 year before entry into the country. This certificate must be accompanied by a notarized translation of the document into German.

Police   Throughout the country, dial ☎ **110** for emergencies.

Rest Rooms   Use the word *Toilette* (pronounced twah-*leh*-teh). Women's toilets are usually marked with an "F" for *Frauen,* and men's toilets with an "H" for *Herren.* Germany, frankly, doesn't have enough public toilets, except in transportation centers. The locals have to rely on bars, cafes, or restaurants—and using them isn't always appreciated if you're not a paying customer. Toilets often have attendants who expect a small tip; if you need soap and a towel, give something extra.

Safety   Germany is a reasonably safe country in which to travel, although neo-Nazi skinheads, especially in the eastern part of the country, have sometimes attacked black or Asian travelers. One of the most dangerous places, especially at night, is around the large railway stations in such cities as Frankfurt, Munich, Berlin, and Hamburg. Some beer halls get especially rowdy late at night.

Taxes   As a member of the European Union, Germany imposes a tax on most goods and services known as a **value-added tax (VAT),** or in German, *Mehrwertsteuer.* Nearly everything is taxed at 15%. That includes vital necessities such as gas and luxury items such as jewelry. VAT is included in the prices of restaurants and hotels in Germany. Note that goods for sale, such as German cameras, also have the 15% tax already factored into the price; but the listed prices of services, such as getting a mechanic to fix your car, don't include VAT, so an extra 15% will be tacked on to the bill. Stores that display a "Tax Free" sticker will issue you a Tax-Free Shopping Check at the time of purchase. When leaving the country, have your check stamped by the German Customs Service as your proof of legal export. You can then get a cash refund at one of the Tax-Free Shopping Service offices in the major airports and many train stations, even at some of the bigger ferry terminals. Otherwise, you must send the checks to Tax-Free Shopping Service, Mengstrasse 19, 23552 Lübeck, Germany. If you want the payment to be credited to your bank card or your bank account, mention this. There is no airport departure tax in Germany.

Telephone   The country code for Germany is 49. To call Germany from the United States, dial the international access code, which is 011, then 49, then the city code, then the regular phone number. *The phone numbers listed in this book are to be used within Germany; when calling from abroad, you omit the initial 0 in the city code.*

Local and long-distance calls may be placed from all post offices and coin-operated public telephone booths. The unit charge is 0.30DM or three 10-pfennig coins. More than half the phones in Germany require an advance-payment telephone card from **Telekom,** the German telephone company. Phone cards are sold at post offices and newsstands; they cost 12DM ($6.85) and 50DM ($28.50). Rates are measured in units rather than minutes. The farther the distance, the more units are consumed. For example, a 3-minute call to the United States costs 41 units. Telephone calls made through hotel switchboards can double, triple, or even quadruple the regular charge. Therefore, try to make your calls outside your hotel at a pay phone or post office. Post offices can also send faxes for you.

To call the U.S. from Germany, you dial 01 followed by the country code (1 for the States), then the area code, and then the number. Alternatively, you can dial the various telecommunication companies in the States for cheaper rates. From Germany, the access for **AT&T** is ☎ **01300010;** for **MCI** ☎ **800/ 888-8000;** and for **Sprint** ☎ **800/888-0013. USA Direct** can be used with all telephone cards and for collect calls. The number from Germany is ☎ **01-30- 00-10.** Canada Direct can be used with Bell Telephone Cards and for collect calls. This number from Germany is ☎ **01-30-00-14.**

If you're calling from a public pay phone in Germany, you must deposit the basic local rate.

Time   Germany operates on Central European time (CET), which means that the country is 6 hours ahead of eastern standard time (EST) in the United States and 1 hour ahead of Greenwich mean time (GMT). Summer daylight saving time begins in Germany in April and ends in September—there's a slight difference in the dates from year to year—so there may be a period in early spring and in the fall when there's a 7-hour difference between U.S. EST and CET. Always check if you're traveling during these periods, especially if you need to catch a plane.

Tipping   If a restaurant bill says *Bedienung,* that means a service charge has already been added, so just round up to the nearest mark.

If not, add 10 to 15%. Round up to the nearest mark for taxis. Bellhops get 2DM ($1.15) per bag, as does the doorperson at your hotel, restaurant, or nightclub. Room cleaning staffs get small tips in Germany, as do concierges who perform some special favors such as obtaining hard-to-get theater or opera tickets. Tip hairdressers or barbers 5 to 10%.

Water   Tap water is safe to drink in all German towns and cities. However, don't drink from rivers or mountain streams, regardless of how clean the water may appear.

3 Berlin

The reunited city of Berlin is once again the capital of Germany. Berlin was almost bombed out of existence during World War II, its streets reduced to piles of rubble, its parks to muddy swampland. But the optimistic spirit and strength of will of the remarkable Berliners enabled them to survive not only the wartime destruction of their city, but also its postwar division, symbolized by the Berlin Wall. Today, structures of steel and glass tower over streets where before only piles of rubble lay, and parks and gardens are again lush. Nonetheless, even in the daily whirl of working, shopping, and dining along the Ku'damm, Berliners encounter reminders of less happy days. At the end of the street stands the Kaiser Wilhelm Memorial Church, with only the shell of the old neo-Romanesque bell tower remaining. In striking contrast is the new church, constructed west of the old tower in 1961, and nicknamed "lipstick and powderbox" by Berliners because of its futuristic design.

Before the war, the section of the city that became East Berlin was the cultural and political heart of Germany, where the best museums, the finest churches, and the most important boulevards lay. The walled-in East Berliners turned to restoring their important museums, theaters, and landmarks (especially in the Berlin-Mitte section), while the West Berliners built entirely new museums and cultural centers. This contrast between the two parts of city is still evident today, though east and west are more and more coming together within the immense, fascinating whole that is Berlin.

BERLIN TODAY & TOMORROW

Berlin is living up to its reputation as a dynamic, exciting hub of activity as never before. The city's nightlife is among Europe's best and wildest. And now that the German government has been transferred here from Bonn, Berlin is bidding to become the reborn capital not only of Germany but of all Europe.

As befits a new capital, the city is undergoing a major facelift. More than $120 billion has been invested in new streets, buildings, and railways. The former East Berlin is rapidly being restored and gentrified, particularly in the **Mitte** (central) district. Here new luxury hotels and shopping arcades compete with the litter of the Kurfürstendamm. The opening of the Adlon Kempinski Hotel, overlooking the Brandenburg Gate, is particularly notable. **Prenzlauer Berg,** a blue-collar eastern neighborhood that escaped the worst of the wartime bombing, is

The New Millennium in the New Berlin

In a bid not to be outdone by the other European capitals, Berlin has embarked on an 18-month, multi-media arts program called "Das Neue Berlin," which will last until January 2001. Among the events is one called "Berlin Open City," launched in the summer of 1999, which aims to put Berlin itself on exhibit. The city's history from 1949 to 1999 will be illustrated at the renovated Martin-Gropius Building. The same building will also host "Collected Spaces—Collected Dreams," tracing German art from 1960 to 2000. An exhibition called "Seven Hills—Images and Signs of the 21st Century" will survey the intellectual, cultural, and scientific landscapes of Germany at the dawn of the 21st century. Many other artistic and cultural events will take place as well.

becoming a chic district of cafes and boutiques. The downside of all this for Berliners has been the sharp increase in real estate prices, as well as the inconvenience of living in the world's largest construction site.

Many of Berlin's famous buildings have been restored. The rebuilt **Reichstag** has a glittering glass dome; upon the building stands not the old glowering imperial hunter, but the national symbol, the eagle (locals refer affectionately to the statue as "the fat hen"). The Oranienburger Strasse **synagogue,** wrecked on Kristallnacht and finished off by Allied bombers, has been rebuilt in all its splendor. Likewise, **Berlin Cathedral** and the five state museums on **Museum Island** have been painstakingly returned to their original glory.

Visitors often overlook Berlin's **natural attractions.** Few metropolitan areas are blessed with as many gardens, lakes, woodlands, and parks—these cover an amazing one-third of the city. First-time visitors are often surprised to learn that small farms with fields and meadows still exist within the city limits.

1 Orientation

ARRIVING

BY PLANE   Tegel is the city's busiest airport, serving most flights from the west. Historic **Tempelhof** (made famous as the city's lifeline during the Berlin Airlift) has declined in importance, although it's still used for flights from Basel, Brussels, Copenhagen, Prague, and many cities within Germany. **Schönefeld,** the airport in the eastern sector, is used primarily by Russian and eastern European airlines. Private bus shuttles among the three airports operate constantly, so you can make connecting flights at a different airport.

Lufthansa (☎ 800/645-3880) does not have direct transatlantic flights into Berlin; instead, it routes transatlantic passengers through its hubs at Frankfurt and Munich. Frequent connections can also be made into Berlin from dozens of other German and European gateways, including Paris, Rome, and Stockholm. Lufthansa offers 100 or more flights into Berlin every day from about a dozen German and European cities.

Delta (☎ 800/241-4141) has daily flights to Berlin-Tegel every evening from New York's JFK International Airport and from Atlanta.

British Airways (BA) (☎ 800/247-9297) offers four direct flights every day from London's Heathrow and Gatwick airports to Berlin-Tegel. BA also flies nonstop to Berlin six times a week from Birmingham. From North America, BA is the most frequent flyer into Britain. The many price wars that offer travelers affordable fares can

Berlin at a Glance

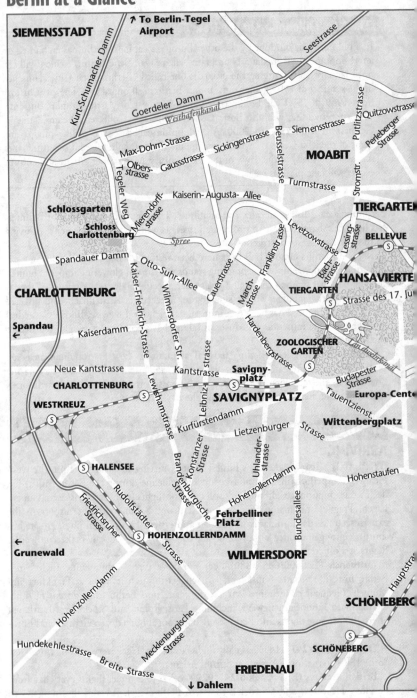

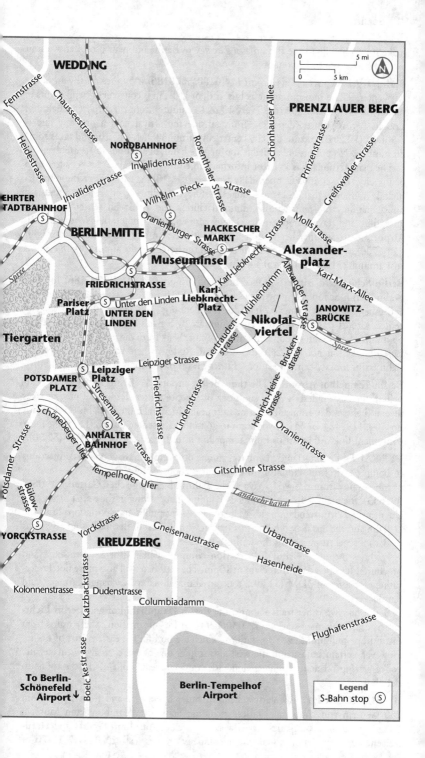

make it worthwhile to use Britain as a gateway to Berlin and may also offer, without extra cost, a stopover in London.

Berlin-Tegel Airport   This airport (☎ 0180/5000186) is 5 miles northwest of the city center. Public transportation by bus, taxi, or U-Bahn is convenient to all points in the city. BVG bus no. 109 runs every 10 to 15 minutes from the airport to Bahnhof Zoo in Berlin's center, departing from outside the arrival hall; a one-way fare is 3.90DM ($2.20). A taxi to the city center costs from 30DM ($17.10) and takes some 20 minutes. No porters are available for luggage handling, but pushcarts are free.

The main terminal has a **visitor information counter** where you can get a free map of the city. The counter is open daily from 5am to 10pm. Facilities at the terminal include money-exchange centers, luggage-storage facilities (and locker rentals), a police station, auto-rental kiosks, dining facilities, and a first-aid center. Shops sell gifts, film, and travel paraphernalia. There's also an airport hotel, the **Novotel Berlin Airport,** Kurt-Schumacher-Damm 202, 13405 Berlin (☎ 030/41060; fax 030/410-6700), with a connecting shuttle between the hotel and the airport. Its 184 rooms cost around 271DM ($154.45) a night.

Berlin-Schönefeld Airport   Once the main airport (☎ 0180/5000186) for East Berlin, Berlin-Schönefeld now receives many flights from Asia, as well as from Russia and other European countries. It lies in Brandenburg, 12 miles southeast of the city center. Airport transfers into the city center are by S-Bahn lines 9 and 45 (trip time: 55 min.). The S-Bahn station is about a 5-minute walk from the main arrival hall. You can also take bus no. 171 from the airport to Rudow, where you can transfer to U-Bahn trains for city-center locations. Either means of transport costs 4DM ($2.30).

Berlin-Tempelhof Airport   The third Berlin airport (☎ 0180/5000186) is Tempelhof, the city's oldest, 4 miles southeast of the city center. Tempelhof now receives several flights a day from German or European cities. Take the U-Bahn (U6) or bus no. 104, 119, 184, or 341. If you want to go to the city center, bus no. 119 is the most convenient link. All bus trips from Tempelhof into the center cost 3.90DM ($2.20).

BY TRAIN   Frankfurt and Hamburg, among other cities, have good rail connections to Berlin. A trip from Frankfurt to Berlin takes about 7 hours.

Most trains from the west arrive at the **Bahnhof Zoologischer Garten** (☎ 085/996633), the main train station, called "Bahnhof Zoo." Lying in the center of the city, close to the Kurfürstendamm, it's well connected for public transportation. Both the U-Bahn and the bus network link this station with the rest of Berlin. Bus no. 109 runs to Berlin-Tegel Airport from the station.

Facilities include a **visitor information counter,** which dispenses free maps and brochures. It's open daily from 5am to 10pm. The staff here will also make hotel reservations for a fee of 3DM ($1.70). You can also mail letters, exchange currency, and rent lockers.

Berlin has two other train stations, the **Berlin Hauptbahnhof** and **Berlin Lichtenberg.** Call the main station (☎ 030/1-94-19) for information. Many trains from east Europe pull into these two stations, which are both in the eastern part of Berlin. However, certain trains from the west also stop at one of these, so always make sure you're getting off at the right station. S-Bahn 5 connects both of these stations to Bahnhof Zoo.

BY BUS (COACH)   Regularly scheduled buses operate to and from Berlin from 250 German and continental cities, including Frankfurt, Hamburg, and Munich. Long-distance bus companies servicing Berlin include **Autokraft GmbH** and **Haru-Reisen.** For information about either company's routes, call ☎ 0431/7-10-70 or

0130/866662. Another company, **Bayern Express & P. Köhn** (☎ **030/8-60-96-0** or 030/8-60-21-1), also operates bus service to Berlin.

Arrivals are at the **ZOB Omnibusbahnhof am Funkturm,** Messedamm 8 (☎ **030/ 3-01-80-28** for reservations, schedules, and information). Taxis and bus connections are available at the station, or you can link up with the U-Bahn at the nearby Kaiserdamm station.

BY CAR   From Frankfurt, take the E451 north until it connects with the E40 going northeast. Follow this Autobahn past Jena and then head north on the E51 into Berlin. From Nürnberg, also take the E51 into Berlin. From Dresden, take the E55 north to Berlin. Expect heavy traffic on the Autobahns on weekends and sunny days when everybody is out touring.

VISITOR INFORMATION

For visitor information and hotel bookings, head for the **Berlin Tourist Information Center** (☎ **030/25100125**), Europa-Center (near Memorial Church); the entrance is on the Budapesterstrasse side. It's open Monday to Saturday from 8am to 10pm and on Sunday from 9am to 9pm. There's also a branch (☎ **030/264-74-80**) at the south wing of the Brandenburg Gate, open daily from 9:30am to 6pm.

CITY LAYOUT

Berlin is one of the largest and most complex cities in Europe. Since it's so spread out, you'll need to depend on public transportation. No visitor should try to explore more than two neighborhoods a day, even superficially.

The center of activity in the western part of Berlin is the 2½-mile-long **Kurfürstendamm,** called the Ku'damm by Berliners, who seem to have a habit of irreverently renaming every street and building in the city. Along this wide boulevard you'll find the best hotels, restaurants, theaters, cafes, nightclubs, shops, and department stores. It's the most elegant and fashionable spot in Berlin, but still, like much of the city, it combines chic with sleaze in places. Walkers can stop off at one of the popular cafes lining the boulevard.

From the Ku'damm you can take Hardenbergstrasse, which crosses Bismarckstrasse and becomes Otto-Suhr-Allee, which will lead to the **Schloss Charlottenburg** area and its museums, one of your major sightseeing goals. The **Dahlem Museums** are in the southwest of the city, often reached by going along Hohenzollerndamm.

The huge **Tiergarten** is the city's largest park. Running through it is **Strasse des 17 Juni,** which leads to the famed **Brandenburg Gate** (just south of the Reichstag), which once separated the two Berlins. On the southwestern fringe of the Tiergarten is the **Berlin Zoo.**

The Brandenburg Gate is the start of eastern Berlin's most celebrated street, **Unter den Linden,** the cultural heart of Berlin before World War II. It runs from west to east, leading to **Museumsinsel,** or Museum Island, where the most outstanding museums of eastern Berlin, including the Pergamon Museum, are situated.

Unter den Linden crosses another major eastern Berlin artery, **Friedrichstrasse.** If you continue south along Friedrichstrasse, you'll reach the former location of **Checkpoint Charlie,** a famous border site of the Cold-War days. No longer a checkpoint, it now has a little museum devoted to memories of the Berlin Wall.

Unter den Linden continues east until it reaches **Alexanderplatz,** the center of eastern Berlin, with its towering television tower (Fernsehturm). A short walk away is the newly restored **Nikolai Quarter (Nikolaiviertel),** a neighborhood of bars, restaurants, and shops that evoke life in the prewar days.

FINDING AN ADDRESS   As for the numbering of streets, keep in mind that the city sometimes assists you by posting the range of numbers that appears within any particular block, at least within major arteries such as the Kurfürstendamm. These numbers appear on the street signs themselves, which is a great help in finding a particular number on long boulevards. You won't find these numbers on street signs of smaller streets. Although some streets are numbered with the odds on one side and the evens on the other, many (including the Ku'damm) are numbered consecutively up one side of the street and back down the other.

Warning: The names of some eastern Berlin streets and squares with links to the old East German regime have been changed.

MAPS   Good maps of Berlin can be purchased at bookstores or news kiosks, such as the Europa Press Center (a magazine and newspaper store in the Europa-Center). One of the best maps is the **Falk** map, which offers full-color detail and comprehensive indexes (consequently, it's sometimes awkward to unfold and refold). Be sure to obtain an up-to-date map showing the most recent changes.

Neighborhoods in Brief

Charlottenburg   Despite being renamed by Berlin wits as Klamottenburg (Ragsville) after the bombings of World War II, this is still the wealthiest and most densely commercialized district of western Berlin. Its centerpiece is Charlottenburg Palace.

Savignyplatz   This tree-lined square is just a few blocks north of the Ku'damm. The square and the nearby streets offer a profusion of bars and restaurants, an engaging aura of permissiveness, and some of the most popular nightclubs and cafes in Berlin.

Tiergarten   The name Tiergarten (which means "Animal Garden") refers both to a massive urban park and to a residential district of the same name. The park was originally intended as a backdrop to the grand avenues laid out by the German kaisers. The neighborhood contains the Brandenburg Gate, the German Reichstag (Parliament), the Berlin Zoo, and some of the city's grandest museums.

Hansaviertel   This neighborhood, north of Tiergarten park, contains a series of residential buildings designed by a different architects (including Le Corbusier, Walter Gropius, and Alvar Aalto).

Dahlem   The university district of Berlin, it was originally established as an independent village to the southwest of Berlin's center.

Kreuzberg   Originally built during the 19th century to house the workers of a rapidly industrializing Prussia, this has traditionally been the poorest and most overcrowded of Berlin's districts. Today, at least 35% of its population is composed of guest workers from Turkey, the former Yugoslavia, and Greece. Recently, the district has become headquarters for the city's artistic counterculture.

Schöneberg   Like Kreuzberg, it was originally an independent suburb of workers' housing, but after the war it was rebuilt as a solidly middle-class neighborhood. It lies south of the Tiergarten and is rarely visited by foreign visitors.

Grunewald   Many newcomers are surprised by the sheer sprawl of Grunewald's 19 square miles of verdant forest. The area serves as a green lung for the urbanites of Berlin. It lies northwest of the city center.

Berlin-Mitte (Center)   Originally conceived as the architectural centerpiece of the Prussian kaisers, this district fell into the eastern zone during the division of Berlin after World War II. Its fortunes declined dramatically as the Communist regime infused it with many starkly angular monuments and boring buildings. Although many of Berlin-Mitte's grand structures were destroyed in the war, unification has opened up to the world its remaining artistic and architectural treasures. Its most famous street is Unter den Linden.

Alexanderplatz   This square at the eastern end of Unter den Linden once sheltered the kaiser's residence, but the former East German regime destroyed the palace and made Alexanderplatz the centerpiece of its government. Today the large and sterile square is dominated by the tallest building in Berlin, the Sputnik-inspired TV tower.

Museumsinsel (Museum Island)   This island in the Spree River hosts a complex of museums housed in neoclassical buildings. Its most famous museum, the Pergamon, contains magnificent reconstructions of entire ancient structures.

Nikolaiviertel   This is where Berlin began during the 1200s. Located conveniently close to Alexanderplatz, the Nikolaiviertel is the most perfectly restored medieval neighborhood in the city and a triumph of the restoration skills of the former East German regime.

Spandau   Set near the junction of the Spree and Havel Rivers, about 6 miles north-west of the city center, Spandau boasts a history of medieval grandeur. Though it merged with Berlin in 1920, its Altstadt (old city) is still intact. The legendary Spandau prison was demolished in the early 1990s.

2 Getting Around

BY PUBLIC TRANSPORTATION   The Berlin transport system consists of buses, trams, and U-Bahn (underground) and S-Bahn (above ground) trains. The network is run by the **BVG** or Public Transport Company Berlin-Brandenburg. Public transportation throughout the city operates from about 4:30am to 12:30am daily (except for some 62 night buses and trams, and U-Bahn lines U-9 and U-12). For information about public transport, call ☎ **030/250025.**

The **BVG standard ticket** *(Einzelfahrschein)* costs 3.90DM ($2.20) and is valid for 2 hours of transportation in all directions, transfers included. A 24-hour ticket for the whole city costs from 7.80DM to 8.50DM ($4.45 to $4.85) depending on the zone. Only standard tickets are sold on buses. Tram tickets must be purchased in advance. All tickets should be kept until the end of the journey; otherwise you'll be liable for a fine of 60DM ($34.20).

If you're going to be in Berlin for 3 days, you can purchase for 29DM ($16.55) a **Berlin-Potsdam WelcomeCard,** which entitles holders to 72 free hours on public transportation in Berlin and Brandenburg. You'll also get free admission or a price reduction of up to 50% on sightseeing tours, museums, and other attractions, and a 25% reduction at 10 theaters as well. The card is sold at many hotels, visitor information centers, and public-transportation sales points. It's valid for one adult and three children under the age of 14.

Two **excursion bus lines** make some beautiful scenic spots accessible. Bus line no. 218 operates from the Theodor-Heuss-Platz U-Bahn station (located near the radio tower) via Schildhorn, Grunewald Tower, and Wannsee Beach to the Wannsee S-Bahn station, and bus line no. 216 runs from the Wannsee S-Bahn station to Pfaueninsel via Moorlake.

BY TAXI   Taxis are available throughout Berlin. The meter starts at 4DM to 6DM ($2.30 to $3.40), with additional kilometers costing from 1.70DM to 2.30DM (95¢ to $1.30) each. The longer the ride, the cheaper the price per kilometer. Visitors can

Berlin U-Bahn & S-Bahn

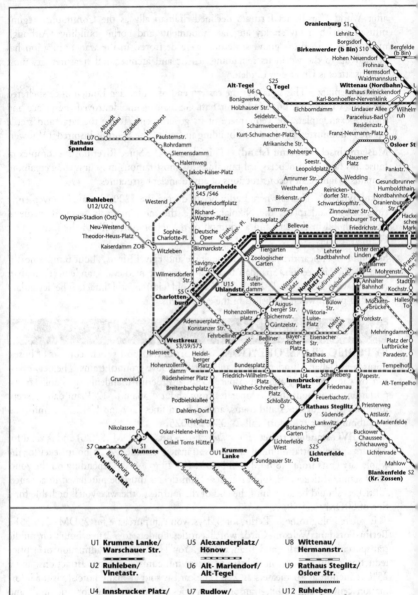

U1 **Krumme Lanke/ Warschauer Str.**

U2 **Ruhleben/ Vinetastr.**

U4 **Innsbrucker Platz/ Nollendorf-platz**

U5 **Alexanderplatz/ Hönow**

U6 **Alt- Mariendorf/ Alt-Tegel**

U7 **Rudlow/ Rathaus Spandau**

U8 **Wittenau/ Hermannstr.**

U9 **Rathaus Steglitz/ Osloer Str.**

U12 **Ruhleben/ Warschauer Str.**

U15 **Uhlandstr./ Wittenbergplatz (Warschauer Str.)**

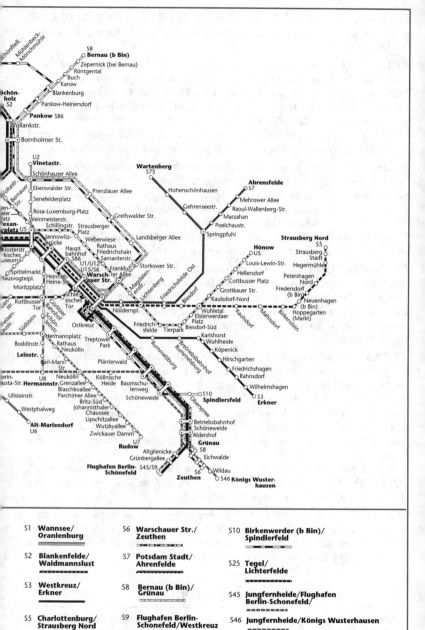

S1 **Wannsee/ Oranienburg**

S2 **Blankenfelde/ Waidmannslust**

S3 **Westkreuz/ Erkner**

S5 **Charlottenburg/ Strausberg Nord**

S6 **Warschauer Str./ Zeuthen**

S7 **Potsdam Stadt/ Ahrenfelde**

S8 **Bernau (b Bin)/ Grünau**

S9 **Flughafen Berlin- Schonefeld/Westkreuz**

S10 **Birkenwerder (b Bin)/ Spindlerfeld**

S25 **Tegel/ Lichterfelde**

S45 **Jungfernheide/Flughafen Berlin-Schonefeld/**

S46 **Jungfernheide/Königs Wusterhausen**

S75 **Westkreuz/ Wartenberg**

57

flag down taxis that have a T-sign illuminated. To call a taxi, try ☎ **21-02-02,** 6-90-22, or 26-10-26. If you call ☎ **21-02-02,** you'll get a taxi company that lets you pay by credit card.

BY CAR   U.S. rental companies have outlets in Berlin. If possible, you should make reservations in advance; however, should you need to rent a car in Berlin, you'll find **Hertz** at Berlin-Tegel Airport (☎ **030/41-01-33-15**) and at Budapesterstrasse 39 (☎ **030/2-61-10-53**). **Avis** is also at Berlin-Tegel (☎ **030/4-10-13-148**) and at Budapesterstrasse 44 (☎ **030/2-61-18-81**).

But in general, touring Berlin by car is not recommended. Traffic is heavy and parking is very difficult to come by. Use the excellent public transportation network instead.

Parking   If you're driving into Berlin, chances are that you'll want to safely store your car once you arrive. Many hotels offer parking facilities; otherwise, you'll find parking garages that remain open throughout the day and night. Those located near the Ku'damm and the Europa-Center include the **Parkhaus Metropol,** Joachimstaler Strasse 14–19; **Parkhaus Los-Angeles-Platz,** Augsburger Strasse 30; **Parkhaus Europa-Center,** Nürnberger Strasse 5–7; and the **Parkhaus am Zoo,** Budapesterstrasse 38. Charges start at 3DM ($1.70) per hour.

City Driving   One problem that often infuriates drivers in Berlin is that it's almost impossible to turn left on major avenues (except at major intersections within the former East Berlin), because of the positioning of metal barriers and tram lines. Oversize signs tell you to drive straight on. Drivers have to make a right-hand turn, swing around the block, and then proceed straight across the tram lines wherever a traffic light will allow.

BY BICYCLE   Bicycling in Berlin's crushing traffic is not a very appealing prospect, but you might want to rent a bike to explore the city's outlying parks and forests. Both the U-Bahn and the S-Bahn provide specific compartments for bicycle transport for an extra 5DM ($2.85). Transport of bicycles, however, is not permitted during rush hour: Monday to Friday before 9am and again in the afternoon between 2 and 5:30pm. In the city and suburbs, try to confine your bicycling to cycle zones, delineated with solid red lines running between the pedestrian sidewalks and the traffic lanes.

A good place for bike rentals is **Hackeschen-Hosen,** Rosenthalerstrasse 40–41 (☎ **030/8599895**), open Monday to Friday 10am to 7pm, Saturday 10am to 4pm. A 24-hour rental costs from 20DM ($11.40) on up.

ON FOOT   Many interesting neighborhoods are great for exploring on foot. Walkers should remember to stay off the bicycle paths, which are marked by red lines adjacent to the sidewalk. Also, neither police nor everyday citizens look favorably on jaywalkers at any time (even when no cars are coming).

Fast Facts: Berlin

American Express   An Amex office is located at Uhlandstrasse 173–174 (☎ **030/8-84-58-80**), just off Kurfürstendamm. Office hours are Monday to Friday from 9am to 5:30pm and on Saturday from 9am to noon. If you have an Amex card or traveler's checks, you can pick up mail here for free; otherwise, a 2DM ($1.15) fee is charged.

Business Hours   Most **banks** are open Monday to Friday from 9am to either 1 or 3pm. Most other **businesses and stores** are open Monday to Friday from 9 or 10am to either 6 or 6:30pm and on Saturday from 9am to 2pm. On *langer*

Samstag, the first Saturday of the month, shops stay open until 4 or 6pm. Some stores close late on Thursday (usually 8:30pm).

Currency Exchange   You can exchange money at all airports, at major department stores, at any bank, and at the American Express office (see above). There is also a currency exchange office at the Bahnhof Zoo; it's open Monday to Saturday from 8am to 9pm and on Sunday from 10am to 6pm.

Dentists/Doctors   The Berlin tourist office in the Europa-Center (☎ 030/264-7480) keeps a list of English-speaking dentists and doctors in Berlin. For an emergency doctor, call ☎ 030/31-00-31.

Drugstores   If you need a pharmacy *(Apotheke)* at night, go to one on any corner and look for a sign in the window giving the address of the nearest pharmacy with nighttime hours (such postings are required by law). For a centrally located pharmacy, go to **Europa-Apotheke,** Tauentzienstrasse 9–12 (☎ 030/2-61-41-42), located near the Europa-Center, in the vicinity of the Bahnhof Zoo; it's open Monday to Friday from 9am to 8pm and Saturday from 9am to 4pm.

Embassies & Consulates   See "Fast Facts: Germany," in chapter 2.

Emergencies   To call the police, dial ☎ 110. To report a fire or to summon an ambulance, dial ☎ 112.

Eyeglasses   One good bet is **Apollo Optik,** Müllerstrasse 153 (☎ 030/469-0730), open Monday to Friday from 9am to 7pm and Saturday from 9am to 4pm.

Hospitals   Hotel employees are usually familiar with the locations of the nearest hospital emergency room. In an emergency, call ☎ 112 for an ambulance.

Hot Lines   For the Rape Crisis Center call ☎ 030/789-02-600. For problems relating to drug use or drug addiction, call the drug help line (☎ 030/1-92-37). Gays seeking legal help should call Schwüles Überfall (☎ 030/216-33-36).

Internet Cafe   You can check your e-mail at Virtuality Cafe, Lewishamstrasse 1 (☎ 030/32-75-143).

Laundry/Dry Cleaning   Deluxe and first-class hotels offer laundry service, but prices tend to be high. A convenient launderette is the **Wasch Center,** Leibnizstrasse 72 (☎ 030/8-52-37-96), open daily from 6am to midnight.

Lost Property   For items lost on the bus or U-Bahn, go to BVG Fündbüro, Lorenzweg 5 (☎ 030/256-230-40); open Monday to Thursday from 9am to 6pm and on Friday from 9am to 2pm. For items lost on S-Bahn trains, go to Deutsches Bahn AG/8-Bahn Berlin GmbH, Mittelstrasse 20 (☎ 030/2-97-296-12), Monday, Wednesday, or Thursday between 10am and 4pm, Tuesday between 10am and 6pm, or Friday between 8am and noon. The general lost-property office, Zentrales Fündbüro, is at Plaza der Luftbrücke 6 (☎ 030/69-95). Hours are Monday and Tuesday from 7:30am to 2pm, Wednesday from noon to 6:30pm, and Friday from 7:30am to noon.

Luggage Storage   Excess luggage can be stored at the Zoologischer Garten Bahnhof and at the Hauptbahnhof. Lockers cost 2DM ($1.15) and up per day.

Photographic Needs   Film and photo equipment are available at KaDeWe, Wittenbergplatz (☎ 030/2-12-10), open Monday to Friday from 9:30am to 8pm and on Saturday from 9am to 4pm.

Post Office   The post office at the Bahnhof Zoo is open Monday to Saturday from 6am to midnight and Sunday from 8am to midnight. If you have mail sent there, have it marked Hauptpostlagernd, Postamt 120, Bahnhof Zoo, 10612 Berlin. There's also a post office at Hauptbahnhof, open Monday to Friday from 7am to 8pm and on Saturday from 8am to 1pm. Another post office, located at the Berlin-Tegel Airport, is open Monday to Friday from 7am to 9pm and Saturday and Sunday from 8am to 6pm. For postal information, call ☎ **030/ 311-00-20.** You can make long-distance calls at post offices at far cheaper rates than at most hotels.

Radio   Radio programs in English can be heard on 87.9 FM (or 94 on cable) and 1197 AM for the American Forces Network, and on 90.2 FM (87.6 on cable) for the BBC.

Rest Rooms   A rest room is called a *Toilette* and is often labeled WC, with either F (for *Frauen,* "women") or H (for *Herren,* "men"). Public facilities are found throughout Berlin and at all terminals, including the Europa-Center on Tauentzienstrasse. It's customary to tip attendants at least 50pf (30¢).

Safety   One unfortunate side effect of unification has been an increase in muggings, bank robberies, bias crimes, and car break-ins. Residents of Berlin sometimes feel unsafe at night, especially in the dimly lit streets of Kreuzberg. Nonetheless, Berlin is still much safer than most large American cities. In case of a robbery or an attack, report the problem immediately to the police. You'll need a police report for any insurance claims.

Taxis   See "Getting Around," earlier in this chapter.

Telegrams/Fax   These can be sent from the post office (see "Post Office," above).

Water   The tap water in Berlin, as in all German cities, is safe to drink. However, most Berliners prefer to ask for bottled water, either carbonated or noncarbonated, instead.

Weather   For a report on Berlin weather, call ☎ **030/7-91-30-03.**

3 Accommodations

Berlin is the scene of frequent international trade fairs, conferences, and festivals, and during these times, vacancies in the city will be hard to find. The greatest concentration of hotels, from the cheapest digs to the most expensive, lies right in the city center near the **Kurfürstendamm** (Ku'damm), the main boulevard of Berlin. Most good-value pensions and small hotels are in the western part of the city; note that many such accommodations are in older buildings where plumbing is rarely state-of-the-art.

The business convention crowd still anchors primarily in the west, as do the hordes of summer visitors on whirlwind tours of Europe. **Eastern Berlin** often attracts Germans from other parts of the country who want a glimpse of the Berlin that was shut away behind the Wall for so long. The eastern sector still doesn't have the visitor structure and facilities of the west, although several first-class and deluxe hotels have opened up there, notably the Grand, Adlon, and Hilton.

Travelers can also head for hotels in **Grunewald** or **Charlottenburg.** In the former you're close to nature in the Grunewald Forest, and in the later you're near Olympic

Dialing Germany

Remember that the phone numbers in this book contain an initial 0 in the German city code. That 0 is only used within Germany. Omit it when calling from abroad.

🛈 Family-Friendly Hotels

Ahorn Berlin (*see p. 65*)   Families like the large rooms that contain small kitchenettes.

Ambassador Berlin (*see p. 68*)   Kids love the eight-floor heated tropical pool with a retractable dome and a waterfall. Rooms, for the most part, are spacious and exceedingly comfortable for families.

Park. If you like biking, jogging, and breathing fresh air and don't mind the commute into central Berlin for shopping and attractions, you'll enjoy both these areas.

ON OR NEAR THE KURFÜRSTENDAMM
VERY EXPENSIVE

✪ **Bristol Kempinski Berlin.** Kurfürstendamm 27, 10719 Berlin. ☎ **800/426-3135** in the U.S., or 030/88-43-40. Fax 030/883-6075. 301 units. A/C MINIBAR TV TEL. 425DM–560DM ($242.25–$319.20) double; 660DM–2,150DM ($376.20–$1,225.50) suite with special offers available. AE, DISC, MC, V. Parking 35DM ($19.95). U-Bahn: Kurfürstendamm.

The "Kempi" enjoys a position in Berlin similar to that of the Waldorf-Astoria in New York. Its only rival is the Grand Hotel Esplanade, but the Kempinski remains the classic choice for luxury and style.

The glass-enclosed winter garden of the recently expanded lobby sets the relaxed mood. Here, amid beige marble and hundreds of potted plants, guests sip tea, cocktails, or sherry in comfortable armchairs. The more expensive Bristol rooms are also more generous with space and better appointed than the regular rooms; the finest accommodations of all are the Kempinski rooms. Visitors should note that the cheapest rooms, called the Berlin rooms, are on the second, fourth, and fifth floors. The furnishings consist of high quality reproductions, antiques, and art deco objects. All units have sound insulation, superb lighting, the town's finest mattresses, and spacious bathrooms with dual basins, scales, shoehorns, hair dryers, and a deluxe set of toiletries.

Dining/Diversions: Elegant and expensive, the Kempenski Grill is one of the best hotel dining rooms in Berlin. Somewhat less formal is the Kempenski Eck, an upscale bistro whose most pleasant feature is an outdoor terrace, where you can get coffee, drinks, and sandwiches and watch the people on the Ku'damm below. The low-key Bristol Bar has a pianist playing soft background music.

Amenities: Room service, laundry, dry cleaning, outdoor pool, recreation center with sauna, massage facilities, steam baths, solarium, fitness center, and an indoor pool with a pool bar. The Kempinski Limousine Service offers an old-fashioned, chauffeur-driven Daimler limousine for airport transportation or sightseeing tours.

Grand Hotel Esplanade. Lützowufer 15, 10785 Berlin. ☎ **030/25-47-80.** Fax 030/2-65-11-71. www.esplanade.de. E-mail: info@esplanade.de. 400 units. A/C MINIBAR TV TEL. 430DM–559DM ($245.10–$318.65) double; from 780DM ($444.60) suite. AE, DC, MC, V. Parking 24DM ($13.70). U-Bahn: Kurfürstenstrasse, Nollendorfplatz, or Wittenbergplatz.

The Grand Hotel Esplanade competes with the more traditional Bristol Kempinski and also attracts the cultural elite. The Esplanade's public and guest rooms are filled with contemporary art, some of it museum caliber. Its art library contains some 4,000 monographs. The uncompromisingly modern rooms are well furnished, bright, and cheerful, and contain sound insulation. There are 33 rooms for nonsmokers. No other hotel in Berlin, not even the front-ranking Kempinski, caters so well to a client's needs.

Western Berlin Accommodations

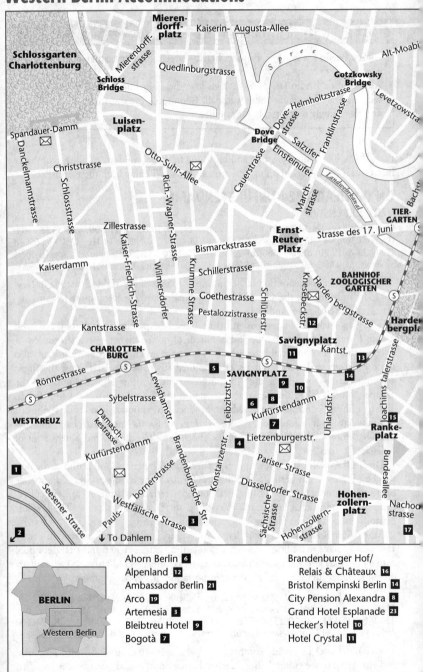

Schlossgarten Charlottenburg

Mierendorff-platz

Kaiserin- Augusta-Allee

Mierendorffstrasse

Quedlinburgstrasse

Spree

Alt-Moabi

Gotzkowsky Bridge

Levetzowstra

Dove- Helmholtzstrasse strasse

Franklinstrasse

Schloss Bridge

Luisen-platz

Spandauer-Damm

Danckelmannstrasse

Christstrasse

Schlossstrasse

Zillestrasse

Otto-Suhr-Allee

Rich.-Wagner-Strasse

Dove Bridge

Salzufer

Cauerstrasse

Einsteinufer

Marchstrasse

Landwehrkanal

Bachst.

TIER-GARTEN

Kaiserdamm

Kaiser-Friedrich-Strasse

Wilmersdorfer

Krumme Strasse

Bismarckstrasse

Schillerstrasse

Goethestrasse

Pestalozzistrasse

Schlüterstr.

Ernst-Reuter-Platz

Strasse des 17. Juni

BAHNHOF ZOOLOGISCHER GARTEN

Knesebeckstr.

Harden bergstrasse

Harden-bergpla

Kantstrasse

CHARLOTTEN-BURG

Rönnestrasse

Levishamstr.

Sybelstrasse

WESTKREUZ

Darnaschkestrasse

Kurfürstendamm

Brandenburgische Str.

bornerstrasse

Westfälische Strasse

Pauls-

↓ To Dahlem

5

Leibzitzstr.

Konstanzerstr.

6

Kurfürstendamm

9 **10**

8

7

Lietzenburgerstr.

4

Pariser Strasse

Düsseldorfer Strasse

Sächsische Strasse

Hohenzollern-strasse

SAVIGNYPLATZ

Savignyplatz

11

Kantst.

Uhlandstr.

13

14

Joachims talerstrasse

15

Ranke-platz

Bundesallee

Hohen-zollern-platz

Nachoo strasse

17

12

1

2

3

BERLIN

Western Berlin

Ahorn Berlin **6**	Brandenburger Hof/
Alpenland **12**	Relais & Châteaux **16**
Ambassador Berlin **21**	Bristol Kempinski Berlin **14**
Arco **19**	City Pension Alexandra **8**
Artemesia **3**	Grand Hotel Esplanade **23**
Bleibtreu Hotel **9**	Hecker's Hotel **10**
Bogotà **7**	Hotel Crystal **11**

62

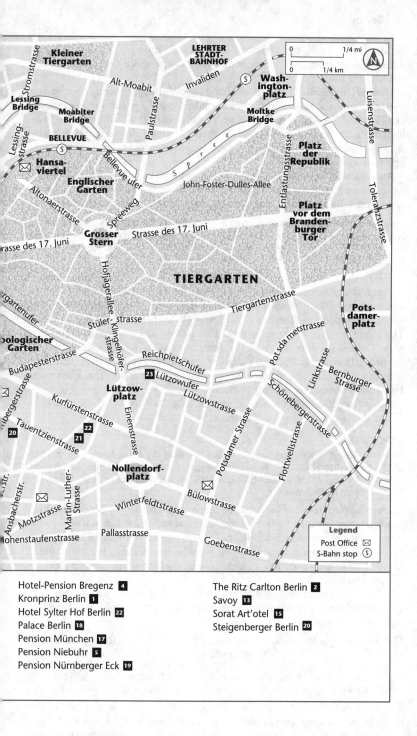

Hotel-Pension Bregenz **4**
Kronprinz Berlin **1**
Hotel Sylter Hof Berlin **22**
Palace Berlin **18**
Pension München **17**
Pension Niebuhr **5**
Pension Nürnberger Eck **19**

The Ritz Carlton Berlin **2**
Savoy **13**
Sorat Art'otel **15**
Steigenberger Berlin **20**

Bathrooms are among the city's most spacious and luxurious, with hair dryers and robes. When reserving, ask for one of the corner rooms, which are the most spacious and have the best views of Berlin.

Dining/Diversions: The Esplanade has some of Berlin's best food. There's a beer-restaurant with a neon-encrusted Würlitzer jukebox, and a gourmet restaurant called Harlekin (see "Dining," below) that was recently awarded a Michelin star. A lavish breakfast buffet is served in the festive Orangerie. The hotel also has its own restaurant ship, the *Esplanade*, with docking space in front of the hotel. See "Berlin After Dark," below, for Harry's New York Bar.

Amenities: 24-hour room service, laundry and dry cleaning, in-house doctor and nurse, valet parking, massages, baby-sitting, triangular indoor pool, whirlpool, solarium, sauna, and full-service hairdressing salon offering hair, nail, and facial treatments.

Steigenberger Berlin. Los-Angeles-Platz 1, 10789 Berlin. ☎ **800/223-5652** in the U.S. and Canada, or 030/2-12-77-07. Fax 030/2-12-71-17. www.steigenberger.com. 397 units. A/C MINIBAR TV TEL. 470DM ($267.90) double; from 750DM ($427.50) suite. AE, DC, MC, V. Parking 28DM ($15.95). U-Bahn: Kurfürstendamm.

It's hardly the most elegant or best Steigenberger in Germany, but still, this hotel is a lot more charming than its plain, rather bleak facade suggests. We prefer it to the Berlin Hilton, a hotel of comparable rating. The decor is tastefully contemporary. Recent renovation has brought a new Executive Club lounge to the executive floor. The rooms are state-of-the-art, with double-glazed windows that minimize street noise. Old-fashioned touches, such as a shoe-shine service, are still maintained.

Dining/Diversions: The hotel's excellent Park Restaurant offers both classical and modern cuisine. The less expensive Berliner Stube serves Prussian fare. The art-deco Hallencafé/Pianobar has excellent pastries.

Amenities: 24-hour room service, dry cleaning, laundry, baby-sitting, in-house doctor, massage, pool, sauna, and solarium.

EXPENSIVE

Bleibtreu Hotel. Bleibtreustrasse 31 (1 block south of the Kürfurstendamm). ☎ **030/ 88474-0.** Fax 030/88474-444. www.bleibtreu.com. E-mail: info@bleibtreu.com. 60 units. MINIBAR TV TEL. 262DM–341DM ($149.35–$194.35) double. Rates include breakfast. AE, MC, V. U-Bahn: Kurfürstendamm.

This special place is one of the latest "boutique hotels" to open in Berlin. The simple facade left over from the 1800s conceals a chic and minimalist Italian interior, which features soft lighting and terrazzo floors. Guest rooms are furnished in natural materials, such as wool, glass, and cotton. The rooms are comfortable, but a bit cramped. Extras include data ports and cordless phones. Bathrooms are well-designed and equipped with hair dryers.

A flower shop and a homeopathic practice are on the premises, and an espresso bar abuts the sidewalk. The restaurant serves an organic international cuisine. There's also an outdoor dining area.

✪ Brandenburger Hof/Relais & Châteaux. Eislebener Strasse 14, 10789 Berlin. ☎ **030/ 21-40-50.** Fax 030/21-40-51-00. www.brandenburger-hof.com. E-mail: info@branden-burger-hof.com. 86 units. A/C MINIBAR TV TEL. 340DM–455DM ($193.80– $259.35) double; 725DM ($413.25) suite. Rates include breakfast. AE, CB, DC, MC, V. Parking 20DM ($11.40). U-Bahn: Kurfürstendamm or Augsburger Str. S-Bahn: Zoologischer Garten.

This hotel on a dignified street in the commercial heart of the city was built in 1991 in the classic Bauhaus style beloved by so many Germans. Its status as a Relais et Châteaux property means it offers better food, service, and amenities than most hotels of its price. The units range from medium-sized to spacious and are among the most stylish in the city. The decor, with its torchère lamps, black leather upholstery, and platform beds, may appear a touch minimalist to some, but everybody will appreciate the original artworks that adorn the walls. Another bonus is the state-of-the-art security system and the French doors that open up onto balconies on all but the top floor. The spacious bathrooms have large shower/tub combinations, plenty of shelf space, scales, and hair dryers. The housekeeping here is among the finest in Berlin. The "Wintergarten," just past the lobby, is an unusual combination of Italian monastery garden and Japanese garden; it's a popular gathering place for guests.

Dining/Diversions: Die Quadriga, a Frank Lloyd Wright design with cherry-wood walls and chairs, boasts French cuisine with an Asian influence and has received a Michelin star. The adjoining Wintergarten functions as both a restaurant and a piano bar.

Amenities: Room service (7am to 10pm), concierge, dry cleaning, laundry, twice-daily maid service, car-rental and tour desk, baby-sitting.

✪ **Savoy.** Fasanenstrasse 9–10, 10623 Berlin. ☎ **800/223-5652** in the U.S. and Canada, or 030/31-10-30. Fax 030/31-10-33-33. www.savoy-hotels.com. E-mail: info@savoy-hotels.com. 140 units. MINIBAR TV TEL. 289DM–389DM ($164.75–$221.75) double; 520DM–900DM ($296.40–$513) suite. Children under 13 stay free in parents' room. AE, DC, MC, V. U-Bahn: Kurfürstendamm.

If you don't demand grand, full-service facilities, this might be the hotel for you. Built in 1929, the quiet, unassuming Savoy is a reliable and durable favorite. It's better than many in its category, and although it has lost some of its old-world Berlin flavor, it remains the choice for the die-hard traditionalist. Its beautifully furnished rooms and luxurious suites come complete with generous desk space, upholstered armchairs, and even cocktail tables as well as the usual hair dryers and trouser presses. There are also such amenities as private safes and double-glazed windows.

Dining/Diversions: A breakfast buffet is served in the street-level restaurant, or on a sixth-floor roof terrace in warm weather. The Savoy's restaurant is Belle Epoque. The hotel's Times Bar is recommended in "Berlin After Dark," below.

Amenities: Room service, laundry, baby-sitting, sauna, fitness club.

MODERATE

Ahorn Berlin. Schlüterstrasse 40 (near the Ku'damm), 10707 Berlin. ☎ **030/8-81-43-44.** Fax 030/8-81-65-00. www.members.aol.com/dglau55015. E-mail: hotel-ahorn@t-online.de. 27 units. MINIBAR TV TEL. 140DM–210DM ($79.80–$119.70) double; 160DM–240DM ($91.20–$136.80) triple; 15DM ($8.55) supplement for kitchenette. Discounts sometimes granted in Dec and Aug. Rates include continental breakfast. AE, DC, MC, V. Parking 10DM ($5.70). U-Bahn: Adenauerplatz. S-Bahn: Savignyplatz.

This simple, clean, cost-conscious hotel is typical of those built during the Cold War era. You stay here more for the price than for any grand comfort, but bedrooms are inviting nonetheless, with good though much-used furnishings, excellent mattresses, and tidy maintenance. The optional kitchenettes are very functional. Families often check in here, not only for the kitchenettes, but because so many rooms are suitable for three. Nearby are many *Kneipen* (bars) and restaurants.

✪ **Artemisia.** Brandenburgischestrasse 18 (near the Ku'damm), 10707 Berlin. ☎ **030/8-73-89-05.** Fax 030/8-61-86-53. E-mail: frauenhotel-berlin@t-online.de. 8 units, 6 with shower or bathroom. TV TEL. 170DM ($96.90) double without shower or bathroom; 200DM–220DM ($114–$125.40) double with shower or bathroom. Children under 8 stay free in mother's room. Rates include continental breakfast. AE, DC, MC, V. Free parking. U-Bahn: Konstan-zerstrasse.

This hotel *for women only* occupies the fourth and fifth floors of a residential building with an elevator. In cold weather, there's often a cozy fire in one of the sitting rooms.

You'll usually find a temporary exhibition of art in the public rooms. Women's conferences and consciousness-raising sessions sometimes take place here. Bedrooms are medium in size and meticulously maintained, each with a quality mattress and fine linen, plus a good-sized bathroom with a hair dryer. On the premises are a bar and a rooftop terrace where a buffet breakfast is served on summer mornings. Children, including boys up to age 14, can stay here with their mothers.

Kronprinz Berlin. Kronprinzendamm 1, 10711 Berlin. ☎ **030/89-60-30.** Fax 030/8-93-12-15. www.kronprinzhotel.de. E-mail: reception@kronprinzhotel.de. 68 units. MINIBAR TV TEL. 260DM ($148.20) double; 380DM ($216.60) suite. Children 12 and under stay free in parents' room. Rates include buffet breakfast. AE, DC, MC, V. Free parking. Bus: 104, 110, 119, 129, or 219.

This hotel is located away from Berlin's center at the far western edge of the Ku'damm. It's about a half-hour walk from the Gedächtniskirche (although linked by bus). In spite of its many discreet charms and features, it remains relatively little known or publicized. All rooms have balconies and fine appointments (often tasteful reproductions of antiques). If you want a little extra comfort, ask for one of the Bel-Etage rooms. Many guests congregate in the cozy in-house bar, or in the garden under the chestnut trees in summer. Laundry and dry cleaning are available, as well as baby-sitting.

INEXPENSIVE

Alpenland. Carmerstrasse 8 (near the Ku'damm), 10623 Berlin. ☎ **030/3-12-39-70.** Fax 030/3-13-84-44. 40 units, 25 with bathroom (5 with shower only). TV TEL. 110DM ($62.70) double without bathroom, 130DM–190DM ($74.10–$108.30) double with bathroom. Rates include breakfast. MC, V. S-Bahn: Savignyplatz. Parking 15DM ($8.55). U-Bahn: Zoologischer Garden.

This hotel is housed in a century-old building that was once an opulent private home. It's convenient to theaters, museums, and pubs and restaurants. Outside, it's ornately decorated with carvings and figures, though the stripped-down interior is almost monastically simple. Mattresses and towels are a bit thin, but there is reasonable comfort here, enhanced by the good maintenance. On the ground floor is a restaurant serving conservative German food that caters to local office workers. There's also a pleasant terrace where guests can enjoy a drink as they watch the sun set over the city. Be warned that the building's four floors are not yet accessible via elevator; however, hotel management plans to have one installed in 2000.

Bogotà. Schlüstrasse 45, 10707 Berlin. ☎ **030/8-81-50-01.** Fax 030/8-83-58-87. www.bogota.de. E-mail: hotel.bogota@t-online.de. 130 units, 65 with bathroom (12 with shower but no toilet). TEL. 110DM ($62.70) double without bathroom; 140DM ($79.80) double with shower but no toilet; from 170DM ($96.90) double with bathroom. Rates include continental breakfast. AE, CB, DC, MC, V. Parking 15DM ($8.55). U-Bahn: Adenauerplatz or Uhlandstr. S-Bahn: Savignyplatz.

The Bogotà is one of the town's most popular budget hotels, though its facilities are less than state-of-the-art. The elevator and floor lobbies are old-fashioned, if not outdated. Bedrooms are small but tidy. Although well maintained, they're a bit dowdy. Bathrooms, though small, are efficiently organized. The best units open onto an inner courtyard and are less noisy than the front rooms. There's a cozy TV room. For an extra 5DM ($2.85) per night you can have a TV in your room.

City Pension Alexandra. Wielandstrasse 32, 10692 Berlin. ☎ **030/8-81-21-07.** Fax 030/88-57-78-18. 9 units, 4 with shower only. TV TEL. 120DM ($68.40) double with shower only, 185DM ($105.45) double with bathroom. Rates include buffet breakfast. AE, DC, MC, V. Parking 10DM ($5.70). S-Bahn: Savignyplatz.

This hotel is comfortable, centrally located, and quiet. The breakfast room, where a buffet is served, is lined with photographs of old Berlin—perfect for acquainting yourself with what to look for as you tour the streets of the city. Most guest rooms have modern furniture; some are more classic. The hotel provides laundry service, and baby-sitting is also available.

Hotel Crystal. Kantstrasse 144, 10623 Berlin. ☎ **030/312-90-47.** Fax 030/3-12-64-65. 33 units, 21 with bathroom (5 with shower only). TEL. 90DM ($51.30) double without bathroom, 110DM ($62.70) double with shower only, 130DM–150DM ($74.10–$85.50) double with bath. Rates include breakfast. AE, MC, V. Parking free. S-Bahn: Savignyplatz.

This hotel has a 1950s middle-European ambience. It's owned and operated by American John Schwarzrock and his German wife, Dorothée; the couple is always glad to welcome American visitors. Guest rooms, although very basic, are comfortable and extremely clean, with eclectic furniture that you might think was gathered piecemeal from all sorts of sources. There's a small bar just off the lobby where guests can have a drink with other travelers. Be warned that unless the Schwartzrocks are personally on the premises, you're likely to find the staff a bit blasé.

Hotel-Pension Bregenz. Bregenzer Strasse 5, 10707 Berlin. ☎ **030/8-81-43-07.** Fax 030/ 8-82-40-09. 14 units, 10 with bathroom. MINIBAR TV TEL. 110DM ($62.70) double without bathroom, 160DM ($91.20) double with bathroom. Rates include breakfast. MC, V. Parking 5DM ($2.85). S-Bahn: Savignyplatz. U-Bahn: Adenauerplatz.

This dignified pension occupies the fourth and sunniest floor of a four-story turn-of-the-century apartment building, accessible by elevator. The owner, Mr. Zimmermann, works hard to maintain the cleanliness and charm of his comfortably furnished, relatively large bedrooms. Double doors help to minimize noise from the public corridors outside. A continental breakfast is served each morning in a small dining area. The staff gladly assists guests in reserving tickets for shows and tours.

Pension München. Guntzelstrasse 62 (close to Bayerischer Platz), 10717 Berlin. ☎ **030/ 8-57-91-20.** Fax 030/85-79-12-22. 8 units, 4 with bathroom. TV TEL. 90DM ($51.30) double without bathroom, 130DM ($74.10) double with bathroom. AE, DC, MC, V. Parking is available on the street. U-Bahn: Guntzelstrasse.

This pension occupies only part of the third floor of a massive four-story building (with an elevator) erected as an apartment house in 1908. It offers a simple but tasteful decor of modern furnishings accented with fresh flowers. Bedrooms are clean and color-coordinated, with contemporary furniture and prints and engravings by local artists. Look for sculptures by the owner, an artist, in some of the public areas as well. Note that if there are no rooms available at this place, you're likely to be recommended to a similar pension, **Pension Güntzel** (☎ **030/8-57-90-20**), on the building's street-level floor and cellar.

Pension Niebuhr. Niebuhrstrasse 74, 10629 Berlin. ☎ **030/3-24-95-95.** Fax 030/3-24-80-21. 12 units, 7 with bathroom. 120DM ($68.40) double without bathroom, 170DM ($96.90) double with bathroom. Rates include breakfast. AE, MC, V. Parking 5DM ($2.85). S-Bahn: Savignyplatz.

Clean, safe, and sophisticated, this gay-friendly hotel occupies one and a half floors of a turn-of-the-century apartment building. Willi Heidasch is your amiable host, maintaining simple but clean rooms, seven with phone and TV. Beds are a bit worn but still have comfort in them, and bathrooms are small. Paintings by aspiring Berlin artists (many are for sale) decorate the public areas. Breakfast is served in your room anytime after 7am and is the only meal offered. About half the clientele is gay, a percentage that's growing, according to the owner.

Pension Nürnberger Eck. Nürnberger Strasse 24a (near the Europa-Center), 10789 Berlin. ☎ **030/2-35-17-80.** Fax 030/2-14-15-40. 8 units, 5 with bathroom. TV TEL. 120DM ($68.40) double without bathroom, 160DM ($91.20) double with bathroom. MC, V. Rates include breakfast. Parking 5DM ($2.85). U-Bahn: Kurfürstendamm.

This reliable pension is refreshingly old-fashioned. It occupies the second floor of a four-story building on a relatively quiet side street. Bedrooms are large, with high ceilings, massive doors, and in many cases, reproductions of Biedermeier-style furniture, including comfortable beds with soft mattresses. This is the kind of place where Christopher Isherwood's Sally Bowles character from *Goodbye to Berlin/Cabaret* might have stayed.

NEAR THE MEMORIAL CHURCH & ZOO
VERY EXPENSIVE

Palace Berlin. Im Europa-Center, opposite the Memorial Church, Budapesterstrasse 43, 10789 Berlin. ☎ **800/457-4000** in the U.S. and Canada, or 030/2-50-20. Fax 030/2-502-1161. www.palace.de. E-mail: sales@palace.de. 325 units. A/C MINIBAR TV TEL. 410DM–590DM ($233.70–$336.30) double; from 650DM ($370.50) suite. AE, DC, MC, V. Parking 30DM ($17.10). U-Bahn: Zoologischer Garten.

Although not at the level of the Bristol Kempinski or the Grand Hotel Esplanade, the stylish Palace outranks such landmarks as the Berlin Hilton and the Steigenberger Berlin. The hotel is much improved over past years. It offers many different styles of accommodations and state-of-the-art maintenance. The best rooms, with all-marble bathrooms and separate showers and tubs, are in the newer Casino Wing. In some rooms, even the good double glazing on the windows is unable to entirely shut out noise from the adjacent Europa-Center. All of the seventh and part of the sixth floor are set aside for nonsmokers. Extras include hair dryers and trouser presses. The staff is extremely pleasant. Bedrooms range from medium to spacious in size, and all have fine beds, superb lighting, and quality carpeting. The bathrooms mostly feature a combination tub and shower (but some have shower stalls only). Each bathroom also contains a hair dryer.

Dining/Diversions: Despite a lot of competition from restaurants nearby, the hotel maintains its own elegant dining room, the First Floor. It also operates two convivial bars and the Alt Nürnberg restaurant, located in the Europa-Center. (See "Dining," below for both restaurants).

Amenities: Room service, laundry, dry cleaning, massage, secretarial services, concierge, baby-sitting; adjacent to the hotel is the Thermen am Europa-Center, a large health club with indoor and outdoor pools, exercise equipment, and a sauna. Admission is free to hotel guests.

EXPENSIVE

Ambassador Berlin. Bayreutherstrasse 42–43 (near Wittenbergplatz), 10787 Berlin. ☎ **030/21-90-20.** Fax 030/21-90-23-80. www-ambassador-berlin.de. E-mail: info@ambassador-berlin.de. 199 units. MINIBAR TV TEL. 280DM–380DM ($159.60–$216.60) double. Rates include buffet breakfast. AE, DC, MC, V. Parking 18DM ($10.25). U-Bahn: Wittenbergplatz.

This hotel is an attractive choice if you'd like to lodge near the Ku'damm. The heated tropical pool on the eighth floor, with its retractable dome and a waterfall, is an unusual feature. Rooms are, for the most part, spacious and exceedingly comfortable and include traditional furnishings, plush carpets, and extras like trouser presses, robes, and hair dryers. Bathrooms are rather small, and only a fifth have showers; the rest have tubs. Readers' reactions to staff attitude have ranged from "hostile" to "exceedingly charming." We guess it depends on who's waiting (or not waiting) on you. Soundproof windows are always a relief in noisy central Berlin, and nonsmokers get a floor to themselves. The hotel is sometimes overrun with large groups.

Dining/Diversions: The elegant Schöneberger Krug restaurant serves tasty regional and international dishes. The hotel's Bar Ambassador is an attractive rendezvous.

Amenities: Same-day laundry, valet, baby-sitting, massage; heated tropical pool, sun lounge, Finnish sauna, solarium, pool bar.

Hecker's Hotel. Grolmanstrasse 35 (near the Ku'damm), 10623 Berlin. ☎ **030/8-89-00.** Fax 030/8-89-02-60. www.heckers-hotel.com. E-mail: info@heckers-hotel.com. 72 units. A/C MINIBAR TV TEL. 260DM–370DM ($148.20–$210.90) double; 260DM–390DM ($148.20–$222.30) junior suite or studio. AE, CB, DC, MC, V. Parking 15DM ($8.55). U-Bahn: Uhlandstrasse. Bus: 109 from Berlin-Tegel Airport to Uhlandstrasse.

For years this establishment enjoyed a reputation as a small, private hotel, but now it's been expanded. Although not in the same league as the Sorat (see below), this is still a winning choice. It's conveniently located near the Ku'damm and the many bars, cafes, and restaurants around Savignyplatz. The original 42 rooms are smaller than the newer units, which are medium-sized. The rather severe and somewhat somber modern style may not suit everyone—certainly not those seeking romantic ambience. Some rooms are exclusively for nonsmokers. There is a sterility here but also up-to-date comfort and top-notch maintenance.

Dining/Diversions: The hotel maintains a small restaurant and bar. The rooftop terrace is available for dining in summer, and provides a great view of Berlin at night.

Amenities: Concierge, room service, dry cleaning and laundry, car-rental and tour desk, baby-sitting and secretarial services.

⭐ **Sorat Art'otel.** Joachimstalerstrasse 28–29 (near the Ku'damm), 10719 Berlin. ☎ 030/ 88-44-70. Fax 030/88-44-77-00. 133 units. A/C MINIBAR TV TEL. 220DM–415DM ($125.40–$236.55) double. Rates include buffet breakfast. AE, DC, MC, V. U-Bahn: Kurfürstendamm.

Chic, discreet, and avant-garde, the Sorat is unlike any other Berlin hotel. The location is ideal, in the heart of cosmopolitan Berlin, with the Ku'damm action virtually outside the front door. The decor, which is strictly minimalist in design, includes touches from top designers. You'll find Philippe Starck–designed bar stools, chairs by Arne Jacobsen, and artwork by Berlin artist Wolf Vostell gracing the bedroom walls. Modernists will be at home here, amid the pedestal tables evoking cable spools and the chrome-legged furnishings. Traditionalists might not be so pleased. The rooms are all comfortable, however, with soundproofing, deluxe mattresses on the large beds, private safes, and tasteful lighting. Bathrooms are generous in size. The service here is among Berlin's finest.

Dining/Diversions: The Anteo restaurant, adjacent to the hotel, is known for both its creative cuisine and its avant-garde decor.

Amenities: Concierge, room service, car-rental, laundry.

MODERATE

Hotel Sylter Hof Berlin. Kurfürstenstrasse 114–116, 10787 Berlin. ☎ **030/2-12-00.** Fax 030/2-14-28-26. 161 units. MINIBAR TV TEL. 186DM ($106) single; 282DM ($160.75) double; 293DM–426DM ($167–$242.80) suite. Rates include buffet breakfast. CB, DISC. Parking 16DM ($9.10). U-Bahn: Wittenbergplatz. Bus: 100 or X9.

Sylter Hof, built in 1966, offers rich trappings at good prices. The main lounges are warmly decorated in Louis XV style, with chandeliers, provincial chairs, and antiques. Well-maintained rooms—the majority of which are singles—may be too small for most tastes but are good for business travelers. The bar-lounge features velvet armchairs and Persian rugs. The more conservative dining room, called the Friesenstube, serves Prussian and continental cuisine. The hotel also has an American-style coffee shop that serves fresh-baked cakes and daily specials at reasonable rates. On the premises is a nightclub featuring burlesque shows (with discreet nudity). The staff pays special attention to your comfort.

INEXPENSIVE

Arco. Geisbergstrasse 30 (near Wittenbergplatz), 10777 Berlin. ☎ **030/2-35-14-80.** Fax 030/2-11-33-87. E-mail: arco/hotel@t-online.de. 22 units, 18 with bathroom (3 with shower only). TV TEL. 140DM–180DM ($79.80–$102.60) double. Rates include breakfast. AE, DC, MC, V. U-Bahn: Wittenbergplatz.

This hotel is in a four-story turn-of-the-century building. Most of its bedrooms are on the ground floor and the floor above, although an additional half-dozen are in privately owned apartments on the upper floors. Bedrooms are a bit plain but comfortable, each fitted with a good mattress on a twin or double bed. A small terrace surrounded by a tree-lined garden gives guests a sense of solitude in the midst of a busy city. The friendly staff is glad to help guests arrange theater tickets or restaurant reservations. Discounts of around 10% are offered for stays of more than 3 nights, or on 1-night stays between October and April if business is slow.

IN GRUNEWALD

✪ **The Ritz Carlton Berlin.** Brahmsstrasse 10, 14193 Berlin-Grunewald. ☎ **030/89-58-40.** Fax 030/89-58-48-07. www.ritzcarlton.com. 54 units. A/C MINIBAR TV TEL. 494DM– 755DM ($281.60–$430.35) double; 895DM–5,500DM ($510.15–$3,135) suite. AE, DC, MC, V. Parking 29DM ($16.55).

A stay here offers a rare opportunity to live within an Italian Renaissance–style palace, where Kaiser Wilhelm II was once a guest. If you don't mind the commute, it's even more enchanting than the Seehof. The lavish new decor is by German-born fashion superstar Karl Lagerfeld. The structure's monumental staircase, minstrel's gallery, and other belle epoque trappings remain, but Mr. Lagerfeld's contributions have added an undeniable gloss to the hotel's interior. Beds are sumptuous, with deluxe mattresses, great pillows, fine linen, and elegant fabrics. Bathrooms have marble surfaces, shower and tub combos, plush towels, radiantly heated floors, slippers, and scales, along with robes.

   Dining: The hotel contains a pair of restaurants; Vivaldi is the more unusual (see "Dining," below).

   Amenities: Concierge, 24-hour room service, twice-daily maid service, health club with Jacuzzi and sauna, conference rooms, beauty salon and boutique, sundeck, babysitting, secretarial service, in-room massage, dry cleaning and laundry service.

IN BERLIN-MITTE
VERY EXPENSIVE

Berlin Hilton. Mohrenstrasse 30, 10117 Berlin. ☎ **800/445-8667** in the U.S. and Canada, or 030/2-02-30. Fax 030/20-23-42-69. www.infoberlin/hilton.com. 502 units. A/C MINIBAR TV TEL. 465DM–550DM ($265.05–$313.50) double; 650DM–1,500DM ($370.50–$855) suite. Krone Wing 255DM–375DM ($145.35–$213.75) double. Special weekend packages available. AE, MC, V. Parking 22DM ($12.55). U-Bahn: Stadtmitte.

This deluxe hotel was the first to open in what was East Berlin following the collapse of the Berlin Wall. Today it's the third largest hotel in the city and one of the most popular. The location is excellent. The seven-floor hotel contains enough accessories, bars, and facilities to keep you jumping for a week. Units come with double-glazed windows, comfortable beds, bedside controls, private safes, and well-equipped bathrooms with tub and shower combos and hair dryers. At least half the units overlook the twin churches of one of the city's most dramatic squares, the Gendarmenmarkt.

Berlin-Mitte Accommodations & Dining

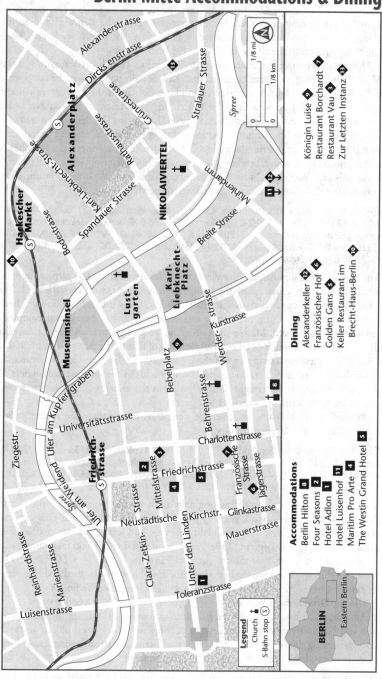

Accommodations

Berlin Hilton **8**
Four Seasons **2**
Hotel Adlon **1**
Hotel Luisenhof **11**
Maritim Pro Arte **4**
The Westin Grand Hotel **5**

Dining

Alexanderkeller **12**
Französischer Hof **6**
Golden Gans **5**
Keller Restaurant im
Brecht-Haus-Berlin **10**

Königin Luise **9**
Restaurant Borchardt **7**
Restaurant Vau **3**
Zur Letzten Instanz **13**

BERLIN
Eastern Berlin

Legend
✝ Church
Ⓢ S-Bahn stop

71

In the same complex is a less lavish, three-star annex, the Berlin Hilton Krone Wing. Rooms here have fewer accessories, but they're less expensive. Krone Wing guests are entitled to use all the facilities of the Berlin Hilton.

Dining/Diversions: Restaurants include The Fellini, an Italian restaurant, and the Mark Brandenburg, with traditional cuisine. La Coupole, named after the famed cafe in Paris, offers good food in a relaxed atmosphere. Beletage is the breakfast restaurant with a large American-style breakfast buffet. In the Wintergarten, you can order drinks, traditional snacks, light meals, and cakes. Restaurant Gendarmenmarkt is self-service. Bars include the Kaminbar, which has an open fireplace, and the Mundi Bar, an artists' bar with an interior design by Charlotta Janse. For more raucous fun, there's a beer pub, Kaktus, with a bowling alley, and a disco is open from dusk until dawn.

Amenities: Concierge, 24-hour room service, laundry, baby-sitting, health club, saunas, pool with Jacuzzi, rooftop squash courts, bowling alley.

✪ **Four Seasons.** Charlottenstrasse 49/Am Gendarmenmarkt, 10117 Berlin. ☎ **800/ 332-3442** in the U.S., or 030/2-03-38. Fax 030/203-36-009. www.fourseasons.com. E-mail: kerstin.pundt@fourseasons.com. 204 units. A/C MINIBAR TV TEL. 395DM–545DM ($225.15–$310.65) double; from 800DM ($456) suite. AE, CB, DC, MC, V. Parking 40DM ($22.80). U-Bahn: Französifchestrasse.

The world's most sophisticated travelers come here demanding and getting supreme service and luxury. Once inside the lobby, opulence reigns, with crystal chandeliers imported from Vienna, silk-covered chairs, and antiques throughout Europe. Bedrooms are furnished with timeless taste and elegance. Many open onto the complex's serene central courtyard. Marble walls surround walk-in showers and deep tubs, and the fine selection of toiletries reflects the pleasures of home. The best rooms, in the 22, 23, and 24 series, open onto views of the French cathedral and the Gendarmenmarkt.

Dining/Diversions: A crackling fire in winter adds to the intimate atmosphere of the excellent Seasons Restaurant. Guests gather in the lounges or bars for afternoon tea, cocktails, or some of Germany's best beers.

Amenities: Health club, room service, concierge, twice-daily maid service, newspaper delivery, dry cleaning, laundry.

✪ **Hotel Adlon.** Unter den Linden 77, 10117 Berlin. ☎ **800/426-3135** or 030/22-61-0. Fax 30/22-61-1116. www.hotel-adlon.de. E-mail: adlon@kempinski.com. 337 units. A/C MINIBAR TV TEL. 490DM–660DM ($279.30–$376.20) double; from 800DM ($456) suite. AE, DC, MC, V. Parking 40DM ($22.80) per day. S-Bahn: Unter den Linden.

This grand and historic hotel was originally built by the legendary hotelier Lorez Adlon in 1907. Public rooms, some of them illuminated with stained-glass cupolas, contain coffered ceilings, mosaics, inlaid paneling, and lots of Carrara marble. The guest rooms are mostly large and have cherry-wood and myrtle-wood furnishings, rich fabrics, and lots of state-of-the-art electronic amenities, such as CD players. The rooms on the top floor have the best views but are a bit more cramped and lack some amenities. Overall, this hotel is one of the premier addresses of Berlin.

Dining/Diversions: There are two restaurants, two bars, and a coffee shop.

Amenities: 24-hour room service, hair dryers, massage, spa services (including skin care and beauty treatments), concierge, supervised aerobics classes, indoor and outdoor swimming pools, health club, jogging path across the street, and access to bicycling, golf, and horseback riding within the city limits of Berlin.

Maritim Pro Arte. Friedrichstrasse 150–153 (across from the Friedrichstrasse train station), 10117 Berlin. ☎ **030/2-03-35.** Fax 030/20-33-42-09. 403 units. A/C MINIBAR TV TEL. 259DM–519DM ($147.65–$295.85) double; 530DM ($302.10) apt; 1,800DM ($1,026) executive suite; 2,700DM ($1,539) presidential suite. AE, DC, MC, V. Parking 25DM ($14.25). S-Bahn: Friedrichstrasse.

This "designer hotel" is a short walk from Unter den Linden. Works by noted artists are exhibited throughout the hotel. The furniture was created by Phillipe Starck. Bedrooms are individually designed, and are soothing and comfortable. All units have built-in safes, fine linen on the beds, and a "lazy chair," and most provide a fax outlet.

Dining/Diversions: There are three restaurants: Bistro Media, the less formal Galerie Restaurant, and the premier à la carte restaurant, Atelier. There's also a bar.

Amenities: Room service, laundry, baby-sitting, indoor pool, fitness studio, sauna, solarium.

✪ **The Westin Grand Hotel.** Friedrichstrasse 158–164, 10117 Berlin. ☎ **800/843-3311** in the U.S., or 030/2-02-70. Fax 030/20-27-33-62. www.westin.com. E-mail: info@westin. com. 358 units. A/C MINIBAR TV TEL. 305DM–530DM ($173.85–$302.10) double; 750DM ($427.50) junior suite; 900DM–1,200DM ($513–$684) apt suite; 3,400DM ($1,938) presidential suite. AE, DC, MC, V. Parking 25DM ($14.25). U-Bahn: Französische Strasse. S-Bahn: Friedrichstrasse.

Amazingly, this monument to capitalistic decadence was first constructed on socialist soil. Now that it's shed the former East German stiffness and formality, it's one of Berlin's finest hotels. Belle epoque features blend contemporary styling. The rooms rise, atrium-style, above an octagonal lobby with a lavender-and-pink skylight of intricate stained glass. Rooms come in a wide range of styles, from beautifully appointed standard singles and doubles all the way up to the Schinkel Suite. The beds come with wonderfully soft linens, down pillows and comforters, and firm mattresses. Other features include chrome fixtures, terry-cloth robes, thick towels, and fresh flowers.

Dining/Diversions: Don't miss the public rooms one flight above lobby level. There's the convivial Peacock Bar, and the impressive Club Diana, a faithful copy of the great room of a Teutonic hunting lodge. The hotel also offers the Coelln restaurant, on lobby level; the Forellen Quintet, a seafood restaurant; the Stammhaus, a beer pub; a cocktail bar named Bar 35; and Le Grand Café.

Amenities: 24-hour room service, fitness club, whirlpool, marble pool, saunas, solarium, deluxe hairdressing salon.

EXPENSIVE

✪ **Hotel Luisenhof.** Köpenicker Strasse 92, 10179 Berlin. ☎ **030/2-41-59-06.** Fax 030/ 2-79-29-83. www.luisenhof.com. E-mail: info@luisenhof.de. 27 units. MINIBAR TV TEL. 250DM ($142.50) double; 450DM ($256.50) suite. Rates include breakfast. AE, DC, MC, V. Parking 14DM ($8). U-Bahn: Märkisches Museum.

This is one of the most desirable small hotels in Berlin's eastern district. It lies within a severely dignified house, originally built in 1822. Its five floors of high-ceilinged bedrooms have been outfitted in a conservative and traditional style, a welcome escape from modern Berlin. The upgraded units range in size from small to spacious, but all are equipped with fine beds, safes, and individual fax machines. Bathrooms, though small, are beautifully appointed and tiled. The neighborhood around this hotel, like many other parts of the once-dour eastern zone, is undergoing a rapid renovation.

Dining/Diversions: Beneath the vaulted ceilings in the cellar, you'll find a very appealing restaurant, the Alexanderkeller (see "Dining" below).

Amenities: Room service from 6am to midnight, laundry and dry cleaning, concierge.

4 Dining

If it's true that optimism and appetite go hand in hand, Berliners must be among the most optimistic people in Europe. But just because Berliners like to eat, doesn't mean

Tipping

If a restaurant bill says *Bedienung*, that means a service charge has already been added, so just round up to the nearest mark.

that they like to spend a lot on food. Locals know that you can often have a memorable dinner here in an unheralded wine restaurant or sidewalk cafe. Rising food costs in the east, however, mean that in the new Berlin, the eastern section can no longer be viewed as a bargain basement in the food department.

Examples of typical dishes are the Berliner *Schlachteplatte* (cold plate), pigs' trotters cooked with sauerkraut and pea puree, and *Eisbein* (pickled knuckle of pork with sauerkraut). Venison, wildfowl, and wild boar also appear frequently, as do carp and trout, along with an infinite variety of sausages.

But Berlin does not limit itself to traditional cuisine. A new wave of restaurants has swept across the city, from east to west. More and more are going ethnic, everything from Indonesian to French to Thai or Japanese. Eastern European wines are now almost as popular as those from Germany itself.

ON OR NEAR THE KURFÜRSTENDAMM
VERY EXPENSIVE

✪ **Bamberger Reiter.** Regensburgerstrasse 7. ☎ **030/2-18-42-82.** Reservations required. Main courses 52DM–62DM ($29.65–$35.35); 6- or 7-course fixed-price menu 165DM–195DM ($94.05–$111.15). AE, DC, MC, V. Tues–Sat 6pm–1am (last order 10pm). U-Bahn: Spichernstrasse. CONTINENTAL.

Bamberger Reiter, serving French, German, and Austrian dishes in the style of *neue Deutsche Küche,* is still the choice of savvy local foodies. Don't judge it by its location in an undistinguished 19th-century apartment house. The quality is beyond question here—only Rockendorf's or Alt Luxemburg can even pretend to have better food. The menu changes daily according to the availability of fresh ingredients and the inspiration of the chef, but might include a roulade of quail, bass with Riesling sauce, cream of fresh asparagus soup, lamb with beans and potato croutons, and date strudel with almond ice cream. The decor evokes old Germany, with lots of mirrors and fresh flowers. The wine list is enormous, with around 20 varieties of champagne alone.

✪ **First Floor.** In the Palace Hotel, Budapesterstrasse 42. ☎ **030/25-02-10-20.** Reservations recommended. Main courses 45DM–65DM ($25.65–$37.05); set menus 78DM ($44.45) at lunch only, and 130DM–169DM ($74.10–$96.35) at lunch and dinner. AE, DC, MC, V. Sun–Fri noon–2:30pm, Sun–Sat 6–11pm; closed August. U-Bahn: Zoo. REGIONAL GERMAN/FRENCH.

This is the Palace Hotel's showcase restaurant, one floor above street level. It features smoothly orchestrated service and the cuisine of master chef Rolf Schmidt. A battalion of wine stewards and wait staff are on hand to smooth your path to a sumptuous meal. Menu items include a terrine of veal with arugula-flavored butter; sophisticated variations of Bresse chicken; guinea fowl stuffed with foie gras and served with a truffled vinaigrette sauce; cassoulet of lobster and broad beans in a southwestern French style; fillet of sole with champagne sauce; and mascarpone mousse with lavender-scented honey.

EXPENSIVE

✪ **Harlekin.** In the Grand Hotel Esplanade, Lützowufer. ☎ **030/25-47-88-58.** Reservations recommended. Main courses 44DM–49DM ($25.10–$27.95); 4- to 6-course menu

⊕ Family-Friendly Restaurant

Funkturm Restaurant (*see p. 81*)   Kids delight in ascending this radio tower on Messedam, open daily from 10:30am to 11pm. The food at the restaurant is good, and later you can go to the observation platform for a truly grand view. The elevator costs 6DM ($3.40) for adults, 3DM ($1.70) for children.

130DM–165DM ($74.10–$94.05). AE, DC, MC, V. Tues–Sat 6–11pm. Closed 3½ weeks in July. U-Bahn: Nollendorfplatz or Wittenbergplatz. FRENCH/INTERNATIONAL.

This restaurant's rise to prominence chagrined jealous chefs at old favorites like the Bristol Kempinski. The menu is perfectly balanced between tradition and innovation. For example, appetizers are likely to include such dishes as calves' consommé with crayfish or osso bucco consommé with lobster Spïtzle. For your main course, you might be won over by the saddle of lamb baked in a spring roll or turbot roasted with mixed root vegetables. All dishes are made with fresh local produce and are perfectly prepared. Set menus are always delightful and often pleasantly surprising.

Paris Bar. Kantstrasse 152 (between Savignyplatz and Gedächtniskiche). ☎ **030/3-13-80-52.** Reservations recommended. Main courses 40DM–55DM ($22.80–$31.35). AE. Daily noon–1am. U-Bahn: Uhlandstrasse. FRENCH.

This French bistro has been a local favorite since it cheered up the postwar years in dismal bombed-out Berlin. It's crowded with elbow-to-elbow tables like a Montmartre tourist trap, but is a genuinely pleasing little place on the see-and-be-seen circuit, close to the Theater des Westens. The food is invariably fresh and well prepared, but not particularly innovative.

MODERATE

La Table. Damaschkestrasse 26. ☎ **030/3-23-14-04.** Reservations required. Main courses 12.50DM–36DM ($7.10–$20.50). MC. Mon–Sat 5pm–midnight. U-Bahn: Adenauerplatz. GERMAN.

La Table has gained a reputation as a select dining spot and social center. Your host is Mr. Seidler, who has a devoted local following among theater and media personalities. Savor the *Kohlroulade*, a stuffed cabbage roll—few chefs would want to compete with it. The *Tafelspitz*, boiled beef with vegetables, would have pleased Emperor Josef of Austria (it was his favorite dish). Another highlight is the rack of lamb with honey onions and rosemary potatoes. Look also for market-fresh daily specials. The chef believes in strong flavors and good hearty cookery. The ambience is that of a Berlin bistro, charmingly cluttered with kitsch from all over the world.

✪ Marjellchen. Mommsenstrasse 9. ☎ **030/8-83-26-76.** Reservations required. Main courses 18.50DM–39.50DM ($10.55–$22.50). AE, DC, MC, V. Mon–Sat 5pm–midnight. Closed Dec 23, 24, and 31. U-Bahn: Adenauerplatz or Uhlandstrasse. EAST PRUSSIAN.

This is the only restaurant in Berlin specializing in the cuisine of Germany's long-lost province of East Prussia, along with the cuisines of Pomerania and Silesia. The restaurant's unusual name comes from an East Prussian word meaning "young girl." Ramona Azzaro, whose East Prussian mother taught her many of the region's famous recipes, is the creative force here. Amid a Bismarckian ambience of vested waiters and oil lamps, you can enjoy a savory version of red-beet soup with strips of beef, East Prussian potato soup with shrimp and bacon, *Falscher Gänsebraten* (pork spare ribs

Western Berlin Dining

Mierendorff-platz

Kaiserin- Augusta-Allee

Alt-Moabi

Schlossgarten Charlottenburg

Mierendorffstrasse

Quedlinburgstrasse

Spree

Gotzkowsky Bridge

Levetzowstra.

Schloss Bridge

Dove-Helmholtzstrasse

Franklinstrasse

Spandauer-Damm

Luisen-platz

Dove Bridge

Salzufer

Christstrasse

Otto-Suhr-Allee

Cauerstrasse

Einsteinufer

Landwehrkanal

Dranckelmannstrasse

Schlossstrasse

Rich.-Wagner-Strasse

March-strasse

Bach-

TIER-GARTEN

Zillestrasse

Bismarckstrasse

Ernst-Reuter-Platz

Strasse des 17. Juni

Kaiserdamm

Kaiser-Friedrich-Strasse

Wilmersdorfer

Krumme Strasse

Schillerstrasse

Schlüterstr.

BAHNHOF ZOOLOGISCHER GARTEN

Goethestrasse

Knesebeckstr.

Harden bergstrasse

Harde bergpla

Pestalozzistrasse

Kantstrasse

CHARLOTTEN-BURG

Savignyplatz

Kantst.

Rönnestrasse

Lewishamstr.

SAVIGNYPLATZ

Leibzitzstr.

Kurfürstendamm

Uhlandstrasse

Joachims talerstrasse

WESTKREUZ

Sybelstrasse

Damasch-kestrasse

Rankeplatz

Kurfürstendamm

Brandenburgische Str.

Konstanzerstr.

Lietzenburgerstr.

Bundesallee

bornerstrasse

Pariser Strasse

Westfälische Strasse

Düsseldorfer Strasse

Hohen-zollern-platz

Nachod strasse

Seesener Strasse

Pauls-

Sächsische Strasse

Hohenzollern-strasse

↓ To Dahlem

BERLIN

Western Berlin

Alt Luxemburg ④	Daitokai ㉒
Alt Nürnberg ㉔	Ernst-August ⑨
Ana e Bruno ②	First Floor ㉑
Arc ⑯	Funkturm Restaurant ⑦
Bamberger Reiter ⑪	Hard Rock Café ⑮
Bierhaus Luisen–Bräu ①	Hardtke's ⑭

76

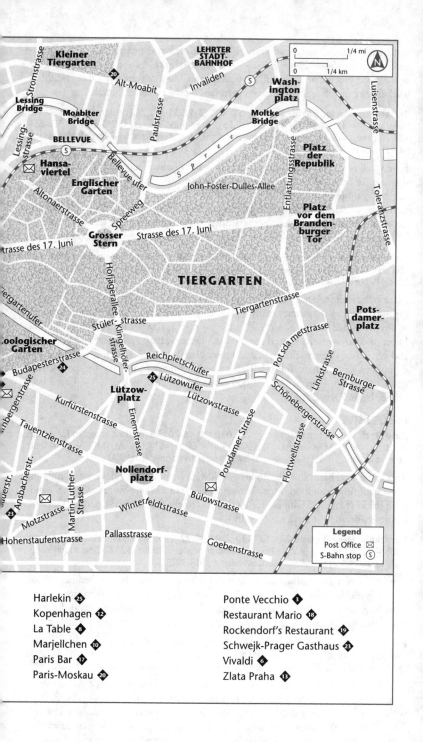

Harlekin 🔵25
Kopenhagen 🔵12
La Table 🔵8
Marjellchen 🔵10
Paris Bar 🔵17
Paris-Moskau 🔵20

Ponte Vecchio 🔵3
Restaurant Mario 🔵18
Rockendorf's Restaurant 🔵19
Schwejk-Prager Gasthaus 🔵23
Vivaldi 🔵6
Zlata Praha 🔵13

stuffed with prunes and bread crumbs "as if the cook had prepared a goose"), marinated elk, and *Mecklenburger Kümmelfleisch* (lamb with chives and onions). This is the type of food Goethe or Schiller liked; perhaps you'll be a convert too. Of course, Marjellchen isn't the place if you want to keep tabs on the cholesterol intake.

Restaurant Mario. Carmerstrasse 2. ☎ **030/3-12-31-15.** Reservations recommended. Main courses 15DM–35DM ($8.55–$19.95); fixed-price menus 45DM–60DM ($25.65–$34.20). AE, MC, V. Mon–Fri noon–midnight, Sat 4pm–1am. S-Bahn: Savignyplatz. NORTHERN ITALIAN.

Here you'll find Berlin's most imaginative northern Italian food. The innovative chefs shop for the best and most market-fresh ingredients. Begin with a platter of the most delectable antipasti in town. At least two different kinds of pastas are offered nightly, including a favorite made with a green-pepper pesto. Also on hand are more traditional dishes such as chicken breast stuffed with mozzarella and herbs, tantalizing herb-seasoned lamb cutlets, and fresh fish simply grilled and perfectly seasoned.

Zlata Praha. Meinekestrasse 4. ☎ **030/8-81-97-50.** Reservations recommended. Main courses 17DM–35DM ($9.70–$19.95). AE, MC, V. Daily 5–11:30pm. U-Bahn: Ulan Strasse. BOHEMIAN/HUNGARIAN.

Zlata Praha is the top place for Bohemian cuisine. Many of the dishes evoke childhood memories for the restaurant's many regular clients. The Szegendiner goulash is as fine as any we've had during a tour of Hungary. Other specialties include as "Bohemian forest" goulash with spätzle and green salad, fillet stroganoff Paprikaschnitzel (an original version of Wiener schnitzel), and honey-glazed roast duck with red cabbage and dumplings. If you have room left after the gigantic portions, try the poppy seed strudel. German, French, and Austrian wines are featured, as well as the Czech beer Pilsner Urquell das Echte.

INEXPENSIVE

Hard Rock Cafe. Meinekestrasse 21. ☎ **030/88-46-20.** Reservations accepted for groups of 10 or more. Main courses 14.50DM–30DM ($8.25–$17.10). AE, MC, V. Sun–Thurs noon–midnight, Fri–Sat noon–2am. U-Bahn: Kurfürstendamm. AMERICAN.

This is the local branch of the familiar worldwide chain that mingles rock 'n' roll nostalgia with American food. Menu choices range from a veggie burger to a "pig" sandwich (hickory smoked pork barbecue) that you might find in rural Georgia. The food is unexceptional, but service is friendly.

Hardtke's. Meinekestrasse 27A. ☎ **030/8-81-98-27.** Reservations required. Main courses 15DM–25DM ($8.55–$14.25); 3-course fixed-price menu 40DM ($22.80). No credit cards. Daily noon–midnight. U-Bahn: Kurfürstendamm. BERLINER.

Hardtke's serves the most authentic German cooking in town. The true Berliner will ask for the *grosse Schlachteplatte*—fresh black pudding and liver sausage (fresh from the in-house butcher shop), small pickled knuckle of pork, liver dumpling, shredded pickled white cabbage, mashed peas, and boiled potatoes. German retirees love dining here.

Kopenhagen. Kurfürstendamm 203–205. ☎ **030/8-81-62-19.** Reservations recommended. Main courses 20DM–35DM ($11.40–$19.95); smorgasbord 15DM–25DM ($8.55–$14.25). AE, DC, MC, V. Daily 11am–1am. U-Bahn: Kurfürstendamm. DANISH.

This restaurant operates out of a long, narrow, bistro-style room, with a glass-enclosed entrance overlooking the Ku'damm. Its most famous specialty is smorgasbord, piled with everything from a slice of Danish cheese to steak tartare crowned by a raw egg. The selection of smorgasbord is so huge that you may spend half your lunchtime deciding what to order. We prefer the marinated herring and roast beef with rémoulade sauce, the liver pâté, or the special aquavit cream cheese. Naturally, you'll want to accompany your meal with a Danish Carlsberg beer. Hot main dishes, Danish-style, are featured as well, including lobster soup, game pie with Cumberland sauce and Waldorf salad, and broiled salmon or fried herring with dill-flavored tartar sauce.

NEAR THE MEMORIAL CHURCH & ZOO
EXPENSIVE

Daitokai. Berlin Europa-Center. ☎ **030/2-61-80-99.** Fixed-price meals 30DM–55DM ($17.10–$31.35) at lunch, 65DM–100DM ($37.05–$57) at dinner. AE, DC, MC, V. Tues–Sun noon–2:30pm and 6–10:30pm. U-Bahn: Kurfürstendamm. JAPANESE.

Think of it as a less-institutionalized Benihana's. Vermilion carp lanterns illuminate the labyrinth of reflecting pools. Chefs prepare the meals before your eyes at several long tables. This teppanyaki restaurant offers some of the city's finest grilled steak—tender, juicy, and never overcooked. The seafood and vegetables are served with an artistic flair, and the fish is always fresh and beautifully presented. Quality is never skimped. The flawless service features kindly, almost overly polite waitresses in kimonos. To dine here inexpensively and still eat well, take advantage of the set luncheons.

INEXPENSIVE

Alt Nürnberg. Berlin Europa-Center. ☎ **030/2-61-43-97.** Reservations recommended on weekends. Main courses 14DM–34DM ($8–$19.40). AE, DC, MC, V. Sun–Thurs 11:30am–11pm, Fri–Sat 11:30am–midnight. U-Bahn: Kurfürstendamm or Zoologischer Garten. GERMAN/BAVARIAN.

This ground-level restaurant handsomely captures the ambience of an old Bavarian tavern. The food is solid German fare, standard and reliable, though hardly exciting. The house specialty is *Nürnberger Rostbratwürstl.* You might begin with a typical Berlin pea soup or Hungarian *Goulashsouppe.* The Wiener schnitzel is always reliable, as are the herring salad and the pork fillet in pepper sauce with broccoli. Inexpensive platters are usually a meal in themselves.

Arc. Fasanenstrasse 81A. ☎ **030/3-13-26-25.** Reservations recommended. Main courses 18.10DM–32.50DM ($10.30–$18.50). AE, DC, MC, V. Daily 10am–2pm (breakfast); noon–midnight (lunch and dinner); 8pm–2am (bar). U-Bahn: Kurfürstendamm. INTERNATIONAL/GERMAN/FRENCH.

Its name comes from its position underneath a brick-and-concrete overpass for a train line. Inside, you'll find a warm and accommodating cafe/restaurant favored by the city's gay and gay-friendly residents. People here like to chat over mugs of beer. You can have an English breakfast, complete with bacon, fried eggs, and beans for 12DM ($6.85). Lunches and dinners are based on organically grown ingredients. Menu items include Greek salads, carrot soup with coriander, pastas, Baden-style potato soup with sausages, and Barbary duck with cassis sauce.

Schwejk-Prager Gasthaus. Ansbacherstrasse 4 (near the Memorial Church). ☎ **030/2-13-78-92.** Reservations recommended. Main courses 15DM–30DM ($8.55–$17.10). AE, DC, V. Daily 5pm–midnight, Sat noon–midnight. U-Bahn: Wittenbergplatz. CZECH.

The taste of eastern Europe is alive and flourishing at this bistro, where Bohemian specialties are served in very generous portions. This place doesn't quite match the standards of Zlata Praha (see above), but still, meals here are one of the best bargains in town. The bistro has a kind of neighborhood-tavern ambience of well-scrubbed tables and regular clients. The food tastes even better when washed down with the Czech beer Pilsner Urquell or the original Czech Budweiser. Typical specialties are crackling pork steak on toast topped with grilled cheese, half roast duck with dumpling sauerkraut, a Russian "Borsch" soup with sour cream, and fried crumbed cheese with rémoulade sauce and fried potatoes.

TIERGARTEN

Paris-Moskau. Alt-Moabit 141. ☎ **030/3-94-20-81.** Reservations recommended. Main courses 34DM–43DM ($19.40–$24.50); fixed-price menus 90DM–140DM ($51.30–$79.80). No credit cards. Daily 6–11:30pm. S-Bahn: Bellevue. INTERNATIONAL.

The grand days of the 19th century are alive and well at this restaurant in the beautiful Tiergarten area, where good dining spots are scarce. Menu items are both classic and more cutting-edge. The fresh tomato soup is excellent. Some of the dishes are mundane—the grilled fillet of beef in mushroom sauce comes to mind—but other lighter dishes with delicate seasonings are delightful. We recommend the grilled North Sea salmon with herbs accompanied by basil-flavored noodles. The chef should market his recipe for saffron sauce, which accompanies several dishes. You'll receive attentive service from the formally dressed staff.

IN GREATER CHARLOTTENBURG
VERY EXPENSIVE

✪ **Alt-Luxemburg.** Windscheidstrasse 31. ☎ **030/3-23-87-30.** Reservations required. 3-course menu 105DM ($59.85); 4-course menu 120DM ($68.40); 5-course menu 135DM–155DM ($76.95–$88.35). AE, DC, MC, V. Mon–Sat 7–11pm. U-Bahn: Sophie-Charlotte-Platz. CONTINENTAL.

Bamberger Reiter is still the leader among Berlin restaurants, but Alt-Luxemburg is nipping at its heels. Karl Wannemacher is one of the outstanding chefs of Germany. Try the honey-glazed duck breast or the saddle of venison with juniper sauce. His Bavarian cream of eel and sturgeon terrine is also excellent. For dessert, don't miss the memorable semolina dumplings with orange ragout or the orange sorbet. The service is both unpretentious and gracious. The dark paneling, evenly spaced mirrors, antique chandeliers, and old-fashioned ambience create a belle epoque aura.

EXPENSIVE

Ana e Bruno. Sophie-Charlotten-Strasse 101. ☎ **030/325-71-10.** Reservations recommended. Main courses 45DM–52DM ($25.65–$29.65); fixed-price menu 115DM–130DM ($65.55–$74.10). AE. Tues–Sat 6:30pm–midnight. U-Bahn: Bismarckstrasse. ITALIAN.

This is one of Berlin's most charming Italian restaurants. Ana and Bruno turn out a delectable cuisine that takes full advantage of the freshest ingredients and produce in any season. *Nuova cucina* is emphasized here more strongly than traditional Italian classics, and the chefs like to experiment. The combinations of food offer delicious flavors and the creations a harmonious medley. Expect dishes such as a radicchio-studded pasta with perfectly cooked shrimp or an Italian fillet of veal with a tuna sauce. Regular customers and gourmets keen on experimenting always seem satisfied with the results here. A large wine selection, most of it reasonable in price, complements the well-chosen menus.

MODERATE

Bierhaus Luisen-Bräu. Luisenplatz 1, Charlottenburg (close to Charlottenburg Castle). ☎ 030/3-41-93-88. Reservations recommended on weekends. Salads, snacks, and platters 20DM–40DM ($11.40–$22.80). MC, V. Sun–Thurs 9am–1am, Fri–Sat 9am–2am. U-Bahn: Richard-Wagner-Platz. GERMAN.

One of the city's largest breweries, Luisen-Bräu, established this restaurant in 1987. The decor includes enormous stainless-steel vats of the fermenting brew, from which the waiters refill your mug. There is no subtlety of cuisine here; it's robust and hearty fare. You serve yourself from a long buffet table. The seating is indoor or outdoor, depending on the season, at long picnic tables that encourage a sense of beer-hall *Bruderschaft* (camaraderie).

Ernst-August. Sybelstrasse 16. ☎ **030/3-24-55-76.** Reservations required. Main courses 22DM–32DM ($12.55–$18.25). No credit cards. Wed–Sun 6:30pm–1am (kitchen stops serving hot food at midnight). Closed July 15–Aug 15. U-Bahn: Adenauerplatz. FRENCH/INTERNATIONAL.

Although outclassed by dozens of grander establishments, this restaurant still maintains a special niche. It's the type of place a local might take a friend from out of town. The setting is quiet and unobtrusive. Antique bric-a-brac adorns the walls. The chef might prepare one of two variations of hare, a longtime German favorite in which he takes a special pride. Even a simple rump steak gets care and attention here.

Funkturm Restaurant. Messedamm 22. ☎ **030/303-829-96.** Reservations not necessary. Set-price lunch 52DM ($29.65); set-price dinner 80DM ($45.60). Main course 23DM–38DM ($13.10–$21.65). AE, DC, V. Tues–Sun noon–3pm and 6–10pm. U-bahn: Kaiserdamm.

This restaurant at the radio tower's midway point (213 feet high) provides both good food and sweeping, high-altitude views. You'll first have to pay 3DM ($1.70) for the elevator ride up. Inside the restaurant's metallic, glossy interior, every table sits near a window. Menu items include saddle of lamb with vegetables, pepper steak, and seafood. If you just want to enjoy the view without the food, consider paying 6DM ($3.40) for a ride up to the observation platform near the top of the tower (446 feet high). The higher platform is open daily from 10am to 11pm. For information about the tower and its upper-tier observation platform, call ☎ **030/38-19-05.**

Ponte Vecchio. Spielhagenstrasse 3. ☎ **030/3-42-19-99.** Reservations required. Main courses 30DM–45DM ($17.10–$25.65). DC. Wed–Mon 6:30–11pm. Closed 4 weeks in summer. U-Bahn: Bismarckstrasse. TUSCAN.

We've dined here many times before and were moderately pleased, but the place has so improved that we now view it as the finest Italian restaurant in Berlin. Market-fresh ingredients produce a winning cuisine with a Tuscan focus. If you don't opt for the excellent fresh fish of the day, you'll find any number of other tempting dishes, such as several variations of veal. Shellfish is deftly handled according to Tuscan style, with fresh basil and olive oil. For a pasta that's succulent, savory, and spicy, we'd recommend the *penne all'arrabiata*, that old Roman favorite.

IN GRUNEWALD

✪ **Vivaldi.** In the Ritz Carlton Berlin, Brahmsstrasse 10. ☎ **030/89-58-40.** Reservations recommended. Main courses 61DM–69DM ($34.75–$39.35). Set-price 4-course dinner 155DM ($88.35); set-price 6-course dinner 196DM ($111.70). AE, DC, MC, V. Daily 6– 10:30pm. Parking 12DM ($6.85). INTERNATIONAL.

This restaurant is the culinary showcase of one of the most unusual small hotels in Berlin, a neo-Renaissance palace built in 1912. Vivaldi serves, with panache, some of the most elegant hotel food in Berlin, although it's not quite in the same league as the Harlekin at the Grand Hotel Esplanade. Most diners opt for one of two set-price menus, although there's also a limited à la carte list. A clear soup of lentils with smoked duck breast might be followed by gratinated oysters and scallops resting on a bed of spinach salad. Turbot coated with coconut is a delectable surprise. The saddle of venison with chervil is a triumph of subtle flavors. For the perfect finish, try orange slices in a puffy pastry on a whipped-cream base with a punch parfait.

IN NORTH BERLIN

✪ **Rockendorf's Restaurant.** Düsterhauptstrasse 1. ☎ **030/4-02-30-99.** Reservations required. Fixed-price meals at lunch 75DM–140DM ($42.75–$79.80), at dinner 140DM–198DM ($79.80–$112.85). AE, DC, MC, V. Tues–Sat noon–2pm and 7–9:30pm. Closed July 15–30. S-Bahn: Waidmannslust. CONTINENTAL.

Rockendorf's is in a 19th-century art-nouveau villa in north Berlin, a 20-minute taxi ride from the city center. It's the only restaurant that mounts a serious challenge to Bamberger Reiter and Alt-Luxemburg. Chef Siegfried Rockendorf achieves a happy wedding between nouvelle cuisine and classic specialties. Perhaps you'll try his memorable fresh jellied aspic with cucumber sauce. Other standbys include a fillet of turbot in Ricard sauce, and goose-meat pâté in Sauterne with cranberries. The service is exquisitely refined—attentive without being cloying. Everything is served on fine porcelain. Some of Germany's most visible names in showbiz, journalism, and politics come here. Warning: Don't confuse this restaurant with others with similar names—this is the most elegant of three restaurants whose names contain the word *Rockendorf.*

IN BERLIN-MITTE

For a map of restaurants in Berlin-Mitte, see page 71.

EXPENSIVE

Königin Luise. In the Opernpalais, Unter den Linden 5. ☎ **030/20-26-83.** Reservations recommended. Main courses 38DM–42DM ($21.65–$23.95). Set menus 85DM–110DM ($48.45–$62.70). AE, DC, MC, V. Tues–Sat 6pm–midnight. Closed Jan 1–13 and June 30–Aug 12. S-Bahn: Friedrichstrasse. GERMAN.

This is the most formal of five restaurants in an ornate, restored 17th-century palace that was rebuilt as a historic showcase by the East German regime. When you enter the building, bypass the concierge and head for the second floor. To start, we suggest the consommé of guinea hen with goose-liver ravioli. An escalope of salmon is served in a delicate saffron sauce with wild rice. The chefs haven't forgotten their longtime German standbys—veal and venison appear together in a blackberry sauce with leek noodles and glazed carrots.

Restaurant Borchardt. Französische Strasse 47. ☎ **030/20-39-71-17.** Reservations recommended. Daily specials 18DM ($10.25); main courses 32DM–48DM ($18.25–$27.35). AE, V. Daily noon–midnight. U-Bahn: Französische Strasse. FRENCH.

This restaurant is elegant, lighthearted, and popular with the city's artistic movers and shakers. It occupies a monumental dining area, complete with marble accents and partially gilded columns. You can order anything from a simple salad (as supermodel Claudia Schiffer often does) to more substantial fare, such as cream of potato soup with bacon and croutons, fillet of carp prepared with Riesling and herbs and finished with champagne, foie gras served with caramelized apples, chicken stuffed with morels and served with cream-and-herb sauce, and a pistachio mousse garnished with essence of fresh fruit.

✪ **Restaurant Vau.** Jägerstrasse 54 (near the Ritz Carlton and the Gendarmenmarkt). ☎ **030-202-9730.** Reservations recommended. Main courses 36DM–64DM ($20.50–$36.50). Set-price lunches 55DM ($31.35); set-price dinners 98DM–179DM ($55.85–$102.05). AE, DC, MC, V. Mon–Sat noon–2:30pm and 7–10:30pm. S-Bahn: Hausvoigteiplatz.

This restaurant is the culinary showcase of up-and-coming chef Kolja Kleeburg. You can select from a menu based on fresh and seasonal ingredients. Choices include terrine of salmon and morels with rocket salad; smoked sturgeon with white beans and caviar; aspic of suckling pig with sauerkraut; salad with marinated red mullet, mint, and almonds; crisp-fried duck with marjoram; ribs of suckling lamb with thyme-flavored polenta; and desserts such as woodruff soup with champagne-flavored ice cream. The wine list is international and well chosen.

MODERATE

Französischer Hof. Jagerstrasse 56. ☎ 030/2-04-35-70. Reservations recommended. Main courses 29DM–42DM ($16.55–$23.95). AE, DC, V. Daily 10am–1am. Closed Dec 24. U-Bahn: Hausvogteiplatz. GERMAN.

If you want a reasonable meal in a relaxed atmosphere, this is the place. Französischer Hof fills two floors connected by a belle epoque staircase, evoking a turn-of-the-century Parisian bistro. The kitchen may not be the finest, but ingredients are fresh and deftly handled. One recent memorable dinner included roast duck breast with calvados along with zucchini and potato pancakes. You can begin with the delectable selection of fish canapés. Saddle of lamb is always admirably done, although you may prefer the rather theatrical flambéed fillet Stroganoff with almond-studded dumplings.

Zur Letzten Instanz. Waisenstrasse 14–16 (near the Nikolaikirche). ☎ **030/2-42-55-28.** Soup 8DM–10DM ($4.55–$5.70); main courses 25DM–35DM ($14.25–$19.95); fixed-price dinner from 25DM ($14.25). AE, DC, V. Mon–Sat noon–1am; Sun noon–11pm. S-Bahn: KlosterStrasse. GERMAN.

Reputedly Berlin's oldest restaurant, dating from 1525, Zur Letzten Instanz has been frequented by everybody from Napoléon to Beethoven. Prisoners used to stop off here for one last beer before going to jail. The place is located on two floors of a baroque building just outside the crumbling brick wall that once ringed medieval Berlin. Double doors open on a series of small woodsy rooms, one with a bar and ceramic *Kachelofen* (stove). At the back, a circular staircase leads to another series of rooms, where every evening at 6pm, food and wine (no beer) are served. The menu is old-fashioned, mainly limited to Berlin staples.

INEXPENSIVE

Alexanderkeller. In the cellar of the Hotel Luisenhof, Köpenicker Strasse 92. ☎ **030/ 2-75-01-42.** Main courses 18DM–35DM ($10.25–$19.95). MC, V. Daily 7am–midnight. U-Bahn: Märkisches Museum. GERMAN.

This reasonably priced, unpretentious restaurant is a lunchtime favorite of neighborhood residents and office workers. The generous meals might include fillet of roast beef served with potatoes and artichoke hearts; fillet of zander with parsley and new potatoes; or roast pork with red-wine sauce. Food is rich and the meat dishes heavy, but the people in this area love this type of food—many remember when they couldn't get much of it.

✪ Golden Gans. In the Westin Grand (1 flight above the lobby), Friedrichstrasse 158. ☎ **030/2027-3246.** Reservations recommended. Main courses 16DM–30DM ($9.10–$17.10). AE, DC, MC, V. Daily 6–11pm. S-Bahn: Friedrichstrasse. GERMAN.

Its name means the "Golden Goose," which is appropriate—this restaurant serves the best goose dishes in Berlin. The rustic place stands in deliberate contrast to the beaux arts glamour of the hotel containing it. Inside, there's a wooden ceiling, colorfully embroidered napery, and an open-to-view kitchen. The cuisine is based on Thuringian recipes vividly evocative of old Germany. The star item is the goose, which comes in three preparations. Other menu items include roast pork with onions and hot potato salad, tenderloin of venison with port sauce, and a simple platter of grilled sausages with mashed potato. Cholesterol watchers should beware—the kitchen's special appetizer (it doesn't appear on the menu) is goose fat with mixed pickles and freshly baked rolls.

Keller-Restaurant Im Brecht-Haus-Berlin. Chausseestrasse 125. ☎ **030/2-82-38-43.** Reservations recommended. Main courses 17DM–37DM ($9.70–$21.10). AE, DC, MC, V. Daily 11am–midnight. U-Bahn: Oranienburger Tor. SOUTH GERMAN/AUSTRIAN.

From 1953 until his death in 1956, Bertolt Brecht lived with his wife, Helene Weigel, here on the second floor of what was a turn-of-the-century apartment house. Today the building houses the Brecht-Weigel-Museum (see below). The restaurant downstairs, with white plaster and exposed stone, is decorated with photographs of the playwright's family, friends, and theatrical productions. No one will mind if you just stop in for a glass or two of wine—the place specializes in eastern German wines, as well as French and New World wines. Traditional south German and Austrian food is also served, such as an Austrian recipe for *Fleisch Laberln,* meatballs made from minced pork, beef, green beans, and bacon and served with dumplings. In good weather, the seating area includes an enclosed courtyard upstairs.

5 Attractions

THE TOP MUSEUMS

The great art collections of old Berlin suffered during and after World War II. Although many paintings were saved by being stored in inoperative salt mines during the bombings, many larger works, including eight paintings by Rubens and three by Van Dyck, were destroyed by fire. Part of the surviving art stayed in the east, including a wealth of ancient treasures that remind us of the leading role played by German archaeologists during the 19th and early 20th centuries. The paintings that turned up in the west and were passed from nation to nation in the late 1940s like so many playing cards have nearly all been returned to Berlin.

MUSEUMS IN DAHLEM

✪ **Dahlem Museums.** Arnimallee 23–27. ☎ **030/8-30-11.** Combination ticket to all Dahlem museums 4DM ($2.30) adults, 2DM ($1.15) children. All collections, Tues–Fri 9am–5pm, Sat–Sun 10am–5pm. U-Bahn: Dahlem-Dorf.

Dahlem is home to several important galleries, although its major museum of yesterday, the Gemäldgalerie (Picture Gallery) has now moved to the Tiergarten. The ✪ **Museum für Völkerkunde** (Museum of Ethnography), Lansstrasse 8 (☎ **030/ 83011**), is one of the world's greatest ethnological collections, totaling some 500,000 artifacts from all continents, even prehistoric America. Many of the figures are grotesquely beautiful ritualistic masks. The Incan, Mayan, and Aztec stone sculptures are as good as those of the finest museums of Mexico. But the highlight here is the collection of boats in their actual sizes, as well as homes and facades gathered from around the globe. There's also an intriguing assemblage of pre-Columbian relics, including gold objects and antiquities from Peru. The museum's Department of Music allows visitors to hear folk music recordings from around the globe.

The **Skulpturengalerie** (Sculpture Gallery), Arnimallee 23–27 (☎ **030/83011**) is currently in the Dahlem, though sometime in 2000 or 2001 it will be moved into newer and more spacious quarters. This gallery is celebrated for its collection of

Potsdam

The best day trip from Berlin is to the town of Potsdam, sometimes called "Germany's Versailles." It's only about half an hour away by rail, S-Bahn, bus, or car. See chapter 4.

Dahlem Museums

TOP FLOOR
(not shown)
Prints and Drawings
Collection
Museum of Ethnography
(East Asia)

UPPER FLOOR

3 Museum of Ethnography
  (South Seas)
4 Sculpture Gallery
5 Picture Gallery
6 Museum of Ethnography
  (Africa)
7 Museum of Islamic Art
8 Museum of East Asian Art
9 Museum of Ethnography
  (South Asia)
10 Special exhibitions

GROUND FLOOR

1 Museum of Indian Art
2 Museum of Ethnography
  (America archaeology)
3 Museum of Ethnography
  (South Seas)
4 Sculpture Gallery
5 Picture Gallery

LOWER FLOOR

A Lecture Room
B Young People's Museum
C Cafeteria
D Museum for the Blind

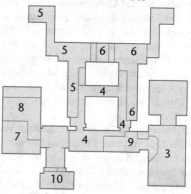

UPPER FLOOR

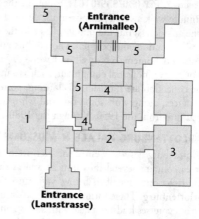

GROUND FLOOR

Entrance
(Arnimallee)

Entrance
(Lansstrasse)

LOWER FLOOR

Byzantine and European sculptures that range from the 3rd to the 18th centuries. Included in its collection are many masterpieces, including Donatello's *Madonna and Child,* sculpted in 1422. In all, there are some 1,200 works. Many carvings are by some of Germany's best-known artists, including Tilman Riemenschneider. The ivory and bronze collections are world class.

The **Museum für Ostasiatische Kunst** (Museum of Far Eastern Art), Lanstrasse 8 (☎ **030/8301-382**), is devoted primarily to Japan, Korea, and China. This gem of a museum has artifacts dating from 3,000 B.C. It presents an overview of some of the most exquisite religious and decorative art to come out of the Far East. In essence, the collection consists of loot garnered during a massive "shopping expedition" the Germans made in Asia, where they even managed to snatch up the 17th-century imperial throne of China, all lacquered and inlaid with mother-of-pearl. The Japanese woodblock prints, each more exquisite than the last, seem reason enough to visit.

The **Museum für Islamische Kunst** (Museum of Islamic Art), Lansstrasse 8 (☎ **030/83011**), traces the culture of Islam around the world. A virtual Arabian Nights fantasyland comes alive here, with carpets, glass, jewelry, pottery, and examples of Arabic script. Artifacts and art from all the Islamic countries are on display, spanning the period from the 8th to the 18th centuries. Some of the Persian carpets are among the finest in the world. Tapestries and rare illuminated manuscripts are also on display.

The **Museum für Deutsche Volkskunde** (Museum of German Ethnology), Im Winkel 6–8, (☎ **030/839-0101**), is outside the Dahlem museum complex, but only a 5-minute walk away. This museum is devoted to the German people themselves—not the aristocrats, but the middle class and the peasants who built the country. It is a true "museum of the people." The exhibits go back 4 centuries, illuminating how artisans and homemakers lived and worked. Household items are displayed along with primitive industrial equipment, such as a utensil for turning flax into linen. Also in the collection are furnishings, clothing, pottery, and even items used in religious observances, along with some fun and whimsical exhibits, including depictions of pop culture from the 1950s through the 1980s.

CHARLOTTENBURG PALACE & MUSEUMS

Charlottenburg lies just west of the Tiergarten. Plan on spending the day here, since the area contains several museums as well as the royal apartments. After seeing the main attractions, described below, you can enjoy a ramble through **Schlossgarten Charlottenburg.** These formal gardens look much as they did in the 18th century. A grove of cypresses leads to a lake with swans and other waterfowl.

North of the palace stands the **Mausoleum,** which holds the tombs of King Friedrich Wilhelm II and Queen Luise, sculptured by Rauch, as well as several other interesting funerary monuments of the Prussian royal family.

✪ **Schloss Charlottenburg.** Luisenplatz. ☎ **030/32091-275.** Combined ticket for all buildings and historical rooms 15DM ($8.55) adults, 10DM ($5.70) children under 14. English translation of guide's lecture on sale at the ticket counter. Guided tours of the Historical Rooms (in German), Tues–Fri 9am–5pm, Sat–Sun 10am–5pm (last tour at 4pm). U-Bahn: Sophie-Charlotte-Platz or Richard-Wagner-Platz.

Schloss Charlottenburg, one of the finest examples of baroque architecture in Germany, was built by Sophie Charlotte. This beautiful and intelligent woman, a patron of philosophy and the arts, was the wife of Frederick I, The Great Elector, who was crowned as the first "king in Prussia" (as opposed to "of") in 1701. (An elector was one of the princes of the Holy Roman Empire who took part in the election of an emperor.) He nearly bankrupted the state with his extravagant ways.

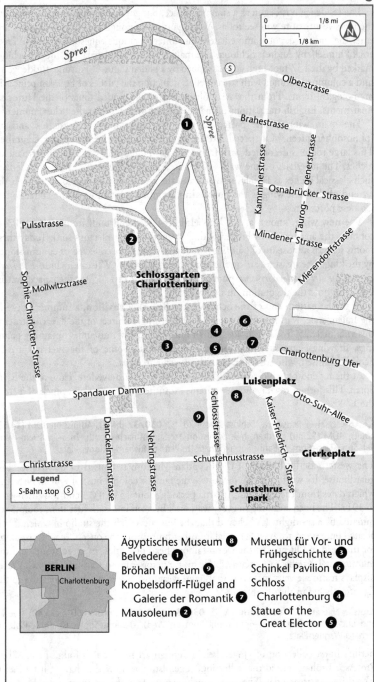

Ägyptisches Museum **8**
Belvedere **1**
Bröhan Museum **9**
Knobelsdorff-Flügel and
   Galerie der Romantik **7**
Mausoleum **2**

Museum für Vor- und
   Frühgeschichte **3**
Schinkel Pavilion **6**
Schloss
   Charlottenburg **4**
Statue of the
   Great Elector **5**

The residence was begun as a summer palace, but got out of hand until it grew into the massive structure you see today. When you pass through the heavy iron gates and enter the courtyard, you'll immediately encounter a baroque equestrian statue of Frederick I himself, by Andreas Schlüter. The main entrance to the palace is directly behind, marked by the 157-foot-high cupola capped by a gilded statue of Fortune. Inside, you'll find a columned rotunda with stucco reliefs depicting the virtues of Prussian princes in mythological terms. From this vestibule, you can take guided tours of the Historical Apartments. English translations of the guide's lecture are sold at the ticket counter.

The main wing of the palace contains the apartments of Frederick and his "philosopher queen." Of special interest in this section is the **Reception Chamber.** This large room is decorated with frieze panels, vaulted ceilings, and mirror-paneled niches. The tapestries on the walls (1730) are based on Plutarch's Lives; included are such classical scenes as Pericles in battle and the sacrifice of Theseus on Delos. At the far end of the west wing is the **Porcelain Chamber,** containing a fine collection of Chinese porcelain.

The **new wing,** known as the Knobelsdorff-Flügel and built from 1740 to 1746, contains the apartments of Frederick the Great (the Great Elector's son). Today these rooms serve as a museum of paintings, many of which were collected or commissioned by the king. The treasures are on the upper floor. Works by Watteau include *The Trade Sign of the Art Dealer Gersaint,* purchased by Frederick in 1745 for the palace's music hall. Also note the decoration on the walls and ceilings.

At the far eastern end of the Schloss is the **Schinkel Pavillon,** a summer house in the Italian style. Karl Friedrich Schinkel, the leading architect of the day, constructed this villa in 1825. Today it holds a small but noteworthy museum, containing paintings, drawings, and sketches from the early 1800s. Some of the sketches are by Schinkel himself, who was both an architect and an artist.

At the far end of Schlossgarten Charlottenburg is the **Belvedere,** close to the River Spree. This former royal teahouse contains exquisite Berlin porcelain, much of it from the 1700s.

✪ **Ägyptisches Museum.** Schloss-strasse 70. ☎ **030/32-09-11.** Admission 8DM ($4.55) adults, 4DM ($2.30) children; free admission 1st Sun of each month. Tues–Fri 10am–6pm, Sat–Sun 11am–6pm. U-Bahn: Sophie-Charlotte-Platz or Richard-Wagner-Platz.

The western Berlin branch of the Egyptian Museum is housed in the palace's east guardhouse. It's worth the trip just to see the famous colored bust of Queen Nefertiti, which dates from the Egyptian Amarna period (about 1340 B.C.) and was discovered in 1912. The bust, stunning in every way, is all by itself in a dark first-floor room, illuminated by a spotlight. It's believed that the bust never left the studio in which it was created but served always as a model for other portraits of the queen. In addition, look for the head of Queen Tiy, the world-famous head of a priest in green stone, and the monumental Kalabasha Gateway, built by Emperor Augustus around 30 B.C. Other displays feature jewelry, papyrus, tools, and weapons, as well as objects relating to the Egyptian belief in the afterlife.

Bröhan Museum. Schlossstrasse 1A. ☎ **030/3-21-40-29.** Admission 6DM ($3.40), free 11 and under. Tues–Sun 10am–6pm (until 8pm on Wed). U-Bahn: Sophie-Charlotte-Platz or Richard-Wagner-Platz.

Berlin's finest collection of "Jugendstil" (German art nouveau) is found here. When Professor Bröhan started the collection, Jugendstil was viewed as having little merit. It's a different story today. The objects include glass, furnishings, silver and gold, paintings, and vases. The outstanding porcelain collection ranges from Gallé to Sèvres and Meissen to Royal Copenhagen.

Attractions in Berlin-Mitte

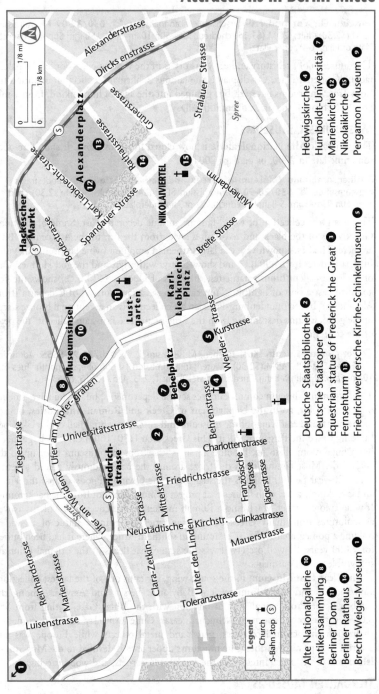

Alte Nationalgalerie 🔟
Antikensammlung 🕗
Berliner Dom ⓫
Berliner Rathaus ⓮
Brecht-Weigel-Museum ➊

Deutsche Staatsbibliothek ➋
Deutsche Staatsoper ➏
Equestrian statue of Frederick the Great ➌
Fernsehturm ⓭
Friedrichwerdersche Kirche-Schinkelmuseum ➎

Hedwigskirche ➍
Humboldt-Universität ➐
Marienkirche ⓬
Nikolaikirche ⓯
Pergamon Museum ➒

Legend
✝ Church
🏛
Ⓢ S-Bahn stop

89

Museum Für vor und Frühgeschichte. Langhansbau. ☎ **030/32-09-11.** Admission 4DM ($2.30)adults, 2DM ($1.15) children. Tues–Sun 10am–6pm. U-Bahn: Sophie-Charlotte-Platz or Richard-Wagner-Platz.

This museum of prehistory and early history is in the western extension of the palace, facing Klausener Platz. On display is the famous Schliemann collection of antiquities from Troy. The rooms have exhibits grouped into the ages of humankind, from 1 million B.C. through the first millennium A.D.

MUSEUMINSEL MUSEUMS

The venerable **Alte Nationalgalerie** is now closed for renovations. It should re-open sometime late in 2000, or perhaps 2001.

Antikensammlung (Museum of Greek and Roman Antiquities). Bodestrasse 1–3, Museumsinsel. ☎ **030/20-90-50.** Admission 8DM ($4.55) adults, 4DM ($2.30) children. Tues–Sun 9am–5pm. S-Bahn: Friedrichplatz or Alexanderplatz.

This is a great collection of world-famous antique decorative art. Some of the finest Greek vases of the black-and-red-figures style, from the 6th to the 4th century B.C., are here. The best-known vase is a large Athenian amphora (wine jar) found in Vulci, Etruria. It dates from 490 B.C. and shows a satyr with a lyre and the god Hermes. One of several excellent bronze statuettes, the Zeus of Dodone (470 B.C.) shows the god about to cast a bolt of lightning. You can also see a rare portrait of Cleopatra (from Alexandria). In the Brandenburg-Prussian art collection is an exceptional bronze statue of the goddess Luna descending from the firmament. The Prussians called it "the pearl of the collection."

✪ **Pergamon Museum.** Kupfergraben, Museumsinsel. ☎ **030/20-90-5555.** Admission 8DM ($4.55) adults, 4DM ($2.30) children; free admission 1st Sun of each month. Tues–Sun 10am–6pm. U Bahn/S-Bahn: Friedrichstrasse. Tram: 1, 2, 3, 4, 5, 13, 15, or 53.

The Pergamon Museum complex houses several departments, but if you have time for only one exhibit, go to the **Department of Greek and Roman Antiquities,** housed in the north and east wings of the museum, and enter the central hall of the U-shaped building to see the Pergamon Altar. This Greek altar (180–160 B.C.) is so large that it has a huge room all to itself. Some 27 steps lead from the museum floor up to the colonnade. Most fascinating is the frieze around the base, tediously pieced together over a 20-year period. It shows the struggle of the Olympian gods against the Titans and is strikingly alive, with figures that project as much as a foot from the background. If you explore further, you'll find a Roman market gate discovered in Miletus as well as sculptures from many Greek and Roman cities, including a statue of a goddess holding a pomegranate (575 B.C.), found in southern Attica, where it had been buried for 2,000 years. So well preserved was the statue that flecks of the original paint are still visible on her garments.

The **Near East Museum,** in the south wing, contains one of the largest collections anywhere of antiquities from ancient Babylonia, Persia, and Assyria. Among the exhibits is the Processional Way of Babylon with the Ishtar Gate, dating from 580 B.C., and the throne room of Nebuchadnezzar. Cuneiform clay tablets document a civilization that created ceramics, glass, and metal objects while Europe was still overrun with primitive tribes. The museum's upper level is devoted to the **Museum of Islamic Art.** Of special interest are the miniatures, carpets, and wood carvings.

TIERGARTEN MUSEUMS

✪ **Gemäldegalerie (Picture Gallery).** Mattäiskirchplatz 4. ☎ **030/20-90-55-55.** Admission 8DM ($4.55) adults, 4DM ($2.30) children. Tues–Fri 10am–6pm, Sat–Sun 11am–6pm. U-Bahn: Kurfürstenstrasse, then bus 148. Bus 129 from Ku'damm (plus a 4-min. walk).

Attractions Around the Tiergarten

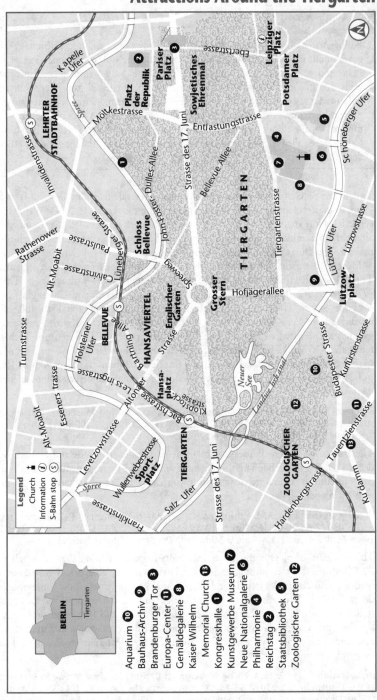

Legend

- ✝ ■ Church
- ⓘ Information
- Ⓢ S-Bahn stop

Aquarium ⑩
Bauhaus-Archiv ⑨
Brandenburger Tor ③
Europa-Center ⑪
Gemäldegalerie ⑧
Kaiser Wilhelm
Memorial Church ⑬
Kongresshalle ①
Kunstgewerbe Museum ⑦
Neue Nationalgalerie ⑥
Philharmonie ④
Reichstag ②
Staatsbibliothek ⑤
Zoologischer Garten ⑫

BERLIN
Tiergarten

A New Wall

Berliners aren't likely to forget the Berlin Wall any time soon, but just in case, their government has reconstructed a partial stretch of the wall at Bernauer Strasse and Ackerstrasse, at a cost of $1.3 million. The 230-foot long memorial consists of two walls that include some of the fragments of the original wall (those fragments not bulldozed away or carried off by souvenir hunters). The memorial is mostly made of mirrorlike stainless steel. Slits allow visitors to peer through. A steel plaque reads: "In memory of the division of the city from 13 August 1961 to 9 November 1989." Critics have called the construction "a sanitized memorial," claiming it does little to depict the 255 people shot trying to escape its predecessor.

This is one of Germany's greatest art museums. Several rooms are devoted to early German masters, with panels from altarpieces dating from the 13th, 14th, and 15th centuries. Note the panel of *The Virgin Enthroned with Child* (1350), surrounded by angels that resemble the demons in the works of Hieronymus Bosch. Eight paintings make up the Dürer collection, including several portraits.

Most of the great masters from other European countries are also represented. The Italian collection contains five Raphael madonnas, along with works by Titian *(The Girl with a Bowl of Fruit)*, Fra Filippo Lippi, Botticelli, and Correggio *(Leda with the Swan)*. There are early Netherlands paintings from the 15th and 16th centuries (Van Eyck, Van der Weyden, Bosch, and Brueghel) as well. And several galleries are devoted to Flemish and Dutch masters of the 17th century, with no fewer than 15 works by Rembrandt, such as his famous *Head of Christ. The Man with the Golden Helmet,* long famous as a priceless Rembrandt, was proven in 1986 to be by another hand. This remarkable painting is now accepted as a fine independent original.

Bauhaus Archiv Museum für Gestaltung (Bauhaus Design Museum). Klingelhofer-strasse 14. ☎ **030/2-54-00-20.** Admission 5DM ($2.85) adults, 2.50DM ($1.40) children. Wed–Mon 10am–5pm. U-Bahn: Nollendorfplatz.

The Bauhaus Museum houses a permanent exhibition of photos and architectural designs relating to the Bauhaus movement. Even if you're not a student of architecture, this museum is fascinating; it will bring you closer to the ideas and concepts that inspired modern design.

Kunstgewerbemuseum. Matthäikirchplatz (opposite the Philharmonie), Tiergartenstrasse 6. ☎ **030/2-66-29-02.** Admission 4DM ($2.30) adults, 2DM ($1.15) children. Tues–Fri 10am–6pm, Sat–Sun 11am–6pm. U-Bahn: Kurfürstenstrasse. S-Bahn: Potsdamer Platz.

This museum displays applied arts and crafts from the Middle Ages through the 20th century. Its outstanding exhibition is the Guelph Treasure, a collection of medieval church articles in gold and silver. The basement rooms show contemporary design from the Bauhaus movement to Charles Eames and Memphis. Venetian glass, Italian majolica, German Renaissance goldsmiths' work, and 18th-century porcelain figurines are also displayed. Notable are such art-nouveau works as a translucent opal-and-enamel box by Eugène Feuillâtre. There's a cafeteria inside, open from 10am to 4:30pm.

Neue Nationalgalerie (Staatliche Museum zu Berlin). Potsdamerstrasse 50 (just south of the Tiergarten). ☎ **030/2-66-26-62.** Permanent collection, 8DM ($4.55) adults, 4DM ($2.30) children; temporary exhibitions, 12DM ($6.85). Tues–Fri 10am–6pm, Sat–Sun 11am–6pm. Closed Jan 1, Dec 24–25 and 31, and the Tues after Easter and Whitsunday. U-Bahn: Kurfürstenstrasse. S-Bahn: Potsdamer Platz.

⭐ Frommer's Favorite Berlin Experiences

Strolling along Unter den Linden and the Kurfürstendamm. You can't know Berlin until you've strolled the Ku'damm, that glossy, store-lined showcase of Western capitalism, and Unter den Linden, the Prussian centerpiece of the Berlin-Mitte district.

Kneipen Crawling. This is the Berlin version of "pub crawling." Whether you want breakfast or a beer at 4am, there's always a Kneipe waiting to claim you, no matter what neighborhood you're in.

A Touch of Culture. The baton of the late Herbert von Karajan is no longer raised, but the Berlin Philharmonic is still one of the world's leading orchestras.

Wandering the Nikolai Quarter. A symbol of Berlin's desire to bounce back after war damage, this charming 16th-century neighborhood has been completely rebuilt. Period taverns and churches make it ideal for a leisurely stroll down narrow streets illuminated by gas lanterns.

Picnicking in the Tiergarten. What better place for a picnic than the former hunting grounds of the Prussian electors? Wander through this 412-acre park until you find the ideal spot, but first stop off at KaDeWe's sixth-floor food emporium at Wittgenbergplatz, 20 minutes away, for the makings of a memorable meal.

In its modern glass-and-steel home designed by Ludwig Mies van der Rohe (1886–1969), the Neue Nationalgalerie is a sequel of sorts to the art at Dahlem. It contains a continually growing collection of modern European and American art. Here you'll find works of 19th-century artists, with a concentration on French impressionists. German art starts with Adolph von Menzel's paintings from about 1850. The 20th-century collection includes works by Max Beckmann and Edvard Munch, and E. L. Kirchner's *Brandenburger Tor* (1929), as well as a few paintings by Bacon, Picasso, Ernst, Klee, and American artists such as Barnett Newman. There's food service in the cafe on the ground floor. Hot meals are served from 10:30am to 6pm.

OTHER MUSEUMS & SIGHTS

Deutsche Guggenheim Berlin. Unter den Linden 13–15 (at the intersection with Charlottenstrasse). ☎ **030/2020930.** Admission 8DM ($4.55) adults, 5DM ($2.85) children. Daily 11am–8pm. U-Bahn: Stadtmitte.

This state-of-the-art museum is devoted to modern and contemporary art. The exhibition space is on the ground floor of the newly restored Berlin branch of Deutsche Bank. The Guggenheim Foundation presents several exhibitions at this site annually, and also displays newly commissioned works created specifically for this space by world-renowned artists. The bank supports young artists from the German-speaking world by purchasing their work and displaying them throughout the company's offices and public spaces. Exhibitions have ranged from the most avant-garde of modern artists, to Picasso, Cézanne, and Andy Warhol. Amazingly, it was along this same street that Hitler denounced modern art as degenerate.

Die Sammlung Berggruen: Picasso und Seine Zeit (The Berggruen Collection: Picasso and his Era). Schlosstrasse 1 (entrance across from the Egyptian Museum, in Charlottenburg). ☎ **030/830-1466.** Admission 8DM ($4.55) adults, 4DM ($2.30) students and children. Tues–Fri 9am–5pm, Sat–Sun 10am–5pm. Closed Mon. U-Bahn: Sophie Charlotte Platz, followed by a 10-min. walk.

This unusual private museum displays the awesome collection of respected art and antiques dealer Heinz Berggruen. A native of Berlin who fled the Nazis in 1936, Berggruen later established a miniempire of antique dealerships in Paris and California before returning, with his collection, to his native home in 1996. Sometime during your visit, there's a good chance that 80-year-old Mr. Berggruen, who has an apartment nearby, will be conducting a lecture here on his favorite painter, or spontaneously strolling among his paintings. The setting is a renovated army barracks designed by noted architect August Stütler in 1859. Although most of the collection is devoted to Picasso, there are also works by Cézanne, Braque, Klee, and van Gogh. The Picasso collection alone, which covers all his major periods, is worth the trip.

Friedrichswerdersche Kirche-Schinkelmuseum. Werderstrasse (at the corner of Niederlagstrasse). ☎ 030/2-08-13-23. Admission 4DM ($2.30) adults, 2DM ($1.15) children. Tues–Sun 10am–6pm. U-Bahn: Hausvogteiplatz.

This annex of the Nationalgalerie is located in the deconsecrated Friedrichswerdersche Kirche, which was designed by leading architect Karl Friedrich Schinkel in 1828. It lies close to Unter den Linden, not far from the State Opera House. The twin Gothic portals of the old church shelter a bronze of St. Michael slaying a dragon. Inside, the museum is devoted to the memory of Schinkel, who designed many of Berlin's great palaces, churches, and monuments. Memorabilia and documents record his great accomplishments. There are also exhibitions of neoclassical sculptures, portraits, and tombs by Johann Gottfried Schadow, Christian Daniel Rauch, Friedrich Tieck, and Berthel Thorvaldsen, the Danish sculptor.

Käthe-Kollwitz-Museum. Fasanenstrasse 24. ☎ **030/8-82-52-10.** Admission 8DM ($4.55) adults, 4DM ($2.30) children and students. Wed–Mon 11am–6pm. U-Bahn: Uhlandstrasse or Kurfürstendamm.

This museum has been called a personalized revolt against the agonies of war. Many works express the sorrow of wartime separation of mother and child, inspired in part by the artist's loss of a son in World War I and a grandson during World War II. Berlin-born Käthe Kollwitz was an ardent pacifist and socialist whose works were banned by the Nazis. The first woman ever elected to the Prussian Academy of the Arts, she resigned her position in 1933 to protest Hitler's rise to power. Her husband, Karl Kollwitz, was a physician who chose to practice among the poor on a working-class street (now called Kollwitzstrasse). In 1943, Allied bombing drove Käthe to the countryside near Dresden, where she died in 1945, a guest of the former royal family of Saxony in their castle at Moritzburg.

The lower floors of the museum are devoted to woodcuts and lithographs, the upper floors to particularly poignant sculptures. *Note:* The collection is closed twice a year for special exhibits.

Martin-Gropius-Bau. Stresemannstrasse 110. ☎ **030/25-48-60.** Admission 8DM ($4.55) adults, 4DM ($2.30) children. Tues–Sun 10am–8pm. S-Bahn: Anhalter Bahnhof. U-Bahn: Kochstrasse.

When this gallery opened in 1981, the *New York Times* called it one of the "most dramatic museums in the world." It contains the **Museum Berlinische Galerie,** with works of art, architecture, and photography from the 19th and 20th centuries; the **Jewish Museum;** and the **Werkbund Archiv.** On the ground floor are changing exhibitions. The building lies near the site of the former Berlin Wall, and its eastern section opens onto the leveled former Gestapo headquarters. It's fascinating to look at the adjoining building with its unrestored exterior terra-cotta friezes—damaged, destroyed, or left intact.

Museum Haus am Checkpoint Charlie. Friedrichstrasse 44. ☎ **030/253-7250.** Admission 8DM ($4.55) adults, 5DM ($2.85) children and students. Daily 9am–10pm. U-Bahn: Kochstrasse or Stadtmitte.

Exhibits in this small building evoke the tragic events connected with the former Berlin Wall. You can see some of the instruments of escape used by East Germans, including chairlifts, false passports, hot-air balloons, and even a minisub. Photos document the construction of the wall, the establishment of escape tunnels, and the postwar history of both parts of Berlin from 1945 until today, including the airlift of 1948 to 1949. One of the most moving exhibits is the display on the staircase of drawings by school children, who, in 1961 to 1962, were asked to depict both halves of Germany in one picture.

Olympia-Stadion. Olympischer Platz 3. ☎ **030/30-06-33.** Admission 1DM (55¢). June–Sept daily 9am–5pm; off-season daily 8am–4pm. U-Bahn: Olympia-Stadion.

Built in 1936 by Werner March for the XI Summer Olympic Games, the Olympia-Stadion, which seats 100,000 people, was the first in Europe to supply all the facilities necessary for modern sports. Hitler expected to see his "master race" run off with all the medals in the 1936 Olympics, but his hopes were dashed when an African American, Jesse Owens, took four golds for the U.S. team.

The stadium area covers a total of 330 acres, but the main attraction is the arena. The playing field in its center lies 47 feet below ground level. For a panoramic view of Berlin, take the elevator to the top of the 260-foot platform, where the Olympic bell hangs. Sporting or cultural events are still presented here about once a week during spring, summer, and autumn. For a 1DM (55¢) fee, you can see the vast interior. For ticket sales and information for sporting events within the stadium, call **Herta-BSC (Herta-Berlin Soccer Club)** at ☎ **030/3-00-92-80.** For information about the occasional live concerts, call **Conzert Concept** at ☎ **030/81-07-50.**

Schöneberg Rathaus. John-F.-Kennedy-Platz. ☎ **030/7-87-60.** Free admission. Daily 10am–6pm. Tower closed Nov–Mar. U-Bahn: Rathaus Schöneberg.

This former political and administrative center of West Berlin is of special interest to Americans. It was the scene of John F. Kennedy's memorable (if grammatically shaky) *Ich bin ein Berliner* speech on June 26, 1963. Berliners have renamed the square around the building the John-F.-Kennedy-Platz. From the 237-foot-high hall tower, a Liberty Bell replica is rung every day at noon. This Freedom Bell, a gift from the American people in 1950, symbolized U.S. support for the West Berliners during the Cold War. The document chamber contains a testimonial bearing the signatures of 17 million Americans who gave their moral support to the struggle.

EXPLORING BERLIN-MITTE

The best street for strolling in eastern Berlin is the famous **Unter den Linden** (see the "Walking Tour," below), beginning at Brandenburg Gate.

Berliner Rathaus, Jüdenstrasse (☎ **030/2-40-10**), appears to be a replica of an Italian palace. This building, constructed between 1861 and 1869, is called the "Red City Hall," not because of its former ideology but because it was built of red bricks. Look for the "stone chronicle" outside, 36 bas-reliefs depicting important moments in Berlin's history. The building is open Monday to Friday from 9am to 6pm, and admission is free.

Alexanderplatz, named for Russian Czar Alexander I, was the center of activity in the old East Berlin. This square has brightened considerably since reunification, though aesthetically speaking it's got a long way to go. Neon lights and bright murals now coexist alongside the dull and fading GDR-era structures, and street musicians and small markets give the area new life. Information and tickets to events in Berlin are available at the **Hekticket** on the square. This office opens at 4pm to sell last-minute tickets for events occurring that same evening; call ☎ **030/24-31-24-31.**

The massive **Fernsehturm (TV tower)** on Alexanderplatz is the second-highest structure in Europe (1,100 feet). It's worthwhile to take the 60-second elevator ride to the observation platform, 610 feet above the city. From this isolated vantage point you can clearly distinguish most landmarks, and on the floor above, you can enjoy cake and coffee as the Tele-Café slowly revolves. The elevator to the top costs 8DM ($4.55) for adults and 4DM ($2.30) for children. The tower is open daily March through October from 9am to 1pm, and November through February daily from 10am to midnight; U-Bahn or S-Bahn: Alexanderplatz.

At the foot of the Fernsehturm stands Berlin's second-oldest church, the brick Gothic **Marienkirche (St. Mary's Church),** Karl-Liebknecht-Strasse 8 (☎ **030/2-42-44-67**), dating from the 15th century. Inside is the 1475 wall painting *Der Totentanz (The Dance of Death),* discovered in 1860 beneath a layer of whitewash in the church's entrance hall. Also worth seeing is the marble baroque pulpit carved by Andreas Schlüter (1703). The cross on the top of the church annoyed the Communist rulers of the former East Germany—its golden form was always reflected in the windows of the Fernsehturm. The church is open Monday to Thursday from 10am to noon and 1 to 4pm, Friday to Sunday from noon to 4pm. Free tours are offered Monday to Thursday at 1pm and again on Sunday at 11:45am.

Brecht-Weigel-Museum. Chausseestrasse 125 (near the Berlin-Friedrichstrasse station). ☎ **030/283-0570-44.** Admission 6DM ($3.40) adults, 3DM ($1.70) children and students. Tues–Wed and Fri 10am–11:30am, Thurs 10am–noon and 5–6:30pm, Sat 9:30am–1:30pm, Sun 11am–6pm visits available only with a tour. U-Bahn: Zinnowitzer Strasse.

This building was occupied by poet and playwright Bertolt Brecht (1898–1956) and his wife, noted actress Helene Weigel, from 1953 until their deaths. Brecht, who lived in the United States during World War II, returned to East Berlin after the war. Here he created his own "epic theater" company, the acclaimed Berliner Ensemble. The museum is in an old apartment house. It now displays the artists' living and working rooms and the Brecht and Weigel archives, containing 350,000 manuscripts, type-scripts, collections of his printed works, press cuttings, and playbills. All visitors are guided around the museum by an attendant. There's a restaurant downstairs (see "Dining," above).

THE HISTORIC NIKOLAI QUARTER

The historic ✪ **Nikolaiviertel** (U-Bahn: Klosterstrasse) was restored in time for the city's 750th anniversary in 1987. Here, on the banks of the Spree River, is where Berlin was born. Many of the medieval and baroque buildings in the neighborhood were completely and authentically reconstructed after World War II. Some of the city's old flavor has been recaptured here.

The area is named for the **Nikolaikirche (Church of St. Nicholas),** Nikolaikirch-platz, off Spandauerstrasse (☎ **030/3-33-80-54**). The church, the oldest in Berlin, was originally constructed in the 14th century on the remains of a 13th-century Romanesque church. The restored building now displays the finds of postwar archae-ological digs; during the reconstruction, 800-year-old skeletons were found. It's open on Sunday from 2pm to 4pm and Saturday from noon to 3pm; on weekdays, if you call in advance, a visit can be arranged. Admission to the church is free, but admission to the tower is 2DM ($1.15).

OTHER ARCHITECTURAL SIGHTS

Just north of the Tiergarten is the **Hansaviertel,** or Hansa Quarter (U-Bahn: Hansaplatz). The architecture of this area was an outgrowth of the great INTERBAU 1957 (International Builder's Exhibition), when architects from 22 nations designed buildings for the totally destroyed quarter. The diversity here is exciting: 50 architects took part, including Gropius, Niemeyer, and Duttman.

Le Corbusier also submitted a design for an apartment house for INTERBAU 1957, but the structure was so gigantic that it had to be built near the **Olympic Stadium** (U-Bahn: Olympia-Stadion). The **Corbusier House,** called *Strahlende Stadt* (radiant city), is one of Europe's largest housing complexes—its 530 apartments can house up to 1,400 people. Typical of the architect's style, this tremendous building rests on stilts.

The architects of rebuilt Berlin were also encouraged to design centers for the performing arts. One of the most controversial projects was the **Congress Hall (Kongresshalle),** on John-Foster-Dulles-Allee, in the Tiergarten, just west of Brandenburg Gate. This building was conceived as the American contribution to INTERBAU 1957. The reinforced concrete structure has a 60-foot-high vaulted ceiling that reminds some viewers of an oversized flying saucer. Irreverent Berliners immediately christened it "The Pregnant Oyster." The building today is used mainly for conventions. More successful was the **Philharmonie,** new home of the Berlin Philharmonic, and its adjacent chamber-music hall, next to the Tiergarten. The tentlike roof arches up in a bold curve, and the gold-colored facade glitters.

Berlin's tallest building sits in the midst of the city's busiest area. The 22-story **Europa-Center,** just across the plaza from the Kaiser Wilhelm Memorial Church, is the largest self-contained shopping center and entertainment complex in Europe. This town-within-a-town opened in 1965 on the site of the legendary Romanisches Café, once a gathering place for actors, writers, and artists in the flamboyant 1920s. Berliners immediately dubbed it "Pepper's Manhattan," after its owner, K. H. Pepper. In addition to three levels of shops, restaurants, nightclubs, bars, and cinemas, it contains dozens of offices, a parking garage, and an observation roof. At the Tauentzienstrasse entrance, you can find two pieces of the former Berlin Wall. The building is open daily from 9am to midnight (to 10pm in winter). Admission to the observation roof is 3DM ($1.70). U-Bahn: Kurfürstendamm.

SIGHTS IN THE ENVIRONS

Haus der Wannsee-Konferenz. Am Grossen Wannsee 56. ☎ **030/80-50-01-0.** Free admission. Mon–Fri 10am–6pm, Sat–Sun 2–6pm. S-Bahn: Wannsee, then bus 114.

This was the site of one of the most notorious conferences in history: a meeting of Nazi bureaucrats and SS officials to plan the annihilation of European Jewry. The minutes of the conference were kept by Adolf Eichmann, the sallow-faced SS functionary who later mapped out transport logistics for sending millions of Jews to their deaths.

The villa is now a memorial to the Holocaust. It includes a selection of photographs of men, women, and children who were sent to concentration camps. This exhibit is not for the squeamish. Nearly all the pictures on display are official Nazi photographs, including some of Nazi medical experiments. As noted at the trials at Nürnberg, "No government in history ever did a better job of photographing and documenting its crimes against humanity."

Jüdischer Friedhof (Jewish Cemetery). Herbert-Baumstrasse, Weissensee (a suburb east of Berlin). ☎ **030/9-25-33-30.** Mar–Nov daily 8am–5pm; Dec–Feb Mon–Thurs 8am–4pm, Fri 8am–3pm. Tram: 23 or 24, or taxi.

This famous Jewish cemetery was opened in 1880. It contains 110,000 graves of Jewish residents of Berlin. Many distinguished artists, musicians, and scientists, as well as religious leaders, are buried here. Some tombs are of Jewish soldiers who fought for Germany in World War I. Back then, of course, many Jews were filled with a strong sense of German nationalism and showed great bravery at the front. A memorial honors Jewish victims murdered during the Nazi era. You may have a hard time finding the cemetery on your own, so we recommend that you take a taxi.

Spandauer Zitadelle (Spandau Citadel). Am Juliusturm. ☎ **030/3-39-12-97.** Admission 8DM ($4.55) adults, 2DM ($1.15) children. Tues–Fri 9am–5pm, Sat–Sun 10am–5pm. U-Bahn: Zitadelle.

The citadel stands at the confluence of the Spree and Havel Rivers in northwestern Berlin. The Hohenzollern electors of Brandenburg used it as a summer residence, and in time it became the chief military center of Prussia. The Juliusturm (Julius Tower) and the Palas, constructed in the 13th to 15th centuries, are the oldest buildings still standing. The main building, accessible by footbridge, houses a local-history museum. The citadel has been besieged by everybody from the French to the Prussians.

THE PARKS & ZOO

The huge **Botanischer Garten (Botanical Garden),** Königin-Luise-Strasse 6–8 (☎ **030/83-00-60**), near the Dahlem Museums, contains vast collections of European and exotic plants. The big palm house is one of the largest in the world. There's a large arboretum here as well as several special collections, such as a garden for blind visitors and another with water-plants. Admission is 6DM ($3.40) for adults, 3DM ($1.70) for children, and free for children under 6. The garden is open daily from 9am to 8pm (it closes at dusk in winter); the museum, Tuesday to Sunday from 10am to 5pm. Free admission to the museum only. S-Bahn: Botanischer Garten or Rathaus Steglitz.

The ✪ **Tiergarten** is the largest green space in central Berlin, covering just under 1 square mile, with more than 14 miles of meandering walkways. It was originally laid out as a private park for the electors of Prussia, by a leading landscape architect of the day, Peter Josef Lenné. The park was devastated during World War II—the trees that remained were chopped down for fuel as Berlin shivered through the winter of 1945–46. Beginning in 1955, trees were replanted, and walkways, canals, ponds, and flower beds were restored to their original patterns. The park is popular with joggers and (sometimes nude) sunbathers. Inside the park is the Berlin Zoo (see below).

Among the park's monuments is the **Siegessäule (Victory Column),** a golden goddess of victory perched atop a soaring red-granite pedestal. The monument stands in

---

Fun for Kids

Children love the **Berlin Zoo-Aquarium** (see below). Its most famous residents, the giant pandas, are perennial favorites. The zoo also has playgrounds and a children's section, where the animals welcome a cuddle. Another place to take the kids is **Grips-Theater,** Altonaerstrasse 22 (☎ **030/3-91-40-04**), known for its bright, breezy productions. Children are sure to enjoy the music and dancing (if not the simple German dialogue). Tickets cost 25DM to 30DM ($14.25 to $17.10) for adults, 15DM ($8.55) for students, and 10DM ($5.70) for children. Call to ask about current productions and performance times. Closed from late June to early August; U-Bahn: Hansaplatz.

the center of the wide boulevard (Strasse des 17 Juni) that neatly bisects the park. A 157-foot-high observation platform can be reached by a climb up a 290-step spiral staircase. It's open on Monday from 3 to 6pm and Tuesday to Sunday from 9:30am to 6:30pm. Admission is 2DM ($1.15) for adults and 1DM (55¢) for children. For information, call ☎ **030/391-29-61.**

The **Zoologischer Garten Berlin (Berlin Zoo-Aquarium),** Hardenbergplatz 8 (☎ **030/25-40-10**), founded in 1844, is Germany's oldest zoo. It occupies almost the entire southwest corner of the Tiergarten. Until World War II, the zoo boasted thousands of animals—many were familiar to Berliners by nickname. By the end of 1945 only 91 animals had survived. The city has been rebuilding its large and extensive collection; today more than 13,000 animals live here, many of them in large, open natural habitats. The most valuable residents are giant pandas. The zoo also has Europe's most modern birdhouse, with more than 550 species.

The **aquarium** is as impressive as the adjacent zoo, with more than 9,000 fish, reptiles, amphibians, insects, and other creatures. The terrarium within is inhabited by crocodiles, Komodo dragons, and tuataras. You can walk on a bridge over the reptile pit (but don't lose your balance). There's also a large collection of snakes, lizards, and turtles. The "hippoquarium" is a new attraction.

Admission to the zoo is 12DM ($6.85) for adults and 6DM ($3.40) for children; to the aquarium, 12DM ($6.85) for adults and 6DM ($3.40) for children. A combined ticket costs 19DM ($10.85) for adults and 9.50DM ($5.40) for children. The zoo is open April through October daily from 9am to 6:30pm; November through March, daily from 9am to 5pm. The aquarium is open year-round daily from 9am to 6pm.

Walking Tour: From the Site of the Berlin Wall to Unter den Linden

Start: Moritzplatz.
Finish: Nikolaikirche.
Time: 4 hours.
Best Time: Daylight hours. After dark, bad lighting and frequent construction projects make access hazardous.

In August 1961, the Berlin Wall was hastily erected between East and West Berlin. For more than 28 years, the Wall dramatized a nation's division. As you take this tour, bear in mind that there were actually two walls, separated by a desolate and very dangerous "no-man's land." In some places, the two barriers were only a few yards apart; in others, spaces the size of a football field separated them.

In 1989, the Berlin Wall started to fall. By 1990, its demolition was in full swing, much to the delight of souvenir hunters around the world. Collectors purchased pieces of the wall for as much as $100,000 and hauled them off as relics of a dying era.

Today, the former no-man's land between the eastern and western zones is prized real estate. Consortiums of German and foreign companies have begun constructing office buildings here, so you'll sometimes walk beneath makeshift tunnels because of construction projects.

Your tour begins in the district of Kreuzberg, in what was formerly the western zone, at:

1. Moritzplatz, which was known before World War II as the publishing center of the German-speaking world. Its importance, however, dried up almost overnight after the Communist regime suppressed newspapers. During the Cold War, Moritzplatz served as the only authorized gateway to and from East Berlin for West Germans not residing in Berlin. The neighborhood was viewed as a wasteland of border controls.

From here, walk a few paces west along Oranienstrasse; then veer right (north) onto:

2. Stallschreiber Strasse. Within less than a block, this street will traverse what was known for almost 30 years as the "Death Zone;" it claimed the lives of all but a lucky handful of people trying to escape from East Berlin. Turn left at Alter-Jakob-Strasse, a residential street once divided midway along its length by the Berlin Wall. Vestiges of the street's past are quickly being swept away.

Turn right onto Kommandanten, then left onto Lindenstrasse. At the corner of Lindenstrasse (a small length of which was renamed "Axel Springer Strasse" in honor of its most famous corporate resident) and Oranienstrasse, you'll see the headquarters of:

3. Axel Springer Verlag (Axel Springer Publishers). The company's pugnacious director deliberately constructed this building adjacent to the Berlin Wall, as a symbol of defiance against the East German regime. Today, the expanded structure houses the executive offices for three of Germany's most powerful newspapers and magazines: ***Berliner Morgenpost, Bild,*** and ***Die Welt.***

Now, retrace your steps north for a block along Lindenstrasse, turning left (west) onto Zimmerstrasse. Here, both walls ran along the entire length of the street, separated by only a few feet of tightly patrolled space. Within 3 blocks, at the:

4. Corner of Zimmerstrasse and Charlottenstrasse, you'll see the site where one of the most widely publicized dramas of the Cold War occurred. A cross, a plaque, and, sometimes, bouquets of faded flowers mark the spot where, in 1962, 18-year-old Peter Fechter was shot as he attempted to climb over the Berlin Wall, within sight of a horrified crowd of West Berliners, photojournalists, and U.S. soldiers.

From here, walk another block west to the corner of Zimmerstrasse and Friedrichstrasse, where you'll see the:

5. Site of Checkpoint Charlie/American Business Center. For decades, this spot was perhaps the most famous border crossing in the world. Checkpoint Charlie (named for Brig. Gen. Charles Frost Craig, commander of U.S. forces in Berlin) was created in 1961, when U.S. tanks moved up Friedrichstrasse and a crane lowered a prefabricated metal-sided hut into the middle of the street. The action provoked three of the tensest weeks of the Cold War, as U.S. and Soviet troops stared at each other over the armor of their tanks. During Checkpoint Charlie's long years of operation, merchants, spies, and members of the non-German public came through a forbidding series of double-locked doors, past television monitors, luggage inspectors, and humorless, heavily armed guards. Ironically, Charlie was the only border crossing between the two Germanys forbidden to all Germans. In 1992, the much-photographed metal hut was sold to a group of American investors for its souvenir value. While here, you might visit the **Checkpoint Charlie Museum** (Museum Haus am Checkpoint Charlie), Friedrichstrasse 44 (☎ **030/253-7250**), described in "Other Museums & Sights," above.

One of the most expensive German-American real estate ventures in history, the **American Business Center** (also known as **Checkpoint Charlie, K.G.**),

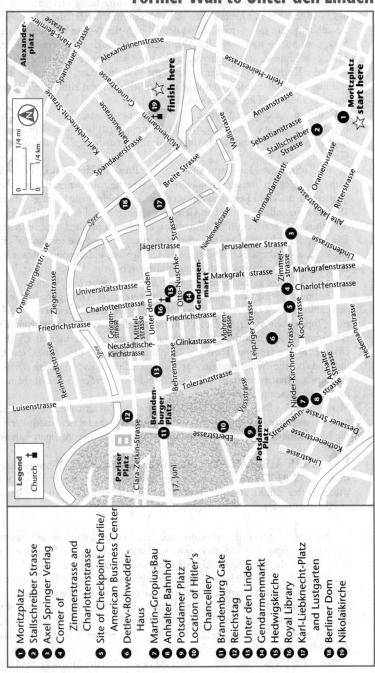

Legend
✝ Church

finish here ⭐

start here ⭐

1 Moritzplatz
2 Stallschreiber Strasse
3 Axel Springer Verlag
4 Corner of Zimmerstrasse and Charlottenstrasse
5 Site of Checkpoint Charlie/ American Business Center
6 Detlev-Rohwedder-Haus
7 Martin-Gropius-Bau
8 Anhalter Bahnhof
9 Potsdamer Platz
10 Location of Hitler's Chancellery
11 Brandenburg Gate
12 Reichstag
13 Unter den Linden
14 Gendarmenmarkt
15 Hedwigskirche
16 Royal Library
17 Karl-Liebknecht-Platz and Lustgarten
18 Berliner Dom
19 Nikolaikirche

Friedrichstrasse 50 (☎ 030/22-33-450), is currently being erected amid the blocks adjacent to this historic site. Today three of the five buildings planned—a combination of commercial and residential high-rises—have been completed. Now, continue to walk west along Zimmerstrasse, looking for occasional remnants of the ruined, once-mighty wall. The street will eventually change its name to Nieder-Kirchner-Strasse after it crosses the Wilhelmstrasse. (Some street signs and maps may refer to this section of the Wilhelmstrasse as either the Toleranz-strasse or the older Otto-Grotewohl-Strasse.)

Continue walking west along Nieder-Kirchner-Strasse. On its right-hand (northern) edge, you'll see the gray-colored (unmarked) back side of one of the largest, most architecturally boring, and most transmogrified buildings in German history, the:

6. **Detlev-Rohwedder-Haus** (also known as the **Prussian Herrnhaus**). Filling an entire city block, its bureaucratic-looking bulk was originally designed as the headquarters for the Third Reich's air ministry, directed by Hermann Göring. Between 1945 and the collapse of the East German regime, it served as the regime's Haus der Ministerien (cabinet offices). After that, its offices supervised the transition of East German industry to the free-market economy. During the rebellion of June 16, 1953, it was the site of some of the fiercest fighting and consequently some of the most brutal repression by the communist government. At this writing, it was being reconfigured as the home of the new German Ministry of Finance.

Continue walking west along Nieder-Kirchner-Strasse. During the lifetime of this edition, the city of Berlin will probably transform a small temporary exhibition "Topography of Terror" into a full-fledged, albeit very small, museum. The exhibition is located within the basement of what was once used as a torture chamber by the Gestapo. There was no phone number at press time. Near the junction of the Wilhelmstrasse, at Neiderkirchnerstrasse 7, (with another entrance at Stresemannstrasse 110), you'll find the entrance to one of the most interesting museums in Berlin, the:

7. **Martin-Gropius-Bau** (☎ **030/25-48-60**). This unusual art collection was deliberately constructed near the site of the Wall, adjacent to the former headquarters of the Nazi Gestapo. For more information, see "Other Museums & Sights," above.

☕ **TAKE A BREAK**   The **Martin-Gropius-Bau Café,** Niederkirchner-strasse 7, (☎ **030/25-48-60**), a cafe inside this museum (see above), serves sandwiches, coffee, drinks, and platters of food in a setting enriched with the ironies of 20th-century art.

After your visit, exit the museum onto Stresemannstrasse, turn left (south), and walk for about 2 blocks. You'll soon see the markings for the S-Bahn station of Anhalter Bahnhof. A short distance to the east of the S-Bahn station lies the site of what during the 1920s was the third-largest railway station in Europe, the:

8. **Anhalter Bahnhof.** During the rule of the German kaisers, this railway station received many of the crowned heads of Europe on official visits. Later, it was used as the setting for many of Hitler's propaganda films. When the Berlin Wall blocked most of the station's feeder lines and access routes, West Berlin officials demolished those parts of the station that weren't already devastated by the wartime bombings. Today, the premises contain an S-Bahn Station, lots of ugly concrete, and little more than memories of the elaborate ceremonies that used to be held here.

Now, retrace your steps and walk north along Stresemannstrasse. Bypass the Martin-Gropius-Bau, site of your earlier visit, and continue on past a landscape that alternates roaring traffic with Cold-War wastelands and what seems like an unending cycle of urban renewal. Soon, you'll reach what before the war was one of the most glamorous addresses in Europe:

9. Potsdamer Platz. The hotels, cafes, and town houses of this square were once legendary bastions of privilege and chic. During its heyday, more than 550 trams passed through the Platz every hour. Its street lamps were Europe's first electric illumination, and in 1920, Germany's first traffic light was installed here. During the height of the Third Reich, the Platz bordered the most important power centers of the Nazi empire, including the now-demolished chancellery. Most of its monuments and all its grandeur were bombed into dust in Allied air raids. During the Cold War, any hope of rebuilding the area was squashed by its division into three occupied zones—American, British, and Soviet. For decades it languished, little more than a depressing expanse of shattered concrete and busy traffic.

Since the collapse of the Wall, Potsdamer Platz has been the site of one of the most impassioned controversies in Berlin. Despite the hope of civic planners to return the plaza to its prewar glory, at least half the surrounding landscape was snapped up in 1990 at deflated prices by Daimler Benz, and the remainder by such companies as Sony and ABB. The square quickly became one of Europe's largest construction sites. If all goes as planned, in the next year or two the square and the surrounding streets will be a city within a city, a 21st-century complex of apartment buildings, restaurants, shops, theaters, and corporate headquarters of several multinational corporations. The **Info-Box Potsdamer Platz,** Leipziger Platz 21 (☎ **030/2-26-62-40**), inside a bright-red temporary building, contains scale models, drawings, and photographs of the way Potsdamer Platz used to look and the way it will look at the dawn of the millennium. The Info Box is open daily from 9am to 7pm (on Thursday, to 9pm). A visit to the viewing terrace costs 2DM ($1.15).

☕ **TAKE A BREAK**   On the third floor of the Info-Box, there's an all-day cafe and restaurant serving coffee, sandwiches, and platters of food.

After your refueling stop, exit from the Potsdamer Platz and walk north along the eastern edge of Ebertstrasse. During World War II, the neighborhood you're traversing was filled with the densest concentration of Nazi administrative buildings in Germany, known collectively as the Regierungsviertel (Government Quarter). As you continue walking along Ebertstrasse, look eastward at the massive changes that are transforming this former wasteland. Straight ahead of you rises the monumental dome of the Reichstag.

Throughout the Cold War, one of the most politically sensitive areas in Berlin was an understated bump in the hard-packed earth located east of Ebertstrasse and beside the northern edge of Vossstrasse. Although recent increases in the land's value and massive urban development have obliterated the once-famous mound almost completely, the site is remembered as the:

10. Location of Hitler's Ruined Chancellery. From here during World War II, Hitler directed the German military machine. In 1945, reluctant to have the site of Hitler's suicide canonized by defeated Germans, the Soviets demolished the massive building brick by brick and in its place established what became, during the Cold War, the broadest point of the impassable no-man's land. According to Soviet legend, none of the guard dogs patrolling the site during the Cold War would ever go near where the chancellery had stood unless forced to do so, and no vegetation ever grew in the poisoned soil around it. The city of Berlin is planning to build a Holocaust Memorial somewhere near this site.

At this point, facing north along Ebertstrasse, you'll be within sight of the world-famous:

11. **Brandenburg Gate (Brandenburger Tor).** This monument was inspired by the Propylea of the Acropolis in Athens. It was originally constructed in 1789 as a focal point for the grand avenues that radiate from it; later, its neoclassical grandeur marked the boundary between East and West Berlin. Ironically, the monument represents an early act of cooperation between the sectors of the once-divided city. When the Quadriga (a chariot drawn by four horses) atop the gate was destroyed during the war and the gate badly damaged, the West Berlin senate arranged for a new Quadriga to be hammered in copper as a gift to the administration of East Berlin.

From the base of the Brandenburg Gate, walk north a short distance, toward the Spree River, to the large square called Platz der Republik. At the eastern edge of the square rises the:

12. **Reichstag (Parliament).** This building is now once again the official seat of the German government. It was designed in the late 19th century in a neo-Renaissance style and rebuilt in a more streamlined style after World War II. The Reichstag, despite a rich history that predates the rise of Hitler, continues to evoke memories of the Nazi period. In 1933, a fire mysteriously broke out in its chambers and nearly destroyed the building. Hitler blamed Communist enemies of Germany for the blaze, and used it as an excuse to assume dictatorial powers. Many historians believe that the Nazis themselves were the arsonists; at any rate, the Reichstag was not repaired during the Nazi period.

Except by special appointment, most of the building, including the chambers of government, is off-limits to visitors. The building's dome, however, can be climbed by means of a winding staircase, every day from 8am to 10pm. For information, call ☎ **030/227-321-30.**

Now retrace your steps south to the base of the Brandenburg Gate, and notice to the east the broad stretch of one of the most famous thoroughfares in Europe:

13. **Unter den Linden.** The palaces and cafes that once stood along this boulevard were legendary throughout Europe for hosting virtually every famous artist and politician in the German-speaking world. The street is lined with symmetrical rows of trees, so admired by the Great Elector, Friedrich Wilhelm, that he decreed that anyone cutting down one of his lindens should have his hand amputated. (Hitler, in defiance of the monarchical tradition, cut all of them down to widen the boulevard for his military parades.) The East Germans replanted the trees after World War II and restored many of the neoclassical palaces and Humboldt University buildings that you see along the street today. Despite these efforts, the prewar gaiety and glamour of Unter den Linden has never returned. Much of the east-to-west expanse remains monumental, monotonous, and lifeless, though not without a formal beauty. One of most famous landmarks here is the **equestrian statue of Frederick the Great.** In 1945, this statue was shipped to Potsdam, but it was returned in 1980.

☕ **TAKE A BREAK**   The most famous coffeehouse of prewar Berlin, the **Operncafé** (or Opern Palais Caf), Unter den Linden 5 (☎ **030/20-26-83**), occupied a section of a palace destroyed during Allied bombing raids. Now restored, the cafe has plenty of old-world charm and dispenses all sorts of drinks, light meals, snacks, and ice cream. It also offers a big breakfast buffet for 25DM ($14.25), every day from 9am to noon. It's open daily from 9am to midnight. Check out the beautiful terrace in the summer. Upstairs, you can order complete lunches and dinners.

At Unter den Linden 8 is the **Deutsche Staatsbibliothek** (National Library) (☎ **030/2660**), which was constructed in a neobaroque style between 1903 and 1914, and contains more than 8.7 million volumes. It's open Monday to Friday from 9am to 9pm and on Saturday from 9am to 5pm. A guided tour is conducted at 10:30am on the first Saturday of the month in building Fjon, and at 10:30am on the third Saturday of the month in building 2.

Turn right at the third street on your right, Charlottenstrasse, which within 3 blocks runs into one of the most monumental squares in the former eastern section:

14. Gendarmenmarkt. Frederick the Great designed this graceful baroque square in the 1780s. Despite its antique appearance, the Genarmenmarkt was reduced to a pile of rubble during World War II and later restored by the East Germans. The square's centerpiece remains the neoclassical theater (Schauspielhaus) designed by Karl Friedrich Schinkel in 1821. It now serves as a concert hall. Restoration of the French Cathedral here was completed in 1983, and the property was returned to the French Reformed Church.

Exit from the square's northeast corner and walk east for a short block along Französische Strasse. Turn left at Hedwigskirchgasse. When it funnels into Bebelplatz, admire the enormous dome of the baroque:

15. Hedwigskirche (☎ **030/2-03-48-70**), which now functions as the Roman Catholic cathedral of the Berlin diocese. Begun in 1747 by Frederick the Great, probably as a gesture to appease his troublesome subjects in Catholic Silesia, it was the only Catholic church in Berlin until the mid-1880s. Architect Georg Wenzeslaus von Knobelsdorf modeled it on the Pantheon in Rome, adding a copper-sheathed dome. Because of the structural problems that plagued the building early in its construction, it's much simpler than what Frederick originally hoped for. The restoration done between 1952 and 1963 preserved the original structure of the dome, although the interior is modern. The church is open Monday to Saturday from 10am to 5pm and on Sunday from 1 to 5pm.

Also on Bebelplatz, across from the cathedral, is the:

16. Königliche Bibliothek (Royal Library), part of Humboldt University, which was completed in 1780. The library is modeled on the Royal Palace (Hofburg) in Vienna. Its curved wings prompted Berliners to christen it the Kommode (chest of drawers). Despite its illustrious contribution to German scholarship over the years, the library is most remembered as the site of Hitler's infamous book burnings. On the eastern edge of Bebelplatz rises the Berlin State Opera (Staatsoper), and on the northern edge of the square you'll once again see Unter den Linden.

Continue your walk east along Unter den Linden, which becomes narrower as it crosses over a branch of the Spree River and then ends at:

17. Karl-Liebknecht-Platz and the Lustgarten. Before reunification, their boundaries were collectively known as Marx-Engels-Platz. Once the much-heralded site of the Kaiser's Palace, which was completely demolished by the Communists as a symbol of bourgeois decadence, the square is now a monument to the bad architectural taste of the defunct East German regime. Many of the graceless and angular buildings here were declared unfit for use after reunification because of the massive amounts of asbestos used in their construction during the 1960s and 1970s.

To the east is the:

18. **Berliner Dom,** constructed in the style of the High Renaissance from 1894 to 1905. It's the largest Protestant cathedral in Germany. Visitors are asked for a 5DM ($2.85) donation for ongoing restoration. The main church is open Monday through Saturday from 9am to 7:30pm and Sunday from 11:30am to 7:30pm. The imperial staircase is open Monday through Saturday from 9am to 6pm and on Sunday from 11:30am to 6pm. Visits to the dome gallery depend on weather conditions.

Exit from Karl-Liebknecht-Platz and the Lustgarten by walking northeast along Karl-Liebknecht-Strasse. (This boulevard is the eastward continuation of Unter den Linden.) After a few blocks, turn right onto Spandauerstrasse. Within 2 blocks you'll reach one of Germany's proud achievements in historic restoration—a neighborhood called the **Nikolaiviertel** (see "Exploring Berlin-Mitte," above), which is quickly blossoming into a haven of coffeehouses, art galleries, and nightspots.

The neighborhood's most prominent building and centerpiece is the:

19. **Nikolaikirche.** Berlin's oldest parish church was built in the 14th century. It has two spires, which have become the symbol of the reunited city. The interior is refreshingly simple. On this site, in 1307, Berlin and its neighbor, Cölln, decided to unite their borders and form a single city.

6 Organized Tours

ON FOOT   For an excellent introduction to Berlin and its history, try one of the walking tours offered by **Berlin Walks** (☎ 030/301-9194 or e-mail: Berlin_Walks@ compuserve.com for information). "Discover Berlin" is a 3-hour introductory tour that takes you past the New Synagogue, the Reichstag, and the Brandenburg Gate, among other major sites. This walk starts daily at 10am and 2:30pm (in winter at 10am only). "Infamous Third Reich Sites" focuses on the sites of major Nazi buildings in central Berlin, such as Goebbels' Propaganda Ministry and Hitler's New Reichschancellery; it starts at 10am, on Saturdays, Sundays, Tuesdays, and Thursdays in summer, less frequently in the off-season. "Jewish Life in Berlin" takes you through the pre-war Jewish community; sights include the Old Cemetery and the former Boys' School. The tour starts at 10am Monday and Thursday, from April through mid-October. For all tours reservations are unnecessary—simply meet the guide, who will be wearing a Berlin Walks badge, outside the main entrance to Bahnhof Zoologischer Garten (Zoo Station), at the top of the taxi stand. Tours last from 2½ to 3 hours and cost 13DM ($7.15) for those under 26 and 18DM ($9.90) for everyone else. This summer, Berlin Walks will be inaugurating a new 5-hour tour to Potsdam, starting every Wednesday and Saturday at 9am; meet at the same place.

BY BUS   Berlin is a far-flung metropolis whose interesting neighborhoods are often separated by extended areas of park, monumental boulevards, and Cold-War wastelands. Because of these factors, organized bus tours can be the best way to navigate the city.

Some of the best tours are operated by **Severin+Kühn,** Kurfürstendamm 216 (☎ 030/88-04-190), located on the second floor of a building across from the Bristol Hotel Kempinski. This agency offers a half dozen tours of Berlin and its environs. Their 2-hour "12-Stops-City Tour" departs daily every hour April to October from

10:15am to 6:15pm and November to March from 10:15am to 5:15pm. Tickets are 30DM ($17.10) per person. The tour passes 12 important stops in Berlin, including the Europa-Center and the Brandenburg Gate, provides taped audio commentary in several languages, and offers the option of getting on and off the bus at any point during the tour. Retain your ticket stub for readmittance to the bus.

Severin+Kühn also offers the 3-hour "Big Berlin Tour," which departs at 10am and 2pm daily and costs 39DM ($22.25) per person. This tour incorporates more sites than the 12-Stops Tour, including the Grunewald Forest.

One of the most interesting tours visits Potsdam, site of the famed World War II conference and of Sans Souci Palace, former residence of Frederick the Great. The price is 59DM ($33.65) per person. Departures are Tuesday to Sunday at 10am May to September and Saturday and Sunday at 2:15pm April to October.

BY BOAT   It may not be the obvious choice for transportation in Berlin, but a boat ride can offer visitors a good change of pace. The networks of canals that bisect the plains of what used to be known as Prussia were an engineering marvel when they were completed in the 19th century. Today, transport through the lakes, locks, and canals around Berlin retains its nostalgic allure, and affords unusual vistas that aren't available from the windows of more conventional modes of transport. Berliners boast that their city has more bridges than Venice. Local waterways include the Spree and Havel Rivers—ranging in size from narrow channels to large lakes—as well as many canals. During the Cold War, many waterways were blocked, but now they're open again. You can take short tours that offer close-up views of the city or daylong adventures along the Spree and Havel; the latter often turn into beer-drinking fests.

The city's best-known boat operator is **Stern- und Kreisschiffahrt,** Pushkinallee 60–70 (☎ **030/5-36-36-00**). Since Germany's reunification, the company has absorbed the piers and ferryboats of its former East German counterparts. "Historische Stadtfahrt" is a ride along the banks of the Spree, the river that helped build Berlin. Two, three, and four-hour tours (in German only) depart at 10am and 2pm from a quay near Berlin's cathedral, Am Palast Ufer. These trips offer good views of the Reichstag, the Pergamon Museums, the Königliche Bibliothek (Royal Library), and the monumental heart of the former East Berlin. The 1-hour tour costs 25.50DM ($14.55) per person.

Stern- und Kreisschiffahrt also has a novelty lake steamer shaped like a whale and called *Moby Dick.* It departs from a point near the terminus of U-Bahn Line no. 6 at Tegel, on the city's northwestern edge. Walk for about 10 minutes through the suburb of Tegel to the Greenwich promenade and then to the Stern- und Kreisschiffahrt pier. Boats head southward from Tegel, passing through a series of long, narrow lakes, as well as the Hohenzollernkanal, the Ploetzensee locks, the Charlottenburger Lake, the Havel Lake, and the lake port of Wannsee on Berlin's southwestern perimeter. Passengers can also opt for an additional ride to Potsdam, farther along the length of the chain of lakes.

Reservations are usually necessary for all boat rides described here. Rides operate only between April and late October. Prices and actual itineraries change seasonally; call for more details.

7 Sports & Outdoor Pursuits

BIKING   The best place to rent a bike is **Hackeschen-Hosen Bike Rentals and Sales,** Rosenthalerstrasse 40–41 (☎ **030/2-859-9895**). Rentals begin at 20DM ($11.40) per day. Another good outlet is **Berlin by Bike,** Möckernstrasse 92 (☎ **030/ 28-59-98-95**), in Kreuzberg, open 10am to 7pm. Here rentals cost from 25DM ($14.25) per day. You can also rent bikes at major hotels for about 30DM ($17.10) per day. There are bike paths, marked by red bricks on the walkways, through the central core of Berlin and in its parks. Bike-rental outlets carry a Berlin biker's atlas to help you find the paths. The best places for biking are the Tiergarten in central Berlin, and farther afield in the Grunewald Forest, which can be reached by taking the S-Bahn to Grunewald.

JOGGING   Head for the vast and verdant leafiness of the **Grunewald,** on the city's western edge, which is crisscrossed with pedestrian and cyclists' paths. This area is appropriate for very long endurance tests. Closer to the center is the **Tiergarten,** which allows you to soak up a little history on your morning jog thanks to its many monuments and memorials. The grounds of **Schloss Charlottenburg** are also good for jogging.

SPECTATOR SPORTS   Among Berliners, **soccer** is the most popular sport. For information about which teams are playing, ask your hotel receptionist, or refer to a daily newspaper or the weekly magazine *Berlin Programm.*

SWIMMING & SAUNAS   Berlin has dozens of pools. One of the best equipped is the **Sports and Recreation Center,** Landsberger Allee 77 (☎ 030/42-18-23-20). Here you'll find a swimming pool, a diving pool, a wave pool, an assortment of waterfalls, a jet pool, sauna and solarium facilities, a weight room, about half a dozen restaurants and snack bars, and a bowling alley. The cost is 6DM ($3.40) for adults and 3DM ($1.70) for children for 2 hours of swimming.

A worthy competitor (located just east of Tempelhof Airport; take U-Bahn 6 to Grenzallee) is the **Club Paradise,** Buschkrugallee 65 (☎ 030/6-06-60-60), which has indoor and outdoor pools, saunas, a steam room, solariums, and a 120-meter water slide. Its latest attraction, called "Crazy River," sends you down a river in water tubes. A 4-hour pass costs 21DM ($11.95) for adults and 16DM ($9.10)for children ages 2 to 12. It's open daily from 10am to 11pm.

At the Europa-Center, a company called **Thermen,** Nürnberger Strasse 7 (☎ 030/2-61-60-32), offers an array of heated pools, saunas, massage facilities, and solariums. The cost for using all the facilities is 30DM ($17.10) for 3 hours or 34DM ($19.40) for all day. Both men and women can use the saunas. Massages cost extra—38DM ($21.65) for 30 minutes. Hours are Monday to Saturday from 10am to midnight and Sunday from 10am to 9pm.

For outdoor swimming during the hot months, head to one of Europe's largest lake beaches at **Wannsee.** Take the S-Bahn to the Nikolaisee and follow the hordes of bathers heading toward the water's edge.

TENNIS & SQUASH   At **Sports Treffe,** Buschkrugallee 84 (☎ 030/6-06-60-11), indoor courts rent for 29DM to 53DM ($16.55 to $30.20) for 45 minutes, depending on when you play. There are also about a dozen squash courts that rent for between 10DM and 29DM ($5.70 and $16.55) per 45-minute session. Closer to Berlin's center is **Squash & Tennis Center,** Treuenbrietzenerstrasse 34 (☎ 030/4-15-30-11), which has similar rates. There are also courts in the **Preussen Park,** Kamenzerstrasse 34, Lankwitz (☎ 030/7-75-10-51), open during the day from April through October with rates beginning at 34DM ($19.40) per hour.

8 Shopping

The **Ku'damm** (or "Kurfürstendamm") is the Fifth Avenue of Berlin. It's filled with quality stores but also has outlets hustling cheap souvenirs and T-shirts. Although Berliners themselves shop on the Ku'damm, many prefer the specialty stores on the side streets, especially between **Breitscheidplatz** and **Olivaer Platz.** You might also want to check out **Am Zoo** and **Kantstrasse.**

Another major shopping street is the **Tauentzienstrasse** and the streets that inter-sect it: **Marburger, Ranke,** and **Nürnberger.** This area offers a wide array of stores, many specializing in amusing German fashions for women. Stores here are often cheaper than on the Ku'damm because the rents are lower. Also on Tauentzienstrasse (near the Ku'damm) is Berlin's major indoor shopping center, the **Europa-Center** (☎ 030/3-48-00-88), with around 100 shops, as well as restaurants, cafes, and a casino. At the end of this street lies the **KaDeWe,** the classiest department store in Berlin and the biggest in continental Europe.

A new, upmarket version of the Europa-Center is the **Uhland-Passage,** at Uhland-strasse 170, which has some of the best boutiques and big-name stores in Berlin. Shop-pers interested in quality at any price should head to **Kempinski Plaza,** Uhlandstrasse 181–183, a pocket of posh with some of the most exclusive boutiques in the city. Haute-couture women's clothing is a special feature here. More trendy and avant-garde boutiques are found along **Bleibtreustrasse.**

If it's serious bargains you're looking for, head to **Wilmersdorferstrasse.** Here you'll find a vast number of discount stores, although some of the merchandise is second-rate. Try to avoid going on a Saturday morning, when it's often impossibly overcrowded.

In eastern Berlin, not that long ago, you couldn't find much to buy at all except a few souvenirs. All that is changed now. The main street of east Berlin, **Friedrich-strasse,** now offers some of Berlin's most elegant shopping. Upmarket boutiques—selling everything from quality women's fashions to Meissen porcelain—are found along **Unter den Linden.** The cheaper stores in eastern Berlin are around the rather bleak-looking open-air expanse of **Alexanderplatz.** Many specialty and clothing shops are open in the old restored **Nikolai quarter.** The largest shopping mall in eastern Berlin, with outlets offering a little bit of everything, is at the **Berliner Markthalle,** lying at the corner of Rosa-Luxemburg-Strasse and Karl-Liebknecht-Strasse.

Most stores in Berlin are open Monday to Friday from 9 or 10am until 6 or 6:30pm. Many stay open late on Thursday evenings, often until 8:30pm. Saturday hours are usually 9 or 10am until 2pm.

ANTIQUES

Astoria. Bleibtreustrasse 42. ☎ **030/8-83-81-81.**

Astoria, whose buyers frequently scour the antique markets of France, England, and Germany, pays homage to the decorative objects of the 1920s and 1930s. You'll find antique mirrors, lamps, tables, and jewelry here, as well as a handful of reproductions.

Harmel's. Damaschkestrasse 24. ☎ **030/3-24-22-92.**

Most of Harmel's inventory was gathered in England and France, a commentary on the relative scarcity of genuine German antiques because of wartime bombing. The carefully chosen collection stresses furniture, jewelry, and accessories from the Victo-rian and Edwardian eras.

L. & M. Lee. Kurfürstendamm 32. ☎ **030/8-81-73-33.**

This is one of several sophisticated antiques stores on the Kurfürstendamm's eastern end. The inventory includes mostly German-made porcelain, silver and glass from the early 20th century, and an assortment of 19th-century pieces from other European countries.

ART GALLERIES

Galerie Brusberg. Kurfürstendamm 213. ☎ **030/8-82-76-82.**

One of Germany's most visible and influential art galleries, Galerie Brusberg was established in 1958 by Dieter Brusberg. The gallery has handled the work of Max

Treasures in the Barn District

At the very heart and soul of Berlin's fashion and art revival is the Scheulenviertel, or "barn district." The name comes from a period in the 17th century, when hay barns were built far from the city center for fear of fires. In time the city's growth overtook the area, and it became Berlin's Jewish quarter. For some reason, many of its oldest buildings survived World War II bombing assaults.

The remains of a grand 1909 shopping arcade—which occupies most of the block formed by Oranienburger, Rosenthaler, Grosse Hamburger Strasse, and Sophienstrasse—have been turned into a series of galleries, studios, and theaters. Worth a visit is **Tacheles,** 53–56 Oranienburger Strasse (☎ 030/282-61-85), or "talking turkey" in Yiddish. It's an alternative arts center. You'll also find here the city's best avant-garde women's designer, **Lisa D** (☎ 030/282-9061).

The more prestigious galleries are found along Auguststrasse. **Galerie Wohn-maschine,** 34–36 Tucholskystrasse (☎ 030/3087-20-15), became the area's first gallery when it opened in 1988. Some of the best artists in the city are on exhibit here, mostly of a Conceptual or Minimalist bent. Another gallery of note, **Galerie Eigen & Art,** 26 Auguststrasse (☎ 030/280-6605), displays the most avant-garde paintings of artists from the old East Germany and other former Eastern Bloc countries.

Other shopping highlights include **Tools & Gallery,** 34–35 Rosenthaler Strasse (☎ 030/2859-9343), which sells both formal and elegantly casual clothes for both sexes, including exclusive labels such as Givenchy, Balenciaga, and Kenzo. **Johanna Petzoldt,** 9 Sophienstrasse (☎ 030/282-6754), sells hand-crafts from the old Erzebig region, including wooden toys and assorted curiosi-ties, such as scenes fitted into a matchbox.

Ernst, Salvador Dalí, Paul Delvaux, Henri Laurens, Pablo Picasso, and René Magritte, plus German artists Altenbourg, Antes, and Klapheck. Long before unification, it pro-moted painters of the old Eastern bloc, notably Bernhard Heisig, Harald Metzkes, and Werner Töbke. No one will mind if you drop in just for a look.

Galerie Pels-Leusden and Villa Grisebach Auktionen. Fasanenstrasse 25. ☎ 030/8-85-91-50.

This building, constructed in the 1880s by architect Hans Grisebach as his private home, is a historic monument in its own right. Two floors are devoted to 19th- and 20th-century art, mainly German. Prices begin at 150DM ($85.50) for the least expensive lithograph, and go much higher. The building also functions as headquar-ters and display area for an auction house. Sales are held every spring and fall.

Galerie Springer. Fasanenstrasse 13. ☎ 030/3-12-70-63.

The list of talent showcased in this gallery in recent years reads like a who's who of Central European artists: Dieter Appelt, François Bouillon, Christa Dichgans, Piero Dorazio, Agnes Maels, Vladimir Skoda, and two who prefer to be identified only by their first names: Marwan and Lucebert.

BOOKSHOPS

This literate and culture-conscious city boasts lots of bookshops catering to a multi-lingual clientele. For English and American literature and recent periodicals, go to the **British Bookshop,** Mauerstrasse 83–84 (☎ 030/2-38-46-80). An outfit richly stocked with works from German publishing houses is **Literaturhaus Berlin,** Fasa-nenstrasse 23 (☎ 030/8-82-50-44). The leading gay bookstore of Berlin, containing both erotica and upscale literature in several different languages, is **Prince Eisenherz,** Bleibtreustrasse 52 (☎ 030/3-13-99-36).

CHINA & PORCELAIN

✪ **KPM.** Kurfürstendamm 27 in the Bristol Kempinski, Berlin. ☎ **030/88-67-21-10.**

This prestigious emporium was founded in 1763, when Frederick the Great invested his personal funds in a lackluster porcelain factory, elevated it to royal status, and gave it a new name: **Königliche Porzellan-Manufaktur (Royal Porcelain Factory).** It was Prussia's answer to Meissen in Saxony. Since then, the factory has become world famous for its artistry and delicacy. Each exquisite, hand-painted, hand-decorated item is carefully packed in almost-unbreakable formats that can be shipped to virtually any-where in the world. Patterns are based for the most part on traditional 18th- and 19th-century designs. All objects carry a distinctive official signature, an imperial orb, and the letters KPM. There's also an array of high-quality trinkets for tourists.

You can also visit the **factory** itself at Wegelystrasse 1 (☎ 030/39-00-90). Guided tours let you look at the craftsmanship of the employees, and you can also buy pieces here. Tours are provided once a day from Monday to Thursday at 10am. The charge is 5DM ($2.85), which is applied to any purchase. Children under 16 are prohibited, as are video cameras and photography.

Meissener Porzellan. Am Kurfürstendamm 214. ☎ **030/88-68-35-30.**

This is one of the most famous porcelain outlets in Europe. It offers the finest array of exquisite Meissen dinner plates in Berlin, and also displays and sells sculptures and chandeliers. For a Meissen factory tour, see chapter 4.

Rosenthal. Kurfürstendamm 226. ☎ **030/8-85-63-40.**

Head here for contemporary Rosenthal designs from Bavaria. In addition to Rosenthal porcelain, you'll find Boda glassware, along with elegantly modern tableware.

DEPARTMENT STORES

Kaufhaus des Westens (KaDeWe). Wittenbergplatz (about 2 blocks from the Ku'damm). ☎ **030/2-12-10.**

This huge luxury department store, known popularly as KaDeWe (pronounced kah-day-vay), was established some 90 years ago. It's best known for its sixth-floor food department, where more than 1,000 varieties of German sausages are displayed along with delicacies from all over the world. Sit-down counters are available. After fortifying yourself here, you can explore the six floors of merchandise. KaDeWe is more than a department store—one shopper called it a "collection of first-class specialty shops."

Wertheim. Kurfürstendamm 231 (near the Europa Center). ☎ **030/88-00-30.**

This centrally located store is good for travel aids and general basics. It sells perfumes, clothing for the entire family, jewelry, electrical devices, household goods, photog-raphy supplies, and souvenirs. It also has a shoe-repair section. Shoppers can fuel up at a large restaurant with a grand view over half the city.

FASHION

Bogner-Shop Zenker. Kurfürstendamm 45. ☎ **030/8-81-10-00.** S-Bahn: Savignyplatz.

This three-story shop has sold garments to three generations of clients. Its selection of women's clothing includes everything from formal evening gowns to sportswear. Many of the items are made in Germany, Austria, or Italy.

Modenhaus Horn. Kurfürstendamm 213. ☎ **030/8-81-40-55.**

Berlin is one of the world's most fashion-conscious cities, and here you'll see examples of what's *au courant* for chic women.

Sonia Rykiel. Kurfürstendamm 186. ☎ **030/8-82-17-74** for women, or 030/882-28-85 for children.

This stylish showcase is the only shop in Germany devoted exclusively to Ms. Rykiel, the successful French fashion mogul. She designed the store's interior herself. Beware: even a Sonia Rykiel T-shirt is expensive. There's both a children's shop and a women's shop.

Triebel. Schönwalder Strasse 12, Spandau. ☎ **030/3-35-50-01.**

This elegant store offers everything you might need for a weekend retreat at a private hunting lodge, such as clothing, shoes, boots, or sporting equipment. If you dream of looking like the lord of a Bavarian manor in a loden coat and feather-trimmed hat, or if you've been invited on a spontaneous fox hunt, come here first. The inventory includes a selection of hunting rifles and shooting equipment.

JEWELRY

Galerie Lalique. Bleibtreustrasse 47. ☎ **030/8-81-97-62.**

One of the more unusual jewelry stores in Berlin, this emporium stocks the original designs of about 50 German-based designers. Most pieces are modern interpretations, using diamonds and other precious stones. Even though the store's name is similar to that of the French glass designer, no crystal or glassware is sold here.

Würzbacher. Kurfürstendamm 36. ☎ **030/8-83-38-92.** S-Bahn: Savignyplatz. U-Bahn: Uhlandstrasse.

Everything this small store sells is crafted on site from either gold or platinum, often with accents of precious or semiprecious stones. Most designs are modern and streamlined. Some pieces are noteworthy for their heft. Most of the jewelry here is for women, although a scattering of rings, tie clips, and cuff links are for men.

KITCHENWARE

WMF. Kurfürstendamm 229. ☎ **030/8-82-39-41.**

Its inventory is a restaurant owner's fantasy, with appealing kitchen gadgets that cooks will love. Be warned that most appliances here are incompatible with American electric current. But if you're interested in glassware (from Nachtmann and Eich), porcelain, stoneware, kitchen cutlery, and porcelain figurines by Hummel and Goebel, you'll find this place fascinating.

MARKETS

Antik & Flohmarkt. Friedrichstrasse S-Bahn station, Berlin-Mitte. ☎ **030/2-08-26-45.**

You might want to check out the finds at this flea market in the S-Bahn station in the old East Berlin. Some 100 vendors try to tempt buyers with assorted bric-a-brac, including brassware and World War II mementos.

Berliner Trödelmarkt. Strasse des 17 Juni. ☎ **030/26-55-00-96.**

This flea market lies near the corner of the Bachstrasse and the Strasse des 17 Juni, at the western edge of the Tiergarten, adjacent to the Tiergarten S-Bahn station. It's the favorite weekend shopping spot of countless Berliners, who come here to find an appropriate piece of nostalgia, a battered semiantique, or used clothing. The market is held every Saturday and Sunday (also Easter Monday) between 10am and 5pm.

MILITARY FIGURES
Berliner Zinnfiguren. Knesebeckstrasse 88. ☎ **030/315-700-0.**

A mecca for collectors since 1934, this shop carries an impressive inventory of German-language books on military history and more than 10,000 different pewter figurines of soldiers from many different imperial armies, up to the Franco-Prussian War of 1870. Also included are hand-painted models of Roman and ancient Greek foot soldiers. Flat, hand-painted pewter figures are sold only in sets of 12 or more and cost from 150DM to 200DM ($85.50 to $114); fully detailed depictions of Prussian soldiers from the 1870s can range as high as 250DM to 300DM ($142.50 to $171) each, or even 1,800DM ($1,026) for special pieces.

PERFUME
Harry Lehmann. Kantstrasse 106. ☎ **030/3-24-35-82.**

This is the kind of shop where German mothers and grandmothers might have bought their perfume between the two world wars. Don't expect a standardized list of the big names you'd find at a duty-free airport shop. Most scents here are family recipes, distilled from flowers, grasses, and leaves. The reasonable prices might surprise you—10 grams for as little as 4.5DM ($2.55). Coming here is a cheap and amusing way to experience the scents of a Prussian spring.

SCULPTURE
Gipsformerei der Staatlichen Museen Preussischer Kulturbesitz. Sophie-Charlotte-Strasse 17. ☎ **030/3267690.** S-Bahn: West-End.

This company has duplicated Europe's great sculptures as plaster casts since 1819. Today, there's an inventory of more than 6,500 of them, everything from busts of Queen Nefertiti to a faithful reproduction of the Farnese Bull. Prices begin at 25DM ($14.25). Objects can be crated and shipped around the world.

9 Berlin After Dark

In Berlin, nightlife runs around the clock, and there's plenty to do at any time. There are at least three magazines that list happenings in the city. The monthly English-language *Checkpoint Berlin* is available free at hotel reception desks and tourist offices and sold at news kiosks. The German-language *Berlin Programm* is available at newsstands. The most detailed listings are found in *zitty,* a biweekly publication in German.

Berlin is famous not only for its opera, classical music, and theater, but also for its cabaret and nightclub entertainment. If you'd like to arrange tickets from America for shows and entertainment in Berlin, contact **Global Tickets,** (☎ **800/223-6108** or 212/332-2435; fax 914/328-2752; www.globaltickets.com). This company can mail actual tickets to your home in most cases, or leave tickets at the box office for you. There's a 20% markup (more for opera and ballet) over the box office price, plus a U.S. handling charge of up to $8. Tickets are available for musicals, cabaret, opera, and dance.

THE PERFORMING ARTS
OPERA & CLASSICAL MUSIC
✪ **Berliner Philharmonisches Orchester (Berlin Philharmonic).** Matthäikirchstrasse 1. ☎ **030/25-48-80.** Tickets 26DM–180DM ($14.80–$102.60).

The Berlin Philharmonic, now directed by Claudio Abbado, is one of the world's premier orchestras. Its home is the Philharmonie, noted for its excellent acoustics and unconventional interior design—the orchestra is in the middle of rising tiers of seats, and none of the 2,200 seats is more than 100 feet from the podium. Tickets for performances can be purchased at the office in the orchestra hall's main lobby Monday to Friday from 3:30 to 6pm and on Saturday and Sunday from 11am to 2pm. You can't place orders by phone, but if you're staying in a first-class or deluxe hotel, the concierge can usually get seats for you.

✪ **Deutsche Oper Berlin.** Bismarckstrasse 35. ☎ **030/3-43-84-01.** Tickets 26DM–116DM ($14.80–$66.10). U-Bahn: Deutsche Oper and Bismarckstrasse.

This opera company performs in Charlottenburg in one of the world's great opera houses, a notable example of modern theater architecture that seats 1,885. The company is willing to tackle a Puccini favorite, a Janácek rarity, or a modern work, and has a complete Wagner repertoire. A ballet company performs once a week. Concerts, including Lieder evenings, are also presented on the opera stage.

Deutsche Staatsoper (German State Opera). Unter den Linden 7. ☎ **030/20-35-45-55.** Tickets, opera 12DM–300DM ($6.85–$171); concerts 15DM–65DM ($8.55–$37.05) U-Bahn: Französische Strasse. S-Bahn: Friedrichstrasse.

The German State Opera performs in the Staatsoper Unter den Linden. This was for years the showcase of the opera scene of East Germany. Originally constructed in 1743 and destroyed in World War II, the house was rebuilt in the 1950s, reproducing as closely as possible the designs of Georg Knobelsdorff, the original architect. Some of the world's finest opera as well as concerts and ballet are presented here. The box office is open Monday to Friday from 10am to 6pm and noon to 6pm on Saturday and Sunday. The opera closes from June 22 to August 28.

Komische Oper Berlin. Behrensstrasse 55–57. ☎ **030/47997400.** Tickets 15DM–108DM ($8.55–$61.55). U-Bahn: Französische Strasse. S-Bahn: Friedrichstrasse or Unter den Linden.

The Komische Oper has become one of the most highly regarded theater ensembles in Europe, presenting many avant-garde opera productions as well as ballet and musical theater. The box office is open Monday to Saturday from 11am to 7pm and on Sunday from 1pm to 1½ hours before performance.

Konzerthaus Berlin. In the Schauspielhaus, Gendarmenmarkt. ☎ **030/20-30-921-00.** Tickets 12DM–125DM ($6.85–$71.25). U-Bahn: Französische Strasse.

This 1821 building was created by Friedrich Schinkel. It offers two venues for classical concerts, the Grosser Konzertsaal for orchestra and the Kammermusiksaal for chamber music. Its organ recitals are considered the finest in Germany. Performances are often daring and innovative. The Deutsches Sinfonie-Orchester is also based here.

THEATER

Berlin has long been known for its theater. Even if you don't understand German, you may enjoy seeing a production of a familiar play, or attending a musical.

Perhaps the most famous theater is the **Berliner Ensemble,** Am Bertolt-Brecht-Platz 1 (☎ **030/28-40-81-55**), founded by the late playwright Bertolt Brecht. Brecht's wife, the great actress Helene Weigel, played an important role in the theater's founding and was the ensemble's longtime director. Works by Brecht and other playwrights are presented here. Seats are reasonably priced. U- or S-Bahn: Friedrichstrasse.

The most important German-language theater in the country is **Schaubühne am Lehniner Platz,** Kurfürstendamm 153 (☎ **030/89-00-23**), at the east end of the Ku'damm, near Lehniner Platz. There are three different stages here. U-Bahn: Adenauerplatz.

Finally, **Theater des Westens,** located between the Berlin Zoo and the Ku'damm at Kantstrasse 12 (☎ **030/31-90-30**), specializes in plays, musical comedies, and the German equivalent of Broadway extravaganzas. The theater was built in 1896.

The Love Parade

The Love Parade is the techno bash to end all bashes. On the second weekend of July, around 600,000 (mostly) young people converge in the center of Berlin for 48 decidedly hedonistic hours. What began in 1988 as a DJ's birthday party with about 150 friends has grown into an immense corporate event that wreaks havoc on the rest of the city's usually impeccable organization (particularly the public transportation system).

The center of Berlin becomes awash with litter and good-natured debauchery. Because of the frenzied jiggling, gyrating, and very noisy good times, anyone wanting an even remotely peaceful weekend should follow the little old ladies and rock fans on the fast train out of town. The event starts off on Saturday afternoon, when a booming caravan of floats carries the best DJs in Europe from Ernst-Reuter-Platz to the Brandenburg Gate. If you want to see the procession, come early and grab as high a view as possible.

Everything imaginable is imbibed in huge quantities, and every year serious worries are voiced over the deluge of urine in the Tiergarten, site of the evening celebrations. The entire city, in fact, transforms itself into a huge party. The BVG (public transport system) offers a 10DM ($5.70) "no limit" ticket to speed you from one rave to another. Traveling revelers should note that club prices skyrocket during the weekend.

Lots of fuss and bother or a really good time? It all depends on your point of view. This is a must for anybody with a love of synthesizers and a lot of steam to let off. The Love Parade has become an international fixture to rival Mardis Gras around the world.

Performances are held Tuesday to Saturday at 8pm and Sunday at 6pm. Ticket prices range from 35DM to 89DM ($19.95 to $50.75).

THE CLUB & MUSIC SCENE
CABARET

Very popular among visitors to Berlin is the kind of nightspot depicted in the musical *Cabaret,* with floor-show patter and acts that make fun of the political and social scene.

Die Stachelschweine. Tauentzienstrasse and Budapester Strasse (in the basement of Europa-Center). ☎ **030/2-61-47-95.** Cover 22DM–40DM ($12.55–$22.80). U-Bahn: Kurfürsten-damm.

Since the beginning of the Cold War, the "Porcupine" has poked prickly fun at the German and the American political scene. The performance is delivered in rapid-fire German and evokes the legendary Berliner sense of satire, which can often be scathing in its humor. Although you need to understand German to really appreciate what goes on here, you'll still recognize some of the names (Newt Gingrich, Jesse Helms, "Bubba" Clinton), and there's likely to be a deliberately corny selection of popular ditties ("Life is a cabaret, old chum") thrown in. Shows take place Tuesday to Friday at 7:30pm and Saturday at 6pm and 9:15pm. The box office sells tickets Tuesday to Friday from 10am to 2pm and 3 to 7:30pm and Saturday from 2 to 6:30pm. It's closed in July.

Wintergarten. Potsdamer Strasse 96. ☎ **030/23-08-82-30.** Cover Fri–Sat 74DM–98DM ($42.20–$55.85), Sun–Thurs 35DM–80DM ($19.95–$45.60) per person, depending on the seat. U-Bahn: Kurfürstenstrasse.

The largest and most nostalgic Berlin cabaret, the Wintergarten offers a variety show every night, with magicians, clowns, jugglers, acrobats, and live music. The most expensive seats are on stage level, where tiny tables are available for simple suppers costing from 20DM to 40DM ($11.40 to $22.80). Balconies have conventional theater seats, but staff members pass frequently along the aisles selling drinks. Shows last around 2¼ hours each and begin Monday to Friday at 8pm, Sunday at 6pm, and Saturday at 6 and 10pm.

DANCE CLUBS

Big Eden. Kurfürstendamm 202. ☎ **030/8-82-61-20.** Cover 12DM ($6.85) Fri–Sat (includes 1 drink). Sun–Thurs 9pm–5am, Fri–Sat 9pm–6am. U-Bahn: Uhlandstrasse.

Everyone from Paul McCartney to Sylvester Stallone has danced here. This club accommodates some 1,000 dancers nightly on its huge dance floor. Top DJs play the latest international hits. The light effects and superstereo are impressive. There's a nightly happy hour.

Café Keese. Bismarckstrasse 108. ☎ **030/3-12-91-11.** No cover, but a drink minimum of 10DM ($5.70) Fri and Sun, 14DM ($8) Sat. U-Bahn: Ernst-Reuther-Platz.

This dance club caters to a more traditional clientele. Here women can ask the men to dance, and the management even reserves the right to kick out any male patron who turns down a request. The orchestra plays a lot of slow music and the place is often jammed, especially on Saturday night. The Keese sees itself as something of a matrimonial bureau, and is always announcing statistics about the number of people who met on its premises and got married. Formal attire is requested. Open Tuesday to Thursday from 8pm to 3am, Friday and Saturday from 8pm to 4am, and Sunday and Monday from 4pm to 1am.

Chip. In the Berlin Hilton, Mohrenstrasse 30. ☎ **030/2-02-30.** Cover 10DM ($5.70). U-Bahn: Stadtmitte.

Chip is an unusual and appealingly glossy dance club. It features a high-tech battery of accessories—laserlike lights, video clips, and a fog machine that adds a surreal mist to the crowded dance floor. Open Wednesday to Saturday from 9pm until 4am.

Clärchen's Ballhaus. Auguststrasse 24–25. ☎ **030/2-82-92-95.** Cover 7.40DM ($4.20). U-Bahn: Rosenthaler Platz. S-Bahn: Oranienburger Strasse.

This place has been around since 1913, and it's schmaltzy enough to remind sentimental newcomers of the nostalgic old-time days. A renewed interest in ballroom dancing has kept it going. Live music from a dance band is the norm, with recorded music to fill in when the band takes a break. On Wednesday, women are encouraged to ask men to the dance floor. Open Tuesday, Wednesday, Friday, and Saturday from 8:30pm until around 3am.

E-Werks. Wilhelmstrasse 43. ☎ **030/617-93-70.** Cover 15DM ($8.55) Fri, 20DM ($11.40) Sat. U-Bahn: Mohrenstrasse.

This is a center of the Berlin techno culture. A former power station, E-Werks features an interior of industrial machines and colored strobe lights. The place really starts to jump after 1am. If you need a break, you can escape to the outside courtyard. Many gay people show up on Saturday. The club is open Friday and Saturday from 11pm until 5am and often until 10am.

Far Out. Kurfürstendamm 156. ☎ **030/320-00-717.** Cover 6DM–10DM ($3.40–$5.70). U-Bahn: Adenauerplatz.

Large and artfully drab, this industrial-looking disco plays danceable rock from the '70s to the '90s for hundreds of high-energy dancers. You'll see lots of students and artists, many dressed up in artfully bizarre clothing. The place only really comes alive after midnight. Open Tuesday to Sunday 10am to between 4 and 6am, depending on the crowd.

Metropole. Nollendorfplatz 5, Schöneberg. ☎ **030/2-17-36-80.** Cover 20DM ($11.40). U-Bahn: Nollendorfplatz.

This club, located in an old theater, is open only on weekends. Its atmosphere is appealingly *laissez-faire.* Most of the patrons are in the 18-to-38 age group. The place hosts live concerts and offers special events for gay people, including Valentine's Day tea dances. Open Friday and Saturday from 9pm to dawn.

SO 36. Oranienstrasse 190. ☎ **030/6-14-01306** or 030/6-18-45-80. Cover 8DM–15DM ($4.55–$8.55). U-Bahn: Görlitzer Bahnhof.

A vibrant selection of Kreuzberg youths—gay, straight, and in-between—shows up here for wild action and frantic dancing into the wee hours. The scene changes nightly: Wednesday is strictly gay and lesbian; Thursday features hard-core, ska, and metal; and Friday and Saturday are "really wild, man," to quote the bartender. Open Wednesday to Saturday from 10pm until "we feel like closing," and on Sunday from 5pm to 1am.

Tresor. Leipzigerstrasse 8.l. ☎ **030/2-29-04-14.** Cover 20DM ($11.40) Wed, 25DM ($14.25) Fri–Sun. U-Bahn: Mohrenstrasse.

One of Berlin's best techno venues, this club really packs them in. The building was once part of Globus Bank; downstairs there's a bunkerlike atmosphere, with prison-type metal bars and harsh acoustics. The spacious dance floor upstairs has lighter house sounds. There's a bar in the back. In summer, tables are placed outside, and food is served. The club is open from 10pm Wednesday and from 11pm Friday to Sunday. It's closed on other nights.

LIVE MUSIC

A Trane. Bleibtreustrasse 1. ☎ **030/3-13-25-50.** Cover 15DM–20DM ($8.55–$11.40). Music begins around 10pm. S-Bahn: Savignyplatz.

This small and smoky jazz house is an excellent choice for either beginning or ending an evening of bar-hopping in the neighborhood. It features musicians from all over the world. Open daily from 6pm.

Ewige Lampe. Niebuhrstrasse 11A. ☎ **030/3-24-39-18.** Cover 10DM–15DM ($5.70–$8.55). S-Bahn: Savignyplatz.

This popular, well-managed place is known for its international jazz acts. Originally, it was a working-class restaurant, but in the late '80s, it was transformed into a club for hard-drinking enthusiasts who like New Orleans jazz and blues. Open Wednesday to Sunday 8pm to 2am.

Knaack-Klub. Greifswalderstrasse 224. ☎ **030/4-42-70-60.** Cover 10DM ($5.70). S-Bahn: Alexanderplatz.

This four-story club features a live-music venue, two floors of dancing, and a games floor. There are usually four live rock shows a week, with a fairly even split between German and international touring bands. Show days vary. There's dancing on Wednesday, Friday, and Saturday nights. Hours are Monday to Friday from 10pm to 4am and Saturday and Sunday from 10pm to 7am.

Oxymoron. In the courtyard of the complex at Rosenthaler Strasse 40–41. ☎ **030/283-91-88-5.** S-Bahn: Hackeschen Höfe.

The red velvet decor here evokes jazz age decadence. The site is primarily a restaurant and bar, although some form of live music begins most evenings at 8pm. Menu items are international and the food is good as well as reasonably priced. Themes range from "gangster nights" to just dancing and jazz. The club is open daily from 11am to 1am (for dining), although the bar doesn't shut down until 3am.

Quasimodo. Kantstrasse 12A. ☎ **030/3-12-80-86.** Cover 20DM ($11.40). U-Bahn: Bahnhof Zoo.

This is the top Berlin jazz club. Although many different styles of music are offered here, including rock and Latin, jazz is the focus. Local acts are featured on Tuesday and Wednesday, when admission is free. Summer visitors should check out the "Jazz in July" festival. The club is open Tuesday to Saturday from 9pm to 2am, with shows beginning at 10pm.

Wild at Heart. Wienerstrasse 20. ☎ **030/6-11-70-10.** Cover 7DM ($4) for concerts only. U-Bahn: Görlitzer Bahnhof.

This club, with its kitschy knickknacks, colored lights, and wine-red walls, is dedicated to the rowdier side of rock. Hard-core punk, rock, and rockabilly bands from Germany and elsewhere are featured. Live performances take place Wednesday to Saturday nights. It's open Monday to Friday from 8pm to 4am and Saturday and Sunday from 8pm to 10am (yes, you may miss breakfast).

DRAG SHOWS

Chez Nous. Marburgerstrasse 14. ☎ **030/2-13-18-10.** Cover 20DM ($11.40), which includes first drink. U-Bahn: Wittenbergplatz.

The famous show at Chez Nous is played to an essentially straight crowd in a mock Louis XIV setting. Some of the world's best transvestite acts appear here, from a sultry, boa-draped star from Rio de Janeiro to a drag queen who looks like a gun moll from the 1940s. Shows are nightly at 8:30 and 11pm. An occasional late show at 1am is offered on Saturday night (call first).

La Vie en Rose. Europa-Center, Tiergarten. ☎ **030/3-23-60-06.** Cover 35DM–60DM ($19.95–$34.20). U-Bahn: Zoologischer Garten.

This club offers a highly polished, Vegas-style revue to a straight clientele, often businessmen. This is where "Barbra," "Dolly," and "Judy" are likely to appear. The box office is open daily from 10am to midnight. Shows start at 9pm Sunday to Thursday and at 10pm on Friday and Saturday.

GAY & LESBIAN BERLIN

Traditionally, lesbian and gay life centered around the **Nollendorfplatz,** the so-called "Pink Village." There is a history of homosexuality here at the **Schwules Museum,** Mehringdamm 61 (☎ **030/693-11-72**), open Wednesday to Sunday from 2 to 6pm. Admission is 7DM ($4) adults, 4DM ($2.30) students. The **Spinnboden-Lesbenarchiv,** Anklamerstrasse 38 (☎ **030/448-58-48**), caters to all sorts of lesbian cultural events. **Man-o-Meter,** Motzstrasse 5 (off Nollendorfplatz) (☎ **030/216-80-08**), is a gay information center.

Today, Motzstrasse is the location of many gay and lesbian bars. A trio of popular gay bars, **Tom's,** the **Pool Disco,** and the **Knast Bar,** are sometimes referred to as "the Bermuda triangle."

In the latter half of June, the **Lesbisch-schwules Stadtfest** (Lesbian Street Fair) takes place at Nollendorfplatz. This is topped in size, though not in exuberance, the following week by the **Christopher Street Day** parade on June 26, when 200,000 people congregate to have fun and drop inhibitions.

Andreas Kneipe. Ansbacher Strasse 29. ☎ **030/2-18-32-57.** Daily 11am–4am. U-Bahn: Wittenbergplatz.

In case you want to see the world.

At American Express, we're here to make your journey a smooth one. So we have over 1,700 travel service locations in over 130 countries ready to help. What else would you expect from the world's largest travel agency?

do more

Travel

Call 1 800 AXP-3429 or visit
www.americanexpress.com/travel

In case you want to be welcomed there.

We're here to see that you're always welcomed at establishments everywhere. That's why millions of people carry the American Express® Card – for peace of mind, confidence, and security, around the world or just around the corner.

do more

To apply, call 1 800 THE-CARD

Cards

In case you're running low.

We're here to help with more than 190,000 Express Cash locations around the world. In order to enroll, just call American Express at 1 800 CASH-NOW before you start your vacation.

do more

AMERICAN EXPRESS

Express Cash

And in case you'd rather be safe than sorry.

We're here with American Express® Travelers Cheques. They're the safe way to carry money on your vacation, because if they're ever lost or stolen you can get a refund, practically anywhere or anytime. To find the nearest place to buy Travelers Cheques, call 1 800 495-1153. Another way we help you do more.

do more

Travelers Cheques

Warm, cozy, and appealing, this is the oldest gay bar in Berlin. The clientele is varied enough so that everyone can find someone to talk to before an evening's end. Few people dance, and no food is served, so it's a place just to talk and drink in a convivial setting.

Begine Café-und-Kulturzentrum für Frauen. Potsdamerstrasse 139. ☎ **030/2-15-14-14.** No cover. Daily 6pm–1am. U-Bahn: Bulowstrasse.

This is a center for feminists and one of Berlin's best places for women to meet other women. It has a changing array of art exhibitions, and features poetry readings, German-language discussions, lectures, and other social events. Call in advance for the schedule. The premises are occasionally transformed into a disco.

Connection Disco. Fuggerstrasse 31-33. ☎ **030/2-181-432.** Cover 12DM ($6.85) with drink. Fri–Sat 10pm–6am. U-Bahn: Wittenberg.

This spacious, two-floor disco is a fashionable weekend spot for men and a good place for romantic encounters. The crowd ranges from teenagers to those in their early 40s. There's a jeans-and-leather touch to the ambience but nothing heavy. The music is soft techno and trance.

Kit Kat Klub. Glogauerstrasse 2. ☎ **030/6-11-38-33.** Cover 10DM–20DM ($5.70–$11.40). U-Bahn: Hermannplatz.

This fluorescent dance club, popular with both straights and gays, is renowned for its sex scene. You're told to check your inhibitions at the door. For hard-core male action, show up for the men-only Crisco Club night on Thursday. The club is open Tuesday to Sunday from 11pm on.

Knast Bar. Fuggerstrasse 34. ☎ **030/2-18-10-26.** Daily 9pm–dawn. U-Bahn: Wittenbergplatz.

The Knast is the leading leather bar in Berlin. Beer costs from 3.50DM ($2) upwards.

Kumpelnest 3000. Lützowstrasse 23. ☎ **030/2-61-69-18.** U-Bahn: Kurfürstenstrasse.

Gay or straight, you're welcome here. All that's asked is that you enjoy a kinky good time in what used to be a brothel. This crowded and chaotic place is really a bar now, but there's also dancing to disco classics. Berliners often show up here for early morning fun after they've exhausted the action at the other hot spots. Open daily from 5pm to 5am, and even later on weekends.

Tom's Bar. Motzstrasse 19. ☎ **030/2-13-45-70.** Daily 10pm–6am. U-Bahn: Nollendorfplatz.

Tom's becomes crowded after 11pm with young gay men. Upstairs, the porno action is merely on the screen; downstairs it's real. Monday nights feature two-for-one drinks. There's a cover charge for special occasions only.

THE BAR & CAFE SCENE
BEER GARDENS & WINE CELLARS

Historischer Weinkeller. Alt-Pichelsdorf 32 (about a mile west of the Olympia-Stadion). ☎ **030/3-61-80-56.** Reservations required. U-Bahn: Olympia-Stadion.

This squat and unpretentious inn might be the site of one of your more interesting evenings in Berlin. The setting is a highly atmospheric vaulted cellar. In winter the staff performs the medieval ceremony of "burning the punch," during which a sugar cone is lighted in your punch. As it burns, you're supposed to make a wish. The ritual takes place three times a week on Wednesday, Friday, and Saturday between 11 and midnight. The punch, a kind of hot spiced wine, costs 10.50DM ($6) per glass. You can also order beer or one of more than 100 German wines, as well as full meals that cost 26DM to 42DM ($14.80 to $23.95). (If you plan to dine, make reservations in advance.) During summer months, an outdoor rustic beer garden is open. Open daily noon to midnight.

Joe's Beer Haus. Hardenbergstrasse 29 (opposite the Kaiser Wilhelm Memorial Church). ☎ **030/2-62-10-20.** U-Bahn: Zoologischer Garten.

This cozy pub in the city center is attractively decorated with traditional Teutonic accessories. Even in winter, when you're snug and warm inside, you get the feeling you're sitting out under the chestnut trees. There's a live band on Friday, Saturday, and sometimes Sunday nights. Tuesday night brings karaoke. The kitchen offers good plain German food, including Bavarian specialties, and some Italian dishes. Open Monday to Saturday from 11am to 4am and Sunday from 11am to 1am; the best time to come here is from 7pm to midnight.

Loretta Im Garten (Pupasch). Lietzenburgerstrasse 89. ☎ **030/8-82-33-54.** U-Bahn: Uhlandstrasse.

This surprisingly rustic indoor/outdoor beer garden is large, sometimes rowdy, and very German. It's outfitted with durable wooden banquettes, battered accessories, a large outdoor area, and a children's play area with its own Ferris wheel. Menu items include platters of sausage with sauerkraut and potatoes, spareribs, and stuffed baked potatoes. There's no live music; this a place for talk, gossip, and beer drinking. Many locals also come here for lunch. Open only from April to early October, daily from 11am to 3am.

ELEGANT BARS

Harry's New York Bar. In the Grand Hotel Esplanade, Lützowufer 15. ☎ **030/25-47-88-21.** U-Bahn: Nollendorfplatz, Wittenbergplatz, or Kurfürstenstrasse.

Harry's is an aggressively stylized bar with minimalist decor, pop art, and photographs of all the American presidents. It's modeled after that famous watering hole, Harry's Bar in Paris. Its drink menu is a monument to the oral traditions of the IBF (International Bar Flies) Society, and includes such favorites as "Mizner's Dream" (created in 1962 for the Boca Raton Hotel Club in Florida) and the 1964 classic, "The Petrifier" (ingredients unlisted), for two. The menu lists almost 200 drinks, as well as a limited selection of food. Open daily noon to 2am.

Times Bar. In the Savoy Hotel, Fasanenstrasse 9–10. ☎ **030/31-10-30.** U-Bahn: Bahnhof Zoo.

The cozy and intimate Times Bar has a quiet charm reminiscent of a wood-paneled private library in someone's home. The bar is dedicated to the *Times* (of London), whose latest edition is often displayed in the window. Guests sit in leather upholstered chairs and read English-language newspapers. Light meals, costing about 25DM ($14.25), and drinks are available. Menu items range from lobster soup to ice cream. Open daily from 5pm to 2am.

FINDING A KNEIPE

A *Kneipe* is a cozy rendezvous place, the equivalent of a Londoner's local pub. The typical Berliner has a favorite Kneipe for relaxing after work and visiting with sympathetic friends. There are hundreds in Berlin. Here's a handful to get you started.

Ax-Bax Corsica. Leibnizstrasse 34. ☎ **030/31-50-95-33.** S-Bahn: Savignyplatz.

This bar draws an arts-oriented crowd. On the facade you'll see only a very discreet sign and a neon-illuminated food menu. Many people come in just for a drink or two, but if you're interested in dining, you'll find an appealing list of European specialties mainly from France, the owner's homeland. The most popular time to arrive is around 9pm. If you want a table, reserve one in advance. Main courses range in price from 15DM to 19DM ($8.55 to $10.85). Open Monday to Friday from noon to 3am and Saturday to Sunday from 5pm to 2am.

Gaststätte Hoeck (Wilhelm Hoeck). Wilmersdorferstrasse 149. ☎ **030/3-41-81-74.** U-Bahn: Bismarckstrasse.

The oldest Kneipe in Charlottenburg (1892) still sports original wood panels with inlaid glass on the walls. It also has a brightly illuminated facade jammed with local beer slogans. You (and half of the neighborhood) can have a drink in the very rowdy, sometimes raucous bar area, where (among other oddities) a clown may be playing the harmonica. The separate dining room serves traditional food. More than a dozen kinds of beer are offered (if in doubt, just ask for our favorite, Pilsner Urquell), as well as wine by the glass. Meals cost 10DM to 20DM ($5.70 to $11.40); hot food is served Monday to Saturday from 11am to 11pm. Regular hours, however, are from 8am to midnight.

Lutter und Wegner 1811. Schlüstrasse 55. ☎ **030/8-81-34-40.** S-Bahn: Savignyplatz.

This place was named after a gastronomic and social landmark, Lutter und Wegner, a hangout for actors in the 19th century. You can have a drink in the stand-up bar, or make reservations in advance to dine. Try the local specialty, Königsberger Klopse, with potatoes and a fresh salad. The wide selection of drinks ranges from single-malt Scottish whiskies to Italian grappas. Meals range from 28DM to 40DM ($15.95 to $22.80). The restaurant is open daily from 6pm to midnight; the bar is open daily from 6pm until 1:30am or even later, depending on business. In summer, you can sit on a terrace and observe the passing parade.

Zwiebelfisch. Savignyplatz 7–8. ☎ **030/3-12-73-63.** S-Bahn: Savignyplatz. Bus: 149.

Zwiebelfisch has long been a favorite hangout of artists, writers, and journalists. It also attracts U.S. jazz musicians after their evening gigs. Friends are easily made here. There's a limited dining menu. Light meals cost from 8DM to 14DM ($4.55 to $8). Open daily from noon to 6am.

CAFE LIFE

At its mid-19th-century zenith, Berlin was famous for its cafes. Max Krell, an editor, once wrote: "Cafes were our homeland. They were the stock exchange of ideas, site of intellectual transactions, futures' market of poetic and artistic glory and defeat." They've changed with the times, but cafes are still going strong in Berlin—particularly, these days, in what used to be East Berlin. In the heart of the old East German capital is a complex of about 30 bars, shops, and restaurants called *Die Hackenschen Höfe* (see Oxymoron, above). This stylish mini-mall attracts hip counter-culture denizens who wander between galleries, boutiques, and fashionable cafes. It has become one of the most prominent places in the city to go drinking. To get there, take the S-Bahn to Hackescher Markt.

Café Adlon. Kurfürstendamm 69. ☎ **030/8-83-76-82.** U-Bahn: Adenauerplatz.

At the turn of the century, Café Adlon's imposing neoclassical decor, overstuffed sofas, and formal waiters made it one of the most prestigious spots in the neighborhood. The clientele is a bit less formal today, and the whole place is somewhat tattered around the edges, but the cafe still offers charming summertime vistas from its sidewalk tables. Inside, there's a collection of Berlin kitsch. Open Sunday to Thursday from 8am to midnight and Friday and Saturday from 8am to 11pm.

Café/Bistro Leysieffer. Kurfürstendamm 218. ☎ **030/8-85-74-80.** U-Bahn: Kurfürsten-damm.

This cafe opened in the early 1980s in what used to be the Chinese embassy. Some of the embassy's ornate moldings and lighting fixtures are still in place; a pair of gilded lions still guards the entrance. On the street level is a pastry and candy shop, but you can climb the flight of stairs to a marble-and-wood-sheathed cafe with a balcony over-looking the busy Ku'damm. The elegant breakfast menu here features Parma ham, smoked salmon, freshly baked baguettes, French butter, and, to round it off, cham-pagne. Meals range from 18DM to 26DM ($10.25 to $14.80). Open Monday to Thursday from 10am to 8pm, Friday and Saturday from 10am to 10pm, and Sunday from 10am to 7pm.

✪ **Café Kranzler.** Kurfürstendamm 18–19. ☎ **030/8-82-69-11.** U-Bahn: Kurfürsten-damm.

The Kranzler was one of the most famous cafes on Unter den Linden, where it first opened in 1825. A century later, it relocated—taking along its art-oriented clientele—to what was then a less imposing district around the Ku'damm. Like almost everything else in the area, it rose from the ashes of World War II to thrive in what became the center of West Berlin. Today you'll find an unabashedly modern establishment with striped canopies, two floors of densely packed tables, and one of the busiest "see-and-be-seen" outdoor terraces in the city. Ice cream, pastries, coffee, and drinks are avail-able. The menu is Swiss, and meals cost 18DM to 35DM ($10.25 to $19.95). Open daily from 8am to midnight.

Café Möhring. Kurfürstendamm 213. ☎ **030/8-81-20-75.** U-Bahn: Uhlandstrasse.

Set behind a belle epoque awning, this cafe is the survivor of a political and literary tra-dition that began in 1898. The fresh flowers and the many older women who linger over pastries give the place the air of a bygone era. Breakfast starts at 10.80DM ($6.15), and lunch and dinner range from 11.50DM to 15.50DM ($6.55 to $8.85). Open Monday to Thursday from 7am to midnight and Friday and Saturday from 7am to 1am.

Café Silberstein. Oranienburger Strasse 27. ☎ **030/2-81-20-95.** S-Bahn: Oranienburger Strasse.

From the outside, this place looks like an art gallery, but once inside, you'll see that it's an artsy cafe, one of Berlin's trendiest, with sushi, ambient music, and an ultrahip clientele. This is one of the best places to enjoy "new Berlin" in the formerly grim eastern sector. Open Monday to Friday from 9pm to 4am and Saturday and Sunday from noon to 5am.

Operncafé. In the Opernpalais, Unter den Linden 5. ☎ **030/20-26-83.** S-Bahn: Friedrich-strasse.

This cavernous place is another leading cafe in eastern Berlin, linked to memories of the academic and intellectual life that flourished in the neighborhood a century ago. Hundreds of patrons come each day. In summer, tables are set up outside on the wide sidewalks of Berlin's most evocative boulevard. The freshly baked pastries here are famous. A grand buffet breakfast costing 16DM ($9.10) is served until noon. Open daily from 9am to midnight.

Operncafe is part of a complex of dining and drinking choices. There's a street-level piano bar, **Opernschänke,** open Thursday to Saturday from 8pm to 2am and Sunday from 11am to 6pm; an upmarket restaurant, **Königin Luise** (see "Dining," above); and the less formal Keller restaurant, **Fridericus,** where old-fashioned German dishes cost from 45DM ($25.65).

A CASINO

Spielbank. Marlene Dietrich Platz 7 (1 floor above street level), Potsdamer Platz. ☎ **030/ 255990.** Cover 5DM ($2.85). U-Bahn: Mendelssohn-Bartholdy-Platz.

This casino has tables for roulette, baccarat, blackjack, and other games. The minimum bet is 5DM to 50DM ($2.85 to $28.50) depending on the game. Berlin's longest bar is inside. A restaurant serves expensive international cuisine. Male guests should wear jackets and ties (no jeans or tennis shoes are allowed). It's important to bring along your passport, driver's license, or ID card. Open daily from 3pm to 3am.

4

Saxony & Thuringia

To go to the regions of the former East Germany today can be an adventure in travel. Many famous cities, closed to the West during the Cold War, can again be visited: Dresden, destroyed during World War II and poignantly restored at least in part; Leipzig, where Johann Sebastian Bach spent most of his musical life as cantor (choirmaster) of St. Thomas Church; Meissen, famous for exquisite porcelain; Potsdam, once the residence of the Prussian kings; and Weimar, still glowing from its 1999 designation as European City of Culture. In addition, unspoiled scenery and medieval towns like Quedlinburg invite you to wander off the beaten track.

Since reunification, many visitors have come from around the world to explore the new political landscape and to honor the memory of the intellectual giants who once made East Germany their home—Goethe, Luther, Bach, Schiller, and Brecht, among others. Hotels are being built and tourist facilities developed. But the traveler should still take care in this rapidly changing terrain. The state of politics here is sometimes erratic and unpredictable, and the economy is weaker than in western Germany. The fears and frustrations of the population have given rise to small neo-Nazi groups. Some of them have been known to assault nonwhite foreigners and members of certain religious groups (notably Muslims), embarrassing the millions of other tolerant and liberal Germans.

Eastern Germany today is a region in transition. Its long isolation also means that you'll find here some of Germany's most unspoiled countryside and untouched villages, where rural traditions that have disappeared from most of western Europe still linger. A visit can provide you with unforgettable new experiences and stories you can tell your grandchildren.

EXPLORING SAXONY & THURINGIA   Getting around eastern Germany is easier than it has ever been. Some 1,000 miles of Autobahns and about 7,000 miles of secondary highways cut across the region. Train schedules are a bit chaotic, as the German government incorporates the former East German system into its vast national network. Since 1991, long-distance bus service has linked Berlin with Dresden and Leipzig. Service is still not frequent, however, as buses exist mainly to supplement the rail network.

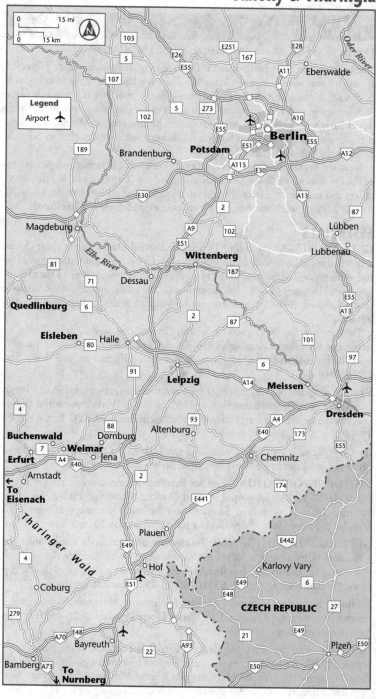

0   15 mi
0   15 km

Legend
Airport ✈

103
5
107
E26
E55
E251
167
E28
A11
Eberswalde
Oder River

102
5
273
189
E55
A10
Brandenburg
Potsdam
Berlin
E55
E51
A115
E30
A12

E30
2
A13
Magdeburg
A9
102
E51
Elbe River
Wittenberg
87
Lübben
Lubbenau
E55
A13

81
71
Dessau
187
6
2
E55

Quedlinburg
6
Eisleben
80
Halle
87
101
97

91
6
Leipzig
A14
Meissen
Dresden
E55

4
88
93
A4
Dörnburg
Altenburg
E40
173
Buchenwald
7
Weimar
Jena
Chemnitz
Erfurt
A4
E40
Arnstadt
← **To**
Eisenach
2
174

Thüringer Wald

4
E441
Plauen
E49
E442
Hof
Karlovy Vary
Coburg
E51
E49
6
279
E48
CZECH REPUBLIC
27
A70
E48
Bayreuth
22
A93
21
E49
Plzeň
E50
Bamberg
A73
↓ **To**
Nurnberg
E50

125

1 Potsdam

15 miles SW of Berlin, 87 miles NE of Leipzig, 92 miles NE of Magdeburg

The best day trip from Berlin is to the baroque town of Potsdam on the Havel River. It's often been called Germany's Versailles. The town has many historic sights, as well as parks and a beautiful chain of lakes formed by the river. It was beautifully planned architecturally, with large parks and many green areas. The palaces and gardens of **Sans Souci Park,** which lies to the west of Potsdam's historic core, are the major attractions here. A mile northwest of Sans Souci is the **Neuer Garten** on the Heiliger See, which contains the **Schloss Cecilienhof.**

From the beginning of the 18th century Potsdam was a residence and garrison town of the Prussian kings. Soviet propagandists called it a "former cradle of Prussian militarism and reactionary forces." World attention focused on Potsdam from July 17 to August 2, 1945, when the Potsdam Conference helped shape postwar Europe.

ESSENTIALS

GETTING THERE   By Train   Potsdam Hauptbahnhof is on the major Deutsche Bundesbahn rail lines, with 29 daily connections to the rail stations in Berlin (23 min. to Bahnhof Zoo and 54 min. to the Hauptbahnhof). There are also 14 trains daily to and from Hannover (3 to 3½ hr., depending on the train), and 15 daily trains to and from Nürnberg (6 to 6½ hr.). For rail information and schedules, call ☎ **1805/ 996633.**

Potsdam can also be reached by S-Bahn Lines S3, S4, and S7 from Berlin, connecting at Wannsee station with Lines R1, R3, and R4. Travel time on these lines from Berlin to Potsdam is 30 minutes. For more information, call **BVG Berlin** (☎ **030/19-449**).

By Bus   Regional bus service with frequent connections between Berlin and Potsdam is available at Wannsee station (bus no. 133) in Berlin. **Verkehrsverbund Potsdam** provides the service. For travel information and schedules, call **BVG Berlin** (☎ **030/ 19-449**).

By Car   Access is via the E30 Autobahn east and west or the E53 north and south. Allow about 30 minutes to drive here from Berlin.

VISITOR INFORMATION   Contact **Potsdam-Information,** Friedrich Strasse 5 (☎ **0331/27-55-80**), open April through October, Monday to Friday 9am to 8pm, Saturday 10am to 6pm, and Sunday 10am to 4pm; November through March, Monday to Friday 10am to 6pm and Saturday and Sunday 10am to 2pm.

GETTING AROUND   By Public Transportation   Ask at the tourist office about a **Potsdam billet,** costing 8.50DM ($4.85) and good for 24 hours on the city's public transportation. In Potsdam, **bus line A1,** leaving from the rail station, will deliver you to the Potsdam palaces. Call ☎ **0331/2-80-03-09** for more information.

By Boat   Since the area around Potsdam is surrounded by water, boat tours in fair weather are a popular diversion. Call **Weisse Flotte Potsdam** at ☎ **0331/29-15-27** for more information.

By Bicycle   You can rent a bicycle from **City Rad Potsdam,** at the Potsdam-Stadt Station (☎ **0331/619052**), but you can't ride your bike on the grounds of Sans Souci Park. The rental shop is open May through October, Monday to Friday from 9am to 7pm and Saturday and Sunday from 9am to 8pm. Bicycles rent for 15DM ($8.55) per day.

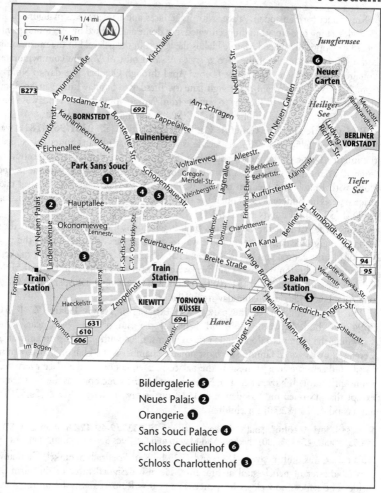

Bildergalerie **5**

Neues Palais **2**

Orangerie **1**

Sans Souci Palace **4**

Schloss Cecilienhof **6**

Schloss Charlottenhof **3**

EXPLORING THE PARKS & PALACES

A British air raid on April 14, 1945, destroyed much of the center of the old city, but the major attraction, Sans Souci Park and its palace buildings, survived.

✪ **Sans Souci Park.** Zur historischen Mühle. ☎ **0331/9-69-41-90.** Daily 8am–8pm. Tram: 94 or 96. Bus: 612, 614, 631, 632, 692, or 695 to reach the sights in the park.

Sans Souci Park, with its palaces and gardens, was the work of many architects and sculptors. The park covers an area of about a square mile. Its premier attraction is the palace of Frederick I ("the Great"), **Sans Souci,** meaning "free from care." Frederick was one of the most liberal and farsighted of the Prussian monarchs. He was a great general, but he liked best to think of himself as an enlightened patron of the arts. Here he could get away from his duties, indulge his intellectual interests, and entertain his friend Voltaire. The style of the buildings he had constructed is called "Potsdam rococo," and is primarily the achievement of Georg Wenzeslaus von Knobelsdorff.

Sans Souci (or Sanssouci) Palace, with its terraces and gardens, was inaugurated in 1747. It's a long one-story building, crowned by a dome and flanked by two round pavilions. The elliptically shaped Marble Hall is the largest in the palace, but the music salon is the supreme example of the rococo style. A small bust of Voltaire commemorates Voltaire's sojourns here. The palace is open April through October, Tuesday to Sunday from 9am to 5pm; November through January, Tuesday to Sunday from 9am to 3pm; and February and March, Tuesday to Sunday from 9am to 4pm; closed Monday. Admission is 10DM ($5.70) for adults and 5DM ($2.85) for children and students.

Bildergalerie (Picture Gallery), Östlicher Lustgarten (☎ 0331/9694181), was built between 1755 and 1763. Its facade is similar to that of Sans Souci Palace, and the interior is one of the most flamboyant in Germany. On display is a collection of some 125 paintings, with works from the Italian Renaissance and the baroque period along with Dutch and Flemish masters. Concerts of the Potsdam Park Festival take place here. The Bildergalerie is open the same hours as Sans Souci Palace. Admission is 4DM ($2.30) for adults and 2DM ($1.15) for children.

West of the palace is the **Orangerie,** built between 1851 and 1864. It was based on Italian Renaissance designs. Its purpose was to shelter southern plants during the cold months. In the central core is the Raphael Hall, which holds 47 copies of that master's paintings. In addition, you can visit five lavishly decorated salons. Admission is 5DM ($2.85) for adults and 3DM ($1.70) for children. The Orangerie is open mid-May to mid-October, Friday to Wednesday from 10am to 5pm.

The largest building in the park is the extravagant **Neues Palais** (☎ 0331/9694255), built between 1763 and 1769, at the end of the Seven Years' War. Crowning the center is a dome. The rococo rooms, filled with paintings and antiques, were used by the royal family. The most notable chamber is the Hall of Shells, with its fossils and semiprecious stones. At the palace theater, concerts take place every year from April through November. The Neues Palais has the same hours as the Sans Souci, except that it's open on Monday and closed on Friday. It charges 8DM ($4.55) for adults and 4DM ($2.30) for children.

Schloss Charlottenhof. South of Okonomieweg. ☎ 0331/9-69-42-28. Admission 8DM ($4.55) adults, 4DM ($2.30) children. Mid-May to mid-Oct Tues-Sun 9am-5pm. Tram: 1 or 4.

This palace was built between 1826 and 1829 by Karl Friedrich Schinkel, Germany's greatest master of neoclassical architecture. He also designed most of the furniture inside. The schloss now closes in winter. The nearby **Roman Baths** are on the north of the artificial lake known as *Maschinenteich* (machine pond). These baths, constructed between 1829 and 1835, were built strictly for the romantic love of antiquity and have no practical purpose.

Neuer Garten. On Heiliger See, about a mile northwest of Sans Souci. ☎ 0331/2-31-41. Free admission. Same hours as Sans Souci. Bus: 695.

On Heiliger See, or "holy lake," in the northern part of Potsdam, lies the Neuer Garten. The nephew and successor to Frederick the Great, Frederick William II, had these gardens laid out.

Schloss Cecilienhof. In Neuer Garten. ☎ 0331/9-69-42-44. Admission 8DM ($4.55) adults, 6DM ($3.40) students with guided tour (2DM less without), free for children under 6. Tues-Sun 9am-12:30pm and 5-7pm. The guided tour is only from Oct 15 to May 15. Bus: 695.

This palace was completed in the style of an English country house. We recommend it not only as an attraction but also as a hotel and a luncheon stopover (see "Where to Stay," below). Kaiser Wilhelm II had it built between 1913 and 1917 for Crown Prince Wilhelm. The palace was occupied as a royal residence until March 1945, when the crown prince and his family fled to the West. In addition to the regular guided tour, offered in summer, there is a new tour of the private rooms of Crown Prince Wilhelm and Princess Cecilie on the upper story. The tour takes place at 11am and 2pm and costs 3DM ($1.70) adults and 2DM ($1.15) students and children.

Cecilienhof was the headquarters of the 1945 Potsdam Conference, attended by the heads of the allied powers, including Truman, Stalin, and Churchill. You can visit the studies of the various delegations and see the large round table, made in Moscow, where the actual agreement was signed.

WHERE TO STAY

Arkona Hotel Voltaire. Friedrich-Ebert-Strasse 88, 14467 Potsdam. ☎ **0331/2-31-70.** Fax 0331/2-31-71-00. www.hotelvoltaire.potsdam.de. E-mail: hotelvoltaire@potsdam.de. 143 units. MINIBAR TV TEL. 234DM–274DM ($133.40–$156.20) double; from 375DM ($213.75) suite. AE, DC, MC, V. Parking 20DM ($11.40). Tram: 92.

This hotel, the newest and best in Potsdam, is a radical renovation of the Brühlsche Palace, formerly a dour and crumbling relic built in 1732. Only the palace's baroque facade has been retained. The site belongs to the small Arkona hotel chain. Bedrooms are scattered over three floors and, in almost every case, overlook the quiet precincts of a pleasant garden in back. All rooms have safes.

Dining/Diversions: On the premises is a well-run restaurant, Hofgarten.

Amenities: Concierge, room service, hair dryers, dry cleaning, laundry, newspaper delivery, baby-sitting, secretarial services, valet parking, courtesy car, bike rental, children's programs.

Hotel Mercure. Lange Brücke, 14467 Potsdam. ☎ **0331/27-22.** Fax 0331/29-34-96. 210 units. MINIBAR TV TEL. 150DM–204DM ($85.50–$116.30) double; 247DM ($140.80) suite. AE, DC, MC, V. Free parking. Tram: 91 or 96.

This high-rise hotel lies at the entrance to the city on the route nearest Berlin, rising over the Havel River by the site of the Schloss Cecilienhof. It's rather colorless, but the bedrooms are streamlined and comfortable, if a bit small and unimaginative. The main hotel dining room offers a standard international cuisine.

✪ **Hotel Schloss Cecilienhof.** Neue Garten, 14469 Potsdam. ☎ **0331/3-70-50.** Fax 0331/29-24-98. 46 units. MINIBAR TV TEL. 290DM–370DM ($165.30–$210.90) double; 550DM–850DM ($313.50–$484.50) suite. Rates include buffet breakfast. AE, DC, MC, V. Free parking. Bus: 695.

Many visitors don't realize that the lovely Schloss Cecilienhof is also an accommodations option. It stands in a tranquil park bordering a lake, about a 15-minute stroll from Sans Souci. The German government converted a residential wing into one of the most charming hotels in the country. Bedrooms are traditionally designed and spacious, and maintenance is state-of-the-art.

Dining/Diversions: Residents can take their meals in the palace dining room, enjoying a first-class cuisine of both international and regional specialties, including some Ukrainian dishes.

Amenities: Concierge, room service, dry cleaning, laundry, newspaper delivery, baby-sitting, secretarial services, valet parking, free coffee in lobby, jogging track.

WHERE TO DINE

✪ **Juliette.** Jägerstrasse 39. ☎ **0331/2701-791.** Reservations required. Main courses 29DM–34DM ($16.55–$19.40). Fixed-price menus 59DM–76DM ($33.65–$43.30). AE, V. Daily noon–11pm. FRENCH.

At last, Potsdam has a world-class restaurant. The cozy and intimate Juliette lies in the center of the restored Holländisches Viertel (Dutch Quarter), 3 blocks north of the Altar Markt. You'll feel at home the moment you enter this restored old house, with its blazing fireplace, low ceilings, and tiny little windows. There is no more romantic choice in the city. Most of the excellent waiters are from France. Menu items include saddle of boar in cranberry sauce, fresh grilled fish, and some wonderful chicken dishes. All the desserts are freshly made on-site.

Villa Kellerman. Mangerstrasse 34–36. ☎ **0331/29-15-72.** Reservations recommended. Main courses 16DM–32DM ($9.10–$18.25); fixed-price menu 70DM ($39.90). AE, DC, MC, V. Tues–Sun noon–midnight. S-Bahn: Potsdam Stadt. Bus: 92 or 93. ITALIAN.

One of the most talked-about restaurants in Potsdam is in an 1878 villa, once occupied by author Bernhardt Kellerman. The Italian cuisine here attracts a diverse clientele from finance and the arts. Your meal might include marinated carpaccio of sea wolf; ravioli stuffed with cheese, spinach, and herbs; John Dory in butter-and-caper sauce; and an array of veal and beef dishes. The wine list is mostly Italian.

2 Weimar

162 miles SW of Berlin, 14 miles E of Erfurt

Weimar, a beautiful 1,000-year-old town on the edge of the Thuringian Forest, is an important destination for those interested in German history and culture. Unlike many cities in the former East Germany, Weimar still retains much of its old flavor. Many of its important historical monuments were spared from the bombings of World War II. Its atmospheric, narrow, winding streets, lined with houses with high-pitched gables and roofs, seem left over from the Middle Ages. A 19th-century writer called Weimar "one of the most walkable towns of Europe," and so it remains today.

Weimar's history as a cultural center is centuries old. Lucas Cranach the Elder worked here in the 16th century. From 1708 to 1717, Bach was court organist. In 1775, the great Goethe came to reside at the court of Dowager Duchess Anna Amalia and her son, Charles Augustus II, and he attracted such notables as Herder and Schiller.

Later in the 19th century, Franz Liszt was musical director of the National Theater; under his auspices, Wagner's *Lohengrin* had its first performance. It was also at Weimar that the German national assembly met in February 1919, in the aftermath of World War I, to draw up the constitution for what was to be called the Weimar Republic.

ESSENTIALS

GETTING THERE **By Train** **Weimar Hauptbahnhof** is on the major Deutsche Bundesbahn rail lines, which link Erfurt and Leipzig with Dresden. There are frequent daily connections in both directions. For rail information and schedules, call ☎ 1805/996633.

By Bus Regional buses to all parts of the city and the surrounding area are run by **Verkehrsgesellschaft Weimar** (☎ **03643/2-42-00**).

By Car Access is via the E40 Autobahn east and west.

VISITOR INFORMATION Head first for Weimar's tourist agency, the **Tourist-Information Weimar,** Am Markt 10 (☎ **03643/2-40-00**). The office is open April through October, Monday to Friday 10am to 6pm, Saturday and Sunday 10am to 4pm; November through March, Tuesday to Friday 9am to 6pm and Saturday 9am to 1pm.

EXPLORING THE TOWN

Weimar enjoys a picturesque location on the Ilm River, set against the backdrop of the Ettersberg and Vogtland hills. The city has many popular sights, but perhaps the best

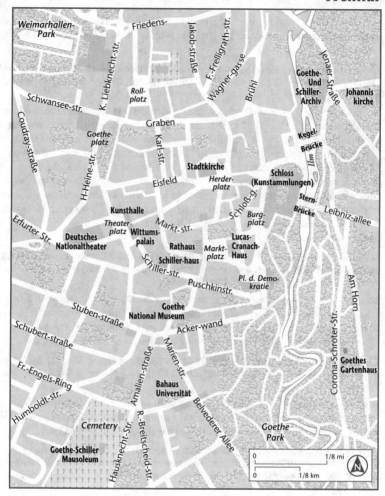

thing to do here is simply to wander about on foot. A walk at night through the old streets that once felt the footsteps of Goethe, Bach, Wagner, and Schiller is particularly rewarding.

The town's main square, called the **Marktplatz,** or market square, retains the old flavor of the city. Instead of breakfast at your hotel, visit one of the bakeries near the square and compose your own breakfast, the way many locals do. The daily produce market still takes place on the Marktplatz. The painter Lucas Cranach the Elder lived here during his last years, from 1552 to 1553; you can view the richly decorated **Lucas Cranach the Elder House.**

For a midday break from sightseeing, we suggest a visit to Park an der Ilm or **Goethe Park,** flanking the river. Goethe himself actually landscaped this park. It sports numerous 18th-century pavilions, and is the best place in Weimar for a picnic.

If you've had a little too much Schiller and Goethe, flee the inner city and escape to **Baushaus Universität** on Marienstrasse, just across the footpath in front of the Bauhaus building. Here you can meet Weimar students, nearly all of whom speak English.

In the evening, head for one of the smoky beer halls near **Herderplatz,** keeping in mind that Nietzsche, who spent the last 3 years of his life here, discovered them long before you.

✪ **Goethe National Museum.** Am Frauenplan 1. ☎ **03643/54-53-20.** Admission 8DM ($4.55) adults, 5DM ($2.85) students, 2.50DM ($1.40) children. Mar–Oct Tues–Sun 9am–4pm; Oct 26–Mar 14 Tues–Sun 10am–4pm. Bus: 1, 4, 6, 8, or 71.

Weimar's principal attraction is the Goethe National Museum, housed in the building where the poet lived from 1782 to 1832. It's a typical example of a German nobleman's baroque house. There are 14 exhibition rooms, some pretty much as Goethe and his wife, Christiane Vulpius, left them. The library contains more than 5,000 volumes. The writer's mineral collection is here also, as well as much original art. Although Goethe's reputation rests today on his writing, his interests and occupations ranged widely. You can see evidence in these rooms of his interest in science (he was an early advocate of the belief in the common origin of all animal life, for example). Goethe even held the post of minister of state in the government. He died in Weimar on March 22, 1832.

Goethes Gartenhaus. Im Park an der Ilm. ☎ **03643/54-53-75.** Admission 4DM ($2.30) adults, 3DM ($1.70) students and senior citizens, 1.50DM (85¢) children. Mar 15–Oct 25 Wed–Mon 9am–6pm; Oct 26–Mar 14 Wed–Mon 10am–4pm.

In a park on the Ilm River stands a plain cottage with a high-pitched roof. Goethe selected this house as his first residence when he came to Weimar. Even after he moved to other quarters, he still came here in summer to find peace and tranquillity. He described the park around him as "infinitely beautiful," and so it remains today.

✪ **Schillerhaus.** Schillerstrasse 9. ☎ **03643/54-53-50.** Admission 5DM ($2.85) adults, 4DM ($2.30) students and senior citizens, 2DM ($1.15) children. Mar 15–Oct 25 Wed–Mon 9am–6pm. Bus: 1, 4, 6, 8, or 71.

After his friend Goethe, Schiller is the greatest name in German literature. He lived here with his family from 1802 to 1805, and wrote his last works here, including *Wilhelm Tell.* The attic rooms have been furnished as they were in Schiller's day.

Liszt House. Marienstrasse 17. ☎ **03643/54-53-88.** Admission 4DM ($2.30) adults, 3DM ($1.70) students, 1.50DM (85¢) children. Jan 7–Mar 14 9am–4pm, Mar 15–May 9 9am–6pm, May 10–Aug 29 9am–7pm, Aug 30–Oct 24 9am–6pm, Oct 25–Dec 31 9am–4pm. Closed daily 1–2pm. Bus: 4, 6, 8, or 71.

Franz Liszt (1811–86), the Hungarian composer and pianist, spent the last period of his life here. You'll find several mementos, both personal and musical, from the composer's life, including letters exchanged between Liszt and his son-in-law, as well as the piano at which he played and taught his pupils. The house was also once the home for the royal gardeners of Weimar.

Kunstsammlungen zu Weimar. Burgplatz 4. ☎ **03643/54-60.** Admission 6DM ($3.40) adults, 3DM ($1.70) children. Self-parking 2DM ($1.15) hourly. Apr–Oct Tues–Sun 10am–6pm, Nov–Mar Tues–Sun 10am–4:30pm. Bus: 5.

This structure was begun under the guidance of Goethe in 1789, and completed in 1803. The previous castle had burned down in 1774; only a tower survived. In one of the wings is a series of galleries dedicated not only to Schiller and Goethe but also to two other famous names associated with Weimar: Johann Gottfried Herder (1744–1803), the German critic and philosopher who was a pioneer of the *Sturm und Drang* ("Storm and Stress") literary movement, and Christoph Martin Wieland (1733–1813), the poet and critic who wrote the satirical romance *The Republic of Fools.* The museum has a shop, which is open from April to October, 10am to 6pm.

The ground floor displays works by Lucas Cranach the Elder. On some of the upper floors you can see exhibits from Walter Gropius's Bauhaus movement, which started in Weimar. The primary aim of this movement was to unify arts and crafts within the context of architecture. Its appeal derived from the changing sensibilities of the Industrial Age, as well as from the need for inexpensive construction techniques in an era of rising costs and exploding demand for housing. Followers around the globe may have been impressed, but not the good people of Weimar. They "tolerated" Gropius's school of design until 1925, and then bombarded it in the press, until it finally moved to Dessau. There it stayed until the Nazis closed it in 1933, claiming it was a center of "Communist intellectualism."

Wittumspalais. Am Palais 3. ☎ **03643/54-53-77.** Admission 6DM ($3.40) adults, 4DM ($2.30) students and senior citizens, 2DM ($1.15) children. Mar 15–Oct 25 Tues–Sun 9am–6pm; Oct 26–Mar 14 Tues–Sun 10am–4pm. Bus: 4, 6, or 8.

If you follow Rittergasse to the end, you will come upon the 1767 Wittumspalais, once the residence of Dowager Duchess Anna Amalia, who presided over the German Enlightenment, which brought a stark rationalism to literature and the arts. The old ducal dower house is devoted to mementos of the movement.7

Stadtkirche St. Peter and Paul. Herderplatz 8 (follow Vorwerksgasse). ☎ **03643/ 85-15-18.** Free admission. Apr–Oct Mon–Sat 10am–noon and 2–4pm, Sun 11am–noon and 2–3pm; Nov–Mar Mon–Sat 11am–noon and 2–3pm, Sun 2–3pm. Bus: 1 or 6.

The origins of this church date from the founding of Weimar itself. The present building consists of three naves designed in a late Gothic style. Its most precious treasure is an altar painting begun by Lucas Cranach the Elder in the last year of his life and completed by his son.

Schloss Belvedere (Château of Belvedere). Belvedereallee. ☎ **03643/54-61-62.** Admission 5DM ($2.85) adults, 3DM ($1.70) children. Apr–Oct Tues–Sun 10am–6pm; closed Nov–Mar. Bus: 12. From Weimar, follow the Belvedereschlossallee south for 2 miles.

The baroque Schloss Belvedere was a favorite retreat of Anna Amalia and the "enlightened" Weimar set. It has an orangerie, along with the open-air theater and an English-style park. Inside the château are displays of dainty rococo art and a collection of historical coaches.

Schloss Tiefurt. On the outskirts of Weimar in the village of Tiefurt. ☎ **03643/85-06-66.** Admission 6DM ($3.40) adults, 4DM ($2.30) students and senior citizens, 2DM ($1.15) children. Mar 15–Oct 25 Tues–Sun 9am–6pm; Oct 26–Mar 14 Tues–Sun 9am–4pm. Bus: 3 from Goetheplatz; Tiefurt is the last stop. Go east along Tiefurter Allee.

This was formerly the site of another summer retreat of Duchess Anna Amalia. Guests today can wander through its pavilions and gardens. Coming here is a good excursion on a lovely day if you have extra time.

MORE SIGHTS

In the **cemetery,** south of the town center, Am Posseckschen Garten, you can see the controversial **Denkmal der März Gefallenen,** a monument to the revolutionaries whose slaughter in 1919 so affected Gropius and his Bauhaus followers. But most interesting today is the grand ducal family vault, where Goethe and Schiller, friends in life, lie side by side in death. The **Goethe-Schiller Mausoleum,** once the family vault of the Weimar dynasty, is on a terrace above the steps. It was built from 1825 to 1826 according to plans drawn up by Coudray, who consulted Goethe on the design and construction. Schiller was entombed here in 1827 and Goethe in 1832, both in oak coffins. Visiting hours are daily from 9am to 1pm and 2 to 5pm. Admission is free.

Goethe Gets a Touch-Up

The news out of Weimar is weird but true: Someone's been fiddling with Goethe. Around thirty years ago, the city's most famous corpse suffered the indignity of being dug up, loaded onto a cart, and pulled off to the nearby Goethe Museum. Why? Well, in the fall of 1970, shortly before the dirty deed was done, local authorities discovered that Goethe's sarcophagus had a broken lock. When they took a look inside, they saw that his corpse was in a bad state of decomposition. Weimar was an important weapon in East Germany's propaganda war against the cultural decadence of West Germany. Communist higher-ups decided that something had better be done soon or the great "Kulturstadt" (city of culture) would be shamed by its mistreatment of the great scribe's remains.

So the national poet and creator of *Faust* was removed from his comfortable resting place and brought to the museum, where the corpse's remaining fragments of flesh were removed by means of a process called "maceration." A special preserving agent was then applied to the bones to strengthen them. The laurel wreath around Goethe's head was likewise doused and strengthened.

Unfortunately, all did not run smoothly. The shroud Goethe was wearing was sent off for examination but, typically, got tangled up in bureaucratic red tape and didn't arrive back in Weimar in time for his reburial. It has since been kept hidden in the Schiller Museum (talk about dirty linen). The report outlining this skullduggery was only made public in 1999.

A **chapel** in Russian-church style is on the south side of the mausoleum. It was built in 1859 for Maria Pavlovna, daughter-in-law of Duke Carl August.

BUCHENWALD   The Buchenwald bus (no. 6) from Weimar's Hauptbahnhof goes 4 miles northwest of Weimar to **Gedenkstätte Buchenwald** (☎ 03643/ **43-00**), the site of the concentration camp. It is estimated that a quarter of a million Jews, Slavs, Gypsies, homosexuals, political prisoners, prisoners of war, and others were confined here from 1937 until the camp's liberation by the U.S. Army in 1945. Buchenwald was officially a work camp, so many fewer people were killed here than at Auschwitz. Nonetheless, 56,000 people died in this camp, and many, many thousands of others were sent on from here to the death camps in the east. Furthermore, atrocities practiced in Buchenwald have made its very name synonymous with human perversity.

A memorial with a cluster of "larger-than-life" people, representing victims of fascism, was created by Prof. Fritz Cremer to honor the people from 32 nations who lost their lives here.

Buchenwald's sad history continued when Soviet occupation forces used the site as an internment camp from 1945 to 1951. It's believed that they sent thousands of prisoners here to die. All this was kept quiet until the winter of 1989. Before that time, the Soviets had attempted to exploit the Buchenwald museum as a showcase illustrating "the suffering of Soviet soldiers and the German Communists." The museum now reflects both the Soviet and the Nazi past of the camp.

You can visit Buchenwald May through September, Tuesday to Sunday from 9:45am to 6pm; October through April, Tuesday to Sunday from 8:45am to 5pm. Admission is free.

SHOPPING

A visit to Weimar's antique stores offers a chance to buy porcelain, silver, crystal, and furniture that survived the devastation of World War II. The most interesting shops include **Antikitäten am Palais,** Schillerstrasse 22 (☎ **03643/59625**), and its immediate neighbor, **Kaiser Antikitäten,** Schillerstrasse 22 (same phone). Also appealing are **Antikitäten am Schloss,** Obereschlossgasse 2 (☎ **03643/51-29-93**), **Goethe-Antiquariat,** Kaufenstrasse 7 (☎ **03643/40-25-67**); and **Thiersch Antikitäten,** Bräuhausgasse 15 (☎ **03643/40-25-40**).

WHERE TO STAY
EXPENSIVE

✪ **Kempinski Hotel Elephant Weimar.** Am Markt 19, 99423 Weimar. ☎ **03643/80-20.** Fax 03643/80-26-10. 102 units. MINIBAR TV TEL. 310DM–390DM ($176.70–$222.30) double; 480DM–580DM ($273.60–$330.60) suite. AE, DC, MC, V. Free parking. Bus: 10, 11 or 71.

The Elephant is Weimar's most famous hotel, although it's actually inferior to the Hilton (see below). Many celebrities have stayed at this hotel, including Tolstoy and Bach; the most notorious guest was Adolf Hitler. The Elephant became best known in Germany through Thomas Mann's novel *Lotte in Weimar* (published in English as *The Beloved Returns).*

The elegant facade of this building (ca. 1696) is set off by a beautifully weathered terra-cotta roof, a series of elongated bay windows stretching from the second to the third floors, and, best of all, a frontage onto the old marketplace, which contains a dried-up fountain dedicated to Neptune. An art-deco decor and bold color schemes make the rooms dramatically appealing. (The bedside reading lamps are a bit dim, however.) The tiled bathrooms have marble countertops.

Dining/Diversions: The hotel maintains two restaurants, The Kempinski Hotel Elephant Weimar Restaurant (see "Where to Dine," below), and the more formal Anna Amalia.

Amenities: Concierge, room service, dry cleaning, laundry service, twice-daily maid service, baby-sitting, secretarial services, conference rooms; a health club is located nearby.

Weimar Hilton. Belvederer Allee 25, 99425 Weimar. ☎ **800/445-8667** in the U.S. and Canada, or 03643/72-20. Fax 03643/72-27-41. www.hilton.com. 306 units. A/C MINIBAR TV TEL. 300DM–345DM ($171–$196.65) double; from 580DM ($330.60) suite. AE, DC, MC, V. Parking 16DM–20DM ($9.10–$11.40). Bus: 1.

Ironically, credit for the excellence of the hotel's construction and the lavishness of its materials is due to the former East German government, which designed and supervised the building of this hotel a few months before reunification. The hotel, now run by Hilton, stands beside Goethe Park, a swath of greenery with posh residences and embassies left over from the Weimar Republic. The lobby is dramatic, with sun-flooded skylights and glass walls. The guest rooms are small but comfortable. Two floors are rented to nonsmokers, and two rooms are suitable for those with disabilities.

Dining/Diversions: The Kolonnaden Bar services the fine Restaurant Esplanade/Trattoria Esplanade. The Biergarten is also popular.

Amenities: 24-hour room service, hair dryers, concierge (who can arrange local sightseeing tours), baby-sitters, massage, impressive indoor pool, two saunas, cosmetic salon, health club.

MODERATE

Amalienhof. Amalienstrasse 2, 99423 Weimar. ☎ **03643/54-90.** Fax 03643/54-91-10. www.vch.de/amalienhof. E-mail: amalienhof.weimar@t-online.de. 31 units. 170DM ($96.90) double; 250DM ($142.50) suite. Rates include buffet breakfast. AE, MC, V. Free parking. Bus: 1.

This hotel was originally constructed in 1826 in neoclassical style. Today, its small, modern bedrooms are comfortably furnished and well maintained. The hotel has a great location, lying directly south of Goethe National Museum, within an easy walk of the town's historic core and major attractions. The breakfast buffet, the only meal served here, is decent.

Russischer Hof. Goetheplatz 2, 99423 Weimar. ☎ **03643/77-40.** Fax 03643/902337. 124 units. TV TEL. 170DM–260DM ($96.90–$148.20) double. Rates include buffet breakfast. AE, DC, MC, V. Parking 10DM–15DM ($5.70–$8.55). Bus: 11 or 71.

Russischer Hof was built in 1805 by Russian aristocrats for their visits to the court of Weimar. It sports a dark green and white facade and opens onto an important square in the center of town. Inside, the pastel-colored public rooms are elegant and intimate, but the guest rooms are in a somewhat lackluster modern annex behind the hotel.

INEXPENSIVE

Thüringen. Brennerstrasse 42, 99423 Weimar. ☎ **03643/903-675.** Fax 03643/903-676. 36 units. 150DM ($85.50) double. Rates include buffet breakfast. AE, MC, V. Bus: 1 and 7.

This affordable hotel in the center of town dates from 1897 but has been completely renovated and restored in modern style. The small bedrooms are clean and simply but adequately furnished. The focal point of the public rooms is a glassed-in winter garden. The hotel is known for its *gutbürgerlich* (home-style) cookery, which one reader described as "just like my Saxon mother used to cook."

WHERE TO DINE

Kempinski Hotel Elephant Weimar. Am Markt 19. ☎ **03643/80-26-39.** Reservations recommended. Main courses 36DM–41DM ($20.50–$23.35); 3-course fixed-price lunch 48DM ($27.35); 5-course fixed-price dinner 97DM ($55.30). AE, DC, MC, V. Anna Amalia 6:30–10:30pm daily, and noon–3pm on weekends only in winter and daily in summer. Elephantenkeller Mon–Sat 12:30pm–3am, Sun 12:30–3pm. Bus: 11 or 71. GERMAN/INTERNATIONAL.

There are two restaurants in this previously recommended hotel. The more formal, Anna Amalia, is modern, skylit, and airy, with spacious tables, a garden terrace, and good service. Its German and international dishes are among the very best in the city. The chefs have an unerring sense of flavor and proportion, as well as a fertile imagination. They use only the finest of ingredients available at the local markets. Fillet Stroganoff, pork medallions, and sauerbraten are among the menu items. Goethe and Schiller wined and dined here, as did Bach, Liszt, and Wagner.

You can reach the historic **Elephantenkeller** (Elephant Cellar) by a flight of stone steps at a separate entrance. It's decorated in a rustic style, with square travertine columns. An autumn specialty is *Zwiebelmarkt* salads, made from onions from the famous October onion market, a tradition dating from 1653.

Ratskeller. In the Stadthaus, Markt 10. ☎ **03643/85-05-73.** Reservations recommended. Main courses 15DM–9DM ($8.55–$16.55). AE, MC, V. Daily 11:30am–midnight. Bus: 7 or 71. THURINGIAN.

A flight of stairs leads into a pair of dining rooms. The first is vaulted and white, the second more modern, paneled, and with a prominent bar. Everything is clean, correct, and proper. You might begin with goose liver on toast, followed with schnitzel, goulash with mixed salad, or pork cutlets prepared four different ways. These dishes

The Thuringian Forest: Germany's Green Heart

"There is indeed no forest on all the earth as beautiful as the Thuringian," wrote the Danish poet Martin Anderson Nexö in his tale *The Doll.* Trekkers and nature lovers have long extolled the scenic beauties of this region, which has often been called "the green heart of Germany." The *Thüringer Wald* was the former stamping ground of such philosophers and artists as Goethe, Friedrich Schiller, Martin Luther, Ludwig Bechstein, and Bach.

The mountains within the forest, though not nearly as tall as the German Alps, are geological highlights. The highest peaks (around 3,230 ft.) are composed of gneiss, porphyry, and granite; the foothills are made of softer strata of sandstone and sedimentary limestone.

The scenic, 100-mile, northwest-to-southeast ramble known as the "Thuringian High Road" was one of the most popular destinations anywhere for East German schoolchildren and campers before reunification. You can take a lowland driving version by following route 88 between Eisenach and Ilmenau, a city that Goethe loved.

Just as attractive as the region's scenic beauty are the dozens of unspoiled, charming medieval villages that pepper the landscape. **Dornburg** has a series of three palaces, perched high above the River Saale. **Altenburg,** directly south of Leipzig, is the home of a hilltop castle. Finally, **Arnstadt,** founded in 704, is the oldest town in the Thuringian Forest. It lies just beyond Erfurt. Today, the town's medieval walkways and buildings are being restored to their former glory.

---

aren't dazzling, but they're very satisfying. The venison, when in season, is excellent, and the wild boar and duck in red-wine sauce is reason enough for a meal here.

Weissen Schwan. Am Frauenplan (in the center of the town near Goethe House). ☎ **03643/20-25-21.** Reservations recommended. Main courses 16DM–35DM ($9.10–$19.95); fixed-price menus 40DM–120DM ($22.80–$68.40). AE, DC, MC, V. Sun and Tues–Thurs noon–11pm, Fri–Sat noon–midnight. Bus: 7 or 71. THURINGIAN/INTERNATIONAL.

This leading restaurant specializes in regional cuisine, using fresh produce and the best of the local beef, game, and poultry. It's in a building that dates from the early 16th century. The library is still preserved. The atmosphere is mellow. Along with Thuringian specialties, somewhat standard international dishes are also offered.

WEIMAR AFTER DARK

A good national theater, live music venues, and dance clubs provide a variety of choices for nightly entertainment. The city's bars and outdoor cafes are good places to drink and talk. Just walk down Schillerstrasse or along the Theaterplatz. All of the bars and cafes in this area carry free copies of *Schlagseite* and *Boulevard,* local entertainment papers. *Takt* is another good resource; you can save 5DM ($2.85) by picking it up in the tourist office (see above), the only place where it's free.

Weimar's main performance venue, which reopened in 1999, is the **Deutsches Nationaltheater,** Theaterplatz (☎ 03643/75-53-34), where Franz Liszt and Richard Strauss once conducted. Call the box office or the tourist office for information about schedules.

C-Keller Galerie, Markt 21 (☎ 03643/50-27-55), combines an art gallery with a cafe that serves beer, wine, tea, and light meals. It's a popular place to unwind. The art gallery has works for sale by local, national, and European artists. The cafe is open daily from noon to midnight. Its most visible competitor is **Galerie C-1,** Karl-August-Allee 1 (☎ **03643/50-23-01**), which presents good food, fresh from the nearby marketplace, along with an oft-changing exhibition of modern paintings. **Cranach Galerie,** Cranach Haus, Marktplatz 12 (☎ **03643/903768**) is a more formal gallery with a wider range of works. It's open Tuesday to Friday from 10am to 8pm.

The most popular and animated disco in Weimar isn't exactly cutting edge—it's more like Hannover than Hamburg or Berlin. But if you're interested in hearing a medley of disco favorites from the '70s and '80s, head for **Bistro Corona-Sthröter,** Goethe-Platz 5 (☎ **03643/515308**). It's open daily from 9pm to midnight. Admission costs 5DM ($2.85) per person.

A three-story medieval tower, **Studentclub Kasseturm,** Goetheplatz (☎ **03643/904323**), has a beer hall on the first floor, live music on the second, and dancing on the third. As the name suggests, students flock to this place. The cover ranges from 5DM ($2.85) to as much as 25DM ($14.25), if there's a particularly well-known band. There's no cover on Monday, Tuesday, and Thursday. The club opens Monday to Saturday at 8pm, with no set closing time.

The most popular place in Weimar for punk and alternative rock is **Haus für Socio-Kultur,** Gerberstrasse 3 (☎ **03643/51-27-14**), a large, loud rock club (or a pub, depending on the evening) with a graffiti-art exterior. Hours are daily from 8pm to 3am. There is no cover charge, but customers pay an extra 0.50DM (30¢) on each drink during performances.

SIDE TRIPS FROM WEIMAR
ERFURT

The small, 1,254-year-old city of Erfurt, on the Gera River, is one of the most visited cities of eastern Germany, because it still exudes the spirit of a medieval market town. Erfurt is filled with historic houses, bridges, winding cobblestone alleys, and church spires reaching toward the skyline, as well as decorative and colorful Renaissance and baroque era facades. The city emerged from World War II relatively unscathed, and remains one of the best places to see what yesterday's Germany looked like. Nearly everything of interest is concentrated in the Altstadt (Old Town) area. It's well worth your time to take 2 or 3 hours to walk around this city of "flowers and towers."

Why flowers? Erfurt is a center of the German horticultural trade. It's also Europe's largest vegetable seed producer. One of Europe's biggest horticultural shows, the *Internationale Gartenbauaustellung,* is held here in the Cyriaksburg Park every year from the end of March through September.

GETTING THERE   You can reach Erfurt after a 15-mile train ride from the Weimar Hauptbahnhof; there are frequent connections. For rail information and schedules, call ☎ **1805/996633.** Access by car is via the E40 Autobahn east and west and State Highway 4. After arriving, head for the **Erfurt Tourist-Information** at Kräerbrücke (☎ **0361/6-6400**). It's open Monday to Friday from 10am to 6pm, Saturday from 10am to 4pm, and Sunday from 10am to 1pm.

Exploring the City

Well-preserved patrician mansions built in both the Gothic and Renaissance style are the town's dominant feature. Many of the narrow streets are lined with old half-timbered houses. One of Erfurt's curiosities is the **Krämerbrücke** (Shopkeepers' Bridge), which has spanned the Gera since the 14th century. It has houses on both sides, nearly three dozen in all, and is filled with book stalls, cafes, and antiques shops. You'll certainly want to spend some time here browsing.

The ecclesiastical center is the **Domberg,** where two Catholic churches stand side by side, their 15th-century walls almost closing in on each other. The **Dom (cathedral)** (☎ **0361/6461-265**), on Domplatz, was begun in the 12th century and later rebuilt in the 14th century in the Gothic style. Its stained-glass windows above the choir date from 1370 to 1420 and are unusual in Germany for depicting scenes of everyday life. The interior of the cathedral is richly baroque, but also has some notable works from 1160: a Romanesque alter of the Virgin and the statue-candelabra known as "the Wolfram." Note also the 13th-century tombstone of the count of Gleichen and his two wives. One version of a local legend says that the second woman wasn't his wife at all, but a Saracen beauty from the Holy Land who had saved his life under mysterious circumstances. The Dom is open May to October, Monday to Friday from 9 to 11:30am and 12:30 to 5pm, Saturday from 9 to 11:30am and 12:30 to 4:30pm, and Sunday from 2 to 4pm; November through April, Monday to Saturday from 10 to 11:30am and 12:30 to 4pm, and Sunday from 2 to 4pm.

Its neighbor is the gothic **Church of St. Severi,** a "hall type" church with 5 naves. Don't miss seeing its extraordinary font, a masterpiece of intricately carved sandstone, rising practically to the roof. You might also look for a notable sarcophagus of the saint (circa 1365) in the southernmost aisle. St. Severi is linked to the Dom by a 70-step open staircase. It's open May through October, Monday to Friday from 9am to noon and 1:30 to 5pm, Saturday from 9 to 11:30am and 12:30 to 4:30pm, and Sunday from 2 to 4pm; November through April, Monday to Saturday from 10 to noon and 1:30 to 4pm, and on Sunday from 2 to 4pm. Admission is free. For information, call ☎ **0361/6-46-12-56.**

The most beautiful churches of Erfurt are the Romanesque **Peterskirche,** dating from the 12th and 14th centuries, and the 13th-century **Predigerkirche,** of the Order of Mendicant Friars. There are also three churches that date from the early Middle Ages: **Agidienkirche, Michaeliskirche,** and **Allerheiligengeistkirche.** The tourist office (see above) will give you a map pinpointing all the locations. Most can be reached on foot.

Where to Stay & Dine

Dorint Hotel. Meienbergstrasse 26–27, 99084 Erfurt. ☎ **0361/5-94-90.** Fax 0361/5-94-91-00. 142 units. MINIBAR TV TEL. 208DM–268DM ($118.55–$152.75) double; 420DM ($239.40) suite. AE, DC, MC, V. Parking 16DM ($9.10).

Erfurt's newest hotel, in the heart of town, was built as a sophisticated enlargement of an inn *(Gasthaus)* from the 1300s. The medieval part of the hotel—which was meticulously conserved and restored—faces onto a side street, the Futterstrasse. Otherwise, the hotel is modern, restrained, and tasteful. Most bedrooms here correspond to middle-to-upscale chain-hotel standards. An additional 13 retain the wood paneling and architectural quirks of their original medieval construction, and are more interesting. On the premises you'll find a Jacuzzi, steam room, sauna, and solarium. The in-house restaurant, Rebstock, the nerve center of the hotel's medieval section, is cozy and appealing. Lunch and dinner are served here daily. Main courses range from 18.50DM to 34DM ($10.55 to $19.40) each.

Radisson SAS Hotel Erfurt. Halfway between the station and the town center, Juri-Gagarin-Ring 127, 99084 Erfurt. ☎ **0361/5-51-00.** Fax 0361/551-02-10. www.radisson.com. E-mail: js@erfzh.rdsas.com. 317 units. MINIBAR TV TEL. 210DM–265DM ($119.70–$151.05) double. Rates include buffet breakfast. AE, DC, MC, V. Parking 15DM ($8.55).

The Radisson SAS Hotel Erfurt is one of the town's better addresses. Its modern bedrooms are comfortable but a bit cramped. The bathrooms are very compact and have inadequate shelf space. The hotel restaurant offers Thuringian specialties as well as international dishes. A wide selection of wines is also available.

EISENACH

This town lies on the northwestern slopes of the Thuringian Forest, at the confluence of the Nesse and Horsel Rivers, 30 miles west of Erfurt. Eisenach, once a center of the East German auto industry, is not particularly charming, but it does have one of the region's finest castles, and a few sights associated with Luther and Bach, who was born here. Its ancient market square is ringed by half-timbered houses.

GETTING THERE   Many trains from Erfurt (see above) arrive every day. For rail information and schedules, call ☎ **03691/1805/996633.** Access by car is via the A4 Autobahn east and west. For tourist information, contact **Eisenach-Information,** Markt 3 (☎ **03691/79230**), open Monday to Friday from 9am to 6pm and Saturday from 10am to 2pm. Here you can pick up a map with the locations of all the tourist sites.

Exploring the Town

Eisenach is best known as the site of ✪ **Schloss Wartburg,** Schlossberg 2 (☎ **03691/ 7-70-73**), reached only after a rigorous climb up a 600-foot hill. Hitler called Wartburg Castle "the most German of German castles" and engaged in a battle with local authorities to take down its cross and replace it with a swastika. This ancient castle belonged to the landgraves of Thuringia and once hosted the medieval Minnesinger poets, immortalized by Wagner in *Tannhäuser.* This was also where Martin Luther hid upon his return from the Diet of Worms in 1521, so he could complete his translation of the Bible—he is said to have "fought the Devil with ink" at Wartburg. The castle has now been turned into a regional museum. It's open April to October daily from 8:30am to 4:30pm, November to March daily 9am to 3:30pm. Admission to the palace, museum, and Luther's room is 11DM ($6.25) for adults, 8DM ($4.55) senior citizens, 6DM ($3.40) for students and children.

Eisenach is also the birthplace of Johann Sebastian Bach. **Bachhaus,** Am Frauenplan 21 (☎ **03691/20-37-14**), contains many mementos of the Bach family, along with a collection of musical instruments. It's open April through September, Monday from noon to 6:45pm and Tuesday to Sunday from 9am to 6:45pm; October through March, Monday from 1 to 5:45pm and Tuesday to Sunday from 9am to 5:45pm. Admission is 5DM ($2.85) for adults, 4DM ($2.30) for students and children. Bus: 3.

You can also visit the **Lutherhaus,** home of the Cotta family, Lutherplatz 8 (☎ **03691/2-98-30**). Martin Luther stayed here as a schoolboy. It's open daily from 9am to 5pm. Admission is 5DM ($2.85) for adults and 2DM ($1.15) for children and students. Bus: 1 or 5.

Where to Stay & Dine

Arkona Hotel Thüringer Hof. Near the railway station, Karlsplatz 11, 99817 Eisenach. ☎ **03691/280.** Fax 03691/281-900. E-mail: 03691280-7@t-online.de. 127 units. MINIBAR TV TEL. 195DM–235DM ($111.15–$133.95) double; 335DM ($190.95) suite. AE, DC, MC, V. Parking 12DM–18DM ($6.85–$10.25).

This hotel was originally a very glamorous inn in the early 19th century. Today it's a part of the nationwide Arkona chain. It boasts six floors of well-designed but small bedrooms. The bathrooms are compact. On the premises are a bar and a well-managed and cozy restaurant, the Wintergarten. The hotel is located near almost every site of historic interest in town.

Romantik Hotel Kaiserhof. Wartburger Allee 2, 99817 Eisenach. ☎ **03691/21-35-13.** Fax 03691/20-36-53. 64 units. MINIBAR TV TEL. 170DM–280DM ($96.90–$159.60) double. Rates include buffet breakfast. AE, DC, MC, V. Free parking. Bus: 3.

Romantik Hotel Kaiserhof is the best hotel in town. The rooms are furnished in traditional style, but also contain modern conveniences, such as hair dryers. You can dine either in the Turmschanke, which serves a substantial regional cuisine, or in the Zwinger. There's also a gift shop.

3 Leipzig

102 miles SW of Berlin, 68 miles NW of Dresden, 78 miles NE of Erfurt

If you have limited time and have to choose between Dresden and Leipzig, make it Dresden. But if you can work Leipzig into your itinerary, you'll be richly rewarded.

More than any other city in former East Germany (except Berlin, of course), Leipzig brings you into the Germany of today. This once-dreary city is taking on a new life and vitality; a visit here can be absolutely invigorating. Glassy skyscrapers and glitzy nightlife add a cosmopolitan flavor that you don't encounter in much of the rest of the region. The approximately 20,000 students who study in the area, as did Nietzsche, Goethe, and Leibniz, help add a spark. One resident put it this way: "Our grunge and metal bands are just as good as those of Berlin, and our cafes just as super cool."

Leipzig is also famous for more traditional music. Johann Sebastian Bach is closely associated with Leipzig; Mozart and Mendelssohn performed here; and Wagner was born here in 1813.

Because of its strategic value as a rail center, both the RAF and the U.S. Air Force bombed the city heavily in World War II, but it's been rebuilt, more or less successfully. It still has some narrow streets and houses from the 16th and 17th centuries, as well as some Jugendstil (art nouveau) flair. And Leipzig is once again a major rail terminus. From its Hauptbahnhof—with 26 platforms, the largest in Europe—lines radiate to all the chief German cities and to the rest of the continent.

ESSENTIALS

GETTING THERE   By Plane   The **Leipzig-Halle International Airport** lies 7 miles northwest of the city center. About 50 airlines link Leipzig with major German cities, such as Munich and Frankfurt, and also some continental destinations. For complete information, call **Airport Information** at ☎ **0341/2241155.** A bus runs between the airport and the Leipzig Hauptbahnhof every 30 minutes, Monday to Friday from 4am to 8pm and Saturday and Sunday from 4:30am to 8pm (trip time: 40 min.). The fare is 10DM ($5.70). Taxis are also available, meeting all arriving planes, but the 25- to 30-minute ride to the city center will cost from 50DM ($28.50) and up.

By Train   The **Leipzig Hauptbahnhof,** Willy-Brandt-Platz, lies on the major Deutsche Bundesbahn rail line, with frequent connections to German cities. 17 trains arrive daily from Berlin (trip time: 2 hr. and 10 min. to 2 hr. and 50 min., depending on the train); 23 trains from Dresden (1 hr. and 35 min. to 2 hr.); and 15 trains from Frankfurt (5 hr.). For rail information and schedules, call ☎ **1805/996633.** The **Hauptbahnhof** has recently been restored, and contains many cafes, shops, and restaurants; it's one of the most happening places in Leipzig.

By Bus   Long-distance bus service to such cities as Berlin is provided by **Leipzieger Verkehrsbetriebe.** Buses depart from the east side of the main rail station. For bus information and schedules, call ☎ **0341/29-17-77.**

By Car   Access is via the Halle-Dresden Autobahn east and west or the E51 Autobahn north and south.

VISITOR INFORMATION   Contact the **Tourist-Information** office at Richard Wagner Strasse 1 (☎ **0341/7104260**), Monday to Friday 9am to 7pm; Saturday 9:30am to 4pm and Sunday 9:30am to 2pm. The office can supply a map pinpointing the major sights. This place becomes a beehive of activity at the time of the annual trade fairs.

SPECIAL EVENTS   Upon arrival, be sure to drop in at the tourist office and see if any festivals are taking place. In late June, for example, during the **Leipziger Jazztage,** the churches, the student clubs, and the opera house fill with music. In early June, the city stages its official **Street Music Festival,** when musicians—some good, some surprisingly good, many awful—play in the area of the Markt, the parks, and other outdoor venues. Sometime during the second week of June, the **Leipziger Stadtfest** turns Sachsenplatz and Grimaische Strasse into one big carnival.

GETTING AROUND   A public transit system of trams, light railways, and buses provides frequent service to all parts of the city.

EXPLORING THE CITY

Goethe, who was a student at Leipzig, called the city *klein Paris,* or a miniature Paris. We wouldn't go quite that far, but Leipzig definitely has its charms. One of the best things to do is to explore the handsomely restored art nouveau **Arkaden** (arcades) that thread through the historic core of the city center. "Mädler Mall" is Leipzig's finest arcade. This is the site of the famous **Auerbachs Keller** (see "Where to Dine," below), which was the setting for one of the scenes of Goethe's *Faust.* A bronze group of characters from Faust, sculpted in 1913, beckon you down a stone staircase into the cellar restaurant. Nearby is a lovely art nouveau coffee shop called **Mephisto,** decorated appropriately in devilish reds and blacks. All through the Mädlerpassage you can find boutiques as chic and sophisticated as those in Berlin.

A gateway leads to **Nasch Markt,** which occupies the space behind the Altes Rathaus. If you walk around the front of the Altes Rathaus, you'll find yourself within Am Markt, the city's best-known square, at the edge of which stands the **Königshaus.** Originally built in the late 1700s on the site of an even older building, the Königshaus at one time functioned as the city's official guest house for VIPs; it housed both Napoléon and Richard Wagner during their sojourns here.

Neues Rathaus on Burgplatz was erected on the site of the old Pleissenburg, the citadel where Martin Luther held a momentous disputation in 1519. The best place in Leipzig to go people-watching is on **Peterstrasse,** below Markt.

THE TOP ATTRACTIONS

✪ **Thomaskirche (St. Thomas Church).** Thomaskirchhof 18 (just off Marktplatz). ☎ **0341/9-60-28-55.** Free admission. Apr–Oct daily 8am–6pm, Nov–Mar daily 9am–5pm. Tram: 4, 6, 8, 10, 11, or 13.

Leipzig's most famous resident, Johann Sebastian Bach (1685–1750) was cantor here from 1723 until his death. He spent his most creative years as choirmaster at this church, and is buried just in front of the altar. Both Mozart and Mendelssohn performed in the Thomaskirche as well, and Richard Wagner was christened here in 1813. The church was built on the site of a 13th-century monastery, and was heavily restored after World War II. Its high-pitched roof dates from 1496. The city's Thomaner Choir presents concerts every Sunday morning and Friday evening, when it's in residence—the choir is often on tour.

Altes Rathaus. Markt 1. ☎ **0341/96-51-30.** Admission 5DM ($2.85) adults, 2.50DM ($1.40) children. Tues 2–8pm, Wed–Sun 10am–6pm.

The 16th-century Town Hall stands on the 12th-century Renaissance Markt. Allied bombs rained down on the building, but it has been carefully restored. Inside, you'll find the Stadtgeschichtliches Museum, chronicling the city's history, both cultural and political.

Leipzig

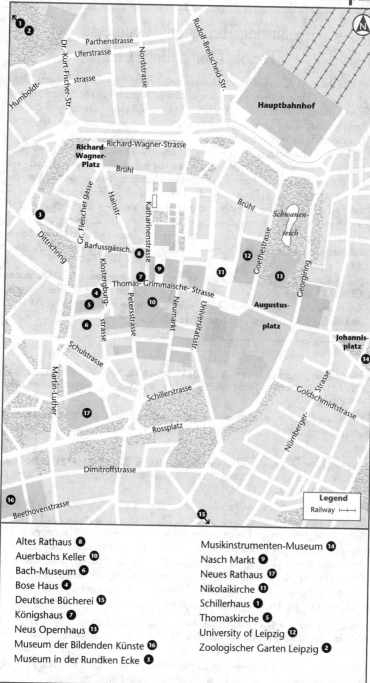

Altes Rathaus **8**

Auerbachs Keller **10**

Bach-Museum **6**

Bose Haus **4**

Deutsche Bücherei **15**

Königshaus **7**

Neus Opernhaus **13**

Museum der Bildenden Künste **16**

Museum in der Rundken Ecke **3**

Musikinstrumenten-Museum **14**

Nasch Markt **9**

Neues Rathaus **17**

Nikolaikirche **11**

Schillerhaus **1**

Thomaskirche **5**

University of Leipzig **12**

Zoologischer Garten Leipzig **2**

Singing Through the Centuries: The St. Thomas Boys' Choir

While the Boys' Choir of Vienna gained worldwide fame, the St. Thomas Choir of Leipzig (Thomasknabenchor) languished in obscurity in the eastern zone in recent times. Now all that is changing. Any musical expert can tell you that the Leipzig choir has plenty of talent, and as it tours more and more widely in Europe, its fame will no doubt grow.

The choir has been here since the 13th century. The boys sang on every occasion in the Middle Ages—city celebrations, the installation of bishops, and even executions. Today, members of the choir still follow an almost medieval regime within a distinctive subculture that's a world unto itself. Each newcomer is assigned a "mentor" from among the trusted older members of the choir, and all members are required to eat, sleep, study, and rehearse according to a semi-monastic regimen. The most famous member was none other than Johann Sebastian Bach. He wrote his great cantatas for this choir and was cantor (choirmaster) for 27 years.

The setting for this venerable musical force is the **Thomaskirche (St. Thomas Church),** whose severely dignified walls have been restored after wartime destruction. Mozart and Felix Mendelssohn both performed their works here, and Richard Wagner was christened here in 1813.

Bach-Museum. Thomaskirchhof 16. ☎ **0341/96-44-10.** Admission 4DM ($2.30) adults, 2.50DM ($1.40) children, 10DM ($5.70) family ticket. Daily 10am–5pm. Guided tours at 11am and 3pm.

This museum stands in the shadow of the Thomaskirche. It contains the largest collection of Bach archives in Germany. Many mementos of the composer are also found here.

Museum der Bildenden Künste. Grimmaische Strasse 1–7. ☎ **0341/21-69-90.** Admission 5DM ($2.85) adults, 2.50DM ($1.40) children. Tues and Thurs–Sun 10am–6pm, Wed 1–10pm. Tram: 4, 6, 8, 10, 11, 13, 15, or 20.

The 2,500 paintings and sculptures in this museum of art include works by Dürer, Rubens, Rembrandt, Rodin, and van Eyck. The building was constructed in 1888 as the home of the Supreme Court of the Reich and changed into a museum in 1952. One section displays exhibits relating the story of Georgi Dimitroff, once head of the Communist party in Bulgaria. Hitler accused Dimitroff and other Communist leaders of responsibility for the Reichstag fire. Hermann Goering himself interrogated Dimitroff, but the trial in Leipzig resulted in an acquittal. In the carefully preserved courtroom, tapes of the Reichstag trial are played (in German).

Museum in der Runden Ecke. Dittrichring 24 (north of Thomaskirche). ☎ **0341/96-12-44-3.** Free admission. Wed–Sun 2–6pm. Tram: 1, 2, 4, 6, 15, 17, 21, or 24 to Goerderlerring or Thomaskirche.

This museum, one of Leipzig's newest, could hardly have been imagined a few years ago. The building was the headquarters of the dreaded Stasi, the East German Ministry for State Security. One exhibition, called "The Power and Banality of the East German Secret Police," documents the meticulous and paranoid methods by which the police monitored every exchange of information in the country. They constantly seized private letters and listened in on phone conversations—at times monitoring up to 2,000 calls at once. The exhibition also traces the steps local people took to throw off the Communist regime and end Stasi terror. On the nights of December 4 and 5, 1989, local citizens seized the building. Leipzig is called *Heldenstadt,* or "city of heroes," for its role in toppling the government of East Germany.

Musikinstrumenten-Museum (Museum of Musical Instruments). University of Leipzig, Täubschenweg 2C. ☎ **0341/21420.** Admission 5DM ($2.85) adults, 2DM ($1.15) children. Tues–Sat 10am–5pm, Sun 10am–2pm. Tram: 4, 6, 15, or 20.

This museum exhibits musical instruments, chiefly Italian, German, and French treasures of the 16th to the 19th centuries. You might be able to attend one of the occasional performances, when the historical instruments are played.

Schillerhaus. Menckestrasse 42, Gohlis. ☎ **0341/5-66-21-70.** Admission 4DM ($2.30) adults, 1DM (55¢) children. Oct–Apr Tues–Wed and Fri 10am–5pm, Thurs 10am–4pm, Sat 11am–5pm; May–Sept Tues–Sun 11am–6pm. Tram: 6, 20 or 24.

In this small farmhouse in Gohlis, a suburb about 20 minutes from the center of Leipzig, Johann Christoph Friedrich von Schiller, the greatest name after Goethe in German literature, wrote his "Ode to Joy" in 1785. Beethoven incorporated the poem into the great final movement of his Ninth Symphony.

Zoologischer Garten Leipzig. Pfaffendorfer-Strasse 29. ☎ **0341/5-93-35-00.** Admission 11DM ($6.25) adults, 6DM ($3.40) children and students. Nov–Mar daily 9am–5pm; Apr and Oct daily 9am–6pm; May–Sept daily 9am–7pm. Tram: 20 or 24.

This zoo breeds animals to help conserve endangered species. It was founded in 1878 and is internationally known for the breeding of carnivores. The biggest aquarium in eastern Germany is also here.

MORE SIGHTS & ACTIVITIES

This city has long been closely linked with the names of eminent personages. The reconstructed **Bose House** (☎ **0341/964-4135**) was once the home of the Bach family and is now a Bach museum. Open daily 10am to 5pm; admission is 4DM ($2.30). The German Museum of Books and Scripts, the **Deutsche Bücherei,** Deutscher Platz 1 (☎ **0341/2-27-12-23**), is the central archive of German literature. You can visit it free, but only with special permission, Monday to Saturday from 9am to 4pm. The archive was established in 1912 to showcase the fine art of German printing and bookbinding. It's said to possess every item of German literature ever published. It also has a copy of *Iskra,* the Bolshevik newspaper that Lenin came here to print secretly in 1900. Take tram no. 21.

Contrary to popular belief, Thomaskirche isn't the oldest church in Leipzig. That distinction belongs to **Nikolaikirche,** on Nikolaistrasse, erected in 1165. Many works by Bach, including the *St. John Passion,* were first performed here.

If the weather is fair, head for the **Leipzig University Tower,** near Nikolaikirche. This metal and glass tower overlooks street performers who take over on summer weekends. It's the greatest free show in Leipzig. (Well, not exactly free—the performers will pass the hat at the end of their acts.) Just beware of the skateboard warriors, who make walking about a bit perilous. The **Universität Leipzig,** founded in 1409, has contributed greatly to the cultural growth of the city. The East German government rechristened it Karl Marx University, but the old name was restored in 1990. **Augustplatz** is the ideal center to rub elbows with the thousands of students who study at Leipzig.

To escape the fumes and noise of the city, head for such "green lungs" as **Johanna-park** on Karl-Tauchnitzstrasse, or one of the wildly overgrown cemeteries by the **Völk-erschlachdenkmai.** On hot days, the fountains in **Sachsenplatz** often become a spectacle of pasty white skin splashing about.

SHOPPING   Leipzig has emerged as the art-buying capital of the former East Germany. Galleries hold rich inventories of paintings and sculpture by artists whose works were once unknown to western consumers. **Galerie für Zeitgenössische Kunst,** Karl Tauchnitz Strasse 11 (☎ **0341/140-810**) displays international art, showing about 14 exhibitions a year. It also charges admission: 5DM ($2.85) for adults, 3DM ($1.70) for students and children (free for those 10 and under). Other good galleries include **ARTCO Galerie für Zeitgenössische Kunst,** Ferdinand Rhodestrasse 14 (☎ **0341/ 960-38-51**); **Galerie Eigen Art,** Barfussgassen 2–8 (☎ **0341/960-78-86**); and **Galerie Michael Beck,** Gottschedstrasse 12 (☎ **0341/862-25-50**).

If you're looking for examples of the antique furniture and art objects that many Leipziegers have dragged down from their attics since reunification, head for any of the dozen or so antiques dealers conducting business within the town's core. Antiques shops catering to walk-in clients include **Musik-Antiquariat,** Thomaskirchhof 15 (☎ **0341/960-48-63**), which is devoted entirely to musical instruments; **H. Beier,** Nikolaistrasse 55 (☎ 0341/960-1038); and **Zentralantiquariat Leipzig GmbH,** at Talstrasse 29 (☎ **0341/216-170**).

WHERE TO STAY

Holiday Inn Garden Court. Rudolf-Breitscheid-Strasse 3 (opposite the main station), 04105 Leipzig. ☎ **0341/1-25-10.** Fax 0341/12-51-10-0. www.holiday-inn.com. 129 units. A/C MINIBAR TV TEL. 139DM–250DM ($79.25–$142.50) double; 200DM–250DM ($114–$142.50) suite. Rates include buffet breakfast. AE, CB, DC, MC, V. Parking 15DM ($8.55). Tram: 11, 15, 16, or 28.

Although this hotel is a top choice, it still ranks below the Inter-Continental. Rooms are brightly decorated and well-furnished, with cherry-wood desks. Each has a safe, satellite TV, and VCR. No-smoking rooms are available. The public rooms are brightly decorated with original and limited-edition prints by Peter Kuckei, a fascinating and internationally acclaimed artist.

Dining/Diversions: The hotel has one of the best restaurants in the area, with a chef who vows he "will not tolerate monotony." He offers a richly varied cuisine, with a focus on local delicacies and produce.

Amenities: Room service, hair dryers, laundry, baby-sitting; health club with sauna, steam bath, and workout equipment.

Inter-Continental Leipzig. Gerberstrasse 15 (5 min. from Altes Rathaus), 04105 Leipzig. ☎ **800/327-0200** in the U.S. and Canada, or 0341/98-80. Fax 0341/9-88-12-29. www.interconti.com. E-mail: leipziginterconti.com. 468 units. MINIBAR TV TEL. 290DM–410DM ($165.30–$233.70) double; from 550DM ($313.50) suite. Special offers on weekends. AE, CB, DC, MC, V. Parking 20DM ($11.40). S-Bahn: Hauptbahnhof.

This silver-and-concrete high-rise, the city's tallest building, stands today as the finest hotel in Leipzig. It's much improved in the last few years, and now receives guests from all over the world. The lobby is spacious and elegant. Rooms are comfortably furnished, with marble bathrooms.

Dining/Diversions: The Brühl Restaurant, which contains a piano bar and wine cellar, offers breakfast and à la carte dining in the evening. Low-priced Saxon dishes are served in the Bierstube. The Yamato Restaurant features sushi, sashimi, and teppanyaki. The hotel also has a casino, lobby bar, and cafe lounge.

Amenities: 24-hour room service, hair dryers, same-day laundry, massage, hairdresser, florist, health club with indoor pool, solarium, sauna, fitness machines, two bowling lanes, car-rental desk, business center, beauty salon.

✪ **Kempinski Hotel Fürstenhof.** Tröndlinring 8, 04105 Leipzig. ☎ **800/426-3135** or 0341/14-00. Fax 0341/1-40-37-00. E-mail: reservationlpz@kempinski.com. 92 units. A/C

MINIBAR TV TEL. 390DM–510DM ($222.30–$290.70) double; from 650DM ($370.50) suite. AE, DC, MC, V. Parking 35DM ($19.95). Tram: 15.

This hotel, located in a historic 18th-century building, is the best in Leipzig. Its interior has been redecorated to reflect the building's original, almost-forgotten neoclassical theme. A corps of English and Swedish designers have outfitted the bedrooms in a modern interpretation of neoclassical style. The ballroom (the Serpentinensaal) and a monumental staircase date from the 19th century.

Dining/Diversions: The hotel maintains a good restaurant that serves full breakfast, lunch, and dinner.

Amenities: Concierge, room service, hair dryers, dry cleaning, laundry service, twice-daily maid service, baby-sitting, rock-ringed swimming pool, secretarial services, health club with Jacuzzi and sauna, conference rooms, business center.

Zum Goldener Adler. Portitzer Strasse 10 (in the Sellerhausen district), 04318 Leipzig. ☎ **0341/24-40-00.** Fax 0341/2440084. 20 units. TV TEL. 140DM ($79.80) double, Fri–Sun 160DM ($91.20) double. AE, MC, V. Tram: 6.

This is a good bet for unpretentious, cost-conscious lodging. The hotel is about a mile northeast of Leipzig's center, easily reached by tram or taxi. Bedrooms offer a simple but appealing decor of dark woods and uncomplicated designs. Rooms are small but reasonably comfortable. There's a bar and an unpretentious, sometimes moderately rowdy bistro that specializes in beer, burgers, steaks, wursts, and pastas.

WHERE TO DINE

Alt-Leipzig. Franz List Strasse 16. ☎ **0341/211-8390.** Reservations recommended. Main courses 15DM–28DM ($8.55–$15.95). AE, DC, MC, V. Daily 11am–midnight. GERMAN.

Because of its old-world decor, you might think this place is more ancient than it is. Within its cozy premises, you can drink foaming mugs of beer, select from a list of German wines, and order from a tried-and-true menu, with items such as roulades of beef, wursts, schnitzels, trout with almonds, roasts, and fried fillets of flounder with tartar sauce.

Apels Garten. Kolonnadenstrasse 2. ☎ **0341/9-60-77-77.** Reservations recommended. Main courses 15DM–30DM ($8.55–$17.10); fixed-price menus 28DM–40DM ($15.95–$22.80). AE, MC, V. Mon–Sat 11:30am–midnight, Sun 11:30am–3:30pm. Tram: 4, 6, 8, 10, 11, or 13. GERMAN.

Its name commemorates the site of a 400-year-old garden, no longer in existence. Today you'll find a modern mid-1980s building with a conservatively decorated street-level restaurant known for its home-style German food. Specialties include wild-duck soup with homemade noodles, roast goose with potatoes and vegetables, grilled wurst with potatoes and red cabbage, and sauerbraten with onions and red cabbage. The cuisine is more robust than refined, but it's very filling.

✪ **Auerbachs Keller.** Mädler Passage (off the market square, close to the Altes Rathaus), Grimmaischestrasse 2–4. ☎ **0341/21-61-00.** Reservations recommended. Historic Rooms, main courses 30DM–40DM ($17.10–$22.80); fixed-price menu 89DM ($50.75). Big Room, main courses 18DM–35DM ($10.25–$19.95). AE, MC, V. Historic Rooms Mon–Sat 6pm–midnight. Big Room daily 11:30am–midnight. S-Bahn: Hauptbahnhof. GERMAN/INTERNATIONAL.

Many visitors to Leipzig eat at their hotels. However, we suggest that you escape for at least 1 night to dine at the famous Auerbachs Keller, the restaurant and tavern where Goethe staged the debate between Faust and Mephistopheles in his play *Faust*. The cellar dates from 1530 and has a series of murals from the 16th century representing the *Faust* legend. The chefs prepare mainly regional cuisine of Saxony, along with a selection of international dishes. Some of the most tempting offerings are fillet of veal, beef, or saddle of lamb, prepared with special sauces and served with seasonal vegetables. The menu changes every 2 months. You can also order from a fine selection of wines and beers. Guests have a choice of dining in the Historic Rooms (dinner only) or in the Big Room, which has a different menu.

Between 11:30am and 6pm, Monday to Saturday, visitors can see the Historic Rooms for a charge of 1.50DM (85¢).

Paulaner Palais. Klostergasse 3–5. ☎ **0341/2-11-31-15.** Reservations recommended, especially Mon–Fri. Main courses 15DM–29DM ($8.55–$16.55). AE, DC, MC, V. Daily 11am–11pm. GERMAN/BAVARIAN/AUSTRIAN.

This large restaurant is on the street level of a fine rococo 18th-century building. One section is decorated like a typical Bavarian inn; others are dedicated to the style of Meissen (known for porcelain), Leipzig itself, and Sans Souci (known for rococo extravagance). More seats are in a summer courtyard. A continental cuisine is served. Although there's an excessive emphasis on boiled meats such as *Tafelspitz* (beef) and heavy sauces, the place remains an enduring local favorite. Wiener schnitzel and braised veal shank are two of the chef's other specialties. Foaming mugs of only one kind of beer are served: Paulaner Bier, brewed in Munich, the hometown of the owner.

LEIPZIG AFTER DARK

Leipzig's active nightlife offers something for everyone. The area around the Markt is full of bars, cafes, and other entertainment options; it's a good place to kick off your search for a nightspot.

THE PERFORMING ARTS　The **Leipzieger Oper** is one of Germany's most acclaimed opera companies. Its home is the **Neues Opernhaus,** 8 Augustus-Platz (☎ **0341/126-12-61**), opposite Das Gewandhaus (see below). The box office is open Monday to Friday from 10am to 8pm, and Saturday from 10am to 4pm. Tickets range from 18DM to 60DM ($10.25 to $34.20), with students getting up to one-third off, depending on the performance. The smaller **Kellertheater** (☎ **0341/1261261**) presents small ensemble progressive performances of all types. Call the box office for information.

The home of the famous ✪ **Gewandhaus Orchestra** is a modern concert hall built in 1981, **Das Gewandhaus** (☎ **0341/1-27-02-80**), which faces the Neues Opernhaus across Augustus-Platz. Founded in 1781, the orchestra saw some of its greatest days under the baton of Felix Mendelssohn, who died in Leipzig in 1847. Other notable conductors have included Wilhelm Furtwängler, Bruno Walter, and Kurt Masur. Concerts, ballets, organ recitals, and other events are staged here. Tickets range from 25DM to 70DM ($14.25 to $39.90) Tram: 4, 5, 12, 13, or 15.

The main theater is the **Schauspielhaus,** Bosestrasse 1 (☎ **0341/12680**), home to several arts companies which jointly stage an eclectic mix of theatrical and musical productions. Tickets cost from 20DM to 50DM ($11.40 to $28.50), and are half-price for students. The box office is open weekdays from 10am to 6pm, Saturday from 10am to 1pm, and 1 hour before show time.

BARS　On the street level of the Auerbachskeller is the **Mephisto Bar,** Mädlerpassage (☎ **0341/216100**), which honors Goethe and the Faust legend. It is also happens to be the hippest bar and cafe in Leipzig, and the best seat for people-watching in the historic core.

Within a decor whose colors (black, red, orange, and green) emulate the fires of hell, you can sit at cramped tables, stand amid the crowd of trendies, and sip cocktails, beer, or wine, or order simple platters such as Camembert with grapes, soups, salads, or pâtés with toast. The most popular cocktail is the "Mephisto Feuer" (Satan's fire), made from a combination of schnapps, orange juice, and sekt. There's live music presented, without a cover charge, usually Thursday through Saturday, beginning around 8pm. Open daily 1pm to midnight.

Another favorite Leipzig watering hole is the **Letterman Bar,** Gottsched Strasse 1 (☎ **0341/961-1293**), which is laid back and appealingly but discreetly permissive.

DANCE CLUBS **Tanzpalast,** Bosestrasse 1 (☎ **0341/960-05-96**), features three discos and seven bars. On the terrace, steaks and barbecue are served. There's live music Wednesday and Friday. The place opens nightly at 11pm and might close anytime between from 4 to 10am. The cover is 5DM ($2.85). Leipzig's newest and trendiest disco is **Distillery,** Kurt Eisner Strasse, at the corner of Lösmiger Strasse (☎ **0341/963-8211**). The cutting-edge scene here resembles Berlin or Hamburg more than staid eastern Germany. It's open Friday 11pm to 6am, Saturday 11pm to 9am. The cover is 8DM ($4.55) on Friday and 10DM to 15DM ($5.70 to $8.55) on Saturday.

LIVE MUSIC Built against the old city wall, **Moritzbastei,** Universitätsstrasse 9 (☎ **0341/702590**), is an all-in-one complex that houses three music halls, a pub with six bars, and a cafe. It's popular with students. On Wednesday, Friday, and Saturday evenings, DJs play African, heavy metal, and rock mixed with contemporary dance music from 8pm to 5am; the cover is 4DM to 10DM ($2.30 to $5.70). Other nights, live bands play jazz and blues, and the cover ranges from 10DM to 25DM ($5.70 to $14.25). During the summer, foreign movies are shown on the roof for 10DM ($5.70). The place also serves a buffet dinner that costs 4DM to 10DM ($2.30 to $5.70) per person. Open 10am until midnight, or until 5am on dance nights.

For more blues, jazz, and the occasional presentation of German-language satire and cabaret, head to **Pfeffermühle,** Thomaskirchhof 16 (☎ **0341/960-31-96**), on Monday night, when the bands start up at 10pm. Other nights, people gather to drink and talk. The courtyard here is very popular during warm weather.

GAY BARS & CLUBS The friendly, ultracool bar **RosaLinde,** Lindenauer Markt 21 (☎ **0341/484-15-11**), is the central focus of gay Leipzig. It's open nightly at 8pm. Come here for a drink and to find out what's happening around town. A gay bar and disco, **Kutsche,** Brandenburger Strasse 9 (☎ **0341/211-43-74**), hosts dancing on Friday and Saturday nights. Other nights, it's a popular drinking spot. The cover on dance nights is 7DM ($4). Night owls come to **Vis à Vis,** Rudolf-Breitscheid-Strasse 33 (☎ **0341/980-37-47**), because it's open around the clock. During the evening, especially between 7pm and 6am, its clientele is predominantly gay.

VARIETY The best cabaret in town, **Gohglmohsch,** Markt 9 (☎ **0341/9-61-51-11**), presents a nightly German-language show of satire and music that can get quite bawdy and extremely critical of the modern German state and the foibles of the bourgeoisie. The cafe here is open daily from 5pm to 3am, and the show starts at 8pm. (Its tongue-in-cheek name, incidentally, translates from a medieval Saxon dialect as "Rubbish.") Tickets cost 25DM ($14.25), but students get discounts of around 17DM ($9.70), depending on the show. **Schaubühne Lindenfels,** Karl-Heine-Strasse 50 (☎ **0341/484620**), offers alternative theater and cinema in a laid-back cafe-bar complex. Open daily from 10am to 1am. Tickets for nightly movies cost 7DM to 9DM ($4 to $5.15). Theater productions, which cost 12DM to 16DM ($6.85 to $9.10), run Thursday to Saturday and sometimes Sunday. Call for information.

SIDE TRIPS FROM LEIPZIG
LUTHERSTADT WITTENBERG

This is the city associated with **Martin Luther,** leader of the German Reformation. It attracts pilgrims from all over the world. Wittenberg's other famous son was humanist

Philipp Melanchthon (1497–1560), a Protestant reformer and scholar and a friend of Luther's and later of Calvin's. Both are honored with statues in front of the Rathaus. Wittenberg is a handsome enough city, but a stop here isn't a must unless you're particularly interested in Luther.

Wittenberg lies 42 miles northeast of Leipzig and 62 miles southwest of Berlin. Access by car is via the A9 Autobahn north and south, Route 187 east, and Highway 2 north and south. The Wittenberg Bahnhof is on the major Deutsche Bundesbahn rail line (Halle-Berlin), with frequent connections. It's an hour by train from Leipzig. For travel information, contact **Wittenberg-Information,** Schloss-strasse 2 (☎ 03491/49-86-10), open Monday to Friday from 9am to 6pm, Saturday from 10am to 2pm, and Sunday from 11am to 3pm.

Both Luther and Melanchthon are buried in the **Schlosskirche,** Friedrichstrasse 1a (☎ 03491/40-25-85), which dates from the 15th century but was rebuilt in the 19th century. It was on the Schlosskirche doors that Luther nailed his "Ninety-Five Theses" in 1517. The bronze doors were added in 1858 and bear the Latin text of the theses. The church is open November through April, Tuesday to Saturday from 10am to 5pm, and Sunday from 11:30am to 5pm; May through October, it's open Monday from 2 to 5pm, Tuesday to Saturday from 10am to 5pm, and Sunday from 11:30am to 5pm. Services are held Sunday at 10am and Wednesday at noon. There's an organ concert every Tuesday at 2:30pm. Admission is free; a guided tour costs 2DM ($1.15).

Part of an Augustinian monastery in which Luther lived has been turned into the **Lutherhalle Wittenberg,** Collegienstrasse 54 (☎ 03491/40-26-71). The parish church here, where Luther preached, dates from the 14th century. An oak tree marks the spot outside the Elster gate where Luther publicly burned his papal bull of excommunication in 1520. It's open November through March, Tuesday to Sunday from 10am to 5pm; April through October, Tuesday to Sunday from 9am to 6pm. Admission is 7DM ($4) for adults, 4DM ($2.30) for students, 2DM ($1.15) for children 7 to 18, and free for children 6 and under.

You can also visit the **Stadtkirche,** Kirchplatz (☎ 03491/40-44-15), where Luther did the majority of his preaching. It's called the "Mother Church of the Reformation." Sections date to the 13th century, making it the oldest structure in Wittenberg. The altar is by Lucas Cranach the Elder, who was once Bürgermeister of Wittenberg and a friend to Luther. It's open Monday to Saturday from 9am to noon and 2 to 5pm and Sunday from 11am to noon and 2 to 5pm. Admission is free.

Where to Stay & Dine

Park Inn. Neustrasse 7–10, 06886 Wittenberg. ☎ **0049/46-10.** Fax 0049/46-12-00. E-mail: plwittenberg@parkhtls.com. 171 units. MINIBAR TV TEL. 140DM–300DM ($79.80–$171) double. Rates include buffet breakfast. AE, CB, DC, DISC, MC, V. Parking 13DM ($7.40).

This is one of the best hotels in town, located in the historic city center on a pedestrian mall. It's often filled in summer with pilgrims coming to pay their respects to Martin Luther. Rooms are comfortable but a bit lackluster, with modern furnishings, compact bathrooms, and rather thin towels. The hotel restaurant serves both regional and international dishes, and there's also a bar.

QUEDLINBURG

In 1994, UNESCO cited Quedlinburg as "an extraordinary example of a medieval European city," and added it to its list of world cultural treasures.

Quedlinburg, which survived World War II intact, is nestled at the foot of a rock pinnacle, and crowned by a castle and an abbey church. It has origins going back to a Saxon settlement in the early 10th century. Here you'll see an architectural masterpiece, the church of St. Servatius, as well as a well-preserved castle and cobbled lanes with half-timbered houses dating from the 16th and 17th centuries.

There are three trains a day from Leipzig (travel time: 3 hr.). Call ☎ **1805/996633** for information and schedules. Access by car is along B6. For tourist information, contact **Quedlinburg-Information,** Markt 2 (☎ **03946/77-30-10**), open May through September, Monday to Friday from 9am to 8pm and Saturday and Sunday from 9am to 6pm; October, March, and April, Monday to Friday from 9am to 6pm and Saturday and Sunday from 10am to 3pm; November through February, Monday to Friday from 9am to 5pm and Saturday and Sunday from 10am to 3pm.

Begin your tour in the **Altstadt (Old Town),** site of the **Markt (Marketplace).** The **Rathaus,** in the Renaissance style of the 1600s, was originally built in 1310. The statue (ca. 1420) on the left of the facade is of Roland, Charlemagne's knight. The buildings on the other three sides of the Markt are from the 1600s and 1700s. Branching off the square are small cobblestone lanes right out of the Middle Ages. The area around Breitstrasse has several colorful alleyways.

Take the ramp up to the castle to the broad terrace that offers a panoramic view of the medieval town. Here, on the site of the original 9th-century church, stands Quedlinburg's major attraction, the **Stiftskirche St. Servatius,** one of the architectural masterpieces of the Romanesque era. The church was started in 1070 but wasn't consecrated until 1129. Craftsmen from northern Italy were imported to create the friezes and capitals above the central nave. Three aisles with diagonal rib vaulting divide the crypt beneath the chancel. The aisles are adorned with frescoes depicting scenes from the Bible.

The church is filled with treasures, including a treasury (Domschatz) with manuscripts from as far back as the 10th century. In 1990, a number of ecclesiastical artifacts that had disappeared from the treasury after the war turned up in Texas, when the heirs of a U.S. Army officer tried to sell them. The purloined art treasures have been returned, after many legal battles, and are now on permanent display. The church is open from May to October, Tuesday to Saturday from 10am to 6pm; off-season, Tuesday to Saturday from 10am to 4pm and on Sunday from noon to 4pm. Admission is 5DM ($2.85) for adults and 3DM ($1.70) for children.

Burgberg Schloss (☎ **03946/27-30**), crowning the hill (Schlossberg), was once part of an abbey. A Saxon stronghold in the 10th century, the castle was expanded from the late 16th to the mid-17th centuries. The castle complex includes the Schlossmuseum, which displays 16th- and 17th-century Italian and Flemish paintings as well as exhibits on the history of the town. A Princes' Hall from the mid-1700s and the throne room can also be visited. The castle is open May through September, Tuesday to Sunday from 10am to 6pm; off-season, Tuesday to Sunday from 10am to 5pm. Admission is 5DM ($2.85) for adults and 3DM ($1.70) for children.

Where to Stay

✪ **Am Brühl.** Billungstrasse 11, 06484 Quedlinburg. ☎ **03946/9-61-80.** Fax 03946/9-61-82-46. 47 units. MINIBAR TV TEL. 170DM–200DM ($96.90–$114) double; 290DM ($165.30) suite. Rates include buffet breakfast. AE, DC, V. Free parking.

This romantic and tranquil hotel is run by the Schmidt family. Some of the bedrooms open onto views of the castle. Bedrooms come in a variety of shapes and sizes, and all are well furnished with first-rate mattresses and fine linens. Virtually all the major attractions are within walking distance. The hotel offers good dining facilities. There's a sauna and a solarium on the premises.

Theophano. Markt 13–14 (on the marketplace), 06484 Quedlinburg. ☎ **03946/9-63-00.** Fax 03946/96-30-36. 22 units. TV TEL. 150DM–240DM ($85.50–$136.80) double. Rates include buffet breakfast. AE, MC, V. Parking 12DM ($6.85).

Two old guild houses, each about 350 years old, were completely renovated and combined into one hotel. Each small bedroom is brightly furnished, individually decorated, and often outfitted with antiques. Some accommodations have canopied beds. The location is central for sightseeing. The hotel's Weinstube is open Monday to Saturday from 6pm to midnight, serving a regional cuisine. In summer, guests can sit in the courtyard.

Zum Goldenen Sonne. Steinweg 11 (a 5-min. walk from the railway station), 06484 Quedlinburg. ☎ **03946/9-62-50.** Fax 03946/96-25-30. www.hotel-glb.de. 27 units. MINIBAR TV TEL. 140DM–170DM ($79.80–$96.90) double. Rates include buffet breakfast. AE, MC, V. Parking 5DM ($2.85).

This hotel, which dates from 1671, is a good traditional choice. It stands near the Mathildenbrunne, a landmark fountain. The building's wood-beam construction is typical of this part of Germany. The small bedrooms are cozily furnished in rustic style. The restaurant serves international and regional cuisine, daily from 11am. In summer, the beer garden is popular with locals and visitors alike.

Where to Dine

Ratskeller. Markt 1 (in the Rathaus). ☎ **03946/27-68.** Reservations recommended. Main courses 18DM–32DM ($10.25–$18.25); fixed-price menu 21DM–36DM ($11.95–$20.50). AE, DC, MC, V. Thurs–Tues 11:30am–10:30pm. Closed Jan. GERMAN/INTERNATIONAL.

This longtime favorite is within walking distance of the railway station. Wine buffs should order the rare Saxon wine. The food is hearty and regional. Many of the meat and game specialties are served with wine sauerkraut and dumplings. In season, venison is likely to be on the menu.

4 Dresden

123 miles S of Berlin, 69 miles SE of Leipzig

Dresden, once known as "Florence on the Elbe," was celebrated throughout Europe for its architecture and art treasures. Then came the night of February 13, 1945, when Allied bombers rained down phosphorus and high-explosive bombs on the city, which had no military targets. By morning, the Dresden of legend was but a memory. No one knows for sure how many people died, but the number is certainly in the tens of thousands, and perhaps more. If you're interested in the subject, you might want to read Kurt Vonnegut's novel *Slaughterhouse Five.*

Today Dresden is undergoing a rapid and dramatic restoration, and is once again a major sightseeing destination. For example, its once-fabled Schloss (castle), for decades only a few blackened walls, is scheduled to be completely rebuilt by the year 2003. Dresden also boasts beautiful churches and palaces, as well as many an array of world-class museums (among the finest in all of Germany); the best is the Zwinger (see "The Major Museums," below).

City officials want the entire city rebuilt by the year 2006 in time for Dresden's 800th anniversary. Even though that dream is a long way from being realized, much has already been accomplished. Thankfully, the work has proceeded along sensible lines, and has none of the unreal, Disney-like feeling that some restorations produce. Wherever you go you will not be allowed to forget the Allied bombings of February 1945, which destroyed about three-quarters of the Altstadt.

Regrettably, the city has recently become a center for neo-Nazi skinheads, who occasionally single out foreigners as targets of attack. Be especially careful walking the streets at night. The area north of the Elbe has seen the most violence.

Dresden

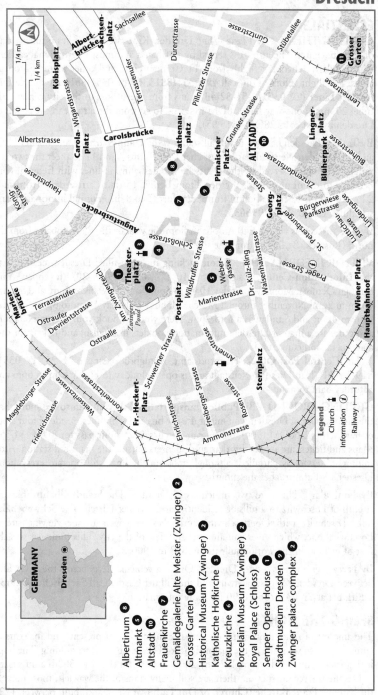

Legend
✝ Church
ⓘ Information
⊢⊢ Railway

GERMANY
Dresden ◉

Albertinum ❽
Altmarkt ❺
Altstadt ❿
Frauenkirche ❼
Gemäldegalerie Alte Meister (Zwinger) ❷
Grosser Garten ⑪
Historical Museum (Zwinger) ❷
Katholische Hofkirche ❸
Kreuzkirche ❻
Porcelain Museum (Zwinger) ❷
Royal Palace (Schloss) ❹
Semper Opera House ❶
Stadtmuseum Dresden ❾
Zwinger palace complex ❷

ESSENTIALS

GETTING THERE By Plane The **Dresden-Klotsche** airport lies 6 miles north of the city center. The airport is served by Lufthansa and most international carriers, with regularly scheduled flights from 11 German cities and other major European cities. For flight information, call ☎ **0351/8813360** or 0351/8810. A shuttle bus, **Airport Liner** (☎ **0351/2-51-82-43**), runs from the airport to the city center (trip time: 20 min.); one-way fare is 8DM ($4.55). To go from the airport to the center of Dresden by taxi costs 28DM ($15.95).

By Train Dresden has two main rail stations, the **Hauptbahnhof**, on Wiener Platz, and the **Dresden-Neustadt**, at Schlesischer Park. Trams 3 and 11 connect the two terminals. The city is served by the Deutsche Bundesbahn rail line, with frequent connections to major and regional cities. From Berlin, 15 trains arrive daily (trip time: 2 hr., 20 min.); 12 trains pull in from Frankfurt (7 to 8 hr.). For rail information and schedules, call ☎ **1805/996633.**

By Car Access is via the E40 Autobahn from the west or the E5 Autobahn from the north (Rostock, Berlin) or from the south.

VISITOR INFORMATION Before tackling museum-filled Dresden, head first to the **Information-Center,** Pragerstrasse 10 (☎ **0351/49-19-20**). It's open April through October, Monday to Friday 10am to 8pm, Saturday 9am to 4pm, and Sunday 10am to 2pm; November through March, Monday to Friday 10am to 6pm, Saturday 9am to 4pm, and Sunday 10am to 2pm. Here you can book your accommodations and purchase a map of Dresden, information booklets in English, and tickets for theater, opera, and concerts.

The **Central Post Office,** Hauptpostamt, Königbrückerstrasse 21–29 (☎ **0351/819-13-70**), is in Dresden-Neustadt and is open Monday to Friday 8am to 6pm and Saturday 8am to noon.

GETTING AROUND By Public Transportation If you plan to see more than the historic core of Dresden, you might use the bus and tram lines. A ride of four stops or fewer costs 1.60DM (90¢), or you can purchase a 24-hour pass for 8DM ($4.55). Maps and tickets are sold at Fahrkarten dispensers outside the main rail station. After midnight, service is curtailed, although most major lines still operate every hour. Dresden's S-Bahn reaches the suburbs.

By Funicular There are two funiculars in Dresden. The **Standseilbahn** links the suburb of Loschwitz to a hillside residential area, Weiber Hirsch. The **Schwebebahn** links Loschwitz with Oberloschwitz, and takes passengers to the viewing site at Loschwitzhöhe, which gives you an excellent view of the city. This funicular was the first of its kind in the world, built from 1898 to 1900.

By Ferry Five ferries service Dresden. One is a vehicular ferry across the River Elbe between Dresden-Kleinzschachwitz and the Pillnitz Castle. Call **Sächsischer Dampf-schiffahrt** at ☎ **0351/86-60-90** for more information.

SEEING THE SIGHTS

The amount of restoration going on here is tremendous. At present, and for years to come, expect to see some of the major sights of Dresden behind scaffolding. The hope is that everything will be completed by 2006, in time for the city's 800th anniversary.

Despite the reconstruction, there are still many ruins of the war left, most notably the baroque **Frauenkirche (Church of Our Lady),** at Neumarkt, built between 1726 and 1743 and once known throughout Europe for its cupola. The East German government deliberately let the blackened hulk remain, as a reminder of the horrors of modern warfare. But today the church is slowly being rebuilt.

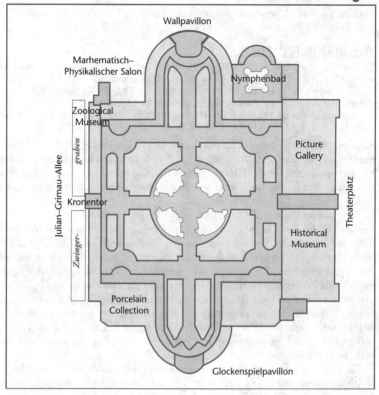

The restored **Katholische Hofkirche** (Catholic Court Church), Schlossplatz (☎ **0351/4992112**), is the biggest church in Saxony. It was built by the son of August the Strong, Frederick Augustus II, who ruled from 1733 to 1763. The church's facade has 38 biblical and historical figures in the high baroque style. Inside, you can see the crypt with the tombs of 49 rulers of Saxony and a box allegedly containing the heart of August the Strong. On the main floor you can see a beautiful stone pulpit by the royal sculptor, Balthasar Permoser (1651–1732), one of the leading sculptors of his time in Saxony. There's also a church organ from the 18th century. Admission is free. This church, which is also known as the Cathedral of St. Trinitas, is open Monday through Saturday from 9am to 5pm, Saturday 10am to 5pm, and Sunday noon to 5pm.

The **Kreuzkirche (Church of the Cross)** stands at the Altmarkt, or old market square. This church is the home of the Kreuzchor, the famous boys' choir of Dresden. Its architecture is a combination of baroque and art nouveau. The present building is from the late 18th century, although a church on this spot stood here as early as the 13th century. You can also view the reconstructed **Rathaus** (town hall) and the 18th-century **Landhaus,** which today contains a minor museum, **Museum für Geschichte der Stadt Dresden** (☎ **0351/498660**), displaying the artifacts of Dresden over the centuries. The museum is open Saturday through Thursday from 10am to 6pm; on Wednesday from May through September, it's open until 8pm. It charges 3DM ($1.70) for admission.

Of Dresden's many parks and gardens, the best and most popular is the **Grosser Garten,** to the southeast of the Altstadt. This park, which was mapped out in 1676, contains a zoo and a botanical garden. In the center is a Lustschloss (pleasure palace) built in 1670.

THE MAJOR MUSEUMS

✪ **Zwinger.** Theaterplatz 1. ☎ **0351/4-91-46-19.** Gemäldegalerie Alte Meister 7DM ($4) adults, 4DM ($2.30) children and senior citizens; Rüstkammer 3DM ($1.70) adults, 2DM ($1.15) children and senior citizens; Porzellansammlung 3DM ($1.70) adults, 2DM ($1.15) children and senior citizens. You may visit all museums for 12DM ($6.85) adults, 7DM ($4) for children and senior citizens. Tues–Sun 10am–6pm. Porzellansammlung closed Thurs also. Tram: 1, 2, 4, 7, 8, 11, 12, or 14 and bus 82, 86, 94 to Postplatz.

Augustus the Strong, elector of Saxony (he was also king of Poland), built this baroque masterpiece, modeled after Versailles, in 1719. Here he staged tournaments and kept his dozens of concubines. His physique was called Herculean, his temperament Rabelaisian, but he also had a great love for the arts. Today this complex of baroque buildings holds a collection of museums.

The Zwinger was initially conceived by M. D. Pöppelmann (1662–1736) as the forecourt of the castle. In the center of the large quadrangle are formal gardens, fountains, and promenades, forming a deep curving bay enclosed by pavilions. Notable are the Wallpavilion in the center of the semicircular arched gallery in the west end, and the Nyphenbad (Bath of Nymphs) with its graceful fountains and mythological figures by Balthasar Permoser, who helped Pöppelmann in the construction of the Zwinger. On the northeast side is a Renaissance-style building, added in 1846 by Gottfried Semper (1803–79). Semper's two-story pavilions are linked by one-story galleries. The architectural critic, Sir Nikolaus Pevsner, once wrote: "What exultation in these rocking curves, and yet what grace! It is joyful but never vulgar; vigorous, boisterous perhaps, but never crude."

The most important museum in the complex is the **Gemäldegalerie Alte Meister,** which has its entrance at Theaterplatz 1. This gallery, one of the best on the continent, has as its showpiece Raphael's *Sistine Madonna.* You'll also find Giorgione's *Sleeping Venus,* Antonello da Messina's *The Martyrdom of St. Sebastian,* Titian's *Tribute Money,* and many famous works by Veronese, Tintoretto, Correggio, and Annibale Carracci. You'll also see Flemish, Dutch, and German paintings by Van Dyck, Vermeer, Dürer, and Rembrandt, among others. The Rubens collection includes his spectacular *Neptune,* full of rearing horses, and an exquisite *St. Jerome.*

A Cruise on the Elbe

You can take a cruise on the historic River Elbe from central moorings below the Brühl Terrace. **Sächsischer Dampfschiffahrt** (☎ 0351/86-60-90) offers a 4½-hour cruise along the Elbe from Dresden to the border of the Czech Republic. These trips take you through some of the finest river scenery in eastern Germany, including an area known as "Swiss Saxony," one of Germany's most popular natural wonders. It's a land of table-shaped outcrops, isolated pillars, deep gorges, and sheer sandstone cliffs. The upper reaches of the Elbe flow in wide curves through these fantastically shaped rock formations. Between April and October, departures are twice daily. The cost of a round-trip is 28DM ($15.95) per person.

Even if you don't make a river trip, it's exciting to watch the boats lower their funnels to pass under the bridges. The *Blaues Wunder* (Blue Wonder), one of Dresden's most celebrated bridges, is a beautiful expression of the bridge-building genius that flourished here at the turn of the century.

The **Porzellansammlung (Porcelain Museum)** holds one of the world's great porcelain collections. Dresden was famous for this form of art; the very first European porcelain was made here in 1707. The swan service here is especially dazzling, as is the parade of Meissen figurines—everything from kings to shepherds, court jesters, and street vendors. Ming and Ching Chinese porcelain is also on display.

The **Rüstkammer (Historical Museum)** displays a collection of weaponry from the 15th to 18th centuries.

✪ **Albertinum.** Brühl Terrace. ☎ **0351/4-91-47-14.** Admission 7DM ($4) adults, 4DM ($2.30) children and students. Fri–Wed 10am–6pm. Tram: 1, 3, 5, 7, or 8 to Rathenau Platz.

This imposing imperial structure houses one of Germany's great galleries. It's named for the Saxon King Albert, who between the years of 1884 and 1887 converted this former royal arsenal into a home for a vast collection of art and precious jewelry from his kingdom. The most famous exhibition is the extraordinary **Grünes Gewölbe (Green Vaults),** a dazzling collection of jewelry and other treasures from the 16th to the 18th centuries: rococo chests, ivory carvings, jewelry, intricately designed mirrors, and priceless porcelain. Many pieces were created by the craftspeople of local guilds; others were acquired from the far corners of the earth.

On the remaining two floors is the **Gemäldegalerie Neue Meister,** a collection of 19th- and 20th-century art, from Corot to Otto Dix. We are especially fond of the desolate and haunting landscapes of Caspar David Friedrich, the German Romantic artist. Impressionists and post-impressionists are well represented, including Gauguin, Degas, Manet, Monet, Corinth, Liebermann, Klimt, and van Gogh. Antifascist artists, whose works were either destroyed or banned in the Nazi era, are also on display.

Stadtmuseum Dresden. Wilsdruffer Strasse 2. ☎ **0351/49-86-60.** Admission 4DM ($2.30) adults, 2DM ($1.15) children. Sat–Thurs 10am–6pm. Tram: 3 or 5.

This museum contains a rich display of Dresden's history. Especially fascinating are the photographs of the controversial 1945 Allied bombings. Most Germans view the air raids as pointless destruction; one British historian claims they were "Churchill's revenge for the Nazi bombing of the civilian population of Coventry."

SHOPPING

Perhaps because of Dresden's destruction in the final days of World War II, there's an emphasis here on collecting the high-quality antiques that remain. You'll find many antiques dealers in the city. Most of the inventory has been culled from homes and estate sales in the relatively unscathed surrounding hamlets. Some of the most appealing shops line either side of a lane called **Am Goldenen Reiter,** accessible via Hauptstrasse 17–19. Here, look for a roster of handcrafted goods and gift items. If you're seeking antiques and artwork, pay a visit to **Antikitäten und Kunst,** Obergraben 19 (☎ **0351/801-4331**), and its similarly named competitor, **Kunst und Antikitäten,** Görlitzerstrasse 39 (☎ **0351/804-5658**). An especially convenient antique gallery is **Antikitäten,** on the lobby level of the Kempinski Hotel Taschenbergpalais, Am Taschenberg (☎ **0351/490-1519**).

The oldest manufacturer of porcelain in Dresden is **Wehsener Porzellan,** 3 miles southeast of the center at Donaustrasse 72 (☎ **0351/470-73-40**). Its hand-painted objects are the most charming and interesting in Dresden. Anything you buy can be shipped. You can also take a free tour of the studios and factory.

And don't overlook the city's role as a purveyor of modern painting and sculpture. Two of the most interesting art galleries are **Galerie Gebrüder Lehmann,** Gorlitzerstrasse 21 (☎ **0351/801-1783**), and **Galerie am Blauen Wünder,** Pillnitzer Landstrasse 2 (☎ **0351/268-40-20**).

WHERE TO STAY

Since reunification and the amazing increase in tourism, Dresden's hotel prices have soared, as has the demand for rooms. Even so-called "budget" hotels can command 250DM ($142.50) a night for a double.

VERY EXPENSIVE

✪ **Kempinski Hotel Taschenbergpalais.** Am Taschenberg, 01067 Dresden. ☎ **0351/4-91-20.** Fax 0351/4-91-28-12. www.lhw.com/dresden/taschenmbergpalais.html. 213 units. A/C MINIBAR TV TEL. 460DM–580DM ($262.20–$330.60) double; from 630DM ($359.10) suite. AE, DC, MC, V. Parking 2DM ($1.15). Tram: 5 or 8.

Few hotels of post-reunification Germany have sparked as much pride among local citizens as this one. Its history dates from the early 18th century, when the elector of Saxony (and king of Poland) built a baroque castle for his favorite mistress, the Countess Cosel, who for mysterious reasons was later banished from his court. For 250 years, the palace was the pride of Dresden, a site visited almost as much as the Zwinger. But Allied bombing raids left it a smoldering ruin. Only the surreal remains of a massive marble staircase survived.

In 1993, a Frankfurt-based real-estate developer spent $175 million on transforming the ruin into Dresden's finest hotel, restoring the five-story baroque, sculpture-dotted facade to its original opulence. The bedrooms here are the most opulent in town. Rooms on the west and north sides overlook the Zwinger or the Opera. The bathrooms are quite opulent as well, with black granite surfaces, heated floors, heated racks of plush towels, robes, hair dryers, and both tubs and shower stalls. Today, a tiny ruined portion of the structure has been artfully retained as a reminder of the bombs of 1945.

Dining/Diversions: A restaurant, the Intermezzo, overlooks the hotel's garden-style courtyard. It serves some of the finest meals in Dresden. There's also a piano bar.

Amenities: Health club with swimming pool and sauna, concierge, 24-hour room service, twice-daily maid service; dry cleaning, laundry, in-room massage, baby-sitting, and secretarial services are all available at an additional charge.

EXPENSIVE

✪ **Bülow Residenz.** Rähnitzgasse 19 (near the Opera), 01097 Dresden. ☎ **0351/8-00-30.** Fax 0351/8-00-31-00. www.buelow-residenz.de. E-mail: info@buelow-residenz.de. 30 units. MINIBAR TV TEL. 370DM ($210.90) double; 460DM–600DM ($262.20–$342) suite. AE, DC, MC, V. Parking 15DM ($8.55). Tram: 6, 7, 8, or 9.

This hotel, with a restored facade from the 1700s, has been a success since its opening in the early 90s. The art-deco lounge, with its plush seating, sets the tone. A garden patio is the perfect place to be on a summer day. Individually decorated bedrooms are unusually spacious, compared to most in Dresden. Oversize beds and contemporary redwood furnishings, along with soothing pastels, make for a restful ambience. The marble bathrooms have hair dryers, gold-plated fixtures, and sandals.

Dining/Diversions: The hotel restaurant serves exceptional meals, specializing in regional, British, and various international dishes.

Amenities: Concierge, dry cleaning, laundry, twice-daily maid service, and baby-sitting.

✪ **Dresden Hilton.** An der Frauenkirche 5, 01067 Dresden. ☎ **800/445-8667** in the U.S. and Canada, or 0351/8-64-20. Fax 0351/8-64-27-25. www.hilton.com. E-mail: dresden-hilton@e-online.de. 345 units. MINIBAR TV TEL. 410DM–445DM ($233.70–$253.65) double; 750DM–900DM ($427.50–$513) suite. AE, DC, MC, V. Parking 25DM ($14.25). Tram: 3, 5, 7, 8, or 12.

This hotel is one of the best in the region. Its conservative mansard-roofed facade blends harmoniously with the baroque buildings on the nearby Neumarkt. A glassed-in passageway connects the hotel to a 19th-century building, the Sekundogenitur, which contains two restaurants and an array of banqueting and conference rooms. Guest rooms are mid-sized and short on style, but well maintained. Baths are small, and have hair dryers. Double-glazed windows cut down on the noise. The rooms facing the Frauenkirche are the best.

Dining/Diversions: There are 11 restaurants and cafes. The Rossini is recommended in "Where to Dine," below; others include a bistro, a Bierclub, a Viennese coffeehouse, and a Saxon-style wine cellar.

Amenities: Concierge (to arrange city tours), room service (6am to midnight), laundry, baby-sitting, fitness club (with pool, whirlpool, sauna, and solarium).

✪ **Villa Emma.** Stechgrundstrasse 2, 01324 Dresden. ☎ **0351/26-48-10.** Fax 0351/ 2-64-81-18. www.prima-hotels.com/gdresden.htm. 21 units. TV TEL. 310DM–450DM ($176.70–$256.50) double. Rates include buffet breakfast. AE, DC, MC, V. Tram: 11.

This special boutique hotel is the best place for those who don't want to stay at the big chain hotels. It lies 5½ miles east of the city center in a forest park of oak, beach, and birch, ideal for walking or jogging. In many ways it has more grace and charm than the highly rated Bülow Residenz. The house is styled with art-deco touches, and rooms are spacious and well lit. The sunny bedrooms are extremely luxurious, with custommade furnishings and even some original stained-glass windows. The bathrooms have massaging showerheads. Amenities include room service, dry cleaning, laundry service, and a sauna. There's also a good restaurant on the premises.

Westin Bellevue. Grosse Meissner Strasse 15, 01097 Dresden. ☎ **0351/8050.** Fax 0351/8051609. www.westin.com. 344 units. MINIBAR TV TEL. 240DM–454DM ($136.80–$258.80) double; from 400DM ($228) suite. AE, DC, MC, V. Parking 20DM ($11.40). Tram: 4 or 5.

The Bellevue stands by the most attractive part of the Elbe. If you look out the hotel's windows or from its terraces to the opposite riverbank, you'll know you're in the spot where Canaletto painted his magnificent scenes. The ornate walls of a pair of courtyards that survived the 1945 bombings have been integrated into the structure; they're now a protected monument. Some rooms overlook these courtyards; others are in modern wings that often open onto the Elbe. Whether you stay in the old part of the building or in the new, you'll find well-appointed, air-conditioned rooms with armchairs. The bathrooms, however, are far from grand, with cheap wall coverings and inadequate towels. All rooms offer better views than those of the Hilton.

Dining/Diversions: Five eating places offer a variety of cuisines, together with consistently good service. Guests can enjoy drinks in the foyer bar.

Amenities: Room service, laundry, baby-sitting, shopping arcade, fitness club with indoor pool, solarium, "bronzarium," and saunas.

MODERATE

Hotel Coventry. Hülsestrasse 1, 01237, Dresden-Altreick. ☎ **0351/28260.** 53 units. MINIBAR TV TEL. 150DM–180DM ($85.50–$102.60) double; 210DM–250DM ($119.70–$142.50) suite. AE, MC, V. Take the train from the Alstadt Hauptbahnhof for 2 miles southwest to the suburb of Altreick, or take trams 9 or 13 to the Hülsestrasse stop.

This inviting new four-story hotel is in the suburb of Altreick, about a 20-minute drive from the city center. The location may seem far flung, but it's an easy trip to the center, and many visitors prefer the tranquillity of the place. Bedrooms are comfortable, cozy, and artfully decorated with a soothing, modern simplicity. Many of the units open onto balconies. The in-house restaurant, Coventry Gardens, is a real gem. There's also a piano bar.

Martha Hospiz. Nieritzstrasse 11, 01097 Dresden-Neustadt. ☎ **0351/8-17-60.** Fax 0351/176222. 50 units. TV TEL. 190DM–230DM ($108.30–$131.10) double. Rates include buffet breakfast. AE, MC, V. Free parking. Tram: 3, 5, 7, 8, 10, or 11.

This simple but comfortable four-story hotel is a quiet 5-minute walk from the commercial heart of modern Dresden. It's a great value. The conservatively modern guest rooms are spotlessly maintained. Bathrooms are a bit small but neatly organized. The hotel contains few amenities other than its rustic restaurant, Potatocellar.

✪ **Seidler Art'otel.** Ostra-Allee 33, 01067 Dresden. ☎ **0351/4-92-20.** Fax 0351/4-92-27-77. 117 units. MINIBAR TV TEL. 265DM ($151.05) double, 365DM ($208.05) suite. Rates include buffet breakfast. AE, DC, MC, V. Parking 15DM ($8.55). Tram: 8, 9, 11, or 26.

The six floors of this dramatic postmodern hotel are the most self-consciously "arty" of any hotel in Dresden. They were designed by Denis Santachiara, whose work has been heralded in Munich, Milan, New York, and Paris. One floor is an art gallery that focuses on striking contemporary paintings and sculpture by German artists. Bedrooms are warmer and more comfortable than you might expect, with cool neutral colors and lots of carefully crafted wood paneling and trim. There's a sauna on the premises, but only a limited roster of exercise equipment. The staff is very conscious of cutting-edge trends in German cities. The hotel's bar and restaurant is called The Factory.

WHERE TO DINE
EXPENSIVE

✪ **Fischgalerie.** Maxstrasse 2 (a 10-min. walk from both the Zwinger and the Kempinski Hotel). ☎ **0351/4-90-35-06.** Reservations recommended. Main courses 26DM–49.50DM ($14.80–$28.20); fixed-price menus 45.50DM–52.50DM ($25.95–$29.90). AE, MC, V. Tues–Fri noon–3pm, and Tues–Sat 6–11pm. Tram: 8, 9, or 26. SEAFOOD.

This is the best seafood restaurant in town. Its culinary pizzazz stems directly from the chef's experience in upscale restaurants in Berlin and other cities. The interior, with its dramatic lighting, minimalist design, and blue-black color scheme, will remind you of a sophisticated enclave in Milan. There's a small aperitif bar near the entrance, and a theatrical-looking open-view kitchen. Menus change every week, depending on the season, availability of ingredients, and the inspiration of the chef. Fresh seafood dishes might include salmon with fresh spinach and champagne sauce; grilled fillet of zander with red risotto; a combination of scampi with John Dory, served with tomato-flavored *spaghettini;* and crepes stuffed with diced crabmeat. As an appetizer you might try the fresh oysters from Brittany, or marinated herring served with coarsely textured black bread. On Wednesday and Friday nights, there's an assortment of very fresh sushi. Live jazz is presented on the 2nd and 4th Tuesday of each month.

Rossini. In the Dresden Hilton, An der Frauenkirche 5. ☎ **0351/8-64-20.** Main courses 19DM–42DM ($10.85–$23.95); fixed-price menu 57DM–90DM ($32.50–$51.30). AE, DC, MC, V. Daily noon–3pm and 6–11:30pm. Tram: 3, 5, 7, 8, or 12. ITALIAN.

Rossini offers Italian cuisine in a stylish setting, one floor above the lobby of the Dresden Hilton (see above). Menu items might include chicken-liver pâté in marsala wine, a buffet of Sicilian antipasti, carpaccio of swordfish marinated in marsala vinaigrette, Sicilian-style fish soup, or grilled lamb with anchovy sauce. Dessert might be cassata made with ricotta cheese and candied fruit, or a *granita* (sorbet) of oranges and lemons floating on white wine.

MODERATE

Brauhaus am Waldschlösschen. Am Brauhaus 8B (in the Neustadt district, a mile northeast of the city center). ☎ **0351/811-990.** Reservations not accepted. Main courses 8DM–27DM ($4.55–$15.40). AE, DC, MC, V. Daily 11am–1am. Bus: 92. Tram: 11, 52. GERMAN.

This is a newly built replica of the old-fashioned beer halls and beer gardens that played such an important role in Dresden's past. Around 250 diners and drinkers can cram themselves into a series of dining rooms, and another 800 can be accommodated within the sprawling garden (open April to October) in back. Expect heaping platters of such time-tested Teutonic favorites as roast pork shank, sautéed fish with parsley and onions, schnitzels, soups, wursts, and roasts. Live music, usually from a jazzy pianist, is presented every evening from 6 to 10pm, and on Saturday and Sunday, a full oompah band plays music throughout the afternoon. Beer (Waldschlösschen) is brewed on the premises, and comes in several degrees of darkness.

Kügelgen Haus Restaurant. Hauptstrasse 13. ☎ **0351/8-04-27-91.** Reservations recommended. Main courses 20DM–29DM ($11.40–$16.55). AE, DC, MC, V. Daily 8am–midnight. SAXON/GERMAN.

This restaurant is in the vaulted cellar of a museum devoted to the paintings of three members of the von Kügelgen family, whose portraits and landscapes were important in Germany's romantic age. The kitchen serves up ample portions of such rib-sticking fare as pork cutlets with braised mushrooms and onions, Zigeuner-steak with mushrooms and roast potatoes, and platters of wurst with potatoes and salad. The dining complex also includes a cafe and a little beer bar.

The museum is often ignored by visitors, but the collection upstairs is an interesting diversion. Admission is 5DM ($2.85); it's open Wednesday to Sunday from 10am to 5pm.

INEXPENSIVE

Miguel's. Louisenstrasse 11. ☎ **0351/804-6072.** Reservations not necessary. Crepes 4.50DM–12DM ($2.55–$6.85). No credit cards. Mon–Fri noon–midnight, Sat–Sun 6pm–midnight. Tram: 7, 8. CREPES.

This restaurant is in the Neustadt district of Dresden. The interior resembles a small, cozily decorated living room in a private home. On the walls is an array of contemporary paintings for sale. Most people come just for a drink or two, although the place does a respectable business as an unpretentious creperie. Choices of fillings range from savory (ham, cheese, broccoli, mushrooms) to sweet (chocolate, ice cream, honey). Every Thursday evening beginning at 8pm, the site hosts German-language lectures, usually on some esoteric arts- or history-related issue.

DRESDEN AFTER DARK

Dresden is Saxony's cultural center. There's always a variety of options for nightlife here, whether you're looking for drama, classical concerts, punk-rock shows, dancing, or just a good place to drink.

THE PERFORMING ARTS Between the Elbe River and the Zwinger, on the western side of Theaterplatz, stands the ✪ **Semper Opera House,** Theaterplatz 2 (☎ **0351/49110**). Both Wagner and Weber conducted here. The building was designed by Gottfried Semper, the same architect who mapped out the famous picture gallery in the Zwinger. Restorers have brought the Renaissance-style two-tiered facade and the interior of the building back to life. Careful attention was paid to the replacement of Semper's original paintings and decorations. More importantly, the fine acoustics for which the opera house was known have been reestablished. Good seats can be had for 15DM to 120DM ($8.55 to $68.40). The opera company takes a vacation from mid-July to September. Tram: 1, 2, 4, 7, 8, 11, 12, 14, or 17.

The **Dresden Philharmonic** appears at the **Kulturpalast,** in the Altmarkt (☎ 0351/486-6306). Tickets cost 18DM to 38DM ($10.25 to $21.65). Concerts are also performed in summer in the courtyards of the Zwinger.

For musical theater, come to the **Staats Operette,** Pirnaer Landstrasse 131 (☎ 0351/207-9929), which mainly performs works from the 19th and early 20th centuries. The box office is open Sunday 1 hour before the show, Monday from 11am to 4pm, Tuesday to Friday from 11am to 7pm, and Saturday from 4 to 7pm. Tickets cost 10DM to 34DM ($5.70 to $19.40) each.

The classical stage for drama in the city is **Schauspielhaus,** Postplatz (☎ 0351/4913565), where dramas by Goethe, Schiller, and Shakespeare (in German) are performed. Performances usually start at 7:30pm. The box office is open Monday to Friday from 10am to 6pm, and Saturday and Sunday from 10am to 2pm. Tickets range from 18DM to 24DM ($10.25 to $13.70). The Schauspielhaus box office also handles tickets and inquiries for the **Residenzteater im Schloss,** Schlossplatz (☎ 0351/4913565), a small theater focusing on modern drama and small ensemble pieces. The price of tickets ranges from 18DM to 24DM ($10.25 to $13.70). Both theaters are closed during July and August.

For a family theater experience, check out **Theater Junge Generation,** Meissner Landstrasse 4 (☎ 0351/421-45-67), which interprets Shakespeare and fairy tales in a way that both kids and parents can enjoy. The box office is open Monday to Saturday from 10am to noon, Wednesday from 12 to 6pm, Friday from 2 to 7pm, and 1 hour before performances. Ticket prices range from 10DM to 50DM ($5.70 to $28.50). In summer, some members of the troupe bring their acts outdoors, usually to the courtyard in front of the Staffhof, an imposing building originally intended as a stable.

Tickets for classical concerts, dance, and opera are available from the tourist office or the **Schinkelwache** box office, Theaterplatz (☎ 0351/491-920), a historic building that was originally a guardhouse for the nearby castle.

BARS A small, low-key bar, **Café Hieronymous,** Louisenstrasse 10 (☎ 0351/8-01-17-39), is the place to go if you don't want to deal with intrusive music or patrons. Daily hours are from 7pm to 2am. **Die 100,** Alaunstrasse 100 (☎ 0351/801-3957), is a cheap and trendy drinking place, set in a cellar under a vaulted arch. It's popular with students and artists. Open daily from 5pm to 3am. At **Planwirtschaft,** Louisenstrasse 20 (☎ 0351/801-3187), an upstairs cafe is open from 8am to midnight, but at the downstairs bar, you can drink until 3am on weekends. It doesn't look like much, but **Raskolnikoff,** Böhmische Strasse 34 (☎ 0351/804-5706), is a hip dive with sand-covered floors. Artists, intellectuals, and wanna-bes tend to congregate here. It's open Sunday to Thursday from 10am to 2am and Saturday from 7pm to 2am.

CLUBS A dance club with room for everyone is **DownTown and Groove Station,** Katherinenstrasse 11–13 (☎ 0351/801-18-59). Monday is gay and lesbian night, and on Sunday there's dinner and dancing. Open daily from 9pm "until everybody leaves." The cover is 8DM ($4.55).

Four nights of live music are balanced by three nights of dancing at **Studentklub Barenzwinger,** Bruhlisseher Garten 1 (☎ 0351/4-95-14-09), a club built into a tunnel under the street. But even the discos here, held on Wednesday, Friday, and Saturday, tend to favor big-beat sounds like reggae and heavy metal. The club is open from 8pm until midnight on Tuesday and Thursday, until 3am on Wednesday (if the evening goes well), until 1 or 2am on Friday, and until 3 or 4am on Saturday. On Sunday it holds a bierabend (beer evening), and on Monday there's a concert or movie. The cover is 10DM to 20DM ($5.70 to $11.40) for bands and 5DM to 8DM ($2.85 to $4.55) for the disco. **AZ Conni,** Conradstrasse 18 (☎ **0351/8-02-56-91**), caters to a young crowd. The doors open at 8pm. On Thursday there's a disco and on the weekend usually parties or bands. Cover is 5DM to 8DM ($2.85 to $4.55).

JAZZ   Projekttheater Dresden, Louisenstrasse 47 (☎ **0351/804-30-41**), a publicly funded organization, usually, but not always, gives a live jazz performance at 9pm Tuesday to Sunday, and also maintains separate areas for the presentation of avant-garde films, lectures, and art exhibitions. Don't expect a nightclub-style cabaret, as no drinks are served. Tickets, available at the box office 1 hour before show time, cost 15DM to 20DM ($8.55 to $11.40). Call to see if there is a performance scheduled. All types of jazz bands hit the stage at **Tonne,** Am Brauhaus 3 (☎ **0351/802-6017**), on Friday and Saturday nights, when the music starts at 9pm. Check on other nights for infrequent shows. The club is open daily from 8pm to 1am. Tickets range from 15DM to 25DM ($8.55 to $14.25).

VARIETY   You'll find a wide variety of concert, theater, and dance performances at **Scheune,** Alaunstrasse 36 (☎ **0351/804-55-32**), which also serves drinks and Indian food. It's open Monday to Friday from 4pm to 2am and Saturday and Sunday from 11am to 2pm. The cover charge ranges from 15DM to 25DM ($8.55 to $14.25). A busy and often aggressively promoted cultural complex, **Reisa Efau,** Adlergasse 14 (☎ **0351/866-02-11**), provides several options. It has two rooms where punk and other music shows are held at 9pm nightly for a 10DM ($5.70) cover. A movie theater charges 7DM ($4) for screenings held at 9pm in the summer and 8pm in the winter. The bar on-site is open daily from 11pm to 1am. Finally, gallery space here often hosts one-artist shows; viewing hours are Monday to Thursday from 10am to 6pm, Friday from 5 to 9pm, and Saturday from 2 to 6pm. Also, check to see what's happening at **Theater 50,** Fechtnerstrasse 2 (☎ **0351/8491925**), a loud and usually irreverent cabaret. The entrance fee costs 15DM to 20DM ($8.55 to $11.40), and usually includes the first drink.

A SIDE TRIP TO THE SPREEWALD & SORB COUNTRY

A fascinating side trip, about an hour's drive north of Dresden, is to the history-rich Sorb country of Spreewald (Forest of the Spree), nearly 100 square miles of woodland, pastures, and canals. The flat, water-soaked landscape has an eerie beauty, and legends abound about spirits that inhabit the thick forests. Over a period of at least a thousand years, the people of the region channeled the marshlands into a network of canals, streams, lakes, and irrigation channels, building their houses, barns, and chapels on the high points of otherwise swampy ground. Ethnologists consider this area a distinctive human adaptation to an unlikely landscape, and botanists appreciate the wide diversity of bird and animal life that flourishes in the lush and fertile terrain.

The area is inhabited by the Sorbs, descendants of Slavic tribes who settled here in the 6th century. They speak a language similar to Czech and Polish. Over the years, they have often faced tremendous persecution, but have never succumbed. The Sorbs were targeted by the Nazis, who outlawed their language and killed many of them. It's estimated that there are still 100,000 Sorbs living in Germany, 30,000 of whom inhabit the Spreewald. They grow vegetables and fruit in a protected landscape, using labor-intensive methods even today.

The Spreewald is at its most appealing in early spring and autumn, when the crowds of sightseers depart and a spooky chill descends with the fog over these primeval forests and shallow medieval canals. To get here from Dresden, take Autobahn 13 north until you come to either the first turnoff, to Lübbenau, or the second turnoff, 6 miles farther, to Lübben. From either hamlet, drive toward the port *(Hafen)*. From there, tour companies will take you through the canals via a shallow-draft boat propelled by a long pole, like a Venetian gondola. The guide is often a woman in traditional dress. Several waterside cafes along the canals serve food and drink.

Boat tours cost about 10DM ($5.70) for 3 hours. Your best bet is simply to wander down to the piers near the hamlet's center and hop aboard the next departure. Few people speak English. The boat tour companies operate only between May and early October, with departures scheduled every day between 9am and 4pm. The companies include **Fahrmannsverein Lübben/Spreewald,** Ernst-von-Houwald Damm 16 (☎ 03456/2225), and **Kahnfahrhafen Flottes Rudel,** Eisenbahnstrasse 3 (☎ 03546/8269), both in Lübben; and, in Lübbenau, **Kahn Fahr GmbH,** Dammstrasse (☎ 03542/2225).

If you're interested in paddling around the Spreewald on your own, head for **Bootsverleih Gebauer,** Lindenstrasse, Lübben (☎ 03546/7194), where canoes can be rented for around 20DM ($11.40) an hour. *Note:* The tourist office in Lübben, the main point of departure for most Spreewald cruises, is on Ernst von Houwald Damm 16 (☎ 03546/3090). The tourist office in Lübbenau, a secondary point of departure, is at Am Weg 15 (☎ 03542/3668).

5 Meissen

14 miles NW of Dresden, 108 miles S of Berlin, 53 miles E of Leipzig

This "city of porcelain" is most often visited on a day trip from Dresden, although since reunification it now has suitable accommodations for those who'd like to spend the night and get acquainted with the area.

Meissen lies on both banks of the Elbe, with the Altstadt on the left bank. It's a very old town, dating from A.D. 929. Since 1710, Meissen has been known around the world as the center for the manufacture of Dresden china. The early makers of this so-called "white gold" were virtually held prisoner here, because the princes who ruled the city wanted to keep their secrets to themselves. Today, shoppers can find here the greatest selection of porcelain in all of Germany. However, not wanting to undercut their distributors in such cities as Munich or Berlin, Meissen porcelain manufacturers keep their prices about the same as elsewhere.

ESSENTIALS

GETTING THERE   By Train   Meissen Bahnhof is on the Deutsche Bundesbahn rail line, with frequent connections to Dresden and other major and regional cities. For rail information, call ☎ 1-94-19.

By Bus   Regional buses connecting Dresden with Meissen are operated by **Verkehrsgesellschaft Meissen.** Consult the tourist office in Meissen for a schedule of connections, or ask at the tourist office in Dresden.

By Car   Access is via the E40 Autobahn from Dresden or the E49 from Leipzig.

By Boat   If you're in Dresden in summer, you can go to Meissen by boat in about an hour and enjoy the scenery along the Elbe. The **Sächsischer Dampfschiffahrt** (☎ 0351/86-60-90) leaves on Saturday and Sunday at 9:30am from Dresden's Brühl Terrace, the fortified embankment on the other side of the Hofkirche.

VISITOR INFORMATION   Contact **Tourist-Information Meissen,** Markt 3 (☎ 03521/45-44-70), November through March, Monday to Friday 10am to 5pm and Saturday 10am to 3pm (closed Saturday in January); April through October, Monday to Friday 10am to 6pm and Saturday and Sunday 10am to 3pm.

Wine in Meissen

The terraces of the nearby vineyards in the Elbe Valley produce fine wines, for which Meissen has been known for 1,000 years. Look for the hard-to-obtain Meissner Domherr.

EXPLORING THE TOWN

Towering over the town is the Gothic-style **Dom,** Domplatz 7 (☎ **03521/45-24-90**), one of the smallest cathedrals in Germany, built between 1260 and 1450. Until the year 1400, the bishops of the diocese of Meissen had their seat next to the cathedral. Later, Saxon rulers were buried here, the first in 1428. Inside are works of art, including a painting by Lucas Cranach the Elder, along with rare Meissen porcelain. The cathedral has been Protestant since the 16th century. It's open April through October daily from 9am to 6pm (until 4pm from November through March). Admission is 3.50DM ($2).

Sharing the castle quarter with the cathedral is **Albrechtsburg Castle,** Domplatz 1 (☎ **03521/47-07-10**), where the first Meissen porcelain was made. Construction of the castle began in 1471 and went on intermittently until 1525. From 1710 to 1864 it was the site of the Meissen Porcelain Manufactory. It's open daily from 10am to 6pm; closed January 8 to January 16. Admission is 6DM ($3.40) for adults, 3DM ($1.70) for children 6 to 16, and free for children 5 and under. Guided tours cost 8DM ($4.55) for adults and 5DM ($2.85) for children.

But the prime attraction in town is the ✪ **Porzellan-Manufaktur,** Talstrasse 9 (☎ **03521/46-87-00**). At this factory, you can see how the centuries-old process of making Meissen china is still carried on, using the same traditional designs. Guided tours depart at 30-minute intervals every Monday to Friday from 9am to 4:30pm, and cost 6DM ($3.40) per person. On the premises you can visit the **Porcelain Museum,** with 3,000 pieces, plus the workshop. Admission is 9DM ($5.15) for adults and 6DM ($3.40) for students.

The original factory was established back in 1710, not long after Johann Friedrich Böttger first succeeded in producing fine red stoneware in 1707 and then, in 1708, European white hard-paste porcelain. Böttger, then an apprentice pharmacist, had taken up alchemy and claimed to be able to make gold. When the Elector Augustus the Strong heard about this, he had Böttger put behind bars and ordered him to prove his claim. Böttger labored for many years, eventually producing "white gold," or porcelain. It wasn't long before Meissen porcelain was sought after in every great palace of Germany. The two most famous designers responsible for the classic Meissen motifs were Johann Gregorious Höroldt (1720–55), who produced the renowned blue onion pattern, and Johann Joachim Kändler (1706–75) who created figurines, giant animals, and elegant table services.

SHOPPING   At **Porzellan-Manufaktur** (see above), you can purchase recently crafted, hand-painted porcelain, which the outfit can ship home for you. The staff are experts at packing fragile objects. However, don't expect prices here to be much cheaper than in other German cities. If you're looking for 18th- or 19th-century porcelain (and can afford it), or for antique furniture, bibelots, and artworks, head for **Meissener Antikitäten,** Holweg 4 (☎ **03521/45-37-52**).

WHERE TO STAY

Parkhotel Pannonia Meissen. Hafenstrasse 27 (on the Elbe, directly across the water from the castle), 01662 Meissen. ☎ **03521/7-22-50.** Fax 03521/72-29-04. 101 units. TV TEL. 197DM–232DM ($112.30–$132.25) double; 252DM–312DM ($143.65–$177.85) suite. Rates include buffet breakfast. AE, DC, MC, V. Parking 5DM ($2.85).

For decades, Meissen didn't have a suitable hotel, but this art nouveau villa filled the void in the early '90s. You can request a bedroom in the original villa, although most accommodations are in the more sterile modern annexes. A suite on the top floor under the eaves is perfect for romantic couples. Most of the rooms open onto panoramic vistas.

Dining/Diversions: Both regional specialties and international dishes are served in the dining room. Even if you're not a guest, consider having a meal here. Lunch is served daily from noon to 2pm and dinner daily from 6 to 10pm. The hotel is also the site of frequent chamber-music concerts in the evening.

Amenities: Room service, laundry, baby-sitting, fitness room, sauna, solarium, whirlpool.

WHERE TO DINE

✪ **Vincenz Richter.** An der Frauenkirche 12 (uphill from Meissen's Marktplatz) ☎ **03521/ 45-32-85.** Reservations recommended. Main courses 18DM–40DM ($10.25–$22.80); fixed-price menus 39DM–48DM ($22.25–$27.35). AE, DC, MC, V. Tues–Fri 11am–4pm, Sat 11am–midnight, Sun noon–5pm. SAXON.

This charming, hearty, and traditional restaurant is in a vine-sheathed 1523 building. It has a hardworking, devoted staff and a cozy setting of Germanic charm. The bar stocks an impressive inventory of local wines, while the kitchens serve ample portions of well-flavored Saxon food.

Franconia & the German Danube

The Renaissance swept across all of Germany, but it concentrated its full force on that part of northern Bavaria that had once been a Frankish kingdom. Franconia today holds many of Germany's greatest medieval and Renaissance treasures. Its hillsides are still dotted with well-preserved medieval castles, monasteries, and churches. From the region's feudal cities sprang some of Germany's most significant artists—Albrecht Dürer, Lucas Cranach, Veit Stoss, Adam Krafft, and many others. Today Franconia draws music lovers from all over the world to its annual **Mozart Festival** in Würzburg and **Wagner Festival** in Bayreuth.

Franconia owes much of its beauty to the limestone range along the southern edge of the province. Between these hills and the edge of the Bavarian Forest is the upper **Danube,** which begins about 20 miles from Regensburg. The Danube gradually builds force from the smaller streams flowing out of the Alps and Swabian Jura, and by the time it reaches the Austrian border, at Passau, it's large enough to carry commercial ships and barges. Although not as important to the German economy as the Rhine, the Danube was responsible for the growth of several influential towns.

Franconia's countryside is equally compelling, especially the forest called **Frankenwald.** This scenic region stretches from the Bohemian Forest on the border of the Czech Republic in the east to the fringes of Frankfurt in the west. The most beautiful part is called Frankisches Schweiz, the "Switzerland of Franconia." It's bounded by Bamberg on the west, Bayreuth in the east, and Kulmbach in the north.

OUTDOORS IN FRANCONIA The best **hiking** is found in the northern stretches of the province. Even the Germans themselves, who rush to the Bavarian Alps, often overlook hiking possibilities in this region. It's estimated that there are some 25,000 hiking trails in Franconia. Local tourist officials can provide details of the best hikes in their region. The most trails are found in the largest park in Germany, **Altmühltal Nature Park,** and in the Frankenwald. If you're a serious hiker, consider contacting **Fremdenver-kehrsverbund Franken** at ☎ **0911/26-42-02** for complete information about the hiking trails of Franconia.

Franconia can also be explored by **bike.** At all train stations in the area, you can rent a bike for 12DM ($7.20) per day or for half-price if you have a valid train ticket. Local tourist offices can supply information on the best biking routes. The **Danube Bicycle Path** cuts right through Regensburg; cyclists can ride along its 400 miles from the river's source to Passau. The Regensburg tourist office (see below) is the most helpful source to contact to organize a biking trip. You can even go as far as Vienna. There's also the **Five Rivers Bicycle Path,** a circular route through the valleys of the Danube, Naab, and Vils that takes 3 to 5 days to complete. This path links Regensburg with Amberg and Nürnberg. Maps and further information about these cycling tours can be obtained from the local tourist information offices.

Exploring the Region by Car

Because of its location, **Ulm** is best explored while visiting Augsburg (see chapter 6, "The Romantic Road"). To see the real heart of Franconia, we suggest the following driving route.

Day 1   The traditional start of the Franconia tour is **Bayreuth** (pronounced By-roit), the city of Wagner. It was here that the great musician finally settled, building the Festspielhaus, a theater appropriate for his grand-scale operas. Ever since 1876, hordes of opera buffs from around the world have poured in for the annual Wagner festival, but the cultural scene in Bayreuth makes it a fascinating place to visit at any time of the year.

Day 2   Take B22 40 miles west of Bayreuth to **Bamberg,** one of Germany's great historic cities. The monumental center, where you'll want to spend the most time, is actually a small island in the river. Be sure to check out the cathedral, transitional Gothic in style, and the Diocesan Museum.

Day 3   From Bamberg, take the A73 Autobahn 38 miles south to **Nürnberg,** an easy trip that will leave you time for a full day of sightseeing. Here you can take in the German National Museum, the Albrecht Dürer House, the Kaiserburg, or the St.-Sebaldus-Kirche, consecrated in 1273.

Day 4   From Nürnberg, take the E56 for 62 miles to **Regensburg.** One of the best-preserved cities in Germany, Regensburg has an old quarter that requires half a day to explore. See St. Peter's Cathedral, the Altes Rathaus, and St. Ulrich's Diocesan Museum.

Day 5   For a final look at life along the Danube, continue on E56 to **Passau,** 73 miles southeast of Regensburg. This frontier town, located between Bavaria and Austria, lies at the junction of the Danube, the Ilz, and the Inn Rivers. Spend the day exploring its old town and patrician houses.

1 Bayreuth

143 miles N of Munich, 40 miles E of Bamberg, 57 miles NE of Nürnberg

Bayreuth lies in a wide valley on the upper basin of the Roter Main River. In the town's early years, the counts of Andechs-Meranien gave it the protection of a fortified castle. In the Middle Ages, Bayreuth became the property of the Hohenzollerns and grew into one of the leading centers of this part of Germany. It's now the capital of the district of upper Franconia.

Bayreuth is forever associated with the memory of **Richard Wagner** (1813–83). The town is worth a visit for its baroque and rococo architectural treasures even if you're not interested in its favorite son, but most people come here because it's the annual home of the Wagner opera festival, and the premier location for Wagnerian performance in the world. Bayreuth is "Valhalla" to Wagner enthusiasts.

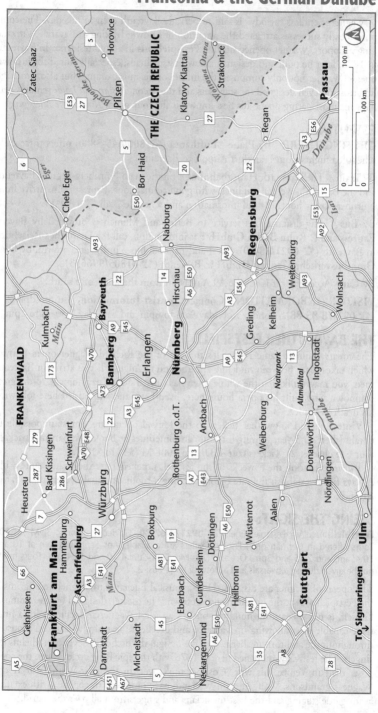

Wagner's "endless melody" is said to pervade Bayreuth even to this day. The composer's early successes attracted the attention of Ludwig II, king of Bavaria. With the king's support, Wagner opened his first **Festspielhaus** in an old residence in Bayreuth in 1876; later he built and designed a new Festspielhaus, especially suited for his own operas. Wagner not only composed the music for his music dramas but also wrote the librettos and even designed the stage sets and the decor. *Tristan and Isolde* remains perhaps his most daring opera; his best known is the four-opera *Ring of the Niebelungs.*

ESSENTIALS

GETTING THERE   By Plane   Lufthansa (☎ 800/645-3880) offers three daily scheduled flights from Frankfurt Airport to Bayreuth.

By Train   The **Bayreuth Hauptbahnhof** is on the main Nürnberg-Pegnitz-Bayreuth and the Bayreuth-Weiden rail lines, with good connections. Express trains arrive from Nürnberg every hour. For rail information and schedules, call ☎ 1-94-19.

By Bus   Long-distance bus service to Berlin and Munich is provided by **Bayern Express** and **P. Kuhn Berlin GmbH.** For information, call the **Deutsches Reisebüro** in Bayreuth (☎ 0921/88-50). Local and regional buses in the area are run by **OVF Omnibusverkehr Franken GmbH** in Bayreuth (☎ 01805/996633).

By Car   Access by car is via the A9 Autobahn from the north and south.

VISITOR INFORMATION   Contact **Tourist-Information,** Luitpoldplatz 9 (☎ 0921/8-85-88), Monday to Friday 9am to 6pm and Saturday 9:30am to 1pm.

THE BAYREUTHER FESTSPIELE

The town's claim to fame is that it's the site of the Richard Wagner opera festival, which takes place between mid-July and the end of August. If you arrive in Bayreuth then, you may think that the whole town has turned out to pay homage to the great composer, who built his opera house here, lived here, and was buried here following his death in Venice.

Visitors should know that tickets to the festival operas are almost impossible to obtain (there's a 5-year waiting list) but can sometimes be booked as part of a package tour (see chapter 2). Tickets cost 40DM to 300DM ($24 to $180).

Warning: During the 5 weeks of the festival, hoteliers raise their rates quite a bit. Always firmly establish the rate before booking a room, and make reservations far in advance.

SEEING THE SIGHTS

Festspielhaus. Am Festspielhügel. ☎ **0921/7-87-80.** Guided tour only, 3DM ($1.80). Tours offered in German only; English leaflets are available. Apr–Sept Tues–Sun at 10 and 10:45am, and 2:15 and 3pm. Oct and Dec–Mar Tues–Sun at 10 and 10:45am. Tours might not be given during rehearsals and at festival time. Bus: 2.

The operas of Wagner are dispensed like a musical Eucharist to Wagnerian pilgrims at the Festspielhaus, at the northern edge of town. The theater, designed by the composer himself, is not a beautiful building, but it's an ideal Wagnerian facility, with a huge stage capable of swallowing up Valhalla, and excellent, beautifully balanced acoustics throughout the auditorium. Because of the design, the orchestra never overwhelms the singers. The festival was opened here in 1876 with the epic Ring cycle. When the composer died in Venice, his wife, Cosima, took over. In the post-World War II era, Wagner's grandsons, Wolfgang and Wieland, have produced the operas, with exciting avant-garde staging and the best musicians and singers from all over the world.

Franz-Liszt-Museum. Wahnfriedstrasse 9. ☎ **0921/7-57-28-18.** Admission 3DM ($1.80). Daily 10am–noon and 2–5pm. Bus: 2 to Villa Wahnfried.

A Woman of Culture

The Margravine Wilhelmine (1709–1758) was Frederick the Great's sister and a life-long friend of Voltaire. She was also one of the most cultivated women of the 18th century. Wilhelmine was in line for the Prussian throne, but instead married the Margrave Friedrich of Brandenburg-Bayreuth, although shortly thereafter decided he was rather dull. ("Margrave" and "Margravine" are titles of nobility similar to Marquess.) She turned her attention to culture and ushered in the most brilliant period in Bayreuth's history, bringing in composers, decorators, writers, and artists. Wilhelmine personally spearheaded a movement that became known as "Bayreuth rococo." This style of architecture, characterized by garlands and flowers, differed markedly from the more rustic French rococo, which was in vogue at the time.

Wagner's father-in-law was Franz Liszt (1811–86), the great Hungarian-born composer and piano virtuoso who revolutionized the technique of piano playing. His daughter, Cosima, married Wagner. Liszt is buried in the Bayreuth cemetery. The museum, which opened on October 22, 1993 (Liszt's birthday), shows the room where the composer died. It also displays memorabilia related to his life and work.

Markgräfliches Opernhaus. Opernstrasse. ☎ **0921/75-96-90.** Guided tours (in German only) 3DM ($1.80) adults, 2DM ($1.20) children. Apr–Sept Tues–Sun 9–11:30am and 1:30–4:30pm; Oct–Mar Tues–Sun 10–11:30am and 1:30–2pm. Bus: 2.

This is the only authentic baroque theater in Germany. It's still in its fine original condition. Behind its weathered wooden doors is a world of gilded canopies and columns, ornate sconces, and chandeliers. The house was built under the auspices of the Margravine Wilhelmine, who was known for her taste and her cultivation of the arts; her name has been given to a special baroque style called *Wilhelmian*. Her brother Frederick the Great formally opened the theater in 1748. Up until that time, operas (notably those of Telemann) had been performed in the court theater.

Today, the opera house, which seats only 520, is used for Bayreuth's "second" festival: the **Franconian Weeks' Festival,** usually held late in May. Concerts are also given during the summer.

Neues Schloss (New Palace). Ludwigstrasse (1 block from the Markgräfliches Opernhaus). ☎ **0921/75-96-90.** Guided tours (in German, with English leaflets available) 5DM ($3) adults, free for children. Tours given Apr–Sept Tues–Sun 10am–noon and 1:30–4:30pm; Oct–Mar Tues–Sun 10am–noon and 1:30–3pm. Bus: 2.

The well-preserved Neues Schloss in the center of town also shows the influence and enlightened taste of the talented and cultured Wilhelmine (1709–1758). This baroque palace dates from the mid-18th century. The apartments of Wilhelmine and her husband, Margrave Friedrich, are decorated in a late-rococo style with period furnishings.

Richard-Wagner-Museum (Wahnfried). Richard-Wagner-Strasse 48 (south of the town center). ☎ **0921/7-57-28-16.** Admission 4DM ($2.40), 5DM ($3) at festival time. Apr–Oct daily 9am–5pm (to 8pm Tues and Thurs). Nov–Mar daily 10am–5pm. Bus: 2.

Wagner lived here from 1874, and the house remained in his family until as recently as 1966. Only the front of the original Wahnfried—which means "illusory peace"—remains intact. On display is a wide range of Wagner memorabilia, including manuscripts, pianos, furnishings, artifacts, and even a death mask. If you walk to the end of the garden, fronting the rotunda, you'll see the graves of the composer and his wife.

Altes Schloss Ermitage (Hermitage). On Rte. 22, 3 miles northeast of Bayreuth toward Weiden. ☎ **0921/799-97-0.** Gardens free; palace 5DM ($3) adults, free for children.

Gardens daily 24 hours. Palace Apr–Sept Tues–Sun 9–11:30am and 1–4:30pm; Oct–Mar Tues–Sun 10–11:30am and 1–2:30pm. Bus: 22 (runs every 20 min. during the day).

The margraves of Bayreuth also had a pleasure palace outside the city, reached via a road lined with chestnut trees that were planted in honor of Frederick the Great. Georg Wilhelm built it in 1718 as a retreat. The structure looks as if it had been hewn out of a rock, but the interior felt the touch of Margravine Wilhelmine. Seek out the Japanese salon and the rococo music room. The castle is set in a park, full of formal as well as English-style gardens. In them, you can see the New Palace of the Hermitage, built around 1750. Its columns are covered with polychrome pebbles in mosaic style, a unique structural element in German architecture. A part of the palace becomes a cafe in summer, and sometimes hosts painting exhibitions.

SHOPPING The **Hofgarten Passage,** an arcade off Richard-Wagner-Strasse, full of upscale shops, is worth a stop just to admire the ornate decoration. Locally crafted pewter is available at **Sturm,** Hohenzollernring 62 (☎ **0921/6-48-25**). **Herteis,** Maxstrasse 40 (☎ **0921/5-30-00**), the local department store, is a good place for souvenirs.

WHERE TO STAY
EXPENSIVE

Bayerischer Hof. Bahnhofstrasse 14 (in front of the train station), 95444 Bayreuth. ☎ **0921/7-86-00.** Fax 0921/7-86-05-60. E-mail: 100332.1776@compuserve.com. 56 units. MINIBAR TV TEL. 205DM–266DM ($123–$159.60) double; 486DM–666DM ($291.60–$399.60) suite. Rates include buffet breakfast. AE, DC, MC, V. Parking 10DM ($6). The train and bus stations are opposite.

Bayerischer Hof, near the Hauptbahnhof, is equaled only by the Hotel Königshof (see below) in style and amenities. This hotel combines contemporary and traditional furnishings. Some guest rooms have French pieces; others are Nordic and modern in design.

Dining/Diversions: Each of the hotel's three dining areas has a distinctive character, though the menu is the same (see "Where to Dine," below). Entertainment is sometimes provided in the Lounge Bar, which is open from 6pm to midnight.

Amenities: Room service, laundry, baby-sitting, indoor pool, sauna, sundeck, conference rooms.

Hotel Königshof. Bahnhofstrasse 23, 95444 Bayreuth. ☎ **0921/2-40-94.** Fax 0921/1-22-64. 36 units. TV TEL. 180DM–320DM ($108–$192) double; from 250DM ($150) suite. Rates include buffet breakfast. AE, DC, MC, V. Take any bus to the Hauptbahnhof.

The stylish opulence of this hotel's gilded, paneled, rococo interior would have suited Frederick the Great. The virtues of another age live on here. Each of the guest rooms is individually decorated, sometimes with antique furniture and a scattering of fine carpets. In July and August, Wagner opera buffs fill the hotel.

Dining: In the formal dining room, crystal chandeliers and gilt trim complement well-prepared Franconian and continental meals and elaborate desserts.

Amenities: Concierge, room service, laundry service.

MODERATE

Goldener Anker. Opernstrasse 6 (next door to the Markgräfliches Opernhaus), 95444 Bayreuth. ☎ **0921/6-50-51.** Fax 0921/6-55-00. 43 units. TEL. 170DM–220DM ($102–$132) double; 350DM ($210) suite. Rates include continental breakfast. AE, DC, MC, V. Closed Dec 20–Jan 10. Parking 15DM ($9). Bus: 2.

Goldener Anker is extremely popular locally, although it doesn't have the amenities, services, and style of either the Bayerischer Hof or the Königshof. It has hosted distinguished composers, singers, and conductors for more than 200 years. The framed photographs on the time-seasoned oak-paneled walls are museum treasures. The guest book includes signatures of notables like Richard Strauss, Arturo Toscanini, Fritz Kreisler, Bruno Walter, William Saroyan, Lauritz Melchior, and Patrice Chereau. Furnishings include fine antiques and Oriental rugs. The guest rooms are individually designed.

INEXPENSIVE

Brauerei-Gasthof Goldener Löwe. Kulmbacher Strasse 30, 95445 Bayreuth. ☎ **0921/ 74-60-60.** Fax 0921/4-77-77. 12 units. TEL. 130DM–140DM ($78–$84) double. Rates include continental breakfast. AE, DC, MC, V. Free parking. Bus: 2.

This is an unpretentious, well-managed inn, the town's best affordable choice. The facade is set off by window boxes loaded with flame-red geraniums. Rooms have a Bavarian theme of checker-patterned down comforters and light-grained pinewood trim. The bedrooms and bathrooms are small but comfortable. This atmosphere is informal and homelike. The smiling staff is very hospitable. In the tavern bar you can drink beer or perhaps join in a game of cards before heading for the dining room for a selection of Klössen (Franconian dumplings).

Hotel-Gasthof Spiegelmühle. Kulmbacher Strasse 28, 9445 Bayreuth. ☎ **0921/4-10-91.** Fax 0921/4-73-20. 13 units. TV TEL. 129DM–139DM ($77.40–$83.40) double. Rates include continental breakfast. AE, DC, MC, V. Free parking. Bus: 6.

This high-ceilinged building, which dates from 1555 and was once a working mill, has been transformed into a hotel. The place is modest and unassuming, although clean and comfortable. In spite of its lack of pretensions, well-known conductors and singers often stay here during the festival. Many of the rooms are small but quite adequate. Do not count on anybody speaking English. There's a bar, plus a breakfast room and a Bierstube/Biergarten, serving good traditional Bavarian and international food.

WHERE TO DINE
EXPENSIVE

✪ **Schloss Tiergarten.** Oberthiergartener Strasse 36 (4 miles south of Bayreuth center), 95406 Bayreuth. ☎ **09209/98-40.** Fax 09209/9-84-13. Reservations recommended. Main courses 35DM–48DM ($21–$28.80); fixed-price menus 105DM ($63). AE, DC, MC, V. Daily 11am–2pm, 6–10:30pm. Bus: 11. CONTINENTAL.

This building with a hexagonal baroque tower was constructed as a private hunting lodge. There are two dining rooms, the Kamin (meaning "fireplace") and the Venezianischersalon, where the Venetian chandelier is more than 300 years old. The cuisine is in the culinary traditions of France, Italy, and Germany. Menu items might include lobster risotto with basil, stuffed halibut with caviar sauce and kohlrabi noodles, and terrine of sweetbreads. There's an impressive wine list.

The establishment is also a cozy hotel with eight large rooms boasting all the modern accoutrements. Doubles run 220DM to 290DM ($132 to $174), including breakfast.

MODERATE

Bayerischer Hof. Bahnhofstrasse 14 (in front of the train station). ☎ **0921/7-86-00.** Reservations recommended. Main courses 20DM–40DM ($12–$24). AE, DC, MC, V. Daily 7am–1am. FRENCH.

This previously recommended hotel has a selection of restaurants offering both French and Franconian cooking. The Hans-Sachs-Stube, an air-conditioned replica of an old inn, has walls covered with pictures of famous opera singers who have performed in Bayreuth or dined here. The food is superbly precise and refined, combining inventive

French dishes with the best of Franconian taste. You can also dine at the hotel's bistro, Spanische Stube, or at Gendarmerie, the main à la carte restaurant. Each dining room has a different decor, although the seasonally adjusted menu is the same in all three.

INEXPENSIVE

Braunbierhaus. Kanzleistrasse 15. ☎ **0921/6-96-77.** Main courses 9DM–23DM ($5.40–$13.80). AE, DC, MC, V. Mon–Sat 11:30am–2pm and 5:30–10:30pm, Sun 11:30am–2pm. Bus: 3. FRANCONIAN.

The oldest house in Bayreuth, Braunbierhaus was built in 1430, with foundations that date from the 13th century. It offers inexpensive and down-to-earth food as well as its own beer. The specialty of the kitchen is a *Holzfäller* steak, which means "woodcutter's steak," served with hash-brown potatoes and a fresh salad. Portions are large, appetites are hearty, and the special house beer is consumed in mass quantities. No one puts on airs here.

2 Bamberg

148 miles NW of Munich, 38 miles NW of Nürnberg, 60 miles NE of Würzburg

This little city is one of the gems of Franconia, although visitors often pass it by. Bamberg is set in the rolling Franconian hills where the Regnitz River flows into the Main. It's loaded with attractions, including numerous architectural treasures, and suffered very little damage in World War II.

In the Middle Ages Bamberg was a powerful ecclesiastical center. Originally, it was actually two towns divided by the river: the ecclesiastical town of the prince-bishopric, of which it was the capital for 800 years, and the secular town of the burghers. Bamberg's architecture reflects over 1,000 years of building, with styles ranging from Romanesque to Gothic, Renaissance to baroque, up to the eclecticism of the 19th century. There are narrow cobblestone streets, ornate mansions and palaces, and impressive churches.

Today, Bamberg and beer go together like barley and hops. The town has been called "a beer drinker's Eden." The average Bamberger drinks 50 gallons of beer a year, making the rest of the German people look like teetotalers by comparison. There are more breweries here than in Munich. Beer lovers come from afar for Rauchbier, a smoked beer first brewed in 1536.

ESSENTIALS

GETTING THERE   By Train   The **Bamberg Bahnhof** is on two major rail lines—the Stuttgart-Hof and the Berlin-Munich, with frequent connections in both directions. Most visitors arrive by rail from Nürnberg (see below) in just 1 hour. For rail information and schedules, call ☎ **01805/99-66-33.**

By Bus   Bamberg has bus links with Bayreuth five times daily. The trip takes 1 hour and 40 minutes and costs 15DM ($9) one-way. Contact **Omnibus Verkehr Franken** (☎ **09561/76009**).

By Car   Access by car is via the B22 from Würzburg or the A73 from Nürnberg.

VISITOR INFORMATION   Contact the **Bamberg Tourist Information Office,** Geyerswörthstrasse 3 (☎ **0951/87-11-61**). Office hours are Monday to Friday from 9am to 6pm, Saturday until 3pm, and Sunday from 10am to 2pm May to October.

EXPLORING THE CITY

The center square is dominated by the **Alte Hofhaltung,** the Renaissance imperial and episcopal palace, with a courtyard surrounded by late-Gothic framework buildings.

Inside the palace are the remains of the original *diet* (assembly) hall, built in the 11th century. Elaborately decorated and furnished, the palace is noted for its frescoed Kaisersaal and its Chinesisches Kabinet, the latter covered with walls of marquetry. Don't miss the rose garden.

Among other places of interest is the **Altes Rathaus,** the strangest town hall in Germany. Determined not to play favorites between the ecclesiastical and secular sections of the city, the town authorities built this Gothic structure on its own little island in the middle of the Regnitz River, halfway between the two factions—a true middle-of-the-road (or river) political stand. From the island, you get the best view of the old fisher's houses along the banks in the section called "Little Venice."

E. T. A. Hoffmann Haus. Schillerplatz 26. ☎ **0951/20-31-22.** Admission 2DM ($1.20) adults, 1DM (60¢) children. May–Oct Tues–Fri 4–6pm, Sat–Sun 10am–noon. Bus: 10.

This was the home of the writer and poet from 1809 to 1813. The little narrow-fronted house is filled with mementos and memorabilia of the man whose strange tales formed the basis of Jacques Offenbach's famous opera *The Tales of Hoffmann.*

Kaiserdom (Imperial Cathedral). Domplatz. ☎ **0951/50-23-30.** Admission free. Apr–Oct daily 9am–6pm; Nov–Mar daily 9am–5pm. Diözesanmuseum 4DM ($2.40) adults, 2DM ($1.20) students, 1DM (60¢) children over 15, free for children under 15. Diözesanmuseum open May–Oct, Tues–Sun 9am–6pm; Nov–Apr, Tues–Sun 10am–5pm. Bus 10.

This cathedral on a hillside was begun in 1215 in Romanesque and early-Gothic style. It has a double chancel, the eastern one raised on a terrace to compensate for the slope. The massive towers at the four corners of the church dominate Bamberg's skyline. The interior contains some fine religious art. Best known is the 13th-century equestrian statue, the **Bamberger Reiter,** which represents the idealized Christian king of the Middle Ages. Among the many tombs is that of Emperor Heinrich II, who erected the original cathedral; sculptor Tilman Riemenschneider labored more than a decade over this masterpiece of a tomb, as well as the one devoted to the emperor's wife, Kunigunde (who was suspected of adultery, commemorated in a scene on the tomb). In the west chancel is the only papal tomb north of the Alps, containing the remains of Pope Clement II, who died in 1047. The rich cathedral treasury may be seen in the adjoining **Diözesanmuseum.**

✪ **Neue Residenz.** Domplatz. ☎ **0951/5-63-51.** Admission 5DM ($3) adults, 4DM ($2.40) children. Apr–Oct daily 9am–noon and 1:30–5pm; Nov–Mar daily 9am–noon and 1:30–4pm. Bus: 10.

Opposite the Alte Hofhaltung is the 17th-century Neue Residenz, the much larger palace of the prince-bishops, showing both Renaissance and baroque influences. This was the site of one of the most famous unsolved mysteries in Germany. In 1815, a corpse found beneath the windows of the palace turned out to be the body of Marshal Berthier, who retired in Bavaria after the return of Napoléon from the Isle of Elba. No one knows if Berthier was murdered or committed suicide.

Upstairs, you can view works by German masters, including the fine *Master of the Life of the Virgin* by Hans Baldung Grien. On the second floor are the former **Imperial Apartments,** with Gobelin tapestries, baroque furnishings, and parquet floors. Notable is the **Emperors' Hall,** with allegorical frescoes and portraits of who was who yesterday.

SHOPPING   The primary shopping district in Bamberg is around the cathedral, where you will find stores of all kinds, including more than a dozen antiques shops and numerous galleries. An antiques store that has it all, **Sebok,** Untere Königstrasse 21 (☎ **0951/20-25-93**), offers paintings, books, furniture, fine jewelry, silver, glass, toys, watches, clocks, and more. Auctions are held every 2 months, with the summer auction falling in July. **Manger,** Grüner Markt 7 (☎ **0951/2-34-54**), is a kitschy souvenir shop. If you're interested in local ceramics, go to **Topferladen,** Untere Brücke 1 (☎ **0951/5-69-13**), where you'll find candleholders, cups, dinnerware, vases, and garden statuary.

WHERE TO STAY
EXPENSIVE

✪ **Bamberger Hof Bellevue.** Schönleinsplatz 4, 96047 Bamberg. ☎ **0951/9-85-50.** Fax 0951/98-55-62. www.sskba.de/wrb/bbghof. E-mail: bbghof.wrb@sskba.de. 50 units. MINIBAR TV TEL. 220DM–320DM ($132–$192) double; 850DM ($510) suite. Rates include buffet breakfast. AE, DC, MC, V. Parking 15DM ($9). Bus: 8 or 12.

This hotel plays a bit of second fiddle to the Residenzschloss Bamberg (see below), but the service and accommodations of both are roughly on a par. A great old palace of stone, crowned by a tower and facing a little park, it's the choice for soaking up the mellow atmosphere of yesteryear. Try to book one of the large guest rooms with sitting areas.

Dining: The Bamberger Hof, the hotel's first-class restaurant, serves international cuisine with attentive service.

Amenities: Concierge, hair dryers, room service, laundry, dry cleaning service.

Residenzschloss Bamberg. Untere Sandstrasse 32, 96049 Bamberg. ☎ **0951/6-09-10.** Fax 0951/6-09-17-01. E-mail: info@hotel-residenzschloss.de. 185 units. MINIBAR TV TEL. 295DM–335DM ($177–$201) double; 500DM–590DM ($300–$354) suite. Rates include buffet breakfast. AE, DC, MC, V. Bus: 8.

This elegant hotel is on a bank of the Regnitz, less than 300 yards from the edge of the Altstadt and across from the Bamberg Symphony Orchestra building. This is the preferred choice in town, a blend of old and new. The building, with its ocher-colored baroque walls, was constructed by the local archbishop in 1787 as a hospital. Today, the original hospital chapel continues to host local weddings. A less-glamorous modern annex is connected to the main building by a glass-sided breezeway. Bathrooms are a bit small but tidily kept. The hotel is popular with conventioneers.

Dining: The hotel's most elegant restaurant, the Fürstbischof von Erthal, is open for dinner only, nightly from 6 to 10pm, and serves a menu of Neuer Küche dishes. Buffet breakfasts and lunches are served in the garden-inspired decor of the Orangerie.

Amenities: Steam bath, sauna, solarium, exercise bikes, weight-lifting equipment.

St. Nepomuk. Obere Mühlbrücke 9, 96049 Bamberg. ☎ **0951/9-84-20.** Fax 0951/9-84-21-00. www.hotel-nepomuk.de. E-mail: preuner@hotel-nepomuk.de. 50 units. MINIBAR TV TEL. 200DM–280DM ($120–$168) double, 300DM–480DM ($180–$288) suite. DC, MC, V. Parking 10DM ($6). Bus: 18.

Many discerning travelers actually prefer the charming and tranquil St. Nepomuk to the more highly rated Residenzschloss or Bamberger Hof Bellevue. This hotel is one of the little gems of Bamberg. Its well-furnished rooms are quite comfortable, with sleek modern styling. Some overlook the Regnitz. Most of the staff speaks English.

Dining: The hotel operates a small dining room serving Franconian and international cuisine.

Amenities: Room service and laundry service (for a surcharge); conference rooms and secretarial services are available; a park is nearby.

MODERATE

Barock Hotel am Dom. Vorderer Bach 4, 96049 Bamberg. ☎ **0951/5-40-31.** Fax 0951/5-40-21. 19 units. MINIBAR TV TEL. 155DM–175DM ($93–$105) double. Rates include buffet breakfast. AE, CB, DC, MC, V. Closed Feb 1–Mar 1. Bus: 8 or 12.

Barock Hotel am Dom offers you some of the same style, tradition, and romance of the pacesetters above, but at a better price. The owners of this symmetrical building have retained every detail of the original ornamented facade and renovated key areas of the interior. The result is a winning combination of baroque elements in a well-lit modernized building. Each room is attractively furnished, although a bit cramped. Reservations are important. The rates include a nourishing breakfast (the only meal available) of wurst and cheese, served in the most unusual breakfast room in Bamberg—the old cellar, where tables with colorful napery are set up under the plastered stone vaulting.

Hotel Brudermühle. Schranne 1, 96049 Bamberg. ☎ **0951/95-52-20.** Fax 0951/9-55-22-55. www.brudermuehle.de. E-mail: info@brudermuehle.de. 16 units. TV TEL. 180DM ($108) double. Rates include continental breakfast. DC, MC, V. Bus: 8 or 12.

The Hotel Brudermühle is a traditional German city inn without pretense or glamour. Reasonable rates, good local cookery, and a hospitable, family-style welcome make this a worthwhile choice for those who like no-frills functionality. Bedrooms are tiny, but housekeeping is good. The functional modern furnishings are less interesting than the views of the old town through the bedroom windows. The building itself dates from 1314, when it was constructed as a mill powered by the Regnitz River. The hotel couldn't be more centrally located; it's within a few blocks of the cathedral.

National. Luitpoldstrasse 37, 96052 Bamberg. ☎ **0951/2-41-12.** Fax 0951/2-24-36. 44 units. MINIBAR TV TEL. 145DM–169DM ($87–$101.40) double; 195DM–220DM ($117–$132) suite. Rates include buffet breakfast. AE, DC, MC, V. Parking 9DM ($5.40). Bus: 5.

The National is still a favorite, though it no longer enjoys the renown it used to. Modernization has removed some of its quaint charm, and the hotel lacks the style of the Romantik Hotel-Weinhaus Messerschmitt (see below), but the price is right, the food is good, and the bedrooms are first rate. With its black mansard roof, iron balconies, baroque and classical detailing, and opulent public rooms, the hotel is attractive, if small. It has well-maintained and traditionally furnished guest rooms, a bar, and a formal restaurant that serves good continental and Franconian specialties. Room service, laundering, and dry cleaning are available.

✪ **Romantik Hotel-Weinhaus Messerschmitt.** Langestrasse 41, 96047 Bamberg. ☎ **0951/2-78-66.** Fax 0951/26-14-1. 18 units. MINIBAR TV TEL. 255DM ($153) double; 265DM ($159) triple. Rates include buffet breakfast. AE, DC, MC, V. Parking 7.50DM ($4.50). Take any bus going to Central Station.

This old hotel, beloved by traditionalists, is Bamberg's most romantic choice. The building itself dates from 1422, making it one of the oldest structures in the area. The present exterior is 18th century, a gabled expanse of pale blue and yellow with window frames carved in baroque style. Inside, paneling, ceramic ovens, and antiques make a mellow decor. Many of the beds upstairs have meticulously crafted headboards. The owner and his staff do everything to be helpful. The exceptional kitchen serves both Franconian and international dishes. Locals love the platter of eels in dill sauce; the gastronomically timid might settle for the local duck instead.

INEXPENSIVE

Hotel Garni Graupner. Langestrasse 5, 96047 Bamberg. ☎ **0951/98-04-00.** Fax 0951/98-04-040. www.bamberginfoline.de/gutnacht/graupner.htm. E-mail: www.hotel-grupner@t-online.de. 30 units, 26 with bathroom. TEL. 85DM ($51) double without bathroom, 110DM–130DM ($66–$78) double with bathroom. Rates include continental breakfast. AE, MC, V. Parking 12DM ($7.20). Bus: 1, 2, 4, 5, 8, or 16.

Much renovated, rebuilt, and overhauled over the years, this hotel has accepted overnight guests since the 14th century. It's your best bet if you can't afford the properties outlined above. You can usually get a room here, perhaps with a view over the Altstadt, and it will be clean and decent, although short on charm. If the main hotel is full, guests are directed to the lackluster 1960s annex, about 8 blocks away across the canal. It offers 10 modern rooms for the same price charged in the main hotel, each with private bathroom. Locals frequent the big-windowed cafe and pastry shop on the ground floor, open daily from 7am to 7pm. The same family also owns a rose-garden cafe, a stone's throw from the cathedral.

WHERE TO DINE

Historischer Brauereiausschank Schlenkerla. Dominikanerstrasse 6. ☎ **0951/5-60-60.** Main courses 10DM–18DM ($6–$10.80). No credit cards. Wed–Mon 10:30am–11pm. Closed Jan 7–21. Bus: 8 or 12. FRANCONIAN.

Diners congregate here much as they did in 1678, when the place was a brewery. The decor is rustic, with long wooden tables and smallish chairs. The price is right, and the cozy, *gemütlich* atmosphere is genuine. Wholesome and unpretentious Franconian fare is served here. You can sample such local dishes as *Bierbrauervesper* (smoked meat and sour-milk cheese) and *Rauchschinken* (smoked ham). Patrons wash down these dishes with a hearty malt, Rauchbier, which has an intense smoky aroma and flavor.

Romantik Restaurant-Weinhaus Messerschmitt. Langestrasse 41. ☎ **0951/2-78-66.** Main courses 27DM–42DM ($16.20–$25.20); fixed-priced menus 42DM–74DM ($25.20–$44.40) and 35.50DM ($21.30) with champagne on Sunday only. AE, DC, MC, V. Daily 11am–2pm and 6–10pm. Buses 1, 2. FRANCONIAN/INTERNATIONAL.

You can dine better here, and in a more refined atmosphere, than anywhere else in town. This pleasant restaurant is more than 160 years old. The cuisine is presented simply, but is remarkably well crafted. Menu items depend on shopping—in spring you get fresh white asparagus. Freshwater fish are kept in an aquarium. Game is another specialty. Veal and lamb dishes are prepared with exquisite care. Some of the offerings, such as eels in dill sauce, may be a bit too regional for you, but the Franconian duck is an exquisite choice.

BAMBERG AFTER DARK

Sinfonie an der Regnitz, Mussstrasse 7 (☎ **0951/9-64-71-00**) is in residence from September 11 to July 17. From the last week in June to mid-July there's a summer festival with weekend symphonic concerts. Tickets range from 35DM to 60DM ($21 to $36).

The **Hofburg Repertory Theater** performs at the **E.T.A. Hoffman Theater,** Schillerplatz 5 (☎ **0951/87-14-33;** box office 0951/87-14-31). Its season runs from September to July 24. The productions range from 18th-, 19th-, and 20th-century classics to contemporary musicals. The box office is open daily from 10am to 1pm and from 1 hour prior to show time (also from 4 to 6pm on Wednesday). In June and July, the company moves outdoors, performing a series of German-language drama within the courtyard of the Alte Hofaltung (see above). Tickets for both indoor and outdoor performances range from 18DM to 35DM ($10.80 to $21), but students with a valid ID card pay only half price. For more information about these and other cultural events in Bamberg, contact the Tourist Information Office (see "Visitor Information," above).

A young crowd gathers at **Jazzclub,** Obere Sandstrasse 18 (☎ **0951/5-37-40**), to listen to punk, gothic, and alternative music on Tuesday and Thursday nights from 9pm to 1am, when the cover charge is 5DM ($3). Between mid-September and April, the club opens its cellar for live jazz on Friday and Saturday from 9pm to 2am, when the cover ranges from 10DM to 50DM ($6 to $30), depending on the group.

3 Nürnberg (Nuremberg)

105 miles NW of Munich, 140 miles SE of Frankfurt, 127 miles NE of Stuttgart

When this city celebrated its 900th birthday in 1950, the scars of World War II were still fresh. Nürnberg was once the ideal of medieval splendor, but that legacy was lost in the ashes of war. With the exception of Dresden, no other German city suffered such devastation in a single air raid. On the night of January 2, 1945, 525 British Lancaster bombers rained fire and destruction on this city, the ideological center of the Third Reich.

Nürnberg today has regained its vitality. Now it's a symbol of postwar prosperity, employing more than 250,000 workers. The largest city in Franconia, Nürnberg is swarming with people, both longtime residents and *Gastarbeiter* (foreign workers), who have flooded the city in recent years—many from the old Soviet bloc countries to the east. For most of the year the city is thronged with visitors, too. It's a notable industrial center, still associated with its traditional gingerbread products and handmade toys. The first pocket watches, the Nürnberg eggs, were made here in the 16th century.

Centuries of art and architecture made Nürnberg a treasure. During the 15th and 16th centuries, Nürnberg enjoyed a cultural flowering that made it the center of the **German Renaissance,** bringing together Italian Renaissance and German Gothic traditions. In the artists' workshops were found such great talents as Veit Stoss, Peter Vischer, Adam Krafft, Michael Wolgemut, and above all, Albrecht Dürer. Koberger set up his printing press here, and Regiomontanus built an astronomical observatory. Here, too, flourished the guilds of the Meistersingers, composed of prosperous artisans; Wagner made their most famous member, Hans Sachs, the hero of his opera *Die Meistersinger von Nürnberg.*

Many of Nürnbeg's most important buildings here, among them some of the finest churches in Germany, have been restored or reconstructed. The old part of the city, the **Altstadt,** lies mainly within a pedestrian zone. Today's visitors can see the ruins of the ramparts that once surrounded the city in addition to more modern sites, such as the **Justice Palace,** where the War Crimes Tribunal sat in 1946.

Visitors can also see the **Zeppelinfeld arena,** the huge amphitheater where, from 1927 to 1935, Hitler staged those dramatic Nazi rallies that were immortalized by Leni Riefenstahl in *Triumph des Willens (Triumph of the Will).* Hitler's architect, Albert Speer, constructed what has been called a "concrete mecca," whose grounds today have been turned into a park with apartment blocks, a trade fair, and a concert hall. Speer's Congress Hall, larger than the Colosseum in Rome, has become a recording studio and warehouse.

ESSENTIALS

GETTING THERE   By Plane   Nürnberg Flughafen is 4 miles north of the city center. Despite its relatively small size (it's only the ninth busiest in Germany), this airport is served by 14 airlines in scheduled flights to dozens of destinations throughout Europe. These are supplemented by charter flights. For information and schedules, call ☎ **0911/9-37-00.**

By Train   The **Nürnberg Hauptbahnhof** lies on several major German rail lines, with frequent connections to big cities and many smaller regional towns. Travel time to Frankfurt is 2 hours and 8 minutes; to Berlin, 6 hours; and to Munich, 1 hour and 40 minutes. For rail information and schedules, call ☎ **01 805/99-66-33.**

By Bus   Long-distance bus service from such cities as Munich and Frankfurt is provided by Europabus Lines 183 and 189E of Deutsche Touring GmbH, operating out of Frankfurt. For information in Nürnberg, call **Reisebüro Olcay** (☎ **0911/22-69-92**).

Regional bus service with frequent connections to neighboring towns is offered by **OVF Omnibusverkehr Franken GmbH,** Kopernikusplatz 14 in Nürnberg (☎ **0911/ 4-39-06-66**).

By Boat The Main-Danube Canal links the Rhine, the Main, and the Danube. For information about riverboat connections, call the **Hafenver-Waltung Nürnberg** (☎ **0911/64-29-40**).

By Car From Munich, take the A9 Autobahn north; from Frankfurt, head southeast along the A3 Autobahn; from Berlin, take the A9 Autobahn south.

VISITOR INFORMATION Contact **Tourist Information,** in the Hauptbahnhof (☎ **0911/2-33-61-32**), Monday to Saturday from 9am to 7pm. An additional branch in the **Rathaus** (☎ **0911/2-33-61-35**) is open Monday to Saturday 9am to 6pm and also Sundays in May from 10am to 1pm and 2 to 4pm.

GETTING AROUND Nürnberg and nearby towns, such as Fürth and Erlangen, are linked by a public transport system. Local and regional services, including subways, trams, buses, and trains, are interconnected. The same ticket can be used for all services. A one-way ticket for travel within the central area costs 3.30DM ($2). If you plan to do much traveling, consider a discount ticket, costing 6.60DM ($3.95) for a full day—a worthy investment. For more information, call ☎ **0911/27-07-99.** To summon a taxi, call ☎ **0911/1-94-10.** Many hotels can arrange bike rentals; otherwise, contact **Fahrradkiste,** Knauerstrasse 9 (☎ **0911/2-87-90-64**). The best cycling paths are along the Pegnitz River.

EXPLORING THE CITY

You can easily spend a full day here seeing the sights. Begin at the central market square, **Hauptmarkt,** the most colorful place in Nürnberg, filled with kiosks stacked tall with fresh produce brought in from the countryside. Nearly all the city's attractions lie nearby within the **medieval fortifications,** parts of which still remain. Between the main wall (which has rampart walks) and the secondary wall once ran the waters of a protective moat. Set at the "corners" of the Altstadt are the massive stone towers, still intact, of the city gates. The remains of dozens of other gateway towers still exist along the ramparts. Crowning the northern periphery of the Altstadt is the **Kaiserburg.**

The best example of Nürnberg's aesthetic passion is the **Beautiful Fountain** on Marktplatz. This stone pyramid, 60 feet high, dates from 1396 and is adorned with 30 figures arranged in four tiers. Within it is enclosed the symbol of Nürnberg, the journeyman's ring.

At some point in your day wander over to **Handwerkerhof,** near the main train station. In this mall, you can see artisan after artisan creating the products for which Nürnberg has been known since the Middle Ages: glassware, pewter (often in the form of beer mugs), intricate wood carvings, and toys. Naturally, this mall is busiest at Christmastime.

If you're interested in a famous landmark of World War II, visit the **Justizgebäude,** Fürtherstrasse 22, where the "Judgment of Nürnberg," took place. Here in room 600, the surviving leaders of the Third Reich stood trial in October of 1946 for crimes against humanity. Afterwards, 10 were hanged. The building still serves as a courthouse, and you'll have to ask the guard at the door if you can enter. To reach the courthouse, take the U-Bahn 1 to Bärenschanze.

✪ **Albrecht Dürer House.** Am Tiergartnertor, Albrecht-Dürer-Strasse 39. ☎ **0911/ 2-31-54-20.** Admission 5DM ($3) adults, 2.50DM ($1.50) students and children 6–15, free for children 5 and under. Tues–Wed and Sun 10am–5pm; Thurs 10am–8pm; Sun 10am–5pm. Tram 4. Bus: 36.

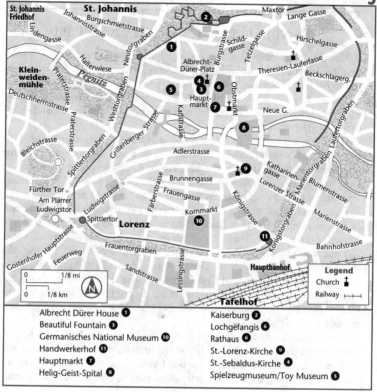

St. Johannis
Friedhof

St. Johannis

Maxtor
Lange Gasse

Johannisstrasse

Burgschmietstrasse

Lindengasse

Neutorgraben

Burgstrasse

Schild-gasse

Tetzelgasse

Hirschelgasse

Klein-weiden-mühle

Hallerwiese

Praterstrasse

Pegnitz

Wettlorstraben

Albrecht-Dürer-Platz

Theresien-Lauferfasse

Beckschlagerg.

Deutschherrnstrasse

Praterstrasse

Karlstrasse

Haupt-markt

Obstmarkt

Neue G.

Bleichstrasse

Spittlertorgraben

Grillenberger Strasse

Adlerstrasse

Katharinen-gasse

Lauferforgraben

Blumenstrasse

Fürther Tor
Am Plärrer
Ludwigstor

Ludwigstrasse

Färberstrasse

Brunnengasse

Frauengasse

Lorenzer Strasse

Marientorgraben

Spittlertor

Lorenz

Kornmarkt

Königstrasse

Marienstrasse

Gostenhofer Hauptstrasse

Feuerweg

Frauentorgraben

Sandstrasse

Lessingstrasse

Königstorgraben

Bahnhofstrasse

Hauptbahnhof

Legend
Church †
Railway

Tafelhof

Albrecht Dürer House ❶		Kaiserburg ❷
Beautiful Fountain ❸		Lochgëfangis ❻
Germanisches National Museum ❿		Rathaus ❻
Handwerkerhof ⓫		St.-Lorenz-Kirche ❾
Hauptmarkt ❼		St.-Sebaldus-Kirche ❹
Helig-Geist-Spital ❽		Spielzeugmuseum/Toy Museum ❺

The town's most popular shrine is the Albrecht Dürer House, just up the cobblestoned Bergstrasse from the Dürer Monument and St. Sebald Church. This site is well worth the short walk up the hill. Typical of the half-timbered burghers' houses of the 15th century, the structure is the only completely preserved Gothic house in Nürnberg. The first floors are sandstone, surmounted by two half-timbered stories and a gabled roof with a view of the town below. Exhibits inside the house are devoted to Dürer's life and works. Many of the rooms are furnished with important historical pieces and contain original etchings and woodcuts, plus copies of Dürer's paintings.

✪ **Germanisches Nationalmuseum (Germanic National Museum).** Kartäusergasse 1 (near the Hauptbahnhof). ☎ **0911/1-33-10.** Admission 6DM ($3.60) adults, 4DM ($2.40) children. Tues and Thurs–Sun 10am–5pm, Wed 10am–9pm. U-Bahn 2: Opernhaus.

The largest museum of German art and culture is just inside the south section of the medieval city walls. It covers the entire spectrum of German craftsmanship and fine arts from their beginnings to the 20th century. The prehistoric and early historical section contains finds from the Stone Age and from the burial sites of the Merovingians. The extensive painting and sculpture sections include works by Albrecht Dürer and Veit Stoss, a sculptor and wood-carver known for his "nervous" angular forms and realism. The boundless variety and richness of German handcrafts is fully evident in this museum. There's also an important library and archive here.

Kaiserburg. Burgstrasse. ☎ **0911/22-57-26.** Admission (including all parts of the castle) 9DM ($5.40) adults, 8DM ($4.80) students, free for children 15 and under. Apr–Sept daily 9am–5pm; Oct–Mar daily 9:30am–4pm. Bus: 36 or 46.

Albrecht Dürer & the German Renaissance

If Albrecht Dürer's father had had his way, his son would have become a gold-smith. Fortunately, that didn't happen. Dürer began his artistic career as apprentice to Michael Wolgemut, then the leading artist in Nürnberg, in 1468. There he learned to excel in woodcutting and engraving. Almost everyone is familiar with the sketch he made of praying hands—it's been reproduced so often it's become a greeting-card cliché.

Dürer was not content to stay at home in Nürnberg. Beginning in 1490, he embarked on a series of travels that eventually took him to Italy, where he came into contact with the artists of the Renaissance. On his return to Nürnberg, he brought their ideas back with him. Dürer was thus largely responsible for pulling art north of the Alps out of the medieval world and into the new era.

Dürer was the first major world master to paint an acknowledged self-portrait. In fact, he painted three of them, and his very first known drawing is a sketch of himself at the age of 13. These paintings show clearly how he saw the artist's role, and the importance of his own mission. The last self-portrait (in the Alte Pinokothek in Munich), shows Dürer in an almost Christlike stance, representing the artist as an elevated figure concerned with the expression of universal ideas. Other important paintings of his include the portrait of *Charlemagne* at the Germanisches Nationalmuseum in Nürnberg, and his *Four Apostles,* commissioned for the Nürnberg Rathaus.

A restless man, Dürer was always probing into the world about him; he produced several theoretical works on art, on architecture, and on the science of proportion. Even more interesting, at one point he invented a mechanical device for drawing a picture that was a first step toward the principle of the photographic camera.

The Burg looms above the city from its hilltop at the northern edge of the Altstadt. From 1050 to 1571, it was the official residence of the German kings and emperors, including Frederick Barbarossa, the zealous crusader who entertained the emperor of Byzantium and the sultan of Tyre within its walls. The castle is divided into three complexes: the Kaiserburg (Imperial Castle), the Burgraves' Castle, and the Municipal Buildings of the Free City.

The oldest portion is the **Pentagonal Tower** (1050). It probably dates from the previous palace of the Salian kings, over which the Burgraves' Castle was constructed. Although the **Burgraves' Castle** has been in ruins since it was destroyed by fire in 1420, the remains offer the visitor an interesting look into the layout of a feudal castle. The watchmen and guards used the heavy ramparts with the parapet walks and secret passages to protect the burgraves and the emperors, who lived in the inner core of the castle complex.

The **Kaiserburg,** grouped around the inner court within the ramparts of the Burgraves' Castle, was the residence of the kings and emperors of Germany. Most of the buildings were constructed during the 12th century, centered around the once magnificent Palas built by Konrad III in 1138. The great Knights' Hall on the ground floor and the Imperial Hall on the floor above look much as they did when King Frederick III rebuilt them in the 15th century, with heavy oak beams and painted ceilings. The rooms are decorated with period Gothic furnishings. Adjoining the Palas is the Imperial Chapel, which actually consists of two chapels, one above the other in cross section but united at the center by an open bay. Thus, the emperor could worship with his court in the upper chapel to the same liturgy as the lesser members of his retinue in the lower chapel.

The third set of buildings, outside the Burgraves' Castle, was erected by the council of Nürnberg in the 14th and 15th centuries when it took over the responsibility of protecting the emperor. This section includes the imperial stables (now housing a youth hostel), the massive bastions of the fortress, the Tiefer Brunnen (Deep Well), and the castle gardens. Even more impressive than the fortress is the view of the roofs and towers of Nürnberg from its terraces.

The complex also includes the new **Kaiserburg Museum** (☎ 0911/13-310), which contains antique weaponry, armor, and paintings, and explains the history of the castle.

Lochgefängnis. Rathausplatz. ☎ **0911/2-31-26-90.** Admission 4DM ($2.40) adults, 2DM ($1.20) children. Tues–Sun 10am–4pm. Closed Jan–Mar and Oct–Nov. Bus: 36, 46, or 47.

Under the Altes Rathaus is a medieval prison with its original cells and torture chamber, a gruesome attraction. Opposite the torture chamber lie the remnants of a room that once hid the city council's treasures and important documents during times of war and emergency. An underground passage from the dungeons to the outside world existed from 1543 until 1945, when bombings rendered it impassable.

St.-Lorenz-Kirche. Lorenzer Platz 10. ☎ **0911/20-92-87.** Free admission. Mon–Sat 9am–5pm, Sun 2–4pm. U-Bahn 1: Lorenz-Kirche.

Across the Pegnitz River is the largest and stateliest church in Nürnberg. Begun in 1270, it took more than 200 years to complete, but the final result is one of Gothic purity, inside and out. The twin towers flank the west portal. The portal's sculptures depict the theme of redemption, from Adam and Eve through the Last Judgment. Upon entering the church, note the color and detail in the stained-glass rosette above the portal. Much of the church's stained and painted glass dates from the 15th century. The interior is marked by pillars that soar upward to become lost in the vaulting shafts above the nave. Each pillar is adorned with sculptures carrying on the theme introduced at the entrance. The oldest of these is *Mary with Child*, created around 1285. The continuing theme of the sculptures urges you toward the single east choir, the last portion of the church to be completed (1477). *The Angelic Salutation* (1519), carved in linden wood by Veit Stoss, is suspended from the roof of the church just behind the Madonna Chandelier. To the left of the altar is the Gothic Tabernacle, hewn from stone by Adam Krafft (1496), its upthrusting turret repeating the vertical emphasis of the church. Above the high altar is another masterpiece by Stoss, a carved crucifix. The painted panels at the beginning of the choir are by Michael Wolgemut, Dürer's teacher.

Spielzeugmuseum (Toy Museum). Karlstrasse 13–15. ☎ **0911/2-31-31-64.** Admission 5DM ($3) adults, 2.50DM ($1.50) children. Tues and Thurs–Sun 10am–5pm, Wed 10am–9pm. Bus: 36.

Nürnberg is a major toy center, so it's only fitting that the city devotes a museum to this industry. Toys, both hand- and machine-made, fill three floors. Some date from medieval times. The collection of old dollhouses is vastly amusing, as is a mechanical Ferris wheel. You'll often see adults here (even without children).

✪ **St.-Sebaldus-Kirche.** Sebalderplatz. ☎ **0911/22-45-72.** Free admission. Mar–May daily 9:30am–6pm; June–Oct daily 9:30am–8pm; Nov–Feb daily 9am–4pm. Sunday services at 8:30 and 10am. U-Bahn 2: Lorenz-Kirche.

Consecrated in 1273, this church is a fine example of 13th-century transition from Romanesque to German Gothic styles. The nave and west choir are late Romanesque, with a narrow chancel containing a simple altar and an ancient bronze baptismal font. The larger east choir, consecrated in 1379, is pure Gothic and contains the most important treasures of the church. Between the two east pillars is a huge 16th-century crucifixion group dominated by a life-size crucifix by Veit Stoss. Just behind the altar is the elaborate shrine of St. Sebald, whose remains are encased in a monument cast in brass by Peter Vischer in 1519. It's supported by an array of escargots and dolphins and adorned with a host of statuettes. The nave of the church also holds several important works of art, including 14th-century statues of St. Catherine and St. Sebald and the *Madonna with a Halo* (artist unknown, 1440).

SHOPPING

Located near the railway station in the center of the city, **Handwerkerhof** is a crafts mall in a medieval castle setting, where Franconian artisans create and sell a wide range of handicrafts. It's open from March 20 to December 23. Weekday hours are 10am to 6:30pm; Saturday hours are 10am to 4pm. In December, it opens on Sunday from 10am to 6:30pm.

Obletter, 2 Königstrasse (☎ **0911/2-14-99-90**), near the town center, has been the largest store for children's toys and playthings in Nürnberg for 20 years. Toys, many of them computerized, cover two floors (street level and cellar) of a building near the town center. For policy reasons, you'll find few of the war games that you'd expect in an equivalent Stateside store, a credit to the establishment's enlightened management. Be warned: Some of the devices, although intended for use by children and teens, might even appeal to adults.

Hofman, Rathaus Platz 7 (☎ **0911/20-48-48**), is devoted entirely to tin figures. The owner paints his historic soldiers, Christmas decorations, and other objects while manning the store.

At **Kistner,** Weinmarkt 6 (☎ **0911/20-34-82**), you can step back in time. This wonderful store is full of antique books, prints, and engravings, including some by Dürer, Rembrandt, and other masters. The owner, Herr Kistner, is an expert in the field.

Villeroy & Boch, 13 Königstrasse (☎ **911/22-31-82**), sells sets of china, crystal ware, and porcelain trinkets that make good souvenirs.

The largest department store in the city, **Karstadt,** Königstrasse 14 (☎ **0911/21-30**), carries clothing, housewares, and other home furnishings.

If you're hungry, stop by **Lebkuchen Frauenholz,** Bergstrasse 1 (☎ **0911/24-34-64**), a bakery that sells fresh gingerbread and honey packed in a container that looks like a half-timbered 18th-century German building.

Adding variety to prudence, **Condomi,** Ludwigstrasse 57 (☎ **0911/23-27-84**), sells condoms in various colors, textures, flavors, and scents. It also has postcards and T-shirts.

WHERE TO STAY
EXPENSIVE

Atrium Hotel. Münchenerstrasse 25 (5 min. drive from the city center), 90478 Nürnberg. ☎ **0911/4-74-80.** Fax 0911/4-74-84-20. E-mail: atrium.nbg@t-online.de. 200 units. MINIBAR TV TEL. 290DM ($174) double; from 590DM ($354) suite. Rates include buffet breakfast. Children under 12 stay free in parents' room. AE, DC, MC, V. Parking 18DM ($10.80). Tram: 9. Bus: 36.

The Atrium is not as grand as Le Meridien Grand Hotel or even the Maritim, but it's close to the top of the heap. This hotel is one of the most modern in town; it looks like a four-story collection of concrete cubes set up on stilts. Inside, it's flooded with natural light, with many windows offering views of the landscaped park around it. The rooms and the bathrooms are spacious. The hotel is directly connected to the Meistersingerhalle, where concerts and conventions take place.

Dining/Diversions: An attractive and formal restaurant, the Parkrestaurant Meistersingerhalle specializes in continental and Franconian food. The Rôtisserie Médoc features international grill specialties. The Terrace Restaurant is open from May through September, weather permitting. There's also a dignified bar called Henry's.

Amenities: Room service, laundry, dry cleaning, indoor pool, three specially designed rooms for travelers with disabilities.

Le Meridien Grand Hotel. Bahnhofstrasse 1–3 (across from the Hauptbahnhof), 90402 Nürnberg. ☎ **800/367-8340** in the U.S., or 0911/2-32-20. Fax 0911/2-32-24-44. 182 units. A/C MINIBAR TV TEL. 330DM–390DM ($198–$234) double; 660DM–1,100DM ($396–$660) suite. AE, DC, MC, V. Parking 20DM ($12). U-Bahn 1 and 2: Hauptbahnhof.

This old-world palace is the best place to stay in Nürnberg; it's superior to its rival, the Maritim. The Grand is a solid, six-story blockbuster built "when hotels were really hotels"—that is, before World War I. It's located opposite the train station, at the entrance of the old city. The rooms are the finest and most spacious in town. Stylish fabrics highlight the classic decor. Many rooms have a private sitting area. The best bathrooms are marble and have a stylish decor. Smoke-free rooms are available, and a trained staff is always there to assist you.

Dining/Diversions: The hotel restaurant, Brasserie, offers formal dining, with a cuisine both Franconian and international. It's a worthy choice for dining even if you're not staying here. A cozy pub, Opus, serves wine and beer, local specialties, and light snacks.

Amenities: Room service, laundry, dry cleaning, sauna, health club, solarium.

Maritim. Frauentorgraben 11, 90443 Nürnberg. ☎ **0911/2-36-30.** Fax 0911/2-36-38-36. www.maritim.de. 325 units. A/C MINIBAR TV TEL. 256DM–404DM ($153.60–$242.40) double; from 360DM ($216) suite. AE, DC, MC, V. Parking 18DM ($10.80). U-Bahn 2: Hauptbahnhof.

Maritim attracts those who prefer modern convenience to old-world charm. It used to be the city's most stylish hotel, until the Meridien chain upgraded the Grand. Rooms here are good-sized, although not as spacious as the Grand's. Large beds and many extra amenities complement the thick, posh carpets and lavish adornment of chintz. Try an upper-floor room for a panoramic view over Nürnberg's medieval fortifications and busy traffic artery.

Dining/Diversions: The hotel's restaurant, the Nürnberger Stuben, serves local and international cuisine. Live piano music is played nightly in the elegant hotel bar, Nürnberger Treff.

Amenities: Room service, laundry, dry cleaning, indoor pool, solarium, sauna, steam bath, newsstand.

MODERATE

Burghotel-Grosses Haus. Lammsgasse 3, 90403 Nürnberg. ☎ **0911/20-44-14.** Fax 0911/22-38-82. 46 units. MINIBAR TV TEL. 175DM–291DM ($105–$174.60) double. Rates include continental breakfast. AE, DC, MC, V. Parking 15DM ($9). Tram: Tiergärtnertor. Bus: 36.

This reliable hotel provides good solid comfort for the travel-weary. Sure, it's a ways down the pecking order among local hotels, but its limited facilities remain a good value. This unusual hotel offers the luxury of a heated indoor pool opening onto a tile bar area furnished with plants, antiques, and bar stools; here you can sip your favorite drink and pretend you're in the Caribbean. Even better, your door will practically open into one of the most historic parts of the old city—you're right next to Dürer's house. The room furnishings feature Laura Ashley fabrics.

Carlton Hotel Nürnberg. Eilgutstrasse 13–15, 90443 Nürnberg. ☎ and fax **0911/2-00-66.** 130 units. MINIBAR TV TEL. 122DM–375DM ($73.20–$225) double; from 325DM ($195) suite. AE, DC, MC, V. Parking 16DM ($9.60). U-Bahn 2: Hauptbahnhof.

This first-class hotel is still among the best in Nürnberg. It's every bit as good as the Atrium, for a lower price. It stands on a quiet street a block from the Hauptbahnhof. Some doubles have a pair of L-shaped sofas with coffee tables, so they can serve as combined living/sleeping rooms. Other rooms are smaller. Although the Carlton has a well-known restaurant, the Zirbelstube, many prefer to have lunch on the stone terrace with its umbrella-shaded tables and flower garden. Amenities include room service, laundry, dry cleaning, health club, sauna, and solarium.

Dürer-Hotel. Neutormauer 32, 90403 Nürnberg. ☎ **0911/20-80-91.** Fax 0911/22-34-58. 107 units. MINIBAR TV TEL. 215DM–300DM ($129–$180) double. Rates include buffet breakfast. AE, DC, MC, V. Parking 13DM ($7.80). Tram: 4 or 9. Bus: 36 or 46.

The Dürer has steadily grown in prestige since it opened in the late '80s. It stands beside the birthplace of its namesake, right under the castle and near all the major sightseeing attractions. The ambience is one of cozy antique charm, combined with modern amenities. Many of the rooms have quite a bit of character. The Dürer offers the Bistro Bar, a fitness center, and a garage. The only meal served is breakfast, but you're a short walk from restaurants and cafes. Laundry service and dry cleaning are also available.

INEXPENSIVE

City Hotel. Königstrasse 25–27 (near St.-Lorenz-Kirche), 90402 Nürnberg. ☎ **0911/22-56-38.** Fax 0911/20-39-99. 20 units. TV TEL. 180DM ($108) double. Rates include continental breakfast. AE, DC, MC, V. Closed for 2 weeks after Christmas. Parking 14DM ($8.40). U-Bahn 2: Lorenz-Kirche.

This serviceable if unspectacular hotel provides good value. It occupies the third, fourth, and fifth floors of an old-fashioned building, on a wide pedestrian thoroughfare. You can take a small elevator upstairs to the third-floor reception area, where the efficient owner will show you one of her simple, cramped, but immaculate rooms. The tiny bathrooms have shower stalls and rather thin towels.

Deutscher Kaiser. Königstrasse 55, 90402 Nürnberg. ☎ **0911/20-33-41.** Fax 0911/2-41-89-82. 51 units. TEL. 169DM–189DM ($101.40–$113.40) double. AE, DC, MC, V. U-Bahn 2: Hauptbahnhof.

This attractive, gray-stone, 19th-century building, with steep gables and a high-pitched roof studded with dormers, stands at the top of a pedestrian mall. Three Romanesque-style arches lead into the main lobby. The general effect is one of comfort in immaculate surroundings. Rooms are small but have comfortable beds. The bathrooms are also cramped and have rather thin towels. This hotel is crowded during December and February, when it's a popular off-season retreat for German visitors. The breakfast room is rather simple, yet fresh and clean. In the basement is a cafe-restaurant.

Drei Linden. Aussere-Suizbacher-Strasse 3, 90489 Nürnberg. ☎ **0911/53-32-33.** Fax 0911/55-40-47. 28 units. MINIBAR TV TEL. 170DM–180DM ($102–$108) double. Rates include buffet breakfast. AE, MC, V. Parking 15DM ($9). Tram: 8. Bus: 45.

This old-fashioned renovated guest house first opened in 1877. Today it provides small but comfortable rooms with tiny bathrooms. Its restaurant has a good reputation and is often frequented by locals.

Weinhaus Steichele. Knorrstrasse 2–8 (near Jakobsplatz), 90402 Nürnberg. ☎ **0911/20-22-80.** Fax 0911/22-19-14. 50 units. TV TEL. 170DM–200DM ($102–$120) double. Rates include buffet breakfast. AE, DC, MC, V. Parking 15DM ($9). U-Bahn 2: Weisser Turm.

This small and charming hostelry retains its old-fashioned allure. It's located on a tranquil street, but not far from the bustling activity of the train station, just outside the city wall. The building is a beautifully balanced and handcrafted structure of heavy stone blocks with a curved sloping roofline. Any overflow of guests spills into a modern annex next door that blends harmoniously with the older building. Rooms are decorated in a rustic Bavarian style.

WHERE TO DINE
EXPENSIVE

✪ **Die Entenstub'n.** Güntersbühlerstrasse 145, Erlenstegen (4½ miles north of Nürnberg). ☎ **0911/5-98-04-13.** Reservations required. Jacket and tie required for men. Main courses 44DM–49DM ($26.40–$29.40); fixed-price 4-course lunch 68DM ($40.80); fixed-price 6-course dinner 98DM ($58.80). AE, MC. Tues–Fri noon–2pm; Tues–Sat 6–10pm. Bus: 8. CONTINENTAL.

Food critics often single out Die Entenstub'n as the best dining spot in Nürnberg. It's in the village of Erlenstegen, but the trip is worth it—no restaurant in or around Nürnberg offers finer food or service, not even front-runner Essigbrätlein. The upscale continental *cuisine moderne* is inventive and refreshing. Carpaccio of beef, presented in truffle-flavored oil, is a delectable choice, or you might opt for pungent medaillons of sea wolf in champagne sauce. Desserts are scrumptious, including a hazelnut torte with fresh fruit. The "Duck Tavern" is decorated like an elegant salon from the 1700s—it was once the hunting lodge of Ludwig III, the Bavarian king.

✪ **Essigbrätlein.** Weinmarkt 3. ☎ **0911/22-51-31.** Reservations required. Main courses 42DM ($25.20); fixed-price lunch 68DM ($40.80) for 3 courses, 78DM ($46.80) for 4 courses; fixed-price dinner 110DM ($66). AE, DC, MC, V. Tues–Fri noon–1:30pm; Tues–Sat 7–9:30pm. Closed Jan 1–15 and 2 weeks in Aug (dates vary). U-Bahn 2: Karstadt. FRANCONIAN/ CONTINENTAL.

This restaurant may not be as highly rated as Die Entenstub'n on the outskirts of town, but it's the finest within the city proper. It's gone through so many managers that critics say it's slipped, but we found it as solidly reliable as always. The cuisine is still an outstanding blend of the continental with the Franconian. The building is said to date from 1550, when it was mentioned for the first time in a chronicle of the city. The chef believes firmly in market-fresh ingredients.

Goldenes Posthorn. Glöckleingasse 2. ☎ **0911/22-51-53.** Reservations required. Main courses 12DM–36DM ($7.20–$21.60); fixed-price meals 28DM ($16.80) at lunch, 60DM–75DM ($36–$45) at dinner. AE, DC, MC, V. Mon–Sat noon–2:30pm and 6–11:30pm. U-Bahn 2: Lorenz-Kirche. FRANCONIAN.

Goldenes Posthorn claims to be in the oldest house in Germany. Among its mementos are a drinking glass used by Albrecht Dürer and a playing card belonging to Hans Sachs from about 1560. Although the restaurant's glory days—it was once celebrated as among the finest in Germany—are now long gone, no other place can match its antique atmosphere. Its modern Franconian cuisine is based on regional products. The menu features such old-fashioned but satisfying dishes as quail stuffed with goose liver and nuts, venison in red wine with plums, fresh carp (in winter), and wurst with a mixture of onions and vinegar. Two special fixed-price dinners are offered, a four-course house menu and a five-course Franconian menu. There are also fine wines dating from 1889.

MODERATE

Heilig-Geist-Spital. Spitalgasse 16. ☎ **0911/22-17-61.** Main courses 12DM–30DM ($7.20–$18); 3-course fixed-price menu 23DM–40DM ($13.80–$24). AE, DC, MC, V. Daily 11:30am–11pm. Bus: 46 or 47. FRANCONIAN.

You wouldn't want to get much more Franconian than this. Heilig-Geist-Spital, Nürnberg's largest historical wine house, in business for 650 years, is entered through an arcade above the river. The main dishes are typical Franconian fare, hearty and filling. Carp is a specialty, as is pork knuckle—we're sure no one has altered this recipe since the days of Dürer himself. In season, you can order leg of venison with noodles and berries. The wine list is abundant and excellent, with more than 100 vintages.

Weinhaus Steichele. Knorrstrasse 2. ☎ **0911/20-22-80.** Main courses 12DM–40DM ($7.20–$24). AE, DC, V. Mon–Sat 11am–midnight. U-Bahn 2: Weisser Turm. FRANCONIAN/ BAVARIAN.

Steichele's walls are covered with polished copper pots, antique display cases lit from within, and hanging chandeliers carved into double-tailed sea monsters and other mythical beasts. The specialties here are a delight, and the wine list is superb. Try roast shoulder of pork with potato balls and sauerkraut, or *Husarenspiess*, with onions, ham, paprika, cucumbers, hot sauce, French fries, and salad. Surely if former patron Hermann Hesse himself returned today, he would notice no major alteration in the cuisine. Amid all the change going on in Nürnberg, this place still respects older times.

INEXPENSIVE

Bratwurst-Häusle. Rathausplatz 1 (opposite the Rathaus). ☎ **0911/22-76-95.** Main courses 12.50DM–18DM ($7.15–$10.25); fixed-price meals 18DM ($10.80) at lunch. AE, MC, V. Mon–Sat 10am–10:30pm. U-Bahn 1: Lorenz-Kirche. FRANCONIAN.

This is the most famous bratwurst eatery in the city. You might make it a luncheon stopover as you explore historic Nürnberg. Prices are kept at a 1970s level, but portions are as large as ever. In winter, you'll find an open hearth to warm you; in summer, this is a refreshingly cool retreat from the heat. Fixed-price menus also include Franconian specialties; most diners, however, especially the large student clientele, prefer simply a platter of bratwurst and beer.

Historische Bratwurst-Glöcklein. Im Handwerkerhof. ☎ **0911/22-76-25.** Reservations recommended. Main courses 9.50DM–14.40DM ($5.70–$8.65). Fixed menu 23DM–39DM ($13.80–$23.40). No credit cards. Mon–Sat 10:30am–9pm. U-Bahn 1 and 2: Hauptbahnhof. FRANCONIAN.

If you want to try bratwurst in all its variations, this place is for you. Nürnbergers refer to it as their Bratwurst-Lokale, and it's the only serious rival to Bratwurst-Häusle (see above). The kitchen prepares a bratwurst as a main course, with traditional side dishes, all served on tin plates. Since beer goes perfectly with wurst, you'll enjoy sampling some of the brews on tap while admiring the craftsmanship of the room, which dates from the Middle Ages. Ham hocks are a specialty. Be careful that you don't spend your entire afternoon on the sun terrace—it's that tempting.

NÜRNBERG AFTER DARK

A theater complex offering quality productions of drama and opera, the **Städtische Bühnen,** Richard-Wagner-Platz 2-10 (☎ **0911/2-31-38-08**), houses the Kammerspiele, Operhaus, and Schauspielhaus. The box office is open Monday to Friday from 9am to 6pm, with ticket prices ranging from 41DM to 52DM ($24.60 to $31.20). Students get half-price admission, and the general public can check on discounted seats at the box office 1 hour before each performance.

Touring cabaret acts play at the **Loni-Ubler-Haus,** Marthastrasse 60 (☎ **0911/ 54-11-56**), on Saturday and Sunday at 8pm. The box office is open Tuesday to Friday from 9am to 11pm, and ticket prices range from 15DM to 90DM ($9 to $54). The city's premier outdoor venue, **St. Katarina,** is located in the ruins of the Katharinenkirche, Katherinenkloster 1 at Peter-Vischer-Strasse. It hosts concerts by an eclectic mix of international musical acts. Call the box office (☎ **0911/2-31-25-30**), Monday through Thursday from 10am to 1pm and Friday from 10am to noon, for recorded show listings and ticket information.

A garden house glowing in blue light marks the rear entrance to **Starclub,** Maxtorgraben 33 (☎ **0911/55-16-82**), the "House of 11 Beers." Brews start at 4.20DM ($2.50), accompanied by baguette sandwiches 5DM ($3) and other cheap snacks. Students come around for backgammon and darts or animated conversation on the patio out front. It's open daily from noon to 1am. An artists' hangout, **Triebhaus,** Karl-Griolenberger-Strasse 28 (☎ **0911/22-30-41**), opens early for big breakfasts that run from 6.50DM to 16.50DM ($3.90 to $9.90), and offers soup, salad, and sandwich specials from 6.50DM to 12.50DM ($3.90 to $7.50) throughout the day. At night it dims the lights and keeps serving drinks. It's open from Sunday to Wednesday 8am to 1am, and from Thursday to Saturday until 2am. Food is served until 11:30pm and breakfast is served all day.

Another low-key arts scene, **Café Ruhestörung,** Tetzelgasse 21 (☎ **0911/22-19-21**), offers some of the best people-watching in the city. Just sit on the patio and order a drink or a sandwich and watch the world waltz past. Draft beers range from 4.20DM to 5.50DM ($2.50 to $3.30). Open Monday to Wednesday from 7:30am to 1am, Thursday and Friday from 7:30am to 2am, Saturday 9am to 2am, and Sunday 9am to 1am.

The dimly lit **Lizard Lounge,** Katharinengasse 14 (☎ **0911/22-33-52**), plays a wide range of dance music from 10pm to 3am on Sunday and Tuesday to Thursday, staying open until 7am on Friday and Saturday. The cover charge is 5DM ($3). Open Saturday and Sunday only, **Forum,** Regensburgerstrasse 334 (☎ **0911/4-08-97-44**), is a two-story club split between indie rock and house dancing on Fridays, and techno raves and live bands on Saturday. Admission ranges from 10DM to 15DM ($6 to $9). At **Mach I,** Kaiserstrasse 1-9 (☎ **0911/203030**), Thursday and Friday move from disco to hip-hop, warming up for Saturday's big house party. The cover charge is 8DM ($4.80) on Thursday, 10DM ($6) on Friday, and 15DM ($9) on Saturday. It's open Thursday and Friday 10pm to 4am, and Saturday 10pm to 5am.

A popular gay bistro, **Cartoon,** An der Sparkgasse 6 (☎ **0911/22-71-70**), serves beer, wine, and light meals on Monday to Saturday from 11am to 1am, and on Sunday from 2pm to 1am. For later hours, hit the dance clubs, all of which have both gay and straight clientele.

4 Regensburg

76 miles NE of Munich, 62 miles SE of Nürnberg, 71 miles NW of Passau

Regensburg is one of Germany's best-preserved cities, relatively undamaged by World War II bombings. Despite this, it remains relatively obscure to many foreign visitors. Even if you don't have time to explore the city's museums or the interiors of its many historical monuments, try to take in the view of the Danube from one of its bridges, especially at sunset.

Regensburg started as a Celtic settlement called Radespona, around 500 B.C. The Romans later took it over, renamed it Castra Regina, and made it their center of power on the upper Danube. From the 7th century, the town was the center from which Christianity spread over southern Germany. The architecture of Regensburg testifies to its long history and past grandeur, which reached its peak by the beginning of the Gothic era. Its buildings and towers offer an unspoiled glimpse into history, and many of its ancient structures are still in active use today. The best example is the **Stone Bridge,** built in 1146 on 16 huge arches, in continuous service for more than 800 years.

ESSENTIALS

GETTING THERE   By Train   The **Regensburg Hauptbahnhof** is on major rail lines, including Passau-Regensburg-Nürnberg and Munich-Landshut-Regensburg, with frequent connections in all directions. From Munich, 20 trains arrive daily (trip time: 1½ hr.), and from Frankfurt, 10 trains daily (3¼ hr.). The trip from Nürnberg takes only an hour; from Passau (see below), 1½ hours. For rail information and schedules, call ☎ **01805/99-66-33.**

By Bus   Regional buses service the nearby towns. Call ☎ **0941/58-50-00** for information. For bus runs to such cities as Munich or Nürnberg, service is provided by **Firma Watzinger** in Bad Albach (☎ **09405/12-01**).

By Car   (☎ **09405/95-94-0**) Access by car is via the A3 Autobahn from east and west and the A93 from north and south.

VISITOR INFORMATION   Contact **Tourist-Information,** Altes Rathaus (☎ **0941/5-07-44-10**). Hours are Monday to Friday 8:30am to 6pm, Saturday 9am to 4pm, and Sunday 9:30am to 4pm.

SEEING THE SIGHTS

Regensburg is a city of churches; it was once the focal point from which Christianity spread throughout Germany and even into Central Europe via the Danube. The most majestic of these churches is the towering **Dom St. Peter's,** on Domplatz (☎ **0941/ 5-97-1002**), which was begun in the 13th century on the site of an earlier Carolingian church. Because it was constructed with easily eroded limestone and green sandstone, this French Gothic-style edifice is constantly being restored. The massive spires of the two western towers, added in the mid-19th century, were almost completely replaced in 1955 with a more durable material. The well-preserved stained-glass windows in the choir (14th century) and south transept (13th century) are impressive. Most of the pillar sculptures in the aisles of the nave were made in the cathedral workshop in the mid-14th century. The two little sculptures in the niches on opposite sides of the main entrance are called *The Devil* and *The Devil's Grandmother* by the townsfolk. The cathedral is home to a famous boys' choir, the Dompatzen, which performs every Sunday morning at mass at 9am. The performance is open to all. From May through October, the cathedral is open to visitors Monday to Saturday from 8am to 6pm and Sunday from noon to 6pm; November through April, Monday to Saturday from 8am to 4pm and Sunday from noon to 4pm. Admission is free. Bus: 1, 2, or 3.

You can also visit the cathedral treasures at the **Domschatzmuseum,** Krautermarkt 3 (☎ **0941/5-76-45**), which displays goldsmiths' work and splendid textiles from the 11th to 20th centuries. Entrance is through a portal in the north aisle of the cathedral. It's open April through October, Tuesday to Saturday from 10am to 5pm and on Sunday from noon to 5pm; December through March, generally only on Friday and Saturday from 10am to 4pm and on Sunday from noon to 4pm; closed in November. The charge is 3DM ($1.80) for adults and 1.50DM (90¢) for children. You can also buy a combination ticket to the Domschatzmuseum and the Diozesanmuseum St. Ulrich (see below) that costs 5DM ($3) for adults and 7DM ($4.20) for a family. (Admission to the cloister isn't included with this ticket.) Bus: 1, 2, or 3.

The permanent collection of the **Diozesanmuseum St. Ulrich** is on exhibit in the former Church of St. Ulrich, an early Gothic building to the side of the cathedral, Domplatz 2 (☎ **0941/5-10-68**). Sculptures, paintings, and goldsmiths' work form a representative selection of religious art in the diocese from the 11th to 20th centuries.

Of particular interest are various works on loan from the monastic foundations of the diocese. The museum is open April through October, Tuesday to Sunday from 10am to 5pm. Admission costs 3DM ($1.80) for adults and 1.50DM (90¢) for children, under 6 free. Bus: 1, 2, 6, or 11.

Crossing the cathedral garden, you enter the **cloister** with its Romanesque All Saints' Chapel and St. Stephen's Church. The ancient frescoes on the walls of the chapel depict liturgical scenes from All Saints' Day. The 11th-century church of St. Stephen contains an altar made of a hollowed limestone rock with openings connecting to early Christian tombs. You can only visit the cloister and St. Stephen's Church on one of the guided tours, which are given from May through October Monday to Saturday at 10 and 11am and 2pm and on Sunday and holidays at noon and 2pm; from November through April Monday to Saturday at 11am and on Sunday and holidays at noon. The charge is 4DM ($2.40) adults, 2DM ($1.20) students and children, free for children under 6. Bus: 1, 2, or 3.

Of all the remnants of Roman occupation of Regensburg, the ancient **Porta Praetoria** behind the cathedral is the most impressive, with its huge stones piled in the form of an arched gateway. Through the grille beside the eastern tower you can see the original level of the Roman street, nearly 10 feet below (which is why you often have to step down into the churches of Regensburg).

Of the four **Museen de Stadt Regensburg,** the most important is **Kunst- und Kulturgeschichtliche Sammlungen,** Dachauplatz 2–4 (☎ **0941/5-07-24-48**). This is not only the main museum of the city, but also one of the most notable in East Bavaria. Its displays show major developments in the history of the region from the earliest days up to the present. You'll see relics of the Roman period, such as a stone tablet marking the establishment of a garrison at Regensburg in the 2nd century. There's also a stone altar to the Roman god Mercury, as well as several Christian tombstones. The museum is open Tuesday to Sunday from 10am to 4pm. Admission is 4DM ($2.40) for adults and 2DM ($1.20) for children.

No town hall in Germany has been preserved better than Regensburg's **Altes Rathaus,** Rathaus Platz (☎ **0941/5-07-44-10**). This Gothic structure, begun in the 13th century, contains a Reichssaal (Imperial Diet Hall), where the Perpetual Diet sat from 1663 to 1806. In the basement of the Rathaus are the dungeons, with the torture chamber preserved in its original setting. The Altes Rathaus is open daily. Guided tours in German are conducted every 30 minutes from 9:30am to noon and from 2 to 4pm Monday to Saturday; on Sunday and holidays, every 30 minutes from 10am to noon. Guided tours in English are offered Monday to Saturday at 3:15pm only from May to September. The cost is 5DM ($3) for adults and 2.50DM ($1.50) for children. Take bus 1, 2, or 3.

A SIDE TRIP TO WALHALLA

An interesting excursion is to **Walhalla** (☎ **0941/96-16-80**), which lies on the steep northern bank of the Danube. This Greek-like temple was constructed between 1830 and 1842 on orders of Ludwig of Bavaria. It honors great Germans, most of them in the arts. The attraction itself isn't that spectacular—most visitors come for the view and the lovely ride down the river. Walhalla is open April to September daily 9am to 5:45pm, October daily 9am to 4:45pm, and November to March daily 10 to 11:45am and 1 to 4:45pm. There's a boat to Walhalla from Regensburg April to October daily at 10:30am and 2pm, with an additional departure from May to September Tuesday to Sunday at noon. The ride takes 45 minutes and costs 11DM ($6.25) each way for adults, and 5DM ($2.85) for children. For information about departures, call **Regensburger Personen Schiffahrt,** Werftstrasse 8 (☎ **0941/553-59**).

WHERE TO STAY

EXPENSIVE

Parkhotel Maximilian. Maximilianstrasse 28, 93047 Regensburg. ☎ **0941/5-68-50.** Fax 0941/5-29-42. www.maximilian-hotel.de. E-mail: pmaximilia@aol.com. 55 units. MINIBAR TV TEL. 210DM–288DM ($126–$172.80) double; 350DM–450DM ($210–$270) suite. Rates include breakfast. AE, DC, MC, V. Parking 18DM ($10.80). Bus: 1, 2, 3, or 6.

The next best thing to staying in one of Mad King Ludwig's palaces is to check into the Parkhotel Maximilian, an exquisitely renovated neo-rococo building. Its facade and public rooms have been classified as a public monument. The main salon, with a ceiling supported by columns of polished red stone, continues the theme of 18th-century opulence coupled with 20th-century convenience. The rooms are attractively furnished.

Dining: The indoor day cafe is a Bavarian fantasy in soft colors, crystal chandeliers, and elaborate plaster detailing, sometimes illuminated with gilt paint. There's also a German restaurant offering hearty Bavarian dishes.

Amenities: Room service, laundry, dry cleaning.

MODERATE

Bischofshof am Dom. Krautermarkt 3, 93047 Regensburg. ☎ **0941/5-90-86.** Fax 0941/5-35-08. 54 units. TV TEL. 195DM–295DM ($117–$177) double. AE, DC, MC, V. Parking 12DM ($7.20). Bus: 1.

This hotel was constructed as an ecclesiastical academy by the bishops of Regensburg in 1810. Today it blends the 19th-century monastic with the modern secular. Many of the units have hosted princes and even emperors. The bedrooms are attractively furnished; some have minibars. Bathrooms are a bit small but well maintained. Part of the hotel takes in a piece of a Roman gateway. Behind the building is one of Regensburg's most popular sun terraces. The hotel restaurants offer French, Bavarian, and international dishes. There's *gutbürgerlich* (home-cooked) cuisine at lunch, and a gourmet menu for dinner. Guests can also sit in the hotel's Weinstube, or in one of the 350 seats in the beer garden. The beer comes from a brewery dating from 1649.

Kaiserhof am Dom. Kramgasse 10, 93047 Regensburg. ☎ **0941/58-53-50.** Fax 0941/5-85-35-95. 30 units. TV TEL. 145DM–225DM ($87–$135) double. Rates include buffet breakfast. AE, DC, MC, V. Parking 10DM ($6). Closed Dec 23–Jan 28 and sometimes for a week in Jan. Bus: 1, 2, 3, or 6.

This hotel has a gabled roof with iron ice-catchers. The interior is nothing short of elegant, with a beamed ceiling in the dining room and a reading room with carved sandstone ribs supporting the plaster vaulted ceiling. From the sun terrace and from many of the hotel's windows you'll have a view of the Dom. The small rooms are soothingly lit and tastefully decorated.

Karmeliten. Dachauplatz 1, 93047 Regensburg. ☎ **0941/5-43-08.** Fax 0941/56-17-51. 80 units. TV TEL. 165DM–220DM ($99–$132) double; from 230DM ($138) suite. Rates include buffet breakfast. AE, DC, MC, V. Parking 10DM ($6). Closed Dec 20–Jan 20. Bus: 1, 2, or 3.

In spite of its 130 years of tradition, the Karmeliten has a young, modern look. It's set on a square about 3 blocks from the river and a 4-minute walk from the Dom, reached via an open-air fruit-and-vegetable market. The bedrooms, the public lounges, and the breakfast rooms have a homelike atmosphere. The rooms and the bathrooms are a bit cramped. The restaurant, open 24 hours, serves good Spanish and German specialties.

INEXPENSIVE

Straubinger Hof. Adolf-Schmetzer-Strasse 33 (a 15-min. walk east of the cathedral), 93055 Regensburg. ☎ **0941/60030.** Fax 0941/79-48-26. 60 units. 160DM–180DM ($96–$108) double. Rates include breakfast. AE, DC, MC, V. Bus: 1. Free parking.

This attractive, unpretentious hotel is little publicized, but bargain-hunters should seek it out. The small rooms are simple but satisfactory, with lots of sunlight, unadorned wood-grained armoires, and pleasing color schemes. Most rooms contain a minibar, TV, and phone. Bathrooms are tiny and towels are rather thin. Inexpensive and satisfying lunches and dinners, both German and regional, are served in the dining room.

WHERE TO DINE

You can satisfy your sweet tooth by stopping by **Princess Konditorei,** Rathaus Platz 2 (☎ 0941/5-76-71), which has a tempting array of homemade pastries and candies.

Gänsbauer. Keplerstrasse 10. ☎ **0941/5-78-58.** Reservations recommended. Main courses 19.50DM–34DM ($11.70–$20.40); fixed-price dinner from 45DM–100DM ($27–$60). AE, DC, MC, V. Daily 6pm–1am. Bus: Fischmarkt. BAVARIAN/INTERNATIONAL.

For elegant dining, call for a table at Gänsbauer, one of the best restaurants in the city. The setting is mellow and old-fashioned, but the cuisine is strictly *neue Küche—cuisine moderne* with a continental influence. Well-known Bavarian dishes are given a lighter touch. Only the freshest ingredients are used. Our recently sampled baby turbot in a Pernod sauce was superb in every way. The desserts are often exotic. The restaurant occupies a 500-year-old building with an open space where you can sit in fair weather. The street in front is a pedestrian zone, and there are tables here in summer, too.

✪ Historisches Eck. Watmarkt 6. ☎ **0941/5-89-20.** Reservations required. Main courses 39DM–45DM ($23.40–$27); fixed-price dinners 90DM–120DM ($54–$72); fixed-price lunch 55DM ($33). AE, DC, MC, V. Tues–Sat 11:30am–1:30pm (last order) and 6:30–9:30pm (last order). GERMAN.

This is the most elegant and charming restaurant in town, located midway between the cathedral and the town hall (Rathaus), and convenient to virtually every historic monument. It occupies what was originally a chapel built around 1250, and retains today the high vaulted ceilings and solid ornamentation of its original construction. Try the roast pigeon with chives, asparagus, and Bohemian-style noodles, or fish *(waller)* from the Danube served on a bed of hot sprouts. The menu has such refreshing change-of-pace fare as sliced tongue of veal with ratatouille, or—only for the adventurous—a well-flavored ragout of freshwater fish with eels, served with a beet-flavored cream-and-red-wine sauce. The wine list is the finest in the region. Your welcome here will be remarkably warm.

Historische Wurstküche. Thundorferstrasse 3. ☎ **0941/5-90-98.** Soup 4.80DM ($2.90); sausages 6 for 10.80DM ($6.50). No credit cards. Daily 9am–7pm. Bus: 1, 2, 6, 11. FRAN-CONIAN.

The owners will tell you that this is one of the oldest Bratwurst-Stuben in the world. Much of the decor is original. Only homemade potato soup, sauerkraut as a side, and pork sausages are served here. A large beer costs 4.60DM ($2.75) and up. In summer, guests can sit outside overlooking the Danube and an old stone bridge.

Ratskeller. Rathausplatz 1 (5 min. from the Dom). ☎ **0941/5-17-77.** Reservations recommended. Main courses 18DM–38DM ($10.80–$22.80); fixed-price lunch 22DM–30DM ($13.20–$18). AE, DC, MC V. Tues–Sun 10:30am–3pm; Tues–Sat 5:30pm–midnight. Bus: 1, 2, 3, or 6. FRANCONIAN.

Traditional and unspoiled—that describes the Ratskeller. Here you'll get some of the best meals for your money in Regensburg. This comfortable middle-class establishment consists of two dining rooms with vaulted ceilings, paneled walls, and painted crests. The Germanic cuisine is good, with other internationally inspired offerings that add variety and flair. The best buy is the fixed-price luncheon. The Franconian soups are good and hearty. You can also try schnitzel cordon bleu or, for an exotic touch, an Indonesian *nasi-goreng*.

REGENSBURG AFTER DARK

The town's cultural center, **Alte Mälzerei,** Galgenberger Strasse 20 (☎ 0941/7-57-49), hosts concerts and theater productions, as well as a rundown bar and beer garden which serves cheap drinks from 6pm to 1am daily. In the same complex, **Cartoon,** Galgenberger Strasse 20 (☎ 0941/7-57-38), has live reggae, blues, and rock bands on the main floor and a disco in the cellar. The club opens daily at 11am (2pm on week-ends), and begins its entertainment at 8pm. The nighttime cover ranges from 20DM to 30DM ($12 to $18). Closing hours vary. The only late-night bar in town, **Wunderbar,** Keplerstrasse 11 (☎ 0941/5-31-30), serves drinks until 3am 7 nights a week.

Südhaus Dance Theatre, Untere Bachgasse 8 (☎ 0941/5-19-46), is the best of the local dance clubs. Easy to spot, its entrance is marked by a statuary angel holding a lit bar sign. It's open Tuesday and Thursday 11pm until 3am, and Friday and Saturday 11pm to 4am. On Thursday night, it's the town's best lesbian and gay rendezvous. Admission is 50DM ($30) on Tuesday and 6DM ($3.60) on other nights. Trendier and snottier is **Scala,** Gesandtenstrasse 6 (☎ 0941/5-22-93), where the dance floor is hemmed in by three bars. This club attracts an under-35 crowd. It's open Wednesday to Sunday from 11pm to 3am (until 4am on Friday and Saturday). Admission ranges from 3DM to 7DM ($1.80 to $4.20).

If the weather's right when you reach Regensburg, head for the town's oldest inn, the **Goldene Ente,** Badstrasse 32 (☎ 0941/8-54-55), which has a beer garden at the end of Eisernen Steg Brücke (along the Danube). Under the chestnut trees, you can sample spareribs, Würstchen, grilled schnitzel, and, of course, that famous brew. Beer prices range from 4.20DM to 4.40DM ($2.50 to $2.65).

5 Passau

119 miles E of Munich, 73 miles SE of Regensburg

For year, Passau languished in a lost corner of West Germany. But since reunification, the beauty and nostalgia of this old city has been appreciated more and more. With its romantic river setting and stately streets, Passau is a city of great harmony. It's located at the confluence of the Danube and two of its tributaries, the Ilz and Inn Rivers. Passau's bustling port is worth a visit in itself.

ESSENTIALS

GETTING THERE   By Train   Since Passau is a German border station, **Inter-City** trains stop here, with frequent daily arrivals from such cities as Nürnberg, Munich, and Vienna. The other major rail links to Passau include the Frankfurt-Nürnberg-Passau-Vienna line and the Nürnberg-Regensburg-Passau line, with frequent connections. Trip time from Nürnberg is 2 hours; from Frankfurt, 4½ hours; from Munich, 1 hour; from Regensburg, 1 hour; and from Vienna, 3¼ hours. For rail information and schedules, call ☎ 01805/99-66-33.

By Bus   There are no long-distance buses serving Passau. However, buses service the outskirts of the city. For a recorded list of schedules (in German), call ☎ 0851/7-34-35.

By Car   Access is by the A3 Autobahn from the north or south.

VISITOR INFORMATION   For information, contact the **Tourist Information Office,** Bahnhof 36 (☎ 0851/95-59-80). April through October, hours are Monday to Friday 9am to 6pm and Saturday and Sunday 10am to 2pm; November through March, Monday to Thursday 9am to 5pm and Friday 8:30am to 4pm.

GETTING AROUND   A local bus, called **City-Bus,** runs through Passau from the Rathaus (Town Hall) to the Hauptbahnhof (train station) every 15 minutes. It connects all the places recommended below. Call the tourist office for schedule information.

CRUISING THE DANUBE

One reason for visiting this *Dreiflüssestadt* (town of three rivers) on the Austrian frontier is to take one of the numerous boat tours along the Danube and its tributaries, the Inn and the Ilz. Trips range from a 45-minute three-river tour to a steamer cruise downriver to Vienna. The cruises depart from Fritz-Schäffer Promenade. Many passengers prefer to go by boat and then take a train back.

You might also be tempted to board one of the passenger ferries that make runs (May to October only) every day from Passau downstream to the Austrian city of Linz. The trips take 5 hours each way, cost 34DM ($20.40) per person, and depart from the city's riverfront piers at 9am and at 1:10pm.

If you're interested in gaining even greater insights into life along the Danube, you can continue by train from Linz to Vienna, buying a ferryboat, train, and hotel package priced at a reasonable 249DM ($149.40) per person, which will include round-trip transit by boat and train to Vienna, via Linz, from Passau, and 1 night's stay at a four-star hotel in Vienna. For information about either the day trip to Linz or the overnight sojourn in Vienna, contact the **Donau-Schiffahrt Line** through its local representative, Würm & Koeck, Höllgasse 26, 94032 Passau (☎ **0851/ 929-292**).

SEEING THE SIGHTS

The **Altstadt** is built on a rocky spur of land formed by the confluence of the Inn and the Danube. To best appreciate its setting, cross the Danube to the **Veste Oberhaus,** St. Georg Berg 125, a medieval episcopal fortress towering over the town and the river. Note how arches join many of the houses, giving them a unity of appearance. As you view the town, you can sense that the architecture here is more closely allied to northern Italy and the Tyrolean Alps than to cities to the north. Veste Oberhaus houses a museum of regional history (☎ **0851/4933512**), going back to medieval times. It's open March through January, Tuesday to Thursday 9am to 5pm, Friday 9am to 7pm, and Saturday and Sunday 10am to 5pm. Admission is 7DM ($4.20) for adults and 4DM ($2.40) for children. Take the shuttle bus to the castle.

Dominating the town are the twin towers of the **Dom (St. Stephen's Cathedral),** Domplatz 9 (☎ **0851/39-33-74**). The original Gothic plan of the church is still obvious in spite of its 17th-century reconstruction in grand baroque style. Its most unusual feature is the octagonal dome over the intersection of the nave and transept. The interior of the cathedral is mainly Italian baroque—almost gaudy, with its many decorations and paintings. Of particular interest is the choir, which remains from the Gothic period. A newer addition is a huge organ, said to be the largest church organ in the world, built in 1928 and placed in an 18th-century casing. Concerts are given May to October Monday to Saturday at noon, costing 4DM ($2.40) for adults and 3DM ($1.80) for children and students, and also at 7:30pm on Thursday, costing 10DM ($6) for adults, 5DM ($3) for children. The Dom is open Monday to Saturday from 8 to 11am and 12:30 to 6pm. Admission is free. Take the City-Bus.

Below the cathedral, on the bank of the Danube, is the **Marktplatz** and the 13th-century **Rathaus,** with a facade decorated with painted murals depicting the history of the town. Inside, the huge knights' hall contains two large 19th-century frescoes illustrating incidents from the legend of the Niebelungen. The Town Hall has a Glockenspiel in its tower that plays at 10:30am, 2pm, and 7:25pm; on Saturday there's an additional performance at 3pm.

Next to the Rathaus, the **Glasmuseum (Glass Museum),** Rathausplatz (☎ 0851/ 3-50-71), features an impressive array of glassware from the 1700s to the 1930s, collected from Bavaria, Austria, Bohemia, and other parts of Europe. In all, there are 30,000 items on display, including the world's largest collection of Bohemian glass. The Biedermeier period of 1840 and the Jugendstil period of 1910 are particularly emphasized. The museum is open April through September, daily from 10am to 4pm; October through March, daily from 1 to 4pm. Admission is 5DM ($3) for adults, 3DM ($1.80) for students and older children, and free for children under 12.

WHERE TO STAY

EXPENSIVE

Holiday Inn. Bahnhofstrasse 24 (across from the Hauptbahnhof), 94032 Passau. ☎ 0851/ 5-90-00. Fax 0851/5-90-05-29. www.holiday-inn.com. 131 units. A/C TV TEL. 140DM–375DM ($84–$225) double; 330DM ($198) suite. AE, DC, MC, V. Parking 17DM ($10.20). Take the City-Bus.

The Holiday Inn is rather sterile, but it's the best hotel in Passau. It's been integrated into the city's largest shopping center. Its bedrooms all have up-to-date amenities and tiny bathrooms.

Dining/Diversions: There's a good restaurant, Batavia, serving both international and regional specialties, and an intimate bar, the Amadeo.

Amenities: Room service, laundry, health club, swimming pool, sauna, solarium.

MODERATE

Passauer Wolf. Rindermarkt 6, 94032 Passau. ☎ 0851/9-31-51-10. Fax 0851/9-31-51-50. 40 units. MINIBAR TV TEL. 160DM–280DM ($96–$168) double. Rates include breakfast. AE, DC, MC, V. Parking 17DM ($10.20). Take the City-Bus.

This hotel on the banks of the Danube has an elegant baroque facade. It isn't as up-to-date as the Holiday Inn but has better food and more character. Inside are modern and comfortable bedrooms. Service is efficient. Room service and laundry service are available.

The hotel's **Passauer Wolf Restaurant** is one of the most distinguished in town; you may want to dine here even if you're not a guest. It serves classic dishes and regional specialties. It's open Monday to Friday from noon to 2pm and from 6 to 10pm, and Saturday from 6 to 10pm only.

Weisser Hase. Ludwigstrasse 23 (off Ludwigsplatz, halfway between the Dom and the Hauptbahnhof), 94032 Passau. ☎ 0851/9-21-10. Fax 0851/9-21-11-00. 108 units. TV TEL. 180DM–250DM ($108–$150) double. Rates include buffet breakfast. AE, DC, MC, V. Parking 15DM ($9). Take the City-Bus.

Weisser Hase straddles the peninsula between the Danube and the Inn Rivers, in the heart of Passau. Some prefer this hotel to the more highly rated Passauer Wolf, because it provides more value for your money. The rooms have modern furnishings. There's a Weinstube with Bavarian-Austrian decor—carved wood and provincial chairs. The sauna is free to guests.

INEXPENSIVE

✪ **Altstadt-Hotel Laubenwirt.** Bäugasse 27–29, 94032 Passau. ☎ 0851/33-70. Fax 0851/33-71-00. www.alstadt-hotel.de. E-mail: info@alstadt-hotel.de. 56 units. TV TEL. 140DM–230DM ($84–$138) double. Rates include buffet breakfast. AE, DC, MC, V. Parking 10DM ($6) in underground garage. Take the City-Bus.

The waters of the Danube, the Ilz, and the Inn converge at a point just a few steps from the foundations of this hotel. You'd stay here just for the view, but it's also a very well-run hotel for a good price. Many guests who could afford the Holiday Inn seek out this little charmer for its ambience. The bedrooms are comfortably furnished in traditional style; a number of them overlook the confluence of the rivers. The in-house pub is a popular gathering spot for locals. The hotel also has a good restaurant, the Donaustuben, which has a fresh catch of fish delivered to the chef daily. In summer, guests can enjoy breakfast or other meals on the terrace.

Hotel König. Untere Donaulande 1, 94032 Passau. ☎ **0851/38-50.** Fax 0851/38-54-60. 41 units. TV TEL. 160DM–200DM ($96–$120) double. AE, V. Parking 10DM ($6). Take the City-Bus.

This hotel is located at the edge of a spit of land separating the Danube and Inn Rivers. It stands behind massive stucco-covered buttresses and a salmon-colored facade. Despite its fortresslike appearance, it has an interior that's comfortably up-to-date. Each of the well-scrubbed bedrooms has pinewood accents. The best ones open onto views of the Danube or the Inn, although the location isn't as scenic as that of the Altstadt-Hotel Laubenwirt (see above). A sauna and solarium are available.

WHERE TO DINE

For another dining option, head to the **Passauer Wolf** hotel (see above), which has one of the better restaurants in town.

Heilig-Geist-Stift-Schenke. Heiliggeistgasse. ☎ **0851/26-07.** Reservations recommended. Main courses 14DM–25DM ($8.40–$15); fixed-price menus 23DM–33DM ($13.80–$19.80). AE, DC, MC, V. Thurs–Tues 11am–1am. Closed Jan. Take the City-Bus. BAVARIAN/AUSTRIAN.

Each year we hope for the opening of a first-class restaurant in Passau, but until that great day comes, this little inn born in 1358 remains the top choice in town, with its hearty, stick-to-the-ribs fare. In summer, you can sit in a beautiful wine garden under chestnut trees. Indoors, the dining room has an open fireplace, decorated with old tools used to press grapes. The restaurant has its own vineyard, and you can order its wines under the label "Grüner Veltliner." The ancient kitchen serves up many good, low-cost regional dishes, including boiled rump steak Austrian-style and roast suckling pig. *Passauer Schlosserbaum* is a dessert specialty (the waiter will explain). Bavarian, Austrian, and international dishes are featured.

PASSAU AFTER DARK

Combining quality drama with a dramatic setting, the **Stadttheater Company** is housed in the **Stadttheater Passau,** Gottfried-Schäffer-Strasse (☎ **0851/9-29-19-10**), a beautiful baroque opera house built by the local prince-bishops. Call for performance schedules and ticket prices. Summertime brings drama, pantomime, opera, jazz, and classical concerts to town, scheduled as part of the **Europäische Wochen (European Weeks) Festival,** which runs from June to early August. Call ☎ **0851/ 560960** for information; for schedules, tickets, or reservations, contact the **Kartenzentrale der Europäischen Wochen Passau,** Dr.-Hans-Kapfinger-Strasse 22 (☎ 0851/752020; fax 0851/7560207).

Home to Passau's popular cabaret company, **Theater im SchaarfrichterHaus,** Milchgasse 2 (☎ **0851/3-59-00**), is open from September through July. It also hosts a series of jazz concerts throughout the year. Contact the theater for schedules, prices, and ticket availability. On June 25, 26, and 27, nearby **Vilshofen** is holding its annual **jazz festival,** which takes place in a tent on the banks of the Danube. Friday and Saturday performances highlight German and international jazz ensembles, Saturday night focuses on dance music, and Sunday is dedicated to jazz, swing and Dixieland.

Tickets for Friday are 45DM ($27), for Saturday 60DM ($36), and for Sunday 15DM ($9). A 3-day pass is 100DM ($60). Call the festival organizers at ☎ **0851/3-59-00** or 085141/20-81-6 for details.

Café Innsteg, Innstrasse 15 (☎ **0851/5-12-57**), housed in a bungalow hanging over the Inn River, offers the town's most scenic setting in which to relax with a drink. Like every other cafe-bar in town, it's open from midmorning until 1am. **Café Kowalski,** Obere Sandstrasse 1 (☎ **0851/24-87**), is less dramatic but also has balcony views of the river. Underground, across the river, **Joe's Garage,** Lederergasse 38 (☎ **0851/3-19-99**), is a friendly student dive named after a Frank Zappa album.

6 Ulm

60 miles SE of Stuttgart, 86 miles W of Munich

Visit Ulm for its architectural heritage and its history—not for great shopping, nightlife, or even an exciting local life. Ulm is a bit sleepy, smug, and satisfied with its monuments, especially its undeniably magnificent cathedral, praised by none other than Hermann Hesse. The town is situated at a strategic spot on the Danube. Ulm's importance as a commercial river port has made it a prosperous city ever since the Middle Ages. Today, Ulm is a center of scientific and technological research, as befits the birthplace of Albert Einstein, who started life here in 1879. The old, narrow alleyways of the Altstadt lead to a modern city of riverbank promenades, beer gardens, spacious squares, and pedestrian zones.

ESSENTIALS

GETTING THERE   By Train   The **Ulm Hauptbahnhof** is on several major and regional rail lines, with frequent connections in all directions. More than 40 trains per day arrive from Munich (trip time: 45 min.) and some 50 or more from Stuttgart (67 min.). Daily trains also arrive from Cologne (4 hr., 6 min.). From Frankfurt (2 hr., 20 min.), you can take an ICE (InterCity-Express), the fastest and most comfortable way to travel by rail. For rail information and schedules, call ☎ **01805/996633.**

By Bus   There are no buses from major cities; local buses service only satellite towns—mostly bedroom communities of Ulm.

By Car   Access by car is via the A8 Autobahn east and west or the A7 north and south. It takes about 1½ hours to drive to Ulm from Munich and about 3 hours to drive from Frankfurt.

VISITOR INFORMATION   Tourist-Information, Münsterplatz (☎ **0731/1-61-28-30**), is open Monday to Friday 9am to 5pm and Saturday 9am to 1pm.

SEEING THE SIGHTS

If you approach the town from the Stuttgart-Munich Autobahn, you'll miss the best view. So sometime during your visit, you should cross the Danube into Neu Ulm for a look at the gables and turrets of the Altstadt, which line the north bank of the river. Here is the **Fisher's Quarter,** with its little medieval houses and tree-shaded squares. Nearby are the elaborate Renaissance patrician houses and the Gothic Renaissance **Rathaus.**

✪ **Ulm Münster.** Münsterplatz 1. ☎ **0731/15-11-37.** Münster free; tower 4DM ($2.40) adults, 2.50DM ($1.50) children. Nov–Feb daily 9am–4:45pm; Mar daily 9am–5:45pm; Apr and Sept daily 8am–6:45pm; May–June daily 8am–6:45pm; July–Aug daily 8am–7:45pm; Oct daily 8am–5:45pm. Buy tickets an hour before the climb. Bus: 2, 7, or 9.

Before you even get close to the city, you'll see the towering Ulm Münster on the skyline. Its 530-foot steeple is the tallest of any cathedral in the world, and the Ulm Münster itself is second only to Cologne Cathedral in size. Without the pews, the nave of the church could hold nearly 20,000 people, more than twice the population of Ulm at the time the cathedral was begun in 1377. When Ulm joined the Protestant movement in 1531, work on the building was suspended, not to be continued until 1844; it was completed in 1890. Miraculously, the cathedral escaped serious damage during World War II.

The exterior is almost pure German Gothic, even though bricks were often used in the walls along with the more typical stone blocks. The unusual feature of the Münster is that its architects placed as much emphasis on horizontal lines as on the vertical. Before entering, stop to admire the main porch whose three massive arches lead to two 15th-century doors. This section dates from the 14th and 15th centuries and contains a wealth of statues and reliefs.

The five aisles of the cathedral lead directly from the hall below the tower through the nave to the east chancel. The conspicuous absence of a transept heightens the emphasis on the chancel and also increases the length of the nave. Huge pillars towering into steep arches enclose each of the five aisles. The ceiling is swept into net-vaults so high that any of Germany's church steeples could sit comfortably beneath them. The nave is so large that, even with pews, it can accommodate more than 11,000 people at one service.

You can climb the tower as far as the third gallery (768 steps), where you can look out on the town and surrounding countryside over the Danube plain as far as the Alps.

Rathaus. Marktplatz 1. ☎ **0731/16-10.** Free admission. Mon–Fri 8am–6pm.

The Rathaus was built in 1370 as a warehouse but has served as the town hall since 1419. It contains some ornate murals dating from the mid-16th century. On the south gable hang coats of arms of cities and countries with which Ulm is linked by commerce. On the east gable is an astronomical clock from 1520. Above the interior staircase is a reproduction of the flying machine constructed by A. L. Berblinger, called "the tailor of Ulm." In 1811, he was one of the first people to make a serious attempt at flight.

Ulmer Museum. Marktplatz 9 (near the cathedral). ☎ **0731/1-61-43-12.** Admission 5DM ($3) adults, 3DM ($1.80) children. Tues–Wed and Fri–Sun 11am–5pm, Thurs 11am–8pm. Bus: 2, 5, or 6.

The Ulm Museum contains an important collection of arts and crafts produced in Ulm and upper Swabia from medieval times onward. There are also successive exhibitions of both ancient and modern art and artifacts, ranging from the region's prehistory up to the 20th century, with works by Klee, Kandinsky, and Picasso.

WHERE TO STAY

Goldenes Rad. Neuestrasse 65, 89073 Ulm. ☎ **0731/6-70-48.** Fax 0731/6-14-10. 21 units, 15 with private bath. MINIBAR TV TEL. 140DM–185DM ($84–$111) double; 230DM ($138) suite. Rates include buffet breakfast. AE, DC, MC, V. Free parking. Bus: 2, 3, 4, or 14.

This hotel doesn't have grand style and amenities, but its location by the cathedral makes it a winning choice nonetheless. The rooms are small and rather standard but hospitable. The beds are very good. The bathrooms, however, are a little too cramped and have rather thin towels.

Neu-Ulm Mövenpick Hotel. Silcherstrasse 40, 89231 Neu Ulm. ☎ **0731/8-01-10.** Fax 0731/8-59-67. 135 units. MINIBAR TV TEL. 235DM–280DM ($141–$168) double; 250DM–290DM ($150–$174) suite. AE, DC, MC, V. Parking 6DM–12DM ($3.60–$7.20). Bus: 2, 3, or 7.

This hotel beside the Danube contains rather bland, but well-maintained, guest rooms. Many rooms feature views of the river. On the premises you'll fine a cafe, a pub, and a Swiss-inspired restaurant with a salad buffet. The English-speaking staff is helpful. Room service and laundry service are available.

Further up the Danube: Sigmaringen

Schloss Sigmaringen (☎ 07571/729-110), one of the most impressive castles in Germany, lies about 60 miles southwest of Ulm, dramatically situated on a rock above the Danube. Inside, the rooms are filled with period furniture, porcelain objects, and works of art. The castle also holds displays of 15th and 16th century paintings and one of the biggest private collections of arms in Europe. Schloss Sigmaringen is open November and February to April, daily 9:30am to 4:30pm; May to October, daily 9am to 4:45pm; December and January, only by private arrangements. To get to Sigmaringen from Ulm, take a train on the Ulm-Frieberg line, or drive southwest on the B311 and then west on the B32. From the north, take the B313. There are also trains from Stuttgart.

Ulmer Spatz. Münsterplatz 27 (just beside the cathedral), 89073 Ulm. ☎ **0731/6-80-81.** Fax 0731/6-02-19-25. 35 units. TV TEL. 150DM–160DM ($90–$96) double. Rates include continental buffet breakfast. AE, MC, V. Bus: 2, 3, or 4.

The Ulmer Spatz is a corner stucco hotel-and-restaurant combination, with most of its simply furnished rooms overlooking the cathedral tower. This is an exceedingly modest but clean and comfortable place. Its chief recommendation is its location in the center of Ulm. The rooms are a bit cramped. The little Weinstube serves tasty Franconian meals in a mellow setting.

WHERE TO DINE

Zur Forelle. Fischergasse 25. ☎ **0731/6-39-24.** Reservations recommended. Main courses 18DM–44DM ($10.80–$26.40); fixed-price menus 44DM ($26.40) and 86DM ($51.60). AE, DC, MC, V. Mon–Sun noon–2pm and 6pm–midnight. Bus: 2, 3, or 4. SWABIAN/CONTINENTAL.

The cuisine here, although not grand, has enough imagination and flair to keep the locals returning again and again. Both nouvelle and Swabian regional specialties are featured. Owners Renate and Guido Heer have created a cozy environment; there are only 10 tables. Menu items include homemade parfait of eel, lobster, goose, and stag, or fillet of trout (*forelle*) in puff pastry with mushrooms and slices of smoked ham.

Zum Pflugmerzler. Pfluggasse 6. ☎ **0731/6-80-61.** Reservations recommended. Main courses 18DM–38DM ($10.80–$22.80). No credit cards. Mon–Fri 11am–2pm and 6–11pm, Sat 11am–3pm. Closed last 2 weeks in July and 1st 2 weeks in Aug. Bus: 2, 3, or 4. GERMAN/INTERNATIONAL.

Although not the equal of Zur Forelle (see above), this intimate restaurant is a winning choice for stick-to-the-ribs fare. Since it's open later than most restaurants in Ulm, it's a good place for an after-concert supper in an old-world setting. The kitchen turns out home-style Swabian, Bavarian, and international meat and fish dishes. A specialty is Swabian *Fischmaultasche,* which looks like large ravioli, usually stuffed with a spinach-and-ricotta mixture. *Tafelspitz,* the famed boiled beef dish, is served with either a horseradish sauce or a green-herb sauce.

ULM AFTER DARK

The two best beer halls in town are **Barfusser,** Lautenberg 1 (☎ **0731/6-02-11-10**), a brew pub that also makes its own pretzels; and **Erstes Ulmer Weizenbierhaus,** Kronengasse 12 (☎ **0731/6-24-96**), which serves more than 20 varieties of Weizenbier and also has a menu of Franconian dishes that range in price from 5.50DM to 12.80DM ($3.30 to $7.70).

The Romantic Road

The aptly named Romantic Road, or *Romantische Strasse,* is one of Germany's most popular tourist routes. The road stretches for 180 miles between Würzburg in the north and Füssen in the foothills of the Bavarian Alps. Strung along the way is a series of medieval villages and 2,000-year-old towns. Frankfurt and Munich are convenient gateways for exploring the road by car, coach, or rail.

Another way to tour the route is by **bicycle.** Cyclists can begin at Würzburg and follow the bike path along the Main River. Tourist offices along the road provide cycling maps and other helpful information. Campgrounds are generally 6 to 12 miles apart. Bikes can be rented at any train station along the Romantic Road for 12DM ($7.20), or 6DM ($3.60) with a valid train ticket.

The Romantic Road is more than just a scenic route—it's also a powerful marketing organization composed of 26 municipalities, each of which would love to welcome you for a visit. The Romantic Road Association will provide information on sights and attractions and mail information packs in English. Contact it at the **Romantische Strasse Arbeitsgemeinschaft,** Marktplatz, 91550 Dinkelsbühl (☎ 09851/9-02-71).

THE TOWNS OF THE ROMANTIC ROAD Every town on the road has its special charms and attractions—and its drawbacks. **Rothenburg,** for example, is a perfect museum town but is overwhelmed with tourists. **Dinkelsbühl** is less perfect—it doesn't do as good a job of transporting you into the past—but at least it has an integrity of its own, independent of tourists. **Nördlingen** is less romantic even than Dinkelsbühl, but is more real. **Augsburg** is Bavaria's third largest city (after Munich and Nürnberg) but still has a rich medieval past. **Würzburg,** traditionally the first town on the route, is the bustling center of the Franconian wine region and home to one of Germany's greatest palaces.

BUS TOURS OF THE ROMANTIC ROAD Green-and-white buses make three runs a day among all the member towns. From April through October, a deluxe motor coach equipped with reclining seats and toilets departs from Frankfurt every morning at 8am, making stops on the main squares of 26 towns en route, eventually pulling into Füssen at 8:40pm. One-way transit between Frankfurt and Füssen costs 129DM ($77.40), but you can get off the bus and reboard it later at any town en route. Buses also run the other way, from Füssen to

Frankfurt, following more or less the same schedule. Make advance reservations by phoning **Deutsche Touring GmbH** (☎ **069/7-90-35-0**), Amrömerhof 17, Frankfurt.

1 Würzburg

174 miles NW of Munich, 74 miles SE of Frankfurt, 68 miles NW of Nürnberg

For Germans, the south begins at Würzburg, one of the loveliest baroque cities in the country. Würzburg is the best starting point for the Romantic Road. This city on the Main is young and lively (and often crowded in summer), and has a population of some 50,000 students, who give it a German version of *joie de vivre*. It's also a center of the Franconian wine region.

Würzburg remained faithful to the Roman Catholic Church throughout the Reformation. It's has been called "the town of Madonnas" because of the more than 100 statues of its patron saint that adorn the house fronts. The best known of these statues is the baroque *Patrona Franconiae*, also known as the "Weeping Madonna," which stands among other Franconian saints along the buttresses of the 15th-century Alte Mainbrücke, Germany's second-oldest stone bridge.

On March 16, 1945, Würzburg was shattered by a bombing raid. In a miraculous rebuilding program, nearly every major structure has been restored.

ESSENTIALS
GETTING THERE **By Train** The **Würzburg Hauptbahnhof** lies on several major and regional rail lines, with frequent connections to all major German cities. From Frankfurt, 30 trains arrive per day (trip time: 1½ hr.); from Munich, 20 trains (2½ hr.); from Nürnberg, 30 trains (1 hr. and 10 min.); and several trains from Berlin (5 hr. and 50 min.). For rail information and schedules, call ☎ **01805/99-66-33.**

By Bus For bus service along the Romantic Road, see "Bus Tours of the Romantic Road," at the beginning of this chapter.

By Car Access is via the A7 Autobahn from the north and south or the A3 Autobahn from the east and west. The A81 Autobahn has links from the southwest.

VISITOR INFORMATION Contact the **Tourist Information Office,** Pavillon vor dem Hauptbahnhof (☎ **0931/37-33-55**). It's open Monday to Saturday from 10am to 6pm.

SEEING THE SIGHTS
In spring and summer, the liveliest place in town is the **Markt,** or central marketplace. Here street performers entertain and vendors hawk their wares, ranging from fresh fruit to souvenir trinkets. You can also stroll down the traffic-free **Schönbornstrasse,** with its modern boutiques and cafes. The wine merchants here will sell you a *Bocksbeutel,* the emerald-green, narrow-necked wine bottle that's native to the region. It's said that the shape came about because wine-drinking monks found it the easiest to hide under their robes.

Mainfränkisches Fortress (Festung Marienburg). ☎ **0931/4-30-16.** Admission 3.50DM ($2.10) adults, free for children under 14. Admission including the Fürstenbaumuseum 6DM ($3.60) adults, free for children under 14. Apr–Oct Tues–Sun 10am–5pm; Nov–Mar Tues–Sun 10am–4pm.

Marienberg Fortress, located across from the Altstadt, over the stone bridge, was the residence of the local prince-bishops from 1253 to 1720. Although portions of the stronghold have been restored, the combination of age and wartime destruction has taken a serious toll on its thick walls and once-impenetrable ramparts. But what

The Romantic Road

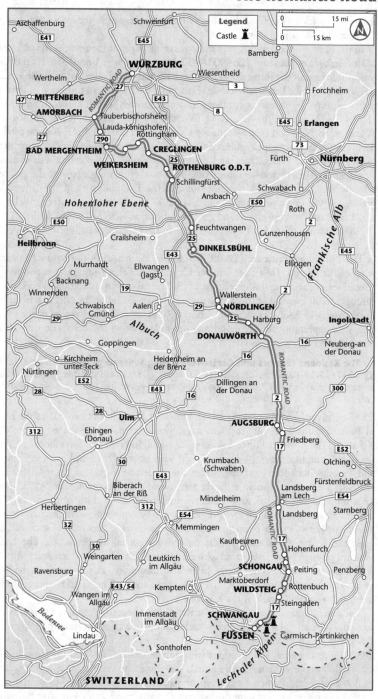

remains is worth a visit. The 8th-century **Marienkirche,** one of the oldest churches in Germany, stands within its walls.

In the former arsenal and Echter bulwark, to the right of the first courtyard, is the **Mainfränkisches Museum** (☎ 0931/4-30-16), housed here since 1946. It's the historical museum of the former Bishopric of Würzburg and Dukedom of Franconia as well as the provincial museum of lower Franconia. On display is a collection of important sculptures by the great flamboyant Gothic master, Tilmann Riemenschneider (1460–1531), called "the master of Würzburg." The sculptor came to live in Würzburg in 1483 and even was the town's mayor in 1520 and 1521. Never a totally decorative artist, Riemenschneider concentrated on the reality of people's appearance, highlighting their hands, faces, and even their clothing. The museum also displays paintings by Tiepolo and sandstone figures from the rococo gardens of the prince-bishops' summer palace. A tribute to one of the few industries of the city, wine making, is paid in the press house, which contains historic casks and carved cask bases and a large collection of glasses and goblets. Admission is 3DM ($1.80) adults, 2DM ($1.20) students; children 14 and under are free. Open Tuesday to Sunday from 10am to 5pm.

The **Fürstenbaumuseum** (☎ 0931/4-38-38) is situated in the restored princes' wing of the fortress. Here the visitor gets a glimpse of the living quarters and living conditions of the prince-bishops up to 1718. The urban-history section offers a stroll through 1,200 eventful years of Würzburg's history, including an exhibit relating to the discovery of X-rays by Wilhelm Conrad Röntgen in 1895. A model of the town shows its appearance in 1525, and another model shows the destruction after the bombing of 1945.

✪ **The Residenz (Schloss und Gartenverwaltung Würzburg).** Residenzplatz 2, Tor B. ☎ 0931/35-51-70. Admission 8DM ($4.80) adults, 6DM ($3.60) students, free for children under 15 and seniors. Apr–Oct Tues–Sun 9am–5pm; Nov–Mar Tues–Sun 10am–4pm. Tram: 1 or 5.

The Residenz of Würzburg is the last and finest of a long line of baroque castles built in Bavaria in the 17th and 18th centuries. This great horseshoe-shaped edifice was begun in 1720 to satisfy Prince-Bishop Johann Philipp Franz von Schönborn's passion for elegance and splendor. Its design was the joint effort of the best Viennese, French, and German architects working under the leadership of an architect of genius, Balthasar Neumann. Both an architect and an engineer, Neumann (1687–1753) was known for his technical virtuosity and the inbuilt harmony of his compositions. He stands today as one of the towering figures of the baroque movement in architecture. This castle shows a unity of purpose and design unusual in structures of such size.

At the center of the castle is the masterful Treppenhaus (staircase). The high, rounded ceiling above is decorated with a huge fresco by Tiepolo. At its center, Apollo is seen ascending to the zenith of the vault. The surrounding themes represent the four corners of the world, the seasons, and signs of the zodiac. The painting appears to be overflowing onto the walls of the upper hall.

The other important attraction in the Residenz is the court chapel, in the southwest section. Neumann placed the window arches at oblique angles to coordinate the windows with the oval sections, thus creating a muted effect. The rectangular room is divided into five oval sections, three with domed ceilings. Colored marble columns define the sections, their gilded capitals enriching the ceiling frescoes by Johann Rudolf Byss, a leading fresco artist. At the side altars, Tiepolo painted two important works: *The Fall of the Angels* on the left and *The Assumption of the Virgin* on the right.

During the summer, a **Mozart festival** is held in the upper halls. For information, call **0931/35-51-70.**

Würzburg

Legend
Church ✝
Information ⓘ

MORE SIGHTS & ACTIVITIES

Cathedral of St. Kilian (Dom). Domstrasse (at the end of Schönbornstrasse). ☎ **0931/5-36-91.** Free admission. Easter–Oct, Mon–Sat 10am–5pm, Sun 1–6pm; Nov–Easter, Mon–Sat 10am–noon and 2–5pm, Sun 12:30–1:30pm and 2:30–6pm.

This cathedral, begun in 1045, is the fourth-largest Romanesque church in Germany. The interior was adorned with high-baroque stucco work, done after 1700. The imposing row of bishops' tombs begins with that of Gottfried von Spitzenberg (ca. 1190), who was one of the first prince-bishops to rule over the town. Look for three sandstone tombstones by Riemenschneider, constructed between 1502 and 1506. The Dom is dedicated to St. Kilian, an Irish missionary to Franconia in the 7th century.

A DAY TRIP FROM WÜRZBURG

The most interesting excursion in the area is to the **Veitshöchheim,** Hofgarten 1 (☎ **0931/9-80-27-40**), about 5 miles away. You can take a Main River excursion (about 30 min.) to this delightful summer retreat of the 17th- and 18th-century prince-bishops. The palace here contains rococo and Empire furniture. But it is the fantastic rococo park that makes the trip worthwhile. Take time to wander among the fine and sometimes comical statues along shaded walks and avenues bordered by lime trees. The park is open daily from 7am to dusk. The palace can be visited April through October, Tuesday to Sunday from 9am to noon and 1 to 5pm. Admission to the park is free, but a visit to the palace costs 3DM ($1.80) for adults, 2DM ($1.20) for children and seniors, free for children under 15.

WHERE TO STAY
EXPENSIVE

Hotel Maritim. Pleichertorstrasse 5, 97070 Würzburg. ☎ **0931/3-05-30.** Fax 0931/3-05-39-00. 287 units. A/C MINIBAR TV TEL. 199DM–327DM ($119.40–$196.20) double; 450DM–550DM ($270–$330) suite. Rates include buffet breakfast. AE, DC, MC, V. Parking 24DM ($14.40). Tram: 1 or 5.

Nothing in Würzburg can match this hotel for comfort and style, not even the closest contender, Rebstock (see below). The Maritim has views over the Main River and is linked to the city convention center. Its modern and imposing yellow facade is topped by a baroque-style mansard roof. The good-sized guest rooms are well upholstered and comfortable.

Dining/Diversions: A Weinstube and a cafe are on the premises, but the Palais is the place for gourmets. Shining crystal and an amber glow from the lamps combine to create the most elegant restaurant in town. Dinner is served nightly from Tuesday to Saturday. The refined continental menu changes frequently, but typical dishes are rabbit fillet with figs, marinated salmon with coriander, and breast of goose in orange-and-mustard sauce. Reservations are necessary. The hotel also has a large terrace and bar.

Amenities: Room service, hair dryers in room, laundry, dry cleaning, sauna, solarium, and indoor pool.

Hotel Rebstock. Neubaustrasse 7, 97070 Würzburg. ☎ **800/528-1234** in the U.S., or 0931/3-09-30. Fax 0931/3-09-31-00. www.rebstock.com. E-mail: rebstock@rebstock.com. 72 units. MINIBAR TV TEL. 284DM–310DM ($170.40–$186) double; 360DM–380DM ($216–$228) suite. Rates include buffet breakfast. AE, DC, MC, V. Parking 18DM ($10.80). Tram: 1, 3, or 5. Closed Jan 4–25.

The impressive Rebstock is housed in a palace that dates from 1408. It's not as stylish as the Maritim, but it appeals to those nostalgic for a taste of old Germany. Through a classical doorway, you enter a wide foyer with carved wooden doors and an old Spanish sea chest. The interior is tasteful. The guest rooms are equipped with wall-to-wall draperies and matching sofas, as well as hair dryers. 30 rooms are air-conditioned. A winter garden with a fountain, chimney, and bar replaces an old courtyard.

Dining/Diversions: Gourmet cuisine is served in the main parquet-floor restaurant. The Fränkische Weinstube has oak beams, stark-white walls, and a gilded baroque painting along with a carved Madonna. Guests gather to drink local wine.

Amenities: Room service, laundry, health club, dry cleaning; car-rental and bicycle-rental facilities are also available.

Walfisch. Am Pleidenturm 5, 97070 Würzburg. ☎ **0931/3-52-00.** Fax 0931/3-52-05-00. www.hotel-walfisch.com. E-mail: walfisch@hotel-walfisch.com. 41 units. MINIBAR TV TEL. 225DM–285DM ($135–$171) double. Rates include breakfast. AE, DC, MC, V. Parking 15DM ($9). Tram: 1, 3, or 5.

From the windows of this inn's modernized guest rooms, you can gaze across the Main as far as Marienberg Castle, high on the opposite hill. Bedrooms have been greatly improved following renovations, making Walfisch a good third choice after the Maritim and Rebstock. Furnishings are typically Franconian: heavy draperies, provincial cupboards, and flowery fabrics. The rooms range from small to medium in size; most are air-conditioned.

Dining/Diversions: The highlight of staying here is ordering your breakfast while overlooking the banks of the Main. In the timbered but modern dining room, generous portions of traditional German food are served. The Weinstube serves a good selection of wine.

Amenities: Room service.

MODERATE

Franziskaner. Franziskanerplatz 2, 97070 Würzburg. ☎ **0931/3-56-30.** Fax 0931/3-56-33-33. 47 units. TV TEL. 165DM–185DM ($99–$111) double. Rates include buffet breakfast. AE, DC, MC, V. Closed Dec 23–Jan 6. Tram: 1 or 5.

For homespun cleanliness, this hotel is a winner—and the price is right, too. You'll receive a hearty welcome from the staff. The lobby has attractive black panels surrounded with natural wood; the breakfast room has fine large windows looking out to the greenery beyond. The guest rooms are well furnished; 40 of them have a TV. The hotel itself serves only breakfast, but an on-site restaurant under separate management offers Franconian specialties.

Gasthof Greifenstein. Hafnergasse 1 (just off the Marienkapelle and its food market), 97070 Würzburg. ☎ **0931/3-51-70.** Fax 0931/5-70-57. 40 units. A/C MINIBAR TV TEL. 155DM–200DM ($93–$120) double. Rates include continental breakfast. AE, DC, MC, V. Parking 10DM ($6). Tram: 1, 3, or 5.

The 300-year-old Greifenstein, which was recently renovated, has been faithfully restored to its original design after 1945. It's a true tavern, abounding in village atmosphere. The upper-floor rooms have a private entrance and are calm and quiet; they have views over a pedestrian walkway in back. Some rooms are quite small and cramped, but all are reasonably comfortable, clean, and cozy. The economical restaurant offers hearty German cuisine.

Hotel und Weinrestaurant Schloss Steinburg. Auf dem Steinberg, 97080 Würzburg. ☎ **0931/9-70-20.** Fax 0931/9-71-21. 50 units. MINIBAR TV TEL. 190DM–260DM ($114–$156) double. Rates include buffet breakfast. AE, CB, DC, MC, V. Free parking and a garage for 10DM ($6). Take Rte. 27 2 miles toward Fulda.

This turreted castle and its outbuildings sprawl high on a hill overlooking Würzburg. The foundations of the castle date from the 13th century, but what you see was largely rebuilt around 1900. It's a good choice for motorists, offering a tranquil setting and reasonable rates. From the sun terrace, guests can view the Main River, the acres of vineyards surrounding the property, and the web of rail lines that carry cargo far into the distance. Guest rooms have a country nostalgia. Each comes with a hair dryer. The hotel has an indoor pool and a sauna.

INEXPENSIVE

Schönleber. Theaterstrasse 5, 97070 Würzburg. ☎ **0931/1-20-68.** Fax 0931/1-60-12. 34 units, 27 with bathroom. TV TEL. 110DM ($66) double without bathroom, 120DM–170DM ($72–$102) double with bathroom. Rates include buffet breakfast. AE, DC, MC, V. Parking 16DM ($9.60). Closed Dec 22–Jan 6. Tram: 1, 2, 3, or 5.

You'll find the salmon-colored facade of this family hotel in the central part of historic Würzburg. The ground floor is rented to boutiques that monopolize the two enormous arched windows facing the sidewalk. The upper floors offer smallish but comfortable rooms. The bathrooms are very cramped and have rather thin towels. The staff is friendly and helpful.

St. Josef. Semmelstrasse 28, 97070 Würzburg. Tel **0931/30-86-80.** Fax 0931/3-08-68-60. 38 units. MINIBAR TV TEL. 147DM–167DM ($88.20–$100.20) double. Rates include buffet breakfast. AE, MC, V. Parking 12DM ($7.20). Closed Dec 22–Jan 5. Tram: 1, 2, 3, or 5.

St. Josef is the best inexpensive accommodation in the Altstadt. Its owner has been successful in bringing it up-to-date. All rooms, though small, are pleasantly furnished and well maintained. Breakfast is the only meal offered, but there are many Weinstuben and restaurants in the area. Fresh flowers add a personalized touch to this well-run establishment.

WHERE TO DINE

Try the local specialty, *Zwiebelkuchen,* which is like a quiche Lorraine, and also look for a fish specialty, *Meerfischle.* White Franconian wine goes well with the local sausage.

Backöfele. Ursulinergasse 2. ☎ **0931/5-90-59.** Reservations recommended. Main courses 10.50DM–35DM ($6.30–$21). AE, MC, V. Mon–Sat 11:30am–1am, Sun 11:30am–midnight. Tram: 1 or 4. FRANCONIAN.

Since this place is a short walk from both the Residenz and the Rathaus, you'll probably eat here at least once while you're in Würzburg. Even the locals don't really know whether to call it a beer hall, a wine cellar, or a restaurant. Regardless, the place serves well-prepared traditional food in copious quantities.

Ratskeller Würzburg. Langgasse 1 (near the Alte Mainbrücke). ☎ **0931/1-30-21.** Reservations required Sat–Sun. Main courses 10DM–32DM ($6–$19.20). AE, DC, MC, V. Daily 11:30am–2:30pm and 5:30pm–midnight. Tram: 1, 2, 3, or 5. FRANCONIAN/FRENCH.

This Ratskeller, some 500 years old, is part of the Rathaus in the center of Würzburg. It's not only an interesting place to visit, but also serves tasty Franconian fare at reasonable prices. Country cookery is an art here, as you'll discover if you order the boiled breast of beef with horseradish sauce and noodles. The English-speaking host will help you with menu selections. Game is featured in season. The place also specializes in local beer and Franconian white wines.

✪ Weinhaus Zum Stachel. Gressengasse 1. ☎ **0931/5-27-70.** Reservations required. Main courses 13.50DM–45DM ($8.10–$27). MC, V. Daily 11am–1am. Tram: 1, 3, 4, or 5. FRANCONIAN.

No other wine house in Würzburg is as old as this one, which dates to 1413. Seats and walls have been burnished by the homespun clothing of many hundreds of drinkers and diners during the past 500 years. The portions are generous. Try veal cordon bleu, a tender pepper steak aromatically flavored with cognac, or the more prosaic rump steak with onions. Some dishes, such as chateaubriand, are so elaborate that they're prepared only for two. The chef is proudest of his freshwater fish prepared according to old family recipes. In summer, you can dine in a vine-draped outdoor courtyard. Wines are from the restaurant's own vineyards.

Weinstuben Juliusspital. Juliuspromenade 19. ☎ **0931/5-40-80.** Reservations required. Main courses 15.90DM–30DM ($9.55–$18). No credit cards. Thurs–Tues 10am–midnight. Tram 1, 3, or 5. FRANCONIAN.

One of the best known of Würzburg's Franconian wine taverns, the Juliusspital is decorated with traditional paneling and a beamed ceiling. It's distinguished by its wide range of regional dishes. The restaurant is a top address for wine connoisseurs, with an array of characteristic Franconian vintages.

Wein- und Fischhaus Schiffbäuerin. Katzengasse 7. ☎ **0931/4-24-87.** Reservations recommended. Main courses 24DM–42DM ($14.40–$25.20). No credit cards. Tues–Sun 11am–2:30pm; Tues–Sat 5:30–11pm. Closed Jan 4–11, and mid-July to mid-Aug. Tram: 3 or 4. SEAFOOD.

One of the best dining spots in the region is this combined wine-house/fish restaurant, across the river in an old half-timbered building on a narrow street, about 1 minute from the old bridge. The house specializes in freshwater fish, such as pike, carp, char, tench, trout, wels, and eel. Most of these dishes are priced per 100 grams (3.5 oz.). Soup specialties are fish, snail, lobster, and French onion.

WÜRZBURG AFTER DARK

Much of Würzburg's nightlife takes place in its numerous Weinstuben, many of which have an interesting character. For music and cultural happenings, scan the flyers posted in the *Studentenhaus* on Am Exerzierplatz at Münzstrasse.

A one-stop entertainment complex, **Autonomes Kulturzentrum Würzburg,** Frankfurter Strasse 87 (☎ **0931/41-78-00**), houses a bar and beer garden and offers a disco during the week. Saturday and Sunday, it hosts concerts, and sometimes a theater production. The complex is open Monday to Wednesday 6pm to 7am, Thursday to Saturday 6pm to 3am, Sunday 3pm to 1am. There's a 48DM ($28.80) cover charge Monday to Friday, and an admission fee of around 20DM ($12) on weekends, depending on the performance scheduled. Call for listings and ticket information.

The city's oldest jazz cellar, **Omnibus,** Theaterstrasse 10 (☎ **0931/5-61-21**), has been packing it in for live acts for nearly 3 decades. This is also where people come to drink and play chess. It's open Monday to Thursday from 8pm to 1am and Friday and Saturday from 9pm to 2am. The cover charge for performances ranges from 14DM to 18DM ($8.40 to $10.80). A place for a cheap meal or a drink, **Standard,** Oberthurstrasse 11a (☎ **0931/5-11-40**), is open daily from 11am to 1am. It occasionally has a live band on the weekend. **Kult Stattkneipe,** Landwehrstrasse 10 (☎ **0931/5-31-43**), keeps the stereo cranking. It's open 9am to 1am Monday to Friday, and 10am to 1am on weekends.

2 Miltenberg

18 miles S of Mespelbrunn, 44 miles W of Würzburg

This riverside town, along with Amorbach (see below), is located to the west of the traditional route of the Romantic Road, but it's very popular and well worth a visit. Miltenberg is sleepy, traditional, and full of half-timbered buildings. If you're looking for a medieval town, but want to avoid the tour-bus hordes that overrun places like Rothenburg (see below), Miltenberg is for you.

The town, which is still enclosed within its walls and gate towers, is attractively situated under a steep wooded hill crowned by a castle. Its municipal charter dates from 1237, but the place was actually settled centuries earlier by the Romans. The best way to appreciate Miltenburg's charm is with a fast drive-through, with a pedestrian detour through its charming **Marktplatz.** Here, on steeply sloping terrain centered around a Renaissance-era red sandstone fountain and a wealth of flowers, you'll find a phalanx of half-timbered houses, and one of the oldest inns in Germany, the **Haus zum Reisen.**

ESSENTIALS

GETTING THERE   By Train   Three or four trains per day arrive from Würzburg, 90 minutes away, and about a dozen come every day from the important railway junction of Aschaffenburg, 45 minutes away. For railway information, call ☎ **06021/ 19419** in Aschaffenburg or ☎ **01805/996633.**

By Car   From the north, take Route B469 into town (it's signposted). From Würzburg, take the A3 west and then minor roads.

VISITOR INFORMATION   The **tourist office,** Engelplatz 69 (☎ **09371/ 400119**), offers pamphlets describing brief walking tours through the town. It's open Monday to Friday 9am to 5:30pm.

A Local Wine House

During your explorations of Miltenburg, don't overlook the oldest and most historic bar in town, a 500-year-old hangout that locals refer to simply as **Weinhaus,** Marktplatz 185 (☎ **09371/5500**). Here, every evening between 5pm and midnight, you can order any of the local vintages, at a per-glass price of 5DM to 8DM ($2.85 to $4.55).

SEEING THE SIGHTS

Park your car in the first convenient parking lot and walk into the center of town—don't attempt to drive. Other than the above-mentioned Marktplatz, the main attraction in town is **Schloss Miltenburg.** (Be warned in advance that this castle is sometimes rather confusingly identified simply as "Miltenburg.") Don't expect a rich tour of a medieval-looking interior, as all but a fraction of the castle's inside (a cafe) has been closed for a long-standing series of renovations. You can visit the courtyard, however, and climb to the top of a watchtower for a sweeping view over the surrounding forest. The courtyard, the tower, and the cafe that's associated with the site are open only between May and October, Tuesday to Sunday from 10:30am to 5:30pm. Admission costs 2DM ($1.20) per adult, 1DM (60¢) for children under 12.

Beer-lovers might want to take a guided tour through one of the town's breweries, such as **Brauhaus Faust,** Hauptstrasse 219 (☎ **09371/97130**), or **Kalt-Loch Brauerei,** Hauptstrasse 201 (☎ **09371/2283**). These tours, given in German, take you through the full range of the hops-gathering and brewing processes and include several mugs' worth of tasting. The cost is 5DM ($3) per participant. If you like tasting more than touring, just sit down at any restaurant or pub in town—they all serve ample quantities of these breweries' products. A particularly good cafe is the **Café Bauer,** Hauptstrasse 41 (☎ **09371/2384**).

WHERE TO STAY & DINE

✪ **Haus zum Riesen.** Hauptstrasse 99. ☎ **09371/67238.** Fax 09371/67176. 15 units. TV TEL. 120DM–175DM ($68.40–$99.75) double; 200DM ($114) suite. Rates include breakfast. No credit cards.

This awesomely historic hotel is permeated with a polite sense of modern management. Its origins date back to 1190, just before it hosted Frederick Barbarossa during his expeditions in this part of Germany. During the Thirty Years' War, it housed VIPs from both sides, depending on who was in control at the moment. Today, this hotel is the most evocative in town, graced with charmingly old-fashioned bedrooms, usually with a beamed ceiling.

However, the place is probably more famous as a restaurant than as a hotel. Inside the old dining room, you can order such medieval-sounding dishes as roasted bear steak (the bear is imported from Russia), as well as a dish that we've seen in no other restaurant in Germany, *Ochsenfetzen* ("Torn-apart ox"). This delicacy, which has been the subject of many articles in culinary reviews and is based on authentic medieval scholarship, uses brisket of beef marinated for 2 weeks in marinades that change every 2 days. A hearty red wine is the best accompaniment for this age-old dish. Main courses cost from 17DM to 35DM ($9.70 to $19.95) at lunchtime, and from 17DM to 48DM ($9.70 to $27.35) at dinner. Meals are served Wednesday to Monday from 11am to 9pm, and Tuesday from 11am to 6pm.

Hotel Altes Bannhaus. Hauptstrasse 211, 63897 Miltenberg. ☎ **09371/3061.** Fax 09371/68754. 10 units. MINIBAR TV TEL. 174DM–184DM ($99.20–$104.90) double. AE, MC, V.

This medieval hotel is set on the main street of town, behind a severely dignified stone facade that's graced with an elaborate iron bracket. The place treads the fine line between authentically historical and merely dowdy. Overall, however, its vaulted stone cellars and massive masonry are charming. Bedrooms are more angular and modern looking than the authentically antique public rooms. Each room has functional furniture, small windows, and vestiges of the early 1960s. The restaurant here is open daily for lunch and dinner.

3 Amorbach

7 miles S of Miltenberg, 57 miles SW of Würzburg.

This little town shouldn't take up too much of your time, but it does offer a few rewarding sights, notably the Abtai Kirch of St. Maria, and it also contains one of the finest hotels in the region. As you wander about Amorbach's center, note the way that local homeowners have dotted many of the half-timbered facades with flower boxes.

ESSENTIALS

GETTING THERE   By Train or Bus   Three or four trains arrive every day from Würzburg (90 min. away), and 12 arrive from Aschaffenburg (45 min.). For railway information, call ☎ **06021/19419** in Aschaffenburg or ☎ **01805/996633.**

BY CAR   From Miltenberg, follow route 469 south for 7 miles.

VISITOR INFORMATION   The Stadt Verkehrsarnt, at the Rathaus, Marktplatz 1 (☎ **09373/20940**), is open Monday to Friday 9am to 5:30pm.

SEEING THE SIGHTS

Much of the fun of a visit to Amorbach lies simply in wandering through the streets of the old town, where half-timbered medieval buildings, some of them a bit artfully askew, still evoke old Germany.

The town's most important monument is the **Abtai Kirche St. Maria,** Kirchplatz (☎ **09373/971545**). This impressive church underwent at least a half-dozen enlargements and alterations between the 8th and the 18th centuries, but it still manages to retain a degree of charm and cohesiveness. The interior is a mass of ornate baroque stucco, centering around one of the most impressive baroque-era organs in Germany. Entrance is free, but a guided tour, conducted in German, costs 4.50DM ($2.55) per person. It's open daily from 9:30am to noon and from 1:30pm till between 4 and 6pm, depending on the season and schedule of religious services and maintenance inside.

A small museum called **Sammlung Berger** (The Berger Collection), Wolkmannstrasse 2 (☎ **09373/618** or 09373/20940), holds around 17,000 teapots, many from the U.S. and Britain. Part of the funding of this museum comes from a local teapot manufacturer, whose wares are for sale in the museum shop. Entrance is free. It's open only between April and October, Tuesday to Sunday from 1 to 6pm.

Three miles southeast of Amorbach lie the ruined remains of **Wildenberg Castle,** Odenwald (☎ **09373/20940**). Originally built a thousand years ago, it's now little more than a jumble of impressive medieval-looking rock piles. The restored watchtower, however, can be climbed every Sunday, between 10am and 5pm, for a fee of 2.50DM ($1.40). The view over the Odenwald Forest is excellent.

WHERE TO STAY & DINE

✪ **Der Schafhof Amorbach.** Odenwald, ☎ **09373/97330.** Fax 09373/4120. E-mail: Der.Schafhof.Amorbach@t-online.de. 23 units. MINIBAR TV TEL. 660DM–720DM ($376.20–$410.40) double, 800DM ($456) suite. Prices reduced on selected midwinter weekends to

450DM–490DM ($256.50–$279.30) double and 650DM ($370.50) suite. Rates include breakfast. AE, DC, MC, V. From Amorbach, follow the N47 (the Niebelungenstrasse) west for 3 miles.

The most reliable and carefully manicured hotel in the district lies within what was originally a Benedictine monastery (around 1450) and later (in 1721) rebuilt in a country-baroque style. The more historic rooms lie within the former abbey; more modern, better-equipped units are within a well-built modern annex. Our favorite rooms lie under the eaves of the main building, and are crisscrossed with a labyrinth of hand-hewn ceiling beams. All rooms are stylishly and comfortably outfitted in a plush but conservative style.

Dining/Diversions: Two good restaurants serve both lunch and dinner. The Benedicter Stube, located within what was originally the monastery's winepress, is open daily except Wednesday and Thursday. The more formal Aptstube, within the masonry walls of the building's oldest section, serves more upscale cuisine at both lunch and dinner; it's open daily except Monday and Tuesday.

4 Bad Mergentheim

29 miles S of Würzburg, 66 miles NE of Stuttgart

Most of this spa town's fame derives from its role during and after the Renaissance as the home, beginning in 1525, of the Teutonic Knights, one of the most durable orders of feudal knights. From their base in Bad Mergentheim, they received tributes and pledges of allegiance from as far away as Lithuania. The knights' way of life ended abruptly in 1809, when Napoléon forcibly disbanded the order, consequently threatening the very existence of the town.

But Bad Mergentheim's fortunes were reversed in 1826, when a shepherd discovered rich mineral springs a short walk north of the town center during the time when Germany's spas were expanding at a rapid pace. The water turned out to be the strongest sodium sulfate water in all of Europe; it was said to have health-giving properties, especially in the treatment of digestive disorders. With the knights gone, the little town had discovered the key to its future prosperity.

ESSENTIALS

GETTING THERE By Train or Bus Access by train is easier and more convenient than by bus. From Würzburg, trains arrive almost every hour (trip time: 40 min.). From Stuttgart, they arrive at intervals of between 90 and 120 minutes (trip time: 90 min.). For information about **railway schedules,** call ☎ 0931/19419 (Würzburg Railway station), or ☎ 01805/996633. For bus service along the Romantic Road, see "Bus Tours of the Romantic Road," at the beginning of this chapter.

By Car From Würzburg, head south along Route 19.

VISITOR INFORMATION The Tourist Office, called **Kultur und Verkehrsamt,** is at Marktplatz 3 (☎ 07931/5713). It's open Monday to Friday 8:30am to 5:30pm, Saturday 10am to noon.

SEEING THE SIGHTS

The best way to see the town is to wander through its historically evocative streets, most of which radiate outward from the meticulously restored **Marktplatz.** Schloss Park leads to the spa establishments on the right bank of the Tauber. The Kursaal is a pump room with both a visitors' center and bathing facilities.

The most impressive structure in town is the somewhat sterile and barren-looking **Munster Kirche Sankt Johannes,** Ledermarkt 12 (☎ 07931/1250), which was begun around 1250 and completed several centuries later. It's noted for its relatively large size. It's open daily from 9am to dusk; entrance is free. More interesting is the medieval castle that once served as the Teutonic Knights' home base, the **Deutschordenschloss,** site of the **Deutschordensmuseum,** Schloss 16 (☎ **07931/52212**). Inside, you'll find a sweeping retrospective of chivalry's preconceptions and preoccupations, with all the requisite displays of suits of armor and weapons. Surprisingly, this medieval order of knights has been restored today, and now serves as a religious and charitable organization. Note the corner towers in the inner courtyard, which are furnished with Renaissance spiral staircases. In the 18th century the castle park was landscaped in the English manner. The building is open Tuesday to Sunday from 10am to 5pm, charging an entrance of 6DM ($3.40), and an additional 9DM ($5.15) for a German-language guided tour.

A second-tier attraction that's a lot less worthwhile than a promenade through the town itself is the **Wildpark Bad** (Bad Mergentheim Game Preserve; ☎ **07931/41344**), 3 miles east of the town center. It contains wild animals both in cages and roaming within natural environments. From mid-March to October, it's open daily from 9am to 6pm; from November to mid-March, it's open only Saturday and Sunday from 10am to 5pm. Entrance costs 11DM ($6.25) for adults, 6DM ($3.40) for children.

WHERE TO STAY & DINE

Haus Bundschu. Cronbergstrasse 15, 97980 Bad Mergentheim. ☎ **07931/9330.** Fax 07931/933-633. 33 units. MINIBAR TV TEL. 150DM–190DM ($85.50–$108.30). Rates include breakfast. AE, DC, MC, V.

Stylish, understated, and cozy, this hotel was built about 15 years ago in a style that incorporated a masonry-covered courtyard, lots of exposed wood, and touches of Romantic Road nostalgia. It lies within a 5-minute walk of the town center. Bedrooms are sunny, thanks to big windows, and well maintained. The hotel contains an excellent restaurant, where set-price menus cost 69DM ($39.35) each.

✪ **Hotel Victoria.** Poststrasse 2–4, 97980 Bad Mergentheim. ☎ **07931/593-0.** Fax 07931/593-500. E-mail: Hotel-victoria@t-online.de. 78 units. MINIBAR TV TEL. 218DM–286DM ($124.25–$163) double. 314DM–423DM ($179–$241.10) suite. Half board 45DM ($25.65) extra per person. AE, DC, MC, V. Parking 16DM ($9.10) per day.

The best hotel in town occupies a stately, five-story, ocher-colored building. Inside, the color scheme is an oft-repeated and very pleasing combination of champagne, beige, yellow, and black. Bedrooms are modern and plush, with lots of concealed, very elegant lighting and supremely comfortable mattresses. The in-house restaurant prepares succulent, sometimes splendid food. A full range of massage and health programs is available.

AN EXCURSION TO STUPPACH

The agrarian village of **Stuppach** (population 500), located 7 miles southeast of Bad Mergentheim, is the site of one of the region's most important artistic treasures, the **Stuppacher Madonna** by Matthias Grünewald (ca. 1475–1528). This dark, brooding work is firmly opposed to the lighter motifs of such contemporaneous artists as Dürer. It's the artistic centerpiece of the village's only church, the **Fahrkirche Maria Krönung,** Kirchplatz (☎ 07931/2615), which can be visited, without charge, daily from 9am to dusk.

5 Weikersheim

6 miles E of Bad Mergentheim, 25 miles S of Würzburg

The architecture of this riverside town is consistently 18th century; it's one of the most stylistically unified towns on the Romantic Road. Weikersheim also boasts one of the mightiest castles on the Romantic Road.

ESSENTIALS

GETTING THERE **By Train or Bus** Trains pull into Weikersheim from Würzburg at intervals of between 60 and 120 minutes throughout the day (trip time: 40 min.). From Stuttgart, they arrive at intervals of between 90 and 120 minutes (trip time: 90 min.). For information about railway schedules, call the station at ☎ 0931/8315.

By Car Take the B232 from Bad Mergentheim.

VISITOR INFORMATION The Tourist Office at Marktplatz 7 (☎ 07934/10255) is open Monday to Friday 9:30am to 5pm.

SEEING THE SIGHTS

During its formative years, the very existence of the town was dependent on its castle, **Schloss Weikersheim,** Schlossstrasse (☎ 07934/8364). It was begun in 1586 and completed a century later in a severely dignified style that had nothing to do with the baroque style then popular in other parts of Germany. When Count Ludwig II re-established Weikersheim as his family's main residence, he ordered that the old moated castle be replaced with a magnificent new Renaissance palace.

You can visit the castle's interior for a cost of 4DM ($2.30) per person, every day between 9am and noon and 1 and 5pm. Its architectural and decorative highlight is the **Rittersaal** (Knight's Hall), which was completed in 1603 and shows the transition between the baroque and the earlier Renaissance style. This is the most sumptuous banqueting hall ever built in Germany. Note the bas-reliefs of game animals lining the walls. The entrance doorway is carved with a scene of a battle against the Turks. The gigantic chimneypiece is adorned with an allegory illustrating the motto, "God gives luck." Also, allow some time to wander through the well-preserved **gardens,** with their chestnut trees and formal clipped hedges offset by the fiery color of flower arrangements.

To one side of the castle is the **Marktplatz,** a semi-circular market square that opens onto sweeping vistas. It was laid out in the early 18th century.

WHERE TO STAY & DINE

Flair Hotel Laurentius. Marktplatz 5, 97990 Weikersheim. ☎ 07934/91080. Fax 07934/910818. 11 units. TV TEL. 155DM–165DM ($88.35–$94.05) double. AE, DC, MC, V.

The most appealing hotel in town is an old-fashioned monument to the art of hospitality. It's an ideal stopover along the Romantic Road, either for a meal or an overnight stay. Its vaulted, street-level area is the site of a cozy restaurant and wine bar, where set-price menus range from 44DM to 110DM ($25.10 to $62.70). Upstairs, a series of high-ceilinged bedrooms contain a pleasing, unpretentious mix of good reproductions and genuine antiques. Bathrooms are quirkily old-fashioned, but not without charm. There's also a sauna on the hotel's premises as well.

6 Creglingen

12 miles E of Weikersheim, 25 miles S of Würzburg

The history of Creglingen goes back more than 4,000 years. Originally, it was an important Celtic stronghold. Later on, around the year 1000, it was mentioned in written sources as a wine-growing site. By 1349, the town had gained the right to call itself a "city." Around the same time, Creglingen became an important pilgrimage site, thanks to the legend of a local farmer who claimed to have seen Jesus and a phalanx of angels plowing his fields.

Today, Creglingen is one of the quietest hamlets along the Romantic Road, with a tiny but colorful inner core of buildings that evoke Germany of long ago, and a charming but substandard set of accommodations, usually in local farmhouses. The surrounding countryside is called "The Lord God's Little Land"—locals believed that it resembled the Garden of Eden. You might think so too if you explore the local streams and lakes, where anglers fish for pike, carp, trout, eel, or perch.

ESSENTIALS

GETTING THERE   By Train or Bus   Rail connections from Würzburg arrive about once every 2 hours, pulling into the hamlet of Steinach, about 12 miles from Creglingen. At the station, an employee will call a local taxi to carry you the rest of the way into Creglingen. For railway information, call the information service for the local train lines at ☎ **07951/19419.** For bus service along the Romantic Road, see "Bus Tours of the Romantic Road," at the beginning of this chapter.

By Car   Follow the signs west from Weikersheim.

VISITOR INFORMATION   Tourist information is available at Bad Mergentheimer Strasse 14 (☎ **07933/631**), available Monday to Friday 9am to 5:30pm.

SEEING THE SIGHTS

Creglingen is home of one of the most quirky museums in Germany, the **Fingerhutmuseum** (Thimble Museum), Herrgottstal (☎ **07933/370**). Here, sociologists have accumulated the largest collection of thimbles in Europe. Some of them are bone rings dating from prehistoric times; others are made of brass that was smelted in Creglingen during the Middle Ages. Between April and October, it's open daily from 9am to 6pm; the rest of the year, it's open Tuesday to Sunday from 10am to noon, and 1 to 4pm.

More stately is the **Feuerwehrmuseum** (Fire-Brigade Museum), in the Schloss Waldmannshofen, in the nearby hamlet of Waldmannshofen (for information, call either the tourist office or ☎ **09355/674**). Inside, you'll find a collection of implements and tools used since medieval times to fight the scourge of fire. It's open only from Easter to late October, daily from 10am to noon and from 2 to 4pm. Entrance is free.

The most important local attraction is the **Herrgottskirche** (Chapel of our Lord; for information, contact the tourist office at ☎ **07933/631**), which is set 2 miles south of Creglingen within the Gerrgottstal Valley. It's clearly posted from the village center. The chapel was built by the counts of Hohenlohe around 1525. Its enormous altarpiece, a 33-foot-tall structure showing the ascension of Mary, was decorated in the 16th century by master craftsman Tilman Riemenschneider and members of his workshop. All the artist's sensitivity is translated into the expression of the Virgin. The work, Riemenschneider's masterpiece, is set in a filigree shrine specially constructed to catch the day's changing light effects. The chapel can be visited without charge. Between April and October, it's open daily from 9:15 to 5:30pm; from November to March, daily from 1 to 4pm.

WHERE TO STAY

Accommodations are not plentiful in Creglingen; most visitors are merely passing through. However, there is one truly offbeat choice.

Heuhotel Ferienbauernhof. Weidenhof 1, 97993 Creglingen. ☎ **07933/378.** Fax 07933/7515. 6 units with shower and toilet; 25 sleeping places in a hayloft with communal bathrooms. 60DM ($34.20) double, with breakfast included; 28DM ($15.95) per person for a sleeping site in the hayloft, with a cold supper included. No credit cards. From Creglingen, drive 6 miles, following the signs to the hamlet of Weidenhof.

Don't expect plush comforts here; the allure of this place derives from its close links to nature and its age-old sense of Teutonic virtue. It lies within a solid-looking German farmhouse owned by the Stahl family. The six Spartan rooms each have a thin but passably comfortable mattress and a stripped-down bathroom. More folkloric is the establishment's barn, where a hayloft provides a soft, sweet-smelling bed for clients who enjoy as close a contact with nature as possible. Don't expect privacy, as the only barriers between the sleeping sites are burlap bags, sewn together and stretched on ropes as a kind of privacy screen. Your comfort here is enhanced by the warm welcome from the owners.

7 Rothenburg ob der Tauber

73 miles NE of Stuttgart, 32 miles SE of Würzburg

If you have time for only one town on the Romantic Road, make it Rothenburg. Admittedly, if you arrive at Rothenburg's Bahnhof, at the northeast corner of town, you may find it hard to believe that this is the best-preserved medieval city in Europe. Contemporary life and industry have made an impact, and as you leave the station you'll first see factories and office buildings. But don't be discouraged. Inside those undamaged 13th-century city walls is a medieval town seemingly untouched by the passage of time.

The only drawback to this gem of a city is that it suffers from serious overcrowding, especially in summer. (The Rothenburg locals go so far as to put bumper stickers on their cars proclaiming in German, "I'm not a tourist—I actually live here.") Ironically, Rothenburg for centuries was impoverished and forgotten. It was first mentioned in written records in 804 as Rotinbure, a settlement above ("ob" in German) the Tauber River. The town grew to be a free imperial city, reaching its apex of prosperity under Burgermeister Heinrich Toppler in the 14th century.

ESSENTIALS

GETTING THERE **By Plane** The nearest regional airport is Nürnberg (see chapter 5); from there it's a 2-hour train ride to Rothenburg.

By Train You can reach Rothenburg via a daily train from Frankfurt (trip time: 3 hr.), from Hamburg (5½ hr.), or from Berlin (7 hr.). Rothenburg lies on the Steinach-Rothenburg rail line, with frequent connections to all major German cities, including Nürnberg and Stuttgart. For information, call ☎ 01805/996633.

By Bus For bus service along the Romantic Road, see "Bus Tours of the Romantic Road," at the beginning of this chapter. Regular long-distance buses (Lines EH 190 and 190A) service Rothenburg from Frankfurt, Würzburg, Augsburg, and Munich, as well as Füssen. For information and reservations, call ☎ 069/79-03-50 in Frankfurt. Regional bus service is provided by **OVF Omnibusverkehr Franken GmbH,** Kopernikusplatz 14, 90459 Nürnberg (☎ 0911/4-39-06-66).

By Car Access by car is via the minor road south from Creglingen, or the A7 Autobahn on the Würzburg-Ulm run.

VISITOR INFORMATION Contact **Stadt Verkehrsamt,** Rathaus (☎ 09861/4-04-92). November through April, it's open Monday to Friday 9am to 12:30pm and 1 to 5pm and Saturday 10am to 7pm; May through October, it's open Monday to Friday 9am to 6pm and Saturday 10am to 3pm.

SPECIAL EVENTS The cultural event of the year is the **Meistertrunk festival,** held the second weekend of September; it celebrates the entire history of the town, with more than 1,000 participants in costume. Concerts, historical exhibitions, a parade, and a play about the Burgermeister Nusch's wager (see the listing for the

Rothenburg ob der Tauber

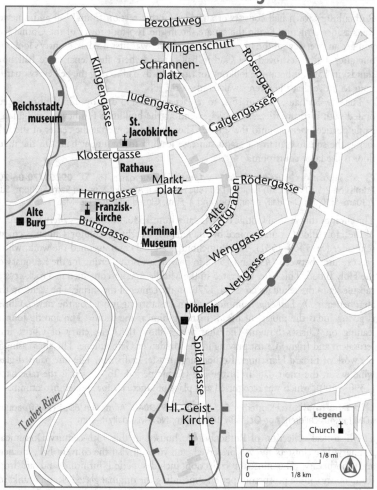

Reichsstadtmuseum, below) are the festival's highlights. The play is also staged in July and October. For details, contact the visitor information office (☎ 09861/4-04-92).

EXPLORING THE TOWN

For an excellent view, take a walk on the town walls. The wall tour, from the massive 16th-century Spitaltor (at the end of the Spitalgasse) to the Klingentor, takes about a half hour.

If you want to escape the tourist hordes, you can rent a bike at **Hermann Kat's,** Galgengasse 33 (☎ **09861/6111**), or at **Rad und Tat,** Bensenstrasse 17 (☎ **09861/87984**), for about 20DM ($12) per day. Get a map from the tourist office and head out along the Tauber River. Of course, it's best if you bring a picnic lunch to enjoy in some romantic spot on the water.

✪ **Rathaus.** Marktplatz. ☎ **09861/4-04-92.** Rathaus free; tower 1DM (60¢) adults, 50pf (30¢) children. Rathaus Mon–Fri 8am–6pm. Tower Apr–Oct daily 9am–12pm and 1–5pm; Nov–Mar usually closed although occasionally open on weekends.

Rothenburg's town hall consists of an older Gothic section from 1240 and a newer Renaissance structure facing the square. From the 165-foot tower of the Gothic hall you get an overview of the town below. The tower was first used as a sentry's lookout, but after a fire destroyed the Gothic hall's twin (where the Renaissance hall now stands) in 1501, it became a lookout for fire. Guards had to ring the bell every quarter hour to prove that they were awake and on the job.

The new Rathaus, built in 1572 to replace the portion destroyed in the fire, is decorated with intricate friezes, an oriel extending the building's full height, and a large stone portico opening onto the square. The octagonal tower at the center of the side facing the square contains a grand staircase leading to the upper hall. On the main floor is the large courtroom.

✪ **St.-Jakobskirche (Church of St. James).** Klostergasse 15. ☎ **09861/70-06-20.** Admission 2.50DM ($1.50) adults, 1DM (60¢) children. Apr–Oct Mon–Fri 9am–5:30pm, Sun 7:30am–5:30pm; Dec daily noon–2pm and 4–5pm. Closed Nov and Jan–Mar.

The choir of this vertical Gothic church dates from 1336. In the west gallery is the Altar of the Holy Blood, a masterpiece by the famous Würzburg sculptor Tilman Riemenschneider (ca. 1460–1531). The Rothenburg Council commissioned the work, which was executed between 1499 and 1505, to provide a worthy setting for the Reliquary of the Holy Blood. This relic, venerated in the Middle Ages, is contained in a rock-crystal capsule set in the reliquary cross (ca. 1270) in the center of the shrine. The scene on the altar beneath *The Last Supper* immediately makes a strong impact on the viewer. Christ is giving Judas the morsel of bread, marking him as the traitor. The apostle John is leaning on Christ's bosom. The altar wings show (left) the entry of Christ into Jerusalem and (right) Christ praying in the Garden of Gethsemane. The altar casing is the work of Erhard Harschner, Rothenburg's master craftsman. The fine painted-glass windows in the choir date from the late-Gothic period. To the left is the tabernacle (1390–1400), which was recognized as a place of sanctuary for condemned criminals.

Reichsstadtmuseum. Klosterhof 5. ☎ **09861/939043.** Admission 6DM ($3.60) adults, 4DM ($2.40) children. Apr–Oct daily 10am–5pm; Nov–Mar daily 1–4pm.

The historical collection of Rothenburg is housed in this 13th-century Dominican nunnery. The cloisters are well preserved, and you can visit the convent hall, kitchen, and apothecary. The museum collection includes period furniture and art from Rothenburg's more prosperous periods, including the original glazed elector's tankard, and a new section of archaeological objects from prehistoric times up to the Middle Ages. Among the artistic exhibits is the 1494 *Rothenburg Passion* series, 12 pictures by Martinus Schwartz that depict scenes from the suffering of Christ. You can also see the works of English painter Arthur Wasse (1854–1930), whose romantic pictures manage to capture the many moods of the city. Finally, there's a Jewish section, with gravestones from the Middle Ages and some cult objects.

But perhaps the most interesting object on display is an enormous tankard that holds 3½ liters—more than 6 pints. You'll find echoes of its story all over the city. In 1631, during the Thirty Years' War, the Protestant city of Rothenburg was captured by General Tilly, commander of the armies of the Catholic League. He promised to spare the town from destruction if one of the town burghers could drink down the huge tankard full of wine in one draught. Burgermeister Nusch accepted the challenge and succeeded, thus saving Rothenburg. Look for the clock on the Marktplatz with mechanical figures representing this event.

Kriminal Museum. Burggasse 3. ☎ **09861/53-59.** Admission 5DM ($3) adults, 3.50DM ($2.10) children under 13. Apr–Oct daily 9:30am–6pm, Nov and Jan–Mar daily 2–4pm, Dec daily 10am–4pm.

The only museum of its kind in Europe, the Kriminal Museum is housed in a structure built in 1395 for the Order of the Johanniter, who cared for the sick. The building was redone in 1718 in the baroque style; it's the only example of baroque architecture in town. The museum's four floors provide an insight into the life, laws, and punishments of medieval days. You'll see chastity belts, shame masks, a shame flute for bad musicians, and a cage for bakers who baked bread too small or too light.

SHOPPING

Kunstwerke Friese, Grüner Markt (☎ 09861/71-66), specializes in cuckoo clocks, and also carries Hummel figurines, pewter beer steins, music boxes, and dolls. It's Christmas every day at **Weihnachtsdorf** (Christmas Village), in the market square, which is filled with shops carrying everything from clothing and accessories to cuckoo clocks, but the real attractions are locally made toys and Christmas ornaments. If you collect teddy bears, you'll love **Teddyland,** Herrengasse 10 (☎ 09861/89-04), which stocks more than 5,000 of them. Bear images are printed on everything from T-shirts to bags and watches.

WHERE TO STAY
EXPENSIVE

✪ **Burg Hotel.** Klostergasse 1–3, 91541 Rothenburg o.d.T. ☎ **09861/9-48-90.** Fax 09861/ 94-89-40. 19 units. MINIBAR TV TEL. 180DM–300DM ($108–$180) double; from 250DM–320DM ($150–$192) suite. Rates include buffet breakfast. AE, DC, MC, V. Parking 10DM ($6).

Although it ranks beneath the Bären and the Eisenhut, this inn is full of German charm. It lies at the end of a cul-de-sac in an old-fashioned timbered house that overlooks the Tauber Valley—just the kind of place Red Riding Hood might have visited to see Grandma. Parking is in a historic garage—the barn of a former Dominican monastery. Rooms are spread across three floors (no elevator), with a great decor of antiques, carpets, and tastefully selected fabrics. There are many extras, such as private safes and spacious bathrooms with large mirrors and a hair dryer. Any bedroom is likely to please you, but for the best views, ask for numbers 7, 12, or 25. The inn also boasts state-of-the-art housekeeping.

    Dining: The hotel is classified as a "garni" inn, meaning it serves breakfast only, but there are many fine dining spots within a few minutes' walk (see below).

    Amenities: Since this is really just a glorified B&B, it does not have many amenities, though it does offer bike rentals.

✪ **Eisenhut (Iron Helmet).** Herrengasse 3–5 (across from the Rathaus), 91541 Rothenburg ob der Tauber. ☎ **09861/70-50.** Fax 09861/7-05-45. www.eisenhut.com. E-mail: hotel@eisenhut.rothenburg.de. 80 units. MINIBAR TV TEL. 285DM–385DM ($171–$231) double; 530DM–650DM ($318–$390) suite. AE, DC, MC, V. Parking 15DM ($9).

Eisenhut is the most celebrated inn on the Romantic Road and the finest small hotel in Germany. It's also the most expensive hotel in town, but it's worth the money. Even though some other properties, such as the Hotel Bären, have style and tradition, none can match the Eisenhut. If this hotel has a problem, it might be its very popularity. The staff appears forever overworked.

    The hotel is composed of four medieval patrician houses joined together. The main living room has a beamed ceiling, Oriental carpets, ecclesiastical sculpture, and a grandfather clock. The guest rooms range from medium in size to spacious, and all are individualized. Yours may contain hand-carved and monumental pieces or have a 1940s Hollywood touch with a tufted satin headboard. All rooms are enhanced by well-chosen fabrics, heavy draperies, spacious marble bathrooms, and ample closet space. Bedside controls, hair dryers, and private safes are some of the in-room amenities.

Dining/Diversions: There's a three-story, galleried dining hall, as well as a multi-tiered flagstone terrace on the Tauber. Meals are served à la carte from noon to 2pm and from 6:30 to 9:30pm. There's also a piano bar and a Bavarian beer garden.

Amenities: Room service, dry cleaning, laundry service, baby-sitting, secretarial services, concierge, jogging track, and nature trails. Bicycle rentals are available for 20DM ($12) per day.

Goldener Hirsch. Untere Schmiedgasse 16–25 (off Wenggasse), 91541 Rothenburg o.d.T. ☎ **09861/70-80.** Fax 09861/70-81-00. www.goldenerhirsch.rothenburg.de. 72 units. MINIBAR (in some) TEL. 190DM–320DM ($114–$192) double. Rates include breakfast. AE, DC, MC, V. Parking 4DM ($2.40).

This is one of the leading inns of Rothenburg, in the same class as the Burg and Bären. It looks a bit more austere than some of the other inns, and lacks a certain coziness. Nevertheless, it's extremely pleasant and well maintained. Because of its popularity, this hotel annexed another patrician house across the street. In spite of the age of the building, the bedrooms are very modern, with built-in furniture, evoking Scandinavia more than Bavaria. Try for one of the older units, which are larger and furnished in a more Bavarian motif. Bathrooms are tiny and lack adequate shelf space; only the most superior rooms here have hair dryers.

Dining/Diversions: The Blue Terrace offers a panoramic view of the Tauber Valley, or you can have dinner in the wood-paneled, cozy Ratsherrenstube. The hotel also maintains a bar.

Amenities: Room service, baby-sitting, and concierge.

✪ **Hotel Bären.** Hofbronnengasse 9 (directly south of the Rathaus), 91541 Rothenburg o.d.T. ☎ **09861/9-44-10.** Fax 09861/8-66-88. 35 units. MINIBAR TV TEL. 250DM–330DM ($150–$198) double. Rates include buffet breakfast. AE, MC, V. Parking 8DM ($4.80). Closed Jan 4–Mar 15.

Dating from 1577, this is one of the oldest inns along the Romantic Road. Only the Eisenhut is a better choice than this. Although modernized by the Müller family, it still has 15-inch oak beams and ornate wainscoting. A major improvement was to reduce the number of guest rooms and enlarge the rest. Each room is styled differently; all have fine carpets, both antique and contemporary furniture, and coordinated colors. The good mattresses and the fine bed linen make for a good night's sleep.

Dining: The owner is a gifted chef who offers excellent food. Three dining rooms with varied cuisine serve both Bavarian and international dishes. See "Where to Dine," below for more details.

Amenities: Baby-sitting.

Hotel Tilman Riemenschneider. Georgengasse 11–13, 91541 Rothenburg o.d.T. ☎ **09861/97-90.** Fax 09861/29-79. www.rothenburg.de/progast/html/tilman.html. E-mail: hotel@tilman.rothenburg.de. 65 units. TV TEL. 220DM–380DM ($132–$228) double, 420DM ($252) suite. Rates include buffet breakfast. AE, DC, MC, V. Parking 10DM ($6).

The prominent Tilman Riemenschneider, named for the famous sculptor, has a half-timbered facade rising directly above one of Rothenburg's most visited historic streets. However, its rear courtyard, adorned with geraniums, offers a cool and calm oasis from the busy pedestrian traffic in front. Inside, the hotel contains alpine-inspired furniture (often painted with floral motifs), stone floors, mountain-style accessories, and an occasional porcelain stove set into a wall niche. Some of the rooms are quite stylish, and all are comfortable and traditionally furnished. Most of the bedrooms are medium in size, though a few are small (usually taken by single travelers). All have exceedingly comfortable mattresses and generous bed linens, including duvets, in the Bavarian style.

Dining: The hotel's restaurant serves old-fashioned food in generous portions.

Amenities: Room service, hair dryers, laundry service, a fitness center with a sauna, a solarium, and two whirlpool baths.

Romantik Hotel Markusturm. Rödergasse 1, 91541 Rothenburg o.d.T. ☎ **09861/9-42-80.** Fax 09861/26-92. www.romantikhotels.com/markusturm. E-mail: markusturm@t-online.de. 25 units. TV TEL. 180DM–290DM ($108–$174) double; 350DM ($210) suite. Rates include buffet breakfast. AE, DC, MC, V. Free parking.

Markusturm is a park of the city's history. When it was built in 1264 next to St. Mark's Tower, it incorporated one of Rothenburg's defensive walls. Today that city wall is gone—except for the section that remains part of the hotel. Although the Markusturm cannot rival the splendor of the Eisenhut, it's a close competitor of the Burg Hotel and the Hotel Bären. Its bold, masculine style may be a welcome relief from the many cute and cozily cluttered inns. Much of the hotel dates from 1988. Local art adds color and interest to the whitewashed walls, and Oriental rugs provide warm touches. Guest rooms have been modernized but are furnished in a traditional style with high-quality antique and rustic furniture. Some rooms have four-post beds. Many tradition-minded guests request room 30, a cozy attic unit. The staff is one of the most helpful in town.

Dining: The German/Bavarian cuisine of the hotel's restaurant is well regarded. Unlike the rest of hotel, it's closed for a month from mid-January to mid-February.

Amenities: Concierge, room service, dry cleaning, laundry, and baby-sitting; tennis courts on site.

MODERATE

Hotel Reichs-Küchenmeister. Kircheplatz 8 (near St.-Jakobskirche), 91541 Rothenburg o.d.T. ☎ **09861/97-00.** Fax 09861/869-65/87-04-09. www.hotelreichskuechenmeister.rothenburg.de. E-mail: hotel@reichskuechenmeister.rothenburg.de. 53 units. TV TEL. 120DM–250DM ($72–$150) double; 250DM ($150) suite for 2, 330DM ($198) for 5. Rates include buffet breakfast. AE, CB, DC, DISC, MC, V. Parking 6DM ($3.60) lot, 10DM ($6) garage.

We like this hotel a lot. It's one of the town's oldest structures and was salvaged from a World War II firestorm through a massive, thoroughly sensitive restoration. It's both stylish and well equipped. Rooms are furnished with regional wooden furniture; some also contain minibars. The bathrooms are a bit small, but maintenance is tidy. Facilities include a Finnish sauna, whirlpool, solarium, and Turkish bath; use of the sauna costs 15DM ($9) extra. Seventeen rooms are available in the annex across the street. For its restaurant, see "Where to Dine," below.

INEXPENSIVE

Bayerischer Hof. Ansbacherstrasse 21, 91541 Rothenburg o.d.T. ☎ **09861/60-63.** Fax 09861/8-65-61. 9 units. TV TEL. 120DM–150DM ($72–$90) double. Rates include breakfast. AE, MC, V. Closed Jan. Free parking.

This little B&B doesn't even try to compete with the grand inns of the town. The Bayerischer Hof stands midway between the Bahnhof and the medieval walled city. Petra and Harald Schellhaas welcome guests to their recently renovated, clean, and well-furnished accommodations. . The exterior looks somewhat sterile, but inside the hotel is full of cozy Bavarian touches, like the traditional painted furniture. Beds are comfortable, though mattresses are a bit thin. Rooms and bathrooms are small, but the housekeeping is excellent and the staff is most hospitable. The food is very good.

Gasthof Goldener Greifen. Obere Schmiedgasse 5 (off Marktplatz), 91541 Rothenburg o.d.T. ☎ **09861/22-81.** Fax 09861/8-63-74. 21 units, 15 with shower or bathroom. 74DM ($44.40) double without bathroom, 135DM ($81) double with shower or bathroom. Rates include buffet breakfast. AE, MC, V. Closed Aug 22–Sept 2 and Dec 22–Feb 7.

Don't expect glamour and glitz here—just home-style warmth and comfort. Located in a patrician 1374 house, this hotel stands next door to the prestigious Baumeister-haus restaurant (see "Where to Dine," below). The rooms are simple but cozy and comfortable. The staff is will to help in any way. You can order your morning coffee in the garden amid roses and geraniums. The dining room is closed Monday.

WHERE TO DINE
EXPENSIVE

✪ **Louvre.** Klingengasse 15. ☎ **09861/87809.** Reservations required. Main courses 34DM–44DM ($20.40–$26.40); fixed-price menu 98DM ($58.80), surprise menus 50DM–100DM ($30–$60). Daily 6–11pm. NEW GERMAN.

At long last, Michelin has recognized that Rothenburg serves some of the best cuisine in this part of Germany. It has finally awarded a star to the Louvre. Chef Berhard Reiser is a man of multiple talents, and he has brought a lighter touch to the kitchens of Rothenburg with his *Neuer Küche* (new cuisine) style of cookery. While most Rothenburg chefs stick to the tried-and-true dishes, Herr Reiser is limited only by the availability of produce. His appetizers are dazzling, especially the goose liver terrine with huckleberries and white port or his consommé of crayfish with ravioli. For a main course, try the perfectly cooked halibut with a potato sauce or else the roulade of guinea fowl with herb-infused cabbage and white-flour dumplings. The elegant cuisine is served against a mainly black decor with high-tech lighting and paintings on display. The wine list, for the most part, is good and fairly priced.

✪ **Restaurant Bärenwirt.** In the Hotel Bären, Hofbronnengasse 9. ☎ **09861/9-44-10.** Reservations recommended. Main courses 25DM–89DM ($15–$53.40). AE, MC, V. Daily 6–10pm. FRANCONIAN/INTERNATIONAL.

The *VIF Gourmet Journal* has cited the "Bear" as one of the finest restaurants in all of Germany. The decor is elegantly subdued and the service impeccable. The food and wine served here have never been better. On occasion, the chef is known to serve a historical menu from the Middle Ages—highly appropriate for a hotel (see above) that has been around since 1577. Menu changes are based on the season and the chef's inspiration.

MODERATE

Baumeisterhaus. Obere Schmiedgasse 3 (right off Marktplatz). ☎ **09861/9-47-00.** Reservations required for courtyard tables. Main courses 12.50DM–35DM ($7.50–$21). AE, DC, MC, V. Daily 10am–9pm. FRANCONIAN.

The Baumeisterhaus is housed in an ancient patrician residence, built in 1596. It contains Rothenburg's most beautiful courtyard (which only guests can visit). The patio has colorful murals, serenely draped by vines. Frankly, although the menu is good, the romantic setting is the main attraction here. One of the chef's best dishes is sauerbraten (braised beef marinated in vinegar and served with spätzle, small flour dumplings). The food, for the most part, is the rib-sticking fare beloved by Bavarians, including roast suckling pig with potato dumplings or roast pork shoulder. Apple strudel is everybody's favorite dessert.

Hotel Gasthof Glocke. Am Plönlein 1. ☎ **09861/958990.** Reservations recommended. Main courses 15DM–66DM ($9–$39.60). AE, DC, MC, V. Daily 11am–2pm; Mon–Sat 6–9pm. Closed Dec 23–Jan 7. FRANCONIAN.

The dining room in this guest house serves regional specialties along with a vast selection of wine produced by the staff. Meals emphasize seasonal dishes. Service is polite and attentive. Guests enjoy the family atmosphere and coziness here.

Ratsstube. Marktplatz 6. ☎ **09861/92411.** Reservations recommended. Main courses 18DM–32DM ($10.80–$19.20). MC, V. Mon–Sat 9am–11pm, Sun noon–6pm. Closed Jan 7–Mar 1. FRANCONIAN.

The Ratsstube enjoys a location right on the market square, one of the most photographed spots in Germany. It's a bustling center of activity throughout the day, beginning when practically every Rothenburger stops by for a cup of morning coffee. Inside, a true tavern atmosphere prevails, with hardwood chairs and tables, vaulted ceilings, and pierced copper lanterns. On the à la carte menu are many Franconian dishes, including sauerbraten and venison, both served with fresh vegetables and potatoes. For dessert, you can order homemade Italian ice cream and espresso. This place is a longtime favorite of those who prefer typical Franconian cookery without a lot of fuss and bother. If you arrive at 9am, you can order an American breakfast.

Reichs-Küchenmeister. Kircheplatz 8 (near St. Jakobskirche). ☎ **09861/97-00.** Reservations required. Main courses 18.80DM–42DM ($11.30–$25.20). AE, DC, MC, V. Daily 11:30am–2pm and 6–9:30pm. FRANCONIAN.

The food served here is perfect for cold days. Liver-dumpling or goulash soup, sauerbraten, or pork tenderloin are typical dishes. We recently discovered that the chef makes one of the best Wiener schnitzels in town. White herring and boiled salmon are usually available. The restaurant has a typical Weinstube decor, along with a garden terrace and a Konditorei (cake shop). The service is warm and efficient.

ROTHENBURG AFTER DARK

Count Picasso among those who have enjoyed the show at the **Figurentheater,** am Burgtor at Herrengasse 38 (☎ **09861/73-54** or 09861/33-33). Puppet shows are presented year-round Monday to Saturday at 8pm, and from June 15 through September, also at 3pm. The evening shows cost 15DM ($9) for adults and 12DM ($7.20) for students. Matinee tickets are 10DM ($6) for adults, with children and student tickets costing 7DM and 8DM ($4.20 and $4.80) respectively.

The most idyllic place to go in the evening is **Unter den Linden** (☎ **09861/59-09**), at Detwang. This is a cafe-bar on the River Tauber. You reach it by going under the arch at St. Jakobskirche and following Klingengasse through the town gate, heading down a path to Detwang. The cafe is open April through October daily from 10am to 10pm, but it reduces its hours in winter, depending on weather conditions. If you'd like to sample some local wine, try **Zur Hölle,** Burggasse 8 (☎ **09861/42-29**), a mellow place in the town's oldest house. A wide assortment of Franconian and international wines is offered at 6.50DM and 9.50DM ($3.90 and $5.70) per glass.

8 Dinkelsbühl

58 miles SW of Nürnberg, 71 miles NE of Stuttgart, 65 miles SE of Würzburg

Still surrounded by its medieval walls and towers, Dinkelsbühl is straight out of a Brothers Grimm story, even down to the gingerbread, which is one of the town's main products. Behind the 10th-century walls, the town retains its quiet, provincial attitude in spite of the many visitors who come here. The cobblestone streets are lined with fine 16th-century houses, many with carvings and paintings depicting biblical and mythological themes.

ESSENTIALS

GETTING THERE   By Train   The nearest train station is in Ansbach, which has several trains daily from Munich, Nürnberg, and Stuttgart. From Ansbach, Dinkelsbühl can be reached by bus. Train rides from Munich or Frankfurt take about 2½ to 3 hours, depending on the connection. For rail information, call ☎ **01805/996633.**

By Bus   For bus service along the Romantic Road, see "Bus Tours of the Romantic Road," at the beginning of this chapter. Regional buses link Dinkelsbühl with local towns. There are three to five buses a day to Rothenburg and five to six buses a day to Nördlingen.

By Car   Access is via the A7 Autobahn or Route 25.

VISITOR INFORMATION   Contact **Stadt Verkehrsamt,** Marktplatz (☎ **09851/ 9-02-40**), open Easter through October, Monday to Friday 9am to noon and 2 to 6pm, Saturday 10am to 1pm and 2 to 4pm, and Sunday and holidays 10am to 7pm; November through March, Monday to Friday 9am to noon and 2 to 5pm, and Saturday 10am to 1pm.

SPECIAL EVENTS   This dreamy village awakens once a year for the **Kinderzeche (Children's Festival),** held from July 14 to 23. This festival commemorates the saving of the village by its children in 1632. According to the story, the children pleaded with conquering Swedish troops to leave their town without pillaging and destroying it—and got their wish. The pageant includes concerts given by the local boys' band dressed in historic military costumes.

EXPLORING THE TOWN

Dinkelsbühl is a lively, wonderfully preserved medieval town, full of narrow, cobblestone streets. You might begin your explorations at the 14th-century gateway, **Rothenburger Tor,** and then head down the wide Martin Luther Strasse to the market square. Along the way you can take in the town's fine collection of early Renaissance burghers' houses. Dinkelbühl's main attraction is the late-Gothic **Georgenkirche,** on Marktplatz, built between 1448 and 1499. The church contains a carved Holy Cross Altar and pillar sculptures, many from the 15th century. The best evening activity here is to take a walk around the ramparts. There's even a nightwatchman making the rounds about town, as in medieval times.

WHERE TO STAY & DINE

✪ **Blauer Hecht.** Schweinemarkt 1, 91150 Dinkelsbühl. ☎ **09851/58-10.** Fax 09851/58-11-70. 44 units. TV TEL. 150DM–180DM ($90–$108) double. Rates include continental breakfast. AE, DC, MC, V. Closed Jan. Parking 15DM ($9).

This up-to-date inn is the best in town. The elegant ochre building dates from the 17th century and has three hand-built stories of stucco, stone, and tile. Although the place is centrally located, rooms are tranquil. Most are medium in size, although there are some small singles. Amenities include a small fitness center with a sauna, solarium, and indoor pool. The hotel restaurant serves a good regional cuisine. Meals range from 35DM to 65DM ($21 to $39).

Deutsches Haus. Weinmarkt 3, 91550 Dinkelsbühl. ☎ **09851/60-58.** Fax 09851/79-11. 15 units. TV TEL. 165DM–210DM ($99–$126) double; 240DM ($144) triple. Rates include continental breakfast. AE, DC, MC, V. Closed Dec 23–Jan 6. Parking 15DM ($9).

The facade of Deutsches Haus, which dates from 1440, is rich in painted designs and festive wood carvings. A niche on the second floor of the arched entrance houses a 17th-century Madonna. Each room in this casually run hotel is different—you may find yourself in one with a ceramic stove or in another with a Biedermeier desk. For the tradition-minded, there are no finer bedrooms in town. Cozy comfort is the rule here.

Even if you don't stay here, you may want to dine in the Altdeutsches Restaurant, one of the finest in Dinkelsbühl. It's intimate and convivial, and serves Franconian and regional specialties daily from 11:30am to 2pm and 6 to 9:30pm. Meals cost from 15DM to 30DM ($9 to $18) for main courses and 32DM to 60DM ($19.20 to $36) for menus. In the afternoon, many visitors drop in for coffee and freshly baked pastries.

✪ **Eisenkrug.** Dr. Martin-Luther-Strasse 1, 91550 Dinkelsbühl. ☎ **09851/57700.** Fax 09851/577070. 23 units. MINIBAR TV TEL. 135DM–170DM ($81–$102) double. Rates include continental breakfast. AE, DC, MC, V. Parking 10DM ($6).

The sienna walls of this centrally located hotel were originally built in 1620. Today the Eisenkrug's forest-green shutters are familiar to everyone in town; many celebrate family occasions at the hotel restaurant. There's even a cafe with alfresco tables in warm weather. The stylish rooms are wallpapered with flowery prints and filled with engaging old furniture. An additional nine rooms are in an equally fine guest house nearby, where doubles cost 125DM to 135DM ($75 to $81). The newer wing contains the most contemporary guest rooms, all rather standardized and modern looking. The older rooms offer more charm, although some tend to be smaller. Some of the beds are canopied. Bathrooms range from small to spacious.

Zum kleinen Obristen serves a gourmet international cuisine. The chef takes an indigenous Franconian-Swabian approach, with many innovative touches. The superior wine cellar has some really unusual vintages. À la carte meals cost 35DM to 65DM ($21 to $39). The restaurant is open noon to 2pm and 6 to 10pm; closed Monday and Tuesday evenings.

9 Nördlingen

81 miles NW of Munich, 59 miles SW of Nürnberg

Nördlingen is one of the most irresistible medieval towns along the Romantic Road. It's still encircled by well-preserved fortifications from the 14th and 15th centuries. Things are rather tranquil around Nördlingen today; nonetheless, the town still employs sentries to sound the reassuring message, *So G'sell so* (all is well), as they did in the Middle Ages.

The area wasn't always so peaceful. The town sits in a gigantic crater called the Ries. Once thought to be the crater of an extinct volcano, it is now known that the Ries was created by a meteorite at least half a mile in diameter. It struck the ground some 15 million years ago at more than 100,000 miles per hour. Debris was hurled as far as Slovakia, and all plant and animal life within a radius of 100 miles was destroyed. Today the Ries is the best preserved and most scientifically researched meteorite crater on earth. The American astronauts from *Apollo 14* and *Apollo 17* did their field training in the Ries in 1970. Contact the **Rieskrater-Museum** (see below) for tours of the crater.

ESSENTIALS

GETTING THERE   By Plane   The nearest major airport is in Nürnberg; from there you can make either bus or rail connections to Nördlingen.

By Train   Nördlingen lies on the main Nördlingen-Aalen-Stuttgart line, with frequent connections in all directions. Call ☎ **0185/996633** for schedules and more information. Nördlingen can be reached from Stuttgart in 2 hours, from Nürnberg in 2 hours, and from Augsburg in 1 hour.

By Bus   For bus service along the Romantic Road, see "Bus Tours of the Romantic Road," at the beginning of this chapter.

By Car   Access by car is via the A7 Autobahn north and south and Route 29 from the east. From Dinkelsbühl, take Route 25 south.

VISITOR INFORMATION   Contact the Verkehrsamt, Marktplatz 2 (☎ **09081/4 3-80**), open Easter to October, Monday to Thursday 9am to 6pm, Friday 9am to 4:30pm, and Saturday 9:30am to 7pm; November to Easter, Monday to Thursday 9am to 5pm and Friday 9am to 3:30pm.

EXPLORING THE TOWN

You can walk around the town on the covered parapet on top of the perfectly preserved walls. Along the way, you'll pass 11 towers and five fortified gates. At the center of the circular Altstadt, within the walls, is **Rübenmarkt.** If you stand in this square on market day, you'll be swept into a world of the past—the country people here have preserved many traditional customs and costumes, which, along with the ancient houses, evoke a living medieval city. Around the square stand a number of buildings, including the Gothic **Rathaus.** An antiquities collection is displayed in the **Stadtmuseum,** Vordere Gerbergasse 1 (☎ **09081/2738230**), open Tuesday to Sunday from 1:30 to 4:30pm; closed November to February. Admission is 5DM ($3) for adults and 1.50DM (90¢) for children, students, travelers with disabilities, and seniors.

The **St. Georgskirche,** on the square's northern side, is the town's most interesting sight and one of its oldest buildings. This Gothic Hall Church is from the 15th century. Plaques and epitaphs commemorating the town's more illustrious 16th- and 17th-century residents decorate the fan-vaulted interior. Although the original Gothic altarpiece by Friedrich Herlin (1462) is now in the Reichsstadtmuseum in Rothenburg, a portion of it, depicting the Crucifixion by Nikolaus Gerhart van Leydeu, remains in the church. Above the high altar today stands a more elaborate baroque altarpiece. The church's most prominent feature, however, is the 295-foot French Gothic tower, called the "Daniel." At night, the town watchman calls out from the steeple, his voice ringing through the streets. The tower is accessible October to March daily from 9am to 5:30pm and April to October daily from 9am to 8pm. Admission to the tower is 3DM ($1.80) for adults and 2DM ($1.20) for students and children. It's free to visit the church, which is open Easter to October, Monday to Friday from 9:30am to 12:30pm and 2 to 5pm, and Saturday and Sunday from 9:30am to 5pm.

The **Rieskrater-Museum,** Eugene Shoemaker Platz 7 (☎ **09081/2738220**), documents the impact of the stone meteorite that crashed into the earth here on the Alb plateau, nearly 15 million years ago. Hours are Tuesday to Sunday from 10am to noon and 1:30 to 4:30pm. Admission is 5DM ($3) for adults and 2.50DM ($1.50) for children and students.

WHERE TO STAY

Astron Hotel Klösterle. Am Klösterle 1, 86720 Nördlingen. ☎ **09081/8-80-54.** Fax 09081/2-27-40. 90 units. MINIBAR TV TEL. 202DM–256DM ($121.20–$153.60) double. Rates include continental breakfast. AE, DC, MC, V. Parking 15DM ($9).

The accommodations here are the best and most luxurious in town. This historic, white-sided, red-roofed building was originally constructed as a monastery in the 1200s. Since then, its ziggurat-shaped gables and steep roof have been an essential part of Nördlingen's medieval center. The hotel offers elevator access, a cozy bar (the Tarantelstube), and a hardworking, polite staff. Under the sloping eaves of its top floor are a sauna, a fitness center, and a series of conference rooms. The bedrooms have dark-wood fixtures, modern upholstery, lots of electronic extras, and larger-than-expected bathrooms. The restaurant, richly paneled with dark-grained wood and filled with modern art, serves lunch and dinner daily from 11:30am to 2pm and 6 to 10pm.

Kaiser Hotel Sonne. Marktplatz 3, 86720 Nördlingen. ☎ **09081/50-67.** Fax 09081/2-39-99. www.eurotravel-guide.de/hotel/n001.htm. E-mail: kaiserhof-hotel-sonne@T-online.de. 43

units (35 with bathrooms). MINIBAR TV TEL. 125DM ($75) double without bathroom; 175DM ($105) double with bathroom. Rates include breakfast. AE, MC, V. Free parking.

The Sonne is in a bull's-eye position next to the cathedral and the Rathaus. It has a heady atmosphere from having entertained so many illustrious personalities since it opened as an inn in 1405. Among its guests have been emperors, kings, and princes, including Frederick III, Maximilian I, and Charles V, the great poet Goethe, and, in more recent times, American astronauts. Many of the rooms contain hand-painted four-post beds. In the hotel's restaurant, you can order main courses such as rump-steak Mirabeau and caloric German desserts. It's all quite casual; the waitresses even urge you to finish all the food on your plate.

WHERE TO DINE

Meyers-Keller. Marienhöhe 8. ☎ **09081/44-93.** Reservations required. Main courses 25DM–40DM ($15–$24); fixed-price menu 45DM–135DM ($27–$81). AE, MC, V. Tues 5–11pm and Wed–Sun 11am–2pm and 5–11pm. Local bus to Markplatz. Closed last 2 weeks of Feb. FRENCH.

The conservative, modern decor here seems a suitable setting for the restrained Neuer Küche style of the talented chef and owner, Joachim Kaiser. The cuisine changes according to the availability of ingredients and the inspiration of the chef; typical selections are likely to include roulade of sea wolf, salmon with baby spinach and wild rice, and John Dory with champagne-flavored tomato sauce. There's also an impressive array of European wines, many reasonably priced. The chef is adroit with both rustic and refined cuisine.

Meyers-Keller also has a cheaper section, featuring local cuisine, with a combination of Bavarian, Swabian, and Franconian specialties. Here you can order main courses for 9DM to 20DM ($5.40 to $12), with a fixed-price menu costing 40DM ($24). There's also a small bar on site, where light meals range from 6DM to 15DM ($3.60 to $9).

10 Donauwörth

25 miles N of Augsburg, 7 miles S of Harburg, 59 miles NW of Munich.

Visitors come to Donauwörth for its architecture and sense of history, rather than for specific attractions. The town is located on what was the last navigable point on the Danube, which led to its becoming a key stop on the trade route between Augsburg and Nürnberg. Its attempted capture by the Imperial party in 1608 led directly to the division of Germany into warring Protestant and Catholic military alliances, leading to the Thirty Years' War.

The oldest part of town sits on an island in the middle of the stream, access to which is via the oldest surviving gate in town, the **Riederstor,** which funnels traffic along the island's most historic and evocative street, the **Reichsstrasse.** Donauwörth was badly damaged in 1945 in World War II bombing raids, but it has been carefully restored. Part of the town's fortifications survived.

ESSENTIALS

GETTING THERE   By Train   Trains arrive from Augsburg at 30-minute intervals throughout the day (trip time: 35 to 45 min.). Trains also come hourly from Munich (trip time: 90 min.). For railway information call ☎ **0906/5040** in Donauwörth or **01805/996633.**

By Bus   For bus service along the Romantic Road, see "Bus Tours of the Romantic Road," at the beginning of this chapter.

By Car   From Augsburg, follow Route 2 north. From Nördlingen, take Route 25.

VISITOR INFORMATION   Tourist-Information is at Rathausgasse 1 (☎ **0906/ 789145**), open Monday to Friday 9am to 5:30pm.

EXPLORING THE TOWN

The town is dominated by the Heiligeskreuz or Holy Cross Church, a large 1720 baroque building with concave interior galleries. It's an outstanding example of the distinctive churches built and decorated by the craftsmen of Wessobrunn.

The site that draws the greatest numbers of visitors is the **Käthe-Kruse-Puppen-Museum,** Pflegstrasse 21A (☎ **0906/789185**). Inside, you'll find a small-scale collection of the dolls and dollhouses that were designed by master artisan Käthe-Kruse, whose most prolific period during the 1950s and 1960s has been called a high point in the history of doll making. Between May and September, it's open Tuesday to Sunday from 11am to 5pm; from October to April, it's open Tuesday to Sunday from 2 to 5pm. Entrance costs 4.50DM ($2.55) for adults, half-price for children under 12.

WHERE TO STAY & DINE

Posthotel Traube. Kapellstrasse 14–16, 86609 Donauwörth. ☎ **0906/706-440.** Fax 0906/706-5180. 42 units. 135DM–150DM ($76.95–$85.50) double; 185DM ($105.45) suite. AE, DC, MC, V.

This hotel has a history going back to the 1600s and a guest list that included Goethe and Mozart. Despite its modern conveniences, there's still the definite sense of old Mittel-Europe here, thanks to a somewhat creaky staff and a no-nonsense approach to innkeeping. Bedrooms are nostalgically outfitted with engravings and prints of old-fashioned Germany. On the premises is a worthy, solid-looking restaurant serving conservative and traditional German food items every day at lunch and dinner, with set menus priced from 25DM to 35DM ($14.25 to $19.95) each.

11 Augsburg

42 miles NW of Munich, 50 miles E of Ulm, 100 miles SE of Stuttgart

Augsburg's 2,000 years of history have made it one of southern Germany's major sightseeing attractions. It's the Romantic Road's largest town and serves also as a gateway to the Alps and the south.

Augsburg was founded under Emperor Tiberius in 15 B.C., though little remains from the early Roman period. The wealth of art and architecture from the Renaissance, on the other hand, is staggering. Over the years, Augsburg has hosted many distinguished visitors and boasts an array of famous native sons, including painters Hans Holbein the Elder and the Younger and playwright Bertolt Brecht. In 1518, Martin Luther was summoned to Augsburg to recant his 95 theses before a papal emissary. Today, Augsburg, with a population of about 250,000, is an important industrial center and Bavaria's third largest city, after Munich and Nürnberg.

ESSENTIALS

GETTING THERE   **By Train**   Ninety **Euro** and **Inter-City** trains arrive here daily from all the important German cities. For railway information, call ☎ **01805/ 996633.** Sixty trains per day arrive from Munich (trip time: 30 to 50 min.) and 35 from Frankfurt (3 to 4½ hr.).

By Bus   For bus service along the Romantic Road, see "Bus Tours of the Romantic Road," at the beginning of this chapter.

By Car   Access is via the A8 Autobahn east and west. From Donauwörth, take Route 2 south.

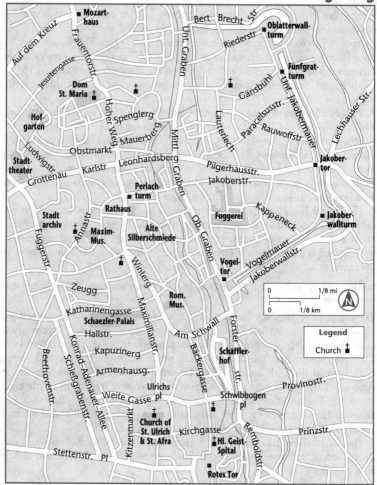

VISITOR INFORMATION Contact **Tourist-Information,** Rathaus Platz and Bahnhafstrasse 7 (☎ **0821/50-20-70**), open October 15 to May, Monday to Friday 9am to 5pm and Saturday 10am to 1pm; May to October 14, Monday to Friday 9am to 6pm, Saturday 10am to 4pm, and Sunday 10am to 7pm.

GETTING AROUND The public transportation system in Augsburg consists of four tram lines and 31 bus lines. It operates from 5am to midnight daily and is provided by **Verkehr gemeinschaft Augsburg Vga** (☎ **0821/3245888**). **Augsburger Verkehrsverbund AVV** (☎ **0821/15-70-07**) provides the service for transport outside the city.

SEEING THE SIGHTS

Extending southward from the Rathaus is the wide **Maximilianstrasse,** lined with shops and old burghers' houses and studded with fountains by the Renaissance Dutch sculptor Adrien de Vries.

✪ **The Fuggerei.** At the end of Vorderer Lech. ☎ **0821/3-08-68.** Museum 1DM (60¢) adults, 70pf (40¢) students and children. Museum Mar–Oct daily 9am–6pm. Tram: 1.

During the 15th and 16th centuries, Augsburg became one of Europe's wealthiest communities, mainly because of its textile industry and the political and financial clout of its two banking families, the Welsers and the Fuggers. The Welsers have long since faded away. But the founders of the powerful Fugger family have established themselves permanently by an unusual legacy, the Fuggerei, established in 1519 by Jakob Fugger the Rich to house poorer Augsburgers. It's Europe's oldest welfare housing.

The basic features of the establishment, laid down in 1521, are still in force today. The nominal rent of 1.72DM ($1.05) per annum (formerly one Rheinish guilder) has not changed in more than 450 years. The only obligation is that tenants pray daily for the souls of their founders. The Fuggerei is a miniature, self-contained town with its own gates, which are shut from 10pm to 5am and guarded by a night watchman. Franz Mozart, a master mason fallen on hard times—great-grandfather of Wolfgang Amadeus Mozart—once lived at Mittlere Gasse 14.

The Fugger Foundation owns the Fuggerei. A house at Mittlere Gasse 13, next to the one once occupied by Mozart's ancestor, is now the Fuggerei's museum. The rough 16th- and 17th-century furniture, wood-paneled ceilings and walls, and cast-iron stove, as well as other objects of everyday life, show what it was like to live here in earlier times.

Dom St. Maria. Hoher Weg. ☎ **0821/3-16-63-53.** Free admission. Mon–Sat 7am–6pm, Sun noon–6pm. Tram: 2.

The cathedral of Augsburg has the distinction of containing the oldest stained-glass windows in the world. These Romanesque windows, dating from the 12th century, are in the south transept, and depict Old Testament prophets in a severe but colorful style. They are younger than the cathedral itself, which was begun in 944, and partially Gothicized in the 14th century. The 11th-century bronze doors, leading into the three-aisle nave, are adorned with bas-reliefs of a mixture of biblical and mythological characters. The cathedral's interior, restored in 1934, contains side altars with altarpieces by Hans Holbein the Elder and Christoph Amberger. You'll find the ruins of the original basilica in the crypt beneath the west chancel.

The cathedral stands on the edge of the park, which also fronts the Episcopal Palace, where the basic creed of the Lutheran Reformation was presented at the Diet of Augsburg in 1530.

Rathaus. Am Rathausplatz 2. ☎ **0821/32-41.** Admission 3DM ($1.80) adults, 1DM (60¢) children 7–14, free for children 6 and under. Daily 10am–6pm. Tram: 1 or 2.

In 1805 and 1809, Napoléon visited the Rathaus, built by Elias Holl in 1620. Regrettably, the building was also visited by an air raid in 1944, leaving it a mere shell of what had once been a palatial eight-story monument to the glory of the Renaissance. Its celebrated "golden chamber" was left in shambles. But now, after a costly restoration, the Rathaus can again be visited by the public, on walking tours that offer a view of the "golden chamber" as well as other rooms. Tours take place May to October 18 daily at 2pm, costing 12DM ($7.20) for adults and 9DM ($5.40) for children.

Church of St. Ulrich and St. Afra. Ulrichplatz 19. ☎ **0821/34-55-60.** Free admission. Daily 9am–6pm.

Near the southern end of Maximilianstrasse is the Hercules Fountain, and behind it, the most attractive ecclesiastical compound in Augsburg. The churches of St. Ulrich and St. Afra were constructed between 1476 and 1500 on the site of a Roman temple. As a tribute to the 1555 Peace of Augsburg, which recognized two denominations, one Roman Catholic and the other Lutheran, these two separate churches—Catholic St. Afra and Protestant St. Ulrich—stand next to each other. The churches are mainly

15th-century Gothic with baroque overlays. St. Afra is the most elaborate, with a magnificent altar and finely carved baroque railings bordering the entrance. St. Ulrich is the former monastery assembly hall, taken over by the Lutherans. The shared crypt contains the tombs of the two namesake saints. The lance and saddle of St. Ulrich are displayed in the sacristy.

Schaezlerpalais. Maximilianstrasse 46 (facing the Hercules Fountain). ☎ **0821/3244102.** Admission 4.50DM ($2.70) adults, 2DM ($1.20) children and students. Wed–Sun 10am–4pm.

The Schaezlerpalais, a 60-room mansion constructed between 1765 and 1770, contains an amazing art collection. Most of the works in the collection are by German artists of the Renaissance and baroque periods, including Hans Holbein the Elder and Hans Burgkmair. One of the most famous paintings is Albrecht Dürer's portrait of Jakob Fugger the Rich. Rubens, Veronese, Tiepolo, and others are also represented. The palace-gallery also contains a rococo ballroom, with gilded and mirrored wall panels and a ceiling fresco, *The Four Continents.* Here, on April 28, 1770, Marie Antoinette danced the night away.

WHERE TO STAY
EXPENSIVE

✪ **Steigenberger Drei Mohren.** Maximilianstrasse 40, 86150 Augsburg. ☎ **800/ 223-5652** in the U.S. and Canada, or 0821/5-03-60. Fax 0821/15-78-64. 107 units. MINIBAR TV TEL. 299DM–379DM ($179.40–$227.40) double; 450DM–550DM ($270–$330) suite. Rates include buffet breakfast. AE, DC, MC, V. Parking 22DM ($13.20). Tram: 1.

The original "Three Moors," dating from 1723, was one of the most renowned hotels in Germany before its destruction in a 1944 air raid. In 1956, it was reconstructed in a modern style in four- and five-story buildings. It remains the premier hotel in town in spite of increasing competition from Romantik Hotel Augsburger Hof. The interior combines stylish contemporary pieces with traditional furnishings. The drawing room contains a slatted natural-wood ceiling and wall, along with a room-wide mural of Old Augsburg. The decor in the rooms is comfortable and inviting, with thick carpets, subdued lighting, double glazing at the windows, and such extra amenities as private safes, hair dryers, and trouser presses. Rooms vary in size and appointments, however, ranging from small economy specials to spacious and luxurious suites.

Dining: The formal dining room offers international cuisine. On the breakfast terrace, umbrellas and garden chairs overlook flower beds and three free-form fountains.

Amenities: Room service, laundry, dry cleaning; staff can arrange golf nearby. Within walking distance is the Original Art Nouveau Baths, with massage facilities, steam bath, sauna, and solarium.

MODERATE

Dom Hotel. Frauentorstrasse 8, 86152 Augsburg. ☎ **0821/34-39-30.** Fax 0821/34-39-32-00. E-mail: domhotel.augsburg@t-online.de. 43 units. TV TEL. 150DM–210DM ($90–$126) double. Rates include buffet breakfast. AE, DC, MC, V. Free parking; 8DM ($4.80) garage. Tram: 2.

The Dom Hotel lacks the decorative flair of the Steigenberger Drei Mohren, but it does have an indoor pool. That, combined with the moderate rates, makes this one of the most appealing choices in town. The 15th-century half-timbered structure rises imposingly beside Augsburg's famous cathedral. You don't get a lot of style here but you do get comfort. Rooms on most floors are medium in size and nicely appointed, although we prefer the smaller attic accommodations, where you can rest under a beam ceiling and enjoy a panoramic sweep of the rooftops of the city. Breakfast is the only meal served; during warm weather it can be enjoyed in a garden beside the town's medieval fortifications.

Hotel Am Rathaus. Am Hinteren Perlachberg 1, 86150 Augsburg. ☎ **0821/34-64-90.** Fax 0821/346-4-999. www.pyramide.de. 32 units. MINIBAR TV TEL. 240DM ($144) double. Rates include buffet breakfast. AE, DC, MC, V. Parking 12DM ($7.20). Tram: 1.

This contemporary hotel's location is its best asset—it's adjacent to the back of Augsburg's famous town hall. It may be short on style, but it offers good value. The lobby is traditional, with Oriental carpets and comfortable chairs. Rooms are accented with darkly stained wood and range in size from small to medium. The breakfast buffet is well stocked. There's no restaurant or bar on the premises.

Romantik Hotel Augsburger Hof. Auf dem Kreuz 2, 86152 Augsburg. ☎ **0821/31-40-83.** Fax 0821/3430555. 36 units. MINIBAR TV TEL. 130DM–250DM ($78–$150) double. Rates include buffet breakfast. AE, DC, MC, V. Parking 10DM ($6). Tram: 2.

This hotel was originally built in 1767 in a solid, thick-walled design with exposed beams and timbers. It's a favorite for its romantic and traditional atmosphere, its good location in the town center, and its excellent food. The bedrooms are completely up to date but not as romantic as the name of the hotel suggests. They range from small to spacious. Some of the bathrooms seem crowded in as an afterthought, but each is beautifully maintained and contains a hair dryer. The rooms overlooking the tranquil inner courtyard are more expensive than ones facing the street. The on-site restaurant serves German and international food.

INEXPENSIVE

Hotel Garni Weinberger. Bismarckstrasse 55 (about 2 miles west of town center, along Augsburgerstrasse), 86391 Stadtbergen. ☎ **0821/24-39-10.** Fax 0821/43-88-31. 31 units (26 with bathroom). 130DM ($78) double without bathroom; 150DM ($90) double with bathroom. Rates include buffet breakfast. No credit cards. Closed Aug 15–30. Free parking. Tram: 2.

The Weinberger is one of the best budget accommodations in the area. Rooms are small but well kept. The private bathrooms are rather cramped. Corridor bathrooms are adequate and tidy. Many of the patrons are Germans, who know a good bargain. The hotel's cafe is one of the most popular in the area for snacks.

WHERE TO DINE

Die Ecke. Elias-Holl-Platz 2. ☎ **0821/51-06-00.** Reservations required. Main courses 18DM–45DM ($10.80–$27); fixed-price dinner 65DM ($39) for 4 courses, 98DM ($58.80) for 6 courses; fixed-price lunch 36DM ($21.60). AE, CB, MC, V. Daily 11:30am–2:30pm and 5:30pm–1am. Tram: 2. FRENCH/SWABIAN.

This restaurant's guests have included Hans Holbein the Elder, Wolfgang Amadeus Mozart, and, in more contemporary times, Rudolf Diesel of engine fame and Bertolt Brecht. The Weinstube ambience belies the skilled cuisine of the chef—the elegant fare here is rivaled only by the Oblinger. Breast of duckling might be preceded by a pâté or pheasant. The fillet of sole in Riesling is a classic, and venison dishes in season, a specialty, are the best in town.

Fuggerei Stube. Jakoberstrasse 26. ☎ **0821/3-08-70.** Reservations recommended. Main courses 18.50DM–28DM ($11.10–$16.80); set-price menu 36DM ($21.60). AE, MC, V. Tues–Sun 11:30am–2pm; Tues–Sat 6:30pm–1:30am. GERMAN/SWABIAN.

This affordable restaurant can fit 60 persons at a time into its large, *gemütlich* dining room. Expect generous portions of well-prepared food such as sauerbraten, pork schnitzel, game, and fish dishes. The beer foaming out of the taps here is Storchenbräu; most visitors find that it goes wonderfully with the conservative German specialties that are this establishment's forte.

✪ Oblinger. Pfärrle 14 (near the cathedral). ☎ **0821/3-45-83-92.** Reservations required. Main courses 17DM–30DM ($10.20–$18); fixed-price menu 49DM ($29.40). AE, DC, MC, V.

Tues–Sun 11:30am–2pm; Tues–Sat 6–11pm. Closed Aug 1–19. Tram: 2. CONTINENTAL/
SEAFOOD.

Oblinger is the best in Augsburg's center. It's a charming, intimate, 20-seat restaurant
offering a changing array of seasonal specialties. The surroundings are unpretentious,
the waiters are attentive, and the cuisine has real personality. Recently we enjoyed the
goose-liver terrine with mushrooms and cabbage, and then an equally well-prepared
sole roulade with crepes. The turbot with chanterelles or the stuffed Bresse pigeon are
excellent as well. There's also a superb selection of more than 350 varieties of wine.

Welser Kuche. Maximilianstrasse 83. ☎ **0821/3-39-30.** Reservations required. Feasts
54DM ($32.40) Thurs only, 69DM ($41.40) for 6 courses, and 79DM ($47.40) for 8 courses,
without drinks. AE, DC, MC, V. Dinner seatings are daily at 8pm. Located close to the rail station. Tram: 2. SWABIAN.

Come to the Welser Kuche for a medieval feast on wooden tables. The traditional menu
is served nightly by *knechte* and *mägde* (knaves and wenches) in 16th-century costumes.
Fixed-price menus, called "Welser Feast," are eaten with a dagger and your fingers for
cutlery. Stone walls, knotty-pine paneling, and stucco arches frame the wooden tables.
Recipes are from a cookbook, discovered in 1970, that belonged to Philippine
Welser (b. 1527), Baroness of Zinnenburg and wife of Habsburg archduke Ferdinand
II. It takes about 3 hours to eat a meal here. Sometimes parties of two or four can be
seated at the last minute, but reservations should be made as far in advance as possible.
To reserve by phone, call ☎ **08231/9-61-10** or fax 08231/96-11-28. The reservations
office is open Monday to Friday from 8am to 6pm and Saturday from 8am to noon.

AUGSBURG AFTER DARK

Kongresshalle, Güggingerstrasse 10 (☎ **0821/3-24-23-48;** information line 0931/5-
86-86), presents concerts by the local ballet and opera companies and the chamber
and symphony orchestras. Call for schedules, prices, and reservations. It's closed in
August. The internationally renowned **Mozart Festival** is held in Augsburg every September. Contact the Tourist-Information office (see above) for details. In the courtyard of the Fugger Palace, the city hosts a **musical theater** production each June and
July. Tickets run 20DM to 64DM ($12 to $38.40). Information and reservations are
available by calling ☎ **0821/3-66-04** Tuesday to Sunday 11:30am to 1pm and
Tuesday to Friday 4:30 to 6pm.

   Maximilianstrasse, the main shopping street, continues to be the focus of nightlife
after the shops close, with its many cafes. **Brauereigasthaus Drei Königinnen,**
Meister-Veits-Gässchen 32 (☎ **0821/15-84-05**), doubles as an art gallery, has a
pleasant beer garden that's open until 11pm, and has a main bar that closes at 7am.
Another garden/bar combo that keeps the same hours is **Thorbräu-keller,** Heilig-
Kreuz-Strasse 20 (☎ **0821/51-19-91**). **Liliom,** Unterer Graben 1 (☎ **0821/51-
40-84**), is equipped with a good stereo system to go with drinks and conversation;
here, too, local artwork is often available for purchase. The bar is open Monday to
Thursday 7pm to 7am and Friday to Sunday 6pm to 7am.

12 Füssen

57 miles S of Augsburg, 74 miles SW of Munich

Füssen is situated in the foothills of the Bavarian Alps, at the end of the Romantic
Road. The town is mainly a base for those going on to the castles at Neuschwanstein
and Hohenschwangau, but it also has a number of attractive buildings, including a
15th-century castle once used by the bishops of Augsburg as a summer palace. In addition, Füssen is ideally located for excursions into the surrounding countryside.

ESSENTIALS

GETTING THERE   By Plane   The nearest major airport is in Munich.

By Train   Trains from Munich and Augsburg arrive frequently throughout the day. For information, call ☎ **01805/99-66-33.** Train time from Munich is 2½ hours; from Frankfurt, 6 to 7 hours.

By Bus   For bus service along the Romantic Road, see "Bus Tours of the Romantic Road," at the beginning of this chapter. Regional service is provided by **RVA Regionalverkehr Schwäben Allgau GmbH** in Füssen (☎ **08362/3-77-71**). This company runs at least 14 buses a day to the royal castles (see below). A one-way ticket costs 2.50DM ($1.50).

By Car   Access by car is via the A7 Autobahn from the north and also the B17 from Augsburg.

VISITOR INFORMATION   Contact the **Kurverwaltung,** Kaiser-Maximilian-Platz 1 (☎ **08362/93-85-0**). Hours vary but are usually in summer Monday to Friday 8:30am to 6:30pm and Saturday 9am to 2:30pm; and in winter, Monday to Friday 9am to 5pm and Saturday 10am to 1pm.

EXPLORING THE TOWN

Füssen's main attraction is the **Hohes Schloss,** Magnusplatz (☎ **08362/90-31-64**), one of the finest late-Gothic castles in Bavaria. It was once the summer residence of the prince-bishops of Augsburg. Inside you can visit the Rittersaal or "Knight's Hall," known for its stunning coffered ceiling. There's also a collection of Swabian art work from the 1400s to the 1700s. The castle is open Tuesday to Sunday 11am to 4pm, and charges 3DM ($1.70) for admission.

Immediately below the castle lies the 8th-century **St. Mangkirche** and its **abbey** (☎ **08362/48-44**), which was founded by the Benedictines and grew up on the site where St. Magnus died in 750. In the 18th century it was reconstructed in the baroque style, and in 1803 it was secularized. Free tours of the abbey are given July to September on Tuesday and Thursday at 4pm and on Saturday at 10:30am; May, June, and October on Tuesday at 4pm and Saturday at 10:30am; and January to April on Saturday at 10:30am.

Within the abbey complex, signs point the way to the **Chapel of St. Anne,** where you can view the macabre *Totentanz* or "dance of death," painted by an unknown local artist in the early 15th century. It has a certain bizarre fascination. The chapel is open April to October Tuesday to Sunday 2 to 4pm. Admission is free. Nearby is the **Museum of Füssen** (Heimatmuseum; ☎ **08362/90-31-45**), which displays artifacts relating to the history and culture of the region, including a collection of musical instruments. It keeps the same hours as the chapel, and charges 3DM ($1.70) to enter.

The principal shopping spot in town is the **Reichenstrasse,** which was known in Roman times as the Via Claudia. This cobblestone street is flanked with houses from the Middle Ages, most of which have towering gables.

OUTDOOR PURSUITS

The lakes around Füssen are good for **windsurfing** and **sailing.** Dinghies and windsurfing boards can be rented from **Selbach Bootsvermietung** at either the Hopfensee or Weissensee boathouse. Call ☎ **08362/1487** or 08364/1487 for more information. The best **hiking** in the often flat region is in the mountains around Füssen and Schwangau. Contact **Kurverwaltung Füssen** at ☎ **08362/93-85-0** for maps, guide services, and other data.

Winter **skiing** is also possible in the Schwangau or Füssen region. Tourist offices locally supply information. For instruction, contact **Skischule Tegelberg-Füssen** at

Schwangau (☎ 08362/98-36-0), during the skiing season. Off-season this number is for hang-gliding instruction and for the cable car, which operates all year when the weather is fine.

A ROCOCO MASTERPIECE

From Füssen, you can take a fascinating side trip to the ✪ **Wieskirche** (☎ 08862/ 501), one of the most extravagant rococo buildings in the world, a masterpiece by Dominikus Zimmermann. The Wieskirche is a noted pilgrimage church, drawing visitors from all over the globe. It's located on the slopes of the Ammergau Alps between Ammer and Lech, in an alpine meadow just off the Romantic Road near Steingaden, where there is a visitor information office (☎ 08862/200). The staff at the office can give you a map and confirm that the church is open.

With the help of his brother, Johann Baptist, Zimmermann worked on this church from 1746 to 1754. The ceiling is richly frescoed. It's amazing that so much decoration could be crowded into so small a place. The great Zimmermann was so enchanted with his creation that he constructed a small home in the vicinity and spent the last decade of his life here. A bus heading for the church leaves Füssen Monday to Friday at regular intervals (less often on the weekend). Visitors should check the timetable at the station for bus information or ask at the Füssen tourist office (see above). The trip takes 1 hour and costs 10DM ($6) round-trip.

WHERE TO STAY

Fürstenhof. Kemptenerstrasse 23, 87629 Füssen. ☎ **08362/70-06.** Fax 08362/3-90-48. 15 units. TV TEL. 110DM–130DM ($66–$78) double. Rates include continental buffet breakfast. AE, MC, V. Closed Nov 7–Dec 24. Free parking.

This hotel offers small but well-furnished and well-maintained rooms. The ceilings are of massive exposed paneling, with full-grained beams set into modern stucco. Breakfast is the only meal served.

Hotel Christine. Weidachstrasse 31 (5-min. ride from the train station), 87629 Füssen. ☎ **08362/72-29.** Fax 08362/94-05-54. 13 units. TV TEL. 160DM–250DM ($96–$150) double. Rates include continental breakfast. No credit cards. Closed Jan 15–Feb 15. Free parking.

The Christine is one of the best local choices. The staff spends the long winter months refurbishing the rooms so they'll be fresh and sparkling for spring visitors. Breakfast, the only meal served, is presented on beautiful regional china as classical music plays in the background. A Bavarian charm pervades the hotel, and the small- to medium-sized rooms are very cozy, though hardly fit for King Ludwig were he to return. Bathrooms are a bit cramped.

Hotel-Schlossgasthof Zum Hechten. Directly below the castle, Ritterstrasse 6, 87629 Füssen. ☎ **08362/9-16-00.** Fax 08362/91-60-99. www.hotel-hechten.com. E-mail: hotel.hechten@t-online.de. 35 units, 25 with shower or bathroom. 100DM ($60) double without shower or bathroom, 110DM–130DM ($66–$78) double with shower or bathroom, 140DM ($84) suite. Rates include buffet breakfast. AE, MC, V. Free parking outside.

The family owners have maintained this impeccable guest house for generations. Today it has some of the area's most comfortable lodgings. You'll open your window in spring to a flower box of geraniums. Rooms are small to medium in size, and the bathrooms are spotless but a bit cramped. The family's hospitality is boundless. There are two restaurants (one a buffet dining room), where typical Swabian and Bavarian cuisine are served, with plenty of dishes for vegetarians as well.

Seegasthof Weissensee. An der B-310, 87629 Füssen-Weissensee (4 miles from central Füssen on B310). ☎ **08362/9-17-80.** Fax 08362/91-78-000. 19 units. MINIBAR TEL. 130DM ($78) double. Rates include breakfast. No credit cards. Free parking.

The paneled rooms at this hotel have sliding-glass doors opening onto a balcony overlooking the lake. Breakfast is an appetizing and generous meal of cheese, cold cuts, bread, pastry, eggs, and beverages. The fish that your obliging hosts serve you for dinner might have been caught in the ice-blue waters of the nearby lake, whose far shore you can see from the dining room. Owners take extra care for the comfort of their guests. Rooms and bathrooms are a bit small.

Steig Mühle. Alte Steige 3, 87629 Füssen-Weissensee. ☎ **08362/91-76-0.** Fax 08362/31-48. 13 units. TV TEL. 100DM–110DM ($60–$66) double. Rates include buffet breakfast. No credit cards. Free outside parking, 4.50DM ($2.70) in garage. Mid-Nov to mid-Dec. From Füssen, take Rte. 310 toward Kempten, a 5-min. drive.

Owners and hosts Gunter and Hedwig Buhmann like things to be cozy—their chalet-like guest house is almost a cliché of Bavarian charm. The rooms open onto a view of the lake or mountains, and many have their own balconies. They're furnished in a neat, functional style and kept immaculately clean. There aren't a lot of frills here, but the place offers one of the best values in the area. The public rooms are paneled in wood and decorated with local objects.

WHERE TO DINE

Fischerhütte. Uferstrasse 16, Hopfen am See (3 miles northwest of Füssen). ☎ **08362/9-19-70.** Reservations recommended. Main courses 16DM–42DM ($9.60–$25.20). AE, MC, V. Daily 11:30am–2pm and 6–9:30pm. Closed Tues in Jan–Mar. SEAFOOD.

This restaurant is at the edge of the lake, within sight of dramatic mountain scenery. There are four gracefully paneled, old-fashioned dining rooms, along with a terrace in summer. As its name (Fisherman's Cottage) suggests, the establishment specializes in seafood. Menu items read like an international atlas: one-half of an entire Alaskan salmon (for two); North Atlantic lobster; a garlicky version of French bouillabaisse; fresh alpine trout, prepared pan-fried or with aromatic herbs in the style of Provence; and grilled halibut. A limited array of meat dishes is also offered, as well as succulent desserts. In summer, a beer garden serves simple Bavarian specialties.

Zum Schwanen. Brotmarkt 4. ☎ **08362/61-74.** Reservations required. Main courses 11DM–32DM ($6.60–$19.20). AE. Tues–Sun 11:30am–2pm; Tues–Sat 5:30–9pm. SWABIAN/BAVARIAN.

A conservative yet flavorful blend of Swabian and Bavarian specialties is served to the loyal clients of this small, attractively old-fashioned restaurant. Specialties include homemade sausage, roast pork, lamb, and venison. Service is always helpful and attentive, and you get good value here, along with generous portions.

13 Neuschwanstein/Hohenschwangau

2 miles E of Füssen, 72 miles SW of Munich

Just east of Füssen are the two "Royal Castles" of Hohenschwangau and Neuschwanstein, among the finest in Germany. Hohenschwangau, the more sedate of the two, was built by Maximilian II in 1836; Neuschwanstein was the brainchild of his son, "Mad" King Ludwig II. The extravagant King Ludwig was responsible for two other architectural flights of fancy besides Neuschwanstein: the Linderhof, near Oberammergau, and Herrenchiemsee, on an island in Chiemsee (see chapter 8). Ludwig died under mysterious circumstances in 1886 (see box below).

After you've fought the crowds to get into these royal castles (in summer, the lines to get in can seem endless), you can spend the remaining time hiking around the surrounding alpine peaks and valleys for what might be some of the most memorable walks of your life. For one of the grandest panoramas in all of the Alps (in any

The Fairy-Tale King

Ludwig II, often called "Mad King Ludwig" (although some Bavarians hate that label), was born in Munich in 1845, the son of Maximilian II. Only 18 years old when he was crowned king of Bavaria, handsome Ludwig initially attended to affairs of state, but he soon grew bored and turned to less subtle pursuits. Ludwig was a loner who never married. As time went on, he became more and more obsessed with acting out his grand and extravagant fantasies.

At the baroque palace of **Nymphenburg,** the summer residence of the Bavarian rulers, you can still see in the Marstall Royal Stables the richly decorated coaches and sleighs in which young Ludwig loved to travel, often at night, with his spectacular entourage. His crown jewels can be admired in the treasury in the Königsbau wing of the **Residenz** palace, in the heart of Munich. See chapter 7.

Ludwig had a long association with Richard Wagner and was both a great fan and a benefactor of the composer. The king had Wagner's operas performed for his own pleasure and watched them in royal and solitary splendor. At Linderhof, the first romantic palace that he built, he went so far as to reconstruct the Venus grotto from the Munich opera stage design for *Tannhäuser.*

Ludwig's architectural creations are legendary. To construct his own Versailles, he chose one of Germany's most beautiful lakes, Chiemsee. He called the palace **Herrenchiemsee** in homage to Louis XIV, the Sun King. Today, visitors can enjoy the castle's Versailles-style Hall of Mirrors and its exquisite gardens (see chapter 8). **Linderhof,** in the Graswang Valley near Oberammergau, was a smaller creation but became his favorite castle; it was the only one completed by the time of his death (see chapter 8).

Nestled in a crag high above the little town of Hohenswangen is the most famous of the royal designer's efforts, the multiturreted Disney-like **Neuschwanstein.** From a distance, the castle appears more dreamlike than real. It's the most photographed castle in Germany. The king's study, bedroom, and living room sport frescoes of scenes from Wagner's operas *Tristan and Isolde* and *Lohengrin* (see below).

Finally, Ludwig's excesses became too much, and he was declared insane in 1886 when he was 41 years old. Three days later, he was found drowned in Lake Starnberg on the outskirts of Munich. He may have committed suicide, or he may have been murdered. A memorial chapel lies on the bank of the lake. Ludwig is buried along with other royals in the crypt beneath the choir of St. Michael's Church.

country), hike up to the ✪ **Marienbrücke** (the trail is signposted), which spans the Pöllat Gorge behind Neuschwanstein Castle. If you're properly dressed and have stout boots, continue uphill from the gorge for another hour for the most splendid view possible of Mad King Ludwig's fantasy castle.

ESSENTIALS

GETTING THERE   By Bus   Ten buses a day arrive from Füssen (see above).

By Car   Head east from Füssen along the B17.

VISITOR INFORMATION   Information about the castles and the region in general is available at the **Kurverwaltung,** Rathaus, Münchenerstrasse 2, in Schwangau (☎ **08362/8-19-80**), open Monday to Friday 8am to 5pm.

VISITING THE ROYAL CASTLES

Be prepared for very long lines (sometimes up to an incredible 4 or 5 hours) at the castles in the summer, especially in August. On some days, 25,000 people visit.

✪ HOHENSCHWANGAU

Not as glamorous or spectacular as Neuschwanstein (see below), the neo-Gothic **Hohenschwangau Castle** nevertheless has a much richer history. The original structure dates from the days of the 12th-century knights of Schwangau. When the knights faded away, the castle began to fade too, helped along by the Napoleonic Wars. When Ludwig II's father, Crown Prince Maximilian (later Maximilian II), saw the castle in 1832, he purchased it and in 4 years had it completely restored. Ludwig II spent the first 17 years of his life here and later received Richard Wagner in its chambers.

The rooms of Hohenschwangau are styled and furnished in a much heavier Gothic mode than those in Neuschwanstein. Many are typical of the halls of knights' castles of the Middle Ages in both England and Germany. There's no doubt that the style greatly influenced young Ludwig and encouraged the fanciful boyhood dreams that formed his later tastes and character. Hohenschwangau, unlike Neuschwanstein, has a comfortable look about it, looking more like an actual home than just a museum.

Among the most attractive chambers is the **Hall of the Swan Knight,** named for the wall paintings depicting the saga of Lohengrin. Note the Gothic grillwork on the ceiling, with the open spaces studded with stars.

Hohenschwangau, Alpseestrasse (☎ 08362/8-11-27), is open March 15 through October 15, daily from 8:30am to 5:30pm; October 16 through March 14, daily from 9:30am to 4:30pm. Admission is 12DM ($7.20) for adults and 9DM ($5.40) for students and children 6 to 15; children 5 and under enter free. There are several parking lots that serve both castles.

✪ NEUSCHWANSTEIN

Neuschwanstein was King Ludwig II's fairy-tale castle. Construction lasted for 17 years until the king's death, when all work stopped, leaving a part of the interior uncompleted. From 1884 to 1886, Ludwig lived in these rooms on and off for a total of only about 6 months.

The doorway off to the left side of the vestibule leads to the king's apartments. The **study,** like most of the rooms, is decorated with wall paintings showing scenes from the Nordic legends. The theme of the study is the Tannhäuser saga. The only fabric in the room is hand-embroidered silk, used in curtains and chair coverings, all designed with the gold-and-silver Bavarian coat of arms.

From the vestibule, you enter the **throne room** through the doorway at the opposite end. This hall, designed in Byzantine style by J. Hofmann, was never completed. The floor is a mosaic design, depicting the animals of the world. The columns in the main hall are the deep copper red of porphyry. The circular apse where the king's throne was to have stood is reached by a stairway of white Carrara marble. The walls and ceiling are decorated with paintings of Christ in heaven looking down on the 12 apostles and six canonized kings of Europe.

The **king's bedroom** is the most richly carved in the entire castle—it took 4½ years to complete this room alone. The walls are decorated with panels carved to look like Gothic windows, as well as with a mural depicting the legend of Tristan and Isolde. In the center is a large wooden pillar completely encircled with gilded brass sconces. The ornate bed is on a raised platform with an elaborately carved canopy. Through the balcony window you can see the 150-foot waterfall in the Pollat Gorge, with the mountains in the distance.

The fourth floor of the castle is almost entirely given over to the **Singer's Hall,** the pride of Ludwig II and all of Bavaria. Modeled after the hall at Wartburg, where the legendary song contest of Tannhäuser supposedly took place, the Singer's Hall is decorated with marble columns and elaborately painted designs interspersed with frescoes depicting the life of Parsifal.

The castle, located at Neuschwansteinstrasse 20 (☎ **08362/8-10-35**), can be visited year-round. In September, visitors have the additional treat of hearing Wagnerian concerts along with other music in the Singer's Hall. For information and reservations, contact the tourist office, **Verkehrsamt,** at the Rathaus in Schwangau (☎ **08362/ 8-19-80**). Tickets go on sale in early June, and sell out rather quickly. The castle can only be visited on one of the guided tours, which are given year-round, except November 1, December 24 to 25 and 31, January 1, and Shrove Tuesday. From April to October, tours are given from 9am to 5:30pm; November to March, from 10am to 4pm. Admission is 12DM ($7.20) for adults, 9DM ($5.40) for children and students, free for children 15 and under.

Reaching Neuschwanstein involves a steep half-mile climb from the parking lot at Hohenschwangau Castle (see above). This can be a 25-minute walk for the athletic, an eternity for those less so. To cut down on the climb, you can take a bus to Marienbrücke, a bridge that crosses over the Pollat Gorge at a height of 305 feet. From that vantage point, you, like Ludwig, can stand and meditate on the glories of the castle and its panoramic surroundings. If you want to photograph the castle, don't wait until you reach the top, where you'll be too close for a good shot. It costs 3.50DM ($2.10) for the bus ride up to the bridge or 2DM ($1.20) if you'd like to take the bus back down the hill. From Marienbrücke, it's a 10-minute walk to Neuschwanstein castle. This footpath is very steep.

The most traditional way to reach Neuschwanstein is by horse-drawn carriage; this costs 8DM ($4.80) for the ascent and 4DM ($2.40) for the descent. Some readers have complained about the rides being overcrowded and not at all accessible for visitors with disabilities.

WHERE TO STAY & DINE NEARBY

Hotel Lisl and Jägerhaus. Neuschwansteinstrasse 1–3, 87643 Hohenschwangau. ☎ **08362/88-70.** Fax 08362/8-11-07. 47 units. TV TEL. 180DM–280DM ($108–$168) double; 320DM–470DM ($192–$282) suite. AE, DC, MC, V. Free parking.

This graciously styled villa, with an annex across the street, provides views as well as comfort. Both houses sit in a narrow valley, surrounded by their own gardens. Most rooms have a view of at least one of the two royal castles; some superior rooms open onto views of both. We prefer the rooms in the main building to the more sterile annex. Two pleasant dining rooms in the main house serve good meals..

Hotel Müller Hohenschwangau. Alpseestrasse 16, 87645 Hohenschwangau. ☎ **08362/ 8-19-90.** Fax 08362/81-99-13. E-mail: hotel-mueller@T-online.de. 44 units. TV TEL. 240DM–300DM ($144–$180) double; 350DM–600DM ($210–$360) suite. Rates include buffet breakfast. AE, DC, MC, V. Closed Jan 3–Feb 29. Free parking. Füssen bus.

The location of this hospitable inn, near the foundations of Neuschwanstein Castle, makes it very alluring. The rooms are comfortable and have lots of rustic accessories. Bedrooms are inviting and have a bit of Bavarian charm. On the premises, you'll find a well-maintained restaurant lined with burnished pinewood and a more formal evening restaurant with views over a verdantly planted sun terrace. Nature lovers especially enjoy hiking the short distance to nearby Hohenschwangau Castle.

7 Munich

The people of Munich never need much of a reason for celebrating. If you arrive here in late September, you'll find them in the middle of the **Oktoberfest,** which draws more than seven million people every fall and lasts for 16 days, ending on the first Sunday in October. Although Oktoberfest, when beer flows as freely as water, is the most famous of Munich's festivals, the city is actually less inhibited during the more interesting pre-Lenten **Fasching** (see chapter 2). Even the most reserved Germans get caught up in this whirl of colorful parades, masked balls, and revelry.

Munich is a lively place all year—fairs and holidays seem to follow one on top of the other. But this is no "oompah" town. Here you'll find an elegant and tasteful city with sophisticated clubs and restaurants, wonderful theaters, fine concert halls, and fabulous museums. According to various polls, it's also the Germans' first choice as a place to live.

1 Orientation

Munich is just slightly smaller than Berlin or Hamburg. You can explore the heart of Munich on foot, but many attractions are in the environs, so you'll have to rely on a car or public transportation.

ARRIVING

BY PLANE The **Franz Josef Strauss Airport** (☎ **089/97-52-13-13**), inaugurated in 1992, is among the most modern, best-equipped, and most efficient airports in the world. It handles more than 100 flights a day, serving 60 cities worldwide. Passengers can fly nonstop from New York, Miami, Chicago, and Toronto. The airport lies 18 miles northeast of central Munich at Erdinger Moos.

S-Bahn (☎ **089/22-33-12-56**) trains connect the airport with the Hauptbahnhof (main railroad station) in downtown Munich. Departures are every 20 minutes for the 40-minute trip. The fare is 15DM ($8.55); Eurailpass holders ride free. A taxi into the center costs about 120DM ($68.40). Airport buses, such as those operated by Lufthansa, also run between the airport and the center.

BY TRAIN Munich's main rail station, the **Hauptbahnhof,** on Bahnhofplatz near the city center, is one of Europe's largest. It contains a hotel, restaurants, shopping, car parking, and banking facilities. All major German cities are connected to this station. Some 20 daily trains connect Munich to Frankfurt (trip time: 3¾ hr.), and 23 to Berlin (trip time: 8 hr.).

The rail station is connected with the **S-Bahn** rapid-transit system, a 260-mile network of tracks, providing service to various city districts and outlying suburbs. The **U-Bahn** (subway) system serving Munich is also centered at the rail station. In addition, buses fan out in all directions. For information about long-distance trains, call ☎ **01805/996633;** for S-Bahn trains, call ☎ **089/22-33-12-56.**

BY BUS   Munich has long-distance bus service from many German and European cities. Buses depart from the section of the Hauptbahnhof called the West-Wing-Starnberger Bahnhof. For information about connections, tariffs, and schedules, call **Deutsche Touring GmbH,** Arnulfstrasse 3 (☎ **089/54-58-70-11**). **Bayern Express Reisen,** Arnulfstrasse 16–18 (☎ **089/55-30-74**), offers daily service to Berlin, Leipzig, and Dresden via Nürnberg.

VISITOR INFORMATION

The main tourist office, **Fremdenverkehrsamt,** at the Hauptbahnhof (Bahnhofplatz 2; ☎ **089/22-33-02-56**), is found at the south exit opening onto Bayerstrasse. It offers a free map of Munich and will also reserve rooms (see "Accommodations," later in this chapter). Its hours are Monday to Saturday 10am to 8pm and Sunday 10am to 6pm.

CITY LAYOUT

Munich's **Hauptbahnhof,** or rail station, lies just west of the town center and opens onto Bahnhofplatz. From there you can take Schützenstrasse to one of the major centers of Munich, **Karlsplatz** (nicknamed *Stachus*). Many tram lines converge on this square. From Karlsplatz, you can continue east along the pedestrians-only Neuhauserstrasse and Kaufingerstrasse until you reach **Marienplatz,** which is located deep in the **Altstadt** (old town) of Munich.

From Marienplatz you can head north on Dienerstrasse, which will lead you to Residenzstrasse and finally to **Max-Joseph-Platz,** a landmark square, with the Nationaltheater and the former royal palace, the Residenz. East of this square runs **Maximilianstrasse,** the most fashionable shopping and restaurant street of Munich, containing the prestigious Hotel Vier Jahreszeiten Kempinski München. Between Marienplatz and the Nationaltheater is the **Platzl** quarter, where you'll want to head for nighttime diversions; here you'll find some of the finest (and also some of the worst) restaurants in Munich, along with the landmark Hofbräuhaus, the most famous beer hall in Europe.

North of the old town is **Schwabing,** a former bohemian section whose main street is Leopoldstrasse. The large, sprawling municipal park grounds, the **Englischer Garten,** are due east of Schwabing.

FINDING AN ADDRESS/MAPS   In the Altstadt, "hidden" squares may make finding an address difficult; therefore, you may need a detailed street map, not the more general maps handed out free by the tourist office and many hotels. The best ones are published by Falk, and they're available at nearly all bookstores and at many newsstands. These pocket-size maps are easy to carry and contain a detailed street index at the end.

Neighborhoods in Brief

Altstadt   This is the historic part of Munich, the site of the original medieval city. The Alstadt is bounded by the Sendlinger Tor ("Tor" means gate) and Odeonsplatz to the north and the south, and by the Isar Tor and Karlstor to the east and west. The

Munich Orientation

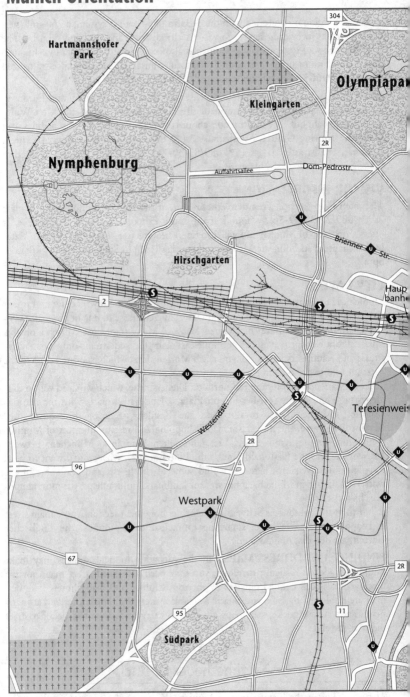

Legend

Church ✝
S-Bahn ─Ⓢ─
U-Bahn ─Ⓤ─

To Airport

Luitpold park

Englisher

Schwabing

Garten

Arabellapark

Museum Quarter

Königsplatz

Odeonsplatz

Hofgarten

Bogenhausen

Karlsplatz (Stachus)

Residenz

Max-Joseph-Platz

Maximilianstr.

Lehel

Neuhauserstr.

Marien platz

Altstadt

Platzl

Maximilians-brücke

englinger or Platz

Isatorplatz

Ludwigsbrücke

Gasteig

Gärtner-platz

Haidhausen

Frühlings-anlagen

cher

Hellabrun Tierpark (Zoo)

⭐ Frommer's Favorite Munich Experiences

A Morning at the Deutsches Museum. It would take a month to see all of the largest technological museum in the world, but a morning will at least whet your appetite. Everything is here: the first automobile by Benz (1886), the original V-2 rocket (Hitler's secret weapon), the first diesel engine, and plenty of buttons to push.

An Afternoon at Nymphenburg Palace. The Wittelsbach family considered this the best place to be on a hot afternoon—and so might you. The grounds of Germany's largest baroque palace are filled with lakes, waterfalls, and pavilions.

A Night at the Opera (Cuvilliés Theater). It's the most beautiful rococo theater in the world: a small, elaborately gilded tier-boxed structure from the mid-18th century.

A Day in the Beer Gardens. Münchners gather on weekends in summer to down huge *masse* of beer and watch the world go by, especially at Chinesischer Turm in the Englischer Garten.

---

hub is **Marienplatz,** with its Rathaus (Town Hall) and its Glockenspiel performance. You can walk across the district in about 15 minutes.

Schwabing   This is a large northern section. After 1945 it became known as the bohemian district of Munich, similar to Greenwich Village in New York. **Leopoldstrasse** makes almost a straight axis through its center. The Englischer Garten forms its eastern border, the Studentenstadt is to its north, and Olympiapark and Josephplatz mark its western border.

Olympiapark   Host to rock and pop concerts on weekends, this residential and recreational area was the site of the 1972 Olympics, which is remembered for the terrorist attack by the Arab "Black September" group against Israeli athletes.

Museum Quarter   Between the Altstadt and Schwabing is the museum district, containing such great museums as the **Alte Pinakothek** (see "Attractions," later in this chapter). Bordered by Briennerstrasse and Theresienstrasse, it actually covers only 2 blocks, but it could take days to explore in depth if you visit all the state-owned museums.

Nymphenburg   Take the U-Bahn to Rotkreuzplatz, then tram no. 12 to reach the Nymphenburg district, about 5 miles northwest of the city center, site of the summer palace of the Wittelsbach dynasty and the famous porcelain manufacturer (see "Attractions," later in this chapter).

2 Getting Around

BY PUBLIC TRANSPORTATION   The city's underground rapid-transit system, the **U-Bahn** or Untergrundbahn network, is modern and relatively noise-free. The above-ground **S-Bahn,** or Stadtbahn, services suburban locations. At the transport hub, Marienplatz, U-Bahn and S-Bahn rails crisscross each other.

The same ticket entitles you to ride both the U-Bahn and the S-Bahn, as well as **trams** (streetcars) and **buses.** The U-Bahn is the system you will probably use most frequently. You're allowed to use your Eurailpass on S-Bahn journeys, as it's a state-owned railway. Otherwise, you must purchase a single-trip ticket or a strip ticket for several journeys at one of the blue vending machines positioned at the entryways to the stations.

Munich U-Bahn & S-Bahn

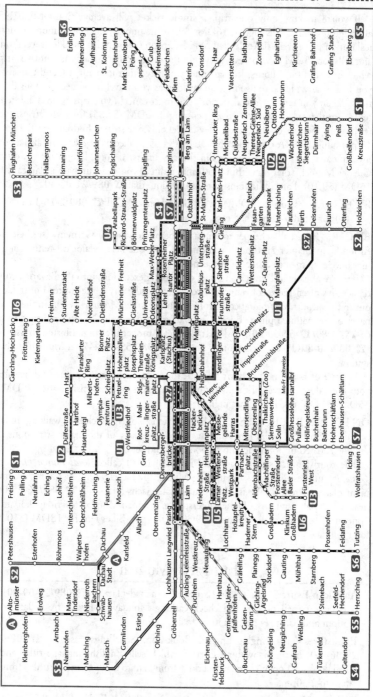

245

If you're making only one trip, a **single ticket** will average 3.40DM ($1.95), although it can reach as high as 16DM ($9.10) to an outlying area. A more economical option is the **strip ticket,** called *Streifenkarte* in German. It's good for several rides and sells for 15DM ($8.55). A trip within the metropolitan area costs you two strips, which are valid for 2 hours. In that time, you may interrupt your trip and transfer as you like to any public transportation, as long as you travel in one continuous direction. When you reverse your direction, you must cancel two strips again. Children 4 to 14 use the red *Kinderstreifenkarte,* costing 8.50DM ($4.85) for eight strips; for a trip within the metropolitan area, they cancel only one strip. Children over the age of 15 pay adult fares. A **day ticket** for 8DM ($4.55), called a *Tageskarte,* is also a good investment if you plan to stay within the city limits. If you'd like to branch out to Greater Munich (that is, within a 50-mile radius), you can purchase a day card for 16DM ($9.10). For public transport information, dial ☎ **089/21-03-30.**

BY TAXI   Cabs cost 2.20DM ($1.25) per kilometer. Call ☎ **089/2-16-11** or 089/1-94-10 for a radio-dispatched taxi.

BY CAR   It's usually cheaper to rent a car before leaving for Germany (see "Getting Around," in chapter 2), though you can also rent one here. Major car-rental companies have easy-to-spot offices at the airport.

If you're already in Munich and plan on making excursions into the Bavarian countryside, it's often more convenient to rent a car in the city center instead of trekking out to the airport. Car-rental companies are listed under *Autovermietung* in the yellow pages of the Munich phone book. Companies include **Avis,** Nymphenburger Strasse 61 (☎ **089/12-60-00-20**), and **Sixt/Budget Autovermietung,** Einsteinstrasse 106 (☎ **089/40-80-05-0**), with another branch (☎ **089/55-02-447**) at Munich's railway station.

Because of heavy traffic, don't attempt to see Munich itself by car. And beware if your hotel doesn't have parking. Parking garages tend to be expensive, often 20DM to 35DM ($11.40 to $19.95) per night.

ON FOOT & BY BICYCLE   The best way to explore Munich is by walking. In fact, because of the vast pedestrian zone in the center, many of the major attractions can only be reached on foot. Pick up a good map and set out.

The tourist office sells a pamphlet for 50pf (30¢) called *Radl-Touren für unsere Gäste;* it outlines itineraries for touring Munich by bicycle. One of the most convenient places to rent a bike is **Aktiv-Rad,** Hans-Sachs-Strasse 7 (☎ **089/26-65-06**), near the U-Bahn station at Frauenhoferstrasse. It's open Monday to Friday 9:30am to 1pm and 2 to 6pm, and on Saturday 9:30am to 1pm. Bikes rent for 18DM ($10.25) for a full day.

Fast Facts: Munich

American Express   American Express, Promenadeplatz 6 (☎ **089/29-09-00**), is open for mail pickup and check cashing Monday to Friday from 9am to 5:30pm and Saturday from 9:30am to 12:30pm.

Bookstores   Try Anglia English Bookshop, Schellingstrasse 3 (☎ **089/28-36-42**), in the Schwabing district, which sells English-language titles and travel books. It's open Monday to Friday from 9am to 6:30pm and Saturday from 10am to 2:30pm.

Business Hours   Most **banks** are open Monday to Friday from 8:30am to 12:30pm and 1:30 to 3:30pm (many banks stay open until 5:30pm on

Thursday). Most **businesses** and **stores** are open Monday to Friday from 9am to 6pm (many stay open until 8 or 9pm on Thursday) and Saturday from 9am to 2pm. On *langer Samstag* (the first Saturday of the month) stores remain open until 6pm.

Consulates   See "Embassies & Consulates" in "Fast Facts: Germany," in chapter 2.

Currency Exchange   You can get a better rate at a bank than at your hotel. On Saturday and Sunday or at night, you can exchange money at the rail station exchange, in Bahnhofplatz; it's open daily from 6am to 11:30pm.

Dentists   For an English-speaking dentist, go to Klinik und Poliklinik für Kieferchirurgie der Universität München, Lindwurmstrasse 2A (☎ **089/ 51-60-29-11**), the dental clinic for the university. It deals with emergency cases and is always open.

Doctors   The American, British, and Canadian consulates keep a list of recommended English-speaking physicians.

Drugstores   For an international drugstore where English is spoken, try International Ludwig's Apotheke, Neuhauserstrasse 11 (☎ **089/2-60-30-21**), in the pedestrian shopping zone. It's open Monday to Friday 9am to 8pm, and Saturday 9am to 4pm.

E-mail   Head for the **Internet Café,** Nymphenburger Strasse 145, corner of Landshutter Allee (☎ **089/129-47-44**). This is not only a cyber cafe but also a bar, disco, bistro, pastry shop, and pizzeria. Its Web site is **www.icafe.space.de.**

Emergencies   For emergency **medical aid,** call ☎ **089/55-17-71.** For the police, call ☎ **110.**

Eyeglasses   Frames and contact lenses are available from **Söhnges Optik,** Kaufingerstrasse 34 (☎ **089/2-90-05-50**), and Briennerstrasse 7 (☎ **089/ 2-90-71-00**).

Laundry/Dry Cleaning   A good dry-cleaning establishment is **Paradies Reinigung,** Octtingenstrasse 29 (☎ **089/22-34-65**). Look in the Yellow Pages under either *Wascherei* or *Waschsalon* for a coin-operated laundry near your hotel.

Lost Property   Go to the local lost-and-found office at Ötztalerstrasse 17 (☎ **089/23-34-59-00**). It's open Monday to Friday 8:30am to noon; on Tuesday it's also open 2 to 5:30pm. If you should lose an item on a German train, go to the lost-and-found office at Track 24 in the Hauptbahnhof (☎ **089/12-88-44-09**); it's open Monday to Friday 8am to 5:30pm and Saturday 8am to 11:45pm.

Luggage/Storage Lockers   Facilities are available at the Hauptbahnhof on Bahnhofplatz (☎ **089/13-08-50-47**), open daily 6am to 11pm.

Post Office   The **Postamt München** (main post office) is across from the Hauptbahnhof, at Bahnhofplatz 1 (☎ **089/60-10-60-4**). If you want to have your mail sent to you, have it addressed Poste Restante, the Postamt München, Bahnhofplatz 1, 85521 Ottobrunnz, for general delivery. Take along your passport to reclaim any mail. The office is open Monday to Saturday 8am to 12:30pm and 2 to 6pm, closed Sunday and holidays. You can also make long-distance calls here (far cheaper than at your hotel).

Radio   Bayern 2 at 88.4 FM presents news in English, French, and Italian from Monday to Friday at 8:50am. You can also listen to the Voice of America at 1197 AM.

Rest Rooms   Use the word *toilette* (pronounced twa-*leht*-tah). Rest rooms may be labeled WC, or "H" (for *Herren,* men) and "F" (for *Frauen,* women). In the center of Munich are several clean, safe, and well-kept public facilities.

Safety   Munich, like all big cities, has its share of crime, especially pickpocketing and purse- and camera-snatching. Most robberies occur in the much-frequented tourist areas, such as the areas around Marienplatz and the Hauptbahnhof, which is particularly dangerous at night. Many tourists lose their valuables when they carelessly leave clothing unprotected as they join the nude sunbathers in the Englischer Garten.

Shoe Repairs   Offering the quickest service is Mister Minit, at the Hertie department store, Bahnhofplatz 7 (☎ 089/5-51-20).

Telegrams/Telex/Fax   These can be sent from the main post office at Bahnhofplatz 1 (☎ 089/599-0870).

Television   There are two national TV channels, ARD (Channel 1) and ZDF (Channel 2). Sometimes these stations show films in the original language (most often English). The more expensive hotels often have cable TV, with such channels as CNN.

3 Accommodations

There are many rooms available in Munich, though most are costly. Bargains are few and hard to find—but they do exist.

For help in finding accommodations, there are two options. The **Munich Tourist Information Office** on Platform 12 at the Hauptbahnhof (☎ 089/2-33-03-00), open daily from 10am to 8pm, is especially good if you arrive in Munich without a hotel reservation. Here, Bavarian personnel (most speak English), with some 34,000 listings in their files, will help you find a place to stay. Tell them what you can afford, and for a 5DM ($2.85) fee, they'll book you a room and even give you a map with instructions on how to reach it. Keep your receipt. If you don't like the room, go back to the tourist office, and they'll book you another at no extra charge. These offices are open Monday to Friday from 9am to 3pm. You can book a room by fax at ☎ 089/23-33-02-33.

The other option is **Advance Reservations Citi Incoming,** Mullerstrasse 11 (Postfach 140163),80451 München (☎ 089/2-60-69-14; fax 089/2-60-64-84), which offers a free, more personal service and is especially good for making reservations from home. Although Citi Incoming works with hotels on a commission basis, it guarantees that travelers never pay more than if they had made the bookings themselves. In some cases, Citi Incoming can even get you a better rate than off-the-street bookings, because hotels give them special offers. There are no fixed open hours, but you can call or fax at any time. The company also provides this service for other areas of Germany and for neighboring countries such as Austria and Switzerland. Both long-term bookings and last-minute requests are handled. If no one is in the office, leave a message on their machine, or visit their Web site at **home.t-online.de/home/citi-incoming,** or e-mail your reservations to citi-incoming@t-online.de.

Dialing Germany

Remember that the phone numbers in this book contain an initial 0 in the German city code. That 0 is only used within Germany. Omit it when calling from abroad.

> ### ⓘ Family-Friendly Hotels
>
> **Gästehaus Englischer Garten** (*see p. 255*)   This ivy-covered villa oasis of calm and tranquillity provides old-fashioned family atmosphere.
> **Hotel Jedermann** (*see p. 255*)   Families on a budget like this hotel, which supplies cribs or cots.

IN CENTRAL MUNICH
VERY EXPENSIVE

✪ **Bayerischer Hof & Palais Montgelas.** Promenadeplatz 2–6, 80333 München. ☎ **800/223-6800** in the U.S., or 089/2-12-00. Fax 089/2-12-09-06. www.lhw.com/munich/bayerischerhof.html. E-mail: hbh@compuserve.com. 445 units. MINIBAR TV TEL. 466DM–522DM ($265.60–$297.55) double; 854DM–1,950DM ($486.80–$1,111.50) suite. AE, DC, MC, V. Parking 33DM ($18.80). Tram: 19.

The Bayerischer Hof hotel and the 17th-century Palais Montgelas combine to form a Bavarian version of New York's Waldorf-Astoria. This establishment has been beneficiary of zillions of marks worth of improvements and is now better than ever, a rival even of the front-ranking Kempinski Hotel Vier Jahreszeiten (see below). It's been a favorite ever since King Ludwig I used to come here to take a bath (the royal palace didn't have bathtubs back then). Rooms range from medium size to extremely spacious. The decor styles range from Bavarian provincial to British country house chintz. Many beds are four-posters. The large marble bathrooms have a private phone and plenty of shelf space. Palais Montgelas has 20 of the most upscale rooms as well as conference and banqueting rooms.

Dining/Diversions: The major dining room, the Garden-Restaurant, evokes the grandeur of a small palace, with an ornate ceiling, crystal chandeliers, and French provincial chairs. Generous drinks and charcoal specialties from the rotisserie are served in the clublike bar. There's also the Kleine Komödie Theater, a Trader Vic's, and the best nightclub in Munich (see "Munich After Dark," below).

Amenities: Room service, laundry, baby-sitting, rooftop pool and garden with bricked sun terrace, sauna, massage rooms, shopping mall with boutiques and salons.

✪ **Kempinski Hotel Vier Jahreszeiten München.** 80539 München. ☎ **800/426-3135** in the U.S., or 089/2-12-50. Fax 089/21-25-20-00. www.kempinski.com. E-mail: reservation. hvj@kempinski.com. 364 units. A/C MINIBAR TV TEL. 510DM–810DM ($290.70–$461.70) double; from 1,320DM ($752.40) suite. AE, DC, MC, V. Parking 30DM ($17.10). Tram: 19.

This grand hotel is not only the most elegant in Munich, but it's also Germany's most famous and distinctive, and among the finest in the world. Its tradition stretches back to 1858. Guest rooms and suites—which have hosted royalty, heads of state, and famed personalities from all over the world—combine the charm of days gone by with modern amenities. The antique-style beds feature fine linen on sumptuous mattresses. The large bathrooms are equipped with all sorts of special treats, including luxurious bathrobes. The windows opening onto Maximilianstrasse are double-glazed to keep out the noise.

Dining/Diversions: The Restaurant Vier Jahreszeiten (open daily) is recommended in "Dining," below. The Four Seasons lies under a magnificent glass roof above the lobby. In the Jahreszeiten Bar, piano music plays nightly during the cocktail hour, and an international trio performs until 2am. The completely refurbished Bistro Eck has a modern yet classical atmosphere.

Munich Accommodations

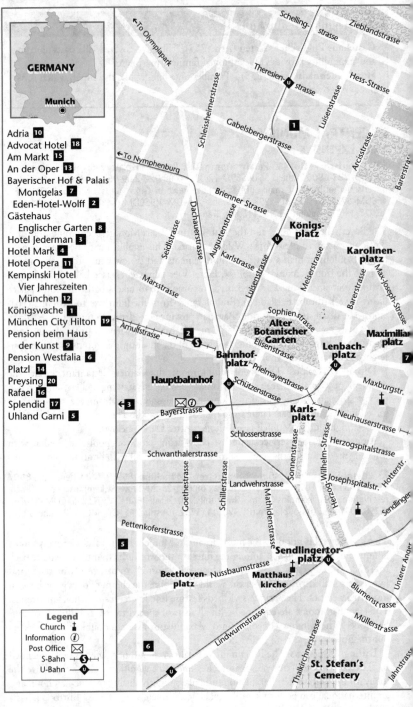

GERMANY

Munich

To Olympiapark

To Nymphenburg

Schelling-strasse

Zieblandstrasse

Theresien-strasse

Hess-Strasse

Gabelsbergerstrasse

Luisenstrasse

Arcisstrasse

Barerstr.

Schleissheimerstrasse

1

Brienner Strasse

Königs-platz

Karolinen-platz

Dachauerstrasse

Augustenstrasse

Karlstrasse

Meiserstrasse

Barerstrasse

Max-Joseph-Strasse

Seidlstrasse

Marsstrasse

Luisenstrasse

Sophien-strasse

Alter
Botanischer
Garten

Maximilian
platz

Arnulfstrasse

2
S

Bahnhof-
platz

Elisenstrasse

Prielmayerstrasse

Lenbach-
platz

7

Hauptbahnhof

Schützenstrasse

Maxburgstr.

Bayerstrasse

3

Karls-
platz

Neuhauserstrasse

4

Schlosserstrasse

Herzogspitalstrasse

Hotterstr.

Schwanthalerstrasse

Sonnenstrasse

Wilhelm-Strasse

Josephspitalstr.

Herzog

Sendlinger

Goethestrasse

Schillerstrasse

Landwehrstrasse

Mathildenstrasse

Pettenkoferstrasse

5

Sendlingertor-
platz

Unterer Anger

Beethoven-
platz

Nussbaumstrasse

Matthäus-
kirche

Blumenstrasse

Lindwurmstrasse

Müllerstrasse

6

Thalkirchnerstrasse

St. Stefan's
Cemetery

Jahnstrasse

Legend
Church ✝
Information ⓘ
Post Office ✉
S-Bahn Ⓢ
U-Bahn Ⓤ

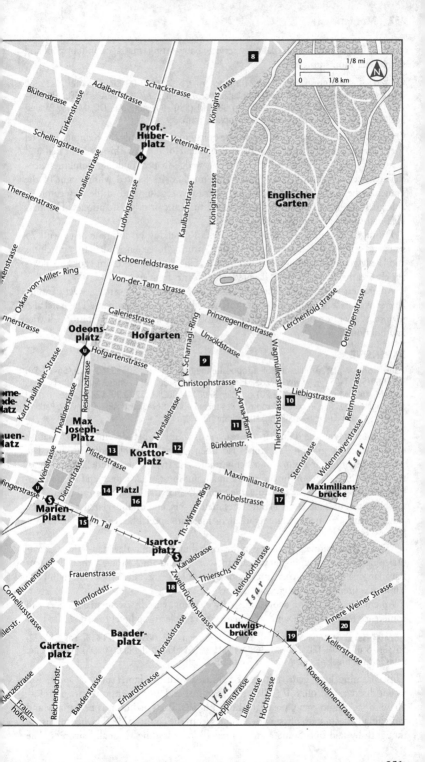

251

Amenities: Room service, laundry service, baby-sitting, massages; indoor pool and sauna, solarium, sun terrace.

✪ **Rafael.** Neuturmstrasse 1, 80331 München. ☎ **089/29-09-80.** Fax 089/22-25-39. www.hotelrafael.com. E-mail: info@hotelrafael.com. 81 units. A/C MINIBAR TV TEL. 680DM–750DM ($387.60–$427.50) double; from 880DM ($501.60) suite. AE, DC, MC, V. Parking 36DM ($20.50). U-Bahn or S-Bahn: Marienplatz. Tram: 19.

One of Munich's smaller hotels is also one of its most posh. Only the Kempinski Hotel Vier Jahreszeiten München and the Bayerischer Hof outclass this sophisticated and luxurious winner. The stylish and elegant wedge-shaped building combines neo-Renaissance, neoclassical, and Biedermeier touches. It's located within sight of the Frauenkirche at Marienplatz. A marble staircase sweeps upward to the very comfortable guest rooms, each with specially crafted furniture or original antiques. The marbled bathrooms are well appointed.

Dining: The culinary showplace is Mark's Restaurant, an intimate place with 75 seats and a piano bar. Its setting is elegant, featuring rose-colored damask tablecloths and Wedgwood china along with Beard silver. Chef Dirk Schlottborn cooks up a dazzlingly creative Italian cuisine, flavored with accents from Asia.

Amenities: Concierge, 24-hour room service, laundry, baby-sitting, valet parking. The service staff is among the most professional in southern Germany. The hotel also maintains a rooftop pool (May through October) with a view over the historic district and boutiques.

EXPENSIVE

Eden-Hotel-Wolff. Arnulfstrasse 4–8 (opposite the train station), 80335. ☎ **089/55-11-50.** Fax 089/55-11-55-55. www.ehw.de. E-mail: sales@ehw.de. 211 units. MINIBAR TV TEL. 280DM–460DM ($159.60–$262.20) double; 370DM–500DM ($210.90–$285) suite. 1 child up to age 6 stays free in parents' room. Rates include buffet breakfast. AE, DC, MC, V. Parking 20DM ($11.40). U-Bahn or S-Bahn: Hauptbahnhof.

If you must stay in the train station area, this is your best bet, despite the fact that it's often booked by groups. The stone-clad Eden-Hotel-Wolff misleads with its sedate exterior. The interior is done in a richly traditional style, with chandeliers and dark-wood paneling. A few of the rooms are small, but most are spacious, and all are tastefully furnished in a decor that runs the gamut from extremely modern to rustic. The marble bathrooms are large. Private safes, hair dryers, and double-glazed windows are added features. Some units are hypo-allergenic, with special beds and a private ventilation system.

Dining/Diversions: The theme in the main dining room is Bavarian—there's a natural pine ceiling, gleaming brass lantern sconces, and thick stone arches. Excellent Bavarian dishes and a savory international cuisine are the fare. On a cold night, the bar with a fireplace is a snug, cozy retreat.

Amenities: Concierge, baby-sitting, dry cleaning, laundry, secretarial services and conference rooms; bicycle and car rentals are available at the hotel tour desk.

Hotel Opera. St-Anna Strasse 10, 80538 München. ☎ **089/2255-3336.** Fax 089/22-55-38. 25 units. TV TEL. 280DM–360DM ($159.60–$205.20) double; 400DM ($228) suite. Rates include breakfast. AE, MC, V. U-Bahn: U5 to Lehel.

This charming little gem (not to be confused with the Hotel an der Opera) is a recent discovery of ours. It's filled with comfort and an authentic Bavarian atmosphere so lacking in many postwar Munich hotels. Each bedroom is beautifully and individually decorated, often with antiques from the countryside. The bedrooms are thoughtfully laid out. Some contain French doors leading to small balconies. The bathrooms are relatively small but well-maintained. The rooms at the rear on the third and fourth floors are more tranquil, although they're slightly smaller than those fronting the street. The location is desirable, too, only a 12-minute walk from the chic Maximilianstrasse, with some of the city's major attractions virtually at your doorstep.

Dining: The hotel serves breakfast only but does operate a bar 24 hours. Many good restaurants lie within walking distance.

Amenities: Jacuzzi, concierge, room service, dry cleaning, laundry, roof garden, garden terrace.

Platzl. Sparkassenstrasse 10, 80331 München. ☎ **089/23-70-30.** Fax 089/23-70-38-00. www.platzl.de. E-mail: info@platzl.de. 167 units. MINIBAR TV TEL. 314DM–434DM ($179–$247.40) double. Rates include buffet breakfast. AE, DC, MC, V. Parking 20DM ($11.40). U-Bahn: U3 or U6 to Marienplatz.

This restored hotel, owned by the Aying brewery, is centrally located in the historic Altstadt, opposite the world-famous Hofbräuhaus and close to Marienplatz. It's the beer-drinker's favorite—more beer is consumed in and around this hotel than at any other place in Europe. It's one of the best choices in Munich for a real taste of home-style German hospitality. Many of the bedrooms are quite small and are decorated in a rustic Bavarian motif. Next door is the folk theater, Platzl's Theaterie.

Dining: The hotel's restaurant, Pfistermühle, serves Bavarian cuisine.

Amenities: Room service, laundry, dry cleaning, sauna and Jacuzzi, conference rooms for business travelers, boutique.

MODERATE

Adria. Liebigstrasse 8a, 80538 München. ☎ **089/29-30-81.** Fax 089/22-70-15. 47 units. MINIBAR TV TEL. 190DM–280DM ($108.30–$159.60) double. Rates include buffet breakfast. AE, MC, V. Closed Dec 23–Jan 6. Free parking. U-Bahn: 4 or 5. Tram: 17.

Adria offers many special touches and has an inviting, friendly atmosphere. The lobby sets the stylish, contemporary tone. The bedrooms are among the best in town for this price range. All have such extra furnishings as armchairs and small sofas, along with desks. Breakfast, served in the garden room, consists of a buffet, with waffles, cakes, homemade rolls, health-food selections, and even sparkling wine—smoked salmon is an added treat on Sunday. Services include money exchange, laundry, theater tickets, and arrangements for sightseeing tours. For 50DM ($28.50), the hotel will give you a "license" allowing you to park free in the neighborhood; when you return the license at checkout time, the fee is returned.

Advocat Hotel. Baaderstrasse 1, 80469 München. ☎ **089/21-63-10.** Fax 089/21-63-190. E-mail: advokathot@aol.com. 50 units. MINIBAR TV TEL. Fri–Sun 215DM ($122.55) double, Mon–Thurs 295DM ($168.15) double. S-Bahn: Isartor.

This hotel occupies a six-story apartment house originally constructed in the 1930s. Its stripped-down, streamlined interior borrows in discreet ways from Bauhaus and minimalist models. One Munich critic said the rooms look as if Philippe Starck had gone on a shopping binge at Ikea. The result was an aggressively simple, clean-lined, and artfully Spartan hotel with very few amenities and facilities. The German government gave it three stars. The Advocat lies around the corner from its more upscale neighbor, the Hotel Admiral, with which it shares the same management, but whose rooms cost 50DM ($28.50) more, double occupancy, per category. There's no restaurant on the premises and no particular amenities to speak of other than a cozy in-house bar. But the prices are reasonable, and the staff is helpful.

An der Oper. Falkenturmstrasse 11 (just off Maximilianstrasse, near Marienplatz), 80331 München. ☎ **089/2-90-02-70.** Fax 089/29-00-27-29. 55 units. MINIBAR TV TEL. 250DM–320DM ($142.50–$182.40) double. Rates include buffet breakfast. AE, MC, V. Tram: 19.

This hotel is superbly located for sightseeing or shopping in the traffic-free malls, and it's just steps from the Bavarian National Theater. In spite of its basic decor, there are touches of elegance, such as crystal chandeliers in the little reception area. Guest rooms, which range in size from small to medium, have such amenities as double-glazed windows, a small sitting area with armchairs, and a table for those who want breakfast in their rooms.

Hotel Mark. Senefelderstrasse 12 (near the Hauptbahnhof's south exit), 80336 München. ☎ **089/55-98-20.** Fax 089/55-98-23-33. 90 units. MINIBAR TV TEL. 200DM–230DM ($114–$131.10) double. Rates include buffet breakfast. AE, DC, MC, V. Parking 15DM ($8.55). U-Bahn or S-Bahn: Hauptbahnhof.

This hotel offers decent comfort at a moderate price. The guest rooms are modern and functionally furnished, although a bit cramped. Breakfast is the only meal served.

Königswache. Steinheilstrasse 7, 80333 München. ☎ **089/5-42-75-70.** Fax 089/5-23-21-14. 40 units. MINIBAR TV TEL. 290DM ($165.30) double. Rates include buffet breakfast. AE, MC, V. Parking garage (reservation required) 12DM ($6.85). U-Bahn: U2 to Königsplatz.

The Königswache has much to recommend it, in spite of its sterile facade. The location, about a 10-minute ride from the Hauptbahnhof and only 2 minutes from the technical university, is between Karlsplatz and Schwabing—a district safer at night than the railway-station area. The staff speaks English. The rooms are modern and comfortable and contain writing desks. The bathrooms are small.

Splendid. Maximilianstrasse 54, 80538 München. ☎ **089/29-66-06.** Fax 089/2-91-31-76. 36 units, 30 with bathroom. TV TEL. 165DM–235DM ($94.05–$133.95) double without bathroom, 205DM–315DM ($116.85–$179.55) double with bathroom; 265DM–495DM ($151.05–$282.15) suite. AE, DC, DISC, MC, V. U-Bahn: 4 or 5. Tram: 17 or 19.

The Splendid is one of the most attractive old-world hotels in Munich. Antiques, Oriental rugs, and chandeliers decorate the public rooms. Each room has the aura of a country home. Most are decorated in a style known as "Bavarian baroque," although two recently remodeled rooms are in the Louis XVI style. You can order breakfast—the only meal served—in your room if you wish, or else have it on a trellised patio. Room prices are scaled according to size, furnishings, and time of year, with the highest prices charged at fair and festival times. Room service is provided.

INEXPENSIVE

Am Markt. Heiliggeiststrasse 6, 80331 München. ☎ **089/22-50-14.** Fax 089/22-40-17. 32 units, 13 with bathroom. TV TEL. 112DM ($63.85) double without bathroom, 160DM ($91.20) double with bathroom. Rates include continental breakfast. No credit cards. Parking 12DM ($6.85). S-Bahn: From the Hauptbahnhof, take any S-Bahn train headed for Marienplatz, a 2-stop ride from the station.

This popular, though not luxurious, Bavarian hotel stands in the heart of the older section. Owner Harald Herrler has maintained a nostalgic decor in the lobby and dining room. Behind his reception desk is a wall of photographs of friends or former guests, including the late Viennese chanteuse Greta Keller. As Mr. Herrler points out, when you have breakfast here, you're likely to find yourself surrounded by opera and concert artists; the hotel is close to where they perform. The guest rooms are quite small but trim, modern, and neat. Mattresses are well worn but still comfortable. All units, even those without private bathrooms, have sinks with hot and cold running water.

Hotel Jedermann. Bayerstrasse 95, 80335 München. ☎ **089/53-32-67.** Fax 089/53-65-06. www.hotel-jedermann.de. E-mail: hotel-jedermann@cube.net. 55 units, 34 with shower and toilet. TV TEL. 95DM–140DM ($54.15–$79.80) double without bathroom; 130DM–240DM ($74.10–$136.80) double with shower and toilet; 110DM–185DM ($62.70–$105.45) triple without bathroom; 155DM–265DM ($88.35–$151.05) triple with shower and toilet. Rates include buffet breakfast. MC, V. Parking 10DM ($5.70). 10-min. walk from Hauptbahnhof (turn right on Bayerstrasse from south exit).

This pleasant, cozy spot has been deftly run by the Jenke family since 1961. Its central location and good value make it a desirable choice, especially for families (cribs or cots are available). The old-fashioned Bavarian rooms are generally small, but cozy and comfortable. Most rooms have a private safe. A generous breakfast buffet is served in a charming room.

Pension beim Haus der Kunst. Bruderstrasse 4, 80538 München. ☎ **089/22-21-27.** Fax 089/22-26-97. www.major.com/bronchen/pension/pension-gb.htm. 9 units, 1 with bathroom. 95DM ($54.15) double; 220DM ($125.40) apt for 4. Rates include breakfast. No credit cards. U-Bahn: Lehel.

This pension is like an old-fashioned Bavarian boarding house, so don't expect luxury. Nonetheless, the place offers an ideal location near the Englischer Garten, copious breakfasts, and warm hospitality. There's only one private bathroom, but the corridor baths are adequate. The towels you're given are rather thin. There's free parking on the street, when available.

Pension Westfalia. Mozartstrasse 23, 80336 München. ☎ **089/53-03-77.** Fax 089/5-43-91-20. 19 units, 11 with bathroom. TV TEL. 90DM ($51.30) double without bathroom; 115DM–130DM ($65.55–$74.10) double with bathroom. Rates include buffet breakfast. AE, V. U-Bahn: 3 or 6 to Goetheplatz. Bus: 58 from the Hauptbahnhof.

This four-story town house near Goetheplatz is one of Munich's best pensions. It faces the meadow where the annual Oktoberfest takes place. Rooms are rather functional, and short on extras, but well maintained. Owner Peter Deiritz speaks English. Parking is free on the street, when available.

Uhland Garni. Uhlandstrasse 1, 80336 München. ☎ **089/54-33-50.** Fax 089/54-33-52-50. www.hotel-uhland.de. E-mail: hotel-uhland@compuserve.com. 30 units. MINIBAR TV TEL. 150DM–290DM ($85.50–$165.30) double. Rates include buffet breakfast. AE, DC, MC, V. Free parking. Bus: 58.

Located in a residential area, just a 10-minute walk from the Hauptbahnhof, the Uhland could easily become your home in Munich. It offers friendly, personal service. The stately town mansion, built in art-nouveau style, stands in its own small garden. Its bedrooms are soundproof; all are snug, traditional, and cozy. The bathrooms contain hair dryers. Only breakfast is served.

IN SCHWABING

✪ **Gästehaus Englischer Garten.** Liebergesellstrasse 8, 80802 München-Schwabing. ☎ **089/3-83-94-10.** Fax 089/38-39-41-33. 25 units, 19 with bathroom. MINIBAR TV TEL. 130DM ($74.10) double without bathroom, 156DM–194DM ($88.90–$110.60) double with bathroom. No credit cards. Parking 10DM ($5.70). U-Bahn: U3 or U6 to Münchener Freiheit.

This oasis of charm and tranquillity, close to the Englischer Garten, is one of our preferred stopovers in Munich. For some 2 decades now, Frau Irene Schlüter-Hubscher has operated this ivy-covered hotel. The decor of the bedrooms, ranging from small to medium, has been called "Bavarian grandmotherly;" furnishings include genuine antiques, old-fashioned but exceedingly comfortable beds, and Oriental rugs. Bathrooms are small and not one of the hotel's stronger features, but their maintenance is first rate. Fifteen units are across the street in an annex; these are small apartments, each with a bathroom and a tiny kitchenette. Try for rooms 16, 23, 26, or especially 20. In fair weather, breakfast is served in a rear garden.

IN HAIDHAUSEN

München City Hilton. Rosenheimerstrasse 15, 81667 München. ☎ **800/455-8667** in the U.S. and Canada, or 089/4-80-40. Fax 089/48-04-48-04. www.hilton.com. E-mail: munich-city@ hilton.com. 499 units. A/C MINIBAR TV TEL. 390DM–550DM ($222.30–$313.50) double; from 600DM ($342) suite. AE, DC, MC, V. Parking 26DM ($14.80). S-Bahn: S1, S2, S3, S4, S5, S6, S7, and S8 stop directly under hotel.

The München City Hilton lies beside the Deutsches Museum and the performing arts center, Gasteig. This low-rise hotel, designed with red brick, shimmering glass, and geometric windows, is reminiscent of a Mondrian painting. Munich's historic center is an invigorating 25-minute walk across the river. The guest rooms contain modern adaptations of Biedermeier furniture and plush carpeting. The well-stocked bathrooms contain hair dryers, luxurious bathrobes, and large, sumptuous towels.

Dining/Diversions: The Hilton offers good drinking and dining facilities, including Zum Gasteig, a Bavarian restaurant decorated in typical style; Löwen-Schanke, a Bavarian pub; and Café Metropolitan, where you can order a leisurely breakfast or afternoon tea.

Amenities: 24-hour room service, laundry, dry cleaning, baby-sitting; flower shop, newsstand.

Preysing. Preysingstrasse 1, 81667 München. ☎ **089/45-84-50.** Fax 089/45-84-54-44. 81 units. A/C MINIBAR TV TEL. 328DM ($186.95) double; 375DM–540DM ($213.75–$307.80) suite. Rates include breakfast. AE, DC, MC, V. Closed Dec 23–Jan 6. Parking 20DM ($11.40). Tram: 18.

If you want a quiet location and don't mind a hotel on the outskirts, consider the Preysing, located across the Isar near the Deutsches Museum. (A short tram ride will whisk you into the center of the city.) When you first view the building, a seven-story modern structure, you may feel we've misled you. However, if you've gone this far, venture inside for a pleasant surprise. The hotel's style is agreeable, with dozens of little extras to provide homelike comfort. Fresh flowers are everywhere, and the furnishings have been carefully selected. Fresh fruit is supplied daily. The spacious bathrooms have hair dryers and deluxe toiletries. The staff is one of the most thoughtful in Munich.

Dining: Preysing's restaurant is one of Munich's best (see "Dining," below).

Amenities: Room service, laundry, baby-sitting, indoor pool, sauna, solarium, whirlpool.

4 Dining

Munich is one of the very few European cities that has more than one "three-star" restaurant. This is the place to practice *Edelfresswelle* ("high-class gluttony"). The classic local dish, traditionally consumed before noon, is *Weisswurste*, herb-flavored white-veal sausages blanched in water. Sophisticated international cuisine is popular throughout the city, too.

IN CENTRAL MUNICH

VERY EXPENSIVE

✪ **Garden Restaurant.** In the Bayerischer Hof Hotel, Promenadeplatz 2–6. ☎ **089/ 21200.** Reservations recommended. Main courses 35DM–56DM ($19.95–$31.90). Fixed-price lunch 59DM–98DM ($33.65-$55.85); fixed-price dinners 69DM-98DM ($39.35–$55.85). AE, DC, MC, V. Daily noon–3pm and 6–11:30pm. Tram: 19. MEDITERRANEAN/ INTERNATIONAL.

Cafe Culture

You can follow the German custom of dining on coffee and cake in the afternoon at one of Munich's fine cafes. The famous **Café Luitpold,** Briennerstrasse 11 (☎ **089/ 29-28-65**), open since 1888, attracted such notables as Ibsen, Kandinsky, and Johann Strauss the Younger. It's open Monday to Friday 9am to 8pm and Saturday 8am to 7pm. From **Café Glockenspiel** on the Marienplatz (☎ **089/26-42-56**), you can watch the miniature tournament staged each day by the mechanical clock on the Rathaus facade. It's open daily 10 to 1am. Two famous purveyors of fine chocolate and pastry are **Confiserie Reber,** Herzogspitalstrasse 9 (☎ **089/26-52-31**), and **Confiserie Kreutzkann,** Maffeistrasse 4 (☎ **089/29-32-77**), which has a cafe on the premises that's open 8am to 6:30pm.

This showcase restaurant within one of the showcase hotels of Munich looks like a miniature pastel-colored palace. It's set in a solemnly hushed room filled with blooming plants off the otherwise bustling lobby of the hotel. Upscale food is served to a cosmopolitan crowd. Menu items are about as cultivated and esoteric as you can find in Munich. Examples include thin noodles with strips of quail and mushroom sauce, a bouquet of salad greens "land and sea" accented with lobster meat and calves' liver, a soup of exotic mushrooms in puff pastry, and fillet of beef stuffed with goose liver and fresh mushrooms. Despite the elaborate menu, one of the most sought after dishes is fillet of Dover sole in lemon-butter sauce, served simply but flavorfully with fresh spinach and boiled potatoes. Desserts are appropriately lavish, and wine choices are among the most varied in Munich.

✪ **Hilton Grill.** In the Hilton Munich Park, Am Tucherpark 7. ☎ **089/3845-0.** Reservations recommended. Main courses 42DM–65DM ($23.95–$37.05); fixed-price lunch 62DM ($35.35); fixed-price dinner 92DM–145DM ($52.45–$82.65). AE, DC, MC, V. Sun–Fri noon–2:30pm and 7–10:30pm; Sat 7–10:30pm. U-Bahn: U3 or U6 to Giselastrasse, then bus 54. CONTINENTAL.

This sophisticated restaurant is like a richly paneled private club that just happens to be open to the public. The place has charm, panache, and flair. Tables are elaborately decorated. Dishes combine traditional and modern European and North American cuisine. Management offers a free bottle of champagne if the set luncheon is not served within an hour of a patron's arrival. Luncheons might include salmon carpaccio with a white-asparagus vinaigrette, spaghettini with morels in an herb sauce, monkfish on lentils with crispy Parma ham, or one of Munich's best Bavarian-style duck dishes, on white cabbage with dumplings. Dinners are even more elaborate; the pièce de résistance is wood pigeon with foie gras and artichokes set in Madeira-flavored aspic, followed by a lavish tray of desserts.

Restaurant Königshof. In the Hotel Königshof, Karlsplatz 25 (Am Stachus). ☎ **089/ 55-13-60.** Reservations required. Main courses 46DM–68DM ($26.20–$38.75); fixed-price menu 144DM–174DM ($82.10–$99.20). AE, DC, MC, V. Daily noon–2:30pm and 6:45pm–midnight. S-Bahn: S3, S7, or S8 to Karlsplatz. Tram: 19. INTERNATIONAL.

This is no longer the finest hotel dining room in Munich, that honor having passed to the Hilton Grill, but it's still near the top. The Geisel family has made major renovations to the dining room, with its oyster-white panels of oak, polished bronze chandeliers, silver candelabra, and porcelain. The waiters are polite and skilled. The chefs here are highly inventive. They like extremely fresh ingredients, and the food here reflects this passion. If available, try the foie gras with sauternes, lobster soufflé, loin of lamb with fine herbs, lobster with vanilla butter, or sea bass supreme.

Munich Dining

GERMANY

Munich

Alois Dallmayr **21**
Andechser am Dom **19**
Asam Schlössel **10**
Austernkeller **32**
Bamberger Haus **29**
Bar-Restaurant Morizz **11**
Biergarten
   Chinesischer Turm **28**
Buon Gusto **36**
Café Glockenspiel **15**
Café Luitpold **24**
Der Katzlmacher **27**
Donisl **17**
Galleria **34**
Garden Restaurant **4**
Gästhaus Glockenbach **9**
Gaststätte zum Flaucher **10**
Hilton Grill **29**
Hirschgarten **1**
Hundskugel **8**
Hunsiger's Pacific **3**
Käfer Am Hofgarten **23**
Käfer-Schänke **30**
Kay's Bistro **12**
Locanda Picolit **25**
Mark's Restaurant **35**
Nürnberger Bratwurst
   Clockl am Dom **18**
Preysing-Keller **31**
Prinz Myshkin **16**
Ratskeller München **20**
Restaurant Königshof **6**
Restaurant Lenbach **5**
Restaurant Vier
   Jahreszeiten **37**
Spago **2**
Spatenhaus **22**
Straubinger Hof **13**
Tantris **26**
Weinbauer **26**
Weinhaus Neuner **7**
Weisses Brauhaus **33**
Zum Alten Markt **14**

Legend
Church
Information
Post Office
S-Bahn
U-Bahn

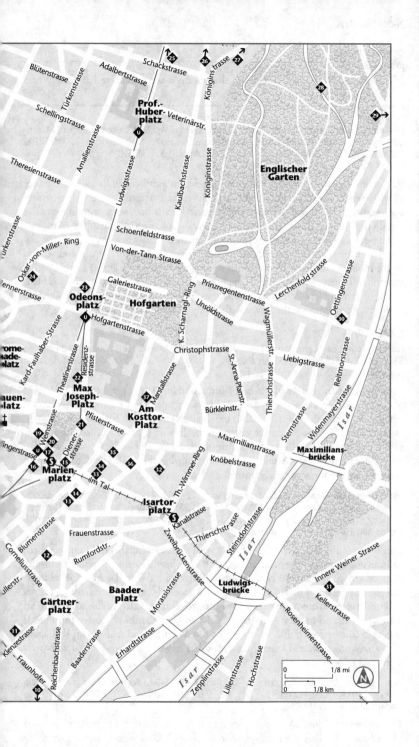

Blütenstrasse
Adalbertstrasse
Schackstrasse 25
26
Königinstrasse
27

Türkenstrasse
Schellingstrasse
Prof.-
Huber-
platz
Veterinärstr.

Amalienstrasse
Theresienstrasse

Englischer
Garten

28

29

Ludwigstrasse
Schoenfeldstrasse
Von-der-Tann Strasse

Kaulbachstrasse
Königinstrasse

Oskar-von-Miller- Ring

Galeriestrasse
24

Odeons-
platz 23

Hofgarten

Prinzregentenstrasse

Lerchenfeld strasse

Oettingenstrasse

Reitmorstrasse

Wiennerstrasse

0 Hofgartenstrasse
Kard-Faulhaber-Strasse

Unsöldstrasse
Christophstrasse

K.-Scharnagl-Ring

30

rome-
ade-
latz

Theatinerstrasse
Residenz-
strasse
22

Max
Joseph-
Platz

Marstallstrasse

St.-Anna-Pfarrstr.

Liebigstrasse

Thierschstrasse

Wagmüllerstr.

auen-
latz

21
Pfisterstrasse

37
Am
Kosttor-
Platz

Bürkleinstr.

Maximilianstrasse

Sternstrasse

Widenmayerstrasse

Isar

Maximilians-
brücke

Weinstrasse

19
20

35
36
32

Knöbelstrasse

Th.-Wimmer-Ring

ingerstrasse
17
15
16
Marien-
platz

Diener-
strasse

33 34

Im Tal

18 14
Isartor-
platz
5

Frauenstrasse

Kanalstrasse
Thierschstrasse

Zweibrückenstrasse

Steinsdorfstrasse

Isar

Innere Weiner Strasse

Cornelliusstrasse
Blumenstrasse
12
Rumfordstr.

Morassistrasse

Ludwigs-
brücke

31

Kellerstrasse

üllerstr.

Gärtner-
platz

Baader-
platz

Rosenheimerstrasse

7

Klenzestrasse

Reichenbachstrasse

Baaderstrasse

Erhardtstrasse

Isar

Zepplinstrasse
Lillenstrasse
Hochstrasse

Fraunhofer

10

0   1/8 mi
0   1/8 km
N

Tipping

If a restaurant bill says *Bedienung*, that means a service charge has already been added, so just round up to the nearest mark.

Restaurant Vier Jahreszeiten. In the Kempinski Hotel Vier Jahreszeiten München, Maximilianstrasse 17. ☎ **089/2-12-50.** Reservations required. Main courses 39DM–58DM ($22.25–$33.05); 5-course fixed-price menu 108DM ($61.55). AE, DC, MC, V. Daily 6–11pm. Closed Aug. Tram: 19. INTERNATIONAL.

Restaurant Vier Jahreszeiten is in a quiet and elegant location within walking distance of the opera house. The atmosphere is dignified and refined, the service extremely competent, and the food prepared along classic French lines with many imaginative variations. The menu changes every 4 to 6 weeks, but appetizers are likely to include mushroom soufflé served with artichoke-cream sauce, freshly made vegetable soup flavored with pesto, or turbot encased in basil-flavored crust. For a main course, you might try breast of Bresse chicken with scampi, flavored with a ginger sauce; or roast medaillons of venison with cherry-pepper sauce. Another main-dish specialty is blanquette of veal and lobster. Desserts include such specialties as strawberries Walterspiel, or, for two, tangerine soufflé served with foamy vanilla sauce.

EXPENSIVE

Austernkeller. Stollbergstrasse 11. ☎ **089/29-87-87.** Reservations required. Main courses 33DM–49DM ($18.80–$27.95). AE, DC, MC, V. Daily 5pm–1am. Closed Dec 23–26. U-Bahn: Isartorplatz. SEAFOOD.

This "oyster cellar" is a delight to both visitors and locals. You get the largest selection of oysters in town, from raw oysters to elaborate preparations such as oysters Rockefeller. A delectable dish to start with is the shellfish platter with fresh oysters, mussels, clams, scampi, and sea snails. Or you might begin with a richly stocked fish soup or cold hors d'oeuvre. French meat specialties are also offered, but the focus is seafood—everything from lobster thermidor to shrimp grilled in the shell. The decor is elegant and refined, and the service is attentive.

Galleria. Ledererstrasse 2 at Sparkassenstrasse. ☎ **089/29-79-95.** Reservations recommended. Main courses 15DM–42DM ($8.55–$23.95); fixed-price lunch 50DM ($28.50); fixed-price dinner 78DM ($44.45). AE, DC, MC, V. Mon–Sat noon–3pm and 6pm–midnight. Closed Aug 10–30. U-Bahn: Marienplatz. ITALIAN.

This is one of the most appealing of the several Italian restaurants in Munich's center, and the one that takes the greatest risks with experimental Italian cuisine. It provides gracious service and a roster of dishes that change with the availability of ingredients and the inspiration of the chefs. Examples are poached sea wolf with fresh vegetables in fennel sauce; an aromatic guinea fowl scented with lavender; homemade spaghetti with white, Italian truffles; herb-flavored risotto with chunks of lobster and braised radicchio (the best such dish we've ever had in Munich); and roasted soft-shell crabs with a light onion sauce. Dessert might include a smooth zabaglione served with pears marinated in port wine.

Kay's Bistro. Utzschneiderstrasse 1. ☎ **089/2-60-35-84.** Reservations required. Main courses 38DM–45DM ($21.65–$25.65). AE, MC. Daily 7pm–1am. U-Bahn: U2 or U3 to Marienplatz. INTERNATIONAL.

This restaurant, Munich's most sophisticated, is located off the historic market, the Viktualienmarkt. This is an "in" place to be, and it's filled nightly with a glamorous (sometimes media-related) clientele. Kay Wörsching personally greets his guests. The decoration changes several times a year—perhaps you'll be there when the walls sport Hollywood souvenirs. Staff outfits, and even the food, reflect the restaurant's decorative motif. The international cuisine is light, nouvelle, and avant-garde; many ingredients are bought fresh daily.

Marks Restaurant. In the Hotel Rafael, Neuturmstrasse 1. ☎ **089/290980.** Reservations recommended. Fixed-price lunch in Mark's Corner 53DM ($30.20). Fixed-price dinner in Mark's Restaurant 116DM–149DM ($66.10–$84.95). Main courses in Mark's Restaurant 35DM–65DM ($19.95–$37.05). AE, DC, MC, V. Daily 11am–2pm and 7–11pm. U-Bahn: Marienplatz. CONTINENTAL.

This restaurant, in the prestigious Hotel Rafael, is appropriately elegant with impeccably trained staff. If you come here, don't ask to meet a chef named Mark (the place was named after the owner's son). Lunch is served in a small, cozy enclave off the lobby, Mark's Corner, and is usually limited to a set price menu favored by business people. Dinners are swankier and more elaborate; they're served one floor above street level in a formal dining room that overlooks a monumental staircase and the lobby below. On Sunday and Monday night only, the formal dining room is closed, and dinner is served in Mark's Corner.

  Menu items change according to the season and the inspiration of the chef. Many dishes are somewhat experimental but still succeed beautifully. Examples include fillet of beef with a ragout of artichokes and potatoes and deep-fried baby garlic buds; a terrine of goose liver with stewed apricots and garden greens; and pan-fried monkfish with Provençal vegetables and balsamic sauce. Dessert might include gratin of rhubarb with house-made vanilla ice cream.

MODERATE

✪ **Alois Dallmayr.** Dienerstrasse 14–15. ☎ **089/2-13-51-00.** Reservations required. Main courses 30DM–43DM ($17.10–$24.50). AE, DC, MC, V. Mon–Wed 9:30am–7pm, Thurs–Fri 9:30am–8pm, Sat 9am–4pm. Tram: 19. CONTINENTAL.

Alois Dallmayr, which traces its history back to 1700, is the most famous delicatessen in Germany. After looking at its tempting array of delicacies from around the globe, you'll think you're lost in a millionaire's supermarket. Dallmayr has been a purveyor to many royal courts. Here you'll find Munich's most elegant consumers.

  The upstairs dining room serves a subtle German version of continental cuisine, owing a heavy debt to France. The food array is dazzling, ranging from the best herring and sausages we've ever tasted to such rare treats as perfectly vine-ripened tomatoes flown in from Morocco and papayas from Brazil. The famous French poulet de Bresse, beloved of gourmets, is also shipped in. The smoked fish is a taste sensation, and the soups are superbly flavored, especially the one made with shrimp. If you're dining alone, you might prefer to sit at the counter instead of a table. This bustling restaurant is crowded at lunchtime.

Buon Gusto (Talamonti). Hochbruckenstrasse 3. ☎ **089/296-383.** Reservations recommended. Main courses 20DM–42DM ($11.40–$23.95). AE, MC V. Mon–Sat noon–11pm. U-Bahn or S-Bahn: Marienplatz. TUSCAN/ITALIAN.

Devotees claim that this is the finest Italian restaurant in Munich. Its interior features two dining areas: a simple, rustic-looking bistro whose sight lines extend over an open kitchen, and a more formal dining room. Menu items and prices are identical in both areas. Owned and managed by an extended family, the Talamontis, whose members are likely not to speak English, the site emphasizes fresh ingredients, strong and savory flavors, and food items inspired by the Italian provinces of the Marches and Tuscany. Delectable examples include ravioli stuffed with mushrooms and herbs, roasted lamb with potatoes, lots of different forms of scallopini, and fresh fish served simply, with oil or butter and lemon. The various risottos are especially flavorful. During Okto-berfest and trade fairs, the place is mobbed.

✪ **Hunsiger's Pacific.** Maximilliansplatz 5 (entrance is on the Max-Joseph-Strasse). ☎ **089/5502-9741.** Main courses 19DM–42DM ($10.85–$23.95). AE, DC, MC, V. Mon–Fri noon–2:30pm, daily 6–10:30pm. Closed Sun May–Sept. U-Bahn: Stachus/Odeonsplatz. INTERNATIONAL.

This restaurant offers great value on excellent food. The menu is the creative statement of one of the city's most innovative young chefs, Werner Hunsiger. Fish is the premier item here—often flown in from Pacific waters just hours after it's caught. Preparation is based on classic French-inspired methods, but many of the innovative flavors come from Malaysia (coconut milk), Japan (wasabi), Thailand (lemongrass), and India (curry). You could begin with a tuna carpaccio with sliced plum, fresh ginger, and lime. Main courses include a succulent version of bouillabaisse with aïoli, which you might follow with cold melon soup garnished with a dollop of tarragon-flavored granita. Fried monkfish in the Malaysian style and turbot in chili and ginger sauce are evocative of Hawaii.

Käfer Am Hofgarten. Odeonsplatz 6–7. ☎ **089/290-7530.** Reservations recommended. Main courses 19.50DM–39.50DM ($11.10–$22.50). AE, V. Mon–Thurs 11am–1am, Fri 11am–3am, Sat 9:30am–3am, Sun 9:30am–1am. S-Bahn: Odeonsplatz. ITALIAN/FRENCH.

This likable and stylish bistro and bar is set midway between the imposing bulk of the Residenz and the Bavarian Ministry of Finance. It's a replica of something you might find in Paris or Lyon. There are outdoor terraces both in front and in back. Staff members are attentive and polite. A live pianist bashes out cabaret and jazz tunes every night throughout the dinner service. Tables are spaced close to one another, which enhances the sense of intimacy, though your dialogue is likely to be overheard by your immediate neighbors. Menu items change daily according to the season and the inspiration of the chefs, but might include carpaccio of beef with olive oil and aromatic herbs; pressed fillet of duck prepared with braised cabbage, apples, *Rösti*, and noodles; pastas with seafood; succulent and very fresh salads; and seasonal rabbit braised with a medley of fresh root vegetables.

Nürnberger Bratwurst Glöckl am Dom. Frauenplatz 9. ☎ **089/29-52-64.** Reservations recommended. Main courses 29DM–35DM ($16.55–$19.95). No credit cards. Daily 9am–1am. U-Bahn: U2 or U3 to Marienplatz. BAVARIAN.

This place, a short walk from Marienplatz, facing the cathedral, is the coziest and warmest of Munich's local restaurants. You sit in chairs that look as if they were made by a Black Forest wood-carver. Upstairs is a dining room decorated with reproductions of Dürer prints. The restaurant has a strict policy of shared tables. The plates are tin. The homesick Nürnberger comes here just for one dish: Nürnberger Schweinwurstl mit Kraut (those delectable little sausages). Last food orders are at midnight.

Ratskeller München. Im Rathaus, Marienplatz 8. ☎ **089/2-19-98-90.** Reservations required. Main courses 15DM–33DM ($8.55–$18.80). Fixed-price menus 30DM–35DM ($17.10–$19.95). AE, MC, V. Daily 10am–midnight. U-Bahn: U2 or U3 to Marienplatz. BAVARIAN.

Throughout Germany you'll find Ratskellers, traditional cellar restaurants in Rathaus (city hall) basements, serving inexpensive good food and wine. Munich is proud of its Ratskeller. The decor is typical: dark wood and carved chairs. The most interesting tables, the ones staked out by in-the-know locals, are in the semiprivate dining nooks in the rear, under the vaulted painted ceilings. Bavarian music adds to the ambience. The menu, generally a showcase of regional fare, also includes some international

---

ⓗ **Family-Friendly Restaurants**

Tower Restaurant, Olympiapark (*see p. 280*)   For a panoramic view of the Alps as well as the Olympic grounds, take your kids here to dine and, later, out onto one of the observation platforms.

Nürnberger Bratwurst Glöckl am Dom (*see p. 262*)   Hot dogs will never taste the same again after your child has tried one of those delectable little sausages from Nürnberg.

Café Glockenspiel (*see p. 257*)   Your kids can down delectable Bavarian pastries while enjoying the miniature "tournament" staged each day near the clock on the Rathaus facade.

---

dishes, many of them vegetarian, which is unusual for a Ratskeller. There's always a salad bar, as well as a freshly made soup of the day. Many of the dishes are heavy, but you can find lighter fare if you search the menu carefully.

Restaurant Lenbach. Ottostrasse 6. ☎ **089/549-1300.** Reservations recommended for dinner. In restaurant, main courses 22DM–120DM ($12.55–$68.40); in cafe-bistro, main courses 16DM–27DM ($9.10–$15.40); 2-course set lunch 24DM ($13.70). AE, DC, MC, V. Restaurant daily 6pm–midnight, cafe-bistro daily 11am–midnight; bar daily 11am–1am (till 3am Thurs–Sat). S-Bahn: Karlsplatz. EUROPEAN/MEDITERRANEAN.

One of the most appealing restaurant newcomers in Munich occupies the grandiose premises of a 19th-century palace (the Bernheimerpalais am Lenbachplatz). This stylish emporium of food, wine, sensuality, and conviviality evokes hip New York or Los Angeles. The decorative theme revolves around the Seven Deadly Sins, albeit with a decidedly stylish, and highly permissive, twist. Adultery is represented by a provocative large-scale pre-Raphaelite painting behind the bar. The theme within the ultracomfortable drinking lounge is Sloth. Vanity is represented by a catwalk, illuminated by tricolored strobe lights, where you'll promenade, fashion-model style, high above other diners. Even the toilet is accessorized with jailhouse bars and manacles, to represent Wrath. Other "sins" await your own discovery. Food items seem less important than the decor, but are likely to include a "seven sins" platter that contains foie gras, lobster, carpaccio of beef, and mozzarella tarts; lamb loin "Lenbach style" served with a gratin of potatoes and zucchini; salmon-trout *en papillote;* and heaping platters of fresh shellfish.

Spatenhaus. Residenzstrasse 12. ☎ **089/2-90-70-60.** Reservations recommended. Main courses 24.50DM–42.50DM ($13.95–$24.20). AE, MC, V. Daily 9:30am–12:30am. U-Bahn: U3, U4, or U6 to Odeonsplatz or Marienplatz. BAVARIAN/INTERNATIONAL.

The Spatenhaus, one of Munich's best-known beer restaurants, has wide windows overlooking the opera house on Max-Joseph-Platz. You can sit in an intimate, semi-private dining nook or at a big table. Spatenhaus has old traditions, typical Bavarian food, and generous portions at reasonable prices. If you want to know what all this fabled Bavarian gluttony is all about, order the "Bavarian plate," which is loaded down with various meats, including pork and sausages. (After that, you'll have to go to a spa.) Of course, to be loyal, you should order the restaurant's own beer, Spaten-Franziskaner-Bier, with your meal.

Weinhaus Neuner. Herzogspitalstrasse 8. ☎ **089/2-60-39-54.** Reservations recommended. Main courses 24DM–33DM ($13.70–$18.80); fixed-price menus 34DM–58DM ($19.40–$33.05). AE, MC, V. Mon–Sat 11:30am–3pm and 5:30pm–midnight. U-Bahn: U4 to Stachus. S-Bahn: All trains to Stachus. BAVARIAN.

This is an *Ältestes Weinhaus Münchens,* one of the city's landmark taverns. It dates from the late 15th century and is the only building in Munich that has its original Tyrolean vaults. The place brims with warmth and charm. Once young priests were educated here, but after Napoléon brought secularization, the place became a wine tavern and a meeting place for artists, writers, and composers, including Richard Wagner. Its rooms have been renovated and its paintings restored. The casual Weinstube is the less-expensive section; it has lots of local atmosphere, and you can order typical Bavarian dishes such as home-smoked beef. The restaurant section is elegant, with candles and flowers. The chef happily marries nouvelle cuisine and regional specialties.

Zum Alten Markt. Am Viktualienmarkt, Dreifaltigkeitsplatz 3. ☎ **089/29-99-95.** Reservations recommended. Main courses 20DM–38DM ($11.40–$21.65). No credit cards. Mon–Sat noon–10pm. U-Bahn: U2 or U3 to Marienplatz. Bus: 52. BAVARIAN/INTERNATIONAL.

Snug and cozy, Zum Alten Markt serves beautifully presented fresh cuisine at a good price. Located on a tiny square just off Munich's large outdoor food market, the restaurant has a mellow charm and a welcoming host, Josef Lehner. The interior decor, with its intricately coffered wooden ceiling, came from a 400-year-old Tyrolean castle. In summer, tables are set up outside. Fish and fresh vegetables come from the nearby market. You might begin with a tasty homemade soup, such as cream of carrot, or perhaps black-truffle tortellini in cream sauce with young onions and tomatoes. The chef makes a great *Tafelspitz* (the elegant boiled-beef dish so beloved by Emperor Franz Josef of Austria). You can also order classic dishes such as Bavarian goose and a savory roast suckling pig.

INEXPENSIVE

Andechser am Dom. Weinstrasse 7a. ☎ **089/29-84-81.** Reservations recommended. Main courses 17.50DM–28DM ($10–$15.95). AE, DC, MC, V. Daily 10am–midnight. U-Bahn and S-Bahn: Marienplatz. GERMAN.

This restaurant and beer hall is set on two floors of a postwar building adjacent to the back side of the Frauenkirche. It serves large amounts of a beer brewed in a monastery near Munich (Andechser), as well as generous portions of German food. No one will mind if you order a snack, a full meal, or just a beer. Menu items are often accompanied with German-style potato salad and green salad and include such dishes as veal schnitzels, steaks, turkey croquettes, roasted lamb, fish, and several kinds of sausages that taste best with tangy mustard. In good weather, tables are set up both on the building's roof and on the sidewalk in front, both of which overlook the back of one of the city's finest churches.

Bar-Restaurant Morizz. Klenzestrasse 43. ☎ **089/201-6776.** Reservations recommended on weekends. Main courses 16DM–29DM ($9.10–$16.55). MC. Sun–Thurs 7pm–12:30am, Fri–Sat 7pm–1:30am. U-Bahn: Fraunhoferstrasse. CONTINENTAL/THAI/INTERNATIONAL.

This is the hip gay restaurant of Munich. As estimated by the staff, it has a 70% gay male clientele; lesbian women and gay-friendly straights make up the rest of the clients. Part of the space is devoted to a sprawling, attractive bar, where red leather chairs, mirrors, and an impeccably trained staff evoke a Paris hotel bar of the 1920s. You can enjoy at least 40 single malt whiskies, a half dozen single-barrel bourbons, and a wide array of unusual wines. The adjacent dining room offers an appealing combination of international and continental food, prepared by a central-European staff whose interpretation of Thai cuisine is especially enjoyable. Try the *vorspeisen-teller* of mixed Thai specialties; some fans find the lemongrass almost addictive. Other choices include veal preparations, fresh fish, pastas, and salads (including one garnished with strips of confit of duckling).

Donisl. Weinstrasse 1. ☎ **089/22-01-84.** Reservations recommended. Main courses 12DM ($6.85). AE, DC, MC, V. Daily 9am–midnight. U-Bahn: U3 or U6 to Marienplatz. BAVARIAN/INTERNATIONAL.

Donisl is Munich's oldest beer hall, dating from 1715. Readers have praised this Munich-style restaurant as *gemütlich*, with its relaxed and comfortable atmosphere, although the seating capacity is about 550. In summer you can enjoy the hum and bustle of the Marienplatz by dining in the garden area out front. The restaurant has two levels, the second of which is a gallery. English is spoken. The standard menu offers traditional Bavarian food as well as a weekly changing specials menu. A specialty is *Weisswürste*, the little white sausage that has been a decades-long tradition of this place. The chef also prepares a good duck. Select beers from Munich's own Hacker-Pschorr Brewery top the evening. A zither player at noon and an accordion player in the evening entertain diners.

Hundskugel. Hotterstrasse 18. ☎ **089/26-42-72.** Reservations required. Main courses 16DM–38DM ($9.10–$21.65). No credit cards. Daily 10am–midnight. U-Bahn: U2 or U3 to Marienplatz. BAVARIAN.

The city's oldest tavern, Hundskugel dates from 1440, and apparently serves the same food it did back then. Why mess with success? The alpine-style building is within easy walking distance of Marienplatz. Perhaps half the residents of Munich at one time or another have made their way here. The cookery is honest Bavarian with no pretensions. Although the chef makes a specialty of *Spanferkel* (roast suckling pig with potato noodles), you might prefer *Tafelspitz* (boiled beef) in dill sauce or roast veal stuffed with goose liver. To begin, try one of the hearty soups, made fresh daily.

Prinz Myshkin. Hackenstrasse 2. ☎ **089/26-55-96.** Reservations recommended. Main courses 16DM–30DM ($9.10–$17.10); fixed-price meals 13.80DM–28.50DM ($7.85–$16.25). AE, MC, V. Daily 11am–1am. U-Bahn: U2 or U3 to Marienplatz. VEGETARIAN.

This popular vegetarian restaurant near the Marienplatz offers freshly made salads with names like "Aphrodite" and "Barbados." Indian and Thai vegetarian dishes are also available, as well as vegetarian *involtini* (stuffed roll ups) and casseroles, soups, and zesty pizzas, many of which are excellent. Wine and beer are sold as well. Smaller portions of many items are available for 8.50DM ($4.85).

Straubinger Hof. Blumenstrasse 5. ☎ **089/2-60-84-44.** Reservations necessary only for 4 or more. Main courses 18DM–28DM ($10.25–$15.95). AE, V. Mon–Sat 9am–9:30pm (last order). U-Bahn: Marienplatz. BAVARIAN.

Consistently crowded, this restaurant in the Altstadt is a well-managed, unpretentious, traditional place sponsored by the brewers of Paulaner beer. No one will mind if you stop in just for a brew in the morning and afternoon, although during peak lunch and dinner hours, it's good form to order at least a small plate of cheese or wurst, or a steaming platter of Tafelspitz (boiled beef with horseradish) or roasted knuckle of pork. The food here caters to nostalgia—you may see the term *Grossmutter Art* ("in the style of grandmother") on the menu. The restaurant is close to the Viktualienmarkt, guaranteeing, at least in theory, ultrafresh produce. Portions are ample and prices are reasonable. In summer, seating spills out onto the pavement. For a traditional Bavarian dessert, try the old-fashioned house specialty, *Apfelschmarrn.*

Weisses Bräuhaus. Tal 7. ☎ **089/29-98-75.** Reservations recommended, especially for the back room. Main courses 20DM–32DM ($11.40–$18.25). No credit cards. Daily 8am–midnight. U-Bahn: Marienplatz. BAVARIAN.

Weisses Bräuhaus is big, bustling, and Bavarian with a vengeance. Not for the pretentious, this informal place does what it's been doing for centuries: It serves home-brewed beer. At one time the famous salt-trade route between Salzburg and Augsburg passed by its door, and salt traders were very thirsty back then. The front room, with smoke-blackened dark-wood paneling and stained glass, is for drinking and informal eating; the back room has white tablecloths and black-outfitted waiters. You can sample typical Bavarian dishes: smoked fillet of trout, rich potato soup, roast pork with homemade potato dumplings and cabbage salad, or Viennese veal goulash with mushrooms and cream sauce. You'll have to share your table, but that's part of the fun here.

NEAR THE SÜDBAHNHOF

✪ Gästhaus Glockenbach. Kapuzinerstrasse 29, corner of Maistrasse. ☎ **089/53-40-43.** Reservations recommended. Main courses 36DM–55DM ($20.50–$31.35); fixed-price menus 40DM–150DM ($22.80–$85.50). AE, MC, V. Tues–Sat noon–2pm (last order); Tues–Sat 7–10pm (last order). Closed 1 week at Christmas. U-Bahn: U3 or U6 to Goetheplatz. MODERN CONTINENTAL.

This unpretentious restaurant is capable of holding its own against more expensive, more *grand bourgeois* establishments, such as Tantris (see below). The setting is a 200-year-old building close to a tributary (the Glockenbach) of the nearby Isar. The dignified country-baroque interior is accented with vivid modern paintings and the most elegant table settings in town, including a lavish array of porcelain by Hutchenreuther, a company not well known in the New World. Cuisine changes with the season. You'll find imaginative preparations of venison and pheasant in autumn, lamb and veal dishes in springtime, and shellfish whenever in season. Ultrafresh vegetables and exotica are imported from local farms and from sophisticated purveyors worldwide. Wines are mostly European, with representatives from Italy, France, and Austria.

NEAR THE ISAR, SOUTH OF CENTER

Asam Schlössl. 45 Maria-Einsiedel-Strasse. ☎ **089/7-23-63-73.** Main courses 20DM–30DM ($11.40–$17.10). AE, DC, MC, V. Daily 11am–1am. U-Bahn: Thalkirchen. BAVARIAN/INTERNATIONAL.

This Augustiner brewery restaurant offers a relaxed, relatively informal hideaway amid the congestion of Munich. The building was built as a private villa in 1724. Some of the original castlelike design remains, though the structure has been expanded and renovated over the years. All brews offered are products of Augustiner, including both pale and dark versions of Weissebier, beer fermented from wheat. Menu items include such typical Bavarian fare as beef braised in red wine *(Böffla-mott)* with *Semmelknödel* (bread dumplings), and a dish beloved by the last of Austria's Habsburg emperors, *gesottener Tafelspitz mit frischen Kren,* a savory form of the familiar boiled beef with horseradish.

IN SCHWABING

This district, which was called "bohemian" in the 1940s, overflows with restaurants. Many of them are awful, but there are several good ones, some of which attract a youthful clientele. The evening is the best time for a visit.

VERY EXPENSIVE

✪ Tantris. Johann-Fichte-Strasse 7, Schwabing. ☎ **089/36-19-59-0.** Reservations required. Fixed-price 5-course lunch 148DM ($84.35); fixed-price dinner 192DM ($109.45) for 5 courses, 218DM ($124.25) for 8 courses; special 5-course dinner Tues–Thurs (including wine) 225DM ($128.25). AE, DC, MC, V. Tues–Sat noon–3pm and 6:30pm–1am. Closed public holidays and annual holidays in Jan and May. U-Bahn: U6 to Dietlindenstrasse. FRENCH/INTERNATIONAL.

Tantris serves Munich's finest cuisine. Chef Hans Haas was voted the top chef in Germany in 1994, and, if anything, he has refined and sharpened his culinary technique since then. The setting is unlikely: a drab commercial area, with bare concrete walls and a garish decor. But once you're inside, you're transported by the fine service and excellent food that's a treat to the eye as well as the palate. The choice of dishes is wisely limited, and the cooking is both subtle and original. There's an eight-course menu that changes daily, plus a five-course table d'hôte served at noon. You might begin with a terrine of smoked fish served with green cucumber sauce, then follow with classic roast duck on mustard-seed sauce, or perhaps a delightful concoction of lobster medaillons on black noodles.

MODERATE

Der Katzlmacher. Kaulbacherstrasse 48. ☎ **089/348129.** Reservations recommended. Main courses 28DM–39DM ($15.95–$22.25). Fixed-price lunches 40DM–50DM ($22.80–$28.50); fixed-price dinners 60DM–90DM ($34.20–$51.30). AE, MC, V. Tues–Sat noon–3pm and 6:30pm–1am. U-Bahn: Universität. ITALIAN.

Few Italian restaurants would have had the nerve to adopt as their name a pejorative German term referring to Italians. This one did, however, and its sense of humor has helped make it beloved by loyal local fans. The setting is a postwar building whose two dining rooms are evocative of a mountain lodge high in the Italian Alps. Starched white napery contrasts pleasantly with the rustic setting. The cooking is based on the culinary traditions of the Italian Marches, Friulia, and Emilia-Romagna, all known for their fine cuisines and agrarian bounty. Menu specialties might include calzone stuffed with spinach and pine nuts, a commendable grilled swordfish with red wine vinaigrette, eel with champagne sauce, and a succulent version of *fritto misto del pesce* based on whatever is in season.

⊘ **Locanda Picolit.** Siegfriedstrasse 11. ☎ **089/396447.** Reservations recommended. Main courses 29DM–43DM ($16.55–$24.50); fixed-price menu 79DM ($45.05). AE, DC, V. Mon–Fri noon–2:30pm and daily 4–11pm. U-Bahn: U3 or U6 to Münchner Freiheit. ITALIAN.

If you come here in the summer and sit on the outdoor terrace with a view over a garden, it's easy to believe that you've suddenly been transported to the Mediterranean world. The interior is full of streamlined furnishings and dramatic, oversized modern paintings. Menu items come from all over Italy, but the favorites are those from the owner's native Friuli district, near Venice. There's a lavish use of in-season asparagus, arugula, shellfish, rabbit, wild mushrooms, and venison in such alluring preparations as ravioli stuffed with lobster, tagliatelle, rotini, linguini with braised radicchio and shellfish, and, when available, *saltimbocca* (veal with ham).

Spago. Neureutherstrasse 15 at Arcisstrasse. ☎ **089/271-2406.** Reservations recommended. Main courses 25DM–39DM ($14.25–$22.25). Fixed-price lunch 39DM ($22.25); fixed-price dinner 59DM ($33.65). AE, DC, V. Mon–Fri 12:30–4:30pm and daily 6:30–11:30pm. U-Bahn: U2 to Josephsplatz or U3 to Universität. ITALIAN.

Less self-conscious and self-promotional than its Los Angeles namesake, this amiable multilingual Italian restaurant still offers lots of Italian pizzazz as well as good, upscale Italian food. Some of the dishes are tagliatelle with porcini mushrooms, braised breast of chicken stuffed with herbs and spinach, ravioli with artichoke hearts or with potatoes and chanterelles, an especially delectable fish baked with herbs in a salt crust and wild mushrooms sautéed with herbs and arugula, a perfectly prepared suckling lamb with mint and balsamic vinegar, and an array of desserts as beautiful as they are tasty.

INEXPENSIVE

Weinbauer. Fendstrasse 5. ☎ **089/39-81-55.** Reservations recommended. Main courses 10.50DM–26.50DM ($6–$15.10). No credit cards. Mon–Fri 11am–midnight, Sat 3pm–midnight. U-Bahn: U3 or U5 to Münchner Freiheit. BAVARIAN.

Just off Leopoldstrasse is this small, relatively untrammeled and affordable restaurant. The decor evokes a small-town dining room in the Alps. The food is reliable but hardly spectacular. Menu items include Wiener schnitzel, Nürnberger wurst'l with sauerkraut, sirloin steak with an herb-butter sauce, goulash soup, and *Blutwurst* and *Leberwurst* platters. Any of these might be washed down with a half liter of draft beer.

IN HAIDHAUSEN

✪ **Preysing-Keller.** Preysingstrasse 1. ☎ **089/45-84-52-60.** Reservations recommended. Main courses 32DM–46DM ($18.25–$26.20); fixed-price menus 89DM–125DM ($50.75–$71.25). AE, DC, MC, V. Mon–Sat 6pm–1am. Closed Dec 23–Jan 6. Tram: 18. GERMAN/INTERNATIONAL.

Preysing-Keller is a "find," but you have to cross the Isar to discover its superb cookery and wines. It's connected to the Preysing hotel (see "Accommodations," above). You'll dine in a 300-year-old cellar, with massive beams and high masonry arches; the decor is simple, with wooden tables and chairs. Everything on the menu is seductively fresh. The staff makes daily excursions to the market. Fish and seafood are stored in aquariums on the premises before cooking. The cuisine is based on classic Bavarian dishes made new—the chef knows how to transform them with inventive touches. Specialties include goose-liver pâté, lobster in butter sauce, and steak tartare of venison.

IN BOGENHAUSEN

Käfer-Schänke. Prinzregentenstrasse 73. ☎ **089/4-16-80.** Reservations required. Main courses 39DM–92DM ($22.25–$52.45); fixed-price lunch 43DM ($24.50). AE, DC, MC, V. Mon–Sat 11:30am–midnight. Closed holidays. U-Bahn: U4 to Prinzregentenplatz. Bus: 55. GERMAN/INTERNATIONAL.

This is a great spot for casual dining with elegant style, in a setting that evokes a chalet. It's located on the second floor of a famous gourmet shop called Käfer. The cuisine roams the world for inspiration—from Lombardy to Asia. You select your hors d'oeuvres from the most dazzling display in Munich. Often Käfer-Schänke devotes a week to a particular country's cuisine. On one visit, we enjoyed the classic soup (sea bass) with fennel, as presented on the French Riviera. The salads have what one reviewer called "rococo splendor." From a cold table, you can choose smoked salmon or smoked eel. Venison, quail, and guinea hen are also regularly featured.

BEER GARDENS

If you're in Munich anytime between the first sunny spring day and the last fading light of a Bavarian-style autumn, you should head for one of the city's celebrated beer gardens (Biergartens). Traditionally, beer gardens were simply tables placed under chestnut trees planted above the storage cellars to keep beer cool in summer. (Lids on beer steins, incidentally, were meant to keep out flies.) It's estimated that today Munich has at least 400 beer gardens and cellars. Food, drink, and atmosphere are much the same in all of them. For information on Munich's other favorite drinking spots, beer halls, see "Munich After Dark," below.

Bamberger Haus. Brunnerstrasse 2. ☎ **089/3-08-89-66.** AE MC V. Restaurant daily 11am–10pm, beer hall daily 11am–midnight. U-Bahn: U3 or U6 to Scheidplatz.

Bamberger Haus, located northwest of Schwabing at the edge of Luitpold Park, is named after a city noted for mass consumption of beer. The street-level restaurant serves Bavarian and international specialties: well-seasoned soups, grilled steak, veal, pork, and sausages. If you only want to drink, you might visit the rowdier and less-expensive beer hall in the cellar. Main courses in the restaurant range from 15.50DM–32DM ($8.85–$18.25). A large beer costs 4.80DM ($2.75).

✪ **Biergarten Chinesischer Turm.** Englischer Garten 3. ☎ **089/3-83-87-30.** AE MC V. May–Oct, daily 11am–9pm; Nov–Apr daily but hours vary. U-Bahn: U3 or U6 to Giselastrasse.

Englischer Garten, the park lying between the Isar River and Schwabing, is home to several beer gardens. This is our favorite. It's the largest and most popular of its kind in Europe, taking its name from its location at the foot of an easy-to-find pagoda-like tower. Beer and Bavarian food, and plenty of it, are what you get here. A large glass or mug of beer (ask for *ein mass Bier)*, enough to bathe in, costs 10DM ($5.70). It will likely be slammed down, still foaming, by a server carrying 12 other tall steins. The food is cheap—a simple meal begins at 15DM ($8.55). Homemade dumplings are a specialty, as are all kinds of tasty sausages. You can also get a first-rate *Schweinbraten* (a braised loin of pork served with potato dumpling and rich brown gravy), which is Bavaria's answer to the better-known sauerbraten of the north. Huge baskets of pretzels are passed around, and they're eaten with *Radi*, the large, tasty white radishes famous from these parts. Oompah bands often play, adding to the festive atmosphere. The place is open every day, but November through April, its hours depend on the weather and the number of guests.

Gaststätte zum Flaucher. Isarauen 8. ☎ **089/7-23-26-77.** No credit cards. Bus: 52 from Marienplatz.

If you're going to the zoo, you might want to stop at this nearby beer garden for fun and food. Gaststätte is mellow and traditional, with tables set in a tree-shaded garden overlooking the river. Here you can order the local specialty, *Leberkäse*, a large loaf of sausage eaten with freshly baked pretzels and plenty of mustard. Beer costs 9.50DM ($5.40) for a large mug, and the most expensive food platter goes for 16DM ($9.10). Main courses in the restaurant cost from 9.50DM to 24.50DM ($5.40 to $13.95). From May through October it's open daily from 10am to 10pm; from November through April, only on Friday, Saturday, and Sunday from 10am to 8pm.

Hirschgarten. Hirschgartenstrasse 1 (in Nymphenburg Park, near the palace). ☎ **089/ 17-25-91.** MC. S-Bahn: Laim. Tram: Romanplatz.

This place is the largest open-air restaurant in Munich, capable of seating more than 8,000 beer drinkers and merrymakers. Full meals cost 9DM to 30DM ($17.10). A 1-liter stein of Augustiner beer goes for 9.50DM ($5.40). It's open daily from 10am to midnight.

5 Attractions

Munich is stocked with so many treasures that any visitor who plans to "do" the city in a day or two will not only miss out on many major sights but will also fail to grasp the city's spirit and absorb its special flavor. There are, however, a few vital highlights.

THE TOP ATTRACTIONS
THE CITY CENTER

Marienplatz is the heart of the Altstadt, or Old City. On its north side is the **Neues Rathaus** (New City Hall), built in 19th-century Gothic style. Each day at 11am and also at noon and 5pm in the summer, the Glockenspiel on the facade performs a miniature tournament, with enameled copper figures moving in and out of the archways. You may wish to climb the 55 steps to the top of the Rauthaus's tower (an elevator is also available) for a good view of the city center. The **Altes Rathaus** (Old City Hall), with its plain Gothic tower, is to the right. It was reconstructed in the 15th century, after being destroyed by fire.

Munich Attractions

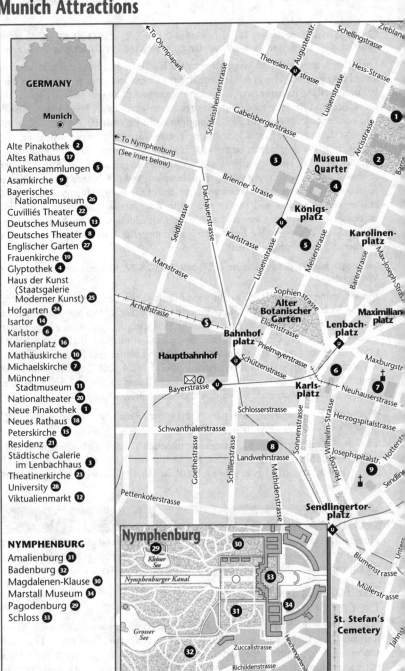

GERMANY

Munich

To Olympiapark

← To Nymphenburg
(See inset below)

Schleissheimerstrasse

Schellingstrasse

Zieblan

Theresien- strasse

Augustenstr.

Hess-Strasse

Gabelsbergerstrasse

Luisenstrasse

Arcisstrasse

❶

Brienner Strasse

❸

Museum
Quarter

❹

❷

Königs-
platz

Karolinen-
platz

Dachauerstrasse

Karlstrasse

Meiserstrasse

❺

Barerstrasse

Max-Joseph-Stra

Seidlstrasse

Luisenstrasse

Marsstrasse

Sophienstrasse

Maximilian
platz

Arnullstrasse

Alter
Botanischer
Garten

Lenbach-
platz

❺

Elisenstrasse

Bahnhof-
platz

Prielmayerstrasse

Maxburgstr

Hauptbahnhof

Schützenstrasse

❻

Neuhauserstrasse

✉ ⓘ

Bayerstrasse

Karls-
platz

❼

Herzog Wilhelm-Strasse

Schlosserstrasse

Herzogspitalstrasse

Schwanthalerstrasse

Goethestrasse

Schillerstrasse

Sonnenstrasse

Josephspitalstr.

Hötters

❾

Landwehrstrasse

❽

Mathildenstrasse

Sendlin

Pettenkoferstrasse

Sendlingertor-
platz

Unter

Blumenstrasse

Müllerstrasse

St. Stefan's
Cemetery

Jahns

Nymphenburg

㉙
Kleiner
See

㉚

Nymphenburger Kanal

㉝

❸❸

Grosser
See

㉛

㉞

㉜

Zuccalistrasse

Hacklergartenstr.

Richildenstrasse

Nymphenburger Kanal

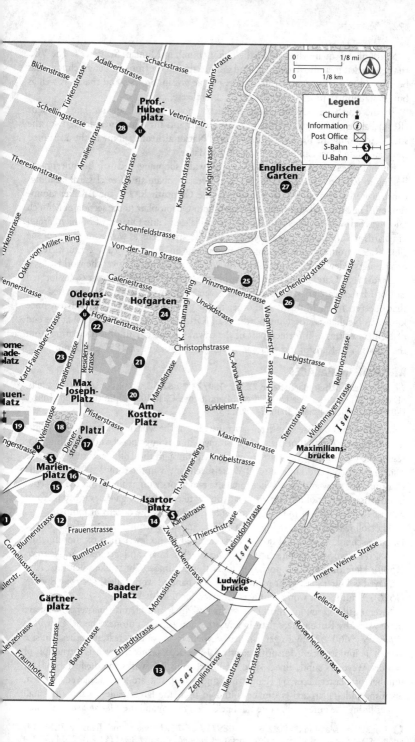

Blütenstrasse
Adalbertstrasse
Schackstrasse
Schellingstrasse
Türkenstrasse
Königins trasse
Prof.-Huber-platz
Veterinärstr.
28 Ⓤ
Amalienstrasse
Ludwigstrasse
Theresienstrasse
Kaulbachstrasse
Königinstrasse
Englischer Garten 27
Oskar-von-Miller- Ring
Schoenfeldstrasse
Von-der-Tann Strasse
Prinzregentenstrasse 25
Lerchenfeld strasse
26
Oettingenstrasse
Türkenstrasse
iennerstrasse
Galeriestrasse
Odeons-platz Ⓤ
Hofgarten 24
Hofgartenstrasse
K. Scharnagl-Ring
Unsöldstrasse
22
Kard.-Faulhaber-Strasse
Theatinerstrasse
Residenz-strasse
Christophstrasse
St.-Anna-Pfarrstr.
Wagmüllerstr.
Thierschstrasse
Liebigstrasse
Reitmorstrasse
rome-ade-latz
23
21
Sternstrasse
Widenmayerstrasse
Isar
auen-latz
†
Max Joseph-Platz
20
Marstallstrasse
Bürkleinstr.
Am Kosttor-Platz
Pfisterstrasse
Maximilianstrasse
Maximilians-brücke
19
18
Weinstrasse
Platzl
17
Diener-strasse
Knöbelstrasse
ingerstrasse Ⓤ
Marien-platz 16
Ⓢ
15
Im Tal
Th.-Wimmer-Ring
Isartor-platz
14 Ⓢ
Kanalstrasse
Steinsdorfstrasse
1
Blumenstrasse
12
Frauenstrasse
Zweibrückenstrasse
Thierschstrasse
Isar
Cornelliusstrasse
Rumfordstr.
Morassistrasse
Innere Weiner Strasse
illerstr.
Baader-platz
Ludwigs-brücke
Kellerstrasse
Gärtner-platz
Reichenbachstrasse
Baaderstrasse
Erhardtstrasse
Zepplinstrasse
Lillenstrasse
Hochstrasse
Rosenheimerstrasse
nzestrasse
Fraunhofer
13
Isar

Legend
Church   †
Information   ⓘ
Post Office   ⊠
S-Bahn   —Ⓢ—
U-Bahn   —Ⓤ—

0   1/8 mi
0   1/8 km

South of the square you can see the oldest church in Munich, **St. Peter's.** The **Viktualienmarkt,** just off Marienplatz and around the corner from St. Peter's church, has been a gathering place since 1807. Here, people gossip, browse, and snack, as well as buy fresh country produce, wines, meats, and cheese.

To the west lies **Odeonsplatz,** Munich's most beautiful square. The Residenz (Royal Palace) is just to the east of Odeonplatz, and the **Theatinerkirche** is to the south. Adjoining the Residenz is the restored **Nationaltheater,** home of the acclaimed Bavarian State Opera and Bavarian National Ballet.

Running west from Odeonsplatz is the wide shopping avenue, Briennerstrasse, leading to **Königsplatz.** Flanking this large Grecian square are three classical buildings constructed by Ludwig I—the **Propyläen,** the **Glyptothek,** and the **Antikensammlungen.** The busy Ludwigstrasse runs north from Odeonsplatz to the section of Munich known as **Schwabing.** This is the Greenwich Village or Latin Quarter of Munich, proud of its artistic and literary heritage. Ibsen and Rilke lived here, as well as members of the Blue Rider group, which influenced abstract art in the early 20th century. Today Schwabing's sidewalk tables are filled with young people from all over the world.

Isartor (Isar Gate) is one of the most-photographed Munich landmarks. It's located east of Marienplatz at Isartorplatz. This is the only tower left from the fortified wall that once encircled Munich. The other major gate of Munich is the **Karlstor,** once known as Neuhauser Tor, lying northeast of Karlsplatz (also called Stachus) at the end of Neuhauserstrasse. It formed part of the town's second circuit of walls, dating from the 1500s. The Karlstor lost its main tower (built 1302) in an 1857 explosion.

MUSEUMS & PALACES

✪ **Alte Pinakothek.** Barerstrasse 27. ☎ **089/23-80-52-16.** Admission 7DM ($4) adults, 4DM ($2.30) students, free for children 14 and under. Daily 10am–5pm (until 8pm Thurs). U-Bahn: U2 to Königsplatz. Tram: 27. Bus: 53.

This is one of the most significant art museums in the world. The nearly 900 paintings on display (30,000 of them are in storage) in this huge neoclassical building represent the greatest European artists of the 14th through the 18th centuries. Begun as a small court collection by the royal Wittelsbach family in the early 1500s, the artistic treasure trove grew and grew. There are only two floors with exhibits, but the museum is immense; we do not recommend that you try to cover all the galleries in 1 day. You'd be wise to get a map of the gallery to guide you through the dozens of rooms.

The following are a few highlights. The landscape painter *par excellence* of the Danube school, Albrecht Altdorfer, is represented by no fewer than six monumental works. The works of Albrecht Dürer include his final, and greatest, *Self-Portrait* (1500). Here the artist has portrayed himself with almost Christ-like solemnity. Also displayed is Dürer's last great painting, his two-paneled work called *The Four Apostles* (1526). A number of works by Lucas Cranach include his *Venus.*

Several galleries are given over to works by Dutch and Flemish masters. There are more works by Rubens here than in any other museum in Europe. The *St. Columbia Altarpiece* (1460–62), by Roger van der Weyden, is one of the greatest of these, in size as well as importance. Measuring nearly 10 feet across, this triptych is a triumph of van der Weyden's subtle linear style, and one of his last works (he died in 1464). A number of masterpieces by Rembrandt and Van Dyck are also displayed. French, Spanish, and Italian artists can be found in both the larger galleries and the small rooms lining the outer wall. Note Raphael's *Holy Family* and the *Madonna* by da Vinci.

✪ **Residenz.** Max-Joseph-Platz 3. ☎ **089/29-06-71.** Museum and Treasury 7DM ($4) adults, 5DM ($2.85) students and seniors; Old Residenz Theater 3DM ($1.70), 2DM ($1.15) students; free for children 15 and under. Combined ticket 12DM ($6.85) adults, 8DM ($4.55)

The Residenz

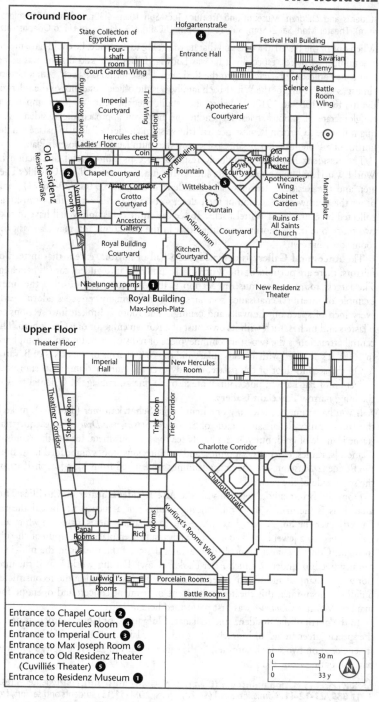

Ground Floor

Hofgartenstraße

State Collection of Egyptian Art

Four-shaft room

Court Garden Wing

Stone Room Wing

Imperial Courtyard

Trier Wing

Hercules chest

Ladies' Floor

Coin Collection

Old Residenz

Residenzstraße

Chapel Courtyard

Antler Corridor

Vestment rooms

Grotto Courtyard

Ancestors Gallery

Royal Building Courtyard

Nibelungen rooms

Royal Building

Max-Joseph-Platz

Entrance Hall

Apothecaries' Courtyard

Festival Hall Building

Bavarian Academy of Science

Battle Room Wing

Old Residenz Theater

Foyer Courtyard

Apothecaries' Wing

Cabinet Garden

Ruins of All Saints Church

Marstallplatz

Tower Building

Fountain

Wittelsbach Fountain

Antiquarium

Courtyard

Kitchen Courtyard

Treasury

New Residenz Theater

Upper Floor

Theater Floor

Theatiner Corridor

Stone Room

Imperial Hall

New Hercules Room

Trier Room

Trier Corridor

Charlotte Corridor

Charlottentrakt

Kurfürst's Rooms Wing

Rooms

Papal Rooms

Rich Rooms

Ludwig I's Rooms

Porcelain Rooms

Battle Rooms

Entrance to Chapel Court ❷
Entrance to Hercules Room ❹
Entrance to Imperial Court ❸
Entrance to Max Joseph Room ❻
Entrance to Old Residenz Theater
   (Cuvilliés Theater) ❺
Entrance to Residenz Museum ❶

0		30 m
0		33 y

students and children. Museum and Treasury Tues–Sun 10am–4:30pm (last tickets sold at 4pm); Theater Mon–Sat 2–5pm, Sun 10am–5pm. U-Bahn: U3, U4, U5, or U6 to Odeonsplatz.

When one of the Bavarian royals said that he was going to the castle, he could have meant any number of places, especially if he was Ludwig II. But if he said that he was going home, he could only be referring to the Residenz. This enormous palace, with a history almost as long as that of the Wittelsbach family, was the official residence of the rulers of Bavaria from 1385 to 1918. Added to and rebuilt over the centuries, the complex is a conglomerate of various styles. Depending on how you approach the Residenz, you might first see a German Renaissance hall (the western facade), a Palladian palace (on the north), or a Florentine Renaissance palace (on the south facing Max-Joseph-Platz).

The Residenz has been completely restored since its almost total destruction in World War II and now houses the Residenz Museum, a concert hall, the Cuvilliés Theater, and the Residenz Treasury. The **Residenz Museum** (☎ **089/29-06-71**) comprises the southwestern section of the palace, some 120 rooms of art and furnishings collected by centuries of Wittelsbachs. To see the entire collection, you'll have to take two tours, one in the morning and the other in the afternoon. You may also visit the rooms on your own.

The **Ancestoral Gallery** is designed like a hall of mirrors, except that instead of mirrors, there are portraits of the Wittelsbach family, set into gilded, carved paneling. The largest room in the museum section is the **Antiquarium,** possibly the finest example of interior Renaissance secular styling in Germany. Frescoes adorn nearly every inch of space on the walls and ceilings. The room is broken into sections by pilasters and niches, each with its own bust of a Roman emperor or a Greek hero. The central attraction is the two-story chimneypiece of red stucco and marble, completed in 1600. It's adorned with Tuscan pillars and the coat of arms of the dukes of Bavaria.

On the second floor of the palace, directly over the Antiquarium, is an enormous collection of Far Eastern porcelain. Note also the fine assemblage of Oriental rugs in the long, narrow **Porcelain Gallery.**

If you have time to view only one item in the **Schatzkammer** (Treasury), make it the 16th-century Renaissance statue of *St. George Slaying the Dragon.* This equestrian statue is made of gold, but you can barely see the precious metal for the thousands of diamonds, rubies, emeralds, sapphires, and semiprecious stones embedded in it. Both the Residenz Museum and the Schatzkammer are entered from Max-Joseph-Platz on the south side of the palace.

From the Brunnenhof, you can visit the **Alte Residenztheater** or **Cuvilliés Theater.** This is Germany's most outstanding example of a rococo tier-boxed theater. Directly over the huge center box, where the royal family sat, is a crest in white and gold topped by a jewel-bedecked crown of Bavaria held in place by a group of cherubs in flight. Court architect François de Cuvilliés designed the theater in the mid-18th century (see box under "Munich After Dark," below). During World War II the interior was dismantled and stored. After the war, it was reassembled in the reconstructed building. In summer, this theater is the scene of frequent concert and opera performances. Mozart's *Idomeneo* was first performed here in 1781.

To the north of the Residenz, the Italianate **Hofgarten,** or Court Garden, is one of the special "green lungs" of Munich. The garden was laid out between 1613 and 1617. It's enclosed on two sides by arcades; in the center is the Hofgarten temple, a 12-sided pavilion dating from 1615.

✪ **Bayerisches Nationalmuseum (Bavarian National Museum).** Prinzregenten-strasse 3. ☎ **089/21-12-41.** Admission 3DM ($1.70) adults, 2DM ($1.15) students and seniors, free for children under 15, free for all Sun. Tues–Sun 9:30am–5pm. U-Bahn: U4 or U5 to Lehel. Tram: 17. Bus: 53.

In 1855, King Maximilian II began an institution to preserve Bavaria's historic and artistic treasures. The collection grew so rapidly that it had to be moved to larger quarters several times over the past 100 years. Its current building, near the Haus der Kunst, contains three vast floors of sculpture, painting, folk art, ceramics, furniture, and textiles, as well as clocks and scientific instruments.

After entering the museum, turn to the right into the first large gallery, the **Wessobrunn Room,** devoted to early church art from the 5th through the 13th centuries. Some of the museum's oldest and most valuable works are here, including ancient and medieval ivories. The most famous is the Munich ivory from about A.D. 400. At the crossing to the adjoining room is the stone figure, the *Virgin with the Rose Bush,* from Straubing (ca. 1300), one of the few old Bavarian pieces of church art influenced by the spirit of mysticism.

The **Riemenschneider Room** is devoted to the works of the great sculptor Tilman Riemenschneider (1460–1531) and his contemporaries. Characteristic of the sculptor's works is the natural, unpainted wood of his carvings and statuary. Note especially the *12 Apostles from the Marienkapelle in Würzburg* (1510), the central group of the high altar in the parish church of Münnerstadt (1490–92), and the figure of St. Sebastian (1490).

The second floor contains a fine collection of stained and painted glass—an art in which medieval Germany excelled. Other rooms on this floor include baroque ivory carvings, Meissen porcelain, and ceramics. Also on display are famous collections of arms and armor from the 16th to 18th centuries, and the collection of antique clocks, some dating from the 16th century.

✪ **Deutsches Museum (German Museum of Masterpieces of Science and Technology).** Museumsinsel 1 (on an island in the Isar River). ☎ **089/2-17-91.** Admission 10DM ($5.70) adults, 7DM ($4) seniors, 4DM ($2.30) students, 3DM ($1.70) children 6–12, free for children 5 and under. Daily 9am–5pm (closes at 2pm the 2nd Wed in Dec). Closed major holidays. S-Bahn: Isartor. Tram: 18.

This is the largest technological museum in the world. Its huge collection of priceless artifacts and historic originals includes the first electric dynamo (Siemens, 1866), the first automobile (Benz, 1886), the first diesel engine (1897), and the laboratory bench at which the atom was first split (Hahn, Strassmann, 1938). There are hundreds of buttons to push, levers to crank, and gears to turn, as well as a knowledgeable, English-speaking staff to answer questions and demonstrate how steam engines, pumps, or historical musical instruments work.

Among the most popular displays are those on mining, with a series of model coal, salt, and iron mines, as well as the electrical power hall, with high-voltage displays that actually produce lightning. There are also exhibits on transportation, printing, photography, and textiles, and halls devoted to air-and-space and high-tech themes. Activities include glassblowing and paper-making demonstrations. The astronomy exhibition is the largest in Europe. A good restaurant and a museum shop are on the premises.

✪ **Schloss Nymphenburg.** Schloss Nymphenburg 1 (5 miles northwest of the city center). ☎ **089/17-90-86-68.** Admission to all attractions 8DM ($4.55) adults, free for children 14 and under. Nymphenburg palace, Amalienburg, Marstallmuseum, and museum of porcelain 6DM ($3.40) adults, free for children 14 and under. Apr–Sept Tues–Sun 10am–noon and 1:30–5pm; Oct–Mar Tues–Sun 10am–noon and 1:30–4pm. Parking beside the Marstallmuseum. U-Bahn: U1 to Rotkreuzplatz, then tram 17 toward Amalienburgstrasse. Bus: 41.

In summer, the Wittelsbachs would pack up their bags and head for their country house, Schloss Nymphenburg. A more complete, more sophisticated palace than the Residenz, it was begun in 1664 by Elector Ferdinand Maria in Italian-villa style and took more than 150 years to complete. The final palace plan was created mainly by Elector Max Emanuel, who in 1702 decided to enlarge the villa by adding four large pavilions connected by arcaded passageways. Gradually the French style took over, and today the facade is a subdued baroque.

The palace interior is less subtle, however. Upon entering the main building, you're in the **great hall,** decorated in rococo colors and stuccos. The frescoes by Zimmermann (1756) depict incidents from mythology, especially those dealing with Flora, goddess of nymphs, for whom the palace was named. Concerts are still presented here in summer.

From the main building, turn left and head for the **arcaded gallery** connecting the northern pavilions. The first room in the arcade is the Great Gallery of Beauties, painted in 1710. More provocative, however, is Ludwig I's Gallery of Beauties in the south pavilion. Paintings by J. Stieler (from 1827 to 1850) include the *Schöne Münch-nerin (Lovely Munich Girl)* and a portrait of Lola Montez, the dancer whose affair with Ludwig caused such a scandal.

To the south of the palace buildings, in the rectangular block of low structures that once housed the court stables, is the **Marstallmuseum.** In the first hall, look for the glass coronation coach of Elector Karl Albrecht, built in Paris in 1740. From the same period comes the hunting sleigh of Electress Amalia, with the statue of Diana, goddess of the hunt; even the sleigh's runners are decorated with shellwork and hunting trophies.

The coaches and sleighs of Ludwig II are displayed in the **third hall.** His constant longing for the grandeur of the past is reflected in his ornately designed state coach, which was meant for his marriage to Duchess Sophie of Bavaria, a royal wedding that never took place. The fairy-tale coach wasn't wasted, however, since Ludwig often used it to ride through the countryside to one of his many castles, creating quite a picture. The coach is completely gilded, inside and out. In winter the king would use his state sleigh, nearly as elaborate as the Cinderella coach.

Nymphenburg's park stretches for 500 acres. A canal runs through it from the pool at the foot of the staircase to the cascade at the far end of the English-style gardens. A number of delightful pavilions are in the park: the Amalienburg, Electress Amalia's hunting lodge; the Badenburg Pavilion, a bathing pavilion near the lake of the same name; the Pagodenburg, decorated in chinoiserie style; and the Magdalenenklause (Hermitage), meant to be a retreat for prayer and solitude.

✪ **Staatsgalerie Moderner Kunst (State Gallery of Modern Art).** Haus der Kunst, Prinzregentenstrasse 1. ☎ **089/21-12-71-37.** Staatsgalerie, 6DM ($3.40) adults, 3.50DM ($2) students and seniors. Tues–Wed and Fri–Sun 10am–5pm, Thurs 10am–8pm. Closed some holidays. U-Bahn: Odeonsplatz. Bus: 53.

Munich's State Gallery of Modern Art is housed in the west wing of the massive Haus der Kunst, which was constructed in 1937. It contains a comprehensive collection of 20th-century art and sculpture. The largest section is devoted to modern German art. You'll see paintings by Klee, Marc, Kirchner, and Beckmann, and by Italian stars such as Marino Marini and Renato Guttoso, as well as works of American abstract expressionism, minimalist art, and more.

The east wing of the **Haus der Kunst,** Prinzregentenstrasse 1 (☎ **089/21-12-71-13**), is entered separately and requires a separate ticket. It's devoted to changing exhibitions, which often feature exciting new artists whose canvases are for sale when on display. Traveling exhibitions of worldwide importance stop here. Admission ranges from 8DM to 12DM ($4.55 to $6.85) for adults, depending on the exhibition, and 4DM ($2.30) for children 6 to 18; children 5 and under free. Open Tuesday to Thursday from 10am to 10pm and Friday to Monday from 10am to 6pm.

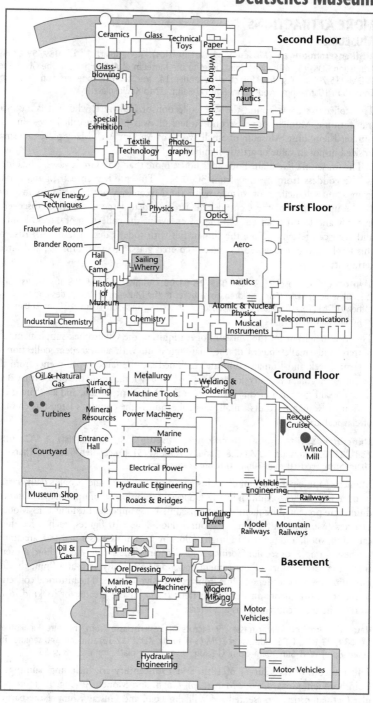

Deutsches Museum

Second Floor

Ceramics | Glass | Technical Toys | Paper
Glass-blowing
Writing & Printing
Aero-nautics
Special Exhibition
Textile Technology | Photo-graphy

First Floor

New Energy Techniques
Fraunhofer Room
Brander Room
Physics
Optics
Aero-nautics
Hall of Fame
Sailing Wherry
History of Museum
Industrial Chemistry
Chemistry
Atomic & Nuclear Physics
Telecommunications
Musical Instruments

Ground Floor

Oil & Natural Gas
Surface Mining
Metallurgy
Welding & Soldering
Turbines
Mineral Resources
Machine Tools
Power Machinery
Rescue Cruiser
Entrance Hall
Marine Navigation
Wind Mill
Courtyard
Electrical Power
Museum Shop
Hydraulic Engineering
Roads & Bridges
Vehicle Engineering
Railways
Tunneling Tower
Model Railways
Mountain Railways

Basement

Oil & Gas
Mining
Ore Dressing
Marine Navigation
Power Machinery
Modern Mining
Motor Vehicles
Hydraulic Engineering
Motor Vehicles

MORE ATTRACTIONS

MUSEUMS

Antikensammlungen (Museum of Antiquities). Königsplatz 1. ☎ **089/59-83-59.** Admission 6DM ($3.40) adults. Joint ticket to the Museum of Antiquities and the Glyptothek 10DM ($5.70) adults, free for children under 14, free for everyone on Sun. Tues and Thurs–Sun 10am–5pm, Wed 10am–8pm. U-Bahn: U2 to Königsplatz.

This collection grew around the vase collection of Ludwig I, who had fantasies of transforming Munich into a second Athens. It was originally called the Museum Antiker Kleinkunst (Museum of Small Works of Ancient Art). Many pieces are small in size but not in value or artistic significance.

The museum's five main-floor halls house more than 650 Greek vases. The oldest is "the goddess from Aegina" from 3000 B.C. This pre-Mycenaean figure, carved from a mussel shell, is on display with the Mycenaean pottery exhibits in room I. The upper level of the Central Hall is devoted to large Greek vases discovered in Sicily and to Etruscan art. On the lower level is the collection of Greek, Roman, and Etruscan jewelry. (Note the similarities with today's design fashions.) Also on this level are rooms devoted to ancient colored glass, Etruscan bronzes, and Greek terra-cottas.

Glyptothek. Königsplatz 3. ☎ **089/28-61-00.** Admission 6DM ($3.40) adults, 3DM ($1.70) seniors, 1DM (55¢) children. Joint ticket to the Museum of Antiquities and the Glyptothek 10DM ($5.70) adults, free for children under 14. Tues–Sun 10am–4:30pm. U-Bahn: U2 to Königsplatz.

The ideal neighbor for the Museum of Antiquities, the Glyptothek supplements the pottery and smaller pieces of the main museum with an excellent collection of ancient Greek and Roman sculpture. Included are the famous pediments from the temple of Aegina, two marvelous statues of *kouroi* (youths) from the 6th century B.C., the colossal figure of a *Sleeping Satyr* from the Hellenistic period, and a splendid collection of Roman portraits. In all, this collection is the country's largest assemblage of classical art.

Münchner Stadtmuseum (Municipal Museum). St. Jacobs-Platz 1. ☎ **089/ 233-22370.** Admission 5DM ($2.85) adults, 2.50DM ($1.40) children. Tues and Thurs–Sun 10am–5pm, Wed 10am–8:30pm. U-Bahn: Marienplatz.

Munich's Municipal Museum offers insight into city history and people's daily lives. A wooden model shows Munich in 1572. Special exhibitions about popular arts and traditions are presented frequently. The museum's most important exhibit is its Moorish Dancers (Moriskentanzer) on the ground floor. These 10 figures, each 2 feet high, carved in wood, and painted in bright colors by Erasmus Grasser in 1480, are among the best examples of secular Gothic art in Germany. The second-floor photo museum traces the early history of the camera back to 1839. Daily at 6 and 9pm, the film museum shows two different films from its extensive archives. The historical collection of musical instruments on the fourth floor is one of the greatest of its kind in the world. The main courtyard has a cafeteria.

Neue Pinakothek. Barerstrasse 29 (across Theresienstrasse from the Alte Pinakothek). ☎ **089/23-80-51-95.** Admission 7DM ($4) adults, 4DM ($2.30) students and seniors. Tues 10am–8pm, Wed–Sun 10am–5pm. U-Bahn: U2 to Königsplatz. Tram: 27. Bus: 53.

This museum offers a survey of 18th- and 19th-century art, including paintings by Gainsborough, Goya, David, Manet, van Gogh, and Monet. Among the more popular German artists represented are Wilhelm Leibl and Gustav Klimt. Note particularly the genre works by Carl Spitzweg, whose paintings poke gentle fun at everyday life in Munich.

Stadtische Galerie im Lenbachhaus. Luisenstrasse 33. ☎ **089/23-33-20-00.** Admission 8DM ($4.55) adults, 4DM ($2.30) students and children 6–12, free for children 5 and under. Tues–Sun 10am–6pm. U-Bahn: U2 to Königsplatz.

This gallery is in the ancient gold-colored villa of portrait painter Franz von Lenbach (1836–1904). It's devoted both to his work and that of other artists. Enter through the gardens. You'll first be greeted by ,a large collection of early pieces by Paul Klee (1879–1940). There's also an outstanding group of works by Kandinsky, leader of the Blue Rider movement in the early 20th century, and many 19th- and 20th-century paintings throughout the villa. The enclosed patio is pleasant for a coffee break.

Churches

Munich has many beautiful churches in addition to those listed below. Visitors should not miss the **Asamkirche,** on Sendlinger Strasse (S-Bahn: Marienplatz), a beautiful rococo church built between 1733 and 1746 and dedicated to St. John of Nepomuk. The **Michaelskirche,** or St. Michael's Church, Neuhauserstrasse 52 (U-Bahn: Marien-platz), is the largest Renaissance church north of the Alps. It was built by Duke William the Pious from 1583 to 1597. Lastly, the **Matthäuskirche,** or St. Matthew's Church, Nussbaumstrasse 1 (U-Bahn: Sendlinger-Tor-Platz), is a modern Evangelical cathedral completed in 1955.

✪ **Frauenkirche (Cathedral of Our Lady).** Frauenplatz 12. ☎ **089/29-00-82-0.** Free admission. Daily 7am–7pm. U-Bahn or S-Bahn: Marienplatz.

When the smoke cleared from the 1945 bombings, only a fragile shell remained of Munich's largest church. Workmen and architects who restored the 15th-century Gothic cathedral used whatever remains they could find in the rubble, along with modern innovations. The overall effect of the rebuilt Frauenkirche is strikingly simple, yet dignified. The twin towers with their onion domes, which remained intact, have been the city's landmark since 1525. Instead of the typical flying buttresses, huge props on the inside, which separate the side chapels, support the edifice. Twenty-two simple octagonal pillars support the Gothic vaulting over the nave and chancel.

Entering the main doors at the cathedral's west end, your first impression is that there are no windows (most of them are hidden by the enormous pillars). According to legend, the devil laughed at the notion of hidden windows and stamped in glee at the stupidity of the architect—you can still see the strange footlike mark called "the devil's step" in the entrance hall. In the chapel directly behind the high altar is the cathedral's most interesting painting: *The Protecting Cloak,* a 1510 work by Jan Polack, showing the Virgin holding out her majestic robes to shelter all humankind. The col-lection of tiny figures beneath the cloak includes everyone from the Pope to peasants.

Peterskirche (St. Peter's Church). Rindermarkt 1 (near the Rathaus). ☎ **089/2-60-48-28.** Church free; tower 2.50DM ($1.40) adults, 1.50DM (85¢) students, 50pf (30¢) children. Apr–Oct daily 9am–7pm (or even longer); Nov–Mar daily 9am–6pm. U-Bahn: Marienplatz.

Munich's oldest church (1180), known locally as Old Peter, has turned over a new leaf, and it's a gold one at that. The white-and-gray interior has been decorated with painted medallions of puce and gilded baroque. It contains a series of murals by Johann Baptist Zimmermann, but nothing tops the attraction of the bizarre relic in the second chapel on the left: the gilt-covered and gem-studded skeleton of St. Mundita. From its resting place on a cushion, it stares at you with two false eyes in its skull. Jewels cover the mouth of its rotten teeth, quite a contrast to the fresh roses usu-ally kept in front of the black-and-silver coffin. The church also has a tall steeple, which you can climb, though it lacks an elevator. Colored circles on the lower plat-form tell you whether the climb is worthwhile: If the circle is white, you can see as far as the Alps.

Theatinerkirche. Theatinerstrasse 22. ☎ **089/21-06-96-0.** Free admission. Church daily 6am–7:30pm; crypt May–Nov 1 Mon–Fri 10am–1pm and 2–4:30pm, Sat 10am–3pm. U-Bahn: Odeonsplatz.

Named for a small group of Roman Catholic clergy (the Theatines), this church, dedicated to Saint Kajetan, is Munich's finest example of Italian baroque. Two Italian architects, Barelli and Zucalli, began building it in 1662. François de Cuvilliés the Elder added the facade a century later, and his son finally completed the structure in 1768. Fluted columns that line the center aisle support the arched ceiling of the nave. Above the transept, dividing the nave from the choir, the ceiling breaks into an open dome, with an ornate gallery decorated with large but graceful statues. Nothing detracts from the whiteness of the interior except the dark wooden pews and the canopied pulpit. Since 1954 the church has been under the care of the Dominican Friars.

PARKS & ZOOS

Munich's city park, the 18th-century **Englischer Garten,** borders Schwabing on the east and extends almost to the Isar River. This is one of the largest and most beautiful city parks in Germany. It was the brainchild of Sir Benjamin Thompson, the English scientist who spent most of his life in the service of the Bavarian government. You can wander for hours along the walks and among the trees, flowers, and sunbathers. Nude sunbathing is permitted in certain areas of the park (some claim these areas are Munich's most popular tourist attraction). For a break, stop for tea on the plaza near the Chinese pagoda, or have a beer at the nearby beer garden. You might also take along a picnic put together at the elegant shop of **Alois Dallmayr,** or less expensive fare from **Hertie,** across from the Hauptbahnhof, from **Kaufhof** at Marienplatz, or from Munich's famous open-air market, the **Viktualienmarkt.**

The **Hellabrunn Zoo** stands in Tierpark Hellabrunn, about 4 miles south of the city center, at Tierparkstrasse 30 (☎ **089/62-50-80**). It's one of the largest zoos in the world, with hundreds of animals roaming in a natural habitat. A walk through the attractive park is recommended even if you're not a zoo buff. There's also a big children's zoo, as well as a large aviary. You can visit the zoo daily from 8am to 6pm (in winter, daily from 9am to 5pm); admission is 10DM ($5.70) for adults, 7DM ($4) for students and seniors, 5DM ($2.85) for children ages 4 to 14, and free for children 3 and under. To reach the park, take bus no. 52 from Marienplatz, or U-Bahn U3 to Thalkirchen.

THE OLYMPIC GROUNDS

The **Olympiapark** (☎ **089/30-67-24-14**), site of the 1972 Olympic Games, occupies 740 acres at the city's northern edge. More than 15,000 workers from 18 countries transformed the site into a park of nearly 5,000 trees, 27 miles of roads, 32 bridges, and a lake. Olympiapark has its own railway station, U-Bahn line, mayor, post office, churches, and elementary school. The planners even broke the city skyline by adding a 960-foot television tower in the center of the park.

The area's showpiece is a huge stadium, capable of seating 69,300 spectators, and topped by the largest roof in the world—nearly 80,000 square yards of tinted acrylic glass. The supports for the stadium are anchored by two huge blocks, each capable of resisting 4,000 tons under stress. The roof serves the additional purpose of collecting rainwater and draining it into the nearby Olympic lake.

Olympia Tower, Olympiapark (☎ **089/30-67-27-50**), is open daily from 9am to midnight. A ticket for a ride up the tower (on the speediest elevator on the continent, no less) costs 5DM ($2.85) for adults and 2.50DM ($1.40) for children under 15. An most exclusive dining spot in the tower is the **Tower Restaurant** (☎ **089/30668585**), which features a selection of international and German dishes. Food is served daily from 11am to 5:30pm and 6:30pm to midnight. A complete dinner costs 65DM to

78DM ($37.05 to $44.45). Before or after dinner, you'll want to take in the extraor-dinary view, which reaches to the Alps. Four observation platforms look out over the Olympiapark. The Tower Restaurant revolves around its axis in 60 minutes, giving guests who linger a changing vista of Munich. American Express, Diners Club, MasterCard, and Visa are accepted.

At the base of the tower is the **Restaurant Olympiasee,** Spiridon-Louis-Ring 7 (☎ **089/30-67-28-08**), serving genuine Bavarian specialties, with meals costing 12.50DM ($7.10) and up. Food is served daily from 9:30am to 7pm (until 9pm in summer). The restaurant is popular in summer because of its terrace. No credit cards are accepted. Take U-Bahn U3 or U8 to Olympiazentrum.

Near Olympiapark, you can visit the **BMW Museum,** Petuelring 130 (☎ **089/38-22-33-07**), where the history of the automobile is stunningly displayed in an atmosphere created by Oscar-winner Rolf Zehetbauer, a "film architect." The exhibi-tion "Horizons in Time," housed in a demisphere of modern architecture, takes you into the future and back to the past. You can view 24 video films and 10 slide shows (an especially interesting one shows how people of yesterday imagined the future). Many of the exhibits are in English. The museum is open daily from 9am to 5pm, charging 5.50DM ($3.15) for adults and 4DM ($2.30) for children. While here, you might also ask about BMW factory tours. Take U-Bahn U3 to Olympiazentrum.

ESPECIALLY FOR KIDS

Of all the museums in Munich, kids will like best the **Deutsches Museum,** Muse-umsinsel 1 (☎ **089/2-17-91**), which has many "hands-on" exhibits. For details, see "The Top Attractions," above.

On the third floor of the **Münchner Stadtmuseum,** St. Jakobsplatz 1 (☎ **089/23-32-23-70**), is an array of marionettes and hand puppets from around the world. Another special department is devoted to fairground art, including carousel animals, shooting galleries, roller-coaster models, and wax and museum figures. The main exhibit contains the oldest-known carousel horses, dating from 1820. For hours and admission fees, see "More Attractions," above.

Spielzeugmuseum, in the Altes Rathaus, Marienplatz 15 (☎ **089/29-40-01**), is a historical toy collection. It's open daily from 10am to 5:30pm. Admission is 5DM ($2.85) for adults, 1DM (55¢) for children, and 10DM ($5.70) for a family.

For a truly charming experience, go to the **Münchener Marionetten Theater,** Blu-menstrasse 32A (☎ **089/26-57-12**), which was established in 1858. It stages, in mar-ionette form, productions from the operas of Mozart and other composers at performances held every Wednesday, Thursday, Saturday, and Sunday at 3pm. There are also evening performances every Saturday at 8pm. Admission costs 8DM ($4.55) for adults during matinees, and 15DM ($8.55) during evening performance; admis-sion for children at both matinees and evenings is 6DM ($3.40). Matinees tend to be more animated and crowded than evening show, and are particularly well-suited for younger children ages 4 and up.

The **Bavaria Film Studio,** Bavariafilmplatz 7, Geiselgasteig (☎ **089/64-99-23-04**), is Europe's largest filmmaking center—Munich's version of Hollywood. Visitors can watch such spine-tingling thrillers as *Adventure in the Devil's Mine* and *Cosmic Pinball.* The Bavaria Action Show features a stunt team demonstrating fist fights and fire stunts, tumbling down staircases, and even taking a 92-foot-high plunge. This show, lasting about 30 minutes, is performed from March through October on Saturday and Sunday. Guided 1½-hour tours (some in English) are given from March through October, daily from 9am to 4pm. Take tram no. 25 to Bavariafilmplatz. Admission is 17DM ($9.70) for adults, 15DM ($8.55) for students and senior citizens, 12DM ($6.85) for children ages 4 to 14, and free for children 3 and under.

Hellabrunn Zoo has a large children's zoo, where kids can pet the animals. For details, see "More Attractions," above.

Older children will enjoy the show at the **Circus Krone,** Marstrasse 43 (☎ **089/ 55-81-66**), when the circus show is presented from December 25 to March 31.

Walking Tour: Munich's Ancient Center

Start: Frauenkirche.
Finish: Königsplatz.
Time: 2½ hours, not counting visits to interiors or shopping.
When to go: Any time except Monday to Friday from 7:30 to 9am and 4:30 to 6pm, when traffic is heaviest.

With a history spanning centuries of building and rebuilding, Munich is one of Europe's most interesting cities, especially for pedestrians.

Begin your tour at the dignified cathedral whose brickwork is among the most impressive in Europe, the:

1. **Frauenkirche.** Built in a mere 20 years, beginning in 1468, on the site of a much older church, this majestically somber building is capped with twin towers, the symbol of Munich.

   After admiring the design, walk for about a block southeast along any of the pedestrian alleyways radiating away from the rear of the church. In about 2 minutes you'll find yourself in the most famous medieval square of Munich:

2. **Marienplatz,** in whose center a golden statue (the Mariensäule) rises above pavement first laid in the 1300s when the rest of the city's streets were a morass of mud and sewage. On the square's northern boundary sits the richly ornamented bulk of the **Neues Rathaus (New City Hall),** built between 1867 and 1908 as a neo-Gothic symbol of Munich's power. On its facade is the famous mechanical clock or Glockenspiel, which performs daily at 11am and also at noon and 5pm in the summer. At the square's eastern border, beyond a stream of traffic, is the simpler and smaller **Altes Rathaus (Old City Hall),** which was rebuilt in its present form in 1470 after fire destroyed an even earlier version.

   From the square, walk south along Rindermarkt, encircling the masonry bulk of the:

3. **Peterskirche.** Its foundations date from 1000. The interior is a sun-flooded fantasy of baroque stucco and gilt. Then walk to the rear of this church, where you'll see the sprawling premises of one of the best-stocked food emporiums in Europe, the:

4. **Viktualienmarkt.** Known as "Munich's stomach," it's packed with opportunities for snacking, picnicking, beer drinking, or watching the ritual of European grocery shopping. At the northern end, at the corner of the streets Rosen Tal and Im Tal, rise the richly ornate baroque walls of the:

5. **Heiliggeist (Holy Ghost) Church.** Its foundations were laid in the 1100s, but the present structure wasn't completed until 1730.

   From here, cross the busy boulevard called Im Tal and walk north along Maderbraustrasse (which within a block will change its name to Orlandostrasse and then to Am Platz). Here, look for the entrance to the most famous beer hall in Europe, the state-owned:

6. **Hofbräuhaus.** For a description, see "Munich After Dark," later in this chapter. For the moment, note its location for an eventual return.

Walking Tour: Munich's Ancient Center

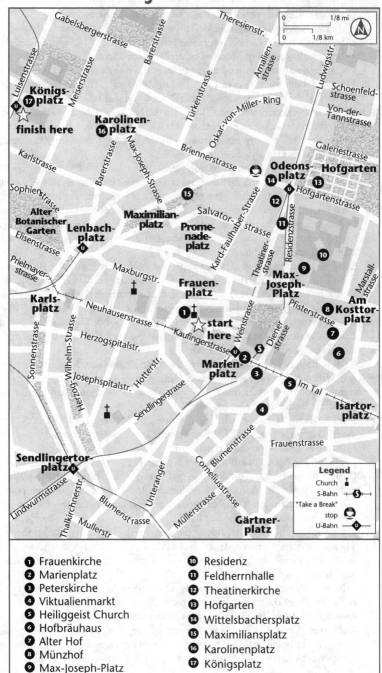

1. Frauenkirche
2. Marienplatz
3. Peterskirche
4. Viktualienmarkt
5. Heiliggeist Church
6. Hofbräuhaus
7. Alter Hof
8. Münzhof
9. Max-Joseph-Platz
10. Residenz
11. Feldherrnhalle
12. Theatinerkirche
13. Hofgarten
14. Wittelsbachersplatz
15. Maximiliansplatz
16. Karolinenplatz
17. Königsplatz

Now, walk east along Pfisterstrasse. To your left are the walls of the:

7. Alter Hof, originally built in 1255. This was once the palace of the Wittelsbachs, although it was eclipsed later by grander residences. Since 1816, it has housed the rather colorless offices of Munich's financial bureaucracies.

On the opposite (northern) edge of Pfisterstrasse rise the walls of the:

8. Münzhof, built from 1563 to 1567. During its lifetime, it has housed the imperial stables, the first museum north of the Alps, and (between 1809 and 1986) a branch of the government mint. Today it's the headquarters for Munich's Landmark Preservation office (Landesamt für Denkmal-Schutz). If it's open, the double tiers and massive stone columns of the building's Bavarian Renaissance courtyard are worth a visit.

Pfisterstrasse funnels into a broader street, Hofgraben. Walk west for 1 block, then turn right (north) along Residenzstrasse. The first building on your right will be the city's main post office (Hauptpost), and a few paces farther you'll reach:

9. Max-Joseph-Platz. Designed as a focal point for the monumental avenue (Maximilianstrasse) that radiates eastward, the plaza was built during the 19th century on the site of a Franciscan convent in honor of Bavaria's first king. At the north edge of the plaza lies the:

10. Residenz. Constructed in different stages and styles from 1500 to 1850, this was the official home of Bavaria's rulers. After the bombings of World War II, it was rebuilt in a design that re-created its original labyrinthine floor plan. The Residenz contains seven semi-concealed courtyards, lavish apartments that have housed foreign visitors such as Elizabeth II and Charles de Gaulle, a number of different museums, the **Cuvilliés Theater,** and the Herkulessaal, a baroque-style concert hall. See "Attractions," above.

Walk from Max-Joseph-Platz north along Residenzstrasse. Make the first left and walk west along Salvatorstrasse; then, within another block, turn right (north) along Theatinerstrasse. On your right you'll immediately notice an important landmark of Munich, the:

11. Feldherrnhalle. This open-air loggia, constructed between 1841 and 1844, was modeled after the Loggia dei Lanzi in Florence. King Ludwig I commissioned the structure as a tribute to the Bavarian army.

The bronze figures honoring Bavarian generals Tilly (1559–1632) and Wrede (1767–1838) were based on drawings by Ludwig Schwanthaler. After the failure of Hitler's putsch in Munich, the Feldherrnhalle became a Nazi rallying point. Today, the area around it is filled with street singers and musicians, who appreciate some marks tossed into their hats.

On the western (opposite) side of the same street (Theatinerstrasse) is the:

12. Theatinerkirche (Church of St. Kajetan). This church has a triple-domed Italian baroque facade. Its crypt contains the tombs of many of the Wittelsbachs. See "Attractions," above.

Now, continue walking north, passing through Odeonsplatz, below which several subway lines converge. On the northeastern side of this square lie the flowers, fountains, and cafes of one of Munich's most pleasant gardens, the:

13. Hofgarten. Originally built for members of the royal court in 1613, it was opened to the public in 1780. Along the edges of the Hofgarten, as well as along the avenues radiating away from it, lie many opportunities for your much-awaited break.

TAKE A BREAK   Do as the Münchners do and enjoy the panorama of Odeonsplatz and the nearby Hofgarten. One particularly attractive choice is

Café Luitpold, Briennerstrasse 11 (☎ **089/29-28-65**), which was rebuilt in a streamlined design after World War II. It has in the past welcomed such cafe-loving habitués as Ibsen, Johann Strauss the Younger, and Kandinsky.

Now, walk westward along Briennerstrasse, through a neighborhood lined with impressive buildings. On your right, notice the heroic statue of Maximilian I, the Great Elector (1597–1651), rising from the center of:

14. **Wittelsbachersplatz.** In a short time, the gentle fork to your left leads into the verdant and stylish perimeter of:

15. **Maximiliansplatz.** Shop at your leisure or plan to return later for a more in-depth sampling of this prestigious neighborhood. For the moment, return to Briennerstrasse, turn left (west), and head toward the 85-foot obelisk (erected in 1833) that soars above:

16. **Karolinenplatz.** Its design commemorates Bavarians killed in Napoléon's invasion of Russia. Continuing west, you'll come upon:

17. **Königsplatz.** In the early 19th century, Crown Prince Ludwig selected its formal neoclassical design after an architectural competition. Its perimeter is ringed with some of Germany's most impressive museum buildings, the Doric-inspired **Propyläen** monument (west side), the **Antikensammlungen** (south side), and the Ionic-fronted **Glyptothek** (north side).

---

6 Organized Tours

ON FOOT Munich Walks (☎ **030/3-01-91-94**) offers two English-language walking tours of Munich. The "Discover Munich" tour takes you past the Sendlinger Tor, the Hofbräuhaus, the Marienplatz, and other major sites. It starts at 10:30am daily April to October, and also at 2:30pm Monday to Saturday May to August. "Infamous Third Reich Sites" features visits to places from Munich's darker past, such as the Feldherrnhalle, where the Beer Hall Putsch was quelled, and the Königsplatz, where the Munich Agreement was signed. Starting times are 2:30pm Saturday in April; 10:30am Monday, Thursday, and Saturday May to August; and 2:30pm Monday and Saturday September to October. Reservations for both tours are unnecessary; simply meet the guide, who will be wearing a Munich Walks badge, at the Hauptbahnhof, outside the EurAide office by track 11. Tours cost 12DM ($6.60) for those under 26 years of age, 15DM ($8.55) for everyone else.

BY BUS Blue buses that give sightseeing tours in both German and English leave from the square in front of the Hauptbahnhof, at Hertie's, year-round. Tickets are sold on the bus; no advance booking is necessary. A 1-hour tour, costing 17DM ($9.70) for adults and 9DM ($5.15) for children 6 to 12, leaves at 10am, 11:30am, 1pm, 2:30pm and 4pm, daily from May through October. Winter departures are November through April, daily at 10am and 2:30pm.

A 2½-hour tour, including the Olympic Tower, costs 30DM ($17.10) for adults and 15DM ($8.55) for children. Departures are at 10am and 2:30pm from May through October and at 10am and 2:30pm from November through April.

A second 2½-hour tour, costing 30DM ($17.10) for adults and 15DM ($8.55) for children, visits the famous Neue Pinakothek (painting gallery), the Frauenkirche, and the chiming clocks at Marienplatz. It departs Tuesday to Sunday at 10am.

A third 2½-hour tour, going for 30DM ($17.10) for adults and 15DM ($8.55) for children, visits Nymphenburg Palace and the Schatzkammer. It departs Tuesday to Sunday at 2:30pm.

If you'd like to go farther afield and visit major attractions in the environs (such as Berchtesgaden or Ludwig II's castles), contact **Panorama Tours.** The office is at Arnulfstrasse 8 (☎ 089/54-90-75-60), to the north of the Hauptbahnhof. Hours are 7:30am to 6pm Monday to Friday, 7:30am to noon on Saturday, and 7:30 to 10am on Sunday and holidays.

BY BIKE   Pedal pushers will want to try Mike Lasher's popular **Mike's Bike Tour,** St. Bonifatiusstrasse 2 (☎ 089/6-51-42-75). His bike-rental services include maps and locks, child and infant seats, and helmets at no extra charge. English and bilingual tours of central Munich run from March through November at 11:30am and 4pm daily (call to confirm). Customers love Mike's charm. Participants meet under the tower of the old town hall, a gray building on the east end of Marienplatz. Mike, the consummate guide, will be here—whistle in mouth—letting everyone know who he is. The tour veers from the bike paths only long enough for a lunch stop at a beer garden. Fear not, fainthearted: the bikes are new and the rides are easy, with plenty of time for historical explanations, photo opportunities, and question-and-answer sessions. Bike rentals for tours without a guide (Mike will supply a map) are 25DM ($14.25) for the day; full-day guided tours are 39DM ($22.25).

7 Sports & Outdoor Pursuits

BEACHES, SWIMMING POOLS & WATER SPORTS   On hot weekends, much of Munich embarks for nearby lakes, the **Ammersee** and the **Starnbergersee,** where bathing facilities are clearly marked. You can also swim at **Maria-Einsiedel,** in the frigid, snow-fed waters of the Isar River. The city has several public swimming pools as well. The largest of these includes the giant competition-size pool in the Olympia-park, the **Olympia-Schwimmhalle** (☎ 089/30-67-20-15). Admission is 13DM ($7.40). Information on both sailing and windsurfing is available from the **Bay-erischer Segler-Verbund,** Georg-Brauchle-Ring 93 (☎ 089/15-70-23-66).

FITNESS CENTERS & HEALTH CLUBS   Several of Munich's larger hotels have installed their own state-of-the-art exercise equipment. There also are gyms and health clubs scattered throughout the city, and many sell temporary passes to new-comers. For information, ask your hotel receptionist or contact the **Bayerischer Landes-sportverbund,** Georg-Brauchle-Ring 93 (☎ 089/15-70-20).

ICE-SKATING   During winter's coldest months, a lake in the Englischer Garten freezes over and is opened to ice-skaters. Also blocked off for skaters is a section of the Nymphenburger Canal, near the palace. Be alert to the GEFAHR ("danger") signs that are posted whenever temperatures rise and the ice becomes too thin. The indoor rink is the **Olympic Icestadium** in the Olympiapark, Spiridon-Louis-Ring 3 (☎ 089/ 30-67-21-50).

JOGGING   Regardless of the season, the most lushly landscaped place in Munich is the **Englischer Garten** (U-Bahn: Münchner Freiheit), which has a 7-mile circumfer-ence and an array of dirt and asphalt tracks. Also appropriate are the grounds of the **Olympiapark** (U-Bahn: Olympiazentrum), or the park surrounding **Schloss Nymphenburg.** More convenient to the center of the city's commercial district is a jog along the embankments of the Isar River.

RAFTING   Raft trips on the Isar River are conducted between the town of Wolfrats-hausen and Munich between early May and late September. Be advised that a raft may contain up to 60 other passengers. If you still want to try it, call **Franz and Sebastian Seitner,** Heideweg 9, 82515 Wolfratshausen (☎ 08171/1-83-20).

ROWING   Rowboats add to the charm of the lakes in the **Englischer Garten.** There's a kiosk at the edge of the Kleinhesseloher See where you can rent them. There are also rowboat rentals on the southern bank of the **Olympiasee,** in the Olympiapark.

SKIING   Because of the proximity of the Bavarian and Austrian Alps, many Munich residents are avid skiers. For information on resorts and getaway snow-related activities, contact the **Bayerischer Segler-Verbund,** Georg-Brauchle-Ring 93,80992 München (☎ **089/15-70-23-66**).

SPECTATOR SPORTS   Munich loves soccer and has one of Europe's outstanding teams, **Bayern München,** which plays at the Olympic Stadium in Olympiapark. If you want to attend a match, call Olympiapark at ☎ **089/30-67-24-24.**

TENNIS   At least 200 indoor and outdoor tennis courts are scattered around greater Munich. Many can be booked in advance through **Sport Scheck** (☎ **089/99-28-74-60**). For information on Munich's many tennis tournaments and competitions, contact the **Bayerischer Tennis Verbund,** Georg-Brauchle-Ring 93,80992 München (☎ **089/15-70-26-40**).

8 Shopping

The most interesting shops are concentrated on Munich's pedestrians-only street, between Karlsplatz and Marienplatz. Store hours in Munich are generally Monday to Friday from 9 or 9:30am to 6pm and Saturday from 9 or 9:30am to 1 or 2pm.

ANTIQUES
Philographikon Galerie Rauhut. Maximilianstrasse 15. ☎ **089/22-50-82.** U-Bahn or S-Bahn: Marienplatz.

This important gallery, set midway between the Hotel Vie Jahreszeiten and the National Opera House, represents one of the most celebrated success stories of Munich's art world. In 1978, Mr. Rauhut, a television producer, transformed his hobby of collecting and categorizing rare engravings and manuscripts into a career by establishing this shop. Here you'll find six rooms on two floors devoted to one of the most comprehensive collections of antique art in Munich. Prices range from 30DM ($17.10) for a 19th-century steel engraving, to hundreds of thousands of deutschmarks for pre-Gutenberg illuminated manuscripts (sold, depending on circumstances, as individual sheets or as entire folios). Other curiosities include antique maps; botanical prints from English, French, and German sources; and a series of rare prints by a Swiss-born engraver, Karl Bodmer, whose depictions in the 1820s of native American Indians are increasingly valuable on both sides of the Atlantic.

Squirrel. Schellingstrasse 54. ☎ **089/2-72-09-29.** U-Bahn: U3 or U6 to Universität.

This unusual shop, established 20 years ago by its charming owners, Urban Geissel and his wife, Gisela, houses a collection of luggage made by English and French purveyors for the aristocrats of the Jazz Age. There are suitcases and steamer trunks from Louis Vuitton; antique pieces by Hermès; and examples from such English makers as Finnegan's and Harrods. Although they tend to be heavy, they're still serviceable and richly imbued with the nostalgia of the great days of oceangoing travel.

ART
Galerie für Angewandte Kunst München. Pacellistrasse 8. ☎ 089/2-90-14-70. U-Bahn: Karlsplatz.

This is the largest, most visible, and most historic art gallery in Germany. The Bavarian government established it in the 1840s as a showcase for local artists. Housed within two interconnected buildings, one a Jugendstil monument and the other "of no artistic importance," the complex contains an upscale art gallery and a sales outlet, the Ladengeschäft, where attractive crafts are sold at prices that begin at 40DM ($22.80). Works by more than 400 artists are displayed and sold here. Examples include sculpture in all kinds of media, crafts, textiles, and woven objects.

BOOKS

Hugendubel. Marienplatz 22. ☎ **089/2-38-91.**

Not only is this Munich's biggest bookstore, but it also enjoys the most central location. It sells a number of English-language titles, both fiction and nonfiction, and also offers travel books and helpful maps.

CHINA, SILVER & GLASS

Georg Jensen. Amiraplatz 1. ☎ **089/29-16-10-84.** U-Bahn: Odeonsplatz.

This is the only outlet in Munich for the most famous and influential silversmith in Denmark. Many of the patterns were first produced shortly after World War I. The inventory includes hollowware, jewelry, cutlery, clocks, and wristwatches.

Kunstring Meissen. Briennerstrasse 4. ☎ **089/28-15-32.** U-Bahn: Odeonsplatz.

During the coldest days of the Cold War, this place was Munich's exclusive distributor of Meissen and Dresden china, which was manufactured behind the so-called iron curtain. With the collapse of the Soviet regime and the rise of the free market in the former East Germany, Kunstring's exclusive access became a thing of the past. Despite that, the shop still contains one of Munich's largest inventories of the elegant porcelain that has intrigued artists, aristocrats, and everyday homeowners since the 18th century.

✪ **Rosenthal.** Dienerstrasse 17. ☎ **089/22-26-17.** U-Bahn or S-Bahn: Marienplatz.

Rosenthal, established in 1879 in the Bavarian town of Selb near the Czech border, is one of the three or four most prestigious names in German porcelain. Much (though not all) of the line today focuses on contemporary design, an approach that separates it from the more traditional ways of Nymphenburg, Sevrès, or Limoges porcelain. The manufacturer pre-establishes prices for Rosenthal patterns and maintains them rigidly, so there are no price breaks at this factory outlet. You will, however, find here the widest array of Rosenthal patterns available in Germany. In addition to porcelain, the line includes furniture, glass, and cutlery, all scattered over two floors of spotlessly maintained showrooms.

CRAFTS

Bayerischer Kunstgewerbeverein (Bavarian Association of Artisans). Pacellistrasse 6–8. ☎ 089/2-90-14-70.

At this showcase for Bavarian artisans, you'll find excellent handcrafts: ceramics, glasses, jewelry, wood carvings, pewter, and seasonal Christmas decorations.

Haertle. Neuhauserstrasse 15. ☎ **089/2-31-17-90.** U-Bahn: Marienplatz or Stachus.

Although much of what this shop sells is crafted from wood, don't look here for carvings of the saints or depictions of woodcutters and alpine farmers. Instead you'll find racks of nostalgic, often kitschy, wooden implements for the home and kitchen. Much of the inventory is rustic, charming, and native to Bavaria. The regional merchandise is offset with racks of porcelain, glassware, and gift items. This shop has thrived at its location in Munich's historic core for more than a century.

✪ **Ludwig Mory.** Marienplatz 8. ☎ **089/22-45-42.** U-Bahn: Marienplatz.

This shop, located in a traditional one-room building near the cathedral, is the most famous purveyor of Bavarian beer steins in Munich, in business since the 1830s. After seeing this place, you'll never want to drink Budweiser from a can again. The steins range from 45DM ($25.65) for an honest but unpretentious souvenir to much more for a richly decorative work of art that might round off a private collection.

Otto Kellnberger Holzhandlung. Heiliggeistrasse 8. ☎ **089/22-64-79.** U-Bahn or S-Bahn: Marienplatz.

This small but choice emporium of traditional wood carvings evokes remote alpine Bavaria. Its inventory features all the folkloric charm and much of the folkloric kitsch you might find in remote Oberammergau.

Prinoth. Guido Schneblestrasse 9A. ☎ **089/56-03-78.** U-Bahn: U4 or U5 to Laimerplatz.

Most of the wood carvings sold here are produced in small workshops in the South Tyrol, that folklore-rich part of Austria that was annexed to Italy after World War I. The selection is wide-ranging, and since the shop is 3½ miles west of Munich's tourist zones, prices are reasonable compared to those of shops closer to the Marienplatz.

✪ **Wallach.** Residenzstrasse 3. ☎ **089/22-08-71.**

We consider Wallach the finest place in Germany for handcrafts, both new and antique, as well as folk art. Shop here for a memorable object to remind you of your trip. You'll find antique churns, old hand-painted wooden boxes and trays, milking stools, painted porcelain clocks, dirndls, leather pants, wooden wall clocks, doilies, napkins, towels, and more.

DEPARTMENT STORES

Hertie. Bahnhofplatz 7. ☎ **089/5-51-20.** U-Bahn: Hauptbahnhof.

This is our favorite department store in Munich, a sprawling four-story-plus basement emporium of all aspects of the German version of the good life. A fixture near the main railway station since the turn of the century, it has survived wars and revolutions with predictable mercantile style.

Kaufhof. Marienplatz. ☎ **089/23-18-51.** U-Bahn: Marienplatz.

This is one of the largest department stores in town. You can wander freely among displays that are art forms in their own right. The inventory is includes virtually everything, from men's, women's, and children's clothing to housewares, and much more.

Ludwig Beck am Rathauseck. Am Marienplatz 11. ☎ **089/23-69-10**.

Most merchandise here is intended for local residents; however, visitors will also be interested in this four-floor shopping bazaar, which sells handmade crafts from all over Germany, both old and new. Items include decorative pottery and dishes, etched-glass beer steins and vases, painted wall plaques, decorative flower arrangements, unusual kitchenware, fashions, textiles, and much more. Within the same block the store has opened two more outlets: **Wäsche-Beck,** which sells lingerie, linens, and curtains; and **Strumpf-Beck,** which offers the town's largest selection of stockings and hosiery.

FASHION

Bogner Haus. Residenzstrasse 15. ☎ **089/2-90-70-40.**

Before you head for the slopes, shop at Bogner Haus for the latest in ski clothing and styles. Willy Bogner, the filmmaker and Olympic downhill racer, sells this flamboyant attire. The store also sells more formal clothing for men and women.

✪ **Dirndl-Ecke.** Am Platzl 1/Sparkassenstrasse 10. ☎ **089/22-01-63.**

One block up from the famed Hofbräuhaus, this shop gets our unreserved recommendation. It's a stylish place specializing in high-grade dirndls, feathered alpine hats, and all clothing associated with the alpine regions. Everything sold is of fine quality—there's no tourist junk. Other merchandise includes needlework hats, beaded belts, and pleated shirts for men. Be sure to see the stylish capes, the silver jewelry in old Bavarian style, the leather shoes, and the linen-and-cotton combinations, such as skirts with blouses and jackets. Bavarian clothing for children is also available.

Exatmo. Franz-Josef-Strasse 35. ☎ **089/33-57-61.** U-Bahn: Giselastrasse.

Only a district like Schwabing could sustain a business like this, one of the most unusual clothiers in Munich. It operates from a showroom complete with mock-medieval murals. Among the racks of clothing are garments inspired by the puffy sleeves and dramatic flair of 17th-century fashions. The store purchases old pieces of linen, such as bed sheets from army surplus inventories across Europe, for reconfiguration into jackets, vests, and ruffled shirts that hang beautifully. Elizabethans would have loved these styles. A second branch, located across from the Hofbräuhaus, is called **Exatmo,** Platzl-Pfisterstrasse 11 (☎ **089/29161531;** U-Bahn/S-Bahn: Marienplatz).

Frankonia. Maximilianplatz 10. ☎ **089/2-90-00-20.**

This store, established in 1907, has Munich's most prestigious collection of traditional Bavarian dress (called *Tracht*). If you see yourself dressed hunter style, or in traditional alpine garb, this place can outfit you well. There's a fine collection of wool cardigan jackets with silvery buttons.

Furore. Franz-Josef-Strasse 41. ☎ **089/34-39-71.** U-Bahn: U3 or U6 to Giselastrasse.

This elegant store has a range of fashionable women's undergarments (brassieres, *bustiers,* slips) by Spain-born André Sard. The designs are tasteful, in some cases filmy and subtly erotic, in silk, cotton, and synthetics. There's also a loungewear collection.

Loden-Frey. Maffeistrasse 7–9. ☎ **089/21-03-90.**

You can see the twin domes of the Frauenkirche above the soaring glass-enclosed atrium of this shop's showroom. Go here for the world's largest selection of loden clothing and traditional costumes, as well as for international fashions from top European designers such as Armani, Valentino, and Ungaro.

Maendler. Theatinerstrasse 7. ☎ **089/2-91-33-22.** U-Bahn: Odeonsplatz.

This store is divided into a series of boutiques well known to virtually every well-dressed woman in Bavaria. You'll find the creative vision of Joop, Claude Montana, New York New York, and Jil Sander here. Looking for that special something for your dinner with the mayor or the president of Germany? Ask to see the formal evening wear of English designer David Fielden. For something more experimental and daring, head for the branch called **Rosy Maendler,** Maximiliansplatz 12 (same phone), where you'll find a more youthful version of the same store.

Red/Green of Scandinavia. Kaufingerstrasse 9. ☎ **089/2-60-64-89.** U-Bahn: Marienplatz.

This shop near the Marienplatz sells relaxed, casual clothing, appropriate for wearing on a private yacht or the local golf links. Most of the inventory comes from Denmark, and since everything was designed to withstand the blustery winds and the clear sunlight of the Baltic, they're study enough for any activity. Garments for men, women, and children are all available.

FOOD

✪ **Dallmayr.** Dienerstrasse 14–15. ☎ **089/2-13-50.** Tram: 19.

What Fortnum & Mason is to London, the venerable firm of Dallmayr is to Munich. Gastronomes as far away as Hamburg and Berlin sometimes telephone orders for exotica not readily available anywhere else. Dallmayr's list of prestigious clients reads like a who's who of German industry and letters. Wander freely among racks of food-stuffs, some of which are too delicate to survive shipment abroad, others of which can be shipped anywhere.

JEWELRY & WATCHES

Carl Jagemann's. Residenzstrasse 3. ☎ **089/22-54-93.** U-Bahn: Marienplatz.

Its reputation for quality and honesty goes back to 1864, as does some (but not all) of the merchandise it sells. It's one of the Altstadt's largest purveyors of new and antique timepieces of all types, ranging from wristwatches to grandfather clocks. There's also a collection of new and antique jewelry.

Hemmerle. Maximilianstrasse 14. ☎ **089/24-22-60-0.**

This is *the* place for jewelry. The original founders of this conservative shop made their fortune designing bejeweled fantasies for the Royal Bavarian Court of Ludwig II. All pieces are limited editions, designed and made in-house by Bavarian craftspeople. The company also designs its own wristwatch, the Hemmerle.

MUSIC

Hieber Musikhaus. In the Rathaus, Landschaftstrasse. ☎ **089/29-00-80-40.** U-Bahn or S-Bahn: Marienplatz.

This is the largest music store in Munich, and with a history going back to 1884, it's also one of the oldest. Its stock of librettos for operas by Wagner, Mozart, Puccini, and Verdi are among the most extensive anywhere.

PORCELAIN

✪ **Nymphenburger Porzellanmanufaktur.** Nordliches Schlossrondell 8. ☎ **089/ 1-79-19-70.**

At Nymphenburg, about 5 miles northwest of the heart of Munich, you'll find one of Germany's most famous porcelain factories, on the grounds of Schloss Nymphenburg. You can visit its exhibition and sales rooms, Monday to Friday from 8:30am to 5pm. Shipments can be arranged if you make purchases. There's also a more central branch in Munich's center at Odeonsplatz 1 (☎ **089/28-24-28**).

TOYS

Münchner Poupenstuben und Zinnfiguren Kabinette. Maxburgstrasse 4. ☎ **089/ 29-37-97.** U-Bahn: Karlsplatz.

This company is Germany's oldest miniature pewter foundry, dating from 1796. Many Germans visit Munich every December to purchase traditional Christmas dec-orations of a type once sold to Maximilian I, king of Bavaria. Managed by matriarchs of the same family, this store is one of the best sources in Germany for the miniature houses, furniture, birdcages, and people, all cunningly crafted from pewter or carved wood. Some of the figures are made from 150-year-old molds that are collector's items in their own right. Anything in this place would make a great gift not only for a child but also for an adult with a nostalgic bent.

Obletter's. Karlsplatz 11. ☎ **089/55089510.** U-Bahn: Karlsplatz.

Established in the 1880s, this is one of the largest emporiums of children's toys in Munich. The five floors of inventory contain everything from folkloric dolls to computer games.

WINE
Geisel's Vinothek. Schützenstrasse 11. ☎ **089/55-13-71-40.** U-Bahn: Hauptbahnhof.

Other than Dallmayr (see "Food," above), which has a much larger scale, this is the most sophisticated wine shop in Munich. Its inventory includes wines from Germany, Austria, Italy, and France, with bottles starting at 15DM ($8.55). The shop also doubles as a restaurant.

9 Munich After Dark

To find out what's happening in the Bavarian capital, go to the tourist office on Platform 12 at the Hauptbanhof (☎ **089/2-33-03-00**) and request a copy of *Monatsprogramm,* costing 2.50DM ($1.40). It contains a complete cultural guide, telling you not only what's being presented—including concerts, opera, special exhibits, and museum hours—but also how to purchase tickets.

THE PERFORMING ARTS
Nowhere else in Europe, other than London and Paris, will you find so many musical and theatrical events. And the good news is that seats don't cost a fortune—so count on indulging yourself and going to several performances. You'll get good tickets for anything from 15DM to 75DM ($8.55 to $42.75).

If you speak German, you'll find at least 20 theaters offering plays of every description: classic, comic, experimental, contemporary—take your pick. The best way to find out what current productions might interest you is to go to a theater-ticket agency. The most convenient one is at Marienplatz at the entrance to the S-Bahn.

For tickets to most events in Munich, and even all throughout Bavaria, head for **WOM (World of Music),** Kaufingerstrasse 15 (☎ **089/2185-1920**). WOM's leading competitors include **München Tickets** (☎ **089/54-81-81-81**) and **Hieber am Dom** (☎ **089/2900-8014**), both of which deal in tickets to basically the same cultural, entertainment, and sporting events within Bavaria, with access to the same computer database. Unfortunately, the use of a credit card for payment, both at WOM and at its competitors, carries a surcharge of at least 20DM ($11.40) per order. Be advised that for some sporting events (such as soccer) and musical events (including most of the operas subsidized by the city of Munich), where season tickets and long-term subscriptions reduce availability, you'll have to go to the venue's box office, as organizers tend not to cooperate with outside ticket agencies.

✪ **Altes Residenztheater (Cuvilliés Theater).** Residenzstrasse 1. ☎ **089/29-16-06-61,** or 089/21-85-19-20 for ticket information. Opera tickets 30DM–255DM ($17.10–$145.35); play tickets 10DM–71DM ($5.70–$40.45).

An attraction in itself (see "Residenz" in "The Top Attractions," above), this is also an important performance venue. The **Bavarian State Opera** and the **Bayerisches Staatsschauspiel** (see below) perform smaller works here, in keeping with the tiny theater's more intimate character. Box-office hours are the same as those for the Nationaltheater (see "Bayerischen Staatsoper," below).

✪ **Bayerischen Staatsoper.** Performing in the Nationaltheater, at Max-Joseph-Platz 2. ☎ **089/2185-1920.** Tickets 8DM–375DM ($4.55–$213.75), including standing room. U-Bahn: Marienplatz.

François Cuvilliés

In the 17th and 18th centuries, Bavaria's rulers were determined to rival Rome itself. They adorned their city with churches, abbeys, and monuments. In the cutthroat competition for commissions that followed, an unlikely candidate emerged for the role of Munich's most brilliant master of the rococo style.

François Cuvilliés (1695–1768) was a dwarf born in Belgium. Like many of his peers, he became first a page boy and later court jester to Max Emanuel, elector of Bavaria. When the elector was exiled, François accompanied him, and in St-Cloud near Paris, he absorbed his patron's interest in the aesthetics of French baroque architecture. Ambitious and witty, he won Max Emanuel's friendship and support. When the elector was reinstated with pomp and ceremony as ruler of Bavaria, François became a draftsman for the court's chief architect.

Cuvilliés proved himself so talented that in 1720 Max Emanuel sent him for a 4-year apprenticeship to one of the leading architects of Paris, Jacques-François Blondel. After his return to Munich, his work soon eclipsed that of his master. By 1745, the former jester had been elevated to the title of chief architect to the Bavarian court.

His commissions between 1726 and his death in 1768 include some of southern Germany's most important rococo monuments, such as the interior of the **Amalienburg Pavilion** in the park of Nymphenburg Palace and the facade of the **Theatinerkirche.** His most famous creation is the remarkable **Altes Residenztheater,** familiarly called by his name. All his work is notable for a flamboyant sinuousness.

Cuvilliés' son, François Cuvilliés the Younger (1731–77), also became an architect, although he never achieved the greatness of his father. Most notably, he put the finishing touches on the facade of the **Theatinerkirche,** which his father had left unfinished at his death.

The **Bavarian State Opera** is one of the world's great companies. The Bavarians give their hearts and souls to opera. Productions here are beautifully mounted and presented, and the company's roster includes some of the world's greatest singers. Hard-to-get tickets may be purchased at the box office Monday to Friday from 10am to 6pm and Saturday from 10am to 1pm, plus 1 hour before each performance. The Nationaltheater is also the home of a younger company, the **Bavarian State Ballet.**

Bayerisches Staatsschauspiel (State Theater). Max-Joseph-Platz. ☎ **089/21-85-19-40.** Tickets 20DM–65DM ($11.40–$37.05).

This repertory company is known for its performances of the classics: Shakespeare as well as Goethe and Schiller, and others. The box office, around the corner on Maximilianstrasse, is open Monday to Friday from 10am to 1pm and 2 to 6pm, Saturday from 10am to 1pm, and 1 hour before any performance.

Deutsches Theater. Schwanthalerstrasse 13. ☎ **089/55-23-42-41.** Tickets 29DM–90DM ($16.55–$51.30); higher for special events. U-Bahn: Karlsplatz/Stachus.

The regular season of the Deutsches Theater lasts throughout the year. Musicals are popular here, but operettas, ballets, and international shows are performed as well. During Carnival in January and February, the theater becomes a ballroom—the regular seats are replaced by tables and chairs for more than 2,000 guests. The costume balls and official black-tie festivities here are famous throughout Europe. Handmade decorations by artists combined with lighting effects create an enchanting ambience. Waiters serve wine, champagne, and food.

Münchner Kammerspiele. Maximilianstrasse 26–28. ☎ **089/23-72-13-28.** Tickets 10.50DM–47.50DM ($6–$27.10). U-Bahn: Marienplatz. S-Bahn: Isartorplatz. Tram: 19 to Maximilianstrasse.

Contemporary plays as well as classics are performed in this theater. The season lasts from early October to the end of July. You can reserve tickets by phone Monday to Friday from 10am to 6pm, but you must pick them up at least 2 days before a performance. The box office is open Monday to Friday from 10am to 6pm and on Saturday from 10am to 1pm, plus 1 hour before performances. There's also a second, smaller theater called **Werkraum,** where new works, mainly from young authors and directors, are presented. The location is at Hildegardstrasse 1 (call the number above for more information).

✪ **Münchner Philharmoniker (Munich Philharmonic Orchestra).** Performing in the Gasteig Kulturzentrum in the Haidhausen district, at Rosenheimerstrasse 5. ☎ **089/54-81-81-81.** Tickets 15DM–80DM ($8.55–$45.60). S-Bahn: Rosenheimerplatz. Tram: 18 to Gasteig. Bus: 51.

This famous orchestra was founded in 1893. Its music director is James Levine, and its home is the Gasteig Cultural Center, where it performs in Philharmonic Hall. The center also shelters the Richard Strauss Conservatory and the Munich Municipal Library, and has five performance halls. You can purchase tickets at the ground-level Glashalle, Monday to Friday from 9am to 6pm and Saturday from 9am to 2pm. The Philharmonic season begins in mid-September and runs to July.

BEER HALLS

The Bierhalle is a traditional Munich institution, offering food, entertainment, and, of course, beer. It is said that Müncheners consume more beer than anyone else in Germany. Bernd Boehle once wrote: "If a man really belongs to Munich he drinks beer at all times of the day, at breakfast, at midday, at teatime; and in the evening, of course, he just never stops." The place where every first-time visitor heads for at least one eating-and-drinking fest is the Hofbräuhaus am Platzl (see below). A liter of beer will generally set you back about 10DM ($5.70). For information on outdoor beer gardens, see "Dining," above.

Augustinerbräu. Neuhäuserstrasse 27. ☎ **089/23-18-32-57.** U-Bahn or S-Bahn: Stachus. Tram: 19.

This beer hall's dark-wood panels and carved-plaster ceilings make the place look older than it is. It's only been around for less than a century, but beer was first brewed on this spot in 1328 (or so they claim). The long menu changes daily, and the cuisine is not for dieters: It's hearty, heavy, and starchy, but that's what customers want. Open daily from 9am to midnight.

✪ **Hofbräuhaus am Platzl.** Am Platzl 9. ☎ **089/22-16-76.** S/Bahn/U-Bahn: Marienplatz.

The state-owned Hofbräuhaus is the world's most famous beer hall. Visitors with only 1 night in Munich usually come here. The present Hofbräuhaus was built in 1897, but the tradition of a beer house on this spot dates from 1589. This one was the setting for the notorious meeting of Hitler's newly launched German Workers party in 1920. Fistfights erupted as the Nazis attacked their Bavarian enemies, right here in the beer palace.

Today, 4,500 beer drinkers can crowd in here. Several rooms, including a top-floor room for dancing, are spread over three floors. With its brass band (which starts playing at 11am), the ground-floor Schwemme is what you always expected of a beer hall—eternal Oktoberfest. In the second-floor restaurant, strolling musicians entertain, and dirndl-clad servers offer mugs of beer between sing-alongs. Every night the Hofbräuhaus presents a typical Bavarian show in its Fest-Hall, starting at 8pm and lasting until midnight. The entrance fee is 9DM ($5.15). The hall is open daily from 9am to midnight.

Max Emanuel Brauerei. Adalbertstrasse 33. ☎ **089/2-71-51-58.** Cover 10DM ($5.70) Wed, 13DM ($7.40) Fri–Sat. U-Bahn: Universität.

Löwenbräu turned this brewery into a beer hall in the 1920s. It still serves steins of beer and platters of filling German grub. On Wednesday, Friday, and Saturday the second floor plays host to a popular salsa disco. Open daily 11am to 1am.

Türkenhof. Türkenstrasse 78. ☎ **089/2-80-02-35.** U-Bahn: Universität.

This beer hall is not the stereotypical schmaltzy old-Bavaria tourist trap. Here you'll find cosmopolitan cuisine made by a Greek co-owner and lively, intelligent conversation flowing among the student patrons. It's a big, fun bar created out of a 150-year-old butcher shop. There are five varieties of Augustiner beer available on tap. Open Sunday to Thursday from 11am to 1am; Friday and Saturday from 11am to 3am.

Waldwirtschaft Grosshesslohe. George-Kalb-Strasse 3. ☎ **089/74994030.** Tram: 7.

This popular summertime rendezvous, located above the Isar River near the zoo, has seats for some 2,000 drinkers. Music ranging from Dixieland to English jazz to Polish is played throughout the week. Entrance is free and you bring your own food. Open daily from 11am to 11pm (they have to close early because neighborhood residents complain).

NIGHTCLUBS

Bayerischer Hof Night Club. In the Hotel Bayerischer Hof, Promenadeplatz 2–6. ☎ **089/2-12-09-94.** Cover 18DM ($10.25) Fri–Sat after 10pm; higher for special events. No cover for hotel guests. Tram: 19.

Here in the extensive cellars of the Bayerischer Hof hotel (see "Accommodations," above) you'll find some of Munich's most sophisticated entertainment. Within one very large room is a piano bar where a musician plays melodies every night between 7 and 10pm. Behind a partition that disappears after 10pm is a bandstand for live orchestras, which play to a crowd of dancing patrons every night between 10pm and 3 to 4am, depending on business. Entrance to the piano bar is free, but there's a cover charge to the nightclub on Friday and Saturday nights. Drinks begin at 15.50DM ($8.85). The club and bar are open daily from 6pm to 3 or 4am. Daily happy hour is at 8:30pm with drinks starting at 9.50DM ($5.40).

Feierwerk. Hansastrasse 39–41. ☎ **089/7-69-36-00.** Cover 10DM–20DM ($5.70–$11.40). U-Bahn: Heimeranplatz.

Whether it's independent theater or rock 'n' roll, the multiple stages inside this complex have hosted it. Entertainment ranges from the commercially viable to the truly underground. In the summer, this already-roomy complex expands outside into circus tents. Open daily from 9pm to 4am.

Kunstpark Ost. Grafingerstrasse 6. ☎ **089/49-00-27-30.** Cover 5DM–10DM ($2.85–$5.70). S-Bahn: Ostbahnhof.

Set within the sprawling premises of what used to be a factory during the heyday of the industrial revolution, this is Munich's newest complex of bars, restaurants, and dance clubs. People tend to move randomly from venue to venue, without any particular loyalty to one or the other. Your best bet is to show up sometime after around 8pm, when all the bars will be functioning. The discos don't get going until at least around 10:30pm. Entrance to most of the bars is free; entrance to the discos usually costs from 5DM to 10DM ($2.85 to $5.70), depending on the night of the week.

Nachtwerk. Landesbergerstrasse 185. ☎ **089/5-78-38-00.** Cover 10DM ($5.70). S-Bahn: Donnersbergerbrücke.

This dance club in a huge factory warehouse also books bands. It's a festive place, not nearly as pretentious as other, more "exclusive" discos. Patrons even dance to rock music. The club is open Thursday from 10pm to 4am and Friday and Saturday from 10:30pm to 4am.

Night Flight. Franz Josef Strauss Airport, Wartungsallee 9. ☎ **089/97-59-79-99.** Cover 6DM ($3.40) Tues–Thurs 9pm–3am, 10DM ($5.70) Fri–Sat. S-Bahn: Flughafen.

This nightclub is located in the midst of enormous airfield hangars; it's designed to highlight the visual effect of airplane departures and arrivals. To get here you'll have to drive 25 miles north of the city or take a 30-minute ride on the S-Bahn. There are three bars, a dance floor, and a restaurant. Frenetic dancing to techno music is the main attraction. In summer, dancers cool off and catch their breath on an outdoor terrace, where the main sport is watching the airport. Open Tuesday to Thursday from 9pm until 3am and Friday and Saturday from 9pm to 6am.

Oklahoma. Schäftlarnstrasse 156. ☎ **089/7-23-43-27.** Cover 10DM–20DM ($5.70–$11.40). U-Bahn: Implerstrasse, then bus 31 or 57.

File under surreal. German and European bands decked out in cowboy hats and boots struggle with the nuances of an extremely foreign musical form. Even when the results are dead-on mimicry, there's something strange about watching German "cowboys" line dance or lean on the bar while guzzling Spaten. The cover charge is usually at the low end of the scale, rising when English and American acts hit the stage. Depending on your mood, this place can be a lot of fun. Pull on your jeans and come on in Tuesday to Saturday from 7pm to 1am.

Parkcafé. Sophienstrasse 7. ☎ **089/59-83-13.** Cover 10DM ($5.70). U-Bahn: Königsplatz.

Male dancers in black leather and feather boas gyrate on elevated platforms, and beautiful people zone out to heavy repetition on the dance floor below them. Who'd ever guess this home to chic freaks was a Nazi hangout in the 1930s? Open Wednesday and Thursday from 10pm to 4am and Friday and Saturday from 10pm to 5am.

Rattlesnake Saloon. Schneeglöckchenstrasse 91. ☎ **089/1-50-40-35.** Cover 5DM–12DM ($2.85–$6.85). S-Bahn: S1 to Fasanerie.

Same owner, same concept as Oklahoma (see above)—the difference is the rib-eye steaks, barbecued pork, chili, and other southern U.S. dishes available to hungry country-music fans. If you never learned line dancing at home, you can give it a chance here under the watchful eye of a Teutonic instructor. Open Wednesday to Sunday from 7pm to 1am.

Welser Kuche. Residenzstrasse 27. ☎ **089/29-65-65.** U-Bahn: U3 to Odeonsplatz.

Welser Kuche offers hearty medieval feasts served by *Magde* and *Knechte* (wenches and knaves) in 16th-century costumes. Guests can begin a meal any night of the week from 8pm, but they must be prepared to stick around for 3 hours. This is a takeoff on the many medieval Tudor banquets that are so popular with visitors in London. Food is served in hand-thrown pottery, and guests eat medieval delicacies with their fingers, aided only by a thin dagger. You can order a 6- or 10-course menu, called a Welser Feast, for 69DM to 79DM ($39.35 to $45.05), respectively. On Tuesday only, a Bürgermahl of five courses costs 59DM ($33.65). Many recipes come from a 16th-century cookbook. The place can be good fun, but it's likely to be overflowing, so reservations are required. Open daily from 7pm to midnight.

Wunderbar. Hochbrückenstrasse 3. ☎ **089/29-51-18.** Cover 7DM ($4). U-Bahn or S-Bahn: Marienplatz.

This is a cellar bar reconfigured into a chrome-laden dance club, where an 18-to-35 crowd sips drinks and cavorts to hip-hop and house music. Open nightly from 9pm to 4am.

JAZZ
Jazzclub Unterfahrt. Kirchenstrasse 96 (in the Haidhausen district). ☎ **089/4-48-27-94.** Cover 5DM–20DM ($2.85–$11.40) Tues–Sat, 10DM ($5.70) Sun jam session. U-Bahn: Ostbahnhof.

This is Munich's leading jazz club. The 120-seat establishment has a cozy ambience of pinewood paneling and flickering candles. Off to one corner is an art gallery, where paintings and sculptures are sold. The club presents live music Tuesday to Sunday from 9pm to 2am (it opens at 8pm). Sunday night there's a special jam session.

Mister B's. Herzog-Heinrichstrasse 38. ☎ **089/53-49-01.** Cover 8DM–10DM ($4.55–$5.70). U-Bahn: U3, U6 or Goetheplatz.

This small, dark club hosts a slightly older, mellower crowd than the rock and dance clubs. Blues, jazz, and rhythm-and-blues combos take the stage Thursday to Saturday. Open Tuesday to Sunday from 8pm to 3am.

Schwabinger Podium. Wagnerstrasse 1. ☎ **089/39-94-82.** No cover. U-Bahn: U3, U4, U5, or U6 to Münchner Freiheit.

This club offers varying nightly entertainment. Oldies and rock 'n' roll dominate some evenings. Open Sunday to Thursday from 8pm to 1am and Friday and Saturday from 8pm to 3am.

Tilt. Helmholtzstrasse 12. ☎ **089/1-29-79-69.** Cover 7DM–12DM ($4–$6.85). S-Bahn: Donnersbergerbrücke.

On weekends, this is the place for acid jazz. It's balanced by world-beat Thursdays and indie Tuesdays. Open Tuesday and Thursday to Saturday from 10pm to 4am.

THE BAR & CAFE SCENE
Alter Simpl. Türkenstrasse 57. ☎ **089/2-72-30-83.** Tram: 18. Bus: 53.

Once a literary cafe, Alter Simpl takes its name from a satirical revue of 1903. Today it attracts a wide segment of locals. The real fun of the place occurs after 11pm, when the iconoclastic artistic ferment begins to resemble Berlin more than Bavaria. Open daily from 11am to 3am, later on weekends.

Café Extrablatt. Leopoldstrasse 7, Schwabing. ☎ **089/33-33-33.** U-Bahn: Universität.

Owner Michael Grater is a prominent Munich newspaper columnist who has created a sprawling, smoke-filled sanctuary for writers, artists, and counterculture observers. Inside, it's decorated with celebrity photos and features a spacious well-designed bar, but the sidewalk tables are preferable during warm weather. Regulars convene here to converse and keep tabs on who's doing what, where. Open 7am to midnight Monday to Thursday, 9am to 1am on Friday and Saturday, and Sunday 9am to midnight.

Café Puck. Türkenstrasse 33. ☎ **089/2-80-22-80.** U-Bahn: Universität.

A dark-paneled retreat for students, artists, and workers, this cafe plays a variety of roles for its diverse crowd. It's a bar to students; a restaurant to the locals, who like the daily menu of German, American, Chinese, and Mexican dishes; and a hangover cure for artists and young people who creep in after mid-day for a big American breakfast. There's usually plenty of conversation and someone who wants to practice English, and there are always German- and English-language newspapers.

Haus der 111 Biere. Franzstrasse 3. ☎ **089/33-12-48.** U-Bahn: Münchener Freiheit.

This unassuming corner bar is the type of small, dark place that adds character to any urban neighborhood. Among the beer selections is the strongest brew in the world: EKU Doppelbock Kulminator, a 22-proof treat. Open Sunday to Thursday 5pm to 1am and Friday and Saturday 5pm to 3am.

Havana Club. Herrnstrasse 30. ☎ **089/29-18-84.** S-Bahn: Isartor.

This is not the spicy Cuban club you might expect. Employees may tell you about the bar's brush with fame, when Gloria Estefan made an appearance here, but its day-to-day function is as a lively singles bar fueled by rum-based cocktails. Open Monday to Wednesday from 6pm to 1am and Thursday to Saturday from 7pm to 2am.

Master's Home. Frauenstrasse 11 (close to the Marienplatz). ☎ **089/22-99-09.** S-Bahn: Marienplatz or Isator.

This is one of the historic core's most animated and convivial bars. It seems to attract a wider range of clients than most other watering holes in Munich. The setting is the ground floor of an imposing 19th-century building, within a large room outfitted with antiques and warm colors. The style evokes an Edwardian-era club in London. The premises also contain a restaurant, where fixed-price seven-course Italian-inspired meals cost 68DM ($38.75). Open nightly from 6:30pm to 3am, with the last order accepted in the kitchen at 1:30am.

Nachtcafé. Maximilianplatz 5. ☎ **089/59-59-00.** Tram: 19.

It hums, it thrives, and it captures everyone's nocturnal imagination. No other nightspot in Munich attracts such an array of soccer stars, film celebrities, literary figures, and, as one employee put it, "ordinary people, but only the most sympathetically crazy ones." Waves of patrons appear at different times of the evening: at 11pm, when live shows here begin; at 2am, when the restaurants close; and at 4am, when die-hard revelers seek a final drink in the predawn hours. There's no cover charge. The decor is updated 1950s; the music is jazz, blues, and soul. Open daily from 9pm to 6am.

O'Reilly's Irish Pub. Maximilianstrasse 29. ☎ **089/29-33-11.** U-Bahn: Marienplatz.

The all-Irish staff lends an air of authenticity to this pub, located in a historic vaulted cellar close to the Hotel Vier Jahreszeiten. Besides the obligatory Irish and German beers, you can also find good brews from England and the Czech Republic, as well as decent Irish stew, steaks, burgers, and mixed grills. Live Gaelic music is performed at irregular intervals throughout the month. Open Monday to Thursday from 4pm to 1am, Friday and Saturday from 4pm to 3am, and Sunday from noon to 1am.

Pusser's. Falkenturmstrasse 9. ☎ **089/22-05-00.** U-Bahn: Marienplatz.

This is the only European franchise of a small, well-run chain of restaurant-bars based in Tortola (in the British Virgin Islands). Its nostalgic decor celebrates the British navy of the 18th and 19th centuries. The specialties are Caribbean-inspired dishes and rum-based drinks. The cellar houses a piano bar. Open Monday to Saturday from 5pm to 3am, Sunday from 5pm to 2am.

Schultz. Barerstrasse 47. ☎ **089/2-71-47-11.** U-Bahn: U3 or U6 to Universität.

Schultz is a New York-style bar in Schwabing. It's popular with theater people, who crowd in as they do at Schumann's (see below) for smoke-filled chatter. The food is uncomplicated, and the decor, as they say here, is "unobvious and understated." Open daily from 5pm to 1am.

Schumann's. Maximilianstrasse 36. ☎ **089/22-90-60.** Tram: 19.

Located on Munich's most desirable shopping street, Schumann's doesn't have to waste any money on decor. The local *beau monde* keep it fully fashionable. In cold weather, guests retreat inside, but in summer, they prefer the terrace that spills out onto the street. Schumann's is known as a "thinking man's bar." Charles Schumann, author of three books, wanted a bar that would be an artistic, literary, and communicative social focus. Popular with the film, advertising, and publishing worlds, his place is said to have contributed to a remarkable renaissance of bar culture in the city. Drinks begin at 8.50DM ($4.85) but can be as steep as 25DM ($14.25). Open Monday to Friday from 5pm to 3am, Sunday from 6pm to 3am. Oddly enough, it's closed on Saturday.

Shalom. Leopoldstrasse 130. ☎ **089/36-66-62.** U-Bahn: Münchener Freiheit.

Over 30 and single? Come to this small room with an even smaller bar. You'll have plenty of time to chat with interesting folks while you wait your turn to order a drink. There's also a dance floor. Open nightly from 9pm to 4am.

Shamrock. Trautenwolfstrasse 6. ☎ **089/33-10-81.** U-Bahn: Universität.

At this beer-lover's bar, you can compare the great brews of Germany with the best of the Irish exports. There's free entertainment every night at 9pm, when a mixed bag of Irish, rock, country, folk, funk, or blues musicians take to the stage. Located near the university, Shamrock gets a fair share of the student crowd. Open Monday to Thursday from 5pm to 1am, Friday from 5pm to 3am, Saturday from 11am to 3am, and Sunday from 11am to 3am.

Tomate Sports. Siegesstrasse 19. ☎ **089/34-83-93.** U-Bahn: Münchener Freiheit.

Why is this bar named after a fruit? That's the only mystery about the place, which upon entrance, is immediately recognizable as a traditional sports bar, with a big-screen television broadcasting an overdose of athletics throughout the evening. Besides the soccer and rugby you might expect, the regulars also watch U.S. events, so stop in if you're a homesick American sports fan. The Paulaner brewery owns and operates this bar. Open Sunday to Thursday from 7:30pm to 1am, and Friday and Saturday from 7:30pm to 3am.

GAY CLUBS

Munich's gay and lesbian scene is centered around the blocks between the Viktualien-markt and Gärtnerplatz, particularly on Hans-Sachs-Strasse.

Moritz. Klenzestrasse 43. ☎ **089/2-01-67-76.** U-Bahn: Frauenhoferstrasse.

This is a stylish gay bar ringed with mirrors. Relax with drinks or food in red leather arm-chairs clustered around marble-topped tables. The eclectic menu includes well-prepared Thai dishes. Full meals, served until midnight, average 50DM ($28.50). Open Sunday to Thursday from 7pm to 2am and Friday and Saturday from 7pm to 3am.

New York. Sonnenstrasse 25. ☎ **089/59-10-56.** No cover Mon–Thurs, 10DM ($5.70) Fri–Sun, including 1st drink. U-Bahn: U1, U2, U3, or U6 to Sendlingertorplatz.

This is Munich's premier gay disco. The strident rhythms and electronic sounds might have been imported from New York, Los Angeles, or Paris. There are also laser-light shows. Clients range in age from 20 to 35; most wear jeans. Open daily from 11pm to 4am.

Soul City. Maximilianplatz 5. ☎ **089/59-52-72.** Cover 10DM ($5.70). U-Bahn: Karlsplatz.

This is a very popular gay dance club. There are nooks and crannies for conversation and one of the best sound systems in the city. The cover charge on Thursday and Friday includes free drinks, and on Saturday you get discount drink coupons. Open Thursday from 10pm until 6am, Friday from 10pm to 4am, and Saturday from 10pm to 9am.

Stadtcafé. Thalkirchnerstrasse 2. ☎ **089/26-69-49.** U-Bahn or S-Bahn: Marienplatz.

Come here for all the latest tips on what's happening in gay Munich, and stay for conversation amid a creative, intellectual crowd. Dialogues spread, from table to table—a distraction that doesn't faze the writers who toil away here. Open Sunday to Thursday from 11am to midnight and Friday and Saturday from 10am to 1am.

Teddy Bar. Hans-Sachs-Strasse 1. ☎ **089/260-33-59.** U-Bahn: Sendlingertor. Tram: 17, 18 or 27.

Teddy Bar is a small, cozy, gay bar decorated with teddy bears. It draws a congenial crowd, both foreign and domestic. There's no cover. Open nightly from 6pm to 3am. From October through April, there's Sunday brunch from 11am to 3pm.

10 Side Trips from Munich

The Bavarian Alps are within easy reach (see chapter 8), or you can head for Neuschwanstein (see chapter 6) to see Ludwig II's fairy-tale castle.

DACHAU

In 1933, what had once been a quiet little artists' community just 10 miles from Munich became a tragic symbol of the Nazi era. Shortly after Hitler became chancellor in March, Himmler and the SS set up the first German concentration camp on the grounds of a former ammunition factory. Countless prisoners arrived at Dachau between 1933 and 1945. The files show a registry of more than 206,000, but the exact number of people imprisoned here is unknown.

Upon entering the camp, **KZ-Gedenkstätte Dachau,** Alte-Roemar-Strasse 75 (☎ **08131/17-41**), you are faced by three memorial chapels—Catholic, Protestant, and Jewish—built in the early 1960s. Immediately behind the Catholic chapel is the "Lagerstrasse," the main camp road lined with poplar trees, once flanked by 32 barracks, each housing 208 prisoners. Two barracks have been rebuilt to give visitors insight into the conditions the prisoners endured.

The museum is housed in the large building that once contained the kitchen, laundry, and shower baths. Photographs and documents show the rise of the Nazi regime and the SS; other exhibits show the persecution of Jews and other prisoners. Every effort has been made to present the facts. The tour of Dachau is a truly moving experience.

You can get to the camp by taking the frequent S-Bahn trains (train no. S2) from the Hauptbahnhof to the Dachau station (direction: Petershausen), and then bus no. 724 or 726 from the station to the camp. The camp is open Tuesday to Sunday from 9am to 5pm; admission is free. The English version of a documentary film, *KZ-Dachau,* is shown at 11:30am and 3:30pm. All documents are translated in the catalog, which is available at the museum entrance.

8

The Bavarian Alps

If you walk into a rustic alpine inn along the German-Austrian frontier and ask the innkeeper if he or she is German, you'll most likely get the indignant response, "Of course not! I'm Bavarian." Some older inhabitants of the region can still remember when Bavaria was a kingdom with its own prerogatives, even while a part of the German Reich (1871–1918).

The huge province of Bavaria includes not only the Alps but also Franconia, Lake Constance, and the capital city of Munich. In this chapter, we'll explore the region of the mountains along the Austrian frontier, a world unto themselves. The hospitality of this area is famous, and the picture of the plump, rosy-cheeked innkeeper with a constant smile is no myth. Many travelers think of the Alps as a winter vacationland, but you'll find that nearly all the Bavarian resorts and villages boast year-round attractions.

Munich is the major driving gateway, with Autobahns leading directly to the Bavarian Alps. If you're beginning your tour in Garmisch-Partenkirchen in the west, you should fly into Munich. However, if your destination is Berchtesgaden in the eastern Alps, then the nearest airport is in Salzburg, Austria.

Note that the town of Oberammergau will be presenting its famous **Passion Play** in the summer of 2000, for the first time since 1990.

OUTDOORS IN THE BAVARIAN ALPS   The Bavarian Alps are both a winter wonderland and a summer playground. The **skiing** here is the best in Germany. A regular winter snowfall in January and February usually measures from 12 to 20 inches. This leaves about 6 feet of snow in the areas served by ski lifts. The great **Zugspitzplatt** snowfield can be reached in spring or autumn by a rack railway. The Zugspitze, at 9,720 feet above sea level, is the tallest mountain peak in Germany. Ski slopes begin at a height of 8,700 feet.

The second great ski district in the Alps is **Berchtesgadener Land,** with alpine skiing centered on Jenner, Rossfeld, Götschen, and Hochschwarzeck. Snow conditions are consistently good until March. Visitors will find a cross-country skiing center, many miles of tracks kept in first-class condition, natural toboggan runs, one artificial ice run for toboggan and skibob runs, and artificial ice-skating and curling rinks.

In summer, **alpine hiking** is a major attraction—climbing mountains, enjoying nature, and watching animals in the forest. Hikers are able at times to observe endangered species firsthand. One of the best areas for hiking is the 4,060-foot **Eckbauer,** lying on the southern fringe of Partenkirchen (the tourist office at Garmisch-Partenkirchen will supply maps and details). Many visitors come to the Alps in summer just to hike through the **Berchtesgaden National Park,** bordering the Austrian province of Salzburg. The 8,091-foot Watzmann Mountain, the Königssee (Germany's cleanest, clearest lake), and parts of the Jenner—the pride of Berchtesgaden's four ski areas—are within the boundaries of the national park, which has well-mapped trails cut through protected areas, leading the hiker through spectacular natural beauty. For information about hiking in the park, contact **Nationalparkhaus,** Franziskanerpl 7, 83471 Berchtesgaden (☎ **08652/ 64343**).

From Garmisch-Partenkirchen, serious hikers can embark on full-day or overnight alpine treks, following clearly marked footpaths and staying in isolated mountain huts. Some huts are staffed and serve meals. For the truly remote unsupervised huts, you'll be provided with information on how to gain access. For information, inquire at the local tourist office or write to the government-subsidized **German Alpine Association,** Am Perlacher Forst 186, 80997 München (☎ **089/651-0720**), which will also direct you to a privately owned tour operator, the **Summit Club,** an outfit devoted to the organization of high-altitude expeditions throughout Europe and the world.

If you're a true outdoorsperson, you'll briefly savor the somewhat touristy facilities of Garmisch-Partenkirchen, and then use it as a base for explorations of the rugged Berchtesgaden National Park, which is within an easy commute of Garmisch. You can also stay at one of the inns in Mittenwald or Oberammergau and take advantage of a wide roster of outdoor diversions there. Any of the outfitters below will provide directions and link-ups with their sports programs from wherever you decide to stay. Street maps of Berchtesgaden and its environs are usually available for free from the **Kurdirektion** (the local tourist office) at Berchtesgaden (☎ **08652/967-0**), and more intricately detailed maps of the surrounding alpine topography are available for a fee.

Another summer activity is **ballooning,** which, weather permitting, can be arranged through **Outdoor Club Berchtesgaden,** Ludwig-Ganghofer-Strasse 201/2 (☎ 08652/50-01). **Cycling** and **mountain biking** are also popular; try the rental facilities of **Full Stall,** Maximilianstrasse 16 (☎ 08652/948450).

Anglers will find plenty of **fishing** opportunities (especially salmon, pike-perch, and trout) at Lake Hintersee and the rivers Ramsauer Ache and Königsseer Ache. To acquire a fishing permit, contact the **Kurdirektion** (tourist office; see above) at Berchtesgaden, which will direct you to any of four different authorities, based on where you want to fish. For fishing specifically within the Hintersee, contact officials at the **Hotel Gamsboch** in Ramsau (☎ **08657/98800**).

Despite the obvious dangers, **hang gliding** or **paragliding** from the vertiginous slopes of Mount Jenner can be thrilling. To arrange it, contact **Full Stall** (see above), or Full Stall's sibling organization, **Berchtesgadener Gleitschirmflieger e.V.,** Königsseestrasse 15 (☎ 08652/23-63).

You can also practice your **kayaking** or **white-water rafting** techniques on one of the area's many rivers (water level permitting), such as the Ramsauer, Königisser, Bischofswiesener, and Berchtesgadener Aches. For information and options, contact the above-mentioned **Outdoor Club Berchtesgaden.**

If you would like to go **swimming** in an alpine lake—not to everyone's body temperature—there are many *"lidos"* found in the Bavarian Forest.

Of course, there's plenty to do outdoors during the winter as well, including some of the greatest **alpine** and **cross-country skiing** in all of Europe. Call the local "Snow-Telefon" at ☎ 08652/967-297 for current snow conditions. There's also skating between October and February at the world-class ice-skating rink in Berchtesgaden. Less reliable, but more picturesque, is skating on the surface of the Hintersee Lake,

The Bavarian Alps

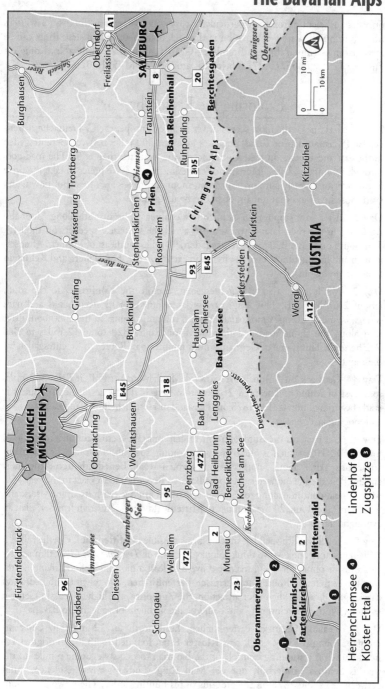

Linderhof ❶
Zugspitze ❸
Herrenchiemsee ❹
Kloster Ettal ❷

once it's sufficiently frozen. A particularly cozy way to spend an hour on a winter's night is to huddle with a companion in the back of a **horse-drawn sled.** Rides can be arranged in Garmisch through Brandtner, GMbH, at the **Café Waldstein,** Königseer Fussweg 17 (☎ **08652/2427**). The cost is around 90DM ($51.30) per hour.

Exploring the Region by Car

Acclaimed as one of the most scenic drives in all of Europe, the ✪ **Deutsche Alpenstrasse (German Alpine Road)** stretches for some 300 miles between Berchtesgaden in the east and Lindau on Lake Constance in the west (see chapter 9). The road goes through mountains, lakes, forests, and "castles in the sky." We prefer to take the drive in early spring or early autumn. In winter, mountain passes are often shut down, and even those highways that remain open can be dangerous.

Day 1   After your stopover in Munich (see chapter 7), head south along Autobahn A8 (drive in the right lane if you want to avoid the hysterical speeders on the left). Turn south on Route B20 for **Berchtesgaden,** 98 miles southeast of Munich. After settling in and having lunch, take an afternoon excursion to **Obersalzberg** and **Kehlstein** (you can go by bus).

Day 2   While still based in Berchtesgaden, explore the **Königssee,** to the south (about 2 hr. by boat). This long, narrow lake, famed for its steep banks and dark waters, is one of Europe's most dramatic and romantic sights. In the afternoon, drive west along the alpine road and then north on Route B20 some 12 miles to **Bad Reichenhall.** This is one of Germany's most famous spas. Return to Berchtesgaden for the night.

Day 3   Get back on Autobahn A8 toward Munich but turn off at **Prien,** 53 miles southeast of Munich. The premier attraction here is the Neues Schloss, a fantastic castle begun by Ludwig II in 1878 on the island of Herrenchiemsee. You can find food and lodging at Prien.

Day 4   Get back on the Autobahn to Munich, but take a cross-country route (472) toward Bad Tölz, which is one of Bavaria's leading spas, although it lacks any major attractions. After about another 9 miles you'll reach **Benediktbeuern,** the most ancient Benedictine monastery in upper Bavaria. Records trace it back to the year 739. After a look, continue along for 4 miles to **Kochel am See,** with its alpine vistas, and from here take Route 20 for 20 miles to **Mittenwald** on the Austrian frontier. Plan an overnight stay.

Day 5   You'll want to spend as much time as possible in **Mittenwald.** Goethe called it a "living picture book"—we think it looks like part of *The Sound of Music* film set. It's also a major center for violin making. Give it at least a morning before driving northwest for 12 miles on Route 2 to **Garmisch-Partenkirchen,** two towns combined. After checking in, head for the major attraction, the **Zugspitze,** the highest peak in German territory. Wear warm clothing. This could be the highlight of your trip to Bavaria.

Day 6   Leaving Garmisch-Partenkirchen, head north for 12 miles to **Oberammergau.** Along the way, you'll pass **Kloster Ettal,** founded in 1330. Its original 10-sided church is a stunning example of the Bavarian rococo style. Some 6 miles to the west is **Schloss Linderhof,** one of "Mad King" Ludwig's royal residences, built between 1874 and 1878 on the grounds of his hunting lodge. These two attractions will take up most of your day, but you'll still arrive in the little old wood-carver's village of Oberammergau, 7 miles northeast of Linderhof, in time to wander about. Later, enjoy a hearty Bavarian dinner before turning in to your alpine bed.

1 Berchtesgaden

98 miles SE of Munich, 11 miles SE of Bad Reichenhall, 14 miles S of Salzburg

Ever since Ludwig I of Bavaria chose this resort as a favorite hideaway, the tourist business in Berchtesgaden has been booming. The village is situated below the many summits of Watzmann Mountain (8,901 ft. at its highest point). According to legend, the mountain peaks were once a royal family who were so evil that God punished them by turning them into rocks.

Berchtesgaden is a quiet old alpine village with ancient winding streets and a medieval marketplace and castle square. Its name is often linked with Hitler and the Nazi hierarchy, but this impression is erroneous. Hitler's playground was actually at Obersalzberg, on a wooded plateau about half a mile up the mountain.

ESSENTIALS

GETTING THERE By Train The **Berchtesgaden Bahnhof** lies on the Munich-Freilassing rail line. Twelve trains a day arrive from Munich (trip time: 1½ hr.). For rail information and schedules, call ☎ **08652/50-74.** Berchtesgaden has three mountain rail lines—the Obersalzbergbahn, Jennerbahn, and Hirscheckbahn—going to the mountain plateaus around the resorts. For more information, contact **Berchtesgadener Bergbahn AG** (☎ **08652/9-58-10**) and **Obersalzbergbahn AG** (☎ **08652/25-61**).

By Bus Regional bus service to alpine villages and towns around Berchtesgaden is offered by **RVO Regionalverkehr Oberbayern** at Berchtesgaden (☎ **08652/54-73**).

By Car Access by car is via the A8 Autobahn from Munich in the north or Route 20 from the south. The drive from Munich takes about 2 hours.

VISITOR INFORMATION Contact the **Kurdirektion,** Königsseerstrasse 2 (☎ **08652/96-70**). It's open Monday to Friday 8am to 5pm and Saturday 9am to noon.

SEEING THE SIGHTS

The Stiftskirche (Abbey Church), dating from 1122, is adjacent to the Königliches Schloss Berchtesgaden. The church is mainly Romanesque, with Gothic additions. One of its ancient twin steeples was destroyed by lightning and rebuilt in 1866. The interior contains many fine works of art; the high altar has a painting by Zott dating from 1669. In the vestry is a small silver altar donated by Empress Maria Theresa of Austria.

Schlossplatz, partially enclosed by the castle and Stiftskirche, is the most attractive plaza in town. On the opposite side of the square from the church is a 16th-century arcade that leads to **Marktplatz,** with typical alpine houses and a wooden fountain from 1677 (restored by Ludwig I in 1860). Some of Berchtesgaden's oldest inns and houses border this square. Extending from Marktplatz is the **Nonntal,** lined with more old houses, some built into rocks of the Lockstein Mountain, which towers above the town.

A minor but interesting museum, **Heimatmuseum,** Schloss Aldelsheim, Schroffenbergallee 6 (☎ **08652/44-10**), is devoted to alpine wood carving. Wood carving as a craft here predates the more fabled wood carving at Oberammergau. Some of the best examples in Germany are on display in this museum. Entry is allowed only as part of a guided tour offered Monday to Friday at 10am and again at 3pm for a charge of 3DM ($1.70).

Königliches Schloss Berchtesgaden. Schlossplatz 2. ☎ **08652/20-85.** Admission 7DM ($4) adults, 3DM ($1.70) children 6–16, free for children 5 and under. Easter–Sept Sun–Fri 10am–1pm and 2–5pm; Oct–Easter Mon–Fri 10am–1pm and 2–5pm. Bus: 9539.

In the Middle Ages, Berchtesgaden grew up around a powerful Augustinian monastery. Its monks introduced the art of wood carving, for which the town is still noted. When the town became part of Bavaria in 1809, the abbey was secularized and eventually converted to a palace for the royal family Wittelsbach. Now it is a museum, mostly devoted to the royal collection of sacred art, including wood sculptures by the famed artists Veit Stoss and Tilman Riemenschneider. There's also a gallery of 19th-century art, a collection of Italian furniture from the 16th century, and a display of 17th- and 18th-century pistols and guns.

Salzbergwerk Berchtesgaden. Bergwerkstrasse 83. ☎ **08652/6-00-20.** Admission 21DM ($11.95) adults, 11DM ($6.25) children. May 1–Oct 15 daily 9am–5pm; Oct 16–Apr 30 Mon–Sat 12:30–3:30pm. Bus: 9539.

These salt mines at the eastern edge of town were once owned by the Augustinian monastery. Operations began here in 1517. The deposits are more than 990 feet thick and are still processed today from four galleries or "hills." Visitors are first given protective miner's clothing. Older children will especially enjoy the guided tours that begin with a ride into the mine on a small wagonlike train. After nearly a half-mile journey, visitors leave the train and explore the rest of the mine, sliding down a miner's slide, and riding on the salt lake in a ferry. The highlight of the tour is the "chapel," a grotto containing unusually shaped salt formations illuminated for an eerie effect. The 1½-hour tour can be taken any time of the year, in any weather.

WHERE TO STAY
MODERATE

Hotel Fischer. Königsseerstrasse 51 (a short uphill walk from the Berchtesgaden railway station), 83471 Berchtesgaden. ☎ **08652/95-50.** Fax 08652/6-48-73. www.hotel-fischer.de. E-mail: hotelfischer@koenigssee.com. 40 units. TV TEL. 162DM–244DM ($92.35–$139.10) double. Half board available for stays of 3 days or more, 182DM–264DM ($103.75–$150.50) double. Rates include buffet breakfast. V. Parking 6DM ($3.40). Closed Nov to mid-Dec and mid-Mar to Apr 10.

This hotel overlooking the town was built in the late 1970s in the Bavarian style. It may be the best choice in town. Fronted with dark-stained wooden balconies against a cream-colored facade, it rambles pleasantly along the hillside. The bedrooms are cozy and traditional, each with a regional theme. On the premises are an indoor swimming pool, a sauna, a solarium, and an alpine-style restaurant and bar.

Vier Jahreszeiten. Maximilianstrasse 20, 83471 Berchtesgaden. ☎ **08652/95-20.** Fax 08652/50-29. E-mail: millers-hotel@online.de. 59 units. TEL. 165DM–260DM ($94.05–$148.20) double. Rates include buffet breakfast. AE, DC, MC, V. Free outdoor parking; 10DM ($5.70) in garage.

Vier Jahreszeiten is an old inn with modern extensions. It's in the heart of the village and has a colorful and distinguished restaurant. The inn has been remodeled and improved over the years and now offers a good level of comfort to its guests, almost rivaling the Fischer. Some of the newer units, with tiny sitting rooms and balconies, resemble suites; most have minibars and TVs. In addition to the main dining room, there's a terrace for summer dining and viewing. The hotel also offers an indoor pool, a sauna, and a solarium.

INEXPENSIVE

Hotel Krone. Am Rad 5, 83471 Berchtesgaden. ☎ **08652/94600.** Fax 08652/946010. 21 units. TV TEL. 100DM–124DM ($57–$70.70) double. 124DM–160DM ($70.70–$91.20) suite. MC. Closed: Nov 1–Dec 20.

One of the most appealing bargains in Berchtesgaden is this well-built chalet-inspired hotel. Operated by live-in managers, the Grafe family, and permeated with a sense of alpine thrift and good cheer, it offers cozy bedrooms sheathed with lots of varnished pine. Each has a balcony or terrace of its own, a comfortable mattress, and a compact bathroom. The dining room, and its adjacent bar, charges only 18DM ($10.25) per person extra for half board, a price so low that it virtually guarantees that most guests will take at least one of their daily meals here.

Watzmann. Franziskanerplatz 2, 83471 Berchtesgaden. ☎ **08652/2005.** Fax 08652/5174. 38 units, 16 with shower. 33DM–69DM ($18.80–$39.35) double without shower, 59DM–72DM ($33.65–$41.05) double with shower. AE, DC, MC, V. Free parking. Closed Nov 1–Dec 25.

This is a good bet for an affordable choice. The Watzmann is located opposite the church on the main square. It has a large outdoor terrace and a cozy Bavarian-inspired decor, with turn-of-the-century artifacts, huge carved wooden pillars, oak ceilings, and wrought-iron chandeliers. Everyone seems to stop here for a beer, coffee, or lunch. The doors of the simply furnished guest rooms are painted with floral murals. Bedrooms are small but well maintained. Rooms with bathrooms have shower stalls; for those without, corridor bathrooms are adequate (you rarely have to wait in line).

Wittelsbach. Maximilianstrasse 16, 83471 Berchtesgaden. ☎ **08652/9-63-80.** Fax 08652/6-63-04. www.urlaubstip.de. E-mail: hotelwittelsbach@t-online.de. 32 units. MINIBAR TV TEL. 100DM–160DM ($57–$91.20) double; 200DM ($114) suite. Rates include buffet breakfast. AE, CB, DC, DISC, MC, V. Free parking.

The Wittelsbach has been stylishly modernized and now offers well-furnished rooms in the heart of Berchtesgaden. The small rooms are quiet and sunny; most have balconies with fine views of the mountains. Breakfast is the only meal served. The hotel also offers a solarium, as well as a bar with a lounge.

WHERE TO DINE

Demming-Restaurant Le Gourmet. Sunklergässchen 2, 83471 Berchtesgaden. ☎ **08652/96-10.** Reservations required. Main courses 13DM–22DM ($7.40–$12.55). AE, DC, MC, V accepted from hotel guests only. Daily 5:30–8:30pm. Closed Oct 26–Dec 10. BAVARIAN/INTERNATIONAL.

The Demming hotel contains one of the town's best restaurants. Only fresh ingredients are used in the well-prepared dishes of hearty mountain fare, including roast beef with chive sauce, and an array of veal and fish choices. Sometimes we wish the chef could be less timid in his cookery, but what you get isn't bad. The hotel rents plainly furnished but comfortable rooms, costing 160DM ($91.20) for a double.

SIDE TRIPS TO KÖNIGSSEE & OBERSALZBERG
✪ KÖNIGSSEE

This is the "jewel in the necklace" of Berchtesgaden. The waters of this scenic lake appear to be dark-green because of the steep mountains that jut upward from its shores. Low-lying land on the lake's northern edge contains a parking lot and a few charming inns and bathing facilities, but the rest of the lake is enclosed by mountains, making it impossible to walk along the shoreline. The only way to explore the waters, unless you're like one of the mountain goats you may see above, is by boat. Electric motorboats—no noisy gas-powered launches allowed—carry passengers on tours around the lake throughout the summer and occasionally even in winter.

The favorite spot on Königssee is the tiny flat peninsula on the western bank, the site of a basilica as early as the 12th century. Today the Catholic **Chapel of St.**

Bartholomew is still used for services (except in winter). The clergy must arrive by boat, since there's no other way to approach the peninsula. The adjacent buildings include a fisher's house and a restaurant, which was once a favored hunting lodge of the Bavarian kings. Here you can sample trout and salmon caught in the crisp, clean waters. At the southern end of the lake you come to the Salet-Alm, where the tour boats make a short stop near a thundering waterfall. If you follow the footpath up the hillside, you'll reach the summer pastures used by the cattle of Berchtesgaden. Just over the hill is **Lake Obersee,** part of Königssee until an avalanche separated them 8 centuries ago. If you prefer a shorter trip, you can take the boat as far as St. Bartholomew and back.

To reach Königssee from Berchtesgaden by car, follow the signs south from the town (only 3 miles). It's also a pleasant hour's walk or a short ride by electric train or bus from the center of town.

For information about boat excursions, call **Schiffahrt Königssee** at ☎ **08652/96-36-13.** An entire tour of Königssee requires about 2 hours. There are boats in summer every 15 minutes, so getting off one boat and climbing aboard another is easy if you want to break up the tour. During the summer, the first boat departs every morning at 7:15am and the last boat leaves at 5:30pm. In winter, boats leave about every 45 minutes. The important stops are at Salet and St. Batholomä. A round-trip fare for a lake tour is 21.50DM ($12.25) for adults and half fare for children.

⊙ OBERSALZBERG

The drive from Berchtesgaden to Obersalzberg at 3,300 feet is one of Bavaria's most scenic routes. Obersalzberg was where Hitler settled down in a rented cottage after his prison term while he completed *Mein Kampf.* After he came to power in 1933, he bought Haus Wachenfeld and had it remodeled into his residence, the **Berghof.** Obersalzberg became the center for holiday living for Nazis such as Martin Bormann and Hermann Göring.

Today, you can walk around the ruins of Hitler's Berghof. This was where the famous 1938 meeting took place between Hitler and British Prime Minister Neville Chamberlain. The result was the Munich Agreement, which Chamberlain so mistakenly declared would bring "peace in our time." The Berghof was destroyed in 1952 by Bavarian government authorities at the request of the U.S. Army—the Americans did not want a monument to Hitler. One of the only fully remaining structures from the Nazi compound is a guest house called the General Walker Hotel that was used by U.S. troops stationed in Europe.

Hitler built the bunkers and air-raid shelter in 1943. Three thousand laborers completed the work in 9 months, connecting all the major buildings of the Obersalzberg area to the underground rooms. Many readers have expressed their disappointment when reaching this site, apparently thinking they would tour Hitler's sumptuously decorated private apartments. The only structures open to visitors are a part of Hitler's air raid shelter system and prison cells used by the Reichssicherheitsdienst (state security police), which were considered a last refuge for Hitler and other high officials. Wear good walking shoes and be prepared to run into some VERBOTEN! signs.

A major point of interest to visitors is the **Kehlstein,** or **Eagle's Nest,** which can be reached only by a thrilling bus ride up a 4½-mile-long mountain road, blasted out of solid rock. This outstanding feat of engineering was begun in 1937 under the leadership of Bormann, who intended it as a 50th-birthday gift for Hitler. The Eagle's Nest was not, as the name may suggest, a military installation. It was a site for relaxation and was not popular with Hitler, who rarely visited it.

To reach the spot, you must enter a tunnel and take a 400-foot elevator ride through a shaft in the Kehlstein Mountain to its summit. The building, with solid granite walls and huge picture windows, houses a mountain restaurant, the Kehlsteinhaus, which is open from mid-May to mid-October. You can enjoy the panoramic view and explore the rooms of the original teahouse, which include Eva Braun's living room. Below you'll have a view of the Obersalzberg area. Nearby is the site of Martin Bormann's house and the SS barracks. To the north you can see as far as Salzburg, Austria; below the mountain to the west is Berchtesgaden, with its rivers dwindling off into threads in the distance.

Eagle's Nest may soon become the centerpiece of a luxurious holiday resort, if the Bavarian Finance Ministry goes through with its plans to lease the 262-acre Berghof site. Jewish groups have attacked the proposal. Shimon Samuels, director of International Liaison for the Simon Wiesenthal Center in Paris, told the press the proposed resort might "turn into a shrine for every lunatic in Europe."

For information about trips to Obersalzberg and Kehlstein, call ☎ **08652/ 54-73.** Local RVO buses based in Berchtesgaden run from the Berchtesgaden Post Office to Obersalzberg-Hintereck. The round-trip journey costs 5.80DM ($3.30). Entrance to the bunker and prison cells is 5DM ($2.85); they're open daily from 9am to 5pm. From Obersalzberg (the Hintereck parking lot), the Kehlstein line operates daily from mid-May to mid-October; during that time full catering services are offered at Kehlsteinhaus. The bus to Kehlstein and elevator ride through the rock costs 20DM ($11.40). If you're up to it, instead of taking the elevator, you can walk the final stretch to the Eagle's Nest from the summit parking lot in about 30 minutes. The Kehlstein road is closed to private vehicles.

Guided tours in English are offered by the American-run **Berchtesgaden Mini Bus Tours,** Königsseerstrasse 2 (☎ **08652/6-49-71**). Tours, including Obersalzberg, Eagle's Nest, and the Bunker System as an afternoon history package, are conducted daily from mid-May to mid-October, starting at the Berchtesgaden tourist office. The service also takes visitors to sights such as the Salt Mines and the Königssee. A 3½-hour tour costs 47DM ($26.80) adults, 13DM ($7.40) under 25, free 6 and under. There's a tour information and ticket booth at the Berchtesgaden tourist office, across the street from the train station. One of the most popular tours offered is the "Sound of Music" tour to nearby Salzburg.

Obersalzberg is also becoming an important health resort; the ruins of Bormann's Gusthof Farm are now the Skytop Lodge, a popular golfing center in summer and a ski site in winter.

WHERE TO STAY

Hotel zum Türken. 83471 Berchtesgaden-Obersalzberg. ☎ **08652/24-28.** Fax 08652/47-10. 17 units, 13 with shower or bathroom. 130DM ($74.10) double without shower or bathroom, 210DM ($119.70) double with shower or bathroom. Rates include continental breakfast. AE, DC, MC, V. Free parking. Closed Tues. Obersalzberg bus from Berchtesgaden.

The Hotel zum Türken, located in Obersalzberg, is legendary. It's designed in the alpine style and has terraces (for hotel guests only) with views. On its facade is a large painted sign of "The Turk"—legend has it that the first owner was a veteran of the Turkish war. In the 1930s, anti-Nazi remarks led to trouble for the proprietor, Herr Schuster, who was arrested. Afterward Bormann used the building as a Gestapo headquarters; it then fell victim to air raids and looting in April 1945. Herr Schuster's daughter, Therese Partner, was able to buy the ruin from the German government in 1949. The small-to-medium-sized rooms are well maintained. They don't have private phones, but there is an international pay phone in the main hallway. There's also a self-service bar on the ground floor.

2 Bad Reichenhall

84 miles SE of Munich, 12 miles SE of Salzburg

The best German spas can call themselves *Staatsbad,* and Bad Reichenhall bears that title with pride. This old salt town is the most important curative spa in the Bavarian Alps. Mountain chains surround it, protecting it from the winds. Its brine springs, with a salt content as high as 24%, are the most powerful saline springs in Europe, and the town has been a source of salt for more than 2,400 years. The combination of the waters and the pure air has made Bad Reichenhall a recognized spa for centuries.

In 1848 King Maximilian of Bavaria stayed here, popularizing Bad Reichenhall as a fashionable resort. Today, visitors come from all over the world to take the waters, which supposedly treat asthma and other respiratory ailments. Treatment sessions take place almost exclusively in the morning at seven resort institutes, the therapy ranging from simply drinking the water to pneumatotherapy—even electronic lungs for the most serious cases. Although Bad Reichenhall takes the medical side of the cure seriously, spa authorities encourage visitors to enjoy its many attractions as well.

ESSENTIALS

GETTING THERE By Train Bad Reichenhall is connected to the airport at Munich (see chapter 7) by frequent train service through Rosenheim. The trip takes about 2½ hours. For information and schedules, call ☎ **01805/99-66-33.**

By Bus Regional bus service to and from Bad Reichenhall is provided by **Regionalverkehr Oberbayers Betrieb** (☎ **08652/54-73** for information). From the spa, you can take a bus to various beautiful spots in the Bavarian Alps, including Berchtesgaden.

By Car Access is by the A8 Autobahn, from Munich in the north and Salzburg in the south. Exit on Federal Highway 21 into Bad Reichenhall.

VISITOR INFORMATION For tourist information, go to the **Kur- und Verkehrsverein im Kurgastzentrum,** Wittelsbacherstrasse 15 (☎ **08651/60-63-03**). It's open Monday to Friday 9am to 5pm and Saturday 9am to 2pm.

SIGHTS & ACTIVITIES

The ideal climate permits a complete spectrum of outdoor events, from excursions into the mountains for skiing or hiking to tennis tournaments. Gardeners and botanists will enjoy the spa gardens; the sheltered location of the town amid the lofty Alps permits the growth of several varieties of tropical plants, giving the gardens a lush, exotic appearance. There's also a wide choice of indoor activities, from symphony concerts to folklore presentations to gambling in the casino.

The great fire of 1834 destroyed much of the town, but many of the impressive churches survived. An outstanding example is **St. Zeno,** a 12th-century Gothic church showing a later baroque influence. Its most remarkable feature is its painted interior, centering on the carved altarpiece of the *Coronation of the Virgin.*

Bad Reichenhaller Saltmuseum, Alte Saline Reichenhall (☎ **08651/7-00-25-1**), just a short walk from the Kurgarten, is the home of the ancient industry responsible for the growth and prosperity of Bad Reichenhall from Celtic times to the present. Parts of the old plant still stand today, but most of it was reconstructed in the mid-19th century by Ludwig I of Bavaria. The large pumps and huge marble caverns are impressive. Tours are offered May 1 to October 31 daily 10am to noon, and 2 to 4pm; November to May 10 Tuesday and Thursday 2 to 4pm. Admission is 8.50DM ($4.85) for adults and 4.50DM ($2.55) for children; 25DM ($14.25) adults and 13DM ($7.40) children if the ticket combines the Saltmuseum with the Salzberwerk Berchtesgaden.

SHOPPING

Shops here are predictably upscale, rather limited in scope, and conservative. The town's only department store, **Kaufhaus Huhasz,** Ludwigstrasse 23 (☎ 08651/9-73-80), stocks some traditional items. About 90% of the resort's shops are in a pedestrian-only zone, which is centered around the **Ludwigstrasse** and the **Salzburgerstrasse.** Since 1856, **Josef Mack Co.,** Ludwigstrasse 36 (☎ 08651/7-82-80), has been the region's best place for medicinal herbs, many of which are grown in the Bavarian Alps.

WHERE TO STAY
VERY EXPENSIVE

✪ **Steigenberger Axelmannstein.** Salzburger Strasse 2–6, 83435 Bad Reichenhall. ☎ **800/223-5652** in the U.S. and Canada, or 08651/77-70. Fax 08651/59-32. 159 units. MINIBAR TV TEL. 355DM–465DM ($202.35–$265.05) double; 590DM–990DM ($336.30–$564.30) suite. Rates include buffet breakfast. AE, DC, V. Parking 10DM ($5.70).

This first-class hotel, set in its own 7½-acre garden, is the best in town for traditional charm and spa conveniences, far superior to its closest rival, the Parkhotel Luisenbad. Public rooms are traditionally furnished with antiques and reproductions. Many of the well-furnished bedrooms have views of the encircling Bavarian Alps. Rooms are generally spacious. Bathrooms are medium in size, and come with hair dryers and deluxe toiletries.

Dining/Diversions: The Parkrestaurant, opening onto a garden, attracts many nonresidents, as does the cozy Axel-Stüberl, with regional dishes. The wood-paneled Axel-Bar features live entertainment daily.

Amenities: Cure department, sauna, solarium, fitness center, cosmetic studio, hairdresser, indoor pool, tennis court, room service, laundry service, and dry cleaning.

EXPENSIVE

Parkhotel Luisenbad. Ludwigstrasse 33, 83435 Bad Reichenhall. ☎ **08651/60-40.** Fax 08651/6-29-28.www.parkhotel.de. E-mail: luisenbad@parkhotel.de. 89 units. MINIBAR TV TEL. 254DM–340DM ($144.80–$193.80) double; 244DM–304DM ($139.10–$173.30) suite. Half board 44DM ($25.10) per person. Rates include continental breakfast. DC, MC, V. Parking 2DM–10DM ($1.15–$5.70).

A world unto itself, Parkhotel Luisenbad is an 1860s hotel with a new guest-room wing in a garden setting. It's a good second choice to the Steigenberger, especially if you like traditional hotels. Its best feature is the indoor pool with a glass wall, bringing the outdoors inside. The more modern rooms are handsome, with bold colors and tasteful furnishings. But many guests prefer the older, more traditional rooms. All rooms range in size from medium to spacious. The bathrooms are well maintained, with hair dryers and deluxe toiletries.

Dining: The lobby and the Restaurant die Holzstube (see "Where to Dine," below) have been renovated in a classic provincial style and decorated in warm colors, making the hotel more attractive than ever.

Amenities: Thermal baths, inhalations, massages, mud baths, Finnish sauna, Jacuzzi, room service, laundry service, dry cleaning.

MODERATE

Hotel Bayerischer Hof. Bahnhofplatz 14, 83426 Bad Reichenhall. ☎ **08651/60-90.** Fax 08651/60-91-11. 64 units. MINIBAR TV TEL. 140DM–220DM ($79.80–$125.40) double. Rates include buffet breakfast. AE, DC, MC, V. Parking 8DM ($4.55).

This modern and inviting hotel is in the center of the spa on Main Street. It has a surprising number of facilities for a small place, although it's hardly in the same league as the Steigenberger or the Parkhotel Luisenbad. The guest rooms are furnished in a well-maintained, functional modern style. The staff is well trained. The hotel is equipped with a roof-garden indoor pool with Finnish sauna, a solarium, a bowling alley, and a salon for massage and cosmetic treatments. In addition to the main restaurant, there's a cafe with live music and a nightclub with international acts. The reception desk is helpful in arranging excursions to Obersalzburg, Berchtesgadener Land, and Salzburg. Guests can also rent bikes. If you visit in winter, the staff will arrange cross-country and downhill skiing.

INEXPENSIVE

Hotel Kurfürst. Kurfürstenstrasse 11, 83435 Bad Reichenhall. ☎ **08651/27-10.** Fax 08651/24-11. 13 units. MINIBAR TV TEL. 104DM–130DM ($59.30–$74.10) double; from 160DM ($91.20) suite. Rates include buffet breakfast. AE, DC, MC, V. Closed Dec 15–Feb 1. Free parking.

Kurfürst is a family-run hotel near the outskirts of Bad Reichenhall, close to the river and about a 10-minute walk to anywhere else in town. A trim and well-maintained modern facade in yellow stucco opens into a lobby with Oriental rugs and a curving staircase. Rooms are spacious and sunny; some have terraces with tables and chairs. Dinner is available to hotel guests only.

Salzburger Hof. Mozartstrasse 7, 83435 Bad Reichenhall. ☎ **08651/9-76-90.** Fax 08651/97-69-99. 25 units. TV TEL. 130DM–160DM ($74.10–$91.20) double. Rates include continental breakfast. AE, MC, V. Parking 5DM ($2.85).

This three-story hotel is one of the best buys in town. Its public rooms are filled with old Bavarian charm. Best of all are the compact guest rooms, most of which contain streamlined sofas, window desks, beds with built-in headboards, and armchairs around a breakfast table; all open onto tiny balconies. The room prices depend on the view.

WHERE TO DINE

Restaurant die Holzstube. In the Parkhotel Luisenbad, Ludwigstrasse 33. ☎ **08651/60-40.** Reservations recommended. Main courses 20DM–30DM ($11.40–$17.10). AE, DC, MC, V. Daily noon–2pm and 6:30–9pm. GERMAN/ITALIAN/INTERNATIONAL.

The old-fashioned tradition and service here attract many regular patrons. This a place where you can watch the flowers bloom and enjoy a world-class cuisine (with many diet-conscious selections). You might try one of the kitchen's own original recipes: for example, marinated and roasted medaillons of venison Königin Luise, served with bacon, chanterelles, and whortleberries.

✪ **Schweizer Stuben.** Kirchberg Schlössl, Thumseestrasse 11, Kirchberg. ☎ **08651/27-60.** Reservations required. Main courses 26DM–44DM ($14.80–$25.10); fixed-price meals 39DM ($22.25) at lunch, 72DM–92DM ($41.05–$52.45) at dinner. AE, DC, MC, V. Thurs–Tues 11am–3pm and 6pm–midnight. INTERNATIONAL.

No restaurant, even those in the luxury hotels, can hold a candle to this place for cuisine. It's located southwest of town in the center of the suburb of Kirchberg. The kitchen prepares light international dishes, along with specialties from Bavaria and the Berchtesgaden region. The decor is appropriately rustic. The chef seems to have a bent for updating contemporary classics. The fixed-price menu at lunch is an especially good value.

BAD REICHENHALL AFTER DARK

Most guests on the nighttime circuit head for the **Bad Reichenhall Casino,** Wittelsbacherstrasse 17 (☎ **08651/40-91**), which offers roulette, American roulette, blackjack, and 50 types of slot machines. You must show your passport if you plan to do any gaming. It's open daily from 3pm to 2am; admission is 5DM ($2.85). Men must wear jackets and ties. A **theater** is also located here at the Kurgastzentrum, site of the casino. This is a setting for operas, operettas, plays, ballets, musicals, symphonies, folk-loric evenings, and chamber musical recitals. The tourism office (see "Visitor Information," above) keeps a complete list of events and ticket prices. When weather permits, performances are staged in an open-air pavilion. Tickets cost from 40DM to 63DM ($22.80 to $35.90).

If you want to hang out with the locals, go to the **Axel Bar,** a woodsy bar in the Steigenberger Axelmannstein Hotel, Salzburgerstrasse 2–6 (☎ **08651/77-70**). Here you can dance to rather sedate disco music interspersed with folk tunes. There's also the **Tiffany Bar** at the Hotel Bayerischer Hof, Bahnhofplatz 14 (☎ **08651/24-80**), where folks sometimes dance to live music but mostly just drink. The Bayerischer Hof's nightclub hosts international acts. Good old-fashioned Bavarian suds is the order of the evening at everybody's favorite beer hall, **Burgerbräu,** Rathausplatz (☎ **08651/60-89**).

3 Chiemsee

Prien am Chiemsee: 53 miles SE of Munich, 14 miles E of Rosenheim, 40 miles W of Salzburg

Chiemsee, known as the "Bavarian Sea," is one of the most beautiful lakes in the Bavarian Alps. It's surrounded by a serene landscape. In the south, the mountains reach almost to the water. Resorts line the shores of this large lake, but the main attraction is its two islands, **Frauenchiemsee** and **Herrenchiemsee,** where Ludwig II built his palace, Neues Schloss.

ESSENTIALS

GETTING THERE   By Train   Prien Bahnhof is on the major Munich-Rosenheim-Freilassing-Salzburg rail line, with frequent connections in all directions. Ten trains arrive daily from Munich (trip time: 1 hr.). For information, call ☎ **01805/99-66-33**.

By Bus   Regional bus service in the area is offered by **RVO Regionalverkehr Oberbayern,** Betrieb Rosenheim (☎ **08031/6-20-06** for schedules and information).

By Car   Access by car is via the A8 Autobahn from Munich.

VISITOR INFORMATION   Contact the **Kur- und Verkehrsamt,** Alte Rathausstrasse 11, in Prien am Chiemsee (☎ **08051/6-90-50**). It's open Monday to Friday 8:30am to 6pm and Saturday 9am to noon.

GETTING AROUND   By Steamer   From the liveliest resort, Prien, on the lake's west shore, you can reach either Frauenchiemsee or Herrenchiemsee via lake steamers that make regular trips throughout the year. The round-trip fare to Herrenchiemsee is 14DM ($8), 16DM ($9.10) to Fraueninchiemsee. The steamers, operated by **Chiemsee-Schiffahrt Ludwig Fessler** (☎ **08051/60-90**), make round-trips covering the entire lake. Connections can also be made from Gstadt, Seebruck, Chieming, Übersee/Feldwies, and Bernau/Felden. Large boats leave Prien/Stock for Herrenchiemsee from May through September, daily, about every 20 minutes between 9am and 5pm. The last return is at 7:25pm.

By Bus   There is also bus service from the harbor to the DB station in Prien (Chiemsee-Schiffahrt) and around the lake by RVO.

EXPLORING THE ISLANDS

FRAUENCHIEMSEE

Frauenchiemsee (or Fraueninsel) is the smaller of the lake's two major islands. On its sandy shore stands a fishing village that holds an elaborate festival at Corpus

Christi (usually in late May). The fishing boats are covered with flowers and streamers, the fishers are outfitted in Bavarian garb, and the young women of the village dress as brides. As the boats circle the island, they stop at each corner for the singing of the Gospels. The island is also the home of a Benedictine convent, Frauenchiemsee Abbey, founded in 782, which makes it the oldest in Germany. The convent is known for a liqueur called *Kloster Likör*—it's supposed to be an "agreeable stomach elixir."

You can walk around the island in about 30 minutes to enjoy panoramic views of the lake. **Torhalle** (☎ 08054/72-56), a summer-only art gallery, is installed in the ancient hall that used to be the gatehouse of the Frauenwörth convent. Admission is 4DM ($2.30) for adults and 1.50DM (85¢) for children.

HERRENCHIEMSEE

Herrenchiemsee (or Herreninsel) is home to the fantastic ✪ **Neues Schloss,** Herrenchiemsee 3 (☎ 08051/30-69), begun by Ludwig II in 1878 (see box "The Fairy-Tale King," in chapter 6). Never completed because of the king's death in 1886, the castle was to have been a replica of the grand palace of Versailles that Ludwig so admired. When work was halted in 1886, only the center of the enormous palace had been completed. Nonetheless, the palace and its formal gardens, surrounded by woodlands of beech and fir, remain one of the grandest and most fascinating of Ludwig's constructions.

The palace **entrance** is lit by a huge skylight over the sumptuously decorated staircase. Frescoes depicting the four states of existence alternate with Greek and Roman statues in niches on the staircase and in the gallery above. The vestibule is adorned with a pair of enameled peacocks, Louis XIV's favorite bird.

The **Great Hall of Mirrors** is unquestionably the most splendid room in the palace and the most authentic replica of Versailles. The 17 door panels contain enormous mirrors reflecting the 33 crystal chandeliers and the 44 gilded candelabra. The vaulted ceiling is covered with 25 paintings depicting the life of Louis XIV.

Practically every inch of the **state bedroom** has been gilded. On the dais, instead of a throne, stands the richly decorated bed, its purple-velvet draperies weighing more than 300 pounds. Separating the dais from the rest of the room is a carved wooden balustrade covered with gold leaf. On the ceiling, a huge fresco depicts the descent of Apollo, surrounded by the other gods of Olympus. The sun god's features bear a strong resemblance to those of Louis XIV.

The **dining room** is a popular attraction for visitors because of the so-called "little table that sets itself." A mechanism in the floor permitted the table to go down to the room below to be cleared and relaid between courses. Over the table hangs an exquisite chandelier of Meissen porcelain, the largest in the world and the single most valuable item in the palace.

You can visit Herrenchiemsee at any time of the year. From April 1 to September 30, tours are given daily from 9am to 5pm; off-season, daily from 10am to 4pm. Admission (in addition to the round-trip boat fare) is 7DM ($4) for adults, 4DM ($2.30) for students, and free for children under 16.

WHERE TO STAY & DINE

Bayerischer Hof. Bernauerstrasse 3, 83209 Prien am Chiemsee. ☎ **08051/60-30.** Fax 08051/6-29-17. 46 units. TV TEL. 165DM ($94.05) double. Rates include buffet breakfast. AE, MC, V. Closed Nov and last week of Jan. Parking 10DM ($5.70).

The Estermann family will welcome you to the Bayerischer Hof. The rustic decor creates the illusion that this relatively severe modern hotel is older than it is. Of particular note is the painted ceiling in the dining room. The rest of the hotel is more streamlined—modern, efficient, and quite appealing, although the Yachthotel

Chiemsee outside of town has more style and flair. Nonetheless, the rooms are very comfortable.

Yachthotel Chiemsee. Harrasser Strasse 49, 83209 Prien am Chiemsee. ☎ **08051/69-60.** Fax 08051/51-71. www.home.t-online.de/home/yachthotel_chiemsee. E-mail: yachthotel_chiemsee@t-online.de. 102 units. MINIBAR TV TEL. 250DM–315DM ($142.50–$179.55) double; 335DM–465DM ($190.95–$265.05) suite. Rates include buffet breakfast. AE, DC, MC, V. Free parking.

The best place to stay on the lake is the Yachthotel Chiemsee, on the western shore of the "Bavarian Sea." This hotel offers attractively furnished rooms, all with balconies or terraces opening onto the water. Lakeside rooms are equipped with two double beds and a pull-out sofa for groups of four or more. Most rooms are fairly spacious.

Dining/Diversions: A choice of restaurants—complete with a lakeside terrace and a marina—awaits you. The most elegant room, with an excellent view, is the Seepavillon. The Seerestaurant is slightly more rustic but still has an elegant flair, and the Zirbelstüberl goes alpine-Bavarian all the way. The menu is the same in all three.

Amenities: Room service (7am to midnight), laundry, baby-sitting, sailing (a two-masted yacht with a skipper is available May through September), rowing, squash, tennis, riding, golf (nearby), horse-drawn carriage trips, spa department, beauty-care center, sauna, solarium, health and fitness center, outdoor whirlpool, indoor pool, hair dryers.

4 Bad Wiessee

33 miles S of Munich, 11 miles SE of Bad Tölz

If you've always believed that the best medicine is the worst tasting, you should feel right at home in Bad Wiessee—the mineral springs of this popular spa on the Tegernsee are saturated with iodine and sulfur. However, the other attractions of this small town more than make up for this healthful discomfort. The spa, with a huge lake at its feet and towering Alps rising behind it, is a year-round resort. In summer, swimming and boating are popular; in winter, you can ski on the slopes or skate on the lake.

The springs are used for the treatment of many diseases, including rheumatism and heart and respiratory conditions. In spite of its tiny size, Bad Wiessee is advanced in its medicinal facilities, as well as in its accommodations and restaurants.

The main season begins in May and ends in October. During these busy times, you should definitely make a reservation. Many hotels close in winter, so be warned if you're an off-season visitor. In recent years the town has become increasingly popular with vacationers from Munich.

From Bad Wiessee, any number of tours are possible, including visits to Munich, Chiemsee, and the castles of Neuschwanstein, Herrenchiemsee, and Linderhof (see chapter 6). You can also visit Salzburg and Innsbruck in Austria. The tourism office (see below) will supply details.

ESSENTIALS

GETTING THERE   By Train   Travelers arriving by train disembark at Gmund, 2 miles away. At the railway station there, a flotilla of buses (between 9 and 11 per day, depending on the day of the week) meet every major train, with easy connections on to Bad Wiessee. For rail information, call ☎ **1805/99-66-33.**

By Bus   Between 3 and 5 buses depart every day for Bad Wiessee from Munich's Hauptbahnhof, with additional stops along the Zweibrückestrasse, adjacent to Munich's Deutsches Museum. Travel time is about 90 minutes. Round-trip transport costs 21DM ($11.95) per person. For bus information, call ☎ **08022/86-03-20.**

By Car   Access from either Munich or Salzburg (Austria) is via the A8 Autobahn. Take the Holzkirchen exit heading toward Bad Wiessee and follow the signs.

VISITOR INFORMATION   For information, go to the **Kuramt,** Adrian-Stoop-Strasse 20 (☎ **08022/8-60-30**). From May through October, the tourism office's hours are Monday to Friday 8am to 6pm and Saturday and Sunday 9am to noon. In the off-season, hours are Monday to Friday 8am to noon and 2 to 5pm.

SIGHTS & ACTIVITIES

Bad Wiesse offers plenty of activities, apart from its health treatments. In summer, visitors can go sailing or windsurfing on the lake, or head to the mountains for mountain biking and hiking. A drive up the **Wallberg Road** winds through the Moorsalm pasture to an altitude of 3,300 feet. There's also plenty of golf and tennis. In winter, experienced alpine skiers are drawn to the Wallberg, and there are many cross-country trails as well. Wintertime hiking is also a possibility, as about 60 miles of paths are cleared of snow. The less adventurous or athletic can enjoy horse-drawn sleigh rides. Finally, you can also take a **mountain cable car,** which travels 5,100 feet high.

The town of Bad Wiesse has an old-world charm. It's best explored via the old-fashioned steam train or by taking a carriage ride. During the annual lake festivals in summer, locals don traditional clothing and parade through the town. Worth the trip is the nearby **Tegernsee Ducal palace,** which contains the former monastery of St. Quinn, founded in A.D. 746.

SHOPPING

You'll find traditional Bavarian souvenirs, loden coats, and lederhosen here. For a full selection of traditional Bavarian clothes, go to **Trachten,** Münchenerstrasse 8 (☎ **08022/8-13-79**), and its competitor, **Friedl Mandel,** Lindenplatz (☎ **08022/ 8-14-58**). If you want to acquire one-of-a-kind wood carvings, either religious or secular, head for the studio of **Franz Trinkl,** Dr. Scheid Strasse 9A (☎ **08022/87-49**), where you'll find a charming and idiosyncratic collection of artfully carved figurines.

WHERE TO STAY & DINE
EXPENSIVE

Hotel Lederer. Am See. Bodenschneidstrasse 9–11, 83707 Bad Wiessee. ☎ **08022/82-90.** Fax 08022/82-92-61. www.lederer.com. E-mail: hotel@lederer.com. 114 units. TV TEL. 160DM–360DM ($91.20–$205.20) double. AE, DC, MC, V. Free parking. Closed Oct–Feb.

This spa and holiday hotel is clearly the most distinguished choice in town. From the balcony of your room, you'll look out onto the Tegernsee and the Lower Bavarian Alps. The atmosphere is pleasant, with good service and attractive, well-maintained rooms, ranging in size from medium to spacious. The hotel stands in a large park, and there's a dock and an indoor pool for swimming, as well as a meadow for sunbathing.

Dining/Diversions: The hotel restaurant turns out an international cuisine of good standard. Sometimes there's a barbecue on the terrace facing the lake, followed by entertainment or dancing in the nightclub.

Amenities: The hotel has its own medical staff and "beauty farm," including a sauna, solarium, and indoor pool. Other amenities include tennis courts, beauty salon, concierge, room service, and dry cleaning and laundry service.

MODERATE

Kurhotel Rex. Münchnerstrasse 25, 83707 Bad Wiessee. ☎ **08022/8-62-00.** Fax 08022/ 8-38-41. 58 units. TV TEL. 194DM–234DM ($110.60–$133.40) double; 264DM ($150.50) suite. No credit cards. Free parking. Closed Nov 1–Apr 5.

A modern hotel with much charm and character, Kurhotel Rex is set against a backdrop of the Lower Bavarian Alps. It's an ideal choice for a vacation by the lake. The decorator tried to make the place as warm and inviting as possible. The well-maintained guest rooms are furnished in Bavarian style. The hotel has good food and caters to special dieters, and its Bierstuberl is a lively gathering place.

Landhaus Hotel Sapplfeld. Im Sapplfeld 8, 83707 Bad Wiessee. ☎ **08022/8-20-67.** Fax 08022/8-35-60. 16 units. TV TEL. 180DM–280DM ($102.60–$159.60) double. Rates include buffet breakfast. MC, V. Free parking. Garage 20DM ($11.40).

This typical Bavarian inn, with geranium-filled balconies and a roof overhang, is a real alpine resort, where people come to have a good time. It attracts scenery lovers in summer, and skiers in winter. The guest rooms are completely modern; each has a balcony. They range from small to medium in size. The hotel has a sauna where, as is usual for Germany, men and women are segregated.

Park Hotel Resi von der Post. Zilcherstrasse 14, 83707 Bad Wiessee. ☎ **08022/9-86-50.** Fax 08022/98-65-65. 27 units. TV TEL. 188DM ($107.15) double; from 218DM ($124.25) suite. Rates include buffet breakfast. AE, DC, MC, V. Free parking.

This enduring favorite has been around much longer than many of its fast-rising competitors. It has been considerably modernized, and now has well-furnished, traditional guest rooms. Bathrooms are a bit cramped. The atmosphere in the hotel's restaurant is often bustling, as diners who live nearby fill up the place; many show up in Bavarian dress. Ask for the special cheese of the Tegernsee district, *Miesbacher.* Make reservations early for this hotel; it's usually booked up for the year by summer.

INEXPENSIVE

Kurhotel Edelweiss. Münchnerstrasse 21 (a quarter-mile north of Bad Weissee's center), 83707 Bad Wiessee. ☎ **08022/8-60-90.** Fax 08022/8-38-83. 40 units. TV TEL. 130DM–160DM ($74.10–$91.20) double. Rates include continental breakfast. No credit cards. Free parking.

This chalet/guest house is ornamented with wooden balconies and painted detailing around its doors and windows. Rooms are functionally but comfortably furnished. Additional but less-desirable units are available in the motel-like outbuildings beside the main structure. The modern public rooms are suffused with a certain German kitsch. The Bavarian-style restaurant is open for hotel guests only.

Wiesseer Hof. Sanktjohanserstrasse 46, 83707 Bad Wiessee. ☎ **08022/86-70.** Fax 08022/86-71-65. 60 units. TV TEL. 140DM–180DM ($79.80–$102.60) double. Rates include buffet breakfast. AE, DC, MC, V. Free parking.

This modern, but still traditional, hotel looks like an overgrown chalet, with four floors of rooms, many with views over a lawn dotted with greenery. The guest rooms are snug and cozy in the alpine tradition, with such amenities as private safes and hair dryers. Most have balconies, festooned in summer with boxes of geraniums. The stuccoed wooden walls of the public rooms create a *gemütlich* warmth. The kitchen features many good Bavarian specialties.

5 Mittenwald

66 miles S of Munich, 11 miles SE of Garmisch-Partenkirchen, 23 miles NW of Innsbruck

The year-round resort of Mittenwald, which lies in a pass in the Karwendel Range, seems straight out of *The Sound of Music.* Especially noteworthy and photogenic are the painted Bavarian houses with overhanging eaves. On the square stands a monument to

Mathias Klotz, who introduced violin making to Mittenwald in 1684. The town is now a major international center for this highly specialized craft.

ESSENTIALS

GETTING THERE **By Train** Hourly train service runs on the express rail line between Munich and Innsbruck, Austria. From Munich, trip time is 1½ to 2 hours. From Frankfurt, trip time is 5 to 6 hours. Call ☎ **1805/99-66-33** for information.

By Bus Regional bus service from Garmisch-Partenkirchen and nearby towns is frequently provided by **RVO Regionalverkehr Oberbayern** at Garmisch (☎ **08821/94-82-74** for schedules and information).

By Car Access by car is via the A95 Autobahn from Munich.

VISITOR INFORMATION Contact the **Kurverwaltung und Verkehrsamt,** Dammkarstrasse 3 (☎ **08823/3-39-81**). It's open Monday to Friday 8am to noon and 1 to 5pm, and Saturday and Sunday 10am to noon.

SIGHTS & ACTIVITIES

The town's museum, which contains a workshop, has exhibits that trace the history of violins and other stringed instruments, from their invention through various stages of their evolution. The **Geigenbau- und Heimatmuseum,** Ballenhausgasse 3 (☎ **08823/25-11**), is open Monday to Friday from 10am to noon and 2 to 5pm, and on Saturday and Sunday from 10am to noon. Admission is 3DM ($1.70) for adults and 1DM (55¢) for students and children. The museum is closed from November 1 to December 22.

In the surrounding countryside, the scenery of the Wetterstein and Karwendel ranges constantly changes. Some 80 miles of hiking paths wind up and down the mountains around the village. You can hike through the hills on your own, take part in mountain-climbing expeditions, or take horse-and-carriage trips and motor-coach tours from Mittenwald to nearby villages. In the evening in the various inns, there's typical Bavarian entertainment, often consisting of folk dancing and singing, zither playing, and yodeling. Concerts during the summer are held in the music pavilion. Mittenwald also has good spa facilities, in large gardens landscaped with tree-lined streams and trout pools. In winter the town is a skiing center.

SHOPPING

The classical stringed instruments crafted here have been sought after by professional musicians for centuries. Prices may be steep for the amateur violinist, but a visit to **Geigenbau Leonhardt,** Mühlenweg 53A (☎ **08823/80-10**), is educational and interesting even if you're just browsing.

If you've ever had the desire to traipse about in a dirndl, embroidered blouse, or lederhosen, head for **Trachtenstubön,** Obermarkt 35 (☎ **08823/85-55**), or **Trachten Werner-Leichtl,** Hochstrasse 1 (☎ **08823/37-85**); both stock a good selection of sizes and styles.

WHERE TO STAY

Alpenrose. Obermarkt 1, 82481 Mittenwald. ☎ **08823/92700.** Fax 08823/3720. 18 units. MINIBAR TV TEL. 124DM–185DM ($70.70–$105.45) double; 192DM ($109.45) suite. Rates include buffet breakfast. AE, DC, DISC, MC, V. Free parking.

This particularly inviting hotel is located in the village center at the foot of a rugged mountain. The facade is covered with decorative designs, and window boxes hold flowering vines. The inn's basic 14th-century structure was once part of a monastery. The hotel's rooms are divided between the Alpenrose (the former monastery) and its annex, the Bichlerhof. Try to stay in the main building, where the rooms have a great deal of charm, with finely woven fabrics, old-fashioned farmhouse cupboards, and plenty of dark wood paneling. Bathrooms in both buildings are a bit cramped. The tavern room, overlooking the street, has many ingratiating features, including hand-made chairs, flagstone floors, and a square tile stove in the center. In the Josefikeller, beer is served in giant steins, and musicians play in the evening. The dining room provides excellent meals, including Bavarian specialties.

Gästehaus Sonnenbichl. Klausnerweg 32, 82481 Mittenwald. ☎ **08823/9-22-30.** Fax 08823/58-14. 20 units. MINIBAR TV TEL. 114DM–160DM ($65–$91.20) double. Rates include buffet breakfast. No credit cards. Closed Nov 1–Dec 15.

One of the more modest inns in town, this chalet nevertheless offers good value and comfort. It has a view of the village set against a backdrop of the Alps. The rooms are freshly decorated in vivid natural colors. They're small but exceedingly well kept. Reserving well in advance is a good idea. Breakfast is the only meal served.

Hotel Post. Obermarkt 9, 82481 Mittenwald. ☎ **08823/10-94.** Fax 08823/10-96. 80 units. MINIBAR TV TEL. 190DM–260DM ($108.30–$148.20) double; 280DM–320DM ($159.60–$182.40) suite. Rates include buffet breakfast. No credit cards. Parking free outside or 8DM ($4.55) inside.

The Post provides Mittenwald's finest lodging. It's the most seasoned and established chalet hotel in the village, dating from 1632, when stagecoaches carrying mail and pas-sengers across the Bavarian Alps stopped here to refuel. A delightful breakfast is served on the sun terrace, with a view of the Alps. On a cool day, take time out to enjoy a beer in the snug lounge-bar, which has an open fireplace. For a night of hearty Bavarian specialties, head for the wine tavern or the Poststüberl. The beds here are among the most comfortable in town, with duvets and beautiful linen. The maids are especially helpful. Amenities include an indoor pool, massage facilities, exercise room, and sauna.

WHERE TO DINE

Restaurant Arnspitze. Innsbruckerstrasse 68. ☎ **08823/24-25.** Main courses 28.50DM–42.50DM ($16.25–$24.20); fixed-price meal 42.50DM ($24.20) at lunch, 82.50DM ($47.05) at dinner. AE. Wed 6–9pm, Thurs–Mon noon–2pm and 6–9pm. BAVARIAN.

This traditionally decorated restaurant, housed in a modern chalet hotel on the out-skirts of town, is the finest in Mittenwald. The cuisine is solid, satisfying, and whole-some. You might order sole with homemade noodles or veal steak in creamy smooth sauce, then finish with one of the freshly made desserts. There's an excellent fixed-price lunch.

6 Garmisch-Partenkirchen

60 miles SW of Munich, 73 miles SE of Augsburg, 37 miles NW of Innsbruck

The twin villages of Garmisch and Partenkirchen make up Germany's top alpine resort. In spite of their urban flair, the towns maintain the charm of an ancient village, especially in Partenkirchen. Even today, you occasionally see country folk in tradi-tional dress, and you may be held up in traffic while the cattle are led from their mountain-grazing grounds down through the streets of town.

ESSENTIALS

GETTING THERE By Train The **Garmisch-Partenkirchen Bahnhof** lies on the major Munich-Weilheim-Garmisch-Mittenwald-Innsbruck rail line, with frequent connections in all directions. Twenty trains per day arrive from Munich (trip time:

Hiking in the Bavarian Alps

Hiking is Bavaria's favorite pastime. Locals believe firmly in the emotional and spiritual benefits of walking and hill climbing and tend to hit the trails the moment the snows melt.

The tourist office in Garmisch-Partenkirchen will point you to hiking trails of varying degrees of difficulty, all with clearly designated signs. The office also offers a brochure outlining the half-dozen best trails. You don't have to be an Olympic athlete to enjoy them. Most hikes will take an energetic 4 to 5 hours, but some of them are shorter and easy enough for children.

An easily accessible destination is the 4,060-foot **Eckbauer** peak that lies on the southern fringe of Partenkirchen. The easy trails on its lower slopes are recommended for first-time alpine hikers. You can even take a chairlift to the top, where, in the real Bavarian style, the Bergasthof will serve you a glass of buttermilk. In less than an hour you can descend on relatively easy trails through a forest. The cable car stretching from Garmisch to the top of the Eckbauer departs year-round from a facility (the Eckbauerbahn) that sits adjacent to the ski stadium in Garmisch. The round-trip costs 19DM ($10.85) for adults, 12DM ($6.85) for children, and 44DM ($25.10) for two adults and a child. For information on the Eckbauerbahn, call ☎ **08821/7970.**

More demanding are the slopes of the rugged ✪ **Alpspitz** region, which begins about a mile southwest of Garmisch. The area is interlaced with wildflowers, unusual geology, alpine meadows, and a network of cable cars and hiking trails spread over a terrain ranging in altitude between 4,600 and 6,300 feet. The highest trails are around the summit of the Alpspitz at 8,541 feet.

One of the most appealing ways to gain a high-altitude panorama over this region is to take a triangular trip up the Alpspitz. Begin your journey at the Kreuzeckbahn/Alpspitzbahn cable car terminus, a mile south of the center of Garmisch. The cable car will carry you uphill along the Kreuzeckbahn for a 4-minute ride across a jagged landscape to the lowest station of the Hochalm cable car. Here the Hochalmbahn will carry you uphill for another 4 minutes to the top of the Osterfelderkopf, 6,300 feet above sea level. Cable cars for both stages of this trip depart at 30-minute intervals every day throughout the year between 8:15am and 5:15pm. After your visit to the Osterfelderkopf summit, you can return to Garmisch via a different route, a direct downhill descent via

1 hr. and 22 min.). For rail information and schedules, call ☎ **1805/996633.** Mountain rail service to several plateaus and the Zugspitze is offered by the **Bayerische Zugspitzbahn** at Garmisch (☎ **08821/79-70**).

By Bus   Both long-distance and regional buses through the Bavarian Alps are provided by **RVO Regionalverkehr Oberbayern** in Garmisch-Partenkirchen (☎ **08821/ 94-82-74**).

By Car   Access is via the A95 Autobahn from Munich; exit at Eschenlohe.

VISITOR INFORMATION   Contact the **Verkehrsamt,** on Richard-Strauss-Platz (☎ **08821/18-06**). It's open Monday to Saturday 8am to 6pm and Sunday and holidays 10am to noon.

the Alpspitzbahn, a 10-minute ride above jagged gorges, soaring cliffs, and grassy meadows. At the points where the cable car lines intersect, you might want to embark on short, high-altitude hikes to observe the unique alpine flora and fauna. Snacks are served at cafes and restaurants at major points on the itinerary.

Round-trip passage along this three-tiered alpine itinerary costs 42DM ($23.95) for adults and 25DM ($14.25) for children 5 to 16; it's free for children 4 and under. These fares and times of departure can fluctuate. For the latest details, call either the information service for the above-mentioned cable cars (☎ **08821/7970**) or check with the tourist office, the **Verkehrsamt,** in Garmisch on Richard-Strauss-Platz (☎ **08821/18-06**).

From Garmisch-Partenkirchen, many other peaks of the Witterstein range are accessible as well, via the 10 funiculars ascending from the borders of the town. From the top of the **Wank** (5,850 ft.) to the east, you get the best view of the plateau on which the villages of Garmisch and Partenkirchen sit. This summit is also a favorite with the patrons of Garmisch's spa facilities because the plentiful sunshine makes it ideal for the *Liegekur* (deck-chair cure).

Another interesting hike is through the **Partnachklamm Gorge,** a canyon with a roaring stream at the bottom and sheer cliff walls rising on either side of the hiking trail. Take the Graseck Seilbahn from its departure point at the bottom of the gorge, less than a half mile south of Garmisch's ski stadium, and get off at the first station, which is adjacent to a cozy hotel, the **Forsthaus Graseck** (☎ **08821/5-40-06**). You might want to get a meal or drink at the Forsthaus first. Afterward descend on foot along narrow paths by the sides of the stream, as it cascades downhill. The path crosses the gorge and returns you to the point where you entered. Many readers have found this one of their most memorable adventures in Bavaria. The experience of walking along a rocky ledge just above a rushing river and often behind small waterfalls, while looking up at 1,200 feet of rocky cliffs, is truly awesome (and sometimes wet).

From its departure point to the Forsthaus, the 3-minute cable car ride costs 5DM ($2.85) per person each way. For information about the Seilbahn, contact Forsthaus Graseck (☎ **08821/5-40-06**). The cable car operates at 20-minute intervals between 8am and 8pm and until 11pm on weekends.

GETTING AROUND   An unnumbered municipal bus services the town, depositing passengers at Marienplatz or the Bahnhof, from which you can walk to all centrally located hotels. This free bus runs every 15 minutes.

EXPLORING THE AREA

Garmisch-Partenkirchen is a center for winter sports, summer hiking, and mountain climbing. The symbol of the city's growth and modernity is the **Olympic Ice Stadium,** built for the 1936 Winter Olympics and capable of holding nearly 12,000 people. On the slopes at the edge of town is the **Ski Stadium,** with two ski jumps and a slalom course. In 1936, more than 100,000 people watched the events in this stadium. Today it's still an integral part of winter life in Garmisch—the World Cup Ski Jump is held here every New Year.

The town and its environs offer some of the most panoramic views and colorful buildings in Bavaria. The pilgrimage **Chapel of St. Anton,** on a pine-wood path at the edge of Partenkirchen, is all pink and silver, inside and out. Its graceful lines are characteristic of the 18th century, when it was built. The **Philosopher's Walk,** in the park surrounding the chapel, is a delightful spot to wander, just to enjoy the views of the mountains around the low-lying town.

This area has always attracted German romantics, including "Mad" King Ludwig (see the box, "The Fairy-Tale King," in chapter 6). Perhaps with Wagner's music ringing in his ears, the king ordered the construction of a hunting lodge here in the style of a Swiss chalet, but commanded that the interior look like something out of *The Arabian Nights.* The lodge, **Jagdschloss Schachen,** is still here. It can only be reached after an arduous climb. The tourist office will supply details. From mid-June to mid-September, tours at 11am and 2pm often leave from the Olympic Ski Stadium heading for the lodge, but check before you go.

TO THE TOP OF THE ZUGSPITZE

From Garmisch-Partenkirchen, you can see the tallest mountain in Germany, the ✪ **Zugspitze,** 9,720 feet above sea level. Ski slopes begin at a height of 8,700 feet. For a panoramic view of both the Bavarian and the Tyrolean (Austrian) Alps, go all the way to the summit. The Zugspitze peak can be reached in one of two different ways from the center of Garmisch. The first way begins with a trip on the cog railway, the Zugspitzbahn, which departs daily from back of the Garmisch's main railway station every hour between 8:35am and 2:35pm. The train travels uphill, past lichen-covered boulders and coursing streams, to a high-altitude plateau, the Zugspitzplatte, where views sweep out all over Bavaria. At the Zugspitzplatte, you'll transfer onto a cable car, the Gletscher Sielbahn, for a 4-minute ride uphill to the top of the Zugspitze. There, far-reaching panoramas, a cafe and restaurant, a gift shop, and many alpine trails await. Total travel time for this itinerary is about 55 minutes, but you may want to linger at the first stop, the Zugspitzplatte, before going on up.

The other way to get to the summit is to take the above-mentioned railway, the Zugspitzbahn, for a briefer trip, disembarking 9 miles southwest of Garmisch at the lower station of the Eibsee Sielbahn (Eibsee Cable Car), next to a clear alpine lake. The cable car will carry you from there directly to the summit of the Zugspitze, for a total transit time of about 38 minutes. The Eibsee Sielbahn makes its run from the lake to the summit at least every half hour from 8:30am to 4:30pm (until 5:30pm in July and August).

Round-trip tickets allow you to ascend one way and descend the other, in order to enjoy the widest range of spectacular views. Between April and October, round-trip fares are 76DM ($43.30) for adults, 67DM ($38.20) for seniors, 53DM ($30.20) for teenagers ages 16 and 17, and 45DM ($25.65) for children ages 5 to 15. A group fare for two adults and a child costs 173DM ($98.60). In winter, the round-trip fares are reduced to 62DM ($35.35) for adults, 44DM ($25.10) for those ages 16 and 17, and 37DM ($21.10) for children ages 5 to 15. For more information, contact the Bayerlsche ugspitzbahn, Olympiastrasse 27, in Garmisch-Partenkirchen (☎ **08821/ 7-97-0;** or 08821/79-97-97 for a recorded message).

SHOPPING

Your best bets are in the traffic-reduced Ludwigstrasse in Partenkirchen and in the almost traffic-free zone from Dr. Richard-Strauss-Platz to Marienplatz in Garmisch. A vast array of stores sells boots, boutique items, clothing, jewelry, art, antiques, and more. An unusual store is **Kaufmann,** Am Kurkpark (☎ **08821/5-52-48**) in Garmisch. This shop not only sells a wide collection of artful lithographs depicting the glories of the Bavarian

Alps but also offers tin-smithy work, glass, ceramics, gold and silver jewelry, and various Bavarian souvenirs. If you like traditional Bavarian dress but don't want to spend a lot of money, head for **Loisachtaler,** Burgstrasse 20 (☎ 08821/ 5-23-90). Here, Petra Ostler has assembled the area's finest collection of secondhand clothing. Take your pick: a jaegermeister loden coat, an alpine hat with pheasant feathers, or a cast-off dirndl. They all look like new.

WHERE TO STAY
EXPENSIVE

Grand Hotel Sonnenbichl. Burgstrasse 97, 82467 Garmisch-Partenkirchen. ☎ **08821/ 70-20.** Fax 08821/70-21-31. www.sonnenbichl.de. E-mail: info@sonnenbichl.de. 93 units. MINIBAR TV TEL. 350DM ($199.50) double; 700DM–950DM ($399–$541.50) suite. Rates include buffet breakfast. AE, DC, MC, V. Free parking. Take Rte. 23 toward Oberammergau.

The most upscale hotel in the area is on the hillside overlooking Garmisch-Partenkirchen, 1 mile from the city center and 2 miles from the Bahnhof. It has excellent views of the Wetterstein mountain range and the Zugspitze (from its front rooms only; those in the rear open onto a rock wall). Some of the spacious bedrooms are showing a bit of wear and tear; a few lack a complete bathtub. The decor is generally art nouveau.

Dining/Diversions: The hotel serves excellent food. You can have light, modern cuisine in the elegant gourmet restaurant, the Blauer Salon, or Bavarian specialties in the Zirbelstube. Afternoon coffee and fresh homemade cake are served in the lobby or on the sunny terrace. Drinks are available in the Peacock Bar.

Amenities: Room service, laundry, dry cleaning, pool, sauna, solarium, fitness and massage rooms.

MODERATE

✪ **Posthotel Partenkirchen.** Ludwigstrasse 49, 82467 Garmisch-Partenkirchen. ☎ **08821/93630.** Fax 08821/93-63-222. 59 units. MINIBAR TV TEL. 200DM–280DM ($114– $159.60) double; 280DM–380DM ($159.60–$216.60) suite. Rates include continental breakfast. AE, DC, MC, V. Free parking.

The Posthotel Partenkirchen, which was founded in 1542, has emerged as one of the town's most prestigious hotels. In recent years, it has even surpassed its major rival, the Reindl's Partenkirchner Hof. Here you'll experience old-world living and personalized service. The U-shaped rooms are stylish, with antiques and elaborately carved furnishings. The sunny balconies overlook a garden and offer a view of the Alps. Bedrooms are generally medium in size, though some are quite spacious.

Dining/Diversions: The restaurant here is unusually fine (see "Where to Dine," below). In the rustic Weinlokal Barbarossa, there are nooks for quiet before- or after-dinner drinks.

Amenities: Room service (7am to 11pm), laundry, golf, tennis, swimming, mountain climbing, skiing, cycling, hiking, horseback riding, paragliding.

Reindl's Partenkirchner Hof. Bahnhofstrasse 15, 82467 Garmisch-Partenkirchen. ☎ **08821/5-80-25.** E-mail: reindl@oberland.net. 88 units. MINIBAR TV TEL. 164DM–223DM ($93.50–$127.10) double; 254DM–430DM ($144.80–$245.10) suite. AE, DC, MC, V. Parking 12DM ($6.85). Closed Nov 9–Dec 15.

Reindl's opened in 1911, and from the beginning it attracted a devoted following. Owners Bruni and Karl Reindl maintain a high level of luxury and hospitality in this special Bavarian retreat. The annexes, the Wetterstein and the House Alpspitz, have balconies, and the main four-story building has wraparound verandas, giving each room an unobstructed view of the mountains and town. The accommodations are among the most attractive in town, often furnished with Bavarian objects, making for a cozy charm. The best rooms are the suites opening onto panoramic views of mountains or the garden. Tasteful pastel fabrics, fine wool carpeting, and rustic pine furniture add to the allure.

Dining: The Reindl's restaurant is well respected (see "Where to Dine," below).

Amenities: Room service, laundry, covered pool, sauna, sun room, health club, open terrace for snacks, two attractive gardens.

✪ **Romantik-Hotel Clausing's Posthotel.** Marienplatz 12, 82467 Garmisch-Partenkirchen. ☎ **08821/70-90.** Fax 08821/70-92-05. 45 units. MINIBAR TV TEL. 160DM– 300DM ($91.20– $171) double; from 400DM ($228) suite. Rates include buffet breakfast. AE, DC, MC, V.

The history and identity of Garmisch are bound up in events that took place at this hotel in the heart of town. It has been here since 1512, when it was a tavern. During the Thirty Years' War, when nearby Munich was ravaged and besieged, the building sheltered refugees within its walls. In 1891, it was bought by the beer baron from Berlin who invented a new brand of beer, Berliner Weissen, which quickly became one of the most popular brands in Garmisch. Nowadays, the upgraded hotel retains its sense of *Gemütlichkeit* comfort. All the rooms successfully mingle Bavarian antique charm with modern comforts. Bedrooms range from spacious to rather small and cozy Bavarian nests. Bathrooms are beautifully kept.

The most glamorous restaurant here is the Stüberl, a paneled enclave of warmth and carefully presented cuisine. The Verandah offers simple platters, drinks, and glassed-in comfort in winter, and open-air access to the bustling Marienplatz in summer. Live music is presented at the Post-Hörnd'l every evening year-round between 6pm and midnight.

INEXPENSIVE

Gasthof Fraundorfer. Ludwigstrasse 24, 82467 Garmisch-Partenkirchen. ☎ **08821/21-76.** Fax 08821/9-27-99. www.gasthof.fraundorfer.de. E-mail: fravendorfer@gap. baynet.de. 30 units. TV TEL. 130DM–170DM ($74.10–$96.90) double; 170DM–325DM ($96.90–$185.25) family room for 2–5 people. Rates include buffet breakfast. AE, MC, V. Free parking.

The family-owned Gasthof Fraundorfer is located directly on the main street of Partenkirchen, just a 5-minute walk from the old church. Its original style has not been updated, so it retains the character of bygone days. There are three floors under a sloping roof, with a facade brightly decorated with murals depicting a family feast. You'll be in the midst of village-centered activities, near interesting shops and restaurants. The guest rooms are furnished with traditional alpine styling, some with four-poster beds. Some larger units are virtual apartments, suitable for up to five guests. Regardless of room assignment, each is fitted with a firm mattress. Bathrooms are compact and tiled with shower stalls and middle-grade towels. Owners Josef and Barbel Fraundorfer are proud of their country-style meals. There's Bavarian yodeling and dancing Wednesday to Monday nights. Dinner reservations are advised.

In addition, the owners operate the Gästehaus Barbara in back, with 20 more beds, including a *Himmelbett* ("heaven bed"). A double in their new house costs 150DM ($85.50).

Haus Lilly. Zugspitzstrasse 20a (a 15-min. walk from the Bahnhof), 82467 Garmisch-Partenkirchen. ☎ **08821/5-26-00.** 8 units. 103DM ($58.70) double; 153DM ($87.20) triple or quad. Rates include buffet breakfast. No credit cards. Free parking.

Many visitors appreciate this spotlessly clean guest house. It wins prizes for its copious breakfasts and the personality of its smiling owner, Maria Lechner, whose English is limited but whose hospitality is universal. Each cozy room includes free access to a kitchen, so in-house meal preparation is an option for guests wanting to save money. Each small bedroom comes with a comfortable bed fitted with a good mattress and covered with a duvet. The linens are fresh and crisp. Bathrooms are small and come with middle-grade towels and shower stalls. Breakfast is a combination of cold cuts, rolls, cheese, eggs, pastries, and coffee, tea, or chocolate.

Hotel Hilleprandt. Riffelstrasse 17 (near the Zugspitze Bahnhof and the Olympic Ice Stadium), 82467 Garmisch-Partenkirchen. ☎ **08821/28-61.** Fax 08821/7-45-48. www.home. t-online.de/home/hotel-hilleprandt. E-mail: hotelhilleprandt@t-online.de. 18 units. TV TEL. 142DM– 178DM ($80.95–$101.45) double; 190DM ($108.30) suite. Rates include buffet breakfast. MC, V. Free parking.

This cozy, tranquil chalet is a good budget choice. Its wooden balconies, attractive garden, and backdrop of forest-covered mountains give the impression of an old-time alpine building. However, a complete renovation has brought streamlined modern comfort. Guests enjoy a fitness room, a sauna, and a pleasant breakfast room. Rooms are small but comfortable. Each has a private balcony.

WHERE TO DINE
EXPENSIVE

Posthotel Partenkirchen. Ludwigstrasse 49, Partenkirchen. ☎ **08821/93630.** Reservations required. Main courses 20DM–30DM ($11.40–$17.10); fixed-price menus 34DM–43DM ($19.40–$24.50). AE, DC, MC, V. Daily noon–2pm and 6–9:30pm. CONTINENTAL.

The restaurant at the Posthotel Partenkirchen (see "Where to Stay," above) is renowned for its distinguished continental cuisine—in fact, its reputation has spread throughout Bavaria. The interior dining rooms are rustic, with a mellow, old-fashioned atmosphere. You could imagine Dürer having a meal here. Everything seems comfortably subdued, including the diners. Perhaps your best choice is to order one of the fixed-price menus, which change daily depending on the availability of seasonal produce. The à la carte menu is extensive, featuring game in the autumn. Other main dishes include schnitzel cordon bleu and mixed grill St. James. The Wiener schnitzel served with a large salad is the best we've had in the resort.

✪ Reindl's Restaurant. In the Partenkirchner Hof, Bahnhofstrasse 15. ☎ **08821/5-80-25.** Reservations required. Main courses 38DM–50DM ($21.65–$28.50); fixed-price meals 38DM–50DM ($21.65–$28.50) at lunch, 50DM–120DM ($28.50–$68.40) at dinner. AE, DC, MC, V. Daily noon–2:30pm and 6:30–11pm. Closed Nov 10–Dec 15. CONTINENTAL.

One of the best places to eat in Partenkirchen is Reindl's, a first-class restaurant in every sense of the word. The seasonal menu offers *cuisine moderne* as well as regional Bavarian dishes. Some famous French wines and champagnes—such as Romanée Conti, Château Lafite Rothschild, and Château Petrus—are on the wine list. As a good opening to a fine repast, we suggest the scampi salad Walterspiel with fresh peaches, lemon, and tarragon, or homemade goose-liver pâté with Riesling jelly. For a main dish, try coq au Riesling (chicken in wine) with noodles or veal roasted with Steinpilzen, a special mushroom from the Bavarian mountains. For dessert, we recommend either the Grand Marnier sabayon with strawberry and vanilla ice cream or something more spectacular: a Salzburger Nockerl for two.

MODERATE

Alpenhof. Am Kurpark 10. ☎ **08821/5-90-55.** Reservations recommended. Main courses 17.50DM–42DM ($10–$23.95); fixed-price lunch 24.50DM–28.50DM ($13.95–$16.25). DC, MC, V. Daily 11:30am–2pm and 5:30–9:30pm. Closed 3 weeks in Nov. BAVARIAN.

Alpenhof is widely regarded as the finest restaurant in Garmisch besides the hotel dining rooms at the Posthotel Partenkirchen and Reindl's Partenkirchner Hof. The cuisine here is neatly grounded in tradition. Renate and Josef Huber offer a variety of Bavarian specialties, as well as trout "any way you want," salmon grilled with mousseline sauce, and ragout of venison. For dessert, try a soufflé with exotic fruits. An exceptional fixed-price meal for 28.50DM ($16.25)—the best for value at the resort—is presented daily. In summer, try for an outside table; in winter, retreat to the cozy interior, which is flooded with sunlight from a greenhouse extension.

INEXPENSIVE

Flösserstuben. Schmiedstrasse 2. ☎ **08821/28-88.** Reservations recommended. Main courses 10DM–32.50DM ($5.70–$18.50). AE, MC. Daily 11:30am–2:30pm and 5–10pm (or as late as 1:30am, depending on business). GREEK/BAVARIAN/INTERNATIONAL.

Regardless of the season, a bit of the Bavarian Alps always seems to flower in this intimate restaurant, close to the town center. On most evenings, the weathered beams above the dining tables reverberate with laughter and good cheer. You can select a seat at a colorful wooden table or on an ox yoke-inspired stool in front of the spliced saplings that decorate the bar. Moussaka and souvlaki, Hungarian goulashes, sauerbraten, and all kinds of Bavarian dishes are abundantly available.

Riessersee. Reiss 6 (2 miles from the center of town). ☎ **08821/9-54-40.** Main courses 10.80DM–36DM ($6.15–$20.50). Tues–Sun 8am–9pm. AE, MC, V. BAVARIAN.

This cafe-restaurant is located on the shores of a small lake with emerald-green water. Stop in here after you explore the Zugspitze. It's the ideal place for a leisurely lunch or afternoon coffee with cakes, ice cream, and chocolates. You may like the place so much you'll stick around for one of the Bavarian dinner dishes. Caviar and lobster are available on occasion, and excellent veal dishes are served all the time.

GARMISCH-PARTENKIRCHEN AFTER DARK

You can test your luck at the town's casino, **Spielbank Garmisch-Partenkirchen,** Am Kurpark 74 (☎ 08821/9-95-90). Admission costs 5DM ($2.85) per person, and presentation of a passport is required. The casino is open daily from 3pm to 2am. Beginning at 7pm, men must wear jackets and ties. Every Friday and Saturday, games of seven-card stud poker are arranged (book in advance).

If you'd like to meet the locals at night, head for one of the taverns for a beer. All major hotels have bars, but for a change of pace go to the **Irish Pub,** Rathausplatz 8 (☎ 08221/7-87-98), and order a Guinness. This pub, in the center of town, attracts one of the most convivial crowds in the area.

Many hotels have dance floors that keep the music pumping into the wee hours, but for dancing of a different sort, check out the summer program of **Bavarian folk music and dancing,** held every Saturday night from mid-May to September in the Bayernhalle, Brauhausstrasse 19. During the same season from Saturday to Thursday, **classical concerts** are held at the Garmisch park bandstand. On Friday, these live shows move to the Partenkirchen bandstand. Check with the local tourist office (see above) for details about these programs as well as a 5-day **Johann Strauss Festival** held in June.

7 Oberammergau

59 miles SW of Munich, 12 miles N of Garmisch-Partenkirchen

In the summer of the year 2000, Oberammergau will once again stage its famous **Passion Play,** which is performed only 1 year out of 10. Surely the world's longest-running show, it began in 1634 when the town's citizens took a vow to give dramatic thanks after they were spared from the devastating plague of 1633. The town will be packed to the gills all summer for this major event.

However, a visit to Oberammergau is ideal at any time, even without the performance. The town is in a wide valley surrounded by forests, green meadows, and mountains. It offers first-class hotels and cozy inns, and has long been known for the skill of its wood-carvers. Numerous hiking trails lead through the nearby mountains to hikers' inns. You can also simply go up to the mountaintops on the Laber cable railway or the Kolben chairlift.

Oberammergau also offers opportunities for tennis buffs, minigolf players, cyclists, swimmers, hang-gliding enthusiasts, and canoeists. The recreation center, Wellenberg, with open-air pools, hot water and fountains, sauna, solarium, and restaurant, is one of the Alps' most beautiful. The surrounding Ammer Valley is a treasure trove for explorers. And Oberammergau is often used as a base for visiting Linderhof Castle, the Benedictine monastery at Ettal, or the fairy-tale Neuschwanstein and Hohenschwangau castles (see chapter 6).

ESSENTIALS

GETTING THERE   By Train   The **Oberammergau Bahnhof** is on the Murnau-Bad Kohlgrum-Oberammergau rail line, with frequent connections in all directions. Through Murnau, all major German cities can be reached. Daily trains arrive from Munich in 2 hours and from Frankfurt in 7 hours. For rail information and schedules, call ☎ **1805/996633.**

By Bus   Regional bus service to nearby towns is offered by **RVO Regionalverkehr Oberbayern** in Garmisch-Partenkirchen (☎ **08821/94-82-74**). An unnumbered bus goes back and forth between Oberammergau and Garmisch-Partenkirchen.

By Car   Many visitors drive here, the trip taking 1½ hours from Munich and 5½ hours from Frankfurt. Take the A95 Munich-Garmisch-Partenkirchen Autobahn and exit at Eschenlohe.

VISITOR INFORMATION   Contact the **Verkehrsbüro,** Eugen-Papst-Strasse 9A (☎ **08822/9-23-10**). It's open Monday to Friday from 8:30am to 6pm and on Saturday from 8:30am to 1pm.

THE PASSION PLAY

The Passion Play depicts the "suffering, death, and rebirth of Jesus Christ." In many ways, it's an authentic recreation of a medieval morality play. Though the theater and production methods are contemporary, the spirit of the play is highly traditional. The whole production is community-based. Locals even do all the acting—the competition for the parts of Jesus and Mary can be fierce. Performances last all day, with a break for lunch. Viewing the production can alternate between tedious and highly dramatic—but it's always fascinating. Where else would you get to witness such a pocket of medievalism in the modern world?

The play is performed at the **Passionspielhaus,** Passionwiese, at the edge of town. This modern, open-air theater, which holds 4,700 spectators, is a wonder of engineering. Performances will take place from May 22 to October 8, 2000, daily except Tuesday and Thursday. A full performance includes a morning session from 9:30am to 11:30 or 11:45am, and an afternoon session from 2:30 to either 5:30 or 6pm. Tickets cost 110DM to 165DM ($62.70 to $94.05) but have been completely sold out far in advance. Your best chance to get them is to book as part of a package deal. For more information, call ☎ **08822/92-31-0** or check out the Web site at **www.oberammergau.de.**

EXPLORING THE TOWN

Oberammergau has much to offer besides the play. Consider taking an excursion to either the **Berg Laber** (Laber Mountain), which rises to the east of the town, or **Berg Kolber** (Kolber Mountain), to the west. Berg Laber, which is slightly more dramatic, is accessible year-round via a cable-gondola (☎ **08822/4770**) that operates year-round from 9am to 11:30am and from 1 to either 5 or 5:30pm. The 10-minute ascent costs 20DM ($11.40) per person. The top of Berg Kolber is accessible via a two-passenger chairlift (☎ **08822/4760**) that operates year-round from 9 to 11:45 am, and from 1 to either 4:30 or 4:45pm. The cost is 10DM ($5.70) round-trip.

Aside from the actors, Oberammergau's most respected citizens are **wood-carvers,** many of whom have been trained in the village wood-carver's school. In the **Pilatushaus,** Ludwig-Thoma-Strasse (☎ **08822/16-82**), you can watch local carvers, as well as painters, sculptors, and potters, as they work. From mid-May to October, their hours are Tuesday to Friday from 1:30 to 6pm. You'll see many examples of their art throughout the town, on the painted cottages and inns and in the churchyard.

The **Heimatmuseum,** Dorfstrasse (☎ **08822/9-41-36**), has a notable collection of Christmas crèches, all hand-carved and -painted, from the 18th through the 20th centuries. It's open May 20 to October 15, Tuesday to Saturday from 2 to 6pm; off-season, only on Saturday from 2 to 6pm. Admission is 4DM ($2.30) for adults, 2DM ($1.15) for students, and 1DM (55¢) for children under 14.

When strolling through the village, note the **frescoed houses** named after fairy-tale characters, such as the "Hansel and Gretel House" and "Little Red Riding Hood House."

SHOPPING FOR WOOD CARVINGS

The region's wood carvings are among the most sought after in the Germanic world, and many an example has graced the mantelpieces and whatnot shelves of homes around the globe. Most subjects are religious, deriving directly from 14th-century originals; however, to cater to the demands of modern visitors, there's been an increased emphasis lately on secular subjects, such as drinking or hunting scenes. Competition is fierce for sales of these wood carvings, many of which are made in hamlets and farmhouses throughout the region. Know before you buy that even some of the most expensive "handmade" pieces might have been roughed in by machine prior to being finished off by hand.

The **Holzschnittschule (Wood Carving School)** here has conditions of study that might remind you of the severity of the medieval guilds. Students who labor over a particular sculpture are required to turn it in to the school, where it's either placed on permanent exhibition or sold during the school's once-a-year sell-off, usually over a 2-day period in July.

Josef Albl, Devrientweg 1 (☎ **08822/64-33**), a taciturn but prestigious wood-carver, specializes in bas-reliefs, some of which are complicated and highly detailed. His subjects are both religious and secular, including hunting scenes. Some of the simple pieces sell for as little as 10DM ($5.70), although commissioned pieces can stretch into the tens of thousands of dollars.

Tony Baur, Dorfstrasse 27 (☎ **08822/8-21**), has the most sophisticated inventory of wood carvings in Oberammergau. The shop employs a small cadre of carvers who usually work from their homes to create works inspired by medieval originals. The outgoing and personable sales staff is quick to admit that the forms of many of the pieces are roughed in by machine, but most of the intricate work is completed by hand. Pieces are crafted from maple, pine, or linden (basswood). Prices start at 20DM ($11.40) and go up to 10,000DM ($5,700). Carvings are in their natural grain, or stained, or polychromed (some of the most charming), and in some instances, partially gilded.

Peter Zwink, Schnitzlergasse 4 (☎ **08822/8-57**), is the place to go for clocks. If you have your heart set on buying a cuckoo clock, you'll probably find one to your liking here, even though, as the staff will point out, the cuckoo clock belongs to the Schwarzwald (see chapter 10), farther to the north. The most simple carved, hand-made clocks are battery-run and cost 120DM ($68.40). More sophisticated clocks with mechanical movement and sound start at 600DM ($342). Look for mantel clocks and floor clocks carved in baroque designs. Some need to be wound only once a year, a tradition that some families carry out as part of their New Year's Day rituals.

SIDE TRIPS FROM OBERAMMERGAU

✪ **SCHLOSS LINDERHOF**   Until the late-19th century, a modest hunting lodge, owned by the Bavarian royal family, stood on a large piece of land 8 miles west of the village. But in 1869, "Mad" King Ludwig struck again, this time creating a French rococo palace in the Ammergau Mountains. This is his most successful creation. Unlike his palace at Chiemsee (see above), Schloss Linderhof was not meant to copy any other structure. And unlike the Neuschwanstein palace (see chapter 6), its con-centration of fanciful projects and designs was not limited to the palace interior. In fact, the gardens and smaller buildings at Linderhof are, if anything, more elaborate than the two-story main structure.

The most interesting rooms are on the second floor, where ceilings are much higher because of the unusual roof plan. Ascending the winged staircase of Carrara marble, you'll find yourself at the **West Gobelin Room** (music room), with carved and gilded paneling and richly colored tapestries. This room leads directly into the **Hall of Mir-rors,** where the mirrors are set in white-and-gold panels, decorated with gilded wood carvings. The hall's ceiling is festooned with frescoes depicting mythological scenes.

The **king's bedchamber** is the largest room in the palace and overlooks the Foun-tain of Neptune and the cascades in the gardens. In the tradition of Louis XIV, who often received visitors in his bedchamber, the king's bed is closed off by a carved and gilded balustrade.

In the popular style of the previous century, Ludwig laid out the **gardens** in formal parterres with geometrical shapes, baroque sculptures, and elegant fountains. The front of the palace opens onto a large pool where, from a gilded statue in its center, a jet of water sprays 105 feet into the air.

The park also contains several other small but exotic buildings, including the **Moorish Kiosk,** where Ludwig often spent hours smoking chibouk and dreaming of himself as an Oriental prince. The unique magic grotto is built of artificial rock, with stalagmites and stalactites dividing the cavelike room into three chambers. In the main chamber, an artificial lake is illuminated from below; in Ludwig's time it had a current produced by 24 dynamo engines. A shell-shaped boat, completely gilded, is tied to a platform called the Lorelei Rock.

Schloss Linderhof, 82488 Ettal-Linderhof (☎ **08822/92030**), is open to the public throughout the year, and makes a good day trip from Munich, as well as from Oberammergau. It's open April through September daily from 9am to 5:30pm; from October through March, the grotto and Moorish Kiosk are closed, but the castle is open daily from 9:30am to noon and from 1 to 4pm. Admission in the summer is 10DM ($5.70) for adults, 7DM ($4) for students, and free for children 14 and under. In winter, admission is 7DM ($4) for adults, 4DM ($2.30) for students, and free for children 14 and under.

Buses run between Oberammergau and Schloss Linderhof seven times per day, beginning at 9am; the last bus leaves Linderhof at 5:35pm. Round-trip passage costs 8.60DM ($4.90). Motorists from Oberammergau should follow the signs to Ettal, about 3 miles away, then go another 3 miles to Draswang, and from there follow the signs to Schloss Linderhof.

✪ **KLOSTER ETTAL**   Kloster Ettal lies in a lovely valley sheltered by the steep hills of the Ammergau lies, on Kaiser-Ludwig-Platz at Ettal (☎ **08822/7-40**). This abbey was founded by Duke Ludwig the Bavarian in 1330. Monks, knights, and their ladies shared the honor of guarding its statue of the Virgin, attributed to Giovanni Pisano. In the 18th century, the golden age of the abbey, there were about 70,000 pilgrims here every year.

The church of Our Lady, within the abbey, is one of the finest examples of Bavarian rococo architecture in existence. The impressive baroque facade was built from a plan based on the designs of Enrico Zuccali. Around the polygonal core of the church is a two-story gallery. Visitors stand under a vast dome, admiring the fresco painted by John Jacob Zeiller in the summers of 1751 and 1752.

The abbey stands 2 miles south of Oberammergau, along the road to Garmisch-Partenkirchen. Admission is free, and it's open daily from 8am to 8pm in summer and to 6pm in winter. Buses from Oberammergau leave from the Rathaus and the Bahnhof once per hour during the day, with round-trip passage costing 5DM ($2.85). Call ☎ **8821/94-82-74** for information.

WHERE TO STAY & DINE

The cost of accommodation in Oberammergau includes a universally imposed kurtaxe (special tax) of 2.50DM ($1.40). This entitles visitors to a card providing small discounts at local attractions. Expect accommodations to be booked well in advance while the Passion Play is being performed.

MODERATE

Hotel Restaurant Böld. König-Ludwig-Strasse 10, 82487 Oberammergau. ☎ **08822/ 91-20.** Fax 08822/71-02. 57 units. MINIBAR TV TEL. 170DM–200DM ($96.90–$114) double. Rates include buffet breakfast. AE, DC, MC, V. Free outdoor parking; 10DM ($5.70) in garage.

This well-designed chalet hotel has steadily improved in quality and now is among the town's premier choices, in a neck-to-neck race with Parkhotel Sonnenhof. It lies only a stone's throw from the river. Comfortable public rooms are located in the hotel's central core; guest rooms are in its contemporary annex. All rooms are well-furnished; most have balconies. A sauna, solarium, and whirlpool are offered for guests' relaxation.

The restaurant features both international and regional cuisine. In the bar, you'll find a tranquil atmosphere and attentive service.

Parkhotel Sonnenhof. König-Ludwig-Strasse 12, 82487 Oberammergau. ☎ **08822/ 91-30.** Fax 08822/30-47. 65 units. TV TEL. 190DM–210DM ($108.30–$119.70) double; 200DM–230DM ($114–$131.10) suite. Rates include buffet breakfast. AE, CB, DC, MC, V.

Short on charm and alpine rusticity, this modern hotel still has a lot going for it. It's placed far enough away from the summer crowds to offer guests peace and tranquillity, but it's still within walking distance of the center. The hotel overlooks the Ammer River and a beautiful *Pfarrkirche* (parish church). Every room has a bedroom balcony with an alpine vista, often of Oberammergau's mountain, the Kobel. The bedrooms, although without old-fashioned charm, are well maintained and filled with first-class comforts. Facilities here are more extensive than at most hotels in the area, including an indoor pool, sauna, and even a bowling alley. There's also a children's playroom. Two restaurants offer many international dishes, although the Bavarian specialties are the better choices.

Schlosshotel Linderhof. Linderhof 14 (near the palace), 82488 Ettal. ☎ **08822/7-90.** Fax 08822/43-47. 29 units. MINIBAR TV TEL. 146DM–166DM ($83.20–$94.60) double. Rates include breakfast. AE, CB, DC, MC, V.

This hotel is designed with gables, shutters, and half-timbering in the style of a Bavarian chalet. The famous palace is only about 400 yards away. The bedrooms are dignified and high-ceilinged, with tasteful hints of 19th-century gentility but also with modern conveniences, such as hair dryers. The hotel's cozy restaurant is responsible for much of its business. It features an array of fixed-price menus, focusing on such standard food as pork schnitzel with mixed salad and cream-of-tomato soup. You can dine on a stone terrace accented with parasols and potted flowers. The restaurant is open daily from 8am to 8pm.

Turmwirt. Ettalerstrasse 2 (5 min. from the town center), 82487 Oberammergau. ☎ **08822/9-26-00.** Fax 08822/14-37. www.minotel.com. E-mail: turmwirt@t-online.de. 22 units. MINIBAR TV TEL. 140DM–190DM ($79.80–$108.30) double. Rates include buffet breakfast. AE, DC, MC, V. Free parking.

A cozy Bavarian-style hotel, the Turmwirt offers small, snug rooms, many with private balconies opening onto mountain views. The present building was constructed in 1889 and has been altered and renovated many times. It's an intricately painted green-shuttered country house with a well-maintained homelike interior. The owners are three generations of the Glas family, who often present Bavarian folk evenings.

Wolf Restaurant-Hotel. Dorfstrasse 1, 82487 Oberammergau. ☎ **08822/30-71.** Fax 08822/10-96. E-mail: hotel.wolf@gap.baynet.de. 32 units. TV TEL. 120DM–180DM ($68.40–$102.60) double. Rates include buffet breakfast. AE, DC, MC, V.

An overgrown Bavarian chalet, Wolf Restaurant-Hotel is at the heart of village life. Its facade, like others in the area, has an encircling balcony, heavy timbering, and window boxes spilling cascades of red and pink geraniums. Inside, it retains some local flavor, although concessions to modernity have been made, such as an elevator, conservative room furnishings, and a dining hall with a zigzag paneled ceiling. Facilities include a sauna, solarium, and outdoor pool. Five of the rooms are singles. Bedrooms range from small to medium in size.

Dining here can be both economical and gracious. The Hafner Stub'n is a rustic place for beer drinking as well as enjoying light meals. There's always a freshly made soup of the day. Main courses, such as Wiener schnitzel or roast pork with dumplings and cabbage, are generous.

INEXPENSIVE

Alte Post. Dorfstrasse 19, 82487 Oberammergau. ☎ **08822/91-00.** Fax 08822/91-01-00. www.altepost.ogan.de. E-mail: altepost@ogan.de. 32 units. TV TEL. 120DM–140DM ($68.40–$79.80) double. Rates include continental breakfast. AE, DC, MC, V. Parking 6DM ($3.40). Closed Oct 25–Dec 19.

Alte Post is a provincial inn located in the village center, built in chalet style. It has a wide overhanging roof, green-shuttered windows painted with decorative trim, a large crucifix on the facade, and tables set on a sidewalk under a long awning. It's the village's social hub. The interior has a storybook charm, with a ceiling-high green ceramic stove, alpine chairs, and shelves of pewter plates. The rustic guest rooms have wood-beamed ceilings and wide beds with giant posts; most have views. Rooms range in size from cozy to spacious. The main dining room is also rustic, with a collection of hunting memorabilia. The restaurant serves excellent Bavarian dishes. There's also an intimate drinking bar.

Hotel Café-Restaurant Friedenshöhe. König-Ludwig-Strasse 31, 82487 Oberammergau. ☎ **08822/35-98.** Fax 08822/43-45. 17 units. TEL. 110DM–170DM ($62.70–$96.90) double. Rates include buffet breakfast. AE, DC, MC, V. Closed Nov–Dec 14.

This villa enjoys a beautiful location. It's one of the town's best bargains, although for quality it's not in the same league as the Böld or the Parkhotel Sonnenhof. It once hosted Thomas Mann, who wrote here. The guest rooms, furnished in tasteful modern style, are well maintained. TVs are available on request. Rooms come in a range of different styles, from rather small singles to spacious doubles. Opt for one of the corner rooms if possible (they're bigger). Bathrooms tend to be too small and come with rather thin towels.

The Bavarian and international cuisine at the restaurant is known for its quality. There's a choice of four dining rooms, including an indoor terrace with a panoramic view and an outdoor terrace.

Hotel Schilcherhof. Bahnhofstrasse 17, 82487 Oberammergau. ☎ **08822/47-40.** Fax 08822/37-93. 26 units. 104DM–150DM ($59.30–$85.50) double. Rates include continental breakfast. AE, V. Closed Nov 15–Christmas. Free parking.

An enlarged chalet with surrounding gardens, the Schilcherhof has a modern wing with snug, good-value rooms. In summer, the terrace overflows with beer and festive living. Five minutes away lies the passion-play theater; also nearby is the Ammer River, which flows through the village. Although the house is built in the old style, with wooden front balconies and tiers of flower boxes, it has a fresh look.

Lake Constance (Bodensee) 9

Mild climate and plentiful sunshine make Lake Constance (*Bodensee* in German) a top vacation spot for lovers of sun and sand, as well as for sightseers and spa-hoppers. The hillsides that slope to the water's edge are covered with vineyards and orchards and dotted with colorful hamlets and busy tourist centers. A network of cruise ships and ferries links every major center around the lake. Even though the 162-mile shoreline of Lake Constance is shared by three nations—Austria, Germany, and Switzerland—the area around the lake is united in a common cultural and historical heritage.

Lake Constance is actually divided into three lakes, although the name is frequently applied only to the largest of these, the Obersee. The western end of the Obersee separates into two distinct branches: One, the Überlingersee, is a long fjord; the other, the Untersee, is more irregular, jutting in and out of marshland and low-lying woodland. The two branches are connected by a narrow channel—which is actually the upper Rhine.

Lake Constance offers a wealth of **activities,** including swimming, sailing, windsurfing, diving, and rowing. Local tourist offices will connect you with various outfitters. You can swim either in the cold waters of the lake itself, or in one of the heated lakeside pools. The Eichwald Lido at Lindau boasts a half-mile-long "beach," with plenty of lawns for sunbathing German-style. The other popular place for lakeside swimming at a heated pool is the Jakob Lido at Constance.

One of the best ways to see the lake is to cycle around it. **Bicycles** can be rented at all the major train stations, including Lindau and Konstanz. Car ferries allow bikes on board.

Sailing on Lake Constance is a major attraction. Some boatyards and sailing schools rent boats; you'll be asked to show some proof of proficiency (a certification from a sailing school, for example). On a more casual level, rowboats and motorboats can be rented at all the major hotels along the lake.

From Munich, motorists should take the B12, via Landsberg and Kempten, to reach the lake. Drivers from Frankfurt head south along the A81 Autobahn to Memmingen, transferring to B18. The nearest international airport to Lake Constance is at Zurich, 49 miles southwest of the town of Konstanz. The Munich airport is about 140 miles north of the lake.

1 Lindau

111 miles SW of Munich, 20 miles S of Ravensburg

Lindau dates from the end of the 9th century. It was a free imperial town of the Holy Roman Empire throughout the Middle Ages and up to 1804, when it became a part of Bavaria. For centuries, it was a center of trade between Bavaria and Switzerland.

Its unique setting on an island at the eastern end of Lake Constance made Lindau a prime tourist attraction. Today this garden city is under landmark protection, and has outgrown its boundaries and spread to the shores of the mainland. It now caters to the tourist's every whim, from bathing to baccarat.

Lindau is a charming city. You can wander at will through the maze of winding narrow streets lined with houses that have stood the test of time. At the harbor stand two **lighthouses:** one, called Mangturm, was built in the 1200s, and the other in 1856. Each tower is some 120 feet tall and can be climbed by the hearty, along narrow spiral staircases. The reward is a panoramic vista of the Alps, both Swiss and Austrian. Another interesting building here is the 15th-century **Rathaus.**

ESSENTIALS

GETTING THERE   Lindau is connected to the mainland by a road bridge and a causeway for walkers and trains. It's a transportation link between the western part of Lake Constance and the towns of Austria and Switzerland, which lie directly across the water. Regional flights come in to the Friedrichshafen airport (see below). The nearest major airport is at Zurich.

By Train   The Lindau Bahnhof is on the major Basel-Singen-Radolfzell-Lindau and Lindau-Kissleg-Memmingen-Buchloe rail lines, with frequent connections in all directions. Call ☎ **01805/996633** for information and schedules.

By Bus   Regional bus service along Lake Constance is offered by **RAB Regionalverkehr Alb-Bodensee GmbH** in Friedrichshafen (☎ **07541/30130**).

By Ferry   Five to seven ferries per day (depending on the season) link Lindau with Konstanz. Before reaching Lindau, boats stop at Meersburg, Mainau, and Friedrichshafen; the entire trip takes 3 hours. Call the tourist office for information and schedules.

By Car   Access by car is via the A96 Autobahn and the B31.

VISITOR INFORMATION   **Tourist-Information** is at Ludwigstrasse 68 (☎ **08382/26-00-30**). From April to September 5, the office is open Monday to Saturday 9am to 7pm; in winter, Monday to Friday 9am to noon and 2 to 5pm.

SEEING THE SIGHTS

A tour of this *Ferieninsel* (Holiday Island) begins with the **old harbor,** seen from the lakeside promenade. The **Mangturm,** the old lighthouse, stands on the promenade as a reminder of the heavy fortifications that once surrounded the city. It also marks the point where Lindau was once divided into two islands. The entrance to the harbor is marked by the 108-foot **New Lighthouse** (19th century) and the **Bavarian Lion,** standing guard as yachts and commercial ships pass by below. From the promenade, you can gaze out past these monuments over the water to the Alps on the opposite side of the lake.

Hauptstrasse, in the center of the town, is the main street of the Altstadt. The most easily recognizable building here is the **Altes Rathaus,** erected in 1422 on the site of a vineyard. The stepped gables are typical of the period, but the building's facade also

Lake Constance (Bodensee)

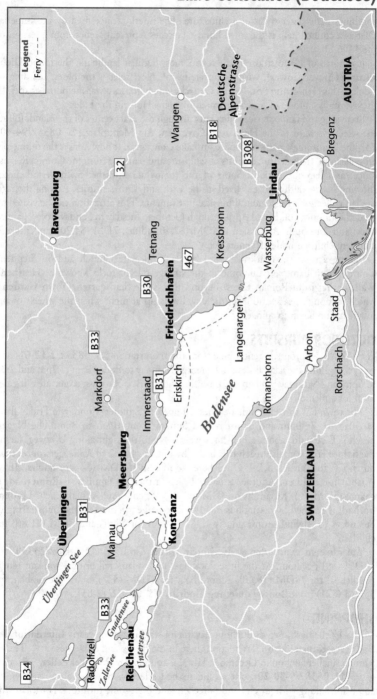

Legend
Ferry - - - -

AUSTRIA

Deutsche Alpenstrasse

B18

B308

Bregenz

Lindau

Wangen

32

Ravensburg

Wasserburg

Kressbronn

Tetnang

467

B30

Friedrichhafen

Langenargen

Staad

B33

Romanshorn

Arbon

Markdorf

B31

Eriskirch

Immerstaad

Rorschach

Bodensee

SWITZERLAND

Meersburg

Überlingen

B31

Konstanz

Überlinger See

Mainau

B33

B34

Gnadensee

Radolfzell

Reichenau

Zellersee

Untersee

335

combines many later styles of architecture. The interior, once used by the Imperial Diet as a council hall, is the town library. Frescoes represent scenes from a session of the 1496 Diet.

Just north of Hauptstrasse is the town's most familiar landmark, the round **Diebsturm (Thieves' Tower),** with its turreted roof. Next to it is the oldest building in Lindau, the 11th-century **St. Peter's Church,** which houses a war memorial chapel. In the church is a group of frescoes painted by Hans Holbein the Elder.

Returning to Hauptstrasse, which cuts through the exact center of the island, follow the street eastward to the **Haus zum Cavazzen,** Am Marktplatz (☎ **08382/94-40-73**), the handsomest patrician house on Lake Constance. It now houses the municipal art collection. Included are exhibits of sculpture and painting from the Gothic, Renaissance, and baroque periods. Some of the rooms are furnished with period pieces showing how wealthy citizens lived in the 18th and 19th centuries. Among the rarities is a collection of mechanical musical instruments. This attraction can be visited by guided tour only, conducted April through October, Tuesday to Sunday from 10am to noon and 2 to 5pm. Admission is 4DM ($2.40) adults, 7DM ($4.20) students and children; children under 10 enter free.

Passing across Am Marktplatz and by the Collegiate Church and St. Stephen's Church, both baroque, you come to the strange pile of rocks known as **Heathen's Wall,** dating from Roman times. Beyond this is the **Stadtgarten (Town Garden),** which, although peaceful during the day, livens up at night when the wheels of the town's casino begin to spin.

OUTDOOR PURSUITS

For 15DM ($9) you can rent a bike from the train station (☎ **08382/2-12-61**) and go cycling along the lake. Bikes can be rented Monday to Friday 9am to 7pm and 2:30 to 6pm, and Saturday 9:30am to 7pm. Lindenhofpark is the most scenic area (it's also ideal for a picnic).

The town has three lakeside beaches, all open in summer Monday to Friday from 10:30am to 7:30pm and Saturday and Sunday from 10am to 8pm. The biggest beach is **Eichwald,** about a half-hour walk away to the right along Uferweg, facing the harbor. You can also reach this beach by bus no. 1 or 2 to Anheggerstrasse, then bus no. 3 to Karmelbuckel. Once here, admission is 5DM ($3) for adults, 3DM ($1.80) for children. Another, smaller beach, attracting families, is **Römerbad;** it charges 5DM ($3) for adults or 3DM ($1.80) for children. A final beach, **Lindenhofbad,** is reached by taking bus no. 1 or 2 to Anheggerstrasse, then transferring to bus no. 4 to Alwind. Admission is 4DM ($2.40) for adults and 3DM ($1.80) for children.

You can rent windsurfers at **Kreitmeir,** In der Grub 17 (☎ **08382/23330**) for 15DM ($9) per hour. At the little dock next to Lindau's rail bridge, you can rent a paddleboat for 14DM ($8.40), a motorboat for 45DM ($27), or an electric boat for 35DM ($21) from **Bootsvermietung Hodrius** (☎ **08382/42-85**).

SHOPPING

Michael Zeller is known throughout Bavaria for staging a twice-yearly **Internationale-Bodensee-Kunstauktion** (art auction) here in the spring and fall (dates vary). There's a much smaller auction in December. His year-round store, **Michael Zeller,** 3 Bindergasse (☎ **08382/9-30-20**), offers Lindau's best selection of watercolors, engravings, and prints, along with jewelry and porcelain, and even some furniture. For the town's best selection of pottery, head for **Angelika Ochsenreiter,** Ludwigstrasse 29 (☎ **08382/2-38-67**), which has teapots, cups, dishes, and animal figures.

WHERE TO STAY
EXPENSIVE

Hotel Bayerischer Hof. Seepromenade, 88131 Lindau. ☎ **800/223-5652** in the U.S. and Canada, or 08382/91-50. Fax 08382/91-55-91. www.gcb.de/lindau/home.html. E-mail: info@ gcb.de. 102 units. MINIBAR TV TEL. 265DM–530DM ($159–$318) double; 750DM–790DM ($450–$474) suite. Accommodation is free for children under 10. Rates include buffet breakfast. AE, CB, DC, MC, V. Parking 10DM–15DM ($6–$9).

This old-world hotel clearly outdistances all others in Lindau. It opens onto the lakeside promenade and looks almost like a hotel on the Mediterranean. The atmosphere and service here are first rate; for real luxury, however, the Steigenberger Insel Hotel at Konstanz (see below) is the grander choice. The large guest rooms are the finest in Lindau, each well furnished with traditional styling. Most of them have good views; the less desirable units overlook a narrow thoroughfare. The public rooms are rather sterile.

Dining/Diversions: The cuisine is the best in town. The formal dining room has wide-screened windows with views of the lake. There's also a lounge and a bar.

Amenities: Room service, hair dryers, laundry and dry cleaning service, twice-daily maid service, massage, baby-sitting, secretarial services, sundeck, conference rooms, business center, and health club with sauna. A beauty salon and boutiques are nearby.

Hotel Reutemann und Seegarten. Seepromenade, 88131 Lindau. ☎ **08382/91-50.** Fax 08382/91-55-91. 64 units. MINIBAR TV TEL. 200DM–370DM ($120.00–$222.00) double. Children under 10 free. Rates include buffet breakfast. AE, CB, DC, MC, V. Parking 10DM–15DM ($6–$9).

Located next to its parent, the superior Bayerischer Hof, this hotel consists of two distinct villas. The Reutemann section has its own waterfront garden, with outdoor furniture, lemon trees, and wisteria vines. Most rooms are large, and some have tile bathrooms, along with heated towel racks, huge tubs, and endless hot water. The Seegarten has the more attractive facade. It's built like a Bavarian villa, with little flower-filled balconies and trailing vines. It, too, has an informal lakefront garden with flower beds and furniture for sunbathing. Public rooms are elegant and the guest rooms are spacious and handsome, especially the lake-view ones (which cost more, naturally).

Dining/Diversions: The romantic Zum Lieben Augustin tavern (closed in winter) is shared with the Bayerischer Hof. It serves good regional and international dishes, along with lots of beer and wine.

Amenities: Concierge, hair dryers, room service, dry cleaning and laundry service, in-room massage, baby-sitting, secretarial services, fitness center with sauna, business center and conference rooms; a beauty salon and boutiques are nearby.

MODERATE

Hotel-Garni Brugger. Bei der Heidenmauer 11, 88131 Lindau. ☎ **08382/9-34-10.** Fax 08382/41-33. 23 units. MINIBAR TV TEL. 150DM–240DM ($90–$144) double. Additional bed 40DM ($24) extra. Rates include continental breakfast. AE, DC, MC, V. Parking 12DM ($7.20).

This modest, charming little hotel is the best affordable choice in Lindau. It's pleasingly proportioned, with a gabled attic and expansive French doors that open onto the balconies in the back. The small rooms are up-to-date, furnished in a functional modern style, with lots of light. The latest innovation is a winter garden filled with potted plants. The location is an easy walk from the lake and casino.

Insel-Hotel. Maximilianstrasse 42 (a quarter-mile from the lake), 88131 Lindau. ☎ **08382/50-17.** Fax 08382/67-56. 28 units. MINIBAR TV TEL. 184DM–188DM ($110.40–$112.80) double. Rates include continental breakfast. AE, CB, DC, MC, V. Parking 18DM ($10.80).

Although not as stylish as its closest competitor (above), the Insel is still a good buy for the area. Its small but comfortable rooms are furnished with modern pieces. The breakfast room opens onto Maximilianstrasse, a pedestrian zone. A small selection of snacks can be ordered daily from 10am to 7pm.

WHERE TO DINE

✪ **Hoyerberg Schlüssle.** Hoyerbergstrasse 64, at Lindau-Aeschach. ☎ **08382/2-52-95.** Reservations required in the restaurant; not required in the cafe. Main courses 44DM–56DM ($26.40–$33.60); fixed-price menus 100DM ($60). AE, DC, MC, V. Restaurant Tues–Sat noon–2pm and 6–10:30pm; cafe Tues–Sat 2–5pm. Closed Jan 15–Feb 28. CONTINENTAL.

The Hoyerberg Schlüssle is the only restaurant on the lake that can rival the superb Seehotel Siber at Konstanz (see below). The inner room is beautifully decorated, with a view of the mountains and lake. You can also dine on the two terraces. Continental delicacies include cream of scampi soup, Bodensee pike-perch stuffed with champagne-flavored herbs, and Allgäuer saddle of venison with small flour dumplings and French beans. Meals here are memorable; the chef has great flair and style—and doesn't oversauce.

Villino. Hoyren (a half-mile east of Lindau's center), Hoyerberg 34, 88131 Lindau. ☎ **08382/934512.** Fax 08382/93450. Reservations recommended. Main courses 50DM–55DM ($30–$33); set-price 5-course menu 126DM ($75.60). MC, V. Tues–Sun 6–10:30pm. ITALIAN.

Set in the suburb of Hoyren, this hotel is better known for its excellent Italian restaurant than for its bedrooms. Only dinner is served, within a comfortable room decorated in high-tech Milanese style. The elegant menu items include pesto-laced spaghetti, Sicilian-style fish soup, a heaping platter of scampi served with stuffed squid and fresh tomatoes, anglerfish and lobster fried with cardamom, filet of *zander* with a ragout of asparagus and new potatoes, and a particularly succulent version of leg of lamb with garlic sauce.

If you're too stuffed to move on after your meal, the establishment maintains 10 bedrooms, priced at 220DM to 360DM ($132 to $216) each, plus six suites at 400DM ($240) each. Each unit has a private balcony, minibar, TV, and telephone. Rates include breakfast, and parking is free.

Zum Sünfzen. Maximilianstrasse 1. ☎ **08382/58-65.** Reservations recommended. Main dishes 18DM–70DM ($10.80–$42). AE, DC, MC, V. Daily 8:30am–11pm. GERMAN/BAVARIAN.

Owned by the same family that runs the Insel-Hotel, this is an old, all-wood house/restaurant serving good food at reasonable prices. Dishes range from roast pork with vegetables to fillet of venison. Fresh fish from Lake Constance is a specialty. The food is the type you might be served in a middle-class private home along the lake.

LINDAU AFTER DARK

Lindau's casino, Oskar-Groll-Anlage 6 (☎ **08382/50-51**), offers slot machines from 3pm to 2am, and blackjack and roulette from 7pm to 2am. The bet ceiling is 12,000DM ($7,200) for roulette. Admission is 5DM ($3), and a passport is required as proof of age. Men should wear a jacket and tie.

SIDE TRIPS FROM LINDAU

WASSERBURG   Four miles west of Lindau lies the town of Wasserburg, which means "water castle." You can wander the traffic-free town's narrow streets, taking in the crooked little medieval houses. Its **fortress,** which stands on a promontory on a loop of the Inn River, is an enchanting discovery. It was sold to the Hapsburgs when its owner, the Fuggers of Augsburg, accumulated serious debts. Eventually the Bavarian government took over.

Head first for the center of the town, Marienplatz, where you can see the tall stepped gables of the Town Hall or **Rathaus.** Guided tours of the second floor Ratssaal are given Tuesday through Friday at 10am, 11am, 2pm, 3pm, and 4pm, and Saturday and Sunday tours at 10am and 11am. Tours cost 2DM ($1.20). The hall is richly adorned with painted panels and carved woodwork. The most interesting church, **St. Jakob,** can be seen on the Kirchplatz. The nave is a masterpiece by the Gothic architect Hans von Burghausen. In the 15th century a chancel and tower were added. If the church is open, you can seek out its elaborate late Renaissance pulpit, another architectural masterpiece.

LANGENARGEN   This town, which lies 5 miles west of Wasserburg, is celebrated for its **Montfort Castle,** Untere Seestrasse 5, which is named for its original founders, the counts of Montfort-Werdenberg. When King Wilhelm I of Württemberg took over, he reconstructed it in a faux-Moorish style. If you climb its tower, you'll be rewarded with a panoramic view of the lake. Hours are 10am to noon and 9am to 5pm but only from Easter through October; admission is 2DM ($1.20) adults, 1DM (60¢) children.

The **Langenargen Stadtmuseum** or city museum, Marktplatz 20 (☎ **07543/ 3410**), is worth a visit if you're interested in some of the slightly more obscure (but still talented) painters of the 20th century. Notable is a series of works by Hans Purrmann (1880–1966), who was a great admirer of Henri Matisse. Purrmann lived at Langenargen from 1915 until 1935. The Nazis denounced his art as "decadent" and prevented it from being seen publicly in Germany until after World War II. The museum is open from April to October Tuesday through Sunday from 10am to noon and 2:30 to 5pm. Admission is 2DM ($1.20).

2 Friedrichshafen

13½ miles W of Lindau; 12 miles S of Ravensburg

Friedrichshafen is set at the northeastern corner of the Bodensee, near the lake's widest point. This mostly modern city was almost completely rebuilt after the devastation of World War II. It's graced with one of the longest waterfront exposures of any town along the lake. Besides that, the town's highlights are two interesting museums and the dome-capped **Schlosskirche,** the premier reminder of Friedrichshafen's baroque past.

ESSENTIALS
GETTING THERE   By Air   The **Friedrichshafen** (☎ **07541/28401**) airport lies 3 miles north of town. Flights come in from Zurich, Frankfurt, Düsseldorf, and Berlin. The nearest major airport is Zurich, 62 miles away.

By Train   Friedrichshafen is the largest railway junction along the northern edge of the Bodensee and serves as a major transfer point for rail passengers going on to other cities and resorts along the lake. The town has two railway stations, the **Stadtbahnhof,** in the center, and the **Hafenbahnhof,** along the Seestrasse, about three-quarters of a mile away. Both of these stations are interconnected with bus nos. 1, 2, 3, 4, 5, 6, and 7. Trains arrive from both Ulm and from Stuttgart at intervals of between 1 and 2 hours throughout the day. For railway information and schedules, call ☎ **01805/ 9 96633.**

By Bus   Regional bus service along Lake Constance is provided by **RAB Region-alverkehr Alb-Bodensee GmbH** in Friedrichshafen (☎ **07541/30130** for more information).

By Car   Friedrichshafen is easily reached from both Stuttgart and Munich. From Stuttgart, follow Autobahn 8 east to the city of Ulm, then turn south onto Route 30 directly into Friedrichshafen. From Munich follow Autobahn 96 west/southwest to Lindau, then head west on Route 31, which runs along Lake Constance to Friedrichshafen.

By Boat   Between April and October, about eight lake steamers travel to and from Friedrichshafen from Lindau, Bregenz (Austria), and Konstanz. For information about departure times and details, call ☎ 07541/201389. A ferry runs year-round between Friedrichshafen and Romanshorn in Switzerland; the trip takes about 40 minutes and costs 9.40DM ($5.65) for adults and 5DM ($3) for children.

VISITOR INFORMATION   The city's **Tourist Information Office** is at Bahnhof-platz 2 (☎ 07541/30010). Between May and September, it's open Monday to Friday 9am to 5pm, Saturday 10am to 2pm. October to April, it's open Monday to Thursday 9am to noon and 2 to 5pm, and Friday 9am to 1pm.

EXPLORING THE TOWN

The best thing to do in town is to stroll the lake-fronting **Seepromenade,** with its sweeping view that extends on clear days all the way to the Swiss Alps. Cycling along the broad Seestrasse is also a delight. A kiosk within the Stadtbahnhof rents bikes for 12DM ($7.20) a day. Contact the tourist office for details.

The town's architectural highlight is the 17th-century **Schlosskirche,** Schlossstrasse 33 (☎ 07541/21422). The palatial ecclesiastical buildings that were once part of the church's monastery were converted in the 1800s into a palace for the kings of Würt-temberg. Today, they're privately owned and can't be entered, but the church itself is well worth a visit. It's open only between Easter and October, daily from 9am to 6pm.

The **Zeppelin-Museum** (☎ 07541/38010), in the Hafenbahnhof, on Seestrasse 22, is a tribute to Count Ferdinand von Zeppelin. This native of Konstanz invented and tested the aircraft that bore his name in the years before and after 1900. Within the museum's premises you'll find a re-creation of the giant and historic Zeppelin called the *Hindenburg,* which exploded in a catastrophic fire in New Jersey in 1937, possibly because of sabotage. In addition to memorabilia associated with Zeppelins and their inventor, the museum also contains a full-scale replica of the passenger cabins aboard the famous blimp. From May to October, it's open Tuesday to Sunday from 10am to 6pm; from November to April, it's open Tuesday to Sunday 10am to 5pm. Admission is 12DM ($7.20) for adults and 6DM ($3.60) for children 16 and under. There's a gift shop as well.

Of interest to students of educational techniques is Friederichshafen's **Schule-museum,** Friedrichstrasse 14 (☎ 07541/32622), which traces the development of education between 1850 (when classes were taught by monks and nuns) and 1930 (when education was the responsibility of the German state). The museum lies near the Schlosskirche in the historic heart of town. Look for the reconstructions of school rooms from various periods in the 19th and 20th centuries. From April through October, the museum is open daily from 10am to 5pm; from November to March it's open Tuesday to Sunday from 2 to 5pm. Admission costs 2DM ($1.20) for adults and 1DM (60¢) for children.

WHERE TO STAY

Hotel Buchhorner Hof. Friedrichstrasse 33, 88045, Friedrichshafen. ☎ **07541/20-50.** Fax 07541/3-26-63. www.buchhorn.de. E-mail: robotbaur@t-online.de. 96 units. MINIBAR TV TEL. 170DM–240DM ($102–$144) double; 260DM–350DM ($156–$210) suite. AE, DC, MC, V. Parking 12DM ($7.20).

This charming four-star lakeside hotel provides a compromise between the luxurious modern comfort of larger hotels and the traditional hospitality of smaller inns. It's housed in the oldest building in town. The rooms are well furnished. The hotel restaurant serves adequate fare at lunch and dinner, and the hotel bar is a cozy retreat. The new fitness center has a sauna, a steam room, a Turkish bath, whirlpools, and a solarium. There's also a bicycle-rental desk.

Hotel City-Krone. Schanzstrasse 7, 88045, Friedrichshafen. ☎ **07541/70-50.** Fax 07541/ 70-51-00. E-mail: citykrone@t-online.de. 86 units. MINIBAR TV TEL. 212DM–272DM ($127.20–$163.20) double. Rates include breakfast. AE, DC, MC, V. Free parking.

This modern building in a lakeside setting isn't very traditional or charming, but it's comfortable and fun. The rooms are adequately furnished, and the lobby is pleasant. The restaurant, Old City, and the bar, Ulf's Nightcafé, are the brightest stars here. Old City turns out reasonable fare of regional specialties and international dishes, and Ulf's Nightcafé gives you an excellent opportunity to mix and mingle with locals, both young and old, who frequent the bar at night. Ask the hotel desk about excursions by bike, train, ship, or foot. Amenities include a sauna, solarium, and swimming pool.

Hotel Goldenes-Rad. Karlstrasse 43, 88045, Friedrichshafen. ☎ **800/528-1234** or 07541/ 28-50. Fax 07541/28-52-85. E-mail: goldenese-rad@t-online.de. 65 units. MINIBAR TV TEL. 196DM–250DM ($117.60–$150) double; 250DM ($150) suite. Rates include buffet breakfast. AE, DC, MC, V. Parking 8DM ($4.80).

Located in the pedestrian center in the middle of town, this traditional hotel is a short walk from Lake Constance, the ferry, and the new Zeppelin Museum. All the rooms are comfortable and modern, with features such as hair dryers, cosmetic mirrors, and safes. The hotel restaurant serves a light cuisine, with many fresh fish specialties and fixed-price menus that change daily. Amenities are surprising for a hotel in this price range, including a gym, sauna, and solarium; massages and bike rentals are also available. The location is not very car-friendly; however, the hotel does have its own parking lot nearby. The English-speaking staff is courteous and helpful.

Seehotel Friedrichshafen. Bahnhofsplatz 2 (near the railway station), 88045 Friedrichshafen. ☎ **07541/30-30.** Fax 07541/30-31-00. 132 units. MINIBAR TV TEL. 265DM ($159) double; 335DM ($201) suite. Rates include buffet breakfast. AE, DC, MC, V. Parking free outside; 10DM ($6) inside.

This is one of the newest and most appealing hotels in town. It's right beside the Seerpromenade—the wide pedestrian parkway that follows the edge of the lake. On the premises are both a bar and a restaurant. The staff is sensitive and well trained. The small rooms are sensibly, even stylishly, decorated. Some have air-conditioning; most have views of the water.

WHERE TO DINE

Hotel-Restaurant Maier. Poststrasse 1–3, Fischbach (4 miles west of Friedrichshafen), 88048 Friedrichshafen. ☎ **07541/40-40.** Reservations recommended. Main courses 20DM–50DM ($12–$30). AE, DC, MC, V. Daily 11am–2pm and 6–10pm. INTERNATIONAL/ GERMAN.

Set at the center of the hamlet of Fischbach, at the edge of the lake, this establishment is better known for its restaurant than for its bedrooms. Local diners appreciate the generous, well-prepared portions, the attentive service, and the sweeping views over the lake. One of the dining rooms is contemporary and modern; the other is a re-creation of a traditional *stube* in the mountains. Menu items include marinated herring, venison in red wine sauce with mushrooms, salmon-trout or pike-perch from the nearby Bodensee, schnitzels, goulash soup, and elaborate pastries for dessert.

The establishment also contains 50 rooms, each with minibar, TV, and telephone. Doubles cost 165DM to 230DM ($99 to $138) and include breakfast and free parking.

Restaurant Kurgarten. Olgastrasse 20. ☎ **07541/3-20-33.** Reservations not necessary. Main courses 15DM–30DM ($9–$18). AE, DC, MC, V. Daily 10am–midnight. INTERNATIONAL.

Depending on the time of day, this place might look like a cafe, a bar, or a restaurant. It has a beautiful view over its own garden and the lake. There's a wide range of tasty menu items. Vegetarian choices include mushrooms stuffed with spinach and zucchini stuffed with ratatouille. Other good options include an Argentine beefsteak with herb butter and grilled scampi on rice with slices of local vegetables and salad.

3 Meersburg

118 miles S of Stuttgart, 89 miles SE of Freiburg

Like the towns of Italy's lake district, this village on the northern shore of Lake Constance cascades in terraces down the hillside to the water. The heart of Meersburg is a pedestrian area. You can drive into town as far as the Neues Schloss; then you must leave your car and explore on foot. In the center, the streets become narrow promenades and steps wander up and down the hillside. From the dock, both large and small boats set out for trips on the water. Many water sports are offered here. One charming little feature of Meersburg is the presence of a town watchman who still makes nightly rounds, keeping alive an ancient tradition.

ESSENTIALS

GETTING THERE   By Plane   Regional flights come in to the Friedrichshafen airport, 12 miles from Meersburg. The nearest international airport is at Zürich, 49 miles away.

By Train   The nearest rail station is in **Überlingen,** 9 miles away, on the Basel-Singen-Radolfzell-Lindau rail line, with frequent connections in all directions. Call ☎ **01805/996633** for more information. From Überlingen train station, buses depart for Meersburg at 30-minute intervals every day between 6:15am and 9:45pm, charging 7DM ($4.20) each way. Buses are marked either "Meersburg" or "Friedrichshafen" but always bear number "7395" on the front.

By Bus   Buses arrive about every 30 minutes throughout the day from Friedrichshafen. Regional bus service along Lake Constance is provided by **RAB Regionalverkehr Alb-Bodensee GmbH** in Friedrichshafen (call ☎ **07541/30130** for more information).

By Ferry   Regular ferry service goes to the town of Konstanz.

By Car   Access by car is via the A7 Autobahn from the north or Highways 31 and 33. You can drive from Munich in about 3 hours; from Frankfurt in about 4½ hours; and from Stuttgart in about 2 hours.

VISITOR INFORMATION   For tourist information, contact the **Kur- und Verkehrsamt,** Kirchstrasse 4 (☎ **07532/43-11-11**). May to October it's open Monday to Friday 8am to 6:30pm and Saturday 10am to 2pm. November to May it's open Monday to Friday 9am to noon and 2:30 to 5pm.

SPECIAL EVENTS   The surrounding vineyards produce excellent wine, and on the second weekend in September wine makers around the lake come to Meersburg for the **Lake Constance Wine Festival.**

EXPLORING THE TOWN

After you enter the town through the ancient **Obertor** (Upper Gate), you'll be on Marktplatz. Here lies the 16th-century **Rathaus,** which contains a typical German

Ratskeller. Leading off from this is **Steigstrasse,** the most interesting artery, passing between rows of half-timbered houses whose arcades serve as covered walkways above the street.

Nearby, at Schlossplatz, is the ✪ **Altes Schloss** (☎ 07532/80000), which dates from 628 and is the oldest German castle still intact. All the relics of a warring age are here—clubs, flails, armor, helmets, and axes—along with 30 fully furnished rooms, decorated with pieces from the various epochs. The bishops of Konstanz lived in this castle until the 18th century, when they moved to the Neues Schloss (see below). The baron of Lassberg, an admirer of medieval romance, then took over, and invited Annette von Droste-Hülshoff (1797–1848), his sister-in-law and Germany's leading female poet, to come as well. She had the castle turned into a setting for artists and writers. You can visit her luxuriously furnished chambers, as well as the murky dungeons and the castle museum with its medieval jousting equipment. The castle is open March through October, daily from 9am to 6:30pm; November through February, daily from 10am to 6pm. Admission is 9DM ($5.40) for adults, 8DM ($4.80) students, and 6DM ($3.60) for children. Next to the castle is the **Castle Mill** (1620), with a 28-foot wooden waterwheel, the oldest of its kind in Germany.

You go from the medieval to the baroque when you enter the **Neues Schloss,** Schlossplatz (☎ 07532/414071), which faces the Altes Schloss. The leading architect of the 18th century, Balthasar Neumann, was responsible for some of the castle's design. Ceiling paintings and frescoes were done by prominent artists and craftsmen. Elegant stucco moldings grace the ceilings and walls. The Spiegelsaal, or Hall of Mirrors, is the setting for an international music festival in summer. On the top floor is the **Dornier Museum,** which traces the history of Germany's aircraft and aerospace industries. Admission for the castle is 5DM ($3) for adults and 4DM ($2.40) for children and students. It's open March to November, daily from 10am to 6pm.

On the promenade below stands the **Great House,** which dates from 1505. It now holds ticket offices for the railway and steamer lines on Lake Constance. Regular ferry service to Konstanz leaves from the dock on the outskirts of town.

OUTDOOR PURSUITS

The rock-strewn beaches lie west of the town center; here you can go swimming or just soak up the sun for free. But you'll find the amenities better at the **Beheiztes Freibad,** Uferpromenade (☎ 07532/41-40-60), east of the harbor. Here you can lie on the grass on a strip of sand adjacent to the lake, or immerse yourself in any of three outdoor swimming pools. There's also a sauna on the premises, plus refreshment stands. Entrance to the compound costs 6DM ($3.60) for adults, 4DM ($2.40) students, 3DM ($1.80) for children; free for children under 4.

If you'd like to cycle along the lakefront promenades, head first to **Sport Pfan,** Unterstadtstrasse 7 (☎ 07532/48873). You can rent one of the shop's 10 bicycles for 15DM ($9) a day. It operates only between April and October.

A Taste of Honey

Just 6 miles from Meersburg is the famous **Wallfahrtskirche** (☎ 07556/9-20-30) at Birnau, 3 miles southeast of Überlingen. This pilgrimage basilica, which dates from the mid–18th century, was built in rococo style, with rose, blue, and beige marble predominating. A celebrated statuette here is called the *Honigschlecker,* or "honey-taster"—it shows a baby sucking a finger as he's yanked out of a nest of bees. It's to the right of the St. Bernard altarpiece. The church is open daily from 7am to 7pm. Admission is free.

WHERE TO STAY

Gasthof zum Bären. Marktplatz 11, 88709 Meersburg. ☎ **07532/4-32-20.** Fax 07532/43-22-44. 20 units. TV TEL. 120DM–185DM ($72–$111) double. Rates include continental breakfast. No credit cards. Parking 8DM ($4.80). Closed mid-Nov to mid-Mar.

This picture-book hotel in the heart of town offers the best value in Meersburg. Its window boxes overflow with red geraniums. There's also an ornately decorated corner tower and a tangle of purple wisteria crawling over most of the facade. The hotel was constructed in 1605 on the foundations of a building dating from 1250 (the cellar of the original Bären is still here and can be visited). The small guest rooms are attractive, snug, and cozily furnished. The innkeepers speak English.

The inn has two good restaurants, serving both regional and international food, including vegetarian dishes. Fish from Lake Constance is a specialty.

Seehotel zur Munz. Seestrasse 7, 88709 Meersburg. ☎ **07532/43590.** Fax 07532/77-85. 11 units. TV TEL. 150DM–190DM ($90–$114) double. Rates include buffet breakfast. AE, MC, V. Parking 10DM ($6) covered; 6DM ($3.60) uncovered.

If you're not looking for glamour or a romantic atmosphere, and want to save some marks, consider checking in here. Only a pedestrian walkway and an iron railing separate this hotel from the tree-lined lakefront. The ambience within lets you forget urban bustle. The Seehotel sur Munz is the simplest of our recommendations, but it's clean, decent, and comfortable in every way.

Strandhotel Wilder Mann. Bismarckplatz 2, 88709 Meersburg. ☎ **07532/90-11.** Fax 07532/90-14. 33 units. TV TEL. 190DM–275DM ($114–$165) double; 350DM ($210) suite. Rates include buffet breakfast. AE, MC, V. Parking 10DM ($6).

This baroque country hotel is just beyond a stone embankment at the edge of the lake. The building's facade is the backdrop for a painted illustration of a traditional folk figure, called *der wilde Mann*. Here he's contemplating whether to have a stag or a unicorn for supper. The small rooms are comfortable and cozily furnished. There's a good view from the lakeside terrace at the restaurant. The hotel is open year-round, though the restaurant is closed from the end of October until the beginning of April.

Weinstube Löwen. Marktplatz 2, 88709 Meersburg. ☎ **07532/4-30-40.** Fax 07532/43-04-10. 21 units. TV TEL. 150DM–220DM ($90–$132) double. Rates include buffet breakfast. AE, MC, V. Parking 8DM ($4.80).

Weinstube Löwen is an old, charming inn on the market square. Its facade has green shutters, window boxes filled with red geraniums, and vines reaching the upper windows under the steep roof. The Fischer family has updated its interior while keeping a homelike ambience. All but a few of the rooms have been modernized in a streamlined functional style. They are, however, a bit cramped. The wood-paneled Weinstube, with a white ceramic corner stove, serves good food and drink. Consider a meal here even if you're not a guest.

WHERE TO DINE

Winzerstube zum Becher. Höllgasse 4 (near the Altes Schloss). ☎ **07532/90-09.** Reservations required. Main courses 20DM–45DM ($12–$27); fixed-price meals 35DM–48DM ($21–$28.80) at lunch, 65DM–100DM ($39–$60) at dinner. AE, DC, V. Tues–Sun noon–2pm and 6–10pm; drinks, snacks, and lunch Tues–Sun 11am–2pm and 5pm–midnight. Closed mid-Dec to mid-Jan. REGIONAL/GERMAN.

Year after year this little independently run restaurant manages to serve better food than any hotel in town. If you've come to Germany with images of a handcrafted Weinstube that radiates warmth, then you should dine here. A pea-green tile oven tucked away in a corner provides heat in winter. The chairs are not that comfortable, but the rest of the flowered, paneled, and happily cluttered room provides a cozy atmosphere. The specialty of the chef is onion-flavored Swabian *Rostbraten* with spätzle, along with a host of other specialties, including fresh fish from Lake Constance. A superb fixed-price dinner cuts down on the cost. The restaurant also offers drinks (mostly wine) and snacks.

MEERSBURG AFTER DARK

The **Spiegelsaal (Hall of Mirrors),** in the Neues Schloss at Schlossplatz (☎ **07532/ 431111**), is the splendid backdrop for an annual international chamber-music festival. It takes place every Saturday from the last week in June to the first week in September. You might hear, for example, two baroque ensembles, a string quartet, and a pianist playing the works of Schumann. Tickets run from 24DM to 28DM ($14.40 to $16.80). Call ☎ **07532/43-11-11** for information.

The **Konstanz Stadttheater,** the oldest theater in Germany, dating from 1609, moves to its summer theater in Meersburg from July through August. For more details about the Meersburg program offerings, call ☎ **07532/43-11-10.**

4 Konstanz (Constance)

111 miles S of Stuttgart, 47 miles NE of Zürich

Crowded against the shores of Lake Constance by the borders of Switzerland, the medieval town of Konstanz had nowhere to grow but northward across the river. Today this resort city lies on both banks of the infant Rhine, as the river begins its long journey to the North Sea. Its strategic position made Konstanz the most important city on the lake. Nowadays tourists come to enjoy the shops, the largest beach in the area, and the magical beauty of nearby **Mainau island.**

Konstanz's history is long and distinguished. Early Celtic dwellings here were possibly fortified by the Romans under Claudius in A.D. 41. In the 3rd century, the fort was seized by the Germanic tribes, who later became Christianized and founded a bishop's see around A.D. 580. In the 12th century, Emperor Frederick I Barbarossa came here to make peace with the Lombard states. Many years later, after the defeat of the Protestant league, which it had supported, Konstanz was ceded to Austria. It remained Austrian territory until 1805, when it was returned to Germany. Although Konstanz never regained the political status it had held in the early part of the 16th century, it is today still the economic and cultural center of the district.

ESSENTIALS

GETTING THERE   By Train   Konstanz is on the main Konstanz-Singen-Villingen-Offenburg rail line, the Schwarzwaldbahn, with frequent connections to the major cities of Germany. For rail information, call ☎ **01805/996633.**

By Bus   Regional bus service around Konstanz is provided by **SBG Südbaden Bus GmbH** at Radolfzell (☎ **07732/9-94-70**). **RAB Friedrichshafen** (☎ **07541/2-20-77**) offers service along the lake going east.

By Boat   Ferry service and lake cruises operate between Konstanz, Mainau Island, Meersburg, Lindau, and Bregenz. The operator is **Bodensee-Schiffsbetriebe,** Hafenstrasse 6 (☎ **07531/28-13-89** for schedules and information).

By Car   Access by car is via the B33.

VISITOR INFORMATION   Contact **Tourist-Information,** Bahnhofplatz 13 (☎ **07531/13-30-30**). April to October, the office is open Monday to Friday 9am to 8pm, Saturday 9am to 4pm, and Sunday 10am to 1pm; November to March, Monday to Friday 9am to noon and 2 to 6pm; it's also open the first four Saturdays of December from 9am to 4pm.

WHAT TO SEE & DO

The best way to see Konstanz is from the water. The **shoreline** is fascinating, with little inlets that weave in and out around ancient buildings and city gardens. Several pleasure ships offer tours along the city shoreline and across the lake to Meersburg and several other destinations. Contact **Bodensee-Schiffsbetriebe,** Hafenstrasse 6 (☎ 07531/28-13-89). Car ferries from Konstanz to Meersburg leave every 15 minutes during daylight hours. From 8:30 to 11pm, service is limited to two ferries per hour, and from 12:05 to 5:30am, one ferry per hour. On Saturday, Sunday, and holidays, service may also be curtailed. For information and schedules, contact **Stadtwerke Konstanz** (☎ 07531/80-33-66).

During the summer, outdoor concerts are presented in the **city gardens.** Below the gardens is the **Council Building,** where the Council of Constance met. The building was originally constructed as a storehouse in 1388, but came to be used for meetings during its early years. The hall was restored in 1911 and decorated with murals depicting the history of the town. On the harbor in front of the building is an obelisk erected in memory of Count Ferdinand Zeppelin, the citizen of Konstanz who invented the dirigible airship in the late 19th century.

The towers of the Romanesque **basilica** rise behind the city garden. Begun in 1052 on the foundations of an older cathedral, this church took centuries to complete. The neo-Gothic spire was added only in 1856. During the Council of Constance, the members of the synod met here. From the top tower, a view opens onto the lake and the city.

MAINAU ISLAND   Four miles north of Konstanz, in the arm of the Bodensee known as the Überlingersee, is the unusual, almost tropical island of Mainau. Here palms and orange trees grow in profusion and fragrant flowers bloom year-round, practically in the shadow of the snow-covered Alps. In the center of this botanical oasis is an ancient castle, once a residence of the Knights of the Teutonic Order, now owned by the Swedish Count Lennart Bernadotte. Only the island's gardens and parks can be visited by the public. They're open March through October daily from 7am to 10pm; in winter, daily from 9am to 5pm.

There are four restaurants on the island, but no overnight accommodations. You can reach Mainau either by tour boat from Konstanz or by walking across the small footbridge connecting the island to the mainland, north of the city. Admission is 16.50DM ($9.90) for adults, 9DM ($5.40) for students, and 5.50DM ($3.30) for children. The island is open year-round, but the flower and garden season lasts only from March through November. For more information, call ☎ **07531/3030.**

OUTDOOR PURSUITS   Strandbad horn, Eichhornstrasse 89 (☎ **07531/ 6-35-50),** at the tip of the peninsula, is the largest and most popular beach in the area. You can rent windsurfers here for 10DM ($6) per hour. The beach is also known for a section where nudity is permitted. From the town center, bus 5 runs here about every 30 minutes.

If you'd like to go biking along the lake, visit **Velotours,** Mainaustrasse 34 (☎ 07531/9-82-80), where rentals cost from 20DM ($12) per day. Open March through October daily from 9am to 5:30pm. Rowboats and paddleboats can be rented at **Am Gondelhafen** (☎ 07531/2-18-81); they cost 14DM to 16DM ($8.40 to $9.60) per hour. Open daily from 10am to dusk April through October.

SHOPPING

The best way to explore the shopping options in this cosmopolitan town is to walk down the main commercial artery, **Hussenstrasse.** Among the best stores are **Jacqueline,** Hussenstrasse 29 (☎ 07531/2-29-90), known for its stylish garments for women over 35; and its immediate neighbor, **Petra,** Hussenstrasse 29 (☎ 07531/ 2-36-86), whose upscale garments are more youthful and sexy. Men can look for tuned-in fashion, both formal and sporty, at **Pierre,** Hussenstrasse 3 (☎ 07531/ 2-21-50); and **Holzherr,** Rossgartenstrasse 32 (☎ 07531/128730). For knit shirts, shorts, and tennis garb, try **La Coste,** Hussenpassage 5 (☎ 07531/2-77-02).

WHERE TO STAY

Buchner Hof. Buchnerstrasse 6 (in Petershausen, across the Rhine from Konstanz), 78464 Konstanz. ☎ **07531/8-10-20.** Fax 07531/81-02-40. 15 units. TV TEL. 140DM–180DM ($84–$108) double; 210DM ($126) suite. Rates include continental breakfast. AE, DC, MC. Closed Dec 23–Jan 7. Free outdoor parking; 10DM ($6) in garage.

Though located in Petershausen, this hotel is just a short walk from most points of interest. The pleasantly furnished rooms range in size from small to medium. Bathrooms are tiny. There's also a sauna and solarium. The hotel is named after composer Hans Buchner, who became organist at the town cathedral in 1510 and was one of the first musicians to arrange and catalog the wealth of Gregorian chants found in the region.

Mago Hotel. Bahnhofplatz 4 (a 2-min. walk from the station), 78462 Konstanz. ☎ **07531/ 2-70-01.** Fax 07531/2-70-03. 34 units. MINIBAR TV TEL. 170DM–210DM ($102–$126) double; 230DM ($138) suite. Rates include buffet breakfast. AE, MC, V. Parking 10DM ($6) in garage.

The Mago is a small hotel with personal service and helpful owners. It was recently much improved. All the small rooms have ceiling fans and TVs with six English-language programs, including CNN and British SKY. Most of the rooms open to the lake. Only breakfast is served.

✪ **Steigenberger Insel Hotel.** Auf der Insel 1, 78462 Konstanz. ☎ **800/223-5652** in the U.S. and Canada, or 07531/12-50. Fax 07531/2-64-02. www.srshotels.com. 115 units. MINIBAR TV TEL. 300DM–410DM ($180–$246) double; 500DM–650DM ($300–$390) suite. Rates include buffet breakfast. AE, DC, MC, V. Parking 10DM ($6).

The Insel started life as a Dominican monastery in the 13th century; now it's the single finest place to stay along the German side of the lake. It has a prime location—on an island, with its own lakeside gardens and dock. The white step-gabled building holds an inner Romanesque cloister. Most of the spacious doubles have a living-room look, with sofas, armchairs, and coffee tables.

Dining/Diversions: The formal Seerestaurant offers an international cuisine. The less-formal Dominikaner Stube specializes in regional cookery. At twilight, guests gather at the intimate, clublike Zeppelin Bar, where the walls are cluttered with framed letters and documents. (The man who pioneered the Zeppelin airship also turned this abbey into a hotel.)

Amenities: Hair dryers, room service, laundry, dry cleaning, baby-sitting, sauna, plus lake facilities for swimming.

WHERE TO DINE

Casino Restaurant am See. Seestrasse 21. ☎ **07531/81-57-65.** Reservations required. Jacket and tie required for men. Main courses 32DM–45DM ($19.20–$27). AE, DC, MC, V. Daily 6–11:30pm. INTERNATIONAL.

If you happen to lose at roulette on one of your casino outings in Konstanz, you can revive your spirits (and drink a few, too) on the lakeside terrace of this casino restaurant. The view is lovely, and the food first rate. The restaurant offers a good choice of dishes; try the fresh fish or saddle of lamb. The food is backed up by a good wine cellar.

✪ **Seehotel Siber.** Seestrasse 25, 78464 Konstanz. ☎ **07531/6-30-44.** Fax 07531/6-48-13. Reservations required. Main courses 52DM–70DM ($31.20–$42); fixed-price menus 75DM–150DM ($45–$90) at lunch, 120DM–350DM ($72–$210) at dinner. AE, DC, MC, V. Daily noon–2pm and 6–10pm. CONTINENTAL.

This outstanding restaurant is the best not only in Konstanz but along the entire lake. Bertold Siber, one of the leading chefs in Germany, is in charge. His establishment occupies an art-nouveau villa near the casino, overlooking the lake. The menu features a conservative version of *cuisine moderne*. Offerings change daily, based on the seasonal availability of ingredients. Your meal might begin with lobster terrine with butter and red basil or freshly caught lake trout with an array of seasonings. Try either the roast Barbary goose with Beaujolais sauce or the stuffed turbot with lobster, if they're available. Most guests opt for one of two fixed-price dinners, although à la carte meals are also offered.

The Seehotel Siber is also a Relais & Châteaux hotel, renting handsomely furnished rooms in a building adjacent to the restaurant. The 11 double rooms cost 270DM to 390DM ($162 to $234), and the one suite goes for 590DM ($354).

NEARBY DINING

Schwedenschenke. Mainau Island. ☎ **07531/30-31-56.** Reservations recommended. Main courses 15DM–25DM ($9–$15) for lunch; 30DM–40DM ($18–$24) for dinner. AE, DC, MC, V. Daily 11am–9:30pm. Bus: 4 from the center of Konstanz. REGIONAL/SWEDISH.

Visitors sometimes make a pilgrimage to Mainau Island in Lake Constance for a meal in this old-fashioned restaurant. The chef's specialty is assorted lake fish, including perch, pike-perch, and trout. You can also try Hungarian goulash, Swedish meatballs in cream sauce, and *Tafelspitz* (boiled beef with horseradish sauce). Pike-perch fillets are served in a spicy sauce of tomatoes, capers, shallots, and mushrooms.

KONSTANZ AFTER DARK

Classical music offerings throughout the year are numerous. The concert season of the **Bodensee Symphony Orchestra** (☎ **07531/59-46-14**), runs from September through April, and a **summer music festival** is held from mid-June to mid-July. There's also an **outdoor music festival** on the Island of Mainau for 3 days in July. Contact the visitor information office (see above) for tickets, schedules, and venues. In May, the **Bodensee Festival** offers a mix of classical concerts and theatrical productions, presented at various locations around the shores of the lake. Tickets range from 15DM to 75DM ($9 to $45). Call the festival office at ☎ **07541/72071** for information.

The **Stadttheater Konstanz** (☎ **07531/130021**) performs at the Stadttheater, Konzilstrasse 11. This is Germany's oldest active theater, having staged plays since 1609. It has its own repertory company. In July and August, the company moves to its summer theater in Meersburg (see "Meersburg," above).

In the main room of the **Konstanz casino,** Seestrasse 21 (☎ **07531/81-57-65**), you try your luck at blackjack, seven-card stud poker, or roulette. Slot machines are located in a side room. Entry into the casino requires a passport as proof of age, and there's a cover charge of 5DM ($3). Men are required to wear jackets and ties at all times. The casino is open daily from 2pm to 2am, closing an hour later on Friday and Saturday. A restaurant on the premises (see "Where to Dine," above) offers continental cuisine from 6 until 11pm.

Those in the party mood should go next door to **Siber,** Seestrasse 19 (☎ **07531/6-30-46**), which offers drinking and dancing, with no cover charge, from 10pm until 3am daily except Tuesday. On weekends, the DJs at **Theatercafé,** Konzilstrasse 3 (☎ **07531/2-02-43**), mix hip-hop and house late into the night. Latin beats play on

Monday, Friday, and Saturday nights at **Rheinterrasse,** Spanierstrasse 5 (☎ 07531/
5-60-93). Good Dixieland jazz and country are found at **Hafenhalle,** Hafenstrasse 10
(☎ **07531/2-11-26**), every Sunday. Call for details.

For a good pub, head to **Brauhaus J. Albrecht,** Konradigasse 2 (☎ 07531/
2-11-26), which has been brewing its own beer for more than 475 years. **Seekuh,**
Konzilstrasse 1 (☎ **07531/2-72-32**), books winter shows to heat up the night. It's
open daily from 6pm until 1am on weekdays and 7pm to 2am on weekends. In the
summer, the beer garden here is a popular hangout.

Two **music festivals** featuring contemporary rock, jazz, and cabaret music are also
held during the summer. From June 23 to July 4, an international menagerie of bands
descends on the town for a series of concerts held in huge tents. Ticket prices range
from 20DM to 47DM ($12 to $28.20), but there are a few free shows, too. Throngs
of revelers flood the town on July 17 for the annual **Rock Am See festival,** where a
64DM ($38.40) ticket buys you admission to an all-day event that draws another
batch of international stars. For information about show schedules, call the festival
office at ☎ **07531/9-08-80.**

5 Reichenau

6½ miles NW of Konstanz

Set within the more southerly of the two arms that stretch westward from the
Bodensee, Reichenau is a small (1 by 2¾ miles) historic island that was only recently
connected to the mainland by a causeway. By the end of the 800s, it was the site of
three separate monasteries, the oldest of which had been established in 724. Later
Reichenau became a political force within the Holy Roman Empire. Today, much of
the island is devoted to the cultivation of vegetables and salad greens, and consequently has a sedate, unflashy aura, much prized by escapists looking for a quiet
getaway.

ESSENTIALS

GETTING THERE   By Train   Reichenau's railway station lies midway between
the much larger railway junctions of Radolfzell (to the west) and Konstanz (to the
east). Trains from throughout Germany and Switzerland make frequent stops at both
those cities, from which passengers heading to Reichenau can transfer onto a small
railway line that makes runs at hourly intervals on to Bahnhof Reichenau. Buses from
Bahnhof Reichenau to Insel Reichenau (the city's historic core), take 10 minutes each
way. For railway information call ☎ **01805/996633.**

By Bus   Bus service to Reichenau is limited and inconvenient. For information, call
SBG GmbH (☎ **07732/19449**).

By Car   From Konstanz, motorists should take Route 33 east to Reichenau.

By Boat   For information about the ferryboats that ply the waters between
Reichenau and the German lakeside hamlet of Allensbach, call ☎ **07533/6361.**

VISITOR INFORMATION   The tourist office is the **Verkehrsbüro,** Mittelzell,
Ergat 5 (☎ **07534/92070**). May through September, it's open Monday to Friday
8:30am to noon and 2 to 6pm, Saturday 9am to noon; October and April, Monday
to Friday 8:30am to noon and 2 to 5pm; November through March, Monday to
Friday 8:30am to noon.

EXPLORING THE TOWN

The island is divided into three separate villages (Oberzell, Mittelzell, and Niederzell),
each of which is centered around the remains of a medieval monastery. The most

impressive of these is the **Münster St. Maria and Markus** Burgstrasse (☎ 07534/276), in Mittelzell. Originally founded in 725, it became one of the most important centers of learning in the Carolingian era. It reached its peak around 1,000, when it was the home of about 700 monks. The structure is beautiful in its simplicity. Entrance is free, but a visit to the treasury costs 2DM ($1.20). The church is open daily, year-round, from 9am to 6pm; its treasury is open only from May to October, Monday to Saturday from 11am to noon and 3 to 4pm. While you're in the vicinity, notice the **Krautergarten** (Herb Garden), in the shadow of the cathedral on the Hermann Contractus Strasse. It emulates the herb and vegetable gardens maintained by monks in the Middle Ages.

The hamlet of Niederzell is home to **Stiftskirche St. Peter and St. Paul,** Eginostrasse (no phone). If it's not open at the time of your arrival, the tourist office will call someone to unlock the gates for you. In 1990, during restorations of the church's apse, a series of Romanesque frescoes were uncovered and are now on view today.

The nearby hamlet of Oberzell is the site of the **Stiftskirche St. George,** Seestrasse (no phone). Rising abruptly from a cabbage field, it has a severely dignified, very simple facade, and a series of charmingly naive medieval frescoes inside. It's open daily from 9am to 6pm. Admission is free.

A final site worth a stop is the **Heimatmuseum,** in the Stadthaus, Ergat 7, in Mittelzell (no phone). This is a showcase for the handcrafts and folklore that developed on Reichenau and the surrounding region. It's open from May to October every Tuesday to Sunday from 3 to 5pm. Entrance costs 3DM ($1.80) adults, 1DM (60¢) children.

SHOPPING

For a sampling of the many wines produced within the Bodenese region, head for **Winzer Vereins,** Munsterplatz (☎ 07534/293), where you'll be able to see rack upon rack of local vintages. You can even get a single glass to decide if you want to buy a whole bottle.

WHERE TO STAY

Seehotel Seeschau. An der Schiffslände, 78479 Reichenau. ☎ **07534/257.** Fax 07534/72-64. www.seeschau.mdo.de. 23 units. MINIBAR TV TEL. 230DM–330DM ($138–$198) double; 420DM ($252) suite for 2. Half board 48DM ($28.80) per person. AE, DC, MC, V. Free parking.

This comfortable, well-maintained hotel is set directly beside the lake. It features good-sized rooms with upscale reproductions of antique furniture, marble-sheathed bathrooms and, in many cases, views over the lake. On the premises are a good restaurant and a bar. This hotel is especially appealing in the midsummer, when the flowers around its windows burst into bloom.

Strandhotel Löchnerhaus. Schiffslände 12, 78478 Reichenau. ☎ **07534/80-30.** Fax 07534/582. www.strandhotelreichenau.mdo.de. 42 units. MINIBAR TV TEL. 210DM–280DM ($126–$168) double. Rates include breakfast. Half board 40DM ($24) per person. Parking 15DM ($9). AE, DC, MC, V. Closed Jan–Feb.

This is a good, well-managed hotel, just a stone's throw from the lakefront. It's set within a pleasant garden, and offers well-maintained bedrooms, many of which have private verandas or terraces and views of the lake. On the premises is a restaurant (see below). Amenities include boats for rent and a private beach.

WHERE TO DINE

Restaurant Strandhotel Löchnerhaus. Schiffslände 12. ☎ **07534/80-30.** Reservations recommended. Main courses 30DM–45DM ($18–$27); set menus 35DM–60DM ($21–$36). AE, DC, MC, V. Daily 11am–9pm. Closed Jan–Feb. GERMAN/INTERNATIONAL.

This restaurant, with its hardworking, kindly staff, is the traditional favorite of many locals. The 1950s-style dining room has views of the sea. Menu items include sea bass cooked either in Riesling sauce or in a potato crust, whitefish from the Bodensee, rack of lamb with horseradish and mint, grilled meats such as steak, and a savory version of goulash.

6 Überlingen

25 miles N of Konstanz; 28½ miles E of Ravensburg, 15 miles W of Friedrichshafen

Locals call the town of Überlingen, founded in the 1200s, a German version of Nice because of its sunny weather and lakeside location. It's also one of the best preserved medieval sites along the Bodensee.

ESSENTIALS

GETTING THERE   By Train   Rail passengers are funneled through nearby Friedrichshafen, from where a smaller rail line goes through Überlingen to Radolfzell. Trains run in either direction along that line at hourly intervals throughout the day. Überlingen's railway station lies on the extreme western edge of town. For rail information call ☎ **01805/996633.**

By Bus   Regional bus service along Lake Constance is provided by **RAB Regionalverkehr Alb-Bodensee GmbH** in Friedrichshafen (call ☎ **07541/30130** for more information).

By Car   Überlingen is off Route 31, just northwest of Konstanz. Route 31 is connected from Stuttgart via Ulm from Route 30 south, which intersects Route 31 at Friedrichshafen. From Munich follow Autobahn 96 west/southwest to Lindau, then head west on Route 31, which runs along Lake Constance to Friedrichshafen and Überlingen.

By Boat   From April to October, between 8 and 10 ferryboats a day carry passengers into Überlingen from Konstanz. The trip takes 1 hour and 20 minutes and costs 14DM ($8.40) each way. For information call the **Weiss Flote,** an armada of lake steamers maintained by the Bodensee Schiffsbetriebe GmbH (☎ **07531/281398**). No cars are carried on any of these ferries.

VISITOR INFORMATION   At this writing, tourist information is available at Steinhausgasse 1, although by early 2000 the office is set to move to permanent quarters in the historic Greth (see below), in Landungsplatz 14 (☎ **07551/991133**). May to October, the office is open Monday to Friday 9am to 6pm, Saturday 9am to 1pm, and Sunday 2am to 5pm; November to April, Monday to Friday 9am to 1pm and 2 to 5pm.

EXPLORING THE TOWN

The most important of the city monuments is the **Münster,** a surprisingly large medieval structure that required 200 years to build. The larger of its two towers functioned during periods of war as a military watchtower and was later capped with an eight-sided Renaissance lantern. The severely dignified exterior is offset by an elaborate and intricate Gothic interior. Take special notice of the main altar piece, carved in the early 1600s by Jorg Zurn. The cathedral is open daily from 8am to 6pm.

On the opposite side of the square is Überlingen's most famous secular building. The **Rathaus** was built in the late 1400s. Most of its interior is devoted to municipal offices, except for the Ratsaal, whose vaulted ceiling and lavishly paneled walls make it the most beautiful public room in town. Notice the coats of arms representing various faction of the Holy Roman Empire. Open Monday to Friday 9am to noon and 2:30 to 5pm, Saturday 9am to noon. Entrance is free.

The city maintains a **Museum of Folklore** (Heimatmuseum) within one of its most prized buildings, the Reichlin-von-Meldlegg Haus, Krummeberggasse 30 (☎ 07551/ 991-079). This building artfully emulates the style of the Florentine Renaissance. Inside you can also visit both a chapel and a lavishly ornate rococo ballroom. The building and its museum are open Tuesday to Saturday 9am to 12:30pm and Sunday 10am to 3pm. Admission is 4DM ($2.40) adults and 3DM ($1.80) children.

Also look for the **Franziskanerkirche,** Spitalgasse. Especially striking is the contrast between its severely dignified exterior and its lavishly baroque interior. Open daily 8am to noon and 2 to 5pm.

The townspeople of Überlingen took great care to ornament the medieval fortifications that protected them from outside invaders. The best preserved of these walls is the **Stadtmauer,** which in recent times was landscaped into a graceful ramble lined with trees and shrubbery. It's part of the encircling walls that flank the north and east side of town.

Along Überlingen's waterfront promenade (Seepromenade), which offers a view of the faraway Swiss Alps, are two of the largest old buildings in town. One of these is the **Greth,** originally a market and storage vault for corn. Today it houses the city's tourist office. Immediately next door is the fanciful Gothic-era **Zeughaus,** Seepromenade (call tourist office for information). It contains a collection of medieval armor and weapons. Admission is 5DM ($3). Open only from Easter to October, Monday to Saturday 10:30am to noon.

Überlingen is also the site of one of the best known medical clinics on the Bodensee. The **Buchinger Clinic,** Willhellmbeckstrasse 27 (☎ **07551/8070**) is expensive, aristocratic, and exclusive. Good spa treatments are available within two of the town's hotels, the Kur und Gasthaus Routher and the Gasthaus Seepark.

WHERE TO STAY & DINE

Landgasthof Adler. Hauptstrasse 44, Lippertsreute (6 miles north of Überlingen center), 8862 Überlingen. ☎ **07553/8-25-50.** Fax 07553/82-55-70. 17 units. TV TEL. 100DM–158DM ($60–$94.80) double. Rates include breakfast. MC. Restaurant Fri–Tues 11:30am–2pm; Fri–Wed 5pm–midnight. Free parking. Closed Nov.

Set within the confines of a bucolic hamlet (Lippertsreute), this hotel and restaurant occupies two antique buildings, the older of which was built 300 years ago. The small bedrooms are cozy, unpretentious, and appealingly (and artfully) rustic.

The establishment's restaurant is well known to locals. It serves heaping, well-prepared portions of time-tested Swabian dishes such as *Spanferkel* (roast suckling pig), *Zweibelrostbraten,* and Bodensee whitefish prepared with white wine sauce. Main courses cost from 10DM to 40DM ($6 to $24) each.

✪ **Parkhotel St. Leonhard.** Obere St. Leonhard-Strasse 71 (a mile north of the center of Überlingen), 8862 Überlingen. ☎ **07551/80-81-00.** Fax 07551/80-85-31. 145 units. MINIBAR TV TEL. 160DM–190DM ($96–$114) double; 360DM–410DM ($216–$246) suite. Rates include breakfast. AE, MC, V. Restaurant open daily 11:30am–2pm and 5:30–11pm. Free parking.

Set a half mile from the edge of the lake on a hilltop, this hotel provides rest and recuperation to urban visitors. The woodsy-looking chalet is flanked on both sides with more angular, modern annexes. The good-sized bedrooms are modern, conservative, comfortable, and well designed. The hotel has its own swimming pool, sauna and exercise room, two restaurants (one of which is a folkloric Weinstube) and a bar. The more formal restaurant (known simply as "The Restaurant") serves main courses priced at 12DM to 58DM ($7.20 to $34.80).

Spitalkeller in Steinhaus. Steinhausgasse 1 (near the Franziskanerkirche). ☎ **07551/ 6-60-20.** Reservations recommended. Main courses 14DM–32DM ($8.40–$19.20). No credit cards. Daily 6pm–midnight. SWABIAN/GERMAN.

The Spitalkeller, which was built in the 1500s, is set in Überlingen's historic core. It has a dining room on each of two levels, plus a garden where tables are laid out during good weather. Menu items are traditional and include savory soups such as goulash, as well as wursts, *Zwiebelrostbraten,* fresh fish, and very good salads.

7 Ravensburg

Ravensburg isn't on Lake Constance, but it's nearby and makes a good side trip. The town boasts one of the most impeccably preserved medieval cores in the region. During the 1400s, the linen trade made Ravensburg into one of the richest in Germany, but economic stagnation set in during the 1600s as a result of the Thirty Years' War. Today this quiet town is a tourist's delight.

ESSENTIALS

GETTING THERE   By Train   Most passengers change trains in nearby Ulm. From there, trains depart at hourly intervals for Friedrichshafen, stopping en route in Ravensburg. For rail information call ☎ **01805/996633.** Transit time from Ulm is about an hour.

By Bus   Most bus routes into Ravensburg start at nearby villages and hamlets. For information, call **0751/2766.**

By Car   From Stuttgart, follow Autobahn 8 east to the city of Ulm, then turn south onto Route 30 directly into Ravensburg. From along Lake Constance, you can take routes B33, B30, or 467 north to Ravensburg.

VISITOR INFORMATION   Head to the **Stadtverkehrsamt,** Kirchestrasse 16 (☎ **0751/82324**). It's open Monday 8am to noon, Tuesday through Friday 8am to 5:30pm, and Saturday 9am to noon.

EXPLORING THE TOWN

You'll appreciate that cars are banned from the narrow labyrinth of alleyways within Ravensburg's historic core. Two of the most evocative streets are **Untere Breite Strasse** and **Charlottenstrasse,** both of which lie near the town's central square. Lining the Marienplatz are the late-Gothic **Rathaus;** the 14th-century **Kornhaus,** which was once one of the largest corn exchanges in the region and is now the town's library; and the **Waaghaus,** which was originally built in the 1400s as a warehouse for municipal supplies and now houses a bank. Look also for the old city **watchtower** and the Renaissance-era **Lederhaus,** which functions today as the town's post office.

Also on the Marienplatz is the **Karmeliteenklosterkirche.** It was originally a monastery in the 14th century and later housed a mercantile association devoted to the promotion of the linen trade. The complex's church can be visited every day from 8am to 6pm. Nearby, at the corner of Kirkstrasse and the Herrenstrasse, is the **Liebfrauenkirche,** the parish church of Ravensburg. Deceptively simple on the outside, the 14th-century structure has been radically but authentically reconstructed on the inside. Look for remnants of the church's original stained glass and a heavy sobriety reminiscent of the Middle Ages.

Part of Ravensburg's allure derives from its well-preserved network of medieval fortifications, studded with defensive towers. The most visible of these is the 170-foot-high **Mehlsack Tower,** which has been adopted as the municipal symbol of Ravensburg itself. You can climb to its heights by means of 240 heavily worn circular steps, but only on the third Sunday of every month between mid-March and mid-October from 10am and noon. Entrance is free. Two other defensive towers can be spotted from the Marienplatz. These are the **Obertor,** the oldest gate in the city walls, accessible via Marktstrasse, and the **Günerturm** (Green Tower), covered with moss-colored ceramic tiles, many of which date from the 14th century. Neither the Günerturm nor the Obertor can be visited.

Ravensburg's only noteworthy museum is its **Heimatmuseum,** devoted to local folklore and handcrafts. It lies within the Folkshaus, Charlottenstrasse 36 (for information contact the tourist office). Open Tuesday to Saturday 3 to 5pm. Admission is 3DM ($1.80).

WHERE TO STAY

Hotel-Gasthof Obertor. Markstrasse 67, 88212 Ravensburg. ☎ **0751/3-66-70.** Fax 0751/3-66-72-00. E-mail: hotelobertor@t-online.de. 44 units. TV TEL. 170DM–210DM ($102–$126) double. Rates include breakfast. AE, DC, MC, V. Free parking.

This hotel was built in the 12th century as a farmhouse and is almost as old as the town of Ravensburg. The house has a lovely garden terrace in front and a park in the back. The rooms vary greatly in size and in personality, so you may want to take a peek at a couple before deciding which to take. Turn-of-the-century antiques abound, mostly made of cherry wood—typical of the Bodense area. The hotel's restaurant has a fine view of the grounds and serves mostly Swabian/regional cuisine. It's open for lunch and dinner. The hotel also offers a small gym with sauna, whirlpool, and solarium.

✪ **Romantikhotel Waldhorn.** Marienplatz 15, 88212 Ravensburg. ☎ **07151/36120.** Fax 07151/3612-100. www.waldhorn.de. E-mail: bouley@waldhorn.de. 35 units. MINIBAR TV TEL. 210DM–280DM ($126–$168) double; 235DM–350DM ($141–$210) suite. Rates include breakfast. AE, DC, MC, V. Parking 15DM ($9).

The most appealing hotel in Ravensburg occupies a late-18th-century building and a more modern annex. Because both buildings lie within the town's all-pedestrian zone, it's easy to get a sense of the relaxed local lifestyle. The rooms are comfortable and cozy, and the staff is very charming. The hotel is also known for its two restaurants. The less expensive of these is a simple and likable Weinstube, the Rebleuterhaus, which serves Swabian specialties such as large ravioli stuffed with meat and spinach and spätzle, which is a thick local pasta. The fixed-price menu is 69DM ($41.40). Open daily from 5pm to 7am. The more expensive, and much more glamorous, of the two restaurants is recommended below.

WHERE TO DINE

✪ **Romantikhotel Waldhorn.** Marienplatz 15. ☎ **0751/36120.** Reservations recommended. Main courses 40DM–60DM ($24–$36). Set menu 169DM ($101.40). AE, DC, MC, V. Tues–Sat 11:30am–2pm and 6–7pm. MODERN INTERNATIONAL.

This sophisticated restaurant is directed by celebrity chef Marcel Bouley. The stylish, gracefully antique dining room has a ceramic *kachelofen* and massive ceiling beams. The Asian-influenced cuisine is among the most subtle, celebrated, and exotic in Germany. Menu items combine eastern and western culinary traditions with verve and zest and change according to the seasons and the inspiration of the much-applauded chef. Your meal might include medaillons of lamb with miso, lemon, and mint tempura; roasted rabbit prepared in the style of Burmese prawns, with pulverized onions and asparagus tips and a warm Asiatic cucumber salad; lobster ravioli with braised sweetbreads, brown butter sauce, and caviar; and rosettes of zucchini.

A SIDE TRIP TO WEINGARTEN

An important archaeological excavation is located within the agrarian hamlet of Weingarten, a sleepy village 3 miles north of Ravensburg. To reach the village, take bus no. 1 or no. 2 from Ravensburg's Marienplatz. In the 1950s, teams of archaeologists discovered one of the richest troves of German graves in the country. Artifacts from the dig lie in the free **Alamannen Museum,** located in Kornhaus, Karlstrasse 28 (☎ **0751/40-51-25**). Open Wednesday, Saturday, and Sunday from 3 to 5pm; closed February and November.

Weingarten is also home to the largest baroque church in Germany, the **Weingarten Basilica** (☎ **0751/40-51-25**), which rises to about 200 feet. It was established in 1056 by the wife of a prominent official in the Guelph dynasty. Inside is one of the holiest relics in Germany, a mystical vial, which, according to legend, contains several drops of Christ's blood. The relic was entrusted to the convent by the sister-in-law of William the Conqueror, the Guelph queen Juditha. Another highlight of the church is the organ, one of the largest in the country; its installation required 13 years, beginning in 1737. Also noteworthy are the ceiling frescoes by Cosmas Damian Asam, one of the leaders of the Baroque School. The church is open daily from 8am to 6pm.

Finally, if you can manage to schedule your visit for the Friday after Ascension (the Thursday 40 days after Easter), you can witness a massive **procession** of pilgrims, at the head of which are more than 2,000 horsemen. The breeding of horses for this procession is a matter of quiet pride among local farmers.

For further information on Weingarten, call the tourist office at ☎ **0751/40-51-25.**

10 The Black Forest (Schwarzwald)

The Black Forest covers a triangular section roughly 90 miles long and 25 miles wide in southwestern Germany. The pine- and birch-studded mountains here are alive with fairy-tale villages, well-equipped spas, and modern ski resorts. The peaks in the southern part of the forest reach as high as 5,000 feet and are excellent for skiing in winter and hiking or mountain climbing in summer. The little lakes of Titisee and Schluchsee are popular for boating, swimming, and ice-skating. Fish abound in the streams and lakes.

GETTING TO THE BLACK FOREST International airports serving the area are located in Stuttgart (see chapter 11) and the Swiss city of Basel. Basel lies only 44 miles from Freiburg in Breisgau, the "capital" of the Black Forest. Trains run north and south through the Rhine Valley, with fast, frequent service to such Black Forest towns as Freiburg and Baden-Baden. Motorists should take the A5 Autobahn, which runs the length of the Schwarzwald. From Lake Constance (see chapter 9), continue along Route 13 for about 40 miles until you reach the Black Forest.

EXPLORING THE REGION BY CAR The roads through the forest are excellent, especially the **Schwarzwald Hochstrasse** (Black Forest High Road or Ridgeway, Route B500). This route runs almost the entire length of the region, from Baden-Baden to Freudenstadt, then resumes at Triberg and goes on to Waldshut on the Rhine. While taking this scenic road, you'll have many opportunities to park your car and explore the countryside or to turn off on one of the side roads leading to hospitable villages, ancient castles, and rolling farmlands.

1 Freiburg im Breisgau

129 miles SW of Stuttgart, 44 miles N of Basel (Switzerland), 174 miles S of Frankfurt

This scenic and interesting city, the largest in the Black Forest region, is often overlooked because of its out-of-the-way location. When approached from the Rhine plain on the west, Freiburg is silhouetted against towering mountain peaks, which are only an hour from the town by funicular or car.

Because of its remarkable climate, Freiberg is a year-round attraction and sports center. The city happens to lie in the path of warm air currents that come up from the Mediterranean through the Burgundy Gap. In early spring, the town is usually bursting into bloom while the

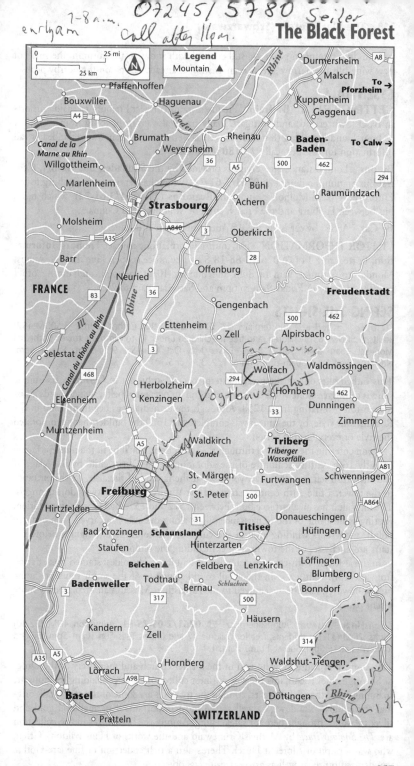

072 45/ 5780 Seiler
earlham 7-8 a.m. Call after 11am.

Legend
Mountain ▲

0 ____ 25 mi
0 ____ 25 km

Durmersheim

Pfaffenhoffen
Malsch
To →
Pforzheim
Bouxwiller
Haguenau
Kuppenheim
Gaggenau

Brumath
Rheinau
Baden-Baden
To Calw →
Weyersheim
Canal de la
Marne au Rhin
Willgottheim

Marlenheim
Bühl
Raumündzach
Achern
Strasbourg
Oberkirch
Molsheim
28

Barr
Offenburg
Neuried
FRANCE
Freudenstadt
Gengenbach
Ettenheim
Zell
Alpirsbach
Selestat
Farmhouses
Wolfach
Waldmössingen
Herbolzheim
Vogtbauernhot
Hornberg
Kenzingen
Dunningen
Elsenheim
Zimmern
Muntzenheim
Waldkirch
Triberg
friendly
Kandel
Triberger
Wasserfälle
St. Märgen
Schwenningen
Furtwangen
Freiburg
St. Peter
Hirtzfelden
Donaueschingen
Schauinsland
Titisee
Hüfingen
Bad Krozingen
Hinterzarten
Staufen
Löffingen
Belchen ▲
Feldberg
Lenzkirch
Blumberg
Badenweiler
Todtnau
Bernau
Schluchsee
Bonndorf
Kandern
Zell
Häusern

Waldshut-Tiengen
Hornberg
Lörrach
Basel
Döttingen
Rhine
Prätteln
SWITZERLAND

Rhine
Moder
Rhine
Canal du Rhône au Rhin
Ill

A8
A4
A35
A5
A840
A81
A864
A98
A35
A5

36
500
462
294
3
36
83
468
3
294
33
31
317
500
500
314
462
462

357

surrounding mountain peaks are still covered with snow. In the autumn, the smell of new wine fills the narrow streets even as snow is already falling on the nearby peaks.

ESSENTIALS

GETTING THERE   By Train   Frequent trains connect Freiburg to major airports in Basel (Switzerland) and Stuttgart. Daily trains also go to Freiburg from Frankfurt (2 hours), and Hamburg (8 hours), as well as Berlin and Zürich, Switzerland. For rail information for the area, call ☎ **01805/996633.**

By Bus   Long-distance bus service is provided by the **Südbaden Bus GmbH,** Central Bus Station, Freiburg (☎ **0761/3-61-72**), which has service from Freiburg to the EuroAirport Basel-Mulhouse, and **EuroRegioBus** (☎ **0761/3-61-72**), which has a bus between Freiburg and the French cities of Mulhouse and Colmar.

By Car   Access by car is via the A5 Autobahn north and south.

VISITOR INFORMATION   For tourist information, contact **Freiburg Information,** Rotteckring 14 (☎ **0761/3-88-18-89**). The office is open June through August Monday to Saturday 9am to 8pm and Sunday 10am to noon, and during other months Monday to Friday 9am to 6pm and Saturday 9am to 2pm.

SEEING THE SIGHTS

Freiburg Cathedral. Münsterplatz. ☎ **0761/20-27-90.** Cathedral free; 3.50DM ($2) adults, 1.50DM (85¢) children, and free for children under 15 to climb the tower. Cathedral Mon–Sat 10am–6pm, Sun 1–6pm. Tower May–Oct Mon–Sat 9:30–5pm, Sun 1–5pm; Nov–Apr, Wed–Sat 9:30am–5pm. Tram: 1, 2, 3, 4, or 5.

This cathedral is one of the great masterpieces of Gothic art in Germany. Its unique spire is of filigree stonework; the steeple sits on an octagonal belfry, which holds a historic 5-ton bell dating from 1258. Although the cathedral was begun in 1200 in the Romanesque style, by the time it was completed in 1620 the builders had incorporated the style of every Gothic period.

Upon entering the cathedral through the south door, you'll be in the transept facing an early 16th-century sculpture of the adoration of the Christ child by the Magi. If you then turn left into the nave, you'll see at the far end of the aisle, by the entrance to the tower, a fine 13th-century statue of the Virgin flanked by two adoring angels. The high altar has an altarpiece built between 1512 and 1516 by Hans Baldung Grien. Resting against one of the Renaissance pillars along the aisle is a carved 16th-century pulpit, with stairs winding around the curve of the column. The figures below the stairs are likenesses of the townspeople, including the sculptor.

In the aisles are 14th-century stained-glass windows. The oldest stained glass, dating from the 13th century, is in the small round windows of the south transept. Some pieces, however, have been removed to the Augustiner Museum and replaced by more recent panels.

Augustiner Museum. Augustinerplatz. ☎ **0761/2-01-25-31.** Admission 4DM ($2.30) adults, 2DM ($1.15) students, free for children 17 and under. Tues–Sun 10am–5pm. Guided tours Wed at 3:30pm, Sun at 11am. Tram: 1.

The Augustiner Museum is housed in the former church and monastery of the Order of St. Augustine. It contains the town's finest collection of art, including religious art spanning more than 1,000 years. Among the treasures are some of the cathedral's original stained-glass windows, as well as the most important of its medieval gold and silver treasures, brought here for safekeeping. Among the best works in the collection are *The Snow Miracle* by Mathias Grünewald and the works of Hans Baldung Grien, who was a pupil of Albrecht Dürer. There's also a rich collection of fine late-Gothic wooden sculpture, as well as art-nouveau glass objects.

Museum für Neue Kunst. Marienstrasse 10A. ☎ **0761/2-01-25-81.** Free admission. Tues–Sun 10am–5pm. Tram: 1, 4, 5, or 6.

This modern art collection was formerly housed in the Augustiner Museum. Painting and sculpture, beginning with examples of German expressionism, Neue Sachlichkeit, and other classic modern works of art, especially by artists of southwest Germany, are displayed here.

MORE SIGHTS IN THE ALTSTADT In Münsterplatz, across from the cathedral, is the **Kaufhaus,** the most colorful building in Freiburg. This Gothic structure, with oriel windows at each end, was originally an ancient emporium, to which a balcony was added in 1550. Above the massive supporting arches, the facade is decorated with the statues of four emperors of the Habsburg dynasty, all but one of whom visited Freiburg during their reigns. The red-painted building is still used as the town's official reception hall.

The **Rathaus,** on the attractive Rathausplatz just west of Münsterplatz, became a happy marriage of two 16th-century merchants' houses when an arcade was built between them in 1900. The Renaissance houses are in good condition. The most remarkable of the decorations on the oriel windows and facades is the relief *The Maiden and the Unicorn.*

WHERE TO STAY
EXPENSIVE

Colombi Hotel. Rotteckring 16, 79098 Freiburg. ☎ **0761/2-10-60.** Fax 0761/3-14-10. 135 units. MINIBAR TV TEL. 390DM–430DM ($222.30–$245.10) double; from 495DM ($282.15) suite. AE, DC, MC, V. Parking 20DM ($11.40). Tram: 10, 11, or 12.

This is the most luxurious hotel in town. Snow-white walls and angular lines make the Colombi easy to spot in the downtown area. Despite its central location, the rooms are quiet and peaceful. Many business conferences take place here, but the Colombi caters to independent travelers as well. The accommodations are well furnished and appointed; the suites are especially luxurious.

Dining: The on-site restaurant (see "Where to Dine," below) is the finest in Freiburg.

Amenities: Concierge, room service, newspaper delivery, beauty parlor, sauna, pool, laundry, hair dyers, and dry cleaning.

MODERATE

Central-Hotel. Wasserstrasse 6, 79098 Freiburg. ☎ **0761/3-19-70.** Fax 0761/3-19-71-00. E-mail: central.hotel@t-online.de. 49 units. MINIBAR TV TEL. 195DM–250DM ($111.15–$142.50) double. Rates include buffet breakfast. AE, CB, DC, MC, V. Parking 10DM–15DM ($5.70–$8.55). Tram: 5 or 6.

Near the pedestrian zone and the cathedral is the modern Central-Hotel, designed with skylights, marble floors, and pleasantly furnished rooms and lobby. Rooms are standard but still quite comfortable. Although maybe a bit bland compared to some of the other hotels reviewed here, this is a decent choice at a good price. A buffet breakfast with a wide choice of dishes is included in the rate. Drinks are offered in a cozy corner bar.

Park Hotel Post. Eisenbahnstrasse 35, 79098 Freiburg. ☎ **0761/38-54-80.** Fax 0761/3-16-80. www.eurohotel.de/park-hotel-post.freiburg.html. E-mail: park-hotel-post-freiburg@t-online.de. 44 units. MINIBAR TV TEL. 219DM–269DM ($124.85–$153.35) double. Rates include continental breakfast. AE, MC, V. Parking 14.50DM ($8.25). Tram: 10, 11, or 12.

This baroque hotel, with an elaborate zinc cap on its octagonal turret, is centrally located, within walking distance of the major attractions and the rail station. This has been one of the leading hotels in town for a long time, although its services, amenities, and style don't match the Colombi. The interior has been entirely renovated, and each unit is attractively furnished and well kept. Rooms come in a variety of shapes and sizes and are among the most comfortable in town. Breakfast is the only meal served.

Victoria. Eisenbahnstrasse 54 (450 ft. from the Hauptbahnhof), 79098 Freiburg. ☎ **0761/ 20-73-40.** Fax 0761/20-73-44-44. E-mail: hotel.victoria@t-online.de. 63 units. MINIBAR TV TEL. 195DM–255DM ($111.15–$145.35) double. Rates include buffet breakfast. AE, DC, MC, V. Parking 6DM–16DM ($3.40–$9.10).

The Victoria is peaceful, thanks to its location fronting Colombi Park. The facade is a symmetrical 19th-century rectangle, with big windows and a wrought-iron balcony above the front door. The public rooms are lavishly paneled. Guest rooms are small but pleasantly furnished. Some are reserved for nonsmokers. Many rooms contain antiques. The hotel also has a cocktail bar, a coffee shop, and an Italian restaurant.

Zum Roten Bären. Oberlinden, 79098 Freiburg. ☎ **0761/38-78-70.** Fax 0761/38-78-87. www.roter-baeren.de. E-mail: info@roter-baeren.de. 25 units. TV TEL. 195DM–350DM ($111.15–$199.50) double. Rates include buffet breakfast. AE, CB, DC, MC, V. Parking 15DM ($8.55). Tram: 1.

This is one of the oldest buildings in Freiburg, with parts dating from 1120. It's said to be the oldest inn in Germany. A modern wing blends in pleasantly. The interior is delightfully decorated, emphasizing original construction elements along with scattered pieces of antique furniture. The rooms are well styled and furnished, some with minibars. Try for one of the rooms in the older section; they have more tradition and atmosphere. The fine restaurant serves traditional food and wine. In summer, you can stop by for a glass of wine or beer on the Weinstube's terrace.

INEXPENSIVE

Rappen. Münsterplatz 13, 79098 Freiburg. ☎ **0761/3-13-53.** Fax 0761/38-22-52. 20 units, 16 with bathroom. MINIBAR TV TEL. 100DM–120DM ($57–$68.40) double without bathroom, 160DM–175DM ($91.20–$99.75) double with bathroom. Rates include buffet breakfast. AE, DC, MC, V. All trams stop 60 feet behind the hotel.

This charming inn in the pedestrians-only Altstadt has a lot more cozy Black Forest ambience than such nearby competitors as the Central. It's marked with a wrought-iron hanging sign, little dormer windows in its steep roof, window boxes, and shutters. The small guest rooms are simply but comfortably furnished; the most desirable have views of the cathedral. There are three dining rooms inside, all with beamed ceilings, leaded-glass windows, and coach lanterns. The cuisine is notable for local dishes, including a goulash of venison.

WHERE TO DINE
EXPENSIVE

✪ **Eichhalde.** Stadtstrasse 91. ☎ **0761/5-48-17.** Reservations required. Main courses 37DM–52DM ($21.10–$29.65); fixed-price menu 43DM ($24.50) for 3 courses, and 86DM–118DM ($49–$67.25) for 4 and 5 courses. MC. Sun–Mon and Wed–Fri noon–2pm; Wed–Mon 6:30–10pm. Tram: 14. FRENCH/GERMAN.

This notable French bistro lies in the Herden district, a long walk from the center. It gets a lot of neighborhood patronage. Fixed-price lunches and dinners are available. The bill of fare is likely to include goose-liver terrine with port aspic, sea bass in thyme sauce, and turbot salad with mustard sauce. The chef has steadily built up a good local reputation, and the food here is always reliable and well prepared.

✪ **Hans-Thoma-Stube/Colombi Restaurant.** In the Colombi Hotel, Rotteckring 16. ☎ **0761/2-10-60.** Reservations required. Main courses 46DM–58DM ($26.20–$33.05);

3-course business lunch 40DM–59DM ($22.80–$33.65); fixed-price dinner 98DM ($55.85) for 4 courses, 158DM ($90.05) for 7 courses. AE, DC, MC, V. Daily noon–3pm and 6pm–midnight. Tram: 10, 11, or 12. REGIONAL/FRENCH.

This is justifiably the most acclaimed restaurant in the area. Gracious and skillful service, along with a sumptuous setting, ensure a memorable meal. Choice ingredients, masterly preparation, and creative presentation delight both the eye and the palate. The chef prepares a light modern cuisine, although many regional dishes are also offered. The menu is ever changing, based on the seasons, but might include a terrine of turbot, chanterelles over fillet of venison, or an array of Atlantic fish dishes perfectly prepared and impeccably served. There are two 1700s-style dining rooms.

Weinstube zur Traube. Schusterstrasse 17. ☎ **0761/3-21-90.** Reservations required. Main courses 38DM–48DM ($21.65–$27.35); fixed-price menus 76DM–110DM ($43.30–$62.70). AE, V. Tues–Sat noon–3pm and 6–10pm. Closed last 2 weeks in Aug. Tram: 10, 11, or 12. FRENCH/SWABIAN.

This 600-year-old Weinstube is the coziest choice in town for tavern dining. The pewter and earthenware dinner services decorating the walls are art objects in their own right, and the ceramic stove is more than 300 years old. The food here is regional and well prepared, emphasizing game, meat, and fish. Try the pike roulade with crab sauce. Fresh ingredients get a lot of respect around here and are deftly handled by the kitchen staff. There's also a fine wine list.

MODERATE

Oberkirchs Weinstuben. Münsterplatz 22, 79098 Freiburg. ☎ **0761/3-10-11.** Fax 0761/3-10-31. Reservations recommended. Main courses 25DM–40DM ($14.25–$22.80). AE, MC, V. Mon–Sat noon–2pm and 6:30–9:15pm. Closed Jan. Tram: 1, 4, or 5. GERMAN.

The innkeeper provides excellent regional cooking and comfortable rooms in this traditional Freiburg establishment. The setting, on a colorful square, is pure picture-postcard. The main Weinstube is old, with a monumental ceiling-high ceramic stove made with ornate decorative tiles. You get good old-fashioned food here—tasty soups, meat dishes, poultry—and plenty of everything. In season, you might try young pheasant. In the rear is a modern complex fronting an open patio with a fish pond.

The Weinstube also has 25 excellent rooms, all with private baths or showers. Doubles cost 230DM to 300DM ($131.10 to $171), with a continental breakfast included.

Wolfshöhle. Konviktstrasse 8. ☎ **0761/3-03-03.** Reservations recommended. Main courses 28.50DM–39DM ($16.25–$22.25); fixed-price menus 40DM–82DM ($22.80–$46.75). AE, DC, MC, V. Summer daily 11am–midnight; off-season Mon–Sat noon–2pm and 6pm–midnight. Tram: 10, 11, or 12. ITALIAN.

Wolfshöhle's warmly paneled ambience might remind you of a cozy inn high in the mountains on the border between Italy and the German-speaking world. The cuisine is sophisticated but fortifying. Choices include veal scaloppini with lemon and fillet of veal delicately seasoned, well-prepared lamb dishes, and calves' liver. You might begin with a hearty soup, or select an appetizer such as veal with tuna, the antipasto of the day, or two different versions of carpaccio.

FREIBURG AFTER DARK

An impressive entertainment complex, the **Konzerthaus** hosts a variety of events, ranging from classic music to theater to pop concerts. In June and July, huge tents are raised to house the annual **Zeltmusik festival,** which emphasizes jazz but includes other musical styles as well. Summer also brings a series of **chamber-music concerts** to the Kaufhaus, in Münsterplatz, and a program of **organ recitals** to the Freiburg

An Excursion to the Upper Black Forest

From Freiburg you can make a 90-mile circuit in 1 day through one of the most scenic parts of the Black Forest, returning in time for dinner. Along the way, you'll pass a trio of the highest summits in the Black Forest, and pass by two of the region's most beautiful lakes.

Head immediately south to **Schauinsland** along a narrow twisting road. At the car park you can climb some 100 steps to the belvedere tower for a panoramic view of the area.

Continuing south, you reach a mountain called **Belchen,** which rises to a height of 4,640 feet. From where the road ends, you can walk to the summit in about 20 minutes. On a clear day, you can look out from the observation platform here and take in a panoramic sweep of the Rhine plain, plus a view of the Alps from Säntis to Mont Blanc.

Upon leaving, continue east to the hamlet of Todtnau, where visitors can walk up a footpath to **The Falls of Todtnau,** about a mile away. Back at Todtnau, continue east along Route 317 to Feldberg. Here a chairlift takes visitors to the **Seebuck** peak (4,750 ft.), which is crowned by the Bismarck monument and offers another sweeping panoramic view of the Black Forest.

Back on the road again, follow Route 317 east until it becomes Route 500 heading south to **Schluchsee,** one of the loveliest lakes of the area and the most important body of water in the Black Forest.

After a visit here, head north along Route 500 to the hamlet of **Lenzkirch,** from which you'll have a view of Lake Titisee. The road then continues to the resort of **Titisee** itself (see below). After a visit you can return to Freiburg by heading west along Route 31.

Cathedral. Information about all venues and events listed above, including program schedules and ticket sales, is available from **Freiburg Verkehrsamt,** Badisches Zeitung, Kaiser Josefstrasse 229 (☎ **0761/496263**).

The city also has a thriving bar and club scene that goes on into the wee hours. Two clubs in one, **Crash,** Schnewlinstrasse 3 (☎ **0761/3-24-75**), serves drinks and plays punk, house, and funk as background music to the lively banter of patrons; in the basement, **Drifler's Club** plays house and techno for dancers. Crash is open Wednesday to Saturday from 10pm until 3:30am, and Drifler's Thursday to Saturday from midnight to 4am. There is no cover charge at either club. **Club Parabel,** Universitätstrasse 3 (☎ **0761/3-06-34**), plays everything from pop to techno. It's open only on Thursday from 11pm to 3am and Friday and Saturday from 11pm to 4am, and also on nights before holidays. The 10DM ($5.70) cover charge includes the price of your first drink.

Jazz Haus, Schnewlinstrasse 2 (☎ **0761/3-49-73**), hosts pop, folk, blues, and jazz shows by international, regional, and local bands. The club is open nightly from 8pm until 1am, with a cover charge ranging from 15DM to 30DM ($8.55 to $17.10). Occasionally bands play jazz or rock at **Le Cher,** Niemensstrasse 8 (☎ **0761/3-28-00**), but usually it's a place just to drink and talk. It's open Monday to Saturday from 11am to 1am and Sunday from 3pm until 1am. Until 8pm, the **Café Atlantik,** Schwabentorring 7 (☎ **0761/3-30-33**), serves up spaghetti platters for 6.50DM ($3.70), but later on, it's mainly a place to drink and listen to the occasional band. Open daily from 11am to 1am.

Hausbrauerei Feierling, Gerberau 46 (☎ **0761/2-66-78**), is a brewery-pub, with a beer garden across the street. It's open daily from 11am until midnight. Those who want a darker, smoky bar, should head to the local Irish pub, the **Isle of Innisfree,** Augustinaplatz 2 (☎ **0761/22984**), which sometimes has live music. **Cafe Brasil,** Wannerstrasse 21 (☎ **0761/28-98-88**) has a tropical feel. It's open daily from 10am to 7am.

2 Badenweiler

22 miles S of Freiburg, 150 miles W of Stuttgart

Badenweiler is one of the smallest, and one of the most charming, spa towns in the Black Forest. It's also known as the site of the best-preserved Roman baths north of the Alps. Town authorities here are intent on keeping their community spotless, squeaky-clean, and steeped in Black Forest myth and legend. Badenweiler is located halfway between Freiburg and Basel, near the Swiss border.

ESSENTIALS

GETTING THERE   By Train   There's no railway station in Badenweiler, so rail passengers should first go to Freiburg, then switch onto any of the dozen-or-so daily trains that carry them to the town of Müllheim. From there, it's easiest to take any of the taxis lined up at the railway station for the 2½-mile eastward trip to Badenweiler. There's also a bus (marked "Badenweiler") from Müllheim; it's timed to coincide with the arrival of trains.

By Bus   Unless you're coming into Badenweiler from one of the nearby communities, bus travel is not convenient.

By Car   From the A5 Autobahn, which runs north to south between Karlsruhe and Basel, exit at the Müllheim/Badenweiler exit, then follow the signs to Badenweiler.

VISITOR INFORMATION   Head for **Kur-Touristik,** Ernst-Eisenlohr-Strasse 4 (☎ **07632/7-21-10**), which is open Monday through Friday 8:30am to noon and 3 to 5pm and Saturday 8:30am to noon.

WHAT TO SEE & DO

The springs that pour water into the spa facilities here are very little changed since Roman days, a fact that the local resort, the **Cassiopeia Therme,** Kurpark (☎ **07632/7990**), won't let you forget. It offers mud packs, massage, sauna, and steam bath treatments. The well-preserved Roman baths, originally built in A.D. 75, still stand today within the Kurpark, or spa gardens. Tours of the ancient Roman baths, complete with descriptions of how the Romans actually bathed, are given Tuesday at 5pm and Sunday at 11:15am. The cost of the tour is 2DM ($1.15) per person. For information, contact the spa directly. The baths are open daily 9am to 10pm. The cost is Monday to Friday 19DM ($10.85) adults, 12DM ($6.85) children; Saturday, Sunday and holidays 16DM ($9.10) adults, 9DM ($5.15) children; two adults and up to 3 children under the age of 18 costs 38DM ($21.65); an evening card for Monday to Friday after 7pm is 10DM ($5.70) for everyone.

In addition to spa treatment, the town offers a wide range of hiking trails through the Black Forest, the most interesting of which is a trek to the **Schloss Bürgeln,** 7846 Schliengen (☎ **07626/237**), 12 miles south of Badenweiler. It's also accessible by car (follow the signs from Badenweiler's center). Schloss Bürgeln was built in 1764 by order of the abbot of St. Blasein. It offers a commanding view of the surrounding countryside; on a clear day, you can see Basel, the Vosges of France, and the bend in the Rhine as it flows into Switzerland. Especially noteworthy are the verdant gardens around the castle. The castle can only be visited between March and November, on one of the guided tours given every day except Tuesday, at 11am, 2pm, 3pm, 4pm, and 5pm. If there are classical concerts there is no 5pm tour. Adults pay 5DM ($2.85), children under 12, 2DM ($1.15).

One of the highlights of Badenweiler's cultural scene is the four-times-per-year concert series conducted inside the town's most prestigious hotel, the Römerbad (see below), in March, June, September, and November. All tickets cost 50DM to 60DM ($28.50 to $34.20) and are sold exclusively by the hotel itself, often as part of overnight packages.

WHERE TO STAY

Hotel Ritter. Friedrichstrasse 2 (a 10-min. walk west from the center), 79410 Badenweiler. ☎ **07632/83-10.** Fax 07632/831299. 65 units. TV TEL. 254DM–368DM ($144.80–$209.75) double; 382DM–400DM ($217.75–$228) suite. Rates include breakfast. Half board is included for 2 or more nights; otherwise it costs 20DM ($11.40) per person. AE, MC, V.

Informal and personal, this hotel is composed of a trio of buildings. The oldest and most traditional looking is a 150-year-old chalet that contains the cheapest of the accommodations. Newer and somewhat more comfortable lodgings lie within a pair of relatively new annexes, the more recent of which was built in the mid-1990s. On the premises, there's a bar and a restaurant, plus an indoor swimming pool, with a glass door overlooking a forest and the carefully maintained lawns. Bedrooms are cozy, simple, modern, and clean.

✪ Hotel Römerbad. Schlossplatz 1, 79410 Badenweiler. ☎ **07632/7-00.** Fax 07632/70200. 110 units. TV TEL. 300DM–400DM ($171–$228) double; 400DM–500DM ($228–$285) suite. Rates include breakfast. AE, DC, MC, V. Parking 7DM ($4).

This is the best, most elaborate, and most historic spa and hotel in town, attracting urbanites in need of R&R from throughout Germany. The staff is steeped in an old-world sense of courtliness. The clientele has included Nietzsche, Thomas Mann, and Andy Warhol. The domes, mansard roofs, and balconies of this bone-white structure inspire a comparison to an elaborate wedding cake. Inside, the place combines an opera-house grandeur with antiques, ornate ceiling medallions, and touches of gilt. Bedrooms are traditionally furnished, often spacious, and beautifully maintained, with sumptuous beds.

The Römerbad is also known for its seasonal presentations of concerts. The hotel's concert hall, built in the early 1800s as a shelter for horses and carriages, is sought out by music lovers throughout the country. A series of classical or jazz concerts, each performed over a period of about 4 days, is presented three or four times a year. For information and schedules, contact the hotel directly.

Dining/Diversions: The Römerbad Restaurant is formal, elegant, and courtly. There's also a paneled bar evocative of a private club.

Amenities: Room service (7am to 10:30pm), massage, concierge, indoor and outdoor swimming pools (linked with a waterfall that re-creates an alpine stream), two tennis courts, small concert hall, easy access to a nine-hole golf course.

✪ Hotel Schwarzmatt. Schwarzmattstrasse 6 (a short walk east of the town center), 79410 Badenweiler. ☎ **07632/8-20-10.** Fax 07632/820120. 41 units. TV TEL. 396DM–446DM ($225.70–$254.20) double; 536DM ($305.50) suite. Rates include breakfast. No credit cards. Indoor parking 12DM ($6.85); outdoor parking free.

Although it ranks behind the Römerbad, this hotel is a consistently popular choice, thanks to its reasonable prices, lack of pretension, comfortable bedrooms, and hard-working, English-speaking staff. The modern, three-story building is adorned with rows of flower boxes along its balconies, and flanked along its sides by verdant ever-greens. There's a well-managed restaurant within an airy, well-lit room on the ground floor (see separate recommendation below), a beauty parlor, massage facilities, and an indoor swimming pool. Bedrooms range from medium to large, and all have a VCR and safe, plus elegant beds and immaculate bathrooms.

Romantik Hotel Sonne. Moltkestrasse 4, 79410 Badenweiler. ☎ **07632/75-08-0.** Fax 07632/75-08-65. E-mail: sonne.romantik.de. 55 units. MINIBAR TV TEL. 170DM–200DM ($96.90—$114) double. Rates include breakfast. Half board 30DM ($17.10) per person. AE, CB, DC, MC, V. Parking 8DM ($4.55) for garage.

Comfortable and cozy, this hotel occupies a rambling chalet that was built in stages beginning around 350 years ago. Bedrooms come in a variety of shapes and sizes and are attractively furnished, with traditional Black Forest motifs and the views of a quiet street near the center of the resort. All are exceedingly comfortable and well-maintained. On the premises is a well-managed restaurant, recommended below.

WHERE TO DINE

Romantik Hotel Sonne. Moltkestrasse 4. ☎ **07632/75-08-0.** Reservations recommended. Main courses 27DM–45DM ($15.40–$25.65). Fixed-price menus 55DM–98DM ($31.35–$55.85). AE, DC, MC, V. Daily noon–2pm and 6–9pm. ITALIAN/GERMAN.

This hotel is more famous among locals for its Italian and German cuisine than for its bedrooms. The Weinstube decor includes old paneling and timbers. Menu items feature a savory mixture of German and Italian cuisine, including braised guinea fowl with arugula, carpaccio of veal with arugula and shaved Parmesan cheese, lobster cocktail, and ravioli stuffed either with lobster and sage, or with ham and ricotta, according to your tastes. In springtime, an entire menu category is devoted exclusively to variations on asparagus.

Schwarzmatt. In the Hotel Schwarzmatt, Schwarzmattstrasse 6. ☎ **07632/8-20-10.** Reservations not necessary. Main courses 39DM–48DM ($22.25–$27.35). Fixed-price menus 85DM–105DM ($48.45–$59.85). AE, MC, V. Daily noon–2pm and 7–10pm. AE, MC, V. REGIONAL/INTERNATIONAL.

There's nothing about this restaurant that's homey or traditional. Instead, you'll find an airy, high-ceilinged, modern decor with views out over the garden of the hotel. The well-prepared food consists of specialties of the Black Forest, as well as such international dishes as steaks, pastas, salads, and casseroles. The menu is ever changing but always good. The kitchen staff is skillful, and the service professional. Every afternoon from 3 to 5pm there's a buffet with an impressive assortment of regional and international cakes and other treats served with coffee.

3 Titisee

33 miles E of Freiburg, 99 miles W of Stuttgart

Titisee is the quintessential German retreat, favored by thousands for its ability to soothe, relax, and refresh the spirit and body. This small lakeside resort, which can be traversed on foot within about 12 minutes, offers access to all the natural bounty of the Schwarzwald. Well-marked hiking trails lead up the hillsides. Motorized vehicles are forbidden on the lake, for the sake of swimmers and general tranquillity. Nearby rises the Feldberg, the highest point in the Black Forest (5,000 ft.).

Titisee has a year-round population of 2,000, although on busy summer days when visitors come in from nearby cities such as Freiburg, the population can easily swell to three times that amount. More facilities are available at the more workaday community of Neustadt, about 4 miles away.

ESSENTIALS

GETTING THERE **By Train** From Freiburg, trains arrive at intervals of every 30 minutes (trip time: 45 min.). The Titisee rail station is on Parkstrasse (☎ 07651/8298). For general information about rail and train schedules to Titisee, call ☎ **01805/996633.**

By Bus Bus connections into Titisee are mostly limited to rural hamlets within the surrounding Schwartzwald. For bus information in Titisee, call the local bus company, **Südbaden Bus GmbH,** at ☎ **07651/5120.**

By Car Titisee is set near the junction of highway B31 and B317. It's clearly marked from each of the larger towns that surround it. Driving time from Freiburg is between 45 and 60 minutes, depending on traffic; from Stuttgart the trip takes 90 minutes.

VISITOR INFORMATION Contact the tourist office at Strandbadstrasse 4 (☎ 07651/98040). From May to October, it's open Monday to Friday 8am to noon and 1:30 to 5:30pm, Saturday 10am to noon and 3 to 5pm, and Sunday 10am to noon. From November to April the same hours apply but for Monday to Friday only. There's another tourist office in nearby Neustadt, at Sebastian-Kneipp-Anlage (☎ **07651/20-62-50**), maintaining the same hours.

WHAT TO SEE & DO

The cold, clear waters of Lake Titisee are among the most sought after in the region. The town's premier bathing spot is **Schwimmbad Titisee,** Strandbadstrasse (☎ 07651/8272), which combines the chlorinated waters of the town's largest swimming pool with immediate access to a sandy beach adjacent to the lake, complete with cabanas, showers, and refreshment stands. Entrance to the complex costs 5DM ($2.85) adults, 2.50DM ($1.40) children and students. It's open daily between May to September 15, from 9am to 7pm.

Except for a handful of medium-sized steamers that slowly circumnavigate the lake (see below), local ordinances allow only rowboats, foot-operated paddleboats, and electric (not gas-operated) motorboats on the water's surface, a rule that keeps noise, pollution, and rowdiness to a minimum. You can rent rowboats and paddleboats for 13DM to 15DM ($7.40 to $8.55) per hour; electric motorboats that putt-putt demurely across the lake rent for 14DM to 19DM ($8 to $10.85) per hour. About a half-dozen purveyors of these rental craft line the edges of the Seestrasse, the town's main lakefront promenade; the two best are **Drubba,** GmbH (☎ **07651/981200**), and **Schweizer-Winterhalder** (☎ **07651/8214**).

Schweizer-Winterhalder also operates **lake steamers,** which provide a more comfortable excursion. Between June and September, they depart during the day at hourly intervals from the company's pier. Trips last about 40 minutes each and are priced at 6DM ($3.40) per person. Don't expect museums or monuments at this outdoorsy resort. Spa clients within Titisee head for the facilities within the **Hotel Brügger,** am See, Strandbadstrasse 14 (☎ 07651/ 8010), which are open to residents of other hotels. In nearby Neustadt, the **Kneipp-Kur,** in the Kurkpark (☎ **07651/1270**), offers an equivalent spa facility, which offers treatments for cardiac and vascular disorders, rheumatism, and intestinal diseases.

Shoppers and boaters head to the stores that line the lakefront **Seestrasse.** In the early evening, a Bavarian-style marching band promenades along the lakefront, its members stopping at various hotels en route.

WHERE TO STAY

Brugger am See. Strandbadstrasse 14, 79822 Titisee. ☎ **07651/80-10.** Fax 07651/82-38. 65 units. TV TEL. 180DM–270DM ($102.60–$153.90) double. Rates include breakfast. Half board 38DM ($21.65) per person. MC, V. Free parking.

This is one of the leading spa hotels around the waterfront. Its allure lies in its relaxation and beauty treatments. The building is a modified chalet, with balconies and an all-window dining room. The rooms are contemporary and mostly good-sized, with exceedingly comfortable furnishings. The hotel restaurant serves classic German fare typical of the region, along with fresh fish from the lake. In addition to cure baths and other spa-related facilities, the hotel also maintains an indoor pool and a salon.

Hotel Rauchfang. Bärenhofweg 2, 79822 Titisee. ☎ **07651/8-25-50.** Fax 07651/8-81-86. 17 units. TV TEL. 159DM–169DM ($90.65–$96.35) double. Prices include breakfast. Half board 50DM ($28.50) per person. AE, MC, V. Free parking.

Rauchfang is one of the best values among pension-hotels in the upper Black Forest region. It's an authentic reproduction of a chalet-style building. The interiors of the public rooms are covered in pine. Although the bedrooms appear somewhat stark and smell, the beds are comfortable; you'll probably spend a very pleasant evening here. Guests can enjoy the indoor pool, sauna, and steam-room, as well as the miles of forest walks stretching in all directions.

Parkhotel Waldeck. Parkstrasse 6, 78922 Titisee. ☎ **07651/80-90.** Fax 07651/8-09-99. E-mail: parkhotel.waldeck@t-online.de. 53 units. MINIBAR TV TEL. 146DM–186DM ($83.20–$106) double; 196DM–320DM ($111.70–$182.40) suite for 2. Rates include buffet breakfast. Half board 29DM ($16.55) per person. AE, DC, MC, V. Parking in garage 8DM ($4.55).

This hotel is extremely popular, and for good reason—it offers tremendous value and numerous amenities. A richly decorated interior with Oriental rugs, hexagonal floor tiles, and a beamed and paneled wooden ceiling greet you when you enter, along with the bright faces of the helpful staff. The exterior of the building is sheltered against a pine-covered hillock. The small rooms are colorful and comfortable—however, you may not spend a lot of time in them. You can swim in the indoor pool, go for a hike on the miles of nearby forest trails, or just relax in the Jacuzzi. There are also two dining rooms and two bars.

✪ **Trescher's Schwarzwaldhotel am See.** Seestrasse 10, 79822 Titisee-Neustadt. ☎ **07651/805-0.** Fax 07651/8116. 101 units. MINIBAR TV TEL. 160DM–220DM ($91.20–$125.40) double; 270DM–350DM ($153.90–$199.50) suite. AE, CB, DC, MC, V. Closed Nov 1–Dec 15. Parking 12DM ($6.85).

This sprawling hotel, right in the center of the resort, is the most comprehensive in Titisee. It's composed of three massive annexes, each of which borders a flowering courtyard constructed on a platform built directly into the waters of the lake. The spacious rooms are graceful and conservatively decorated.

Dining/Diversions: Two bars and three restaurants are on the premises, the most formal of which is the Terrasse. See "Where to Dine," below.

Amenities: The hotel has one of the most appealing indoor swimming pools along the Titisee, as well as facilities for boating, fishing, and tennis. A concierge can arrange virtually anything. There's also room service, laundry, dry cleaning, and hair dryers in the rooms.

WHERE TO DINE

Trescher's Schwarzwaldhotel am See. Seestrasse 10. ☎ **07651/805-0.** Reservations required. Main courses 29DM–42DM ($16.55–$23.95). AE, CB, DC, MC, V. Daily 7am–11pm. Closed Nov 7–Dec 20. INTERNATIONAL/BLACK FOREST.

The formal dining room in this hotel (recommended above), with picture windows opening onto the lake, is the finest choice for cuisine at Titisee. Diners here enjoy refined service and sublime cuisine. Many of the chef's specialties are regional. Appetizers include melon with Black Forest ham and carpaccio of beef with Parmesan. As for main courses, the Black Forest trout is delectably broiled and served with parsley potatoes, and there's also a hunter's plate, Black Forest style, with spätzle (dumplings). A good authentic regional choice is the boiled calf's head and tongue, served in an onion-red wine sauce. For dessert, try the Black Forest cherry bombé.

NEARBY PLACES TO STAY & DINE

Just 3 miles west of Titisee, or 20 miles east of Freiburg, lies **Hinterzarten,** one of the major pockets of posh within the Black Forest. You may want to retreat here instead of Titisee itself, as Hinterzarten is more tranquil and luxurious. In the center of town stands St. Oswald's, a church constructed in 1146. The Park Hotel Adler (see below) was established in 1446.

✪ **Park Hotel Adler.** Adlerplatz 3, 79856 Hinterzarten. ☎ **07652/1270.** Fax 07652/127-717. 90 units. MINIBAR TV TEL. 270DM–450DM ($153.90–$256.50) double; 450DM–620DM ($256.50–$353.40) junior suite; 500DM–960DM ($285–$547.20) suite. Rates include buffet breakfast. AE, DC, MC, V. Parking 10DM ($5.70).

This is one of the great inns of the Black Forest. Chic and country estate-ish, the inn suggests luxury at every turn, with a wealth of leisure facilities. It's located in the middle of a lovely 10-acre park. All the bedrooms are sumptuously appointed and beautifully maintained, and many are quite spacious. The beds are so comfortable you won't want to get out of them, and the beautiful bathrooms are filled with all the amenities. The hotel's family ownership dates from 1446.

Dining/Diversions: This world-famous hotel has seven different restaurants. Each serves a high-quality cuisine based on the freshest ingredients. An orchestra accompanies dinner in the main 17th-century dining room, and later moves into the bar to play for dancing.

Amenities: Indoor pool, sauna, tennis courts, driving range, Jacuzzi, sauna, beauty salon, hairdresser, open-air tennis courts, bike rentals, golf courses nearby, concierge, room service, baby-sitting, laundry, dry cleaning.

Hotel Reppert. Adlerweg 21–23, 79856 Hinterzarten. ☎ **07652/1208-0.** Fax 07652/1208-11. www.reppert.de. E-mail: hotel@reppert.de. 44 units. MINIBAR TV TEL. 270DM–410DM ($153.90–$233.70) double; 360DM–420DM ($205.20–$239.40) suite. Rates include buffet breakfast. Half board 25DM–42DM ($14.25–$23.95) per person. AE, DC, MC, V. Closed Nov 24–Dec 12. Garage parking 15DM ($8.55).

Although not rated as highly as the Park Hotel Adler, this is a good second choice, a luxurious and traditional four-star hotel in a sunny and central location in a church meadow. Its many rooms open onto balconies, each shaded by an umbrella. The stylish hotel also fronts the village pond. A rich, warm ambience inhabits the comfortable, well-furnished rooms. The traditional lobby is filled with antiques.

Dining: The hotel's restaurants are among the finest in the area for atmosphere, efficient service, and cuisine.

Amenities: Concierge, room service, baby-sitting, faxes, hair dryers, laundry and dry cleaning. The thermae is a unique pool and sauna combined; it was once voted best in the nation. Other facilities include swimming pool, two Jacuzzis, aromatherapy rooms, sauna, steam bath, massage, bike rentals, tennis, riding, water sports, and a hotel program that features guided walks.

4 Triberg

86 miles SW of Stuttgart, 30 miles NE of Freiburg

Triberg, deep in the heart of the Black Forest, is home to the highest waterfall in the country. It also claims to be the birthplace of the cuckoo clock. If you're looking for

Wunderhiking in the Black Forest

You can see the loveliest parts of the Black Forest by hiking the ancient trail of the cuckoo-clock traders. Really. The marked trail follows the route of the traders who, centuries ago, carried the famous Black Forest clocks across Europe. Along the village-to-village journey, you'll pass through deep, fragrant pinewoods and sunny pastures where farmhouses are set scenically on the hillsides.

The circle trail starts at Triberg, with its waterfalls. An arrangement with a series of hotels along the trail, beginning with the **Parkhotel Wehrle** (see below), allows you to hike with only a small rucksack; vans haul your luggage on to the next hotel. You can hike anywhere from 1 or 2 to 10 days and more if you have the time (but most hikers have their fill long before this). Distances for a day's hike between hotels can be anywhere from 12 to 17 miles.

Clearly marked signs guide you across this easy trail, and the Parkhotel Wehrle provides detailed road descriptions and a road map, with instructions in English, to set you on your way. Restaurants and farmhouses offering food and refreshment are not far apart, and the area is quite safe, even for a woman walking alone.

an interesting traditional timepiece, this is the place to find it. You'll also find many little shops selling wood carvings, music boxes, and other traditional crafts.

ESSENTIALS

GETTING THERE By Plane The nearest major airport is at Stuttgart, 2½ hours away by train.

By Train Trains arrive daily from Munich (trip time: 4½ hr.) and from Frankfurt (trip time: 3 hr.). The **Triberg Bahnhof** is on the Konstanz-Singen-Villingen-Offenburg Schwarzwaldbahn rail line, with frequent connections in all directions. Call ☎ **01805/996633** for schedules and information.

By Bus Regional bus service in the Black Forest area is provided by **SBG Südbaden Bus GmbH** in Villingen (☎ **07721/9-28-521**).

By Car Access is via the A5 Autobahn north and south; exit at Offenburg and then follow the signs along Route 33 south.

VISITOR INFORMATION For tourist information, contact the **Kurverwaltung,** Kurhaus (☎ **07722/95-32-30**), open year-round Monday to Friday 9am to 5pm and from May to October also Saturday 10am to noon.

EXPLORING THE AREA

The waterfall, called the **Gutach Falls,** is exceptional, but be prepared to walk an hour or so to reach it. The falls drop some 530 feet, spilling down in seven stages. To get there, you park your car in a designated area near the Gutach Bridge (in the town center) and then walk along a marked trail. It's open daily from 9am to 6pm in summer, and costs 2.50DM ($1.40) adults, 1DM (55¢) children. At the bottom of the falls is a year-round cafe/restaurant serving the famed Black Forest cake for which, by then, you'll have worked up an appetite.

The **Schwarzwald-Museum of Triberg,** Wallfahrstrasse 4 (☎ **07722/44-34**), brings the olden days of the Black Forest vividly to life, with displays of dresses, handcrafts, furnishings, bird music boxes, and, of course, clocks and clock making. You can also see the famed Schwarzwaldbahn railway, which really works, a

---

Stop for Clocks

You may want to make a stop along the B33 between Triberg and Hornberg at the **Haus der 1000 Uhren (House of 1,000 Clocks),** An der Bundesstrasse 33, 78098 Triberg-Gemmelsbach (☎ 07722/96300). You'll recognize the shop immediately because of the giant cuckoo clock and waterwheel in front. A painter of clock faces, Josef Weisser, launched the business in 1824; today his great-great-grandson owns the place. The shop is open Monday to Saturday from 9am to 5pm. It ships to the United States and Canada and takes all major credit cards. There's another branch in the center of Triberg, near the entrance to the waterfall.

---

mineral exhibit of the area, and Europe's largest barrel organ collection. The museum is open May to October, daily 9am to 6pm; November to April, Monday to Friday 9am to 6pm and Saturday and Sunday 10am to 5pm. Admission is 7DM ($4) for adults, 4DM ($2.30) for students, and 3DM ($1.70) for children.

One of the most beautiful churches in the Black Forest, the **Wallfahrtkirche Maria in der Tannen (Church of Our Lady of the Fir Trees),** is within easy reach. Built in the early 18th century, it has superb baroque furnishings, including a remarkable pulpit.

After a visit to the church, you may want to drive to the **Freilchtmuseum Schwarzwälder** in Gutach (☎ 07831/2-30), which contains original Black Forest homes as many as 4 centuries old. In summer, guides may demonstrate weaving on some of the looms and other skills. The museum is open April to October, daily from 8:30am to 6pm. Admission is 8DM ($4.55) for adults and 4DM ($2.30) for children and students. From the A5, turn off at the Offenburg exit and follow B33 toward Gengenbach, Hausach, and Triberg; at Hausach, turn right to Gutach.

A 10-mile drive south of Triberg is the **Deutsches Uhrenmuseum (German Clock Museum),** Gerwigstrasse 11, in Furtwangen (☎ 07723/92-01-17). It's open daily 10am to 5pm from November to April and 9am to 6pm from May to October. Admission is 5DM ($2.85) for adults and 3DM ($1.70) for children. This museum presents a history of timepieces, including displays of a wide variety of Black Forest clocks, some from the early 18th century. Many are elaborate and complicated. Look for the mechanical music automata and the cuckoo clocks.

WHERE TO STAY

Parkhotel Wehrle. Gartenstrasse 24 (1 mile from the train station), 78098 Triberg. ☎ 07722/86-02-0. Fax 07722/86-02-190. 52 units. TV TEL. 195DM–340DM ($111.15–$193.80) double; from 420DM ($239.40) suite. Rates include buffet breakfast. AE, DC, MC, V. Free parking outdoors; 10DM ($5.70) in garage.

Built in the early 1600s, Parkhotel Wehrle was acquired around 1730 by the family that has owned it ever since. Its lemon-yellow walls and gabled mansard roof occupy one of the most prominent street corners in town. The main house offers an old-world atmosphere, but forest-loving vacationers often request accommodation near the woods in a separate chalet, where a pool and breeze-filled balconies create a modern sylvan retreat. The good-sized guest rooms are beautifully furnished and individually decorated, sometimes with antiques. Some rooms have minibars; all have hair dryers. The hotel restaurant is the finest in the area (see "Where to Dine," below). Amenities include indoor and outdoor pools, sauna, fitness room, room service, and laundry.

Römischer Kaiser. Sommerauerstrasse 35 (just over a mile outside Triberg), 78098 Triberg-Nussbach. ☎ 07722/44-18. Fax 07722/44-01. 26 units. TV, TEL. 112DM–122DM ($63.85–$69.55) double. Rates include continental breakfast. AE, DC, MC, V. Closed Nov 15–Dec 7. Free parking.

This comfortable, charmingly preserved hotel has been owned by several generations of the same family since 1840. The exterior has lots of exposed wood. Guest rooms come in a wide range of shapes and sizes, but all are pleasant and well maintained. The bathrooms are roomy.

The very popular restaurant here serves fresh fish throughout the year. Menu items include lake trout served with watercress mousse and wild salmon with lobster-cream sauce and fresh asparagus. The food is not on par with that served at the more glamorous Parkhotel Wehrle, but it's satisfying in every way, and your bill will be a lot cheaper.

WHERE TO DINE

✪ **Parkhotel Wehrle.** Marktplatz. ☎ **07722/8-60-20.** Reservations required. Main courses 23DM–40DM ($13.10–$22.80); fixed-price meals 70DM–118DM ($39.90–$67.25). AE, DC, MC, V. Daily noon–2pm and 6–10pm. CONTINENTAL.

People come from great distances to eat at this fine, famous restaurant. Meals here are accompanied by the ticking of a stately grandfather clock; meanwhile, the clientele relaxes in the comfort of cane-bottomed French-style armchairs. The cuisine is intelligent and imaginative, with a focus on natural flavors. Even simple dishes have a certain flair. Try the trout or saddle of venison with juniper berry cream sauce and spätzle. A traditional dessert is apples baked with pine honey and flambéed with Kirschwasser. Some of the game specialties are prepared for two.

5 Freudenstadt

57 miles N of Freiburg

One of the most important transportation hubs in the northern tier of the Black Forest is Freudenstadt, a riverside town known for clear air, streaming sunshine, and a sense of cleanliness and conservatism. Originally founded in 1599 by Duke Friedrich I of Württemberg, Freudenstadt provided a home at the time for Protestants fleeing religious persecution within Carinthia, in southern Austria. French troops set most of the town ablaze in the closing days of World War II, but it was completely rebuilt, more or less to the original plans, before 1950.

ESSENTIALS

GETTING THERE   By Train   Trains from Frankfurt, 3½ hours away, arrive at hourly intervals throughout the day. There are also 10 trains per day from Munich (about 4½ hours away). Freudenstadt has two railway stations, the **Stadtbahnhof** (☎ 07441/4554 for information), in the center of town, and the **Hauptbahnhof** (☎ 07441/2015 for information), about a mile south of the center. Most trains stop at both. For general rail information and schedules, call ☎ **01805/996633.**

By Bus   Bus travel tend to be convenient only for those coming from surrounding hamlets. Buses stop at both the Bahnhofplatz and the Marktplatz. For information, call ☎ **07441/1555.**

By Car   Driving distance from Stuttgart, following the B28, takes about 1¼ hours; from Karlsruhe via the B462, about 1½ hours.

VISITOR INFORMATION   The **Tourist Information Office** is at Promenade-platz 1 (☎ 07441/86-40). It's open year-round Monday to Friday 9am to 6pm, Saturday 10am to 1pm.

EXPLORING THE TOWN

Freudenstadt's appeal lies not so much in the town itself, as in its ideal location in the midst of the best hiking and camping country in the Black Forest. Trails wind for hundreds of miles through the nearby hills. In winter the snow-covered paths are great for skiing.

Unlike many German towns, Freudenstadt has no castle overshadowing it, but it certainly does have an enormous castle square. This plot of land, the largest market-place in Germany, was laid out in the 16th century for a castle that was never built. History's loss is today's gain. The market square that greets the visitor to Freuden-stadt is a maze of lawns and concrete, broken by patches of flowers and kiosks. The buildings surrounding the square are mainly postwar, since the air raids and fires of World War II almost completely destroyed the city. A few of the old Renaissance structures on the square have been reconstructed, up to their neat little archways and gabled roofs.

The town takes pride in its **Stadtkirche,** Marktplatz (☎ 07441/6087), dating from the 17th century. The unusual L-shaped architecture of the church brings the two main aisles together at right angles. Over the entrance stand identical towers, topped with rounded domes and narrow spires. The church's most important treasure is the 12th-century reading desk, supported by carved and painted likenesses of the writers of the four Gospels. The church is open daily from 10am to 5pm. Entrance is free.

Regrettably, Freudenstadt doesn't have any other museums or attractions worth mentioning, with the exception of a small regional folk and crafts museum, the **Heimatmuseum,** in the Stadthaus, Marktplatz (☎ 07441/6177). It's open Monday 3 to 6pm, Tuesday and Wednesday 9 to 11am and 3 to 6pm, Thursday 9 to 11am and 3 to 7pm, Friday 3 to 6pm, and Sunday 10am to noon; closed on Saturday. Entrance is free.

WHERE TO STAY

Hotel Baren. 33 Langestrasse (near the Marktplatz), 72250 Freudenstadt. ☎ **07441/ 27-29.** Fax 07441/2881. 24 units. TV TEL. 150DM–180DM ($85.50–$102.60) double; 200DM ($114) suite. MC, V. Free parking.

This establishment is best known for its well-managed restaurant, separately recom-mended below, but it's also an eminently respectable hotel. The cozy interior, lined with old panels and capped with heavy ceiling beams, might remind you of the inside of a prosperous local farmhouse. The small bedrooms are cozy, traditionally decorated, and well maintained. The staff is charming and polite, managing to convey a nostalgic sense of traditional Germany.

Hotel Hohenried im Rosengarten. Zeppelinstrasse 5 (about a mile south of Freudenstadt's center), 72250 Freudenstadt. ☎ **07441/24-14.** Fax 07441/25-59. 27 units. TV TEL. 150DM–180DM ($85.50–$102.60) double; 220DM ($125.40) suite. AE, DC, MC, V. Bus 14.

This three-story hotel is designed like a modern version of an alpine chalet. The garden contains more than 2,000 well-tended rose bushes. Views from the windows of the comfortable and contemporary-looking bedrooms overlook a golf course and stately trees. Most rooms are medium in size and well furnished with modern pieces. In summertime, the balconies are adorned with flower boxes that bloom with gera-niums. The hotel also has a pleasant restaurant that charges from 20DM to 30DM ($11.40 to $17.10) for main courses at lunch and dinner. On the premises are an indoor pool, a sauna, and a solarium. The staff is polite and English speaking.

Luz Posthotel. Stuttgarterstrasse 5, 72250 Freudenstadt. ☎ **07441/8970.** Fax 07441/84533. 52 units. TV TEL. 140DM ($79.80) double; 180DM ($102.60) suite. Rates include breakfast. AE, DC, MC, V. Free parking.

This hotel, built in 1809, was almost demolished during World War II and then was reconstructed along more modern lines shortly thereafter. Since then, strands of climbing ivy have added to a more antique-looking appearance. Today, this comfortable, contemporary, four-story hotel combines touches of Black Forest nostalgia with a smooth, conservatively modern decor. Many of the civic-minded organizations of Freudenstadt (including the Lion's Cub and the Rotarians) meet within this hotel's restaurants at regular intervals. The medium-sized bedrooms are clean, tastefully modern, and comfortable. On the premises, you'll find a bar, a woodsy-looking *stube*, and a modern, international-looking dining room, the Restaurant Posthotel, where main courses cost from 9.50DM to 32DM ($5.40 to $18.25).

WHERE TO DINE

✪ Hotel Baren. 33 Langestrasse. ☎ **07441/27-29.** Reservations recommended. Main courses 15DM–30DM ($8.55–$17.10). Set menus 30DM–40DM ($17.10–$22.80). MC, V. Sun–Thurs 11am–3:30pm and 6–10pm, Fri 11am–3:30pm. SWABIAN/GERMAN.

This is an attractive, pleasingly proportioned 200-year-old inn. The warmly decorated, richly beamed and paneled interior will soothe urban hearts. The well-prepared cuisine emphasizes fresh Atlantic and Mediterranean fish. Look for fillet of monkfish with garlic and parsley, fillets of sole with a Riesling sauce, spicy fish soup redolent with saffron and garlic, savory game dishes, and beer and wine from every part of Germany.

Jägerstüble. Marktplatz 12. ☎ **07441/23-87.** Reservations recommended. Main courses 14DM–35DM ($8–$19.95). MC, V. Tues–Sat 11am–2pm and Tues–Sun 7–9pm. SWABIAN/GERMAN.

Like most of the buildings around it, this is an excellent re-creation of a medieval house that was severely damaged during World War II. Inside, foaming mugs of beer and hardworking waitresses in folkloric costumes contribute to an unpretentious re-creation of the Germany of another era. The hearty and savory dishes include *Eisbein* (veal shank) with sauerkraut, farmer's omelets, venison steak prepared with garlic and red wine, and goulash of venison.

NEARBY ACCOMMODATIONS

If you want to experience the Schwarzwald at its most isolated and remote, consider a stay at either of the following two hotels, the Bareiss and the Traube Tonbach, which are positioned south and north of the hamlet of Baiersbronn, respectively. Baiersbronn lies 4 miles northwest of Freudenstadt. Trains arrive in Baiersbronn about once an hour from Stuttgart and Karlsruhe, stopping in Baiersbronn before continuing south for another 4 miles to Freudenstadt. Local buses (marked "Baiersbronn") depart from the Marktplatz in Freudenstadt for Baiersbronn, but there are only about four a day, and they won't take you anywhere near either of the two hotels we recommend. For the short distance involved, it's a lot more convenient to take any of the taxis lined up in Freudenstadt's Marktplatz.

✪ Hotel Bareiss. Gärtenbühlweg 14, 072270 Baiersbronn/Mitteltal. ☎ **07442/470.** Fax 07442/47320. 100 units. MINIBAR TV TEL. 210DM–298DM ($119.70–$169.85) double; 258DM–381DM ($147.05–$217.15) apt, from 363DM ($206.90) suite. Rates include breakfast. AE, DC, MC, V. Garage parking 9DM ($5.15). From the center of Baiersbronn, follow signs pointing to Hotel Bareiss for 6 miles, heading south.

This five-star resort hotel is equivalent in most ways to the Hotel Traube Tonbach (see below), but it's a bit less formal and a lot less stiff. It provides a soothing, carefully orchestrated, well-manicured environment, where peace, quiet, and access to the surrounding forest are fiercely guarded. You'll find lots of urban refugees on site, recuperating from stressful careers. The spacious bedrooms are carefully maintained, conservatively modern, and very comfortable. All have views over the forest.

Dining: The formal dining room is reserved exclusively for guests. There are also three other restaurants. The Restaurant Bareiss serves sublime French food at dinner only, every day except Monday and Tuesday. The cuisine here is among the finest in Germany, although the Schwarzwaldstube in the Hotel Traube Tonbach is even better. The hotel's middle-bracket choice is the cozy-looking Kaminstube, offering German and Alsatian food. There's also a budget-conscious Bierstube on the premises, featuring Black Forest and international food.

Amenities: On the premises are an indoor/outdoor swimming pool; a tennis court; a health club with an exercise room, sauna, whirlpool, and massage facilities; a "beauty farm" with massage, skin, and hairstyling facilities; a concierge; and facilities for bicycle rentals. Services include room service, dry cleaning, and laundry.

✪ **Hotel Traube Tonbach.** Ortsteil Tonbach, Tonbacherstrasse 237, 07442 Baiersbronn. ☎ **07442/4920.** Fax 07442/492-692. 175 units. MINIBAR TV TEL. 173DM–379DM ($98.60–$216.05) double; 359DM–495DM ($204.65–$282.15) suite. Rates include breakfast and parking. Half board 45DM ($25.65) per person. AE, DC, MC, V. Parking 7DM–14DM ($4–$8).

In 1957, this establishment was massively enlarged into the stately looking, many-balconied resort you see today, and immediately attracted one of the grandest resort clienteles in Germany. Set closer to Baiersbronn (only about a mile north of town) than its competitor, the Bareiss (see above), the Traube Tonbach prides itself on its conservatism, its strictly enforced sense of peace and quiet, and the glamour of its very upscale clientele. The good-sized bedrooms are solid, well built, quiet, and very, very comfortable. Service is good. You'll find a safe and secure sense of well-upholstered, well-managed grandeur throughout. Ask the staff for advice on nearby hiking trails.

Dining: The resort contains three recommended restaurants, the most formal of which, the Schwarzwald Stube, is one of the best in all of Germany. Less formidably grand are the Köhlertube, serving German and international food, and a congenial Bierstube, the Bauernstube, specializing in Swabian food.

Amenities: Three separate swimming pools, sauna, whirlpool, beauty salon, exercise facilities, massage, indoor bowling alley, tennis courts, concierge, room service, laundry, dry cleaning.

6 Calw

12½ miles S of Pforzheim, 41 miles N of Freudenstadt

Many residents of other parts of Germany call Calw the most appealingly folkloric town in the Black Forest. Hermann Hesse, who was born here in 1877, described Calw as "the most beautiful place I know."

ESSENTIALS

GETTING THERE **By Train** Trains arrive at Calw's Bahnhof at hourly intervals from both Stuttgart and Karlsruhe. Both cities are about an hour away. For railway information, call ☎ **01805/996633.**

By Bus Buses that travel between Horb, Nagold, and Pforzheim make stops at Calw's Bahnhofplatz. For information, call ☎ **07051/968850.**

By Car Calw lies midway between Pforzheim and Nagold, along Highway B463. From the A8 Autobahn, exit at the signs indicating Calw.

VISITOR INFORMATION The **Tourist Information office** in Calw is at Marktbrücke 7 (☎ **07051/96-88-66**). It's open Monday through Friday 9am to 12:30pm and 2 to 5pm (to 6:30pm on Thursday), and also on Saturday from April to October 9:30am to 12:30pm.

EXPLORING THE TOWN

Calw's allure derives from its impressive and meticulously maintained roster of late 17th- and early 18th-century houses, whose half-timbered facades add an undeniable charm to such sites as the Marktplatz. The town's most prominent bridge, the 14th-century **Nikolausbrücke,** in the center, merits a stroll in admiration of its carefully chiseled masonry.

The birthplace of Herman Hesse, the **Hesse Haus,** Marktplatz 30 (☎ 07051/ 7522), is a literary shrine for scholars and fans. Entrance is 5DM ($2.85) adults, 3DM ($1.70) children and students. The only other formal attraction in town is a free small-scale folklore museum called **Palais Vischer,** Bischofstrasse 10 (same phone as Hesse Haus).

The environs of Calw also merit some attention if you have the time. Of exceptional interest is the hamlet of **Zavelstein,** which is signposted in Calw. Follow the road south for 3 miles. A drive to this little hamlet is especially interesting in late March and April, when the meadows blossom with edelweiss and crocuses. You might want to continue south in the direction of Talmühle-Seitzental, where you'll see a sign pointing along a twisting road leading to **Neubulach.** Until it closed in the mid-1920s, this was one of the most active silver mines in the Black Forest. Long after it was abandoned, the medical profession learned that its dust-free interior was beneficial in the treatment of asthma. A therapy center is located inside. The mine's ancient shafts can be visited on guided tours given daily from April to November 10am to noon and 2 to 4pm, costing 4DM ($2.30) for adults and 2DM ($1.15) for children.

WHERE TO STAY

Hotel Kloster Hirsau. Ortsteil Hirsau, Wildbacher Strasse 2, 75365 Calw. ☎ **07051/ 5621.** Fax 07051/967469. 42 units. MINIBAR TV TEL. 145DM–195DM ($82.65–$111.15) double. Rates include breakfast. Half board 35DM ($19.95) per person. AE, DC, MC, V. Free parking; parking in garage 5DM ($2.85).

Parts of the foundation of this historic hotel date from 1092, when the site functioned as a monastery that was noted for housing overnight visitors. Today the establishment retains its medieval touches and antique charm. The good-sized bedrooms have lots of Schwarzwald-inspired features, including pinewood trim and reproductions of traditional furniture. The oldest rooms are numbers 114 to 235. The hotel also offers a beauty salon, sauna, and swimming pool.

WHERE TO DINE

Ratstube. Marktplatz 12, 75365 Calw. ☎ **07051/1864.** Reservations recommended. Main courses 20DM–30DM ($11.40–$17.10). Daily noon–2:30pm and 5:30–9:30pm. AE, DC, MC, V. SWABIAN/INTERNATIONAL.

This is the most popular and reliable restaurant in town—a kind of civic staple in Calw. The interior is a labyrinth of masonry-sided rooms. The well-prepared, but not particularly innovative dishes include *Zwiebelrostbraten,* fillet of sole in wine sauce; stingray in black butter sauce; trout with almonds or meunière-style; and an array of sausages served with cabbage and roasted potatoes. Service is competent.

The inn also rents the best rooms within the town center. A double costs 165DM ($94.05).

Restaurant Klosterschanke. Wildbader Strasse 2. ☎ **07051/96740.** Reservations recommended. Main courses 30DM–70DM ($17.10–$39.90). DC, V. Lunch noon–2pm, *Kafe mit Kuchen* (coffee and cakes) 2–5pm, dinner 6–11pm. SWABIAN/INTERNATIONAL.

Cozy and historically authentic, this restaurant occupies a trio of dining rooms whose beamed and/or vaulted ceilings in some cases are hundreds of years old. Menu items include fresh house-marinated sardines; rack of lamb with white beans; *Zwiebelrost-*

braten; monkfish braised in olive oil with herbs; and several kinds of schnitzel. Although cuisine here never reaches the sublime, it's always fresh and competently prepared.

7 Pforzheim

22 miles S of Karlsruhe, 33 miles SW of Stuttgart

Set at the northern edge of the Black Forest, at the junction of three rivers (the Würm, the Enz, and the Nagold), Pforzheim is one of the Schwarzwald's largest settlements. It was founded by the Romans as a fortified camp, and developed into an important mercantile center during the Middle Ages. Key industries have traditionally included the crafting of jewelry and clock making. Although most of it was severely damaged by bombs during World War II, Pforzheim is a worthwhile site for an overnight stay between forays into the Black Forest.

ESSENTIALS

GETTING THERE   By Train   Trains pull into Pforzheim at least once an hour from Munich (3 hours by train), Frankfurt (2 hours by train), and Stuttgart (1½ hours by train). The railway station lies within an 8-minute walk of the center. For rail information, call ☎ **01805/996633.**

By Bus   Bus travel to Pforzheim is a lot less practical than rail travel. The bus stop is at Leopoldsplatz, in the town center.

By Car   Pforzheim lies beside the high-speed A-8 Autobahn that stretches between Munich and Karlsruhe. Transit from Stuttgart takes between 75 and 90 minutes, from Munich around 2½ hours, and from Frankfurt around 2 hours.

VISITOR INFORMATION   Head to **Stadinformation,** Marktplatz 1 (☎ 07231/ 1454560), open Monday to Friday 9am to 6pm.

EXPLORING THE TOWN

Much of Pforzheim was demolished by Allied bombs during World War II. Of the limited number of buildings that have been restored to their former grandeur, the **Sankt Michaelerskirche** (St. Michael's Church), Schlossberg 10 (☎ 07231/102484), is the most dramatic. It was built in stages between the 1200s and 1400s, and combines aspects of both Romanesque and Gothic architecture. It's open daily from 8:30am to 6pm. A fine example of a more modern church is the **Stadtkirche,** on Melanchthonstrasse (no phone), in the town center across from the Parkhotel. Rebuilt from the town's rubble during the 1950s, this is a symbol of Pforzheim's rebirth from the devastation of World War II.

For insights into the role that clock making has always played in Pforzheim, head for the city's **Technisches Museum,** Bleichstrasse 81 (☎ 07231/392869), where souvenirs and mementos of the clock-making trade commemorate humankind's painstaking efforts to organize time. On the premises is a reconstruction of a clock-making studio from the early 1800s. The museum is open every Wednesday from 9am to noon and 3 to 6pm, and every 2nd and 4th Sunday of the month from 10am to 5pm. Admission is free, although donations are appreciated.

The equally nostalgic **Schmuckmuseum,** Jahnstrasse 42 (☎ 07231/392-126), is devoted to Pforzheim's jewelry-making trade. Its collection includes ornaments from the 3rd century B.C. to modern times, and is one of the most unusual anywhere. The museum is open Tuesday to Sunday from 10am to 5pm. Admission is free.

If you're passionate about botany or gardening, you might enjoy a visit to the **Alpengarten (Alpine Garden),** Auf dem Berg 6 (☎ 07231/70590), in which about

100,000 varieties of high-altitude plants are grown in a natural-looking milieu. It's set adjacent to the banks of the Würm River, about 2 miles south of Pforzheim's center, and is open April to November, daily 8am to 7pm. Admission costs 4DM ($2.30). To reach it from Pforzheim, follow the signs pointing to Würm.

WHERE TO STAY

Hotel Royal. Wilhelmbeckerstrasse 3A (less than a mile north of the center), 75179 Pforzheim. ☎ **07231/14250.** Fax 07231/142599. 43 units. MINIBAR TV TEL. 185DM–195DM ($105.45–$111.15) double. Rates include breakfast and free parking. AE, DC, V. Bus: 29.

Equivalent in most ways to the Parkhotel (see below), the Royal's only drawback is its location on the outskirts of town. It was built in 1995 in a two-story, modern format. The small to medium-sized bedrooms are contemporary, sunny, comfortable, clean and utterly without pretension. On the premises are a bar and a restaurant, Etagen. The staff is polite and well trained.

Parkhotel. Deimlingerstrasse 36, 75175 Pforzheim. ☎ **07231/1610.** Fax 07231/161690. E-mail: parkhotelpforzheim@s-direktnet.de. 144 units. A/C MINIBAR TV TEL. 268DM ($152.75) double Sun–Thurs; 198DM ($112.85) double Fri–Sat. Rates include breakfast. AE, CB, DC, DISC, MC, V.

Set in the center of town, the four-story, contemporary Parkhotel is the meeting place for most of the civic and charitable organizations in Pforzheim. Inside, you'll find a streamlined, tasteful decor with lots of exposed wood and stone. On the premises, there's a sauna, Jacuzzi, fitness center, bar, and two restaurants, the less pretentious of which is recommended below. The good-sized bedrooms are airy, contemporary, soothing, and comfortable.

WHERE TO DINE

Parkrestaurant. In the Parkhotel, Deimlingerstrasse 36. ☎ **07231/1610.** Reservations not necessary. Main courses 25DM–40DM ($14.25–$22.80). AE, CB, DC, DISC, MC, V. Open daily noon–3pm and 6–10pm. GERMAN.

This well-managed restaurant offers solid home-style cuisine, a view over the Stadt Theater and the banks of the Enz River, and a polite, well-trained staff. We prefer this place to the Galarestaurant, its more upscale sibling within the same hotel. Menu items include schnitzels, stews, roulades and grills, soups, salads, and hearty, regional desserts layered with chocolate and whipped cream.

A MEDIEVAL EXCURSION FROM PFORZHEIM

One of the Schwarzwald's most evocative sights lies 11 miles to the northeast of Pforzheim, within the agrarian hamlet of Maulbronn. **Maulbronn Monastery** (☎ **07043/926610**) has been called the best-preserved medieval monastery north of the Alps. Most of its more than 30 stone-sided buildings were constructed between 1150 and 1390, within an encircling wall that protected the monks and their allies from outside attackers. The most visible of the buildings is the compound's church, which combines aspects of both Romanesque and Gothic architecture, and which influenced the design of later structures throughout central and northern Europe. Look for the complicated irrigation system, still intact, which distributed water to key elements within the compound. Most visitors arrive by car or taxi from the center of Pforzheim, although there's also a bus that departs for Maulbronn from Pforzheim's Leopoldplatz at 50-minute intervals throughout the day. The monastery is open from March to October daily 9am to 5:30pm; from November to February Tuesday to Sunday 9:30am to 5pm. Admission is 8DM ($4.55) adults, 4DM ($2.30) children and students.

8 Baden-Baden

69 miles W of Stuttgart, 69 miles NE of Freiburg, 108 miles S of Frankfurt

Baden-Baden, where the bath-conscious Roman emperor Caracalla once came to ease his arthritic aches, was rediscovered in the 19th century by the nobility of Europe. Swanky clients such as Queen Victoria, Kaiser Wilhelm I, Napoléon III, Berlioz, Brahms, and Dostoyevsky helped make Baden-Baden the most elegant and sophisticated playground in Germany. Tolstoy set a scene in *Anna Karenina* here, though he gave the town a different name. Today the clientele may have changed, but Baden-Baden still evokes an aura of 19th-century privilege, combined with the most up-to-date facilities. More recent clients have included everybody from the late Frank Sinatra to Barbra Streisand and Yasser Arafat.

Baden-Baden is the ideal choice for sports and outdoor enthusiasts. Golf, tennis, and horseback riding are all popular here. Lovers of horse racing will enjoy the international racing season each August at Iffezheim Track. The surrounding countryside is good for hiking and mountain climbing. During the winter, Baden-Baden is a convenient center for skiing. After a day on the slopes, you can return to a soothing swim in a thermal pool and a night out at the casino.

ESSENTIALS

GETTING THERE **By Train** Baden-Baden is on major rail lines connecting Frankfurt and Basel, and Stuttgart and Munich. There are 20 trains daily from Stuttgart (trip time: 1 hr., 15 min.); 25 from Munich (4 hr., 10 min.), and 45 from Frankfurt (3 hr.). For information, call ☎ **01805/996633.** The railway station is at Baden-Oos, north of town; regrettably, it's an expensive 20-minute taxi ride from the town center.

By Bus Long-distance bus service is provided to Freudenstadt and Tübingen (Line 1070), operated by **Deutsche Touring GmbH** (☎ **0721/30804** for information).

By Car Access to Baden-Baden is via the A5 Autobahn north and south or the A8 Autobahn east and west. The drive south from Frankfurt takes 2 hours; from Munich, about 4 hours.

VISITOR INFORMATION For information, contact **Tourist-Information,** Schwatzwaldstrasse 7 (☎ **07221/27-52-00**), daily from 9am to 7pm.

TAKING THE WATERS

The center of Baden-Baden activity is **Lichtentaler Allee,** the park promenade along the bank of the Oosbach River (affectionately called the Oos—pronounced ohs), which runs through the center of town. As you stroll along this walk, you'll be amazed at the variety not only of exotic shrubs and trees but also of the rhododendrons, azaleas, and roses. At the north end of the park, on the banks of the stream, are the buildings of the **Kurgarten,** including the classical Kurhaus, used as an entertainment complex.

Your hotel can give you full information on the facilities available at both the Friedrichsbad and the Caracalla, which are in the heart of the Altstadt.

Caracalla-Therme. Römerplatz 1. ☎ **07221/27-59-40.** Admission 19DM ($10.85)for 2 hours. Daily 8am–10pm. Bus: 1.

Caracalla-Therme has been made more pleasing visually by the addition of a round colonnaded extension with splashing and cascading pools. You can decide on your own bath system here. Medicinal treatment includes mud baths, massages, and whirlpools. The slightly radioactive water, rich in sodium chloride, comes from artesian wells 6,000 feet under the Florentiner Mountain. Its temperature is around 160°F. Bathers usually

Mark Twain Abroad

Mark Twain, who stopped here on his tour of Europe, didn't think much of Baden-Baden, although he must have liked the baths: "I fully believe I left my rheumatism in Baden-Baden," he wrote, adding that Baden-Baden was welcome to it.

begin in cooler pools, working up to the warm water. The baths also have a sauna area, with foot baths and sun baths; sauna temperatures go from 185°F to 200°F. You must wear bathing suits in the pools, but everyone goes nude in the saunas. Also offered are group water gymnastics. Caracalla has a bar and a cafeteria as well.

Friedrichsbad. Römerplatz 1. ☎ **07221/27-59-20.** Reservations recommended. Admission 36DM ($20.50) without soap-brush massage, 48DM ($27.35) with soap-brush massage. Mon–Sat 9am–10pm, Sun 9am–8pm (last admission always 7pm).

It's likely that the waters that did Mark Twain so much good were those of the Friedrichsbad, also known as the Old Baths, built from 1869 to 1877 at the behest of Grand Duke Friedrich von Baden. Following the Roman-Irish method, it takes about 2 hours to have the complete bath program, which involves a shower, two saunas (from 130°F to 160°F), a brush massage soaping, thermal steam baths, and three freshwater baths ranging from warm to 60°F. After a 30-minute period of rest and relaxation, wrapped in a sheet or blanket, you're supposed to feel rejuvenated. Other types of therapy, including massage, electrotherapy, and hydrotherapy, are also offered. Massages are 33DM ($18.80) for 20 minutes and 66DM ($37.60) for 40 minutes.

Pump Room (Trinkhalle). Kaiserallee 3. ☎ **07221/9070.** Free admission. Apr–Oct daily 10am–5:30pm. Bus: 1.

The spa gardens contain the Pump Room *(Trinkhalle)*, where visitors can sip the water. The loggia of the hall is decorated with frescoes depicting Black Forest legends. The springs of Baden-Baden have been recognized for more than 2,000 years, and their composition is almost the same today as when the Romans built their baths here in the 3rd century.

THE CASINO
Spielbank. Kaiserallee 1. ☎ **07221/2-10-60.** Bus: 1.

The Spielbank, open year-round, is the oldest casino in Germany, popular for more than 200 years. Dostoyevsky is said to have written *The Gambler* after he lost his shirt, and almost his mind, at the tables here. The various casino rooms were designed in the style of an elegant French château. Jackets and ties for men are mandatory, as is evening wear for women. To enter the casino during gambling hours, you must possess a valid passport or identification card and be at least 21 years old.

The historic gaming rooms may be viewed daily from 10am to noon on a conducted tour costing 6DM ($3.40). For those who want to gamble later, a full day's ticket is available for 10DM ($5.70). The minimum stake is 10DM ($5.70), but visitors are not obligated to play. Hours are daily from 2pm to 2am (3am on Friday and Saturday). Admission is 5DM ($2.85) Sunday to Thursday, rising to 10DM ($5.70) on Friday and Saturday.

SPORTS & OUTDOOR PURSUITS
For an entirely new perspective on the area, go hot-air ballooning. **Balloon 2000** offers rides between the Black Forest and the Vosges. Contact pilot Jean-Marc Culas (☎ **07223/6-00-02**) for details. A 2-hour, champagne breakfast trip over the Rhine Valley goes for 500DM ($285) per person.

For a more up-close and personal experience, rock climbing at all levels and altitudes can be enjoyed on the Battert rocks directly over the city. For a climber's guide, contact the **German Alpine Club,** Rathausplatz 7 (☎ 07221/1-72-00). You can also walk the 5-mile nature trail from the Strouzda chapel via Friesenberg to Fremersberg.

Horse races are another diversion. **The International Club,** Lichtentaler Allee 8, invites all comers to the "Spring Meeting" May 27 to June 4 and to the "Grand Week" from August 25 to September 3. Call ☎ 07221/2-11-20 for details. Those not content to watch can ride on a 1-kilometer (0.62-mile) track, provided by **Equestrian Hall,** Gunzenbachstrasse 4A (☎ 07221/949625) from 25DM ($14.25) per hour. Instruction is also available.

Many other outdoor sports are offered as well. The local 18-hole course in Fremersberg is one of the most scenic in Europe; contact the **Baden-Baden Golf Club** at ☎ 07221/2-35-79. For tennis, contact either **TH 365,** Rheinstrasse (☎ 07221/6-78-08), which serves up two indoor courts under a retractable roof, or **Red-White Tennis Club** at Lichtentaler Allee 5 (☎ 07221/2-41-41), which offers 10 outdoor courts. Swimmers can take a dip in the indoor and outdoor **swimming pools** in Bertholdbad at Ludwig-Wilhelm-Strasse 24 (☎ 07221/93-26-11), at a cost of 4.50DM ($2.55) for adults and 3DM ($1.70) for students per day. There's also swimming at **Sandweier Beach,** at the converted gravel pit at Kühlsee, from mid-May to mid-September. For information, call ☎ 07221/5-14-33.

SHOPPING

A flower-flanked pedestrian zone includes **Sophienstrasse** and **Gernsbacher Strasse.** These streets are lined with upscale boutiques, among the most expensive in Germany. Women's clothing by one of Germany's most emulated designers is available at **Escada Boutique,** Sophienstrasse 18 (☎ 07221/39-04-48). Another shop, **Münchner Moden,** Lichtentalerstrasse 13 (☎ 07221/3-10-90), carries women's designs in loden-colored wool during autumn and winter, and offers Austrian and Bavarian silks, linens, and cottons during warmer months. The best men's store, **Herrenkommode,** Sophienstrasse 16 (☎ 07221/2-92-92), is a bit more international, focusing on the collections of Giorgio Armani and Renee Lazard.

Leather goods by Gold Pfiel and other manufacturers are sold at **Inka,** Sophienstrasse 26 (☎ 07221/2-39-55), where the inventory includes luggage, wallets, and handbags. Cuckoo clocks, puppets, and other locally produced items can be found at **Boulevard,** Lichtentaler Strasse 21 (☎ 07221/2-44-95). **Gaisser,** Langestrasse 22 (☎ 07221/2-43-93), carries crystal and glass, along with some flatware and utensils. An intriguing antique store is **Peter Liebman,** Sophienstrasse 13 (☎ 07221/3-13-33), which specializes in baroque furniture from the 18th century and Biedermeier furniture from the 19th century, plus a wide array of other German antiques from silver to lamps.

Among the beeswax- and honey-based products available at **Schwarzwald Bienen-Honig-Haus,** Langestrasse 38 (☎ 07221/3-14-53), are candles, cosmetics, candies, schnapps, and wine. Several varieties of bottled honey are sold as well. A multitude of libations are available by the bottle at **Schulmeister,** Maria Victoria Strasse 13-A (☎ 07221/2-41-70), but especially tasty are the house cherry or raspberry *eau de vie,* clear brandies. A 400-year-old wine tavern and shop, **Nägelsförster Hof,** Nägelsförst 1 (☎ 07221/3-55-50), conducts daily wine tastings of the vintages available for purchase.

WHERE TO STAY
VERY EXPENSIVE

✪ **Brenner's Park Hotel & Spa.** An der Lichtentaler Allee, 76530 Baden-Baden. ☎ 07221/90-00. Fax 07221/3-87-72. 100 units. MINIBAR TV TEL. 420DM–890DM ($239.40–$507.30) double; 1,200DM–2,200DM ($684–$1,254) suite. AE, DC, MC, V. Parking 28DM ($15.95). Bus: 1.

This sumptuously furnished hotel is one of the finest in the world, far outdistancing the two Steigenberger properties (see below). It lies in a large private park facing the River Oos and Lichtentaler Allee. The spa facilities here, Baden-Baden's best, are a major draw. Some of its international habitués wouldn't dare let a year go by without making an appearance at this glamorous place. The hotel's guest rooms and suites are the last word in luxurious appointments. Beds are sumptuous and the marble bathrooms are state of the art.

Dining/Diversions: A pianist plays every afternoon in the lounge and in the evening at the Oleander Piano Bar. There's gourmet dining in the main restaurant, Park, and in the Schwarzwald-Stube.

Amenities: Room service, laundry, dry cleaning, hair dryer in room, pool, sauna, solarium, massage-and-fitness studio, beauty spa, modern facilities for diagnosis and therapeutics. The staff includes an expert team of beauticians and masseurs. Golf, tennis, riding, climbing, and walking on marked paths and promenades can be arranged.

EXPENSIVE

✪ **Der Kleine Prinz (The Little Prince).** Lichtentalerstrasse 36, 76530 Baden-Baden. ☎ **07221/34-64.** Fax 07221/3-82-64. www.derkleineprinz.de. E-mail: info@derkleineprinz.de. 40 units. A/C MINIBAR TV TEL. 285DM–305DM ($162.45–$173.85) double; 305DM–505DM ($173.85–$287.85) suite. Rates include buffet breakfast. AE, CB, DC, MC, V. Parking 15DM ($8.55).

This small hotel is located in a century-old baroque building in the central pedestrian zone, a short walk from the casino and the thermal baths. Two elegant city mansions were combined to form this winning address, the most personalized, cozy, and intimate nest at the spa. Norbert Rademacher, who owns the hotel with his wife, has had 25 years of hotel experience in the United States as director at the Waldorf-Astoria and then at the New York Hilton. He and his wife have totally renovated and upgraded the hotel. Each of the good-sized rooms has its own special feature: an open fireplace, a tower, a balcony, or a whirlpool bathtub. Some have air-conditioning. The furnishings are antiques or Portuguese pine. Personalized service adds to the attractiveness of this intimate, immaculate hotel.

Dining/Diversions: The small ground-floor restaurant is an elegant place for a four-course dinner; you can have drinks at the adjacent lobby bar.

Amenities: Concierge, room service, dry cleaning and laundry service, twice-daily maid service, baby-sitting, secretarial services, business center, and conference rooms. A health club, tennis, and racquetball courts are nearby.

Privahotel Quisisana. Bismarckstrasse 21 (an 8-min. walk from the town center), 76530 Baden-Baden. ☎ **07221/36-90.** Fax 07221/36-92-69. 69 units. TV TEL. 340DM–400DM ($193.80–$228) double; from 500DM ($285) suite. Rates include continental breakfast. AE, MC, V. Free parking.

Although Brenner's Park Hotel and even the Steigenberger properties are far superior, this runner-up is more tranquil. It's set in a spacious park, 8 minutes away from the town center by foot. Annexes radiate from the core of a 19th-century villa. Some of the most up-to-date health facilities in the Black Forest are here. You can spend an early morning in group calisthenics, for example, followed by treatments with any one of a dozen skin- and muscle-toning techniques. One of the more unusual facilities is the tepidarium, where a room is warmed to body temperature as you sit and listen to meditation music. Rooms are beautiful, well kept, spacious, and well appointed, furnished with both traditional and modern styling.

Dining: The elegant restaurant serves excellent international and regional cuisine from the world-class kitchens.

Amenities: Room service, laundry, dry cleaning, swimming pool, sauna, "beauty farm," various medical treatments.

Steigenberger Badischer Hof. Langestrasse 47, 76530 Baden-Baden. ☎ **800/223-5652** in the U.S. and Canada, or 07221/93-40. Fax 07221/93-44-70. 139 units. MINIBAR TV TEL. 310DM–450DM ($176.70–$256.50) double; 550DM–850DM ($313.50–$484.50) suite. Rates include buffet breakfast. AE, DC, MC, V. Parking 20DM ($11.40).

A Baden-Baden landmark, this famed traditional hotel isn't quite as highly rated as Brenner's, but it's in a neck-and-neck race with its sibling, the other Steigenberger, the Europäischer Hof. Badischer Hof is on a busy street in the center of town, but in the back you'll find an elegant garden with a wide balustraded terrace, flower beds, and a lawn around a stone fountain. The hotel began its career as a social center for famous personalities, who came here for "the season," beginning in 1809. The four-story-high colonnaded hallway, with its great staircase and encircling balustraded balconies, is the hotel's most distinguishing feature. The public rooms are attractive and old world. The well-furnished guest rooms are priced according to size and view. Many have private balconies. Each is elegantly appointed with tasteful fabrics and comfortable beds. Those in the monastery building have thermal water piped into the baths.

Dining: Dining is in the Park Restaurant, where a first-class international cuisine is served. Vegetarian food and regional specialties are also featured.

Amenities: Room service, hair dryer in room, laundry, dry cleaning, swimming pool, thermal spring pool, open-air thermal pool, sauna, beauty and health center, medical baths, physiotherapy.

Steigenberger Europäischer Hof. Kaiserallee 2 (opposite the Kurgarten and the casino), 76530 Baden-Baden. ☎ **800/223-5652** in the U.S. and Canada, or 07221/93-30. Fax 07221/2-88-31. 145 units. MINIBAR TV TEL. 308DM–454DM ($175.55–$258.80) double; from 555DM–2,000DM ($316.35–$1,140) suite. Rates include buffet breakfast. AE, DC, MC, V. Parking 30DM ($17.10).

This is the liveliest and most social of the centrally located hotels, with a far more bustling atmosphere than Brenner's or the other Steigenberger (see above). The elegant Europäischer Hof is adjacent to the Oos River, which runs at the edge of the Kurpark. Actually, the hotel consists of a pair of joined structures that were built back when spacious living facilities were more affordable. Its colonnaded central hallway is stunning. Many suites and rooms open onto balconies. The staff is a bit too formal but highly efficient.

Dining: In the restaurant, formal old-world service combines with a sweeping view of the park.

Amenities: Room service, laundry, dry cleaning; a hairdresser and beauty parlor are also on site.

MODERATE

Bad-Hotel zum Hirsch. Hirschstrasse 1, 76530 Baden-Baden. ☎ **800/223-5652** in the U.S. and Canada, or 07221/93-90. Fax 07221/3-81-48. 58 units. ☎ 250DM–290DM ($142.50–$165.30) double. Rates include buffet breakfast. AE, CB, DC, DISC, MC, V. Parking 22DM ($12.55).

This beautiful old-fashioned hotel is a tranquil compound of several buildings. Its antique furnishings make it a living museum of fine period pieces. The formal dining room is dominated by crystal chandeliers and paneled walls; the Blauer Salon is equally attractive, with blue-velvet provincial armchairs and classic draperies. The interesting old-style guest rooms are individually furnished, as if in a country home; some offer minibars and TVs. All rooms have piped-in thermal water.

The restaurant is reserved for guests. In summer, you can drink coffee on the wisteria-shaded terrace. Amenities include a newsstand, dry cleaning, laundry, sauna, beauty salon, social program, hair dryers in room, and adapter plugs.

Haus Reichert. Sophienstrasse 4, 76530 Baden-Baden. ☎ **07221/2-41-91.** Fax 07221/2-95-34. 26 units. MINIBAR TV TEL. 236DM–336DM ($134.50–$191.50) double. Rates include continental breakfast. AE, DC, MC, V. Parking 10DM ($5.70).

Haus Reichert is an inviting place to stay in a central location, not far from the casino. Inside this five-floor 19th-century hotel, the good-sized rooms are high-ceilinged and comfortable, although practically none of the original furniture or detailing has survived the many renovations. Most of the rooms are priced at the lower end of the scale. There is limited room service confined to drinks and snacks. Exercise equipment, a pool, a sauna, and a beauty farm are at your disposal.

INEXPENSIVE

Hotel am Markt. Marktplatz 18, 76530 Baden-Baden. ☎ **07221/27-04-0.** Fax 07221/27-04-44. 27 units, 12 with bathroom or shower. 110DM ($62.70) double without bathroom or shower; 140DM ($79.80) double with bathroom or shower. Rates include continental breakfast. AE, MC, V.

Hotel am Markt, on the old marketplace, is far removed from the grander social life of Baden-Baden and its deluxe palace hotels. But though it may be at the bottom of the pecking order, it's number one in town for economy. The location is first rate, with the quiet interrupted only by chimes from the church across the square. A tiny terrace cafe in front has window boxes of petunias. There's no lounge to speak of, but there is a tavern dining room with a relaxed and informal atmosphere. Innkeeper Herr Bogner offers small and simply furnished but comfortable rooms. A restaurant is open for house guests from 6 to 9pm daily.

WHERE TO DINE

Münchner Löwenbräu. Gernsbacher Strasse 9 (in the Altstadt). ☎ **07221/2-23-11.** Main courses 14DM–32DM ($8–$18.25). AE, DC, V. Daily 10am–11pm. GERMAN/BAVARIAN.

Baden-Baden has many fine restaurants dispensing haute cuisine, but this isn't one of them—the food here is simple and affordable. The terrace is beneath a copse of clipped and pruned linden trees, and the indoor dining room (open year-round), with its curved glass walls, is up a flight of stone steps at the rear. Many kinds of German sausage are offered, along with Bavarian specialties and a wide selection of cheeses. Regional devotees order pork knuckles fresh from "the pork-knuckle grill." Regulars often ask for the "Löwenbräu platter of bites," which is a hearty plate with everything from black pudding to sliced pork. For dessert, we'd suggest the apple fritters. The restaurant also has a popular beer garden.

Park-Restaurant. In Brenner's Park Hotel, Schillerstrasse 6 (at the corner of Lichtentaler Allee). ☎ **07221/90-00.** Reservations required. Main courses 36DM–65DM ($20.50–$37.05); fixed-price menus 120DM–140DM ($68.40–$79.80). AE, DC, MC, V. Daily 7–11am, noon–2pm and 7:30–9:30pm. INTERNATIONAL/RHINELAND.

Park-Restaurant serves the best food in the center of Baden-Baden, although its cuisine is not quite as refined as that of Zum Alde Gott on the outskirts. This is one of the renowned spa dining rooms of Europe, and the cuisine and service are definitely worth the high price. The emphasis is on French (Alsatian) dishes, along with regional Badish and Rhine Valley foods. Specialties include pâté of quail and goose liver and roast saddle of venison or lamb noisettes with tarragon sauce. For dessert, try an ice-cream soufflé. No matter who is in charge of the kitchen here, the same superb standards are always maintained.

Stahlbad. Augustaplatz 2. ☎ **07221/2-45-69.** Reservations required. Main courses 29DM–55DM ($16.55–$31.35); fixed-price menu 65DM ($37.05) for 4 courses, 130DM ($74.10) for 6 courses. AE, DC, MC, V. Tues–Sun noon–2pm and 6–10pm. CONTINENTAL.

Stahlbad is a luxury restaurant with an elegant decor. Although its food may not be as good as the Brenner's Park Hotel's, it's the most tranquil and charming choice in the center of town, mainly because of its garden terrace. The owner, Frau Uschi Mönch, welcomes you in the dining room. The decor and atmosphere evoke a tavern, with prints, copper vessels, antique pewter plates, mugs, and engravings. Continental specialties are pepper steak and venison steak (in hunting season), fresh fish, and lobster thermidor (very expensive). The homemade fettuccine Alfredo with white truffles (in season) is as good as any you'll have in Rome.

Zum Nest. Rettigstrasse (Near Leopoldsplatz). ☎ **07221/2-30-76.** Reservations recommended. Main courses 12DM–31DM ($6.85–$17.65); fixed-price menus 22DM–33DM ($12.55–$18.80). AE, DC, MC, V. Daily 11:30am–2pm and 5:30–10pm. REGIONAL/CONTINENTAL.

Zum Nest consistently serves some of the finest inexpensive food in the Altstadt. The kitchen is noted for its assorted noodle dishes. Try noodles with mushrooms, fresh tomatoes, garlic, and parsley. Black Forest ham with spätzle is always a good choice. Grilled fish dishes are also excellent. In summer, guests can sit on a veranda overlooking a garden.

DINING AT NEUWEIER

It's traditional for Baden-Baden's visitors to dine at the satellite resort of Neuweier, 6 miles southwest via Fremersbergstrasse. Here are two suggestions:

Schloss Neuweier. Mauberbergstrasse 21. ☎ **07223/96-14-99.** Reservations required. Main courses 42DM–54DM ($23.95–$30.80); 3-course fixed-price lunch 85DM ($48.45); 3- or 4-course gourmet dinner menu 85DM ($48.45); 5-course menu 125DM ($71.25). AE, MC. Wed–Mon noon–2pm and 6:30–9:30pm. Bus: 6. INTERNATIONAL.

Schloss Neuweier is a small 12th-century castle entirely surrounded by defensive water fortifications and vineyards belonging to the estate. Its restaurant is not large but offers impeccable service in a decor of tile walls hung with portraits of former inhabitants. The house proudly serves local wines, including an excellent Riesling, and practices international cookery with flair. Try the brisket with horseradish sauce or the baked ray. The kitchen is consistent, and dishes are well prepared.

✪ Zum Alde Gott. Wienstrasse 10. ☎ **07223/55-13.** Reservations required. Main courses 49DM–55DM ($27.95–$31.35); fixed-price meals 58DM–80DM ($33.05–$45.60) at lunch, 115DM–140DM ($65.55–$79.80) at dinner. AE, DC, MC, V. Fri–Wed noon–3pm and 6:30–11pm. Bus: 6. BADISCHE.

Here's where the true gourmand comes to dine. In this attractive and very old wine cellar, Wilfried Serr, the most distinguished chef in the Baden-Baden area, mixes his palette of flavors with astounding skill and imagination. Wild game in season is a fine art here. Try also the Black Forest trout or the sea bass. There are only 12 tables, in soft green and white, and the ambience is bright and cheerful. An added bonus is an open-air terrace.

BADEN-BADEN AFTER DARK

A busy annual schedule of concert, dance, and dramatic performances entertains locals and visitors alike. The centerpiece for most of the resort's cultural activities is the oft-photographed **Kurhaus,** Kaiserallee 1 (☎ **07221/353207**). Originally built in the 1870s as the focal point of the resort, the Kurhaus does not, as its name implies, contain spa facilities, but is rather a catch-all entertainment complex. In the same building is Baden-Baden's casino, the **Spielbank** (for more information, see "The Casino," above.

The **Theater am Goetheplatz,** Goetheplatz (☎ **07221/93-27-00**), is a well-maintained and beautiful baroque-style theater that presents opera, ballet, and drama productions. It opened auspiciously with the world premiere of the Berlioz opera *Beatrice et Benedict* in 1862. A month-long celebration of music is held during the summer, when the **Musikalischer Sommer Festival** brings a series of concerts to venues scattered throughout the town. For dates, schedule, and ticket information, contact the **Philharmonic Orchestra of Baden Baden** at Schloss Solms, 76530 Baden Baden (☎ **07221/93-27-00**), or the tourist information office (see "Visitor Information," above).

Bars in the resort hotels often have low-key entertainment. Try the **Jockey Bar,** in the lobby of the Steigenberger Badischer Hof (tel **07221/93-4484**), or the **Oleander Bar** in Brenner's Park Hotel, Lichtentaler Allee (☎ **07221/9000**).

11 Heidelberg, Stuttgart & the Neckar Valley

Ancient castle ruins in the midst of thick woodlands, quiet university towns, busy manufacturing centers—you'll find all these in the countryside of southwestern Germany. The area extends along the Neckar River from Heidelberg past medieval towns and modern cities as far as Tübingen. The Neckar flows between the Black Forest and the Schwäbische Alb. Although the river is open to commercial shipping vessels as far as Stuttgart, much of the valley has remained unspoiled. The castles that rise around every bend in the river were once home to the German royal families of Hohenstaufen and Hohenzollern. Some of these ruins were the summer palaces of kings and emperors. Today, castles and country palaces sometimes offer bed and board to travelers.

1 Heidelberg

75 miles NW of Stuttgart, 12 miles SE of Mannheim, 55 miles S of Frankfurt

Summertime in Heidelberg, according to the song from the operetta *The Student Prince,* is a time for music and romance. Today, it's also a time when droves of visitors invade this beautiful city. Heidelberg is one of the few German cities that was not leveled by air raids in World War II, and therefore still has original buildings from the later Middle Ages and early Renaissance. Modern Heidelberg is centered around Bismarckplatz at the foot of the Theodore-Heuss-Brücke; in this part of the city, you'll find many of the best hotels and restaurants. The tall buildings and shopping plazas here contrast with the Altstadt nearby. Across the Neckar are sports grounds, a zoo, and a large botanical garden.

Heidelberg is, above all, a university town, and has been since 1386. Students make up much of the population. The colorful atmosphere that university life imparts to the town is felt especially in the old student quarter, with its narrow streets and lively inns. This oldest university in Germany is officially named **Ruprecht-Karl-University,** honoring both its founder, Elector Ruprecht I of the Palatinate, as well as the man who, in 1803, made it the leading university in the state of Baden, Margrave Karl Friedrich. The school was founded after the Great Schism of 1378, when conflicting claims to the papacy created unrest, and German teachers and students fled the Sorbonne in Paris.

The university grew rapidly. At first monastic in character, it changed in the 16th century with the appointment of a married rector. The so-called Old University was built in the early 18th century; the New University was constructed nearby from 1930 to 1932. Funds for this structure came from American sources, including Henry Ford.

Today, lecture halls, institutes, seminar buildings, and clinics are scattered all over town, but a new university quarter has been developed on the plain in the Neuenheim district, with multistory buildings and a modern cancer-research center.

ESSENTIALS

GETTING THERE **By Plane** The nearest major airport is Frankfurt (see chapter 12), with a direct bus link to Heidelberg. The shuttle bus between Frankfurt and Heidelberg costs 45DM ($27) per person. Call ☎ **06221/77-00-77** for information about the shuttle.

By Train Heidelberg's Hauptbahnhof is an important railroad station, lying on the Mannheim line, with frequent service to both regional towns and major cities. From Frankfurt, 40 trains arrive per day (trip time: 1 hr.); from Stuttgart, 30 trains (trip time: 45 min.). Travel time to and from Munich is about 3½ hours. For rail information, call **01805/996633.**

By Bus Regional bus service is provided by **BRN Busverkehr Rhein-Neckar** at Heidelberg (☎ **06221/606220**).

By Car Motorists should take the A5 Autobahn from the north or south.

VISITOR INFORMATION Contact **Tourist-Information,** Pavillon am Hauptbahnhof (☎ **06221/1-94-33**). It's open Monday to Saturday 9am to 7pm and Sunday 10am to 6pm. Here visitors can purchase a Heidelberg Card, which provides discounts on attractions and free use of public transportation. It costs 19DM ($11.40) for an adult and two children for up to 2 days or 34DM ($20.40) for up to 4 days.

EXPLORING THE TOWN

✪ TOURING HEIDELBERG CASTLE You can reach the huge red-sandstone Heidelberg Castle (☎ **06221/53-84-0**), set amid woodlands and terraced gardens, by several routes. Either take a 2-minute cable-car ride, or drive up the winding Neue Schlosstrasse past the old houses perched on the hillside, or walk. Walking is the most rewarding approach because of the constantly changing scenic view of the town and surrounding countryside. You can take the more gradual slope from the Klingentor, or make the shorter walk up the steep Burgweg from Kornmarkt. The cable car leaves from the platform near the Kornmarkt, and costs 5.50DM ($3.30) round-trip for adults and 3.50DM ($2.10) for children.

The castle is a dignified ruin today, but even in its deteriorated state, it's one of the finest Gothic-Renaissance castles in Germany. Entering the castle walls at the main gate, you first come upon the huge **Gun Park** to your left, from which you can gaze down upon Heidelberg and the Neckar Valley. Straight ahead is the **Thick Tower,** or what remains of it after its 25-foot walls were blown up by the French in the late 17th century. Leaving the Gun Park via Elizabeth's Gate (erected by Friedrich V in 1615 for his Scottish wife, Elizabeth Stuart, daughter of James I), you come to the Bridge House and the bridge crossing the site of the former moat.

Along the north side of the courtyard stretches the stern **palace of Friedrich IV,** erected from 1601 to 1607. The palace is less damaged than other parts of the castle, and its rooms have been almost completely restored, including the gallery of princes and kings of the German empire from the time of Charlemagne. The palace has its own terrace, the Altan, which offers a panoramic view of the plain of the Neckar. The ancient bell tower, at the northeast end of the Altan, dates from the early 1500s.

At the west end of the terrace, in the cellars of the castle, is the **Wine Vat Building,** built in the late 16th century and worth a visit for a look at the Great Cask, symbol of the abundant and exuberant life of the Rhineland-Palatinate. This huge barrel-like monstrosity, built in 1751, is capable of holding more than 55,000 gallons of wine.

Heidelberg

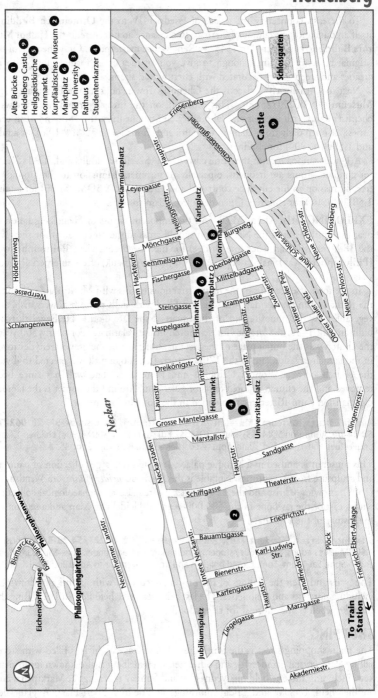

1 Alte Brücke
9 Heidelberg Castle
5 Heiliggeistkirche
8 Kornmarkt
3 Kurpfäalzisches Museum
6 Marktplatz
7 Old University
7 Rathaus
4 Studentenkarzer

To the east, connecting the palace of Friedrich IV to the **Ottheinrich Building,** itself an outstanding example of German Renaissance architecture, is the **Hall of Mirrors Building,** constructed in 1549—a Renaissance masterpiece. Only the shell of the original building remains, enough to give you an idea of its former glory, with its arcades and steep gables decorated with cherubs and sirens.

Next to Ottheinrich's palace is the Chemist's Tower, housing the **Pharmaceutical Museum** (☎ 06221/25880). This museum, on the tower's ground floor, shows a chemist's shop with utensils and laboratory equipment from the 18th and 19th centuries. It's open daily from 10am to 6:30pm, and admission is 3DM ($1.80) for adults and 1.50DM (90¢) for children.

A 1-hour guided tour of the castle costs 4DM ($2.40) for adults and 2DM ($1.20) for children. Tours are frequent, especially in summer. Admission to the grounds is free; admission to the entrance courtyard and Great Cask is 3DM ($1.80) for adults, 1.50DM (90¢) for children. Open daily from 8am to 6pm.

EXPLORING THE ALTSTADT All the important sights of Heidelberg lie on or near the south bank of the Neckar. You should cross to the other side of the river (via the 18th-century Karl Theodore Bridge) for the best overall view. **Philosophenweg (Philosopher's Way),** halfway up the hill on the north bank, offers an especially good vista.

In the town itself, a tour of the main attractions begins with **Marktplatz** in front of the Rathaus. On market days the square is filled with stalls of fresh flowers, fish, and vegetables. At the opposite end of the square is the late-Gothic **Heiliggeistkirche,** built around 1400, the largest Gothic church in the Palatinate. For nearly 300 years, the church was the burial place of the electors, but most of the graves were destroyed in the French invasion late in the 17th century. In 1706, a wall was erected to divide the church between Roman Catholics and Protestants. The wall has since been removed and the church restored to its original plan. Around the corner is the famous old mansion **Zum Ritter,** recommended in the hotel listings below.

Kurpfälzisches Museum (Museum of the Palatinate). Hauptstrasse 97. ☎ **06221/58-34-00.** Admission 5DM ($3) adults, 3DM ($1.80) students, 1.50DM (90¢) children 17 and under. Tues and Thurs–Sun 10am–5pm, Wed 10am–9pm. Bus: 10, 12, or 35.

This museum is housed in a baroque palace. It contains a large collection of painting and sculpture from 6 centuries. Notable is the *Riemenschneider Altar* from Windsheim (1509), showing Christ and the 12 Apostles. There's also an archaeological collection with a cast of the jawbone of the 500,000-year-old Heidelberg Man and a section on the history of the Palatinate.

Studentenkarzer (Student Jail). Augustinergasse 2. ☎ **06221/54-23-34.** Admission 1.50DM (90¢) adults, 1DM (60¢) students and children 14 and under. Tues–Sat 10am–noon and 2–5pm, Sat 10am–1pm. Closed holidays and from November to April. Bus: 10, 12, or 35.

The walls and even the ceilings of the prison are covered with graffiti and drawings, including portraits and silhouettes. The last prisoners were held here in 1914. Ring the caretaker's bell (same address) for admission.

SHOPPING

The main shopping street is the traffic-free **Hauptstrasse,** which is filled with stores selling glass, crystal, handcrafts, and other items. Heidelberg is also known for its markets, including the one held on Wednesday and Sunday mornings at Marktplatz, and another held Tuesday and Friday mornings at Friedrich-Ebert-Platz. A giant flea market sprawls along Guteramtsstrasse near the Customs office one Saturday a month, but there isn't a designated week within which it falls.

In a city of this size, there are lots of stores to choose from. **Michael Kienscherff,** Hauptstrasse 177 (☎ **06221/2-42-55**), offers a wide assortment of handcrafts from all over Germany: music boxes, nativity scenes, nutcrackers, and glass and crystal ornaments. The two branches of **Gätschenberger,** Hauptstrasse 6 and 42 (☎ **06221/ 1-44-80**), share a telephone, but no. 42 is known for its array of fine linens and embroideries for bed, bath, and table, whereas no. 6 sells men's and women's undergarments. An oddly named toy store, **Muckels Maus,** Plöck 71 (☎ **06221/2-38-86**), is the place to find beautifully handcrafted puppets, including replicas of characters from the operas of Mozart, antique-looking and ultramodern dolls, and wooden blocks and figures.

Other shops of interest include **Unholtz,** Hauptstrasse 160 (☎ **06221/2-09-64**), which carries Solingen cutlery, tableware, and scissors; **Spiess & Walther,** Friedrich-Ebert-Anlage 23a (☎ **06221/2-22-33**), which features exclusive designs in contemporary furniture, antiques, and textiles; and **B&B Antiques,** Sofienstrasse 27 (☎ **06221/2-30-03**), which stocks paintings, silver, clocks, jewelry, glass, and porcelain from different eras. For all things leather, stop by **Leder-Meid,** Hauptstrasse 88 (☎ **06221/2-25-70**), which sells the crafts of German and other manufacturers. **Tischer,** Hauptstrasse 73 (☎ **06221/1-48-00**), carries quality cooking items.

If you want more variety under one roof, go to either of Heidelberg's two best department stores, **Kaufhof,** Hauptstrasse 22–32 (☎ **06221/50-40**), or **Horten,** Bergheimerstrasse 7 (☎ **06221/91-60**).

WHERE TO STAY
EXPENSIVE

✪ **Der Europäische Hof-Hotel Europa.** Friedrich-Ebert-Anlage 1, 69117 Heidelberg. ☎ **800/223-4541,** 800/223-6800 in the U.S. and Canada, or 06221/515513. Fax 06221/ 51-55-56. www.europaeischerhof.com. E-mail: europa@cubus.de. 120 units. A/C MINIBAR TV TEL. 320DM–510DM ($192–$306) double; 530DM–850DM ($318–$510) suite. AE, DC, MC, V. Parking 25DM ($15). Tram: Bismarckplatz.

This glamour hotel is by far the best in Heidelberg. It fronts the city park in the heart of town, within walking distance of the castle and the university. Its interior is like that of a gracious home, with antiques, crystal chandeliers, and Oriental rugs. Some rooms and several suites face a quiet inside garden; the front rooms in the oldest section tend to be noisy (from traffic). Each room is individually decorated with rich, traditional taste and has a hair dryer, room safe, and trouser press. Most are air-conditioned, and the more expensive doubles contain alcoves. Nineteen have whirlpool tubs.

Dining/Diversions: Meals are served in the Louis XVI restaurant, the Garden Room, or the finely paneled Kurfürstenstube. Before dinner, guests congregate around the curved bar in the wood-paneled lounge. In summer, meals are served on the open terrace with a view of the water fountains.

Amenities: Room service, laundry, dry cleaning, shopping arcade.

✪ **Hotel Hirschgasse.** Hirschgasse 3, 69100 Heidelberg. ☎ **06221/45-40.** Fax 06221/ 45-41-11. www.hirschgasse.de. E-mail: ekraft@compuserve.com. 20 units. MINIBAR TV TEL. 295DM ($177) junior suite for 2; 350DM–450DM ($210–$270) senior suite for 2; 450DM–550DM ($270–$330) salon suite for 2. AE, DC, MC, V. Free parking.

This historic country home-style hotel, nestled on the hillside of a historic lane adjoining Philosopher's Way, is tops in Heidelberg for its tranquil and romantic setting. It dates from 1472 and has lodged such impressive figures as Mark Twain and Bismarck. Its guest rooms are all suites decorated in Laura Ashley designs. Each has a salon, hair dryer, and Jacuzzi. For American guests, there's cable-TV news from home.

Dining/Diversions: Regional, traditional, and modern cuisine is offered in Le Gourmet, which since 1472 has been attracting diners from Europe and abroad. The Mensurstube keeps alive the atmosphere of the old student fraternities.

Amenities: Room service, laundry, baby-sitting, terrace garden; horseback riding and golf can be arranged.

✪ **Hotel Zum Ritter St. Georg.** Hauptstrasse 178, 69117 Heidelberg. ☎ **06221/13-50.** Fax 06221/13-52-30. www.ritter-heidelberg.de. 40 units. MINIBAR TV TEL. 275DM–375DM ($165–$225) double; 430DM ($258) suite. Rates include buffet breakfast. AE, DC, MC, V. Bus: 10, 11, or 12.

A glorious old inn right out of the German Renaissance, the Zum Ritter is a well-preserved rarity, although it's inferior to the Hirschgasse (see above) in comfort and antique charm. Built in 1592 by the Frenchman Charles Bèlier, it's now listed among the major sightseeing attractions of this university town. There are no public lounges. Furnishings are in a traditional, often German Romantic style. Many rooms are somewhat cramped, but the beds are most comfortable and all the bathrooms have been renewed.

Dining: The hotel's restaurant (see "Where to Dine," below), which serves an eclectic fare of German and international dishes, actually outshines the accommodations.

Amenities: Dry cleaning, laundry service, conference rooms; a shopping arcade is within walking distance.

MODERATE

Alt Heidelberg. Rohrbacher 29, 69115 Heidelberg. ☎ **800/528-1234** in the U.S. and Canada, or 06221/91-50. Fax 06221/16-42-72. 79 units. MINIBAR TV TEL. 258DM ($154.80) double; 308DM ($184.80) triple. Rates include buffet breakfast. AE, DC, MC, V. Parking 15DM ($9). Tram: 1. Bus: 41, 42.

This five-story hotel is set on a street corner in the commercial center of Heidelberg's old town. The interior is streamlined and a bit sterile. The bedrooms are individually decorated and contain double-paned windows to insulate against noise from the traffic outside. The bar has occasional live piano music. A well-managed restaurant, the Graimberg, serves French and German cuisine.

Heidelberg Renaissance Hotel. Vanerowstrasse 16, 69115 Heidelberg. ☎ **06221/90-80.** Fax 06221/90-85-08. www.marriott.com. 251 units. A/C MINIBAR TV TEL. 199DM–260DM ($119.40–$156) double; 290DM ($174) junior suite; 390DM ($234) suite. AE, DC, MC, V. Parking 20DM ($12).

This hotel sits on the banks of the Neckar, just a few minutes from the Altstadt and the main train station. Although it doesn't have the flair and traditional style of Der Europäische Hof, it's far superior to its nearest rival, Holiday Inn Crowne Plaza at Kurfürstenanlage 1. The exit from the Autobahn is only minutes away, making it convenient for motorists. The rooms are comfortably furnished and newly renovated, many with views over the river or the hills beyond. As a special service, the hotel operates a Lufthansa check-in counter, and a Lufthansa airport bus operates between the Frankfurt International Airport and the hotel 18 times per day.

Dining/Diversions: The elegant Globetrotter Restaurant, with a terrace on the Neckar, features international dining, popular buffet lunches, and Sunday brunch. The Pub Pinte serves not only draft beer but also regional dishes, and the lobby bar offers snacks and drinks.

Amenities: Room service, laundry, dry cleaning, health club, indoor swimming pool, sauna, solarium, massage, hair and beauty salon, gift shop, business center.

Neckar-Hotel Heidelberg. Bismarckstrasse 19, 69115 Heidelberg. ☎ **06221/905-150.** Fax 06221/9051510. 35 units. TV TEL. 180DM–240DM ($108–$144) double. Rates include continental breakfast. AE, MC, V. Free parking. Closed Dec 20–Jan 7. Bus: 10, 12, or 35.

If the Parkhotel Atlantic and Alt Heidelberg are full, this hotel is a good bet in this price range. It enjoys an enviable position on the Neckar River near the center of the university town. There's no garden, but there is a superb view of the Odenwald Forest. The facilities are substantial, and the spacious guest rooms are fitted with modern furnishings. Breakfast is the only meal served.

Parkhotel Atlantic. Schloss-Wolfsbrunnen-Weg 23, 69117 Heidelberg. ☎ **06221/60-42-0.** Fax 06221/60-42-60. 23 units. MINIBAR TV TEL. 180DM–220DM ($108–$132) double. Rates include buffet breakfast. AE, DC, MC, V. Free parking. Bus: 11, 12, 33. Head east from the Hauptbahnhof, along Kurfürstenanlage going through the tunnel, and take the 2nd right, bringing you to Heidelberg Castle; continue straight beyond the castle to the hotel.

This grand hotel on the wooded outskirts of Heidelberg, near the castle, offers modern comfort in annexes built around the core of an older villa. Visitors are assured calm and comfort, and can take advantage of the many woodland trails extending through the Neckar Valley. This hotel's setting makes it the best in its price range; hotels in the city center, unless soundproofed, get a lot of traffic noise. The rooms are decorated in 1965-ish modern style but are quite comfortable, though not large.

INEXPENSIVE

Hotel Anlage. Friedrich-Ebert-Anlage 32, 69117 Heidelberg. ☎ **06221/2-64-25.** Fax 06221/16-44-26. 20 units. TV TEL. 149DM–189DM ($89.40–$113.40) double. Rates include continental breakfast. AE, DC, MC, V. Bus: 11, 12, or 33. Parking 9DM ($5.40).

Hotel Anlage is one of Heidelberg's best affordable hotels. It's located in the heart of the city, on the street leading up to the castle. It occupies one wing of a lavishly built, late-19th-century palace of orange brick and carved stone. The small guest rooms are cozy and have cable TV (with English programs). The pleasant restaurant is reserved for guests.

Hotel Vier Jahreszeiten. Haspelgasse 2 (near the Alte Brücke), 69117 Heidelberg. ☎ 06221/2-41-64. Fax 06221/16-31-10. 22 units, 19 with bathroom. TV TEL. 130DM ($78) double without bathroom, 195DM–215DM ($117–$129) double with bathroom. Rates include continental breakfast. AE, DC, MC, V. Parking 15DM ($9). Closed Dec 24–Jan 10. Bus: 33, 34.

This hotel is a worthy choice for any of the "four seasons." It's located near the starting point for many interesting walks. Several famous student inns and the castle are also nearby. The hotel has been improved over the years, and the small rooms are comfortable, if rather plain. Mattresses and towels are a bit thin, but the price and the location are hard to beat.

WHERE TO DINE
EXPENSIVE

✪ **Kurfürstenstube.** In Der Europäische Hof-Hotel Europa, Friedrich-Ebert-Anlage 1. ☎ **06221/51-50.** Reservations required. Main courses 45DM–55DM ($27–$33); fixed-price meals from 79DM ($47.40). AE, DC, MC, V. Daily noon–3:30pm and 6:30–11:30pm. Tram: Bismarckplatz. FRENCH.

The best dining spot in Heidelberg is in the ground-floor wing of this deluxe hotel. The wood-paneled grill room is attractively decorated with provincial furnishings. The menu is in English, but the cuisine is mainly French, with both fixed-price and à la carte meals. Only the highest quality seasonal ingredients are used, so you never know what's likely to be featured on the menu. Perhaps it'll be roast John Dory with garlic-flavored cream sauce and braised peppers and tomatoes, or saddle of Limousin lamb with a coating of herbs, essence of basil, green beans, and pesto-flavored polenta. The chef never oversauces or overseasons a dish. For a spectacular finish, try the crepes flambée with bananas and maple sauce. The wine list is the most impressive in town.

Simplicissimus. Ingrimstrasse 16. ☎ **06221/18-33-36.** Reservations required. Main courses 35DM–39DM ($21–$23.40); fixed-price menu 85DM ($51). AE, MC, V. Wed–Mon 6–11pm. Closed 1 week in Mar and 1st 3 weeks in Aug. Bus: 11, 12, 33, 35, 41. FRENCH.

This elegant spot is ideal for a gourmet rendezvous. Johann Lummer, one of the finest chefs in Heidelberg, prepares a *cuisine moderne* with consummate skill. His restaurant in the Altstadt is decorated simply but with taste and style, with white paneling, globe lights, and touches of crimson. *Gourmet* magazine said that Herr Lummer "paints with food," and we agree. Not only are his dishes delectable to the taste buds, but their presentation is equally pleasing. The menu varies but is likely to include fresh mushrooms in cream sauce with homemade noodles, or crayfish with fresh melon and herb-flavored cream sauce.

Zum Ritter St. Georg. Hauptstrasse 178. ☎ **06221/1-35-0.** Reservations recommended. Main courses 18DM–65DM ($10.80–$39); fixed-price menus 38DM–58DM ($22.80–$34.80). AE, DC, MC, V. Daily noon–2pm and 6–10pm. Bus: 10, 11, or 12. GERMAN/INTERNATIONAL.

Zum Ritter is popular with both students and professors, who know that they can get not only good German cooking here but also the wonderful Dortmunder Actien-Brauerei beer. It's located in a hotel that's one of the most famous Renaissance buildings in Heidelberg. You dine either in the first-class Great Hall (the Rittersaal) or in the smaller Councillors' Chamber. We like the elegant larger room, with its sepia ceilings, wainscoting, and Oriental rugs. The house specialty is saddle of Odenwald venison for two (in season); when this dish is offered, locals flock here. A good beginning might be game soup St. Hubertus with brandy foam, and crêpes suzette is a fine dessert.

✪ **Zur Herrenmühle.** Hauptstrasse 237–239. ☎ **06221/60-29-09.** Reservations recommended. Main courses 47DM–55DM ($28.20–$33); fixed-price menus 65DM–110DM ($39–$66). AE, DC, MC, V. Mon–Sat 5:30pm–midnight. Bus: 33. FRENCH.

You'll quickly realize that this family-owned restaurant is in a 17th-century house, thanks to the thick walls and the antique paneling. The sophisticated maître d' adds both glamour and an appropriate theatricality. The succulent classical cuisine is based on fresh ingredients. Try the rack of lamb with herbs and homemade green noodles, or the roast roebuck with a vinegar-and-honey sauce. The desserts make better use of fresh fruit than any other place in town; try the sorbet flavored with blood oranges and served with a parfait of mandarin oranges. The service here is equaled only at the Kurfürstenstube.

MODERATE

Kurpfälzisches Museum Restaurant. Hauptstrasse 97. ☎ **06221/2-40-50.** Reservations required. Main courses 16DM–40DM ($9.60–$24). AE, DC, MC, V. Daily 11am–10pm. Bus: 1, 35, 97. GERMAN.

This quiet culinary oasis at the museum makes an interesting stopover for lunch. The baroque palace setting is sometimes more interesting than the food. You can order such dishes as rump steak Madagascar with green pepper while you enjoy the view of the little garden and splashing fountain. The food is satisfying, though hardly a challenge to the chefs at Kurfürstenstube or Simplicissimus.

✪ **Mensurstube.** In the Hotel Hirschgasse, Hirschgasse 3. ☎ **06221/45-40.** Reservations recommended. Main courses 25DM–33DM ($15–$19.80). AE, DC, MC, V. Daily noon–2pm and 6–10pm. GERMAN/REGIONAL.

No other place in Heidelberg captures bygone days quite like this one. In this rustic and cozy spot, you sit at tables more than 2 centuries old—you can still see where Count Bismarck and many others have carved their names. Swords hang from the ceiling—in the past, when dueling was the regular sport of the student fraternities, many duels were fought in what is now the dining room. Traditional recipes are served; the menu is limited but all the ingredients are fresh. Potato soup is a good starter, followed by homemade noodles, oxtail, and lamb shank. Rinderfilet (fillet of beef) is often served with bone marrow and a red-wine sauce with potatoes gratin. Almost everything is best accompanied by fresh-draft Pils.

INEXPENSIVE

Konditorei-Café Schafheutle. Hauptstrasse 94. ☎ **06221/1-46-80.** Main courses 15DM–17.50DM ($9–$10.50). V. Mon–Fri 9:30am–7pm, Sat 9am–6pm. Closed holidays. Bus: 10 or 12. PASTRIES/GERMAN.

Rain need never ruin your summer outing in this partially roofed cafe garden. You can order light meals here, and there's also a large choice of pastries. Service is attentive. This is a good choice for afternoon coffee or for a quick bite as you're dashing up to Heidelberg Castle.

HEIDELBERG AFTER DARK

Nights here are alive with the youthful enthusiasm of Heidelberg's students. Early evenings often start in the bars along Hauptstrasse; then late nights get rolling in the clubs around Marktplatz and the Karlstorbahnhof.

THE PERFORMING ARTS   The main performance stage is **Theater der Stadt,** Friedrichstrasse 5 (☎ 06221/58-35-02), where nightly entertainment includes plays, opera, and dance productions. The avant-garde theater is the **Zimmer Theater,** Hauptstrasse 118 (☎ 06221/2-10-69). Information and tickets for both are available by contacting **Theaterkasse,** Theaterstrasse 4 (☎ 06263/771). From June 7 to August 31, the **Schlossfest-Spiele** festival brings performances of opera, classical music, jazz, and theater to venues around the area, including Heidelberg Castle. Contact the main festival office at ☎ 06274/1440 for full details.

HISTORIC STUDENT DRINKING CLUBS   Heidelberg's most famous and revered student tavern, ✪ **Zum Roten Ochsen (Red Ox Inn),** Hauptstrasse 217 (☎ 06221/2-09-77), opened in 1703. For six generations it has been in the Spengel family, who have welcomed everybody from Bismarck to Mark Twain to Cardinal Spellman. It seems that every student who has attended the university has left his or her mark (or initials) on the walls. Other distinguished patrons of yore have left mementos, often framed photographs of themselves. The series of rooms, where revelers sit at long oak tables under smoke-blackened ceilings, is arranged in horseshoe fashion; the U part has a pianist who sets the musical pace. As the evening progresses, the songs become louder and louder—by midnight the place can be heard blocks away. Motherly looking waitresses bring in huge steins of beer and plates of food. A mug of beer costs 4.30DM ($2.60) and up. Meals go from 19.50DM to 38DM ($11.70 to $22.80). The place is open daily from 11:30am to 2pm and 5 to 11pm (sometimes to midnight). Closed mid-December to mid-January. Bus: 33.

Next door is **Zum Sepp'l,** Hauptstrasse 213 (☎ 06221/2-30-85), the second most famous drinking club in Heidelberg. It's also filled with photographs and carved initials of former students, along with memorabilia that range from old Berlin street signs to Alabama license plates. The building itself dates from 1634. Meals cost 15DM to 30DM ($9 to $18). A mug of beer goes for 5.80DM ($3.50). There's live piano music daily from 8pm to midnight. When the university is closed, the activity here dies down considerably. It's open April through October daily from 11am to midnight; November through March, Monday to Friday from 4pm to midnight and Saturday and Sunday from 10am to midnight. Bus: 12 or 33.

Exploring on Two Wheels

Unique in Germany, the **Neckar Valley Cycle Path** allows you to ride all the way from the source of the Neckar in Villingen-Schwenningen to the confluence of the Rhine at Mannheim. The path is marked with a signpost showing a green bicycle and a red wheel mark. The route follows the river the whole way, though many cyclists go only as far as Heidelberg. Along the way, you'll pass castles, manor houses, vineyards, country inns, and such old towns as Rottweil and Esslingen. Most German cyclists average about 30 miles per day on the trail.

Suggested stopovers along the way are Sulz, Tübingen, and Heilbronn. In the town of Neckarsulm, you can make a stop to visit the **German Bicycle Museum,** housed in Deutschorden Castle. It's close to the cycle path. Here you can see the original "dandy horse," the first bicycle, invented in 1819.

BARS & CAFES   Students also like to drink beer at **Reichsapfel,** Unterestrasse 35 (☎ **06221/2-79-50**), a popular hangout for more than 300 years. It sells nothing but beer. Open daily from 6pm until 1am. **Max Bar,** Marktplatz 5 (☎ **06221/2-44-19**), is another beer-drinker's bar, but you can also get a baguette or croissant to soak up some of the alcohol. There's indoor and patio seating. Open daily from 8pm to 7am. When you tire of beer and want a more spirited drink, wander over to **Sonder Bar,** Unterestrasse 13 (☎ **06221/2-52-00**), which stocks more than 150 brands of whisky, 10 kinds of vodka, and sundry other potions, besides its 11 types of beers. Open daily from 7pm to 1am.

Catch up on the latest news and trends at **Café Journal,** Hauptstrasse 172 (☎ **06221/16-17-12**), where drinkers linger over beer while scanning newspapers and magazines from all over Europe and the United States. Daily hours are 8am to 1am. The familiar **Hard Rock Cafe,** Hauptstrasse 142 (☎ **06221/2-28-19**), has a branch here, open from 10am to 1am. A popular bar with a mixed gay crowd, **Mata Hari,** Oberbadgasse 10 (☎ **06221/18-18-08**), is a mellow place to meet and drink. Open 9pm and 3am nightly.

LIVE MUSIC & CLUBS   The **Schwimmbad Musik Club,** Tiergartenstrasse 13 (☎ **06221/47-02-01**), which features trendsetting local and international bands, is open Wednesday and Thursday from 8pm to 3am, Friday and Saturday from 8pm to 4am. The cover charge ranges from 7DM to 20DM ($4.20 to $12), depending on the act. At **Dr. Flotte,** Hauptstrasse 130 (☎ **06221/2-05-69**), jazz bands appear on Sunday from September to May, from 4 to 7pm. A variety of music is featured at other times. Open daily from 11am to 1am.

Named after a barbecue sauce from Texas, **Ziegler-Bräu/Billy Blue's,** Bergheimer Strasse 1B (☎ **06221/2-53-33**), serves up barbecue in the front room while local and international bands kick out soul, funk, and blues in the back from Wednesday to Saturday nights. Daily hours are 5pm to 3am; the cover is 8DM ($4.80) Wednesday to Thursday, 15DM to 25DM ($9 to $15) on weekends. Known as the oldest jazz club in Germany, **Cave 54,** Kramergasse 2 (☎ **06221/2-78-40**), now hosts live blues, funk, and rock acts on Tuesday night and jazz bands on Sunday. The rest of the week, it's a '70s-style disco. It opens nightly at 8:30pm when bands are playing at 10pm on other nights. The cover charge is 12DM ($7.20) for dancing and 20DM ($12) for bands. The DJs at **Club 1900,** Hauptstrasse 117 (☎ **06221/2-01-76**), play a mix of music to keep dancers guessing and coming out to one of the city's most popular clubs.

2 The Neckar Valley

Heidelberg is a good point from which to explore the romantic Neckar Valley. From April to early October, you can take a boat tour along the river as far as Neckarsteinach and back. There are usually four or five round-trips daily, and you need not return on the same boat. Boats are operated by the **Rhein-Neckar-Fahrgastschiffahrt GmbH,** Stadthalle, Heidelberg (☎ **06221/2-01-81**). Trips between Heidelberg and Neckarsteinach cost 16DM ($9.60) round-trip, and those between Heidelberg and Hirschhorn (which operate from June 17 to September 30) cost 22DM ($13.20) round-trip. You can order drinks or snacks on the boat. Some of the people who take visitors on this pleasant trip are descended from the Neckar fishers who helped Mark Twain when he rafted down from Hirschhorn. The same families have been working the Neckar since the early 1600s.

You can also see the many attractions along the banks of the Neckar by car, driving eastward along the right bank of the river.

HIRSCHHORN

This medieval town, 16 miles east of Heidelberg, is known as the gem of the Neckar Valley. It obtained municipal rights in 1391. Overlooking the town and the river from a fortified promontory is the 18th-century **Hirschhorn Castle.** The castle defenses are from the 14th century, and wall paintings from that period can be seen in the chapel. The castle is now a hotel and restaurant (see below). For a view of the sharp bend of the Neckar below the town, climb to the top of the tower.

GETTING THERE   Access by car is via Route 45 east from Heidelberg. Hirschhorn lies on the Neckarelz-Heidelberg rail line with frequent local service between the two towns. For rail information, call ☎ **01805/996633.**

WHERE TO STAY & DINE

Schloss-Hotel. Auf Burg Hirschhorn (on Route B37), 69434 Hirschhorn. ☎ **06272/13-73.** Fax 06272/32-67. 25 units. MINIBAR TV TEL. 180DM–243DM ($108–$145.80) double; 243DM ($145.80) suite. Rates include continental breakfast. AE, DC, MC, V. Free parking. Closed mid-Dec through Jan.

This hotel offers rooms in a hilltop castle looming over the center of town. Each unit has a river view and a collection of good antiques. Some rooms are in a guest-house annex, but those in the castle itself have more space, style, and tradition. Central heating and an elevator have been installed. The restaurant serves traditional dishes to nonresidents, but you have to phone in advance. Specialties include various kinds of game, smoked trout, and home-baked bread. Food service is daily from 8 to 10am, noon to 2pm, and 6 to 9:30pm. Meals begin at 80DM ($48).

EBERBACH

Seven miles farther along the Neckar is the Imperial City of Eberbach, established in 1227. Its castle, which dates all the way from 1190, was mostly destroyed in the 15th century, but its ivy-covered ruins attract many visitors today. The old Pfarrhof, the medieval center of the town, is within the city walls. Eberbach is proud to be the city where Queen Victoria was conceived; the event is commemorated by a plaque outside her parents' home, Haus Thalheim.

GETTING THERE   Routes 37 and 45 connect to the A5 Autobahn heading north and south or the A6 going east and west. From Heidelberg, head east along Route 37. Eberbach lies on the Neckarelz-Heidelberg rail line, with frequent service. Call ☎ **01805/996633** for rail information.

VISITOR INFORMATION   Contact the **Kurverwaltung,** Im Kuzentrum, Kellereistrasse 32 (☎ **06271/48-99**), Monday to Friday 8am to noon and 2 to 5:30pm, and also Saturday from May 15 to October 15 from 8:30am to noon.

WHERE TO STAY & DINE

Hotel Krone-Post. Hauptstrasse 1, 69412 Eberbach. ☎ **06271/20-13.** Fax 06271/16-33. 45 units. MINIBAR TV TEL. 224DM ($134.40) double. Rates include continental breakfast. AE, DC, MC, V. Free parking.

The central core of this structure was built during the 1600s as a coach-and-buggy station for passengers and mail routes. Today the place operates as a spacious and well-maintained hotel. The guest rooms are conservatively furnished. The in-house restaurant serves well-prepared, traditional food, with many regional dishes; there's a flowering outdoor terrace for warm-weather dining. Meals range from 34DM to 71DM ($20.40 to $42.60).

Hotel zum Karpfen. Am Alten Markt 1–4, 69412 Eberbach. ☎ **06271/7-10-15.** Fax 06271/71010. 68 units. 150DM ($90) double, 220DM ($132) suite. Rates include buffet breakfast. AE, MC, V. Free parking.

This is the best and most colorful hotel in town. On its facade are authentic *sgraffiti* (scratched-on paintings) depicting the story of Eberbach. The building is more than 2 centuries old. The small guest rooms are well maintained and furnished, most with phones and about half with TVs. The old-world restaurant serves well-prepared meals daily from 7am to noon.

HEILBRONN

Heilbronn is today a major commercial and cultural center. It was made an Imperial City by Emperor Karl IV in 1371; however, documents show that a Villa Heilbrunna existed here in A.D. 741. The town owes its name to a holy spring (Heiligbronn) that bubbled up from beneath the high altar at **St. Killian's Church,** the city's most important monument. The old city was largely destroyed in World War II, but the church has been rebuilt in its original Gothic and High Renaissance style. The church's 210-foot-high tower is the earliest example of Renaissance architecture in Germany. Inside are excellent original wood carvings, preserved during the war, including an elaborate choir and altar.

Opposite the church is the **Rathaus,** also reconstructed, a combination of Gothic and Renaissance architecture. On its balcony is an astronomical clock dating back to 1580. It was designed by the best-known horologist of the time, Isaak Habrecht, who created the famous clock inside the cathedral at Strasbourg, France.

Heilbronn is the largest producer of wine in the Neckar Valley, growing mainly Trollinger and Riesling grapes. The 550 acres of vineyards around the town yield about 5 million liters of wine annually. Every September, a large arena around the Rathaus is converted into a **"wine village."** At various booths you can sample the vintage, often at bargain prices. Merriment and music fill the air. Local food is sold as well, including *Zwiebelkuchen* (onion cake) and *Dicker Hund,* which has been compared to a "pork hamburger" (don't order it rare).

Perhaps to compensate for all the wine and beer drinking, the town definitely believes in keeping fit. Some 10,000 acres of wooded parkland surround the city, accessible by footpaths and nature trails.

GETTING THERE   Access by car is via the A6 Autobahn east and west and the A81 north and south. From Heidelberg, drive south along Route 45, then take A6 east. Heilbronn lies on the major Stuttgart-Würzburg rail line with frequent service. Call ☎ **01805/996633** for rail information. Bus service to Stuttgart is provided by

Regional Bus Stuttgart GmbH at Heilbronn (☎ **07131/6-24-50** for more information). For local transport information, call Heilbronner Verkehrbund at ☎ **07131/78560.**

TOURIST INFORMATION   Contact the **Stadtisches Verkehrsamt,** Rathaus, Marktplatz 7 (☎ **07131/19433**), Monday to Friday 9am to 4pm and Saturday 9am to 7pm.

WHERE TO STAY

Insel Hotel. Friedrich-Ebert-Brücke, 74072 Heilbronn. ☎ **07131/63-00.** Fax 07131/62-60-60. 120 units. TV. 228DM–268DM ($136.80–$160.80) double; 320DM–430DM ($192–$258) suite. Rates include buffet breakfast. AE, DC, MC, V. Free parking.

This modern hotel stands on an island (*Insel* in German) in the middle of the river, right in the heart of Heilbronn. Rooms range from medium in size to spacious. Most have balconies opening onto a view of weeping willows in the hotel's park. The buffet breakfast features rolls, cheeses, sausages, juices, cereals, and fruits. The front terrace is the beer and gossip center of town. Inside, there's the cozy Swabian Restaurant, where you can have homemade spätzle and other specialties. The Insel also has an indoor pool, a sauna, and a solarium.

WHERE TO DINE

Ratskeller. Im Rathaus, Marktplatz 7. ☎ **07131/8-46-28.** Reservations recommended. Main courses 14.50DM–36DM ($8.70–$21.60). AE, MC, V. Mon–Sat 11am–11pm. Closed 10 days in Sept. GERMAN/SWABIAN.

This is your best bet for dining in Heilbronn. It's an authentic Ratskeller, unlike so many others, but it's been given the modern treatment, with upholstered banquettes and wrought-iron grillwork. The rib-sticking fare here is solid and reliable. Main dishes include goulash, pepper steak with French fries and salad, and grilled sole. Fish specialties and vegetarian meals are also featured. There's an impressive wine list, although many diners consider the "wine of the cellar" (house wine) perfectly adequate.

3 Stuttgart

126 miles SE of Frankfurt, 138 miles NW of Munich, 78 miles SE of Heidelberg

Unlike many large, prosperous industrial centers, Stuttgart is not a city of concrete—on the contrary, two-thirds of the land inside the city limits is devoted to parks, gardens, and woodland. Yet Stuttgart is one of Germany's largest manufacturing cities, the home of Mercedes and Porsche cars, Zeiss optical equipment, and many other industrial concerns. It's also the site of international trade fairs and congresses.

As a cultural center, it's without peer in southwestern Germany. The Stuttgart Ballet is known throughout the world; its State Opera and Philharmonic Orchestra are also highly regarded. In addition, Stuttgart boasts an abundance of theater groups, cultural festivals, and museums, and is also the largest wine-growing city in Germany.

The name "Stuttgart" comes from a stud farm owned by one of the dukes of Swabia, son of Emperor Otto the Great; a horse can be seen today in the city's coat of arms. By 1427, Stuttgart had become the capital and residence of the counts of Württemberg. The city grew and prospered under the reign of Kaiser Wilhelm I (1816–64). At the turn of the 20th century it had a population of 175,000. By the beginning of World War I, Stuttgart had reached out to embrace several districts, notably ancient Cannstatt, so that its landmass extended as far as the Neckar River.

In World War II, 53 bombing attacks leveled 60% of Stuttgart's buildings. Not one of its landmarks or historic structures came through intact. After the war, Stuttgart became the capital of the newly formed state of Baden-Württemberg (many still prefer to call it "Swabia"). Stuttgart's population today is about 580,000.

ESSENTIALS

GETTING THERE   By Plane   The **Stuttgart Echterdingen Airport** (☎ 0711/ 948-33-88) is 9 miles south of the city near Echterdingen. The airport has connections with most major German and European cities. Trip time by air from Frankfurt is 50 minutes; from Hamburg or Berlin, it's 1¼ hours. The commuter train to Stuttgart's main rail station leaves from below the arrival level of Terminal 1. Trains depart every 20 minutes, taking 27 minutes to reach the heart of Stuttgart. A one-way fare is 4.60DM ($2.75). A taxi to the center of the city costs from 40DM ($24).

By Train   Stuttgart has rail links to all major German cities, with frequent connections. The train station is directly north of the historic area. Forty-five daily trains run from Munich (trip time: 2 to 3 hr., depending on the train), and 30 trains run from Frankfurt (trip time: 1½ to 2 hr.). For Stuttgart rail information, call ☎ 01805/ 996633.

By Bus   Long-distance bus service from several major German cities, including Frankfurt, is provided by Europabus Line 1012. Call **Deutsche Touring GmbH** in Stuttgart (☎ 0711/2265881) or in Frankfurt (☎ 069/7-90-35-0) for information.

By Car   Access by car is via the A8 Autobahn east and west or the A81 north and south.

VISITOR INFORMATION   Information about transportation, sightseeing, and hotels is available at the **Touristik-Zentrum,** Königstrasse 1A (☎ 0711/2-22-82-40), which is open Monday to Friday 9:30am to 8:30pm and Saturday 9:30am to 6pm. Sunday hours are 11am to 6pm from May 1 to October 31, and 1 to 6pm from November through April.

GETTING AROUND   Stuttgart has a streamlined bus and streetcar system, as well as a modern U-Bahn, with more lines planned for the future. A 3-day pass, called a *Tageskarte,* costs 20DM ($12). It allows visitors to travel on all city transportation facilities. For information, call ☎ 0711/19449.

EXPLORING THE CITY

Many of the most remarkable structures in today's Stuttgart are of advanced design, created by such architects as Ludwig Mies van der Rohe, Walter Gropius, Hans Scharoun, and Le Corbusier. The **Liederhalle,** Schlossstrasse, constructed in 1956 of concrete, glass, and glazed brick, is fascinating inside and out. The hall contains three auditoriums so well soundproofed that all three can stage concerts at the same time and not disturb the others.

The town's older section is clustered around **Schillerplatz** and the statue of the great German poet and dramatist, Schiller. **Neues Schloss,** on Schlossplatz, can be visited only by group tour. It was originally constructed between 1746 and 1807 and rebuilt beginning in 1958. Today it houses state government rooms. The modern **Rathaus** faces the old Marktplatz, where flowers, fruit, and vegetables are sold in open stalls.

For the best view of Stuttgart, climb to the top of the 1,680-foot **Birkenkopf,** west of the city. The hill was created from the debris of Stuttgart dumped here after air raids in World War II. After the 20-minute walk to the top, you'll be rewarded by a view of the city and the surrounding Swabian Hills, covered with vineyards and woods.

A free organized walking tour through historical Stuttgart leaves from the inner courtyard of the Altes Schloss on Schillerplatz on Saturday at 10am, lasting until about 12:30pm. There's also a bus tour, starting at 1pm and continuing until 3:30pm, which winds its way through the city. The cost is 32DM ($19.20) for adults and 25DM ($15) for children, if they need a seat. For tickets, contact the tourist office (☎ 0711/ 2-22-82-40).

Stuttgart

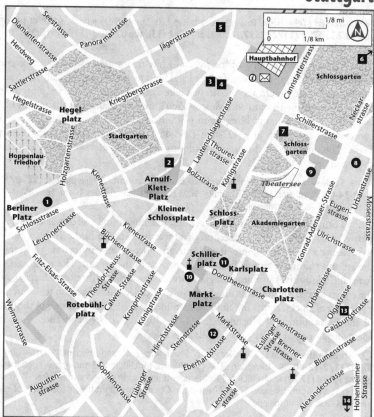

Hauptbahnhof

Accommodations
City Hotel **13**
Hotel Ruff **2**
Hotel am Schlossgarten **7**
Hotel Wörtz-Zur
  Weinsteige **14**
Mack und Pflieger **5**
Park Hotel Stuttgart **6**
Rieker **3**
Steigenberger Hotel
  Graf Zeppelin **4**

Attractions
Altes Schloss **11**
Liederhalle **1**
Neues Schloss **10**
Rathaus **12**
Staatsgalerie
  (State Gallery
  of Stuttgart) **8**
Staatstheater **9**

GERMANY

● Stuttgart

Legend
Church ✝
Information ⓘ
Post Office ✉

Fernsehturm (Television Tower). Jahnstrasse 120, Stuttgart-Degerloch, south of the city, just off B3. ☎ **0711/232597.** Admission 5DM ($3) adults, 3DM ($1.80) children. Daily 9am–10:30pm.

This 712-foot tower, capped with a red-and-white transmitter, soars above a forested hillock south of Stuttgart. It was designed and built in 1956 using radically innovative applications of aluminum and pre-stressed reinforced concrete, and served a prototype for larger towers in Toronto and Moscow. You'll find a restaurant at the tower's base, and a cafe, bar, restaurant, observation platform, and information about the tower's construction at the top of a 492-foot elevator. Food is served daily from 10am to 11pm. Look outside for the mobile platforms used by window washers. Views from the top are panoramic.

Altes Schloss and Württembergisches Landesmuseum. Schillerplatz 6. ☎ **0711/ 2-79-34-00.** Admission 5DM ($3) adults, 3DM ($1.80) children. Tues 10am–1pm, Wed–Sun 10am–5pm. U-Bahn: Schlossplatz.

One of Stuttgart's oldest standing structures, this huge ducal palace was originally a moated castle built in the 13th century and was later redone in the 16th century in Renaissance style. Now it houses the Württembergisches Landesmuseum, which traces the art and culture of Swabia from the Stone Age to the present. The most valuable items include a survey of European glass through the ages, the ducal art chamber, and the crown jewels. The museum also houses a large collection of Swabian sculptures; an exhibition of clocks, coins, and musical instruments; the famous treasures of the tomb of the Celtic prince of Hochdorf (ca. A.D. 530); and a large collection from the Merovingian period in the early Middle Ages.

✪ **Staatsgalerie (State Gallery of Stuttgart).** Konrad-Adenauer-Strasse 30–32. ☎ **0711/2-12-40-50.** Admission 3DM ($1.80), free for children 13 and under; special exhibitions 12DM ($7.20) adults, 8DM ($4.80) students and children. Wednesday is free. Wed and Fri–Sun 10am–6pm, Tues and Thurs 10am–8pm. Open to midnight the first Saturday of each month. U-Bahn: Staatsgalerie.

The city's finest art museum exhibits works spanning some 550 years. However, the best collection is from the 19th and 20th centuries, especially the works of the German expressionists–Kirchner, Barlach, and Beckmann–as well as representatives of the Bauhaus movement and Blue Rider group, such as Klee and Feininger. There are also good examples of French art of the 19th and 20th centuries and of the European and American postwar avant-garde.

Mercedes-Benz Museum. Mercedesstrasse 136, Stuttgart-Cannstatt. ☎ **0711/1-72- 25-78.** Free admission. Tues–Sun 9am–5pm. S-Bahn: 1 to Gottlieb-Daimler-Stadion; then walk to the entrance of the plant, where you'll be taken on a special bus to the museum.

This museum honors the oldest automobile factory in the world and the invention of the motorcar by Carl Benz and Gottlieb Daimler. Nearly 75 historical vehicles are shown, including a Daimler Reitwagen from 1885, the first motor bicycle. You can also see the Daimler company's first Mercedes of 1902. Race cars on display date from 1899, and include the Blitzen-Benz, the Silver Arrow, the Sauber Mercedes, the Indy car, and some vehicles built especially to achieve speed records.

SHOPPING

Home to clothing designers Hugo Boss and Ulli Knecht, Stuttgart has its fair share of boutiques that range from interesting to elegant. **Klett Passage,** located across from the train station, is an underground mall full of upscale shops. If you follow the Königstrasse from the station for about half a mile, you'll likely find anything you want in one of the retail stores that line the street. There are boutiques along the Calwer Strasse, especially in the gleaming chrome-and-glass arcade, **Calwer Passage.**

Bargains galore can be found at the Saturday morning **flea market** held on the Karlsplatz between the old castle and the new palace, where clothes, books, furniture, household items, art, and just about anything else is likely to turn up.

The latest styles for men can be found at **Holy's,** Königstrasse 54A (☎ **0711/ 22-29-44-4**), which carries the work of local heroes Boss and Knecht as well as other leading international designers, from Prada to Dolce Gabbana. The real men's-clothing deals lie south of the city in the suburbs, where you'll find the **Hugo Boss factory outlet,** Kanalstrasse, Metzingen (☎ **07123/9-40**), featuring suits, coats, jackets, and shirts at discount prices. North of the city, **Salamander,** Stammheimerstrasse 10, Kornwestheim (☎ **07154/1-50**), has a factory outlet selling shoes for the whole family in styles ranging from fun and functional to more conservative. Women can find fashions for all occasions at the trendy **Hennecke,** Zellerstrasse 26 (☎ **0711/ 2369492**).

Gunter Krauss, Kronprinzstrasse 21 (☎ **0711/29-73-95**), has won numerous design awards for its interior of white marble, mirrors, and gilded fixtures; it houses an impressive array of designer jewelry. In business since 1723, **Tritschler,** Am Marktplatz (☎ **0711/29-15-82**), stocks glass, porcelain, and fine china as well as cutlery and decorative housewares. **Pavillon,** Eberhardstrasse 31–33 (☎ **0711/24-31-34**), specializes in silver from the 19th and 20th centuries, and also sells glass, crystal, Meissen porcelain, and a few paintings.

Hans Rehn, Buchsenstrasse 25–31 (☎ **0711/2-26-23-61**), sells German-made pens and stationery, leather wallets, and other small well-made items. A fantasyland of playthings, **Kurtz,** Am Marktplatz 10 (☎ **0711/23-85-20**), sells puzzles, games, dolls, and toys for children of all ages. The city's largest bookstore, **Wittwer,** Königstrasse 30 (☎ **0711/2-50-70**), carries many books in English and has tables placed throughout the store so you can comfortably scan potential purchases. For a bit of everything, head to the city's largest department store, **Breuninger,** Marktstrasse 3 (☎ **0711/ 21-10**), where glass elevators whisk you through several floors of housewares, furnishings, and fashion. Take a break for chocolate or gingerbread at **Susi,** Königstrasse 1 (☎ **0711/2-26-41-15**), and you'll feel well rewarded no matter how the shopping is going.

WHERE TO STAY

No matter when you come to Stuttgart, you'll probably find an international trade fair in progress, from the January glass-and-ceramics exposition to the December book exhibition. (Stuttgart is also southern Germany's most important publishing center.) Good accommodations may be difficult to find at almost any time, so you should reserve in advance.

EXPENSIVE

Hotel am Schlossgarten. Schillerstrasse 23 (on the Hauptbahnhof square), 70173 Stuttgart. ☎ **0711/2-02-60.** Fax 0711/2-02-68-88. www.summithotels.com. 120 units. MINIBAR TV TEL. 385DM–470DM ($231–$282) double; 480DM–520DM ($288–$312) suite. Rates include buffet breakfast. AE, DC, MC, V. Parking 15DM ($9). U-Bahn: Hauptbahnhof.

This tasteful 10-floor hotel isn't splashy, but it offers very good conveniences and comfort. The good-sized guest rooms are well furnished, with wool carpets, satellite TVs, hair dryers, and feather comforters.

Dining/Diversions: The bar is warm and cozy, but even more intimate is the Zirbelstube, with knotty-pine walls and birch armchairs. More formal and elegant is the Restaurant Schlossgarten. Both serve the same menu of German and Swabian dishes.

Amenities: Room service, laundry, dry cleaning, Jacuzzi, sauna, terrace garden, conference facilities.

✪ **Steigenberger Hotel Graf Zeppelin.** Arnulf-Klett-Platz 7 (at the Hauptbahnhof), 70173 Stuttgart. ☎ **800/223-5652** in the U.S. and Canada, or 0711/2-04-80. Fax 0711/2-04-85-42. www.steigenberger.com. 195 units. A/C MINIBAR TV TEL. 345DM–445DM ($207–$267) double; from 450DM ($270) suite. AE, DC, MC, V. Parking 25DM ($15). U-Bahn: Hauptbahnhof.

This is the best hotel for those who come to wheel and deal with Stuttgart business-people. Although situated right at the train station, it's not only attractive but also dignified and stylish, once you get by its plain postwar exterior. The spacious soundproof guest rooms are colorfully decorated.

Dining/Diversions: Guests congregate in the Zeppelin-Bar. Restaurant Graf Zeppelin features a lunch buffet, the Zeppelin-Stüble serves Swabian dishes, the Maukenescht is the wine bar, and the ZEPP 7 bistro-cafe has a fish menu only. The Gourmet Restaurant has the best and most expensive cuisine.

Amenities: Room service, laundry, dry cleaning, hair dryer in room, Jacuzzi, men-only beauty salon, sauna, indoor pool with wood-paneled waterside lounge.

MODERATE

City Hotel. Uhlandstrasse 18 (directly west of Charlottenplatz), 70182 Stuttgart. ☎ **0711/21-08-10.** Fax 0711/2-36-97-72. 31 units. MINIBAR TV TEL. 185DM–220DM ($111–$132) double. Rates include buffet breakfast. AE, DC, MC, V. Free parking. U-Bahn: Olgaeck.

The City is a renovated bed-and-breakfast-type hotel, within walking distance of the sights in the city center. It offers pleasantly furnished but hardly spectacular bedrooms equipped with private showers (no bathtubs), radios, hair dryers, and direct-dial telephones. The generous breakfast buffet, the only meal served, is offered in a sunny winter garden.

Hotel Ruff. Friedhofstrasse 21 (about a mile from the rail station), 70191 Stuttgart. ☎ **0711/2-58-70.** Fax 0711/2-58-74-04. 90 units. MINIBAR TV TEL. 200DM–390DM ($120–$234) double. Rates include buffet breakfast. AE, DC, MC, V. Parking 15DM ($9). U-Bahn: U15 from the Hauptbahnhof.

This hotel, although not as centrally located as the City Hotel, has a lot more style and better bedrooms. Other side benefits are an attractively tiled indoor pool with a sauna and a manicured garden where a waiter will take your drink order. Guest rooms, furnished with a blend of contemporary and traditional pieces, are well maintained and inviting, and a good value for the price. Most rooms are medium in size, although some are quite small. The attractive dining room serves both Swabian and international food.

Park Hotel Stuttgart. Villastrasse 21, 70190 Stuttgart. ☎ **0711/2-80-10.** Fax 0711/2-86-43-53. www.parkhotel-stuttgart.de. 69 units. MINIBAR TV TEL. 240DM ($144) double; 260DM ($156) suite. Rates include buffet breakfast. AE, DC, MC, V. Parking 12DM ($7.20). Tram: 1, 2, or 14.

If you're looking for a first-class accommodation in a secluded and quiet area, this is your place. It's outside the center in the gardens of the Villa Berg, within walking distance of a mineral-water pool surrounded by a park. The good-sized rooms are well designed and have a decidedly personal air. Amenities include hair dryers, room service, laundry, and dry cleaning services. There are two on-site restaurants. The Villa Berg serves a German/international menu in a colorful setting. The less-formal and less expensive Radio-Stüble offers Swabian dishes.

Rieker. Friedrichstrasse 3 (across the street from the Hauptbahnhof), 70174 Stuttgart. ☎ **0711/22-13-11.** Fax 0711/29-38-94. 63 units. TV TEL. 198DM–258DM ($118.80–$154.80) double. Rates include breakfast. AE, DC, MC, V. Parking 15DM ($9). U-Bahn: Hauptbahnhof.

This well-furnished hotel offers a convenient location and a certain charm. Its public rooms have lots of comfortably upholstered armchairs and Oriental rugs scattered over the parquet or terrazzo floors. Some of the virtually soundproof guest rooms are designed with sleeping alcoves and draw curtains. It's only a 1-minute walk from Stuttgart's Municipal Air Terminal, where buses leave frequently for Echterdingen Airport. Amenities include a concierge, hair dryers, dry cleaning, laundry service, a car-rental desk, and a tour desk.

INEXPENSIVE

Hotel Wörtz-Zur Weinsteige. Hohenheimerstrasse 30, 70184 Stuttgart. ☎ **0711/ 2-36-70-00.** Fax 0711/2-36-70-07. www.hotel-woertz.de. E-mail: hotelwoertz@t-online.de. 25 units, 22 with bathroom or shower. TV TEL. 130DM ($78) double without bathroom or shower, 160DM–260DM ($96–$156) double with bathroom or shower. Rates include buffet breakfast. AE, DC, MC, V. Parking 5DM ($3). S-Bahn: Dobelstrasse.

The amber lights of a Weinstube welcome visitors to this local favorite in Stuttgart, which has the best rooms and the best food of all local hotels in this price range. The small guest rooms are paneled and sometimes have massive hand-carved armoires; all are soundproof. The Weinstube evokes the feeling of a remote corner of Swabia—it's perfect for relaxing after a long trip. The hotel is known for its garden terrace. See our recommendation of the hotel's restaurant in "Where to Dine," below.

Mack und Pflieger. Kriegerstrasse 7–11 (an 8-min. walk from the Hauptbahnhof), 70191 Stuttgart. ☎ **0711/29-19-27.** Fax 0711/29-34-89. 40 units, 25 with bathroom or shower. TV TEL. 210DM ($126) double with bathroom or shower. Rates include buffet breakfast. AE, DC, MC, V. Free parking. U-Bahn: Hauptbahnhof.

This hotel, behind an uninspired modern facade, is actually two in one. Hotel Mack and Hotel Pflieger stand close to each other and are under the same management. Check in at the Mack, since there's always someone there at the reception desk. Homelike and cozy, the hotel offers up-to-date bedrooms that are small and basic but still quite adequate. The least expensive rooms are singles without bathroom or shower.

WHERE TO DINE
EXPENSIVE

✪ **Délice.** Hauptstätter Strasse 61. ☎ **0711/6-40-32-22.** Reservations recommended. Main courses 47DM–63DM ($28.20–$37.80); fixed-price menu 130DM ($78). Mon–Fri 6:30pm–midnight. No credit cards. U-Bahn: Österreichischer Platz. Closed 2 weeks in June. AUSTRIAN/INTERNATIONAL.

A 200-year-old vaulted ceiling arches over the tables of this sophisticated cellar-level restaurant. Its appealing interior features fresh flowers, skillful and dramatic lighting, and plush upholstery. This icon of *neue Küche* is a showcase for the cuisine of Vienna-born Friedrich Gutscher, whose alchemy in the kitchen can be observed from some of the tables. Amateurs and professional chefs alike claim to have improved their methods by watching him at work.

The menu changes virtually every week. Starters might include a summer version of cream of cucumber soup, or its midwinter counterpart, consommé of pigeon with truffles. A succulent main course might be a fillet of Brittany sea wolf marinated in lemon juice and olive oil and served with a salad of warm asparagus and exotic mushrooms. A nougat truffle, or a traditional Austrian treat called Topfenknoedel (a cottage cheese dumpling) are excellent desserts. The wine list here is almost overwhelming; it's the creative statement of a team of knowledgeable sommeliers, and has selections from virtually every wine-producing region in Europe.

MODERATE

Aldos Pinocchio. Hohenheimerstrasse 64. ☎ 0711/24-08-21. Reservations required. Main courses 18DM–42DM ($10.80–$25.20). No credit cards. Daily 6pm–1am; Sept 7–May 7 daily noon–2pm and 6pm–2am. S-Bahn: Bopser. SWABIAN/ITALIAN.

Rustic and cozy are the key words here, from the filtered light streaming in through the bull's-eye glass in the leaded windows to the sympathetic chatter of the other guests. The restaurant features Swabian and Italian food, with a heavy emphasis on fish. Menu items include osso bucco and veal Parmesan as well as sauerbraten, roulade of beer, and pork schnitzel with dumplings. Salmon in a butter-and-dill sauce is a good bet.

Alte Kanzlei. Schillerplatz 5A. ☎ **0711/29-44-57.** Reservations recommended. Main courses 14DM–35DM ($8.40–$21). AE, DC, MC, V. Daily 11am–11pm. U-Bahn: Schlossplatz. SWABIAN/INTERNATIONAL.

This popular folkloric restaurant is in the section of the old castle (Altes Schloss) originally built in 1533. One of the most popular Swabian specialties is Maultaschen, the Stuttgart version of ravioli, stuffed with ham or spinach. Equally popular is Stuttgarter Ratsherrenteller, fillets of pork and beef served with spätzle (dumplings), fresh vegetables, and mushroom gravy. To accompany your meal, ask for the local Pils beer or some of the region's fine wines, such as the pale rosé known as Tuniberg or one of the full-bodied red wines made from the Trollinger grape.

Zeppelin-Stüble. In the Steigenberger Hotel Graf Zeppelin, Arnulf-Klett-Platz 7. ☎ 0711/ 20-48-184. Fax 0711/2048-542. Reservations recommended. Main courses 16.20DM–36DM ($9.70–$21.60); fixed-price menus 45DM–100DM ($27–$60). AE, DC, MC, V. Mon–Fri 11:30am–2:30pm and 6–11:30pm. U-Bahn: Hauptbahnhof. SWABIAN.

In this elegantly appointed restaurant furnished with Swabian antiques, each dish is individually prepared from fresh ingredients, according to the season. Swabian specialties like *Rostbraten* (roast beef) and *Maultaschen* (Stuttgart's version of ravioli) are offered. Although many restaurants in Stuttgart have abandoned true Swabian cuisine for more international fare, the chefs here still turn out the old-fashioned specialties preferred by locals. The kitchen does an excellent *Schwäbischer* sauerbraten with spätzle and salad.

Zur Weinsteige. In the Hotel Wörtz, Hohenheimerstrasse 30. ☎ **0711/2-36-70-00.** Fax 0711/2367007. Reservations recommended. Main courses 13.50DM–46DM ($8.10–$27.60); business lunch 18DM ($10.80); fixed-price menus 46DM–79.50DM ($27.60–$47.70). AE, CB, DC, MC, V. Tues–Sat noon–2pm and 6–10pm. Closed holidays, 3 weeks in Jan, and 3 weeks in Aug. S-Bahn: Dobelstrasse. INTERNATIONAL.

The interior of this place is a celebration of German handcrafts. Everything looks handmade, from the handblown leaded glass in the small-paned windows to the carved columns and tables and chairs. International cuisine, with numerous Swabian specialties, is offered. In summer, you'll be tempted to sit among the grapevines stretching over the sun terrace. Also worth seeing is the wine cellar, well stocked with the best regional wines and a good selection of German and international wines, about 15,000 bottles in all. You can even buy wine directly from the hotel's vineyards. Next to the cellar is a room for sitting and tasting the wines.

STUTTGART AFTER DARK

Listings of the various cultural events as well as tickets are available from the tourist office (see above). A magazine called *Lift*, available at newsstands, lists all the happenings around Stuttgart.

THE PERFORMING ARTS **Staatstheater,** Oberer Schlossgarten (☎ 0711/ 20-20-90), is the leading cultural venue in Stuttgart. The theater consists of a Grosses Haus for opera and ballet, a Kleines Haus for theater, and the Kammer-theater, which puts on experimental works. This is home to the world-class **Stuttgart Ballet,** established by the American choreographer John Cranko in the 1960s, and now led by artistic director Reid Anderson. It also houses the respected **Staatsoper (State Opera).** Tickets range from 16DM to 140DM ($9.60 to $84), and can be purchased at the Staatstheater box office. Closed August and September.

Classical and other concerts may be heard in the three halls of the **Liederhalle,** Schloss-Strasse (☎ 0711/2167110), which is home to the **Stuttgarter Philharmoniker,** under the baton of Jörg Peter Weigle, and the **Radio Symphony Orchestra,** which can be contacted at ☎ 0711/9290. Tickets for all concerts are on sale at **SKS** Russ, Charlottenplatz 17 (☎ 0711/1635321). Prices range from 15DM to 40DM ($9 to $24). Oratorical works are performed six times a year by the **Gächinger Kantorei** and **Bach Collegium** choral ensembles in the **Internationale Bachakademie,** Johann-Sebastian-Bach-Platz 1 (☎ 0711/61-92-10). Tickets range from 30DM to 110DM ($18 to $66). Each summer from August 28 to September 11, this venue also hosts a musical festival, with tickets to the nightly performances costing 18DM to 100DM ($10.80 to $60). In 2000, this festival will celebrate the 250th anniversary of Bach's death.

Political satire is the specialty of the cabaret presented nightly at **Renitenz-Theater,** Eberhardstrasse 65 (☎ 0711/29-70-75). Admission to these 8:30pm performances costs 25DM to 33DM ($15 to $19.80). The oldest stage in the city, the **Wilhelma Theater,** Neckartalstrasse 9, Bad Cannstatt (☎ 0711/54-39-84), is now a student-production facility for Stuttgart's college of music.

THE BAR, CAFE & CLUB SCENE You might start your evening with a drink at **Amadeus,** Charlottenplatz 17 (☎ 0711/29-26-78), where students and locals gather. It's open 11am to 2am on Monday and Tuesday, 11am to 3am on Wednesday and Thursday, and 11am to 4am on Friday and Saturday. For a trendier locale, head to **Palast der Republik,** Friedrichstrasse 27 (☎ 0711/2-26-48-87), a 100-year-old bar that attracts an artsier crowd. DJs here play funk and soul. It's open Monday to Wednesday from 11am to 2am, and Thursday to Saturday from 11am to 3am.

Café Stella, Hauptstätter Strasse 57 (☎ 0711/6-40-25-83), hosts local jazz bands on the first Monday of the month. It's open Monday to Thursday from 9am until 1am, Friday and Saturday from 9am until 2am, and Sunday from 9am to 10pm. Once one of Germany's bizarre versions of a country-and-western bar, the **Longhorn,** Heiligenwieses 6 (☎ 0711/4-09-82-90), has retained its name but broadened its horizons. Now, the mix includes indie, pop, and rock bands. Sunday to Tuesday brings a mix of German and international acts; on Wednesday the stage hosts local bands. Open Thursday to Tuesday from 9pm to 3am and Wednesday from 8pm until midnight. On Friday and Saturday only, the cover charge is 10DM ($6). The eclectic **Café Merlin,** Augustenstrasse 72 (☎ 0711/57766), hosts live jazz, plays, and cabaret. It's open Tuesday to Sunday from 10am until midnight, and the cover charge is 10DM to 25DM ($6 to $15).

The top dance club in Stuttgart is **Perkin's Park,** Stresemannstrasse 39 (☎ 0711/ 2-56-00-62), where two sizable rooms provide an eclectic mix of '70s to '90s dance music. It's open Wednesday to Sunday from 9pm until 4 or 5am, with a cover charge of 8DM to 15DM ($4.80 to $9). Gay men dance at **King's Club,** Calverstrasse 21 (☎ 0711/2-26-45-58), until Sunday, when they're booted for a women-only night.

The club is open Wednesday to Sunday from 10pm to 6am, with a 10DM ($6) cover charge on Saturday. **Laura's,** Rotebühlplatz 4 (☎ **0711/29-01-60**), is a lesbian and gay bar with a dance floor. It's open Thursday to Sunday 10pm to 5am; admission is 10DM ($6).

4 Tübingen

29 miles S of Stuttgart, 95 miles NE of Freiburg

Though it's often compared to Heidelberg, this quiet old university town on the upper Neckar has a look and personality all its own. Gabled medieval houses are crowded against the ancient town wall at the bank of the river. In summer, the only movement that disturbs this peaceful picture is from the students, who pole gondola-like boats up and down the river. This far upstream, the Neckar is too shallow for commercial vessels, so Tübingen has been spared the industrial look of a trading community.

Progress has not passed the city by, however. In spite of its medieval aspect, it has a new residential and science suburb in the shadow of the Schoenbuch Forest north of the city, with medical facilities, research institutes, and lecture halls affiliated with the university. The buildings of the old university, founded in 1477, are located north of the botanical gardens. The humanist Melanchthon taught here in the 16th century, and later on Schiller, Hegel, and Hölderlin were students.

ESSENTIALS

GETTING THERE **By Air** The nearest major airport, at Stuttgart (see above), has good connections to Tübingen, including a direct bus link.

By Train The Stuttgart-Tübingen rail line offers frequent service. Tübingen also has good rail ties to other major cities in Germany, including Frankfurt (trip time: 3½ hr.), Berlin (11 hr.), and Hamburg (8½ hr.). For rail information, call ☎ **01805/996633.**

By Bus Long-distance buses link Tübingen with major German cities, like Stuttgart. For information, call **Deutsche Touring GmbH** in Frankfurt (☎ **069/23-07-35**) or in Stuttgart (☎ **0711/226588**).

By Car Access is via Route 27 west from the A8 Autobahn running east and west or Route 28 east from the A81 Autobahn running north and south.

VISITOR INFORMATION Contact the **Verkehrsverein,** An der Eberhardsbrücke (☎ **07071/9-13-60**), open Monday to Friday from 9am to 7pm and Saturday from 9am to 5pm.

SEEING THE SIGHTS

An unusual feature of Tübingen is an artificial island in the Neckar. Through it runs a promenade, known as **Platanenallee,** always alive with summer strollers who cross over to the island via the wide Eberhardsbrücke. From there, you get a panoramic view of the town, with its willows and houses reflected in the river. Towering above the other buildings is the Renaissance castle, which is now used by the university. It's worth climbing up to the castle for the dramatic view from the terraces.

The narrow streets of the Altstadt wind up and down the hillside, but they all seem to lead to **Marktplatz,** where festive markets are held on Monday, Wednesday, and Friday. You'll feel as if you're stepping into the past when you come upon the scene of country people selling fruit and vegetables in the open square. In the center of all this activity stands the softly murmuring Renaissance fountain of the god Neptune. Facing the square is the **Rathaus,** which dates from the 15th century but also has more recent additions, including the 19th-century painted designs on the facade.

On a hillside above Marktplatz is **Stiftskirche,** Holzmarkt, the former church of the Stift, an Augustinian monastery. The monastery became a Protestant seminary in 1548, and its church became the Collegiate Church. Worth seeing inside are the tombs of the dukes of Württemberg in the chancel and the 15th-century French Gothic pulpit and rood screen. The church is open daily from 9am to 5pm. You can climb the tower (entrance on the left of the chancel) for a panoramic view. The chancel and tower are open April to November daily 10:30am to 5pm. Admission to the tower is 2DM ($1.20) for adults and 1DM (60¢) for children.

Hölderlinturm, Bursagasse 6 (☎ **07071/2-20-40**), lies at the end of a walk by the Neckar River. This was the home of the lyric poet, Friedrich Hölderlin, who resided here with the Zimmer family from the onset of his mental illness at age 36 until his death in 1843. Hölderlin is not well known outside Germany, but we highly recommend that you read a few of his poems in translation. Most tours of the museum are in German, but you can request one in English; otherwise you won't understand many of the exhibits. The house is open Tuesday to Friday from 10am to noon and 3 to 5pm and Saturday and Sunday from 2 to 5pm. Admission is 2DM ($1.20) adults, 1DM (60¢) children and students.

WHERE TO STAY

Hotel am Bad. Am Freibad 2, 72072 Tübingen. ☎ **07071/79740.** Fax 07071/7-53-36. 36 units. MINIBAR TV TEL. 140DM–175DM ($84–$105) double. Rates include buffet break-fast. AE, MC, V. Closed Dec 20–Jan 10. Free outdoor parking; 7DM ($4.20) in garage.

This hotel, located in the center of one of Tübingen's well-maintained public parks, offers woodland calm not far from the city center. Its rambling rose-colored exterior complements the masses of red flowers on the sun terrace. Rooms are modest and a bit small but still comfortable. The hotel has one bar and one restaurant, specializing in Bavarian food. There's also an Olympic-size pool practically at its back door.

Krone Hotel. Uhlandstrasse, 72072 Tübingen. ☎ **07071/1-33-10.** Fax 07071/13-31-32. www.tuebingen-info.de/hotels/krone/index.htm. 50 units. TV TEL. 200DM –310DM ($120–$186) double; from 320DM ($192) suite. Rates include buffet breakfast. AE, DC, MC, V. Closed Dec 23–31. Parking 14DM ($8.40).

The town's most prestigious hotel is located right off the river, in the heart of Tübingen. The place is traditional and conservative, with a homelike atmosphere. The decor includes a liberal use of antiques or good reproductions. The rooms are all per-sonalized; many are decoratively tiled.

The owners, Karl and Erika Schlagenhauff, provide some of the best meals in town (recommended even if you're not staying here). There are three dining rooms: the formal dining salon; the Uhlandstube, with an old tavern atmosphere; and a country-style room—all served by one kitchen. The menu is international; typical dishes include fillet of sole in butter, Wiener schnitzel, and tournedos Rossini. Service is daily from noon to 2:15pm and 6 to 10:30pm.

WHERE TO DINE

In addition to the restaurants below, the Krone Hotel (see above) is a good dining spot.

Restaurant Museum. Wilhelmstrasse. ☎ **07071/2-28-28.** Reservations recommended. Main courses 17DM–42DM ($10.20–$25.20). AE, MC, V. Daily 11:30am–2:30pm; Tues–Sun 6:30pm–11:30pm. INTERNATIONAL/SWABIAN.

This is one of Tübingen's foremost restaurants. It's a pleasant place to dine on inter-national specialties, such as Marseille snail soup, or regional dishes, such as Swabian medaillons of veal. The lunches here are considered by many locals (including stu-dents) to be not only the best meals in town but also the best value.

Restaurant Rosenau. Beim Neuen Botanischen Garten. ☎ **07071/6-64-66.** Reservations recommended. Main courses 20DM–35DM ($12–$21); fixed-price menu 49DM ($29.40). AE, DC, MC, V. Tues–Sun 11am–midnight. GERMAN/SWABIAN.

This restaurant, near the botanical gardens, has the finest food within the town center, though it's not as good as at the Gasthof Waldhorn (see below), on the outskirts. Landgasthof Rosenau is like a roadhouse with a cafe annex. The owner serves superb Swabian specialties along with modern cuisine. The typical regional fare is listed under the gutbürgerlich selections. Try the tasty and filling Swabian hot pot with spätzle (dumplings) and fresh mushrooms. From the section of the menu "reserved for gourmets," you might choose a delectable veal steak with morels. Desserts are often elaborate concoctions. In fair weather, guests can order drinks out in the sun.

NEARBY DINING

✪ **Gasthof Waldhorn.** Schönbuchstrasse 49 (4 miles from the town center). ☎ **07071/6-12-70.** Reservations required. Main courses 35DM–58DM ($21–$34.80); business lunch 98DM ($58.80); fixed-price menus 98DM–160DM ($58.80–$96). AE. Wed–Sun noon–2:30pm and 6:30pm–midnight. Closed Aug 18–30. GERMAN/FRENCH.

The finest restaurant in the area is not in Tübingen but on its outskirts, at Tübingen-Bebenhausen. The place is decorated like a farmhouse. Herr and Frau Schilling offer a light German and French cuisine based on regional ingredients, backed up by an impressive wine list (with many half bottles). This restaurant truly deserves its star. The chef combines inventiveness with a solid technique. The menu changes daily but is likely to include trout terrine and wild venison with forest mushrooms, along with whatever vegetable is in season. The dessert specialty is a soft cream concoction flavored with rose hips. Behind the house is a garden area with five tables for summer dining.

TÜBINGEN AFTER DARK

Student-inspired nightlife makes this old town very young at heart. Just head into the Marktplatz at night and follow the sound of revelry. You can order a beer and read the comics hanging on the walls of **Marktschenke,** Am Markt 11 (☎ **07071/2-20-35**), then join the students spilling outside into the square. Daily hours are 9am to 1am. Or you might start your evening in the ancient **Boulanger,** Collegiumsgasse 2 (☎ **07071/2-33-45**), where you could offer to pick up Hegel's bar tab, which has gone unpaid for more than 200 years. A riverside retreat, **Neckarmüller,** Gartenstrasse 4 (☎ **07071/2-78-48**), has a barroom, but more inviting in nice weather are the picnic tables on the banks of the river. It's open daily from 11am to 1am. Also on the Neckar, **Ammerschlag,** Ammergasse 13 (☎ **07071/5-15-91**), has live music one Sunday a month, ranging from blues to rap. Hours are daily from 3pm until 1am.

Located next to the Stiftskirche steps, **Tangente-Night** (☎ **07071/2-30-07**) is a place to dance to techno, acid jazz, and house at night. It's open daily from 10am until 3am. Dancing is also top priority at **Zentrum Zoo,** Schleifmuhleweg 86 (☎ **07071/9-44-80**), open Tuesday and Thursday to Saturday from 9pm until 2am; Sunday from 8:30pm to 1am. The cover charge is 6DM ($3.60).

5 Schwäbisch Hall

60 miles NE of Stuttgart, 86 miles W of Nürnberg

Technically, this medieval town is not in the Neckar Valley; however, if you skip it in your travels through this region, you'll have missed one of the treasures of southwestern Germany. Schwäbisch Hall is located in the heart of the forests of the Schwäbische Alb, where it clings to the steep banks of the Kocher River, a tributary of the Neckar. The houses of the Altstadt are set on terraces built into the hillside; from the opposite bank they appear to be arranged in steps, overlooking the old wooden river bridges.

ESSENTIALS

GETTING THERE   By Train   Trains run daily from Stuttgart and Nürnberg into the Bahnhof Schwäbisch Hall. For information call ☎ **01805/996633.**

By Bus   Regional bus service in the area is offered by **Stuttgart GmbH** (☎ **07131/ 6-24-50** for schedules and information).

By Car   Access is via the A6 Autobahn running east and west, or Route 14 from the east and Route 19 from the north.

VISITOR INFORMATION   The **Verkehrsverein** is at Am Markt 9 (☎ **0791/ 75-12-46**). Open October through April, Monday to Friday 9am to 5pm; May through September, Monday to Friday 9am to 6pm and Saturday 10am to 3pm.

SEEING THE SIGHTS

Marktplatz is perhaps the most attractive market square in all of Germany. Flanking the sloping square are fine half-timbered patrician houses, and at the lower end stands the baroque Rathaus. In the center of the square is a 16th-century Gothic fountain adorned with statues of St. Michael with St. George and Samson. The Marktplatz is the scene of festive occasions, such as the annual Kuchenfest, celebrating the ancient salt industry that grew around the salt springs in Schwäbisch Hall.

On the north side of Marktplatz, facing the Rathaus, are 54 large, imposing, delicately curved stone steps leading to **Michaelskirche.** This cathedral is a 15th-century Gothic Hallenkirche with a 12th-century tower. Many pews date from the 15th century, as does St. Michael's altarpiece in the side chapel. The church is open on Monday 2 to 5pm, Tuesday to Saturday 9am to noon and 2 to 5pm, and Sunday 11am to noon and 2 to 5pm.

WHERE TO STAY & DINE

Der Adelshof. Am Markt 12 (on Marktplatz), 74523 Schwäbisch Hall. ☎ **0791/7-58-90.** Fax 0791/60-36. 49 units. TV TEL. 195DM ($117) double; 435DM ($261) suite. Rates include breakfast. AE, DC, MC, V. Free parking.

The Adelshof is in an attractive stone building, much of it dating from 1400. Its advantage is its location, right in the center of town. Bedrooms are clean and comfortable, if a bit small. The hotel also contains a small fitness room, with sauna and solarium available for an extra charge. Downstairs, the restaurant, open Tuesday to Sunday evenings, serves some of the best food in town. The recently refurbished, 500-year-old Kellerbar has become one of the town's most popular bars; it's open daily from 7pm to 3am.

Hotel Garni Scholl. Klosterstrasse 3, 74523 Schwäbisch Hall. ☎ **0791/9-75-50.** Fax 0791/97-55-80. E-mail: hotelscholl@t-online.de. 32 units. TV TEL. 170DM ($102) double. Rates include buffet breakfast. AE, MC, V. Parking free overnight until 9am and then 5DM ($3).

Three very old half-timbered houses, beautifully situated on the medieval square at the side of St. Michael's, were combined to create this hotel. One is pumpkin colored, another olive green. The guest rooms are nicely furnished, but cramped. You'll find plenty of visitors enjoying the cafe's front terrace, overlooking Marktplatz.

Hotel Hohenlohe. Am Weilertor 14, 74523 Schwäbisch Hall. ☎ **0791/7-58-70.** Fax 0791/75-87-04. 113 units. MINIBAR TV TEL. 218DM–268DM ($130.80–$160.80) double; 298DM–470DM ($178.80–$282) suite. Rates include buffet breakfast. AE, DC, MC, V. Parking 10DM ($6) inside and free outside.

The Hohenlohe is on the left bank of the Kocher River, in the historic Freie Reichsstadt district opposite the town center. The rooms are pleasant and compact, with bright color accents. Many have good views. Breakfast is served on an open-view roof deck. The hotel's restaurant offers regional meals; a cafeteria and a bar are also on the premises. Other facilities include two indoor pools and a saltwater outdoor pool, a sauna, a solarium, a bowling alley, and a massage parlor.

A NEARBY PLACE TO STAY & DINE

✪ **Wald und Schlosshotel Friedrichsruhe.** 74639 Friedrichsruhe-Zweiflingen. ☎ **07941/6-08-70.** Fax 07941/6-14-68. www.relaischateaux.fr/waldschloss. E-mail: schlosshotel_friedrichsruhe@t-online.de. 48 units. TEL. 295DM–395DM ($177–$237) double; 490DM–590DM ($294–$354) suite. Rates include continental breakfast. AE, CB, DC, MC, V. Parking 15DM ($9). Take a train from Schwäbisch Hall to Öhringen; then take either a taxi, or a bus marked ZWEIFLINGEN.

This hotel is about 17 miles from Schwäbisch Hall on the Hohenlohe plateau, about 4 miles north of the little village of Öhringen. One of the hotel's three buildings was constructed between 1712 and 1719 as a three-story hunting lodge. A second building, added in 1953, about a 3-minute walk from the original lodge, was designed to look old, but inside rooms are modern, with up-to-date conveniences, such as hair dryers. Some have a TV and minibar. There are saunas, a heated indoor pool, a jogging track, an outdoor pool, and tennis courts.

This establishment's restaurant facilities are excellent. The more formal choice is The Restaurant, where red walls, white damask napery, and brass chandeliers provide the setting for elegant cuisine. Five- and seven-course fixed-price menus cost 150DM to 200DM ($90 to $120), respectively. À la carte meals begin at around 48DM ($28.80). Less formal (and less expensive) is the richly atmospheric Jägerstube, with a regional decor of mounted antlers, carved-back chairs, and an old porcelain stove. Here, a fixed-price menu for four courses is 75DM ($45).

Frankfurt am Main

The thriving industrial metropolis of Frankfurt, Germany's fifth-largest city, may well be your first glimpse of Germany. Most international flights land here at Frankfurt's huge airport, and its massive 19th-century railway station is the busiest in Europe.

Frankfurt is a heavily industrial city, with more than 2,450 factories operating around the ford *(Furt)* on the Main River, where the Frankish tribes once settled. As the home of the Bundesbank, Germany's central bank, Frankfurt is also the country's financial center. It's been a major banking city ever since the Rothschilds opened their first bank here in 1798. Frankfurt also has a leading stock exchange.

Frankfurt's international trade fairs in spring and autumn bring some 1.2 million visitors to the city and its *Messengelände* (fairgrounds), often causing a logjam at hotels. Fairs include the Motor Show, the Textile Fair, the Chemical Industries Fair, and the Cookery Fair. But the best known is the International Book Fair, which draws some 5,500 publishers from nearly 100 countries and is the most important meeting place in the world for the acquisition and sale of book rights and translations.

1 Orientation

ARRIVING

BY PLANE **Flughafen Frankfurt/Main** (☎ 069/69-01) lies 7 miles from the city center at the Frankfurter Kreuz, the intersection of two major expressways, A3 and A5. This airport, continental Europe's busiest, serves more than 240 destinations in about 110 countries worldwide, including many American cities. It's Germany's major international gateway. All important German airports can be reached via Frankfurt. Flying time from Frankfurt to Berlin and Hamburg is 70 minutes, and to Munich, 60 minutes.

At the Airport Train Station beneath Terminal 1, you can connect to German InterCity trains and S-Bahn commuter trains to Frankfurt and nearby cities. Terminal 2 is linked to Terminal 1 by a people-mover system, Sky Line, which provides quick transfers (the airport's standard connection time is 45 min. maximum).

Train information is available at the **German DB Travel Center** (☎ 01805/996633). **S-Bahn** lines between the airport and Frankfurt center run every 10 minutes and deposit passengers at the main rail station. Take train S-8. Travel time is 11 to 15 minutes. A one-way ticket costs 5.80DM ($3.50); tickets should be purchased before boarding.

Frankfurt Accommodations, Attractions & Dining

Accommodations
Admiral **42**
Am Zoo **41**
An Der Messe **13**
Arabella Sheraton Grand Hotel **40**
Continental **33**
Diana **10**
Falk Hotel **1**
Frankfurt Savoy Hotel **30**
Hotel Hessischer Hof **14**
Hotel Palmenhof **4**
Hotel Robert Mayer **2**
Hotel Westend **12**
Hotelschiff Peter Schlott **34**
Kepinski Hotel Gravenbruch Frankfurt **51**
Le Meridien Parkhotel **31**
Mozart **6**
National **32**
Steigenberger Frankfurter Hof **22**

Attractions
Alte Oper **16**
Deutches Architekturmuseum **27**
Dom St. Bartholomäus **45**
Deutsches Filmmuseum **25**
Goethe-Haus **21**
Liebieghaus **29**
Museum für Kunsthandwerk **24**
Museum für Moderne Kunst **43**
Palmengarten **3**
Römer **23**
Städel Gallery **28**

Dining
Altes Zollhaus **37**
Avocado Bistro **17**
Bistrot 77 **35**
Café Laumer **9**
Café Schwille **18**
Churrasco **46**
Die Gans in Sachsenhausen **36**
Erno's Bistro **8**
Gargantua **5**
Germania **50**
Gilde Stuben **38**
Humperdinck **7**
Jaspers **49**
Jewel of India **11**
Mövenpick am Opernplatz **15**
Premiere **39**
Steinernes Haus **44**
Weinhaus Brückenkeller **47**
Zum Bitburger **19**
Zum Gemalten Haus **26**
Zum Grauen Bock **48**
Zur Hauptwache **20**

BY TRAIN   Frankfurt's main rail station, the **Hauptbahnhof,** the busiest in Europe, is the arrival point for some 1,600 trains per day carrying about 255,000 passengers. A train arrives from most major cities of Germany every hour until 8pm. Many other European cities also have direct rail links with Frankfurt. For travel information, ticket reservations, and seat information, call **Deutsche Bahn** (☎ **01805/996633**).

BY BUS   Frankfurt has long-distance bus service to about 800 German and European cities. Buses depart from the south side of the Hauptbahnhof. For information, contact **Deutsche Touring,** Am Römerhof 17 (☎ **069/230735**).

BY CAR   The A3 and A5 Autobahns intersect at Frankfurt. The A3 comes in from the Netherlands, Cologne, and Bonn, and continues east and south to Würzburg, Nürnberg, and Munich. The A5 comes from the northeast (Hannover, Bad Hersfeld) and continues south to Heidelberg, Mannheim, and Basel (Switzerland). From the west, the A60 connects with the A66, which leads to Frankfurt and the inner city, hooking up with the A3. Road signs and directions are frequently posted.

VISITOR INFORMATION

The **tourist office** is in two locations: the Hauptbahnhof, opposite the main entrance (☎ **069/21-23-88-49**), and im Römer (☎ **069/21-23-87-08**). Both branches open Monday to Friday from 8am to 9pm and on the weekends from 9am to 6pm. **Amerika Haus** is an American cultural institute at Staufenstrasse 1 (☎ **069/9-71-44-80**).

CITY LAYOUT

The Hauptbahnhof, at the western edge of the center of town, opens onto a large street called **Am Hauptbahnhof.** As you walk out of the station, Düsseldorferstrasse will be on your left and Baselerstrasse on your right, heading south toward the Main River. You have a choice of three streets heading east to the center of the **Altstadt** (old town): Taunusstrasse, Kaiserstrasse, and Münchner Strasse. Münchner Strasse leads directly into **Theaterplatz,** with its opera house. Taunusstrasse leads to three of the major Altstadt squares in the southern part of the city: **Goetheplatz, Rathenauplatz,** and (most important) the **Hauptwache,** with its U-Bahn connections. In this section of Frankfurt, along Kaiserstrasse, some of the best shops are found; major attractions, including Goethe-Haus, are also nearby.

The **Main River** flows slightly south of the Altstadt. Many bridges, including the Alte Brücke and the Obermainbrücke, cross this important waterway. On the south bank of the Main is a popular district, **Alt-Sachsenhausen,** center of the apple-wine taverns (more about them later). For other major attractions, you'll have to branch out, heading east to the Frankfurt Zoo or northwest to the Palmengarten (both easily reached by public transportation).

STREET MAPS   Arm yourself with a detailed street map, not the general overview handed out by the tourist office. Maps are sold at most bookstores and news kiosks. See "Bookstores" in "Fast Facts: Frankfurt," below.

2 Getting Around

BY PUBLIC TRANSPORTATION   Frankfurt is linked by a network of fast, modern subways, trams, and buses, all of which are administered by the **RMV** *(Rhein-Main Verkehrsverbund),* Mannheimer Strasse 15 (☎ **069/27-30-70**). All methods of public transport can be used within their respective fare zones at a single price, which includes transfers between any of them. Tickets are purchased at green, coin-operated automatic machines *(Fahrscheine)* that are lined up adjacent to each of the points of departure. The machines accept all denominations of coins, and bills up to

50DM, but be alert that any change you receive will be in coins, so try to use the smallest bills possible. A 24-hour ticket, good for unlimited travel inside Frankfurt's central zone, costs 8DM ($4.80) for adults and 5DM ($3) for children. Zone charts and additional information in six languages are displayed on all the automatic machines. Except for bus travel (where you have the additional option of paying the driver directly for your passage), be sure to buy your ticket before you board any of the public transport conveyances of Frankfurt. If you're caught traveling without the proper ticket, you may be fined 60DM ($36).

If you want to simplify the ticket-buying process, both for public transport and museum admissions within Frankfurt, consider the purchase of a **Frankfurter Tageskarte** (Frankfurt Card) from any branch of the city's tourist office. These cards allow unlimited travel anywhere within the greater Frankfurt area, plus transport on the shuttle bus going to and from the airport, plus half-price admission to any of the city's museums. The cost is 10DM ($6) for a 1-day card and 15DM ($9) for a 2-day card. For more information, contact the tourist office.

BY TAXI   There's no surcharge for calling for a taxi; dial ☎ **069/54-50-11, 069/23-00-33,** or **069/25-00-01.** Otherwise, you can get a cab either by standing at any of the city's hundreds of clearly designated taxi stands, or by hailing one with an illuminated dome light. Taxis charge by the trip and by the carload, without surcharge for pieces of luggage. Some are suitable for carrying up to six passengers, others for a maximum of only four. Regardless of their size, the initial fee you'll pay for a Frankfurt taxi is 3.80DM ($2.30); additional kilometers cost 2.15DM to 2.55DM ($1.30 to $1.55) each, depending on the time of day. The most expensive rates are charged on holidays between the hours of 10pm and 6am; the least expensive are charged between 10am and 4pm.

BY RENTAL CAR   The big rental companies each maintain offices at the airport and at central locations throughout Frankfurt. The most reliable are **Avis,** whose downtown branch is at Schmidtstrasse 39 or inside the Hauptbahnhof (☎ **069/27-99-7010**); and **Hertz,** whose offices are in the Hauptbahnhof (☎ **069/23-04-84**), and on the Hanauer Landstrasse 117 (☎ **069/44-90-90**). Also recommended is **Europcar,** which maintains offices at the Hauptbahnhof (☎ **069/242-9810**) and downtown at Am Industriehof 3–5 (☎ **069/970-6410**).

Fast Facts: Frankfurt

American Express   Centrally located at Kaiserstrasse 8 (☎ **069/2-10-50**), the American Express offices are open Monday to Friday from 9:30am to 6pm and on Saturday from 9:30am to 12:30pm. Unless you have an American Express card or traveler's checks, you'll be charged 2DM ($1.20) for using their mail service.

Bookstores   The best English-language bookstore is **British Bookshop,** Börsenstrasse 17 (☎ **069/28-04-92**). It's open Monday to Friday from 9:30am to 7pm and Saturday from 9:30am to 4pm. Many English-language editions are also for sale at **Sussmann's Presse und Buch,** Zeil 127 (☎ **069/1-31-07-51**), open Monday to Wednesday and Friday from 9am to 7pm, Thursday from 9am to 8pm, and Saturday from 9am to 4pm.

Consulates   See "Fast Facts: Germany," in chapter 2, for a list of consulates in Frankfurt.

Currency Exchange   Go to the Hauptbahnhof's **Reise-Bank AG** kiosk (☎ **069/24-27-85-91** or **069/24-27-85-92**), which is open daily from 7:30am to 10pm. The same bank maintains two separate branches within the Frankfurt airport. The smaller branch (☎ **069/69-07-20-71**) is open daily from 7am to 7pm; the larger (☎ **069/69-03-50-61**) is open daily from 6am to 11pm.

Dentist   For an English-speaking dentist, call ☎ **069/19292** to arrange an appointment.

Doctor   For an English-speaking doctor, call ☎ **069/19292** to arrange an appointment.

Drugstores   For information about pharmacies open near you, call ☎ **069/ 19292.**

E-mail   Head for **Euro-Net,** Willy-Brandt-Platz/Euro-Tower (☎ **069/ 242-9370**), a cybercafe with computers and Internet access, as well as five chic bars and a kitchen serving everything from Spanish-style tapas to sushi until 1am each morning.

Emergencies   Dial ☎ **110** for the police; ☎ **112** for a fire, first aid, and ambulance; ☎ **069/1-92-92** for emergency medical service; and ☎ **6-60-72-71** for emergency dental service.

Eyeglasses   Go to **Hertie,** An der Zeil 390 (☎ **069/92-90-50**), the city's major department store. The optician's hours are Monday to Friday from 9:30am to 8pm and Saturday from 9am to 4pm.

Laundry   Try **SB Wasch Center,** Grosse Seestrasse 46 (☎ **069/77-35-80**), open daily from 6:30am to 10pm.

Lost Property   Go to **Deutsche Bahn Fundstelle,** Hauptbahnhof (☎ **069/ 2-65-48-34**). Open around the clock.

Luggage Storage/Lockers   Lockers can be rented and luggage stored at the Hauptbahnhof.

Photographic Needs   Try **Foto Neithold,** Schillerstrasse 10 (☎ **069/28-25-61**), open Monday to Friday from 9am to 7pm and Saturday from 9am to 3pm.

Post Office   The central post office is at Zeil 108–110 (60001 Frankfurt) near the Hauptwache (☎ **069/21-11**). It's open Monday to Friday from 9am to 6pm and Saturday from 9am to 1pm. Go there to pick up general delivery mail (called *Poste Restante* in Europe). There's also a post office at the Hauptbahnhof 60036 Frankfurt (☎ **069/2-42-42-70**), open Monday to Friday from 6:30am to 9pm, Saturday from 8am to 6pm, and Sunday and holidays from 11am to 6pm.

Rest Rooms   There are many decent public facilities in central Frankfurt, especially in the Altstadt.

Safety   Frankfurt is a relatively safe city, but you should still stay alert at all times. Stay out of the area around the Hauptbahnhof at night, as muggings are frequent.

Taxis   See "Getting Around," earlier in this chapter.

Telegrams/Telex/Fax   You can send all of these at the **post office** at the Hauptbahnhof (☎ **069/2-42-42-70**). See above for office hours.

3 Accommodations

Frankfurt is notorious for room shortages during busy trade fairs. If you have the bad luck to arrive when one of them is scheduled, you might find all the more central hotels fully booked. To find an available room, head to one of the tourist offices. Either branch will charge you 5DM ($3) for a room-finding service.

IN THE CENTER
VERY EXPENSIVE

Arabella Sheraton Grand Hotel. Konrad-Adenauer-Strasse 7, 60313 Frankfurt. ☎ **800/ 637-7200** in the U.S. and Canada, or 069/2-98-16. Fax 069/2-98-18-10. www.rma.de/hotel/ arabella-grand-hotel-frankfurt.htm 78 units. A/C MINIBAR TV TEL. 460DM–690DM ($276–$414) double; from 900DM ($540) suite. AE, DC, MC, V. Parking 30DM ($18). U-Bahn: Konstablerwache.

This hotel in the heart of the shopping district is one of the most modern and glamorous in Frankfurt, though it's not as stylish as either the Steigenberger Frankfurter Hof or the Hessischer Hof. It's designed in the international big-city style, and is a favorite of business travelers. The hotel has an atrium lobby, warmly decorated in brown and white marble. The bedrooms are large and often outfitted with art-deco-inspired furniture. Bathrooms are luxurious.

Dining/Diversions: The hotel boasts one of the best Chinese restaurants in Frankfurt (Dynasty) and operates two Japanese restaurants (Sushi bar and Teppen Yaki), as well. There's also a rustic German restaurant offering regional specialties, as well as a bar and a cafe. For a review of the hotel's main restaurant, Premiere, see "Dining," later in this chapter.

Amenities: 24-hour room service, laundry, baby-sitting, fitness center, sauna, solarium, pool.

✪ **Hotel Hessischer Hof.** Friedrich-Ebert-Anlage 40, 60325 Frankfurt. ☎ **800/223-6800** in the U.S. and Canada, or 069/7-54-00. Fax 069/75-40-29-24. www.heissischer.hof.de. E-mail: info@heissischer.hof.de. 117 units. A/C MINIBAR TV TEL. 545DM–615DM ($327–$369) double; from 635DM ($381) suite. Children 12 and under stay free in parents' room. AE, DC, MC, V. Parking 25DM ($15). S-Bahn: Platz der Republik.

A private and traditional place with an elegant atmosphere, this hotel has first-class style and amenities all the way. It's topped only by the Steigenberger Frankfurter Hof. The hotel is located opposite the trade-fair building. The relatively modest postwar exterior doesn't prepare you for the spacious and glamorous interior. Many of the bedrooms are furnished with antiques. The bathrooms are equipped with perfumed soap and other thoughtful little extras such as luxurious bathrobes and a hair dryer. The hotel staff follows the old European custom of having guests leave their shoes outside the bedroom door at night, to be returned shined the next morning.

Dining/Diversions: Sèvres-Restaurant offers both traditional and modern cuisine. Its walls are decorated with original Sèvres porcelain. Jimmy's Bar is an elegant rendezvous spot in Frankfurt.

Amenities: Room service, daily laundry, baby-sitting, fitness equipment.

Le Meridien Parkhotel. Wiesenhüttenplatz 28–38 (near the Hauptbahnhof), 60329 Frankfurt. ☎ **800/225-5843** in the U.S. and Canada, or 069/2-69-70. Fax 069/2-69-78-84. www. forte-hotels.com. E-mail: GM1275@forte-hotels.com. 296 units. A/C MINIBAR TV TEL. 415DM–715DM ($249–$429) double; 585DM–1,015DM ($351–$609) suite. AE, DC, MC, V. Parking 28DM ($16.80). S-Bahn: 8.

We prefer this hotel over its bigger, more impersonal competitors: the Frankfurt Intercontinental at Wilhelm-Leuschner-Strasse 43 and the Frankfurt Marriott Hotel at Hamburger Allee 2. Le Meridien Parkhotel provides not only warmth but also personal attention for its guests, mainly from the world of commerce. It opens onto a square. The hotel has been built in two sections—an ornately decorated, recently renovated 1905 building and a sleek but duller 1970s wing. In the older part, rooms have a luxurious atmosphere and are individually designed. The newer section's decor is modern. All rooms and suites are in the five-star category. The marble bathrooms are well maintained and have robes, hair dryers, and deluxe vanity items.

ⓘ Family-Friendly Hotels

Admiral (*see p. 422*) This family favorite near the zoo has rooms that are simply furnished but comfortable—and the price is right.

Am Zoo (*see p. 421*) This clean, well-furnished, and comfortable hotel is just across from the zoo entrance in a quiet, safe neighborhood.

Le Meridien Parkhotel (*see p. 419*) Children under 16 stay free in their parents' room at this pricey chain hotel located across from a city park.

Dining/Diversions: Le Park Restaurant offers excellent German regional and international cuisine. The Casablanca Bar has piano music and a lively atmosphere; it attracts both foreign visitors and locals.

Amenities: Room service, laundry, dry cleaning, baby-sitting, overnight shoe shine, sauna, solarium, business center, shopping boutique.

★ **Steigenberger Frankfurter Hof.** Am Kaiserplatz, 60311 Frankfurt. ☎ **800/223-5652** in the U.S. and Canada, or 069/2-15-02. Fax 069/21-59-00. www.steigenberger.com. 369 units. AC MINIBAR TV TEL. 430DM–630DM ($258–$378) double; from 690DM ($414) suite. AE, DC, MC, V. Parking 30DM ($18). U-Bahn: 1, 2, or 3.

This grand hotel, run by the Steigenberger chain, is the number-one choice of traditionalists. Its position in the center of the city is ideal for vacationers and businesspeople alike; it's just a few short blocks from the Hauptbahnhof, near the sights of the Altstadt. Its art collection, featuring Gobelin tapestries, is outstanding. In spite of its size, it offers both well-maintained comfort and a personalized atmosphere. The rooms and suites are furnished in a restrained and dignified modern style. Bathrooms include hair dryers and luxurious robes.

Dining/Diversions: There are a few choices for dining: a Japanese restaurant; the thatch-roofed Hofgarten Restaurant; and the cozy Kaiserbrunnen, which offers light meals, wines, and champagne in a Biedermeier decor. The hotel's Lipizzaner Bar is one of the most elegant in the city. But the best spot in the hotel is the provincial-style Frankfurter Stubb. A pianist plays at teatime in the lobby lounge.

Amenities: 24-hour room service, same-day laundry and valet service, dry cleaning, shoe-shine service, baby-sitting, full business-services center, shopping arcade with hairdresser and beauty parlor, wine and gourmet boutique.

EXPENSIVE

An Der Messe. Westendstrasse 104, 60325 Frankfurt. ☎ **800/221-6509** in the U.S., or 069/74-79-79. Fax 069/74-83-49. E-mail: hotel-messe.frankfurt@eurohotel-online.com. 46 units. MINIBAR TV TEL. 280DM–500DM ($168–$300) double. Rates include breakfast. AE, DC, MC, V. Underground garage parking 20DM ($12). Tram: 16 or 19.

This quiet charmer is the choice of seasoned and discriminating visitors to Frankfurt. It's just a 5-minute walk from the university, the Hauptbahnhof, the banking district, and the fairgrounds. The staff does much to make guests feel comfortable. Rooms are large and stylishly furnished; many have an Asian motif. The bathrooms are luxurious and have hair dryers. A half-dozen singles are rented, but they're hard to come by unless you reserve well in advance.

Dining: Breakfast, the only meal offered, is served in a light, airy room.

Amenities: Concierge, room service, dry cleaning, laundry service, baby-sitting, car rental and tour desk.

Frankfurt Savoy Hotel. Wiesenhüttenstrasse 42 (near the Hauptbahnhof), 60329 Frankfurt. ☎ **069/27-39-60.** Fax 069/27-39-67-95. 144 units. MINIBAR TV TEL. 285DM–390DM ($171–$234) double. Rates include buffet breakfast. AE, DC, MC, V. Parking available in mul-tistory car park nearby for 25DM ($15). S-Bahn: All trains.

This hotel offers first-class comfort and a lighthearted ambience. Swedish furnishings are used throughout. The good-sized guest rooms contain trouser presses and hair dryers.

Dining: The Rhapsody offers a continental menu with many international dishes.

Amenities: Fitness club with an indoor pool, a dry or steam sauna, and a solarium; room service, concierge, dry cleaning, laundry.

Hotel Palmenhof. Bockenheimer Landstrasse 89–91, 60325 Frankfurt. ☎ **069/753-0060.** Fax 069/753-0060. E-mail: hotel.palmenhof@t-online.de. 45 units. MINIBAR TV TEL. Mon–Thurs 290DM–415DM ($165.30–$236.55) double, 385DM–495DM ($219.45–$282.15) suite. Fri–Sun 175DM ($99.75) double, 385DM–495DM ($219.45–$282.15) suite. Rates include breakfast. Parking 18DM ($10.25). AE, DC, MC, V. U-Bahn: Westend.

This hotel, just a short walk from Frankfurt's Botanical Gardens, is set in a much-renovated, five-story art nouveau building, some of whose original architectural details have been carefully preserved. Bedrooms are high-ceilinged and relatively spa-cious, with art nouveau furnishings.

Dining/Diversions: In the hotel's basement is a cozy-looking restaurant, Bastei, that's open Monday to Friday for lunch and dinner. Set-price menus cost from 25DM to 60DM ($14.25 to $34.20).

Amenities: Room service, hair dryer in room, concierge, dry cleaning/laundry.

National. Baselerstrasse 50 (2 minutes from the Hauptbahnhof), 60329 Frankfurt. ☎ **800/528-1234** in the U.S., or 069/27-39-40. Fax 069/23-44-60. www.bestwestern.com. 72 units. MINIBAR TV TEL. 229DM–498DM ($137.40–$298.80) double. Rates include buffet breakfast. AE, DC, MC, V. Parking 25DM ($15). U-Bahn: 1, 2, or 3.

The National has a smaller, more personal ambience that will appeal to the tradition-alist. Antiques and handsome reproductions adorn both the public and private rooms. Many of the comfortable rooms are decorated with Oriental carpeting.

Dining/Diversions: The hotel has a beautifully appointed dining room, with an international menu that features fixed-price meals as well as à la carte selections. The lobby bar is perfect for a comfortable rendezvous before dinner or after the theater.

Amenities: Concierge, dry cleaning, laundry service, conference rooms, tour desk.

MODERATE

Am Zoo. Alfred-Brehm-Platz 6 (across from the zoo entrance), 60316 Frankfurt. ☎ **069/94-99-30.** Fax 069/94-99-31-99. E-mail: hotelamzoo@t-online.de. 85 units. TEL. 189DM ($113.40) double. Rates include continental breakfast. AE, DC, MC, V. Parking behind the hotel 6.50DM ($3.90). Closed Dec 20–Jan 5. Tram: 11, 14, or 16.

This modern hotel is bland on the outside, but welcoming on the inside. The rooms are well maintained, with simple but comfortable modern pieces; 80 contain minibars and TVs. The street-level breakfast room is the hotel's most charming feature, with linen-covered tables and stained-glass windows. Trams stop across the street.

Continental. Baselerstrasse 56, 60329 Frankfurt. ☎ **069/23-03-41.** Fax 069/23-29-14. 84 units. TV TEL. 185DM–398DM ($111–$238.80) double. Rates include buffet breakfast. AE, DC, MC, V. Parking 25DM ($15). U-Bahn: 5; S-Bahn: 1, 2, 3, 4, 5, 6, 7, or 8.

The Continental, the choice of many businesspeople, is a leader among middle-bracket hotels near the Hauptbahnhof. Founded in 1889, it enjoyed its heyday in the belle epoque era. The rooms are modern and comfortable, though the bathrooms are small. Around the corner are lively bars, but serenity prevails inside. The windows have been soundproofed to keep out traffic noise. The hotel has a pleasant restaurant, Conti, with an international cuisine.

Hotel Robert Mayer. Robert-Mayer-Strasse 44, 60486 Frankfurt. ☎ **069/970910.** Fax 069/97091010. www.frankfurt.de/hotel-robert-mayer. 11 units. TV TEL. 230DM–350DM ($131.10–$199.50) double. Rates include breakfast. AE, DC, MC, V. U-Bahn: Bockenheimer Warte.

This is one of the most artfully decorated hotels in town. It's within walking distance of Frankfurt's trade fair complex. Though the building dates from 1905, the rooms date from 1994, when the manager hired 11 lesser-known artists to each impose his or her vision on one of the bedrooms. You might find a thought-provoking jumble of furniture inspired by Frank Lloyd Wright, or an anonymous Milanese postmodernist set adjacent to pop art. Creature comforts, however, remain high. There's no restaurant on the premises, but many dining options lie within a short walk.

Hotel Westend. Westendstrasse 15, 60325 Frankfurt. ☎ **069/746-702.** Fax 069/745-396. 15 units. MINIBAR TV TEL. Mon–Thurs 230DM–290DM ($138–$174) double, Fri–Sun 180DM ($108) double; 320DM–390DM ($192–$234) doubles during trade fairs. U-Bahn: Hauptbahnhof. Free parking. AE, MC, V.

This small-scale hotel, which was built in the late 19th century, is a winner, thanks to its courtly staff and its carefully polished roster of French and German antiques. There's no restaurant on the premises, but few of the clients, many of whom seem involved in some kind of media, seem to mind—dozens of dining options lie within a short walk.

✪ **Mozart.** Parkstrasse 17 (near the Alte Oper), 60322 Frankfurt. ☎ **069/55-08-31.** Fax 069/1568061. 35 units. MINIBAR TV TEL. 220DM ($132) double, 270DM ($162) during trade fairs. Rates include buffet breakfast. AE, DC, MC, V. Closed Dec 24–Jan 1. U-Bahn: Holzhausenstrasse. Bus: 36.

Perhaps the best small hotel in Frankfurt, the Mozart stands on the periphery of the Palmengarten, right off the busy Fürstenbergerstrasse. Its marble facade is softened by curtained windows. Everything inside—walls, furniture, bed coverings—is white or pink. Bedrooms are small but comfortable. The breakfast room, with its crystal chandeliers and Louis XV-style chairs, could pass for an 18th-century salon. The staff is polite and helpful.

INEXPENSIVE

Admiral. Hölderlinstrasse 25, 60136 Frankfurt. ☎ **069/44-80-21.** Fax 069/43-94-02. 67 units. MINIBAR TV TEL. 160DM–220DM ($96–$132) double. Rates include breakfast. AE, DC, MC, V. Parking 10DM ($6). U-Bahn: 6 or 7.

The Admiral is a favorite with families, who like its location near the zoo, a short haul from the center of Frankfurt. The rooms are plainly but comfortably furnished, with a natural-wood, Scandinavian-style decor. The bathrooms are small but adequate. Only breakfast is served.

Diana. Westendstrasse 83, 60325 Frankfurt. ☎ **069/74-70-07.** Fax 069/74-70-79. 26 units. TV TEL. 167DM ($100.20) double; 220DM ($132) triple. Rates include continental breakfast. AE, DC, MC, V. Parking 8DM ($4.80). Bus: 17.

Spotless and homey, the Diana is a leader in its price class. It's a copy of a private villa, with a drawing room and an intimate breakfast salon. It's located in the Westend district on a pleasant residential street. The small bedrooms are rather lackluster but comfortable and clean. The towels are rather thin.

Falk Hotel. Falkstrasse 38A, 60487 Frankfurt. ☎ **069/70-80-94.** Fax 069/70-80-17. 32 units. MINIBAR TV TEL. 160DM–245DM ($96–$147) double. Rates include buffet breakfast. AE, DC, MC, V. Free parking.

The Falk may be stark outside, but it's still a good choice. It's located on a small quiet side street in the center of the city, near the exhibition center, the main railway station, and the university. This hotel is bright and modern but has enough traditional touches to lend warmth and coziness. The small, uncluttered guest rooms are spotlessly maintained.

Hotelschiff Peter Schlott. Mainberg, 65929 Frankfurt. ☎ **069/300-4643.** Fax 069/307-671. 19 units (all with washbasins, 10 with showers, none with toilets). 110DM–120DM ($62.70–$68.40) double without shower; 120DM–150DM ($68.40–$85.50) double with shower. Rates include breakfast. AE, DC, MC, V. S-Bahn: Höchst.

This 1950s riverboat, now permanently moored at the Frankfurt suburb of Höchst, has some of the smallest, but most evocative, hotel rooms in the area. The style evokes life at sea: Everything is tiny and cramped; mattresses are a bit thin; and bath towels are small and not particularly plush. But the unusual nature of the accommodations help soften any disagreeability, and the waters of the Main lap soothingly beneath your portholes. On the premises is a cozy, small-scale restaurant that's open daily for both lunch and dinner. You'll have to exercise caution on this ship's narrow and steep staircases. If you have enormous amounts of luggage, consider a stay in a more conventional hotel.

IN GRAVENBRUCH

✪ **Kempinski Hotel Gravenbruch Frankfurt.** Frankfurt/Neu-Isenburg, 63263. ☎ **800/426-3135** in the U.S. and Canada, or 06102/50-50. Fax 06102/50-59-00. E-mail: hgk@mail.pop-frankfurt.com. 286 units. A/C MINIBAR TV TEL. 458DM–552DM ($274.80–$331.20) double; 687DM–2,303DM ($412.20–$1,381.80) suite. AE, DC, MC, V. Free parking. Free transfers to/from the airport every half hour 7am–9pm. From the city center, it's a 20-min. taxi ride via A3 and B459 across Gravenbruch.

This place in the suburbs, only 15 minutes from the Frankfurt airport, is recommended for guests wanting to escape the bustle of a commercial setting. Here you'll find luxury combined with rural charm. The hotel is set back from Route B459 on 37 acres of parkland, complete with a lake. The structure was built on the foundation and old walls of a former manor house dating from 1568. More modern residential wings are positioned along the lakeshore, but some touches of the old country-mansion character remain, including the large atrium-style courtyards. The bedrooms are attractive and the bathrooms well maintained.

Dining/Diversions: Many in-the-know Frankfurters journey here just to sample the cuisine. The elegant and formal Restaurant Forsthaus opens onto a view of the park. The Forsthaus-Schänke has a stone-slab floor, as well as draft beer from a barrel; it's housed in what in the 16th century were horse stables. The lobby bar offers dancing to music from international entertainers.

Amenities: Room service, laundry facilities, baby-sitting, heated indoor and outdoor pools, fitness center, sauna, solarium, tennis courts, boutiques, hairdressing salon, beauty and fitness farm, massage service, hair dryers, golf and horseback riding available nearby.

4 Dining

As in most German cities, the café here is an important institution, where people read newspapers, enjoy a beer or coffee and cake, and watch the passing parade. Try **Café Laumer** at Bockenheimer Landstrasse 67, in an enviable location between the Palmengarten and the Alte Oper, where habitués often have their favorite marble-topped table. **Café Schwille,** at Grosse Bockenheimerstrasse 50, is the most famous place in Frankfurt for pastries and sweets. 250-year-old **Zur Hauptwache** is the cafe nearly everybody finds without any guidance. It's located in the heart of the Frankfurt pedestrian zone on an der Hauptwache. Sample the special beer, Römer Pilsner.

At some point in your visit, head across the Main River to the Alt-Sachsenhausen district to eat a meal and drink **apple wine,** Frankfurt's specialty.

IN THE CENTER
EXPENSIVE

Avocado Bistro. Hochstrasse 27. ☎ **069/292-867.** Reservations recommended. Main courses 36DM–42DM ($20.50–$23.95). AE, MC, V. Mon–Sat noon–2:30pm and 6–10:30pm. U-bahn: Opernplatz. FRENCH/GERMAN.

This upscale bistro has lots of fresh flowers and a battalion of formally dressed waitstaff providing impeccable service. Overall the setting is romantic and charming—it's a suitable venue for either a seduction or a sales pitch. Menu items might include such well-prepared dishes as quail breast with zucchini flowers, green beans, and a crabmeat-enhanced vinaigrette; carpaccio of tuna with soya; and fillet of pike with green asparagus and salmon-flavored caviar.

Gargantua. Liebigstrasse 47. ☎ **069/720718.** Reservations recommended. Main courses 42DM–55DM ($23.95–$31.35). Set-price lunches 49DM–120DM ($27.95–$68.40); set-price dinners 95DM–120DM ($54.15–$68.40). AE, DC, MC, V. Mon–Sat noon–1:30pm and 6:30–9:30pm. U-Bahn: Westend. GERMAN/FRENCH.

This well-managed, much-talked-about restaurant has a dining room and an outside garden, which can accommodate 30. The owner (Klaus Trebes) writes a well-known food column that appears once a week in the *Frankfurter Allgemeinerzeitung*. Menu items include roasted sea bass with an infusion of clams and artichoke hearts, blackened tuna, venison in port sauce, and anglerfish with a saffron-flavored cream sauce. Overall, this place is stylish, warm, and creative, with generous portions and an undeniable culinary zeal.

Premiere. In the Arabella Sheraton Grand Hotel, Konrad-Adenauer-Strasse 7. ☎ **069/2-98-11-72.** Reservations recommended. Main courses 36DM–68DM ($21.60–$40.80); fixed-price menus 95DM–130DM ($57–$78). AE, DC, MC, V. Mon–Fri noon–2:30pm; daily 6:30–10:30pm. U-Bahn: Konstablerwache. FRENCH/ITALIAN.

One of Frankfurt's most stylish and elegant restaurants lies just above the lobby level of this previously recommended five-star hotel. Mirrors and polished cherry wood adorn the dining room, a favorite of the city's industrial and financial moguls. The chefs call their style *cuisine vitale,* stressing healthful and succulent preparations of fresh ingredients, artfully presented. Examples include liaison of salmon and John Dory with rice in chervil sauce, and a "composition of seafood" featuring several fish and shellfish, served with leaf spinach and two sauces. The dessert menu is appropriately elegant; a particular favorite is the Irish-coffee tart.

✪ **Weinhaus Brückenkeller.** Schützenstrasse 6. ☎ **069/29-80-07-0.** Reservations required. Main courses 39DM–50DM ($23.40–$30). AE, DC, MC, V. Mon–Sat 6:30–11pm. Closed Dec 20–Jan 8. U-Bahn: 1, 2, or 3. GERMAN/INTERNATIONAL.

Weinhaus Brückenkeller, in the heart of the Altstadt, is one of Frankfurt's leading restaurants and a favorite spot of well-heeled North American visitors. Tables are candlelit, and strolling musicians encourage singing. Here the age of Bismarck lives again. Franconian carvings adorn the alcoves, and huge wooden barrels are decorated with scenes from Goethe's *Faust*. The food is light and subtle. A typical meal might begin with cream of sorrel soup or more substantial roast goose liver with green beans, followed by saddle of venison or young lamb. For a perfect finish, you might order a soufflé of strawberries with vanilla sauce. The *Tafelspitz* (boiled beef) is the best in town. The evening meal includes homemade sourdough bread. The wine cellar holds an excellent collection of German wines, 180 in all, including the best from the Rhineland. Personal attention and efficient service are hallmarks.

MODERATE

Jewel of India. Wilhelm-Hauff Strasse 5. ☎ **069/752375.** Reservations recommended. Main courses 15DM–70DM ($8.55–$39.90); set menus 40DM–80DM ($22.80–$45.60). AE, MC, V. Sun–Fri 11:30am–2:30pm; daily 5:30–11:30pm. U-bahn: U6 or U7 to Westend or Messe. INDIAN.

The decor here includes ornate carvings around the windows and black and white paintings accented with semi-precious gemstones. The main draw, however, is the savory Indian cuisine, which includes lots of vegetarian choices, as well as tandoori chicken in a saffron-yogurt marinade, and slow-cooked lamb with cumin and coriander.

Steinernes Haus. Braubachstrasse 35 (around the corner from the Rathaus). ☎ **069/ 28-34-91.** Main courses 20DM–49.50DM ($12–$29.70); daily platters 15DM–20DM ($9–$12). V. Daily 11am–11pm. Tram: 11. GERMAN.

The 500-year-old Steinernes Haus, in the historic heart of Frankfurt, was restored simply and unpretentiously after the war. Locals come here for the good German beer, along with hearty rib-sticking fare. The daily main-dish specialty also includes salad and potatoes. Other choices include a selection of sausages, beef fillet, and such popular German dishes as *Zigeunerhackbraten* (spicy meat loaf) and *Frankfurter Rippchen* (smoked pork). The best choice is a fillet steak cooked on a hot plate right at your table.

INEXPENSIVE

Churrasco. Domplatz 6. ☎ **069/28-48-04.** Reservations recommended. Main courses 15DM–25DM ($9–$15). AE, DC, MC, V. Daily 11am–11:30pm. U-Bahn: 4, 5. ARGENTINE.

Churrasco is where Frankfurters go for succulent Argentinean beefsteak, the best cuts in town. A red sign with a steer marks this dimly lit tavern. Menu items include delicious fillet or T-bone steaks and several styles of grilled salmon and jumbo shrimp. Lower-priced orders of rump steak are also available. All cuts are charcoal grilled to your specifications. Rounding out the menu are fresh salads and a limited list of desserts.

Gilde Stuben. Bleichstrasse 38A. ☎ 069/283-228. Reservations recommended. Main courses 9.90DM–24.90DM ($5.65–$14.20). AE, DC, MC, V. Daily 11am–midnight. U-Bahn: Eschenheimer Turm.

Virtually every member of Frankfurt's Czech and Slovak communities knows about this Bohemian beer tavern, where portions are generous and excellent beer flows constantly. Try the sauerbraten or the *Schweinbraten,* both of which will be accompanied with potatoes and sauerkraut, and a traditional Czech staple known as *Svickova,* consisting of smoked beef in cream sauce with cranberries and dumplings. Mugs of beer, including Budweiser and Pilsner Urquell from the tap, cost 4.50DM ($2.55) each.

Mövenpick am Opernplatz. Opernplatz 2. ☎ 069/2-06-80. Reservations recommended. Main courses 13.50DM–32.50DM ($8.10–$19.50). AE, DC, MC, V. Mon–Sat 8am–11pm, Sun 11am–11pm. U-Bahn: 6, 7 to Hausen. SWISS/FRENCH.

This busy member of a Swiss-owned restaurant chain is clean, efficient, and bustling, partly because of a central location in the commercial heart of Frankfurt, and partly because of a well-maintained setting, good value, and reasonable prices. Within the busy premises you'll find three different areas: a simulation of an outdoor terrace, an informal spot with leather banquettes and a look like a French bistro, and an area that pays homage to the art deco heyday of Hollywood. Try the antipasti buffet, a lavish display containing salads, marinated fish and vegetables, guacamole, small tarts, and an herb-laden roster of Italian dishes; a small platter is 15DM ($9), a large is 20DM ($12). There's also a large selection of salads and pastas, roast rib of Angus beef with horseradish cream sauce, scampi in bordelaise sauce, and more. Everything is competently prepared, but not exactly exciting.

Zum Bitburger. Hochstrasse 54 (near the Alte Oper). ☎ **069/28-03-02.** Reservations required. Main courses 15.50DM–35DM ($9.30–$21). AE, DC, MC, V. Mon–Fri 11:30am–1am. Closed July 16–25. CONTINENTAL.

This brewery-operated restaurant has a long and proud tradition. Waiters somehow manage to slip through the crowds with mugs of beer and hearty platters of food. The standard but well-prepared dishes include grilled rump steak, goulash, and sausages with red cabbage and home-fried potatoes. You can begin with the soup of the day, and there's always a fresh seasonal salad. The kitchen serves hot food until midnight.

IN ALT-SACHSENHAUSEN

Alt-Sachsenhausen has been called the most Frankfurt-ish neighborhood in the city, but now that the main street, Schweizerstrasse, is filled with bistros, cafes, and boutiques catering to tourists, some of the old character is gone. Nonetheless, it remains an interesting place, especially for its many apple-wine taverns.

Bistrot 77. Ziegelhüttenweg 1 (less than a mile from the city center), Frankfurt-Sachsenhausen. ☎ **069/61-40-40.** Reservations required. Main courses 38DM–52DM ($22.80–$31.20); fixed-price meals 60DM ($36); "menu surprise" 120DM ($72). AE, MC, V. Mon–Fri noon–2pm; Mon–Sat 7–10pm. Closed Dec 24–Jan 6. Bus: 62. Tram: 16. FRENCH/ALSATIAN.

Bistrot 77 is one of the most chic of Frankfurt's restaurants. The overall impression is one of light and glass, with a black-and-white tile floor and an airy latticework ceiling. In summer, tables are set on the terrace. Dominique and Guy Mosbach, two French citizens, have made a name for themselves with their contemporary cuisine, a frequently changing array of imaginatively prepared fish and meat dishes, along with intriguing appetizers and desserts.

Die Gans in Sachsenhausen. Schweizerstrasse 76. ☎ **069/62-26-25.** Reservations recommended. Main courses 29DM–40DM ($17.40–$24); fixed-price menus 68DM–98DM ($40.80–$58.80). AE, DC, MC, V. Mon–Sat 6–11pm. Closed Dec 23–Jan 5. U-Bahn: Schweizer Platz. CONTINENTAL/GAME.

Stylish, sophisticated, and relatively casual, this is a refreshing tribute to the combined cuisines of Europe, with a special emphasis on the game dishes that have always been dear to Frankfurt residents. In the intimate, bistrolike dining room, you'll be offered a choice of such dishes as zesty fish soup with strips of smoked salmon; mousse of smoked ham; venison and rabbit; North Atlantic lobster; fish ravioli with spinach sauce; and a perfectly cooked roast rack of lamb with Provençale herbs.

Jaspers. Schifferstrasse 8 (near Affentorplatz), Sachsenhausen. ☎ **069/614-117.** Reservations recommended. Main courses 18DM–38DM ($10.25–$21.65); set-price menu 31DM ($17.65). AE, DC, MC, V. Mon–Sat 6pm–1am. Train 16 or 17 from the Frankfurt Hauptbahnhof to Localbahnhof Sachsenhausen. CONTINENTAL.

This stylish, international bistro is lined with mirrors and art nouveau accessories, with vague references to the bistros of Lyon. The food is more Germanic than French, but still has some Mediterranean overtones. You might try the fish soup, or the snails prepared in calvados and served over a bed of spinach, or the excellent Wiener schnitzel. The roasted lamb is especially succulent as well.

Family-Friendly Restaurants

Churrasco (*see p. 425*)   Kids delight in the atmosphere of the *pampas* at this Argentine restaurant. Children's portions are available.

Zum Gemalten Haus (*see below*)   You can dine early at this apple-wine tavern, where children will discover some of the biggest and tastiest franks they've ever eaten.

THE APPLE-WINE TAVERNS (APFELWEINSTUBEN)

In these taverns you drink local apple wine (like hard cider), which many locals enjoy and many foreigners consider a cousin to vinegar. Our verdict: It's an acquired taste. Tradition says that you won't like the apple wine until you've had three big steins. After that, what does taste matter? Other apple-wine taverns, besides those listed below, include **Mutter Ernst,** Alte Rothofstrasse 12 (☎ 069/28-38-22), and **Apfelwein-wirtschaft Wagner,** Schweizerstrasse 71 (☎ 069/61-25-65).

Germania. Textorstrasse 16, Sachsenhausen. ☎ **069/613-336.** Reservations not accepted. Main courses 7.80DM–25DM ($4.45–$14.25). No credit cards. Daily noon–2pm and 5–10pm. Train 16 or 17 from the Frankfurt Hauptbahnhof to Localbahnhof Sachsenhausen. GERMAN.

Those searching for local authenticity will thrill to the coziness and warmth of this old-fashioned apple wine house, where hearty portions and genuine earthiness are a way of life. Don't even think about ordering beer here, as it simply isn't served. The drink of choice is tart and pungent apple wine, served at 2.80DM ($1.60) per glass. You'll consume it elbow-to-elbow with fellow diners at long trestle tables, probably amid lots of cigarette smoke and conviviality. Menu items include a roster of sausages, as well as herb-enriched pork ribs *(Rippchen mit Kraut)* and a salty version of cheese with onions *(Handkäse mit Musik)* that invariably inspires you to order more drink. Friday night brings fresh fish, especially catfish and whiting, usually served with parsley butter sauce.

Zum Gemalten Haus. Schweizerstrasse 67. ☎ **069/61-45-59.** Reservations recommended. Main courses 10DM–25DM ($6–$15). No credit cards. Wed–Sun 10am–midnight. Tram: 16. HESSIAN.

Chances are you'll share a table here with other patrons, perhaps in the garden if the weather is fair. The kitchen provides ample portions of good Hessian cooking. If you're in a group, try the "Frankfurter Platte," which usually includes liver pâté, blood sausage, the chef's special Frankfurter Wurst, sauerkraut, and perhaps knockwurst with sauerkraut or potato salad. The *Eisbein,* or pork knuckle with mashed potatoes, washed down with apple wine, is the cook's specialty. The apple wine is homemade.

Zum Grauen Bock. Grosse Rittergasse 30–45. ☎ **069/61-80-26.** Reservations recommended. Main courses 14DM–42DM ($8.40–$25.20); 3-course fixed-price menu 25DM–38DM ($15–$22.80). AE, MC, V. Mon–Sat 5pm–1am. U-Bahn: Lokalbahnhof. GERMAN.

Sometimes the communal singing here is so robust that it's necessary to slide back the roof on a summer night. An accordionist goes from table to table, involving everyone in the singing. Featured on the menu is cheese with vinegar, oil, and onions *(Handkas mit Musik),* but you may want to leave the subtle pleasures of this dish to the locals. Instead, try a German specialty, the huge pork shank with sauerkraut and boiled potatoes *(Schweinshaxen).* A good beginning is the liver dumpling soup or the goulash soup.

IN WESTEND

Erno's Bistro. Liebigstrasse 15 (between the Alte Oper and the Palmengarten). ☎ **069/ 72-19-97.** Reservations required. Main courses 48DM–56DM ($28.80–$33.60); business menu 50DM ($30); fixed-price menu 125DM ($75); special dinner with wine 175DM ($105). AE, DC, MC, V. Mon–Fri noon–2pm and 7–10pm. Closed mid-June to mid-July. U-Bahn: 6 or 7 to Westend. FRENCH.

Erno's, a chic midtown rendezvous, draws everybody from visiting film stars to bank executives. This small place with an English-speaking staff offers fine service and appointments, plus a commendable cuisine that seems to improve year after year. The kitchen serves only fish brought fresh by air from European waters. The chef offers both *cuisine moderne* and what is known as *cuisine formidable*. The most exciting (and expensive) appetizer is a version of foie gras. For a main course, we'd suggest the grilled brill, whose flesh is very delicate and light, served with a rare type of mushroom. Another excellent choice is fillet of venison coated with truffles and served with a smooth and creamy savoy cabbage.

✪ **Humperdinck.** Grüneburgweg 95 (near the Palmengarten). ☎ **069/97-20-31-55.** Reservations required. Main courses 48DM–65DM ($27.35–$37.05); fixed-price dinners 145DM–165DM ($87–$99); fixed-price lunch 49DM ($29.40). AE, DC, V. Mon–Fri noon–2pm and Mon–Sat 7–10pm. Closed July–Aug 3. INTERNATIONAL.

If you can afford it, there's no better table waiting for you in Frankfurt today. The setting at this elegant *Neuer Kuche* restaurant is classical, refined, and dignified. Dress as you would to a wedding. The place, by the way, is named not after the British pop singer, but after the composer Engelbert Humperdinck, who once lived at this fashionable address in the western sector of Frankfurt. Patron Alfred Friedrich is clearly a master chef, familiar with cuisines worldwide but thoroughly determined to make his own culinary statement. There is a short à la carte menu, but the set meals are clearly the showcase of the evening. You might see on the menu scampi in truffle sauce with fresh truffles, a rich herb soup with butter croutons, a salmon Schnitzel with vegetable risotto, or even couscous.

IN HEILIGENSTOCK

Altes Zollhaus. Friedberger Landstrasse 531, in Heiligenstock (4½ miles north of Frankfurt). ☎ **069/472-707.** Reservations recommended. Main courses 27DM–38DM ($15.40–$21.65). Set menus 55DM ($31.35). AE, DC, MC, V. Tues–Sun 6–10:30pm. Bus: 30 to Heiligenstock. GERMAN.

This restaurant is set within a 235-year-old half-timbered structure that was originally a tollhouse. Within its timbered and nostalgically antique-looking premises, you can enjoy relatively formal meals whose ingredients change with the seasons. Between October and February, expect a rich assortment of game dishes, especially venison and pheasant, usually cooked with wine sauce and herbs. In spring, look for different combinations of asparagus dishes, including an "asparagus cocktail" garnished with strips of ham and vinaigrette sauce. During warm weather, additional seating is set up within the garden.

5 Attractions

When bombs rained on Frankfurt in 1944, nearly all the old half-timbered buildings were leveled. In what might have been a record reconstruction, however, residents of Frankfurt rebuilt their city into a fine mélange of modern and traditional architecture and faithfully restored some of their most prized old buildings as well.

THE ALTSTADT

The Altstadt centers around three Gothic buildings with stepped gables, known collectively as the **Römer,** Römerberg (☎ 069/21-23-48-14). These houses were originally built between 1288 and 1305 and bought by the city a century later for use as the Rathaus. The second floor of the center house is the **Imperial Hall (Kaisersaal),** lined with the romanticized portraits of 52 emperors; 13 of them celebrated their coronation banquets here. You can visit this hall daily from 10am to 1pm and 2 to 5pm. An hourly tour costing 3DM ($1.80) is obligatory. Tickets can be purchased at the entrance to the Römer.

The elaborate facade of the Römer, with its ornate balcony and statues of four emperors, overlooks **Römerberg Square.** On festive occasions in days gone by, the square was the scene of oxen roasts that featured flowing wine. Today, unfortunately, the Fountain of Justitia pours forth only water, but oxen are still roasted on special occasions.

The dominant feature of the Altstadt is the 15th-century red-sandstone tower of the **Dom St. Bartholomäus,** Domplatz 14 (☎ 069/29703236), in whose chapel the emperors of the Holy Roman Empire were elected and crowned for nearly 300 years. In the cloister of the church is the **Dom Museum** (☎ 069/28-92-29), which exhibits robes of the imperial electors. It's open Tuesday to Friday from 10am to 5pm and Saturday and Sunday from 11am to 5pm. Admission is 2DM ($1.20) for adults and 1DM (60¢) for children.

Alte Nikolaikirche (Old Nicholas Church), Römerberg (☎ 069/292449), is a historic church across from the Rathaus. Originally, it was a court chapel; after the 15th century it served as the church for the city fathers. Today, it's home to the Lutheran St. Paul's congregation. Inside are ancient gravestones as well as a copy of a medieval sculpture, Schmerzensmann, dating from 1370. Outside are Gothic sandstone sculptures portraying St. Nicholas. The 40-bell Glockenspiel plays at 9:05am, 12:05pm, and 5:05pm; a church hymn and a German folk song are played. A number of materials in English, including a church guide and a free walking map, are available at the information table in the church. A musical vespers service is held each Wednesday evening during the summer months (English-German) from 5:30 to 6:30pm, with tea, cookies, and conversation afterward to the accompaniment of the organ. The church is open daily from 10am to 8pm (in winter to 6pm). An American pastor on staff is available to answer questions and give free tours, including a trip to the roof gallery, and to help travelers needing advice or those in emergency situations. Contact the church office just across from the church.

At the northern edge of the Altstadt is **An der Hauptwache,** named for the old guard house *(Hauptwache)* which stands upon it. This square is the heart of modern Frankfurt. Underneath is the main U-Bahn station with a modern shopping promenade.

MUSEUMS

✪ **Goethe-Haus.** Grosser Hirschgraben 23–25. ☎ **069/13-88-00.** Admission 7DM ($4.20) adults, 3DM ($1.80) students, 2DM ($1.20) children. Apr–Sept Mon–Fri 9am–6pm; Sat, Sun, and holidays 10am–4pm. Oct–Mar Mon–Fri 9am–4pm; Sat, Sun, and holidays 10am–4pm. U-Bahn or S-Bahn: Hauptwache.

This house, where Goethe was born in 1749, has been a shrine for Goethe enthusiasts since it opened to the public in 1863. One observer wrote that the postwar restoration was carried out "with loving care and damn-the-expense craftsmanship." The house is decorated in various styles, all reflecting the fashion trends of the 18th century: neoclassical, baroque, and rococo. You can view the library, where Goethe's father worked and often watched the street for the return of his son. A portrait of the severe-looking gentleman hangs behind the door of his wife's room.

On the second floor is an unusual astronomical clock built around 1749 and repaired in 1949 to run for another 200 years. One room contains a picture gallery with paintings collected by Goethe's father. These works, mainly by contemporary Frankfurt artists, influenced Goethe's artistic views for a great part of his life. The poet's rooms contain one of his most important childhood possessions, the puppet theater, which played a significant role in his novel *Wilhelm Meister.*

Annexed to the house is the **Frankfurter Goethe-Museum.** This museum contains a library of 120,000 volumes and a collection of about 30,000 manuscripts, as well as 16,000 graphic artworks and 400 paintings associated in some way with Goethe and his works.

✪ **Liebieghaus.** Schaumainkai 71. ☎ **069/21-23-86-17.** Admission 5DM ($3) adults, 2.50DM ($1.50) seniors, students, and children. Tues and Thurs–Sun 10am–5pm, Wed 10am–8pm. Tram: 16 from the Hauptbahnhof to Otto-Hahn-Platz.

This sculpture museum stands alongside the Bargello in Florence as one of the most important in Europe. The building is an 1896 villa. Its collection includes objects from ancient Egypt, classical Greece and Rome, and medieval and renaissance Europe. Highlights include a small bronze horse from the 8th century B.C., and Roman copies of earlier Grecian works, such as the *Torso* of Polycletus, Praxiteles's *Satyr,* and Myron's *Athena.* Although the most ancient artifacts generate the most excitement, the medieval section is also fascinating. Look for the *Virgin and Child* created in Trier in the 11th century, the head of Bärbel von Ottenheim (attributed to van Leyden in 1462), the Riemenschneider *Madonna,* Andrea della Robbia's altarpiece of the Assumption, and the 16th-century *Black Venus with Mirror.*

✪ **Städel Gallery.** Schaumainkai 63 (on the south bank of the Main). ☎ **069/6-05-09-80.** Admission 10DM ($6) adults, 8DM ($4.80) children 6–16, 3DM ($1.80) children 5 and under, free for everyone Wed. Tues and Thurs–Sun 10am–5pm, Wed 10am–8pm. U-Bahn: 1, 2, or 3 to Schweizer Platz.

This is Frankfurt's most important art gallery, containing a fine collection of most European schools of painting. The first floor features French impressionists such as Renoir and Monet, along with German painters of the 19th and 20th centuries. Note in particular Ernst Ludwig Kirchner's *Nude Woman with Hat.* Also on the first floor is Johann Heinrich Wilhelm Tischbein's portrait of Goethe in the Campagna in Italy. But if you're short on time, go directly to the second floor to view the outstanding collection of Flemish primitives, 17th-century Dutch artists, and German 16th-century masters such as Dürer, Grünewald, Memling, Elsheimer, and many others. One of the most impressive paintings is Jan van Eyck's *Madonna* (1433). Lucas Cranach is represented by a large winged altarpiece and his rather impish nude Venus. Recent acquisitions include Jean Antoine Watteau's *L'Ile de Cythère* (1709). In the Department of Modern Art are works by Bacon, Dubuffet, Tapiès, and Yves Klein.

Deutsches Filmmuseum (German Film Museum). Schaumainkai 41, at the corner of Schweizerstrasse. ☎ **069/21-23-88-30.** Admission 5DM ($3) adults, 2.50DM ($1.50) students, 3DM ($1.80) children; film screenings 8DM ($4.80) adults, 6DM ($3.60) students and children. Tues, Thurs, Fri, and Sun 10am–5pm, Wed 10am–8pm, Sat 2–8pm. U-Bahn: 1, 2, or 3 to Schweizer Platz.

This is the finest film museum in Germany. Old films from the collection are shown continuously on the second floor. The rooms downstairs chronicle the history of the filmmaking industry. Exhibits include Emile Reynaud's 1882 Praxinoscope, Edison's Kinetoscope from 1889, and a copy of the Lumière brothers' Cinematograph from

1895. There are also models illustrating how special effects are shot, including those in *King Kong*.

Deutsches Architekturmuseum. Schaumainkai 43. ☎ **069/21-23-88-44.** Admission 8DM ($4.80) adults, free for children. Tues and Thurs–Sun 10am–5pm, Wed 10am–8pm. U-Bahn: 1, 2, or 3 to Schweizer Platz.

Like the film museum, this museum is the best of its kind in Germany. Exhibits trace the saga of architecture from the Sumerians to today's most modern statements. The displays are arranged in what has been called "a house within a house," that is, a series of intimate galleries encased in a villa. The permanent collection consists of some two dozen commissioned large-scale models, but these are not always on view, since floor space is often needed for temporary exhibitions.

Museum für Kunsthandwerk. Schaumainkai 17. ☎ **069/21-23-40-37.** Admission 8DM ($4.80) adults, 4DM ($2.40) students and children over 5. Tues and Thurs–Sun 10am–5pm, Wed 10am–8pm. U-Bahn: Schweizer Platz.

Frankfurt's Museum of Applied Arts is part of the Museumsufer, a row of museums along the Schaumainkai on the southern bank of the Main. More than 30,000 objects, ranging across Europe and Asia, are exhibited here. Two buildings house the collection: a 19th-century villa and 1985 structure designed by New York architect Richard Meier. The museum has an outstanding collection of German rococo furnishings (called *Mainzer Meistermöbel*) created in Mainz. The glassware is a highlight, with some Venetian pieces from the 15th century. On the second floor, the Far East and Islamic department has a rich collection of Persian carpets and faïence dating from the 9th century. One of Germany's finest porcelain collections is here as well.

Museum für Moderne Kunst. Domstrasse 10 (in the center of the Innenstadt, near Römerberg). ☎ 069/21-23-04-47. Admission 7DM ($4.20) adults, 3.50DM ($2.10) for students and children, free for everyone Wed. Tues and Thurs–Sun 10am–5pm, Wed 10am–8pm. U-Bahn: Rümer. Tram: 11 to Domstrasse.

This museum opened in 1991 in a building created by Hans Hollein, the Viennese architect. The structure is designed like a boat, but in spite of its somewhat bizarre shape, the gallery has a bright, spacious air. (Some unkind critics have claimed that the dazzling architecture is more interesting than the exhibits.) Major artists since the 1950s are displayed here, including Roy Lichtenstein (see his *Brush-stroke)* and George Segal, with his *Jazz Combo.* Modern German artists include George Flintzer, Inge Rambow, August Sambe, Gerhard Richter, and others.

THE PALMENGARTEN

The Palmengarten, Siesmayerstrasse 61 (☎ **069/21-23-39-39**), is a park and a botanical garden. During the last decade, the gardens have been renewed and the conservatories and historic greenhouses completely reconstructed. You can admire a perennial garden, an expanded rock garden, and a beautiful rose garden. The 1869 palm house is now surrounded by a huge gallery that serves as an exhibition hall for flower shows and other botanical exhibitions. In recent years new conservatories have been added: The Tropicarium is a complex for tropical vegetation; the Subantarctic House displays plants from southern Chile, Argentina, and New Zealand; and the Entrance Conservatory houses insectivorous plants and bromeliads. Collections of orchids, palms, succulents, water lilies, and many others are also on display.

Admission to the botanical garden is 7DM ($4.20) for adults and 3DM ($1.80) for children, or 15DM ($9) for a family ticket. It's open March through September daily from 9am to 6pm, October and February daily from 9am to 5pm, and November through January daily 9am to 4pm. (U-Bahn 6 or 7 to Westendstrasse. Bus: 36.) In the park area, there's a small lake where people can row boats. In summer, concerts are given in the band shell; evening events include open-air dancing, jazz, and fountain illumination. There are some facilities for food.

ESPECIALLY FOR KIDS

Children love the **Palmengarten** (see above). Take along a picnic (**Hertie,** at An der Zeil 390, has a good deli), and then rent a rowboat and take the kids on an excursion. Another option is the **Senckenberg Museum of Natural History,** Senckenberg-anlage 25 (☎ **069/7-54-20**), which has an interesting collection of fossils, including dinosaur bones. Admission is 7DM ($4.20) for adults, 3DM ($1.80) for students and children over 3, and free for children 2 and under. Open daily from 9am to 5pm. Children will also enjoy the circus performances at the **Tiger Palast,** Heiligkreuzgasse 16–20 (☎ **069/2-89-69**), which include jugglers, acrobats, and magic acts.

Another interesting possibility is **Struwwelpeter Museum,** Schirm am Römerberg (☎ **069/28-13-33**), which is dedicated to memorabilia associated with one of Germany's most famous children's books, *Struwwelpeter ("Slovenly Peter")*. The story was written and illustrated by a local doctor, Heinrich Hoffman (1798–1874), who opened the first hospital for neurology in Frankfurt. His Slovenly Peter character gained popularity in the United States after Mark Twain translated Hoffman's work into English. On the premises is a museum shop selling posters, postcards, and actual copies of the Struwwelpeter books translated into many different languages. The museum is open Tuesday to Sunday from 11am to 5pm; during July and August, it remains open on Wednesday till 8pm. Entrance is free. The kindly staff members are strictly volunteer.

✪ **Zoologischer Garten.** Alfred-Brehm-Platz 16. ☎ **069/21-23-37-35.** Admission 11DM ($6.60) adults, 5DM ($3) children 6–17, free for children 5 and under. Oct–Mar daily 9am–5pm; Apr–Sept daily 9am–7pm. U-Bahn: 6 or 7.

This zoo is intent on education as well as entertainment, and proves interesting for both young and old. Most animals are in enclosures resembling their native habitats. One of the best examples is the African Veldt Enclosure, landscaped with hills and bushes; antelopes and ostriches roam freely. In the Exotarium, fish and various reptiles live under special climatic conditions. Penguins swim and dive in an artificially cooled polar landscape. There's also an aviary where you can watch birds preparing unusual nests. The building for small mammals, with its nocturnal section, is one of the largest and most diversified of its kind in the world.

Walking Tour—Frankfurt: From Medieval to Modern

Start: Alte Oper (Opera House).
Finish: Goethe-Haus.
Time: 90 minutes.
When to go: Avoid rush hours (Monday to Saturday 8 to 9:30am and 4:30 to 6:30pm).

Despite its modern skyscrapers and daunting traffic, Frankfurt contains charming sights best appreciated on foot. Begin your tour at the:

1. **Alte Oper,** the old opera house, constructed in 1880, destroyed by incendiary bombs in 1944, and rebuilt in 1981. Its portico affords sweeping views of the city.

From Opernplatz's southeast corner, follow Fressgasse, a street lined with specialty food shops, taverns, and cafes. Within 5 blocks, turn left on Börsenstrasse, where, on the right side of the street, you'll see the:

Walking Tour: Frankfurt from Medieval to Modern

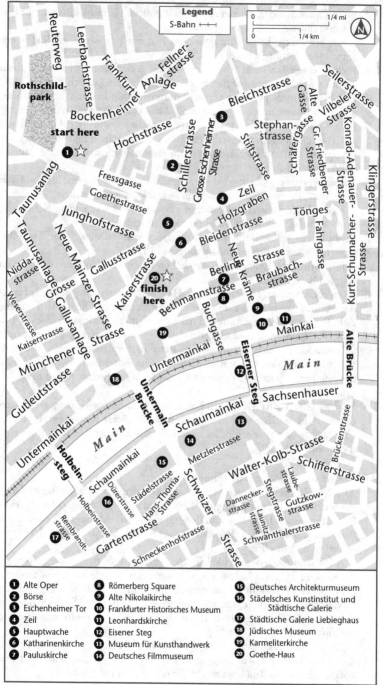

Legend
S-Bahn ├──┤

❶ Alte Oper	❽ Römerberg Square
❷ Börse	❾ Alte Nikolaikirche
❸ Eschenheimer Tor	❿ Frankfurter Historisches Museum
❹ Zeil	⓫ Leonhardskirche
❺ Hauptwache	⓬ Eiserner Steg
❻ Katharinenkirche	⓭ Museum für Kunsthandwerk
❼ Pauluskirche	⓮ Deutsches Filmmuseum

⓯ Deutsches Architekturmuseum
⓰ Städelsches Kunstinstitut und Städtische Galerie
⓱ Städtische Galerie Liebieghaus
⓲ Jüdisches Museum
⓳ Karmeliterkirche
⓴ Goethe-Haus

2. **Börse** (Stock Market), where the economic pulse of Germany throbs to the beat of world finance.

  Just beyond the Börse, turn right onto Taubenstrasse, which will lead to one of the oldest fortified gates of Frankfurt, the:

3. **Eschenheimer Tor.** From here, head southeast along Stiftstrasse, which in about a block will intersect one of the city's legendary shopping streets:

4. **Zeil.** Explore its shops (which at this point run in either direction) at your leisure, but for the moment, turn right and walk 2 blocks until you reach the:

5. **Hauptwache,** a single-story 18th-century building originally constructed as a jail. The adjacent square serves as the public transportation hub of the city. On the square's southern edge rises one of the most noteworthy Protestant churches of Frankfurt, the:

6. **Katharinekirche,** reconstructed after damage from Allied bombs in World War II. In 1522, the first Protestant sermon in Frankfurt was given here.

  After admiring the church's somber grandeur, head south along Kornmarkt, then east along Berliner Strasse to the rounded walls of the:

7. **Pauluskirche,** whose 18th-century walls (redesigned and rebuilt after World War II) were the site of a revolutionary congress in 1848.

  Just beyond the Pauluskirche, turn left on Buchgasse. Very soon, you'll see on your left hand side the larger expanse of:

8. **Römerberg Square.** The Römer (City Hall) at the center of the square is Frankfurt's official symbol. It's composed of three separate buildings (Alt Limpurg, Zum Römer, and Löwenstein) and has a symmetrical facade and an ornate balcony. The Römer was used for ceremonial, commercial, and political functions for centuries. The elegant 16th-century statue in the plaza represents Justice. At the 1612 coronation of Emperor Matthias, wine instead of water flowed from this fountain, a grace note that almost caused a riot as citizens rushed to drink.

☕ **TAKE A BREAK**   You'll find cafes and taverns at virtually every street corner of this walking tour, but your best bet is **Römer Restaurant,** inside the City Hall building, which offers typical Frankfurt dishes and wine from city-owned vineyards.

  After your snack, stop to admire the massive:

9. **Alte Nikolaikirche** (Church of St. Nicholas), rising from the southern edge of the square. It was built during the 12th century as a royal chapel for the Holy Roman emperors. In front is a carillon (Glockenspiel) that rings out every day at 9am, noon, and 5pm. Local citizens set their watches by these chimes. It's worthwhile to stop by to listen.

  A few steps south of the Nikolaikirche, set against the river quays, is the:

10. **Frankfurter Historisches Museum,** which contains scale models of medieval Frankfurt as well as exhibits covering city life from the 1500s to today. The displays of antique silver are especially noteworthy. The medieval fortifications near the riverbank adjacent to the museum once controlled access from the river to the town center.

  About half a block east rise the dignified walls of the:

11. **Leonhardskirche,** a well-maintained building. Parts of the building (most notably, the porch) date from the 1200s; others from the 1500s.

  Take this opportunity to cross over one of Germany's most important rivers, the Main, by traversing the all-pedestrian:

12. Eisener Steg (iron bridge). From its center, you'll appreciate the contrast between medieval and modern Frankfurt. On the southern bank of the Main at this point is the ancient district of Sachsenhausen. Turn right at the far end of the bridge and walk west along Schaumainkai, a tree-lined traffic artery and pedestrian walkway parallel to the south bank. You might want to return for an extended visit later. You'll pass the following museums:

13. Museum für Kunsthandwerk (Museum of Applied Arts), at no. 17, containing exhibits of virtually every handcraft of Europe and Asia. Less than a block to the west is the:

14. Deutsches Filmmuseum, at no. 41, whose exhibits celebrate Germany's fascinating film industry. A short distance to the west is the:

15. Deutsches Architekturmuseum (Museum of German Architecture), at no. 43, with notable displays on the evolution of German architecture. Slightly farther west is the:

16. Städelsches Kunstinstitut und Städtische Galerie (Städel Art Institute and Municipal Gallery), at no. 63, whose august premises shelter an impressive collection of German, Italian, Flemish, and Dutch old masters. A short walk west is the:

17. Städtische Galerie Liebieghaus, at no. 71, originally a private villa built in the 1600s, whose collection of sculpture is one of the best in Germany. Some pieces are displayed in the garden.

Now, backtrack east along Schaumainkai and cross to the northern end of the Untermain Bridge. At the west corner of the bridge's northern terminus rises the:

18. Jüdisches Museum (Jewish Museum), Untermainkai 15, housed in the former Rothschild Palace. Its library and exhibitions spotlight the city's former Jewish population—before World War II it was the second largest in Germany, after Berlin's.

Now, walk east along the river's northern bank, along Untermainkai. Turn left at the first narrow street (little more than an alleyway) and cut almost immediately right onto the somewhat wider Mainzer Gasse. Within a few steps (turn left onto Münzgasse to find its entrance), you'll see the somber masonry walls of the:

19. Karmeliterkirche (Carmelite Church and Monastery). Inside is the largest religious fresco north of the Alps. It was painted in the 1500s by Jörg Ratgeb, who was tortured to death soon after its completion because of his involvement in the Peasant Revolt of 1535. Deconsecrated in 1803, the building now houses the city archives and a small museum devoted to the prehistoric era.

Continue walking north along Münzgasse, crossing through a confusing intersection of east-west streets. (Among them will be both Bethmannstrasse and Berliner Strasse, although from your vantage point their union might resemble nothing more than a giant traffic junction.) Walk north along the first street that intersects Berliner Strasse (Grosser Hirschgraben). Within less than a block, you'll arrive at the building from which Frankfurters draw much of their civic pride, the:

20. Goethe-Haus, Grosser Hirschgraben 23–25. Born here in 1749, Johann Wolfgang von Goethe went on to write the greatest poetry in the German language. Although destroyed during World War II, the building has been reconstructed to look almost exactly as it did when young Goethe played here as a child.

6 Sports & Outdoor Pursuits

BICYCLING   Bicycles can be rented from **Holger's Rad-Laden,** Eschersheimer Landstrasse 470 (☎ **069/522004**), for 15DM ($9) per day.

FITNESS CENTERS & HEALTH CLUBS Many major hotels in Frankfurt maintain health clubs, but if yours doesn't, consider a day ticket to one of the semiprivate health clubs such as **Fitness Company,** Taubenstrasse 9 (☎ **069/28-05-65**), **Sport Fabrik,** Ginnheimerstrasse 47 (☎ **069/970-7210**), or **Sportschule Petrescu,** Bleichstrasse 55–57 (☎ **069/29-59-06**). All three offer roughly equivalent arrays of exercise machines, free weights, saunas, and massage facilities. A day pass ranges from 40DM to 110DM ($24 to $66), depending on what facilities you want to use.

GOLF Golf Anlage im Frankfurter Waldstadion, Morfelder Landstrasse 362, 60528 Frankfurt (☎ **069/69-80-40**), located with the city limits, is open to all. This course has nine holes, plus a floodlit driving range. Open daily from 8am to 8pm.

ICE-SKATING Between November and April, you can skate at the **Eissporthalle,** am Bornheimer Hang 4, Ratsweg (☎ **069/21-23-08-25**). Open Monday to Friday 9am to 9pm, Saturday 10am to 9pm, and Sunday 10am to 8pm. Admission is 8DM ($4.80) for adults and 6DM ($3.60) for children.

JOGGING A good jogging route is along the quays of the River Main, using both sides of the river and the bridges to create a loop. Another choice is the centrally located Gruneberg Park, whose walkways are suitable for jogging.

TENNIS Few of the tennis courts in Frankfurt allow non-members to play. A noteworthy exception is the **Tennisplata Eissporthall,** Am Bornheimer hang, 60486 Frankfurt (☎ **069/41-91-41**), which has a half-dozen courts. They're open between April and October every day from 7am to sundown. The cost is 20DM ($12) per hour.

7 Shopping

When it comes to shopping, Frankfurt has everything. The specialty shops here are so much like those back in the States that most visitors from America will feel right at home. Shops in the central area are open Monday to Friday from 9am to 6:30pm and Saturday from 9am to 2pm (until 4 or 6pm on the first Saturday of the month).

THE SHOPPING SCENE

In Frankfurt, the shopping scene is divided into different regions. On the **Zeil,** a pedestrian zone between the Hauptwache and Konstablerwache, you'll find department stores, clothing shops, shoe stores, and furniture outlets. Once one of the most famous shopping streets on the Continent, the Zeil was destroyed in the war and hasn't regained its former prestige, though it still has the highest sales of any shopping area in Germany. In the 14th century, it was a cattle-round-up market. Nearby is the **Kleinmarkthalle,** a covered market with international grocery products.

The **Hauptwache,** in the center of Frankfurt, has two shopping areas, one above and one below ground. Groceries, book dealers, flowers, clothing, tobacco, photo supplies, recordings, and sporting equipment abound. In the Hauptwache-Passage are restaurants, travel agencies, and banks.

Schillerstrasse, another pedestrian zone, lies between Hauptwache and Eschenheimer Turm, near the stock exchange. Walking from Schillerstrasse northeast toward Eschenheimer Tor, you'll pass many elegant boutiques and specialty shops.

Southwest of the Hauptwache is the Alte Oper. You can reach it by taking either the **Goethestrasse,** with its exclusive stores, evocative of Paris or Milan, or the parallel **Grosse Bockenheimerstrasse,** traditionally nicknamed Fressgasse. Most wine dealers, delis, and butcher shops here look back on a long and venerable past. At **Opernplatz** you'll find a variety of restaurants and cafes.

West of the Hauptwache is Rossmarkt, leading to **Kaiserstrasse.** It passes the BFG skyscraper, which has three floors of exclusive retail stores, boutiques, and restaurants and directly connects the downtown area to the Hauptbahnhof. Kaiserstrasse is also known for its large selection of stores selling clothing, audio and photography equipment, and stainless-steel ware. The heart of the fur trade in Frankfurt is **Düsseldorfer Strasse,** opposite the Hauptbahnhof. Most book dealers are located around the Hauptwache and **Goetheplatz.** Antiques, old books, etchings, and paintings on **Braubachstrasse** can be found near the Römer, at the Dom, and on Fahrgasse.

Art and antiques are the domain of **Alt-Sachsenhausen,** an appealing and original neighborhood. The famous **Frankfurt Flea Market** takes place here every Saturday from 8am to 2pm along the Main River on the Sachsenhausen side. To get there, walk from the Römer toward the river and cross the Eisener Steg bridge.

DEPARTMENT STORES & MALLS   The 45 shops of the **Zeil Galerie,** Zeil 112–114 (☎ **069/92-07-340**), sell everything imaginable. The three best department stores in the city are **Kaufhof,** Zeil 116 (☎ **069/2-19-10**); **Hertie,** Zeil 90 (☎ **069/ 92-90-50**); and Japanese-transplant **Mitsukoshi,** Kaiserstrasse 13 (☎ **069/9218870**), all of which carry the wide variety expected in such establishments.

FOOD & WINE   **Konditorei Lochner,** Karl-Becher-Gasse 10 (☎ **069/9-20-73-20**), specializes in marzipan cookies and creamy Frankfurter Kranz cake, and also has a coffee bar. A small bakery-cafe, **Laumer,** Bockenheimer Landstrasse 74 (☎ **069/72-79-12**), sells a wide variety of sweets and has a popular cafe. Regional wines, including those produced by the city's own vineyards, are available at **Weingutes,** Limpurger Gasse 2 (☎ **069/21-23-36-80**).

JEWELRY   Expensive but worth it, the jewelry found at **Friedrich,** Goethestrasse 9 (☎ **069/28-43-53**), is the product of Cristoph and Stephan Friedrich, two of Germany's best designers. The brothers work with gold, platinum, silver, and assorted gemstones. One of the best centers of elegant jewelry in Frankfurt is **Gerhard Wempe,** An der Hauptwache 7 (☎ **069/29-17-77**). Items start at nearly 1,000DM ($600). The shop also carries about 46 brands of watches.

LEATHER GOODS   **Fink Exklusiv Schuhe,** Goethestrasse 9 (☎ **069/28-99-04**), carries leather clothing and shoes for both men and women.

PORCELAIN, CHINA & CRYSTAL   The porcelain dinnerware, crystal, and glassware at **Rosenthal,** Goethestrasse 1 (☎ **069/28-85-90**), are designed exclusively for the shop, and include classic and original contemporary patterns. Great deals can be found at the factory outlet **Höchster Porzellan Manufaktur,** Berliner Strasse 60, at the Kornmarkt in suburban Höchst (☎ **069/29-52-99**). This is Germany's second oldest porcelain manufacturer after Meissen. Among the items found in the shop are dinnerware, candleholders, vases, figurines, and Austrian glassware.

Lorey, Schillerstrasse 16 (☎ **069/29-99-50**), carries one of the city's best selections of Hummel and Meissen figurines, plus porcelain and china, housewares, crystal, and accessories.

TOYS & CHILDREN'S BOOKS   The best places for children's toys in Frankfurt are the three department stores listed above (in "Department Stores & Malls") and **Behle Spiel & Ferienzeit,** Grosse Friedberger Strasse 7–11 (☎ **069/92-00-850**).

8 Frankfurt After Dark

For details of what's happening in Frankfurt, you can pick up copies of *Journal Frankfurt* at newsstands throughout the city. Also listing events are *Fritz* and *Strandgut,* both free and available at the tourist office.

To purchase tickets for many major cultural events, go to the tourist office at the Hauptbahnhof. The department store **Hertie,** Zeil 90 (☎ **069/294848**), also has a theater ticket office, which is open during regular store hours.

THE PERFORMING ARTS

Theater der Stadt Frankfurt, Untermainanlage 11 (☎ **069/21237999**), has three stages. One belongs to the **Frankfurt Municipal Opera,** whose productions have received worldwide recognition in recent years. Two stages are devoted to drama. If your German is adequate, you might want to see a performance of **Städtische Bühnen/Schauspiel** (☎ **069/21-23-79-99**), a forum for classic German plays as well as modern drama. U-Bahn: Willy-Brandt-Platz. A variety theater, **Kunstlerhaus Mouson Turm,** Waldschmidtstrasse 4 (☎ **069/4058-9520**), hosts plays, classical music concerts, and dance programs almost every night of the week. Tickets run 20DM to 40DM ($12 to $24).

Alte Oper. Opernplatz. ☎ **069/1-34-04-00.** Tickets 30DM–200DM ($18–$120). Box office Mon–Fri 8:30am–8:30pm, Sat 9:30am–2pm. U-Bahn: Alte Oper.

The old opera house is still the pride of Frankfurt, even though opera is no longer presented here. This building was reopened in 1981, following its reconstruction after World War II bombings. The original structure had been officially opened in 1880 by Kaiser Wilhelm I. At that time it was hailed as one of the most beautiful theaters in Europe. Today the Alte Oper is the site of frequent symphonic and choral concerts.

✪ **Oper Frankfurt/Ballet Frankfurt.** Willy-Brandt-Platz (between the Hauptbahnhof and the Innenstadt). ☎ **069/21-23-79-99.** Opera and ballet 20DM–210DM ($12–$126). Box office Mon–Fri 8am–8pm, Sat 8am–6pm. U-Bahn: Willy-Brandt-Platz.

This is Frankfurt's premier showcase for world-class opera and ballet. Acclaimed for its dramatic artistry, the **Frankfurt Opera** is under the charge of conductor Sylvain Cambreling. The world renown **Frankfurt Ballet** is directed by William Forsythe.

English Theater. Kaiserstrasse 52 (near the Hauptbahnhof). ☎ **069/24-23-16-20.** Plays 43DM–50DM ($25.80–$30); reduced student price 20DM ($12); musicals 65DM ($39); reduced student price 40DM ($24). On Tues and Sun prices are 8DM ($4.55) less. Box office daily 10am–7pm. S-Bahn: Hauptbahnhof.

This English-language theater was founded by the actress Judith Rosenbauer, who is still its artistic director. It began in a Sachsenhausen backyard, but was later moved to this location, compliments of the city of Frankfurt. The auditorium, which seats 230, is in the art-deco style and has an adjoining cafe. Musicals, comedies, dramas, and thrillers are produced. During the season (September through July), performances are Tuesday to Saturday at 8pm and Sunday and Wednesday at 6pm.

THE CLUB & BAR SCENE

In a 16-square-block area in front of the Hauptbahnhof, you'll find a rowdy kind of entertainment: what the Germans call *erotische spiele.* Doormen will practically pull you inside to view porno movies, sex shows, sex shops, even discos teeming with prostitutes. *Warning:* This area can be dangerous—don't come here alone.

For less lurid activities in a safer environment, head to the live-music clubs, discos, bars, and cafes across the Main River in the **Sachsenhausen** district. Most gay bars and clubs are located in a small area between Bleichstrasse and Zeil.

DANCE CLUBS

Cooky's. Am Salzhaus 4. ☎ **069/28-76-62.** Cover Sun and Tues–Thurs 11DM ($6.60), Fri–Sat 14DM ($8.40).

Tuesday to Sunday, DJs at Cooky's mix a dance soundtrack of hip-hop and house music. Hours are Tuesday, Thursday, and Sunday from 11pm to 4am, Friday to Saturday 10pm to 6am.

Dorian Gray. O Level of Section C in the Frankfurt airport. ☎ **069/69-02-21-21.** Cover 15DM–20DM ($9–$12).

This popular disco and continental bistro can be reached from the heart of the city in about 15 minutes aboard an S-train, which departs from Hauptbahnhof every 20 minutes. Its well-appointed lounges and club room draw an elegant well-dressed crowd. Open Sunday, Wednesday, and Thursday 9pm to 4am, Friday and Saturday 10pm to 6am.

Nacht Leben. Kurt-Schumacher-Strasse 45. ☎ **069/2-06-50.** Cover 8DM–10DM ($4.80–$6).

This club has a cafe-bar upstairs and a disco downstairs. Here you can either have drinks and conversation, or dance to the throbbing beat of hip-hop, funk, soul, and house. The club occasionally books a live band. Open Monday to Wednesday 11:30am to 2am, Thursday to Saturday 11:30am to 4am.

LIVE MUSIC

An Sibin. Wallstrasse 9. ☎ **069/6-03-21-59.**

This Irish cellar pub is decorated with pushcarts, wagons, and antique instruments. There's a band on most nights; the music is Irish-only on Tuesday. You'll find Guinness on tap, English and Irish pub grub, and a friendly barkeep who'll teach you a few phrases in Gaelic. Open Monday to Thursday 7pm to 2am, Friday to Saturday 7pm to 3am.

Der Jazzkeller. Kleine Bockenheimer 18A, near Goethestrasse. ☎ **069/28-85-37.** Concerts 12DM–40DM ($7.20–$24), disco 9DM ($5.40).

This basement club, established in 1952, is one of the most famous and atmospheric jazz clubs in Germany. Its reputation is as solid as the 200-year-old redbrick walls that surround it. The place has played host to such jazz luminaries as Louis Armstrong, Dizzy Gillespie, and Gerry Mulligan. Wednesday and Friday, patrons dance to the club's "Cool Music Mix." Thursday and Saturday, live music is presented. Open Tuesday to Sunday 9pm to 3am.

Dreikönigskeller. Färberstrasse 71. ☎ **069/62-92-73.**

This tiny place features live performances of any and every pop musical style from the 1940s through the contemporary music scene. It opens daily at 8pm.

Jazz-Kneipe. Berliner Strasse 70. ☎ **069/28-71-73.** Cover 5DM–20DM ($3–$12).

A venue for soloists, duos, and small ensembles, Jazz-Kneipe hosts solo piano or piano/guitar or piano/bass duos Sunday to Wednesday. On Friday and Saturday, trios and quartets perform jazz or blues. Open daily 8pm to 4am.

Sinkkasten. Brönnerstrasse 9. ☎ **069/28-03-85.** Disco 8DM ($4.80), concerts 12DM–40DM ($7.20–$24).

At this live-music institution, regulars show up regardless of who's playing. Rock, reggae, blues, pop, jazz, and African music bands might be found here, except on Thursday, Saturday and late Friday, when the club turns disco. Come early to beat the crowd or you risk being turned away. Open Sunday to Thursday 9pm to 2am, Friday to Saturday 9pm to 3am.

BARS, CAFES & TAVERNS

Jimmy's, in the Hotel Hessischer Hof, Friedrich-Ebert-Anlage 40 (☎ 069/75400), is a luxurious candlelit bar with a whisper of background music. It's a relaxing place to unwind, but it's not cheap—drinks start at 23DM ($13.80) and beers at 11DM ($6.60). One of the best-known beer halls in Frankfurt, **Maier Gustl's Bayrisch Zell,** in the Hauptbahnhof, Münchner Strasse 57 (☎ 069/23-20-92), is a timbered re-creation of a mountain chalet. It has two dance floors, which hold nearly 1,000 people. After hoisting a few steins of brew, exuberant patrons dance to a Bavarian brass band and a modern show band that alternate sets every 30 minutes. Some of the tables have table-to-table telephones, a slightly sleazy nod to the surrounding red-light district. Meals include *Eisbein mit sauerkraut* (leg of pork), the most expensive dish on the menu at 16DM ($9.60). Beers, available in different sizes and brands, run from 6DM to 11DM ($3.60 to $6.60).

Lovers of apple wine should head to **Mutter Ernst,** Alte Rothofstrasse 12 (☎ 069/28-38-22), open daily from 9am to 10pm (until 5am Saturday), and **Apfelweinwirtschaft Wagner,** Schweizerstrasse 71 (☎ 069/61-25-65), open daily 11am to midnight, where you can order traditional German dishes to accompany your beverage.

Club Voltaire, Kleine Hochstrasse 5 (☎ 069/29-24-08), is a place for impromptu poetry readings. You can listen or join in. Full meals at 10DM to 15DM ($6 to $9) draw as many students as the poetry and drinking. Want to hear "Born Free" or the Muzak version of "Hey Jude"? Slip into the comfortable, pastel **Café 5 Bar,** Am Glauburgplatz (☎ 069/55-88-30), where easy listening is the music of choice and a 4DM ($2.40) lager with a 7DM ($4.20) sandwich combo is another incentive. Open Monday to Thursday from 5pm until 1am and Friday and Saturday until 2am.

GAY CLUBS

Blue Angel. Bronnerstrasse 17. ☎ 069/28-27-72. Cover 10DM ($6).

This club was named after gay icon Marlene Dietrich's first movie hit. The DJs keep you guessing by mixing dance styles. The revelry often picks up steam late in the night, so hours generally extend into the early morning. Open daily 10pm to various closing times, usually 4 or 5am.

Harvey's Cafe Bar. Bornheimer Landstrasse 64. ☎ 069/49-73-03.

This indoor/outdoor bistro sometimes has live disco bands on the weekend. It's a pop-ular place for a gay date. Open daily 9am to 1am (until 2am Friday and Saturday).

Lucky's Manhattan. Schäfergasse 27. ☎ 069/28-49-19.

Best described as a gay cafe and bar wrapped into one, Lucky's also has aspects of a conservative tearoom. Most folks come here to drink beer or apple wine, or perhaps to nibble on a limited array of toasts and crepes. It's a worthwhile place to begin, but not to end, an evening on the town. Open daily noon to 2am.

Mr. Dorian's Club. Alte Gasse 34. ☎ 069/29-45-06.

This small but not particularly crowded place caters to a clientele of gay men in their 30s and 40s. Regulars come to talk and have a leisurely drink. Open Sunday to Thursday 6pm to 2am, Friday to Saturday 6pm to 3am.

The Stall. Stiftstrasse 22. ☎ 069/29-18-80.

This is the most visible and crowded leather bar in Frankfurt. It attracts a woodsy, macho-looking set that's been a part of the local gay scene for years. Open Sunday to Thursday 9pm to 4am, Friday and Saturday 9pm to 6am.

9 Side Trips from Frankfurt

Picturesque Aschaffenburg and some of the leading spas of Germany lie on the doorstep of Frankfurt. Another good side trip is to Mainz (see chapter 13).

ASCHAFFENBURG

219 miles NW of Munich, 25 miles SE of Frankfurt, 48 miles NW of Würzburg

Aschaffenburg was originally a Roman settlement on the right bank of the Main River, and later became an important town in the Middle Ages. In recent years, it's grown industrially, but even with 250 garment manufacturers, the town has remained peaceful and provincial. Its many parks and shady lanes make it a fitting gateway to the streams and woodlands of the Spessart Hills. Weekly fairs are held on the square, where fishers along the banks of the Main sell seafood straight from their buckets. Many traditional shops are in a pedestrian zone, with lamps, fountains, and flowers.

ESSENTIALS

GETTING THERE   By Train   The **Aschaffenburg Bahnhof** is on the major Nürnberg-Würzburg-Frankfurt rail line, and on the regional Maintal Aschaffenburg-Mittenburg-Wertheim rail line, with frequent connections in all directions. From Frankfurt, 45 trains arrive daily (trip time: 30 to 45 min., depending on the train). For rail information, call ☎ **01805/99-66-33.**

By Bus   There is no direct bus service between Frankfurt and Aschaffenburg.

By Car   Access by car is via the A3 Autobahn east and west.

VISITOR INFORMATION   Contact **Tourist-Information,** Schlossplatz 1 (☎ **06021/39-58-00**). It's open Monday to Friday 9am to 5pm and Saturday 10am to 1pm.

SEEING THE SIGHTS

The best park in Aschaffenburg is **Schönbusch Park,** Kleine Schönbuschallee 1 (☎ **06021/2-24-17**), located across the Main (2 miles on foot or by car). It's a marvel of planning, using the natural surroundings as a setting for formal 18th-century gardens, shady lanes, temples, and gazebos. At the edge of the mirror-smooth lake is a small neoclassical castle, really a country house, once used by the electors of Mainz. The house is open from April through October, Tuesday to Sunday from 10am to 12:30pm and 2:30 to 5pm. Admission is 4DM ($2.40) for adults, 3DM ($1.80) for students, and free for children under 15. In summer, it's possible to rent a small boat to go on the lake. There's also a cafe-restaurant open daily from 8am to 8pm. Bus: 4.

The most impressive castle in Aschaffenburg is the huge Renaissance **Schloss Johannisburg,** Schlossplatz 4 (☎ **06021/2-24-17**), reflected in the waters of the Main. Erected from 1605 to 1614, it became the residence of the rulers of the town, the prince-electors of Mainz. The red sandstone castle is almost perfectly symmetrical, with four massive lantern towers surrounding an inner courtyard. From January through December, the castle is open from 9am to noon and 1 to 5pm, Tuesday to Sunday; off-season, Tuesday to Sunday from 11am to 4pm. Admission is 5DM ($3) for adults and 4DM ($2.40) for children 14 and under. From the castle gardens you can reach the **Pompeianum,** built by Bavaria's King Ludwig I as a replica of the Castor and Pollux palace discovered among the ruins of Pompeii. The Pompeianum is open mid-March to mid-October, Tuesday to Sunday from 10am to noon and 2:30 to 5pm. Admission is 4DM ($2.40) for adults, 3DM ($1.80) for students, and free for children. Bus: 1, 2, or 8.

Stiftskirche St. Peter and St. Alexander, Stiftsgasse 5 (☎ **06021/2-24-20**), has stood on its hill overlooking the town for 1,000 years. Its architecture has changed over the centuries, however, as it was remodeled and reconstructed, and today it stands as a combination of Romanesque, Gothic, and baroque. Its most precious treasure is the painted retable *The Lamentation of Christ,* by Mathias Grünewald. The interior is decorated with several paintings of the school of Lucas Cranach, as well as a marble-alabaster pulpit by Hans Juncker. One of the oldest pieces is a Roman-style crucifix from 980. Adjacent to the north side of the church is a Romanesque cloister from the 13th century. The church is open Wednesday through Monday from 10am to 1pm and 2 to 5pm. Admission is 3DM ($1.80) adults and 2DM ($1.20) children and students. Bus: 1, 4, or 10.

WHERE TO STAY

Aschaffenburger Hof. Frohsinnstrasse 11, 63739 Aschaffenburg. ☎ **06021/386810.** Fax 06021/2-72-98. 60 units. TV TEL. 148DM–196DM ($88.80–$117.60) double. Rates include breakfast. AE, DC, V. Parking 8DM ($4.80). Bus: 1, 3, 4, 6, or 10.

This establishment offers many thoughtful details. It's housed in a tall yellow building with a single balcony on each floor. The small rooms, although no style-setters, are pleasantly furnished. Each has a small refrigerator. Try for one overlooking the courtyard. The restaurant is locally popular for its fresh, modern cuisine that includes some vegetarian dishes. The hotel offers room service, dry cleaning, and laundry service.

Hotel Post. Goldbacherstrasse 19, 63739 Aschaffenburg. ☎ **06021/33-40.** Fax 06021/ 1-34-83. 71 units. MINIBAR TV TEL. 185DM–199DM ($111–$119.40) double. Rates include breakfast. AE, DC, MC, V. Parking 8DM ($4.80). Bus: 1, 3, 4, 6, or 10.

This is the town's premier hotel, offering greater comfort than its nearest rival, Aschaffenburger Hof (see above). Close to the heart of town, it provides handsome accommodations and some of the best food in Aschaffenburg. Its exterior may be conventional, but there's drama inside. A miniature sitting room is almost New England in character, with natural-pine chairs, hanging oil lamps, and lots of decorative copper. The rooms are well maintained, each individually decorated in traditional style. The dining room is a stylized version of an old posting inn; it includes an original mail coach, timbered walls and ceiling, and leaded-glass windows. Reasonably priced and very good Franconian meals are served here. The hotel offers room service and laundry service, and has a sauna, indoor swimming pool, and solarium.

Hotel-Restaurant Schönbusch. Frohsinnstrasse 11, 63739 Aschaffenburg. ☎ **06021/ 85-60.** Fax 06021/8-02-88. 10 units. TV TEL. 140DM–155DM ($84–$93) double. Rates include buffet breakfast. AE, DC, MC, V. Free parking. Bus: 4.

The Schönbusch dates from 1783. The building was at one time the living quarters of the court gardener, a high official with eight personal servants at his disposal. The Bischofszimmer, the largest room in the house and now the main dining room, once served as the gardener's living room. You can walk in the park with its old and rare trees, including a 2-centuries-old red beech, and take a look at the Lustschlösschen, where King Ludwig I of Bavaria entertained his mistress, the notorious Lola Montez. The bedrooms are attractively furnished and vary in shape and size.

Syndikus. Löherstrasse 35 (a few blocks from the cathedral), 63739 Aschaffenburg. ☎ **06021/2-35-88.** Fax 06021/2-92-80. 27 units. TV TEL. 140DM ($84) double; 160DM– 220DM ($96–$132) suite. Rates include breakfast. AE, CB, DC, DISC V. Parking 6DM ($3.60). Bus: 3 or 6.

An unpretentious three-story facade greets visitors to this hotel. The bar area is rustically decorated with timbered ceilings and wheel chandeliers. All bedrooms are well-maintained and have up-to-date furnishings. Although the hotel is open year-round, its restaurant is closed in August.

WHERE TO DINE

Schlossweinstueben. Schloss Johannisburg. ☎ **06021/1-24-40.** Reservations recommended. Main courses 8DM–32DM ($4.80–$19.20). No credit cards. Tues–Fri 11am–midnight, Sat–Sun 10am–midnight. Bus: 1, 3, or 4. FRANCONIAN/BAVARIAN.

One of the most alluring corners of this historic castle is its popular wine cellar. Here you'll find a wide variety of German wines to complement the conservative but well-prepared menu items. A meal might begin with liver-dumpling soup, then follow with a game specialty (depending on the season). The selection of very fresh fish is likely to include trout and pike. There is no pretension to this cuisine—it's just good, hearty, rib-sticking fare.

WIESBADEN

25 miles W of Frankfurt, 94 miles SE of Bonn

This sheltered valley, between the Rhine and the Taunus Mountains, has held a spa since Roman times. Today Wiesbaden competes with Baden-Baden for the title of Germany's most fashionable resort. Its success is based partly on its 26 hot springs, with temperatures ranging from 117°F to 150°F, and partly on its proximity to Frankfurt's transportation centers, which gives the spa a distinctly international flavor.

Wiesbaden is also a major cultural center. Every spring it plays host to the International May Festival of music, dance, and drama. Most of these cultural activities take place in Wiesbaden's Kurviertel (spa quarter), around the Kurhaus and Kurhauskolonnade, opposite the Theaterkolonnade. The major concert halls are in the **Kurhaus,** a lively, multiroomed structure centered around a cupola-crowned hall. In addition to concerts, the complex hosts plays and ballets, plus a variety of social gatherings, such as international conferences, congresses, exhibitions, and trade fairs. It also holds a casino, a lively restaurant, and an outdoor cafe.

For the more active visitors, Wiesbaden offers horseback riding, a golf course, swimming, tennis, and hiking. The streets of the city are enjoyable for strolling, as is the **Kurpark,** which has a lake surrounded by old shade trees. It's especially beautiful at night, when the lights of the spa are reflected in the water and the huge fountains are lit up. The park stretches for half a mile northward along the Kuranlagen, ending in a fancy residential quarter, the Sonnenberg. People-watching on the **Wilhelmstrasse** is another favorite pastime for both locals and visitors.

ESSENTIALS

GETTING THERE   By Train   Trains run between Frankfurt airport and Wiesbaden about every hour, leaving from the airport's lower level. The trip takes 30 minutes. Tickets can be purchased at automatic machines in the station area or at the airport's railway ticket counter. There's also frequent train service from the center of Frankfurt on the S-Bahn line (trip time: 30 to 40 min.). For rail information, call ☎ **01805/996633.**

By Bus   Deutsche Touring GmbH in Frankfurt (☎ **069/7903261**) operates frequent service to Wiesbaden (Line T81 or T82).

By Car   Wiesbaden lies at a major crossroads, with access via the A3 Autobahn from the north and south, connecting with the A66 Autobahn from the west and east. Travel time by car from Frankfurt (Route 66) is about 20 to 30 minutes, depending on traffic. From the Frankfurt airport to Wiesbaden by car is about 20 minutes.

VISITOR INFORMATION The **Verkehrsbüro,** Marktstrasse 6 (☎ **0611/ 1-72-97-80**), is open Monday to Friday from 9am to 6pm and Saturday 9am to 3pm. Closed on Sundays.

SHOPPING The shopping scene here is prosperous, squeaky-clean, and in the eyes of some, a bit smug. The resort's major shopping artery is **Wilhelmstrasse.** Wiesbaden is also a center for antiques, although we find them too pricey. **Taunusstrasse** is lined with antique shops.

WHERE TO STAY

Zur Rose (see "Where to Dine," below) also rents inexpensive rooms.

Very Expensive

✪ **Hotel Nassauer Hof.** Kaiser-Friedrich-Platz 3–4, 65183 Wiesbaden. ☎ **800/223-6800** in the U.S. or 0611/13-30. Fax 0611/13-36-32. E-mail: hotel-nassauer-hof@t-online.de. 198 units. A/C MINIBAR TV TEL. 435DM–580DM ($261–$348) double; 680DM–2,500DM ($408–$1,500) suite. AE, DC, MC, V. Parking 25DM ($15). Bus: 5, 18, or 25.

The superluxurious Nassauer Hof, often referred to as the "grande dame" of Wiesbaden, is among the most appealing in town. It's an old favorite with up-to-date conveniences. The spacious rooms feature soundproof windows, elegant furnishings, and comfortable mattresses; some have air-conditioning. The bathrooms contain deluxe beauty products, hair dryers, and robes. The hotel stands in the city center, within walking distance of the Kurhaus, Spielbank, theaters, and the shopping area.

Dining/Diversions: The cozy Nassauer Hof Bar has an open fireplace and piano entertainment. Guests usually have an aperitif here before dinner. The bright, sunny Orangerie offers a refined German cuisine at lunch and dinner. The more expensive Ente Restaurant boasts the finest cuisine in Wiesbaden (see "Where to Dine," below). Other choices include the Entenkeller, a wine and beer cellar with a lighter menu, and the Bistro & Gourmet Boutique, open for both lunch and dinner.

Amenities: 24-hour room service, laundry, baby-sitting, Lancaster Beauty Spa, indoor thermal swimming pool, sauna, solarium, fitness room.

Expensive

Hotel Klee am Park. Parkstrasse 4, 65189 Wiesbaden. ☎ **0611/30-50-61.** Fax 0611/ 9001310. www.klee-am-park.de. E-mail: 061190010-001@t-online.de. 54 units. MINIBAR TV TEL. 245DM–320DM ($147–$192) double. AE, DC, MC, V. Free parking. Bus: 2 or 8.

This hotel is highly recommended for those who might find the older, more luxurious Nassauer Hof a bit too monumental. Klee am Park is a square, modern hotel in a tranquil setting at the edge of a park. It's surrounded by its own informal gardens. The theater, casino, and shopping area are nearby. All the guest rooms have French doors opening onto balconies and stylish furniture; some have sitting areas large enough for entertaining.

Dining/Diversions: Guests will find a cafe and restaurant where French cuisine is served, plus a comfortable English-style bar. The hotel's kitchen is known for its excellent and novel fare. Alfresco dining on the summer terrace is an added treat.

Amenities: Concierge, room service, hair dryers, laundry, dry cleaning.

Ramada Hotel Wiesbaden. Abraham-Lincoln-Strasse 17, 65189 Wiesbaden. ☎ **800/ 854-7854** in the U.S. and Canada, or 0611/79-70. Fax 0611/76-13-72. www.ramada.com. 205 units. A/C MINIBAR TV TEL. Mon–Thurs 180DM–271DM ($108–$162.60) double; Fri–Sun 165DM–185DM ($99–$111) double (rate includes breakfast); 270DM–350DM ($162–$210) suite. AE, DC, MC, V. Free parking. Bus: 5, 18, or 25.

Lots of businesspeople stay at the Ramada instead of staying in Frankfurt, as it's only 20 minutes from the Frankfurt airport. It's also a good center for visitors to Wiesbaden, within a 5-minute walk of the Kurhaus and the elegant boutiques and old cafes of the pedestrian zone. The modern guest rooms are comfortably furnished and have small, well-maintained bathrooms.

Dining/Diversions: The restaurant, Abrahams, offers a variety of regional and international dishes. Try a glass of Rhine wine or draft beer in the rustic bar or a snack on the terrace bordering the indoor pool.

Amenities: Pool, sauna, fitness room, solarium, baby-sitting, and laundry service.

Moderate

✪ **Admiral Hotel.** Geisbergstrasse 8 (a 5-min. walk from the Kurhaus), 65193 Wiesbaden. ☎ **0611/5-86-60.** Fax 0611/52-10-53. 27 units. TV TEL. 205DM ($123) double. Rates include buffet breakfast. AE, DC, MC, V. Parking 15DM ($9). Bus: 1 or 8.

The centrally located Admiral is favorite of traditionalists and one of the best values in Wiesbaden. Readers constantly praise the owners for their hospitality. The rooms are furnished in a charmingly old-fashioned way, often with antique brass beds. The bathrooms are small yet clean and contain hair dryers. The hotel offers health food. The owners are a retired U.S. Army officer and his German-born wife.

Hotel am Landeschaus. Mortitzstrasse 51 (within walking distance of the railroad station), 65185 Wiesbaden. ☎ **0611/37-30-41.** Fax 0611/37-30-44. 20 units. TV TEL. 180DM ($108) double. Rates include buffet breakfast. AE, MC, V. Parking 8DM ($4.80). Closed Dec 22–Jan 5. Bus: 10, 14, or 16.

This hotel in central Wiesbaden is one of the spa's best reasonably priced hotels. It's completely modern, but also warm, cozy, and inviting. The rooms are well-kept, with small, clean bathrooms. Guests can enjoy drinks in a rustic ale tavern.

Inexpensive

Hotel Klemm. Kapellenstrasse 9 (near the Kurhaus), 65193 Wiesbaden. ☎ **0611/58-20.** Fax 0611/58-22-22. 55 units. TV TEL. 140DM–180DM ($84–$108) double. Rates include breakfast. AE, DC, MC, V.

This hotel occupies a late-19th-century Jugendstil villa with solid stone walls. Although the setting is well scrubbed and respectable, it has touches of genteel shabbiness that seem to go well with the nostalgia that permeates this part of Wiesbaden. This place enjoys many repeat visitors. Rooms are simple, but comfortable and clean. Only breakfast is served.

WHERE TO DINE

✪ **Ente Restaurant.** In the Hotel Nassauer Hof, Kaiser-Friedrich-Platz 3–4. ☎ **0611/133666.** Reservations required. Main courses 39DM–58DM ($23.40–$34.80); fixed-price dinner 105DM–165DM ($63–$99). AE, DC, MC, V. Restaurant and bistro daily noon–2:30pm and 6pm–midnight. Bus: 5, 18, or 25. CONTINENTAL.

This restaurant has the best food in town. The innovative chef makes sure the meals are as pleasing to the eye as they are to the palate. Cuisine is light and modern. Specialties change from week to week, based on seasonal availability of ingredients. Typical offerings include parfait of duck livers, a whole roast duck for two, roast medaillons of venison with chanterelles, and clams in puff pastry. Desserts alone are reason to visit, especially the lemon soufflé with strawberries and the mountain-honey ice cream. Ente also has one of the best wine lists in Europe, with 1,630 labels. Many of the wines are moderate in price. A boutique, delicatessen, wine cellar, and bistro are also attached.

✪ **Käfer's.** In the Kurhaus, Kurhausplatz 1. ☎ **0611/53-62-00.** Reservations recommended. Main courses 25DM–50DM ($15–$30). AE, DC, MC, V. Daily 11:30am–2am. INTERNATIONAL.

Käfer's is the name of the organization that directs two restaurants within one of the most stately and prestigious buildings in Wiesbaden, the Kurhaus. The more appealing of the two is Käfer's Bistro, a replica of the kind of bustling, upscale, well-run bistro you might find in Lyon or Paris. It features starched napery, wood paneling, framed artwork, and staff dressed in black and white. In an adjoining room is the airier, quieter, and more self-consciously formal Casino Restaurant. The menu and prices are the same as in the bistro, but the atmosphere is calmer and frankly a bit more stuffy. Men are required to wear a jacket and tie. Menu items change every 2 weeks. Examples might include smoked salmon served with a *Rösti* pancake, crème fraîche, and chives; Canadian lobster with yogurt-flavored cocktail sauce and lemon; penne pasta with pesto sauce and grilled giant prawns; vegetarian dishes; and in springtime, asparagus with filet mignon, bacon, or salmon steak. Dessert might be a mousse flavored with three kinds of chocolate.

Zur Rose. Bremthaler Strasse 1 (east of the town center), 65207 Naurod. ☎ **06127/40-06-07.** Reservations recommended. Main courses 35DM–48DM ($21–$28.80); fixed-price menus 54DM–79DM ($32.40–$47.40). AE, DC, MC, V. Daily 11am–midnight. Bus: 21, 22, or 23. FRENCH/GERMAN.

This nearly two-hundred-year-old restaurant, located in a half-timbered building, offers a cozy, nostalgic decor, with a ceramic-tile oven, rose-colored lace tablecloths, and candlelight. You can enjoy freshly baked rolls as you peruse the menu. Begin with cucumber-cream soup with dill-flavored shrimp, then try the Barbarie duck breast with goose-liver sauce. Smoked salmon, trout, and other fresh fish and shrimp are also regularly featured. For dessert, try puff pastry filled with fresh fruits or poppy-seed mousse with rum-marinated fruits.

Zur Rose also rents 10 bedrooms, each with shower, TV, and phone. The charge for a double is 125DM ($75), including breakfast.

WIESBADEN AFTER DARK

Rien ne va plus is the call when the ball starts to roll on the gaming tables at the **Spielbank Wiesbaden,** Im Kurhaus, Kurhausplatz 1 (☎ **0611/53-61-00**). The casino is open daily from 3pm to 3am and charges an admission of 5DM ($3). Roulette, blackjack, and poker are the featured games. The place is located at the end of Wilhelmstrasse, one of the most famous streets in Wiesbaden, and can be reached by bus no. 1, 8, or 16. To enter, you must present a passport or an identification card. Men must wear jackets and ties.

Music and **theater** flourish in Wiesbaden throughout the year. For information on performances during your visit, check at the Wiesbaden tourist office (see "Visitor Information," above). For information about any of the conference and cultural facilities in the **Kurhaus** compound, Kurhaus Platz 1, including the casino and theater, call ☎ **0611/17290.**

Hessisches Staatstheater, Christian-Zais-Strasse (☎ **0611/13-23-25**), built in 1894 by Emperor Wilhelm II, is one of the most beautiful theaters in Germany. It presents a program of operettas, musicals, ballets, and plays. The season lasts from September 15 to June 30; tickets range from 7DM to 70DM ($4.20 to $42).

An important event is the **International May Festival,** which runs throughout the month of May. The festival features concerts, classical in-house drama productions, and a wide selection of guest performances by theaters of international stature. For information and tickets, call ☎ **0611/132325.**

The **Prak Café,** Wilhelmstrasse 36 (☎ **0611/3-93-21**) incorporates a cafe, brasserie, and disco. It's sprawling and often very busy. Much louder is **The Big Apple,**

Kirchgasse 66 (☎ **0611/37-40-33**), where music that will remind you of New York City and Los Angeles is played to a crowd of enthusiastic dancers, mostly in their early 20s. For beer in an appealingly old-fashioned atmosphere, head for the **Ratskeller** (also known as the **Rathsbräu Keller),** Schlossplatz (☎ **0611/300023**), or the **Ratstube,** Matstrasse 8 (☎ **0611/37-25-08**).

BAD HOMBURG
10 miles N of Frankfurt, 28 miles NE of Wiesbaden

Bad Homburg is one of Germany's most attractive spas, still basking in the grandeur left over from turn-of-the-century Europe. The spa's saline springs are used to treat various disorders, especially heart and circulatory diseases. The town has been a popular watering spot since Roman times. Royalty from all over the world have visited and left a mark. King Chulalongkorn of Siam (Thailand) was so impressed that he built a Buddhist temple in the Kurpark. Tsar Nicholas I erected an onion-domed Russian chapel nearby. The name of the town was popularized by Edward VII of England when, as Prince of Wales, he visited the spa and introduced a new hat style, which he called the "homburg." The town became the gaming capital of Europe when the Blanc brothers opened the casino in 1841.

The spa park is a verdant, carefully landscaped oasis in the middle of an otherwise rather commercial-looking town. The actual spa facilities are in the **Kaiser Wilhelms Bad,** im Kurpark (☎ **0611/17290**). They're open Monday to Friday from 6:30am to 7:30pm, Saturday from 6:30am to noon. The immaculately tended gardens in the surrounding Kurpark are filled with brooks, ponds, arbors, and seasonal flowers. The town center has a sprawling pedestrian-only district that offers many shops, restaurants, and cafes.

ESSENTIALS
GETTING THERE   By Train   There's rail service by S-Bahn (S-5) from the center of Frankfurt. Call ☎ **01805/996633** for more information.

By Bus   The **Alpina-Airport-Express** is Bad Homburg's hourly, nonstop shuttle service to and from the Frankfurt airport (see "Orientation," above); trip time is 30 minutes.

By Car   Access by car from the north or south is via the A5 Autobahn, exiting at Bad Homburg.

VISITOR INFORMATION   For information, go to the **Verkehrsamt im Kurhaus,** Louisenstrasse 58 (☎ **06172/675110**). It's open Monday to Friday from 8:30am to 6:30pm and Saturday from 9am to 1pm.

SIGHTS & ACTIVITIES
Bad Homburg Palace. Schlossverwaltung (a few blocks from the spa gardens). ☎ **06172/ 9-26-21-47.** Admission 6DM ($3.60) adults, 4DM ($2.40) children. Palace and formal gardens Mar–Oct Tues–Sun 10am–5pm; Nov–Feb Tues–Sun 10am–4pm.

This palace was the residence of the landgraves of Hesse-Homburg from its construction in 1680 until the mid-19th century. Its builder, Prince Frederick II von Homburg, preserved the White Tower from the medieval castle that stood on the site previously. In the late-19th century, the palace became a summer residence for Prussian kings and, later, German emperors. After World War I the state assumed ownership. The interior contains 18th-century furniture and paintings, including a bust of Prince Frederick II by Andreas Schluter, Germany's greatest baroque sculptor. The former "telephone room of the empress" includes *Cleopatra* by Pellegrini.

Taunus Therme. Seedammweg. ☎ **06172/4-06-40.** Admission Mon–Fri, 23DM ($13.80) for 2 hr., 31DM ($18.60) for 4 hr., 45DM ($27) for all day; Sat–Sun and holidays, 26DM ($15.60) for 2 hr., 35DM ($21) for 4 hr., 49DM ($29.40) for all day; daily, free for children 3 and under. Sun–Tues 9am–11pm, Wed and Fri–Sat 9am–midnight.

A large, fascinating recreation area, Taunus Therme boasts several pools, a sauna, a solarium, and a health center, plus TVs, cinemas, and two restaurants.

WHERE TO STAY
Expensive
Maritim Kurhaus-Hotel. Kurpark, Ludwigstrasse, 61348 Bad Homburg. ☎ **06172/66-00.** Fax 06172/66-01-00. 148 units. MINIBAR TV TEL. 263DM–313DM ($157.80–$187.80) double; 480DM–580DM ($288–$348) suite. AE, DC, MC, V. Parking 20DM ($12).

This hotel near the spa facilities offers visitors plush rooms, many with tall bay windows. As sleek and up-to-date as this hotel is, it's still far outclassed by the Steigenberger Bad Homburg. Double rooms feature king-size beds and deep armchairs in pastel fabrics. Even the single rooms have queen-size beds. All rooms contain outlets for computers. The second and fifth floors are reserved for nonsmokers. Some rooms have balconies or terraces, permitting wide-angle views over the greenery of the surrounding park. The luxurious bathrooms contain hair dryers and plush towels.

Dining: Both international and regional fare are served at the Bürgerstube, which is open daily. Large buffet breakfasts are also offered.

Amenities: Big-windowed indoor pool, sauna, laundry service, room service from 6:30am to 10pm, baby-sitting, concierge.

✪ **Steigenberger Bad Homburg.** Kaiser-Friedrich-Promenade 69–75 (opposite the spa gardens and casino), 61345 Bad Homburg. ☎ **800/223-5652** in the U.S. and Canada, or 06172/18-10. Fax 06172/18-16-30. 169 units. A/C MINIBAR TV TEL. 300DM–430DM ($180–$258) double; 490DM–690DM ($294–$414) suite. AE, DC, MC, V. Parking 20DM ($12).

This the resort's best and most prestigious hotel. Europe's high society used to stroll here in days of yore, and an ambience of luxury still prevails. Guest rooms are beautifully furnished, each with individually adjustable air-conditioning and extra-long beds, along with a large and spacious bathroom containing deluxe luxury items, hair dryers, and sumptuous bathrobes. Fifty-three rooms are reserved for nonsmokers.

Dining: The elegant Parkside Restaurant offers creative contemporary cuisine. There's also the French-style Charly's Bistro.

Amenities: Sauna, steam bath, solarium, beauty center, baby-sitting, 24-hour room service, laundry, dry cleaning.

Moderate
✪ **Hardtwald Hotel.** Philosophenweg 31 (a 20-min. walk from the center of town), 61350 Bad Homburg. ☎ **06172/98-80.** Fax 06172/8-25-12. 42 units. MINIBAR TV TEL. 195DM–355DM ($117–$213) double. Rates include buffet breakfast. AE, DC, MC, V. Parking 15DM ($9). Bus: 3 from the Bahnhof.

This hotel, which resembles a chalet set in a forest, is an ideal retreat near the spa gardens. In spring, flowers overflow from its window boxes. Its rooms overlook the forest. The chef in the excellent, flower-filled dining room uses only the freshest of ingredients to prepare his well-known international and German dishes. In summer, tables are set on the large patio. Next to the hotel is a stable where you can rent horses.

Parkhotel Bad Homburg. Kaiser-Friedrich-Promenade 53–55, Am Kurpark, 61348 Bad Homburg. ☎ **06172/80-10.** Fax 06172/80-14-00. www.Bad-Homburg.de. E-mail: Parkhotel.Bad-Homburg@t-online.de. 122 units. MINIBAR TV TEL. 184DM–358DM ($110.40–$214.80) double; 300DM–400DM ($180–$240) suite. Rates include buffet breakfast. AE, DC, MC, V. Parking 12DM ($7.20). Tram: 5.

This is your best bet for a moderately priced spa vacation. This hotel has an enviable location in the middle of the Kurpark's well-maintained gardens, near the thermal springs. Although its design is modern and angular, its edges are softened with window boxes. The rooms are conservatively furnished. The bathrooms are well kept and contain hair dryers. On the premises are a bar and a sunny room for writing postcards. Restaurant Jade serves Chinese cuisine. Amenities at the hotel include sauna, health club, solarium, and room and laundry service.

Inexpensive

Haus Daheim. Elisabethenstrasse 42 (a short walk from the Kurhaus), 61348 Bad Homburg. ☎ **06172/67-73-50.** Fax 06172/2-58-00. 19 units. TEL. 185DM–265DM ($111–$159) double. Rates include buffet breakfast. AE, DC, MC, V. Parking 15DM ($9). Tram: 5.

When you're trying to save on deutschmarks, head here. This hotel, in a light-blue corner building, is one of the finest small hotels in the town. The comfortable rooms have good beds with firm mattresses. This is an admittedly modest choice after the hotels reviewed above, but for value, it's hard to beat.

Villa Kisseleff. Kisseleffstrasse 19 (in the Kurpark), 61348 Bad Homburg. ☎ **06172/21559.** Fax 06172/21569. 14 units, 9 with shower or bathroom. TV TEL. 160DM ($96) double with bathroom. Rates include continental breakfast. AE, MC, V. Tram: 5.

This 19th-century, baroque-style villa is located near the curative springs. All the rooms are well-furnished, and homelike doubles have private bathrooms or showers. There are also some singles without shower or bathroom. A restful atmosphere pervades the place.

WHERE TO DINE

Casino-Restaurant. Im Kurpark. ☎ **06172/1-70-10.** Reservations required. Jacket and tie required for men. Main courses 17DM–46DM ($10.20–$27.60); fixed-price menus 49DM–53DM ($29.40–$31.80). AE, DC, V. Daily 6–10:30pm. FRENCH/GERMAN.

Until a few years ago, this was the only restaurant in Germany that directly adjoined the gaming tables of a casino. It's one of the finest restaurants in town, although not in the same class as Sängers or Oberle's. The dining room is decorated in a formal, vaguely English style. It offers attentive service and a winning combination of light French and German cuisine. The frequently changing menu features seasonal specialties with the freshest of ingredients—head chef Gunther Schwanitz begins each workday at the local markets. Lobster is a universal favorite here, attracting diners from as far away as Frankfurt. Although the main kitchen service stops at 10:30pm, there's a reduced menu until 12:30am.

Oberle's Restaurant. Obergasse 1. ☎ **06172/2-46-62.** Reservations required. Main courses 39DM–52DM ($23.40–$31.20); fixed-price menus 79DM–110DM ($47.40–$66). AE, MC. Tues–Sun noon–2pm; Tues–Sat 6:30–11:30pm. INTERNATIONAL.

This is the second-best restaurant in Bad Homburg. The kitchen staff prides itself on a superb cuisine. Try the goose-liver mousse, marinated and warmed fillets of salmon served in saffron-and-Pernod sauce, sweetbreads of veal in a sauce of white wine and mustard, or a deliciously caloric version of cream and wild-mushroom soup. The menu is changed according to the season, and only the freshest of ingredients are used. The decor is art nouveau and art deco. In summer, guests can order their meals on a sun terrace.

✪ **Sängers Restaurant.** Kaiser-Friedrich-Promenade 85 (next to the Steigenberger Bad Homburg). ☎ **06172/92-88-39.** Reservations required. Main courses 45DM–55DM ($27–$33); fixed-price meals 55DM ($33) at lunch, 98DM–165DM ($58.80–$99) at dinner. AE, MC, V. Tues–Fri noon–2pm; Mon–Sat 7–11pm. Closed 2 weeks in midsummer. FRENCH.

Local food lovers and spa devotees crowd this restaurant to enjoy the highly personal and inventive cuisine, the best in the spa. The two elegant dining rooms are outfitted in the style of Louis XIV. Menu items might include carpaccio of turbot with Iranian caviar, goose-liver terrine served with brioche and gelatin of wild berries, a foam-capped version of celery soup with quail eggs, roast breast of duck on a bed of rhubarb, and a succulent array of desserts.

BAD HOMBURG AFTER DARK

Spielbank Im Kurpark (☎ **06172/1-70-10**), called the "Mother of Monte Carlo," is the spa's major attraction. This casino opened way back in 1841 and helped make Bad Homburg famous. Roulette, blackjack, and baccarat are the games here. Passports are required for entrance, and men must wear jackets and ties. Admission is 5DM ($3); hours are daily from 2:30pm to 3am.

The most active disco in town is the **Tennis Bar,** Kisseleffstrasse (☎ **06172/2-60-41**), named for the municipal tennis courts in the nearby Kurpark. It offers both recorded and live rock music. If you thought you were too old to hang out in a disco, think again, as this one attracts clients ages 25 and over. It's open from 9pm Tuesday to Saturday, with a varying cover. More traditional is the town's favorite beer hall and Weinstube, **Zum Wasser Weibehen,** Am Mühlberg 57 (☎ **06172/2-98-78**). And about a mile east of the town center, you'll find another folkloric place, **Zum Ruppe Karl,** Hamburgerstrasse 6 (☎ **06172/4-24-84**), whose home-style cuisine is enhanced with the establishment's homemade apple wine. The **Kurhaus** also contains a handful of bars, cafes, and shops that usually stay open late.

BAD NAUHEIM

22 miles N of Frankfurt, 40 miles NE of Wiesbaden

Like many spas throughout Germany, Bad Nauheim became popular in the early part of this century, when the railroad became a convenient and inexpensive means of transportation. Still going strong today, this resort at the northern edge of the Taunus Mountains is a center for golf, tennis, and ice-skating, as well as the starting point for hiking up the 773-foot Joannisberg, which towers over the town.

The warm carbonic-acid springs of the spa are used to treat heart and circulatory disorders and rheumatic diseases. The Kurpark is attractive, well maintained, and filled with promenaders all summer long. The impressive bathhouse here is the single largest complex of Jugendstil architecture in Germany. The Sprudelhof (fountain court), at the center of the complex, stretches from the Hauptbahnhof to the Kurpark and all the way to the Kurhaus. All the important sights, including the bathhouse complex, can be visited in half a day. The resort has a busy activity calendar, with concerts twice daily, along with operas, plays, dances, park illuminations, and fashion shows.

ESSENTIALS

GETTING THERE By Train Bad Nauheim can easily be reached from Frankfurt. Trains arrive at least once per hour (every 30 min. during rush hours) during the day; the trip time is 30 minutes. Service is on the Weatherman line between Frankfurt and Giessen. For information and schedules call ☎ **01805/996633.**

By Car Access is via the A5 Autobahn from the north and the south. Driving time from Frankfurt is about half an hour.

VISITOR INFORMATION For information, go to the Verkehrsverein, Neue Kurolonnade (☎ **06032/21-20**). It's open Monday to Friday 9am to noon and 2 to 5pm, Saturday 9am to noon and 2 to 4pm, and Sunday 10am to noon.

Elvis in Bad Nauheim

Many famous guests have visited this spa, including Otto von Bismarck (1859) and Richard Strauss (1927). Franklin D. Roosevelt spent about 2 years here with his family when he was a small child. Locals believe that Bad Nauheim was spared destruction during World War II, even though a Nazi radio transmitter was installed here, because President Roosevelt had fond memories of the place.

Real fame came to the spa when a private named Elvis Presley arrived in Bad Nauheim and found a home off-base, right next to the Kurhaus. The singer was stationed in nearby Friedberg/Hessen at Ray Barracks Kaserne from October 1958 to March 1960, and his presence had an electrifying effect on the German youth scene. It was here that Elvis fell in love with Priscilla, "my little girl." She was 14 at the time, and when she first drove up to the plain, old-fashioned villa where he lived, the street was full of German girls, waiting by the sign AUTO-GRAPHS BETWEEN 7 AND 8PM ONLY. After that first meeting, she saw him once more, and when he returned to the States he vowed to send for her. Today, the barbershop at Presley's old army post is still operated by the same man who kept the singer's hair trimmed.

Elvis wasn't the only famous American to visit. It was the habit of newspaper magnate William Randolph Hearst to come here every year with his mistress, Marion Davies, and a dozen or so of her women friends—Hearst would rent automobiles and have the women chauffeured around the countryside in style. He firmly believed Bad Nauheim's physicians were the answer to his minor heart problem. Here he had his notorious meetings, with Mussolini in 1931 ("a marvelous man") and Hitler in 1934 (who sent a plane to bring him to Berlin). He claimed that he had done "much good" in advising Hitler to drop his persecution of the Jews, but afterward he spent most of his life trying to live down his image as a supporter of the Nazi cause.

WHERE TO STAY

Hotel Gaudesberger. Hauptstrasse 6, 61231 Bad Nauheim. ☎ and fax **06032/25-08.** 8 units, none with bathroom. TEL. 90DM ($54) double. Rates include continental breakfast. Closed Jan 15–Feb 15. AE, DC, MC, V.

This centrally located hotel is known mainly for its restaurant (see "Where to Dine," below). Its guest rooms are simply furnished. The place is plain and decent, not grand in any way. The staff speaks no English.

Hotel Rosenau. Steinfurther Strasse 1 (west of Grosser Teich, the town lake), 61231 Bad Nauheim. ☎ **06032/9980.** Fax 06032/8-34-17. 54 units. A/C MINIBAR TV TEL. 180DM–248DM ($108–$148.80) double. Rates include continental breakfast. AE, DC, MC, V. Closed Dec 27–Jan 8. Free parking.

This is one of the better choices at the resort, though it's not nearly as good as the Parkhotel am Kurhaus. The Hotel Rosenau is an updated version of a German manor house, with white walls and a red-tiled hip roof. Inside, the decor is one of light-toned wood and pastel colors. Guest rooms are modern and attractive, with such amenities as electric trouser presses. On the premises there's both a good bistro and a fine restaurant, plus a small pool.

Parkhotel am Kurhaus. Nordlicher Park 16, 61231 Bad Nauheim. ☎ **06032/30-30.** Fax 06032/30-34-19. 168 units. MINIBAR TV TEL. 249DM–360DM ($149.40–$216) double;

380DM–480DM ($228–$288) suite. Rates include continental breakfast. AE, DC, MC, V. Parking 10DM ($6).

This modern hotel is the finest in town, with better amenities than the Rosenau. It's located in the middle of the park that rings the resort's thermal springs. Its public rooms are filled with green plants and arching windows. In the traditional bedrooms, with their big sliding glass windows and balconies, you'll find calm, quiet, and conservative comfort. The bathrooms are luxurious and contain deluxe luxury items and hair dryers. There are two restaurants and a cafe, in addition to a Bierstube, wine tavern, and bar. Special diets and vegetarian menus are offered. Amenities include room service, laundry, and baby-sitting. Nonsmoking rooms are available on the third floor.

WHERE TO DINE

Restaurant Gaudesberger. In the Hotel Gaudesberger, Hauptstrasse 6. ☎ **06032/25-08.** Reservations recommended. Main courses 15DM–30DM ($9–$18). AE, DC, MC, V. Thurs–Tues 11:30am–2pm and 5:30–9pm. INTERNATIONAL.

A large menu of well-prepared dishes is offered here in comfortable but simple surroundings. You can stick to the tried-and-true choices, such as chateaubriand with béarnaise sauce or herring fillet in dill sauce, or you can dip into the other specialties, such as pork in curry-cream sauce, ox tongue in Madeira sauce, or trout and salmon prepared in at least four different ways. Ingredients are fresh and everything is prepared home-style. The staff is cooperative and courteous.

Rosenau-La Rose. In the Hotel Rosenau, Steinfurther Strasse 1. ☎ **06032/9980.** Main courses 26DM–42DM ($15.60–$25.20); fixed-price buffet lunch 36DM ($21.60). AE, DC, MC, V. Tues–Sun noon–2pm and 6–10pm. Closed Dec 27–Jan 30. INTERNATIONAL.

This restaurant is known as one of the best in town. It serves a fixed-price lunch plus à la carte evening meals. The flavorful dishes might include cream of tomato and young-vegetable soup, roast breast of young hen, and fillet of salmon with fresh herbs, plus several different pork and game dishes, depending on the season. The cookery is not innovative, but we are impressed with its honesty and freshness. There are no pretensions here.

The Rhineland 13

Few rivers of the world can claim such an important role in the growth of a nation as the Rhine. The Rhine rises in Switzerland and ultimately flows through the Netherlands in its progress to the sea, but most of its 850 miles snake through the mountains and plains of Germany. For more than 2,000 years, it has been a chief trade route, its deep waters enabling modern seagoing vessels to travel downstream from the North Sea as far as Cologne.

From earliest times, the Rhine has also been a main road for religious, intellectual, and artistic ideas. It has been called a "triumphal avenue of the muses," and a trip along its banks today reveals endless treasures. Legend and history wait around every bend of the river.

From Mainz north to Koblenz, the winding river cuts through steep vine-covered hillsides dotted with towns whose names are synonymous with fine German wine. Here you'll find the dramatic Lorelei, the legendary rock from which a siren lured men to their doom. The saga of the *Nibelungenlied,* the best known of the Rhine legends, is associated with the topography from the Siebengebirge (the Seven Mountains) near Bonn, where Siegfried slew the dragon, to the city of Worms, where Brünnhilde plotted against the dragon-slayer.

The Rhine is also the home of many of Germany's largest and most modern cities. **Cologne** (Köln) and **Düsseldorf** vie for trade and tourism. Cologne is also a common starting point for boat tours of the river.

Roadways along the Rhine tend to be heavily trafficked, so allow adequate time. Highways, not Autobahns, hug both the left and right banks of the river, and at many points you'll come across car-ferries that can take you across. The most scenic stretch for driving is the mid-Rhine, between Koblenz and Mainz. EuroCity and InterCity trains connect all the major cities along the Rhine, including Köln, Düsseldorf, Bonn, and Mainz. Rail service also extends as far north as Hamburg and as far south as Munich.

Exploring the Region by Car

Day 1   If you're beginning in the south, your gateway to the Rhine can be the city of **Speyer,** one of the oldest Rhine cities, 58 miles south of Mainz. A morning visit to its Kaiserdom (imperial cathedral) will suffice. You can then continue north on Route 9 to **Worms,** the ancient city where Siegfried began his legendary adventures, as recorded in *The Nibelungenlied*. Worms contains St. Peter's Cathedral, one of the purest Romanesque basilicas in the Rhine valley. Stay overnight here.

Day 2   After Worms, continue north along Route 9 to **Mainz.** There's a lot to see in this 2,000-year-old former Roman city, including the Museum Gutenberg, devoted to the man who invented movable type here in 1440. With its many attractions and good food and wine, Mainz deserves a full day.

Day 3   Take Route B455 toward Wiesbaden. The highway will run into A66, the Autobahn. Go to the western extension of A66, which then changes its name to B42. Continue along this route for some 22 miles to **Rüdesheim** for the night. For dinner, head for one of the wine taverns in the area, preferably along the tiny alley of Drosselgasse. Here you'll not only learn about the history of wine making, you'll also get to taste the best selection of Rhine wines in the area.

Day 4   In the morning, take a side detour north on Route 42 to Assmannshausen via the Niederwald Monument, which commemorates the unification of Germany under Bismarck. Explore the wine town of **Assmannshausen** in the morning. This town produces a red wine called *Spätburgunder,* which you may want to sample at a tavern for lunch.

If you return to Rüdesheim, you can take the car-ferry to Bingen, crossing to the more scenic left bank and continuing along Route 9. Bingen merits only a passing stopover, but outside the town, the highway is celebrated for its scenery, its romantic old castles, and its Rhineland landmarks. This stretch is so filled with castles that you'll despair of ever visiting them all. Keep on B9 for its entire length, some 40 miles to **Koblenz,** where, after the busy day you've had, you'll want to stay overnight.

Day 5   Since Koblenz was bombed almost out of existence in World War II, you may want to pass on after breakfast, getting back on Route B9 and following the signs to **Bonn,** some 39 miles to the northwest. Everyone always talks about how dull Bonn is, but there's still quite a bit to see here, including Beethoven's House. You can also visit a spa called **Bad Godesberg,** southeast of Bonn, where you might spend the night or at least enjoy a meal.

Day 6   From Bonn, and only if you have an extra day, you can continue west toward France for an overnight stay in **Aachen,** an ancient city lying at the frontiers of Belgium, Germany, and the Netherlands. Aachen is inseparably linked with the legend of Charlemagne. Visit its Dom, Rathaus, and Couven Museum.

Day 7   Retrace your route west, toward Bonn. Get on the A3 Autobahn north and continue for some 17 miles to **Cologne** (Köln), which may well be the highlight of your Rhineland motor trip.

Day 8   After Cologne, it's just 25 miles north on A57 to the city of fashion and industry, **Düsseldorf.**

1 Speyer

58 miles S of Mainz, 13 miles SW of Heidelberg

One of the oldest Rhine cities, Speyer celebrated its two-thousandth jubilee in 1990. It became a significant religious center early on. The Diet of Speyer, in 1529, united the followers of Luther in a protest against the Church of Rome.

ESSENTIALS

GETTING THERE   By Train   Trains reach Speyer only by connections at Heidelberg and Mannheim. The trip from Frankfurt takes 2 hours; from Munich, 5 to 6 hours. Call ☎ **01805/996633** for schedules.

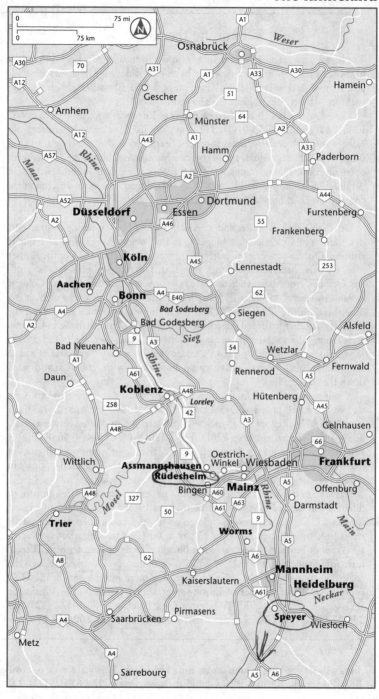

The Rhineland

Cruising the Rhine

The best way to get a really intimate look at the river valley that helped shape the history of Europe is to travel its waters by ship. A wide range of cruises are available from several shipping lines. These range from a 500-mile tour on a luxury yacht to 1-day cruises to historical and artistic sites.

The premier carrier is **KD River Cruises of Europe,** Frankenwerft 15, 50667 Köln 1 (☎ **0221/25-83-01-1**). This company has been running cruises since early in the 19th century; today it owns a fleet of more than 25 vessels. Its river tours, elegant but nonglitzy, are on compact but comfortable ships equipped with open-air pools, dining rooms, bars, and highly competent multilingual staffs. Although a traditional band might play over dinner, the main entertainment comes from chatting with fellow passengers and taking in the sweeping views of the landscape.

Depending on your tastes and schedule, you can book anything from a short day tour from Cologne, to a longer tour that might take 5 days of leisurely cruising. Our favorite excursion from Cologne is a trip past many of the Rhine's most evocative ruins and landscapes, to Mainz. This tour is offered between April and October, every day via a hydrofoil (*Tragflugelboot*) that departs from Cologne at 9am, arriving in Mainz at 1:15pm. We suggest that you spend the night at any of our recommended hotels in Mainz, but if you want to return to Cologne the same day, another hydrofoil departs from Mainz at 2:30pm, arriving in Cologne at 6:05pm. The round-trip cost is 240DM ($136.80) per adult, and 55DM ($31.35) for accompanying children under 14. The arrangement of seats within the hydrofoils is similar to what's within an airplane, with rows of seats divided down the center aisle.

A longer option for cruising down the Rhine is a 6-day cruise between Amsterdam and Basel, priced at 1,456DM to 2,180DM ($829.90 to $1,242.60) per person, double occupancy, all-inclusive. Shorter, 4-day cruises between Strasbourg and Cologne cost from 720DM to 1,120DM ($410.40 to $638.40), per person, double occupancy. During the longer river tours, ships dock at cities of historical or cultural interest. For an additional surcharge, you can participate in motorcoach or walking tours of the city where you're docking.

Day cruises don't stop for very long, but passengers can still often embark or disembark at such historic towns as Bonn, Linz, Bräubach, St. Goarshausen, and Rüdesheim. On day excursions, children up to age 4 and holders of Eurailpasses travel free, and children ages 4 to 13 pay 5DM ($2.85). Tickets for day excursions cannot be reserved and should be bought directly on the pier before departure. Arrangements for cruises of 2 nights or more can be booked through the company's U.S.-based sales representative. For more information in the U.S., contact **KD River Cruises of Europe** (represented within North America by JFO Cruise Service), 2500 Westchester Ave., Purchase, NY 10577 (☎ **800/346-6525**); or 323 Geary St., San Francisco, CA 94102 (☎ **800/858-8587**).

By Bus   About one bus per hour arrives from Heidelberg. Regional service is provided by BRN Busverkehr Rhein-Neckar GmbH at Ludwigshafen (☎ **06231/51-21-22**).

By Car   You can drive from Frankfurt in about an hour. It takes about 4 hours to drive from Munich. Access is by the A61 Autobahn east and west connecting with Route 9, a state highway, south.

VISITOR INFORMATION   For information, go to the **Verkehrsamt,** Maximilianstrasse 11 (☎ **06232/14-23-92**). Open year-round Monday to Friday from 9am to 5pm; from May to October, also open on Saturday from 10am to 4pm and on Sunday from 11am to 3pm; in the off-season, also open on Saturday from 10am to noon.

GETTING AROUND   A blue and white "City Shuttle" (bus) runs from the Speyer Hauptbahnhof through the town to Festplatz near the cathedral, east of the Altstadt. It connects most of the major hotels and restaurants. The bus comes every 10 minutes, and the service runs daily from 7am to 7pm. The trip costs 1DM (55¢) regardless of its length.

THE IMPERIAL CATHEDRAL

Nothing brings back the medieval German empire as much as the ✪ **Kaiserdom (Imperial Cathedral)** in Speyer (☎ **06232/10-22-98**), the greatest building of its time. This cathedral, consecrated in the early 11th century, is the largest Romanesque edifice in Germany. Having weathered damage by fires, wars, and restorations, the cathedral was finally restored to its original shape from 1957 to 1961. When you enter the church through the single west door set in a stepped arch, you're immediately caught up in the vastness of its proportions; the whole length of the nave and east chancel opens up before you, lit by the muted daylight from above. The church contains the royal tombs of four emperors, three empresses, and four German kings, as well as a row of bishops' tombs. Open April through October, Monday to Saturday from 9am to 7pm and Sunday from 1:30 to 6pm; November through March, Monday to Friday from 9am to 5pm, Saturday from 9am to 4pm, and Sunday from 1:30 to 4:30pm.

WHERE TO STAY

Am Wartturm. Landwehrstrasse 28, 67346 Speyer. ☎ **06232/6-43-30.** Fax 06232/64-33-21. 17 units. TEL. 130DM–180DM ($74.10–$102.60) double. Rates include breakfast. No credit cards. Free parking.

In this modern but modest little guest house, the owners, the Heck family, rent simply furnished, comfortable, but rather small units. They also operate a plain but good restaurant, open for both lunch and dinner. Service is polite and attentive. When the weather is cooperative, you can enjoy either lunch, breakfast, or dinner in the hotel's garden, whose centerpiece is a small goldfish pond.

Rhein-Hotel Luxhof. At the Rhine Bridge, just outside the town, 68766 Hockenheim. ☎ **06205/30-30.** Fax 06205/3-03-25. E-mail: luxhof@t-online.de. 45 units. TV TEL. 156DM–160DM ($88.90–$91.20) double. Rates include buffet breakfast. AE, DC, MC, V. Free parking.

This hotel has an unusual character. It's modern in style, but somehow the spirit of a rambling country inn has been retained. The blandly decorated guest rooms are well designed and compact, often featuring small sitting areas that open onto tiny balconies. The dining rooms are charming and colorful, and the hotel has a sauna, a solarium, and other fitness facilities.

Trutzpfaff. Webergasse 5 (near the cathedral), 67346 Speyer. ☎ **06232/6-01-20.** Fax 06232/60-12-30. 8 units. TV TEL. 125DM–135DM ($71.25–$76.95) double. Rates include buffet breakfast. No credit cards.

This conveniently located, family-run guest house offers personalized service from the English-speaking owners, the Peter Hemmler family. The rooms are pleasantly furnished but small, with compact bathrooms. The hotel's Weinstube offers regional dishes and emphasizes whole grains for the health-conscious. Only wines from the region (Pfalz) are served, and bottles are also sold.

WHERE TO DINE

Backmulde. Karmeliterstrasse 11–13. ☎ **06232/7-15-77.** Reservations required. Main courses 38DM–48DM ($21.65–$27.35); fixed-price dinner 72DM–110DM ($41.05–$62.70). AE, DC, MC, V. Tues–Sat 11:30am–2:30pm and 7–11pm. Closed 3 weeks from the end of Aug to mid-Sept. FRENCH/SEAFOOD.

Backmulde is owned by Gunter Schmidt, who has researched the centuries-old recipes of the Rhineland Palatinate, added a modern touch, and come up with a combination that has made this place Speyer's most important restaurant. You can savor such unusual delicacies as gratiné of oysters in champagne sabayon, quail stuffed with well-seasoned sweetbreads, and a meltingly tender roast lamb with freshly picked spinach.

2 Worms

28 miles S of Mainz, 27 miles SW of Darmstadt

This ancient city traces its beginnings from the earliest civilizations. Before the Romans settled here, Germanic peoples had made Worms their capital. Here, Siegfried began his legendary adventures, recorded in *The Nibelungenlied.* Later on, the town's most famous visitor, Martin Luther, arrived under less than desirable circumstances. He was "invited" to appear before the Imperial Diet at Worms, and after refusing to retract his grievances against the Church of Rome, the Holy Roman Emperor Charles V declared him an outlaw. Now that Worms is mainly Protestant, a huge monument to Luther and other giants of the Reformation has been erected.

Worms also makes an excellent base for a tour of the *Deutsche Weinstrasse,* or German Wine Road, a 50-mile route through picturesque local wine towns (see below).

ESSENTIALS

GETTING THERE   By Plane   The nearest airport is at Frankfurt (see chapter 12), 43 miles away.

By Train   Worms enjoys good rail connections to major German cities. It lies on the main Mainz-Mannheim line, with frequent service. For rail information and schedules, call ☎ **1-94-19.**

By Bus   Regional bus service for the area is provided by **BRN Busverkehr Rhein-Neckar GmbH** (☎ 06241/1077028) in Worms.

By Car   From Mainz (see section 3, below), continue south along Route 9.

VISITOR INFORMATION   For tourist information, go to the **Verkehrsverein,** Neumarkt 14 (☎ **06241/2-50-45**). It's open year-round Monday to Friday 9am to 6pm; April through October, also open Saturday 9am to noon.

SEEING THE SIGHTS

Towering physically and historically above all the other ancient buildings of the city is the majestic ✪ **Dom St. Peter,** Lutherring 9 (☎ **06241/61-15**). This basilica is a fine example of High Romanesque style. The east choir, with a flat facade and semicircular interior, is the oldest section, dating from 1132. This was designed as the sanctuary, where the clergy performed the rites of divine service. The chancel glows with the gold and marble of the pillared enclosure of the baroque high altar by the famous 18th-century architect Balthasar Neumann. This opulent work was so large that there was no place for a proper transept. In Gothic times the choir stalls stood in the apse, but later they were built into the transept. The interior has a quiet elegance, with little decoration other than the rosette window and several memorial slabs and monuments. Well worth seeing is the highly decorated 14th-century side chapel of St. Nicholas, with its Gothic baptismal font and new stained-glass windows. The cathedral is open for visitors April through October, daily from 8am to 6pm; in winter, daily from 9am to 5pm. To get here, take bus 2.

North of the Altstadt is the restored **old Jewish quarter.** Before World War II, Worms had one of the oldest Jewish communities in Germany. The **synagogue,** Hintere Judengasse 6 (☎ **06241/853-4701**), which dated from the 11th century, was destroyed in 1938. It has been rebuilt, using some of the original masonry. Inside, you'll find the **Raschi-Haus Museum** (same phone), containing memorabilia from the original synagogue and references to the Holocaust. Both the synagogue and its museum are open May to October, daily from 10am to noon and from 2 to 6pm; November to April, daily from 10am to noon and from 2 to 5pm. Admission is 3DM ($1.70). A staff member inside will point you in the direction of the **Jewish cemetery** (**Judenfriedhof**), off the Lutherrin, one of the oldest and largest in Europe, with hundreds of tombstones, some of them more than 900 years old.

WHERE TO STAY

Central Hotel Worms. Kämmererstrasse 5, 67547 Worms. ☎ **06241/6-45-70.** Fax 06241/2-74-39. 19 units. TV TEL. 145DM–155DM ($82.65–$88.35) double. Rates include buffet breakfast. AE, DC, DISC, MC, V. Closed Dec 20–Jan 6. Parking 8DM ($4.55). Bus: 2 or 4.

This is one of the best small hotels in the city, although it's a modest and unassuming choice. Innkeeper Alexandra Hill rents comfortably furnished but rather small rooms. The reception staff speaks English, and the hotel has an ideal central location, within walking distance of all major historic monuments.

Dom-Hotel. Am Obermarkt 10 (about a block from the cathedral), 67547 Worms. ☎ **06241/69-13.** Fax 06241/2-35-15. 62 units. A/C MINIBAR TV TEL. 160DM–220DM ($91.20–$125.40) double; 230DM ($131.10) suite. Rates include buffet breakfast. AE, DC, MC, V. Free parking.

This is an ideal choice for the in-and-out traveler. This recently renovated, all-purpose hotel is a postwar structure built in a complex of shops and boutiques. Bedrooms are a little bandboxy and functionally furnished, but each is well maintained. The guest lounge is a good place to relax. In the wood-paneled dining room, a breakfast buffet is offered, and later in the day, French cuisine is served.

Hotel Nibelungen. Martinsgasse 16, 67547 Worms. ☎ **06241/92-02-50.** Fax 06241/92-02-55-05. 46 units. MINIBAR TV TEL. 160DM–210DM ($91.20–$119.70) double. Rates include buffet breakfast. AE, MC, V. Parking 5DM ($2.85).

The most modern place to stay in Worms is the Nibelungen, in the center of town. It offers up-to-date comfort behind a rather sterile facade. The well-furnished guest rooms are the best in town and are generally spacious, although devoid of any particular Rhinelander flavor. Breakfast is the only meal served.

WHERE TO DINE

Le Bistro Léger. Siegfriedstrasse 2. ☎ **06241/4-62-77.** Reservations recommended. Main courses 18DM–35DM ($10.25–$19.95). MC. Mon–Sat noon–2pm and 6–11pm. Bus: 2. RHINELAND.

The nostalgically decorated Le Bistro Léger offers a regional cuisine at reasonable prices. An outdoor terrace is a favorite in warm weather. Fresh ingredients go into the food. You might try, for example, veal cutlets prepared in the style of the Rhineland, fish fillet, or oysters (in season). The well-chosen wine list is mostly German.

Rôtisserie Dubs. Kirchstrasse 6, at Rheindurkheim (take Rte. 9 north for 5 miles). ☎ **06242/20-23.** Reservations required. Main courses 38DM–44DM ($21.65–$25.10); fixed-price menu 65DM–125DM ($37.05–$71.25). No credit cards. Fri–Mon 6–10pm; Sun–Mon 11:30am–2pm. CONTINENTAL.

The prices here are a bit steep for the area, but you're paying for imaginative cookery and quality ingredients. Despite rustic ceiling beams and the massive stonework of the fireplace, Rôtisserie Dubs has a feeling of elegant airiness. The light continental cuisine adds to that impression. After traveling through France, the owner, Wolfgang Dubs, decided to feature such dishes as salmon in champagne marinade and delicately seasoned pike-and-cabbage soup. His steak in snail sauce is worth the trip outside of town (it may not sound appealing but is quite sublime). His is a very personal cuisine, and his efforts and hard work pay off, pleasing a set of demanding customers. Regrettably, at this writing, this highly appealing restaurant is open only 2 days a week at lunch, and only 4 days a week for dinner.

WORMS AFTER DARK

The city's most important showcase for music, classical drama (in German only), and opera is the circa 1962 **Städtisches Spiel und Festhaus,** Rathenaustrasse 4 (☎ **06241/22525**). For information about coming events, either contact the theater directly, or call **Theater-Kasse,** Rathenaustrasse 4 (☎ **06241/225-25**) for a list of upcoming events and ticket availability.

Don't expect raucous nightlife in Worms. Our best advice, if you want a drink within cozy circumstances in the town center, is to head for the **Judengasse,** a street with a denser collection of nightlife options than any other in town. One of the most appealing is the **Altstadt Bar,** Judengasse 17 (☎ **06241/222-16**), which opens for business every day at 3pm, carrying on into the wee hours.

A DRIVING TOUR OF THE GERMAN WINE ROAD

Germany's oldest designated tourist route, the *Deutsche Weinstrasse,* runs south for 50 miles from Bockenheim, a small town 8½ miles west of Worms, to Schweigen-Rechtenbach on the frontier with France. This is a land of old castles (most of them in ruins) and venerable vineyards. Most of the wines produced along this scenic stretch are whites, with special emphasis on clear, aromatic Rieslings and Weissburgunders. The area also abounds in old Rhineland Palatinate inns and wine taverns, serving hearty local specialties such as "white cheese."

Armed with a good map, available at the Worms tourist office, you can set out to explore the area beginning in the north at **Bockenheim.** From Bockenheim, follow Route 271 directly south to Grünstadt, where signs point the way to the village of **Neuleiningen,** 6 miles away. The locals here are known rather unflatteringly as *Geesbocke* or "billy goats," a reference to their longtime poverty—goats (supposedly) were the only livestock they could afford. Today the locals bear the label with a certain pride. While here, you can sample the local fare at **Alte Pfarrey,** Untergasse 54, Oberstadt (☎ **06359/86066**), where set-price menus cost 42DM ($23.95) at lunch or 120DM ($68.40) at dinner. Closed Tuesday at noon and all day Monday.

From here, Highway 271 leads south to Kallstadt, a distance of 6 miles, where our next stopover at **Bad Dürkheim** is signposted. This is a main target along the wine road heading south. Here you can view the remains of the **Monastery of Limburg,** once one of the most significant Romanesque structures in the country. The best restaurant here is **Weinrefugium,** Schlachthausstrasse 1A (☎ **06322/6-89-74**), which charges 35DM ($19.95) for a set-price menu of regional food. Closed Monday.

Route A37 en route to Kaiserslautern, west of Bad Dürkheim, leads to **Frankenstein Schloss,** a castle from the Middle Ages (now in ruins). Local legend claims it was this Schloss that inspired Mary Shelley's classic monster.

A journey 5 miles to the south along 271 leads to the **Deidesheim,** the medieval seat of the bishops of Speyer. The grounds that surround their former Schloss, now a picturesque ruin, have been turned into a lovely park. Some of the wine road's most charming half-timbered buildings are found on the main square, Marktplatz.

The most elegant hotel in the neighborhood is the very stylish **Deidesheimer Hof,** Marktplatz 1 (☎ **06326/96870**), where doubles cost 240DM to 285DM ($136.80 to $162.45). Inside are two restaurants, the **Schwarzer Hahn,** where set-price menus go from 149DM to 185DM ($84.95 to $105.45), and the more artfully rustic **St.-Urban,** which charges 105DM ($59.85) for a set-price menu.

From Deidesheim, continue along Route 271 for another 15 minutes, following the signs to **Neustadt-an-der-Weinstrasse,** the largest town on the Weinstrasse, lying at the foot of the Haardt hills. Pass quickly through its ugly suburbs to reach the heart of the old town, with its narrow, often crooked streets, holdovers from the Middle Ages. There are some 5,000 acres of vineyards within the town limits, and the main streets are lined with taverns and wine shops. Neustadt's most appealing restaurant is **Gerberhaus,** Hintergasse 6 (☎ **06321/88700**). Main courses cost 11DM to 18DM ($6.25 to $10.25). Closed Monday and Tuesday.

From Neustadt, you can drive 3 miles south to historic **Schloss Hambach** (☎ **06321/30-881**), half a mile outside the village of Hambach. It's open March to November daily from 9am to 6pm.

A 5-mile drive south takes you into the sleepy hamlet of St. Martin, which for our money is the loveliest village along the wine road, filled with antique houses draped with flowering vines. A castle here, whose nostalgic ruins still tower over St. Martin, happens to have the best food and lodging along the wine road. Its name is **St. Martiner Castell,** Maikammer Strasse 2 (☎ **06323/95-10**), and its 26 bedrooms rent for around 160DM ($91.20) double occupancy, with breakfast included. In its restaurant, set-price menus cost from 65DM to 90DM ($37.05 to $51.30).

Yet another 3 miles south (the road is signposted) takes you to **Gleisweiler,** a wine-producing hamlet known as the warmest village in Germany. Fig trees flourish in its rich soil and almost subtropical climate.

From Gleisweiler, it's 8 miles south along Route B38 to **Annweiler,** site of Burg Trifels, the Rhineland's most fabled castle, set imperiously on a jagged crag. In 1193, Richard the Lionhearted was captured and imprisoned here until he was bailed out with a huge ransom. From the panoramic peak here, you can also view the ruins of Scharfenberg Castle and also Anebos Castle to the south. Burg Trifels (☎ **06346/ 8470**) is open daily from January through March and October through November from 9am to 5pm; from April through September from 9am to 6pm; closed in December.

In Annweiler, if you opt to remain for the night, check out the facilities at **Zum Goldenen Lamm,** Ramberg, 7697 Annweiler (☎ **06345/8286**). Rooms cost 90DM ($51.30) each, with breakfast included. On the premises is a loud and sometimes rowdy, but very good, restaurant, which charges 20DM ($11.40) for a set-price meal.

The B38 leads next to **Klingenmünster,** a journey of only 5 miles south. From here, a sign points the way to the ruins of **Burg Landeck,** reached after a 30- to 40-minute stroll through a chestnut tree forest. At the end, the castle ruins stand at one of the most scenic spots along the wine road, with views extending as far as the Black Forest.

From here, B38 goes yet another 5 miles to reach **Bad Bergzabern,** a picturesque spa, without equal for its old half-timbered houses. The most appealing restaurant here is **Zum Engel,** Königstrasse 45 (☎ **06343/4933**), with set-price meals costing from 20DM to 38DM ($11.40 to $21.65). Closed Monday night and Tuesday.

From Bad Bergzabern, a 6-mile drive along Highway B38 (the final lap of your journey) will deliver you to **Schweigen-Rechtenbach,** a village at the French frontier.

In the summer of 1935, local vintners constructed a gargantuan stone arch here, the **German Wine Gate** (Deutsches Weintor), marking the southern end of this oft-traveled tourist route. From a gallery atop the wine gate, you can view miles of vineyards and even see a panorama of the Vosges in France. Visitors can cross the border, some 250 yards from the arch, to sample the vintages on the French side as well, as there are no border formalities here. You can follow a trail known as the *Weinlehrpfad* (wine inspection path), going on for a mile until you reach the vineyards at the hamlet of Sonenberg. This is one of the most rewarding walks along the wine route.

In Schweigen-Rechtenbach, one of the best values for lodging is found in the town center at **Am Deutschen Weintor,** Bacchusstrasse 1 (☎ **06342/7335**), which charges 90DM to 130DM ($51.30 to $74.10) for a double room. The price includes breakfast. We suggest getting a meal at the **Hotel Schweigenhof,** Hauptstrasse 2, 76889 Schweigen-Rechtenbach (☎ **06342/244**), which charges 25DM to 90DM ($14.25 to $51.30) for a set-price lunch or dinner.

3   Mainz

8 miles S of Wiesbaden, 51 miles NW of Mannheim, 25 miles SW of Frankfurt

Mainz is located on the left bank of the Rhine, across from the Rhine's intersection with the Main River. It is thought that there may have been wine-producing vines in the area even before the coming of the Romans in 38 B.C., although it was from that time that the regions of the Rheingau and Rheinhessen became widely known for fine viticulture.

Christianity came early to Mainz. At the beginning of the Christian era, the settlement on the Rhine's left bank and the Roman fortifications opposite were connected by a bridge. In the 8th century, the town became a primary archbishopric. Over the centuries, church politics and a series of wars shuffled control of the city back and forth between the French (who called it "Mayence") and various German factions. Mainz never became the great commerce center that its location would seem to merit. However, today it's a bustling city, with a prosperous trade in wine and other businesses.

Most visitors will be interested in the relatively compact **Altstadt,** which has been restored with taste and care. The heart of the old town is the Marktplatz, which is dominated by the cathedral.

ESSENTIALS

GETTING THERE   By Plane   The nearest airport is at Frankfurt (see chapter 12). There is direct rail service from the airport (S-14 train) via Wiesbaden to Mainz. For information, call the Mainz Railway Station at ☎ **06131/15107553**.

By Train   From Frankfurt, an express train takes 25 minutes to reach Mainz, while an S-Bahn train arrives in 40 minutes. There are also trains leaving Mainz for Heidelberg and Koblenz (trip time: 1 hr.) or Cologne (2 hr.). Daily trains to and from Munich take about 4½ hours. For more rail information, call ☎ **01805/996633.**

By Bus   Regional bus service is provided by **ORN Omnibusverkehr Rhein-Nahe GmbH,** at Mainz (☎ **06131/67-10-26**).

By Car   Access by car to Mainz is via the A60 east and west, and the A63 south and A643 north.

VISITOR INFORMATION   Go to **Touristik Centrale,** Brückenturm am Rathaus (☎ **06131/28-62-10**). Open Monday to Friday from 9am to 6pm and Saturday from 9am to 1pm.

SPECIAL EVENTS   The most celebrated merrymaking in festive Mainz is the All Fools capers at **Carnival** each spring, on the Monday before Ash Wednesday. This festival is broadcast throughout Germany like the Macy's parade. Each year in June, the **Gutenberg Festival** sponsors a cultural season as a living memorial to the city's favorite son, the inventor of the movable-type printing press. There's also an annual **Wine Fair** in August and September. For information, contact the tourist office at ☎ 06131/286210.

EXPLORING THE TOWN

✪ **Dom und Diözesan Museum.** Domstrasse 3. ☎ **06131/223727** or 06131/253344. Cathedral, free; Diocesan Museum, 5DM ($2.85) adults, 2.50DM ($1.40) children (charge applies to special exhibitions only). Cathedral Apr–Sept Mon–Fri 9am–6:30pm, Sat 9am–4pm, Sun 12:45–3pm; Oct–Mar Mon–Fri 9am–5pm, Sat 9am–4pm, Sun 12:45–3pm. Museum Mon–Wed and Fri 10am–4pm, Thurs 10am–5pm, Sat 10am–2pm. Bus: 1, 7, 13, 17, or 23.

Above the roofs of the half-timbered houses in the Altstadt rise the six towers of St. Martin's Cathedral, the most important Catholic cathedral in the country after Cologne's. It dates from A.D. 975 but was continually rebuilt and restored, reaching its present form mainly from the 13th and 14th centuries. Below the largest dome, which is a combination of Romanesque and baroque styles, is the transept, separating the west chancel from the nave and smaller east chancel. Many of the supporting pillars along the aisles of the nave are decorated with carved and painted statues of French and German saints.

A collection of religious art is housed in the cathedral's **Diocesan Museum.** In it are exhibitions of reliquaries and medieval sculpture, including works by the Master of Naumburg. In the 1,000-year-old cathedral crypt is a contemporary gold reliquary of the saints of Mainz. Among the most impressive furnishings in the sanctuary are the rococo choir stalls and a pewter baptismal font from the early 14th century.

✪ **Gutenberg Museum.** Liebfrauenplatz 5 (opposite the east towers of the cathedral). ☎ **06131/232955.** Admission 5DM ($2.85) adults; 2.50DM ($1.40) children 6–18, seniors, and students; free for children 5 and under. Tues–Sat 10am–6pm, Sun 10am–1pm. Free admission Sun and holidays. Closed Jan. Bus: 1, 7, 13, 17, or 19.

This museum is a unique memorial to the city's most famous son. In the rebuilt Gutenberg workshop, visitors can trace the history of printing, beginning with Johannes Gutenberg's hand press, on which he printed his 42-line-per-page Bible from 1452 to 1455. The collections cover the entire spectrum of the graphic arts in all countries, past and present, as well as printing, illustration, and binding. Two Gutenberg Bibles are the most popular exhibits. Note: The museum has been closed for a period but is scheduled to reopen in February 2000.

Landesmuseum Mainz (Provincial Museum of the Central Rhineland). Grosse Bleiche 49–51. ☎ **06131/232955.** Admission 5DM ($2.85) adults, 2.50DM ($1.40) children under 18, free on Sat. Tues 10am–8pm, Wed–Sun 10am–5pm. Bus: 6, 15, or 23.

It's worth a visit here to get a pictorial history of Mainz and the middle Rhineland ranging from prehistoric times to the present. The Lapidarium shows one of the most important collections of Roman monuments in Europe. The most impressive exhibits are the Roman tombstones of soldiers and civilians of the 1st century A.D., and the towering Column of Jupiter, erected in Mainz at the time of the emperor Nero, from around A.D. 65 to A.D. 68. There's a true-to-life replica of the column in front of the Parliament building.

SHOPPING

The city's most active shopping area is **Am Brand,** a short boulevard near the cathedral that's lined with shops on either side. One of the town's best clothing emporiums is **Peek & Kloppenburg,** Brand 38 (☎ 06131/23-27-61), which sells clothing for men, women, and children, in styles ranging from very formal to chic and casual. For German designer fashions, head to **Sinn,** Am Brand 4 (☎ 06131/27-30), which carries men's and women's clothing, and **Leininger,** Ludwigstrasse 11 (☎ 06131/28-88-20), which sells outfits for women and children.

Whatever you can't find along the Am Brand will almost certainly be available among the vast inventories of Mainz's two most visible department stores, **Kaufhof,** Schusterstrasse 41 (☎ 06131/2541), and **Lang,** Am Schillerplatz 8 (☎ 06131/231549). To find a treasure trove of secondhand goods, shop the **Krempelmarkt flea market,** held along the banks of the Rhine on the first Saturday of each month, February through October.

Many of Mainz's hotels, restaurants, and banks take an interest in modern art. You might also want to visit the city's most prestigious modern art gallery, **Galerie H. G. Lautner,** Augustinerstrasse 52 (☎ 06131/22-57-36). Another place, **Galerie Kreiter-Kuhnt,** Badergasse 22 (☎ 06131/22-98-36), is appealing to aficionados of middle Europe's contemporary art scene. Three additional galleries of distinction are **Atelier 9,** Heidelberger Fassgasse 18 (☎ 06131/23-26-42); **The Art Gallery,** Holzhofstrasse 10 (☎ 06131/28-04-61); and **Brückenturn Galerie der Stadt Mainz,** Am Brandt (☎ 06131/12-25-22).

WHERE TO STAY

EXPENSIVE

Atrium Hotel Kurmainz. Flugplatzstrasse 44, 55126 Mainz-Finthen. ☎ **06131/49-10.** Fax 06131/49-11-28. www.info-mainz.de/atrium. E-mail: atrium-hotel.mainz@t-online.de. 75 units. MINIBAR TV TEL. 270DM–380DM ($153.90–$216.60) double. AE, DC, MC, V. Free parking in the parking lot on the grounds; 15DM ($8.55) per night in the 12-car indoor garage. Bus: 16. Take the A60 and exit at the turnoff for Mainz-Finthen; drive through Finthen; the hotel is the last building on the right.

This modern hotel lies in the midst of orchards in the Rhine Valley. It's convenient to the nearby cities of Frankfurt and Wiesbaden, and only 15 minutes from the Frankfurt airport. The atmosphere is inviting. The bar has an open fireplace, and the atrium garden has a brook, pond, and exotic plants. The bedrooms are among the finest and most spacious in town (although not on the level of the Hilton's), with lots of extra amenities such as hair dryers and personal safes.

Dining/Diversions: There's a French restaurant and a bistro-bar, serving both regional specialties and international dishes.

Amenities: Concierge, room service, laundry, dry cleaning service, and a wide range of sports facilities, including an indoor pool, sauna, steam bath, fitness center, and tennis court.

✪ **Hilton International.** Rheinstrasse 68 (a 5-min. walk from the cathedral), 55116 Mainz. ☎ **800/445-8667** in the U.S. and Canada, or 06131/24-50. Fax 06131/24-55-89. www.hilton.com. 431 units. A/C MINIBAR TV TEL. 250DM–350DM ($142.50–$199.50) double; from 775DM ($441.75) suite. AE, DC, MC, V. Parking 30DM ($17.10). Bus: 7, 13, 17, 34, or 37.

The Hilton, renovated in 1998, is the most imaginatively designed and strikingly modern hotel along the Rhine Valley. It occupies two desirable plots of land near the center of town. Its twin sections are sheathed in reflective mirrors and soaring spans of steel, and are connected by a glass-sided covered walkway above the traffic below. There are enough bars, restaurants, and health-club facilities to keep you busy for a week. The labyrinthine interior has sun-flooded atriums with live plants, piano bars made of polished mahogany and brass, and acres of marble flooring. The guest rooms have lots of amenities and are the most artfully decorated in the region. Both the rooms and bathrooms are spacious.

Dining: The Brasserie is a fine dining place, as is the rustic, French-inspired Römische Weinstube.

Amenities: Room service, laundry, dry cleaning, hairdresser, sauna, supervised health and exercise club.

MODERATE

Hammer. Bahnhofplatz 6, 55116 Mainz. ☎ **06131/96-52-80.** Fax 06131/96-52-88-8. www.hotel-hammer.com. E-mail: info@hotel-hammer.com. 40 units. MINIBAR TV TEL. 168DM–230DM ($95.75–$131.10) double. Rates include buffet breakfast. AE, DC, MC, V. Parking 15DM ($8.55). Bus: 16 or 23.

The Hammer has a bright, inviting lobby and modern furnishings. The rooms are a good size; all come with hair dryers. The staff is excellent and very helpful. There's also a sauna, solarium, and fitness center.

Hotel Mainzer Hof. Kaiserstrasse 98 (a 10-min. walk from the Hauptbahnhof), 55116 Mainz. ☎ **06131/28-89-90.** Fax 06131/22-82-55. www.info-mainz.de/hotel-mainzer-hof. 93 units. MINIBAR TV TEL. 190DM–240DM ($108.30–$136.80) double. Rates include buffet breakfast. AE, DC, MC, V. Parking 8DM ($4.55). Bus: 9.

Mainzer Hof is six floors of modernity directly on the Rhine, almost at the point where some of the boats dock. This hotel is a clean-cut, convenient stopover. The medium-sized rooms are well furnished and maintained and have hair dryers. In the basement is an Italian specialty restaurant; on the sixth floor is the restaurant Panorama Salon, which is reserved for groups. There's an inviting atmosphere in the lobby bar. Room service, laundry, and dry cleaning are provided.

INEXPENSIVE

Hotel Mira. Bonifaziusstrasse 4 (near the Hauptbahnhof), 55118 Mainz. ☎ **06131/96-01-30.** Fax 06131/63-27-00. 34 units, 20 with bathroom. TEL. 95DM–105DM ($54.15–$59.85) double without bathroom, 130DM–150DM ($74.10–$85.50) double with bathroom; 165DM–180DM ($94.05–$102.60) triple with bathroom. Rates include continental breakfast. AE, DC, MC, V. Parking 8DM ($4.65). Bus: 16 or 23.

The delicate beige of the postwar facade hides a quiet but central hotel that beckons warmly to visitors. The hotel staff provides lots of useful information. Bedrooms are small and basic, but well maintained. Twenty have TVs.

WHERE TO DINE

✪ **Drei Lilien.** Ballplatz 2. ☎ **06131/22-50-68.** Reservations required. Main courses 25DM–34DM ($14.25–$19.40); fixed-price menu 55DM–80DM ($31.35–$45.60). AE, DC, V. Tues–Sat noon–2pm and 6:30–10pm. Bus: 15 to Schillerplatz. FRENCH.

Drei Lilien is an excellent place to have a French meal. The chef, H. J. Stuihmillers, practices a form of *cuisine moderne* that he has dubbed *cuisine du marché*, or "market fresh." Everything is cooked with imagination and the freshest seasonal ingredients. The decor of this wood-beamed, chandeliered place could be called "graciously rustic." Linens are impeccable, and the service is deferential. Try grilled steak with wild trumpet mushrooms in cognac sauce with grape leaves, or delicately poached baby turbot in champagne sauce.

Geberts Weinstuben. Frauenlobstrasse 94. ☎ **06131/61-16-19.** Reservations required. Main courses 25DM–40DM ($14.25–$22.80). AE, DC, MC, V. Mon–Fri 11:30am–2pm; Mon–Fri and Sun 6–10pm. Closed mid-July to mid-Aug. Bus: 7 or 21. PALATINATE.

This traditional Weinstube is housed in one of the oldest buildings in Mainz, with a decor that's almost Spartan. But decor is not the reason people come here, and they come in great numbers. Once seated, you're treated to a traditional meal of game, fish, or regional specialties such as goose à l'orange. The menu is robust Palatinate fare.

Langolo. Augustinerstrasse 8. ☎ **06131/23-17-37.** Reservations not necessary. Pizzas and pastas 9DM–16.50DM ($5.15–$9.40); meat platters 18.50DM–18.80DM ($10.55–$10.70). No credit cards. Daily 11am–midnight. Bus: 6, 15, or 23. ITALIAN.

This informal Italian-inspired trattoria is known for its excellent pizza and pasta and congenial staff. You can also order freshly made salads with shrimp or prosciutto, and meat dishes, consisting of escalopes of either pork or veal. Reasonable prices and a full bar generally keep this place packed.

Weinstube Lösch. Jakobsbergstrasse 9. ☎ **06131/22-03-83.** Reservations recommended. Main courses 15DM–40DM ($8.55–$22.80). No credit cards. Daily 5:30pm–1am. Bus: 6, 23. RHINELAND.

This old-fashioned Weinstube in the heart of the Altstadt has been popular for generations, and is rich in tradition. Meals feature both hot and cold dishes, plus lots of Rhine wine. The menu offers regional dishes and interesting salads. The pork schnitzel with mushrooms is particularly savory. There are only 12 tables, but they seat 85 guests. Six additional tables are placed out front in summer on the pedestrian mall.

MAINZ AFTER DARK

The cultural center of the city is **Frankfurter Hof,** Augustinerstrasse 55 (☎ 06131/22-04-38), which stages concerts of classical music, jazz, folk, and pop. The center also hosts an annual tent festival featuring an eclectic mix of international performers. Tickets to all events cost between 10DM and 70DM ($5.70 and $39.90). Call for scheduled shows, festival dates and performers, and ticket information.

Although you can buy tickets at the offices of any of the theaters and entertainment venues in Mainz, a more convenient way is to contact the **Ticket Service,** which is a division of the town's tourist office at Brückenturm am Rathaus, 55116 Mainz (☎ 06131/28-62-10). A privately funded competitor of the city's Ticket Service is **Kartenhaus,** Schillerstrasse 11 (☎ 06131/22-87-29).

In terms of its nightlife, Mainz is sleepy enough to compel many residents to head to Cologne or Düsseldorf after dark. But if you don't want to get too quickly out of town, consider dancing the night away at the **Disco Kuz,** Winterhaven 12 (☎ 06131/28-68-60), where good music and attractive people drink, dance, and talk. It's open nightly from 10pm till at least 2am, charges an 8DM ($4.55) entrance fee, and attracts a crowd aged 20 to around 35. A somewhat snobbier, smaller, and much more formal, nearby competitor is **L'Escalier,** Winterhaven 19 (☎ 06131/23-43-11). It's outfitted in a style that evokes a semiprivate club in London. Open nightly after 10:30pm; 10DM ($5.70) cover. **Chapeau Claque,** Kleine Landgasse 4 (☎ 06131/223-111), is a gay bar that's open nightly from 5pm till 4am.

4 The Rheingau

Legend says that when God was looking for a place to set up Paradise, the sunny slopes between the Taunus Mountains and the Rhine nearly won the prize. Today the Rheingau is the kingdom of another god, Bacchus. Nearly every town and village from Wiesbaden to Assmannshausen, no matter how small, is a major wine producer. The names suddenly seem familiar—Bingen, Johannisberg, Rüdesheim, Oestrich—because we have seen them on the labels of many favorite wines.

The Rheingau is also rich in old churches and castles, as well as landmarks. The **Niederwald Monument,** on a hill halfway between Rüdesheim and Assmanns-hausen—it can be reached by cable car from either town—is a huge statue of Germania, erected by Bismarck in 1883 to commemorate the unification of Germany. Below it, on a small island at the bend of the Rhine, is the **Mäuseturm (Mouse Tower),** where, according to legend, the greedy archbishop of Mainz was devoured by a swarm of hungry mice. But the real attraction of the Rheingau is the cheerful character of the wine villages and their people. Rüdesheim and Assmannshausen are the most visited towns. Assmannshausen is actually part of Rüdesheim—its center lies 3 miles to the northwest of Rüdesheim's center on the Rhine River.

ESSENTIALS

GETTING THERE   By Plane   The nearest airport is at Frankfurt (see chapter 12), 30 miles away.

By Train   The main rail station at Rüdesheim is on the Wiesbaden-Koblenz line, with frequent service to regional towns and connections to all major cities. For rail information and schedules, call ☎ **01805/996633.** Train service from Frankfurt is via Wiesbaden and takes 1 hour.

By Bus   Bus service for the region is provided by **ORN Omnibusverkehr Rhein-Nahe GmbH,** in Wierbaden (☎ **0611/97-75-822**).

By Car   Access by car is via the A61 Autobahn from the west and state highway 42 connecting with the A671 from the west. From Frankfurt, motorists can take the A66 until they reach the junction with Route B42, which will be signposted and lead them right to Rüdesheim. Motorists heading from Koblenz on the west bank of the Rhine can use the A61 to Bingen, then follow the signs for the ferryboats that cross the river to Rüdesheim. For information on the ferry service, call ☎ **06721/1-41-40.** From Koblenz, you can also take B42 along the east bank of the river, which will lead directly into Rüdesheim. Route B42 links Rüdesheim with Assmannshausen.

VISITOR INFORMATION   For information about Rüdesheim and Assmanns-hausen (see below), go to the **Stadt Verkehrsamt,** Rheinstrasse 16 in Rüdesheim (☎ **06722/19433**). It's open year-round Monday to Friday 8:30am to 6:30pm, and May through October also on Saturday 10:30am to 5:30pm and Sunday 11:30am to 3:30pm.

EXPLORING RÜDESHEIM

With its old courtyards and winding alleyways lined with timbered houses, Rüdesheim is the epitome of a Rhine wine town. The vineyards around the village date back to the Roman emperor Probus. The full-bodied Riesling is produced here, as well as brandy and champagne *(sekt).* Rüdesheim is also the scene of the annual August wine festival, when the old taverns on the narrow and very touristy **Drosselgasse** are crowded with visitors from all over the world. Drosselgasse has been called "the smallest but the happiest street in the world." From April through November, you can listen to music and dance in these taverns daily from noon to 1am.

To prove how seriously Rüdesheimers take their wine, they have opened a wine museum in Bromserburg Castle. The **Rheingau- und Weinmuseum,** Rheinstrasse 2 (☎ **06722/23-48**), charges 5DM ($2.85) for adults and 3DM ($1.70) for children under 12, and is open mid-March to mid-November daily from 9am to 6pm. It traces the history of the grape and has an exhibition of wine presses, glasses, goblets, and drinking utensils from Roman times to the present.

WHERE TO STAY & DINE IN RÜDESHEIM
MODERATE

Hotel und Weinhaus Felsenkeller. Oberstrasse 39–41 (in the center of the old town), 65385 Rüdesheim. ☎ 06722/9-42-50. Fax 06722/4-72-02. www.ruedesheim-rhein.com. E-mail: felsenkeller@ruedesheim-rhein.com. 60 units. MINIBAR TV TEL. 148DM–212DM ($84.35–$120.85) double; 190DM–244DM ($108.30–$139.10) triple. Rates include buffet breakfast. AE, MC, V. Closed Nov–Easter. Garage parking 10DM ($5.70).

The beautifully carved timbers on the facade of this 1613 building suggest the traditional aura you'll find inside. A sampling of Rhine wine can be enjoyed in a room of vaulted ceilings and murals with vine leaves and pithy pieces of folk wisdom. In fair weather, guests can eat on the terrace. The small guest rooms are attractively modern and freshly painted; they open onto views of the vineyards surrounding the house.

Rüdesheimer Hof. Geisenheimerstrasse 1 (a 10-min. walk from the Bahnhof), 65385 Rüdesheim. ☎ 06722/91-19-0. Fax 06722/4-81-94. E-mail: ruedesheiner-hof@t-online.de. 42 units. 130DM–160DM ($74.10–$91.20) double. Rates include buffet breakfast. AE, DC, MC, V. Closed Dec to mid-Feb. Free parking.

This village inn, set back from the Rhine, boasts a side garden and terrace where wine tasters gather at rustic tables. Most of the units are roomy and comfortably furnished; 20 have TVs and 30 have telephones. The atmosphere is informal. If you stay here, you can sample the lifestyle of a Rhine village by mingling with the townspeople, eating the regional food, and drinking the Rheingau wines. If you're stopping by just to eat, you'll find meals priced at 29DM ($16.55) and up. Guests dine at cafe tables placed under a willow tree. Food is served daily from 11:30am to 9:30pm.

Rüdesheimer Schloss. Steingasse 10. 65385 Rüdesheim. ☎ **06722/9-05-00.** Fax 06722/4-79-60. www.ruedesheimer-schloss.com. E-mail: ruedesheimer-schloss@t-online.de. 21 units. MINIBAR TV TEL. 190DM–260DM ($108.30–$148.20) double. Rates include buffet and local champagne. AE, DC, MC, V. Closed Dec 22–Jan 5. Free outdoor parking; 15DM ($8.55) in garage.

This hotel is the first choice for staying and dining in the town. The wine cellar dates from 1729. The Breuer family is noted for its wine cellars and plentiful food and drink. The medium-sized guest rooms are immaculately kept, and most are quite spacious, with radio, safe, hair dryer, and floor heating. The hotel staff will prepare for you a tailor-made package of excursions or perhaps a "gastronomic feast" and a musical evening on their premises.

INEXPENSIVE

Gasthof Krancher. Eibinger-Oberstrasse 4 (a 10-min. hike uphill from the town center), 65385 Rüdesheim. ☎ **06722/27-62.** Fax 06722/4-78-70. 62 units. 100DM–120DM ($57–$68.40) double. Rates include buffet breakfast. V. Free parking.

Gasthof Krancher has been in the Krancher family for four generations. It's located next to the inn's own vineyards. Naturally, the Kranchers make their own wines, and they'll gladly show you the cellar where they store bottles that have won gold and silver medals. Everything is decorated in a regional motif. The bedrooms are a bit cramped but reasonably comfortable. None has a telephone, although 10 contain TVs. From your window you can look out on the vineyards. The cuisine is first class, as are the wines.

Hotel Rheinstein. Rheinstrasse 20 (across from the riverside landing stage of the Cologne-Düsseldorf Anlegestelle), 65385 Rüdesheim. ☎ **06722/20-04.** Fax 06722/4-76-88. 40 units. TEL. 100DM ($57) double with shower, 140DM ($79.80) double with bathroom. Half board 65DM–75DM ($37.05–$42.75) per person. Rates include buffet breakfast. AE, DC, MC, V. Closed Dec–Mar.

The Rheinstein's elongated terrace facing the street is one of the most popular gathering places in Rüdesheim. Many locals drop in during the afternoon to enjoy the excellent cakes, all baked on the premises. Irene Gehrig offers small and well-kept rooms furnished with modern styling; some have TVs.

EXPLORING ASSMANNSHAUSEN

This old village at the northern edge of the Rheingau is built on the slopes of the east bank of the Rhine. Its half-timbered houses and vineyards seem precariously perched on the steep hillsides, and the view of the Rhine Valley from here is awe-inspiring. Assmannshausen is known for its fine burgundy-style wine. It lies 3 miles northwest of Rüdesheim and 37 miles west of Frankfurt.

WHERE TO STAY & DINE IN ASSMANNSHAUSEN

Alte Bauernschanke-Nassauer Hof. Niederwaldstrasse 23 (near the church, about ¼ mile from the Rhine), 65385 Rüdesheim-Assmannshausen. ☎ **06722/23-13.** Fax 06722/4-79-12. 52 units. TV TEL. 140DM–180DM ($79.80–$102.60) double, 250DM ($142.50) suite. Rates include buffet breakfast. AE, MC, V. Closed Dec–Feb.

The wine-grower owners have turned two of the oldest mansions in town into a hotel and restaurant. The interior decor is luxurious, the comfort fine, and the welcome hearty. The rooms are beautifully furnished in traditional style. The restaurant has live folk music every night. Try goulash soup, pepper steak with fresh green beans and French fries, and a bottle of the growers' red wine. The set price menu costs from 30DM to 115DM ($17.10 to $65.55); the higher price is for a lavish, eight-course banquet.

Ewige Lampe und Haus Resi. Niederwaldstrasse 14, 65385 Rüdesheim-Assmannshausen. ☎ **06722/24-17.** Fax 06722/4-84-59. 24 units. 100DM–180DM ($57–$102.60) double. Rates include continental breakfast. No credit cards. Closed Jan 6–Feb 6. Free parking.

This hotel is within a few miles of historic vineyards, plus some woodland trails through Rhenish forest. You'll find a lot to do in this wine-producing center. Hosts Engelbert and Renate Uri will welcome you to their cozy, tastefully furnished guest house. Many of the medium-sized rooms have wooden ceilings, some have colorfully tiled bathrooms, and all are impeccably clean. The fortifying breakfast is often served on a sun terrace under parasols. Meals cost 25DM to 65DM ($14.25 to $37.05) per person.

✪ **Krone Assmannshausen.** Rheinuferstrasse 10, 65385 Rüdesheim-Assmannshausen. ☎ **06722/40-30.** Fax 06772/30-49. 65 units. MINIBAR TV TEL. 250DM–320DM ($142.50–$182.40) double; 390DM ($222.30) junior suite; 590DM–780DM ($336.30–$444.60) suite. AE, DC, MC, V. Free parking.

This distinguished hotel offers the most luxurious accommodations in the entire Rüdesheim am Rhein district. It's on the banks of the Rhine, surrounded by lawns, gardens, and a pool. Its origins can be traced back 400 years. The inn is overscale, a great big gingerbread fantasy. A small second-floor lounge is virtually a museum, with framed letters and manuscripts of some of the famous people who have stayed here—Goethe, for one. There's a stack of about 40 autograph books dating from 1893 and signed by writers, painters, diplomats, and composers. You may stay in a medieval, a Renaissance, or a postwar building. The spacious guest rooms have an old-inn character, with traditional furnishings and compact bathrooms.

Dining: Even if you're not overnighting, you should stop to sample some of the finest food served on the Rhine. Specialties are homemade pâtés, fresh salmon or eel from Lake Constance, and saddle of venison in season. For dessert, try the *Eisbecher Krone.* The owners, the Hufnagel family, known for the famous Assmannshauser

Höllenberg Pinot Noir, maintain within the inn one of the finest cellars of Rhine wines in the world. Fixed-price menus cost from 42DM to 78DM ($23.95 to $44.45) for lunch and 135DM ($74.25) for dinner.

Amenities: Room service (breakfast only), hair dryers, laundry, baby-sitting, pool, sauna.

5   Koblenz

55 miles SE of Cologne, 39 miles SE of Bonn, 62 miles NW of Frankfurt

Koblenz has stood at the confluence of the Rhine and the Mosel for more than 2,000 years. Its strategic location in the mid-Rhine region has made the city a vital link in the international river trade routes of Europe. The city is surrounded by vine-covered hills dotted with castles and fortresses. Koblenz is also the place where many cruises through the Rhine begin or end.

ESSENTIALS

GETTING THERE   By Plane   The nearest airports to Koblenz are Frankfurt (see chapter 12) and Cologne (see section 9 below).

By Train   The **Koblenz Hauptbahnhof** lies on a major rail line, with frequent connections to important German cities. For train information, prices, and schedules, call ☎ **01805/996633.** Thirty trains per day arrive from Frankfurt (trip time: 2 hr.) and 16 from Berlin (8½ hr.). Trains also arrive every 30 minutes from Cologne (45 min. to 1 hr.).

By Bus   Rail is by far the best way to get to Koblenz, but information on bus service is available by calling ☎ **0261/303-88-23.**

By Car   Access by car to Koblenz is via the A48 Autobahn east and west, connecting with the A3 north to south.

VISITOR INFORMATION   For information about tours, boat trips on the Rhine, and bus and train connections, contact the **Koblenz Tourist Office,** Löhrstrasse 141 (☎ **0261/3-13-04**). It's open May to September, Monday to Friday 9am to 8pm, Saturday and Sunday 10am to 8pm; October and April Monday to Friday 9am to 6pm, Saturday and Sunday 10am to 6pm; November to March, Monday to Friday 9am to 5pm.

SEEING THE SIGHTS

Koblenz was heavily bombed during World War II, but many of the historic buildings have been restored. For the best overall view of the town, go to the point where the two rivers meet. This is called **Deutsches Eck** ("corner of Germany"). From the top of the base where a huge statue of Wilhelm I once stood, you can see the Altstadt and across the Rhine to the Ehrenbreitstein Fortress.

The focal point of the Altstadt is the **Liebfrauenkirche** (Church of Our Lady), a 13th-century Gothic basilica built on a Romanesque foundation, with twin towers topped by onion-shaped spires. The early-18th-century **Rathaus** was formerly a Jesuit college. In the courtyard behind the hall is a fountain dedicated to the youth of Koblenz called *The Spitting Boy* (*Das Schängelchen*), and that's just what he does. At the edge of the old town, near the Deutsches Eck, is Koblenz's oldest and most attractive church, **St. Castor's,** originally built in 836, though in its present form it dates mostly from the 12th century.

The **Festung Ehrenbreitstein** (☎ **0261/71987**), across the Rhine from Koblenz, can be reached by chairlift. You can also drive there via the Pfaffendorfer Bridge just south of the Altstadt or take bus 8, 9, or 10 from the rail station. The fortress was constructed on a rock and towers 400 feet above the Rhine. The present walls were built in the 19th century. From the stone terrace, you get one of the best views along the Rhine; the panoramic vista includes not only Koblenz but also several castles on the river and many terraced vineyards. To reach the fortress, make the 2DM ($1.15) one-way passage across the river from the main Rhine dock. Ferries operate between mid-April and late November, daily from 9am to 5:15pm. The chairlift *(Sesselbahn)* operates between May and September daily from 9:30am to 6pm. Round-trip tickets cost 10DM ($5.70) for adults, 6DM ($3.40) for children under 14.

WHERE TO STAY
EXPENSIVE

Diehl's. Am Pfaffendorfer Tor 10, Ehrenbreitstein, 56077 Koblenz. ☎ **0261/9-70-70.** Fax 0261/9-70-72-13. www.eurohotel-online.com/diehl.koblenz.html. E-mail: info@diehls-hotel.de. 64 units. MINIBAR TV TEL. 160DM–280DM ($91.20–$159.60) double; 280DM–480DM ($159.60–$273.60) suite. Rates include buffet breakfast. DC, MC, V. Free parking. Bus: 7, 8, 9, or 10.

Diehl's is on the banks of the Rhine; all its public rooms, lounges, dining rooms, and guest rooms face the river directly. This old-style hotel lies below the Ehrenbreitstein fortress, linked by a little ferry boat to the center of town. The place often accommodates groups.

Dining: Elevators connect the hotel floors with the restaurant, Rheinterrasse, which features both Rhineland and international cuisine. The hotel is well known for the quality of its food, and its cellar is filled with some 30,000 bottles of wine from the Rhine and Mosel Valleys.

Amenities: Pool, sauna, Jacuzzi, jogging track, hair dryers, limited room service, laundry service, baby-sitting, and conference rooms.

Mercure. Julius-Wegeler-Strasse 6, 56068 Koblenz. ☎ **0261/13-60.** Fax 0261/1-36-11-99. www.accor.com. 170 units. A/C MINIBAR TV TEL. 258DM ($147.05) double; 500DM ($285) suite. Rates include buffet breakfast. AE, DC, MC, V. Parking 20DM ($11.40).

Glittering and stylish, the Mercure is easily the best hotel in town. It's perched on a hillock at the edge of the Rhine. Its streamlined architecture contrasts with the century-old trees and ancient stones of the medieval town surrounding it. Guest rooms are well-insulated against sound from the street and neighboring rooms; each has a VCR. One of the city's loveliest riverside promenades lies just a short walk away.

Dining/Diversions: The hotel has a restaurant that serves lunch and dinner and a separate breakfast room.

Amenities: Sauna, solarium, hot whirlpool, room service, laundry, dry cleaning, secretarial assistance.

MODERATE

Hotel Brenner. Rizzastrasse 20–22 (near the Kurfürstl Schloss), 56068 Koblenz. ☎ **0261/91-57-80.** Fax 0261/3-62-78. www.eurohotel-de/brenner.koblenz.html. E-mail: brenner.koblenz@eurohotel-online.com. 24 units. MINIBAR TV TEL. 160DM–230DM ($91.20–$131.10) double. Rates include buffet breakfast. AE, DC, MC, V. Parking 10DM–15DM ($5.70–$8.55). Bus: 1 or 5 to Christuskirche.

This hotel is your best bet if you're seeking a good moderately priced choice. The small to medium-sized bedrooms are spotlessly maintained. Each bathroom has a hair dryer. The garden retreat is a good spot for getting back to nature.

Kleiner Riesen. Kaiserin-Augusta-Anlagen 18, 56068 Koblenz. ☎ **0261/3-20-77.** Fax 0261/16-07-25. 27 units. TV TEL. 150DM–180DM ($85.50–$102.60) double. Rates include buffet breakfast. AE, DC, MC, V. Parking 15DM ($8.55).

This is one of the few hotels in central Koblenz that sits directly on the banks of the Rhine. Its dining-room terrace and most of its guest rooms are close enough to view the boats as they go by. Within the city proper, only the Mercure is better. The Kleiner Riesen is a large, overgrown, informal chalet, with several living rooms and comfortable bedrooms. It's away from town traffic, so it has a peaceful small-town quiet.

INEXPENSIVE

Hotel Scholz. Moselweisserstrasse 121 (a 5-min. bus ride from the town center), 56073 Koblenz. ☎ **0261/94260.** Fax 0261/40-80-26. 62 units. TV TEL. 150DM ($85.50) double. Rates include buffet breakfast. AE, DC, MC, V. Free parking. Closed Dec 20–Jan 7. Bus: 6.

Scholz is a personally run family hotel. It offers sparsely furnished units that make for a reasonably priced overnight stopover. Bedrooms are small, as are the bathrooms, but the beds are comfortable and the maintenance is good. Traditional German cuisine is served at the restaurant.

WHERE TO DINE

Gillstuga. In the Mercure, Julius-Wegeler-Strasse 6. ☎ **0261/13-60.** Reservations recommended. Main courses 18DM–45DM ($10.25–$25.65). AE, DC, MC, V. Daily 11:30am–10:30pm. Bus: 1 or 5. RHINELANDER/INTERNATIONAL.

Elegantly modern in both design and flavor, Gillstuga is one of the leading restaurants of Koblenz, though that's not saying much—Koblenz is a notoriously bad restaurant town. You dine on a wide flower-trimmed terrace in summer, with a partial view of the river, or inside in an ambience of pastel and polished wood. Dishes are well prepared, although rarely exciting. Start with smoked salmon in a mustard dill sauce or perhaps a smooth consommé of pink mushrooms. Fish dishes are excellent, especially the fried catfish with a lime sauce or perch Strindberg with onions and mustard. Strips of veal appear in a mushroom cream sauce with potato *Rösti* and a salad from the buffet.

Weinhaus Hubertus. Florinsmarkt 6 (across from the Old Rathaus). ☎ **0261/3-11-77.** Reservations recommended. Snacks 8.50DM–15DM ($4.85–$8.55); glass of wine 3DM–7.50DM ($1.70–$4.25). MC, V. Wed–Mon 4pm–midnight. Bus: 1. GERMAN.

Weinhaus Hubertus looks like a timbered country inn. It's the oldest wine tavern in town, dating from 1696. The place offers German wines accompanied by a choice of homemade dishes—soups, sandwiches, and light platters, all designed to go well with the wines offered. The furnishings and the decor are family style, providing a homelike atmosphere. There's a choice here of 100 wines from all over Germany, 30 of these by the glass. In summer, you can enjoy the view of the Altstadt from the terrace.

KOBLENZ AFTER DARK

THE PERFORMING ARTS   The **Rheinische Philharmonie Orchestra** performs in the **Rhein-Mosel-Halle,** Julius-Wegeler-Strasse (☎ **0261/3012272**), which also hosts other performances. The symphony's season is September through June, and tickets range from 20DM to 110DM ($11.40 to $62.70). Call for listings, dates, and prices of other performances. The **Stadtheater (City Theater),** housed in the **Grosse-haus,** Dinehartplatz (☎ **0261/1292840** from 9am to noon), stages dramas, comedies, and musicals from September through June. The box office is open daily from 8am to noon and 1 to 4pm. Tickets range from 35DM to 75DM ($19.95 to $42.75).

BARS   Three of our favorite bars in Koblenz are devoted to individual themes that local residents embrace with relish. The first is the arts-conscious (and devilish) **Mephisto,** Eltzerhofstrasse 3 (☎ **0261/31735**), the walls of which are covered with photographs of famous German actors dressed for the part of Mephistopheles in various productions of *Faust*. Open Sunday to Friday from 7pm to 1am, and Saturday till 2am. Nearby is another establishment with an almost equivalent theme, the **Faustus Bar,** Eltzerhofstrasse 11 (☎ 0261/17991), which is open from 11am to 4pm and 6pm to 3am and caters to the same clientele.

For a laugh or two as you drink, head for the **Blauer Biwel,** Entenpfuhl 9 (☎ 0261/35577), a bar where local stand-up comics sometime perform. Even if your German isn't up to the challenge, you might like the disco music they sometimes play.

One of Koblenz's most counterculture pubs is **Klepsmühle,** Poststrasse 2A (☎ 0261/3-84-14). The music played here is mostly cutting-edge, with occasional touches of old-fashioned alpine evergreen music (yodeling and such). The pub-oriented clientele is mostly under age 40.

LIVE MUSIC   Pflaumenbaum, Friedrich-Ebert-Ring 32 (☎ 0261/30-90-70), is a smoke-filled, woodsy pub enhanced with live jazz, pop, and other types of music. Open daily from 7pm to 7am. At **Irish Pub Koblenz,** Burgstrasse 7 (☎ 0261/17377), copious amounts of Guinness, Kilkenny, hard cider, and German beers are served as accompaniment to live music, everything from traditional Gaelic songs to progressive rock 'n' roll. Open Sunday to Thursday from 1pm to 1am and Friday and Saturday from 1pm to 2am.

DANCE CLUBS   Koblenz's largest nightlife complex lies 2½ miles north of the town center. **Extra,** August-Horch-Strasse 2 (☎ 0261/809-050) includes a half-dozen movie theaters, and a scattering of bars and dance clubs that play everything from old-time mountain-style evergreen music to the cutting-edge. The best way to experience the complex is to wander through its hallways, popping into whatever place suits your fancy. Entrance to most of the bars is free; cover charge to some of the dance emporiums runs from 5DM to 15DM ($2.85 to $8.55).

6 Bonn

45 miles S of Düsseldorf, 17 miles S of Cologne, 108 miles NW of Frankfurt

Until 1949, Bonn was a sleepy little university town, basking in its 2,000 years of history. Then suddenly it was shaken out of this quiet life and made capital of the Federal Republic of Germany. But in 1991, after the unification of the two Germanys finally took place, Berlin again became the official capital.

Although Bonn is, at least officially, thrilled at reunification, no other cities stand to loose as much, especially in terms of prestige and political influence. However, Bonn will continue to function as a smaller "second capital." Six of the major 15 departments of the German government, including the Defense Ministry, will remain here, although they will also have smaller offices in Berlin.

Bonn has been the brunt of jokes for years because of its small town provincialism. As European capitals went, Bonn was at the bottom of the totem pole. But over the years government workers, civil servants, journalists, lobbyists, think-tank gurus, and others developed a fondness for the place and settled down here. Thousands upon thousands of these people have been most reluctant to rip up roots and relocate to the more bustling city of Berlin. Bonn also remains a leader in technology and international government.

From the 13th through the 18th centuries, Bonn was the capital of the prince-electors of Cologne, who had the right to participate in the election of the emperor of the Holy Roman Empire. The city is also proud of its intellectual and musical history—Beethoven was born here; composer Robert Schumann and his wife, pianist Clara Schumann, lived here; and Karl Marx and Heinrich Heine studied in Bonn's university.

Bonn's latest cultural addition is the "Museum Mile," which includes the **Bundes-kunsthalle** (Federal Art and Exhibition Hall) and the **Kunstmuseum** (Art Museum).

Bonn is also within sight of the **Siebenbirge** ("The Seven Mountains"), a volcanic mountain range rising up on the eastern bank of the Rhine. The entire range is today a national park. The local wine produced on these slopes is known as Drachenblut ("Dragon's Blood").

ESSENTIALS

GETTING THERE   By Plane   The nearest airport is **Flughafen Köln/Bonn** (see section 9, below). Buses from the airport to Bonn's main rail station run every 30 minutes daily from 6am to 10:30pm.

By Train   The **Bonn Hauptbahnhof** is on a major rail line, with connections to most German cities. There are 12 trains daily to Berlin (trip time: 7 hr.), more than 30 trains to Frankfurt (trip time: 2 hr.), and service to Cologne every 15 minutes (trip time: 20 min.). For rail information, call ☎ **01805/996633.**

By Bus   Long-distance bus service goes to such cities as Munich, Stuttgart, Aachen, Brussels, and London. For information and schedules, call **Deutsches Touring GmbH** in Frankfurt (☎ **069/7-90-35-0**). Regional bus service to Bad Godesberg and nearby towns is provided by **Regionalverkehr Köln GmbH at Meckenheim** (☎ **02225/60-87**).

By Car   Access is by the A565 Autobahn connecting with the A3 Autobahn from the north or south.

VISITOR INFORMATION   Go to the **Bonn Tourist Office,** Cassius-Passage, Münsterstrasse 20 (☎ **0228/19433**), which is open Monday to Friday 9am to 6:30pm, Saturday 9am to 4pm, and Sunday 10am to 2pm.

EXPLORING THE TOWN

Residents and tourist officials within Bonn show an extraordinary degree of civic and cultural pride whenever they discuss their city. Part of this manifests itself in **walking tours** that stress the 2,000 years of Bonn's history, with an emphasis on its role as a city of culture during the 19th century, and its changing role within Germany since reunification. From April through October, 2-hour walking tours of Bonn are offered at the following times: Monday to Friday at 2pm, Saturday at 10:30am and 2pm, and Sunday at 10:30pm. Between November and March, there's only one tour a week: Saturday at 2pm. Tours cost 22DM ($12.55) for adults and 11DM ($6.25) for students and children under 16. The meeting point for these tours is the Bonn Tourist Office (see above). Call ☎ **0228/19433** for reservations and advance confirmation.

The **government quarter,** along the west bank of the Rhine, is a complex of modern, rather nondescript white buildings. The two most impressive structures, both along Koblenzerstrasse, are the former residences of the president and chancellor. These empire-style villas are reminiscent of the older Bonn, before it became an international center of diplomatic activity. They are not open to the public. Running north along the Rhine from the government buildings is a tree- and flower-lined promenade, which ends at the **Alter Zoll.** This ruined ancient fortress makes a good viewing point from which visitors can see across the Rhine to the Siebengebirge and the old village of Beuel. These grounds have, in essence, become a city park.

✪ **Beethoven House.** Bonngasse 20 (in the old section of town, just north of the market-place). ☎ **0228/9-81-75-25.** Admission 8DM ($4.55) adults, 6DM ($3.40) students and children. Guided tours by prior arrangement 15DM ($8.55). Apr–Sept, Mon–Sat 10am–5pm, Sun 11am–4pm; Oct–Mar, Mon–Sat 10am–4pm, Sun 11am–4pm. Tram: 61 or 62.

Beethoven House is Bonn's pride and joy. Beethoven was born in 1770 in the small house in back, which opens onto a little garden. On its second floor is the room where he was born, decorated only with a simple marble bust of the composer. Many of Beethoven's personal possessions are in the house, including manuscripts and musical instruments. In the Vienna Room, in the front of the house overlooking the street, is Beethoven's last piano. The instrument was custom-made, with a special sounding board to amplify sound so that the deaf composer could hear it.

Kunstmuseum Bonn. Friedrich-Ebert-Allee 2. ☎ **0228/77-62-60.** Admission 5DM ($2.85) adults, 3DM ($1.70) children. Tues–Sun 10am–6pm, Wed 10am–9pm. U-Bahn: 16, 63, or 66 to Heussallee.

One of the major buildings along the new "Museum Mile," this triangular structure, flooded with light, contains one of the most important art collections along the Rhine. The highlight is the collection of 20th-century art, including works by Rhenish expressionists, most notably the painter August Macke. There are also works by Kirchner, Schmidt-Rottluff, Campen-donk, Ernst, Seehaus, and Thuar.

Haus der Geschichte der Bundesrepublik Deutschland. Adenauerallee 250. ☎ **0228/9-16-50.** Free admission. Tues–Sun 9am–7pm. U-Bahn: Heussallee.

All the sweep and drama of Germany's modern history is brought to life in this museum, in artifacts, photographs, and other displays. Exhibits trace the history of Germany after 1945, up to the breakdown of law and order in the eastern sector that led to reunification. This museum is one of Bonn's most visited.

SHOPPING

Not surprisingly, you'll find lots of shops in town specializing in garments suitable for diplomacy and business. Most of the best are on the **Sternstrasse,** partly a pedestrian-only street for certain times of day. Fanning out from here, you'll find women's clothing at **Beatrix Moden,** Münsterplatz 26 (☎ **0228/63-46-96**); **Boecker,** Wenzelgasse 17 (☎ **0228/98-50-60**); and **La Belle,** Friedrichstrasse 51 (☎ **0228/63-74-75**). For menswear, try **Daniel's,** Münsterplatz (☎ **0228/98350**), which sells an assortment of designer labels, including Boss and Armani.

Two notable shops sell antique German furniture. **Ehlers Antiquitäten,** Berliner Freiheit 28 (☎ **0228/65-72-88**), specializes in 19th- and 20th-century pieces and also sells some English silver and glass. Eighteenth-century German and French furniture as well as Biedermeier is found at **Paul Schweitzer,** Loebestrasse 1 (☎ **0228/36-26-59**), which also handles Oriental carpets, silver, French glass, and estate jewelry. A market called the **Flohmarkt,** at Rheinaue, Ludwig-Erhard-Strasse, is where you'll find all manner of secondhand goods and collectibles. It's held the third Saturday of each month from April through October.

WHERE TO STAY
VERY EXPENSIVE
Günnewig Bristol Hotel. Prinz-Albert-Strasse 2 (near Poppelsdorf Castle), 53113 Bonn. ☎ **0228/2-69-80.** Fax 0228/2-69-82-22. 116 units. A/C MINIBAR TV TEL. 370DM–470DM ($210.90–$267.90) double; 570DM ($324.90) suite. Rates include American breakfast. AE, DC, MC, V. Parking 23DM ($13.10). Tram: 61 or 62.

This somewhat sterile, Cold War-era concrete-and-glass tower is still the best address in town. The graceful interior rooms are decorated with plenty of fresh flowers, Oriental carpeting, and leather chairs. The good-sized bedrooms are the best in Bonn, with such extras as safes, trouser presses, and double-glazing on the windows, along with fashionable and well-equipped marble baths with hair dryers, toiletries, and robes. The staff is also the finest in town.

Dining/Diversions: The food is of a high standard without being exceptional. Diplomats from all over the world patronize the Restaurant Majestic, the Hofkonditorei Bierhoff, and the Walliser Stuben. There's also a cozy lounge bar.

Amenities: Room service, laundry, dry cleaning, heated indoor pool, sauna, solarium.

EXPENSIVE

✪ **Hotel Domicil.** Thomas-Mann-Strasse 24–26 (4 blocks north of the cathedral, near the Hauptbahnhof), 53111 Bonn. ☎ **800/528-1234** in the U.S., or 0228/72-90-90. Fax 0228/69-12-07. 40 units. MINIBAR TV TEL. 280DM–420DM ($159.60–$239.40) double; 480DM ($273.60) suite. AE, DC, MC, V. Free parking.

This modern and convenient hotel, like the Kaiser Karl (see below), is an oasis of charm and grace amid the rather sterile environment of Bonn. It's like an exclusive London townhouse, and provides a viable alternative to staying at the Günnewig Bristol. In the front, a glass-and-steel portico stretches over the sidewalk. The interior is one of the most elegant in the capital, with a stylishly angular lobby and an art-deco bistro. The styles of the handsomely designed and spacious guest rooms range from belle epoque to Italian modern.

Dining/Diversions: You can enjoy a drink in the piano bar before heading for the Krull restaurant, where French and Italian meals are served. The hotel also has a nightclub, called the Joyce Evening Club.

Amenities: Room service, laundry, dry cleaning, sauna, car-rental facilities.

✪ **Kaiser Karl.** Vorgebirgstrasse 56, 53119 Bonn. ☎ **0228/65-09-33.** Fax 0228/63-78-99. 43 units. MINIBAR TV TEL. 290DM–390DM ($165.30–$222.30) double; 450DM–850DM ($256.50–$484.50) suite. AE, DC, MC, V. Parking 20DM ($11.40). Bus: 624 or 634.

Kaiser Karl is one of Bonn's gems. Like the Domicil (see above), it has more style and atmosphere than other luxury leaders. Constructed in 1905 as a private townhouse, it was converted in 1983 into a stylish four-story hotel. The attractive decor includes lacquered Japanese screens, English antiques, Oriental carpets, Venetian mirrors, and Edwardian potted palms. Each beautifully furnished guest room has a safe and phones in both the bedroom and the bathroom.

Dining/Diversions: Breakfast is the only meal served. There's an elegant piano bar and a garden where you can order drinks.

Amenities: Room service, hair dryers, laundry, concierge, dry cleaning.

Steigenberger Hotel Venusberg. An der Casselsruhe 1 (1½ miles southwest of Bonn, via Trierer Strasse), 53127 Bonn. ☎ **800/223-5652** in the U.S. and Canada, or 0228/28-80. Fax 0228/28-82-88. 91 units. MINIBAR TV TEL. 235DM–363DM ($133.95–$206.90) double; from 595DM ($339.15) suite. Rates include continental breakfast. AE, DC, MC, V. Parking 14.50DM ($8.25).

The elegant and intimate Steigenberger is surrounded by the beauty of the Venusberg nature reserve, which is a part of the larger Kottenforst. Built in a style evocative of a French country home, the hotel extends symmetrical wings around either side of a forecourt. There are six air-conditioned suites, and about half the units offer private balconies overlooking the hills. Each unit contains a well-accessorized bathroom in cream-colored or black-and-white marble.

Dining: The gourmet dining room has an outdoor terrace overlooking the seven nearby hills of local legends.

Amenities: Room service, laundry, dry cleaning, hair dryers, sauna, health club, massage facilities.

MODERATE

Sternhotel. Markt 8 (next to the Rathaus), 53111 Bonn. ☎ **0228/7-26-70.** Fax 0228/ 7-26-71-25. www.eurohotel.de/sternhotel.bonn. 79 units. MINIBAR TV TEL. 155DM–295DM

($88.35–$168.15) double. Rates include buffet breakfast. AE, DC, MC, V. Parking 20DM ($11.40) garage. U-Bahn: Uni-Markt. Bus: 624, 625, or 626.

This is one of the best of Bonn's moderately priced hotels. It offers an informal, home-like atmosphere. Furnishings harmoniously blend the traditional and the contemporary. Equally homelike are the guest rooms, the larger of which have sitting areas. International meals are served in the dining room. The warmly decorated Bistro Miebach, under separate management, serves lunch and dinner.

INEXPENSIVE

Haus Hofgarten. Fritz-Tillmann-Strasse 7 (a 5-min. walk from the Hauptbahnhof), 53113 Bonn. ☎ **0228/22-34-72.** Fax 0228/21-39-02. 15 units. TV TEL. 125DM ($71.25) double without bathroom, 185DM ($105.45) double with bathroom. Rates include continental breakfast. AE, DC, MC, V. Parking 5DM ($2.85). Tram: 61 or 62.

A hard-working couple presides over this unique establishment, which offers the charm of another era. It's an excellent value for Bonn. A wide mahogany staircase leads to the cozy rooms, which are simply but comfortably furnished and very well kept. There's also a good-sized breakfast room.

Hotel Beethoven. Rheingasse 24–26 (across the street from the Stadttheater, a 10-min. walk from the Hauptbahnhof), 53113 Bonn. ☎ **0228/63-14-11.** Fax 0228/69-16-29. www. hotel-beethoven-bonn.com. E-mail: hotel-beethoven@t-online.de. 59 units. TV TEL. 165DM–185DM ($94.05–$105.45) double. Rates include buffet breakfast. AE, DC, MC, V. Free parking. Tram: 62; Bus 638.

One of the Beethoven's wings faces the Rhine. The hotel's main attraction is a panoramic view of the river traffic from the high-ceilinged dining room, where first-class meals are served, supervised by the owner. Double-glazed windows prevent urban noises from disturbing the calm in the well-furnished rooms, which range in size from small to medium.

WHERE TO DINE
EXPENSIVE

Le Petit Poisson. Wilhelmstrasse 23A. ☎ **0228/63-38-83.** Reservations recommended. Main courses 50DM–55DM ($28.50–$31.35); fixed-price dinner 65DM–120DM ($37.05–$68.40). AE, DC, MC, V. Tues–Sat 6pm–midnight. Tram: 61 or 62. FRENCH/SEAFOOD.

The food here is the finest in the center of Bonn. All ingredients are fresh, and many dishes are temptingly light and contemporary. Try the cream of fish and mushroom soup. Savory meat and game dishes include venison in vermouth sauce. Many diplomats dine here.

Ristorante Grand'Italia. Bischofsplatz 1 (adjacent to the old market square). ☎ **0228/ 63-83-33.** Reservations recommended. Main courses 29DM–42DM ($16.55–$23.95); set-price menus 37.50DM–72.80DM ($21.35–$41.50). AE, DC, MC, V. Daily noon–3pm and 6–11:30pm. Tram: 62 or 66. ITALIAN/INTERNATIONAL.

This place is one of the most appealing Italian restaurants along the Rhine. Main courses might include a *filletto della casa* (fillet of beef prepared in a "special sauce" whose composition the chefs won't discuss), tagliorini with white truffles, and an autumnal version of roast pheasant. Also look for Roman-style osso bucco (veal shank layered with prosciutto), a succulent risotto Milanese, and such desserts as a velvety version of zabaglione.

MODERATE

Zur Lese. Adenaueralle 37. ☎ **0228/22-33-22.** Reservations recommended for lunch and dinner, not required for the afternoon cafe. Main courses 26DM–39DM ($14.80–$22.25); fixed-price meals 52DM–60DM ($29.65–$34.20); 39DM ($22.25) 3-course, fixed-price menu for lunch. AE, DC, MC, V. Restaurant Tues–Sun 10am–11pm; cafe Tues–Sun 10am–11pm. GERMAN.

This restaurant's polite service and outdoor terrace with a sweeping view over the Rhine attract many local residents, especially in the afternoon, when visitors drop in for coffee, cakes, and glasses of wine after strolling in the nearby Hofgarten. Elegant, well-prepared lunches are also offered. Dinner is served in the cafe. A menu of German specialties (with English translations) includes pork with curry sauce and the chef's superb *Gulasch Lese*. You can also choose rainbow trout or lobster from the terrace aquarium. The food is home-style and hearty, with no pretense.

INEXPENSIVE

Em Höttche. Markt 4 (next to the Rathaus). ☎ **0228/69-00-09.** Reservations not accepted. Main courses 12DM–30DM ($6.85–$17.10). No credit cards. Daily 11am–1am. Tram: 47. Bus: 618. GERMAN.

Em Höttche has a long and colorful history, stretching all the way from 1389. It's fed thousands over the centuries with its rib-sticking fare—perhaps changing the recipes every 100 years or so. The interior has been restored, with carved-wood paneling, natural brick, old beamed ceilings, decoratively painted plaster, and curlicue chandeliers. Favorite dining spots are tables set inside the walk-in fireplace. On the à la carte list, you'll find specialties for two, including entrecôte. Fresh salmon is often available. Complement your meal with a carafe of local wine—the best buy in the house.

Im Bären. Acherstrasse 1–3 (5 min. from the main train station). ☎ **0228/63-32-00.** Reservations recommended. Main courses 10DM–35DM ($5.70–$19.95). No credit cards. Daily 9am–midnight. Tram: 61, 62, or 63. GERMAN.

This historic inn was first mentioned in documents dating from 1385. Today it occupies a prominent position in Bonn's pedestrian zone and is one of the best-known restaurants in town. Most diners head for tables on the street level, although a large additional room is on the second floor. The food is hearty Rhinelander cuisine, including everything from simple wursts with potatoes to more elaborate steaks with béarnaise sauce and salad. Service is bustling, matter-of-fact, and efficient.

Im Stiefel. Bonngasse 30 (a few doors down from the Beethoven House). ☎ **0228/ 630805.** Reservations recommended. Main courses 15DM–35DM ($8.55–$19.95); fixed-price menus 16DM–60DM ($9.10–$34.20). AE, DC, MC, V. Mon–Sat 10am–1am. Tram: 61 or 62. RHINELAND.

This atmospheric restaurant is a local favorite. You dine at bare bleached tables in rooms with wood paneling and stained glass. There's a stand-up bar for mugs of beer. The short menu features down-home Rhineland dishes, including a local dish, *Hämmchen,* served with sauerkraut and mashed potatoes. A specialty is braised beef marinated in almond-raisin sauce.

BONN AFTER DARK

Once considered a dismal place to go out on the town, Bonn now has a thriving fine-arts community and a brisk nightlife. If you're in the area around the first Saturday in May, don't miss the spectacular annual fireworks display, visible for a distance of 16 miles south of the city.

THE PERFORMING ARTS   Bonn has always struggled with the perception that it can't compete with the larger arts communities in Hamburg and Berlin, and consequently it has compensated (or overcompensated) with an impressive roster of cultural events. One of the most visible is "La Scala of the Rhineland," the **Oper der Stadt Bonn,** Am Boselagerhof 1 (☎ **0228/77-36-67**), where ballet and opera are performed at regular intervals between mid-August and June. Box office hours are Monday to Friday 8am to 6pm, Saturday 9am to 4pm, and Sunday 10am to 2pm. Tickets range from 25DM to 175DM ($14.25 to $99.75) each, depending on the event.

The **Bonn Symphony Orchestra** performs in Beethovenhalle, Wachsbleiche 26 (☎ 0228/7222100), also from September through June, with occasional free concerts given on Sunday mornings. Otherwise, tickets cost between 20DM and 110DM ($11.40 to $62.70). On a more intimate scale, chamber music is sometimes presented within a small but charming concert hall within the **Beethoven House** (☎ 0228/ 981-7525 for details).

From mid-May through August, the Bonner Summer Festival takes place, during which an international selection of dance and music groups perform, mostly for free, in open-air locations around the city. Contact ☎ 0228/19433 or 0228/774400 for details. In addition to all this, the **Beethoven Festival,** a rekindling of both the nostalgia and the music associated with Bonn's greatest musical genius, takes place in September of 2000. Contact the visitor information center (see above) for information.

Bonn's **Theater-Kasse,** Mühlheimerplatz 1 (☎ 0228/773-6667), is a well-known and highly resourceful ticket agency associated with the city's tourist office. It has access to tickets for virtually every sporting, entertainment, and cultural venue in Bonn. Also call for information on performers, schedules, and prices.

DANCE CLUBS   **Maxim and Kleopatra Discotheque,** Maxstrasse 18-20 (☎ 0228/65-77-98), features a different mix of music each night. Friday brings house, soul, and funk; on Saturday there's house, reggae, and hip-hop. You can dance Tuesday to Sunday from 9pm to 4am. There's a 8DM ($4.55) cover. Another weekend-only club, **Sharon,** Oxfordstrasse 20–21 (no phone), is straight out of the 1970s, with dancing to soul and funk under a spinning mirror ball and strobe lights. It's open from 10pm to 5am, with a 10DM ($5.70) cover.

LIVE MUSIC & CABARET   Live jazz is featured on Friday and Saturday nights from 8pm till around 4am at **The Jazz Galerie,** Oxfordstrasse 24 (☎ 0228/63-93-24). The cover charge ranges from 12DM to 25DM ($6.85 to $14.25), depending on the band. The **Pantheon Theater,** Bundes-kanzlerplatz (☎ 0228/21-25-21), stages jazz and pop concerts, comedy shows, and political cabaret. Nearly every weekday night there is a performance of some sort. Friday and Saturday nights, the facility becomes a disco. The box office is open Monday to Friday from noon to 6:30pm.

BARS   A small, dark, and smoky bar, **Pinte,** Breitestrasse 46 (no phone), is the kind of place that has a great atmosphere simply because it doesn't try to create one. **Pawlow,** Heerstrasse 64 (☎ 0228/65-36-03), has an alfresco terrace. While here, don't let appearances intimidate you—a sometimes fierce-looking crowd with tattoos and body piercings is actually a bored intelligentsia set at heart. Open daily from 11am to 1am. Candlelit late into the night, **Zur Kerze,** Königstrasse 25 (no phone), is a good conversation spot and a place to order Italian, German, and Greek dishes to go with your beer. Open nightly from 7pm to 5am. **Bräuhaus Bönnsch,** Sterntorbrucke 4 (☎ 0228/65-06-10), serves the very smooth Bönnsch beer, as well as *Bönnsche Flammkuchen,* an old regional recipe for a sort of pizza topped with sour cream, onions, cheese, and meat. Open Sunday to Thursday from 11:30am to 1am and Friday and Saturday from 11:30am to 3am.

GAY BARS   The most crowded gay bar is **Boba's Bar,** Josefstrasse 17 (☎ 0228/ 65-06-85), set near the town's railway station, adjacent to the Rhine. It welcomes a drinking (but not dancing) crowd in their 20s and 30s. It's open Sunday to Tuesday 9pm to 3am and Friday to Saturday 9pm to 5am. Another gay bar is **Charley,** Kölnstrasse at Theaterstrasse (☎ 0228/69-07-61), open Sunday to Thursday 9pm to 3am and Friday to Saturday 9pm to 5am. There's also **Le Copain,** Berliner Platz 5 (☎ 0228/63-99-35), which attracts a somewhat older clientele and is open from 9pm to 2 or 3am.

7 Bad Godesberg

4 miles S of central Bonn

Part of greater Bonn, Bad Godesberg is one of the Rhine's oldest spa towns. It's located just opposite the legendary Siebengebirge (The Seven Mountains), with a view of the crag, Drachenfels (Dragon's Rock), where Siegfried slew the dragon. Dragons are no longer found on the Rhine, but you can still see some ancient castle ruins on the hills. The most interesting is **Godesberg Castle,** built in the 13th century by the electors of Cologne (its ruins have been incorporated into a hotel, described below). From the promenade along the Rhine, you can watch a flow of boats and barges wending their way up and down the river.

Most of the spa's activity centers around the **Redoute Palace,** a small but elegant 18th-century structure. Although the town is mainly a residential center, there is seemingly no end to the entertainment and cultural facilities here. Theaters, concerts, and social functions offer a constant whirl of events.

GETTING THERE You can reach Bad Godesberg from Bonn by taking tram 16 or 63 from Bonn's central rail station. If you're driving from the center of Bonn, take the B9 (driving time: 20 min.). For information about the town, consult the Bonn Tourist Office (see above).

WHERE TO STAY

Günnewig Godesberg Castlehotel. Auf dem Godesberg 5, 53177 Bonn-Bad Godesberg. ☎ **0228/31-60-71.** Fax 0228/31-12-18. 13 units. TV TEL. 170DM ($96.90) double. Rates include continental breakfast. AE, DC, MC, V. Free parking. Tram: 16 or 63 from Bonn.

A winding road leads up to this hilltop castle ruin, now converted to a hotel that we highly recommend. Its tall tower and many of its rugged stone walls were erected in 1210 by the archbishop of Cologne and are still intact. A lounge built against one of the stone walls provides a sunny perch and a view of the spa and river. There's also a roof terrace, with tables for drinks. The small guest rooms are traditionally furnished and well maintained and have picture windows. The food in the restaurant here is especially good.

WHERE TO DINE

✪ **Halbedel's Gasthaus.** Rheinallee 47. ☎ **0228/35-42-53.** Reservations recommended. Main courses 49DM–53DM ($27.95–$30.20); fixed-price menus 99DM–135DM ($56.45–$76.95). AE, MC. Tues–Sun 6–11pm (last order 10:30pm). Closed July–Aug 3. Tram: 16 or 610 from Bonn. CONTINENTAL.

The only restaurant that matches the superior cuisine of this award-winning selection is Le Marron, on the outskirts of Bonn. Here, amid many nostalgic souvenirs and antique tables and chairs, the courtly owners will welcome you to their turn-of-the-century villa. The kitchen prides itself on using mostly German-grown produce. The chefs are true artists, using ingredients of superlative quality to create harmonious flavors and textures. Some of the dishes will be familiar; others are imaginative inventions. Menu choices might include wild mushroom soup, rack of lamb prepared French style, and a salad of dandelion greens and wild lettuce, followed by flavorful desserts.

Zur Korkeiche. Lyngsbergstrasse 104 (½ mile south of Bad Godesberg in the village of Lannesdorf). ☎ **0228/34-78-97.** Reservations recommended. Main courses 30DM–38DM ($17.10–$21.65); fixed-price menus 68DM–78DM ($38.75–$44.45). V. Tues–Sun 6pm–midnight. Closed 2 weeks in October and 2 weeks in April (dates vary). Bus: 14. CONTINENTAL.

Zur Korkeiche is a wine-and-sherry house. It's located in a well-maintained, 150-year-old half-timbered building. There are two stories of cozy comfort and tradition. The decor is rustic in a country-elegant way. The head chef prepares a light cuisine. Menu choices include a delicately seasoned smoked salmon in champagne sauce.

8   Aachen (Aix-la-Chapelle)

40 miles W of Cologne, 50 miles SW of Düsseldorf

The ancient Imperial City of Aachen (Aix-la-Chapelle), at the frontier where Germany, Belgium, and the Netherlands meet, is inseparably connected with Charlemagne. He selected this spot as the center of his vast Frankish empire. History is important at this spa town, but today there's also a youthful *joie de vivre* that attracts young people from all over the world. Visitors also come for the sulfurous hot springs or the magnificent cathedral, or to use Aachen as a launching pad for exploring the Benelux nations.

Aachen has an even longer history as a spa than as an imperial city. Roman legionnaires established a military bath here in the 1st century A.D. By the end of the 17th century, Aachen was known as the "Spa of Kings" because royalty from all over Europe came here to take the cure. In 1742 Frederick the Great came here, and in 1818 the "Congress of Monarchs" brought Tsar Alexander from Russia. After World War II, the spa was rebuilt and today enjoys a mild reputation as a remedial center. Its springs are among the hottest in Europe. The treatment includes baths and the *Trinkkur* (drinking the water). The spa gardens are the center of resort activity, with attractive ponds, fountains, and shade trees.

Aachen can be visited as a sightseeing day trip from Cologne. However, those interested in using the spa facilities should stay at one of the hotels described below.

ESSENTIALS

GETTING THERE   By Train   The Hauptbahnhof at Aachen receives some 200 trains a day from all parts of Germany and from Paris, with easy connections from most major cities as well as nearby Cologne (trip time: 45 min.). Frankfurt is 3½ hours away, and Munich, 7 hours. For rail schedules and information, call ☎ **01805/ 996633.**

By Bus   It's best to take the train, but once you arrive in Aachen, regional bus service is provided by **BVR Busverkehr Rheinland GmbH** at Simmerath (☎ **02473/66-46** for schedules and information).

By Car   Access is by the A4 Autobahn east and west or the A44 north or south. Driving time from Cologne is 50 to 60 minutes, depending on traffic. Frankfurt is 3½ hours away by car; Munich, 6½ hours.

VISITOR INFORMATION   You'll find the **Tourist Office Aachen** on Friedrich-Wilhelm-Platz (☎ **0241/19433**). Office hours are Monday to Friday 9am to 6pm and Saturday 9am to 2pm.

SEEING THE SIGHTS

Aachen's Altstadt is small enough to be covered on foot. **Marktplatz,** in the heart of town, is overshadowed by the Gothic Rathaus, which contains the city archives. From here, you can head down one of the most popular and busiest pedestrian precincts in the city, **Krämerstrasse,** which will lead to Münsterplatz (Cathedral Square) and the famous cathedral (see below), one of the masterpieces of architecture in the Western world. Past the cathedral you reach the **Elisengarten,** bordered on the south by the symbol of Bad Aachen, the Elisenbrunnen, a rotunda with a thermal drinking fountain. From Münsterplatz you can go through the great iron gate to the **Fischmarkt,** with old merchants' houses and the Fischpuddelchen fountain with spouting fish.

The **Wingerstberg Kurgarten** and the **Stadtgarten,** with its thermal bath and casino, lie to the northeast of town, and the **Hauptbahnhof** is on the southern ring, opening onto Römerstrasse.

✪ **Cathedral (Dom).** Klosterplatz 2. ☎ **0241/47-70-91-27.** Cathedral free; treasury 5DM ($2.85) adults, 3DM ($1.70) children. Mon 10am–12:30pm, Tues and Thurs–Sat 10am–5:30pm, Wed 10am–8:30pm, Sun 10am–5:30pm. Bus: 1, 11, or 21.

About A.D. 800 the emperor Charlemagne built the "octagon," the core of the Imperial Cathedral. Within the cathedral stands the marble *Königsstuhl,* Charlemagne's throne, one of the most venerable monuments in Germany. (Visitors to the cathedral can view the throne of Charlemagne only with a guide; request one at the treasury or call ahead.) From 936 to 1531 the Holy Roman emperors were crowned here, until Frankfurt became the coronation city.

The cathedral is an unusual mixture of Carolingian (the well-preserved dome), Gothic (the choir, completed in 1414), and baroque (the Hungarian chapel), all united into a magnificent upward sweep of architecture. The treasury, in the adjoining house (entry: Klostergasse), is the most valuable and celebrated ecclesiastical treasure trove north of the Alps. But the cathedral itself holds its own share of wealth. The elaborate gold shrine (1215) in the chancel contains the relics of Charlemagne. The pulpit of Henry II (ca. 1002) is copper studded with precious gems.

Rathaus. Am Markt. ☎ **0241/4-32-73-10.** Admission 3DM ($1.70) adults, 1.50DM (85¢) children. Daily 10am–1pm and 2–5pm. Closed sometimes for official events. Bus: 4 or 11.

The 14th-century Rathaus was built on the original site of Charlemagne's palace. Part of the ancient palace structure can still be seen in the so-called Granus Tower at the east side of the hall. The richly decorated facade, facing the marketplace, is adorned with the statues of 50 German rulers, 31 of them crowned in Aachen. In the center, standing in relief, are the "Majestas Domini," the two most important men of their time in the Holy Roman Empire, Charlemagne and Pope Leo III.

On the second floor of the Rathaus is the double-naved and cross-beamed Imperial Hall, where coronation banquets took place from 1349 to 1531. Built as the successor to the Carolingian Royal Hall, the hall today contains exact replicas of the imperial crown jewels, true in size and material to the originals, presently in the Vienna Secular Treasury. On the walls are the Charlemagne frescoes, painted in the 19th century by Alfred Rethel, illustrating the victory of the Christian Franks over the Germanic heathens.

Couven Museum. Huhnermarkt 17. ☎ **0241/4-32-44-21.** Admission 2DM ($1.15) adults, 1DM (55¢) children. Tues–Wed and Fri–Sun 10am–5pm, Thurs 10am–1pm. Bus: 1, 11, or 21.

This gracefully designed villa gives you an insight into the decorative traditions of the late 18th and 19th century. It has one of the best collections of antique furnishings of any museum in the region. On the ground floor is a reproduction of a small-scale chocolate factory. You'll find treasures, some of them low-key and discreet, virtually everywhere you look.

Suermondt Ludwig Museum. Wilhelmstrasse 18. ☎ **0241/47-98-00.** Admission 6DM ($3.40) adults, 3DM ($1.70) children. Tues and Thurs–Fri 11am–7pm, Wed 11am–9pm, Sat–Sun 11am–5pm.

The impressive collection of medieval German sculpture here is one of the finest in the land. Highlights are a *Madonna in Robes* from 1420 from the Swabian school and a *Virgin and Child* from the 14th-century Tournai school. The second landing has a good collection of primitive Flemish and German works, along with 17th-century

Dutch and Flemish paintings. Look for works by Van Dyck and Jordaens. The museum also has modern works, especially from the 1920s and 1930s.

WHERE TO STAY

Am Marschiertor. Wallstrasse 1–7, 52064 Aachen. ☎ **0241/3-19-41.** Fax 0241/3-19-44. 50 units. TV TEL. 160DM–195DM ($91.20–$111.15) double. Rates include buffet breakfast. AE, DC, MC, V. Parking 15DM ($8.55), opposite the hotel. Bus: 1, 11, or 21.

This charming hotel stands in the center of Aachen, not far from the Hauptbahnhof and next to the medieval town gate, Marschiertor, for which it's named. This is a beautiful and historic part of town. The hotel is quiet, with a courtyard and a view over the Altstadt and cathedral. The lobby and connecting hall are attractive, with antique furniture. The recently refurbished rooms have a cozy atmosphere, and each accommodation—generally medium in size—is well appointed and maintained.

Aquis Grana City Hotel. Büchel 32, 52016 Aachen. ☎ **0241/44-30.** Fax 0241/44-31-37. 99 units. MINIBAR TV TEL. 215DM–245DM ($122.55–$139.65) double; from 450DM ($256.50) suite. Children up to age 10 stay free in parents' room. Rates include buffet breakfast. AE, CB, DC, MC, V. Parking 10DM ($5.70). Bus: 1, 11, or 21.

Aquis Grana City Hotel is your best bet in the town center. The comfortable rooms offer all the modern amenities (including hair dryers) and range from spacious to medium in size. The staff is very alert to all your needs. Housekeeping rates an A+.

Dining/Diversions: The hotel has a good restaurant, featuring international and regional specialties. Favorite dishes include creamed soup with "herbs from Charlemagne's garden" and roast beef with home-fried potatoes. Low-calorie dishes are also served.

Amenities: There's a direct entrance from the hotel into the spa facilities. Room service, laundry, and dry cleaning can be arranged.

Hotel Benelux. Franzstrasse 21–23 (5-min. walk from the main train station), 52064 Aachen. ☎ **0241/2-23-43.** Fax 0241/2-23-45. 30 units. TV TEL. 165DM–220DM ($94.05–$125.40) double. Rates include continental breakfast. AE, DC, MC, V. Parking 15DM ($8.55).

The warm and inviting Benelux is within walking distance of many major attractions. It's a small family-run hotel, tastefully decorated and personalized. Americans from the Southwest will feel at home in the lobby/reception area—it has probably the only cactus collection in Aachen. Antiques are scattered throughout the corridors. Rooms range from small to medium in size. On the premises is a Chinese/Mongolian restaurant. Other attractive features are a roof garden and a fitness room.

Hotel Brülls am Dom. Hühnemarkt, 52062 Aachen. ☎ **0241/31704.** Fax 0241/404-326. 10 units. TV TEL. 185DM ($105.45) double. No credit cards.

This is a solid, not particularly imaginative hotel that's ruled with a firm grip by the family who owns it. Set within a very short walk from the town center, it was built in the late 1950s in a modern, no-nonsense style consistent with postwar architecture in Germany. Bedrooms are cozy, clean, and small, with rustic furnishings that verge on the kitsch. Set-price lunches here cost 40DM to 64DM ($22.80 to $36.50); set-price dinners 50DM to 100DM ($28.50 to $57).

WHERE TO DINE

La Bécasse. Hanbrucherstrasse 1 (just outside the Altstadt by the Westpark). ☎ **0241/7-44-44.** Reservations recommended. Main courses 43DM–60DM ($24.50–$34.20); fixed-price 6-course menu 102DM ($58.15). DC, MC, V. Daily 7–10:30pm; Tues–Fri noon–2:30pm. Bus: 15, 25, or 35. GERMAN/FRENCH.

This modern restaurant, full of greenery, serves a pleasing combination of light, modern French specialties and traditional German recipes. Although not in the same league as Gala (see below), La Bécasse is a discreetly classy place. Christof Lang, who realized early his "calling" of reproducing the fine foods of France, has been the owner since 1981. The food is imported every day from the wholesale markets at Rungis, outside Paris. Try his ragout of fish or his cassoulet.

Ratskeller. Am Markt (in the Rathaus). ☎ 0241/3-50-01. Reservations recommended. In Postwagen pub, platters 14DM–36DM ($8–$20.50); in Ratskeller Restaurant, main courses 18DM–43DM ($10.25–$24.50). AE, CB, DC, DISC, MC, V. Postwagen Pub daily 10am–11pm; Ratskeller restaurant daily 11:30am–3pm and 6–10pm. Bus: 2, 11, or 25. WESTPHALIAN/ GERMAN.

This is a charming, old-fashioned restaurant that's beloved by many senior citizens and office workers. The less-expensive venue is the Postwagen, a publike setting that serves platters and drinks throughout the afternoon. But we prefer the majesty of the brick-and-stone Ratskeller, where a sense of medievalism is enhanced by solid, conservative fare, such as sauerkraut with wurst; minestrone or potato soup; grilled steaks; fricassée of sole; and fresh berries and pastries for dessert.

Restaurant Elisenbrunnen. Friedrich-Wilhelm-Platz 14. ☎ **0241/297-72.** Reservations recommended. Main courses 21DM–48DM ($11.95–$27.35). Fixed-price lunch 38DM ($21.65). AE, CB, DC, MC, V. Daily 11am–10pm. Bus 15, 25, 55. FISH/FRENCH/WESTPHALIAN.

This stately restaurant occupies the Elisenbrunnen Rotunda, which was built in 1838 to commemorate the visit of a local potentate, Queen Elisen. Today it shares the same site as the city tourist office. It specializes in regional dishes (such as West-phalian green cabbage with *Mattwurst,* or pork sausage); French specialties (*chou-croute garnie* or chateaubriand with béarnaise sauce); and fresh fish. On warm days, you can dine on a large, well-maintained terrace in the shade of the Kaiserdom and the Rathaus.

✪ **Restaurant Gala.** Monheimsallee 44. ☎ **0241/15-30-13.** Reservations required. Main courses 34DM–49DM ($19.40–$27.95); fixed-price menu 55DM–150DM ($31.35–$85.50). AE, DC, V. Tues–Sat 7–10pm. Bus: 13. GERMAN.

The best dining place in Aachen is the elegant Restaurant Gala, which is loosely linked to one of the country's busier casinos. Light plays merrily through the crystal-draped decor onto the oak-paneled walls. Some of the paintings are Salvador Dalí originals. (The restaurant is named for his former wife.) The Gala can soothe the frayed nerves of the most inveterate gamblers. The kitchen turns out modern, lighter interpretations of regional food, including gamecock in calvados-and-mustard sauce or fillet of venison in blood sauce. Ingredients are trucked in daily from the Rungis markets near Paris. The wine list is encyclopedic; the French desserts are delectable.

AACHEN AFTER DARK

For information about what's happening in Aachen, pick up a copy of the booklet *Tourist-Information,* published and given away free by the tourist information office. Alternatively, you can buy a copy of a glossy-looking magazine, *Klenkes,* a monthly publication that's available in news kiosks around the city for 4DM ($2.30) each.

THE PERFORMING ARTS   Classical concerts are presented in the town's con-vention center, **Kongresszentrum Eurogress,** Mondheimsallee 52 (☎ 02451/ 913120), by the local symphony orchestra and by visiting chamber orchestras. The center is well-respected as an all-purpose rendezvous point for all kinds of public functions, and was renovated to a high level of acoustical and engineering standards in 1998. The **Theater Aachen** (formerly known as the Stadttheater) Theater-platz

(☎ **02451/ 4784244**) hosts opera, theater, and dance recitals. Ticket prices in both these places range from around 19DM to 170DM ($10.85 to $96.90).

If you understand German and want to see experimental theater and plays by Bertolt Brecht, head for the small and rather cramped **Aachener Kultur und Theater Initiative,** Gasborn 9–11 (☎ **0241/2-74-58**). Tickets range in price from 30DM to 85DM ($17.10 to $48.45).

For any local sports, entertainment, or cultural event, you can purchase tickets either from the establishment's ticket office or by contacting the tourist office's ticket booth (☎ **02451/180-2965**).

BARS & CAFES   There are at least a half-dozen bars in or around Aachen's Marktplatz. One of the most appealing is the **Martesa Keller,** Martesastrasse (☎ **0241/ 311-10**). This cozy, convivial, wood-paneled place offers live music, usually jazz, on most nights (usually Wednesday to Saturday, beginning around 8:30pm), and a bar that opens every night at 6pm. More youth-oriented is the **Café Kittel,** Pontstrasse 39 (☎ **0241/3-65-60**), which somewhat resembles a greenhouse; its menu concentrates on beer, wine, sandwiches, and quiche. Open Monday to Thursday from 10am to 2am, Friday and Saturday from 10am to 3pm, and Sunday from 11am to 2am. The popular **Aoxomoxoa,** Reihstrasse 15 (☎ **0241/226-22**), has a different theme from night to night; it's open every night except Monday from 5:30pm until around 1am or later, depending on business.

DANCE CLUBS   Friday and Saturday nights, **Rotation,** Pontstrasse 135 (☎ **0241/ 4-88-74**), keeps the dance music cranking until 6am. Other nights, the music provides a background for drinking and socializing. Two things you won't find here are a cover charge and food. Open Sunday to Thursday from 11am to 2am. More formal, stylish, and—according to its detractors—snobbish, is **Disco Zero,** which occupies the cellar of the town's **casino,** Mondheimsallee (☎ **0241/158948**). It's open every day at 3pm as a bar; after 10pm, it becomes a dance club and charges a cover of 15DM to 20DM ($8.55 to $11.40).

LIVE MUSIC   It's Irish in conception, but **Wild Rover,** Hirschgraben 13 (☎ **0241/ 3-54-53**), is a rock club first and foremost. The bands that take the stage nightly range from mainstream to punk. It's open daily from 8pm until 2am, with a 6DM ($3.40) cover charge from Sunday to Thursday, and a 4DM ($2.30) cover on Friday and Saturday. A worthy competitor is the **Exil-Bar,** Schlosstrasse 2 (☎ **0241/51-23-45**), where live music, including jazz and rock, is presented within a small, smoke-filled, and decidedly bohemian venue every night between 6pm and 1am. A final nightlife venue within Aachen is the **Domkeller,** Hof 1 (☎ **0241/3-42-65**), which offers live blues or jazz on some nights, and lots of hubbub every night. Open Monday to Thursday 10am to 1am and until 2am on Friday and Saturday.

9 Cologne (Köln)

17 miles N of Bonn, 25 miles S of Düsseldorf, 117 miles NW of Frankfurt

Cologne, the largest city in the Rhineland, is so rich in antiquity that every time a new foundation is dug, the excavators come up with archaeological finds. Devastating though the World War II bombing of Cologne was—nearly all the buildings of the Altstadt were damaged—reconstruction brought to light a period of Cologne's history that had been a mystery for centuries. Evidence showed that Cologne was as important and powerful during the early Christian era as it was during Roman times and the Middle Ages.

Cologne traces its beginnings to 38 B.C., when Roman legions set up camp here. As early as A.D. 50, the emperor Claudius gave it municipal rights as capital of a Roman province. In the early Christian era, a bishopric was founded here and a number of saints were martyred, including the patron of the city, St. Ursula. During the Middle Ages, as Cologne became a center for international trade, Romanesque and Gothic churches were built with prosperous merchants' gold. Today there is much to see from every period of the city's 2,000-year history—from the old Roman towers to the modern opera house. But Cologne is also a bustling modern city, with a lively population. It's increasingly becoming the fine-art capital of Germany.

The very word *cologne* has been a part of the common language since the introduction to the world many years ago of the scented water called *eau de cologne,* first made by Italian chemist Giovanni Maria Farina, who settled here in 1709. Cologne water is still produced in this city.

ESSENTIALS

GETTING THERE   By Plane   Cologne and Bonn share the same airport, **Flughafen Köln/Bonn Konrad Adenauer,** 9 miles southeast of Cologne. Flights come from most major European cities. For complete information, call ☎ **02203/ 40-40-01.** Bus service 170 from the airport to the center of Cologne operates from the airport every 30 minutes from 6:05am until 7:35am, every 15 minutes to 8:35pm, and then every 30 minutes to 11:05pm. Travel time takes 20 minutes, and the fare is 8.50DM ($4.85) per person. A taxi, suitable for up to four passengers, costs from 50DM to 60DM ($28.50 to $34.20).

By Train   The **Cologne Hauptbahnhof** is in the heart of the city, next to the cathedral. For schedules, call ☎ **01805/996633.** This depot has frequent rail connections to all major German cities and many continental destinations. There are 17 trains per day from Berlin (trip time: 5½ hr.), 31 from Frankfurt (2½ hr.), and 25 from Hamburg (4½ hr.).

By Bus   Cologne is linked to several major cities, including Frankfurt, by bus. For complete information and schedules, call **Deutsche Touring GmbH** (☎ **7-90-35-0**). Regional bus service to nearby cities such as Trier (see chapter 14) is provided by **Regionalverkehr Köln GmbH** at Euskirchen (☎ **02251/12-44-12**).

By Car   Cologne is easily reached from major German cities. It's connected north and south by the A3 Autobahn and east and west by the A4 Autobahn.

VISITOR INFORMATION   For tourist information, go to the **Köln Tourismus Office,** Unter Fettenhennen 19 (Am Dom) (☎ **0221/19433**), a few steps from the cathedral. November to April, it's open Monday to Saturday 8am to 9pm and Sunday 9:30am to 7pm; May to October, Monday to Saturday 8am to 10:30pm, Sunday 9:30am to 10:30pm.

GETTING AROUND   For 3.14DM ($1.80), depending on where you're going, you can purchase a ticket allowing you to travel on Cologne's excellent **bus, tram, U-Bahn,** and **S-Bahn** connections. Tickets are interchangeable. You must stick the ticket into a cancellation machine to show that it's been used. A day ticket, the Kölner Tageskarte, which costs 9DM ($5.15), will allow you to travel throughout the city's transportation network for 4½ hours. For information about public transportation in Cologne, call ☎ **0221/547-3333.**

For a taxi in Cologne, call ☎ **0221/1-94-10** for a recorded message and then press 1 in reply. The meter will start at 3.60DM ($2.05) and rise 2.30DM ($1.30) per kilometer for rides between 6am and 10pm, and 2.50DM ($1.40) per kilometer for rides between 10pm and 6am.

Cologne (Köln)

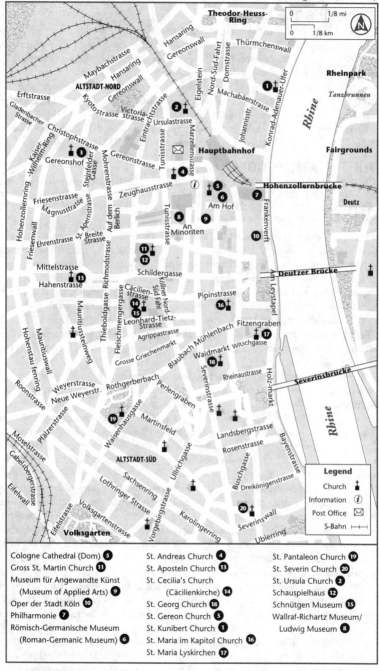

EXPLORING THE CITY

One of the best panoramas over the ancient city of Cologne is available from within one of the cars of the **Rhein-Seilbahn,** the first and only cable car in Europe that was designed to span a major river. The Rhein-Seilbahn stretches between a point near the zoo, in the district of Cologne-Riehl, to the Rhein Park in Cologne-Deutz, a total of about 3,000 feet. You get a good view of the busy river traffic along the Rhine. The cable car operates from April until the end of October, Monday to Friday from 11am to 6pm, Saturday and Sunday from 10am to 6pm. A one-way ticket costs 6.50DM ($3.70) for adults, 3.50DM ($2) for children; a round-trip ticket costs 9.50DM ($5.40) for adults, 5DM ($2.85) for children. For more information, call ☎ 0221/ 76-20-06.

THE TOP ATTRACTIONS

✪ **Cologne Cathedral (Dom).** Domkloster. ☎ **0221/92584720.** Treasury and cathedral tower each 3DM ($1.70) adults, 1.50DM (85¢) children. Cathedral daily 7am–7pm, except during religious services. Cathedral tower daily 9am–5pm. Treasury Mon–Sat 9am–5pm, Sun and holidays 12:30–5pm. U-Bahn: Hauptbahnhof.

This majestic structure is one of the world's great cathedrals—the spiritual and geographical heart of the city. It's the largest Gothic cathedral in Germany. From the top of the south tower, you get panoramic views of the city and surrounding area.

Construction on the cathedral was begun in 1248, in order to house the relics of the three Magi brought to Cologne in 1164 by Archbishop Reinald von Dassel, chancellor to Frederick Barbarossa. After the completion of the chancel, south tower, and north-side aisles (around 1500), work was halted and not resumed until 1823. In 1880, the great enterprise was completed, and unlike many time-consuming constructions that change styles in midstream, the final result was in the Gothic style, true to the original plans.

For the best overall view of the cathedral, stand back from the south transept, where you can get an idea of its actual size and splendor. Note that there are no important horizontal lines—everything is vertical. The west side (front) is dominated by two towering spires, perfectly proportioned and joined by the narrow facade of the nave. The first two stories of the towers are square, gradually merging into the octagonal form of the top three stories and tapering off at the top with huge finials. There is no great rose window, so characteristic of Gothic architecture, between these spires—nothing detracts from the lofty vertical lines.

Entering through the west doors (main entrance), you are immediately caught up in the grandeur of the cathedral. Although this portion of the church is somewhat bare, the clerestory and vaulting give a feeling of the size of the edifice. The towering windows on the south aisles include the Bavarian windows, donated by King Ludwig I of Bavaria in 1848. Like most windows in the nave, they are colored with pigments that have been burned on rather than stained. In the north aisles are the stained-glass Renaissance windows (1507–09).

In the center of the transept is an elegant bronze-and-marble altar that can be seen from all parts of the cathedral. Behind the high altar, in the chancel, is *The Shrine of the Three Magi,* the most important and valuable object in the cathedral. It's designed in gold and silver in the form of a triple-naved basilica, and decorated with relief figures depicting the life of Christ, the Apostles, and various Old Testament prophets. Across the front of the chancel are two rows of choir stalls divided into richly carved partitions. The oak choir dates from 1310 and is the largest extant in Germany.

Surrounding the chancel are nine chapels, each containing important works of religious art. The Chapel of the Cross, beneath the organ loft, shelters the oldest full-size cross in the Occident, the painted, carved oak cross of Archbishop Gero (969–76).

Directly across the chancel, behind the altar in Our Lady's Chapel, is the famous trip-tych masterpiece painted by Stephan Lochner (1400–51). When closed, the so-called *Altar of the City Patrons* shows the *Annunciation,* and when opened, it reveals the *Adoration of the Magi* in the center, flanked by St. Ursula, the patron saint of Cologne, and St. Gereon.

German-language tours of the cathedral are conducted every Monday to Saturday at 11am and 12:30, 2, and 3:30pm, and every Sunday at 2 and 3:30pm. English-language tours are given Monday to Saturday at 10:30am and 2:30pm, and Sunday at 2:30pm. Tours last about an hour, and cost 7DM ($4) for adults, and 4DM ($2.30) for children and students.

Museum für Angewandte Kunst (Museum of Applied Art). An der Rechtsschule. ☎ **0221/22123860.** Admission 5DM ($2.85) adults, 2.50DM ($1.40) children 6–12, free for children 5 and under. Tues–Sun 11am–5pm, Wed 11am–8pm. U-Bahn: Hauptbahnhof.

This is a showcase for the arts and crafts of Germany dating from the Middle Ages, with the 20th century prominently featured. This museum is one of the best of its kind in Germany.

Römisch-Germanisches Museum (Roman-Germanic Museum). Roncalliplatz 4. ☎ **0221/2-21-23-04.** Admission 5DM ($2.85) adults, 2.50DM ($1.40) children, free for children 5 and under. Tues–Sun 10am–5pm. U-Bahn: Hauptbahnhof.

The most compelling treasure in this museum is the Dionysos-Mosaik, from the 3rd century A.D., discovered in 1941 when workers were digging an air-raid shelter. This elaborately decorated and colored mosaic was once the floor of an *oecus* (main room) of a large Roman villa. It depicts Dionysus, the Greek god of wine and dispeller of care. On the second floor of the museum is an unusual collection of Roman antiquities found in the Rhine Valley, including Roman glass from the 1st through the 4th centuries, as well as pottery, marble busts, and jewelry.

Schnütgen Museum. Cäcilienstrasse 29. ☎ **0221/2-21-36-20.** Admission 5DM ($2.85) adults, 2.50DM ($1.40) children. Tues–Fri 10am–5pm and Sat–Sun 11am–5pm. U-Bahn: Neumarkt.

This is Cologne's best collection of religious art and sculpture. It's all displayed in an original setting, St. Cecilia's Church (Cäcilienkirche), which is a fine example of Rhenish-Romanic architecture. The works displayed include several medieval ivories, woodwork, and tapestries, including one showing rosy-cheeked Magi bringing gifts to the Christ child (1470). There are also many Madonnas, of all sizes and descriptions, carved in stone, wood, and metal.

Wallraf-Richartz Museum/Ludwig Museum. Bischofsgartenstrasse 1 (a short walk from Domplatz). ☎ **0221/221-22379.** Admission 10DM ($5.70) adults, 5DM ($2.85) children. Tues 10am–8pm, Wed–Fri 10am–6pm, Sat–Sun 11am–6pm. U-Bahn: Hauptbahnhof.

This is Cologne's oldest museum, begun in the 19th century with a collection of Gothic works by local artists. That group of works is still one of the main attractions. The Wallraf-Richartz shows art from 1300 to 1900, and the Ludwig, art from 1900 until today. Several well-known works from churches are exhibited as well, including the triptych of the *Madonna with the Vetch Flower* (1410). The painting collection represents nearly every period and school, from the Dutch and Flemish masters to the French impressionists to American art of the 1960s and 1970s (the famous Ludwig Donation). Stephan Lochner's *Madonna in the Rose Garden,* painted in 1450, is a fine example of the German Gothic style. The museum also houses Germany's largest collection of works by Wilhelm Leibl as well as paintings by Max Ernst, Paul Klee, and Ernst Ludwig Kirchner.

CHURCHES

Cologne has 12 important Romanesque churches, all within the medieval city wall. Devastated during World War II, they have been almost completely restored and again recapture Cologne's rich early medieval heritage. **St. Panteleon,** Am Pantaleonsberg 2, built in 980, has the oldest cloister arcades remaining in Germany. **St. Gereon,** Gereonsdriesch 2–4 is elliptically shaped, with a decagon between its two towers. It contains the tomb of St. Gereon and other martyrs, and its crypt still has mosaics from the 11th century. **St. Severin,** on Severinstrasse, originated as a late 4th-century memorial chapel; the present church dates from the 13th to the 15th centuries.

The church of **St. Ursula** (1135), on Ursulaplatz, is on the site of a Roman graveyard. St. Ursula, patron saint of Cologne, was supposedly martyred with her 11,000 virgin followers. **St. Maria im Kapitol,** Kasinostrasse 6, is in the place where Plectrudis, wife of Pippin, built a church in the early 8th century. The cloverleaf choir of the present structure was modeled on that of the Church of the Nativity in Bethlehem. **St. Aposteln,** Neumarkt 30, and **Gross St. Martin,** on the Rhine in the Altstadt, also have the cloverleaf choir design.

St. Georg, Am Waidmarkt, the only remaining Romanesque pillared basilica in the Rhineland, contains an impressive forked crucifix from the early 14th century. **St. Cecilia's (Cäcilienkirche),** Cäcilienstrasse 29, near Neumarkt, is the site of the Schnütgen Museum for sacred art (see above). **St. Andreas,** near the cathedral, contains a wealth of late Romanesque architectural sculpture. The remaining two Romanesque churches are on the Rhine: **St. Kunibert,** Kunibertskloster 2, and **St. Maria Lyskirchen,** Am Lyskirchen 12, both of 13th-century origin.

SHOPPING

Shopping is not taken quite as seriously here as in Düsseldorf—with one exception. Increasingly, Cologne is emerging as the capital of contemporary art in Germany. The city is brimming with galleries.

ART GALLERIES   We'll recommend the major ones to get you started, but there are many more. The gallery that launched Cologne as a European art mecca is **Galerie der Spiegel,** Richartstrasse 10 (☎ **0221/25-55-52**). Established amid the ruins of the wartime bombings, in 1945, it was a focal point for the contemporary art that evolved from the shattered dreams of the postwar years. Since then, despite the volcanic changes that have rocked Germany, it has managed to hold its own against rising competition. You might want to walk along **St. Apernstrasse,** where many leading art galleries are located. **Galerie Greve,** Albertusstrasse 18 (☎ **0221/2-57-10-12**), changes its exhibits every season, specializing in international post-war avant-garde painting. Another excellent gallery for both modern and experimental art is **Galerie Werner,** Gertrudenstrasse 24 (☎ **0221/9-25-46-20**), which sells contemporary European painters with a particular emphasis on German artists.

COLOGNE WATER   Eau de Cologne, Glockengasse 4711 (☎ **0221/9-25-04-50**), sells the scented water that was first developed at this address by Italian chemist Giovanni Maria Farina in 1792. Originally employed to hide the stench of aristocrats who rarely bathed, cologne is now simply a sweet-smelling tradition and a cheap way to take home a little piece of Köln. The smallest 25 milliliter flacon costs a mere 7.95DM ($4.55).

OUTDOOR MARKETS   If you're interested in the kitschy artifacts that pour out of estate sales, with items that are slightly damaged, mismatched, or old-fashioned, be alert to the flea markets in Cologne's inner city. The most appealing are held within the **Alter Markt,** at irregular intervals throughout the year, usually at least once a month. More regular are the outdoor food and vegetable markets, the largest of which is held on the **Wilhelmsplatz,** in the Nippes district, every Saturday from 8am to at least 2pm.

WHERE TO STAY
VERY EXPENSIVE

✪ **Dom Hotel.** Domkloster 2A, 50667 Köln 1. ☎ **800/225-5843** in the U.S., or 0221/2-02-40. Fax 0221/2-02-44-44. www.forte-hotels.com. E-mail: gm1304@forte-hotels.com. 125 units. MINIBAR TV TEL. 485DM–685DM ($276.45–$390.45) double. AE, DC, MC, V. Parking 30DM ($17.10). U-Bahn: Hauptbahnhof.

The Dom Hotel's location, in the shadow of Germany's most famous cathedral, assures it of a steady clientele. Few hotels in Germany, however, have been so consistently awarded five stars or maintained such a standard of excellence. We prefer the Excelsior Hotel Ernst, but there are many clients who will stay nowhere else but the Dom. In summer the hotel's side portico overlooking the square to the side of the cathedral is filled with cafe tables. Guest rooms have all the modern conveniences and an interesting collection of period furniture. Try for one of the corner units, which are the most spacious and have the best views. To reach the hotel by car, drive into the square to the side of the Dom's flying buttresses.

   Dining: On the premises is a winter-garden bistro, the only dining facility.

   Amenities: 24-hour room service, laundry, dry cleaning, terrace garden, conference facilities.

✪ **Excelsior Hotel Ernst.** Domplatz (facing the cathedral square), 50667 Köln. ☎ **0221/27-01.** Fax 0221/13-51-50. www.lhw.com. 160 units. MINIBAR TV TEL. 415DM–665DM ($236.55–$379.05) double; 950DM–1,500DM ($541.50–$855) suite. Rates include continental breakfast. AE, DC, MC, V. Parking 35DM ($19.95). U-Bahn: Hauptbahnhof.

Cologne's longtime prestige hotel, with plenty of traditional style and ambience, is in the center of the city's finest shopping and business area, only a couple of hundred yards from the Hauptbahnhof.

In spite of increased competition, notably from the Hyatt Regency, the Excelsior Ernst continues to hold its own as the premier address in Cologne. Founded in 1863, the hotel is known for its Empire-style lobby in bright yellow and gold along with royal blue. The public rooms contain paintings by old masters, including an original work by Van Dyck. Even the breakfast room has a Gobelin tapestry. The guest rooms are spacious, with many amenities, including hair dryers, designer fixtures, marble bathrooms, and satellite TV. Most rooms are air-conditioned.

   Dining/Diversions: The hotel has an outstanding restaurant, Hanse Stube (see "Where to Dine," below), and an intimate and cozy Piano Bar.

   Amenities: Concierge, room service, laundry, dry cleaning, massage, shoe shine, exclusive boutique, whirlpool, fitness area, Roman steam bath, hairdresser, barbershop.

✪ **Hyatt Regency.** Kennedy-ufer 2A (across the Rhine from the Alstadt, a short walk from the train station), 50679 Köln-Deutz. ☎ **800/228-12-34**, or 0221/8281234. Fax 0221/828-13-70. 306 units. A/C MINIBAR TV TEL. 360DM–460DM ($205.20–$262.20) double, from 560DM–3,100DM ($319.20–$1,767) suite. AE, DC, MC, V. Parking 25DM ($14.25). Tram: 1 or 2.

This is the most spectacular and up-to-date hotel in Cologne. It's an architectural triumph: a mixture of reddish granite, huge expanses of glass, and a facade that combines art-deco and neo-Aztec styles. The lobby is dramatic, with a 12-foot waterfall. Each guest room is stylishly furnished with plush carpets and richly grained hardwood furniture. Rooms come with walk-in closets. Bathrooms have a private phone, a deep tub with shower, robes, deluxe toiletries, and a hair dryer. Many of the bedrooms have views of the Rhine and the cathedral on the other side. To get to the Alstadt from here, you can take the Hohenzollernbrücke, a bridge across the Rhine.

Dining/Diversions: Graugans offers a Germanic version of contemporary cuisine, and also has a wonderful Asian-influenced menu. You can also dine in the lobby cafe, with its excellent view of the Rhine and the Alstadt. The intimate bar connects to a garden terrace and serves a selection of international wines, as well as a local beer called Schael Sick.

Amenities: 24-hour room service, business center, laundry, dry cleaning, concierge, and fitness center with pool, sauna, steam room, massage facilities, solarium, and whirlpool.

EXPENSIVE

✪ **Antik-Hotel Bristol.** Kaiser-Wilhelm-Ring 48, 50672 Köln. ☎ **0221/12-01-95.** Fax 0221/13-14-95. www.koeln-hotels.de. E-mail: hotel@antik-hotel-bristol.com.. 44 units. MINIBAR TV TEL. 195DM–350DM ($111.15–$199.50) double; 220DM–380DM ($125.40–$216.60) suite. Rates include buffet breakfast. AE, DC, MC, V. Closed Dec 23–Jan 2. Parking 12DM ($6.85). U-Bahn: Christophstrasse.

The Bristol is exceptional in that each of its rooms is furnished with genuine antiques, either regal or rustic. There's a different antique bed in almost every room, ranging from French baroque and rococo to something reminiscent of High Rhenish ecclesiastical art; the oldest four-poster dates from 1742. The hotel is conveniently located near a U-Bahn stop and is within walking distance of the cathedral. Bathroom amenities include hair dryers and magnifying makeup mirrors. The Bristol stands in a little park, removed from traffic, with lots of greenery, flowers, and fountains.

Dining: The hotel has the Bristol Bar for guests, but breakfast is the only meal served.

Amenities: Concierge, room service, dry cleaning, laundry service, in-room massage, twice-daily maid service, and baby-sitting.

MODERATE

Altstadt-Hotel. Salzgasse (2 min. from the Rhine boat-landing dock), 50667 Köln. ☎ **0221/2-57-78-51.** Fax 0221/2-57-78-53. 29 units. MINIBAR TV TEL. 140DM ($79.80) double; 250DM ($142.50) suite. Rates include buffet breakfast. AE, DC, MC, V. Closed Dec 20–Jan 6. Parking 20DM ($11.40). U-Bahn: Hauptbahnhof.

Guests have passed the word along to their friends, making this place a big success. Herr Olbrich learned about catering to international guests as a steward on the German-American Line. He has furnished his little hotel beguilingly. Each of the restful rooms is individually decorated. Rooms range from small to medium, and each comes with a comfortable bed fitted with crisp white linen and a good mattress, plus a small but well-kept private bathroom, mainly with shower stalls. A sauna is on the premises. Advance reservations are recommended.

Das Kleine Stapelhäuschen. Fischmarkt 1–3, 50667 Köln. ☎ **0221/2-57-78-62.** Fax 0221/2-57-42-32. 31 units, 10 with bathroom. TEL. 125DM ($71.25) double without bathroom, 190DM ($108.30) double with bathroom. Rates include buffet breakfast. AE, MC, V. Parking in garage 25DM ($14.25) nearby. U-Bahn: Heumarkt.

Stapelhäuschen was originally built in the 1100s near where fish were sold by Scottish Benedictine monks. The two tall, narrow town houses are on a corner of a historic square, and their ironwork announces the year of their construction: 1235. Inside you'll find a richly evocative decor and an occasional portrait of Irish-born St. Brigit. Rooms offer an old-fashioned decor of patterned wallpaper and clean, if slightly faded, furniture. On the premises is a good restaurant (see "Where to Dine," below).

INEXPENSIVE

Brandenburger Hof. Brandenburgerstrasse 2–4 (behind the Hauptbahnhof), 50668 Köln. ☎ **0221/12-28-89.** Fax 0221/13-53-04. 45 units, 28 with bathroom. 90DM ($51.30) double without bathroom, 110DM ($62.70) double with bathroom; 105DM ($59.85) triple without bathroom; 125DM ($71.25) quad without bathroom. Rates include continental breakfast. No credit cards. Free parking. U-Bahn: Hauptbahnhof.

In this family-style hotel, all rooms are small, warm, and equipped with running water, and there's a well-kept bathroom on each floor. A full breakfast, including orange juice and eggs, is served in a cozy room or, in summer, in the garden. The hotel is about 3 blocks from the river and within walking distance of the cathedral.

WHERE TO DINE

VERY EXPENSIVE

✪ **Goldener Pflug.** Olpener Strasse 421, Merheim (on the outskirts of Cologne). ☎ **0221/89-55-09.** Reservations required. Main courses 49DM–69DM ($27.95–$39.35); fixed-price meal 65DM ($37.05) at lunch, 125DM–198DM ($71.25–$112.85) at dinner. AE, MC, V. Mon–Fri noon–3pm and 7–11pm, Sat 7–11pm. Tram: 1 to Merheim. FRENCH.

The Goldener Pflug is one of the top restaurants in Germany. The decor of this former tavern is simple, with a golden motif repeated in the walls, draperies, and upholstery. The chef, Herbert Schönberner, takes pleasure in serving demanding clients with jaded palates and sending them away satisfied. Top-quality ingredients are always used in his imaginative blend of classical repertoires. Try, for example, any of the truffled specialties, ranging from soups to a wide choice of delicately seasoned main courses. For dessert, the most exciting choices are apple cake flambé and soufflé à la Rothschild with strawberries. The fixed-price gourmet "surprise" menu consists of seven courses for 198DM ($112.85).

Hanse Stube. On the ground floor of the Excelsior Hotel Ernst, Domplatz. ☎ **0221/27-01.** Reservations recommended. Main courses 50DM–60DM ($28.50–$34.20); 5-course fixed-price menu 120DM–160DM ($68.40–$91.20). AE, DC, MC, V. Daily noon–3pm and 6–11pm. U-Bahn: Hauptbahnhof. FRENCH.

One of Cologne's best restaurants, Hanse Stube offers top-drawer cuisine and service. The food here is better than that served in the dining room of the Dom Hotel. Prodigious talent and imagination go into shaping the cuisine. Of the chef's appetizers, none are better than a variation of salmon on truffled potato salad blended harmoniously with a Pommery mustard sauce. Unusual and tasty main courses include breast of guinea fowl stuffed with herbs or medaillons of venison with savoy cabbage and a sweet corn potato Rösti.

EXPENSIVE

Börsen Restaurant. Unter Sachsenhausen 10–26 (near the stock exchange, a short walk from the cathedral). ☎ **0221/13-30-21.** Reservations recommended. Main courses 40DM–50DM ($22.80–$28.50); fixed-price lunch 60DM–89DM ($34.20–$50.75); fixed-price dinner 75DM–89DM ($42.75–$50.75). AE, DC, MC, V. Mon–Fri noon–2:30pm and Mon–Sat 6–11pm. U-Bahn: Hauptbahnhof. CONTINENTAL.

This busy place, which serves many members of Cologne's financial community, offers not only good value but also a glimpse of everyday Cologne life, particularly at lunch. Seasonally adjusted fixed-price meals feature classic, conservative cookery made from fresh ingredients. The restaurant offers a choice of different dining areas. In the Börsen-Stube, which has the same hours as the main restaurant, main courses range from 25DM to 40DM ($14.25 to $22.80). The Börsen Schanke, open Monday to Friday from 10am to 9:30pm, has meals starting at 15DM to 35DM ($8.55 to $19.95). There is a terrace for this beer restaurant, which serves local dishes.

Le Moissonnier. Krefelder Strasse 25 (across the street from the Schlosspark). ☎ **0221/72-94-79.** Reservations recommended. Main courses 39DM–44DM ($22.25–$25.10); midday plat du jour 21DM ($11.95). No credit cards. Tues–Sat noon–1:45pm and 7–10:45pm. U-Bahn: Hansaring. FRENCH.

This well-maintained and charming brasserie is steeped in the aesthetic and culinary traditions of the early 20th century. It has a turn-of-the-century decor, with mirrors, cove moldings, dark paneling against ocher-colored walls, bentwood chairs, and tiled floors. Here you'll enjoy the carefully crafted cuisine of the restaurant's namesake, Vincent Moissonnier. Menu items change with the season and the inspiration of the chef, but are likely to include risotto with almonds and truffle oil; carpaccio of turbot; and a house specialty that combines braised fillet of goose breast with tarragon and strips of goose liver served with prosciutto-studded mashed potatoes. Salads and fresh fish are all delicious, as are the sauerkraut and a Toulouse-inspired version of cassoulet loaded with pork, small sausages, and white beans.

MODERATE

Brauhaus im Walfisch. Salzgasse 13 (on a narrow street set back from the Rhine, near Heumarkt [Haymarket]). ☎ **0221/2-57-78-79.** Reservations required. Main courses 17DM–37DM ($9.70–$21.10). AE, DC, MC, V. Daily 11am–midnight. U-Bahn: Hauptbahnhof. GERMAN/FRENCH.

Brauhaus im Walfisch isn't easy to find, but it's a good choice for atmospheric dining. This step-gabled inn with a black-and-white timbered facade dates from 1626. More important, it serves excellent food. There are many German specialties, often influenced by French cuisine. You might try the sole meunière or venison for two.

Das Kleine Stapelhäuschen. Fischmarkt 1–3 (a few minutes from the cathedral). ☎ **0221/2-57-78-62.** Reservations recommended. Main courses 20DM–40DM ($11.40–$22.80). AE, MC, V. Daily noon–11:30pm. Closed Dec 22–Jan 10. U-Bahn: Heumarkt. GERMAN.

This is one of the most popular wine taverns in Cologne. It's housed in an office building and opens on to the old fish-market square and the Rhine. The two-story dining room and service bar are antique in style. Provincial cabinets hold a varied wine collection. A wide cantilevered wooden staircase leads to mezzanine tables. Though wine is the main reason for coming here (it's that special), the cuisine is also excellent. A specialty is Rheinischer sauerbraten with almonds, raisins, and potato dumplings. Desserts are appropriately luscious.

Ratskeller. Rathausplatz 1 (in the Rathaus). ☎ **0221/2-57-69-29.** Reservations recommended. Main courses 25DM–35DM ($14.25–$19.95). AE, DC, MC, V. Mon–Sat noon–11pm, Sun 11am–3pm. U-Bahn: Altemarkt/Heumarkt. GERMAN.

This busy and very traditional restaurant occupies a trio of dining rooms in the cellar of Cologne's landmark city hall. It welcomes the city's political, business, and journalistic communities during the lunch hour. Menu items are conservative German, particularly Rhenish, specialties, and include generous portions of sauerbraten, *Schweinshaxen* (roast leg of pork), and *Kalbshaxen* (roast leg of veal). Any of these might be preceded with steaming bowls of *Leberknoedel* soup or goulash, salads, and marinated herring in cream sauce with onions. During warm weather, tables spill out into a courtyard that's protected from the roar of traffic. Look for a lavish lunch buffet every Sunday, and a dinner buffet every Saturday. The price of each of those is 39DM ($22.25) per person.

BEER TAVERNS

Some of the best inexpensive places to eat (and drink) in Cologne are beer taverns.

Alt-Köln am Dom. Trankgasse 7–9 (across from the cathedral and the Hauptbahnhof). Main courses 13DM–30DM ($7.40–$17.10). ☎ **0221/13-74-71.** AE, DC, MC, V. Daily 11am–midnight (kitchen closed at 11:30pm). U-Bahn: Hauptbahnhof.

Alt-Köln is a re-creation of a group of old taverns, including one done in the Gothic style. You can come here for a beer or a good hot meal. The place seems like it could feed half the visitors to Cologne on any busy day. Some of the upper-floor tables provide box-seat views of the cathedral. On the face of the building is a mechanical clock; when it chimes the hours, a parade of figures emerges and disappears. The favorite main dishes include Wiener schnitzel, *Schweinshaxen* (pork knuckle), and a platter of sausage specialties with spicy mustard. Try also the braised beef Rhineland-style.

Bräuhaus Sion. Unter Taschenmacher 5. ☎ **0221/2-57-85-40.** Main courses 12DM–32DM ($6.85–$18.25). No credit cards. Daily 10am–11:30pm. Closed Christmas Eve. Tram: 5 or 7 to Heumarkt.

Come here if you want a traditional local Bräuhaus, where the beer is good, the wood paneling a little smoky with time and frequent polishing, and the food portions inexpensive and generous. The main courses are traditional and filling Westphalian fare, such as pigs' knuckles with sauerkraut and the inevitable bratwurst with savoy cabbage and fried potatoes. But the best traditional dish to order here is *kölsch Kaviar* (blood sausage decorated with onion rings). You can also ask for *halve Hahn,* which translates as "half rooster." On tap is the famed local beer, Kölsch, a light brew with an alcohol content of about 3%. It's served in *Stangen* (rods) about 7 inches tall.

Früh am Dom. Am Hof 12–14 (in the cathedral area). ☎ **0221/2-58-03-97.** Meals 25DM–60DM ($14.25–$34.20). No credit cards. Tavern open 8am–midnight (hot meals served 11:30am–11:30pm). U-Bahn: Hauptbahnhof.

Früh am Dom is the best all-around choice for economy and hearty portions. Well-cooked meals are served on scrubbed wooden tables, with a different German specialty offered every day of the week. The menu is in English. A favorite dish is a Cologne specialty of cured smoked knuckle of pork cooked in root-vegetable broth and served with sauerkraut and potato puree; apple puree and dumplings go well with this dish. Also sample a glass of Früh-Kölsch—a top-fermented brew with a dry, inimitable taste and a 1,000-year-old tradition. In summer, there's a beer garden.

Haus Töller. Weyerstrasse 96 (a 15-min. walk south of the cathedral). ☎ **0221/2-40-91-87.** Main courses 15DM–25DM ($8.55–$14.25). No credit cards. Mon–Sat 5–midnight. U-Bahn: Barbarossaplatz. GERMAN.

This venerable, beer-soaked building has thrived as a brew house since 1876 by selling copious portions of two-fisted Teutonic food and foaming mugs of a local brew, Seon (1DM/55¢ each). No one will mind if you just want to spend a few hours drinking (the beer is very, very good), but if you want a meal, menu items include a local specialty of *Schinkenhempsel* (roast leg of pork), the latter served with sauerkraut and roast potatoes.

COLOGNE AFTER DARK

One of Germany's major cultural centers, Cologne offers a variety of fine arts and nightlife options. Many clubs stay open into the early morning hours. You can pick up a copy of *Stadt Revue* for 4DM ($2.30) or *Kölner* for 4DM ($2.30) to find out what's happening in the city. If you're interested in attending a sports, entertainment-related, or cultural venue within Cologne, you can always head to the box office of whatever stadium or concert hall is producing the event. More convenient, however, is the well-orchestrated services of **Köln-Ticket,** Roncalliplatz 4, next to the cathedral (☎ **0221/28-01**).

THE PERFORMING ARTS

The most impressive grouping of theater space in Cologne is within the **Schauspielhaus,** Offenbachplatz (☎ **0221/28400**), the site of three theaters, each with its own agenda and schedule. Performances range from the avant-garde to the classic. **Der Keller,** Kleingedankstrasse 6 (☎ **0221/31-80-59**), hosts contemporary plays, usually in German, and dance performances. Tickets range from 20DM to 45DM ($11.40 to $25.65) each; call either the number listed above or **Köln-Ticket** (☎ **0221/28-01**) for schedules and show times.

If your German is fluent and you're interested in absorbing some of the counter-culture trends sweeping the country's literature and politics, you might be interested in the **Theater Kaiserhof,** Hohenzollenring (☎ **0221/139-2772**). Performances are sometimes comic, sometimes obscure, sometimes trenchant, sometimes grotesque, sometimes satirical, and often a combination of all of the above. Most shows begin at 8pm. Tickets cost from 25DM to 50DM ($14.25 to $28.50).

Oper der Städt Köln. Offenbachplatz. ☎ **0221/22128400.** Tickets 21DM–106DM ($11.95–$60.40). AE, DC, MC, V. U-Bahn or S-Bahn: Neumarkt.

This is the leading opera house of the Rhineland, known for its exciting productions and innovative repertory of classical and contemporary works. Performances take place almost every evening except Tuesday, usually beginning at 7:30pm. Dance programs are also presented. The box office is open 9am to 6pm Monday to Friday and Saturday 9am to 2pm.

Kölner Philharmonie. Bischofsgartenstrasse 1. ☎ **0221/28-01.** Tickets 15DM–250DM ($8.55–$142.50). U-Bahn: Bahnhof.

This architectural showcase was completed during the late 1980s. The concert hall features a soaring roof, enviable acoustics, and some of the finest classical music along the country's western tier. The building is the home of two separate orchestras, the **Gürzenich Kölner Philharmoniker** and the **Westdeutscher Rundfunk Orchestra.** Pop and jazz programs are also presented. Performances are given almost every night beginning at 8pm, except Monday, when the theater is closed.

THE CLUB & MUSIC SCENE

DANCE CLUBS   Live bands (Tuesday, Thursday, and Saturday) and DJs (Monday, Wednesday, Friday, and Sunday) play for dancers at **MTC,** Zulpicher Strasse 10 (☎ **0221/1-70-27-64**), open 10pm to 3am. Cover is 6DM to 20DM ($3.40 to $11.40).

One of the city's most angular, dramatic, and surreal nightlife options is **E-Werk,** Schanzenstrasse 28 (☎ **0221/96-27-90**), a combination of a disco and a large concert hall. It's housed within what used to be an electrical power plant. Recorded music alternates with live acts. The Backstreet Boys have played here. The place is open every Friday and Saturday night at 10pm.

JAZZ CLUBS   **Klimperkasten** (also known as **Papa Joe's Biersalon**), Alter Markt 50–52 (☎ **0221/258-2132**), is a small and intimate jazz and piano bar open from 11am to 2am, with live music every night beginning around 8pm. The jazz is also hot at **Papa Joe's Jazzlokal,** Buttermarkt 37 (☎ **0221/257-7931**). Sunday, when the music begins at 3:30pm and lasts until 1am, is the best day to come. The club is also open for live jazz Monday to Saturday from 7pm to 2am. Surprisingly, there's never a cover.

LIVE-MUSIC CLUBS   Several times a week, usually at 8pm on Wednesday and Saturday, but with frequent exceptions, the **Underground,** Vogelsanger Strasse 200 (☎ **0221/542326**), hosts rock groups that include relatively unknown local acts as well as high-profile bands. There's a disco on other nights. This place, in the words of a spokesperson, is "very alternative. If you're 40, you're probably too old to appreciate the music here." A food stand inside prepares pastas, burgers, and breakfast items for late-night (or early morning) hunger pangs. The cover charge ranges from 12DM to 20DM ($6.85 to $11.40).

Prime Club (formerly known as Luxor), Luxemburgstrasse 40 (☎ 0221/ 924-460), offers some kind of live music most nights of the week, except Monday, although the schedule varies with the bands. You'll never know what to expect here. The management books unknown, inexperienced bands, some of whom show great promise.

A final contender in Cologne's live-music sweepstakes is **Kantine,** Kempenorstrasse 135 (☎ 0221/9726836), whose musical style, hours, and free-form scheduling policies are similar to those at Prime Club. Kantine also has a beer garden.

BARS

A 110-year-old bar, **Päffgen Bräuhaus,** Friesenstrasse 64–66 (☎ 0221/13-54-61), serves its Kölsch brand of beer, along with regional cuisine. Seating is available indoors and out. Open daily from 10am to midnight. **Altstadt Päffgen,** Heumarkt 62 (☎ 0221/2-57-77-65), also serves the local brew with German dishes. Open Tuesday to Sunday from noon to midnight. **Broadway,** Ehrenstrasse 11 (☎ 0221/ 25-52-14) is a cafe and bar associated with an arts-conscious movie theater. It's decorated with playbills and memorabilia from theater productions of yesteryear. Drinks, coffee, tea, sandwiches, and simple platters of snack food are served. Open daily from 10am to 1am.

A place where you might be tempted to hang out for an hour or two is the **Café Storchen,** Ursula Kloster 4–6 (☎ 0221/13-17-12), which has thrived as an appealingly battered, very informal bar and cafe since the early 1980s. It serves drinks, platters of uncomplicated food, and sandwiches, while patrons listen to recorded music, read newspapers, and play board games. Open Sunday to Friday from 11am to 1am.

A somewhat different setting is **Museum Pub,** Zulpicher Platz 9 (☎ 0221/23-20-98), which makes a living selling foaming mugs of beer to thirsty students. Rock and punk music are usually blaring from the stereo. Some aspects of the place might remind you of student dives in the Latin Quarter of Paris. Open Sunday to Thursday from 6pm to 1am, and Friday and Saturday from 6pm till 3am.

Students who have rediscovered the styles of the 1960s and 1970s lounge about amid a decor of lava lamps, futuristic televisions, and other memorabilia at **Hallmackenreuthur,** Brusseler Platz 9 (☎ 0221/51-79-70). This is a place to drink, eat a late breakfast (served until 4pm), or have a plate of pasta (6 to 11pm). It's open daily from 11am to 1am. A holdover from the Cologne's leftist days is **Hotelux,** Rathenauplatz (☎ 0221/241136). Both its food and scarlet decor are self-consciously Soviet. You can eat platters of Russian food, drink Russian beer or more than two dozen brands of Russian vodka, and sit within a garden whose greenery is thankfully apolitical. It's open daily from 7pm to 1am.

GAY NIGHTLIFE

Cologne offers more diversions and distractions for gay men and women than any other city in the Rhineland. Head either to the Marienplatz area or the "Bermuda Triangle" (see below). A good gay bar for men and women near Marienplatz is **Quo Vadis Pub,** Pipinstrasse 7 (☎ 0221/258-1414), which is open nightly from noon to midnight during the week and 11am to 1am on the weekend. Another gay bar in the Marienplatz area is the men-only leather bar called **Teddy Treff,** Stephansstrasse 1 (☎ 0221/248-310), open daily from 6pm till "late." **Chains,** Stephansstrasse 4 (☎ 0221/23-87-30), opens at 10pm and closes at 2 or 3am. The most sophisticated rendezvous for gays and lesbians in Cologne today is called **Gloria,** Apostelnstrasse 11 (☎ **0221/254433**), which is generally packed with a cruisy crowd. If there's music playing, there's a cover of 10DM ($5.50). Open Sunday to Thursday 9am to 1am, Friday and Saturday 9am to 3am.

If you want to do as the Kölners do, consider a walk through what locals call **"the Bermuda Triangle"** formed by the locations of the four bar/clubs listed below. Visited as an ensemble, they provide plenty of insight into the lifestyle (and limitations) of the gay Rhineland. The first is **Schampanja,** Mauritiuswall 43 (☎ **0221/240-95-44**), a small pub which sometimes books live bands (often punk). Nearby, along the same street, is **The Park,** Mauritiuswall 84 (☎ **0221/21-33-57**), a cafe-style rendezvous point where table-hopping is a way of life. It's open daily from 8am to 3am, but gay life is most visible in the late evening. Two near-neighbors at the opposite end of the Bermuda Triangle are **Café Huber,** Schaafenstrasse 51 (☎ **0221/240-6530**), and **The Corner,** Schaafenstrasse 57–59 (☎ **0221/24-90-61**), where attractively—even conservatively—dressed men drink, smoke, talk, and generally enjoy each other's company. Both are open nightly from 7pm till around 3am, depending on business.

Confused and don't know how to best approach the gay scene of Cologne? Pay a visit to **Checkpoint,** Pipinstrasse 7 (☎ **0221/925-76868**), a privately owned dispenser of information that performs some of its functions in cooperation with the city's official tourism authorities. It's open daily from 5 to 9pm, and has a staff that's ready, willing, and able to tell you what's up in gay Cologne. They'll even sell you memorabilia.

The first weekend in July is devoted to the city's **Gay Pride Parade,** when as many as 500,000 spectators line the parade route for a glimpse of the floats and marchers. For specifics on the parade, contact Checkpoint (see above).

DRAG ACTS

Cologne isn't prudish when it comes to admiring the female figure, even if that figure isn't biologically female. For the most sophisticated drag acts in the Rhineland, head for the **Bar of the Hotel Timp,** Heumarkt 25 (☎ **0221/258-1409**). This tiny spot opens at 11am and presents drag acts every night from 1:30am to 4am (it stays open to 5 or 6am). The cover charge of 15DM ($8.55) gets you views of such camp heroines as the divine Marlene Dietrich, several European starlets, and even Leni Riefenstahl, the controversial *wünderkind* of German movies during the Hitler regime. Those who want a good table should get here early. The Hotel Timp's most appealing competitor is **Star-Treff,** Alte Wallgasse (☎ **0221/25-50-63**), which offers at least one, and sometimes two, shows a night, usually beginning at 7:45pm and 10:45pm and staying open to 4am. Call in advance for the schedule. There's an entrance fee of 15DM to 20DM ($8.55 to $11.40).

10 Düsseldorf

25 miles N of Köln, 143 miles NW of Frankfurt

Düsseldorf is a wealthy city—the richest in Germany. It's big and commercial, full of banks and industrial offices and skyscrapers, but also refreshingly clean. Düsseldorf got its start as a settlement on the right bank of the Rhine, but today it's spread out on both sides—the older part on the right and the modern, commercial, and industrial part on the left. The two sections are connected by five bridges, the most impressive being the Oberkassel. Parks and esplanades line the riverbanks. After 85% of the right bank was destroyed in World War II, the city could easily have grown into just another ugly manufacturing town, but Düsseldorf followed a modern trend in reconstruction, and today it's the most elegant metropolis in the Rhine Valley.

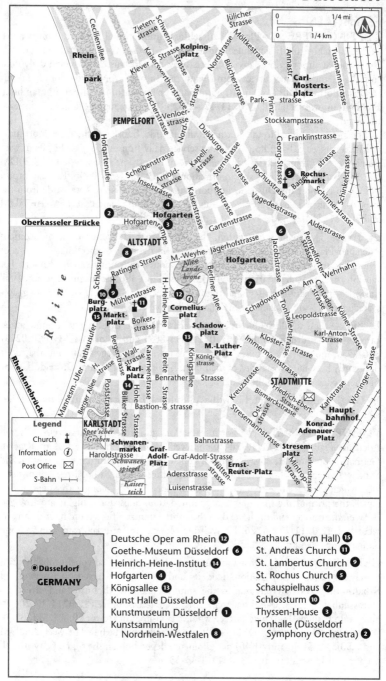

Düsseldorf

Deutsche Oper am Rhein 12
Goethe-Museum Düsseldorf 6
Heinrich-Heine-Institut 14
Hofgarten 4
Königsallee 13
Kunst Halle Düsseldorf 8
Kunstmuseum Düsseldorf 1
Kunstsammlung
  Nordrhein-Westfalen 8

Rathaus (Town Hall) 15
St. Andreas Church 11
St. Lambertus Church 9
St. Rochus Church 5
Schauspielhaus 7
Schlossturm 10
Thyssen-House 3
Tonhalle (Düsseldorf
  Symphony Orchestra) 2

ESSENTIALS

GETTING THERE **By Plane** **Düsseldorf International Airport,** 4 miles north of the city, has regularly scheduled connections to 14 German, 47 European, and 132 international airports. Lufthansa connects New York to Düsseldorf with a daily non-stop flight, and also has service from Miami and Toronto. You can fly from Frankfurt to Düsseldorf on Lufthansa in just 45 minutes or from Munich or Berlin in an hour. For flight information, call ☎ 0211/421-22-23. There are luggage-storage facilities at the airport.

The airport is linked to the **GermanRail** network. Transfer to the Düsseldorf main rail station is via S-Bahn no. 7, offering service daily from 4:03am to 12:30am, with trains every 20 minutes; the trip time is 12 minutes. The one-way fare is 3.20DM ($1.80). For train schedules and information call ☎ 0211/3680596. Regular airport buses also connect the Düsseldorf airport with Bonn and Köln. A taxi ride from the airport to central Düsseldorf takes about 20 to 30 minutes, and costs between 25DM and 30DM ($14.25 and $17.10), depending on traffic.

By Train The main train station, the **Düsseldorf Hauptbahnhof,** on Konrad-Adenauer-Platz in the southeastern sector, offers frequent connections to all major cities. The trip time to Frankfurt is about 2½ hours; to Munich, about 7 hours. For rail information, call ☎ 01805/996633. Düsseldorf also has extensive regional rail links; for information on regional trains or trams, call ☎ 0211/5-82-28. Luggage-storage facilities are available at the Hauptbahnhof.

By Bus Access to Düsseldorf is a lot easier by rail than by bus. The region's largest carriers are **Bandroch GmbH** (☎ 0211/353-862) and **Adorf GmbH** (☎ 0211/320-771), most of whose buses service small towns within the Rhineland that don't necessarily have railway stations of their own. Buses usually pull into Düsseldorf at the northern edge of the Bahnhofplatz.

By Car Access to Düsseldorf is by the A3 Autobahn north and south or the A46 east and west.

VISITOR INFORMATION For information, go to the **Verkehrsverein,** Konrad-Adenauer-Platz (☎ 0211/17-20-20 followed by 0 after the recorded message in German), opposite the railway station. It's open Monday to Saturday 8am to 8pm, and Sunday and national holidays 4 to 8pm. The office also has a hotel reservations service, which charges a one-time booking fee of 5DM ($2.85), along with a deposit that equals the price of the first night's accommodation. Subsequent nights are arranged between the traveler and the hotel directly. For the tourist office's room reservation services, call ☎ 0211/172-0226. It's available Monday to Saturday from 8am to 8pm, Sunday from 4 to 8pm.

GETTING AROUND Düsseldorf is a big, sprawling city, so you'll probably want to rely on public transportation. The city and environs are served by a network of **S-Bahn railways** that fan out to the suburbs, along with **buses** and **streetcars** **(Strassenbahn)** and a **U-Bahn** system. Ask at the tourist office (☎ 0211/17-20-20) about purchasing a **Tagesnetzkarte,** a whole day visitor's ticket, for 10.60DM ($6.05).

Taxi meters begin at 4.90DM ($2.80), after which you'll be billed between 2.30DM and 2.50DM ($1.30 and $1.40) per kilometer, depending on the time of day. To call for a taxi in Düsseldorf, dial ☎ 0211/3-33-33.

EXPLORING THE CITY

As in most German cities, there's an **Altstadt,** with a marketplace, a Gothic **Rathaus** **(Town Hall),** and a few old buildings and churches. Near the Rathaus on Burgplatz are two of the city's most famous landmarks, the twisted spire of **St. Lambertus Church** and the round **Schlosssturm (Castle Tower),** both of 13th-century origin. A short walk to the east takes you to **St. Andreas Church,** one of the most important in Düsseldorf.

The Altstadt has been called "the longest bar in the world" because of the 200-plus bars and restaurants found here. The favorite drink here is a top-fermented Altbier (old beer), a dark, mellow brew that must be consumed soon after it's made.

A walk up **Königsallee,** called the "Kö" by Düsseldorfers, will give visitors a quick overview of the city and its residents. This street flanks an ornamental canal, shaded by trees and crossed by bridges. One bank is lined with office buildings; the other with elegant shops, cafes, and restaurants. Here you'll see women dressed in the very latest styles. Düsseldorf is the fashion center of Germany. It's known for its Fashion Weeks, which attract designers and buyers from all over Europe.

If you walk up the Kö toward the Trident Fountain at the northern end of the canal, you'll reach the **Hofgarten,** a huge rambling park. Here you can wander along the walks or sit and relax amid shade trees, gardens, fountains, and statues, almost forgetting you're in the very center of the city. Among the monuments is one to the poet Heinrich Heine. The Hofgarten is a good central point for seeing the city's major attractions—nearly all museums and cultural attractions are on its perimeter. Towering over the Hofgarten is Düsseldorf's most impressive skyscraper, the **Thyssen-House.** Residents call it the *Dreischeibenhaus* ("three-slice house"), because it actually looks like three huge monoliths sandwiched together. Northeast of the Hofgarten is **St. Rochus,** one of the city's finest modern churches.

Kunstsammlung Nordrhein-Westfalen. Grabbeplatz 5 (opposite the Kunsthalle). ☎ **0211/8-38-10.** Admission 12DM ($6.85) adults, 8DM ($4.55) children over 6 and students, free for children 5 and under. Tues–Sun 10am–6pm (until 8pm Fri). U-Bahn: U-78 or U-79.

This museum has an outstanding collection of modern art, including works by many major French, German, and American artists. The museum architecture itself is impressive. There is an especially large collection of works by Julius Bissier, and also 16 works by Paul Klee—so many, in fact, that the Klee exhibition is rotated at regular intervals since all of it cannot be shown at the same time. Six temporary exhibitions of contemporary art are hosted in the large exhibition hall every year.

Goethe-Museum Düsseldorf. Schloss-Jägerhof (in the Jägerhof Castle at the Hofgarten), Jacobistrasse 2. ☎ **0211/8-99-62-62.** Admission 4DM ($2.30) adults, 2DM ($1.15) children. Tues–Fri 11am–5pm, Sat 1–5pm, Sun 11am–5pm. Tram: 707. Bus: 722.

The Anton and Katharina Kippenberg Foundation sponsors this literary museum dedicated to the memory of Goethe's life and work. It emerged from the Kippenbergs' private collection of some 35,000 items of Goethe memorabilia, including autographs, books, busts, paintings, coins, medals, plaques, and china. About 1,000 pieces of the collection are shown in the permanent exhibition, including first drafts of well-known poems. The displays present a chronology of Goethe's life and work. There are also exhibits on various topics of the Goethe era.

Kunst Halle Düsseldorf. Grabbeplatz 4 (across from the Kunstsammlung Nordrhein-Westfalen). ☎ **0211/327023.** Entrance 10DM ($5.70) adults, 7DM ($4) for students and children over 10. Tues–Sat 11am–6pm (Friday till 9pm). U-Bahn: U-75 or U-76.

The Kunst Hall Düsseldorf is devoted to contemporary art from the Rhineland and throughout Europe. No other museum in the city keeps up with changing trends in art as well as this one. Visiting exhibits of every shape and size, often bizarre, are displayed here. This museum should not be confused with the Kunstmuseum Düsseldorf.

Kunstmuseum Düsseldorf. Ehrenhof 5. ☎ **0211/8-99-24-60.** Admission 5DM ($2.85) adults, 2.50DM ($1.40) students and children. 10DM ($5.70) family ticket. Tues–Sun 11am–6pm. Tram: 701, 706, 711, or 715.

This is one of the largest and most comprehensive museums in the Rhineland. The painting collection includes works by Rubens, Caspar David Friedrich, and the Die Brücke and Der Blaue Reiter schools. The sculpture collection ranges from the late Middle Ages to the 20th century. There are also some 80,000 prints and drawings, as well as early Persian bronzes and ceramics, a glass collection, textiles from late antiquity to the present, and a design collection.

Heinrich-Heine-Institut. Bilkerstrasse 12–14. ☎ **0211/899-2902.** Admission 4DM ($2.30) adults, 2DM ($1.15) children and students, free for children under 10. Tues–Fri and Sun 11am–5pm, Sat 1–5pm. Tram: 704 or 707.

Heinrich Heine (1797–1856) was Germany's greatest lyric poet. More than 10,000 volumes, as well as the manuscript bequest of this Düsseldorf-born poet, are found here at the Heinrich-Heine-Institut. Born into a Jewish family, Heine nominally converted to Christianity so that he could attend law school. He was the author of the famous *Die Lorelei,* and his poems were put to music by Schubert, Schumann, and Hugo Wolf. His work was prohibited during the Nazi era, during which *Die Lorelei* was officially attributed to an unknown author.

In the Altstadt, you visit the house where Heine was born. It's at Bölkerstrasse 53 and is marked by a plaque.

SHOPPING

Düsseldorf is a city of high fashion and high prices. Many chic Europeans visit the city just to shop for what's new and hot. The best and trendiest fashions are sold on the opulent east side of the Königsallee. The two largest concentrations of designer shops are found at the **Kö Galerie,** Königsallee 60, and the **Kö Center,** Königsallee 30. Each gallery has some 100 shops. Those not interested in dishing out big deutschmarks for designer duds should head for the more recently opened **Schadow Arcade,** off Schadowplatz, at the end of the Kö. Fashion here isn't so *haute,* but neither are the prices. Shoppers spend some one billion deutschmarks in the shops on Schadowstrasse annually—more than is spent on any other street in the country.

ANTIQUES Düsseldorf's historic core contains a fine selection of antique stores. **Monika Müser,** Schwanenmarkt (☎ **0211/327-346**), specializes in the intensely fashionable Biedermeier style of the early 18th century. The style's combinations of blond and ebony-colored wood and lines inspired by the aesthetics of ancient Greece and Rome will surely impress you. Antique silver, china, paintings, and other art objects are available from **Lothar Heubel,** Bastionstrasse 10 (☎ **0211/134-103**), which also sells Asian and African antiques, including jewelry, ceramics, and Chinese items from the Han, Ming, and Tang dynasties, mixed in with a handful of antiques from Provence and the south of France.

DEPARTMENT STORES **Carsch Haus,** Heinrich-Heine-Platz (☎ **0211/8-39-70**), carries a good selection of fashions, as well as quality home furnishings, jewelry, and other items.

DESIGNER CLOTHING & ACCESSORIES Designer shopping in Düsseldorf is limited only by your bank account. Two floors of men's casual clothing await you at **Fashonable,** Königsallee 58 (☎ **0211/32-75-66**). Men and women can both browse at **Giorgio Armani,** Königsallee 72 (☎ **0211/32-44-22**), where the best deals are found in early summer, just before the season's new designs come in. **Ritterskamp,** Trinkausstrasse 7 (☎ **0211/32-99-94**), also caters to both sexes, with designers such as Richard Tyler, Gianfranco Ferre, and Donna Karan. **Bogner Shop,** Königsallee 6–8 (☎ 0211/13-42-22), carries functional sportswear that's meant for action on the golf course, tennis court, and ski slopes. The designers have their workshop on the second floor.

   Chanel, Kö Center, Königsallee 30 (☎ 0211/32-59-35), offers the company's complete line of products, from clothing to cosmetics and fragrances. Also in Kö Center, German designer **Jil Sander** (☎ 0211/32-84-44) has set up one of her many shops selling women's fashions. For strictly German fashions, check the racks of women's clothing and accessories at **MCM (Modern Creations Munich)**, Königsallee 68 (☎ 0211/32-23-50).

   Need shoes and accessories to go with your newly purchased outfits? Head for **Anena,** Kö Center (☎ 0211/32-73-03), where one stop gives you access to the products of Calvin Klein, Jil Sander, Sonia Rykiel, Prada, Donna Karan, DUNY, and other designers. Shoes and more shoes fill the racks at **Walter Steiger Schuhe,** Kö Galerie (☎ 0211/13-41-04), the German designer of high-quality, high-fashion footwear. Choose from luggage, handbags, shoes, and other accessories at **Etienne Aigner,** Kö Galerie (☎ 0211/3-23-09-55). In the boutique of **Louis Vuitton,** Kö Center (☎ 0211/32-32-30), leather accessories, luggage, and handbags are sold.

DINNERWARE & KITCHEN ACCESSORIES   A diversity of items and styles can be found at **Georg Jensen,** Kö Galerie (☎ 0211/32-42-81), the shop of the German designer who redefines silver flatware, bowls, candle sticks, coffee pots, and much more.

FURNITURE & DECORATIVE ACCESSORIES   One of Düsseldorf's largest purveyors of art-deco furniture and art objects is **Arts Decoratifs,** Hohestrasse 20 (☎ 0211/32-45-53). Look for lamps, vases, paperweights, and high quality, pre-war costume jewelry, some of which could make good souvenirs.

JEWELRY & WATCHES   Located in the heart of the designer shopping district, **Wempe Juwelier,** Königsallee 14 (☎ 0211/32-72-87), is one of a chain of 23 shops scattered throughout Düsseldorf that carry Swiss watches and jewelry designs in gold, silver, and precious stones.

WHERE TO STAY
VERY EXPENSIVE

Breidenbacher Hof. Heinrich-Heine-Allee 36 (around the corner from Königsallee), 40213 Düsseldorf 1. ☎ **800/223-68-00** in the U.S., or 0211/1-30-30. Fax 0211/1-30-38-30. www. breidenbacherhof.de. E-mail: info@breidenbacherhof.de. 162 units. A/C MINIBAR TV TEL. 480DM–660DM ($273.60–$376.20) double; from 690DM ($393.30) suite. Rates include continental breakfast. AE, DC, MC, V. Parking 35DM ($19.95). U-Bahn: Heinrich-Heine-Allee. Tram: 76, 78, or 705.

This hotel is a citadel of luxury, refined taste, and understatement, imbued with elegance at every corner. Each guest room is individually decorated. Bedrooms are medium in size and are mostly decorated in traditional styling, with original art, elaborate beds, and spacious bathrooms with makeup mirrors, scales, robes, hair dryers, and marble floors. The service is grand, though a bit stuffy.

   Dining/Diversions: The Bar Royal is a small and intimate meeting place, with leather chairs and soft piano music. Next door, the Grill Royal serves a traditional European cuisine and is one of the finest restaurants in Düsseldorf. The Breidenbacher Eck, an informal bistro, offers a full menu at lunch and dinner and snacks throughout the day until late at night. Trader Vic's is a Polynesian restaurant and bar.

   Amenities: 24-hour room service, laundry, nearby health club, car-rental facilities.

Steigenberger Park-Hotel. Corneliusplatz 1 (at the beginning of Königsallee, next to the German Opera), 40213 Düsseldorf 1. ☎ **800/223-5652** in the U.S. and Canada, or 0211/1-38-10. Fax 0211/13-16-79. www.srs-worldhotels.com. E-mail: steigenbergerparkhotel@t-online.de. 147 units. MINIBAR TV TEL. 470DM–620DM ($267.90–$353.40) double; 950DM–1,750DM ($541.50–$997.50) suite. Rates include buffet breakfast. AE, DC, MC, V. Free parking. Tram: 78 or 79. Bus: 778.

This traditional deluxe German hotel is number two in the center, vastly surpassed by the Breidenbacher Hof. It has been completely modernized and re-equipped to meet modern demands. Its central location, overlooking the Hofgarten park, is virtually unbeatable, which may explain why it attracts so many conventions and groups. The Steigenberger maintains a high level of service in the old-world style. All the guest rooms, refitted to the latest standards, are cozy and comfortable. Bathrooms have makeup mirrors, robes, and hair dryers.

Dining/Diversions: The French cuisine at the Menuett attracts gourmets from all over the world. Drinks are served in the Etoile Bar. In summer, you can have a leisurely meal in a terrace overlooking parks and gardens. There's also a little bistro.

Amenities: 24-hour room service, laundry, dry cleaning, shoe-shine service.

MODERATE

Fürstenhof. Fürstenplatz 3, 40215 Düsseldorf 1. ☎ **0211/38-64-60.** Fax 0211/37-90-62. 43 units. MINIBAR TV TEL. 195DM–360DM ($111.15–$205.20) double. Rates include buffet breakfast. AE, DC, MC, V. Closed Dec 24–Jan 2. Tram: 701, 707, or 708. Bus: 725.

This hotel is a good, safe choice in the center of town. It's modern, but not glaringly so. It opens onto a tree-filled square. Guest rooms are handsomely furnished, each ranging in size from medium to spacious. Nonsmoking rooms are available, and half the breakfast room is reserved for nonsmoking guests. There's a sauna and fitness room, and the buffet breakfast is one of the best in town.

Hotel Grosser Kurfürst. Kurfürstenstrasse 18, 40211 Düsseldorf. ☎ **0211/173370.** Fax 0211/16-25-97. 21 units. TV TEL. 145DM–330DM ($84.10–$191.40) double. Rates include continental breakfast. AE, MC, V. Closed Dec 22–Jan 4. Tram: 709 or 719.

Although this modern hotel has some expensive rooms, it's a bargain overall—at least by the pricey standards of Düsseldorf. Rooms are small and sparsely furnished, though well organized. The bathrooms are also small and have somewhat thin towels. Breakfast is the only meal served, but several restaurants are nearby. Facilities include a sauna and a solarium.

INEXPENSIVE

Wurms Hotel. Scheurenstrasse 23 (near Graf-Adolf-Strasse, about 4 blocks from the Hauptbahnhof), 40215 Düsseldorf. ☎ **0211/37-50-01.** Fax 0211/37-50-03. 27 units, 24 with shower and toilet. TV TEL. 160DM–240DM ($91.20–$136.80) double with shower and toilet. Rates include buffet breakfast. AE, MC, V. Parking 15DM ($8.55). Tram: 734, 741, or 752. Bus: 835.

The Wurms Hotel, set in a five-story stucco building, is a good choice. The small guest rooms are done in dark wood offset by bright bedspreads and curtains. Bathrooms are a bit plain but are spotlessly maintained. A few rooms—rented only to singles—are without private bathrooms. The buffet breakfast is the only meal served. The hotel is a short walk from the central landmark square, Graf-Adolf-Platz.

WHERE TO DINE
VERY EXPENSIVE

✪ **Im Schiffchen.** Kaiserwerther Markt 9 (on the outskirts of the city, at Kaiserwerth). ☎ **0211/40-10-50.** Reservations required. Main courses 59DM–100DM ($33.65–$57);

fixed-priced menus 180DM–216DM ($102.60–$123.10). AE, DC, MC V. Tues–Sat 7–9:30pm. Tram: U79 to Klemensplatz. FRENCH/SEAFOOD.

The chefs at Im Schiffchen deliver a refined, brilliantly realized repertoire of the finest cuisine you'll find in any city along the Rhine. The ingredients that go into the meals are unimpeachably authentic—every tomato, every onion, every fish or piece of meat seems to have been thoroughly evaluated for quality before purchasing. The menu is ever-changing, based on seasonal variations, but you might find homemade goose-liver pâté with green peppercorns, a delectable Norwegian salmon in Vouvray sauce, or lobster cooked in chamomile tea. We could return again and again for the pike or perch cooked aromatically in puff pastry. The desserts are luscious; try the granulated fruit mélange with almond cream.

✪ **Victorian Restaurant.** Königstrasse 3A. ☎ **0211/8-65-50-22.** Reservations required for the restaurant, recommended for the bistro. Main courses 42DM–70DM ($23.95–$39.90); fixed-price lunch 55DM–80DM ($31.35–$45.60); fixed-price menus 135DM ($76.95) and 165DM ($94.05). AE, DC, MC, V. Mon–Sat noon–3pm and 7–midnight. Tram: 709 or 719. Bus: 834. FRENCH/GERMAN.

This is the finest restaurant in the city center. The decor features sparkling crystal, black-leather banquettes, and masses of flowers. The food represents the best of both traditional and modern schools. Examples include heavenly deep-fried zucchini flowers stuffed with lobster mousse and flavored with a sauce of champagne vinegar and coriander, apple salad with slices of goose liver, and three-vegetable puree. The delectable desserts change with the inspiration of the pastry chef but might include terrine of oranges served with raspberry liqueur and fresh mint.

Nearby is the **Bistro im Victorian,** decorated in shades of ocean blue with a mini-malist interior design. The kitchen area is wide open, so you can watch for yourself as the fresh ingredients are whipped into meals. Patrons can even discuss their food wishes with the chef himself. Meals in the Bistro begin at 38DM ($21.65).

EXPENSIVE

De' Medici. Amboss-Strasse 3 (on the outskirts, at Oberkassel). ☎ **0211/59-41-51.** Reservations required. Main courses 28DM–45DM ($15.95–$25.65). AE, DC, MC, V. Mon–Fri noon–2:30pm; Mon–Sat 6pm–midnight (last orders 10:30pm). U-Bahn: 74 to Amboss-Strasse. FRENCH/ITALIAN.

De' Medici is elegantly modern, serving two culinary traditions, French and Italian, which are blended harmoniously. The chefs make it their goal to create, startle, and amaze diners with zesty flavors. The oversize menu lists an array of tried-and-true dishes, with concessions to whatever was available in the market that day. The mari-nated sweetbreads over sautéed eggplant or medaillons of veal in puff pastry are both unusual and excellent.

Restaurant Savini. Stromstrasse 47, Unterbilk. ☎ **0211/39-39-31.** Reservations recom-mended. Main courses 37DM–49DM ($21.10–$27.95); fixed-price menus 49DM–98DM ($27.95–$55.85). AE, MC. Tues–Fri noon–3pm; Mon–Sat 7–11pm. Closed 3 weeks in July. Tram 704 or 709 from Graf Adolph Platz; get off at the Unterbilk station. ITALIAN/INTERNATIONAL.

If you don't mind the trip outside the center, this restaurant offers the finest Italian dining in Düsseldorf. The white-walled dining room has tastefully colored banquettes. The creative Italian cuisine uses produce that comes fresh from the market and is deftly handled in the kitchen. Menu items include carpaccio of beef with warm king prawns, black spaghetti with scallops, or sea bass with risotto of mushrooms. The restaurant also has one of the best Italian wine cellars in Germany, with some 500 offerings.

Rheinturm—Top 180 Restaurant. Stromstrasse 20. ☎ **0211/84-85-80.** Reservations recommended. Main courses 33DM–50DM ($18.80–$28.50); 3-course fixed-price lunch 51.20DM ($29.20); 4-course dinner 84.50DM ($48.15). AE, DC, MC, V. Daily noon–2:30pm and 6:30–11:30pm. Tram: 704, 709, or 719. Bus: 725. INTERNATIONAL.

Most of the clientele come here for the view. This futuristic restaurant is set atop the spool-shaped summit of the city's tallest tower, affording a 360° panorama of Düsseldorf's buildings and parks. The competently prepared menu items include grills, game dishes, fish, and soups. Try the slices of smoked duck breast with creamy savoy cabbage or rolls of salmon stuffed with turbot filling and served in Riesling-and-saffron sauce. Vegetarian courses are also featured. Many who share the elevator with you may only be coming for the tower's observation lookout. A trip up the tower costs 5.80DM ($3.30) for adults, 4DM ($2.30) for those 13 to 17, and 3DM ($1.70) for children 6 to 12. Kids 5 and under go free. The tower is open daily from 10am to 11:30pm.

MODERATE

Zum Csikos. Andreastrasse 9. ☎ **0211/32-97-71.** Reservations recommended. Main courses 20DM–40DM ($11.40–$22.80). AE, DC, MC. Daily 5pm–3am. Closed July. U-Bahn: Opernhaus. HUNGARIAN.

When you tire of Germanic cookery, Zum Csikos makes a refreshing change of pace. The restaurant's name, Csikos, translates as "Hungarian cowboy." It's set on three levels of a narrow town house that was originally built in 1697. Candlelight gives the place (and the diners) a mellow glow. The home-style Hungarian food is well prepared, and the portions are hefty. The beef goulash is excellent, as is the chopped liver. The restaurant follows the Hungarian tradition of late-night closings.

✪ **Zum Schiffchen.** Hafenstrasse 5 (a block from the Rhine). ☎ **0211/13-24-21.** Reservations required. Main courses 15.50DM–39.50DM ($8.85–$22.50). AE, DC, MC, V. Mon–Sat noon–midnight, Sat noon–midnight. Tram: 705. RHINELAND.

If you want the most traditional and atmospheric place to dine, come here before anywhere else. Zum Schiffchen, in the heart of the Altstadt, is Düsseldorf's oldest restaurant. A golden model ship on top of the step-gabled building (which dates from 1628) reminds you of its location, near the river. The interior follows the tavern tradition of scrubbed wooden tables and rustic artifacts. Good, hefty portions of regional cuisine are the rule here. The menu is large, and the service by the blue-aproned waiters (called *Köbesse)* is rather hectic. Zum Schiffchen is the perfect place to sample Düsseldorf's local beer. Over the years, the restaurant has attracted a host of famous diners ranging from Napoléon and Heinrich Heine to Arthur Miller.

INEXPENSIVE

Im Alten Bierhaus. Alt-Niederkassel 75 (on the outskirts). ☎ **0211/55-12-72.** Reservations required. Main courses 13DM–17DM ($7.40–$9.70). No credit cards. Tues–Sat 3–11pm, Sun 11am–11pm. Closed 3 weeks in July (dates vary). Bus: 834. RHINELAND.

This place is actually more of a wine tavern than a restaurant. The building dates from 1641. Style connoisseurs will recognize it as typical of the Rhine's left bank (as opposed to the right). Traditional German specialties, many sautéed, are served here. The house specialty is *Speck-Pfannenkuchen,* a bacon pancake; a similar version is made with marmalade. On Sunday the beer drinkers pile in at 11am. The specialty of the house is a local dark and foamy brew called Altbier.

Zum Schlüssel. Gatzweilers beer hall, Bölkerstrasse 43–47. ☎ **0211/32-61-55.** Reservations recommended. Main courses 15DM–50DM ($8.55–$28.50). AE, DC, MC, V. Sun–Thurs 10am–midnight, Fri–Sat 10am–1am. U-Bahn: Heinrich Heine Allee. GERMAN.

This establishment is as Germanic as the Rhine. Zum Schlüssel is located on the original site of the famous Gatzweilers Alt brewery. The decor is that of a classic German Gasthaus, with the aura of a country inn. The service is courteous and swift. The food has both aroma and taste, and there's plenty of it; sample the *Eisbein* (pig's knuckles) or a huge bowl of soup. Wash it all down with the house beer, Gatzweilers Alt.

DÜSSELDORF AFTER DARK

The place to go is the **Altstadt.** This half square mile of narrow streets and alleyways, between Königsallee and the Rhine River, is jam-packed with restaurants, discos, art galleries, boutiques, nightclubs, and some 200 song-filled beer taverns. Düsseldorfers refer to a night cruising the Altstadt as an *Altstadtbummel.*

THE PERFORMING ARTS   Classical music has long had an illustrious association with this city, once home to Brahms, Mendelssohn, and Schumann. Consequently, it's not surprising that both the **Düsseldörfer Sinfonie** and its home, **Tonhalle,** Ehrenhof 2 (box office ☎ **0211/8-99-61-23**), are world-famous. The Tonhalle is perhaps Germany's most successful modern concert hall after Berlin's Philharmonie. The highly regarded orchestra gives about a dozen concerts a year, with tickets running between 36DM and 90DM ($20.50 and $51.30). Call ☎ **0221/1-72-02-23** for the program schedule and ticket information. **Deutsche Oper am Rhein,** Heinrich Heine Allee 16A (☎ **0211/8-90-82-11**), is one of the city's renowned opera and ballet companies. Performances begin between 7 and 8pm, and tickets range from 20DM to 90DM ($11.40 to $51.30).

The city's dramatic venue, **Schauspielhaus,** Gustav-Gründgens-Platz (☎ **0211/ 36-99-11**), is outstanding, known all over Germany. The production and acting here are first-rate. Performances (in German) take place each day from September through June, and tickets cost 20DM to 80DM ($11.40 to $45.60).

BARS & BEER HALLS   The oldest brewery-bar in the city is **Bräuerei Schumacher,** Oststrasse 123 (☎ **0211/326004**), a popular establishment that serves only beer that's brewed by the company that owns it. It's open Sunday to Thursday from 10am to midnight, Friday and Saturday from 10am to 1am. The brewery **Bräuerei zum Uerige,** Berger Strasse 1 (☎ **0211/86-69-90**), serves traditional German dishes along with its house brews. Open Sunday to Thursday from 10am to midnight and Friday and Saturday from 10am to 1am. Two other breweries, each serving beer brewed on the premises, are **Bräuerei im Suchschen,** Ratingerstrasse 28 (☎ **0211/ 137-470**), and **Bräuerei zum Schlüssel,** Bölkerstrasse 43 (☎ **0211/326-155**), both of which also offer platters of German food. Purists in Düsseldorf are quick to point out that the **Bräuerei zum Uel,** Rattingerstrasse 16 (☎ **0211/32-53-69**), is not technically a brewery at all, because beer is not brewed on the premises. Nonetheless, students flock here for the house beers and international dishes. It's open Monday to Saturday 10am to 1am, and Sunday 11am to 1am.

Angel images fill every nook and cranny of **Engelchen** (German for "angel"), Kurzestrasse 15 (☎ **0211/32-73-56**), where an alternative arts crowd gathers for conversation and coffee, beer, or mixed drinks. It's open Monday to Friday 9am to 2am and weekends 9am to 5am. **N.T. Pub,** Königsallee 27 (☎ **0211/138-000**), is a conveniently located and convivial pub, set beside the town's main shopping thoroughfare. It serves cafe-style platters and drinks every day from 9am till after midnight.

DANCE CLUBS   Two hot dance spots, **Tor 3,** Ronsdorferstrasse 143 (☎ **0211/ 7-33-64-97**), and **Stahlwerk,** Ronsdorferstrasse 134 (☎ **0211/7-30-86-81**), face each other across the street. Both intersperse recorded dance music with live acts from throughout Europe. Both draw a mixed, fashion-conscious crowd, are open Friday and

Saturday nights from 10pm until about 5am, and charge 10DM to 35DM ($5.70 to $19.95) as a cover.

The interior of **Checkers,** Königsallee 30 (☎ **0211/32-22-88**), is glossy, contemporary, and urban. There's a dance floor and a busy bar. The cover charge of around 20DM ($11.40) includes the first drink. Open nightly from 10pm to at least 5am, depending on the crowd.

At **Ratinger Hof,** Ratinger Strasse 10 (no phone), Indian accents shine through a postmodern decor. The sound system blares a contemporary techno dance mix. There's an 18DM ($10.25) cover charge. Open Wednesday, Thursday, and Sunday from 10pm to 3am, Friday and Saturday from 10pm to 5am.

JAZZ CLUBS At the small and smoked-filled **Em Pootzke,** Mertensgasse 6 (☎ **0211/32-69-73**), there's no cover charge and no food, just nightly live jazz and drinking from 9pm to 1am.

LIVE-MUSIC CLUBS A popular piano bar, **Bei Tino,** Königsallee 21 (☎ **0211/ 32-64-63**), has music from noon to 3am nightly; guests are often allowed to play the piano. **McLaughlin's Irish Pub,** Kurzestrasse 11 (☎ **0211/32-46-11**), serves Guinness and Murphy's with stew and pies, and presents touring Irish bands on the weekend. It's open Sunday to Thursday 11am to 1am, and Friday and Saturday 11am to 3am. Another pub with a brogue, **Irish Pub Bei Fatties,** Hunsruckenstrasse 13 (☎ **0211/13-31-81**), hosts live blues, rock, jazz, and Irish music on Friday and Saturday. It's open Monday to Friday 2:30pm until 3am, Saturday 1pm to 3am and Sunday noon to 3am.

GAY CLUBS The centerpiece of gay life in Düsseldorf is the **Café Rosa Mond,** Oberbilker Allee 310 (☎ **0211/77-52-42**). It functions as a cafe, a bar, and an organizer of gay-themed entertainment, which changes virtually every night of the week. The staff can direct you to other gay-friendly venues. It's open nightly 8pm to 3am or later.

The Mosel Valley 14

Those returning from Germany singing the praises of the Rhine as the most scenic German river have probably not yet toured the Mosel Valley. The Mosel meanders in a snakelike path through the mountains west of the Rhineland, passing town after town whose sole purpose seems to be to beautify the riverbanks. Nearly every village and hill has its own castle or fortress, often surrounded by vineyards.

The Mosel *(Moselle* in French) begins in the hills of France, but its most scenic portion is the last 120 miles before it enters the Rhine at Koblenz. Visitors to the area enjoy the lively landscapes, the legend-rich countryside, and, of course, the wines. Many of the rich and full-bodied Mosel wines are superior to those of the Rhine Valley.

If you enter Germany via France or Luxembourg, the Mosel route is a good way to begin your tour of the German countryside. You'll arrive first at the major city of **Trier** with its significant Roman ruins before weaving through the Hunsrück and Eifel mountains.

Exploring the Region by Car

The 125-mile drive along the Mosel between the Rhine city of Koblenz (see chapter 13) and the ancient city of Trier is one of the most rewarding in Germany. Although it's a relatively short distance, you should allow at least 3 days to fully enjoy the Mosel River Valley tour. Rustic country inns are scattered along both the left and right banks of the river.

Day 1 Leave **Koblenz** by crossing the Neue Moselbrücke (New Mosel Bridge) on the southern outskirts. Look for the sign pointing to Route 49 and follow the highway along the east bank of the Mosel. Some 10 miles south of Koblenz you come to **Winningen,** a village from the Middle Ages, set against a backdrop of vine-covered hills. Another 6 miles along the route stands **Alken,** a little wine town known for its Thurant Castle. Take the nearby bridge across the Mosel and continue on Route 49 heading south for 6 miles to **Moskelkern,** another wine village. Continue along for another 3 miles to where signs point the way to **Burg Eltz,** the most prominent and most visited castle along the Mosel (there's a picture of this castle on the 500DM banknote).

From Ries, it's another 4 miles—still on the left bank—to **Cochem,** a medieval wine town where you can find food and lodging. You can also take guided tours of its huge castle, Reichsburg Cochem.

If you decide not to spend the night in Cochem, continue along the "wine road" with its panoramic scenery and towering promontories along the river—expect sharp curves in the highway. Vineyards cling to the rock-strewn hillsides. Route 49 goes along the left bank for 3 miles to the Ernest Brücke, where you can cross to the other side of the river. Follow the signposts for 3 miles to **Beilstein,** a market town of cobbled streets left over from the Middle Ages.

Day 2 After checking out Beilstein and its Metternich Castle, get back on Route 49, going for 4 miles to the bridge at Senheim. Here, we recommend that you cross the bridge to the left bank and go another 6 miles to **Alf,** a little village at the foot of Marienburg Palace, which dates from 1127. There are panoramic views of the Mosel and its vineyards here.

Then get on Route 53 and travel for another 5 miles to **Zell,** crossing back to the right bank of the river. To many, Zell is the loveliest of the Mosel wine towns, and you may want to linger. Zell is the headquarters of the producers of the fabled Schwarze Katze or "black cat" wine.

After Zell, go along Route 53 for some 11 miles to the old market town of **Traben-Trarbach,** the headquarters of the Mosel wine trade. After a look, continue south on Route 53 for 15 miles to **Bernkastel-Kues,** two wine villages on opposite sides of the river. A bridge connects the towns. Bernkastel exudes medieval charm. Visit any of its taverns for a glass of the local wine, Bernkasteler Doktor.

After Bernkastel-Kues (where you may decide to overnight), you can go for another 40 or so miles, passing some of the prettiest vineyard landscapes in Germany, to **Trier,** a city dating from prehistoric times, where you can spend the night.

Day 3 You can easily devote an entire day or more to discovering Trier's charms—after all, "Trier stood for 1,300 years before Rome" (or so the local slogan goes). We recommend that you spend another night here, visiting its Roman monuments and strolling its ancient streets.

1 Cochem

57 miles NE of Trier, 32 miles SW of Koblenz

This medieval town, located in one of the best wine regions of the Mosel Valley, is crowded against the left bank of the river by a huge vineyard-covered hill. Because of its large number of inns, Cochem might be your best choice for an overnight stopover between Koblenz and Trier.

The town is a typical wine village, with tastings and festivals. But the biggest attraction is **Reichsburg Cochem** (☎ **02671/255**), a huge castle at the top of the mound behind the town. The original 1027 structure was almost completely destroyed by Louis XIV's army in 1689. It has since been restored according to the original ground plans, and its medieval ramparts and turrets create a dramatic backdrop for the town. To reach the castle, follow the steep footpath from the center of town; the 15-minute walk is well worth it for the views of the town and the Mosel below. Although you can visit anytime, the interior of the castle is open daily from mid-March to November from 9am to 6pm. Guided tours are conducted at regular intervals. Admission is 7DM ($4) for adults and 3DM ($1.70) for children and students.

ESSENTIALS

GETTING THERE **By Train** The Cochem Bahnhof is on the Wasserbillig-Trier-Koblenz rail line, with frequent service between these connecting cities. For information and schedules, call ☎ **01805/996633.**

The Mosel Valley

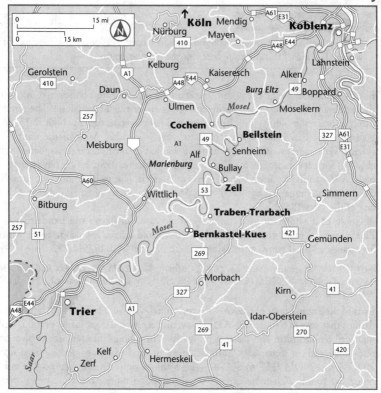

By Bus   Regional bus service along the Mosel is provided by RMV Rhein Mosel Verkehrsgesellschaft (☎ **02671/8976**) and by Moselbahn, GmbH (☎ **0651/ 147750**).

By Car   Access is via the A48 Autobahn on the Koblenz-Trier express highway; exit either at Ulmen or at Kaisersesch.

By Boat   Boat rides on the Mosel River operate between Trier and Cochem. Contact **Mosel Personen Schiffahrt Gebrüder Kolb,** Briedern/Mosel (☎ **02673/1515**).

VISITOR INFORMATION   For tourist information, contact the **Verkehrsamt,** Endertplatz 1 (☎ **02671/60040**), open Monday to Friday 9am to 5pm and, from May to October, also on Saturday 10am to 3pm and Sunday 10am to noon.

SPECIAL EVENTS   During the first week of June, **Mosel-Wein-Woche** begins, celebrating the region's wines with tasting booths and a street fair. The similar **Weinfest** takes place in the last weekend of August. For information on either of these events, contact the tourist office (see above) or the **Weingut Winzerhof** (☎ **02671/72-97**) for details on dates, activities, and accommodations.

SHOPPING   **Die Geschenkidee Heimes,** Herrenstrasse 13 (☎ **02671/9-11-22**), located on the town's main street, sells locally produced arts and crafts.

WHERE TO STAY

✪ **Alte Thorschenke.** Brückenstrasse 3, 56812 Cochem. ☎ **02671/70-59.** Fax 02671/ 42-02. 35 units. MINIBAR TV TEL. 165DM–225DM ($94.05–$128.25) double; 280DM ($159.60) suite. Rates include buffet breakfast. AE, DC, MC, V. Parking 10DM ($5.70) in garage. Closed Jan 5–Mar 15.

Thunderbird It's Not

Mosel wines have the lowest alcoholic content (about 9%) of any white wine in the world. Because of this, they are best enjoyed in their youth.

Both a hotel and a wine restaurant, the centrally located Alte Thorschenke is one of the oldest and best-known establishments along either side of the Mosel. The romantically conceived building, with its timbers and towers, was originally built in 1332. It became a hotel in 1960, when a modern wing was added. Most of the rooms are reached via a cantilevered wooden staircase that has creaked for centuries—and probably will for a few more (there's also an elevator in the rear). Six rooms have four-post beds. A romantic Napoléon suite was recently added. Not to be ignored are meals in the tavern, accompanied by Mosel wine. In summer, guests often take their lunch at one of the sidewalk tables.

Guests of the hotel can visit the 500-year-old **castle of Baron von Landenberg**, in Eller, about 4½ miles from Cochem. Here, in the old cellars, you can taste the wines. To arrange a visit if you're not staying at the hotel, call ☎ **02675/2-77.**

Burg Hotel. Moselpromenade 23, 56812 Cochem. ☎ **02671/71-17.** Fax 02671/83-36. 43 units. TV. 100DM–200DM ($57–$114) double. Rates include buffet breakfast. AE, DC, MC, V. Free parking.

Parts of the ground floor of this cozy riverside hotel were built in the 1500s, atop foundations that stretch back to 886 A.D. Today, the feeling you'll get is one of solid, well-managed conservatism and discreet prosperity. Furnishings throughout the place are traditional and, in some cases, antique. Seven of the bedrooms—those priced from 100DM to 120DM ($57 to $68.40)—lie within a simple nearby annex. The main house has rooms with more expansive balconies and more panoramic views of the river. The hotel offers an indoor pool, sauna, and solarium.

The hotel also contains two restaurants, each serving the same regional and international specialties. The more appealing is on the ground floor and holds a collection of antique weapons and artifacts. Set menus cost 14.50DM to 22DM ($8.25 to $12.55) at lunch and 14.50DM to 95DM ($8.25 to $54.15) at dinner. Typical dishes include specialties of the Mosel Valley. Naturally, a large selection of the best Mosel wine is available to accompany your meal.

Flair Hotel am Rosenhügel. Valwigerstrasse 57, 56812 Cochem-Cond. ☎ **02671/ 9-76-30.** Fax 02671/97-63-63. 23 units. TV TEL. 190DM ($108.30) double. Rates include buffet breakfast. MC, V. Free parking. Closed Dec 15–Jan 3.

The Rupp and Breslauer families are your hosts at this centrally located hotel, which has balconies and a sun terrace overlooking the Mosel. Some of the rooms also offer panoramic views of the castle on the hill. The rooms are modern, simple, and quite comfortable, though a bit small.

Lohspeicher. Obergasse 1, 56812 Cochem. ☎ **02671/39-76.** Fax 02671/17-72. 8 units. A/C TV TEL. 170DM ($96.90) double. Rates include continental breakfast. AE, MC, V. Parking 8DM ($4.55). Closed Feb.

A former warehouse, this generously proportioned 1832 building with hand-hewn beams has been completely renovated into a delightful and centrally located hotel and restaurant. Rooms, though generally a bit small, are comfortably furnished. In the restaurant, gourmet meals are presented at the best table in town (open Thursday to Tuesday from noon to 11pm). Specialties include onion or snail soup, followed by all kinds of fish and game dishes. Try the fillet of venison with wild mushrooms in cream sauce.

WHERE TO DINE

Parkhotel Landenberg. Sehler Anlagen 1 (about a mile from the town's Bahnhof), 56812 Cochem-Sehl. ☎ **02671/71-10.** Fax 02671/83-79. Reservations recommended. Main courses 21DM–52DM ($11.95–$29.65); fixed-price menu 95DM ($54.15). AE, MC, V. Daily noon–2pm and 6–9pm. Closed Jan 5–Mar 15. GERMAN/INTERNATIONAL.

Parkhotel Landenberg offers a pleasing panoramic view over the Mosel. Delectable regional specialties include venison, wild boar, and fish—all best enjoyed with a good bottle of white Mosel wine from the hotel's own cellar.

Weissmühle im Enterttal. Endertstrasse 1. ☎ **02671/89-55.** Fax 02671/82-07. Reservations recommended. Main courses 26DM–39DM ($14.80–$22.25); set menus 48DM–58DM ($27.35–$33.05). DC, MC, V. Daily noon–2pm and 6–9pm. From the center of Cochem, drive toward the Autobahn, following the signs for Koblenz/Trier; the inn is on the left of the road, 1 mile northwest of Cochem. GERMAN/FRENCH.

Set within Cochem's suburb of Enterttal, this respected restaurant is sought out by locals because of its fine cuisine. It offers a friendly welcome and a position in the middle of a little wine-producing village. You can dine within either the Müllerstube, a woodsy, antique-looking room that might remind you of an inn high in the Swiss Alps, or the brighter, sunnier, and larger Sommerrestaurant, where big windows create a greenhouse effect. A trademark dish is fresh trout from the small nearby lake, stuffed with herbs, baked, and kept warm beside your table by a hot stone.

A SIDE TRIP TO BURG ELTZ

The stately castle on the north bank of the Mosel is ✪ Burg Eltz (☎ 02672/95-05-00), set above the village of Moselkern and surrounded by woodlands. It lies 18 miles northeast of Cochem and 18 miles southwest of Koblenz. Access is by the A48 and A61 Autobahns and Route 49. A parking lot, Antoniuskapelle, less than a mile from the castle, can be reached via Münstermaifeld. A bus runs to the castle every 5 minutes.

This is one of the few medieval castles in the region still intact. The original structure, built from the 12th to the 17th centuries, has been preserved in all its glory—the romance of the Middle Ages really comes alive here. The castle houses four separate residences, with original furnishings from the medieval period, including some fine old paintings and tapestries. A treasury contains works by goldsmiths and silversmiths, armor, weapons, and other objects acquired by the family over the centuries. The castle is open daily from April to November 1, from 9:30am to 5:30pm. Admission is 9DM ($5.15) for adults and 6DM ($3.40) for children. If you want to fortify yourself before the trek back to town, stop at one of two small self-service restaurants in the castle.

2 Beilstein

7 miles E of Cochem, 69 miles W of Mainz

This unspoiled medieval wine town on the east bank of the Mosel has an unusual marketplace hewn right into the rocky hillside. Above the town stands the former cloister church and the ruins of the 12th-century **Metternich Castle.**

ESSENTIALS

GETTING THERE   By Train   The nearest rail station is at Cochem (see "Cochem," above).

By Bus   Service from Cochem and other points along the Mosel is available from **RMV Rhein Mosel Verkehrsgesellschaft** (☎ **02671/8976**) and from **Moselbahn, GmbH** (☎ **0651/147750**).

By Car Access by car is via the A48 Autobahn on the Koblenz-Trier run; exit at Kaisersesch.

VISITOR INFORMATION The nearest information office is at Cochem (see above).

WHERE TO STAY & DINE

Haus Burgfrieden. Im Muhlental 63 (a 5-min. walk west of the town center), 56814 Beilstein. ☎ **02673/9-36-39.** Fax 02673/93-63-88. www.f.von.metternich@t-online.de. 72 units. TV TEL. 129DM–140DM ($73.55–$79.80) double. Rates include buffet breakfast. No credit cards. Free parking. Closed Nov–Mar.

This hotel's simple but comfortable bedrooms are outfitted in an uncluttered modern style, with few concessions to traditional accessories. Rooms aren't very spacious, but the maintenance is good. On the premises is a dining room, where the chef offers an international menu specializing in game and fish. Main courses range from 18DM to 25DM ($10.25 to $14.25). Meals are wholesome and unpretentious.

Haus Lipmann. Marktplatz 3, 56814 Beilstein. ☎ **02673/15-73.** Fax 02673/15-21. 5 units. TV. 130DM–160DM ($74.10–$91.20) double. Rates include continental breakfast. No credit cards. Free parking. Closed Nov 1–Apr 1.

You can sample the wines that made Beilstein famous at its favorite inn, Haus Lipmann, in the town center. Time has been kind to this 1795 timbered building. The five guest rooms are located in its main house. They're all small, cozy, and very inviting, with tiny bathrooms.

For six generations, the same family has tended the vast riverside vineyards that have won them acclaim. Try their Ellenzer Goldbäumchen or their Beilsteiner Schlossberg. The various places for drinking and dining are so tempting that it's difficult to choose one over the other. Most popular in summer, however, is the vine-covered terrace with a statue of Bacchus, overlooking the Mosel. Or try the antique-filled tavern or the wood-paneled Rittersaal, with its collection of old firearms and pewter. Candles are lit at night. In the cooler months, fires burn in the tall walk-in fireplace and the tiny open hearth, with its copper kettle on a crane. The Mosel eel in dill sauce is a classic choice, but especially delectable is the fresh wild trout. Meals cost 30DM to 52DM ($17.10 to $29.65); hours are daily from noon to 2pm and 6 to 8pm. Activities get hectic at grape-harvest time.

3 Zell

43 miles NE of Trier, 65 miles W of Mainz, 22 miles S of Cochem

This old town, stretching along the east bank of the Mosel, is best known for its excellent wine, Schwarze Katze ("Black Cat"). The grape is king here, as you'll quickly realize if you visit during the annual autumn wine festival. Nearby, on the left bank of the Mosel, 5 miles from Zell and 20 miles from Cochem, stands the little wine village of **Alf.** The surroundings are idyllic, especially if you climb up to the Marienburg. From here, you get a fine view overlooking the Mosel and the vineyards of Zell.

ESSENTIALS

GETTING THERE **By Train** Zell doesn't have a rail station. The nearest one is at Bullay, some 2½ miles away. For information, call ☎ **01805/996633.**

By Bus Regional bus service is provided by **RMV Rhein Mosel Verkehrsgesellschaft GmbH** (☎ **02671/8976**), and by **Moselbahn, GmbH** (☎ **0651/147750**).

By Car Access by car is via the A1 Autobahn north and south or Route 53 east and west.

VISITOR INFORMATION   Check with **Tourist-Information,** in the Rathaus, Balduinstrasse 44 (☎ **06542/7-01-22**), open Monday to Friday 9am to 5pm.

WHERE TO STAY & DINE

Weinhaus Mayer. Balduinstrasse 15, 56856 Zell. ☎ **06542/45-30** (Apr–Nov) or 06542/57-76 (Dec–Mar). Fax 06542/6-11-60. 30 units. MINIBAR TV TEL. 120DM–160DM ($68.40–$91.20) double. Rates include continental breakfast. V. Free parking. Closed Dec–Mar.

This five-story, rustic, balconied building in the center of town thrives as both a hotel and a wine house. It offers small, simply furnished bedrooms in the main building, which is more than a century old. Some rooms have a view of the Mosel. The less expensive rooms are within a less desirable annex on the same street. The in-house restaurant serves only dinner, daily from 6 to 9pm; you might accompany your meal with one of the restaurant's bottles of Mosel Valley wines. Main courses range from 13.50DM to 25DM ($7.70 to $14.25).

Zur Post. Schlossstrasse 21, 56856 Zell. ☎ **06542/42-17.** Fax 06542/4-16-93. 16 units. 120DM–130DM ($68.40–$74.10) double. Rates include continental breakfast. AE, DC, MC, V. Free parking. Closed Feb to mid-Mar.

This beflowered hotel sits directly on the river. Its small rooms are carpeted, with French doors opening onto balconies. The owner takes pride in looking after her guests and ensuring their comfort. On the inviting sun terrace you can enjoy a glass of Mosel wine while watching the river traffic go by. Or you can sample the local wine in the warmly decorated Weinstube. Meals, served Tuesday to Sunday, cost 28DM to 50DM ($15.95 to $28.50).

4 Traben-Trarbach

37 miles NE of Trier, 64 miles W of Mainz, 11 miles SW of Zell

Thanks to their central location on the Mosel, halfway between Koblenz and Trier, the twin towns of Traben and Trarbach have become the wine capitals of the Mosel Valley. Their gardenlike promenades on both banks of the river are viewpoints for annual international speedboat and waterskiing competitions. The **July wine festival** attracts visitors from all over Europe to the old wine cellars and taverns of the towns.

Traben-Trarbach is also proud of its historic attractions. Above Trarbach, on the east bank of the river, are the remains of the 14th-century **Grevenburg Castle,** which was the scene of hard-fought battles to gain control of its strategic position. On the opposite bank, above Traben, are the ruins of **Mont Royal,** a fortress built in the late-17th century by the invading Louis XIV. You can wander about these testimonials to faded grandeur at any time, without charge. Another attraction, just south of town, is the spa resort, **Bad Wildstein,** with its thermal springs.

ESSENTIALS

GETTING THERE By Train   Rail passengers for Traben-Trarbach can arrive either at Trier or Bullay, then go the rest of the way by bus. Call ☎ **01805/996633** for schedules and times.

By Bus   Regional bus service among the Mosel River towns is provided by **RMV Rhein Mosel Verkehrsgesellschaft** (☎ **06571/7141**) and by **Moselbahn, GmbH** (☎ **0651/147750**).

By Car   Access by car is via the A48 Autobahn (Trier-Koblenz); exit at Wittlich.

VISITOR INFORMATION   For tourist information, contact the **Kurverwaltung und Verkehrsamt,** Bahnstrasse 22, in Traben (☎ **06541/83980**), open Monday to

Friday 8am to noon and 1 to 5pm; during May through October, also on Saturday 1 to 4pm.

WHERE TO STAY & DINE

Hotel Moseltor. Moselstrasse 1, 56841 Traben-Trarbach. ☎ **06541/65-51.** Fax 06541/ 49-22. 11 units. TV TEL. 128DM–188DM ($72.95–$107.15) double. Rates include continental breakfast. AE, DC, MC, V. Parking 12DM ($6.85) in garage.

You'll find this hotel on the outskirts of town at Im Otsteil Trarbach. The exterior of this four-story rectangular building is a masterpiece of 19th-century fieldstone masonry. Inside, a charming combination of new construction and antique elements from the original building creates a warm mixture of comfort and convenience. The inviting bedrooms contain such amenities as satellite TVs, hair dryers, private safes, and trouser presses.

Chef Ruth Bauer's reputation for light cuisine has spread so widely that German urbanites come here for gastronomic weekends. Bauer's restaurant is small, only 11 tables, with fixed-price meals costing 45DM to 65DM ($25.65 to $37.05). It's open Wednesday to Monday from noon to 2pm and 6 to 9pm. The hotel is open year-round, but the restaurant is closed in February.

Rema Jugendstilhotel Bellevue. Am Moselufer, 56841 Traben-Trarbach. ☎ **06541/ 70-30.** Fax 06541/70-34-00. 50 units. MINIBAR TV TEL. 189DM–299DM ($107.75–$170.45) double. Rates include buffet breakfast. AE, DC, MC, V. Free outdoor parking; 10DM ($5.70) in garage.

This art-nouveau castle, right on the riverbank, is one of the finest hotels along the Mosel. It was designed in 1903 by the noted architect Bruno Moehring and features elaborate timberwork, a domed tower, a high-pitched roof, gables, and dormers. The cozy bedrooms are often furnished with antiques. Amenities include an indoor swimming pool and a sauna. The Clauss-Feist Restaurant is a romantic spot for both breakfast and dinner, with stained-glass windows and an old-German ambience. Its high-backed chairs are drawn around fringed parlor tables under a high-vaulted ceiling, and there's a cozy fireplace and intimate wood bar. There's also an ivy-covered terrace for dining outside.

5 Bernkastel-Kues

30 miles NE of Trier, 70 miles W of Mainz

In a valley of wine towns, Bernkastel stands out as the most colorful. Its old Markt-platz is surrounded by half-timbered buildings dating from as early as 1608. In the center of the square stands the 17th-century **St. Michael's Fountain,** which flows with wine during the annual September wine festival. The ruined 11th-century **Landshut Castle** lies on a promontory above the town; it's worth a visit for the view. Like Traben-Trarbach, this town is split into twin villages on opposite banks of the Mosel.

ESSENTIALS

GETTING THERE   By Train   The nearest rail station is the Wittlich Haupt-bahnhof, 12½ miles west, with a bus or taxi connection to Bernkastel-Kues. For sched-ules and information, call ☎ **1-94-19.**

By Bus   Regional bus service along the Mosel River towns is provided by **RMV Rhein Mosel Verkehrsgesellschaft** (☎ **06571/7141**) and by **Moselbahn, GmbH** (☎ **0651/147750**).

By Car   Access by car is via the A48 Autobahn on the Koblenz-Trier run; exit at Wittlich.

VISITOR INFORMATION   Contact **Tourist-Information,** Gestade 5, in Bernkastel (☎ **06531/40-23**), open May through October, Monday to Friday 8:30am to 5pm and Saturday 10am to 4pm; November through April, Monday to Thursday 8:30am to 12:30pm and 1 to 5pm, and Friday 8:30am to 12:30pm and 1 to 3:30pm.

WHERE TO STAY & DINE

Doktor Weinstuben. Hebegasse 5, 54470 Bernkastel-Kues. ☎ **06531/96650.** Fax 06531/62-96. 19 units. TV TEL. 150DM–170DM ($85.50–$96.90) double. Rates include buffet breakfast. AE, DC, MC, V. Free parking.

This intricately half-timbered building in the town center was constructed in 1652. Today it's the most visually interesting hotel in Bernkastel, with more atmosphere than any of its competitors, except Zur Post. Transformed into a tavern back in 1830, it still has many of its original wood carvings. Its public rooms are traditional, and the cozy but often too-small guest rooms are furnished in a simple, modern style.

The inn serves the best food in town, with meals beginning at 35DM ($19.95). Hours are daily from noon to 2pm and from 6 to 10pm. Many guests prefer to sample Mosel wine in the hotel's vine-covered courtyard. Look for the 100-year-old plant called "Blue Rain."

Römischer Kaiser. Markt 29 (on the riverside promenade), 54470 Bernkastel-Kues. ☎ **06531/9-68-60.** Fax 06531/76-72. 38 units. TV TEL. 100DM–160DM ($57–$91.20) double. Rates include buffet breakfast. AE, DC, MC, V. Closed Feb.

The facade of this hotel, covering the corner of two downtown streets, has a view of the Mosel from many of the upper windows. The public rooms are decorated almost like rooms in a private home, with paintings and Oriental rugs. The rooms are rather small but comfortable.

Many visitors come here just to dine; the hotel is well known in the region for its traditional cookery. Like any good restaurant along the Mosel, it features local wines. A separate menu lists all the things that anyone could possibly cook with prawns. The restaurant is open daily from 11am to 9:30pm, with meals costing 20DM to 55DM ($11.40 to $31.35).

Zur Post. Gestade 17, 54470 Bernkastel-Kues. ☎ **06531/9-67-00.** Fax 06531/96-70-50. www.zur.post.bernkastel.de. 42 units. MINIBAR TV TEL. 160DM–190DM ($91.20–$108.30) double. Rates include buffet breakfast. AE, DC, MC, V. Free parking. Closed Jan.

This centrally located hotel was once a stopover for horseback riders on the local postal routes. The well-maintained but small rooms have both traditional and modern furnishings. The bathrooms are both tiny and tidy. The public areas include an elegantly crafted stairwell flanked by half-timbered walls and a paneled, beamed dining room. The restaurant serves excellent regional cookery daily from noon to 2pm and 6 to 9pm. À la carte meals cost 42DM to 65DM ($23.95 to $37.05).

6 Trier (Treves)

77 miles SW of Koblenz, 89 miles SW of Bonn, 120 miles SW of Frankfurt

As the Romans spread over Europe, they established satellite capitals for ruling their distant colonies. Augusta Treverorum (Trier) was founded under Augustus in 16 B.C. It eventually became known as Roma Secunda—the second Rome. For nearly 5 centuries, well into the Christian era, Trier remained one of Europe's political, cultural, and ecclesiastical power centers.

But this city, Germany's oldest, actually dates back much farther. In 2000 B.C., according to legend, the Assyrians established a colony here, and archaeological findings indicate a pre-Roman Celtic civilization. The buildings and monuments still standing today, however, date from Roman and later periods.

Trier is an important gateway, lying only 6 miles from Luxembourg on the western frontier of Germany, where the Ruwer and Saar Rivers meet the Mosel. The city is rich not only in art and tradition, but also, because of its location, in wine—it's one of Germany's largest exporters.

ESSENTIALS

GETTING THERE   By Train   Trier Hauptbahnhof is on the Wasserbillig-Trier-Koblenz "Moselbahn" line and also the Trier-Saarbrücken rail line. Trier has frequent regional connections. There are 20 trains per day to Koblenz (trip time: 1 hr., 20 min.), 20 trains to Cologne (2 hr., 25 min.), and 20 trains to Saarbrücken (1 hr., 20 min.). For rail information, call ☎ **01805/996633.**

By Bus   Buses between Trier and Bullay run along the Mosel River, leaving from the main station in Trier at Bussteig 3. Service is provided by **RMV Rhein Mosel Verkehrs-gesellschaft** (☎ **02671/8976**) and by **Moselbahn, GmbH** (☎ **0651/ 147750**).

By Boat   Boat rides on the Mosel River operate between Trier and Cochem (see section 1). Contact **Mosel Personen Schiffahrt Gebrüder Kolb,** Briedern/Mosel (☎ **02673/1515**).

By Car   Access by car to Trier is via the A1 Autobahn north and south, the A48 east, and Route 51 from the north.

VISITOR INFORMATION   Contact **Tourist-Information,** An der Porta Nigra (☎ **0651/97-80-80**), open Monday to Saturday 9am to 6:30pm and Sunday 9am to 3:30pm.

GETTING AROUND   Most of Trier's attractions are within walking distance of each another, and few visitors need to take the bus. Bus tickets (purchased on the bus) cost 2.50DM ($1.40) within zone 1 (the city). For information, call ☎ **0651/71-72-73.**

SHOPPING   The richest selection of Mosel Valley products and crafts, especially objects involved with wine, is available from the **Welcome Shop,** Simeonstiftsplatz (☎ **0651/994-0540**). If you're interested in seeing the art of glassmaking, head for the glassmaking studio at the Kunsthandwerkerhof, **Simeonstiftsplatz** (☎ **0651/ 4-29-91**), where a small-scale team of glass artisans open their studio for observation, as well as offer their wares for sale.

SEEING THE SIGHTS

Every day between May and October, the tourist office (see above) conducts a 2-hour **walking tour** that departs from the office at 1:30pm. The cost is 10DM ($5.70) per adult, 3DM ($1.70) for children 6 to 14.

EXPLORING THE ROMAN RUINS

When the last Roman prefect departed from Trier in about A.D. 400, he left behind a vast collection of monuments from the centuries of Roman domination. **Porta Nigra (Black Gate)** (☎ **0651/75424**) is the best-preserved Roman structure in Germany,

---

Local Boy

Karl Marx was born and grew up in Trier; his birthplace is now a museum. As a young man, he traveled down the Mosel Valley and was so shocked by the exploitation of vineyard workers that he decided to write an article about their plight. Thus began his career.

the only survivor of the great wall that once surrounded Trier. The huge sandstone blocks, assembled without mortar, were held together with iron clamps—the marks can still be seen. From outside the gate, the structure appeared to be simply two arched entrances between rounded towers leading directly into the town, but intruders soon discovered that the arches opened into an inner courtyard where they were at the mercy of the town's defenders. During the Middle Ages, the Greek hermit Simeon, later canonized, chose the east tower as his retreat. After his death, the archbishop turned the gate into a huge double church. When Napoléon came this way, however, he ordered all the architectural changes to be removed and the original Roman core restored. Porta Nigra is open daily, from April through October, 9am to 6pm; in November and January through March, 9am to 5pm; and in December, 10am to 4pm. Admission is 4DM ($2.30) for adults and 1.50DM (85¢) for children.

The Imperial Palace district, stretching along the site of the former medieval wall of the city, begins with the Roman building known today as the **Basilica,** at Basilikaplatz (☎ **0651/72468**). Although much of the structure has been demolished, the huge hall that remains—believed to be the throne room—gives some idea of the grandeur of the original palace. The hall is 220 feet long, 90 feet wide, and 98 feet high. The two tiers of windows are arranged within high-rising arches in which fragments of the original wall paintings can be seen. Five large heating chambers outside the walls sent warm air through the hollow floor, in the unique method of Roman central heating. Today the Basilica serves as the main Protestant church in the city. It's open Monday to Saturday 9am to 6pm and Sunday 11am to 6pm. Admission is free.

Next to the Basilica stands the 17th-century **Kurfürstliches Palais** (Electral Palace (☎ **0651/94-94-218**), which was built in the German Renaissance style as a residence for the archbishop-electors, the town's governors. The palace cannot be entered because its interior is used for city offices, but it can be admired from the exterior. The adjoining **Palace Gardens** (Palastgarten) are formal gardens full of ponds, flowers, and rococo statues. Admission is free; they're always open.

The **Imperial Baths** (Kaiserthermen; ☎ **0651/44262**), at the south end of Palastgarten, were erected in the early 4th century by Constantine I. Of the huge complex, more than 284 yards long, only the ruins of the hot baths remain. These baths were among the largest in the Roman empire, and although never completed, they were used in connection with the Imperial Palace. Even older Roman baths, the **Baths of St. Barbara** (Barbarathermen; ☎ **0651/762280**) are located on Südallee, near a Roman bridge. Admission to both baths is 4DM ($2.30); they're open daily 9am to 6pm.

The **Amphitheater,** Amphitheaterplatz (☎ **0651/73010**), is the oldest Roman construction in Trier, dating from A.D. 100. The stone seats, arranged in three circles separated by broad promenades, held at least 20,000 people. The ruins are open daily from 9am to 6pm; admission is 4DM ($2.30).

A **collective ticket,** which grants admission to the amphitheater, the two sets of Roman baths, and the Porta Nigra, costs 9DM ($5.15) for adults, and 3DM ($1.70) for children under 18.

MORE SIGHTS & ACTIVITIES

Since medieval times, Trier has served as a warehouse and distribution center for thousands of liters of wine fermented in its underground cellars. At least 40 of these cellars lie beneath the streets of the city and surrounding suburbs and hamlets. The oldest and most venerable of these is **Vereinigte Hospitien,** Krahnen Ufer Strasse 19 (☎ **0651/ 94-50**), which only accepts visitors who phone in advance for a reservation. Be warned that if it's inconvenient for this outfit to receive you, they'll be quick to tell you. The quickest way to arrange a tour of this cellar, or any of its competitors, is to enlist the aid of the tourist office. The staff there knows which group of vintners is receptive to visits; they'll make suggestions as to the best spots for drop-ins.

○ **Dom (St. Peter's Cathedral).** Domfriehof (north of the Palace Gardens and Basilica). ☎ **0651/7-58-01.** Cathedral free; treasury 2DM ($1.15). Cathedral Apr–Oct daily 6am–6pm, Nov–Mar daily 6am–5:30pm. Treasury Apr–Oct Mon–Sat 10am–5pm; Nov–Mar Mon–Sat 10am–noon and 2–5:30pm.

From the outside, this cathedral, with its rough-hewn stonework, looks more like a fortress than a church. This is the third church to stand on the site of the former palace (4th century) of the Empress Helena, mother of Constantine. It was begun in 1035 in Romanesque style. The Gothic and baroque additions in later centuries only helped to pull the ecclesiastical architecture into a timeless unity. The interior combines baroque decoration with Gothic vaulting and archways. On the south aisle is a magnificent tympanum depicting Christ between the Virgin and St. Peter. The Treasury Museum contains many important works of art, including the 10th-century St. Andrew's Altar, an unusual portable altar made of wood and covered with gold and ivory. But its most valuable treasure, the Holy Robe alleged to be the seamless robe of Christ, is so fragile that it was last displayed in 1959.

○ **Liebfrauenkirche.** Liebfrauenstrasse 2. ☎ **0651/4-25-54.** Free admission. Daily 8am–noon and 2–6pm.

This parish church, separated from the cathedral by a narrow passageway, is more pleasing aesthetically than its older neighbor. Begun in 1235, it was among the first examples of French Gothic architecture. The ground plan is in the shape of a Greek cross, creating a circular effect with all points equidistant from the central high altar. The structure is supported by 12 circular columns, rather than the typical open buttresses. The interior is bathed in sunlight, which streams through the high transoms. Although its restoration after the war changed some of the effect of the central construction, this edifice is still unique among German churches.

Some of the church's more important works of art are now in the **Bischöfliches Museum,** Windstrasse 8 (☎ 0651/7-10-52-55). The sepulcher of Bishop Karl von Metternich, who represented the archbishopric during the Thirty Years' War, is among the most interesting of those remaining. The museum is open Monday to Saturday 9am to 1pm and 2 to 5pm, Sunday 1 to 5pm; admission is 2DM ($1.15) for adults and 1DM (55¢) for children.

Karl-Marx-Haus. Brückenstrasse 10. ☎ **0651/4-30-11.** Admission 3DM ($1.70) adults, 2DM ($1.15) children. Apr–Oct Mon 1–6pm, Tues–Sun 10am–6pm; Nov–Mar Mon 3–6pm, Tues–Sun 10am–1pm and 3–6pm. Bus: 1, 2, 3, or 4.

This old burgher's house is where Karl Marx was born in 1818 and where he lived until he finished school in 1835. The museum has exhibits on Marx's personal history, such as his volumes of poetry, original letters, and photographs with personal dedications. There's also a collection of rare first editions and international editions of his works, as well as exhibits on the development of socialism in the 19th century. In the vicinity of the museum is a study center, **Studienzentrum Karl-Marx-Haus,** Johannestrasse 28 (same phone) for research on Marx and Engels.

○ **Rheinisches Landesmuseum.** Weimarer Allee 1 (between the Imperial Baths and the Basilica, at the edge of the Palace Gardens). ☎ **0651/9-77-40.** Admission 5DM ($2.85) adults, 3DM ($1.70) children. Tues–Fri 9:30am–5pm, Sat–Sun 10:30am–5pm. Bus: 2, 6, 16, 26, or 30.

This is one of the outstanding museums of Roman antiquities north of the Alps. Numerous reliefs from funerary monuments show daily life in Roman times. The museum's most popular exhibit is the *Mosel Ship,* a sculpture of a wine-bearing vessel crowning a big burial monument of the 3rd century A.D. Also on display are many mosaics and frescoes, ceramics, glassware, a 2,700-year-old Egyptian casket complete with mummy, an outstanding numismatic collection, and prehistoric and medieval art and sculpture.

BOAT TOURS

Trier owes much of its majesty to the river that nurtured its medieval commerce. You can take a day cruise for a waterside view of its historic banks. Between Easter and October, boats depart daily at 9:15am from the city docks (Zurlauben) for a 4-hour trip along the river to **Bernkastel** (see above), passing by vineyards, wine hamlets, historic churches, and semiruined fortresses en route. Participants spend 2 hours exploring Bernkastel before returning on the same boat to Trier, arriving back at 7:40pm. The cost is 44DM ($25.10) per person.

If you don't want to spend so much time on the river, you can take a shorter, hour-long excursion from Trier to the nearby historic hamlet of **Pfalzel.** Boats depart leave Trier's docks daily between Easter and October at 11am, 12:30pm, 2pm, 3:15pm, and 4:30pm. One-way transit costs 8DM ($4.55); a round-trip ticket is 10DM ($5.70). You can prolong your hour-long experience with a walk along the riverbanks in Pfalzel, or you can return almost immediately after your arrival on the next boat.

For information on either of these boat excursions, contact either the tourist office (see above) or the boat operator **Gebrüder Kolb** (☎ **0651/2-63-17** in Trier, or 02673/15-15 at its corporate headquarters in the nearby town of Briedern).

WHERE TO STAY
EXPENSIVE

Dorint Porta Nigra. Porta-Nigra-Platz 1 (across from the Roman ruins), 54292 Trier. ☎ **0651/2-70-10.** Fax 0651/2-70-11-70. 106 units. MINIBAR TV TEL. 210DM–260DM ($119.70–$148.20) double; 465DM ($265.05) suite. Rates include buffet breakfast. AE, DC, MC, V. Parking 6DM ($3.40). Bus: 3.

The six-story Dorint Porta Nigra combines style, comfort, and location, making it one of the two leading choices in Trier (the other is the Ramada). The interior is decorated with primary colors and contemporary furnishings. Most of the rooms have sitting areas and ornately tiled baths. All were freshly renovated in 1999.

Dining/Diversions: Porta is the hotel's gourmet restaurant, and Forum is where breakfast and lunch are served. International and regional cuisine are featured in both. A cafe with an entire wall of glass provides a view of the Roman ruins. The hotel also has a casino offering roulette and blackjack.

Amenities: Room service, laundry, dry cleaning.

Ramada Hotel Trier. Kaiserstrasse 29, 54290 Trier. ☎ **800/854-7854** in the U.S., or 0651/9-49-50. Fax 0651/9-49-56-66. www.ramada.com. 130 units. MINIBAR TV TEL. 182DM–196DM ($103.75–$111.70) double; 310DM–350DM ($176.70–$199.50) suite. AE, DC, MC, V. Parking 10DM ($5.70) outdoors; 20DM ($11.40) in garage. Bus: 1, 2, or 12.

This is the most important hotel to be built in Trier in many a year. It's located in the heart of the sightseeing zone, near the old Roman monuments. It may be too sleek and impersonal for some tastes, but it's serviceable in every way. The rooms are spacious, with streamlined modern furnishings. Some 42 rooms have air-conditioning.

Dining: The Park Restaurant offers an international cuisine. In summer, you can dine on the terrace.

Amenities: Baby-sitting, laundry, room service, first-aid room.

MODERATE

Kessler. Brückenstrasse 23 (next to the Karl-Marx-Haus), 54290 Trier. ☎ **0651/97-81-70.** Fax 0651/9-78-17-97. 22 units. MINIBAR TV TEL. 140DM–250DM ($79.80–$142.50) double; 250DM–350DM ($142.50–$199.50) triple. Rates include buffet breakfast. AE, MC, V. Parking 5DM ($2.85) outside; 20DM ($11.40) in garage. Bus: 1, 2, 3, or 4 from the Hauptbahnhof.

The sunny Kessler is managed by Jörg Müller, who speaks English and does everything he can do to make your stay pleasant. Rooms are small but attractively maintained and furnished in a clean, modern style. Guests gather in the evening in the hotel's cozy bar. The breakfast is very good.

Petrisberg. Sickingenstrasse 11 (a 10-min. walk from the Altstadt), 54296 Trier. ☎ **0651/46-40.** Fax 0651/4-64-50. 37 units. TV TEL. 160DM–190DM ($91.20–$108.30) double. Rates include continental breakfast. No credit cards. Free outdoor parking; 8DM ($4.55) in garage. Bus: 6.

The Petrisberg is beautifully situated at a point where a forest, a vineyard, and a private park meet. Each room in this intelligently designed four-story hotel has a view of the greenery outside. Furnishings may include seven-foot armoires or reproductions of slant-topped antique desks. The ground-floor Weinstube is the gathering place for many locals, particularly on weekends.

✪ **Römischer Kaiser.** Am Porta Nigra Platz 6, 54292 Trier. ☎ **0651/9-77-00.** Fax 0651/97-70-99. 43 units. MINIBAR TV TEL. 190DM–210DM ($108.30–$119.70) double; 250DM ($142.50) triple. Rates include buffet breakfast. AE, DC, MC, V. Free parking. Bus: 1, 2, 3, or 4.

This hotel offers cozily furnished, turn-of-the-century-style rooms in a prime location. Renovation in the mid-90s restored the building to its original beauty as a 19th-century patrician house. The hotel's restaurant features an international cuisine, with both three-course and à la carte meals. Food is served daily from noon to 10pm. Because of the hotel's location, visitors touring the area often drop in for a meal.

✪ **Villa Hügel.** Bernhardstrasse 14, 54295 Trier. ☎ **0651/3-30-66.** Fax 0651/3-79-58. 34 units. MINIBAR TV TEL. 170DM–240DM ($96.90–$136.80) double. Rates include buffet breakfast. AE, DC, MC, V. Free outdoor parking; 10DM ($5.70) in garage. Bus: 2 or 8.

This lovely, white, art-nouveau villa, built in 1914, has more style and ambience than some of the more highly rated hotels, such as the Ramada. The windows overlook either a private garden with old trees or the city. The sitting room/lobby area is decorated with masonry detailing and Oriental rugs, and the guest rooms are spacious and high-ceilinged. Four double rooms are so large that they're almost suites, making them favorites with families. You can order food and beverages on the two terraces. Facilities include a swimming pool and sauna.

INEXPENSIVE

Hotel Monopol. Bahnhofsplatz 7 (across from the Hauptbahnhof), 54292 Trier. ☎ **0651/71-40-90.** Fax 0651/7-14-09-10. 35 units, 24 with shower or bathroom. 130DM ($74.10) double without shower or bathroom; 150DM ($85.50) double with shower or bathroom. Rates include buffet breakfast. No credit cards. Parking 5DM ($2.85). Bus: 1, 2, or 12.

If you're seeking inexpensive lodging, try the four-story Monopol. It's a completely updated, turn-of-the-century hotel with a cooperative staff. Its rooms are both good-sized and well maintained, although completely sterile in decor. Rooms with shower or bathroom also contain a TV and telephone.

WHERE TO DINE

Palais Kesselstatt. Liebfrauenstrasse 10 (next to the cathedral). ☎ **0651/4-02-04.** Reservations recommended. Main dining room, main courses 27DM–42DM ($15.40–$23.95); fixed-price menus 55DM–85DM ($31.35–$48.45). Weinstube platters

15.50DM–20DM ($8.85–$11.40); wine 3DM–9DM ($1.70–$5.15) per glass. AE, MC, V. Restaurant Tues–Sun 11:30am–2pm and 6–9:30pm. Weinstube, daily 10am–midnight. Bus: 1. GERMAN/INTERNATIONAL.

This is the most unusual and interesting restaurant in Trier. The pink-sided baroque building was originally the residence of the count of Kesselstatt. Inside, the three high-ceilinged dining rooms include the building's former chapel and the Kaminstube (chimney area), which has an enormous fireplace. Menu items are made with fresh ingredients and change with the seasons. They might include fresh greens with slices of duck breast in herb vinaigrette, consommé with strips of fillet steak, fillet of turbot with prawns in a vegetable sauce, and a dessert specialty of Bavarian cream with straw-berry sorbet, served with fresh marinated strawberries.

The restaurant prides itself on stocking only Rieslings produced in nearby vine-yards—an excellent selection. Anyone interested in sampling the region's legendary wines in a less-formal setting can head for the Weinstube. Here you can order glasses of wine, as well as simple platters of traditional German and international food.

✪ **Pfeffermühle.** Zurlaubener Ufer 76, Zurlauben. ☎ **0651/2-61-33.** Reservations required. Main courses 42DM–47DM ($23.95–$26.80); fixed-price menus 85DM–120DM ($48.45–$68.40). MC, V. Tues–Sat noon–2pm; Mon–Sat 6:30–9:30pm. Closed Dec 24–Jan 4. Bus: 5. FRENCH.

This is clearly the best restaurant in Trier. Siegberg and Angelika Walde use fresh ingredients and maintain a bright, well-decorated dining room with a river view. Their nouvelle French cuisine is delectable. Try the assorted fish, cooked à point, with home-made noodles, followed by petit fours. The list of Mosel wines is extensive. In summer, guests can enjoy their meals on a terrace.

Zum Domstein. Hauptmarkt 5. ☎ **0651/7-44-90.** Reservations recommended. Main courses 18DM–30DM ($10.25–$17.10); set menus 45DM–54DM ($25.65–$30.80). MC, V. Daily 9am–midnight, with hot food served daily 11:30am–2pm and 6–9:30pm. Bus: 1, 2, or 12. RHINELAND.

Charming Zum Domstein is permeated with an old-time sense of bounty. It overlooks the flower stands and the fountain of Trier's most central plaza. The three dining rooms are richly accessorized with a collection of antiques. Ask for one of the wine tastings, which will get you either three glasses of wine (from the Mosel, the Ruwer, and the Saar, respectively) for a combined total of 10DM to 15DM ($5.70 to $8.55); or a half-dozen very small glasses showcasing separate regional vintages for a combined total of 12DM ($6.85). In addition, at least 10 regional whites and 6 regional and French reds are sold by the glass, while hundreds more, in bottles, are stored within the cellars.

The food here is as tempting as the wine; a typically savory offering is a platter of fillet of trout in a Riesling sauce or knuckle of lamb with vegetables. All the dishes are redo-lent with old-fashioned flavors; some are even said to have been enjoyed by the Romans, often with rich sauces. In winter, you'll want to find a spot near the huge tiled stove.

You might also want to look at the **Römischer Weinkeller,** in the cellar. Originally built around A.D. 326, it was excavated and restored in 1970. Original Roman arti-facts, many connected with food and cooking, decorate the cellar room. Dishes here are prepared according to recipes attributed to Marcus Gavius Apicius, said to have been the foremost chef at the court of the emperor Tiberius. Set menus in the cellar range from 45DM to 55DM ($25.65 to $31.35).

TRIER AFTER DARK

The cathedral hosts a series of free **organ recitals** in May, June, August, and Sep-tember. Contact the tourist office (see above) for schedules.

Run by students for students, **Textorium,** Wechselstrasse 4 (☎ **0651/4-48-31**), is a bar that hosts bands, art exhibits, and assorted workshops. Next door, **TUFA** (☎ **0651/4-07-17**) presents theater, more established touring bands, and the occasional disco. Another student hangout, **Blaues Blut,** Pferdermarkt (☎ **0651/4-12-53**), features blue lights and tables covered in imported Turkish tile; outside, the terrace includes some of the only shade trees in the entire city (short-sighted architectural designers removed the rest). Open Monday to Saturday from 9am to 2am and Sunday from 10am to 2am. From Thursday to Saturday there's dancing and DJs. A club with a beer garden, **Exhaus,** Zurmainer Strasse 114 (☎ **0651/2-51-91**), has both dancing and bands, usually Wednesday to Saturday. Days vary, but the hours of operation are 8pm to 2am. Call to see what's scheduled. The cover charge ranges from 5DM to 20DM ($2.85 to $11.40).

Jazz aficionados gather at **Milton's Playhouse,** Jakobstrasse 13 (☎ **0651/4-91-32**), which is open daily from 10am to at least 1am. The simply but aptly named **Irish Pub,** Jakobstrasse 10 (☎ **0651/4-95-39**), serves toasted sandwiches, along with Guinness and Harp. Many evenings you'll often find an Irish, English, or German band entertaining a rowdy drinking crowd.

The area's newest nightlife hotspot is **Riverside,** a complex of bars and restaurants on the city's outskirts, about a mile north of the town center. The most popular place here is **Disco Riverside,** Zur Mainer Strasse 173 (☎ **0651/21006**), which draws a high-energy crowd of local dance enthusiasts from Wednesday to Sunday night, beginning around 10:30pm. Entrance costs 15DM ($8.55) and usually includes the first drink.

15

Bremen, Lower Saxony & North Hesse

The area between Frankfurt and Hamburg is Germany's most neglected tourist destination, yet it holds many discoveries. Some of Germany's best-preserved medieval towns, as well as some major spas, lie in the flatlands and rolling hills of Lower Saxony and North Hesse. The character of the area ranges widely, from the bustle of the port of Bremen to the isolation of the Lüneburg Heath.

Here you'll also find the beautiful Harz Mountains, perhaps the country's last stronghold of paganism, still a land of legends and fanciful names. It is said that the last bear was killed in the Harz in 1705, the last lynx in 1817, but there are still wildcats, badgers, deer, and foxes, as well as many limestone caves. The beech tree that grows in the Harz range has an unusual size and great beauty, and walnut trees abound.

Note that in the summer of 2000, Hannover will be hosting Expo 2000, the first World Exposition of the new millennium. Millions of visitors of expected for this exciting event, and hotel rooms in the area will be booked well in advance.

1 Bremen

74 miles SW of Hamburg, 76 miles NW of Hannover

Bremen, Germany's oldest coastal city, is second only to Hamburg among German ports. As soon as you as you arrive at "this ancient town by the gray river," you see how closely Bremen is tied to the sea. The sights and smells of coffee, cacao, tropical fruit, lumber, and tobacco give the city an international flavor.

Bremen grew from a little fishing settlement on a sandy slope on the right bank of the river. It was already a significant port when it was made an episcopal see in 787. In the 11th century, under the progressive influence of Archbishop Adalbert, Bremen became known as the "Rome of the North." During the Middle Ages, it was one of the strongest members of the Hanseatic League, and in 1646 it became a free imperial city. It remains one of Europe's most important port cities. The population of Bremen is about 550,000.

ESSENTIALS

GETTING THERE **By Plane** The **Bremen Flughaven** (☎ 0421/55950) lies only 2 miles southeast of the city center (take S-Bahn no. 5). It is used mainly as a commuter airport for flights within Germany.

By Train　Bremen has excellent rail connections with leading German cities. Its Hauptbahnhof lies on major rail lines, including Hamburg-Bremen-Osnabrück-Münster and Hannover-Bremen-Bremerhaven. Thirty trains arrive daily from Hamburg (trip time: 55 min. to 1 hr.), 35 trains from Hannover (1 hr., 5 min.), 13 trains from Berlin (5 hr.), and 50 trains from Frankfurt (4 hr., 15 min.). For rail information, call ☎ **01805/996633.**

By Bus　Rail travel to Bremen is far more efficient, but the city does have some bus links to other towns. Call ☎ **0421/5363288** for information. The bus station is in front of the railway station.

By Car　Access by car is via the A7 Autobahn east and west and the A27 north and south.

VISITOR INFORMATION　Contact the **Bremen Tourist Center,** Tourist-Information am Bahnhofsplatz (☎ **0421/308000**), open Monday to Wednesday 9:30am to 6:30pm, Thursday and Friday 9:30am to 8pm, and Saturday and Sunday 9:30am to 4pm. There's also a second branch at **Liebrauenkircher Hof,** near Markplatz (same phone and hours as the one in the Bahnhofplatz).

GETTING AROUND　For information about public transportation within Bremen, call ☎ **0421/55-96-333.** A single ticket, good for one trip on the city's network of buses and trams, costs 3.40DM ($1.95) to most destinations. For 8DM ($4.55), two adults and up to five children may ride all day on the network. The meter on local taxis begins at 3.60DM ($2.05).

EXPLORING THE CITY
ORGANIZED TOURS

Bremen has both bus and walking tours of its historic sites. **Bus tours,** conducted in both German and English, depart from the Hauptbahnhof daily at 10:30am. They cost 25DM ($14.25) for adults and 15DM ($8.55) for children under 12. **Walking tours** depart every day at 2pm, last 2 hours, and cost 9DM ($5.15) per participant. The combination of a morning bus tour with an afternoon walking tour offers a broadly comprehensive overview of Bremen. Tickets should be reserved in advance, then picked up at the tourist office (see "Visitor Information," above).

The city also sponsors **boat trips** around the harbor. They depart from the jetty in front of the Martinikirche every day between March and the end of October. You can reach the jetty from Marktplatz by walking southwest along Böttcherstrasse for about 3 minutes. Tours depart at 11:45am, 1:30pm, and 3:15pm. The cost is 13DM ($7.40) for adults and 7DM ($4) for children under 14. For more information, call the tourist office (see above).

THE TOP ATTRACTIONS

The main sights center around **Marktplatz,** the "parlor" of Bremen life for more than 1,000 years. The 30-foot statue (1404) of the city's protector, Roland, still stands today. The knight bears the "sword of justice" and a shield decorated with an imperial eagle. Local legend has it that as long as the statue of Roland stands in the Marketplace, Bremen will survive as a free city. During World War II, when this area was hard hit by Allied bombs, extensive measures were taken, with bomb-proof concrete and mountains of sandbags, to protect the statue.

Across the square from the Rathaus stands another example of a happy merger of Gothic and Renaissance architecture, the **Schötting,** a 16th-century guild hall used by the chamber of commerce. Somewhat in contrast to these ancient masterpieces is the **Haus der Bürgerschaft,** home of Bremen's Parliament, constructed in 1966.

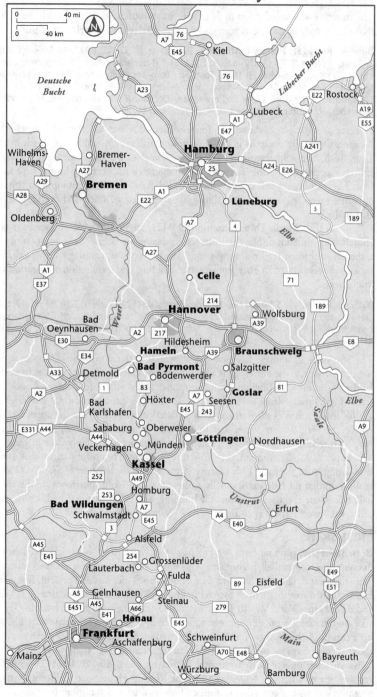

Bremen, Lower Saxony & North Hesse

0   40 mi
0   40 km

Deutsche
Bucht

Lübecker Bucht

A7
76
E45
Kiel
76
A23
E22 Rostock
A19
A1
E55
Lübeck
E47
A241
Hamburg
Wilhelms-
Haven
Bremer-
Haven
A27
25
A24 E26
Bremen
E22 A1
Lüneburg
A29
A28
5
A7
189
Oldenberg
4
Elbe
A27
A1
Celle
71
E37
214
189
Hannover
Wolfsburg
Bad
Oyenhausen
217
A39
Weser
A2
E30
Hildesheim
E8
E34
Hameln
A39
Braunschweig
A33
Bad Pyrmont
Salzgitter
Detmold
Bodenwerder
81
A2
1
83
Elbe
Höxter
A7
Goslar
Bad
Karlshafen
E45
Seesen
Saale
243
E331 A44
Sababurg
Oberweser
A9
A44
Göttingen
Nordhausen
Veckerhagen
Münden
Kassel
252
A49
4
253
Homburg
Unstrut
Bad Wildungen
A7
Erfurt
Schwalmstadt
E45
A4
E40
3
Alsfeld
A45
254
Grossenlüder
E49
E41
Lauterbach
Fulda
89
Eisfeld
A5
Gelnhausen
Steinau
279
E51
E451 A45
A66
Hanau
E45
Frankfurt
Schweinfurt
Main
Aschaffenburg
A70 E48
Bayreuth
Mainz
Würzburg
Bamburg

The structure was scaled down to fit in with its surroundings. Even though the architecture is a maze of glass, concrete, and steel, it doesn't look entirely out of place.

Dom St. Petri (St. Peter's Cathedral). Sandstrasse 10–12. ☎ **0421/36-50-40.** Cathedral free; museum 3DM ($1.70) adults, 2DM ($1.15) students, seniors, and children; tower 1DM (55¢). Cathedral Mon–Fri 10am–5pm, Sat 10am–2pm, Sun 2–5pm. Museum May–Oct Mon–Fri 10am–5pm, Sat 10am–noon, Sun 2–5pm; Nov–Apr Mon–Fri 11am–4pm, Sat 10am–noon, Sun 2–5pm. Cellar and tower May–Oct Mon–Fri 10am–5pm, Sat 10am–noon; closed Nov–Apr. Closed holidays. Bus: 30, 31, or 34.

St. Peter's, set back from the square, towers majestically over all other buildings in the Altstadt. Originally designed in 1043 as the archbishop's church, it was rebuilt in the 13th, 16th, and 19th centuries. The Romanesque east crypt dates from the early church. Another crypt, from the same period, houses a 12th-century bronze baptismal font. There's a bizarre collection in the Bleikeller (Lead Cellar) of mummified corpses of workers who fell from the roof during the construction. Their bodies were discovered in 1695.

You can also visit the **Dom Museum** (☎ **0421/36-50-40**), which is located in the church. The museum displays artifacts found during the large-scale restoration of the cathedral, including medieval tombs and 15th-century wall paintings. Other exhibits include the remains of an early Romanesque building, and a collection of historic altar implements.

Rathaus. Marktplatz. ☎ **0421/36-10.** Admission 5DM ($2.85) adults, 2.50DM ($1.40) children. For tours, inquire at the tourist office (see "Visitor Information," above). Tours generally begin Mon–Sat 11am, noon, 3pm, 4pm; Sun 11am and noon. Tram: 1, 2, 3, or 5. Bus: 30, 31, or 34.

The 560-year-old Rathaus has seen several periods of transformation. Outside, at the west end, is one of the more recent additions, a sculpture of Bremen's visitors from the land of Grimm—the Bremen town musicians. The donkey, dog, cat, and cock are stacked, pyramid style, in a constant pose for the ever-present cameras. The original Gothic foundations of the Rathaus remain basically unchanged, but the upper section reflects the 17th-century Weser Renaissance style in the facade; the tall windows alternate with relief statues of Charlemagne and the electors of the Holy Roman Empire. The upper hall, part of the original structure, contains a beautifully carved oak staircase dating from the early 17th century. A mural of *The Judgment of Solomon* (1537) reminds us that the hall was originally a council chamber and courtroom. In the lower hall, oak pillars and beams support the building, and below that lies the historic wine cellar, the "good Ratskeller of Bremen" (see "Where to Dine," below).

MORE SIGHTS

Böttcherstrasse, running from Marktplatz to the Weser River, is a brick-paved reproduction of a medieval alley, complete with shops, restaurants, museum, and galleries. The street was designed to present a picture of Bremen life, past and present. It was the brainchild of a wealthy Bremen merchant, Ludwig Roselius, and was dedicated in 1926 and rebuilt after World War II. This artery is one of Bremen's biggest attractions. Try to visit around noon, 3pm, or 6pm, when the Meissen bells strung between two gables set up a chorus of chimes for a full 15 minutes. Besides fine handcraft and pottery shops, the street also contains buildings of historical significance. Take tram no. 4.

Kunstsammlungen Böttcherstrasse, Böttcherstrasse 8–10 (☎ **0421/33-65-066**), consists of two adjoining buildings. One, the Roselius House, is a 16th-century merchant's home with a collection of medieval objets d'art and furniture. Next door, the Paula-Becker-Modersohn House is dedicated to Bremen's outstanding painter (1876–1907) and contains many of her best works, including paintings, drawings, and prints. The two upper floors house works of the sculptor, painter, and architect Bernhard Hoetger (1874–1949). The museum is open Tuesday to Sunday from 11am to 6pm. Admission is 8DM ($4.55) for adults and 4DM ($2.30) for children. Take tram no. 4.

Schnoor, the old quarter of Bremen, has undergone restoration by the custodian of ancient monuments. The cottages of this east-end district, once homes of simple fishermen, have been rented to artists and artisans in an effort to revive many old arts and crafts. Sightseers visit not only for the atmosphere but also for the unusual restaurants, shops, and art galleries.

Rampart Walk is a peaceful green park where the ramparts protecting this Hanseatic city used to stand. Its gardens divide the Altstadt from the newer extensions of the city. The park is just a few short blocks from Marktplatz, along the canal (once Bremen's crown-shaped moat). Its major attraction is an ancient windmill that's still functioning.

SHOPPING

Bremen has thrived on the salty air of business and commerce since it was founded. Today, you'll find lots of shopping options along two shopping streets, **Obernstrasse** and **Sögestrasse,** as well as dozens of boutique-inspired gift shops in the **Schnoor.** The city's cutest stuffed teddy bears, available in all sizes and degrees of fuzziness, are sold at **Bärenhaus,** Schnoor 17 (☎ **0421/32-64-03**), for prices that begin at 25DM ($14.25) for your garden-variety bear and can go much, much higher. Next door is **Rapunzel,** Schnoor 17A (same phone), an emporium for gift items, as well as T-shirts, souvenirs, books, and marionettes modeled after figures from the Brothers Grimm.

The best shop for women's fashions is **Roland Kleidung,** Sögestrasse 18–20 (☎ **0421/1-25-36**), although the town's largest department store, **Karstadt,** Obernstrasse 1 (☎ **0421/3-07-10**), also stocks an impressive selection of less expensive garments. Antiques, including some brass fixtures salvaged from old ships, are sold at **Antikitäten B&M,** Fedelhörn 19 (☎ **0421/328282**). Two art galleries that contain sometimes riveting modern art are **Gallery Hubert,** Söge-strasse at Pelzstrasse 4 (☎ **0421/1-65-55-44**); and **Art Gallery,** Böttcherstrasse 8–20 (☎ **0421/33-88-20**), both of which represent artists from the region and throughout middle Europe.

Shoes are the best buy in Bremen, and **Leder-Koopman,** Georgstrasse 56 (☎ **0471/30-28-29**), is the best representative of the trade. The company has been making quality shoes and leather products for 100 years. Visit their shop to admire a level of craftsmanship that has become a rare commodity, and chances are you won't leave empty-handed. Bargain hunters swarm over the city's riverfront **flea markets.** The Weserflohmarkt is held at the Schlactel and Weser promenade every Saturday from 8am to 5pm; on Sunday, the action shifts to Burgerweide from 8am to 2pm.

WHERE TO STAY
VERY EXPENSIVE

✪ **Park Hotel Bremen.** Im Burgerpark, 28209 Bremen. ☎ **0421/3-40-80.** Fax 0421/3-40-86-02. 157 units. MINIBAR TV TEL. 510DM–610DM ($290.70–$347.70) double; from 900DM ($513) suite. Rates include buffet breakfast. AE, DC, MC, V. Free parking in front of the hotel; 30DM ($17.10) in the garage. Tram: 5 or 6. Bus: 26.

This hotel is without question the most outstanding and charming in Bremen. It occupies an enviable site, in a park whose meandering lakes, exotic trees, and zoo are the pride of the city. It's also just a short ride from the center of town. Behind the hotel is a large symmetrical reflecting pool that has a stream of water arching into the sky. The hotel's terra-cotta dome and evenly proportioned side wings were rebuilt in 1955 to emulate a turn-of-the-century pleasure pavilion. Guest rooms are stylishly decorated, with large windows overlooking the park. Rooms are generally spacious and are well appointed.

Dining/Diversions: Among the dignified public rooms are a bar and three restaurants, one of which occupies an elegant terrace overlooking the lake. The hotel's gourmet Park Restaurant serves continental cuisine. There's also an informal bistro, Buten und Binnen.

Amenities: Room service, baby-sitting, laundry, dry cleaning, terrace and garden, jogging track, hair dryers; horseback riding is arranged, and free bicycles are provided.

MODERATE

Hotel Munte am Stadtwald. Parkallee 299 (in the Burgerpark, about 1½ miles from the center), 28213 Bremen. ☎ **0421/2-20-20.** Fax 0421/21-98-76. 134 units. MINIBAR TV TEL. 195DM ($111.15) ground-floor double, 270DM ($153.90) upper-floor double. Rates include buffet breakfast. AE, DC, MC, V. Free outdoor parking; 8DM ($4.55) in garage. Bus: 22 or 23.

You'll think you're in the country at this brick hotel because it fronts directly on one of Bremen's biggest parks. Inside you'll find a wood-ceilinged pool area with a sauna, a steam room, a sympathetic Weinstube (called "The Fox"), a sunny dining room with a panoramic view of the woods, and handsome guest rooms decorated in woodland colors. Bedrooms range from medium to spacious in size.

Hotel zur Post. Bahnhofsplatz 11 (near train station), 28195 Bremen. ☎ **800/528-1234** in the U.S. and Canada, or 0421/3-05-90. Fax 0421/3-05-95-91. 194 units. MINIBAR TV TEL. 190DM–295DM ($108.30–$168.15) double; from 385DM ($219.45) suite. Rates include buffet breakfast. AE, DC, MC, V. Parking 15DM ($8.55). Tram: 1, 5, 6, or 10.

A longtime favorite, Hotel zur Post offers top-notch facilities and comfort, as well as Bremen's leading restaurant, L'Orchidée, and two other dining spots. Rooms are first rate and slightly larger than average. Laundry, dry cleaning, and room service are available, and the hotel also has a tropical fitness club, hairdresser, and beauty salon. It's an ideal choice for train passengers.

INEXPENSIVE

Hotel Mercure Columbus. Bahnhofsplatz 5–7 (near the train station), 28195 Bremen. ☎ **0421/3-01-20.** Fax 0421/1-53-69. 148 units. MINIBAR TV TEL. 160DM–200DM ($91.20–$114) double; 283DM ($161.30) suite. Rates include continental breakfast. AE, DC, MC, V. Parking 12DM ($6.85). Tram: 1, 5, 6, or 10.

Mercure Columbus offers attractive and tasteful rooms. An elegant recent renovation has set a higher standard for this hotel, putting it on the same footing as Munte am Stadtwald or Hotel zur Post. Leisure facilities include a sauna with a relaxing room and a solarium; personal services include dry cleaning, laundry, and room service. The Hanseaten Bar is a popular rendezvous.

Residence. Hohenlohestrasse 42, 28209 Bremen. ☎ **0421/34-10-29.** Fax 0421/34-23-22. 30 units. MINIBAR TV TEL. 169DM–189DM ($96.35–$107.75) double. Rates include buffet breakfast. AE, DC, MC, V. Free outdoor parking; 12DM ($6.85) in garage. Tram: 1, 5, 6, or 10.

Residence advertises itself as an art-deco hotel. The elegant public rooms have high ceilings with polished crisscrossed timbers and chandeliers. On the premises you'll find a sunny breakfast room, as well as a Nordic sauna and a solarium. The rooms are comfortably furnished but small. There's also a 24-hour snack and drink service.

WHERE TO DINE

As a seaport, Bremen has developed its own style of cooking, concentrating much of its effort, naturally, on seafood from Scandinavia and the North Sea.

VERY EXPENSIVE

✪ **L'Orchidée.** In the Hotel zur Post, Bahnhofsplatz 11. ☎ **0421/3-05-98-88.** Reservations required. Main courses 49DM–58DM ($27.95–$33.05); fixed-price dinner 107DM ($61) for 5 courses, 147DM ($83.80) for 7 courses. AE, DC, MC, V. Tues–Sat 6:30–10pm. Closed 2 weeks at Easter and 4 weeks sometime in summer. Tram: 1, 5, 6, or 10. FRENCH/MODERN GERMAN.

L'Orchidée, on the 6th floor of the Hotel zur Post (see above), has an elegantly sophisticated gold, cream, and black decor to go with its candles, silverware, and fine porcelain. Year after year this hotel restaurant emerges at the top in Bremen. Veteran chefs watch over a well-trained kitchen crew, and the service is sophisticated and skillful. The dishes are simply delicious. Try the terrine of smoked eel and shrimps followed either by fillet of turbot with lobster or breast of pigeon in a red-wine sauce. The desserts are made fresh daily, and the wine list is extensive.

EXPENSIVE

Meierei im Burgerpark. Im Burgerpark. ☎ **0421/3-40-86-19.** Reservations required. Main courses 29DM–46DM ($16.55–$26.20); fixed-price menus 29DM and 48DM ($16.55 and $27.35). AE, DC, MC, V. Tues–Sun noon–2:30pm and 6:30–10pm. Tram: 6. CONTINENTAL.

This lovely restaurant in the center of a city park is managed by the Park Hotel (see above). Locals often combine a meal here with a promenade in the park. The restaurant occupies what was originally a local aristocrat's summer house, sheathed in lacy gingerbread and ringed with ornate verandas. It contains four dining rooms furnished in Hanseatic style. The food doesn't match the refined cuisine of the Park Restaurant, but we like the setting. Typical, and very good, dishes include fresh fish, consommé with scallops and saffron, fried breast of duck filled with herbs, sautéed squab with forest mushroom risotto, and medaillons of monkfish with orange butter and basil sauce. Coffee and pastries are served every afternoon.

✪ **Ratskeller.** Am Markt (in the Rathaus). ☎ **0421/32-16-76.** Reservations recommended. Main courses 30DM–35DM ($17.10–$19.95) in the Ratskeller Restaurant; 18.50DM–35DM ($10.55–$19.95) in the Ratskeller Bistro. Set menus 58.50DM–68DM ($33.35–$38.75) in the restaurant. Restaurant daily noon–3pm and 6–11pm; bistro daily 11am–midnight. AE, DC, MC, V. Tram: 1, 3, 5, 24, or 25. GERMAN/INTERNATIONAL.

This Ratskeller is one of Germany's most celebrated—and certainly one of the best. It's traditional for friends to gather in the evening over a good bottle of Mosel or Rhine wine (no beer is served). Appetizers include an assortment of smoked fish as well as creamy fish soup flavored with saffron; main courses often include fried pike-perch in a basil sauce and chicken ragout Bremen-style (in a crayfish sauce with calves' sweetbreads, tongue, mushrooms, sausages, and a vegetable risotto). The wine list is outstanding, one of the longest lists of German vintages in the world. Some of the decorative kegs have contained wine for nearly 200 years. There's also a less formal bistro here, with a limited list of less expensive traditional dishes that include *Laubskaus*, and simple platters of fresh fish.

MODERATE

Alte Gilde. Ansgaritorstrasse 24 (entrance on Hutfilterstrasse). ☎ **0421/17-17-12.** Reservations recommended. Main courses 18DM–25DM ($10.25–$14.25); fixed-price lunch 29DM–47DM ($16.55–$26.80). AE, DC, MC, V. Mon–Sat 11am–11pm. Tram: 2 or 3. Bus: 6, 25, or 26. CONTINENTAL.

Alte Gilde is located in one of the most ornately decorated houses in Bremen. In spite of the new building surrounding it, the 17th-century structure, with its gilt gargoyles and sea serpents, clings tenaciously to the past. The restaurant is in the vaulted cellar. The chef prepares many fresh fish dishes, as well as pork steak à la Kempinski, with poached eggs and béarnaise sauce—a lot of diners still go for this grandmotherly favorite.

✪ **Grashoff's Bistro.** Contrescarpe 80. ☎ **0421/1-47-40.** Reservations recommended. Main courses 40DM–45DM ($22.80–$25.65). Set menu 50DM ($28.50). DC, V. Mon–Fri 10am–6:30pm, Sat 10am–2pm. GERMAN.

This restaurant is well managed, charming, and concerned with quality and ambience. Its only real flaw is that it's never open for dinner—instead, it caters to the mobs of office workers and shoppers at lunchtime. You'll get a distinct sense of the arts here, and a few memories of Paris as well, thanks to dozens of framed pictures hung edge-to-edge across the cream-colored, bistro-inspired walls. Menu items include a succulent version of spaghetti with lobster; flank steak in a pepper sauce; an oft-changing roster of fresh fish, such as turbot and fillet of sole; and desserts such as crème brûlée, fresh pastries, and tarts.

Pappagallo. Goetheplatz 4 (near the town center). ☎ **0421/32-79-63.** Reservations recommended. Main courses 31DM–40DM ($17.65–$22.80). MC, V. Mon–Fri noon–2:30pm; Mon–Sat 6–11pm. Tram: 2 or 3. ITALIAN.

This is the best Italian restaurant in Bremen; it's a welcome break from a steady diet of north German cuisine. It occupies a Tuscan-style manor that was originally built by a local industrialist in 1842. Its interior is decorated in a radically modern style that might have been inspired by Milanese minimalism. The angularity is offset by succulent food prepared in sophisticated but time-tested ways. The menu changes every 2 weeks and reflects whatever is in season. Examples might include Sicily-inspired spaghetti Norma, rich with eggplant and mozzarella and herbs; spaghetti with fresh artichoke hearts and asparagus tips; risotto with scampi; and pasta with Parma ham and asparagus.

BREMEN AFTER DARK

Bremen nightlife offers a full range of activities. Many pubs and clubs, including those geared toward the gay community, are located in the **Ostertorsteinweg** district.

THE PERFORMING ARTS Classical concerts, opera, and dance performances by visiting companies are held in the **Theater am Goetheplatz** complex, Am Goetheplatz 1–3 (☎ 0421/365-3333). Call for a list of scheduled performers, ticket prices, and available seating. One of its stages, Schauspielhaus (☎ 0421/3-65-30), houses a theatrical company that occasionally performs in English. Tickets range from 20DM to 40DM ($11.40 to $22.80) during a season that runs from September through June. Opera and other musical performances are also scheduled in the **Musiktheater,** Am Goetheplatz (☎ 0421/3-65-33-33), where ticket prices range from 20DM to 58DM ($11.40 to $33.05). Experimental theater and modern dance can be found in the **Concordia,** Schwachauser Heerstrasse (☎ 0421/365-30), where a seat costs from 25DM to 45DM ($14.25 to $25.65). To attend productions of the Bremen Shakespeare Company, head for the **Theater am Leibnitzplatz,** Friedrich-Ebert-Strasse (☎ 0421/50-03-33), where tickets also cost from 25DM to 45DM ($14.25 to $25.65).

BARS An early evening bar, **Achims Beck Haus,** Carl-Ronning-Strasse 1 (☎ 0421/1-55-55), is a gathering place for drinks and simple pub fare. Open Sunday to Thursday from 10am to 11pm and Friday and Saturday from 10am to 2am. The oldest brew pub in town, **Schüttinger Brauerei,** Hinter dem Schütting 13 (☎ 0421/37-77-70), serves several tasty home brews along with traditional Bavarian cuisine. A DJ provides a wide range of music to drink by on Saturday night. Open Monday to Thursday from 11am to 1am, Friday and Saturday from 11am to 2am, and Sunday from 11am to midnight. An art-scene hangout with a large street-front terrace and a sometimes rowdy clientele, **Litfass,** Ostertorsteinweg 22 (☎ 0421/ 70-32-92), also has the longest bar in town. It serves breakfast, snacks, coffee, and beer. Open Sunday to Thursday from 10am to 2am; Friday and Saturday 10am to 4am.

CASINO   Bremen's centrally located casino, **Bremer Spielbank,** 3 Boettcher Strasse (☎ 0421/329-3000), contains roulette and blackjack tables. Admission is 5DM ($2.85), and a passport is required, as are jackets and neckties for men. Open daily from 3pm to 3am.

DANCE CLUBS   The place to dance is **Delight,** Am Liebfrauenkirchhof 23 (☎ 0172/42-08-167), a basement club where the DJs play house and hip-hop. Weekends generally bring theme parties. The club opens at 10pm on Wednesday and Thursday and 11pm on Friday and Saturday; there's no set closing time. On weeknights, the cover is 10DM to 12DM ($5.70 to $6.85); on theme nights, it can be as much as 25DM ($14.25). The club is closed in August. In winter, **Modernes,** Neustadtwall 28 (☎ 0421/50-55-53), is a movie house during the week, with dancing and live music shows on the weekend. For the rest of the year, it's a place to dance and watch bands nightly. Bands usually play from 8pm to 11pm; afterwards, the place is a dance club. Dancing costs 10DM ($5.70); admission to live music shows runs from 20DM to 35DM ($11.40 to $19.95). Twice monthly there's a free show.

GAY CLUBS   Much of the gay nightlife in and around Bremen is diverted into the clubs of nearby Hamburg, but there's still a few good spots. **Queen's Bar,** Ausser der Schliefmühle (☎ 0421/32-59-12), attracts a clientele of gay men. **Thealit,** Im Krummen Arm 1 (☎ 0421/70-16-32), is the leading lesbian gathering place in town. It offers platters of German and international food, priced at around 20DM ($11.40) every Wednesday to Saturday from 6pm to 1am. Other gay bars of note, mostly for men, include **Rat und Tat,** Theodor-Körner-Strasse 1 (☎ 0421/70-00-08), and the leather-oriented **The Bronx,** Bohnenstrasse 15 (no phone), where effeminacy is definitely not in vogue. And for dancing, there's **Monopol,** Ostertorwaldstrasse (☎ 0421/32-19-40), which attracts a mixed crowd of gays and straights every night except Sunday from 10pm till around 4 or 5am. The cover charge of 10DM ($5.70) applies only on Friday and Saturday nights.

LIVE MUSIC   For music in a bar setting, check out the band line-up at **Aladin's,** Hannoverschestrasse 11 (☎ 0421/43-51-50), which also houses a two-room disco and a bar with rock 'n' roll memorabilia (it might remind you of a Hard Rock Café). Open Wednesday to Saturday from 8pm to 7am; cover is 6DM ($3.40). **Moments,** Vordem Stein Tor 65 (☎ 0421/78007), hosts live rhythm and blues and jazz for a crowd of loyal regulars. Entrance costs 30DM ($17.10) for most shows. The place functions as a disco on some nights; cover is then 10DM ($5.70). The **Club Kernerwahl,** Kernerwahl 1 (☎ 0421/70-58-52), also has live music. Both Moments and Kernerwahl are open Tuesday to Sunday from 8pm till dawn.

VARIETY   Popular with children and adults, the ambitious puppet theater **Theatrium,** Bleicherstrasse 28 (☎ 0421/361-61-81), produces entertaining interpretations of books, plays, and movies, ranging from classical works to Woody Allen. In the same building, **Theater im Schnoor** (☎ 0421/32-60-54) presents cabaret and underground theater productions.

2 Lüneburg

77 miles NE of Hannover, 82 miles E of Bremen, 34 miles SE of Hamburg

Motorists driving south from Scandinavia through the Baltic port of Lübeck often find themselves on the Old Salt Road leading to the Hanseatic city of Lüneburg. This was the route over which the "white gold" of Lüneburg's salt mines was transported to the Scandinavian countries during the Middle Ages. Because of its heavy salt deposits, Lüneburg became a spa, which it remains today. In the **Kurpark** is a bathing house where visitors can take brine mud baths. In the **spa gardens,** there are indoor swimming pools, sauna baths, and tennis courts.

Lüneburg is also the ideal starting point for excursions into the **Lüneburg Heath,** which is especially beautiful in late summer, when the heather is in bloom.

ESSENTIALS

GETTING THERE **By Train** The **Lüneburg Bahnhof** lies on two major rail lines, the Hamburg-Hannover line and the Lüneburg-Lübeck-Kiel-Flensburg line, with frequent connections. For rail information and schedules call ☎ **01805/996633.**

By Bus Long-distance bus service into Lüneberg is provided by **KVG GmbH** (☎ **04131/87-20-80**) or **VOG GmbH** (☎ **04131/88-07-0**). The bus station is in front of the railway station.

By Car Access is Route 4 from Hamburg.

VISITOR INFORMATION **Lüneburg Tourist Information** is in the Rathaus Am Markt (☎ **04131/207-6620**). It's open Monday to Friday 10am to 7pm (to 6pm between November and April), and Saturday and Sunday 10am to 4pm.

EXPLORING THE AREA

Although most buildings in this 1,000-year-old city are from its most prosperous period, the 15th and 16th centuries, a total of seven centuries of architecture are represented here. The **Rathaus,** Am Markt, reached along Auf der Meere, is a perfect example of several trends in architecture and design. You enter through a Gothic doorway into a Renaissance hall. The Great Council Room is the building's most outstanding feature, with sculptures and bas-reliefs by Albert von Soest (1566–84). Daily guided tours are conducted all year at 11am, 12:30pm, and 3pm. The cost is 6DM ($3.40) for adults and 4DM ($2.30) for children. For information, call ☎ **04131/ 30-92-30.**

In honor of Lüneberg's role as "the Salt City," you might want to visit **Das Salz Museum,** Wandrahm Strasse 1 (☎ **04131/43891**). Inside, a series of exhibitions and artifacts explore life in the Middle Ages and the role of salt in the region's economy and culture. Entrance costs 4DM ($2.30) for adults, 2DM ($1.15) for children. Open Tuesday to Friday from 10am to 4pm, Saturday and Sunday from 11am to 5pm.

SHOPPING

The heath area is known for its craftspeople. Some of the best local arts and crafts are on sale at the tourist office (see above). The town's largest department store is **Karstadt,** Am Markt (☎ **04131/3040**). The main shopping streets are **Bäckerstrasse** and **Grapengiesserstrasse,** both lying in pedestrian zones. There's also an abundance of antique stores, the best of which are **H. Beckhaus,** Am Markt 5 (☎ **04131/3-11-61**), and **Brüning,** Auf der Altstadt 16 (☎ **04131/40-23-03**).

WHERE TO STAY

Bremer Hof. Lünestrasse 13 (a 2-min. walk from Marktplatz), 21335 Lüneburg. ☎ **04131/ 22-40.** Fax 04131/22-42-24. 53 units. 140DM–225DM ($79.80–$128.25) double. Rates include buffet breakfast. AE, DC, MC, V. Parking 6DM ($3.40). Bus: 3.

The logo of this hotel is an illustration of the animal musicians of Bremen, who, with their noise, frightened away the robbers. The facade looks like something out of the 16th century. Rooms are modern and sunny, but a bit small. All but four have phones and TVs. The hotel also has its own restaurant, serving specialties of the Lüneburger Heide region. A bar and a 400-year-old wine cellar are open on weekends.

The Lüneburg Heath

The Lüneburg Heath (in German, *Lüneburger Heide*) is one of the major attractions of northern Germany. The heath covers nearly 300 square miles and includes many beautiful spots. The sandy soil here is mainly covered with brush and heather, although there are a few oak and beech forests in the northern valleys. Toward late summer, the green of the heath flowers turns to purple; August and September are the most beautiful months. The best way to approach the heath is via the old town of Lüneburg, the area's transportation hub.

You'll find dramatic, windswept, and bleakly evocative scenery in the ✪ **Naturschützpark Lüneburger Heide,** a 100-square-mile sanctuary for plants and wildlife. Its highest point is the Wilsederberg, a low-lying peak only 550 feet above sea level, accessible via a network of footpaths from the hamlet of Wilsede. This reserve, in the center of the heath, is a peaceful, pastoral scene of shepherds, sheep, and undulating hills. Strict laws enforce the maintenance of the thatch-roofed houses and rural atmosphere. One of the park's most charming hamlets is **Undeloh,** which has a good hotel called the **Heiderose,** Gästehaus Heideschmiede, Wilseder Strasse 13 (☎ **04189/311**), renting doubles for 180DM ($102.60). There are also a number of villages—listed on only the most detailed of maps—that post *zimmer frei* ("Room for Rent") signs. These accommodations might be on a heath farm or even a horse farm.

For information, contact **Fremdenverkehrsverbund Lüneburger Heide e.V.** Barkhausenstrasse 35, Lüneburg (☎ **04131/7-37-30**), the park's administrative headquarters, which can furnish maps and information on horseback riding and cycling. Open Monday to Friday from 7:30am to 6pm. To reach the park from Lüneberg, drive 22 miles west, following the signs to Salzhausen. After you cross the bridge over the A7 Autobahn, follow the brown-and-white signs to the park. Bicycles can be rented in Lünenberg at **Laden 25,** Am Weder 25 (☎ **04131/ 37960**), for a cost of 12DM ($6.85) per day, plus a refundable deposit of 50DM ($28.50). Some ID is required. Open Monday to Friday 9am to noon and 1 to 5:30pm, and Saturday 9am to 12:30pm.

Hotel Bargenturm. Lambertiplatz, 21335 Lüneburg. ☎ **04131/72-90.** Fax 04131/ 72-94-99. www.hotel-bergenturm.de. E-mail: keil@hotel-burgenturm.de. 40 units. MINIBAR TV TEL. 174DM ($99.20) double; 249 ($141.95) junior suite. DC, MC, V. Parking 10DM ($5.70).

This three-story hotel at the edge of Lüneburg's historic center is one of the most modern in town. Its concrete walls and large expanses of glass make no concessions to the antique architecture of other parts of the city. Circular staircases spiral upward past glass-sided towers. The bedrooms are decorated with a no-nonsense kind of comfortable modernity. The staff is multilingual and efficient. There's a restaurant on the premises, Luna, with its own bar area, serving Mediterranean food and wine.

Residenz-Ring Hotel. Münstermannskamp 10, 21335 Lüneburg. ☎ **04131/75-99-10.** Fax 04131/7-59-91-75. www.ringhotels.de. 35 units. MINIBAR TV TEL. 210DM–240DM ($119.70–$136.80) double. Rates include buffet breakfast. AE, DC, MC, V. Parking 8DM ($4.55). Bus: 1 or 6.

The rooms of this serviceable hotel are so separated from each other that the place will remind you of an apartment building. Since the establishment is right inside the city's Kurpark, there's lots of shady greenery around. Rooms are functionally furnished and rather small but well maintained. The bathrooms are a bit cramped. You'll also find an inviting bar and an up-to-date restaurant, serving rather standard international and regional specialties.

WHERE TO DINE

Ratskeller. Am Markt 1 (on the market square). ☎ **04131/3-17-57.** Reservations recommended. Main courses 40.80DM–54DM ($23.25–$30.80); 4-course fixed-price menus 25DM–60DM ($14.25–$34.20). AE, MC, V. Thurs–Tues 11am–10pm. Closed Jan 6–20. Bus: 3. GERMAN/CONTINENTAL.

This is a good choice for lunch, dinner, or in between. The Ratskeller serves satisfying but unspectacular meals in a town not known for its restaurants. The varied menu includes game and regional specialties, according to the season. You can always count on good home-style cooking in a pleasant setting, backed up by a fine wine list. Parts of the decor date from 1328.

LÜNEBURG AFTER DARK

Students make this a rowdier place with a later nightlife than most other small towns. Bars are located along the river on **Am Stintmarkt.** The most popular place to hang out, drink, and debate, is **Dialog,** Am Stintmarkt 12 (☎ 04131/39-11-39), open daily from noon to 2am. Dancers hit the **Garage,** Auf der Hude 72 (☎ 04131/3-58-79), on Wednesday, Friday, and Saturday. DJs start mixing music at 10pm and stop at 5am. There's an 8DM ($4.55) cover charge.

Another important nightlife area is the **Schroederstrasse,** which is lined chock-a-block with bars and *nacht-cafés,* some of which provide live music. Locals like to duck in and out of as many bars as possible along this street during the course of an evening. Three of the best are **Max Bar,** Schroederstrasse 6 (☎ 04131/47887); **Café Central,** Schroederstrasse 1 (☎ 04131/40-50-99); and **Lillienthal,** Schroederstrasse 8 (☎ 0413/40-11-44).

3 Celle

28 miles NE of Hannover, 69 miles SE of Bremen, 73 miles S of Hamburg

The well-preserved town of Celle stands at the edge of a silent expanse of moorland, looking like something out of a picture book. Its ancient half-timbered houses were untouched by the war, and the legends carved on their beams seem to live on today. Most of the houses date from the 16th and 17th centuries—the oldest was built in 1526—but they're in such good condition that they could have been constructed in the 1900s.

ESSENTIALS

GETTING THERE By Train Celle Hauptbahnhof is on the Hamburg-Hannover rail line, with frequent connections to major German cities. Forty trains arrive daily from Hannover (trip time: 20 to 30 min.), and the same number pull in from Hamburg (1 hr., 10 min. to 1 hr., 30 min.). For rail information and schedules, call ☎ **01805/996633.**

By Bus Long-distance bus connections, from cities such as Hannover, are provided by **Winkermann GmbH** (☎ 05143/98820) and **Lempke & Koschick GmbH** (☎ 05143/46980). Buses arrive in front of the main railway station.

By Car Access by car is via the A7 Autobahn north and south, or Route 214.

VISITOR INFORMATION Contact the **Verkehrsverein,** Markt 6 (☎ 05141/12-12), open mid-November to March, Monday to Friday 9am to 5pm and Saturday

10am to 1pm; and April until mid-October, Monday to Friday 9am to 7pm and Saturday 10am to 4pm.

SEEING THE SIGHTS

Herzogschloss. West of the Altstadt. ☎ **05141/1-23-73.** Admission 5DM ($2.85) adults, 2.50DM ($1.40) children. Guided tour 10DM ($5.70). Tours Apr–Oct Tues–Sun at 10 and 11am, noon, and 2, 3, and 4pm; Nov–Mar Tues–Sun at 11am and 3pm. Bus: 2, 3, or 4.

One of the landmarks of the town, the palace of the dukes of Brunswick and Lüneburg is a square Renaissance castle surrounded by a moat. There's a tower at each corner. The palace's bizarre 16th-century chapel was designed by Martin de Vos, with galleries and elaborate ornamentation. The pride of the castle, and of the town, is its baroque theater, the oldest in Germany (1674), still in regular use today. Call the tourist office (☎ 05141/12-12) to arrange for a tour given by an English-speaking guide.

Bomann Museum. Schlossplatz 7. ☎ **05141/1-23-72.** Admission 4DM ($2.30) adults, 2DM ($1.15) children. Tues–Sun 10am–5pm. Bus: 2, 3, or 4.

For a picture of everyday life from the 16th through the 20th centuries in Celle, visit this fine regional museum with its extensive exhibits illustrating life in the country and in the town. Included is a complete 16th-century farmhouse, as well as rooms from old cottages, period costumes, and Hannoverian uniforms from 1803 to 1866. In the portrait gallery of the Brunswick-Lüneburg dukes, you can see pictures of the electors, later kings of England and Hannover.

WHERE TO STAY

✪ **Fürstenhof Celle.** Hannoverschestrasse 55 (at the edge of town), 29221 Celle. ☎ **05141/20-10.** Fax 05141/20-11-20. www.fuerstenhof.de. E-mail: reservation@ruerstenhof.de. 76 units. A/C MINIBAR TV TEL. 245DM–440DM ($139.65–$250.80) double; 250DM–950DM ($142.50–$541.50) suite. AE, DC, MC, V. Parking 12DM ($6.85). Bus: 3, 5, or 10.

This hotel, quite sophisticated for such a provincial town, is by far the best in Celle. It's a small-scale 17th-century manor house flanked by timbered wings. The brick courtyard in front of the salmon-colored mansion is shaded by a towering chestnut tree. The interior has formal neoclassical paneling and a collection of antiques. The older and more traditional rooms are in the main house; more modern rooms are in an annex beyond the rear courtyard. Rooms range in size from medium to spacious.

Dining/Diversions: The elegant Restaurant Endtenfang, formal yet warm, is one of the best in Lower Saxony (see "Where to Dine," below). The barroom is in the ancient vaults of the mansion. The beer tavern, the Kutscherstube, built into the old coach house, is more formal, with old wooden tables and farm artifacts. The hotel also has a bar, Die Bar im Unterhaus, that often offers dancing, and also an Italian restaurant, Palio.

Amenities: Room service, laundry, baby-sitting, tile pool, sauna, beauty parlor, shops.

Hotel Celler Hof. Stechbahn 11, 29221 Celle. ☎ **05141/2-80-61.** Fax 05141/2-80-65. www.residenzhotels.de. E-mail: reservation@residenzhotels.de. 49 units. MINIBAR TV TEL. 170DM–310DM ($96.90–$176.70) double. Rates include buffet breakfast. AE, DC, MC, V. Parking 12DM ($6.85). Bus: 3, 5, or 10.

Celler Hof is on the street where tournaments were once held. The old-world 1890 architecture of the hotel and its neighboring timbered houses renders the interior furnishings incongruously modern, although quite pleasing. Bedrooms, ranging in size from medium to spacious, have recently been renovated and are of a high standard. Many have a view of the castle. Guests can order lunch at the hotel's Stadtwache daily from 11am to 3pm. No dinner is served, although there is a bar in the lobby.

Hotel Schifferkrug. Speicherstrasse 9, 29221 Celle. ☎ **05141/70-15.** Fax 05141/63-50. 12 units. TV TEL. 120DM–160DM ($68.40–$91.20) double. Rates include buffet breakfast. V. Free parking. Bus: 3, 5, or 10.

The brick-and-timber walls of this comfortable hotel have witnessed more than 3 centuries of innkeeping tradition. The small to medium-sized guest rooms have lace curtains and eiderdowns—old-fashioned comfort just like at Grandma's. There's a bar on the premises, along with a rustic Weinstube and a more formal restaurant serving conservative but tasty German food.

WHERE TO DINE

In addition to the restaurants below, you can stop in at **Café Kief,** Grosserplan 16–17 (☎ **05141/22540**), which serves coffee, pastries, drinks, and platters of hearty German food with democratic, and rather conservative, aplomb every day from 8am to 7pm. **Alex's Antik Café,** Schuhstrasse 6 (☎ **05141/2-36-36**), is open Tuesday to Saturday from 8:30am to 6pm, and Sunday from 9am to 6pm. The youth and arts cultures hang out here.

Historischer Ratskeller. Markt 14. ☎ **05141/2-90-99.** Reservations recommended. Main courses 25DM–35DM ($14.25–$19.95); fixed-price menus 45DM–60DM ($25.65–$34.20). AE, MC, V. Wed–Mon noon–3pm and 6–10pm. Bus: 3, 5, or 10. GERMAN.

Historischer Ratskeller is plusher than the typical Ratskeller and has better fare. Attentive waiters are constantly passing by, carrying silver platters heaped with spicy, flavorful German dishes, such as roast venison with juniper berries, pork schnitzels, and fillet steak with a cognac-cream sauce and peppercorns.

Restaurant Endtenfang. in the Fürstenhof Celle, Hannoverschestrasse 55. ☎ **05141/ 20-10.** Reservations recommended. Main courses 48DM–60DM ($27.35–$34.20). Fixed-price menu 138DM ($78.65). AE, DC, MC, V. Daily noon–2pm and 6:30–10pm. FRENCH.

Celle's most prestigious and stylish restaurant occupies an appealingly old-fashioned dining room on the street level of this previously recommended hotel. You dine in the midst of carefully maintained wooden paneling, expanses of white plaster, and quality furnishings from the late 1800s and the 1950s. Service is efficient, helpful, and friendly. The menu focuses on game dishes, including two succulent versions of duck. (The word *Endtenfang,* which comes from an old regional dialect, means "the hunting reserve for duck-shooting.") Traditional adornments include a pepper-cream sauce, cabbage roulade, a potato and pear gratin, and fresh mushrooms, along with slices of red apples. Other main courses include halibut sautéed with fresh coriander and veal liver cooked with baby onions. The small dumplings that accompany many dishes are light and feathery. Desserts are quite imaginative, and the wine list is the finest in the area.

Ringhotel Celler Tor. Cellar Strasse 2 (about 2 miles outside town), 29229 Celle-Gross Hehlen. ☎ **05141/59-00.** Fax 05141/59-04-90. E-mail: celler.tor@t-online.de. Reservations recommended. Main courses 28.50DM–43.50DM ($16.25–$24.80); fixed-price menus 52DM–87DM ($29.65–$49.60). AE, DC, MC, V. Daily noon–3pm and 6–10pm. Bus: 11. GERMAN/INTERNATIONAL.

The Celler Tor is a cliché of German charm, with its gabled red-tile roof and banks of geraniums. When local residents want to celebrate a special occasion, they head here, knowing they can get a great selection of *gutbürgerlich* fare—that is, the food fondly remembered from childhood. In season, that means wild game, such as ragout of stag with mushrooms. You can also get good shrimp and rice dishes here.

The Celler Tor also rents 70 good guest rooms. A double costs 238DM to 268DM ($135.65 to $152.75), including buffet breakfast; eight suites are also available, at 298DM to 328DM ($169.85 to $186.95) each. Facilities include an indoor saltwater pool, massage facilities, a sauna, a solarium, and a workout room.

4 Hannover

76 miles SE of Bremen, 94 miles S of Hamburg, 179 miles W of Berlin

In the summer of 2000, Hannover will be the center of everyone's attention. From June 1 to October 31, the city is hosting Expo 2000, the first World Exposition of the new millennium, and the first to take place in Germany (see box below). Millions of visitors are expected, both for the exposition itself and for the many collateral cultural events, featuring world-class musicians, artists, and athletes. Be advised that hotel rooms in Hannover, and in many of the towns nearby, will be booked well in advance.

Hannover is one of Germany's hubs of industry, transportation, and commerce. Its annual industrial trade fair is now the largest trade fair in the world, attracting producers and buyers from around the globe. Bombed into oblivion in World War II, Hannover was badly reconstructed. If you want half-timbered houses, head for Celle (see above). Nevertheless, Hannover does have some attractions, including one of the finest baroque gardens in the world.

ESSENTIALS
GETTING THERE   By Plane   Hannover is served by **Hannover-Langenhagen International Airport,** 6 miles north of the city center. Many international airlines fly here, as well as Lufthansa. Flying time between Hannover and Munich is 1 hour and 10 minutes; between Frankfurt and Hannover, 50 minutes. For flight information from the airport, call ☎ **0511/9-77-12-23.** From 5am and 11pm, white shuttle buses run between the airport and the city every 20 minutes, depositing passengers at the Hauptbahnhof. The cost is 10DM ($5.70) each way.

By Train   Hannover lies at the junction of an important network of rail lines linking Scandinavia to Italy and Paris to Moscow. Some 500 trains per day pass through Hannover, with frequent connections to major German and European cities. Nineteen trains arrive daily from Berlin (trip time: 3 hr., 50 min.), 40 trains from Frankfurt (2 hr., 21 min. or 3 hr., 50 min., depending on the train), and 40 trains from Hamburg (1 hr., 11 min. to 1 hr., 30 min.). For rail information, call ☎ **01805/996633.**

By Bus   Long-distance bus service to major German cities is offered by **Deutsche Touring Büro Hannover,** at the Hauptbahnhof (☎ **0511/32-94-19**).

By Car   Access is via the A1 Autobahn north or south and from the A2 east and west.

VISITOR INFORMATION   Contact **Hannover Tourist Information,** located at Ernst-August-Platz 2 (☎ **0511/3-01-40**). Here you can reserve hotel rooms (ask about special weekend packages), book sightseeing tours, obtain general information about the city, and purchase tickets for local events as well as for trains, trams, and buses. The office is open Monday to Friday 9am to 7pm and Saturday 9:30am to 3pm. The organizers of Expo 2000 (see box below) will also be able to supply information and make accommodations reservations.

GETTING AROUND   The local public-transport system includes commuter trains, an extensive underground network, city trams, and bus routes operated by several companies. Service is frequent and extensive. For information and schedules, contact **Regionalverkehr Hannover GmbH** in Hannover (☎ **0511/9-90-01-30**).

EXPLORING THE CITY
Market Church (Marktkirche), the Gothic brick basilica on Marktplatz, is one of Hannover's oldest structures, built in the mid-14th century. **Altes Rathaus,** facing the square, dates from 1425. It was badly damaged in the war, but has been restored and now houses the civic archives.

Millions to Visit Hannover for Expo 2000

The eagerly awaited Expo 2000 will take place in Hannover from June 1, 2000 to October 31, 2000. More than 100 nations and international organizations will take part in this first great gathering of nations in the new millennium. The theme of the Expo is "Mankind-Nature-Technology." More than 15,000 events are planned. Visitors will find most of the fascinating activities taking place at a 400-acre theme park south of town. Organizers expect up to 20 million visitors—perhaps as many as 40 million—boosting tourism (and bringing crowds) not only in Hannover itself but also in the many nearby historic towns and cultural sites.

Expo 2000 will explore ways in which humankind can achieve a new balance with nature through the application of technology. Its aim is to encourage hope and confidence in the future by showing that solutions are being developed for urgent global problems. Themes of the exhibits will include health and nutrition, living and working, environment and development, communications and information, leisure and mobility, and education and culture.

Art, culture, entertainment, and sport are also on the agenda, day and night. Leading international artists, musicians, performers, and athletes will participate, along with spectators, who will be encouraged to join in many events. The world's top tennis players will compete in Hannover, and the Expo Entertainment Park will offer facilities for streetball, go-cart racing, beach volleyball, hockey, and much more. Other events will include "Music and Theatre" performances, including Handel's "Water Music" and "Firework Music," along with the "Festival of Light," a moonlight and fireworks display with the gardens as the backdrop.

Hannover has been busy preparing for the event. The Expo site is being developed on the city's already-existing fairgrounds (Messegalände), about 4½ miles south of the city center. Access is fast and easy by car (follow the signs plastered everywhere), S-Bahn (take the S-Bahn from the town or Hannover airport to the newly built station of Messegalände Brüsseler Strasse), or conventional train.

In addition, SAS Radisson is building a new mega-hotel near the Expo site, to be completed in early 2000. For reservations, call ☎ **800/333-3333** in the U.S. and Canada. All the other hotels in town are also preparing for the deluge. Expo 2000's planners (see below for contact information) will act as reservations agents for accommodations. Starting at around December of 1999, they will be able to direct visitors to available space in hotels, guest houses, private homes, and campsites in and around Hannover. Deutsches Bahn, the German national railway system, is planning to improve the railway lines that run from Hannover to Berlin, Hamburg, Frankfurt, Kassel, and Düsseldorf. Many visitors may prefer to stay overnight outside of Hannover itself.

A day ticket to the Expo will cost 69DM ($39.35), lowered to 24DM ($13.70) for an evening ticket (after 7pm). Children and students will pay 49DM ($27.95) for a day ticket or 15DM ($8.55) for an evening ticket.

For more information, contact Expo 2000 Hannover GmbH, Deutsche Messe A. G., Messegalände, 30510 Hannover (☎ **0511/8404-118;** fax 0511/8404-100), or check out the excellent multilingual Web site at **www.expo. hannover.de**. For information on special packages to Expo 2000, contact **General Tours** in Keene, New Hampshire (☎ **603/357-5033;** fax 603/357-4548), and **DER Travel Services** in Rosemont, Illinois (☎ **847/430-0000**).

⊙ **Herrenhäuser Garten (Royal Gardens of Herrenhäusen).** Herrenhäuser Strasse 4. ☎ **0511/30-14-22.** Admission 3DM ($1.70) adults, free for children. Apr–Sept daily 8am–7pm; Oct–Mar daily 8am–4:30pm. Waterworks display May–Sept Mon–Fri 11am–noon and 3–5pm, Sat–Sun and holidays 11am–noon and 2–5pm. U-Bahn: 4 or 5 to Herrenhäuser Gärten.

No matter where you go in Hannover, you won't be far from a park or garden. But make sure you don't miss this one, the only surviving example of Dutch/Low German early baroque-style gardening. Designers from France, the Netherlands, England, and Italy, as well as Germany, worked together to create this masterpiece of living art. **Grosse Garten,** from 1666, is the largest garden here, consisting of a rectangle surrounded by a moat. Within the maze of walks and trees are examples of French baroque, rococo, and Low German rose and flower gardens. The Grosse Garten also contains one of the highest fountains in Europe, shooting jets of water 236 feet into the air, and the world's only existing baroque hedge-theater (1692), where plays by Shakespeare, Molière, and Brecht are still performed today, along with ballets and jazz concerts. The smaller 17th-century **Berggarten,** across Herrenhäuser Strasse from the Grosse Garten, is a botanical garden with houses containing rare orchids and other tropical flowers.

Niedersächsisches Landesmuseum Hannover (Lower Saxony State Museum). Willy-Brandt-Allee (near the Maschpark). ☎ **0511/9-80-75.** Admission 10DM ($5.70). Tues–Wed and Fri–Sun 10am–5pm, Thurs 10am–7pm. Tram: 1, 2, 4, 5, 6, 7, 8, or 11. Bus: 132, 250, or 267.

The Landesmuseum is one of the most important regional museums in Germany. Its Natural History Department has exhibits on the biology and geology of northern Europe, with special reference to Lower Saxony. The aquarium shows a world of exotic fish, amphibians, and reptiles. In the Department of Archeology, objects from Lower Saxony illustrate the history of this county from the Paleolithic Age up to the Middle Ages. In the newly created Kindermuseum, children can learn about prehistoric times with activities like grinding corn or working stone tools. The Department of Ethnology has a special emphasis on Ethnomedicine and Ethnobotany.

The museum's art gallery contains treasures spanning 7 centuries. A highlight is Meister Bertram von Minden's *Passion Altar* (1390–1400). You'll also see paintings by Rembrandt, Van Dyck, and Rubens (his *Madonna*), as well as the *Four Times of Day* series by Caspar David Friedrich.

Rathaus. Am Maschpark. ☎ **0511/1-68-53-33.** Elevator ride to dome 3DM ($1.70) adults, 2DM ($1.15) students and children. Rathaus Apr–Oct Mon–Fri 9:30am–5:30pm, Sat–Sun 10am–5pm. U-Bahn: Markthalle. Tram: 3, 7, or 9. Bus: 22.

The "new" Rathaus is a large structure, built between 1901 and 1913 on 6,026 beech piles. An inclined elevator—the only one in Europe other than the elevator at the Eiffel Tower—takes visitors up to the 33-foot-high dome. The building is attractive because of its location in the Maschpark, by a small lake. It's just a short distance from the extensive artificial Maschsee, frequented by Hannoverians for its beach, boats, and restaurants.

The House of Hannover

Every student of English history is aware of the role that Hannover played in the history of Great Britain. For more than 100 years, Britain was ruled by monarchs descended from the House of Hannover (or Hanover), who technically also ruled over the German city. The most notorious was George III, the occasionally insane king whose policies provoked the American Revolutionary War.

SHOPPING

Your first destination might be the **Galerie Luise,** a multilevel shopping mall at the corner of Luisenstrasse and Rathenaustrasse, with upscale shops for clothing and home furnishings. Inside the complex is a good place for souvenirs, **Steinhoff** (☎ 0511/32-91-11). **Der Herrenausstatter Hemdenstuhe,** Georgstrasse 42 (☎ 0511/36-38-04), and **Donna-Men,** Krämerstrasse 25 (☎ 0511/32-50-12), are good choices for menswear. Donna-Men has a counterpart for women's clothing known as **Donna,** Lilienplatz (☎ 0511/32-58-75). **Terner,** Luisenstrasse 9 (☎ 0511/36-39-31), and **Joop,** Karmarsch Strasse 18 (☎ 0511/36-78-97-30), have three floors loaded with designer-inspired clothing for men, women, and children. If you want to duplicate the traditional look of rural, agrarian Germany, consider dropping into **trachten Sander,** Seilwinderstrasse 3 (☎ 0511/36-36-55), where dirndls, loden-colored coats, and jaunty-looking hats accessorized with pheasant feathers are all the rage.

Fine needlepoint, including material for curtains or upholstery, is available at **Bertold-Handarbeiten,** Grosse Parkhofstrasse 27 (☎ 0511/3-09-13-00). Souvenirs are sold at **Raachermantel,** Luisenstrasse 1 (☎ 0511/3-63-14-24), which specializes in hand-carved figures, some inspired by German folklore and fairy tales. Also, one of the largest **flea markets** in all of Germany takes place every Saturday from 7am to 4pm along Am Hohen Ufer.

WHERE TO STAY

To escape the clutches of the city's pricey (and rather sterile) hotels, you might stay at a restaurant-hotel—either the Landhaus Ammann or the Georgenhof-Stern (see "Where to Dine," below). During Expo 2000, hotel rooms will be difficult to come by.

EXPENSIVE

✪ **Forum Hotel Schweizerhof.** Hinuberstrasse 6, 30175 Hannover. ☎ **0511/3-49-50.** Fax 0511/3-49-51-23. 203 units. MINIBAR TV TEL. 310DM–599DM ($176.70–$341.45) double; from 775DM ($441.75) suite. Rates include buffet breakfast. AE, DC, MC, V. Parking 19.50DM ($11.10). Tram: 16.

This is one of the most imaginatively designed hotels in Hannover, with a lot more charm and atmosphere than other leading contenders. It sits on a quiet street in the central business district, behind a redbrick facade whose angular lines were inspired by medieval Hanseatic models. Inside you'll find illuminated Plexiglas columns, sweeping expanses of russet-colored marble, and color-coordinated accents of gleaming brass and light-grained wood. The place serves an affluent clientele, often including visiting celebrities. Rooms are spacious and elegantly furnished; 85 are air-conditioned.

Dining: Schu's Restaurant is one of the most stylish in the city. Reservations are important. The hotel also offers the Gourmet's Buffet and the Zirbelstube, serving a regional cuisine.

Amenities: Room service, laundry, dry cleaning, airport pickup if arranged in advance, a terrace garden in summer.

✪ **Kastens Hotel Luisenhof.** Luisenstrasse 1–3 (near the Hauptbahnhof), 30159 Hannover. ☎ **0511/3-04-40.** Fax 0511/3-04-48-07. 165 units. MINIBAR TV TEL. 298DM–598DM ($169.85–$340.85) double; 550DM–950DM ($313.50–$541.50) suite. Rates include buffet breakfast. AE, DC, MC, V. Parking 15DM ($8.55). Tram: 16 to Stadthalle.

This is the leading hotel in town. Its stately glass-and-stone facade is just minutes from the Hauptbahnhof in the city center. A series of modernizations have enhanced comfort while maintaining conservative good taste in its traditional interior. The carefully renovated rooms are spacious, stylishly furnished, and impeccably kept. The English-speaking staff welcomes overseas visitors.

Dining/Diversions: The lobby-level grill room serves superlative food; a few steps away, a cozy modern pub offers drinks and salads.

Amenities: Room service, hair dryers, laundry, dry cleaning.

MODERATE

Hotel Königshof. Königstrasse 12, 30175 Hannover. ☎ **0511/31-20-71.** Fax 0511/31-20-79. 82 units. TV TEL. 178DM–398DM ($101.45–$226.85) double; 540DM ($307.80) suite. Discounts for children under 16 in parents' room. Rates include buffet breakfast. AE, DC, MC, V. Parking 10DM ($5.70). Bus: 20 or 39.

Both the skylights and the modernized crenellations on this hotel's mansard roof make it look like an updated feudal fortress. The hotel was built in 1984 above a glass-and-steel shopping arcade in the town center. Each plushly carpeted room has a couch that converts to a bed. Furnishings are designed more for functional comfort than style. Only breakfast is served at the hotel, but there's an Italian restaurant across the street.

Loccumer Hof. Kurt-Schumacher-Strasse 16 (near the Hauptbahnhof), 30159 Hannover. ☎ **0511/1-26-40.** Fax 0511/13-11-92. 87 units. MINIBAR TV TEL. 180DM–430DM ($102.60–$245.10) double. Higher rates during fairs. Rates include buffet breakfast. AE, DC, MC, V. Parking 10DM–13DM ($5.70–$7.40). Tram: 16.

This is one of the best economy finds in the city. The utilitarian rooms and bathrooms are small. Service and frills are minimal. The standard fare in the hotel's dining room, however, is quite good.

WHERE TO DINE
VERY EXPENSIVE

✪ **Georgenhof-Stern Restaurant.** Herrenha user Kirchweg 20, 30167 Hannover. ☎ **0511/70-22-44.** Fax 0511/70-85-59. Reservations required. Main courses 50DM–70DM ($28.50–$39.90); fixed-price meals 40DM–59.50DM ($22.80–$33.90) at lunch, 89DM–169DM ($50.75–$96.35) at dinner. AE, DC, MC, V. Daily noon–2pm and 6–10pm. Tram: 4, 5, or 6. INTERNATIONAL.

This is Hannover's most famous restaurant, and it's well worth the price. It's in a country inn in a private park near the Herrenhäuser Gardens. International dishes of fresh seafood and game are featured. In summer, tables are set on the terrace, overlooking a garden and pond. The place also rents 14 clean and pleasant rooms, with traditional, handcrafted furniture. Doubles run 255DM to 525DM ($145.35 to $299.25); buffet breakfast is included.

✪ **Landhaus Ammann.** Hildesheimer Strasse 185. ☎ **0511/83-08-18.** Fax 0511/8-43-77-49. Reservations required. Main courses 45DM–65DM ($25.65–$37.05); fixed-price dinners 90DM–193DM ($51.30–$110); fixed-price lunch 63DM–82DM ($35.90–$46.75). Daily noon–2pm and 7–10pm. AE, DC, MC, V. INTERNATIONAL.

This is the only restaurant in Hannover that serves better food and has a more luxurious atmosphere than the Georgenhof-Stern. Service is discreet and efficient, but never stuffy. The chefs turn out a distinguished cuisine, backed up by the city's finest wine cellar. The menu is adjusted seasonally to take advantage of fresh produce. Typical dishes include sea bass with caviar sauce.

The place also rents 15 beautifully furnished bedrooms; a double costs 275DM to 450DM ($156.75 to $256.50), including a buffet breakfast. The setting, near a park, is tranquil, and each accommodation is individually decorated in a traditional motif, with thoughtful extras such as minibars, trouser presses, and hair dryers.

EXPENSIVE

Wichmann. Hildesheimer Strasse 230, at Hannover-Döhren. ☎ **0511/83-16-71.** Reservations required. Main courses 35DM–54DM ($19.95–$30.80); 3-course fixed-price lunch

50DM ($28.50); fixed-price dinner 120DM ($68.40) for 4 courses, 170DM ($96.90) for 7 courses. AE, MC, V. Mon–Sat noon–3pm and 6–11pm. Tram: 1 or 8. GERMAN.

This family-owned, white-walled, shuttered inn, with its slate walks and carefully tended flower beds, is on the eastern edge of Hannover. The garden serves as a pleasant setting for dining in the summer months. The place is an oasis of comfort. Cooking is German *gutbürgerlich*—wholesome and hearty. Try specialties such as fish terrine, rack of lamb, homemade noodles, and wine and cheese from all over Germany.

MODERATE

Altdeutsche Bierstube. Lärchenstrasse 4. ☎ **0511/34-49-21.** Reservations required. Main courses 17DM–35DM ($9.70–$19.95); 3-course fixed-price menu 48DM ($27.35). AE, DC, MC, V. Mon–Fri noon–2pm; Mon–Sat 6–10pm. Closed holidays. U-Bahn: Lister Platz. GERMAN.

With a decor that has changed very little since its original construction around 1860, this old-fashioned Bierstube has remained stable and solid, despite the monumental changes that have transformed the society around it. The unpretentious food is hearty, wholesome, and filling, with the regular fare augmented by seasonal specialties. Three favorites include pork knuckles with sauerkraut, fillet of beef, and mixed grills.

Mövenpick Quartet. Georgstrasse 35. ☎ **0511/32-43-43.** Reservations recommended for the four restaurants, not for the cafe. Main courses 20DM–35DM ($11.40–$19.95). Main courses in the vegetarian restaurant 14DM–35DM ($8–$19.95). AE, DC, MC, V. Restaurants daily 11:30am–midnight. Cafe daily 8am–midnight. Tram: 1, 2, 3, 4, or 5. INTERNATIONAL.

This is a well-managed, bustling restaurant complex whose four separate eating areas are managed by the Swiss-based chain, Mövenpick. The food is a smörgåsbord of international cuisines, including French (in **La Brasserie**); California (salads, seafood soups, and very fresh produce in **Opus 1**); Italian (in the self-service cafeteria, **Pick's**); and vegetarian (in **Grüneschnabel**). All sections, particularly the old-fashioned **Café Kröpcke,** have an elaborate array of high-calorie Central European pastries and desserts.

Steuerndieb. Steuerndieb 1, Hannover-Bothfeld, 30655 Hannover. ☎ **0511/90-99-60.** Reservations not required. Main courses 25DM–40DM ($14.25–$22.80); fixed-price menu 35DM–40DM ($19.95–$22.80) for 3 courses, 105DM ($59.85) for 7 courses. AE, DC, MC, V. Mon–Sat 11am–10pm, Sun 11am–6pm. Tram: 3 or 7. GERMAN.

In 1329, a stone-sided tower was erected about a mile east of central Hannover to guard the lumber produced in Eilenreide Forest. The tower's name, Steuerndieb, translates from the archaic German as "Stop, thieves!" Around 1850 a rustic restaurant was built on the site of that tower, and it has been known ever since for hearty and flavorful food. Many of the specialties are cooked over an open fire, and the restaurant offers a locally inspired menu that, unlike those of many other restaurants, features game year-round. Two popular dishes are venison with red cabbage, dumplings, and black-cherry sauce; and rabbit with black-pepper sauce and red cabbage.

The establishment also has a modern wing containing seven simple, white-walled guest rooms, each with a private bathroom, TV, telephone, and view overlooking the forest. Doubles cost 250DM ($142.50), including a buffet breakfast.

HANNOVER AFTER DARK

Hannover Vorschau, a monthly newspaper devoted exclusively to the city's nightlife and cultural venues, is available for 3.50DM ($2) at news kiosks, but is usually given out free in most of the city's hotels.

THE PERFORMING ARTS The **Nieder Sächsische Stadtstheater Hannover GmbH,** Opernplatz 1 (☎ **0511/32-11-33,** or 0511/3-68-17-11 for tickets and information), was built between 1845 and 1852, and is the region's leading venue for ballet, concerts, and opera. Depending on the performance, tickets cost from 30DM to 95DM ($17.10 to $54.15) each. Less formal, with popular as well as classical offerings, is the **N. D. R. Symphoniker,** Rudolf Benigsen Ufer 22 (☎ **0511/9-88-29-90**), an ugly postwar building whose charm derives from what goes on inside. You can hear poetry readings, jazz and rock 'n' roll concerts, and chamber orchestras. Contact the theaters or the tourist office for schedules. During Expo 2000, there will be numerous additional cultural offerings, including concerts, drama, and even athletic events.

BARS   Oddly, many of Hannover's most appealing bars are Irish pubs. They include **The Irish Pub,** Brüderstrasse 4 (☎ **0511/1-45-89**), which won a 1998 award as the best Irish Pub in Germany, and its most visible competitor, **The Irish Harp,** Schwarzer Bär (☎ **0511/44-70-70**), which has a beer garden in good weather. Both establishments are open daily from 5pm to 2am; serve both Guinness and Murphy's on tap, along with sandwiches, pies, fish-and-chips, and Irish stew; and occasionally book Irish music bands, for which they charge a cover of 10DM to 12DM ($5.70 to $6.85).

Look for the tail of an airplane sticking out over the street to find the entrance to **Boomerang,** Engelbosteler Damm 45. When you step inside, you'll find that the rest of the plane is still attached, suspended above the bar and dining area. Students and locals come here all day, and on Saturday there are restaurant parties and food sales to benefit local causes, from AIDS awareness to city-run children's gardens. Open Monday to Saturday, 10am to 1am; Sunday 10am to 2pm.

DANCE CLUBS   The best place for mainstream dance is **Osho Disco,** Rauschplatz 7L (☎ **0511/34-22-17**), a 14-year survivor of the club scene. It plays funk, house, and other dance music. It's open from 10pm until "whenever," Wednesday to Sunday. The cover charge ranges from 5DM to 8DM ($2.85 to $4.55). One of its leading competitors is **Palo Palo,** Rauschplatz 8A (☎ **051/33-10-73**), where house, funk, blues, reggae, and old-fashioned Motown soul play every night from 9:30pm till dawn, for a cover charge of around 8DM ($4.55) per person.

LIVE MUSIC   An alternative venue, **Café Glocksee,** Glockseestrasse 35 (☎ **0511/1-61-47-12**), stages hard-core, punk, and techno shows Friday and Saturday night starting at 10pm. The cover charge is 6DM ($3.40). It's open daily from 5pm until sometime between 6 and 10am. **Musik Theater Bad,** Am Grossen Garten 60 (☎ **0511/70-34-04** or 0511/70-34-83), is a former swimming pool turned stage. In it, every type of pop music imaginable is explored, glorified, transformed, or mutated. Dancing is held in another part of the complex. Call to see what's scheduled. Hours on concert nights depend on the band; for dancing, the hours are 10pm to 5am. The cover charge ranges from 6DM to 30DM ($3.40 to $17.10).

GAY CLUBS   **Schwul Sau,** Schaufeldstrasse 38 (☎ **0511/7-00-05-25**), hosts discos, theater performances, and private parties, attended by a crowd of gay and straight arts-conscious patrons. It's open Tuesday, Wednesday, and Friday from 8pm to 3am, Saturday from 9pm until at least 7am, and Sunday from 3pm to 2am. The cover charge is 15DM ($8.55) for parties or theater events, and 8DM ($4.55) for dancing. There's no cover Tuesday, Wednesday, or Sunday. A hip and happening dance spot, **Men's Factory,** Engelbosteler Damm 7 (☎ **0511/70-24-87**), is open only on Friday, for a mixed dance night, and Saturday, for gay dance night. The Friday cover is 15DM ($8.55); on Saturday, it's 10DM ($5.70).

A CASINO   The **Spielbank,** Arthur-Menge-Ufer 3 (☎ **0511/98-06-60**), has an impressive roster of blackjack, roulette, and baccarat. It's set within a modern building, with none of the belle epoque trappings or decorations you might have hoped for, and contains both a bar and a restaurant. Men are required to wear jackets and ties, and women are requested to dress appropriately. Open daily from 3pm to 3am. Admission costs 5DM ($2.85), and you must show your passport to enter.

5 Hameln

28 miles SW of Hannover, 30 miles W of Hildesheim

Hameln (Hamelin in English) has many many interesting buildings and a history dating from the 11th century, but its main claim to fame is the folktale about the Pied Piper, which has been immortalized by the Brothers Grimm, Goethe, and Robert Browning, among others. According to legend, in 1284 the town was infested by rats. Soon after, there appeared a piper who offered, for a fee, to lure the vermin into the Weser River. The rat-catcher successfully performed the service, but the stingy denizens of Hameln refused to pay his fee, claiming that he was a sorcerer. So the piper reappeared the next Sunday and played a tune that lured all the town's children, except one lame boy, into a mysterious door in a hill. The children and the Pied Piper were never heard from again.

There is some historical basis for the story. It appears that, several centuries ago, for some unknown reason, the children of Hameln did indeed leave the town. The story of the Pied Piper is retold every summer Sunday at noon in a special performance at the **Hochzeitshaus (Wedding House)** on Osterstrasse. In the town shops, you can buy rat figures made of every conceivable material, even candy.

ESSENTIALS

GETTING THERE By Plane   The nearest major airport is Hannover-Langenhagen, 34 miles away.

By Train   The Hameln Bahnhof lies on the Hannover-Hameln-Altenbeken rail line, with frequent connections. Depending on the train, trip time from Hannover ranges from 45 to 55 minutes. For rail information and schedules, call ☎ **01805/996633.**

By Bus   Local and regional bus service to nearby towns and Hannover is available from **RVH Regional Verkehr** (☎ **05151/811414**). Buses stop in front of the Hauptbahnhof.

By Car   It takes 3 hours to reach Hameln from Frankfurt and some 6 to 7 hours to reach Hameln from Munich. From Frankfurt, head northeast along the A5 Autobahn, then north on the A7, and finally west on A27. From Munich, take the A9 Autobahn north to Nürnberg, the A3 west to Würzburg, then the A7 north toward Hannover, and finally A27 west to Hameln.

VISITOR INFORMATION   Contact the **Verkehrsverein,** Deisterallee (☎ **05151/ 20-26-17**), open May through September, Monday to Friday 9am to 6pm, Saturday 9:30am to 12:30pm and 2 to 4pm, and Sunday 9:30am to 12:30pm; October through April, Monday to Friday 9am to 1pm and 2 to 5pm.

WHAT TO SEE & DO

Hameln's most interesting building is the Gothic **Münster,** at the end of Bäckerstrasse, overlooking the Weser River. Other attractions include the **Rattenfängerhaus** (Rat-Catcher's House; see "Where to Dine," below), on Osterstrasse, with frescoes illustrating the Pied Piper legend, and the **Hochzeitshaus (Wedding House)** on Osterstrasse, with its three attractive gables. The finest houses in the town are built in what is known as the Weser Renaissance style, from the late-16th century. You can admire these nicely sculpted houses as you stroll along the pedestrians-only streets.

SHOPPING   There are lots of opportunities to buy folkloric art objects here. One of the best bets for souvenir and gift hunting, **Renner,** Am Markt 6 (☎ **05151/9-44-20**), has some genuinely charming objects. Antiques that might become part of your family heirlooms are at **Antikitäten Bayer,** Bäckerstrasse 49 (☎ **05151/32-97**), **Antiqutiäten Franke,** Wendenstrasse 4 (☎ **05151/44388**). You also might simply want to window-shop along the town's best shopping streets, the **Osterstrasse** and the **Bäckerstrasse.**

NIGHTLIFE   The town's Weserbergland Festhalle, **Rathausplatz** (☎ **05151/91-62-20**), hosts an array of concerts, opera and ballet performances, and theatrical productions. Call the theater or the visitor information center (see above) for upcoming events and ticket information.

WHERE TO STAY

Dorint Hotel Hameln. 164er Ring 3, 31785 Hameln. ☎ **05151/79-20.** Fax 05151/79-21-91. 105 units. MINIBAR TV TEL. 245DM–424DM ($139.65–$241.70) double. Rates include buffet breakfast. AE, DC, MC, V. Parking 9DM ($5.15). Bus: 1 or 2.

This hotel stands in a park with lots of trees, but is within walking distance of the heart of the Altstadt, at the northern edge of the Burgergarten. It rises like a modern collection of building blocks, with oversize glass walls. Rooms are standard and functional. Guests have access to a pool, sauna, solarium, and massage facilities. There's also an international restaurant, Brochette, plus a beer pub called Alt Hamelin.

Hotel Zur Börse. Osterstrasse 41A, 31785 Hameln. ☎ **05151/70-80.** Fax 05151/2-54-85. 34 units. TV TEL. 145DM–160DM ($82.65–$91.20) double. Rates include buffet breakfast. AE, DC, MC, V. Parking 5DM–7DM ($2.85–$4). Bus: 1 or 2.

This balconied hotel within the walls of the Altstadt can be identified by the four peaks of its modern roofline. The interior is refreshingly uncluttered. The rooms are spacious and well maintained. A restaurant on the premises serves German cuisine.

Komfort-Hotel Garni Christinenhof. Alte Markstrasse 18, 31785 Hameln. ☎ **05151/9-50-80.** Fax 05151/4-36-11. 30 units. MINIBAR TV TEL. 185DM–220DM ($105.45–$125.40) double. Rates include buffet breakfast. AE, MC, V. Closed Dec 20–Jan 6. Free parking. Bus: 1 or 2.

The gabled windows of this half-timbered building, which is more than 300 years old, overlook a cobblestoned street in the middle of the Altstadt. Despite the antique facade, much of the hotel's interior is streamlined and modern, with many conveniences. There's a pool beneath the vaulted stone ceiling of the old cellar, plus a sauna, a solarium, and conference rooms. The rooms are well furnished, though small.

WHERE TO DINE

Klütturm. Auf dem Klütberg. ☎ **05151/6-16-44.** Reservations recommended. Main courses 25DM–40DM ($14.25–$22.80). AE, MC, V. Wed–Mon noon–2:30pm and 6–10pm. Closed Jan–Feb 10. GERMAN/FRENCH.

Even the lovely decor here takes second place to the restaurant's panoramic view of the Altstadt. The cooking is traditional, with special care lavished on the dessert wagon, whose confections change every day. In season, the cook will prepare game dishes, and throughout the year you'll find an aromatically seasoned rack of baby lamb with fresh vegetables, a tender entrecôte of beef with escargots, and Barbary duckling with an orange-pepper sauce. Immediately adjacent to the restaurant is a stone-sided tower, with 99 steps, which was built in the 1820s. It can be climbed, without charge, as part of your dining experience. From the top, panoramic views extend out over the surrounding landscapes.

Rattenfängerhaus. Osterstrasse 28. ☎ **05151/38-88.** Reservations recommended. Main courses 18DM–32DM ($10.25–$18.25). AE, DC, MC, V. Daily 11am–3pm and 6–11pm. Bus: 1 or 2. GERMAN.

Rattenfängerhaus (Rat-Catcher's House) dates from 1603. The outside is well preserved; inside are small wood windows, antiques, and pictures. A meal here is practically like eating in a museum. The place is a little too touristy and crowded for some tastes, but it's an enduring favorite nonetheless. You can order traditional German dishes here, including various kinds of schnitzels, roasted goose, or fillets of salmon with hollandaise sauce. Souvenirs of the Pied Piper are offered.

6 Bad Pyrmont

45 miles SW of Hannover, 30 miles SE of Bielefeld

This attractive spa has enjoyed a good reputation for more than 2,000 years. Its springs vary from the brine variety in the fields to the medicinal iron waters on the southern side of the valley of the Weser Hills. In the center of town you can drink a medicinal cocktail from the fountain at the Hyllige Born spring. Another popular pastime is taking mud baths. But Bad Pyrmont is a good place to vacation even if you don't come to take the waters. Horseback riding in the hills, hiking, tennis, and swimming, as well as concerts and shows, make the resort a lively place.

ESSENTIALS
GETTING THERE **By Train** The nearest airport is at Hannover, where there are good rail connections to Bad Pyrmont. There are frequent trains throughout the day on the Hannover-Paderborn main rail line. For rail information, call ☎ **01805/ 996633**.

By Bus Regional buses run between Hameln (see above) and Bad Pyrmont. The service is provided by **RVH Busline Hameln** (☎ 05151/1-20-15).

By Car From Hannover, Route 217 leads southwest to Bad Pyrmont.

VISITOR INFORMATION Go to **Kur- und Verkehrsverein,** Südstrasse 11 A (☎ 05281/94-05-11), open Monday to Friday 9am to 5pm and Saturday 10am to 12:30pm.

SHOPPING There aren't many shops in this quiet town, but **Hildebrandt,** Hauptallee 3 (☎ 05281/60-99-25), has an appealing collection of German handcrafts.

EXPLORING THE TOWN
The **Kurpark (Spa Park)** is among the most beautiful in Germany, with little temples, flowering trees, and even a palm garden, an unusual touch in this temperate climate. The concert house in the Kurpark has shows during the busy summer. At night, the central promenade is glamorously lit, giving the spa a festive air, while guests sit at sidewalk tables drinking beer.

After a stroll through town in the day, you can visit **Festung und Schloss Pyrmont,** Schloss Strasse (☎ 05281/94-92-48), the town castle, built in 1792. It displays antiques and paintings. Open Tuesday to Sunday from 10am to 5pm; admission is 3DM ($1.70).

WHERE TO STAY
Bad Pyrmonter Hof. Brunnenstrasse 32, 31812 Bad Pyrmont. ☎ **05281/94-10.** Fax 05281/94-12-00. 45 units. TV TEL. 140DM–180DM ($79.80–$102.60) double without bathroom; 150DM–200DM ($85.50–$114) double with bathroom. Rates include continental breakfast. AE, MC, V. Parking 6DM ($3.40).

This hotel is a good economical choice. It provides personal atmosphere and good service and has been considerably modernized. The small guest rooms are immaculate, restful, and suitably furnished. The hotel restaurant is only open to guests.

Bergkurpark. Ockelstrasse 11, 31812 Bad Pyrmont. ☎ **05281/40-01.** Fax 05281/40-04. 49 units. MINIBAR TV TEL. 190DM–380DM ($108.30–$216.60) double; 380DM–400DM ($216.60–$228) suite. Rates include continental breakfast. AE, MC, V. Parking 6DM ($3.40). Bus: 3.

Bergkurpark is not the most distinguished hotel at Bad Pyrmont (that honor goes to the Steigenberger—see below), but it is the most glamorous architecturally. Its entryway has a thatched roof covering a hewn stone and stucco facade with half-rounded picture windows—very dramatic. The hotel rents singles, twin-bedded rooms, and a few suites; all are very comfortable. Your room might be in a modern block with private terraces overlooking a park.

The hotel has its own park, a forest, a heated pool, and a terrace with sun parasols overlooking the garden. There are also exercise rooms and a sauna. Its restaurant serves the best food at the spa (see "Where to Dine," below). There's also an elegant cafe, Sans Souci, and the rustic Wilhelm-Busch-Stube, where beer, wine, and good food are served. Another bar is called Separée. Room service, laundry, and dry cleaning are provided.

Park-Hotel Rasmusen. Hauptallee 8, 31812 Bad Pyrmont. ☎ **05281/9-30-64.** Fax 05281/60-68-72. 12 units. TV TEL. 200DM–230DM ($114–$131.10) double. Rates include continental breakfast. AE, MC, V. Free parking in lot; 9DM ($5.15) in garage.

This gracefully renovated villa stands on a traffic-free promenade in the center of Bad Pyrmont. The spacious rooms are well furnished, with comfortable beds; many have balconies overlooking the promenade. The staff is pleasant. The hotel's tranquil dining room offers moderately priced local and international dishes. Trout and Dover sole are especially good choices. Main courses range from 18DM to 35DM ($10.25 to $19.95), a very low price considering the quality of the food. In truffle season, the chef mingles truffles freely with such costly ingredients as caviar.

Steigenberger Bad Pyrmont. Heiligenangerstrasse 2–4 (in the garden adjacent to the spa), 31812 Bad Pyrmont. ☎ **800/223-5652** in the U.S. and Canada, or 05281/15-02. Fax 05281/15-20-20. 154 units. MINIBAR TV TEL. 290DM–345DM ($165.30–$196.65) double; 460DM–785DM ($262.20–$447.45) suite. Rates include breakfast. AE, DC, MC, V. Parking 16DM ($9.10).

This venerable 19th-century monument is the premier hotel in the spa, drawing people from all over the world. It's the only hotel in town with direct (covered) access to the spa. The calm and quiet rooms have a conservative modern gloss. They're the most comfortable in town. This retreat is well suited to repairing the wear and tear of urban life. Nothing even comes near the Steigenberger for service and amenities.

Dining/Diversions: There's an elegantly formal restaurant, the Palmengarten, and two bars.

Amenities: Modern swimming pool (independent from the spa) sauna, whirlpool, room service, laundry, dry cleaning, baby-sitting, concierge, hair dryers.

WHERE TO DINE

Restaurant Bergkurpark. In the Hotel Bergkurpark, Ockelstrasse 11. ☎ **05281/40-01.** Main courses 25DM–60DM ($14.25–$34.20). AE, MC, V. Daily noon–2pm and 6:30–9pm. INTERNATIONAL.

This restaurant is part of one of the town's finest hotels (see above). In summer, diners like to eat on the beautiful terrace. Otherwise, food is served in an elegantly decorated restaurant that has large, comfortable chairs. We were impressed by the size and cleanliness of the kitchen, which turns out a reliable array of international specialties, with an emphasis on fresh produce. Try the medaillons of veal with cream morels, or salmon with a dill and morel sauce.

8 Goslar

56 miles SE of Hannover, 27 miles S of Braunschweig, 37 miles SE of Hildesheim

In spite of Goslar's growth, the old portion of the town looks just as it did hundreds of years ago. This ancient Hanseatic and imperial town at the foot of the Harz Mountains owed its early prosperity to the Harz silver mines, which were worked as early as 968. The 600-year-old streets here are still in use today, as are the carved, half-timbered houses.

For hikers and other outdoor enthusiasts, Goslar is a good starting point for day trips and excursions into the **Harz Mountains,** where some of the area's best skiing resorts and several spas are found. Bus tours into the Harz Mountains can be booked at the tourist office (see below).

The legends and folklore associated with the Harz Mountains are perhaps more intriguing than the mountains themselves. Walpurgis Eve (the famous Witches' Sabbath), is still celebrated in the hills of the Harz region each year on the night of April 30. The mountain on which the witches supposedly danced in olden times was the **Brocken,** whose granite top has been flattened by erosion. The area around the Brocken is now a national park.

ESSENTIALS

GETTING THERE **By Plane** The nearest major airport is in Hannover.

By Train The **Goslar Bahnhof** is on the Hannover-Hildesheim-Goslar-Bad Harzburg rail line, with frequent connections. It takes about 1½ hours to get to Goslar from Hannover. For rail information, call ☎ **01805/996633.**

By Bus Long-distance bus service to Goslar is available through **Reisebüro Bokermann** (☎ 05321/25138). Regional bus service to all parts of the city and nearby towns is offered by **Regionalbus Braunschweig GmbH,** Geschaftstelle, Goslar (☎ 05321/34310).

By Car Access is via the A7 Autobahn north and south; exit at either Seesen or Rüden.

VISITOR INFORMATION Contact the **Kur- und Fremdenverkehrsgesellschaft,** Markt 7 (☎ **05321/7-80-60**), open November through April, Monday to Friday 9am to 5pm and Saturday 9:30am to 2pm; May through October, Monday to Friday 9am to 6pm, Saturday 9:30am to 4pm, and Sunday 9:15am to 2:15pm.

SEEING THE SIGHTS

To best explore this 1,000-year-old town, park your car, put on a pair of comfortable shoes, and set out on foot through the Altstadt, which has more than 1,000 half-timbered buildings from the 15th to the 18th centuries. Don't miss any of the numerous attractions that await you. The impressive **Rathaus** on the Marktplatz (currently being restored; to open sometime in 2000) was built in 1450. The portico, with Gothic cross-vaulting, opening on to the Marktplatz, was used by merchants for centuries. Above this is the citizens' meeting hall and the councilmen's meeting chamber, lavishly decorated in the early 1300s with a cycle of 55 paintings depicting biblical and heathen iconography and believed to incorporate the zinc miners returning home from the Rammelsberg mines.

Marktplatz, in front of the Rathaus, was for a long time the town's hub of activity. In the center of the large square is a 13th-century fountain with two bronze basins and the German imperial eagle at the top. Many visitors view the performance of the town's **Glockenspiel** here as the highlight of their visit. Every day at noon, 3pm, and 6pm (there's a smaller version of the spectacle at 9am), a procession of mechanized miners, representing the silver trade of long ago, traipses out of the innards of the clock tower.

The churches of Goslar provide a look into the architectural history of the area. Many of the oldest churches—five had already been built by 1200—have been expanded and altered from their original Romanesque style to their current Gothic appearance. The Romanesque **Marktkirche,** just behind the Rathaus, still has its 700-year-old stained-glass windows and a 16th-century bronze baptismal font. From Marktplatz, take Rosentorstrasse north to reach the **Jakobikirche,** which dates from the 11th century. It was later transformed into a Gothic masterpiece, complete with baroque altars. The church contains a *Pietà* by Hans Witten (1520). Farther down the street, the **Neuwerkkirche,** which stands in a garden, has retained its purely Romanesque basilica, and its well-preserved sanctuary contains a richly decorated choir and stucco reliefs. It was originally constructed as a Cistercian convent in the late 1100s.

Frankenberg Kirche, on Bergstrasse, is from the 12th century but was completely remodeled in the 1700s. Over the elaborate baroque pulpit and altars hangs the intricately carved Nun's Choir Gallery, bedecked with gilded saints and symbols.

One of the reminders that Goslar was once a free imperial and Hanseatic city is the **Breites Tor (Broad Gate),** a three-towered town gate with walls up to 13 feet thick. From here you can follow the old town fortifications to the **Kaiserpfalz,** Kaiserbleek 6. A Romanesque palace, the Kaiserpfalz was the ruling seat of the emperors in the 11th and 12th centuries. You can view the 1800s murals that cover its walls and visit the Ulrichskapelle, where the heart of Heinrich III was placed inside a large sarcophagus. The site is open April through October, daily from 10am to 5pm; off-season, daily from 10am to 4pm. Admission is 3.50DM ($2) for adults and 2DM ($1.15) for children.

For a quick and less exhausting look at the history of Goslar, visit the **Goslarer Museum,** at the corner of Abzuchstrasse and Königstrasse (☎ **05321/433-94**), which has displays of the architecture of the early town and several relics of the past. The museum also contains a large geological collection from the Harz Mountains. It's open April through October, Tuesday to Sunday 10am to 5pm; November through March, Tuesday to Sunday 10am to 4pm. Admission is 3DM ($1.70) for adults and 2DM ($1.15) for children.

Just outside Goslar, about a mile south of the town center (follow the signs), you can explore an ancient mine. As early as the 3rd century A.D., lead, zinc, copper, silver, tin, and a little gold were being mined here. The **Rammelsberger Bergbaumuseum,** Bergtal 19, 38640 Goslar (☎ **05321/3-43-60**), conducts guided tours at hourly intervals, on foot or on a small underground train. The museum is open daily from 9am to 6pm. Walking tours cost 8DM ($4.55) for adults and 5DM ($2.85) for children. A train ride is 13.50DM ($7.70) for adults and 11.50DM ($6.55) for children. For more information, call either the museum (see above) or the tourist office in Goslar (☎ **05321/7-80-60**).

WHERE TO STAY

Dorint-Harzhotel Kreuzeck. Am Kreuzeck 1–4, 38644 Goslar-Hahnenklee. ☎ **05325/ 7-40.** Fax 05325/7-48-39. 112 units. MINIBAR TV TEL. 250DM–325DM ($142.50–$185.25) double; 325DM–365DM ($185.25–$208.05) suite. Rates include buffet breakfast. AE, DC, MC, V. Free outdoor parking; 8DM ($4.55) in garage. Bus: 2434 from Goslar. Take the A7 Autobahn and exit at Seesen.

About 9 miles from Goslar is a well-rated, comfortable hotel set directly on a small lake with beautiful mountain scenery. The hotel offers country hospitality and exceptional food, and you may want to drive here for a meal even if you can't stay. The bedrooms, which range from medium to spacious, are comfortable and tranquil, the best in the area. Numerous ski lifts are in the vicinity, as well as an 18½-mile cross-country ski course. Ice-skating rinks are also nearby, and guests can enjoy an old-fashioned ride in a horse-drawn sleigh. In summer, available activities include sailing, windsurfing, hiking, tennis, and cycling.

Goldene Krone. Breitestrasse 46 (near the Breites Tor), 38640 Goslar. ☎ **05321/3-44-90.** Fax 05321/34-49-50. www.touronline.de/harz/hotel/goldkrone. E-mail: Goldene-Kronegoslar@t-online.de. 26 units. TV TEL. 155DM–195DM ($88.35–$111.15) double. Rates include buffet breakfast. AE, DC, MC, V. Free parking. Bus: A or B.

This 300-year-old, recently renovated village inn comes complete with a friendly innkeeper, Herr Dietmar Pflug, who attends to the rooms and the meals. If you enjoy local color, this is a real find. The rooms are small and simple but homelike and clean; they're a great value for the price. The food and drink are good and inexpensive.

Hotel Der Achtermann. Rosentorstrasse 20, 38640 Goslar. ☎ **05321/2-10-01.** Fax 05321/4-27-48. 152 units. TV TEL. 259DM–299DM ($147.65–$170.45) double. Rates include breakfast. AE, DC, MC, V.

This hotel is a bustling but somewhat dowdy three-star hotel whose amenities rival those of four-star hotels nearby. Just after World War II, one of the round-sided 500-year-old watchtowers in the city's wraparound fortifications was enlarged with a white-sided extension, thereby creating an intriguing but rather cumbersome-looking amalgam of old and new architecture. If you're looking for a place to stay within the city itself, this is your best bet. Rooms are well furnished and comfortable, except for a handful that are a bit too small (most, however, are spacious). On the premises are several restaurants and cafes, many of which are especially popular at lunchtime with local workers.

Kaiserworth. Markt 3, 38640 Goslar. ☎ **05321/2-11-11.** Fax 05321/2-11-14. 50 units. TV TEL. 199DM–249DM ($113.45–$141.95) double. Rates include buffet breakfast. AE, DC, MC, V. Parking 7DM ($4). Bus: A or B.

The Kaiserworth is a big, old-fashioned hotel, right in the heart of town. The building dates from 1494 and is a sightseeing attraction in itself. The exterior is Gothic, with an arched arcade across the front, topped by a turreted oriel window facing Marktplatz. The large rooms are designed for comfort; the corner rooms are big enough to be suites. Rooms 102, 106, 110, 202, and 206 offer the best views of the nearby Glockenspiel performance outside. The hotel has a sedate wood-paneled breakfast room and a vaulted dining room, Die Worth. Step through a 1,000-year-old cistern and you'll be in the cellar restaurant, the Dukatenkeller, with stone pillars and ecclesiastical chairs.

WHERE TO DINE

Die Worth. In the Kaiserworth, Markt 3. ☎ **05321/2-11-11.** Main courses 18DM–38DM ($10.25–$21.65); fixed-price lunch 28DM ($15.95). AE, DC, MC, V. Daily noon–2:30pm and 6–11pm. Bus: A or B. NORTH GERMAN.

This is the most rustic and also the most attractive dining room in Goslar. The restaurant is in a Gothic stone crypt with vaulted ceiling and arches, stained-glass windows, wrought-iron lanterns, and trestle tables. The food is good and the portions are hearty, although all the recipes are very familiar. In season, roast game is featured with wild mushrooms, mashed apples, and berries. Rump steak is always an excellent choice, as is the more unusual *Harzer blaubeer schmandschnitzel*, a local recipe that combines pork schnitzel with blueberry-flavored cream sauce.

Goldene Krone. Breitestrasse 46 (on the eastern edge of Goslar), 38640 Goslar. ☎ **05321/ 3-44-90.** Fax 05321/34-49-50. Reservations recommended. Main courses 22DM–32DM ($12.55–$18.25); fixed-price meals 25DM–35DM ($14.25–$19.95) at lunch, 40DM ($22.80) at dinner. AE, MC, V. Daily 11:30am–2pm and 6–9pm. Bus: A or B. INTERNATIONAL/NORTH GERMAN.

It seems like everyone in town knows about this historic Weinstube. The decor is rustic and cozy, and you'll feel at home with the polite service. In addition to the standard north German dishes, occasional international dishes appear on the changing seasonal menu.

The Goldene Krone also has 19 rooms for rent, all of them with showers, TVs, and phones. Doubles are 155DM to 195DM ($88.35 to $111.15).

9 Göttingen

82 miles S of Hannover, 29 miles NE of Kassel, 68 miles SW of Braunschweig

Göttingen was pronounced "famed for its sausages and university" by Heinrich Heine. The university in this Gothic town is one of the oldest and most respected in Germany. It was established in 1737 by George II, king of England and elector of Hannover. In time, Göttingen became the most popular university town in Europe. The university suffered relatively little damage during World War II.

Medieval romanticism and lively student life make Göttingen worth a day's visit. By making a slight detour, you can explore the university town before dipping into the fairy-tale country of the upper Weser Valley. Göttingen is halfway between Bonn and Berlin.

ESSENTIALS

GETTING THERE   By Train   Göttingen has frequent daily rail connections from Munich (trip time: 6 hr.), from Frankfurt (2½ hr.), and from Hannover (1 hr.). It lies on the major Kassel-Bebra-Göttingen-Hannover rail line, with frequent connections in all directions. For rail information and schedules, call ☎ **01805/99633.**

By Bus   Long-distance bus connection, from such cities as Hannover, is provided by **Winkermann GmbH** (☎ **05143/98820**) and **Lempke & Koschick GmbH** (☎ **05143/46980**). Buses arrive in front of the main railway station. Regional bus service to other parts of Lower Saxony is offered by **Regionalbus Braunschweig** (☎ **0551/ 5-06-84-22**).

By Car   Access is via the A7 Autobahn, which runs north to Hannover and Hamburg.

VISITOR INFORMATION   Contact **Tourist-Information,** Altes Rathaus, Markt 9 (☎ **0551/5-60-00**), open November through March, Monday to Friday 9:30am to 6pm and Saturday 10am to 1pm; April through October, Monday to Friday 9:30am to 6pm and Saturday and Sunday 10am to 4pm.

SEEING THE SIGHTS

In the center of Göttingen, you can wander down narrow streets, looking at wide-eaved, half-timbered houses. Many of the facades are carved and painted, and some bear marble plaques noting the famous people who lived inside, such as the more than 40 Nobel Prize winners who temporarily made their home here.

Altes Rathaus was originally built for trade purposes around 1270, but it wasn't completed until 1443. Its highlights are the open arcade, the Gothic heating system, and the Great Hall, in which the people of Göttingen once received princes and dignitaries, held courts of law, and gave feasts. **Marktplatz,** in front of the Town Hall, is the most interesting section of Göttingen. Here, since 1910, stands the "most-kissed girl in the world," the smiling statue of the Ganseliesel on the market fountain. By tradition, every student who attains a degree must plant a kiss on the lips of the little goose-girl. Take bus no. 4, 8, 10, 11, or 14.

Stadtisches Museum, Ritterplan 7–8 (☎ 0551/4-00-28-45), chronicles the history and culture of southern Lower Saxony. The most interesting exhibits are in the Göttingen history wing on the second floor. Surprisingly, the museum takes an uncompromising look at the town's Nazi past—most German towns tend to conceal it. Everything is here, from Hitlerjugend memorabilia to pages ripped from the local Nazi-run newspaper. The museum is open Tuesday to Friday from 10am to 5pm and Saturday and Sunday from 10am to 1pm. Admission is 3DM ($1.70) for adults and 1DM (55¢) for children. Take bus no. 3, 8, or 9.

SHOPPING The commercial heart of town is **Wenderstrasse** and **Grönestrasse,** both of which feature pedestrian malls during most of the shopping day. Here, you'll find an appealing roster of cafes and delicatessens selling sausages and cakes, as well as purveyors of the German-style good life. If you want souvenirs, the local tourist office (see above) sells T-shirts, cigarette lighters, beer mugs, and posters. Antiques are found at **Bohm,** Barfusserstrasse 12 (☎ 0551/5-78-86). Junkier, dustier, less pretentious, and a lot less expensive is **Brocante,** Kurzestrasse 16 (no phone), where the accumulated treasures and debris of estate sales are displayed in an appealingly disorganized jumble. Both of the town's art galleries include worthy statements by local and international painters and sculptors. They are on exhibit at **Galerie Apex,** Burgstrasse 46 (☎ 0551/4-68-86).

WHERE TO STAY

Central Hotel. Judenstrasse 12 (near the university), 37073 Göttingen. ☎ **0551/5-71-57.** Fax 0551/5-71-05. 38 units, 11 with bathroom. TEL. 130DM ($74.10) double without bathroom; 150DM–180DM ($85.50–$102.60) double with bathroom; 250DM ($142.50) suite. Rates include buffet breakfast. AE, DC, MC, V. Parking 7DM ($4). Bus: 4, 8, 10, 11, or 14.

Although this quiet hotel on a pedestrian walkway is centrally located, as its name indicates, its best feature is the imaginative care the designers have used to decorate the bedrooms. For example, one room is flamboyantly wallpapered and curtained in vivid yellow and white tones, and another seems to be covered in pink silk. Some bedrooms have TVs.

Eden-Hotel. Reinhauser Landstrasse 22A (near the new Rathaus), 37083 Göttingen. ☎ **0551/7-60-07.** Fax 0551/7-67-61. www.eden-hotel.gss.de. E-mail: eden-hotel@gass.de. 100 units. MINIBAR TV TEL. 178DM–263DM ($101.45–$149.90) double. Rates include buffet breakfast. AE, MC, V. Parking 10DM ($5.70).

The centrally located Eden-Hotel offers comfortable rooms with private bath or shower, hair dryer, trouser press, and fax outlet. The hotel serves good Italian food in its restaurant, La Locanda, with meals costing 20DM to 38DM ($11.40 to $21.65). It recently opened a German restaurant as well. Service is polite and attentive. Laundry and pressing service are available. Facilities include a sauna, an indoor pool, and a solarium.

Gebhards Hotel. Goethe-Allee 22–23 (in front of the Bahnhof), 37073 Göttingen. ☎ **0551/4-96-80.** Fax 0551/4-96-81-10. 60 units. MINIBAR TV TEL. 210DM–290DM ($119.70–$165.30) double; 310DM–340DM ($176.70–$193.80) suite. Rates include buffet breakfast. AE, DC, MC, V. Free parking. Bus: 4, 8, 10, 11, or 14.

Gebhards is the best hotel in town. It's housed in a grand building that evokes a Tuscan villa, with a modern balconied annex built onto the back. The renovated interior offers high-ceilinged public rooms and a pleasant bar area. The cheapest double has a toilet and shower; the most expensive is an apartment with a complete private bathroom. All the rooms are well designed and furnished.

The attached restaurant has hosted a king of Denmark and a few German presidents. The menu is likely to feature fresh fish and fresh fish terrines, turbot poached in cider, medaillons of quail, and Swabian pork with apple compote. Meals are served daily from noon to 2:30pm and 6pm to midnight.

WHERE TO DINE

Ratskeller. Markt 9. ☎ **0551/5-64-33.** Reservations recommended. Main courses 13DM–40DM ($7.40–$22.80); set menus 21DM–40DM ($11.95–$22.80). AE, DC, MC, V. Daily 11am–11:30pm. Closed Christmas Eve. Bus: 4, 8, 10, 11, or 14. NORTH GERMAN.

This 600-year-old restaurant lies in the historic cellar of the Altes Rathaus. This is the best place to eat in town, although Göttingen is not known for its restaurants. The menu is varied and extensive, with the longest list of soups and hors d'oeuvres in the region. The chef also prepares the best *Tafelspitz* (boiled beef) in the area. Specialties include Old German Farmer's Plate (chicken breast and pork steak with fried potatoes and roast onions) or fresh trout au bleu with parsley potatoes.

Zum Schwarzen Bären (The Black Bear). Kurzestrasse 12. ☎ **0551/5-82-84.** Reservations required. Main courses 15DM–35DM ($8.55–$19.95); fixed-price lunch 20DM–28DM ($11.40–$15.95); fixed-price dinner 40DM ($22.80). AE, DC, MC. Tues–Sun noon–2pm; Tues–Sat 6–10pm. Bus: 4, 8, 10, 11, or 14. NORTH GERMAN.

This fine restaurant is housed in a black-and-white timbered building (ca. 1500). It still has the original stained-glass leaded windows. Inside, the ambience is tavern style, with a ceramic stove in the corner and dining rooms with intimate booths. The innkeeper wisely recommends the brook trout from the Harz Mountains or Bärenpfanne (various fillets with spätzle).

GÖTTINGEN AFTER DARK

Pick up a copy of *Universitätsstadt Göttingen Informationsheft* for a complete rundown of entertainment listings.

THE PERFORMING ARTS   The local symphony orchestra is very active, as is the town's boys choir, and an annual Handel music festival is held in June. Information on schedules, venues, and tickets for all three is available by calling ☎ 0551/5-67-71 or by contacting the tourist office (see above).

For 100 years, the **Deutsches Theater,** Theaterplatz 11 (☎ 0551/4-96-90), has been staging classical and contemporary drama. Its counterpart, the **Junges Theater,** Hospitalstrasse 6 (☎ 0551/5-51-23), has produced experimental works for 40 years. Performances of both are held Tuesday to Sunday, with tickets costing 20DM to 25DM ($11.40 to $14.25) for adults and 13DM to 18DM ($7.40 to $10.25) for students. The box office is open Monday to Saturday from 11am to 1pm and 6 to 8:30pm.

BARS   A small cafe with indoor and outdoor seating, **Schroeder's Kneipe,** Judenstrasse 29 (☎ 0551/5-56-47), serves beer, wine, and coffee, as well as chocolate and other sweets. It also has pinball. Open Sunday to Thursday from 11am to 2am; Friday and Saturday from 11am until 3am. One of the more offbeat social centers of Göttingen is **KAZ (Kommunikations Aktions-Zentrum),** Hospitalstrasse 6 (☎ 0551/5-30-62), where everyone from senior citizens to anarchists meet for drinks in one of the two on-premises pubs. One also serves traditional German cuisine; the other offers sandwiches. Within the complex, political forums, local discussion groups, and cultural associations meet regularly. Opening hours change with the seasons and the scheduling of volunteers and group discussion leaders, but in most cases, the center is open Monday to Thursday, from noon to 2am, Friday from noon to 4pm, and Saturday from 11am to 2am. A jazz soundtrack sets the mood at **Café Kadenz,** Judenstrasse 17 (☎ **0551/4-72-08**), where a mellow crowd meets for beer, wine, coffee, and perhaps a light meal or snack. Daily hours are 11am to 1am.

DANCE CLUBS   One of the oldest nightlife venues in Göttingen, **Die Oper,** Nikolaistrasse 1B (☎ **0551/48-79-98**), was built 150 years ago as a pub. It offers music and dancing for a crowd aged 20 to around 32. Open Wednesday, Friday, and Saturday, from 10pm till 3am; depending on business, it's often open Thursday night (same hours) as well. Expect to pay an entrance fee of 5DM ($2.85).

LIVE MUSIC   Performance jazz is only featured 1 night a week at the excellent **Blue Note,** Wilhelmsplatz 3 (☎ **0551/4-69-07**); on other nights, musicians explore blues, salsa, African, reggae, and other Caribbean forms. Open Sunday to Thursday from 8pm until 2am; on Friday and Saturday, it stays open an hour later. The cover charge for most bands is 20DM to 35DM ($11.40 to $19.95). Popular with locals and students, **Irish Pub,** Muhlenstrasse 4A (☎ **0551/4-56-64**), hosts live music every night of the week, from local rockers to visiting Irish folk bands. The pub serves Guinness, Kilkenny, and hard cider. There's never a cover charge, and it's open nightly from 6pm until 1am.

STUDENT TAVERNS   A visit to Göttingen is traditionally capped by going to one of the student taverns, such as the cramped but convivial **Zum Altdeutschen,** Prinzenstrasse 16 (☎ **0551/5-65-45**), which is open daily from 4:30pm to 1am; or **Trou,** Burgstrasse 20, in the cellar (☎ **0551/4-39-71**), open daily from 7:30pm to 3am.

GAY CLUBS   **Café Kabale,** Geismarlandstrasse 19 (☎ **0551/48-58-30**), is where lesbians gather. **Café Protz** and **Faces,** Nikolaikirchhofstrasse 11 (☎ **0551/5-76-99**) offer a cafe and a bar setting, respectively, that are popular with gay men. Café Kabale and Café Protz are both open from 11am to 2 or 3am daily; Faces is open daily from 5pm to 2 or 3am.

10 Bad Wildungen

27 miles SW of Kassel, 100 miles NE of Frankfurt am Main

Bad Wildungen is more than 700 years old. Its healing mineral springs have long attracted northern Europeans to the rolling hills and deep forests of the Waldeck region, southwest of Kassel. Thousands of annual visitors come here seeking treatment for kidney and gallbladder disorders, or simply for rest and relaxation and the numerous cultural activities.

ESSENTIALS
GETTING THERE   By Train   There's frequent service on the Kassel-Fritzlar line from Kassel. For information and schedules, call ☎ **01805/996633.** The nearest airport is at Frankfurt am Main, 100 miles away.

By Bus   Bus service in the region is provided by **B.K.W. GmbH** (☎ **05621/802810** for schedules and information).

By Car   From Kassel, take Route 49 southwest, then go west on Route 253.

VISITOR INFORMATION   For information, contact the **Kurverwaltung,** Langemarckstrasse 2 (☎ **05621/704113**), open Monday to Friday 8am to 4:30pm and Saturday 8am to noon.

SIGHTS & ACTIVITIES

Rising above the Altstadt is the massive tower of the 14th-century **Stadtkirche,** the most impressive (and oldest) structure in the town, with interesting Hallenkirch architecture. It was restored in 1995. The highlight of the church is its remarkable *Niederwildungen Altarpiece,* one of the best examples of early German painting. Painted in 1403 by Master Konrad von Soest, the wing-paneled altarpiece contains a large, dramatic scene of the crucifixion, flanked by six smaller scenes depicting the birth, passion, and resurrection of Christ. The work shows an obvious French influence in the use of delicate colors and figures, made even more vivid by the use of actual gold. The church is open daily 10:30am to noon and 2 to 5pm. Call ☎ **05621/40-11** for more information.

The **spa gardens** augment the town's natural wooded surroundings with carefully planted flowers from all parts of the world, as well as with several attractive buildings, including two band shells where outdoor concerts are frequently given. The grounds are dotted with lawn chairs. The modern horseshoe-shaped arcade houses the George-Viktor Spring, plus several exclusive shops and a small auditorium.

SHOPPING   Bad Wildungen's shops carry fashion suitable for Germany's most sophisticated cities. Shops line either side of the Brunnenallee. One of the most appealing is **Manhenke,** Brunnenallee 28 (☎ **05621/960253**), which sells clothes and accessories for both men and women.

WHERE TO STAY

Hotel-Pension Die Hardtmühle. Im Urfftal 5-7, 34537 Bad Wildungen. ☎ **05626/99-90.** Fax 05626/7-43. 32 units. TEL. 120DM–160DM ($68.40–$91.20) double; 240DM ($136.80) apt for 4. Rates include buffet breakfast. AE, DC, MC, V. Free parking. 6 miles west of the town center; follow signs to Urfftal.

Don't check into this hotel if you're looking for lots of activities or anything approaching urban diversions. Come here instead for bucolic views of lazy cows grazing in nearby fields, an environment so pressure-free as to be almost somnolent, and access to outdoor pastimes. Accommodations are simple but comfortable, completely unpretentious, and suitable for catching up on the sleep you might have lost in more frenetic environments. Besides the double rooms, there's also one apartment, often rented by families. The family that runs the hotel doesn't speak much English, but this is still a great place for a getaway. There's both a tennis court and an outdoor pool.

Maritim Badehotel. Dr.-Marc-Strasse 4 (at the entrance to the gardens, in the Kurpark), 34537 Bad Wildungen. ☎ **05621/79-99.** Fax 05621/79-97-99. E-mail: reservierung.wil@ maritim.ole. 230 units. MINIBAR TV TEL. 260DM–320DM ($148.20–$182.40) double; 380DM– 900DM ($216.60–$513) suite. Rates include buffet breakfast. AE, DC, MC, V. Parking 15DM ($8.55).

The Maritim Badehotel is located in the center of the town's clinical and cultural activities. No hotel in Bad Wildungen comes close to this one for comfort, style, amenities, and facilities. This place evokes the grandeur of another era. Large and rambling, it branches out in two great wings from the circular domed entrance. The renovated rooms are large, comfortable, sunlit, and airy, all with views of the Waldeck woodlands and spa gardens.

Dining: The hotel's restaurant offers a rich cuisine for those not worried about calories. Special diets are also available, including vegetarian meals. Veal dishes are the specialty; the *Kalbsschnitzel* (veal scallops) cooked with herbs is a tasty choice.

Amenities: Large, heated indoor pool; therapeutic facilities, including carbon-dioxide baths, massages, and complete medical attention by a fine professional staff; room service; baby-sitting; concierge; dry cleaning; laundry; hair dryers.

Treff Hotel Quellenhof. Brunnenallee 54 (across the street from the Kurpark), 35437 Bad Wildungen. ☎ **05621/80-70.** Fax 05621/80-75-00. 112 units. MINIBAR TV TEL. 226DM ($128.80) double. AE, DC, MC, V.

This white-sided hotel has a mansard roof and art nouveau gables. Rooms are international in their decor and carefully outfitted. A stylish restaurant is on the premises (Park Restaurant; see recommendation below). There's also live music at Café Bistrot on Friday night and at the Moltemstoffel Bar on Saturday night. Facilities include a sauna, solarium, and whirlpool. The hotel also contains Bad Wildungen's only casino.

WHERE TO DINE

The hotel dining rooms enjoy a culinary monopoly in Bad Wildungen; there is no major independent restaurant.

Park Restaurant. In the Treff Hotel Quellenhof, Brunnenallee 54. ☎ **05621/80-70.** Reservations recommended. Main courses 12DM–42DM ($6.85–$23.95); set menu 28DM ($15.95). AE, DC, MC, V. Daily noon–2pm and 6–10pm. INTERNATIONAL.

Stylish, airy, and international, this is the showcase restaurant of the Treff Hotel (see above). Though it's a top place to dine, its prices are affordable. The immaculately clean interior is outfitted with lots of green plants. The staff is alert and well trained. Menu items include well-prepared salads, roasted meats, pastas, pastries, and such traditional German dishes as sauerbraten and *Rostbraten.*

BAD WILDUNGEN AFTER DARK

The tourist office keeps a list of special events, which are staged almost every week. Concerts and theater take place usually in the **Neues Kurhaus** in the town center or at the **Kursaal** in Reinhaltshausen, not far from Bad Wildungen. For tickets, call ☎ **05621/70-47-73.**

 Spielbank, Brunnenallee 54 (☎ **05621/96-00-56**), located in the Treff Hotel (see above), is the resort's only casino. It's minor league as Germany's casinos go. Open daily from 2:30 to 10:30pm, with an entrance fee of 5DM ($2.85).

 Nighttime diversions in Bad Wildungen revolve around the **Brunnenallée** and its extension, the **Brunnenstrasse,** in the form of lively bars and cafes that stay open until around 2am. Some of the best include the **Warsteiner** Ecke, Brunnenstrasse 66 (☎ **05621/74172**); the **Ratskeller,** Marktplatz (☎ **05621/71855**); and **Hosenlantz,** Brunnenallée 32 (☎ **05621/92996**), a small, tucked-away bar with occasional live music. The most earthy and rowdy of the town's beerhalls is **Bräuhaus,** Frankenbergerstrasse 2 (☎ **05621/74150**), which is open Monday to Friday noon till 11pm, Saturday 6 to 11pm, and Sunday 8:30am to 3pm.

11 The Fairy-Tale Road

To tour the Fairy-Tale Road (Märchenstrasse) is to take a trip though the land made immortal by the Brothers Grimm. German folklore survived in rural areas at least until the mid-19th century, and much of its charm is still visible and nostalgically remembered today. The Grimm brothers were the earliest scholars of their country's folklore; they traveled to far-flung corners of Germany in the early 19th century to record the tales they heard. Their compendium, *Tales of the Brothers Grimm,* is the world's second most frequently translated book, after the Bible.

 Today you can follow the Fairy-Tale Road, a 370-mile route from Hanau, near Frankfurt, where the Brothers Grimm were born, to Bremen, where the "Town Musicians of Bremen" lived. The route goes through some of the prettiest medieval villages in the country, all listed on the German Tourist Office's maps of the road. In some of the towns, marionette shows (in German, but universal in appeal) are given in summer, and museums keep the legends alive, including the one in Ziegenhain in the Schwalm Valley, where costumes that might have been worn by Little Red Riding Hood and her grandmother are displayed.

Day 1   Begin in **Hanau**, 12½ miles east of Frankfurt. Jakob (1785) and Wilhelm Grimm (1786) were born here, on the River Main. Appropriately, the Fairy-Tale Road starts at a monument to the story-telling brothers at Neustadter Marktplatz. The memorial, erected in 1898, is about all that will interest you in this traffic-clogged suburb of Frankfurt. Hanau was heavily bombed in World War II.

From Hanau, go along B43 about 12 miles northeast to **Gelnhausen,** where the remains of the imperial palace evoke memories of the emperor, Friedrich Barbarossa, and his lover, Beautiful Gela. Barbarossa constructed the castle here on an island in the 12th century.

Continue another 12 miles to **Steinau an der Strasse,** where the Grimm brothers spent their carefree youth. Visit the Amtshaus, the Renaissance palace, and see a performance at the fairy-tale puppet theater. Half-timbered buildings line cobblestone streets. The surrounding woods might have been the home of Snow White. In the center of the main square is a memorial fountain honoring the Grimm brothers.

Continue north on B40 following the directions to **Fulda,** noted for its baroque architecture, as exemplified by the bishops' palace on Schlossstrasse, overlooking the city. The prince-bishops were guardians of the tomb of St. Boniface, the apostle of Germany. Fulda's cathedral dates from 1704, and pilgrims still worship at the tomb of St. Boniface, in a crypt beneath the main altar. Consider staying overnight in Fulda.

Romantik Hotel Goldener Karpfen, Simpliziusbrunner 1 (☎ **0661/8-68-00;** fax 0661/8680100), in Fulda, was built in the baroque era, but the facade is of a later date. Try to arrive for afternoon tea in the hotel's elegant lounge. The place rents 50 cozy and comfortable rooms; a double goes for 300DM to 450DM ($171 to $256.50). The hotel also serves some of the best food in town. Set-price lunches cost 40DM to 64DM ($22.80 to $36.50); set-price dinners 50DM to 100DM ($28.50 to $57).

Day 2   Leave Fulda in the morning and take B254 into the Vogelsberg Mountains, going via Grossenlüder to **Lauterbach,** 15 miles northeast of Fulda. The town is known for its medieval half-timbered houses and its two castles, Eisenbach and Riedesel. In one of the Grimms' tales, the Little Scalawag loses his sock in Lauterbach. After your visit, follow Route 254 northwest to **Alsfeld,** a town of half-timbered houses and cobblestone streets. Its 1512 Altes Rathaus is a showpiece.

Follow the route along the Schwalm River, which the Germans call *Rotkäppchen-land,* or Little Red Riding Hood country. Signs point to **Neustadt,** with its circular tower, from which Rapunzel might have let down her golden tresses. Some 6 miles to the north, **Schwalmstadt** is the capital of the district. Continue north of Schwalmstadt for 12 miles to **Homberg.**

Krone Inn, Marktplatz (☎ 05681/93-07-73), in Homberg, claims to be the oldest inn in Germany. The best of the hearty dishes is the Kronenplatte, which combines three kinds of meat with fresh vegetables, potato croquettes, and salad. Main courses cost from 15DM to 30DM ($8.55 to $17.10). Meals are served daily from noon to 2pm and from 6 to 9:30pm, but you can always stop in for a glass of wine or a foaming mug of beer. Credit cards are not accepted.

From Homberg, follow the signs for 24 miles north to **Kassel,** where you'll want to spend the night. The Waldeck Region and the Reinhards Forest around Kassel were the birthplace of many legends and tales about witches, sleeping princesses, strange beasts, and magic spells. These tales had a profound influence on the Grimm brothers, who lived in Kassel from 1798 to 1830. The **Bruder Grimm Museum,** at Schone Aussicht 2, contains letters, portraits, and mementos.

Schloss Hotel Wilhelmshöhe, Schlosspark 8 (☎ 0561/3-08-80), in Kassel, is not an old castle but a completely modern structure directly across the street from former imperial palaces. The 105-room hotel has many private terraces with views of the rolling castle park and its buildings, which were once a summer residence for the landgraves and electors of Hessen-Kassel. Later the area became the summer residence of Kaiser Wilhelm II. Doubles cost 268DM ($152.75), and meals begin at 45DM ($25.65).

Day 3   Leaving Kassel, go along B3 for some 10 miles north to **Münden** (known more properly as Hannoversch-Münden). The Fulda and Werra Rivers meet here. In the town center are some 700 half-timbered houses built in many styles. Also in Münden is the tombstone of the much-maligned Doctor Eisenbart, who is remembered every year at a folk festival.

Jagshaus Heede, Hermannshager Strasse 81 (☎ 05541/23-95), in Hann-Münden, is inside the town's nature preserve. The 18-room hotel is an enlarged former private house. There's a cafe-style sun terrace on the premises, as well as a children's playground. The dining room serves conservative German cuisine and offers generous portions; set-price meals cost 25DM to 42DM ($14.25 to $23.95); double rooms rent for 120DM ($68.40) each.

From Münden you can detour from the Fairy-Tale Road, taking the Autobahn (E45) to Göttingen (see above), where you may want to spend the night.

Day 4   Return to the Fairy-Tale Road by going back to Münden and then heading north on Route 80. About 6 miles north of Münden in the village of Veckerhagen, go left and follow the signs to Sababurg.

Right outside the village of Sababurg lies **Dornröschenschloss Sababurg,** Hofgeismar (☎ 05671/80-80), a park and castle said to be the setting of the Sleeping Beauty legend. You'll almost start to believe the tale when you see the Italianate turrets of the castle. The park is said to be the oldest zoological garden in the world. The wilderness of ancient oak and beech trees, along with the tall ferns, adds to the fairy-tale atmosphere of the area. In the castle courtyard, where sweet-smelling briar roses still bloom, you half expect to see the prince coming to awaken Sleeping Beauty. The castle here has an excellent restaurant.

After viewing the castle, take the road back to the Weser Valley village of Oberweser and make a left turn onto B80 heading north. After some 8 miles you reach the spa of **Bad Karlshafen,** a resort noted for its baroque buildings.

Hotel Zum Schwan, Conradistrasse 3, Bad Karlshafen (☎ 05672/10-44), is an elegant 32-room spa hotel situated beside the main bathhouse, opposite the town pond. Built in 1765, it has the baroque facade of a palace, with an entrance terrace overlooking the river. Excellent meals are served here, with many regional dishes featured, costing 48DM ($27.35) and up. An attractively furnished double rents for 210DM ($119.70).

Continue on Route 80 north (which becomes Route 83) to **Höxter,** the easternmost town in Westphalia. Among its many Renaissance and baroque buildings, the town's most visited attraction is Dechanei (the Deanery). You can take Corveyer Allee from Höxter for about 2 miles to Corvey, one of the oldest Benedictine abbeys in Germany, planned by Charlemagne and constructed by his son, Ludwig the Pious, in 822.

Follow the Weser River north for some 20 miles to the town of **Bodenwerder,** the birthplace of Lügen Baron, known as the "Liar Baron" von Münchhausen. He's honored by the **Münchhausen Museum,** filled with mementos of his fanciful life.

After Bodenwerder, head northwest on Route 83 for Hameln (see above), where you'll want to spend the night.

Day 5   After a night in Hameln, take Route 83 northwest to the Autobahn (E30) and continue west beyond Osnabruck until you connect with the E37 Autobahn heading northeast to **Bremen** (see above), the final stop of the trip.

Hamburg

16

Hamburg has many faces. A walk down the neon-lit Reeperbahn at night will revive those old memories of "Sin-City Europe." A ride around Alster Lake in the center city will reveal the elegance of its finest parks and buildings. A stroll along one of Hamburg's many canals will show you why this city has been called the "Venice of the North." Contrasts are evident wherever you look. Amid the steel-and-glass structures of the modern city is the old baroque Hauptkirche St. Michaelis. A Sunday-morning visit to the Altona fish market will give you a good look at early shoppers mingling with late-night partyers.

Hamburg has had to be flexible to recover from the many disasters of its 1,200-year history. This North Sea port was almost totally destroyed during World War II. But out of the rubble of the old, the industrious Hamburgians rebuilt a larger and more beautiful city, with huge parks, impressive buildings, and important cultural institutions. Hamburg is today the greenest city in Europe, with nearly 50% of its surface area marked with water, woodlands, farmland, and some 1,400 parks and gardens. Green is, in fact, the city's official color.

Hamburg, the second-largest city of Germany, lies on the Elbe River, 68 miles from the North Sea, 177 miles northwest of Berlin, 74 miles northeast of Bremen, and 93 miles north of Hannover. The city has about 1.7 million inhabitants.

1 Orientation

ARRIVING

BY PLANE The **Airport Hamburg-Fuhlsbüttel,** Paul-Baumer-Platz 1–3, is 5 miles north of center city. It's served by many scheduled airlines and charter companies, with regular flights to major German airports and many European and intercontinental destinations. **Lufthansa** (☎ 01803/80-38-03) offers flights to Hamburg from most major German cities, and many national carriers fly into Hamburg, including Air France from Paris and British Airways from London. United Airlines, Delta, and Lufthansa offer direct flights from the United States. For flight information in Hamburg, call ☎ 040/507-50.

An ultramodern terminal and passenger pier at the airport has a roof shaped like an enormous aircraft wing. This terminal contains an array of interesting shops and boutiques—even a branch of Harrods of London—as well as restaurants and other establishments.

Hamburg Accommodations & Dining

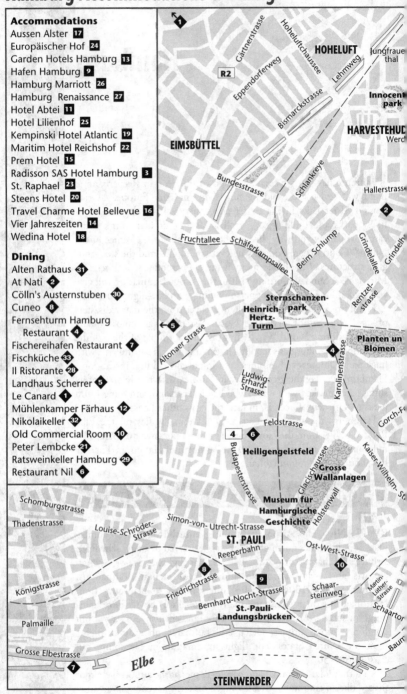

Accommodations
Aussen Alster **17**
Europäischer Hof **24**
Garden Hotels Hamburg **13**
Hafen Hamburg **9**
Hamburg Marriott **26**
Hamburg Renaissance **27**
Hotel Abtei **11**
Hotel Lilienhof **25**
Kempinski Hotel Atlantic **19**
Maritim Hotel Reichshof **22**
Prem Hotel **15**
Radisson SAS Hotel Hamburg **3**
St. Raphael **23**
Steens Hotel **20**
Travel Charme Hotel Bellevue **16**
Vier Jahreszeiten **14**
Wedina Hotel **18**

Dining
Alten Rathaus **31**
At Nati **2**
Cölln's Austernstuben **30**
Cuneo **8**
Fernsehturm Hamburg Restaurant **4**
Fischereihafen Restaurant **7**
Fischküche **33**
Il Ristorante **28**
Landhaus Scherrer **5**
Le Canard **1**
Mühlenkamper Färhaus **12**
Nikolaikeller **32**
Old Commercial Room **10**
Peter Lembcke **21**
Ratsweinkeller Hamburg **29**
Restaurant Nil **6**

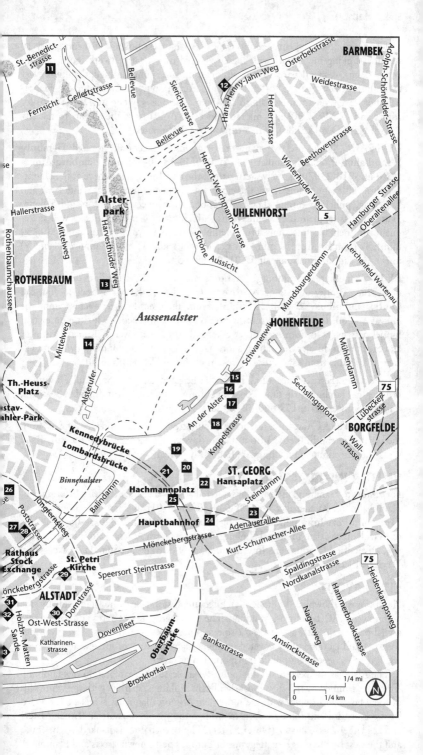

The Hamburger Verkehrsverbund (HVV) **Air Express bus no. 110** runs every 10 minutes, linking the airport with the city's rapid-transit rail network (both U-Bahn and S-Bahn). A bus departs for the airport from the Hamburg Hauptbahnhof every 20 minutes from 5:40am to 9:20pm daily. Airport buses heading for the Hauptbahnhof leave daily from 6:22am to 10:42pm. The one-way fare is 8DM ($4.55) for adults and 4DM ($2.30) for children under 12. A taxi from the airport to the city costs from 40DM ($22.80), with a trip time of 25 minutes.

BY TRAIN   There are two major rail stations, the centrally located **Hamburg Hauptbahnhof,** Hachmannplatz 10 (☎ 040/39-18-30-46), and **Hamburg-Altona** (☎ 040/3918-2387), in the western part of the city. Most trains arrive at the Hauptbahnhof, although trains from the north of Germany, including Westerland and Schleswig, pull into Altona. The two stations are connected by train and S-Bahn. Hamburg has frequent train connections with all major German cities, as well as frequent continental connections. From Berlin, 14 trains arrive daily (trip time: 2 hr., 30 min.), 37 from Bremen (54 min. to 1 hr., 16 min.), and 33 from Hannover (1 hr., 30 min.). For rail information, call ☎ **01805/996633.**

BY BUS   Because of Hamburg's location astride most of the rail lines of north Germany, the majority of passengers arrive by train. But if the bus appeals to you, call **Central Omnibus** (☎ 040/24-75-75). From their headquarters across from the railway station, they'll supply information on fares and schedules for the buses that funnel passengers in from such other cities as Berlin, Hannover, Nürnberg, Munich, and Stockholm. Information about short-haul buses from surrounding towns and villages is available from **Hamburger Verkehrsverbund** (☎ 040/32880).

BY FERRY   Ferry service links Harwich, England and the St. Pauli Landungsbrücken in Hamburg (trip time: 20 hr.). For information, call **Scandinavian Seaways,** Van-der-Smissenstrasse (☎ 040/38-90-30).

BY CAR   The A1 Autobahn reaches Hamburg from the south and west, the A7 from the north and south, the A23 from the northwest, and the A24 from the east. Road signs and directions to Hamburg are frequently posted.

VISITOR INFORMATION

For visitors to Hamburg, information is offered at several centers. **Tourist-Information,** Hauptbahnhof, Kirchenallee exit (☎ 040/30-05-12-01), is open daily from 7am to 11pm; and **Port Information,** St. Pauli Landungsbrücken (☎ 040/30-05-12-00), is open daily from 10am to 7pm. Hamburg also has a North American tourist representative, **Diversified Destinations International,** 38 West 32nd St., Suite 1210, New York, NY 10001 (☎ 212/967-3110).

CITY LAYOUT

Hamburg is a showplace of modern architecture; historic structures stand side by side with towering steel-and-glass buildings. The 4½ square miles of parks and gardens are a vital part of the city, as are the 22 square miles of rivers and lakes. The city is not compact and can't be easily covered on foot. Many sections of interest are far apart; you'll have to depend on public transportation or taxis.

The **Alster** is the perfect starting point for a pleasurable exploration of Hamburg. This lake, rimmed by the city's most significant buildings, sparkles with the white sails of small boats and ripples with the movement of motor launches. The lake is divided by the Lombard and John F. Kennedy bridges into the **Binnenalster (Inner Alster)** and the larger **Aussenalster (Outer Alster).** The Binnenalster is flanked on the south and the west by the **Jungfernstieg,** one of Europe's best-known streets and Hamburg's most vital artery and shopping district. For landlubbers, the best view of the Alster is from this "maiden's path."

From the Hauptbahnhof, on the eastern fringe of the heart of town, in the vicinity of the Binnenalster, two major shopping streets fan out in a southwesterly direction, toward St. Petri Church and the Rathaus. They are **Spitalerstrasse** (reserved for pedestrians) and **Mönckebergstrasse,** paralleling it to the south. These streets contain some of the city's finest stores. Stay on Mönckebergstrasse to reach **Rathausmarkt,** which is dominated by the Rathaus, a Renaissance-style city hall palace.

The center of Hamburg offers fine opportunities for walking; for example, the eastern shoreline of the Binnenalster opens onto **Ballindamm,** which contains many elegant stores. At the foot of this lake is the Jungfernstieg, already mentioned; and along its western shoreline is yet another main artery, the Neuer Jungfernstieg. At the intersection of the Jungfernstieg and Neuer Jungfernstieg is one of the more fascinating streets of Hamburg, the **Colonnaden,** a colonnade of shops and cafes. In this neighborhood stands the Hamburgische Staatsoper, the famous modern opera house.

The **Port of Hamburg** is the world's fifth-largest harbor, stretching for nearly 25 miles along the Elbe River. More than 1,500 ships from all over the world call each month. Since 1189, the stretch of water has been one of the busiest centers for trade on the Continent, making Hamburg one of Germany's wealthiest cities.

Central Hamburg   This is the commercial and shopping district of Hamburg, seat of many of its finest hotels and restaurants. The district centers around Binnenalster and the Rathaus (City Hall). Boat rides on the Alster lakes are a major attraction. Many historic buildings that withstood World War II stand here, including St. Petri, the oldest surviving structure.

The Harbor   Sixty dock basins stretching for some 25 miles of quays, including mooring buoys, constitute one of the world's greatest ports. Maritime vessels from all over Europe and the world carry cargo up the Elbe to dock and unload here.

St. Pauli   This is the nightlife center of Hamburg, with lots of erotica. The district is split by its famous street, the Reeperbahn, neon-lit and dazzling, offering all sorts of nighttime pleasures—cafes, sex shows, bars, discos, and music halls.

Altona   Formerly a city in its own right, this western district is now integrated into Greater Hamburg. It was once populated mainly by Jews and Portuguese. Today it's the scene of Hamburg's famous Fischmarkt, which takes place at dawn every Sunday.

Övelgönne   This region, down the river from Altona, is known for its coterie of sailing freighters. From this river district, you'll have a good vantage point for seeing the maritime vessels on the Elbe heading for port or leaving Hamburg for destinations around the globe.

Pösseldorf   Northwest of Aussenalster, this is a tree-filled residential district, often with villas dating from the 1800s. Many exemplary Jugendstil buildings can be seen here. The district is largely occupied by upwardly mobile professionals, including a lot of media stars.

GETTING AROUND

A word to the wise: Park your car and use public transportation in this busy city.

Practically all public transportation services in the Hamburg area—the **U-Bahn** (subway), **S-Bahn** (city rail), **A-Bahn** (commuter rail), numerous bus routes, and harbor ferries—are run by **Hamburger Verkehrsverbund (HVV),** Steinstrasse 12. For train information, call ☎ **040/32880.** Tickets are sold at Automats and railroad ticket counters.

BY PUBLIC TRANSPORTATION Hamburg's **U-Bahn,** one of the best in Germany, serves the entire central area and connects with the **S-Bahn** surface trains in the suburbs. This network is the fastest means of getting around, but buses offer a good alternative. The advantage of surface travel, of course, is that you get to see more of the city.

Fares for both U-Bahn and bus range from 2.50DM to 15DM ($1.40 to $8.55), depending on the distance. You buy your ticket from the driver or from vending machines at stops and stations. If you plan to make a day of it, you can purchase a **day ticket** for unlimited use of public transportation services, costing 9.50DM ($5.40).

There are also discount cards that offer free travel on all public transport in Hamburg, as well as free admission to 11 Hamburg museums and a 30% discount on city tours, guided tours of the port, and lake cruises. A 1-day card goes for 12.50DM ($7.10) for individuals or 24DM ($13.70) for families. A 3-day card costs 26DM ($14.80) for individuals and 43DM ($24.50) for families.

BY TAXI Taxis are available at all hours; call ☎ 040/44-10-11 or 040/66-66-66. A taxi from the airport to the city center costs 45DM ($25.65). Taxi meters throughout Hamburg begin at 4DM ($2.30) and rise between 2.40DM ($1.35) and 2.50DM ($1.40) per kilometer after that.

BY BIKE Bicycles can be rented at **O'Niel Bikes,** Beethovenstrasse 37 (☎ 040/531-177-44), at a cost of 19DM ($10.85) per day.

Fast Facts: Hamburg

American Express The Amex office in Hamburg is at Ballindamm 39 (☎ 040/30-90-80) and is open Monday to Friday 9am to 5:30pm and Saturday 10am to 1pm.

Bookstores **Frensche,** Landesbank Galerie, Spitalerstrasse 26C (☎ 040/32-75-85), is a good English-language bookstore with a large selection of books and tapes. It's open Monday to Wednesday from 10am to 7pm; Thursday to Friday 10am to 7:30pm; Saturday 10am to 4pm.

Business Hours Most **banks** are open Monday to Friday from 8:30am to 12:30pm and 1:30 to 3:30pm (many banks stay open until 5:30pm on Thursday). Most **businesses** and **stores** are open Monday to Friday from 9am to 6pm and on Saturday from 9am to 2pm (until 4 or 6pm on the first Saturday of the month).

Car Rentals We don't recommend that you rent a car for touring Hamburg, but an automobile is ideal for the environs. Rentals are available at **Avis,** Drehbahn 15–25 (☎ 040/34-16-51), or at **Hertz,** Kirchenallee 34-36 near the main railway station (☎ 040/2-80-12-01-03).

Consulates See "Embassies & Consulates" in "Fast Facts: Germany," in chapter 2.

Currency Exchange The most convenient place for recent arrivals to exchange foreign currency for deutschmarks is the **ReiseBank** at the Hauptbahnhof (☎ 040/32-34-83), which is open daily from 7:30am to 10pm. The same bank maintains a branch at the Altona Station (☎ 040/390-3770), open Monday and Wednesday through Friday 7:30am to 7:30pm, and Tuesday and Saturday 9am to 2pm and 2:45 to 5pm. There's also a branch in Terminal 4 of Hamburg's airport (☎ 040/5075-3374), open daily 6:30am to 10pm.

Dentist   A dental clinic, with English-speaking dentists, is available at **Allgemeines Krankenhaus,** Lohmühlen Strasse 5, 20099 Hamburg (☎ **040/ 28-90-11**).

Doctor   Ask at the British and American consulates or go to **Allgemeines Krankenhaus,** Lohmühlen Strasse 5, 20099 Hamburg (☎ **040/28-90-11**), where you'll find an English-speaking staff.

Drugstores   Pharmacies that stock foreign drugs include **Internationale Apotheke,** Ballindamm 39 (☎ **040/30-96-060**), which is open Monday to Friday from 8am to 7pm and on Saturday from 9am to 3pm. **Roth's Alte Englische Apotheke,** Jungfernstieg 48 (☎ **040/34-39-06**), is open Monday to Friday 8:30am to 6:30pm and Saturday 9am to 2pm.

Emergencies   Dial **110** for the police or an ambulance or emergency doctor or dentist; **112** for the fire brigade; and **01805/10-11-12** for the German Automobile Association (ADAC).

Eyeglasses   One of the city's largest opticians is **Fielmann,** Mönckebergstrasse 29 (☎ **040/300-50-60**), which sells and services both glasses and contact lenses.

Laundry/Dry Cleaning   Your hotel reception desk can often recommend a laundry or dry cleaning place nearby. If not, try Express Wasch-Center, Friedrichstrasse 30 (☎ **040/3-19-14-34**), for both laundry and dry cleaning. Open Monday to Friday 9:30am to 10pm and Saturday 9:30am to 5pm.

Lost Property   Municipal bus, U-Bahn and S-Bahn lost property offices are at Backerbreitergang 73 (☎ **040/35-04-17-35**), open Monday 8am to 4pm, Tuesday and Wednesday 8am to noon, and Thursday 8am to 6pm. For goods lost on railways call ☎ **01805/99-66-33,** Monday to Thursday 9 to 11am and 1 to 3pm and Friday 9 to 11am and 1 to 2pm.

Luggage Storage/Lockers   These are available at the Hamburg Hauptbahnhof, Hachmannplatz 10 (☎ **040/39-18-28-57**). Lockers cost 5DM ($2.85) for 24 hours.

Photographic Needs   Photo Porst, Dammtorstrasse 12 (☎ **040/34-49-16**) is open Monday to Friday 9am to 6:30pm and Saturday 9am to 2pm.

Post Office   The post office at the Hamburg Hauptbahnhof, Hachmannplatz 13 (☎ **040/3-25-51-60**), is convenient. You can make long-distance calls here far cheaper than at your hotel. Telegrams, telexes, and faxes can also be sent. It's open Monday to Friday 8am to 8pm, Saturday 8am to 6pm, and Sunday 10am to 4pm. A branch office located at the airport (☎ **040/5-00-04-85**) is open Monday to Friday 6:30am to 9pm, Saturday 8am to 6pm, and Sunday 10am to 6pm.

Rest Rooms   See "Fast Facts: Germany" in chapter 2. There are several decent public facilities in the center of Hamburg.

Safety   Hamburg, like all big cities of the world, has its share of crime. The major crimes that tourists encounter are pickpocketing and purse and camera snatching. Most robberies occur in the big tourist areas, such as the Reeperbahn and the area around the Hauptbahnhof, which can be dangerous at night, but much less so than in Frankfurt or Munich.

Taxis   See "Getting Around," earlier in this chapter.

Telegrams/Telex/Fax   These can be sent from the post office at the Hamburg Hauptbahnhof, Hachmannplatz 13 (☎ **040/3-25-51-60**).

Transit Information   For U-Bahn and S-Bahn rail information, call the Hamburg Hauptbahnhof, Hachmannplatz 10 (☎ **01805/996633**).

2 Accommodations

Hamburg is an expensive city with an abundance of first-class hotels but a limited number of budget accommodations, especially in the center city. During a busy convention period, you may have trouble finding a room. A department within **Hamburg's Tourist Information Office** (Tourismus Centrale), Steinstrasse 7 (☎ **040/ 30-05-13-00;** fax 040/30-05-13-33), in the city's main railway station, at Kirchenallee in the Wandelhalle, can reserve rooms in Hamburg for visitors who arrive without prebooked accommodations. Rooms from more than 200 hotels in all price categories are available. There's a fee of 6DM ($3.40) per reservation. You can use this agency on a last-minute basis (shortly after your arrival in town), but no more than 7 days in advance of the time you'll need the room.

Hotel-booking desks can also be found at the airport in Arrival Hall A. For a map of hotels in Hamburg, see page 562.

NEAR THE HAUPTBAHNHOF
VERY EXPENSIVE

✪ **Kempinski Hotel Atlantic Hamburg.** An der Alster 72 (near the Aussenalster), 20099 Hamburg. ☎ **800/426-3135** in the U.S., or 040/2-88-80. Fax 040/24-71-29. www.ehi.com/ travel/ehi/germany/hamb0001.html. 267 units. MINIBAR TV TEL. 425DM–495DM ($242.25–$282.15) double; 575DM–1,900DM ($327.75–$1,083) suite. AE, DC, MC, V. Parking 20DM ($11.40). U-Bahn: Hauptbahnhof.

This sumptuous hotel, the Kempinski chain's flagship, is one of the two great hotels of the north. It's in a central location filled with trees and imposing villas and was one of the few buildings in the neighborhood to escape the bombs of World War II. Michael Jackson, the artist formerly known as Prince, and Madonna cast their votes for this hotel, but we still think Vier Jahreszeiten (see below) is number one. The theme here is turn-of-the-century maritime. Some rooms are air-conditioned. Most accommodations are very spacious with high ceilings, private safes, luxury mattresses, and plush carpets, along with large bathrooms dressed in tile or marble with plush towels, hair dryers, and robes.

Dining: The elegant Atrium Bar opens onto a neoclassical fountain; there's also a pub-style restaurant called Atlantic Mühle. The stylish Atlantic Restaurant is one of the finest dining rooms in northern Germany, with some 55 cooks preparing modern haute cuisine that's matched by a superb wine list. Meals are served daily from noon to 3pm and 6pm to midnight.

Amenities: Room service, laundry, dry cleaning, baby-sitting, sauna, solarium, Chanel Institut de Beauté, and a beautifully maintained chlorine-free indoor pool.

EXPENSIVE

Aussen Alster. Schmilinskystrasse 11 (a 5-min. walk from the rail station and a 3-min. walk from the Alster), 20099 Hamburg. ☎ **040/24-15-57.** Fax 040/2-80-32-31. 27 units. TV TEL. 260DM–310DM ($148.20–$176.70) double. Rates include buffet breakfast. AE, DC, MC, V. Closed Dec 22–27. U-Bahn: Hauptbahnhof.

Small and exclusive, and on a quiet residential street, Aussen Alster attracts actors, advertising directors, executives, writers, and artists. Its stylish, ultramodern interior was designed by one of Germany's most famous architects. Its 19th-century facade is painted milk white, capped with an Italianate-inspired frieze. Hamburg film producer

---

⊕ Family-Friendly Hotels

Garden Hotels Hamburg (*see p. 573*)   For the family that can afford it, this traditional hotel in the western sector looks out onto the Outer Alster Lake. Here you'll find cozy comfort in a safe neighborhood.

Radisson SAS Hotel Hamburg (*see p. 572*)   Children will enjoy the setting and the surprising architecture.

Steens Hotel (*see p. 571*)   This simple but clean and safe hotel is great for a family on a budget.

Klaus Feddermann and his partner, Burkhardt Stoelck, manage the place with panache. The lobby walls exhibit works of a number of European artists. The rooms are white-walled, angular, and consciously simple. Everything in the medium-sized rooms is designed for style and comfort, from the luxurious beds to the immaculate bathrooms with hair dryers and plush towels.

Dining/Diversions: Have a drink in the hotel bar, where on cool nights a fireplace burns, and then enjoy the international restaurant, Schmilinsky, where Italian food is a specialty.

Amenities: Room service, laundry, garden (in back), sauna, solarium.

Europäischer Hof. Kirchenallee 45 (across from the Hauptbahnhof), 20099 Hamburg. ☎ **040/24-82-48.** Fax 040/24-82-47-99. 320 units. MINIBAR TV TEL. 250DM–430DM ($142.50–$245.10) double. Rates include buffet breakfast. AE, DC, MC, V. Parking 22DM ($12.55). U-Bahn: Hauptbahnhof.

Europäischer Hof is the largest privately owned hotel in Hamburg. It lacks the atmosphere of the Maritim Hotel Reichshof or the chic of Aussen Alster hotel, although it has its supporters, especially among business clients. The well-furnished and medium-sized rooms, which are always being improved, have soundproof windows; most have tiny art-deco dressing rooms, fax ports, brass lamps, and fine carpets that make for a welcoming ambience.

Dining/Diversions: Two restaurants await visitors, the Chalet and the Burgerstube. A piano bar offers evening entertainment.

Amenities: 24-hour room service, laundry, dry cleaning, sauna, solarium, indoor pool, fitness room.

Maritim Hotel Reichshof. Kirchenallee 34–36 (across from the Hauptbahnhof), 20099 Hamburg. ☎ **040/24-83-30.** Fax 040/24-83-38-88. www.maritum.de. 303 units. MINIBAR TV TEL. 256DM–376DM ($145.90–$214.30) double; from 435DM ($247.95) suite. Rates include buffet breakfast. AE, DC, MC, V. Parking 20DM ($11.40). U-Bahn: Hauptbahnhof.

The Reichshof was built in 1910 across from the ornate spire of the Hamburg Hauptbahnhof. At the time, it was the largest hotel in Europe and boasted a landmark art-deco lobby. In World War II it lost most of its upper floors, but the marble and gilded pilasters of the lobby were left intact. A complete renovation has substantially upgraded the place. Guest rooms are now modern, with reproduction art-nouveau furniture and color TVs with in-house movies. This hotel is a favorite with business travelers, so more than half its rooms are classified as singles. Bedrooms range from medium sized to spacious, and those on the top floor open onto good views of the city. Rooms are no style setters, but they are comfortable and have double glazing on the windows. Bathrooms are small but with up-to-date plumbing.

Dining/Diversions: Tea is served in the lounge. The Piano Bar is open nightly from 5pm to 2am; live piano music begins at 9pm and continues past midnight. The hotel's restaurant, the Classic-Restaurant, is excellent.

Amenities: Room service, laundry, dry cleaning, swimming pool, sauna.

✪ **Prem Hotel.** An der Alster 9, 20099 Hamburg. ☎ **040/24-17-26.** Fax 040/2-80-38-51. 53 units. MINIBAR TV TEL. 340DM–395DM ($193.80–$225.15) double; 580DM ($330.60) suite. AE, DC, MC, V. Free parking. Bus: 108.

This beautifully located mansion-hotel is called the "white house on the Alster." It attracts a well-heeled clientele. The glistening facade overlooks the lake, and the rear faces a quiet garden with umbrella-covered tables. The reception salons show off a personalized collection of French antiques and reproductions. Most of the rooms are furnished with white-and-gold Louis XV-style pieces. The garden-facing accommodations are much quieter than the front rooms on the Alster. Bedrooms are well designed and cared for with luxury mattresses. Some 50% of the bathrooms are well equipped with big mirrors, marble baths, and hair dryers. The rest are a bit cramped with shower stalls and fewer amenities.

Dining: You can enjoy breakfast in the white-and-gold rococo dining room jutting out into the garden. La Mer, the hotel restaurant, is one of the finest in the city, famous for its imperial oysters and salmon roe. Service is formal, and the cuisine is both German and international.

Amenities: 24-hour room service, laundry, dry cleaning, sauna.

✪ **St. Raphael.** Adenauerallee 41, 20097 Hamburg. ☎ **800/528-1234** in the U.S. and Canada, or 040/24-82-00. Fax 040/24-82-03-33. E-mail: raphaelhotels@t-online.de. 130 units. MINIBAR TV TEL. 248DM–308DM ($141.35–$175.55) double; 294DM–444DM ($167.60–$253.10) suite. Rates include buffet breakfast. AE, DC, MC, V. Parking 10DM ($5.70). U-Bahn: Hauptbahnhof.

One of the gems of Hamburg, this Best Western hotel on the famous Adenauerallee is a rival of the Prem, without the Prem's stuffiness. The five-story building is constructed of white brick with soundproof windows. It's so special that it sometimes attracts the kind of clients who stay at the Vier Jahreszeiten or Kempinski. The best rooms are in the Raphael Royale wing, which has a private entrance in the rear. All rooms are beautifully appointed, with plush carpeting, state-of-the-art marble baths, and many extras such as hair dryers and safes.

Dining: A full-service restaurant offers everything from weekly specialties to weekly buffets. The Sunday champagne brunch is a popular affair.

Amenities: Room service, concierge, baby-sitting, dry cleaning, laundry. The hotel also has a rooftop fitness center, with a sauna, solarium, and Jacuzzi, plus a sweeping view of Hamburg.

Travel Charme Hotel Bellevue. An der Alster 14 (facing the Alster, a short ride from the Hauptbahnhof), 20099 Hamburg. ☎ **040/28-44-40.** Fax 040/28-44-42-22. www.top-hotels.de/travelcharme. 93 units. MINIBAR TV TEL. 290DM–330DM ($165.30–$188.10) double; 395DM ($225.15) suite. Rates include buffet breakfast. AE, DC, MC, V. Parking 15DM ($8.55). Bus: 108.

Many theatrical celebrities make this their Hamburg choice. Some of the larger rooms contain traditional furnishings, but the new singles are modern, often Scandinavian style. Many units contain cherry-wood and rattan pieces; all have trouser presses and hair dryers. The front windows open onto the lake, but the back rooms are quieter.

Dining/Diversions: The ground-floor Alster Room serves as a breakfast room. Guests can enjoy international cuisine as well as regional specialties in the restaurant, Alster Charme, which is open for lunch. Another restaurant, Schifferstube, serves dinner. Live piano music is played several nights a week in the bar, after 6pm.

MODERATE

Steens Hotel. Holzdamm 43 (near the Alster), 20099 Hamburg. ☎ **040/24-46-42.** Fax 040/2-80-35-93. 11 units, 2 without bathroom. TV TEL. 135DM–160DM ($76.95–$91.20) double. Rates include continental breakfast. AE, MC, V. U-Bahn: Hauptbahnhof.

Despite its classy location, a short walk from the much more expensive Atlantic Hotel, this century-old house charges reasonable rates. Rooms are carefully maintained but short on style. Each has a private shower; all but two have a private toilet. In 1998 all the bedrooms were renovated and the mattresses upgraded, along with rejuvenated bathrooms to which hair dryers were added. Breakfast is the only meal served.

Wedina. Gurlittstrasse 23 (near the lake, a 5-min. walk from the Hauptbahnhof), 20099 Hamburg. ☎ **040/24-30-11.** Fax 040/2-80-38-94. E-mail: wedina@aol.com. 42 units. TV TEL. 165DM–240DM ($94.05–$136.80) double. Rates include buffet breakfast. AE, DC, MC, V. Parking 15DM ($8.55). Bus: 108.

This recently remodeled 18th-century town house is a quiet retreat. Most of the rooms open onto a small, informal Tuscan-style garden. The rooms are tastefully styled and range in size from small to medium, each with a good bed and a tidy bathroom equipped with a hair dryer. The hotel is owned and run by an English-speaking family.

INEXPENSIVE

Hotel Lilienhof. Ernst-Merck-Strasse 4, 20099 Hamburg. ☎ **040/24-10-87.** Fax 040/2-80-18-15. 24 units, none with private bathroom. TV TEL. 118DM ($67.25) double without shower, 138DM ($78.65) double with shower. Rates include buffet breakfast. AE, DC, MC, V. U-Bahn: Hauptbahnhof.

This unpretentious five-story hotel is a good place to stay for convenience and the economy, but forget grand style. The simple, clean, and rather small rooms have double-insulated windows to keep out some noise from the heavy traffic on the street. The quieter rooms overlook the back of the hotel. None of the rooms contain a toilet, but some have private showers, and adequate toilet facilities are scattered throughout the hallways.

IN BINNENALSTER & NEUSTADT
VERY EXPENSIVE

✪ **Vier Jahreszeiten.** Neuer Jungfernstieg 9–14 (on the Binnenalster), 20354 Hamburg. ☎ **800/223-6800** in the U.S. and Canada, or 040/3-49-40. Fax 040/3-49-46-02. E-mail: vier-jahreszeiten@hvj.de. 181 units. MINIBAR TV TEL. 495DM–625DM ($282.15–$356.25) double; from 990DM ($564.30) suite. AE, DC, MC, V. Parking 30DM ($17.10). U-Bahn: Hauptbahnhof.

This warm, mellow hotel is the finest in Germany and one of the best in the world. It was founded in 1897 by Friedrich Haerlin (today it's run by a Japanese company). Its position is ideal, right on the Binnenalster. Built in the baronial style, it evokes the grand Edwardian hotels. Antiques are used profusely throughout. Despite the large size of the hotel, personal service is a hallmark.

Although no two rooms are alike, they are all beautiful, with period furnishings, Oriental rugs, lavish fabrics, and all the modern amenities, including bedside controls and double glazing on the windows. This is a hotel for connoisseurs.

Dining/Diversions: The hotel's dining room, Haerlin, decked out with old tapestries, gold-framed mirrors, and four Dionysian porcelain cherubs, serves excellent international cuisine. There's also the informal Grill Room, where meats are roasted on spits along one wall. The tearoom, the two-level Condi (Hamburg's answer to Demel's of Vienna), is a favorite rendezvous point. There's also a cocktail bar, a wine shop, and a confectioner's shop selling the chef's own pastry.

Amenities: 24-hour room service, laundry, dry cleaning; horseback riding and golf can be arranged.

EXPENSIVE

Hamburg Marriott. ABC Strasse 52, 20354 Hamburg. ☎ **800/228-9290** in the U.S., or 040/35-05-0. Fax 040/35-05-17-77. www.marriott.com. 277 units. A/C MINIBAR TV TEL. 305DM–380DM ($173.85–$216.60) double; 440DM ($250.80) studio; 495DM ($282.15) suite. AE, DC, MC, V. Parking 25DM ($14.25). U-Bahn: Gänsemarkt.

This traditionally styled hotel is one of the finest in Hamburg. It was built on the site of the old Gänsemarkt, where geese were sold in the Middle Ages. The hotel is also near the Hanse Viertel shopping complex. The fashionable surrounding area is filled with boutiques, wine bars, shops, and restaurants. Rooms, which range in size from small to medium, have bathrooms with marble floors and sinks topped with a slab of polished granite. The lower price is for the standard rooms; the higher rates are charged for studios. Lavish suites are also available. One hundred rooms are reserved for nonsmokers.

Dining/Diversions: Live music begins at 6pm in the lobby-level piano bar. The casual and moderately priced restaurant, American Place, features California wine and cuisine, plus food from New Orleans and Boston. All popular American holidays and events are celebrated here. Service is daily from noon to 3pm and 5:30pm to midnight. A special theater menu is also available.

Amenities: Full concierge services, including baby-sitting and car rental; 24-hour room service; same-day laundry and dry cleaning (Monday to Friday). This is the only downtown hotel with a pool, sauna, whirlpool, and fitness center; it also has the Dominique Beauty Farm, ice machines on all floors, and fax and computer connections in each room.

Hamburg Renaissance Hotel. Grosse Bleichen, Hanse-Viertel, 20354 Hamburg. ☎ **800/228-9290** in the U.S. and Canada, or 040/34-91-80. Fax 040/34-91-84-31. 205 units. A/C MINIBAR TV TEL. 350DM–385DM ($199.50–$219.45) double; from 580DM ($330.60) suite. AE, DC, MC, V. Parking 25DM ($14.25). U-Bahn: Jungfernstieg.

A 19th-century building with 20th-century comfort, the nine-story Renaissance recently affiliated itself with Marriott but has kept its original name. From the sunken, antique-furnished lobby to the carpeted bar area, you'll be feted by the staff and serenaded by a resident pianist. Rooms range from well-appointed doubles to sumptuously upholstered suites. Most of the accommodations are quite spacious, with well-cushioned chairs and sofas and paired queen-sized beds fitted with luxury mattresses, plus large bathrooms with robes, plush towels, makeup mirrors, phones, and hair dryers. The hotel was constructed behind the facade of a historic building, and the entire complex was designed with connections to the Hanse Viertel Galerie Passage, Europe's longest shopping arcade.

Dining/Diversions: After drinks in the lounge bar, you can dine at the Brasserie Noblesse, which offers distinguished French and German cuisine.

Amenities: Room service, laundry, dry cleaning, massage, fitness area.

Radisson SAS Hotel Hamburg. Marseillerstrasse 2 (in the Planten un Blomen Park), 20355 Hamburg. ☎ **040/3-50-20.** Fax 040/35-02-35-30. www.radisson.com. 560 units. A/C MINIBAR TV TEL. 270DM–390DM ($153.90–$222.30) double; from 550DM ($313.50) suite. Business class 340DM–480DM ($193.80–$273.60) double. AE, DC, MC, V. Parking 19DM ($10.85). Bus: 102.

This 32-story high-rise hotel is of real architectural interest. It looks like a collection of narrow black lines banded together vertically. Although it's very professionally run and has many winning features, we'd rank it under the Hamburg Renaissance or the Marriott. The medium-sized rooms are beautifully appointed, many with paneled walls; all contain individually controlled air-conditioning, radios, trouser presses, and hair dryers. One floor is reserved for nonsmokers.

Dining/Diversions: Guests can order South Pacific-style dinners at Trader Vic's, or sample north German and Scandinavian cuisine in the rustic Vier-Landerstuben. For coffee, pastries, or drinks, the Park Bistro and Lobby Lounge are good choices; later, head for the 26th floor to enjoy a view over Hamburg and the harbor in the nightclub/bar, Top of Town.

Amenities: 24-hour room service, express laundry, baby-sitting; heated pool, sauna, solarium, fitness studio.

MODERATE

✪ **Hafen Hamburg.** Seewartenstrasse 9, 20459 Hamburg. ☎ **040/31-11-30.** Fax 040/31-11-3-755. 239 units. TV TEL. 195DM–205DM ($111.15–$116.85) double. Rates include buffet breakfast. AE, DC, MC, V. Parking 12DM ($6.85). U-Bahn: Landungsbrücke.

This Hamburg landmark, constructed in the Wilhelmian style, offers panoramic views of the river and the harbor traffic. This hotel attracts the commercial traveler who's not on an expense account. The functionally furnished rooms are unusually spacious. If they're within your budget, book the more expensive harbor-view rooms. Each accommodation comes with a comfortable bed fitted with a fine mattress, plus a well-equipped private bathroom with plush towels and a hair dryer.

IN HARVESTEHUDE

Garden Hotels Hamburg. Magdalenenstrasse 60 (a mile from Hamburg's center), 20148 Hamburg. ☎ **040/41-40-40.** Fax 040/4-14-04-20. 60 units. MINIBAR TV TEL. 300DM–400DM ($171–$228) double; from 550DM ($313.50) suite. AE, DC, MC, V. Parking 15DM ($8.55). U-Bahn: Hallerstrasse.

This hotel dates from 1791, and over the years it has entertained many luminaries, including King Christian VIII of Denmark in 1824. The location, however, isn't for everyone. It stands in the Hamburg-Harvestehude district on the western sector of the Outer Alster Lake, about a mile from the historic heart of town and some 6 miles from the airport. It attracts many visitors from the publishing industry. Modern art and well-chosen antiques add to the sophisticated comfort of the rooms. Most rooms are generously sized, and the luxurious bathrooms have plush towels and hair dryers.

Dining/Diversions: The hotel, which serves breakfast only, has a bar adjoining the winter garden.

Amenities: 24-hour room service, laundry, dry cleaning, terrace garden, swimming pool, fitness area.

✪ **Hotel Abtei.** Abteistrasse 14 (3 miles north of Hamburg's center), Harvestehude, 20149 Hamburg. ☎ **040/44-29-05.** Fax 040/44-98-20. 11 units. MINIBAR TV TEL. 350DM–500DM ($199.50–$285) double. AE, DC, MC, V. U-Bahn: Klosterstern.

This suburban hotel is small, choice, and engaging, with a discreet and well-trained staff. It occupies a 19th-century villa that was once an opulent private residence. The high-ceilinged bedrooms retain many aspects of a private home, including antique furniture and, in many cases, the building's original elaborate plasterwork and parquet floors. Each room contains its own stereo system. Buildings are configured into various shapes and sizes, but each offers traditional comfort evocative of a London town-house hotel. Every other year mattresses are renewed, and the beds are sumptuous with their elegant fabrics, crisp white linen, feather pillows, and duvets. Marble bathrooms are complete with hair dryers, robes, and lots of marble. The hotel has a fine restaurant.

IN WINTERHUDE

✪ **Hanseatic Hotel.** Sierichstrasse 150, 22299 Hamburg-Winterhude. ☎ **040/48-57-72.** Fax 040/48-57-73. 12 units. TV TEL. 300DM–400DM ($171–$228) double. AE, MC, V. Take the Alster ferry or U-Bahn 3 to Hudt Wackerstrasse.

This hotel, on the banks of the Alster River, close to the Winterhude Market, is the smallest and most delightful place to stay in Hamburg. In summer, a little flower garden blooms in the front. The town house, painted a soothing white, was built around 1930. The interior evokes a gentlemen's club in England, complete with prints of horses, chintz upholstery, and leather-bound books. Bedrooms, ranging in size from small to medium, are furnished in a one-of-a-kind manner, containing many antiques. Breakfast is the only meal served, but there's a bistro next door and other restaurants in the vicinity. Guests meet and mingle as they mix their own drinks at the complimentary bar.

IN NIENSTEDTEN

✪ **Louis C. Jacob.** Elbchaussee 401, 22609 Hamburg. ☎ **040/82-25-50.** Fax 040/82255444. www.hotel-jacob.de. E-mail: jacob_relaischateau.fr. 86 units. A/C MINIBAR TV TEL. 350DM–550DM ($199.50–$313.50) double, from 650DM ($370.50) suite. AE, DC, MC, V. Free parking. Lies 8 miles west via Elbchaussee.

Lying outside the city center along the Elbe, this tranquil deluxe hotel compares to the Vier Jahreszeiten and Kempinski Hotel Atlantic Hamburg. In summer you can sit out under linden trees 2 centuries old and enjoy views of the river traffic. Built in 1791 as a guest house, the hotel has been brought up to stunning modernity after a major overhaul. The owners believe in spectacular luxury and coddling their guests. The hotel owns one of the biggest private art collections in the north of Germany. The medium-sized to spacious guest rooms are elegantly appointed and decorated, with walk-in closets, private safes, data ports, luxury mattresses, and state-of-the-art bathrooms in marble and granite, each with plush towels, toiletries, and a hair dryer.

Dining/Diversions: Even if you don't stay here, consider driving out for the modern French cuisine and a wine list finer than that of any other establishment in Hamburg (according to the *Wine Spectator).* The service is some of the best in the city, and from the truffled scallops to the chocolate mousse cake, the food is impeccable.

Amenities: Room service, laundry/dry cleaning, concierge.

3 Dining

Hamburg life is tied to the sea, and that includes the cuisine: lobster from Helgoland; shrimp from Büsum; turbot, plaice, and sole from the North Sea; and huge quantities of fresh oysters. Of course, there's also the traditional meat dish, hamburger steak, called *Stubenküchen,* and the favorite sailor's dish, *Labskaus,* made with beer, onions, cured meat, potatoes, herring, and pickle. The *Aalsuppe* (eel soup) is the best known of all Hamburg's typical dishes.

For a map of restaurants in Hamburg, see page 562.

NEAR THE HAUPTBAHNHOF

Peter Lembcke. Holzdamm 49. ☎ **040/24-32-90.** Reservations required. Main courses 26DM–72DM ($14.80–$41.05). AE, DC, MC, V. Mon–Fri noon–10:30pm, Sat 6–11pm. U-Bahn: Hauptbahnhof. NORTH GERMAN.

Peter Lembcke is one of Hamburg's leading restaurants, a local favorite since 1910. The good-hearted, helter-skelter service adds to the charm, but the food is the real attraction here. Lembcke specializes in the cuisine of northern Germany, including the most local dish of all, *Labskaus,* or sailor's hash. A house specialty that attracts a loyal following is the eel soup, with dill and fruit swimming in the broth (definitely an acquired taste). Besides the best Kalbs fillet (veal), the restaurant serves excellent steaks. Lembcke's is invariably crowded, so phone ahead.

ⓘ Family-Friendly Restaurants

Fernsehturm Hamburg Restaurant (*see p. 577*)   It's family fun, as diners enjoy good food in a 900-foot revolving television tower.

Schulauer Fährhaus (*see p. 582*)   This establishment stands at Wedel, the "welcome point" for ships arriving in the Hamburg harbor. Children will delight in watching the ships go by as they eat. Afterward, don't miss the downstairs museum of 200 little boats preserved in bottles.

IN BINNENALSTER & NEUSTADT
VERY EXPENSIVE

✪ **Cölln's Austernstuben.** Brodschrangen 1–5. ☎ **040/32-60-59.** Reservations recommended. Main courses 36.80DM–59DM ($21–$33.65); fixed-price menus 88DM–146DM ($50.15–$83.20). AE, DC, MC. Mon–Fri noon–3pm and 6–10pm, Sat 6–10pm. U-Bahn: Rathausmarkt. NORTH GERMAN/CONTINENTAL.

The food here is the best in central Hamburg. This "oyster-eating house" originally opened in 1761 as a waterfront fish house. It now occupies much larger quarters, filling seven dining rooms, and is one of the most stylish and best-liked restaurants in town. It serves oysters, of course, and many other dishes as well—try pheasant in puff pastry with white beans; minestrone studded with lobster meat and served with lobster-stuffed ravioli; schnitzels of salmon in balsamic-vinegar linden-flower sauce; or the breast of goose with wild mushrooms and pepper-flavored Bordeaux sauce.

EXPENSIVE

Fischküche. Kajen 12 (a 1-min. walk from the Elbe). ☎ **040/36-56-31.** Reservations recommended. Main courses 29.50DM–40DM ($16.80–$22.80). AE, DC, MC, V. Mon–Fri noon–3pm and 6–11pm. U-Bahn: Rödingsmarkt. SEAFOOD.

Breezy and unpretentious, this restaurant prides itself on specializing exclusively in fish. It's in a modern building, with a dining room brightly outfitted in bold colors and extravagant chandeliers. Menu items include a changing array of seafood, brought in fresh daily and priced with an eye for good value. Choices vary with the day's catch, but might include several different preparations of clear or creamy fish soup, marinated crabmeat salad, flounder with spaghetti and lemon-butter sauce, codfish with potatoes and onion, and fillet of monkfish in a mustard-herb sauce. It's hardly haute cuisine, but locals flock here for the robust specialties and no-nonsense service.

Il Ristorante. Grosse Bleichen 16. ☎ **040/34-33-35.** Reservations required. Main courses 29.50DM–44.50DM ($16.80–$25.35); fixed-price menu 59DM ($33.65) for 3 courses, 85DM ($48.45) for 5 courses. AE, DC, MC. Daily noon–11pm. U-Bahn: Jungfernstieg. ITALIAN/INTERNATIONAL.

The most fashionable Italian restaurant in Hamburg is located in the heart of town in a very modern building. It's set at the top of a glass-enclosed stairwell, amid seasonal flowering shrubs. The atmosphere is luxurious and formal; and only the freshest ingredients find their way into the kitchen. Even such simple dishes as carrot-and-celery soup have great flavor. After a taste of some well-chosen Italian wine, consider the perfectly prepared crayfish in a saffron sauce, or the marinated salmon with green asparagus mousse. Mellow balsamic vinegar and aromatic fresh herbs lend zest and flavor to many dishes. Impeccably trained waiters provide smooth service even if you aren't a familiar face.

MODERATE

⭐ **Eisenstein.** Friedensallee 9. ☎ **040/3904-606.** Reservations recommended. Main courses 27DM–37DM ($15.40–$21.10). Set-price lunch 23DM ($13.10); set-price dinners 55DM–60DM ($31.35–$34.20). No credit cards. Daily 11am–3pm and 6pm–midnight. U-3 to Altona Bahnhof. INTERNATIONAL.

The food items available here are representative of the wide range of cultures that Hamburgers have been exposed to, thanks to the city's role as a great port. The menu lists specialties from Thailand, Japan (including sushi and sashimi), southern France, and Italy, as well as traditional and very fresh versions of the North German cuisine that Hamburg excels in, particularly fresh Atlantic Sea fish prepared virtually any way you want. The setting is a solid-looking, much-restored factory and former warehouse whose soaring, russet-colored brick walls envelop diners in a cozy womb against the sometimes gray weather outside. The clientele is artsy, hip, and stylish; the staff is cooperative, and the food is surprisingly flavorful, considering its diversity.

Ratsweinkeller Hamburg. Grosse Johannisstrasse 2. ☎ **040/36-41-53.** Reservations required. Main courses 19.75DM–60DM ($11.25–$34.20); fixed-price menus 26.50DM–120DM ($15.10–$68.40). AE, DC, MC, V. Mon–Sat 11am–10:30pm, Sun 11am–4pm. Closed holidays. U-Bahn: Rathausmarkt. HAMBURG/INTERNATIONAL.

The city takes pride in the distinguished Ratsweinkeller Hamburg, in business since 1896. The overall theme is suggested at the entrance, where you'll find a stone statue of Bacchus. The main dining hall has high vaulted ceilings, wood-paneled columns, and large stained-glass windows. The 26.50DM ($15.10) menu is one of the best values in town, and even more wallet-friendly are the large portions, which make appetizers unnecessary. One excellent dish is the halibut steak in curry sauce. The fresh sole *bonne femme* is heavenly and served in large portions; or try the Hamburg crab soup, the best in the city. Listen for the great-grandfather clock to chime the quarter hour, resounding throughout the chambers.

INEXPENSIVE

Alten Rathaus. Börsenbrücke 10 (in the Altstadt). ☎ **040/3751-89-07.** Reservations recommended. Main courses 28DM–32DM ($15.95–$18.25). AE, MC, V. Mon–Sat 11:30am–11pm. U-Bahn: Rathausmarkt. NORTH GERMAN.

This restaurant occupies a carefully preserved mid-19th-century building set close to the mouth of the Elbe, in the most historic part of the Altstadt. The upper floors are a preferred meeting place for civic associations, and a faithful clientele has been coming here for years. Surprisingly for Hamburg, no fish is served. Instead, the chefs prepare some of the town's best grilled meats, along with Argentine beef dishes and some savory chicken or turkey offerings. Scampi salad is a lunch favorite. Finish with the Tyrolean apple pie or vanilla ice cream in a hot strawberry sauce.

Nikolaikeller. Cremon 36. ☎ **040/36-61-13.** Reservations required. Main courses 22DM–34.50DM ($12.55–$19.65). V. Mon–Sat noon–10pm. Bus: 37. HAMBURG.

This is the type of food that brings Hamburg sailors in out of the fog to warm up. You can see the sprawling maritime facilities of Hamburg from the windows of this restaurant, which is often filled with a crowd of local businesspeople and workers. The Hamburg cuisine here includes more than two dozen varieties of herring. You can also order goulash soup Altona-style; bacon pancakes topped with cranberries; fresh sole; or salmon. Ample quantities of local beer are provided in oversize mugs.

IN EIMSBÜTTEL

At Nati. Rutschbahn 11. ☎ **040/410-38-10.** Reservations not required. Main courses 24DM–40DM ($13.70–$22.80). AE, DC, MC, V. Daily 11am–midnight. Metro: Hauptbahnhof. TURKISH.

One of the best choices for a taste of authentic Turkish cuisine is this kebab restaurant, which has been offering delicious and very inexpensive meals from the central region of Anatolia for the last 22 years. The owner and chef, Ali Reza kaya, has maintained a traditional kebab house atmosphere and the restaurant is still very popular. The extensive menu includes various kebabs, lamb fillet with spinach, and scampi with garlic. On the desserts side the baklava and halva are recommended, as are the traditional sweet lemon teas and, of course, the thick, strong Turkish coffee you can stand your spoon up in.

Fernsehturm Hamburg Restaurant. In the television tower in Rotherbaum, Lagerstrasse 2–8. ☎ **040/43-80-24.** Reservations recommended. Main courses 24DM–48DM ($13.70– $27.35). DC, V. Daily noon–2:30pm and 5–11pm. S-Bahn: Sternschanze. U-Bahn: Messehallen. CONTINENTAL.

Fernsehturm, on the 14th floor of Hamburg's revolving 900-foot television tower, offers fine views and a cuisine that's just as good. Inside the tower are six sections, with separate decors inspired by New York, London, Paris, Copenhagen, Rome, and Hamburg. One of Hamburg's best-known chefs is in charge, and popular dishes include Argentine fillet steak and turbot in butter-and-champagne sauce. During the afternoon you can have coffee and cake for 12DM ($6.85). Visitors must purchase a 6.50DM ($3.70) ticket to ascend the tower.

IN ALTONA

✪ **Fischereihafen Restaurant.** Grosse Elbstrasse 143 (a 10-min. taxi ride from the wharf area of Landungsbrücken). ☎ **040/38-18-16.** Reservations required. Main courses 28DM– 68DM ($15.95–$38.75); fixed-price 4-course menu 89DM ($50.75); "Hamburg menu" 65DM ($37.05). AE, DC, MC, V. Sun–Thurs 11:30am–10:30pm, Fri–Sat 11:30am–10pm. S-Bahn: Königstrasse. SEAFOOD.

Fischereihafen, established some 4 decades ago, is the best seafood restaurant in town, if you prefer true local fare rather than the internationally oriented cuisine of the pricey Cölln's Austernstuben. Every day, the staff buys only the freshest fish and shellfish at the Hamburg auction hall. The menu changes daily, depending on what seafood is available. The second floor is said to be full of "fish and VIPs"—the latter have included the likes of Chancellor Helmut Kohl and Tina Turner. Appetizers include fillet of sole and lobster or a plate of fresh oysters, and the house special is turbot with salmon mousse dotted with truffles. Picture windows open onto a view of the Elbe.

✪ **Landhaus Scherrer.** Elbchaussee 130. ☎ **040/8-80-13-25.** Reservations required. Main courses 46DM–68DM ($26.20–$38.75); fixed-price menus 189DM ($107.75) and 198DM ($112.85). AE, DC, MC, V. Mon–Sat noon–2:30pm and 6:30–10:30pm. Bus 135. CONTINENTAL.

Once a brewery, the Landhaus is now a citadel of gastronomy on the Elbe River at Altona. It has gained a reputation for correct service and imaginatively prepared cuisine. The chef's superbly precise, inventive cookery combines the flavors of the home region of northern Germany with those of lands farther afield. The result is an often stunning culinary achievement. Specialties are fresh seafood, as well as excellent meat. An unusual variation might be roast goose with rhubarb in cassis sauce. Dessert might be praline cream or one of 30 types of pastry loading down the sweets trolley. Because of its location in a country house surrounded by trees, this place is also popular with locals for wedding receptions.

✪ **Le Canard.** Elbchaussee 139, Ottensen (southwest of Hamburg's center). ☎ **040/ 8-80-50-57.** Reservations required. Main courses 52DM–79DM ($29.65–$45.05); fixed-price menus 149DM–225DM ($84.95–$128.25). AE, DC, MC, V. Mon–Sat noon–2:30pm and 7–10:30pm. Bus 115. CONTINENTAL.

Le Canard is one of the best restaurants in Germany. Virtually every restaurant critic in the country has lauded the unusual *cuisine moderne* of its imaginative owner/chef, Josef Viehhauser. The unpretentious decor is made more alluring by the soft lighting. The lobster soup is the city's finest, and even the iced soup of potatoes—a kind of vichyssoise—comes graced with caviar. The crisp fried duck with a Bordeaux sauce is the best we've had in Hamburg, but we were especially drawn to an unusual concoction as an appetizer—a terrine of Roquefort with gazpacho jelly and olive bread. Pigeon with chanterelles is a delectable choice, or you can have your chanterelles with a perfectly sautéed turbot. The place isn't so trendy that they're afraid to serve an old-fashioned *Salzburger Nockerl* for dessert.

IN ST. PAULI

Cuneo. Davidstrasse 11. ☎ **040/31-25-80.** Reservations required. Main courses 18DM–39DM ($10.25–$22.25). No credit cards. Mon–Sat 6:30pm–1:30am. Closed 2 weeks in July. U-Bahn: U-3 to St. Pauli. ITALIAN.

Good Italian food at reasonable prices is what you'll find here. Behind an unprepossessing facade, unchanged since 1905, the place opens onto crowded rooms that look like an art director's concept of a Greenwich Village restaurant in the 1930s. Grilled fish is one of the best items on the menu, but you can also order pizza, carpaccio, spaghetti with pesto, gnocchi with Gorgonzola, and Venetian-style liver.

✪ **Old Commercial Room.** Englische Planke 10 (at the foot of St. Michaelis). ☎ **040/36-63-19.** Reservations required. Main courses 18.50DM–60DM ($10.55–$34.20); fixed-price menus 39DM–85DM ($22.25–$48.45). AE, DC, MC, V. Daily noon–midnight. Closed Dec 24. U-Bahn: St. Pauli. NORTH GERMAN.

The Old Commercial Room, founded in 1643, is so tied into Hamburg maritime life that many residents consider it the premier sailors' stopover. It's the best place in town for *Labskaus* (sailor's hash), prepared with devotion by the chef; if you order it, you're given a numbered certificate proclaiming you a genuine Labskaus-eater. You can also order many traditional north German dishes. The restaurant's name, along with that of the street, speaks of the historic mercantile links between Hamburg and England.

Restaurant Nil. Neuer Pferdemarkt 5. ☎ **040/4397-823.** Reservations recommended. Main courses 25DM–38DM ($14.25–$21.65). Set menus 58DM–81DM ($33.05–$46.15). AE, DC, MC, V. Mon–Fri noon–2:30pm, Sun–Thurs 6–11pm, and Fri–Sat 6pm to midnight. U-3 to Feldstrasse. INTERNATIONAL.

Even though the name of this restaurant refers to Egypt's River Nile, don't imagine a decor influenced either by the desert or the Arab world. What you get is upscale French bistro, replete with mirrors, oiled mahogany, and polished brass. The name refers to the bounty provided by the Nile, as interpreted by North German tastes, and the cooking is superb. Clients derive from the worlds of publishing and the arts, with lots of cultural movers and shakers, many of whom have adopted this place as their preferred culinary hangout. Dishes include a carpaccio of beef with a black olive marinade and shiitake mushrooms; saltimbocca of calves' liver prepared with artichoke hearts; braised leg of turkey stuffed with sautéed leeks and served with noodles in an orange-flavored whisky sauce; and beef bourguignonne with braised shallots, mushrooms, and mashed potatoes.

IN UHLENHORST

Mühlenkamper Fährhaus. Hans-Henny-Jahnn-Weg 1 (in the Hamburg-Uhlenhorst district, about a mile east of the railway station). ☎ **040/2-20-69-34.** Reservations required. Main courses 26DM–70DM ($14.80–$39.90); fixed-price lunch 39DM ($22.25). AE, DC, MC, V. Mon–Fri noon–midnight, Sat 6pm–midnight. Bus: 106 or 108. CONTINENTAL/INTERNATIONAL.

This family-owned spot near the Alster Fleet has been a Hamburg landmark for more than 50 years. The restaurant was established in 1916 by the great-grandparents of the present owner. It's a favorite rendezvous of celebrities and the city's most discerning diners. The menu is a virtual encyclopedia of German, French, and international food. The cuisine, reflecting a light touch, but based on north German ingredients, is charming and old-fashioned. The menu changes with the seasons and the availability of ingredients, but might include broiled brisket of beef, fillet of eel in dill-flavored gelatin, lentil soup studded with sausages and boiled bacon, sole meunière, fried turbot with bacon and shrimp, and warm potato salad (one of the house specialties). Three hundred varieties of wine are available. In warm weather, try for a seat on the terrace.

4 Attractions

Before you tour the city, you can get a good overall view of Hamburg from the tower of the finest baroque church in northern Germany, ✪ **Hauptkirche St. Michaelis,** Krayenkamp 4C, Michaeliskirchplatz (☎ **040/3767-8100**). Take the elevator or climb the 449 steps to enjoy the sweeping view from the top of the hammered-copper tower. The crypt is one of the largest in Europe, and contains the tombs of such famous citizens as the composer, Carl Philipp Emanuel Bach, and the church's builder, Ernst Georg Sonnin. There's also an audiovisual show that tells the history of the city. From April to September, hours are daily from 9am to 6pm; from October to March, daily 10am to 5pm. Entrance to the church is free, but to use the stairs or elevator costs 4.50DM ($2.55). A combined ticket for the tower, show, and crypt costs 9DM ($5.15). U-Bahn: Rüdingsmarkt or St. Pauli.

The **Altstadt** actually has little left of the old architecture, but there are a few sights among the canals (fleets) that run through this section from the Alster to the Elbe. The largest of the old buildings is the **Rathaus,** Rathausplatz (☎ **040/36-81-24-70**), which is modern compared with many of Germany's town halls. This Renaissance-style structure was built in the late 19th century on a foundation of 3,780 pinewood piles. It has a sumptuous 647-room interior and can be visited on guided tours costing 3DM ($1.70). Tours in English are given Monday to Thursday, hourly from 10:15am to 3:15pm; Friday to Sunday from 10:15am to 1:15pm; no tours during official functions. The Rathaus's 160-foot clock tower overlooks Rathausmarkt and the **Alster Fleet,** the city's largest canal. A visit to the Rathaus can be combined with a stop at the 16th-century **Hamburg Stock Exchange** on Adolphsplatz 1 (☎ **040/3-61-30-20**), which is back-to-back with the Rathaus. Free guided tours are offered Tuesday and Thursday at 11am and noon. U-Bahn: Rathausmarkt.

A few blocks away is **St. Petri Kirche,** Mönckebergstrasse (☎ **040/32-57-400**), built in the 12th century and renovated in 1842. The lion-head knocker on the main door is the oldest piece of art in Hamburg, dating from 1342. The church is open Monday to Friday 10am to 6pm, Saturday 9am to 5pm, and Sunday 9am to noon and 1 to 5pm. U-Bahn: Rathausmarkt.

The nearby 14th-century Gothic church of **St. Jacobi,** Jakobikirchhof 22, entrance on Steinstrasse (☎ **040/32-77-44**), was damaged in World War II but has been restored. It contains several medieval altars, pictures, and sculptures, as well as one of the largest baroque organs in the world (Arp-Schnitger, 1693). The church is open Monday to Saturday 10am to 5pm, Sunday 10am to noon. Guided tours in English can be arranged. U-Bahn: Mönckebergstrasse.

Hamburg's tallest structure is the 900-foot **Heinrich Hertz-Turm** (the Television Tower), Lagerstrasse 2–8 (☎ **040/43-80-24**). Named after Heinrich Hertz, the Hamburg-born physicist whose work was instrumental in the harnessing of electricity, the tower was inaugurated in 1968 as an answer to a similar tower erected by the East Germans in East Berlin. Today, the structure still appeals, partly as a kitschy reminder of the Cold War and the Age of Sputnik, and partly for its panoramic view over Hamburg. You'll pay a one-time charge of 6.50DM ($3.70) for the elevator ride to the top. There, you'll find a self-service cafeteria and observation platform, open daily from 10am to 6pm, and a more formal restaurant that serves meals from 11am to 11pm. If you want a high-altitude tea, the site features two separate seatings of 1 hour each, at 3:30pm and 4:30pm. You'll get unlimited access to tea, coffee, and a buffet table laden with pastries, all for a price of 12DM ($6.85) per person, plus the cost of the elevator ride described above. U-Bahn: Sternschanze.

THE TOP ATTRACTIONS

✪ **Carl Hagenbeck's Tierpark.** Hagenbeckallee at Steilingen (in the northwest suburbs). ☎ **040/5-40-00-10.** Admission 21DM ($11.95) adults, 16DM ($9.10) children. Free for children under 6. Spring–fall daily 9am–6pm; winter daily 9am–5pm. U-Bahn: The U2 goes almost directly to the Tierpark entrance, with its bronze elephants, in about 20 min.

The Tierpark's zoo, one of Europe's best, was founded in 1848 and today is home to about 2,100 animals. The unfenced paddocks and beautifully landscaped park are world famous. There are sea-lion and dolphin shows, rides on elephants and camels, a train ride through "fairyland," and a spacious children's playground. A restaurant serves well-prepared set menus priced at 18DM to 26DM ($10.25 to $14.80) from 11:30am to closing time.

✪ **Kunsthalle.** Glockengiesser Wall. ☎ **040/24-86-26-12.** Admission 14DM ($8) adults, 7DM ($4) children. Tues–Wed and Fri–Sun 10am–6pm, Thurs 10am–9pm. U-Bahn: Hauptbahnhof.

This is the leading art museum in northern Germany. Outstanding is the altarpiece painted for the St. Petri Church in 1379 by Master Bertram, Hamburg's first painter known by name and a leading master of 14th-century Germany. The 24 scenes on the wing panels are a free adaptation of the medieval text *The Mirror of Human Salvation* and depict the biblical story of humankind from creation to the flight into Egypt. Particularly interesting is the panel showing the creation of the animals, in which a primitive Christlike figure is surrounded by creatures, from the fish of the sea to the fowl of the air. As a sardonic note, or possibly prophetic, one little fox is already chewing the neck of the lamb next to it. The museum also contains works by Master Francke, a Dominican monk. The altar of St. Thomas of Canterbury (1424) is the first work to depict his murder in the cathedral.

The museum collection also includes modern art. From the romantic movement come the distinctive visions of Philipp Otto Runge and Carl David Friedrich. German impressionists Max Liebermann and Lovis Corinth are also here, and the 20th century is represented by Munch, Kirchner, Otto Dix, Beckmann, Kandinsky, and Paul Klee. In addition, the museum has an entire wing devoted to contemporary art, including pop art.

Museum of Hamburg History (Museum für Hamburgische Geschichte). Holsten Wall 24. ☎ **040/35-04-23-80.** Admission 8DM ($4.55) adults, 4DM ($2.30) children, 16DM ($9.10) family ticket. Tues–Sat 10am–5pm, Sun 10am–6pm. U-Bahn: St. Pauli. Bus: 112.

In this museum you'll find a detailed portrait of Hamburg from the 8th through the 20th centuries. Scale models represent the changing face of the port, and reconstructions of various rooms—from the hall of a 17th-century merchant's house to an air-raid shelter from World War II—illustrate the different eras in Hamburg's history.

Attractions in Central Hamburg

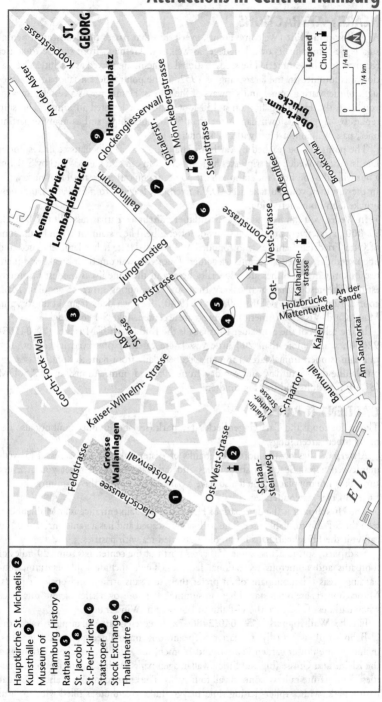

Legend
✝ Church

ST. GEORG
Koppelstrasse
An der Alster
Hachmannplatz
Glockengiesserwall
Spitalerstr.
Mönckebergstrasse
Steinstrasse
Oberbaum-brücke
Brooktorkai
Kennedybrücke
Lombardsbrücke
Ballindamm
Domstrasse
Ost-West-Strasse
Dovenfleet
Jungfernstieg
Poststrasse
Katharinen-strasse
An der Sande
Holzbrücke
Mattentwiete
ABC-Strasse
Gorch-Fock-Wall
Kaien
Kaiser-Wilhelm-Strasse
Schaartor
Martin-Luther-Strasse
Baumwall
Am Sandtorkai
Grosse Wallanlagen
Holstenwall
Feldstrasse
Gladschausse
Ost-West-Strasse
Schaar-steinweg
Elbe

Hauptkirche St. Michaelis ❷
Kunsthalle ❾
Museum of Hamburg History ❶
Rathaus ❺
St. Jacobi ❽
St.-Petri-Kirche ❻
Staatsoper ❹
Stock Exchange ❹
Thaliatheatre ❼

NEARBY ATTRACTIONS

At **Willkomm-Höft** (Welcome Point), every ship that passes this landscaped peninsula is welcomed in its own language, as well as in German, from sunrise to sunset
(8am to 8pm in summer). The ships' national anthems are played as a salute. The station was founded in the late spring of 1952, at the point where a sailor first catches
sight of the soaring cranes and slipways of the Port of Hamburg. As a vessel comes in,
you'll see the Hamburg flag on a 130-foot-high mast lowered in salute. The ship
replies by dipping its own flag. More than 50 arriving ships, and as many departing
ones, pass Willkomm-Höft within 24 hours.

The point can be reached by car from Hamburg via the Elbchaussee or Ostdorfer
Landstrasse to Wedel; the trip takes half an hour. You can also go to Wedel by S-Bahn;
a bus will take you from the station to the point, or you can enjoy the 15-minute walk.
In the summer, you can take a HADAG riverboat, leaving from St. Pauli Landungsbrücken, an hour's ferry ride.

In Wedel, you can have lunch at **Schulauer Fährhaus,** Parnastrasse 29 (☎ **04103/
92-000**), attractively situated on the wide lower Elbe. The restaurant is run by the sons
of Otto Friedrich Behnke, who founded Willkomm-Höft. It has large enclosed and
open verandas, as well a spacious tea garden. Guests are welcomed for breakfast, lunch,
tea, or dinner. Fish dishes are a specialty here, and the wine list is modest but interesting. The restaurant's own bakery turns out a tempting array of goodies. Main
courses run 16DM to 34DM ($9.10 to $19.40). It's open daily from 11am to 9pm.
MasterCard, Visa, and American Express are accepted. Take S-1 to Wedel.

In the cellars of the Schulauer Fährhaus is the **Buddelschiff-Museum** (☎ **04103/
92000**), where more than 200 little vessels are carefully preserved in bottles. The
museum is open from March through October, daily from 8am to 8pm; off-season,
on Wednesday, Saturday, and Sunday from 10am to 6pm. Admission is 2.50DM
($1.40) for adults and free for children.

GARDENS & PARKS

The major zoo is the **Carl Hagenbeck's Tierpark** (see above), but Hamburg also has
many other "green lungs."

Alsterpark lies on the northwest banks of Alster Lake, spread across 175 well-
manicured acres. Beautiful shade trees and cultivated gardens greet you at every
turn. From many places, you'll also have a panoramic view of the Hamburg skyline.
Enter on Harvestehuderweg.

The **Hirschpark** is the deer park of Hamburg. Its main entrance is at Mühlenberg;
take the S-Bahn to Blankensee. The park is landscaped and has a game enclosure. You
can visit the Hirschparkhaus for an old-fashioned tea with pastries.

Stadtpark, spread across some 450 acres north of the center, has some 20 miles of
footpaths and numerous recreational facilities. These include a planetarium, sunbathing areas (Hamburgians often prefer their sun sans attire), and open-air pools.
Music concerts are often staged here in summer. For your own safety, avoid this place
when darkness falls. Take the U-Bahn to Borgweg in Winterhude.

Finally, **Wallringpark** (☎ **040/24864723**), entered at Stefansplatz (also the
U-Bahn stop), is actually a quartet of beautifully maintained parks and gardens,
including the flower garden Planten und Blomen, the Alter Botanischer Garten, and
the Kleine and Grosse (big and little) Wallanlagen parks, with many recreational facilities. A miniature railway connects all four parks. The entire complex is also a popular
leisure park, with a roller-skating rink, playgrounds, greenhouses filled with tropical
plants, restaurants, and an ice-skating rink in winter. A particular highlight is the

illuminated-fountain concert, with classical or pop music, at the onset of darkness—10pm from June through August, earlier as the summer wanes. The largest Japanese garden in Europe is in Planten und Blomen. Here, rock gardens, flowering plants, miniature trees, and winding pathways attract garden enthusiasts.

ESPECIALLY FOR KIDS

Although Hamburg is known for its X-rated entertainment, the city is actually a good place for a family vacation.

Carl Hagenbeck's Tierpark (☎ 040/54000147) is one of Europe's great zoos (see above), and many other parks in Hamburg have amusements for children—the **Wallringpark** has a roller-skating rink. Boat tours of the Alster and more lengthy tours of the Port of Hamburg will also delight kids.

Language is often not a problem for children, so they may enjoy the children's theater, **Theater für Kinder,** Max-Brauer-Allee 76 (☎ 040/38-25-38). All tickets cost 25DM ($14.25). Shows are presented at 4:30pm on Thursday and Friday, at 2:30 and 5pm on Saturday, and at 2:30pm on Sunday.

BOAT TOURS

You can tour Hamburg by water, on both the Inner and the Outer Alster, experiencing all the charm of the Alsterpark, the villas, and the sailing boats set against the panorama of towers and church spires. **ATG-Alster-Touristik,** Am Anleger Jungfernstieg (☎ 040/ 3-57-42-40), has daily departures about every 30 minutes from 10am to 6pm, with trips lasting 50 minutes. Between November and March, tours are greatly reduced in their frequency, departing daily at 10:30am, noon, and 1:30pm. The ships leave from the Jungfernstieg quayside. Cassettes with a description of the tour in English, plus a brochure in four languages (including English), are available from the captain. Trips cost 15DM ($8.55) for adults and 7.50DM ($4.25) for children under 16.

HADAG Seetouristik und Fahrdienst AG, Bei den St. Pauli, Fischmarkt 28 (☎ 040/3-11-70-70), also conducts tours through the watery channels of Hamburg, in a comfortable heated pleasure boat. Tours are conducted in both German and English. Between April and October, they depart at hourly intervals every day between 9am and 6pm. Between November and March, they depart at hourly intervals every day between 10:30am and 3:30pm. Boats leave from the Landungsbrücken, Pier 3. The fare is 15DM ($8.55) for adults and 7.50DM ($4.25) for children under 14.

5 Sports & Outdoor Pursuits

BOATING   A paddle on the Aussenalster (Outer Alster Lake) can be one of the most relaxing and charming warm-weather activities in Hamburg. **H. Pieper** (☎ 040/ 24-75-78), **Alfred Seebeck** (☎ 040/24-76-52), and **Captain Prüsser** (☎ 040/ 31-31-40) rent rowboats, paddleboats, one-occupant sailing dinghies, and small catamarans; prices begin at 19DM to 30DM ($10.85 to $17.10) per hour. Each of these boat rental outfits is open only from April to late September, daily from 10am to 8pm.

GOLF   Hamburg has many golf clubs, including Golf Club auf der Wendlohe, Oldesloerstrasse 251 (☎ 040/5-50-50-14), and Hamburger Golf-Club Falkenstein, In de Bargen 59 (☎ 040/81-21-77). Greens fees range from 75DM to 85DM ($42.75 to $48.45) for 18 holes.

JOGGING   Our personal favorite route, either for long promenades or jogging, is the pedestrian walkway that circumnavigates the Alster lakes. The total perimeter of the larger of the two lakes measures about 4 miles; that of the more congested Binnenalster, about 1 mile. Equally suitable for jogging and pedestrian rambles are the public parks flanking the northwestern edge of the inner city.

SPECTATOR SPORTS   For information about soccer matches and other spectator events, contact the **Hamburger Sportbund (Hamburg Sports Association),** Schäfer-kampsallee 1, 20357 Hamburg (☎ 040/41-90-80).

SWIMMING   The rivers and lakes in Hamburg are being cleaned up, and there are many swimming pools. Two of the most popular are the **Alster-Schwimmhalle,** Ifflandstrasse 21 (☎ 040/22-30-12), and the **Holthusenbad,** Goernestrasse 21 (☎ 040/47-47-54). The latter has the advantage of artificial waves, thermal baths, and steam baths. Alster-Schwimmhalle charges 15DM ($8.55) for all day; Holthusenbad asks 12DM ($6.85) for all day. Newest and biggest of all is the huge **Midsommerland Freibad**, Gotthelfweg (☎ 040/76-31-827), in the suburb of Hamburg-Harburg. (Take S-Bahn S-3 to Harburg, or bus nos. 142 or 143 about 3 miles south of Hamburg's main railway station.) It's open daily from May to September from 8am to 10pm, charging 15DM ($8.55) for a full day's use.

TENNIS   Not surprisingly, the country that gave the world Steffi Graf and Boris Becker has no lack of tennis facilities. For names and addresses of tennis facilities, as well as information about upcoming tournaments, contact the Deutscher Tennis Bund, Hallerstrasse 89 (☎ 040/4-11-78-0).

6 Shopping

Hamburg is a city of merchants. In general, stores are open Monday to Friday from 9am to 6:30pm (some are open till 8pm on Thursday) and on Saturday from 9am to 2pm (until 4 or 6pm on langer Samstag, the first Saturday of the month). Unfortu-nately, the interesting shops are not concentrated in one location. Two of the oldest and most prestigious shopping streets, **Grosse Bleichen** and **Neuer Wall,** run parallel to the canals, connected transversely by Jungfernstieg and Ufer Strasse on the Bin-nenalster. Less expensive shopping streets are Spitalstrasse and Mönckebergstrasse.

Hamburg has nine major shopping malls. Even on the grayest, rainiest day in winter, you can shop in Hamburg in relative comfort. The glass-roofed **Hanse Viertel Galerie Passage** is some 220 yards long. There's a scattering of upscale cafes here, and even a stand-up seafood bar where glasses of beer or Sekt (sparkling wine) are served at tiny tables.

Mönckebergstrasse, a street connecting the main station with the Rathaus, is the city's traditional shopping district, with big department stores such as **Karstadt,** Mönckebergstrasse 16 (☎ 040/30940), part of a chain that carries many of the same brands and items as the other leading department stores, all competitively priced. The store is open Monday to Friday from 9am until 8pm and Saturday from 9am to 4pm. A thrifty alternative, **Kaufhof,** Mönckebergstrasse 3 (☎ 040/33-30-70), carries less-expensive items than the surrounding department stores and also offers better deals on merchandise markdowns. Bargain hunters combing the store are apt to find good values. Hours are Monday to Friday from 9:30am to 8pm and Saturday from 9:30am to 4pm. More fashionable and upscale than any of the three mentioned above is **Alsterhaus,** Jungfernstieg 22 (☎ 040/359011), which some New Yorkers have com-pared favorably to Bloomingdale's (same hours as Karstadt).

If you walk down Bergstrasse to the second part of the city center, you pass along **Jungfernstieg,** with tourist boats of the Alster Fleet on the right and a teeming shop-ping street on the other side. About a block farther along you come to the **Hamburger Hof,** the elegant entrance to one of the most attractive chains of shopping galleries in

Europe. At the end of Jungfernstieg, you can cross Gänsemarkt to **Gänsemarkt Passage,** another shopping gallery, with stores on three levels.

An upmarket and youthfully fashionable shopping area is in **Eppendorf,** Hamburg's oldest village, first mentioned in written history in 1140. Many prosperous and avant-garde Hamburgians live in the stately 19th-century homes and apartments. The shopping district, from Klosterstern to Eppendorfer Markt, has exclusive boutiques selling fashions from Paris, Milan, and New York; colorful shops with odds and ends for your home; antiques shops; and places where you can not only make purchases but watch goldsmiths, hatmakers, potters, and weavers at work.

The Hamburg **Fischmarkt** (fish market), between Hexenberg and Grosse Elbstrasse, is held every Sunday beginning at 5am in summer or 7am otherwise. Flowers, fruit, vegetables, plants, and pets are also for sale at this traditional market, in existence since 1703. It sometimes seems that the fish are just an afterthought nowadays. The nearby taverns are open to serve Fischmarkt visitors and vendors. Take the U-2 to **Landungsbrücken.**

Seifarth and Company, Robert-Koch Strasse 19 (☎ 040/5-24-00-27), is an upscale shop dealing in seafood, among other items. It smokes its own salmon, runs one of the leading mail-order caviar business in Europe, has one of the Continent's largest selections of tea, imports pâté and champagne from France, and stocks lobsters and Alaskan king crab. Everything can be shipped or ordered by mail.

One of the densest concentrations of antiques in Hamburg lies within the **Antik-Center,** Klosterwall 9–21 (☎ 040/32-62-85), a covered passageway loaded with more than 35 dealers and the accumulated loot of estate sales throughout England, Germany, and to a lesser degree, France. It's been compared to Portobello Road in London by aficionados of the trade who value the sheer volumes of objects that glint, sparkle, and evoke the values and aesthetics of other places and other times. U-Bahn: Steinstrasse or Hauptbahnhof.

Jil Sander, Milchstrasse 8 (☎ 040/55-30-21-73), is the best place to go for chic women's styling. Jil Sander burst upon Europe's fashion scene from her native city of Hamburg and has taken special efforts to make this three-floor store the flagship of her increasingly successful operation. Part of the success of her designs derives from their wearability—they are appropriate for the office, the boardroom, or cocktail hour. Another popular choice for women's fashions is **Escada Boutique,** Neuer Wall 32 (☎ 040/36-32-96), owned by the German design company of the same name. This store carries the firm's complete collection of women's sports, evening, business, and knit wear, plus accessories that include hats, bags, gloves, and shoes. A less-expensive division of Escada, **Laural Boutique,** Neuer Wall 41 (☎ 040/3-74-32-70), appeals to an active, younger clientele with alternative takes on casual day and elegant evening wear. If you think that hats have gone out of style, think again. **Monika Flac,** Bleichenhof Passage 35, off Grosse Bleichen (☎ 040/34-54-37), sells all kinds of hats, from serious garden party varieties festooned with cabbage roses to perky numbers that might have been favored by the late Jacqueline Onassis, as well as Homburgs and Stetson-style hats for men.

For high-fashion men's clothing, go to **Thomas-i-Punkt,** Gänsemarkt 24 (☎ 040/7-80-98-80), where you'll find suits, jackets, shirts, shoes, and belts carrying the exclusive Omen label. Ties, handkerchiefs, and other accessories are also available. Shoes, well made and fashionably styled, are sold to both men and women at **Prange Schuhhaus,** Jungfernstieg 38 (☎ 040/34-31-51).

One of the city's leading hairdressers, for both men and women, is **Marlies Müller** at Tesdorpfstrasse 20 (☎ 040/4-44-00-40). Besides hair styling and beauty treatments, a large perfume and cosmetic selection is also offered here.

Brahmfeld & Gutruf, Jungfernstieg 12 (☎ **040/34-61-03**), is one of Germany's oldest jewelers, founded in 1743.

One of Hamburg's biggest selections of books, mostly in German but with lots of English-language texts as well, can be found at **Thalia Buchhandlung,** Spitalerstrasse 8 (☎ **040/30207**). A smaller branch, mostly with German-language titles, of the same outfit is at Hermannstrasse 18–20 (☎ **040-3-02-07-01**).

Two stores of a nautical nature, **Binikowski,** Lokstedter Weg 68 (☎ **040/46-28-52**), established in 1955, is the place to find a *Buddelschiffe* (ship in a bottle), as well as ship models and clocks; while **Captain's Cabin,** St. Pauli Landungsbrücken (☎ **040/31-63-73**), stocks ship models, telescopes, barometers, figureheads, lamps, nautical clothing for the whole family, prints, posters, and more.

Flags in all shapes and sizes fill **Gäth & Peine,** Luisenweg 109 (☎ **040/21-35-99**), where just about every national ensign or known signal banner can be found.

If you've ever fancied yourself as someone who looks best in silk, you might pay a visit to Hamburg's **Haus des Osten,** Jungfernstieg 7 (☎ **040/34-36-80**), which sells only silk clothing imported from Asia (usually the People's Republic of China). There's an appealing collection of shirts and neckties for men, in all degrees of flamboyance and discretion. And for women, check out the kimonos, skirts, jumpers, undergarments, and scarves that fill the medium-sized premises of this well-stocked store.

7 Hamburg After Dark

To find out what's happening in Hamburg, pick up a copy of *Hamburger Vorschau* for 2.30DM ($1.30). Published once a month, it's available at various tourist offices, most hotels, and most newsstands.

THE PERFORMING ARTS

✪ **Hamburgische Staatsoper (Hamburg State Opera).** Dammtorstrasse 28. ☎ **040/35-17-21.** Tickets 8DM–150DM ($4.55–$85.50). U-Bahn: Stefansplatz. S-Bahn: Dammtor.

This modern opera house was built after the bombings of World War II. Its acoustics and technical facilities are among the most advanced in the world. The venue is the home of the **Hamburg State Opera,** and also the **Hamburg Ballet,** directed by Californian John Neumeier. Performances begin at 7:30pm. For tickets, call the number listed above, or head for the building's ticket office at Grosstheaterstrasse 34.

Musikhalle. Johannes-Brahms-Platz. ☎ **040/34-69-20.** Tickets 40DM–120DM ($22.80–$68.40). U-Bahn: Stefansplatz. S-Bahn: Dammtor.

This survivor of Germany's romantic age lies a few steps away from the Hamburg Oper, with which it shares some facilities and staff members. The building was painstakingly restored after World War II. It hosts concerts by the **Hamburg Symphony,** the **Hamburg Philharmonic,** the **NDR Symphony,** and the renowned **Monteverdi-Chor,** known for its interpretations of baroque and Renaissance music. Touring orchestras also perform here. In most cases, tickets don't exceed around 60DM ($34.20) in price. For tickets, call either the number listed above, or the number listed for the Hamburg Oper (see above).

THEATER   Hamburg is blessed with more than 40 theaters, but for most of these, a good knowledge of German is necessary. An exception, the **English Theatre of Hamburg,** Lerchenfeld 14 (☎ **040/2-27-70-89**), is the only English-speaking theater in the northern part of Germany. Tickets range from 20DM to 60DM ($11.40 to $34.20). Performances are Monday to Saturday at 7:30pm; a matinee is presented on Tuesday and Friday at 11am.

Ticket-Buying Tips

Tickets to sporting events, including soccer matches, are best acquired through the **Hamburger Sportbund (Hamburg Sports Association),** Schäferkampsallee 1, 20357 Hamburg (☎ **040/419080**). **Theater-Kasse Reckewell,** Einkaufcentrum shopping mall on Osterfer Landstrasse (☎ **040/80-10-13**), can arrange virtually everything else. A third option for cultural (but not necessarily sporting) events in Hamburg is to contact Hamburg's Tourist Information Office **(Tourismus Centrale),** in the "Wendelhalle" of the city's main railway station (☎ **040/30-05-13-00**).

If you understand German, try the ✪ **Deutsches Schauspielhaus,** Kirchenallee 39 (☎ **040/24-87-12**). It's one of the outstanding theaters in the German-speaking world, performing both the classics and modern plays.

Other theaters are the cutting-edge **Thaliatheater,** Alstertor (☎ **040/32-81-44-44**), and the **Kammerspiele,** Hartungstrasse 9–11 (☎ **040/41-33-4444**). Both stage a wide range of plays as well as musical shows. A new production usually opens every month. Tickets at these theaters range from 20DM to 110DM ($11.40 to $62.70). Small ensemble performances such as *Evening with Marlene Dietrich* are the specialty of the **Schmidt Theater,** Spielbudenplatz 24 (☎ **040/32-77-880**). Its companion, **Schmidts Tivoli,** Spielbudenplatz 27–28 (same phone), hosts musicals and other popular performances. Tickets range from 30DM to 100DM ($17.10 to $57). All of these are closed on Monday.

Two of Hamburg's busiest theaters are the **Neue Flora Theater,** Stresemannstrasse 159A (☎ **01805/4444**), and the **Operettenhaus,** Spielbudenplatz 1 (same phone), which have enjoyed an unprecedented success with *Phantom of the Opera* (at the Neue Flora), and *Cats* (at the Operettenhaus). Performances have run within these theaters for 9 and 13 years, respectively, with only vague hints that they might be nearing the ends of their runs. The cost of seeing either of these shows ranges from 70DM to 230DM ($39.90 to $131.10), depending on your seat and the night you opt to attend.

Hansa Theater, Steindamm 17 (☎ **040/24-14-14**), is a north German variety show that claims to be intelligible to all foreigners. The humor is so broad that that may be true. Each show includes international attractions such as acrobats, clowns, dancers, magicians, and aerialists. There are special tables for smoking and drinking. Two shows are performed daily Monday to Saturday at 4 and 8pm and Sunday at 3 and 7pm. Prices range from 40DM to 70DM ($22.80 to $39.90).

THE CLUB & MUSIC SCENE
JAZZ
Cotton Club. Alter Steinweg 10. ☎ **040/34-38-78.** Cover 8DM–25DM ($4.55–$14.25).

The legendary Cotton Club is the oldest (some 36 years) and best established of the Hamburg jazz clubs. Jazz and Dixieland bands come here from throughout Europe and the United States. Open Friday and Saturday 8pm to 1am and Monday to Thursday 8pm to midnight; from September through April, also open Sunday 11pm to 3am.

Dennis' Swing Club. Papenhuderstrasse 25 (in Uhlenhorst). ☎ **040/2-29-91-92.** Cover 10DM–15DM ($5.70–$8.55); no cover Wed.

The completely informal Dennis' became legendary under the management of Dennis Busby, a transplant from Louisiana. After his death, the club was taken over by Jochen Marcus, a very well-known jazz drummer in the 1950s. Today the club features some of the finest jazz talent in the city and a bilingual German and English format that's

The Reeperbahn: A Walk on the Wild Side

Commercialized sex flourishes in many towns, but hardworking, entrepreneurial Hamburg has succeeded better than almost anywhere else at transforming it into a tourist attraction. The place where it all hangs out is the St. Pauli district (U-Bahn: St. Pauli; S-Bahn: Reeperbahn), just east of the center. St. Pauli's midsection—the "genital-zone," as it's sometimes called—is the Reeperbahn, a half-mile thoroughfare whose name literally translates as "rope street," referring to the massive amounts of hempen rope produced here during the 18th and 19th centuries for ships in Germany's biggest harbor.

In the 19th century, most forms of entertainment, including theaters, were banned from the city's more respectable medieval core. As one resident of the district remarked, "Bourgeois Protestants don't know how to have fun." Consequently, this neighborhood near the great port developed entertainment options of its own, and sailors from around the world were safely channeled into a neighborhood where their recreational activities were out of sight (and out of mind) of the city's sober business establishment. Hamburg's first theater opened on the Reeperbahn in 1842. By the 1860s, the question, "Whatch'a doing, sailor?" became the unofficial motto of an army of prostitutes who set up shop (with the legal sanction of municipal authorities) in the district.

The city's official line is that the Reeperbahn is Hamburg's second greatest attraction and asset (the first is the port itself). The authorities see their policies as a rare instance of civic and moral enlightenment unparalleled in any other city, except for Amsterdam's more sanitized sex scene. They make frequent references to their requirement that every officially sanctioned working girl submit to a medical examination every 2 weeks—and pay income tax on her profits. Hamburg's most talked-about police station, Davidwache, at the corner of the Davidstrasse and the Reeperbahn, provides highly visible and omnipresent police protection.

What are the rules of the game and what should you do to survive such an "in-your-face" neighborhood? Throw your sense of scheduling to the wind and take a nap on the day of your visit. Mornings in St. Pauli are burned-out, unenthusiastic times, when virtually everyone is recovering from the bacchanals of the night before. Midafternoons perk up a bit. But regardless of the fogs that roll in from the Baltic and the damp chill that's an inseparable part of the Hamburg experience, by 8pm the district's bars and theaters (legitimate and otherwise) are roaring away. Between midnight and 5am, you'll find thousands of women and female wanna-bes strutting their stuff along the turf. German enterprise has honored these women (and their reputation for a good time) by naming one of Hamburg's native beers in their honor—the famous "St. Pauli Girl."

There's a distinct pecking order among the working girls, based on the neighborhood, or street, where they're headquartered. The most exclusive and

very familiar with the jazz traditions of both Europe and the U.S. Open Tuesday to Sunday from 8:30pm to 2am.

ROCK

Club Grosse Freiheit. Grosse Freiheit 36. ☎ **040/3177780.** Cover 6DM–40DM ($3.40–$22.80).

expensive area is **Herbertstrasse,** where plate-glass windows allow the women to display their charms to window shoppers. This street is only open to men over the age of 18. Less-expensive rents can be found on the streets near Herbertstrasse: Gunterstrasse, Erichstrasse, Friedrichstrasse, Davidstrasse, and Gerhardstrasse. Lots of the women here are from the Eastern Bloc, and lately there's been a distressing trend for runaway teenagers to join their ranks. Crossdressers, transsexuals, and "shemales" ply their trade here too.

If it's erotic theater you're looking for, you'll have to move a few blocks away to **Grosse Freiheit,** a street whose name appropriately translates as "Great Freedom." Any act of sexual expression, with every conceivable permutation except those that involve animals (bestiality is one of the few things expressly forbidden here) is shown in these theaters. Be it joyful, be it disgusting, it's all here, often performed by artists whose barely concealed boredom sometimes permeates the setting in ways that anywhere else would be embarrassing, but here seems merely surreal.

You aren't likely to be solicited at a performance—municipal regulations forbid prostitution, or overt solicitation, inside erotic theaters. But there's nothing to prevent a member of the audience from suddenly deciding to be a performer—it's been known to happen, if rarely. And there's nothing that prevents performers setting up an off-premises rendezvous. In any event, *caveat emptor.*

If you're subject to sudden fits of guilt in places like this, municipal and religious authorities made provisions long ago. There always seems to be a church nearby, such as the early-18th-century **Kirche St. Joseph,** at 5 Grosse Freiheit. There's also a branch office of the Salvation Army, whose members are ready, willing, and able to fortify your resolve with a cup of coffee and some religious boosterism.

The district also contains a museum dedicated to legitimizing humankind's age-old fascination with sexually explicit materials. It's the **Erotic Art Museum,** Nobistor 10A (☎ 040/31-78-410). This institution is privately owned and funded, and closed to anyone under 16. It manages to present its displays in a way that's both academic and titillating, and it has a street-level gift shop featuring sexual toys and enhancements. Open daily 10am to midnight; entrance is 15DM ($8.55) adults, 10DM ($5.70) students.

Hamburg gay life, however, is centered west of the city's medieval core, within the St.-Georg district (see below). **Absolut,** Hans-Albers-Platz (☎ 040/317-3400) is a St. Pauli bar that caters to a mixed/gay/lesbian crowd. The **Funky Pussy Club,** Grosse Freiheit 34 (☎ 040/314-4266), is mainly for lesbians. In the general free-for-all permissiveness that reigns in this neighborhood, however, sexual pigeonholing of visitors into specific gender preferences seems unnecessary.

This club, now world-famous, is where the Beatles performed in their earliest days. Today, it's a free-for-all venue whose acts change almost nightly, and whose guests in the recent past have included Prince and Willie Nelson. Even the civic and municipal authorities of Hamburg view it as one of their preeminent cultural treasures. For recorded information about upcoming acts, call ☎ 040/3177-7811.

Fabrik. Barnerstrasse 36 (5 min. from Bahnhof Altona). ☎ **040/39-10-70.** Cover 15DM–40DM ($8.55–$22.80).

This cultural center is similar in style to the Markthalle (see below). Originally it was an old ammunition depot (ca. 1830), until it was burned down; later, it was reconstructed in the same style. From 8pm until midnight (later on Saturday and Sunday), Fabrik is a nightclub beloved by those who survived the 1970s more or less intact. It offers a mixed program likely to feature African bands, jazz, and blues.

Finnegan's Wake. Börsenbrücke 4. ☎ **040/3-74-34-33.** Cover 5DM ($2.85) Sun–Thurs, 6DM ($3.40) Fri–Sat.

This place is as Irish as it sounds. English speakers flock here for Guinness and Harp on tap, as well as shepherd's pie, chili, and sandwiches (food is available until 9pm). Every Thursday to Saturday, there's live music of some sort. The pub is open Sunday to Thursday from 11am to 1am and Friday and Saturday from 11am to 4am.

Kaiserkeller. Grosse Freiheit 36 (in the cellar of the Grosse Freiheit concert hall). ☎ **040/317-7780.** Cover 10DM–15DM ($5.70–$8.55).

Kaiserkeller functions both as a stage for live music by not terribly famous bands, and as a disco. Long-time aficionados of the Reeperbahn scene remember it, along with the now-defunct Star Club, whose empty premises stands across the street, as an early venue for performances by the Fabulous Four. The place has a different musical theme on different nights of the week (Sunday is oldies night). Open nightly from 10pm to 4 or 5am.

Logo. Grindelallee 5. ☎ **040/4-10-56-58.** Cover 8DM–30DM ($4.55–$17.10).

Because of its position near Hamburg's university, this club attracts lots of college students, although many Big Chill survivors in their 40s and 50s gravitate here as well. It's a small, informal place that often features rock bands. Sometimes well-known singers appear in concert. Open daily from 8pm (live music begins at 9pm) to 2 or 3am. Audiences often sit on the floor.

Markthalle. Klosterwall 49. ☎ **040/33-94-91.** Cover 20DM–40DM ($11.40–$22.80).

This is one of the most visible live music venues in Hamburg, with a special emphasis on up-and-coming British groups and sometimes heavy metal and high-volume electronics. The building functioned early in the 20th century as a covered marketplace. Inside is an amphitheater with a stage and a large area for standing or sitting on notoriously uncomfortable benches. Performances usually begin at 8pm, with the ticket office opening about an hour before the performance.

EROTIC SHOWS

Off-the-record theaters include **Safari,** Grosse Freiheit 24 (☎ **040/31-32-33**), where you're likely to find the press agent for the city of Hamburg entertaining foreign travel writers. Expect to pay a fixed price of around 45DM ($25.65) for two beers. There's also **Taboo,** Grosse Freiheit 24 (☎ **040/31-32-33**). **Bangkok Star Cabaret,** Grosse Freiheit 17 (☎ **040/3-19-28-73**), stresses an Asian sensuality and aesthetic. A final contender for the voyeuristic fervor of mostly male clients along the Reeperbahn is **Charlie's Nightclub,** Hamburger Berg 29 (☎ **040/31-03-70**), which is open daily from 7am to 4am.

DRAG SHOWS

Pulverfass. Pulverteich 12. ☎ **040/24-97-91.** Cover 27DM–29DM ($15.40–$16.55); first drink 25DM ($14.25).

The best-known drag show in town, Pulverfass is usually featured on the "Hamburg by Night" tours. This place is not for the timid. You might find the shows downright vulgar, especially if you know German. Female impersonators from all over Europe appear here. There are shows nightly at 8:30pm, 11:30pm, and 2:30am (Friday and Saturday only). Within the same building, with a view of the stage, there's a restaurant, **Teatro-café,** which is open daily from 6am to 3pm, and where French and German-inspired set-price menus cost 49DM ($27.95) each.

DANCE CLUBS

After Shave. Spielbudenplatz 7. ☎ **040/3-19-32-15.** Cover 10DM–15DM ($5.70–$8.55).

After Shave features funk, soul, jazz, and fusion. It's a place for dancing and for meeting people, and it attracts the 20-to-30 age group. The dance music is wide-ranging, featuring the latest imports but no hard rock or heavy metal. On Tuesday jazz is featured exclusively. Open on Thursday from 11pm to 4am, Friday from 11pm to 5am, and Saturday from 11pm to 6am.

Café Kesse. Reeperbahn 19-21. ☎ **040/31-08-05.** Cover 15DM ($8.55).

If you're a woman looking for a guy, Café Kesse features the so-called "Ball Paradox" whereby women have the right (and are encouraged) to ask the men to dance, drink, or whatever. There's a doorman who screens the entrance to keep out rowdies, and the place is highly legitimate and very visible on Hamburg's nightlife scene. Live bands alternate with disco, and it's open Wednesday to Saturday from 8:30pm to between 5 and 6am, depending on business.

Madhouse. Valentinskamp 46A. ☎ **040/34-41-93.** Cover 10DM ($5.70) Thurs–Sat, includes first drink.

This dance club, the oldest in Hamburg, has been in business for 30 years, and in 1997 it was voted the best dance club in the city. The artist formerly known as Prince must agree; he's rented it out twice now. The music is a mix of rock, soul, funk, and house, played nightly from 10pm until "whenever."

Mojo Club. Reeperbahn 1. ☎ **040/3-19-19-99.** Cover 10DM ($5.70).

Although located on the Reeperbahn, this nightclub and disco is devoted not to sex but to soul music and acid jazz. It attracts a crowd of mainly straight couples in their 30s. One local TV station called it "the best night club in Germany," but we think that's a bit of an exaggeration.

Molotow. Spielbudenplatz 5. ☎ **040/31-08-45.** Cover 5DM–18DM ($2.85–$10.25).

This is the place to dance to funk—George Clinton and Bootsy Collins have been elevated to god status here. Say you've seen Parliament-Funkadelic, and you may make lifelong friends. It opens Wednesday at 9pm, Thursday to Saturday at 11pm, and Sunday at 9pm; closing time depends on the energy of the dancers.

Top of the Town. On the 26th floor of the Radisson SAS Hotel Hamburg, Marseiller Strasse 2. ☎ **040/35020.** Cover 8DM ($4.55) Fri–Sat only; no cover for guests of the hotel.

This eagle's nest attracts a relatively youthful crowd, many of whom show up without jackets or neckties to dance, drink, and talk. A DJ spins out danceable tunes. This club isn't nearly as wild and crazy as those within less-restrictive parts of town, such as the Reeperbahn. Nonetheless, it can be fun, and there's a gorgeous panorama of North Germany's most dynamic city spread out in front of you. Open every night except Sunday, from 9:30pm to around 4am.

GAY CLUBS

Hamburg, like Berlin, is one of the major gay havens of Europe, with a particularly dense concentration of gay boutiques and cafes along the Lange Reihe in St. Pauli. Try

Absolut, Hans-Albers-Platz (☎ 040/317-3400), a gay and lesbian bar, or the **Funky Pussy Club,** Grosse Freiheit 34 (☎ 040/314-236)—no prize for guessing who this caters to. A little journal, *Dorn Rosa,* distributed at most gay and lesbian bars, lists the clubs, restaurants, bars, and events that cater to a gay, lesbian, and bisexual clientele.

Café Gnosa. Lange Reihe 93. ☎ 040/24-30-34.

More than any other eatery in Hamburg, this comes the closest to fulfilling the need for an official "gay restaurant." Set near the railway station, on a street noted for its gay clientele, it's open Tuesday to Sunday from 11am to 1pm, and Monday from 6pm to 1am. Platters of food range from 8.50DM to 21DM ($4.85 to $11.95) and feature all-day breakfasts, steaks, fish, salads, and all kinds of coffee and drinks.

Bar Tusculum. Kreuzweg 6 (no phone).

Set near the above-mentioned Café Gnosa, this gay bar operates very late, only reaching its queeny, sometimes sarcastic and arch best around 2am till closing around dawn. Don't come looking for redemption or anything approaching churchiness—the venue is jaded, even jejeune. It's open from 8pm nightly.

Chocolate City. Heidenkampsweg 32. ☎ 040/23-25-23. Cover 15DM ($8.55).

In 1997, this big-city bar and disco took over the premises of what had previously been an all-gay club, the Front. Since its takeover, music has included an engaging mixture of swing, soul, R&B, hip-hop, and reggae, and the clientele includes goodly numbers of gay men and women, who move easily (as they do in many clubs throughout Hamburg) within the permissive ambience. It's open Friday to Sunday from 11pm to 5am.

Frauenkneipe. Stresemannstrasse 60. ☎ 040/43-63-77. Cover 6DM–12DM ($3.40–$6.85).

This bar is a major rendezvous point in Hamburg for women only—men are told to do their drinking elsewhere. The clientele is mainly lesbian, though there are a lot of straight women here too. On Sunday, there's ballroom dancing, with a 5DM ($2.85) cover, and Friday is disco night, with a cover of 8DM ($4.55). On other nights, this a good place to visit for a drink. Open Wednesday to Monday from 8pm to 1am.

Pit Club-Saloon/Tom's Bar. Pulverteich 17. ☎ 040/280-30-56. Cover 5DM ($2.85) for cellar leather bar, 10DM ($5.70) for street-level disco and first-floor "jeans bar."

This is the best-established and most popular gay men's bar in Hamburg, known to virtually every gay male in town. Begin your night in the street-level disco, work your way up to a watering hole one floor above, and end your evening in the cellar, where leather is optional but encouraged. Women, if they come here at all (which is rare), usually remain in the street-level disco. At least one part of this place is open every night from 10:30pm till dawn; every Wednesday to Sunday, additional sections open for greater space devoted to a leather bar/dungeon and a disco.

Spundloch. Paulinenstrasse 19. ☎ 040/31-07-98. No cover.

The famous Spundloch is also sometimes patronized by heterosexual couples. Its elegant bar and disco draw a youngish crowd. Open Wednesday, Thursday, and Sunday from 9pm to 4am, and on Friday and Saturday from 10pm to 6am.

THE BAR SCENE

Bayrisch Zell. Reeperbahn 110. ☎ 040/31-42-81. No cover Mon–Thurs; 10DM ($5.70) Fri–Sat, including first drink.

This beer hall, clearly an imitation of Munich's famed Hofbräuhaus, is one of the most popular places in the St. Pauli district. It may be on the Reeperbahn, but you could take your great-aunt here, especially if she likes to dance the polka. The place attracts couples young and old and has plenty of seats (1,200) for all. It also has good food, with meals starting at 10DM ($5.70). If someone catches your fancy from across the room, call him or her from your table—that's what those phones are for. Open 7pm to 3am daily.

Café Schone Aussichten. Gorch-Fock-Wall 4. ☎ **040/34-01-13.**

This is a bar/restaurant/disco. On most nights, the 300-seat beer garden is full of students; if you get hungry, try the southeast Asian dishes. On weekends there's a breakfast bar. Hours are Sunday to Thursday 10am to 2am and Friday and Saturday 10am to 4am.

Gröninger Braukeller. Ost-West-Strasse 47. ☎ **040/33-13-81.**

Gröninger has been making and selling beer here since 1750; today the site consists of two brew pubs flanking a traditional German restaurant. One of the pubs opens at 11am, the other at 5pm, and both close at 1am. If you get hungry, the brewery restaurant serves meals from 11:30am to 11:30pm.

La Paloma. Gerhardstrasse 2, at the corner of Friedrichstrasse. ☎ **040/31-45-12.**

This bar in the heart of the Reeperbahn has nothing to do with the sex trade going on around it. Instead, it's an artists' hangout where the wall space is used for art exhibitions. It's open Tuesday to Thursday 7pm to 1am, and Friday and Saturday 7pm to 4am.

Schwenders. Grossneumarkt 1. ☎ **040/34-54-23.**

This is one of Hamburg's most venerated wine houses. The place today often attracts some 400 or more patrons to its belle epoque setting, filled with nooks and crannies, even though there's room for only 200 to sit down. Musical entertainment might be anything from a Viennese operetta to cabaret, sometimes performed by local (often amateur, or temporarily out-of-work) musicians. Deli cold cuts and excellent cheese will do if you want something to eat with your drinks. Live classical music is played October through March. The bar is open daily from 4pm to 3am.

Shamrock. Feldstrasse 40. ☎ **040/4-39-76-78.**

The oldest Irish pub in Hamburg, the Shamrock has been in business for nearly 2 decades. It's a popular hangout for students and a transient English-speaking crowd that comes to soak up the Guinness, Kilkenney, Harp, and hard cider on tap. Open Sunday to Thursday from 1pm to 2am, and Friday and Saturday from 5pm to 4am.

A CASINO

Spielbank Hamburg. In the Hotel Inter-Continental, Fontenay 10. ☎ **040/44-70-44.** Cover 5DM ($2.85).

This casino offers roulette, blackjack, and baccarat, played according to international rules. You can also enjoy a drink at the bar, taking in the panoramic view over the roofs and lakes of Hamburg. The minimum stake for roulette is 5DM ($2.85), for blackjack 10DM ($5.70). Men should wear jackets and ties. The casino is open daily from 3pm to 3am.

17

Schleswig-Holstein

In this region of Germany, you can walk along the dunes and hear the roaring sea break fiercely on the rocks, or you can lie on a tranquil beach while tiny waves lap at your feet. Sound inconsistent? Not in Schleswig-Holstein. Germany's northernmost province borders both the turbulent, chilly North Sea and the smooth, gentle Baltic. And between these two bodies of water are rolling groves and meadows, lakes and ponds, and little fishing villages with thatched cottages. Fashionable seaside resorts dot both shorelines and nearby islands. Even in the coldest weather you can swim in heated seawater at the resorts of Westerland and Helgoland. In Kiel, you can wander around the harbor and explore Schleswig, with its Viking memories.

If you're flying, Hamburg (see chapter 16) is a good gateway to the region. After that, go to Lübeck, which is easily reached from Hamburg by train or by car, via the A1 Autobahn. Roads are only overcrowded in July and August. Where the trains end, local buses wait to take you the rest of the way, linking small towns and villages.

Exploring the Region by Car

Day 1 Leave Hamburg (see chapter 16) and take the E47 Autobahn to **Lübeck,** a distance of 41 miles to the northeast. Lübeck (see below), the old Hanseatic League capital, still retains its medieval aura, and deserves at least a day of your time.

Day 2 After visiting Lübeck, leave town on Route 207 and turn onto Route 76. This takes you to **Kiel** (a distance of 57 miles) by way of Eutin and Plön. On the way, you pass through a region called Holsteinische Schweiz (the "Switzerland of Holstein"). The district is filled with nearly 150 lakes and many forests. Eutin was the hometown of Carl Maria von Weber. Plön lies on the Plöner Sea (Plöner Lake), the largest lake in Schleswig-Holstein.

Day 3 After visiting Kiel, continue your motor tour northwest along Route 76 for 30 miles until you reach the Viking town of **Schleswig,** the oldest town in Schleswig-Holstein. Schleswig deserves an overnight stopover. Haitabu, southeast of Schleswig on Route 76, can absorb most of your afternoon with its Viking artifacts and lore.

Day 4 From Schleswig, head to the long, narrow island of Sylt and its capital, **Westerland,** only 13 miles west of the border with Denmark. Go west along Route 201 toward Husum; then go north on

Route 5 until Niebüll, where you must put your car aboard a train for the final journey to Westerland. After the short trip, you can explore the island by car.

1 Lübeck

57 miles SE of Kiel, 41 miles NE of Hamburg

It is said that nothing testifies to the wealth of an old European city as much as the size and number of its church spires. If this is so, Lübeck is rich indeed, for no fewer than seven towering steeples punctuate the skyline of this Hanseatic city. Lübeck was made a free imperial city in 1226. From the 13th century on, it was the capital of the Hanseatic League, the association of merchants that controlled trade along the Baltic, as far as Russia. Even today the town retains the name Hansestadt Lübeck.

Today Lübeck is a city of high-gabled houses, massive gates, and strong towers. The Hanseatic merchants decorated their churches with art treasures and gilded their spires to show off their wealth. Many of these survivors of nearly 900 years of history stand side by side today with postwar housing developments, and the neon lights of the business district shine on the streets and narrow passageways of bygone days.

Lübeck has had several famous sons, notably Thomas Mann and Willy Brandt. As a young man, Brandt, who later became West German chancellor and won the Nobel Peace Prize in 1971, opposed the Nazis so vehemently that he had to flee on a boat to Norway. Thomas Mann's novel *Buddenbrooks,* set in his hometown, catapulted the 27-year-old author to international fame in 1902. In 1929, he won the Nobel Prize for literature.

Lübeck's other claim to fame is that it's the world capital of marzipan. According to legend, Lübeckers, riding out a long siege, ran out of flour and started grinding almonds to make bread. So delighted were they with the results that they've been doing it ever since. To sample marzipan on its home turf, go to the Niederegger shop across from the Rathaus.

ESSENTIALS

GETTING THERE   By Train   The **Lübeck Hauptbahnhof** lies on major rail lines linking Denmark and Hamburg, and also on the Hamburg-Lüneburg-Lübeck-Kiel-Flensburg and the Lübeck-Rostock-Stralsund rail lines, with frequent connections. From Hamburg, 40 trains arrive daily (trip time: 40 min.), and 7 from Berlin (4 hr., 40 min.). For rail information, call ☎ **01805/996633.**

By Bus   Long-distance bus service to such cities as Berlin, Kiel, and Flensburg is provided by **Autokraft GmbH** (☎ **0451/89-97-283**).

By Ferry   Ferryboat service from the region around Lübeck to Denmark lies astride the main railway between Hamburg and Copenhagen, and is therefore among the busiest in Europe. Service is offered by **ScandLines** at ☎ **04371/86-51-61,** which has boats leaving across the sound every 30 minutes, 24 hours a day, every day of the year. The port on the German side is in Puttgarden; the one on the Danish side is in Rødbyhaven, a 2-hour train ride from Copenhagen. The trip takes about 75 minutes. Railway cars, trucks, and conventional automobiles are all taken on board. Round-trip transport for a car with up to four passengers averages 55DM ($31.35), with slight variations depending on the season.

TT Saga Line operates between the German port of Travemünde and the Swedish port of Trelleborg. Call ☎ **04502/80181** for bookings and departure times. And for transport by boat between Lübeck and the faraway Baltic port of Helsinki, **Finn Lines** (☎ **0451/1507443**) provides occasional service, usually favored by vacationers during midsummer.

By Car   Access to Lübeck is via the A1 Autobahn north and south.

VISITOR INFORMATION   For tourist information, contact the **Lübeck-Informations-Zentrum,** Breitestrasse 62 (☎ **0451/1-22-81-06**), Monday to Friday 9:30am to 6pm and Saturday and Sunday 10am to 2pm; or the **Touristbüro Beck-ergrube,** Beckergrube 95 (☎ **0451/1-22-1909**), Monday to Friday 8am to 4pm.

SPECIAL EVENTS   Lübeck is the center of the **Schleswig-Holstein Music Festival,** with performances between the end of June and August every year. For more information, contact ☎ **0451/389-5731.** At the **Christmas market,** held mainly during the 3 weeks preceding Christmas, vendors from all over northwestern Germany descend on the town to sell their wares—many of them handmade. You can pick up deals on one-of-a-kind items from toys to pottery.

EXPLORING THE CITY

Lübeck's ✪ **Altstadt** is surrounded by the Trave River and its connecting canals, giving it an islandlike appearance. It suffered heavily during World War II, when about one-fifth of the city was leveled. Today, damaged buildings have been restored or reconstructed, and Lübeck still offers a wealth of historic attractions. To reach the Altstadt and the attractions outlined below, take bus no. 5, 6, 7, 11, 14, or 16.

Just across the west bridge from the Altstadt, the **Holstentor (Holsten Gate)** is the first monument to greet visitors emerging from the Bahnhof. At one time it was the main town entrance, built in the 15th century as much to awe visitors with the power and prestige of Lübeck as to defend it against intruders. To the outside world the towers look simple and defiant, rather like part of a great palace. But on the city side they contain a wealth of decoration, with windows, arcades, and rich terra-cotta friezes. Within the gate is one of the municipal museums, **Museum Holstentor** (☎ 0451/1-22-41-29), housing a model of Lübeck as it was in the mid-17th century. The museum is open Tuesday to Sunday from 10am to 5pm (until 4pm in winter). Admission is 5DM ($2.85) for adults, 3DM ($1.70) for students, and 1DM (55¢) for children 17 and under.

The **Salt Lofts** (Der Salzspeicher) viewed from the riverside, near the Holstentor, are among Lübeck's most attractive sights. In the 16th century, these buildings were used to store the salt from Lüneburg before it was shipped to Scandinavia. Each of the six buildings is slightly different, reflecting several trends in Renaissance gabled architecture.

Rathaus, Rathausplatz (☎ 0451/1221005), traces its origins from 1230. It has been rebuilt several times, but there are remains of the original structure in the vaulting and Romanesque pillars in the cellar and the Gothic south wall. The towering walls have been made with open-air medallions to relieve the pressure on the Gothic-arcaded ground floor and foundations. Tours are conducted Monday to Friday at 11am, noon, and 3pm, costing 4DM ($2.30) for adults and 2.50DM ($1.40) for children.

✪ **Marienkirche** (☎ 0451/74901), across Marktplatz from the Rathaus, is the most outstanding church in Lübeck, possibly in northern Germany. Built on the highest point in the Altstadt, it has flying buttresses and towering windows that leave the rest of the city's rooftops at its feet. Some of its greatest art treasures were destroyed in 1942, but after the fire was put out, an earlier painted decoration on the walls and clerestory was discovered. The bells fell in a World War II air raid and embedded themselves in the floor of the church, where they remain to this day. Organ concerts take place during the summer months, carrying on the tradition established by St. Mary's best-known organist and composer, Dietrich Buxtehude (1668–1707).

Buddenbrookhaus, Mengstrasse 4 (☎ 0451/122-41-92), near Marienkirche, is the house where the grandparents of Thomas Mann lived. It's a big, solid stone structure with a gabled roof and a recessed doorway. Above a leaded-glass fan over the heavy double doors is the date 1758. This is the house Mann described as the home of the family in *Buddenbrooks*. The museum also highlights Thomas's brother, Heinrich Mann, author of *Professor Unrat,* the source of the movie *Der Blaue Engel* (*The Blue Angel*). The house is open daily from 10am to 5pm; admission is 7DM ($4) for adults, 4DM ($2.30) for students, and free for children under 14.

It's estimated that within an area of 2 square miles around the Marktplatz stand 1,000 medieval houses. Nearby is **Petersgrube,** the finest street in Lübeck, lined with restored houses; one is from as early as 1363. A walk through the old streets of Lübeck reveals a continuing use of brick (the city insisted on this after fires in the 13th century). The effect is one of unity among all the houses, churches, shops, and guild halls.

Haus der Schiffergesellschaft (Seamen's Guild House), on Breitestrasse, is one of the last of the elaborate guild houses of Hanseatic Lübeck, built in 1535 in Renaissance style, with stepped gables and High Gothic blind windows. It's worth seeing just for the medieval furnishings and the beamed ceilings in the main hall, now a restaurant (see "Where to Dine," below).

Museen Behnhaus/Drägerhaus, Königstrasse 9–11 (☎ 0451/1-22-41-42), was formed from two patrician houses, both entered on Königstrasse, north of Glockengiesser Strasse. Like many such houses in the town, they are tall and narrow, constructed that way to avoid heavy taxes based on frontage. The museum displays mostly German impressionists and paintings from around 1900. There is an outstanding collection of German Romantic and "Nazarene" paintings and drawings, especially by Johann Friedrich Overbeck and his school. The Behnhaus part of the museum is housed in the city's most important neoclassic building. It has a permanent exhibition of contemporary paintings, including Schumacher, Schultze, Rainer, Antes, and Kirkeby, along with such 20th-century artists as Kirchner, Beckmann, Lehmbruck, and Barlach. Both houses are open April through September, Tuesday to Sunday 10am to 5pm; October through March, Tuesday to Sunday 10am to 4pm. Admission is 5DM ($2.85) for adults, 3DM ($1.70) for children 6 to 18, and free for children under 6.

You can take an excursion boat around **Lübeck Harbor,** departing from Trave Landing, right in front of the Jensen hotel. In season, departures are every half hour, anytime between 10am and 6pm.

SHOPPING   Lübeck is a center for antique stores. Two of the best are **Antique Center im Engelshof,** Engelsgrube 40 (☎ **0451/7-23-38**), and its competitor, **Antiquitäten Gunter Bannow,** Fleischhauerstrasse 87 (☎ **0451/7-73-38**). Both carry antique silver, crystal, porcelain, books, pewter, and English, Danish, and German furniture; any article can be shipped to your home. If you're in the market for antique books, head for the town's largest repository of antique books and folios, **Von Lingelsheim,** Breitestrasse 42 (☎ **0451/74743**), which has everything from obscure volumes of Romantic poetry to arcane Protestant treatises. And if you're looking for souvenirs that celebrate Lübeck's rich maritime traditions, head for the town's most interesting handcrafts shop, **Kunsthaus Lübeck,** Königstrasse 20 (☎ **0451/7-57-00**), where tin, pewter, wood carvings, pottery, and antique books will help you remember your visit. **Breitestrasse,** a pedestrian walkway throughout most of the day, is the main shopping street in town. Much of Lübeck's Altstadt is banned to cars, and makes for a pleasant afternoon of wandering.

WHERE TO STAY
EXPENSIVE

Holiday Inn. Travemünder Allee 3 (near the Burgtor entrance of the Altstadt), 23568 Lübeck. ☎ **0451/3-70-60.** Fax 0451/3-70-66-66. 161 units. A/C MINIBAR TV TEL. 245DM–295DM ($139.65–$168.15) double; 495DM–520DM ($282.15–$296.40) suite. AE, DC, MC, V. Free outdoor parking; 12DM ($6.85) in garage.

This chain hotel is first class. Until 1998, it was the Scandi Crown, and the Swedish aura remains. The hotel is close to the ferry docks, and, as a result, it attracts many Scandinavians as well as businesspeople. The medium-sized rooms are well maintained, furnished with modern pieces including good beds with firm mattresses. Half the rooms are nonsmoking. There are also accommodations for people with allergies.

Dining: The restaurant offers not only north German dishes but regional Swedish seafood recipes as well.

Amenities: Laundry, room service, baby-sitting, pool, fitness center, and sauna.

Radisson SAS Senator Hotel Lübeck. Willy-Brandt-Allee 6 (on the banks of the river, connected to the Altstadt by pedestrian bridge), 23554 Lübeck. ☎ **800/333-3333** or 0451/ 14-20. Fax 0451/1-42-22-22. www.radisson.com/luebeck.de. E-mail: jmh@lbczh.rdsas.com. 231 units. MINIBAR TV TEL. 230DM–320DM ($131.10–$182.40) double; 350DM–890DM ($199.50–$507.30) suite. AE, DC, MC, V. Parking 14DM ($8).

This hotel is the best in town. It's well laid out and well run. Although the bulk of its clients are businesspeople, it has equal appeal to other visitors. The soundproof and medium-sized bedrooms are well kept and attractively furnished, containing such amenities as hair dryers and firm mattresses. The sleekly maintained private bathrooms come with a basket of toiletries.

Dining/Diversions: The Trave Restaurant, serving international cuisine, has distinguished itself since its opening. In addition, the Bierstube Kogge is a popular rendezvous, both for beer at night and afternoon tea or coffee, served with the luscious cakes for which Lübeck is well known. The hotel bar has good views of the Altstadt.

Amenities: 24-hour room service, 190-car garage, laundry, baby-sitting, fitness center with indoor swimming pool, solarium, sauna, steam room, and massage.

MODERATE

Hotel Excelsior. Hansestrasse 3 (near Lindenplatz, opposite the central bus station and next to the train station), 23558 Lübeck. ☎ **0451/8-80-90.** Fax 0451/88-09-99. 61 units. TV TEL. 140DM–190DM ($79.80–$108.30) double; 220DM–250DM ($125.40–$142.50) suite. Rates include buffet breakfast. AE, DC, MC, V. Free outdoor parking; 10DM ($5.70) underground.

This is a good, functional hotel, and not a lot more. It's in a symmetrical baroque building with splendid proportions and an entirely renovated and modernized interior. It's especially convenient if you're traveling to Lübeck by rail. All rooms have shower or bath and a hair dryer, and some are also equipped with a minibar. Accommodations range from small to medium in size, and many units have recently been renovated. A few rooms are designated for nonsmokers.

Jensen. An der Obertrave 4–5 (near the Holstentor), 23552 Lübeck. ☎ **0451/7-16-46.** Fax 0451/7-33-86. www.branchennet.de/hotel-jensen. E-mail: hotel.jensen@t-online.de. 42 units. MINIBAR TV TEL. 170DM–210DM ($96.90–$119.70) double; from 300DM ($171) suite. Rates include buffet breakfast. AE, DC, MC, V. Parking 10DM ($5.70). Bus: 1, 3, or 11.

The Jensen is one of Lübeck's best moderately priced hotels. This family-run place is a good value, if your expectations aren't too high. Its small to medium-sized guestroom windows have fine views of the Hanseatic brick architecture just across the canal. The rooms are modestly furnished in modern style and were recently renovated with new mattresses added and the plumbing upgraded. The buffet breakfast is served in a delightful room with picture windows overlooking the old canal. The warmly decorated, tavern-style restaurant serves good lunches and dinners.

✪ Kaiserhof. Kronsforder Allee 11–13, 23560 Lübeck. ☎ **0451/70-33-01.** Fax 0451/79-50-83. 71 units. MINIBAR TV TEL. 200DM–250DM ($114–$142.50) double; 350DM–440DM ($199.50–$250.80) suite. Rates include buffet breakfast. AE, DC, MC, V. Free outdoor parking; 12DM ($6.85) in garage. Bus: 2, 7, 10, 16, or 32.

The Kaiserhof hotel, frankly, could probably demand a higher price tag for its rooms, as it ranks up near the top with the Senator. Two former patrician town houses have been remodeled into this hotel, located outside the city center on a tree-lined boulevard. The owner has created a fashionable yet homelike environment. Every room is individually furnished, and they come in various shapes and sizes. Some overflow guests are housed in a more sterile but still quite comfortable annex. All the beds contain firm mattresses and fine linens, and bathrooms are tiled, compact, and well equipped with a hair dryer and plush towels. An elaborate and authentic Scandinavian sauna opens off the rear garden, and a large pool, a Roman vapor bath, a fitness center, and a solar studio are available.

Mövenpick Hotel. Willy-Brandt-Allee 1–3 (across from the Holstentor), 23554 Lübeck. ☎ **800/111-2222** in the U.S., or 0451/1-50-40. Fax 0451/1-50-41-11. 197 units. MINIBAR TV TEL. 200DM–240DM ($114–$136.80) double; 260DM–340DM ($148.20–$193.80) suite. Children under 16 stay free in parents' room. AE, DC, MC, V. Parking 10DM ($5.70). Bus: 1, 3, or 11.

This long-established hotel provides great value for the money. It stands by a canal, near the major attractions of the city. The Swiss-owned chain has created a modern, lively atmosphere with plenty of brass and rattan furnishings, along with modern paintings. Guest rooms are compact and furnished in a somewhat bland motel style, but each comes with a good bed with a firm mattress plus a tiled bathroom with plush towels and a hair dryer. Rooms for nonsmokers are available. Amenities include indoor and outdoor parking, Hertz reservation desk, concierge, room service, laundry, and dry cleaning. The restaurant, open from 6:30am to 11pm, offers such Swiss specialties as *Rösti* and venison with lingonberries. The Lysia Bar opens daily at 5pm.

WHERE TO DINE

Das Schabbelhaus. Mengstrasse 48–52. ☎ **0451/7-20-11.** Reservations recommended. Main courses 30DM–42DM ($17.10–$23.95); fixed-price 4-course menu 58DM–63DM ($33.05–$35.90); menu à deux including wine 168DM ($95.75). AE, MC, V. Mon–Sat noon–3pm and 6–11pm. Bus: 5, 7, 11, 12, 14, or 16. NORTH GERMAN/ITALIAN.

A classic example of Hanseatic architecture on a medieval street, the Schabbelhaus is installed in two patrician buildings from the 16th and 17th centuries. A wooden staircase and balcony lead to two rooms devoted to memorabilia of Thomas Mann. In the restaurant, ceiling-high studio windows overlook the small gardens, and a pair of 15-foot-high armoires hold the restaurant's linen and glassware. It's easy to get the impression that the setting competes with the food, but that's not entirely true. Although the cuisine isn't quite as good as the Wullenwever's (see below), it's skillfully prepared with fresh ingredients. Begin with Lübecker crab soup, the finest in town, and follow with one of the fresh fish items from the Baltic. If you wish, the chef will prepare a perfectly cooked steak to your specifications.

Haus der Schiffergesellschaft. Breitestrasse 2. ☎ **0451/7-67-76.** Reservations required. Main courses 17DM–38DM ($9.70–$21.65). No credit cards. Daily 10am–midnight. Bus: 1 or 2. NORTH GERMAN.

Entering this restaurant, with ship models hanging from the ceiling and other nautical memorabilia on the walls, is like going inside a museum of Hanseatic architecture. The restaurant was once patronized exclusively by sailors. Today, good food (and lots of it) is served on scrubbed-oak plank tables with high-backed wooden booths carved with the coats of arms of Baltic merchants. Often, you must share a table here. One of the most expensive items is an elaborate sole meunière (1 lb.) with salad. Many regional dishes are featured, such as baked black pudding with slices of apple and lamb's lettuce. Try the roast pork with fruit, pickled fried herring with home-fried potatoes, or Baltic plaice flavored with bacon. You might want to have a drink in the cocktail bar of the historical Gotteskeller, open Monday to Saturday 6pm to 2am.

Historischer Weinkeller. Heiligen-Geist-Hospital, Koberg 8. ☎ **0451/7-62-34.** Reservations recommended. Main courses 16DM–38DM ($9.10–$21.65). AE, MC, V. Daily noon–midnight. Bus: 1 or 3. INTERNATIONAL.

You'll find this first-class restaurant and 12th-century wine cellar in the basement of one of Lübeck's monuments (Holy Ghost Hospital). This is the number-three dining spot in town, topped only by the Wullenwever, which has better (and more expensive) food, and Das Schabbelhaus, which has a more refined atmosphere. You might begin with North Sea shrimp served with a quail egg and caviar or assorted fish in aspic. Soups can include mussel-cream soup with Pernod or clear soup prepared with Baltic fish. For a main dish, try fillet of cod gratinée with sauerkraut or poached haddock in a mustard sauce. North Sea sole is never better than when it's sautéed simply in butter. A few meat dishes are also featured.

In the basement is a potato cellar, where the potato-based menu items include baked potatoes and potato soufflé, served along with simple meat or fish selections. Main courses here cost 9.50DM to 21DM ($5.40 to $11.95).

Sweet Treats

J. G. Niederegger, Breitestrasse 98 (☎ **0451/5-30-10**), sells that "sweetest of all sweetmeats," famous Lübeck marzipan. It's been right across from the main entrance to the Rathaus since 1806. On the ground floor, you can purchase pastries to take away, or you can go upstairs to a pleasant cafe, where you can order dessert and the best brewed coffee in Lübeck. Ask for their pastry specialty, a nut torte resting under a huge slab of fresh marzipan. You'll pay around 55DM ($31.35) per kilo, which is about 25DM ($14.25) per pound. Open 9am to 6pm daily, no credit cards. Take bus no. 5, 7, 11, 14, or 16.

✪ **Wullenwever.** Beckergrube 71. ☎ **0451/70-43-33.** Reservations required, as far in advance as possible. Main courses 28DM–48DM ($15.95–$27.35); fixed-price menus 88DM–135DM ($50.15–$76.95). AE, DC, MC, V. Tues–Sat noon–2pm and 7–11pm. Closed 2 weeks in Mar and Oct. FRENCH/CONTINENTAL.

Roy Petermann, in his elegant 16th-century house, has established himself as one of the finest chefs in northern Germany. Scion of a distinguished culinary family, Petermann has brought a refined and imaginative cuisine to sleepy Lübeck. Chandeliers and oil paintings enhance the ambience, and in summer, tables overflow onto a flower-filled courtyard. Using only the best and freshest produce, his dishes have subtle depths of flavor and texture. Game is featured in the autumn, and seafood is always available. One recent memorable creation is baked pike-perch fillets in a red-wine sauce.

Zimmermann's Lübecker Hanse. Am Kolk 3–7. ☎ **0451/7-80-54.** Reservations recommended. Main courses 27DM–43DM ($15.40–$24.50); fixed-price lunch 33DM–37DM ($18.80–$21.10); fixed-price dinner 35DM–60DM ($19.95–$34.20). AE, DC, MC, V. Mon–Fri noon–2pm and 7–11pm. Open Sat Nov–Dec. Closed Jan 1–6. Bus: 1, 3, or 11. FRENCH/GERMAN.

This is one of the most praised restaurants of Lübeck. It has an authentically weathered exterior, with dark paneling inside. French food, regional meals, and lots of fresh seafood are offered. You might want to confine yourself to the *plats du jour;* they are invariably fresh and well prepared. Fresh fish from the Baltic is another good choice. In season, wild game is featured.

LÜBECK AFTER DARK

Two newsletters, *Piste* or *Szene Journal,* free at most hotels, have news of local happenings.

Lübeck is known for its organ concerts, and about two a week are presented in various churches in the summer. The tourist office (see above) will provide complete details, or check with **Musik und Kongresshallen Lübeck,** Willy-Brandt-Allee 10 (☎ **0451/79-04-00**), about the many concert and theater opportunities in town. The most important venue is **Theater Combinale,** Huxstrasse 115 (☎ **0451/7-88-17**). Its plays range between the experimental and the classic. Performances are on Friday and Saturday from August through June. Tickets cost 20DM to 30DM ($11.40 to $17.10) for adults and 15DM to 22DM ($8.55 to $12.55) for students and children.

Finnegan, Mengstrasse 42 (☎ **0451/7-11-10**), won a 1997 award from Guinness as the best Irish pub in northern Germany. Naturally, there's Guinness on tap, as well as Kilkenny, other kinds of beers, and five or six whiskies. On Wednesday night, visiting bands play Irish music from 8pm to midnight. The pub is open Monday to Thursday 6pm to 1am and Friday and Saturday 6pm to either 3 or 4am.

Bräuberger, Alfstrasse 36 (☎ 0451/7-14-44), is a restaurant and pub located in the oldest cellar in Lübeck, dating from 1225. Its beer, Zwickel, is brewed on the premises, and it also serves regional dishes and Bavarian specialties. Open Monday to Friday from 5pm to 1am, and on Saturday from 6pm to 2am. Large mugs of beer cost 5.10DM ($2.90) each. Don't overlook this place as a site for a hearty, traditional platter of German food as an accompaniment for your beer. Platters cost from 15DM to 18DM ($8.55 to $10.25) each.

2 Kiel

55 miles SE of the Danish border at Flensburg, 60 miles N of Hamburg, 57 miles NW of Lübeck

Everything about this city reflects the importance the sea has played in its growth and prosperity. Its perfect natural harbor at the end of a 10-mile extension of the Baltic Sea made Kiel a center for commerce with other northern European countries. The opening of the Kiel Canal in 1895 connected the Baltic with the North Sea and Western trade.

Although Kiel celebrated its 750th anniversary in 1992, there is little in the way of streets or buildings to make the casual visitor believe that the town was ever anything other than a modern city. Almost all its buildings were destroyed in World War II, after which the town was rebuilt in an admirable modern style. Kielers are proud of their broad streets, spacious squares, and green parks in the heart of town. Stretches of sandy beach in nearby resorts make this port a Baltic vacation spot as well.

ESSENTIALS

GETTING THERE   By Plane   Lufthansa has flights from Frankfurt to Kiel from Sunday to Friday. There are also daily flights from Munich and Hamburg. Call ☎ 800/645-3880 for flight information. In Kiel, call the airport at ☎ 0431/32-36-56.

By Train   The **Kiel Hauptbahnhof** is on two major rail lines, the Neumünster-Hamburg and the Flensburg-Kiel-Lübeck-Lüneburg lines, with frequent connections. From Hamburg, there are 40 trains daily (trip time: 1 hr., 10 min.). For rail information and schedules, call ☎ 01805/996633.

By Bus   Long-distance bus service to Berlin and Flensburg, as well as local and regional service, is provided by **Autokraft GmbH,** in Kiel (☎ 0431/66-60). Buses pull into the Bahnhofplatz. The tourist office (see below) will provide you with schedules.

By Ferry   Service between Kiel and Oslo, Norway, is provided by **Color Line GmbH,** in Kiel (☎ 0431/97-4090). **Baltic Line,** in Kiel (☎ 0431/98-20-00), offers service between Kiel and Gothenburg (Göteborg), Sweden.

By Car   To reach Kiel from Hamburg, head north along the A7 Autobahn; from Lübeck, take Route 76 west.

VISITOR INFORMATION   Contact **Tourist Information Kiel,** Andreas-Gayk-Strasse 31 (☎ 0431/67-91-00). It's open Monday to Friday 9am to 6:30pm October through April; Monday to Saturday 9am to 6:30pm in May and August through September; and daily 9am to 6:30pm in June and July.

SPECIAL EVENTS   Kiel Week (Kieler Woche), held each June, celebrates the port's close ties to the sea. This week of special events, held for more than 100 years, includes a spectacular regatta in which more than 1,500 yachts race on the water of the Kieler Förde. In 1936 and 1972, the Olympic yacht races were held on the waters at Schilksee. For information, call the **Kieler Wochenbüro** at ☎ 0431/901-24-02).

EXPLORING THE HARBOR & BEYOND

Most attractions in Kiel center around the harbor, which can be reached by bus no. 8 or 18. For the best overall look at the city and the harbor, go to the top of the Rathaus's 350-foot, century-old tower (☎ **0451/9010**), much of which was restored after the devastating bombs of World War II. Between May and September, guided tours of the tower are offered every Wednesday at noon and 6pm, and every Saturday at noon, for a price of 3DM ($1.70) per person. For an even closer view over the harbor, take a stroll along the **Hindenburgufer (Hindenburg Embankment)**, which stretches for 2 miles along the west side of the fjord, opposite the shipyards. Perches along this embankment are especially favored by spectators during regattas.

If you'd like to go to the beach, take a short steamer trip to one of the nearby Baltic towns, such as Laboe, 10 miles to the north. Besides the beach, the town's main attraction is a restored World War II submarine called **U-Boot 995,** Havn (☎ **04343/42700**). Between May and October, you can tour it every day from 9:30am to 6pm (to 4pm between November and April). Admission is 3.50DM ($2) for adults, 2DM ($1.15) for students and persons under 18. To reach this attraction from the main railway station in Kiel, take bus 100.

The open-air **Schleswig-Holsteinisches Freilichtmuseum,** Alte hamburger Landstrasse (☎ **0431/659660**), lies 4 miles south of Kiel. Take bus 502 to reach it. Farms and rustic country homes, dating from the 16th to the 19th centuries, have been assembled here, and craftspeople operate shops while working animals perform their tasks. A half-timbered inn serves tasty lunches to visitors. November through March, the site is open only on Sunday and holidays 11am to 5pm; April through October, it's open Tuesday to Sunday 9am to 6pm, and Monday 9am to 6pm July through September only. Admission is 7DM ($4) for adults, 3.50DM ($2) for children 6 and over, and free for children under 6.

WHERE TO STAY

Hotel Kieler Yacht Club. Hindenburgufer 70, 24105 Kiel. ☎ **0431/8-81-30.** Fax 0431/8-81-34-44. 58 units. MINIBAR TV TEL. 250DM–330DM ($142.50–$188.10) double. Rates include buffet breakfast. AE, DC, MC, V. Parking 15DM ($8.55). Bus: 8 or 18.

This yacht club offers unusually fine guest facilities. It's in an old classical building, standing back from the harbor, with an adjoining contemporary motel annex. Rooms here are comfortable but unexciting. For style, we prefer those in the main building; however, all the units have the standard comforts such as quality mattresses and neatly arranged bathrooms. Mastenkeller, in the basement, is for beer drinking; the restaurant is recommended separately (see "Where to Dine," below).

Hotel Wiking. Schützenwall 1–3, 24114 Kiel. ☎ **0431/67-30-51.** Fax 0431/66-109-66. www.hotel-wiking.de. E-mail: hotelwiking@t-online.de. 42 units. MINIBAR TV TEL. 160DM–195DM ($91.20–$111.15) double. Rates include continental breakfast. AE, DC, MC, V. Parking 10DM ($5.70). Bus: 8 or 18.

The Wiking, in the center of town, offers well-furnished rooms for reasonable prices. The dark facade of this modern hotel is ornamented with heavy-walled balconies painted a vividly contrasting white. Rooms are a bit small but well maintained, each equipped with a comfortable mattress on a good bed, plus a compact tiled bathroom with shower stalls. The restaurant, Pfannkuchen Haus, and breakfast rooms have a warm Nordic ambience. The hotel has a sauna and solarium.

Maritim-Bellevue. Bismarckallee 2, 24105 Kiel. ☎ **0431/3-89-40.** Fax 0431/33-84-90. 89 units. MINIBAR TV TEL. 268DM–450DM ($152.75–$256.50) double; 600DM–650DM ($342–$370.50) suite. Rates include buffet breakfast. AE, DC, MC, V. Parking 15DM ($8.55). Bus: 8 or 18.

Rated "superior first class," the Maritim-Bellevue is a well-appointed convention hotel opening onto the shore promenade of the Baltic. Its most serious rival, to which it plays second fiddle, is the Steigenberger Conti-Hansa (see below). The most expensive doubles are the luxurious corner accommodations, but all rooms—even the medium-sized ones—are well furnished and beautifully maintained.

Dining/Diversions: The hotel is known locally for its Baltic cuisine at two restaurants: the Stockholm and the Oslo. Drinks are served at the Maritim Nightclub.

Amenities: Room service, laundry, and dry cleaning are available.

Steigenberger Conti-Hansa. Schlossgarten 7, 24103 Kiel. ☎ **800/223-5652** in the U.S. and Canada, or 0431/5-11-50. Fax 0431/5-11-54-44. 166 units. MINIBAR TV TEL. 290DM–355DM ($165.30–$202.35) double; 620DM ($353.40) suite. Rates include buffet breakfast. AE, DC, MC, V. Parking 22DM ($12.55). Bus: 1 or 12.

Conti-Hansa, located between the edge of the harbor and a well-groomed city park, is Kiel's premier hotel. The hotel has two separate wings, one with two floors, the other with seven. It's well maintained, modern, and solidly comfortable. The medium-sized bedrooms are outfitted in streamlined contemporary furniture; most of them look out over the harbor or the park. Every room has a trouser press and a hair dryer, and (if requested) air-conditioning.

Dining/Diversions: There's a formal dining room, the Restaurant Jakob (see "Where to Dine," below), as well as a bistro (the Avance) and a bar.

Amenities: Concierge, laundry, baby-sitting, whirlpool, solarium, sauna, car-rental kiosk, easy access to golf, horseback riding, tennis, and boat rentals.

WHERE TO DINE

Kieler Yacht Club. Hindenburgufer 70. ☎ **0431/8-81-34-42.** Reservations recommended. Main courses 28.50DM–39DM ($16.25–$22.25); fixed-price menu 39.50DM ($22.50). AE, DC, MC, V. Daily noon–3pm and 6–10:30pm. CONTINENTAL.

This restaurant is found in a previously recommended hotel. The bar, a local hangout, attracts the yachting set. The food is solid and reliable, though not dazzling. The main attraction, naturally, is seafood. Try the fillet of haddock with mustard sauce and potatoes. Other chef's specialties are saddle of venison with savoy cabbage, roasted lamb in wine sauce with herbs, and an assortment of meal-sized salads.

Restaurant im Schloss. Am Oslokai. ☎ **0431/9-11-55.** Reservations required. Main courses 28DM–48DM ($15.95–$27.35); fixed-price menu 38DM ($21.65) for 3 courses, 98DM ($55.85) for 7 courses. AE, DC, MC, V. Year round, Tues–Fri 11am–3pm; Mon–Sat 6–10:30pm. Sept–May also Sun noon–3:30pm. Bus: 1. CONTINENTAL.

The most elegant formal restaurant in Kiel offers superb cuisine, service, and wine. The Schloss, a stone building overlooking the harbor, looks like a museum set in a park. If you reserve, you can get one of the window tables opening onto the water. The cuisine has a creative and lighthearted style, using the freshest of produce. Many fish dishes are from the north German seas. Try, for example, terrine of salmon and zander in cream sauce, followed by fillet of lamb breast brushed with white bread crumbs and baked with fresh herbs.

Restaurant Jakob. In the Steigenberger Avance Conti-Hansa Hotel, Schlossgarten 7. ☎ **0431/5-11-54-07.** Reservations recommended. Main courses 25DM–35DM ($14.25–$19.95); fixed-price menus 59DM ($33.65). AE, DC, MC, V. Daily noon–3pm and 6–9:30pm. Bus: 1 or 12. CONTINENTAL.

Set on the lobby level of one of Kiel's most comfortable hotels, this restaurant boasts views over the harbor and a plush, modern decor. You might begin your meal with a crepe filled with Jacob mussels served on red lentils, or a soup—perhaps lobster soup with cognac. Main dishes range from the mundane (strips of turkey breast in a curry-

and-yogurt sauce) to the sublime (saddle of boar with a juniper berry sauce). Try the filet of pork medaillons coated in bacon and served with a mustard sauce, or the calves' liver with asparagus and hollandaise. Dessert might be a slice of apricot cake with ice cream.

KIEL AFTER DARK

It's worthwhile just to take a stroll after dark through the salt air and fog of this seafaring city, admiring the Hanseatic architecture and the ever-present sense of gloomy nostalgia. Along the way, you can stop at any of the small bars of the Altstadt, one of the best of which is **Nachtcafe,** Iggirstedtstrasse (☎ **0431/9-55-50**), which attracts night owls beginning at around 7pm. In the cramped basement, there's a bar and a dance floor, with recorded soul, funk, and garage music. Next door, under the same management (same phone) is the town's most popular disco, Velvet. No self-respecting Kieler would consider going into **Velvet** (whose red-and-green interior on two floors has velvet upholstery, as you'd expect) before around 11pm. Entrance here costs 10DM ($5.70). Newer, and more intently geared to the developing (and sometimes cutting-edge) musical tastes of the under-25 crowd,is **Mex Musik Halle,** Eichhof Strasse 1 (☎ **0431/122-9944**). It's open only on Friday, Saturday, and Sunday from 11pm till dawn. Entrance costs 10DM ($5.70) per person.

One of the most visible old-fashioned nightlife options in Kiel is **Klosterbräurei,** Am Alten Markt (☎ **0431/906-290**) which brews and serves, on-site, a medium-dark beer that locals compare to the better-known Düsseldorfer. Most of the clients come just for the beer, but if you're hungry, head for the self-service cafeteria area for heaping platters of sauerkraut, sausage, salads, and prepared meats (try the pig on a spit, tastefully rotating behind glass for your viewing pleasure), which a staff member will weigh for you and charge by the kilo. Expect to pay around 7DM to 16DM ($4 to $9.10) for a platter.

3 Schleswig

30 miles NW of Kiel, 21 miles S of Flensburg

This one-time Viking stronghold on the Schlei (an arm of the Baltic) is Schleswig-Holstein's oldest town, with some 1,200 years of history. Everything here is steeped in the legend, even the seagulls. According to tradition, the birds nesting on Seagull Island in the middle of the Schlei are actually the fellow conspirators of Duke Abel, who in 1250 murdered his own brother, King Eric. The crime was discovered when the king's body, weighted with chains, washed ashore from the Schlei. The duke went mad, eventually died, and was impaled and buried in the Tiergarten. But his followers, according to the story, became seagulls, doomed to nest forever on Seagull Island. Today this sleepy town is visited mainly for its memories.

ESSENTIALS

GETTING THERE By Train   The **Schleswig Bahnhof** is on the Flensburg-Neumünster-Hamburg and Westerland-Hamburg rail lines, with frequent connections. Trains from Hamburg arrive daily (trip time: 2 hr., 20 min.). For information and schedules, call ☎ **01805/996633.**

By Bus   Long-distance bus service to and from Hamburg, Flensburg, and Kiel is provided by **Autokraft GmbH** in Kiel (☎ **0431/71070**).

By Car   Access by car is via the A7 Autobahn north or south.

VISITOR INFORMATION   For information, contact **Tourist-Information,** Plessenstrasse 7 (☎ **04621/2-48-78**). Hours are May through September, Monday to Friday 9am to 12:30pm and 1:30 to 5pm, Saturday 9am to noon; October through April, Monday to Thursday 9am to 12:30pm and 1:30 to 5pm, and Friday 9am to 12:30pm.

EXPLORING THE TOWN

Dom St. Petri (St. Peter's Cathedral). Süderdomstrasse 1. ☎ **04621/96-30-54.** Free admission. May–Sept Mon–Thurs and Sat 9am–5pm, Fri 9am–3pm, Sun 1–5pm; Oct–Apr Mon–Thurs and Sat 10am–4pm, Fri 10am–3pm, Sun 1–4pm. Bus: 1, 2, 3, 4, or 5.

The jewel of Schleswig is St. Peter's Cathedral, a brick Romanesque-Gothic Hallenkirche (hall church) begun in the 12th century. Its towering spire makes the rest of the Altstadt seem like so many dollhouses by comparison. Inside is the outstanding 16th-century *Bordesholm Altarpiece*, a powerful work carved in oak by Hans Bruggeman for the convent at Bordesholm. Its elaborately carved Gothic panels contain nearly 400 figures. The cathedral and cloisters also possess art treasures, including the *Blue Madonna* by J. Ovens and 13th-century frescoes.

Schloss Gottorf. On a small island in the Burgsee, a bay at the west end of the Schlei. ☎ **04621/81-32-22.** Admission (including both museums) 8DM ($4.55) adults, 4DM ($2.30) children. Mar–Oct daily 9am–5pm; Nov–Feb daily 9:30am–4pm. Bus: 1, 2, 3, 4, or 5.

A dam and a bridge connect the island with the town. As you walk around the harbor, the panorama of the Altstadt and the widening bay opens up behind you. The castle is the largest in Schleswig-Holstein. The foundations date from the original 13th-century ducal palace; the present structure was built mainly in the 16th and 17th centuries and has been reconditioned since 1948 to house two museums.

The **Provincial Museum of Archeology** or Archäologisches Landesmuseum (☎ **04621/81-33-00**) has a most remarkable exhibit (in a separate building), the Nydam Boat, a 4th-century ship found in the Nydam marshes in 1863. In the same room are artifacts and weapons discovered with the ship and Viking corpses preserved in the moor, all adding up to one of the major archaeological finds in northern Germany.

Schleswig-Holstein State Museum (☎ **04621/81-32-22**), also housed in the castle, contains an exceptional collection of fine and applied art from medieval times to the 20th century, including painting, sculpture, furniture, textiles, and weapons. Outstanding are the late Gothic King's Hall, the 17th-century ducal living rooms with rich stucco ceilings, and the Renaissance chapel with a private pew for the ducal family, decorated with intricate and elaborate carvings and inlays. Two separate buildings east of the castle house collections of contemporary art, including outstanding works of German expressionism and modern sculpture, plus the ethnological collection of implements and tools used by farmers, artisans, and fishermen.

Wikinger Museum Haithabu. Durchwahl (1½ miles from Schleswig). ☎ **04621/81-33-00.** Admission 6DM ($3.40). Apr–Oct daily 9am–5pm; Nov–Feb Tues–Sun 10am–4pm.

Haithabu was one of the most prominent settlements of northern Europe during the Viking era. This Viking Museum, opened in 1985, contains the finds of archaeological excavations of the Viking-age town of Haithabu. Exhibits cover all aspects of daily life. There's even a Viking long ship.

In summer, you can reach this site by a scenic, 20-minute boat ride. Departures are from Stadthafen, the town quay in Schleswig, south of the cathedral. After you dock, it's a 10-minute walk to the museum. In winter you'll have to take a 2-mile walk from the rail station.

WHERE TO STAY

Hotel and Restaurant Skandia. Lollfuss 89, 24837 Schleswig. ☎ **04621/2-41-90.** Fax 04621/2-99-85. 25 units. 120DM ($68.40) double. Rates include buffet breakfast. AE, MC, V. Bus: 1 or 2.

This is the best budget choice in Schleswig. You'll find a collection of high-ceilinged public rooms, along with small but cozy guest rooms decorated with modern wood-grained pieces, including good beds. The hotel has an excellent kitchen, turning out north German specialties. Set-price menus cost 18DM to 30DM ($10.25 to $17.10). The restaurant serves dinner daily 6 to 10pm.

Hotel Waldschlössen. Kolonnenweg 152 (a mile southwest of town), 24837 Schleswig-Pulverholz. ☎ **04621/38-30.** Fax 04621/38-31-05. 126 units. TV TEL. 145DM–195DM ($82.65–$111.15) double; 370DM ($210.90) suite. Rates include buffet breakfast. AE, DC, MC, V. Free parking.

This elegant country hotel has finer bedrooms and amenities than any of the in-town properties. It's equipped with every convenience to make your stay interesting and comfortable. Outside, there's a rock garden, a gabled house, an elongated annex, and lots of trees. The public rooms are intimately lit and decorated with tasteful carpeting, warm brick detailing, and wood paneling. The pool is centrally heated year-round. Other amenities include a bowling alley, sauna, whirlpool bathtub, and solarium. Many of the rooms contain a minibar and safe. Accommodations range in size from small to medium, each equipped with a firm mattress on a comfortable bed, plus a tiled and compact bathroom.

Strandhalle. Strandweg 2, 24837 Schleswig. ☎ **04621/90-90.** Fax 04621/90-91-00. 25 units. MINIBAR TV TEL. 170DM–210DM ($96.90–$119.70) double. Rates include buffet breakfast. AE, DC, MC, V. Parking 12DM ($6.85). Bus: 1, 2, 3, 4, or 5.

Strandhalle may not be as good as the Waldschlössen, but it still has many winning features, especially for those who'd like to stay within Schleswig and absorb the atmosphere of this ancient town. Actually, this hotel is more of a holiday resort—right on the water, with its own rowboats and indoor pool. The owners maintain an informal atmosphere. Bedrooms are small but neatly kept, each coming with a firm mattress on a good bed, plus a small, somewhat cramped bathroom with shower stalls. Nonetheless, the hotel is good value for the area. Ask for a room opening onto the water, with a view of the yacht harbor.

WHERE TO DINE

Olschewski's. Hafenstrasse 40 (near the waterfront). ☎ **04621/2-55-77.** Reservations required Fri–Sat. Main courses 20DM–40DM ($11.40–$22.80); fixed-price menu 65DM ($37.05). AE, MC, V. Wed–Mon 11:30am–2:30pm; Wed–Sun 5:30–9:30pm. Bus: 1, 2, 3, 4, or 5. CONTINENTAL.

This cozy, well-managed restaurant is the best in town, superior to any of the hotel dining rooms. You can dine in either a glass-sided modern extension or an unpretentious dining room with views of the Schlei. Your choices may include fresh salad in almost any season, cream of tomato soup, salmon with a tangy cream base or a Riesling sauce, fillet of lamb with rosemary, or a perfectly cooked roast goose.

SCHLESWIG AFTER DARK

If you're looking for action, head for **Lollfuss,** running parallel to the Schlei between Schloss Gottorf and a north-side residential area. Many places here are cafes during the day and bars at night. The best and most popular pub of the lot is **Patio,** Lollfuss 3 (☎ **04621/2-99-99**), an intimate two-story structure that usually stays open between midnight and 1am (considered very late in this small town). It also has Schleswig's most popular outdoor terrace. If you get hungry, you'll find pastas, salads, pizzas, and steaks costing from 8DM to 21DM ($4.55 to $11.95).

4 Westerland (Sylt)

13 miles W of the German/Danish border, 120 miles NW of Hamburg

The long, narrow island of Sylt (pronounced *Zoolt*) and its capital, Westerland, form the northernmost point of Germany. Sylt lies in the North Sea off the coasts of Denmark and Schleswig-Holstein. It's the largest island of the Frisian archipelago, which stretches from Denmark to the Netherlands. The "Watt" is the name given to the eastern coast, facing the mainland. Pounding winter storms seem to take more and more of the coastline each year, and there are those who think that Sylt will one day disappear into the sea.

People come here to breathe the iodine-rich air and enjoy a climate the Germans call *Reizklima*. Sylt is today the most exclusive resort in Germany, and its hotel prices reflect its lofty status. Sylt also has a sizable gay and lesbian population, and is often called "The Fire Island of Europe." In the 1960s, Sylt became famous for "the rich and the naked," when the entire island was reportedly an ongoing bacchanalian frenzy. But it's quieted down since then. Temperatures in midsummer are usually in the low 70s, but rain can come at any minute, and winds on the beach are a constant. This has given rise to the Sylt "mink," or yellow oilskin, which chic visitors wear to protect themselves from the elements.

The spa here has facilities for the treatment of everything from heart disease to skin irritations. The basic therapy is sunshine, pure air, and seawater, but in recent years mud baths have also become a method of treatment. Some of the more remote sections of the dunes have been turned into nudist beaches for purists in the art of sunshine therapy. In addition to bathing, there are facilities in and around Westerland for horseback riding, surfing, golf, and tennis, as well as more sedentary entertainment, such as the theater and concerts.

ESSENTIALS

GETTING THERE   **By Plane**   The nearest international airport is at Hamburg (see chapter 16). From there you can fly to the regional **Westland Airport** (☎ **04651/ 92-06-12**). There's also regularly scheduled air service from Berlin, Munich, Frankfurt and Hamburg.

By Train   The only link between the mainland and the island of Sylt is the railroad causeway running from the mainland town of Niebüll. If you wish to bring your car to the island, you'll have to load it on the train at Niebüll for the slow ride (see "By Car," below). No advance booking is necessary—you just arrive and take your chances. Passengers are carried free.

Westerland Bahnhof lies on the Westerland-Hamburg and the Westerland-Lübeck rail lines, with frequent connections. Seventeen trains arrive from Hamburg daily (trip time: 2 hr., 40 min., to 3 hr., 20 min., depending on the train). For rail information and schedules, call ☎ **01805/996633.**

By Car-Ferry   An alternative way of reaching Sylt is to take a car-ferry between the Danish port of Havneby, on the island of Rømo (which is easily accessible via highway from Germany) and the German port of List, at the northern tip of Sylt. There are at least a dozen daily crossings between those points in summer, with a much-reduced schedule in winter. Reservations for your car are possible. For information about these crossings, call the **Rømo-Sylt Line.** In List (Germany), its number is ☎ **04651/ 870475.** In Havneby (Denmark), the number is ☎ **045/74-75-53-04.**

By Bus   The few buses that pull into Sylt are forced to ride the flatcars on the rail line across the Hindenburg Causeway for the final stretch of their journey. Many

A Disappearing Playground

Scientists warn that the western coast of Sylt is one of the most fragile ecosystems in Germany, and like New York's Fire Island, may one day be reclaimed by the sea. The entire island is little more than a strip, only 1,800 feet wide at its narrowest point, that's composed mostly of sand and very little rock. As such, it presents little resistance—especially after it's been stripped of its tenacious salt grasses—to the onslaught of erosion and deterioration. The sand dunes, warmed by the Gulf Stream, are forever shifting, and the winds sweeping in from the North Sea can move them by as much as a dozen feet in only a year. (Locals call these "wandering" sand dunes *Wanderdunen.)* Although the winter months in general, and storms at any time of the year, are highly destructive, it's during strong south winds that most erosion takes place, and on some mornings after violent storms, huge amounts of sand migrate from the beachfront out into the North Sea.

In the 1970s, a series of *tetrapoden* (four-legged concrete structures that look like giant jacks) were built on the sands of Westerland and Hornum beaches, in an unsuccessful attempt to hold back erosion. (They were later judged useless, and their construction discontinued.)

Today, everyone's favorite solution is one of the simplest: Whenever funds are allocated by the municipal budget, you'll see one or more barges moored offshore, pumping sand from deepwater sites back onto beaches of Sylt. There are also severe penalties for anyone removing salt grasses and scrub from the beachfronts, and severe restrictions against building new houses on any land that's deemed as fragile.

A Frisian we met took us for a day's walk to view the desertlike, forlorn beauty of the sand dunes. Deep, windless ridges were everywhere. "Look, the wind, the rain, and the sea are taking my island from me," the man said with a kind of despair. "One day—not in my time, perhaps—but one day it will all be gone. The wind is actually blowing Sylt away. The crashing tides are claiming our coast."

If there is an air of desperation about the Germans who live and frolic in this North Sea playground, it may be because they know they won't be here forever.

passengers prefer to get off their bus in Niebühl and transfer onto one of the passenger trains that make the frequent crossings to Westerland from other parts of Germany and Europe. Rail fare between Niebühl and Westerland costs 22DM ($12.55) per person, round-trip. The ride takes between 30 and 45 minutes each way.

By Car   Construction of a conventional bridge from the mainland of Schleswig-Holstein to Sylt has never really been feasible. Therefore, cars headed to Sylt are loaded onto flatcars at the mainland railway junction of Niebühl and hauled out across the *Hindenburg Damm* (Hindenburg Causeway) to the railway station of Westerland, on Sylt. Drivers remain in their cars, with the doors locked, eventually arriving at Westerland between 30 and 45 minutes later. For information on these and all other (conventional) trains between the German mainland and Sylt, call the **Deutsche Bahn** information service in Westerland at ☎ **01805/99-66-33.** Trains depart at 30-minute intervals daily between 5am and 10pm. No reservations are accepted for hauling your car across. Round-trip transport for most cars costs 140DM ($79.80).

Access to Niebühl is possible via the A7 Autobahn north or south.

VISITOR INFORMATION For information, contact the **Fremdenverkehrszentrale,** Am Bundesbahnhof Westerland (☎ **04651/99-88**). It's open May through October daily 9am to 8pm; November through April, Monday to Saturday 9am to 7pm.

SHOPPING Few other holiday destinations in Germany are as frenetic about clothing as Sylt. Garments are removed and put on again with abandon on this island with fickle weather and an extremely clothes-conscious population. You'll find impressive inventories of expensively casual clothing on Sylt—items that are artfully simple, easy to don, easy to doff, and easy to look at. The island's best shopping streets are the **Friedrichstrasse,** in Westerland, and the **Stroewae,** in Kampen, both lined with boutiques associated with the great names of European fashion.

In Westerland, look for menswear at **The Camel Store,** Friedrichstrasse 32 (☎ **04651/77-79**), and **Heising,** Friedrichstrasse 22 (☎ **04651/2-27-65**); and women's wear at **Marco Polo,** Strandstrasse 3–5 (☎ **04651/61-11**), or at any of the dozens of chic hole-in-the-wall boutiques. In Kampen, on the northern side, both men and women will find the glossy and endlessly tasteful emporium of German luminary **Jil Sander,** Stroewae 7 (☎ **04651/4-54-56**).

The island's art galleries reflect the tastes and preoccupations of big-city Hamburg. Two of the most interesting emporiums for dramatic modern art include the **Galerie Martens,** Keitumerchaussee 20, in Westerland (☎ **04651/98-79-44**); a highly visible competitor is **Galerie Sprotte,** Altdorfstrasse 1 (☎ **04651/4-24-13**), whose exhibition space is mostly devoted to the stylized and often riveting paintings of long-time Sylt resident Siegvard Sprotte. His renderings of the landscapes of Sylt have been influenced by everything from 16th-century Flemish portraits to early 20th-century impressionism.

WHERE TO STAY

Hotel Clausen. Friedrichstrasse 20 (in Westerland's pedestrian zone, a 3-min. walk from the beach), 25980 Westerland/Sylt. ☎ **04651/9-22-90.** Fax 04651/2-80-07. 21 units. TV TEL. 180DM–280DM ($102.60–$159.60) double; 240DM–300DM ($136.80–$171) suite. Rates include buffet breakfast. AE. Parking 10DM ($5.70). Closed Jan 7–21.

This four-story building was originally built around 1950 and radically modernized in 1992. Today, its congenial English-speaking owners occupy the upper (fourth) floor. On the building's lower stories is a series of simple but well-maintained rooms. Rooms are small but tidily maintained, each fitted with a quality mattress on a good bed. Bathrooms are also small and have shower stalls. Breakfast is the only meal served, but many restaurants are nearby.

Hotel Miramar. Friedrichstrasse 43, 25980 Westerland/Sylt.☎ **04651/85-50.** Fax 04651/85-52-22. www.hotel-miramar.de. E-mail: miramar-sylt@t-online.de. 104 units. MINIBAR TV TEL. 280DM–660DM ($159.60–$376.20) double; 450DM–1,190DM ($256.50–$678.30) suite. Rates include buffet breakfast. AE, DC, MC, V.

This hotel, on a bluff just above the beach, is the second best accommodation at Westerland, just below Stadt Hamburg (see below). The Miramar is surrounded by an arched veranda, and its public rooms are graced with enormous arched windows with views of the sea. An octagonal light, left over from the building's 1903 construction, illuminates the salon from above. The high-ceilinged guest rooms are quite comfortable and were recently renovated; each comes with a luxurious bed and a recently renewed bathroom.

Dining/Diversions: Guests relax on the cafe-terrace overlooking the water. The bar is a chic rendezvous spot. The formal restaurant, serving both North German and international dishes, is among the finest on the island.

Amenities: The sunny indoor pool, near the sauna and fitness room, makes swimming an option even in winter. Also, room service, concierge, dry cleaning, laundry.

✪ **Stadt Hamburg.** Strandstrasse 2 (next to the casino), 25980 Westerland/Sylt. ☎ **04651/ 85-80.** Fax 04651/85-82-20. 94 units. TV TEL. 325DM–475DM ($185.25–$270.75) double; 510DM–570DM ($290.70–$324.90) suite. AE, MC, V. Parking 15DM ($8.55).

This is the best hotel on the island, though it looks more like a well-appointed country home than a hotel. The gleaming white entrance is reached through a white picket fence, and its rear windows overlook a well-kept lawn. The bright and cheerful interior has country-estate furnishings, including wing chairs and floral-covered armchairs. Each spacious room is individually furnished, with homelike touches. The mattresses and the linens are the island's finest, and the tiled bathrooms are state of the art, with hair dryers, toiletries, and plush towels.

Dining/Diversions: The charming breakfast room has a blue-and-white ceramic stove. Guests gather on cooler evenings around the open fireplace. The restaurant serves some of the best food at the resort (see below).

Amenities: Concierge, room service, dry cleaning, laundry, newspaper delivery.

Wunschmann Hotel. Andreas-Dirks-Strasse 4, 25980 Westerland/Sylt. ☎ **04651/50-25.** Fax 04651/50-28. 36 units. TV TEL. 206DM–396DM ($117.40–$225.70) double; 490DM– 660DM ($279.30–$376.20) suite. AE. Parking 12DM ($6.85). Closed mid-Nov to mid-Dec.

This hotel is in the heart of the tourist belt of Westerland, yet only minutes from the sand dunes. Rooms are in a complex of modern buildings (with more than two dozen boutiques), but the hotel's interior exudes old-world tranquillity. The medium-sized and one-of-a-kind guest rooms are cheerful, with strong colors and firm mattresses. Two offer minibars.

Dining: The hotel restaurant serves adequate German and international fare for breakfast, lunch, and dinner.

Amenities: Concierge, 24-hour room service, dry cleaning, laundry service, in-room massage, twice-daily maid service, and baby-sitting. A health club is nearby.

WHERE TO DINE

Alte Friesenstube. Gaadt 4, Westerland. ☎ **04651/12-28.** Reservations required. Main courses 29.50DM–49DM ($16.80–$27.95). AE. Tues–Sun 11:30am–2:30pm and 6–10:30pm. Closed Jan. NORTHERN GERMAN/FRISIAN.

This restaurant is refreshingly down-to-earth amid the pretentiousness of Sylt. The thatched building housing this place was constructed in 1648. The menus are written on the wall in a dialect of low German, but someone will gladly assist you in deciphering the offerings, which include regional pork, fish, and beef dishes. Especially popular is duck with orange sauce, and a local saltwater fish (panfische) with roasted potatoes and mustard sauce. No one puts on airs, and the kitchen hardly follows trendy recipes, sticking instead to the robust fare the islanders have been eating for decades.

Hardy auf Sylt. Norderstrasse 65, Westerland. ☎ **04651/2-27-75.** Reservations required. Main courses 26DM–34DM ($14.80–$19.40). No credit cards. Tues–Sun 6pm–midnight. Closed Jan 15–Feb 15 and Nov 30–Dec 20. INTERNATIONAL/NORTHERN GERMAN.

This round, thatched restaurant has a nostalgic interior featuring furniture dating from about 1890. Finely worked columns, old oil portraits, beautiful glass lamps, and skillfully wrought candlesticks combine to create a relaxed, intimate feeling. The menu is adjusted seasonally. There's a fine selection of French and German wine.

✪ **Jörg Müller.** Süderstrasse 8 (a 5-min. walk from the center of Westerland). ☎ **04651/ 2-77-88.** Reservations required. Main courses 52DM–76DM ($29.65–$43.30); fixed-price menus 148DM–178DM ($84.35–$101.45). AE, DC, MC, V. Thurs–Mon 11:30am–2pm; Wed–Mon 6–10pm. Closed Nov 25–Dec 18. CONTINENTAL/FRENCH.

The most elegant dining on the island is at Jörg Müller. The brick building that contains this restaurant is almost a landmark in itself, thanks to its thatched roof, steep gables, and Frisian architecture. The restaurant's fame has eclipsed that of every competitor. Menu items change with the seasons and feature a blend of contemporary continental cuisine with imaginative variations of French recipes, which might include lobster salad with herb-flavored vinaigrette sauce, sliced and braised goose liver with segments of glazed apples, or roast salt-marsh lamb flavored with herbs and served with ratatouille-flavored cream sauce. You can also enjoy local oysters with compote of red shallots and champagne sauce or halibut baked in fennel. For dessert, you might order a compote of fresh fruits with pistachio nuts or feuilleté of chocolate served with both light- and dark-chocolate mousse.

✪ **Restaurant Stadt Hamburg.** Strandstrasse 2, Westerland. ☎ **04651/85-80.** Reservations recommended, especially if you're not a hotel guest. Main courses 39DM–58DM ($22.25–$33.05); fixed-price dinners 69DM–124DM ($39.35–$70.70). AE, MC, V. Daily 6–10pm. Bus: Centrale Omnibus Bahnhof. GERMAN/FRISIAN.

Top-rate cuisine is offered here in an attractive setting. The menu is so wide-ranging it may be hard to make up your mind, but among the à la carte listings, the smoothest beginning is the cream of lobster soup. Many seafood specialties are featured as main courses, such as pan-fried fresh North Sea sole and turbot medaillons in saffron sauce with zucchini. Another good dish is the rack of lamb (raised on the salty grasslands of the island). For dessert, try homemade *rote Grütze*—different kinds of berries and cherries topped with vanilla ice cream.

Web Christel. Süderstrasse 11 (opposite Jörg Müller), Westerland. ☎ **04651/2-29-00.** Reservations recommended. Main courses 33DM–45DM ($18.80–$25.65); fixed-price menus 50DM–99DM ($28.50–$56.45). No credit cards. Fri–Wed 5–11pm. NORTH GERMAN.

Favored by local residents for its reasonable prices and cozy ambience, this restaurant occupies a century-old Frisian house set in the center of Westerland, opposite its more glamorous (and more expensive) rival, Jörg Müller. The three old-fashioned dining rooms are each outfitted with linen napery. Menu items include a wide selection of fish, such as classic versions of turbot in an herb-butter-mustard sauce, and sole prepared in the meuniére style or grilled and served with hollandaise sauce. Roast duck with two different sauces is also available. The staff is warm and polite.

SYLT AFTER DARK

Two contenders on Sylt's nightlife circuit include **Disco Pony,** Strowae, in Kampen (☎ 04651/42182), where both indoor and outdoor bar areas encompass views of the sea and the scrub-covered coastline that flanks it. Attracting for the most part a clientele under 40, it's open nightly beginning around 10:30pm. (It's closed on Monday and Tuesday from October to April.) And for the closest thing to the kind of urban underground life you might have expected in Hamburg or Berlin, head for the **Airport Lounge,** a disco within some of the industrial-looking buildings at the Westerland airport (☎ 04651/92-06-12). Here, loud and highly danceable house and garage music is the norm every Wednesday to Sunday from 10:30pm till at least 3am.

Unless you're a hard-core gambler, the island's bars, cafes, and restaurants are more interesting than its casino, **Spielbank Westerland,** Strandstrasse (☎ 04561/230450), which, ironically, occupies the same premises as Westerland's Rathaus (town hall). There's no maximum limit on how much you can bet, so the activities around the baccarat, roulette, and blackjack tables can get intense, depending on the crowd. Entrance costs 5DM ($2.85) per person. Men are encouraged to wear neckties. Hours are daily from 5pm till at least 3am. On the premises is a sophisticated bar, open during the same hours as the gaming tables.

18

A Scenic Drive Along the Baltic

The Baltic coast is saltier and windier and has a more international outlook than other regions of the former East Germany. Throughout the Cold War, this windswept seaside was a playground for the factory workers and bureaucrats of the now-defunct DDR. For centuries before that, the region thrived as the site of the busy ports of the Hanseatic League, whose lore still permeates the land. Other cultural influences came from the Swedish, Latvian, Lithuanian, and Polish ports with which for many centuries the League did much of its trading.

Since the opening of the border, the district is once again being enjoyed for its nautical history and its old Hanseatic towns. Since the collapse of the East/West border, the Baltic Coast has slowly emerged as a hot spot for Germany's beach-loving throngs, and the entire coastline has benefited from a major restoration of its historic structures, many of which were decaying.

The region is best visited by car, on any of several different driving routes. The ideal departure point for this exploration is Lübeck (see chapter 17). From Lübeck, drive east for 35 miles along Highway 105 (also known as E22). En route, you'll traverse the frontier that separated West from East Germany for more than 45 years and enter the medieval principality of Mecklenburg-West Pomerania. Your first stop will be Wismar.

1 Wismar

37 miles E of Lübeck, 33 miles W of Rostock

Wismar was once an elegant city of the Hanseatic League, the medieval capital of Mecklenburg-West Pomerania. The city became prominent in the early 1200s because of its port facilities. For long periods of its history it was part of the overseas empire of Sweden. Wismar contains the largest market square in Germany (2½ acres), that's surrounded by elegant buildings with architectural styles ranging from 19th-century Romanesque revival to 14th-century North German Gothic. The square's focal point, and one of the town's most frequently photographed objects, is an elaborate wrought-iron fountain imported from Holland in the early 1600s. The silent filmmaker Friedrich Wilhelm Murnau used the twisting streets of Wismar's Altstadt as the backdrop for his classic vampire film, *Nosferatu*.

Unfortunately, your drive into this town's charming core will be dampened by a view of the socialist regime's endless concrete-sided suburbs.

Sites to watch for in the historic city center include the pillared and gabled **Rathaus** (not open to visitors), built on the town's main square in the neoclassical style in 1819. A very old house on the square, **Alter Schwede (The Old Swede),** constructed around 1380, functions as a restaurant (see "Where to Dine," below). The town's most famous church is the **St. Nikolaikirche,** Hinter dem Chor (☎ **03841/21-36-24**), a Gothic brick structure whose high altar dates from 1430. It's open May through October Monday through Saturday 10am to noon and 1 to 6pm, and Sunday 1 to 5pm; in the off-season only on Saturday 11am to 3pm and Sunday 1 to 4pm. Admission is free.

For tourist information in Wismar, contact **Wismar-Informationen,** Am Markt 11 (☎ **03841/1-94-33**), open year-round daily from 9am to 6pm.

WHERE TO STAY

Most visitors come to Wismar only for the day, moving on to overnight accommodations in either Rostock or Schwerin. However, if you choose to stay, try one of these hotels below.

Hotel Stadt Hamburg. Am Markt 24, 23966 Wismar. ☎ **03841/23-90.** Fax 03841/ 23-92-39. www.edition-digital. E-mail: hotelsthh@aol.com. 106 units. TV TEL. 185DM– 245DM ($105.45–$139.65) double. Rates include buffet breakfast. AE, DC, MC, V.

This well-managed hotel, recently renovated, is the best in town. It has three floors, three restaurants, an English-speaking staff, and a desirable location on the main (and most historic) square in Wismar. The no-frills bedrooms are comfortable and contemporary. Each is rather bandboxy, but all are fitted with comfortable mattresses. The hotel's uppermost floor contains a health club that's free for residents but costs 12DM ($6.85) for a 2-hour session for nonresidents. The hotel's most formal restaurant is the Pülergarten; more casual is a simple coffee shop (Café Am Markt). Our favorite spot is the Tittataster (see below).

WHERE TO DINE

Bierkeller Tittataster. Am Markt 24. ☎ **03841/23-90.** Platters 14DM–33DM ($8–$18.80). AE, DC, MC, V. Mon–Sat 5pm–midnight. GERMAN/INTERNATIONAL.

This restaurant in the cellar of the Hotel Stadt Hamburg is workaday and deliberately informal. The vaulting that rises above its battered wooden tables dates from the 14th century. Menu items taste best when consumed with copious amounts of beer. They include an array of snack-style platters and a hearty selection of salads, schnitzels, and roasts. On some nights, the cellar hosts live jazz bands.

Restaurant Alter Schwede. Am Markt 20. ☎ **03841/28-35-52.** Reservations recommended in summer. Main courses 20DM–35DM ($11.40–$19.95); set menu 38DM ($21.65). AE, MC, V. Daily 11:30am–11:30pm. GERMAN.

Constructed in 1380, this building is one of the oldest and most historically evocative in Wismar, so well known that many Germans drive from other parts of the Baltic just to see it. Its name, "The Old Swede," refers to the Swedish invasions of the 1600s, but luckily for sightseers, the building functions as a restaurant. In the high-ceilinged dining room, an old-time staff in black-and-white uniforms bustles back and forth, carrying steaming platters of traditional Germanic food. Menu items include sauerbraten with red cabbage and potatoes, a marinated pork roast known as *Rippenbraten,* all kinds of wursts, salmon roasted in orange sauce, and lots of fish from the Baltic.

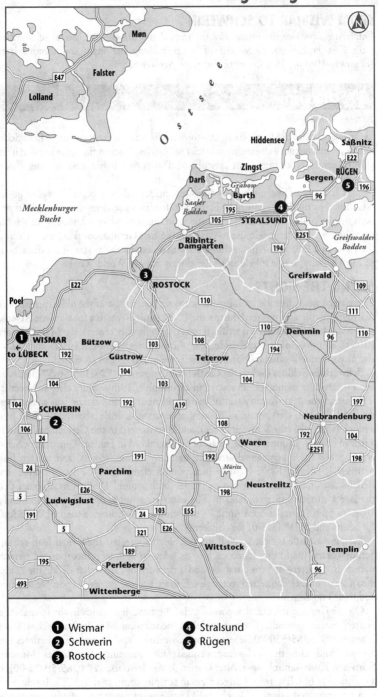

Møn

Falster

E47

Lolland

Mecklenburger Bucht

Poel

E22

1 WISMAR

← to LÜBECK 192

Bützow

Güstrow 104

104

104

2 SCHWERIN

106

24

Ostsee

Hiddensee

Zingst

Darß *Grabow*

Saaler Bodden Barth

195

105 STRALSUND

Ribintz-Damgarten

3 ROSTOCK

110

110

108

Teterow

103

192

A19

103

Saßnitz

E22

RÜGEN

5 196

Bergen

96

E251

Greifswalder Bodden

194

Greifswald

109

111

110

Demmin

96 110

194

104

197

Neubrandenburg

108

192 104

Waren

E251 198

Müritz

191

24

Parchim

E26

Ludwigslust

5

191

24 103

5

321

189

195

493 Wittenberge

Perleberg

E55

E26

192

198

Neustrelitz

Wittstock

Templin

96

---

1 Wismar   **4** Stralsund

2 Schwerin   **5** Rügen

3 Rostock

FROM WISMAR TO SCHWERIN

Our route now detours inland (south) toward the present-day capital of Mecklenburg-West Pomerania. Drive out of Wismar along the main southbound artery (Highway 106) for 19 miles until you reach Schwerin.

2 Schwerin

20 miles S of Wisman

Lying inland from the Baltic coast, this town at the southwestern corner of Lake Schwerin is set in a fertile, well-irrigated district of "lakelets." Schwerin is the industrial and cultural center of an important agricultural district, but it has more to offer visitors than commerce.

This is a city of ancient history and well-entrenched civic pride. It was originally established in the 11th century by Slavs, who fortified a settlement on the island now occupied by Schwerin Castle. Henry the Lion, duke of Saxony, annexed their settlement and used the strategic site to establish the first German-speaking colony east of the Elbe. In 1358, Schwerin was honored with a designation as seat of the ducal court of Mecklenburg, a title it held until the closing days of World War I.

SEEING THE SIGHTS

There aren't many historic buildings in Schwerin, since most of the old structures were destroyed by fire and replaced during the 19th century. Worth a look are the **Arsenal,** set beside the Pfaffenteich (an artificial reservoir in the city center), the **Marstall** (royal stables), and the **Kollegiengebäude,** seat of civic government until 1945 and today a site of government offices. (None of these three buildings can be visited.)

Schweriner Schloss (Schwerin Castle), Lennestrasse 1 (☎ **0385/56-57-38**), is the most spectacular monument in town and a triumph of 19th-century civic architecture. This castle, the 19th-century seat of the Mecklenburg grand dukes, was spared from fires and bombings. It's set on an island that separates a small lake (the Burgsee) from a much larger lake (the Schweriner See), and is connected to the German mainland by a pair of bridges. Inspired by the Château de Chambord in France's Loire Valley, Schweriner Schloss is a pentagonal structure of many domes, towers, and turrets, built between 1843 and 1857. Its style incorporates elements of Gothic, baroque, and Renaissance architecture. The castle's chapel (built around 1560) is much older than the larger structure that contains it. The castle-museum is open Tuesday to Sunday 10am to 5pm (closes at 6pm April 15 to October 14). Entrance costs 6DM ($3.40) for adults and 3DM ($1.70) for children.

Even if the castle is closed, you'll still be able to appreciate the formal 18th-century **Schlossgarten** (park) that flanks each of its sides. Its architects incorporated terraced waterfalls, a battery of heroic statues, and a network of canals that divide the garden into a series of interconnected rectangles. Entrance to the gardens is possible anytime, and there's no admission fee.

On the German mainland, a pair of imposing buildings stands in the former Alter Garten parade grounds. These include the neoclassical **Mecklenburgisches Staatstheater** (☎ **0385/53000**), where dramas, comedies, and operas are sometimes performed, and also the well-recommended state museum, **Staatliches Museum Schwerin-Kunstsammlunger,** Alter Garten 3, Werderstrasse (☎ **0385/59-24-00**), in a neoclassical building resembling a Roman temple, completed in 1785. Inside you'll find a worthy collection of Dutch and Flemish paintings from the 16th century, as well as 18th-century paintings from France and the German-speaking world. Specific examples include *Drinking Boy* and *Boy Holding a Flute* by Frans Hals, and *Home*

Concert by Frans van Mieris. There are also collections from the German Middle Ages, including porcelain (especially Dresden china), 18th-century court paintings, and works by such modern artists as Max Liebermann. It's open Tuesday to Sunday 10am to 5pm. Admission is 7DM ($4) adults, 5.50DM ($3.15) students and children.

Schwerin's **Dom,** Am Marktplatz (☎ **0385/56-50-14**), was begun around 1248. The cathedral is a fine example of brick medieval architecture, designed in the Lübeck Hanseatic Gothic style. Highlights include a Gothic altarpiece, probably carved in Lübeck around 1480. If you'd like a panoramic view of the town and the lake, you can climb to the top of the 320-foot-high tower. The Dom is open June through September, Monday 10am to 1pm, Tuesday through Saturday 10am to 1pm and 2 to 5pm, and Sunday noon to 5pm. During other months, hours are Monday 11am to 4pm, Tuesday to Saturday 11am to noon and 2:30 to 4:30pm, and Sunday 2:30 to 4:30pm. You can enter the church free, but it costs 2DM ($1.15) to go up in the tower.

Several interesting trips are possible from Schwerin. You can take a boat trip (mid-summer only) across the Schweriner See or, if you feel athletic, hike around the lake's southern shore. Information on attractions in and around the town can be obtained at the **City Tourist Office,** Am Markt 10 (☎ **0385/592-52-12**). It's open Monday to Friday 10am to noon and 1 to 5pm, and during summer (May through September), Monday to Friday 10am to 6pm and Saturday 10am to 1pm.

WHERE TO STAY

Crowne Plaza Hotel Schwerin. Bleicher Ufer 23 (a 15-min. walk west of the town center), 19053 Schwerin. ☎ **800/2-CROWNE** or 0385/5-75-50. Fax 0385/5-75-57-77. www.crowneplaza.com. 100 units. MINIBAR TV TEL. 220DM–235DM ($125.40–$133.95) double; 350DM ($199.50) suite. AE, DC, MC, V. Tram: 1 or 2. Bus: 10.

This hotel rises five floors above the shoreline of a freshwater lake (the Ostdorfer See). It's part of a compound of modern, cement-sided buildings that include offices and private apartments. Bedrooms are modern and convenient, although rather bandboxy and furnished in a completely functional way, but the beds are comfortable with good mattresses. Those overlooking the lake are outfitted in blue; those fronting a verdant public park are in deep tones of red. Two of the five floors are reserved strictly for non-smokers. On the hotel's premises is a health club with its own sauna, and just off the marble-sheathed lobby are a bar and a noteworthy restaurant, Marco Polo, which is open daily for lunch and dinner. Set menus cost 42DM to 60DM ($23.95 to $34.20).

Hotel Nordlicht. Apothekerstrasse 2 (one-half mile from Marktplatz), 19055 Schwerin. ☎ **0385/55-81-50.** Fax 0385/5-57-43-83. 5 units. TV TEL. 145DM ($82.65) double. Rates include continental breakfast. MC, V. Free parking. Tram: Marienplatz.

This inexpensive establishment is more like a B&B than a conventional hotel. It's across from the pond *(Pfaffenteich)*, which is encircled by walkways. The hotel, built in 1991, consists of only five rooms furnished in a simple but modern style, each with a good mattress and a cramped bathroom with a shower stall and thin towels. Hot food is served daily from 11:30am to midnight in the restaurant or on the cafe-terrace.

Hotel Plaza Schwerin. Am Grünen Tal (near Schloss Schwerin, 5 min. from the center by car), 19063 Schwerin. ☎ **800/528-1234** or 0385/3-99-20. Fax 0385/3-99-21-88. 79 units. MINIBAR TV TEL. 150DM–200DM ($85.50–$114) double; 250DM ($142.50) suite. AE, DC, MC, V. Free parking. Tram: Zoo.

This hotel is outstanding in many respects, in spite of its unappetizing location in a sea of Sputnik-era apartment blocks. It's a favorite with vacationers and business travelers. Most of the contemporary bedrooms are spacious and all are designed for standard comfort with decent beds and compact little bathrooms with shower stalls.

Amenities include trouser presses, hair dryers, and fax outlets. There's also a sauna and fitness center, and room service and baby-sitting are offered. The hotel's much-awarded restaurant, Primavera, is one of the best along the Baltic (see "Where to Dine," below).

WHERE TO DINE

Primavera. In the Hotel Plaza Schwerin, Am Grünen Tal. ☎ **0385/3-99-20.** Reservations recommended. Main courses 22.50DM–32.50DM ($12.85–$18.50); fixed-price lunch 14.50DM ($8.25), fixed-price dinner 35DM–55DM ($19.95–$31.35). AE, DC, MC, V. Daily 11:30am–midnight. Tram: Zum Zoo. ITALIAN.

This restaurant, in the previously recommended hotel, has consistently been voted the best in the Mecklenburg area. The menu changes with the season. Italian dishes are featured, along with a small regional menu. The service is impeccable, and the food is always good. The fresh fish is often from the North Sea. Arrive early for dinner and enjoy music in the piano bar beginning at 6pm nightly.

Weinhaus Uhle. Schusterstrasse 13–15 (near the castle and the cathedral). ☎ **0385/ 56-29-56.** Reservations recommended. Main courses 25DM–40DM ($14.25–$22.80); daily specials 15DM–20DM ($8.55–$11.40). Daily noon–11pm. INTERNATIONAL.

This wine house in the oldest part of town is set in a building dating from 1751. It's mostly decorated in Jugendstil (art nouveau), but the second floor incorporates a traditional Rittersaal (Knight's Room) with large and ornate windows, metal replicas of knights, and heraldic coats of arms. The chef's specialty is a savory Mecklenburger Ente (duck). A host of other regional dishes, as well as an international mixed grill, are also offered. A small band plays nightly.

A SIDE TRIP TO GÜSTROW

From Schwerin, strike out in a northeasterly direction along a secondary road (Route 104, but be aware that some sections along this road might also be called Route 192). Follow the signs to Brüel and then to the historic town of Güstrow, a distance of 43 miles. En route, you'll pass through villages that haven't really changed very much since the days of the East German regime.

Güstrow, 26 miles south of Rostock, holds one of the district's architectural gems, **Schloss Güstrow,** which rises in imposing 16th-century splendor amid formal French gardens. Also of interest is the town's cathedral, the **Dom** (Am Domplatz), whose decorative highlights are statues of the Apostles, sculptured in oak around 1530.

For information in Güstrow, contact the **tourist information office,** Domstrasse 9 (☎ 03843/68-10-23). It's open May through September, Monday to Friday from 9am to 6pm and Sunday from 9:30am to 1pm; October through April, Monday to Friday from 9:30am to 6pm.

Continue from Güstrow north along Autobahn 19 for another 26 miles into the heart of Rostock, one of the Baltic coast's most historic seaports. To get to Rostock from Schwerin, take route 106 north to Wismar, and then take Route 105 (E22) east.

3 Rostock

73 miles NE of Lübeck.

Rostock is set on a wide and navigable estuary of the Warnow River, about 175 miles northwest of Berlin. Throughout the Cold War, it was the largest and busiest seaport in East Germany, built on a scale to rival Hamburg. The town still bustles with maritime activity, though its importance has declined since reunification. Today visitors come to Rostock to wander its reconstructed Alstadt, which contains major sections of the town's medieval wall, and visit the town's museums and churches.

During the 13th and 14th centuries, Rostock was one of the most important cities of the Hanseatic League, trading and competing with ports in Sweden, Denmark, Estonia, Poland, and Lithuania. Its university (founded in 1419) was the first in any city along the Baltic, and its wealth and strategic location soon provoked the envy of the Scandinavians. Danes and Swedes occupied the city twice, first during the Thirty Years' War (1618–48), and again from 1700 to 1721. Later, the French, under Napoléon, occupied the town for about a decade until 1813. During World War II, Rostock was blasted by British bombers. The monuments and houses lining its principal street, Lange Strasse (Long Street), were completely demolished. Some historic buildings were restored, at great expense, from piles of little more than rubble.

⟫ SEEING THE SIGHTS

Some noteworthy historic buildings stand on Neuer Platz (also known as Ernst-Thalmann-Platz). Among the most prominent is the **Rathaus,** Neuer Markt (☎ 0381/14-16), which manages to incorporate three late–13th- and early–14th-century houses and seven towers into a brick structure linked by an arcaded gallery. Its interior is devoted to municipal offices.

Beginning at the Rathaus's base and extending westward for several historic blocks is Rostock's most photographed street, **Kröpeliner-Strasse,** a pedestrians-only walkway lined with shops and restored buildings constructed between 1500 and around 1850. It runs parallel to the more banal, and much less charming, Lange Strasse, Rostock's principal street. Of particular interest is the **step-gabled presbytery** (ca. 1480), from what used to be a hospital, at Kröpeliner-Strasse 82. The street ends at one of the most instantly recognizable features in town, the **Kröpeliner Tor,** a 14th-century brick gatehouse (the interior is closed to the public).

Among the buildings that survived war damage is the **St-Marien-Kirche (St. Mary's Church),** Am Ziegenmarkt (☎ 0381/4-92-33-96), set on a narrow side street off Lange Strasse. It's one of the finest (and largest) ecclesiastical structures of the Baltic world. It began in the 1200s as a Romanesque Hallenkirche (hall church) and was enlarged and modified around 1398 into a cross-shaped basilica. The huge tower wasn't completed until the late 1700s. From the top there's a sweeping panorama over Rostock's wharves and dock areas. Inside the church is an enormous organ dating from 1770 and an astronomical clock that was originally built in the late 1400s and reconfigured in 1643. The numeration of its calendar will remain valid until 2017. The Marienkirche is open Monday to Saturday from 10am to 5pm. Sunday worship is at 10am. Admission for adults is 2DM ($1.15).

Other churches to be seen include the **Heilig-Kreuz-Kirche (Church of the Holy Cross),** a Gothic Hallenkirche with three naves (or aisles), built of brick in the 14th century. In the Cistercian convent associated with this church is the **Kulturhistorisches Museum,** Universitätsplatz (☎ 0381/45-59-13), containing religious paintings and sacred art from the Middle Ages. It's open Tuesday to Sunday from 10am to 6pm. Entrance is 4DM ($2.30) for adults, 2DM ($1.15) for children.

The **Schiffahrtsmuseum (Navigational Museum),** August-Bebel-Strasse 1, at the corner of Richard-Wagner-Strasse (☎ 0381/4-92-26-97), contains exhibits related to the nautical history of one of Germany's most important seaports, beginning with the Vikings and focusing on the great maritime developments of the 19th and early 20th centuries. It's open Tuesday to Sunday from 9am to 5pm. Admission is 4DM ($2.30) for adults, 2DM ($1.15) students and children.

Rostock's **tourist office,** Schnickmannstrasse 13–14 (☎ 0381/49-79-90), will dispense information on any of Rostock's sights. It's open October through April, Monday to Friday 10am to 6pm and Saturday 10am to 2:30pm; May through September, Monday to Friday 10am to 6pm and Saturday and Sunday 10am to 4:30pm.

The tourist office can also provide information on any boat tours that might be offered at the time of your visit.

WHERE TO STAY

Radisson SAS Hotel Rostock. Lange Strasse 40 (a block from the Kröpeliner Gate), 18055 Rostock. ☎ **0381/4-59-70.** Fax 0381/4-59-78-00. E-mail: guest@zrozh.rdsa3.com. 352 units. MINIBAR TV TEL. 170DM–250DM ($96.90–$142.50) double; 380DM–480DM ($216.60–$273.60) suite. Rates include buffet breakfast. AE, DC, MC, V. Parking 10DM ($5.70) outdoors; 14DM ($8) in garage. Tram: Schröderplatz.

This eight-story high-rise in the center of the city is the largest hotel in town. It used to house the bigwigs of the DDR as well as vacationing East German workers. All the bedrooms are done in a contemporary style, but are strictly functionally furnished, even though the beds are comfortable. The hotel offers two restaurants, the Malmö and the Captain's Corner, featuring both international and regional cuisine. Its bar, the Arkona, is one of the major rendezvous centers in town.

WHERE TO DINE

Mond und Sterne. Strandstrasse 85 (on the harbor). ☎ **0381/4-59-03-44.** Reservations recommended. Main courses 11.50DM–29DM ($6.55–$16.55). AE, MC, V. Daily 11am–midnight. Tram: Lange Strasse. NORTH GERMAN/FISH/GAME.

This establishment has flourished since 1992 because of its well-prepared cuisine and its no-frills, rib-sticking food, rich with the traditions of the Baltic. The decor is inspired by the old Hanseatic League, with timber beams and brass lighting fixtures. The restaurant offers steaming bowls of *Leberknödel* (liver dumpling) soup and goulash soup, platters of fried schnitzels of pork or veal, several preparations of herring and cod, and a house specialty, *Laubskauf*. This traditional dish is a fish hash that was traditionally made with whatever leftovers were in the larder—fish, potatoes, onions, eggs, and perhaps a trace or two of meat. Another chef's specialty is *Edelfischteller*, a platter of four Baltic fish, sautéed and then served with potatoes and chives. This traditional Baltic dish, popular in Denmark as well, is associated with civic and regional culinary pride.

Volldampf. Hannes-Meyer-Platz 18 (4 miles north of Rostock), Dierkow. ☎ **0381/690772.** Reservations recommended. Main courses 12DM–28DM ($6.85–$15.95). AE, DC, MC, V. Daily 10am–midnight. Bus: 2 or 4 from Rostock's center. NORTH GERMAN.

This cozy restaurant is located in a modern 1990s building in the central pedestrian zone of the hamlet of Dierkow. Menu items are served in generous portions, with special emphasis on fish from the Baltic, Laubskauf (see the review above), and a house specialty known as *Volldampf Pfanne*, which includes portions of fried beef, veal, and pork, artfully arranged with potatoes and vegetables onto the same platter. The restaurant's name is an old-fashioned term from the Industrial Revolution that translates as "With Full Steam." Wine and beer taste especially good when accompanied by this restaurant's hearty specialties.

Zur Kogge. Wokrenterstrasse 27 (on the harbor). ☎ **0381/4-93-44-93.** Reservations required at night. Main courses 14DM–32DM ($8–$18.25). AE, DC, MC, V. Daily 11:30am–11:30pm. Tram: Lange Strasse. GERMAN.

This is the oldest sailors' pub in Rostock. The restaurant is decorated with all kinds of nautical marine items, either placed on shelves or hanging from the ceiling. Wednesday to Saturday, there's live music—the German version of New England sea chanteys. Naturally, fish specialties are the chef's best items. Try the *Mecklenburger Fischsuppe* (fish soup) or the various versions of smoked fish.

FROM ROSTOCK TO STRALSUND

To continue our tour of Germany's Baltic coast from Rostock, drive northeast from the center of town along the E22 highway (it's also called Route 105), heading for the next major destination, Stralsund, about 50 miles away. By veering off the highway at any of about five different junctions, you can visit some half-dozen seafront towns, each permeated with the scents and salt air of the Baltic. Many are attractive and, to an increasing degree, open for resort business.

Consider breaking up your trip with a visit to one of the best of these towns, **Ribnitz-Damgarten,** about 16 miles northeast of Rostock, right beside the E22 highway. Its architectural highlight is the **Rostocker Tor,** an imposing tower that symbolized the town itself for many generations. Most visitors opt for only a brief exploration of Ribnitz before continuing on their journey. The **tourist information office** in Ribnitz-Damgarten is at Am Markt 1 (☎ 03821/2201).

From Ribnitz, continue driving east along E22 (also identified at some points as Route 105) until you reach Stralsund.

4 Stralsund

45 miles NE of Rostock

Stralsund has one of the best natural harbors in the Baltic. The town is separated from the island of Rügen by a narrow sea channel, the Strait of Bodden, and makes its living mainly from shipyards, fishing fleets, and, to an increasing degree, tourism. Stralsund boasts a picturesque network of canals, coves, and lakes, as well as more half-timbered 19th-century houses and a more intact sense of history than many other cities on Germany's Baltic coast. With a population of 70,000, it's one of the largest towns in Lower Pomerania.

During the 1200s, it was rivaled in the Hanseatic League only by Lübeck, and enjoyed a rich trade with many of the other cities around the Baltic basin. Perhaps because of its success, the town has been invaded repeatedly throughout its long history, by armies from Denmark, Sweden, Holland, Napoleonic France, Prussia, and, in May 1945, the Soviet Union. By the mid-1960s, much of the inner core of Stralsund had been faithfully rebuilt by the Communist local government, though some historic structures remain.

Many visitors use Stralsund as the takeoff point for the flat and sandy Baltic island of Rügen (see below), which is joined to Stralsund by a 1¼-mile-long bridge.

SEEING THE SIGHTS

Buildings of historic interest are mostly of Lower German Gothic brick construction. They include a series of medieval defenses whose ramparts are best viewed on the town's western edge. Also important is the **Rathaus,** Alter Markt (☎ 03831/25-20), which dates from the 13th century. It's one of the most imposing examples of the North German secular brick Gothic architecture. Other than the Rathaus, Stralsund's other attractions are mostly ecclesiastical buildings. **St. Nikolaikirche** (on Alter Markt, with an entrance on Badenstrasse), whose design was based on models in Lübeck, has a very high nave built in the 13th and 14th centuries in the Hallenkirche style. It's open May through October, Tuesday to Saturday 10am to 5pm and Sunday noon to 5pm; November through April, Tuesday to Friday 10am to noon. Entrance is free. Call ☎ 03831/29-71-99 for more information.

Also of interest is the **Marienkirche,** Neuer Markt (☎ 03831/29-35-29), with an entrance on Bleistrasse. It was begun in the late 1200s, and had a soaring tower added to it in the mid-1400s. Open Monday through Saturday from 10am to 4pm and Sunday from 11:30am to 4pm. If you don't mind climbing 349 steps, you'll be rewarded with a view of the old town, the coastline, and even Rügen Island. It costs 2DM ($1.15) to climb the tower. Another church, the **Jacobikirche** on Böttchrstrasse, was transformed into a three-nave basilica in the 14th century. It has a high altar with baroque mountings and paintings by J. H. Tischbein, one of the foremost ecclesiastical artists of his day. The **Heiligengeistkirche (Church of the Holy Ghost),** on Wasser-strasse (☎ 03831/29-04-46), is noteworthy for its inner courtyard ringed with wooden galleries and is open July and August, Monday to Saturday from 10am to noon and 3 to 6pm. Admission is free.

Stralsund's cultural museum, **Kulturhistorisches Museum,** Mönchstrasse 25–27 (☎ 03831/29-21-80), contains sacred art from the Middle Ages and exhibits relating to the history of Stralsund. It's open Tuesday to Sunday from 10am to 5pm. Admission is 4DM ($2.30) for adults and 1.50DM (85¢) for students and children. There's also the **Deutsches Museum für Meereskunde und Fischerei (Oceanographic Museum and Aquarium),** Mönchstrasse 25 (☎ 03831/26500), in a complex of buildings that was originally part of a 15th-century abbey, the Katharinenkloster. The museum features exhibitions pertaining to the sea life of the Baltic and the distillation of its seawater into salt during the Middle Ages. A very large aquarium (11,000 gal.), containing exhibitions of tropical fish, is housed in the cloister's medieval crypt. The complex is open November through April, Tuesday to Sunday from 10am to 5pm; in May, June, September, and October, daily from 10am to 5pm; and July and August, Monday to Thursday from 9am to 6pm and Friday to Sunday from 10am to 5pm. Admission is 7DM ($4) for adults and 3.50DM ($2) for students.

For more information about the town and its monuments, contact the **tourist office,** Ossenrexerstrasse 1–3 (☎ 03831/2-46-90). It's open Monday to Friday from 10am to 5pm and Saturday from 10am to noon.

WHERE TO STAY

Hotel an den Bleichen Garni. An den Bleichen 45 (a 10-min. walk west of the historic center), 18435 Stralsund. ☎ **03831/39-06-75.** Fax 03831/39-21-53. 23 units. TV TEL. 125DM–145DM ($71.25–$82.65) double. Rates include buffet breakfast. AE, MC, V.

This hotel is a three-story, family-run establishment similar to many that have blossomed across Germany's eastern region since reunification. Built in 1993, it features pale-colored bedrooms outfitted with oak and mahogany furnishings, a simple but tasteful decor, and hardworking on-site owners. Both the bedrooms and bathrooms are rather small but still quite comfortable; everything is neatly maintained. No meals are served other than breakfast, but many restaurants are within a short walk, and there's a bar on the premises.

Norddeutscher Hof. Neuer Markt 22, 18439 Stralsund. ☎ and fax **03831/29-31-61.** 13 units. TV TEL. 160DM ($91.20) double. Rates include buffet breakfast. AE, MC, V. Bus: 3.

This small and charming inn, built around the turn of the century, is set in the heart of Stralsund's old town. On its street level, it contains a simple restaurant that's popular with local residents. Full meals are served every day at both lunch and dinner; the chef specializes in Baltic cuisine. The small bedrooms are outfitted with old-fashioned, not particularly valuable furniture whose slightly battered look adds to the establishment's time-tested charm.

WHERE TO DINE

Wulflamstuben. Alter Markt 5 (within the Wulflamhaus). ☎ **03831/29-15-33.** Reservations recommended. Main courses 13DM–24DM ($7.40–$13.70). AE, DC, MC, V. Daily 11am–11pm. Bus: 3. NORTH GERMAN.

This restaurant was established in 1991 within the historic walls of a town monument (the Wulflamhaus), which was originally built in 1370. It's set on the ground floor and features a carefully preserved decor of ornate carvings and old-fashioned engravings of local folklore and architecture. In many ways this place is a civic showcase of the town's culinary bounty. The focus is almost exclusively on the food of Mecklenburg and Lower Pomerania. Menu items include Stralsunder Aal Suppe (eel soup in the style of Stralsund), Eisbein (veal shank in the style of Berlin), stuffed goose in the style of Mecklenburg, and roast duckling stuffed with apples, black bread, and plums. There's also a choice of fish from local waters.

5 Rügen

2½ miles NE of Stralsund

Rügen is the largest island in Germany, but in many ways it's more Scandinavian than German in its climate, flavor, and feel. Riddled with saltwater lagoons and radically indented coves and harbors, it lies just off the northwestern coast of what used to be Pomeranian Prussia, joined to the town of Straslund by a 1¼-mile-long bridge. From north to south, it stretches for 32 miles, covering a landmass of 358 square miles—mostly scrubland, windswept forests, and dunes.

Don't come here for monuments or museums; nature is the main attraction, as well as seaside bathing (often nude) in summer. Highlights include geological features such as the chalk cliffs of Stubbenkammer and the Königstuhl Rock on the island's northeastern tip. Kap (Cape) Arkona, a Baltic Gibraltar, is the most northerly point of what used to be East Germany.

WHERE TO DINE

Uns Fischerhaus. Waldstrasse 4, Sellin. ☎ **038303/86635.** Reservations recommended July–Aug. Main courses 15DM–31DM ($8.55–$17.65). No credit cards. Sat and Sun 11am–3pm; Mon–Fri 4pm–midnight. NORTH GERMAN/SEAFOOD.

This restaurant celebrates the sandy, windy landscapes of Rügen and caters to a crowd of vacationers. It's a relaxing, unpretentious, sunny place, with an outdoor terrace for warm-weather dining. There's very little that's historic about the restaurant, which occupies a simple 1989 building overlooking a forest, near the heart of town. The food, however, is better than average, usually based on fresh ingredients and a roster of fish hauled in that day: halibut, eel, stingray, flounder, herring, and zander. The fish is often prepared with butter, white wine, and liberal doses of herbs and fresh vegetables.

EXPLORING THE ISLAND

Of architectural interest is **Schloss Spyker (Spycher Castle),** Schlossallee, 18551 Spyker (☎ **038302/5-33-83;** fax 038302/53-386), a baronial building now functioning (somewhat erratically) as a restaurant and hotel. The island's most unusual building is the **Jagdschloss Granitz (Granitz Hunting Lodge),** in the village of Binz (☎ **038393/22-63**), an ornate neofeudal castle built in 1836 by Prince Wilhelm Malte I of Putbus. One of its most unusual features is a corkscrew-inspired stone staircase winding gracefully up 154 steps to the top of the building's massive central tower. The lodge is open October through April, Tuesday to Sunday from 9am to 4pm; May to September daily 9am to 5:30pm. Admission is 5DM ($2.85) for adults and 2.50DM ($1.40) for children.

Although the island's capital is Bergen, most of the population is centered around the seasonal coastal resorts of Ostseebad Göhren, Ostseebad Baabe, Ostseebad Sellin, and Ostseebad Binz, all of which lie on the island's eastern edge. Of the above-mentioned villages, Ostseebad Binz (referred to locally simply as Binz) is the most interesting and most charming. Of special interest to bird-watchers are the shores of the island's vast inland sea, beautiful **Jasmunder Bodden.**

The coast of Rügen contains some of the island's finest scenic beauty. To get to Kap (or Cape) Arkona, the Baltic Gibraltar, go northeast from Bergen on Route 96, until you come to a small secondary road signposted Kap Arkona. A lighthouse stands at the cape, next to a restored watchtower, which you can climb for a view of the Danish island of Moen. Near the lighthouse stand the ruins of the ancient fortress of Jarosmarburg, constructed by the Slavs but destroyed by invading Vikings in 1168. All around the cape, chalky cliffs rise to 170 feet above the water.

After viewing the cape, drive back to Route 96, but instead of returning immediately to Bergen, follow this route east (it's signposted) to another end of the line, the towering chalky cliffs of Stubbenkammer, which lie 6 miles north of the small port of Sassnitz. Stubbenkammer is one of the most photographed sights on the island. From here, a steep trail leads down to a Baltic Beach.

For **tourist information** on the island, go to the office at Markt 11 in Bergen (☎ **03838/25-60-95**). From June through October, it is open Monday to Friday 10am to 8pm and Saturday 10am to 2pm. Off-season hours are Monday to Friday 10am to 6pm.

WHERE TO STAY

Hotel Nordperd. Nordperdstrasse 11, 18586 Göhren-Rügen. ☎ **038308/70.** Fax 038308/71-60. www.top-hotels.de. 70 units. TV TEL. 160DM–310DM ($91.20–$176.70) double. Rates include buffet breakfast. AE, DC, MC, V.

This four-story hotel is unusual for the island in that it remains open all year, even after the vacationers have gone home. It offers modern design and simple comfort.

The rooms in front have coastal views; all have streamlined furniture, including firm mattresses on comfortable beds. There's a restaurant on the premises that offers well-prepared regional food even when virtually everything else on Rügen is closed. It's open for dinner only, daily from 6 to 10:30pm.

Appendix A: Germany In Depth

This appendix will introduce you to Germany's history, artistic and cultural traditions, and cuisine. We'll also recommend some books to help you get even better acquainted with this fascinating country.

1 History 101

EARLY DAYS "A large build, very strong in the attack, but not suitable to the same extent for heavy work" was how Tacitus, the Roman historian, described the Teutons in A.D. 60. The Romans had been trying to push the borders of their empire up to the Rhineland, with mixed success, since 9 B.C. But the Teutonic tribes fought back ferociously. The first recognized German national hero was Arminius, who led his tribe (the Cherusci) in defeating three Roman legions near modern-day Bielefeld in A.D. 9.

After the deterioration of the Roman Empire, the Franks ruled much of what we now know as Germany. In 800, a Frankish king, Charlemagne, extended the Carolingian empire from the Pyrenees to Saxony and Bavaria. His rule marks the high point of cultural and political development of that period. He divided the empire into counties, each with an administrator directly responsible to him, and promoted education, scholarship, and the revival of Greek and Roman culture.

THE HOLY ROMAN EMPIRE After Charlemagne's death, the Carolingian empire fell apart. In 843, the Treaty of Verdun granted the empire's eastern territory to Louis the German, marking the beginning of German history.

Dateline

- **9 B.C.–A.D. 9** Romans attempt to conquer Teutonic tribes.
- **486** Clovis founds Frankish kingdom, ruling from Paris.
- **496** Franks are converted to Christianity.
- **800** Charlemagne is crowned in Rome by the pope.
- **962** Pope crowns Otto I as Holy Roman Emperor.
- **1152–1190** Frederick Barbarossa's reign leads to a greater centralization of power, but his invasion of Italy is beaten back by the Lombard League.
- **1158** Munich founded by Henry the Lion, duke of Saxony.
- **1241** Hanseatic League founded to protect the trade of such cities as Bremen, Hamburg, and Lübeck.
- **1432** Maximilian I, "last of the German knights," becomes Holy Roman Emperor, marking the beginning of the hegemony of the Hapsburgs.
- **1456** Johannes Gutenberg prints the first book in Europe using movable type.

continues

- **1517** Martin Luther nails his "Ninety-Five Theses" to a church door in Wittenberg, beginning the Protestant Reformation in Germany.
- **1618–48** Thirty Years' War devastates Germany, as Protestant forces defeat Catholic Hapsburgs.
- **1740–86** Prussian might grows under Frederick the Great in the Age of Enlightenment.
- **1806** Armies of Napoléon invade Prussia, which is incorporated briefly into the French Empire.
- **1813** Prussians defeat Napoléon at Leipzig.
- **1815** At the Congress of Vienna, the German Confederation of 39 independent states is created.
- **1862** Otto von Bismarck (1815–98) becomes prime minister of Prussia.
- **1871** Wilhelm I is crowned emperor of the newly created German Empire; Bismarck becomes chancellor.
- **1890** Bismarck is dismissed by Kaiser Wilhelm II, who launches an aggressive foreign policy.
- **1907** Russia, Great Britain, and France form the Triple Entente, against the Triple Alliance of Germany, Austria-Hungary, and Italy.
- **1914** Assassination of Archduke Franz Ferdinand launches World War I.
- **1918** Germany is forced to sign the Treaty of Versailles, accepting responsibility for starting World War I.
- **1923** Hitler's "Beer Hall Putsch," a rightist revolt, fails in Munich.
- **1925** Hitler publishes *Mein Kampf*.
- **1926** Germany is admitted to the League of Nations, in the heyday of the Weimar Republic.
- **1933** Hitler becomes chancellor.

continues

In 962, the pope officially recognized Otto I as Emperor of what was later called the Holy Roman Empire. This new political entity was formed both to impose unity on the European political world and to create a bulwark against the invasion of non-Christian tribes. It claimed direct links both to the grandeur of ancient Rome and to the more contemporary might of the Church.

Unity, however, did not prevail. The empire splintered into a bickering alliance of dukedoms, bishoprics, and principalities. The emperor's authority was often dependent on German nobles and the pope. A capital city that could have served as a center of power was never established (the monarch would simply move from one city to another, mustering an army and collecting revenue wherever he could), so the possibilities for dynastic intrigues were endless. In subsequent jockeying, the church itself was a voracious competitor for power. This broke out into open conflict in 1076, when Pope Gregory VII excommunicated the emperor Henry IV, who was forced to stand humiliatingly barefoot in the snow outside Canossa, awaiting a repeal.

To strengthen their position as the Holy Roman Empire declined, the emperors turned to alliances with the wealthy, independent trading ports to the north and east, under the federation of the Hanseatic League. Such German cities as Hamburg, Lübeck, and Bremen grew in both economic and political power. Eventually the league controlled trade as far as Novgorod in Russia.

THE REFORMATION & THE RELIGIOUS WARS When an Augustinian monk, Martin Luther, nailed his theological and political complaints to a church door in Wittenberg in 1517, he set off a political and religious wildfire that spread across the landscape of Europe. He was not the first religious reformer. In the early 15th century, John Wyclif had translated the Bible into English, and Jan Hus of Prague had become a martyr to his beliefs at the Council of Constance. However, the fragmented political situation in Germany played into Luther's hands—for every prince who condemned him he could find one to protect him. Luther's Reformation fanned the flames around Germany's political factions. The new conflict between Catholics and Protestants set the stage for the devastation of the Thirty Years' War

(1618–48), which only entrenched the divided sensibilities of the splintered German nation.

The only powerful German state to emerge from these conflicts was the little kingdom of Prussia, in the northeast on the Baltic Sea. The rise of Prussian power continued throughout the 18th century until, led by that talented soldier and patron of the Enlightenment, Frederick the Great, Prussia became a major kingdom, with Berlin as its capital.

NAPOLÉON ARRIVES

After the French Revolution, Napoléon and his new political ideas swept across Europe. The left bank of the Rhine came under French control. Under these pressures, the Holy Roman Empire officially came to an end in 1806. Around the same time, Napoléon's armies invaded Prussia, making it, for a brief time, a part of the French empire. But Napoléon was defeated at Leipzig in 1813, and 2 years later Britain and Prussia crushed him forever at the Battle of Waterloo.

BISMARCK & PRUSSIA

The Congress of Vienna (1814–15) redrew the map of Germany after Napoléon's defeat, giving more territory to Prussia but making Austria the leader in a German Confederation. During this time, there was a rising spirit of nationalism, exploited to good effect by Prince Otto von Bismarck when he became Prussia's prime minister in 1862. Prussia triumphed in the Austro-Prussian War of 1866, and after the subsequent Franco-Prussian War, when Prussia laid siege to Paris, Bismarck succeeded in his goal. Wilhelm I was made emperor of all Germany in 1871. A strong, unified Germany had at last taken shape. Under Bismarck's leadership, Germany adopted an advanced social welfare system and brought its military and industrial production as well as technical and scientific achievements to new heights.

WORLD WAR I

By 1907, Europe was divided into two armed camps: the Triple Alliance (Germany, Austria-Hungary, and Italy) and the Triple Entente (France, Great Britain, and Russia). The match that ignited the powder keg was struck at Sarajevo in 1914, with the assassination of Austrian Archduke Franz Ferdinand, heir to the throne of the Austro-Hungarian Empire. The subsequent German invasion of France launched the bloodiest war the world had ever seen. A new and particularly demoralizing form of battle

- **1934** President von Hindenburg dies and Hitler declares himself Führer (leader) of the Third Reich.
- **1935** Nuremberg Laws deprive Jews of citizenship and forbid marriage between Jews and non-Jewish Germans.
- **1936** Germany militarizes the Rhineland in violation of the Treaty of Versailles, and Hitler signs agreements with Italy and Japan to form the Axis.
- **1938** Germany occupies Austria and the Sudetenland in Czechoslovakia.
- **1939** Hitler signs a non-aggression pact with the Soviet Union in August, and on September 1 invades Poland, launching World War II.
- **1940–45** After early successes, German armies are forced back by the Soviet Union in the east and Allied troops in the west; Germany is in ruins by 1945.
- **1945** The Yalta Conference divides Germany into zones of occupation.
- **1948–49** The Soviet Union attempts by blockade to exclude the Allies from Berlin; the city is saved by a massive airlift.
- **1949** Soviets establish the country of East Germany, the German Democratic Republic (DDR in German); Konrad Adenauer becomes chancellor of newly established West Germany, known formally as the Federal Republic of Germany.
- **1950** West Germany's "economic miracle" begins to take hold.
- **1957** West Germany becomes a founding member of the European Economic Community (now European Union).

continues

- **1961** The Berlin Wall divides the city.
- **1989** Refugees from East Germany flood into West Germany; Communist power collapses in the east, and the Berlin Wall comes down.
- **1990** East Germany and West Germany unite; five German states are created out of the old DDR.
- **1991** Berlin is chosen as the capital of the united Germany.
- **1992** Unemployment and disillusionment sweep across East Germany as unification costs mount.
- **1995** Bundestag approves German participation in NATO Bosnia mission.
- **1997** German government and private companies tally up the cost of rebuilding eastern Germany: $1 trillion U.S. dollars to date.
- **1998** Chancellor Kohl is defeated in election, bowing to Gerhard Schröder.
- **1999** The German seat of government is returned to Berlin, as the Reichstag.

known as "trench warfare" produced staggering casualties. On August 8, 1918, the Allies, now joined by the United States, penetrated German lines, and the German high command realized that the situation was hopeless.

In an attempt to get more favorable treatment from the Allies, the Germans voluntarily declared a parliamentary democracy, ending the reign of the kaiser. Despite that concession, in 1918 Germany was forced to sign the humiliating Treaty of Versailles, surrendering strategic territories including beloved Alsace-Lorraine, just west of the Rhine. The Allies—especially the French—also demanded huge monetary reparations.

WEIMAR REPUBLIC In the turbulent years following World War I, Weimar became the headquarters of a new German democracy. Its constitution was immediately hailed as the most progressive in the world. The selection of Weimar as the capital was a symbolic gesture. It had been a center of the Enlightenment in the 18th century, home to some of the greatest voices in German literature and music, including Goethe and Schiller.

But in the defeated and humiliated postwar Germany, extremists from both the left and the right launched savage attacks against the inexperienced and idealistic government. The enormous payments demanded by the Allies crippled the German economy. When reparations from Germany couldn't be made, France retaliated by occupying the Ruhr, one of Germany's most valuable industrial resources. Inflation—perhaps the worst in history—destroyed what was left of the German economy.

THE RISE OF NAZISM This was just the right climate for the rise of Adolf Hitler and the Nazi Party. The Nazis believed in the superiority of the Aryan race over all other people, particularly Jews, and in the necessity for German expansion and adherence to a supreme leader. At first Hitler's anti-Semitic, nationalist ideas failed to gain popular support, even with right-wingers. Nazi membership in the *Reichstag* (parliament) went from 25 in 1925 to only a dozen following the elections of 1928.

In 1932, Hitler lost the electoral race for president against the compromise candidate of the democratic parties, the war hero Paul von Hindenburg. Nevertheless, Hitler's power increased, and on January 30, 1933, Hindenburg, submitting to rightist pressure, appointed him chancellor. Upon Hindenburg's death in 1934, Hitler declared himself *Führer* (leader) of a new German empire he called the "Third Reich." Protected by hastily drafted laws and regulations, he made his power absolute.

The horrors of unchecked Nazi rule lasted until the end of the Third Reich. The Gestapo, or secret police, launched one of the most notorious reigns of terror in history. Those the Nazis considered enemies, or simply undesirables— which included Communists, Social Democrats, homosexuals, political dissidents, and many others—were persecuted. Jews were disenfranchised, terrorized, deprived of property, and forced into ghettos and concentration camps.

On June 30, 1934, Hitler disposed of any opposing elements in his own party in the "Night of Long Knives," when hundreds were massacred, including Ernst Röhm, chief of his notorious brownshirts. Heinrich Himmler's black-shirted *Schutzstaffel* (SS) became a powerful political force. Surrounded by adoring fans (or, at best, passive witnesses), Hitler now viewed his empire as a worthy successor to those of Charlemagne and Bismarck.

In 1936, Hitler remilitarized the Rhineland and signed agreements with Japan and fascist Italy, forming the Axis alliance. In 1938, he enforced the *Anschluss* (annexation) of Austria and marched triumphantly into the country of his birth. That same year, he occupied the German-speaking Sudetenland in Czechoslovakia, an act the other Western powers could not summon the will to oppose.

WORLD WAR II   In late August 1939, Hitler signed a nonaggression pact with the Soviet Union that gave him free reign to launch an invasion of Poland, which he did on September 1. France and Britain, honoring their agreements with Poland, declared war on Germany. Germany scored early victories, and in one of the most stunning campaigns of the 20th century, invaded and occupied France in June 1940. In 1941, Hitler chose not to invade England but instead to attack his nominal ally, the Soviet Union. Around the same time, the Nazis implemented the "final solution" to the "Jewish Question," carrying out the systematic extermination of millions of Jews. The mass murders of homosexuals, Gypsies, Communists, Slavs, and other enemies were less systematic but also numbered in the millions.

On December 7, 1941, Japan, pursuing its own agenda, attacked Pearl Harbor and brought the United States into the war. After defeats in North Africa in 1942 and at Stalingrad in 1943, the recurrent theme became one of Nazi retreat. The D-Day landings on June 6, 1944 along the coast of Normandy began the steady advance of the Allied armies from the west, while Soviet armies relentlessly marched toward Berlin from the east. Hitler committed suicide in Berlin in April 1945. His country, along with much of Europe, lay in rubble.

DIVISION OF GERMANY   At war's end, Germany and its capital city were divided. The nation shrank in size, losing long-held territories (among them East Prussia). The United States, Great Britain, France, and the Soviet Union divided the country into four zones of occupation. Berlin, in the heart of the Soviet district, was also divided among the four powers. In the late 1940s, the Soviet Union tried to cut off all Allied access to Berlin, but a massive U.S.-sponsored airlift into the beleaguered city thwarted the attempt. In 1961, the Soviet-directed German Democratic Republic sealed off its borders and erected the Berlin Wall, a stark symbol of the Cold War itself.

FALL OF THE WALL & UNIFICATION   1989 was a year of change and turmoil. In the wake of the collapse of Communist power across eastern Europe, the Berlin Wall also fell. The following year was perhaps the most significant in postwar German history. The two German nations announced economic unification in July, followed by total unification—with its thousands of inherent problems and headaches—on October 3, 1990. In 1991, Parliament voted to quit Bonn, seat of the West German government, and reestablish the once-mighty capital of Berlin.

After the first heady period of reunification, disillusionment set in, especially in eastern Germany, which was riddled with unemployment and unrealized expectations. Resentment against immigrant workers led in some instances to violent neo-Nazi marches, bombings, and physical assaults. However, most Germans rose up in revulsion to condemn the ultrarightists and the sporadic violence.

Psychic and emotional differences between the two zones were almost overwhelming, as were the vast disparities in industrial development. As the influential newspaper *Frankfurter Rundschau* editorialized, "The terms of east and west are not so much geographical expressions as they are descriptions of states of mind."

GERMANY TODAY But despite the enormous problems of reunification, progress is being made. Construction in the eastern part of the country proceeds at an incredible pace, particularly in Berlin, which is once again the seat of German government. Meanwhile, Chancellor Gerhard Schröder, who defeated longtime chancellor Helmut Kohl in 1998, when the Social Democrats swept into power, continues to place Germany squarely in the vanguard of a united Europe. Despite its problems, Germany remains the continent's premier economic power, and its citizens are looking with hope to its future in the new millennium.

2 In Pursuit of Artistic Excellence

ARCHITECTURE

ROMANESQUE German architecture first flowered in the 10th and early 11th centuries—an era called the Ottonian period, in honor of Emperor Otto I. German architects, virtually all anonymous, built churches on principles adapted from the basilicas developed centuries earlier by the ancient Romans. Noteworthy features included barrel vaults, rounded arches, very thick walls, and (usually) symmetrical, rather squat towers. Today, the few Romanesque buildings that remain intact are among the most cherished in Germany. Cologne contains many important examples (see chapter 13).

GOTHIC New developments in the Middle Ages such as "broken" (pointed) arches and flying buttresses permitted a world of new structural possibilities. Architects could now build bigger and more impressive buildings, higher and thinner walls, taller belfries, and spacious windows. This Gothic architectural style flowered in Europe, especially in northern France, between the 13th and 16th centuries.

The Romanesque influence remained pervasive, however, and Gothic design never established as strong a foothold in Germany as it did in France and England. Most representative of the German Gothic style is the hall-type church *(Hallenkirche)*, which originated in Westphalia. It was characterized by aisles constructed at the same height as the nave, separated from the nave by tall columns. A good example is **St. Georgskirche** (Church of St. George) in **Nördlingen** on the Romantic Road (see chapter 6).

The greatest of the German Gothic cathedrals, the **Dom** at **Cologne,** was begun in 1284 but not completed, as astonishing as it may sound, until 1880 (see chapter 13). High Gothic is best represented by the cathedral at **Freiburg im Breisgau** (see chapter 10), famous for its pierced octagonal belfry crowned by a delicate openwork spire.

RENAISSANCE In southern Germany, Italian-inspired Renaissance motifs were installed in **Augsburg** in the **funerary chapel** of **Fugger the Rich** (see chapter 6) and in **Munich** in **St. Michael's Church** (see chapter 7). Overall, however, the emerging Protestant principalities of northern Germany tended to reject Italian influences as being too closely tied to the Catholic sensibility. In the north, motifs from Flanders and Holland were much more popular. The finest German Renaissance towns are **Rothenburg** (see chapter 6) and **Celle** (see chapter 15). As the prosperity of the rich trading centers of the Hanseatic League grew, they adopted a distinctive design, the so-called "Weser Renaissance," almost never seen in the south

FROM BAROQUE TO NEOCLASSICISM

The Baroque style, an Italian import whose influence in Germany began around 1660 and continued into the 18th century, brought a different kind of renaissance to southern Germany, especially Bavaria. Architectural forms no longer followed regular patterns, as individual artists and craftsmen were granted increased freedom and more variety in design. **Würzburg** is one of Germany's most beautiful baroque cities (see chapter 6). The baroque movement eventually led to the greater freedom and gaiety of the rococo. Outstanding examples are **Kloster Ettal,** near **Oberammergau** (see chapter 8), and the **Cuvilliés Theater** and **Asamkirche** in **Munich** (see chapter 7).

By the 19th century, many members of the rising and prosperous middle class in Germany favored the **Biedermeier style** of furniture and decoration, with its lighter designs and carefully balanced symmetry. **Neoclassicism,** with its references to the grandeur of ancient Greece and imperial Rome, gained favor as well. Once again, the south of Germany brought a lighter touch to this style than did the north. Ludwig I of Bavaria built the **Alte Pinakothek** and the **Glyptothek** in **Munich** (see chapter 7), in an effort to make the city into a "new Athens."

ROMANTICISM

The romantic movement was full of implications for Germany's sense of national identity. For inspiration in this neo-Gothic era, architects looked back to a rose-colored image of Germany's medieval history, myth, and folklore. There was an almost obsessive rebirth of interest in Teutonic lore, as rediscovered by the Brothers Grimm and reinterpreted by Richard Wagner. The imitation Florentine loggia in **Munich,** the **Feldherrnhalle,** brings all these ideas together.

German architecture in the latter 1800s is often termed **Historicism.** No one represented this flamboyant and eclectic movement better than Ludwig II of Bavaria. His unfinished **Neues Schloss** at **Herrenchiemsee** (see chapter 9) is an elaborate and romanticized interpretation of Versailles. But his completed palace, **Neuschwanstein** (see chapter 6), best represents the movement. Outrageously ornate, with all the fairy-tale ornamentation of a Teutonic version of Disneyland, it's one of the major tourist attractions of modern Germany.

FROM JUGENDSTIL TO MODERNISM

By the end of the 19th century, the art-nouveau movement—called *Jugendstil* in German, after the magazine Jugend (Youth)—was sweeping the country. *Jugendstil,* which was characterized by mass production and solid construction, marked the beginning of contemporary architecture. Its practitioners used such materials as glass, steel, and concrete, often shaping them into curved lines inspired by the sinuous forms of nature.

In the aftermath of World War I, Walter Gropius (1883–1969) gained prominence as leader of the **Bauhaus movement.** The primary aim of this movement was to unify arts and crafts within the context of architecture. Its appeal derived from the changing sensibilities of the Industrial Age, as well as from the need for inexpensive construction techniques in an era of rising costs and exploding demand for housing. Founded at Weimar and directed there by Gropius from 1919, the Bauhaus moved to Dessau in 1925. (Gropius eventually settled in the United States.) For a variety of personal and political reasons, the movement was formally dissolved in 1933, but not before its influence had been felt around Europe.

By 1935, the so-called National Socialist, or "Third Reich," style of architecture was virtually the law of the land. Under Hitler and such designers as Albert Speer, architecture became a propaganda tool. It was pompous, monumental, innately frightening, and devoid of any real humanity. After the war, cities scrambled to hide the origins of some of these buildings. A good example is **Munich's Haus der Kunst** (see chapter 7), which houses the State Gallery of Modern Art. Its angular fascist architecture seems curiously appropriate for the starkly modern painting it showcases today—ironically, everything now in it would have been anathema to Hitler.

DESTRUCTION & RENEWAL   One of the legacies of World War II was the leveling of many of Germany's greatest architectural treasures by Allied bombing raids. Notable among these was the destruction of **Dresden,** until 1945 one of the most beautiful cities in Europe. More than 50 years after its firebombing by British and American planes, its loss is felt more poignantly than that of any other city, though some of its buildings have been restored.

In the years after the war, both Germanys, East and West, set for themselves the formidable task of rebuilding. In some cases, the architectural rubble of the past was swept away, never to be restored. However, many cathedrals, churches, town halls, and other buildings were laboriously (and at enormous expense) reconstructed in the original style, notably **the Zwinger** in **Dresden** (see chapter 4). Other careful and tasteful city restorations were those of **Cologne** (see chapter 13) and of **Munich** (see chapter 7). Some cities, like **Düsseldorf,** opted to become strikingly modern (see chapter 13).

Berlin, once reduced to rubble, is today undergoing a massive rebuilding project. A previous restoration effort was made in 1957, when architects from 22 nations were invited to design homes, schools, and apartment buildings in Berlin's **Hansaviertel,** or Hansa Quarter (see chapter 3). The resulting works, by Gropius, Niemeyer, Duttman, and many others, created an exciting diversity.

MUSIC

Music is an important and pervasive facet of German life. German disunity over the centuries actually helped foster German music. The many small principalities and bishoprics that split up the German-speaking world meant that there were many courts to offer opportunities to musicians, both composers and instrumentalists. As a result, the German-speaking nations produced more composers of indisputable greatness than any other.

Today, the musical scene in Germany is as vibrant as ever. Every major city has an opera house and an orchestra, many of them of world renown. New composers are encouraged, and productions are often at the cutting edge.

MUSIC FESTIVALS   Major music festivals take place in the summer, but music lovers can pretty well take their pick all year of what they want to hear. The most famous festival, of course, is the **Bayreuth Festival,** instituted by Richard Wagner, which made the town of Bayreuth a musical landmark (unfortunately, tickets are very hard to come by). But all major cities, including Munich and Berlin, have music festivals at various times. Contact German tourist offices, within the country and abroad, for the latest information and dates.

Since reunification, **Dresden,** for example, has emerged as a major center for music. The Dresden Music Festivals, held each year at the end of May and the beginning of June, bring together not only local ensembles but prominent German and international artists. The Dresden Festival of Contemporary Music is presented in October. And a Dixieland Festival, a tradition since 1971, transforms Dresden into a city of jazz in May.

Other world-class festivals include the **Mozart Festival** at **Würzburg** in June; the **Berliner Festwochen** in September; and the **Jazz-Fest Berlin** in November.

MUSICAL MUSEUMS   The true devotee of German music may want to visit cities and towns where the masters lived and wrote their music. Some of the homes of former composers have been turned into museums, such as the home of **Franz Liszt** in **Weimar** and of **Richard Wagner** in **Bayreuth.** To see where the great Beethoven lived, head for the former German capital of Bonn. Actually, considering how many famous musicians lived and composed in Germany, the country has surprisingly few museums devoted to these great artists. Blame it on wartime devastation.

A HISTORY OF GERMAN MUSIC

BAROQUE MUSIC   The greatest composer of the baroque era was **Johann Sebastian Bach** (1685–1750), who was a supreme master of all musical forms of his time. Bach produced many church cantatas, especially for St. Thomas's Lutheran Church in Leipzig (see chapter 4), where he served as cantor. His compositions were technically outstanding, vigorous, and profound. Little of his music was published during his lifetime, but after his death, his influence steadily grew, especially that of his organ works. The musical tradition in his large family was maintained by two of his talented sons, Philipp Emanuel Bach and Johann Christian Bach.

A contemporary, **George Frideric Handel** (1685–1759), was another great composer. His best-known work today is his oratorio, *Messiah.* He first rose to prominence as musician of the court of Hannover, a post that he left to become composer at the court of St. James of England. He was a leading composer of operas and instrumental music for the court.

THE CLASSICAL PERIOD   **Wolfgang Amadeus Mozart** (1756–91), although an Austrian, cannot be omitted from any discussion of German music. His operas *The Marriage of Figaro* and *Don Giovanni,* with their contemporary themes and lively musical characterizations, paved the way for later composers. **Franz Joseph Haydn** (1732–1809), another Austrian, also exerted great influence on German music, especially instrumental music.

THE 19TH CENTURY & ROMANTICISM   The 19th century was rich in musical genius. **Ludwig van Beethoven** (1770–1827) was the composer who ushered in romanticism. His works included symphonies, piano concertos, piano sonatas, quartets, and many others. He greatly expanded and developed the orchestra. Tragically, he completely lost his hearing in 1819. However, the chamber music he wrote after this event shows an even greater depth and complexity.

Other great composers of the era include Franz Schubert (1797–1828), who developed the song *(Lied)* to a high art; **Robert Schumann** (1810–56), who represents the apex of the romantic period; and **Johannes Brahms** (1833–97), a profound and complex composer.

The giant of the 19th-century opera world was **Richard Wagner** (1813–83). His theories of music drama exerted a tremendous influence on everyone who followed him, even his detractors. Perhaps his greatest work is his cycle *The Ring of the Nibelungs.* His influence can best be heard in the music of the later romantic composer **Richard Strauss** (1864–1949). Strauss's operas *Salome* (based on a work by Oscar Wilde) and *Elektra* carry Wagner's ideas of character development to greater psychological depth. Strauss also developed the symphonic poem.

THE 20TH CENTURY   During the Nazi era, many composers fled their homeland. Among them were **Kurt Weill** (1900–50), who wrote the music for Brecht's *The Threepenny Opera,* and Austrian-born composer **Arnold Schoenberg** (1874–1951), best known for his 12-tone system of musical structure. Other composers, like Hans Pftzer and Richard Strauss, remained in Germany in an uneasy relationship with the Nazis.

Today, at the end of the 20th century, important composers such as **Karlheinz Stockhausen, Hans Werner Henze,** and **Wolfgang Rihm** carry on the traditions of Germany's musical past.

3 A Taste of Germany

Traditional Germans like to eat, but don't like to count calories. Cholesterol-conscious Americans may recoil at the sight of heavy dumplings, wurst (sausages), and pastries. The beer that often accompanies meals is not in the "light" category, and helpings of food are not small. And even the heaviest meals do not keep many Germans from their cake and coffee break, considered a compulsory afternoon event.

However, Germans get German cooking at home, and so more and more restaurants are offering foreign foods and *neue Küche (cuisine moderne).* Young people are becoming increasingly health conscious and are eschewing the rich fare of their parents. Young chefs trained in Switzerland, France, or Italy are returning to Germany to open continental restaurants. Italians, many of whom originally came to Germany as "guest workers," have stayed to open up trattorias. Even health-food shops are beginning to pop up.

REGIONAL SPECIALTIES

Every region has its own specialties, ranging from *Aalsuppe,* or eel soup, in Hamburg, to *Zwiebelbrot,* or onion bread, in the Black Forest.

- **Bavaria & Franconia:** In southern Germany, you can feast on such hearty fare as *Leberkäs* (minced pork, beef, and liver prepared as a galantine); lots of *Knödel* (dumplings or soaked bread); gigantic *Haxen* (pork or veal trotters, most often consumed with sauerkraut); *Roastbratwürste* (small finger sausages); and *Leberknödel* (large liver dumplings in a clear broth). *Schweinwürstl mit Kraut* (pork sausages with sauerkraut) is another unforgettable local dish.

- **Lower Saxony & Schleswig-Holstein:** Here in northwest Germany, with its maritime tradition, one of the most typical local dishes is *Aalsuppe,* sweet and sour eel soup flavored with bacon, vegetables, and sometimes even pears and prunes (or perhaps other fruits). The eternal sailor's favorite is *Labskaus,* a ground-together medley of pork, salt herring, and beef, along with potatoes and beets. The traditional topping is a fried egg and a side dish of cucumbers. *Bruntes Huhn* is salt beef on a bed of diced vegetables, a robust winter favorite. *Rollmops,* pickled herring rolled in sour cream, is another local specialty, as is *Finkenwerder Scholle* (plaice) and oysters, raw or baked with cheese.

- **Berlin:** During those cold nights in old Prussia, Berliners took comfort in their soups, notably *Kohlsuppe* (cabbage soup) and *Erbensuppe* (pea soup), along with dark bread, especially Westphalia pumpernickel. *Hase im Topf* is a delicious rabbit pâté. Other favorites are *Bratwurst,* a pork sausage; and *Regensburger,* a spicy pork sausage. For dessert, Berliners like *Kugelhupf,* a marvelous coffee cake; and *Käsekuchen* or cheesecake. But probably the most typical Berlin delicacy is *Eisbein* or pigs' knuckles.

The Best of the Wurst

The German love affair with *wurst* (sausage) dates from the dawn of history. Every region of Germany has its own specialty, but everybody's favorite seems to be bratwurst from Nürnberg, made of seasoned and spiced pork. Germans often take their wurst with a bun and a dab of mustard (often smoky). White sausage, called *Weisswurst,* is a medley of veal, calves' brains, and spleen. Tradition has it that this sausage should be eaten only between midnight and noon. *Bauernwurst* (farmer's sausage) and *Knockwurst* are variations of the frankfurter, which originated (naturally) in Frankfurt. (Oddly enough, small frankfurters, which are called wieners or Vienna sausages in the United States and *Wienerwurst* in Germany, are known simply as frankfurters in Austria.) *Leberwurst* is a specialty of Hesse. *Rinderwurst* and *Blutwurst* (beef sausage and blood sausage) are specialties of Westphalia and are often consumed with *Steinhager* (corn brandy).

- **Hassen & Westphalia:** Famed for its hams, this region of Germany eats food guaranteed to put hair on your chest. To go totally native, sample their *Sulperknochen,* made from the pig's trotters, ears, and tail, and served traditionally with peas pudding and pickled cabbage. Or try *Tüttchen,* a ragout of herb-flavored calf's head and calf's brains. Not into any of the above? You might settle for the local favorite *Pickert,* sweet potato cakes flavored with raisins.
- **Baden-Württemberg:** Here in southern Germany, in the region centered around Stuttgart, you can begin with such dishes as *Schneckensuppe* (snail soup), *spätzle* (egg-based pasta), or perhaps *Maultaschen* (ravioli stuffed with ground meat, spinach, and calf's brains). A main dish beloved in the area and widely consumed is *Geschnetzeltes* (slices of veal in a cream sauce). The favorite local dish in Stuttgart itself is *Gaisburger Marsch,* a beef stew. Another commonly served dish is *Roastbraten,* braised beef, invariably accompanied by *Sauerkraut,* or else *Linsen mit Saiten,* lentil stew cooked with sausages.
- **Saxony & Thuringia:** In what used to be East Germany, you can feast on everything from *Linsensuppe mit Thüringer Rotwurst* (lentil soup with Thuringian sausages) to *Rinderzunge in Rosinen-Sauce* (calf's tongue in grape sauce). *Kartoffelsuppe* (potato soup) remains a favorite of the district, as does a baked appetizer, *Quarkkeulchen,* made from curd, boiled potatoes, flour, sugar and raisins, topped with cinnamon, and served with applesauce. Each city in the district also has its own popular local dishes. Leipzig, for example, has its *Leipziger Allerlei,* a blend of carrots, peas, asparagus, cauliflower, mushrooms, crayfish, tails, bits of veal, and dumplings.

BEER & WINE

BEER   For variety and quality, German beer is unmatched. The world's oldest brewery is in Bavaria, but other regions in Germany have proud beer-making traditions. Export beers and the rather more bitter *Pils,* the most popular type of beer, are also produced in Berlin, Hamburg, the Ruhr, Hesse, and Stuttgart. *Altbier,* a very early product of the brewer's art, can be found today all over Germany. *Berliner Weisse* is made from wheat, like a Bavarian white beer, but with a dash of raspberry or woodruff syrup. Dark and sweet, malt beer contains hardly any alcohol, whereas "March beer" is also dark but considerably stronger.

In Germany, if you go into a beer hall and ask the bartender for *ein Bier,* you'll probably get the standard stock beer, *Vollbier,* which is 4% alcohol. More potent is *Export* at 5% or *Bockbier* at 6%. *Helles Bier* is light and brewed from malt dried and baked by the local brewery, or *Brauerei.* When the malt has been darkly roasted and fermented for much longer, it becomes *dunkles Bier,* or dark beer. *Pils,* or *Pilsener,* beers are light and contain more hops. Dortmund has earned a reputation in this field.

Many inns today actually brew their own beer. In summer, Germans, particularly Bavarians, flock to beer gardens to enjoy their local brews, which are sometimes accompanied by white or red radishes and crisp pretzels.

WINE   Germany has produced delightful wines for centuries, but sometime in the 1970s German wine became the butt of jokes. The post-war German economic miracle had led to a boom in wine production. Many new vineyards sprung up suddenly, and quality was not always their first priority. Cheap, cloyingly sweet table wines flooded the market. One label in particular, *Liebfaumilch,* began to sully the reputation of the entire industry; the mere mention of its name to anyone in the know met with a knowing titter or contemptuous sneer. These days, however, German viticulture has been saved by smaller producers who have exploited their potential by producing excellent, unique wines.

Good German wine is renown for its natural lightness and its delicate balance of sweetness and acidity. Most vineyards flourish on steep hillsides, protected from harsh winds by wooded neighboring hills, especially on the banks of the Rhine and the Mosel Rivers and their many tributaries. The vineyards profit from the warmth reflected off the sunlit water. The slow maturing of the grapes gives German wines their typical fresh, fruity acidity.

Germany does produce red wine, but as a rule it's better to stick to white or perhaps a rosé, if recommended. The words *trocken* (dry) or *halbtrocken* (semidry) are often given on the labels; look for them if you want to escape anything sweet. This avoidance, however, should not extend to the delicious dessert wines, which resemble nectar as opposed to syrup.

The overload of information on a German wine label is often puzzling to foreigners, but it's not really that hard to decipher. First of all, the grape variety should be indicated. Legally, German wines are only required to contain 85% of the declared variety. The classic is *Riesling,* which can range widely in taste, from fruity to even spicy. Other grapes include *Weisburgunder,* used to make dry wines, often with an aroma of melon or pear, and *Scheurebe,* which produces delicious, high-quality wine with the aroma of red currant. No grape reference on the label often means a poorly blended, inferior quality; these wines should be kept at an arm's length.

The term "vintage" refers to when the grapes were grown (not harvested). The question of origin is also something to keep an eye on. It's best if the label gives a single vineyard, but these can only be distinguished from the less specific vineyard zones if you are in the know or can consult a pocket guide, such as Johnson's.

Next, check for the level of ripeness. German law distinguishes between *tafelwein* (table wine) and *qualitatswein* (quality wine). QbA on a bottle means the wine is made from the approved grape varieties, which will give it the particular and traditional taste of its region. QmP refers to *qualitatswein mit*

O' Zapfstisl ("The Barrel Is Tapped")

Much of the world seems to think that the Germans invented beer, but the drink has actually has been around for thousands of years, at least since the days of ancient Egypt and Babylon. But if the Germans didn't exactly invent beer, they certainly perfected the process of making it. Just ask them!

At Weilhenstephan, a former Benedictine monastery 18 miles northeast of Munich in Old Bavaria, stands the oldest brewery in the world. It dates from the year 1040, although there is evidence that a hop garden already existed near the grounds of the monastery in A.D. 768. The monks here brought beer to the masses in Europe. Even today, the oldest brewery within Munich itself, Augustiner, reflects brewing's monastic heritage.

Over the centuries monks brewed a strong beer for consumption during the fasting period of Lent, during which they were technically supposed to drink only water. The story goes that the pope heard about this custom and ordered that the beer be transported to Rome for him to sample. When the pope finally tasted the beer (which didn't have preservatives back then) after its long journey, he couldn't imagine why anyone would want to drink it and decreed that the beer was strong enough punishment for the Bavarian monks to drink it during Lent. Today, all Munich breweries brew this strong beer during Lent. The beer always ends with an "ator" in its name; Salvator and Triumphator are the best-known brands.

To go into a German beer hall and ask simply for a beer would brand you a beer illiterate. Connoisseurs specify the type of beer they want and often the brewery. The following is a bit of beer vocabulary. *Dunkel* is a generic designation for all dark beers. *Doppelbock* is an extra dark beer with a 6% alcoholic content. *Hell*, believe it or not, is the name for light-colored beers. Many Germans, especially the citizens of Bamberg, like their beer "smoked." If that appeals to you, request *Rauchbier*. In nearby Bayreuth, Richard Wagner's old hometown, locals prefer a "steam beer" known as *Dampfbier*. The denizens of Düsseldorf and Frankfurt can often be heard requesting *Alt*, a brown, barley-malt brew. *Kolsch* is a light beer drunk mainly in Cologne in tall fluted glasses. *Hefe-Weizen* is a yeasty wheat beer consumed often with a squeeze of lemon. Finally, *Starkbierzet* is a powerful beer served when the barrels are opened after the post-Lenten celebrations in March. It has the highest alcohol content of them all.

What to consume with this brew? Germans prefer white and red radishes, chives on buttered bread, cold sausages, and, you guessed it, pretzels. What about a main course? One old Bavarian who starts drinking beer at 7 in the morning (and has ever since he was 16) says there is only one "acceptable" dish—ox from the spit with a potato and cucumber salad. Many Germans, especially Bavarians, see nothing wrong with drinking beer in the morning, often along with a hearty second breakfast of white sausages.

Although beer festivals are common around the world, none has ever equaled Munich's renowned **Oktoberfest.** This massive celebration lasts 16 days and lures some 7 million visitors yearly; some 1½ million gallons of beer are consumed. Of course, if you attend the right beer party in Germany, any night can be Oktoberfest.

pradikat (wine with distinction) and carries one of six special attributes. These, in order of ascending price, are *Kabinett, Spatlese, Auslese, Berrenauslese* (BA), *Eiswein,* and the exclusive *Trockenbeerenauslese* (TBA).

As a classification, *Kabinett* was first used by Eberbach Abbey in 1712 to denote quality. This wine is especially good as an apertif, with light snacks and also veal. The mildly sweet and fruity *Auslese* from the Mosel-Saar-Ruwer region and the rich *Spätlese* are well suited to richer dishes such as duck, smoked fowl and oysters. Those *trocken* and *halbtrocken* Rieslings from the Rheingau and Mosel-Saar-Ruwer are perfect with pork, sausages, and sauerkraut as well as with mild cheeses. A fuller-bodied Riesling *Spätlese* and *Auslese Trocken* from Rheingau or Pfalz goes excellently with wild boar and lobster. The rarest vintages, those sweet wines carrying the BA and TBA designations, are best left for anything oily or pungent in flavor, such as goose liver pâté or rich cheeses. They are also wonderful with desserts.

Many visitors to Germany tour one of the wine-growing districts. Since reunification, a number of wine districts have emerged in eastern Germany, but the traditional German wine country, which stretches from the middle Rhine at Bonn down to Lake Constance on the Swiss border, is still the most charming, with its classic scenery of imposing castle ruins, elegant spas, and Brothers Grimm villages, replete with spires and black-and-white gabled houses.

4 Recommended Books

BIOGRAPHY

Riefenstahl, Leni. *Leni Riefenstahl: A Memoir.* St. Martin's Press, 1993. This autobiography by the aging photographer and former film director has been both praised and condemned by critics. Known as the "Führer's moviemaker" because of her 1934 Nazi propaganda film *The Triumph of the Will,* Riefenstahl has been the subject of lurid speculation concerning her personal and professional life. She answers her critics in this account of her life.

Taylor, A.J.P. *Bismarck: The Man and the Statesman.* Random House, 1967. This is the story of the "Iron Chancellor," who was instrumental in unifying the German states into the German empire.

Trevero-Roper, Hugh. *The Last Days of Hitler.* Macmillan, 1986. This is an insightful reconstruction of the twilight of the Third Reich.

FICTION

Goethe, Johann Wolfgang von. *The Sorrows of Young Werther.* Random House, 1990. This is required reading for every German schoolchild. Goethe explored the theme of suicide in this early epistolary novella.

Grass, Günter. *Dog Years* (Harcourt Brace Jovanovich, 1989), *The Tin Drum* (Random House, 1990), and *The Flounder* (Harcourt Brace Jovanovich, 1989). Grass's works deal with the German psyche coming to terms with the dreadful legacy of Nazism and World War II. His latest book, *The Call of the Toad* (Harcourt Brace Jovanovich, 1993), is a good read—part love story and part political lampoon.

Hesse, Hermann. *Narcissus and Goldmund.* Batman, 1981. This book tells the story of two monks in Germany in the Middle Ages.

Isherwood, Christopher. *The Berlin Stories.* New Directions, 1954. Isherwood lived in Berlin from 1929 to 1933. His most famous story was "Good-bye to Berlin," which became the source of the stage and film versions of *Cabaret.*

Mann, Thomas. *The Magic Mountain.* Random House, 1969. This is Mann's most celebrated masterpiece.

Nebenzal, Harold. *Café Berlin*. Avon, 1994. Nebenzal has attracted a lot of world attention with this kaleidoscopic work, his first novel. Its intrigue unfolds against the backdrop of the 1930s nightlife of Berlin.

Remarque, Erich Maria. *All Quiet on the Western Front*. Fawcett, 1987. This is a classic novel of World War I.

FOLKLORE & LEGENDS

Grimm, Jacob, and Wilhelm Grimm. *Complete Grimm Tales*. Pantheon, 1974. This is the world's most famous collection of folktales, with a cast of characters that includes everybody from Little Red Riding Hood to Tom Thumb.

The Nibelungenlied. Penguin, 1965. The great German epic.

HISTORY

Ash, Timothy Garton, *In Europe's Name: Germany and the Divided Continent*. Random House, 1993. This book tells a tale filled with paradoxes and ironies of how a divided Germany achieved unification. Ash, a British journalist and scholar, drew part of his information from declassified files of East Germany's secret police.

Darnton, Robert. *Berlin Journal 1989–90*. W. W. Norton, 1991. This American scholar writes of the near-bloodless revolution that led to the unification of Germany.

Schneider, Peter. *The German Comedy: Scenes of Life After the Wall*, translated by Leigh Hafrey and Philip Boehm. Farrar, Straus & Giroux, 1992. Comic absurdities surrounding the collapse of the Wall fill this book, but Schneider (author of *The Wall Jumper*) also explores resurgent anti-Semitism and how Germans are coping with the flood of refugees from the east.

Shirer, William L. *The Rise and Fall of the Third Reich: A History of Nazi Germany*. Simon & Schuster, 1959–60. This story has never been told better—the complete saga of Hitler's empire from beginning to end.

West, Rebecca. *A Train of Powder*. Viking, 1955. This English novelist and historian covered the Nürnberg Trials for the *Daily Telegraph*. She provides a keen insight into the moral and legal judgments rendered there.

TRAVEL

Twain, Mark. *A Triumph Abroad*. Hippocrene Books, 1989. The American humorist's travels through Germany are humorously detailed here. Read also his comments on "The Awful German Language."

Appendix B:
Useful Terms & Phrases

1 Glossary

GENERAL TERMS

Altstadt   old part of a city or town
Anlage   park area
Apotheke   pharmacy
Bad   spa (also bath)
Bahn   railroad, train
Bahnhof   railroad station
Bergbahn   funicular (cable railway)
Hauptbahnhof   main railroad station
Seilbahn   cable car
Stadtbahn (S-Bahn)   commuter railroad
Strassenbahn   streetcar, tram
Untergrundbahn (U-Bahn)   subway, underground transportation
   system in a city
Berg   mountain
Brücke   bridge
Brunnen   spring or well
Burg   fortified castle
Damm   dike, embankment
Diet   a policy meeting of church officials
Dom   cathedral
Domplatz   cathedral square
Drogerie   shop selling cosmetics, sundries
"Evergreen"   traditional alpine music
Fleet   canal
Gasse   lane
Gastarbeiter   foreign worker
Gasthof   inn
Gemütlichkeit (adj. Gemütlich)   comfort, coziness, friendliness
Graben   moat
Gutbürgerliche Küche   (German)
   home-cooking
Hotelgarni   hotel that serves no meals or serves breakfast only
Insel   island
Jugendstil   art nouveau
Kai   quay
Kaufhaus   department store
Kloster   monastery

Kneipe   bar for drinking, may serve snacks

Konditorei   cafe for coffee and pastries

Kunst   art

Marktplatz   market square

Messegelände   exhibition center, fairgrounds

Neue Küche   cuisine moderne

Neustadt   new part of city or town

Oper   opera

Platz   square

Rathaus   town or city hall

Altes Rathaus   old town hall

Neues Rathaus   new town hall (currently used as such)

Ratskeller   restaurant in Rathaus cellar serving traditional German food

Reisebüro   travel agency

Schauspielhaus   theater for plays

Schloss   palace, castle

See   lake *(der See)* or sea *(die See)*

Spielbank   casino

Stadt   town, city

Steg   footbridge

Strasse   street

Tor   gateway

Turm   tower

Ufer   shore, riverbank

Verkehrsamt   tourist office

Weg   road

Weinstube   wine bar or tavern serving meals

ART & ARCHITECTURE TERMS

Apse   domed or arched area at the altar end of a church

Baroque   ornate, decorated style of art and architecture in the 18th century; characterized by elaborate gilding and ornamentation

Bauhaus   style of functional design for architecture and objects, originating in the early–20th century in Germany

Biedermeier   solid, bourgeois style of furniture design and interior decoration in the mid–19th century

Chancel   part of a church that contains the altar, with seats for the clergy and choir

Clerestory   an outside wall, rising above an adjoining roof, that contains windows

Cloister   covered walkway, usually enclosed by columns, around a quadrangle

Finial   an ornament at the top of a column or some upper extremity in Gothic architecture

Nave   the central part of a church

Ottonian   a Romanesque style of the 10th and early–11th centuries, named for the first Holy Roman emperor, Otto I

Reliquary   a container or shrine for sacred relics

Retable   a raised shelf above an altar for a cross

Rococo   a highly decorative development of baroque style

Transept   the part of a Gothic cross-shaped church at right angles to the nave

Vault   an arched structure of masonry forming a ceiling or roof

Wilhelmian   decorative style of the 18th century

2 Menu Terms

SOUPS (SUPPEN)

Erbsensuppe   pea sou
Gemüsesuppe   vegetable soup
Kartoffelsuppe   potato soup
Gulaschsuppe   goulash soup
Linsensuppe   lentil soup
Nudelsuppe   noodle soup

MEATS (WURST, FLEISCH & GEFLÜGEL)

Aufschnitt   cold cuts
Brathuhn   roasted chicken
Bratwurst   grilled sausage
Deutsches beefsteak   hamburger steak
Eisbein   pigs' knuckles
Ente   duck
Gans   goose
Geflügel   poultry
Kalb   veal
Kassler rippchen   pork chops
Lamm   lamb
Leber   liver
Ragout   stew
Rinderbraten   roast beef
Rindfleisch   beef
Schinken   ham
Schweinebraten   roast pork
Truthahn   turkey
Wiener schnitzel   veal cutlet
Wurst   sausage

FISH (FISCH)

Forelle   trout
Hecht   pike
Karpfen   carp
Krebs   crawfish
Lachs   salmon
Makrele   mackerel
Rheinsalm   Rhine salmon
Schellfisch   haddock
Seezunge   sole

EGGS (EIER)

Eier in der schale   boiled eggs
Mit speck   with bacon
Rühreier   scrambled eggs
Spiegeleier   fried eggs
Verlorene eier   poached eggs

SALADS (SALAT)

Gemischter salat   mixed salad
Gurkensalat   cucumber salad
Rohkostplatte   raw vegetable platter

SANDWICHES (BELEGTE BROTE)

Käsebrot   cheese sandwich
Schinkenbrot   ham sandwich
Schwarzbrot mit butter   pumpernickel with butter
Wurstbrot   sausage sandwich

VEGETABLES (GEMÜSE)

Artischocken   artichokes
Blumenkohl   cauliflower
Bohnen   beans
Bratkartoffeln   fried potatoes
Erbsen   peas
Grüne bohnen   string beans
Gurken   cucumbers
Karotten   carrots
Kartoffelbrei   mashed potatoes
Kartoffelsalat   potato salad
Knödel   dumplings
Kohl   cabbage
Reis   rice
Rote Rüben   beets
Rotkraut   red cabbage
Salat   lettuce
Salzkartoffeln   boiled potatoes
Spargel   asparagus
Spinat   spinach
Steinpilze   boletus mushrooms
Tomaten   tomatoes
Vorspeisen   hors d'oeuvres

DESSERTS (NACHTISCH)

Blatterteiggebäck   puff pastry
Bratapfel   baked apple
Käse   cheese
Kompott   stewed fruit
Obstkuchen   fruit tart
Obstsalat   fruit salad
Pfannkuchen   sugared pancakes
Pflaumenkompott   stewed plums
Torten   pastries

FRUITS (OBST)

Ananas   pineapple
Apfel   apple
Apfelsine   orange
Banane   banana
Birne   pear
Erdbeeren   strawberries
Kirschen   cherries
Pfirsich   peach
Weintrauben   grapes
Zitrone   lemon

Useful Terms & Phrases

BEVERAGES (GETRÄNKE)

Bier   beer
Ein dunkles   a dark beer
Ein helles   a light beer
Eine tasse kaffee   a cup of coffee
Eine tasse tee   a cup of tea
Milch   milk
Rotwein   red wine
Schokolade   chocolate
Tomatensaft   tomato juice
Wasser   water

CONDIMENTS & TABLE ITEMS

Brot   bread
Bötchen   rolls
Butter   butter
Eis   ice
Essig   vinegar
Gabel   fork
Glas   glass
Löffel   spoon
Messer   knife
Platte   plate
Pfeffer   pepper
Sahne   cream
Salz   salt
Senf   mustard
Tasse   cup
Zucker   sugar

COOKING TERMS

Gebacken   baked
Gebraten   fried
Gefüllt   stuffed
Gekocht   boiled
Geröstet   boiled
Gut durchgebraten   well done
Heiss   hot
Kaltes   cold
Nicht durchgebraten   rare
Paniert   breaded

Frommer's Online Directory

By Michael Shapiro and Karen Pojmann

Michael Shapiro is the author of *Internet Travel Planning* (The Globe Pequot Press). Karen Pojmann contibuted the Germany listings to this directory.

Frommer's Online Directory is a new feature designed to help you take advantage of the Internet to better plan your trip. Part I lists general Internet resources that can make any trip easier, such as sites for booking airline tickets. It's not meant to be a comprehensive list—it's a discriminating selection of useful sites to get you started. In Part II, you'll find some top online guides for Germany.

1 The Top Travel-Planning Web Sites

Among the most popular sites are online travel agencies. The top agencies, including Expedia, Preview Travel, and Travelocity, offer an array of tools that are valuable even if you don't book online. You can check flight schedules, hotel availability, or car rental prices, or you can even get paged if your flight is delayed.

While online agencies have come a long way over the past few years, they don't always yield the best price. Unlike a travel agent, for example, they're unlikely to tell you that you can save money by flying a day earlier or a day later. On the other hand, if you're looking for a bargain fare, you might find something online that an agent wouldn't take the time to dig up. Because airline commissions have been cut, a travel agent may not find it worthwhile spending half an hour trying to find you the best deal. On the Net, you can be your own agent and take all the time you want.

Online booking sites aren't the only places to book airline tickets—all major airlines have their own Web sites and often offer incentives, such as bonus frequent flyer miles or Net-only discounts, for buying online. These incentives have helped airlines capture the majority of the online booking market. According to Jupiter Communications, online agencies such as Travelocity booked about 80% of tickets purchased online in 1996, but by 1999 airline sites (such as **www.ual.com**) were projected to own about 60% of the online market, with online agencies' share of the pie dwindling each year.

WHEN SHOULD YOU BOOK ONLINE?

Online booking is not for everyone. If you prefer to let others handle your travel arrangements, one call to an experienced travel agent should suffice. But if you want to know as much as possible about your options, the Net is a good place to start, especially for bargain hunters.

Editor's Note: What You'll Find at Frommer's Site

We highly recommend Arthur Frommer's Budget Travel Online (**www. frommers.com**) as an excellent travel planning resource. Of course, we're a little biased, but you will find indispensable travel tips, reviews, monthly vacation give-aways, and online booking.

Subscribe to Arthur Frommer's Daily Newsletter (**www.frommers.com/ newsletters**) to receive the latest travel bargains and inside travel secrets in your mailbox every day. You'll read daily headlines and articles from the dean of travel himself, highlighting last-minute deals on airfares, accommodations, cruises, and package vacations. You'll also find great travel advice by checking our Tip of the Day or Hot Spot of the Month.

Search our Destinations archive (**www.frommers.com/destinations**) of more than 200 domestic and international destinations for great places to stay, tips for traveling there, and what to do while you're there. Once you've researched your trip, you might try our online reservation system (**www.frommers.com/ booktravelnow**) to book your dream vacation at affordable prices.

One of the most compelling reasons to use online booking is to take advantage of last-minute specials, such as American Airlines' weekend deals or other Internet-only fares that must be purchased online. Another advantage is that you can cash in on incentives for booking online, such as rebates or bonus frequent flyer miles. Unfortunately for travelers to Germany, online booking works best for trips within North America—for international tickets, it's usually cheaper and easier to use a travel agent or consolidator. Going online is, however, a good way to research current airfares before talking to an agent.

Keep in mind that the pace of evolution on the Net is relentless, so some of the sites below may have made advancements (or at least changes) by the time you go online.

LEADING BOOKING SITES

Below are listings for the top travel booking sites. The starred selections are the most useful and best designed sites.

Cheap Tickets. www.cheaptickets.com
Essentials: Discounted rates on domestic and international airline tickets and hotel rooms.

Sometimes discounters such as Cheap Tickets have exclusive deals that aren't available through more mainstream channels. Registration at Cheap Tickets requires inputting a credit card number before getting started, so many people elect to call the company's toll-free number rather than booking online. Cheap Tickets actually regards this policy as a selling point, arguing that "lookers" who don't intend to buy will be scared off by its "credit card first" approach and won't bog down the site with their queries. Despite its misguided credit card policy, Cheap Tickets is worth the effort because its fares can be substantially lower than those offered by its competitors.

✪ **Expedia. expedia.com**
Essentials: Domestic and international flight hotel and rental car booking; late-breaking travel news, destination features, and commentary from travel experts; deals on cruises and vacation packages. Free registration is required for booking.

Airline Sites

Below are the Web sites for the major airlines serving Germany's airports. These sites offer schedules and flight booking, and most have pages where you can sign up for e-mail alerts listing weekend deals and other late-breaking bargains.

Air Canada. **www.aircanada.ca**
Air France. **www.airfrance.com**
American Airlines. **www.aa.com**
British Airways. **www.british-airways.com**
Continental Airlines. **www.flycontinental.com**
Delta Air Lines. **www.delta-air.com**
Lufthansa. **www.lufthansa-usa.com**
KLM. **www.klm.com**
Northwest Airlines. **www.nwa.com**
TWA. **www.twa.com**
US Airways. **www.usairways.com**

Expedia makes it easy to handle flight, hotel, and car booking on one itinerary, so it's a good place for one-stop shopping. Expedia's hotel search offers crisp, zoomable maps to pinpoint most properties; click on the camera icon to see images of the rooms and facilities. But like many online databases, Expedia focuses on the major chains, such as Hilton and Hyatt, so don't expect to find too many one-of-a-kind resorts or B&Bs here.

Once you're registered (it's only necessary to do this once from each computer you use), you can start booking with the Roundtrip Fare Finder box on the home page, which expedites the process. After selecting a flight, you can hold it until midnight the following day or purchase it online. If you think you might do better through a travel agent, you'll have time to try to get a lower price. And you may do better with a travel agent because Expedia's computer reservation system does not include all airlines.

Expedia's World Guide, offering destination information, is a glaring weakness—it takes a lot of page views to get very little information. However, Expedia compensates by linking to other Microsoft Network services, such as its Sidewalk city guides, which offer entertainment and dining advice for many of the cities they cover.

Preview Travel. www.previewtravel.com
Essentials: Domestic and international flight, hotel, and rental car booking; Travel Newswire lists fare sales; deals on cruises and vacation packages. Free (one-time) registration is required for booking. Preview offers express booking for members but at press time, this feature was buried below the fold on Preview's reservation page.

Preview features the most inviting interface for booking trips, though the wealth of graphics involved can make the site somewhat slow to load. Use Farefinder to quickly find the lowest current fares on flights to dozens of major cities. Carfinder offers a similar service for rental cars, but you can only search airport locations, not city pick-up sites. To see the lowest fare for your itinerary, input the dates and times for your route and see what Preview comes up with.

Preview has a great feature called the Best Fare Finder; after it searches for the best deal on your itinerary, it will check flights that are a bit later or earlier to see if it might be cheaper to fly at a different time. While these searches have become quite sophisticated, they still occasionally overlook deals that might be uncovered by a top-notch

---

---

travel agent. If you have the time, see what you can find online and then call an agent to see if you can get a better price.

With Preview's Fare Alert feature, you can set fares for up to three routes and you'll receive e-mail notices when the fare drops below your target amount. For example, you could tell Preview to alert you when the round-trip fare from New York to Berlin drops below $600. If it does, you'll get an e-mail telling you the current fare.

Minor quibbles: When you search for a fare, hotel, or car (at least when we went to press), Preview launches an annoying little "Please Wait" window that gets in the way of the main browser window, even when your results begin to appear. The hotel search feature is intuitive, but the images and maps aren't as crisp as those at Expedia. Also: All sorts of extraneous information that's irrelevant to most travelers is listed on maps.

Note to AOL Users: You can book flights, hotels, rental cars, and cruises on AOL at keyword: Travel. The booking software is provided by Preview Travel and is similar to Preview on the Web. Use the AOL "Travelers Advantage" program to earn a 5% rebate on flights, hotel rooms, and car rentals.

Priceline.com. **www.priceline.com**
Launched in 1998 with a $10 million ad campaign, Priceline lets you "name your price" for domestic and international airline tickets. In other words, you select a route and dates, guarantee with a credit card, and make a bid for what you're willing to pay. If one of the airlines in Priceline's database has a fare that's lower than your bid, your credit card will automatically be charged for a ticket.

But you can't say when you want to fly—you have to accept any flight leaving between 6am and 10pm, and you may have to make a stopover. No frequent-flyer miles are awarded, and tickets are nonrefundable and can't be exchanged for another flight. So if your plans change, you're out of luck. Priceline can be good for travelers who have to take off on short notice (and who are thus unable to qualify for advance purchase discounts). But be sure to shop around first—if you overbid, you'll be required to purchase the ticket and Priceline will pocket the difference.

Travelocity. **www.travelocity.com**
Essentials: Domestic and international flight, hotel, and rental car booking; deals on cruises and vacation packages. Travel Headlines spotlights latest bargain airfares. Free (one-time) registration is required for booking.

Travelocity almost got it right. Its Express Booking feature enables travelers to complete the booking process more quickly than they could at Expedia or Preview, but Travelocity gums up the works with a page called "Featured Airlines." Big placards of several featured airlines compete for your attention—if you want to see the fares for all available airlines, click the much smaller box at the bottom of the page labeled "Book a Flight."

Some have worried that Travelocity, which is owned by American Airlines' parent company AMR, directs bookings to American. This doesn't seem to be the case; I've booked there dozens of times and have always been directed to the cheapest listed flight, for example on Tower or ATA. But this "Featured Airlines" page seems to be

Check Your E-Mail at Internet Cafes While Traveling

Until a few years ago, most travelers who checked their e-mail while traveling carried a laptop, but this posed some problems. Not only are laptops expensive, but they can be difficult to configure, incur expensive connection charges, and are attractive to thieves. Thankfully, Web-based free e-mail programs have made it much easier to stay in touch.

Just open an account at a freemail provider, such as Hotmail (hotmail.com) or Yahoo! Mail (mail.yahoo.com), and all you'll need to check your mail is a Web connection, easily available at Net cafes and copy shops around the world. After logging on, just point the browser to www.hotmail.com, enter your username and password and you'll have access to your mail.

Internet cafes have become ubiquitous, so for a few dollars an hour you'll be able to check your mail and send messages back to colleagues, friends, and family. If you already have a primary e-mail account, you can set it to forward mail to your freemail account while you're away. Freemail programs have become enormously popular (Hotmail claims more than 10 million members), because they enable everyone, even those who don't own a computer, to have an e-mail address they can check wherever they log onto the Web.

Travelocity's way of trying to cash in with ads and incentives for booking certain airlines. (*Note:* It's hard to blame these booking services for trying to generate some revenue; many airlines have slashed commissions to $10 per domestic booking for online transactions, so these virtual agencies are groping for revenue streams.) There are rewards for choosing one of the featured airlines. You'll get 1,500 bonus frequent-flyer miles if you book through United's site, for example, but the site doesn't tell you about other airlines that might be cheaper. If the United flight costs $150 more than the best deal on another airline, it's not worth spending the extra money.

On the plus side, Travelocity has some leading-edge tools. Exhibit A is Fare Watcher E-mail, an "intelligent agent" that keeps you informed of the best fares offered for the city pairs (round-trips) of your choice. Whenever the fare changes by $25 or more, Fare Watcher will alert you by e-mail. Exhibit B is Flight Paging: If you own an alphanumeric pager with national access that can receive e-mail, Travelocity's paging system can alert you if your flight is delayed. Finally, though Travelocity doesn't include every budget airline, it does include Southwest, the leading U.S. budget carrier.

FINDING LODGINGS ONLINE

While the services above offer hotel booking, it can be best to use a site devoted primarily to lodging because you may find properties that aren't listed on more general online travel agencies. Some specialize in a particular type of accommodation, such as B&Bs, which you won't find on the more mainstream booking services. Other services, such as TravelWeb, offer weekend deals on major chain properties, which cater to business travelers and have more empty rooms on weekends.

All Hotels on the Web. www.all-hotels.com

Well, this site *doesn't* include all the hotels on the Web, but it does have tens of thousands of listings throughout the world. Bear in mind that each hotel listed has paid a small fee ($25 and up) for placement, so it's not an objective list; it's more like a book of online brochures.

InnSite. www.innsite.com

B&B listings for inns in all 50 U.S. states and dozens of countries around the globe. Find an inn at your destination, have a look at images of the rooms, check prices and availability, and then send e-mail to the innkeeper if you have further questions. This is an extensive directory of B&Bs, but it only includes listings if the proprietor submitted one (*note:* it's free to get an inn listed). The descriptions are written by the innkeepers, and many listings link to the inn's own Web sites, where you can find more information and images.

Places to Stay. www.placestostay.com

Mostly one-of-a-kind places in the U.S. and abroad that you might not find in other directories, with a focus on resort accommodations. Again, listing is selective—this isn't a comprehensive directory, but it can give you a sense of what's available at different destinations.

✪ TravelWeb. www.travelweb.com

TravelWeb lists more than 16,000 hotels worldwide, focusing on chains such as Hyatt and Hilton, and you can book almost 90% of these online. TravelWeb's Click-It Weekends, updated each Monday, offers weekend deals at many leading hotel chains. TravelWeb is the online home for Pegasus Systems, which provides transaction processing systems for the hotel industry.

LAST-MINUTE DEALS & OTHER ONLINE BARGAINS

There's nothing airlines hate more than flying with lots of empty seats. The Net has enabled airlines to offer last-minute bargains to entice travelers to fill those seats. Most of these are announced on Tuesday or Wednesday and are valid for travel the following weekend, but some can be booked weeks or months in advance. You can sign up for weekly e-mail alerts at airlines' sites (for airline's Web site addresses, see above) or check sites such as WebFlyer (see below) that compile lists of these bargains. To make it easier, visit a site (see below) that will round up all the deals and send them in one convenient weekly e-mail. But last-minute deals aren't the only online bargains—other sites can help you find value even if you can't wait until the eleventh hour.

✪ 1travel.com. www.1travel.com

Deals on domestic and international flights, cruises, hotels, and all-inclusive resorts such as Club Med. 1travel.com's Saving Alert compiles last-minute air deals so you don't have to scroll through multiple e-mail alerts. A feature called "Drive a little using low-fare airlines" helps map out strategies for using alternate airports to find lower fares. And Farebeater searches a database that includes published fares, consolidator bargains, and special deals exclusive to 1travel.com. *Note:* The travel agencies listed by 1travel.com have paid for placement.

Handy Tip

While most people learn about last-minute weekend deals from e-mail dispatches, it can be best to find out precisely *when* these deals become available and check airlines' Web sites at this time. To find out when deals become available, check the pages devoted to these deals on airlines' Web pages. Because these deals are limited, they can vanish within hours, sometimes even minutes, so it pays to log on as soon as they're available.

Go4less.com. www.go4less.com

Specializing in last-minute cruise and package deals, Go4less has some eye-popping offers, such as off-peak Caribbean cruises for under $100 per day. The site has a clean design, but the bargains aren't organized by destination. However, you avoid sifting through all this material by using the Search box and entering vacation type, destination, month, and price.

Moment's Notice. www.moments-notice.com

As the name suggests, Moment's Notice specializes in last-minute vacation and cruise deals. You can browse for free, but if you want to purchase a trip you have to join Moment's Notice, which costs $25.

Smarter Living. www.smarterliving.com

Best known for its e-mail dispatch of weekend deals on 20 airlines, Smarter Living also keeps you posted about last-minute bargains on everything from Windjammer Cruises to flights to Iceland.

✪ WebFlyer. www.webflyer.com

WebFlyer is the ultimate online resource for frequent flyers and also has an excellent listing of last-minute air deals. Click on "Deal Watch" for a round-up of weekend deals on flights, hotels, and rental cars from domestic and international suppliers.

TRAVELER'S TOOLKIT

Seasoned travelers always carry some essential items to make their trips easier. The following is a selection of online tools to smooth your journey.

ATM LOCATORS

Visa. www.visa.com/pd/atm/
MasterCard. www.mastercard.com/atm

Find ATMs in hundreds of cities in the U.S. and around the world. Both include maps for some locations and both list airport ATM locations, some with maps.

Intellicast. www.intellicast.com

Weather forecasts for all 50 states and cities around the world. Note that temperatures are in Celsius for many international destinations.

✪ MapQuest. www.mapquest.com

Specializing in U.S. maps but capable of generating maps for dozens of international cities, MapQuest enables you to zoom in on a destination and locate restaurants, hotels, and other attractions on maps.

✪ Net Café Guide. www.netcafeguide.com

Locate Internet cafes at hundreds of locations around the globe. Catch up on your e-mail, log onto the Web and stay in touch with the home front, usually for just a few dollars per hour.

TheTrip: Airport Maps and Flight Status. www.thetrip.com

At this business travel site you can find out when an airborne flight is scheduled to arrive. Click on "Guides and Tools" to peruse airport maps for more than 40 domestic cities.

Universal Currency Converter. www.xe.net/currency

See what your dollar or pound is worth in more than a hundred other countries.

U.S. Customs Traveler Alerts. www.customs.gov/travel/travel.htm

Wondering what you're allowed to bring into the U.S.? Check at this thorough site, which includes maximum allowance and duty fees.

2 The Top Web Sites for Germany

Note: If you open a site that's in German and it's all Greek to you, don't panic. Many of them provide English translations. Look for the little British or American flag, or the word "English."

GENERAL GUIDES FOR GERMANY

A to Z Hotels. reisen-mit-preisen.de
Within this chartreuse and typographically hip site are listings for 44,000 German hotels (or so it claims). Search by price and region, or link directly to the guide's half-dozen favorites.

Eat Germany. www.eat-germany.net
Get started on the appealing, if daunting, task of eating Germany with help from this dining guide. Search for a schnitzel-filled *gasthaus* or other eatery by city, price, ethnicity, child-friendliness, level of festivity, wheelchair accessibility, or any of a slew of other criteria.

Frankfurt Airport. www.frankfurt-airport.de
It helps to have a lot of computer memory or a little patience when using this directory for Germany's main airport. Once it's loaded, though, you can easily find running announcements of arrivals and departures and a thorough guide to the terminal and its facilities. See below for sites for the Munich and Stuttgart airports.

German National Tourist Board. www.germany-tourism.de
This site gives you an online tour of several quaint, window-box-filled cities, and highlights attractions for educational excursions, romantic vacations, or youth trips. You can also access facts on weather, transportation, language, currency, accommodations, events, and so forth.

IHA Hotelverband Deutschland Hotel Guide. www.hotels-germany.com
Book a room at any of more than 750 German hotels through this site. Conduct a search according to location and amenity preferences, or check out the page of special offers for accommodations conducive to family, cultural activities, sports, biking, special events, or last-minute travel.

BERLIN

✪ Berlin.de. www.berlin.de
Sporting a trendy Euro design, this guide to Germany's capital city features a cyber tour of more than two dozen Berlin attractions, complete with virtual-reality panoramic images. The site also provides an online hotel reservation service, a virtual ticket counter for all kinds of shows and cultural events, and a wealth of information about Berlin's government, economy, ecology, and public services.

Berlin Hotel Discounts and City Guide. www.worldexecutive.com/cityguides/berlin
You can get discounts at Berlin luxury hotels when you book through this site. The guide also offers transportation and etiquette tips for travelers as well as photographs and attraction-marked maps of the city.

Berlin Info. www.berlin-info.de
Though some sections of this Berlin guide are available only in German, others, such as the online sightseeing tour and the searchable accommodations directory, are full of useful information for English-speaking tourists.

Metropolis Berlin Scene. www.zitty.de/metact/m_guide2.htm
Metropolis magazine recommends Berlin hotels and hostels, bars, book stores, cafes, night clubs, markets, restaurants, ticket agencies, car rental businesses, and tours. Each entry comes with a short but clear description of the establishment's attributes.

Public Transport and Traffic in Berlin. verkehr.epilog.de/traffic.htm
Whether you're traveling by plane, train, or automobile in Berlin, this site can help. You'll find road maps, bus fare rates, train and subway schedules, airport information, and many phone numbers.

Net 4 Berlin. www.net4berlin.com
This frills-free city guide encompasses the city's history, population, architecture, and culture. The site also gives tips on getting around and finding low-cost hostels and boarding houses. Best of all, Net 4 Berlin breaks the city down into districts and describes the atmosphere and scene, as well as the best bars and restaurants, of each one.

Time Out Berlin: The Living Guide. www.timeout.com/berlin/index.html
The comfortable design of this Berlin travel site makes it easy to navigate. Check the front page to see what's going on in the city this month, or click on the sidebar menu for self-contained, extensive guides to accommodations, sightseeing, entertainment, kids' stuff, shopping, dining, and gay and lesbian culture. You can also check the weather and exchange rates or book a flight, hotel room, or rental car.

SAXONY & THURINGIA

Dresden Online. www.dresden-online.de
This guide provides a photo and short history of each of Dresden's important sights. You'll also find a simple directory of theaters and museums alongside searchable guides to hotels and restaurants.

Leipzig. www.leipzig.com
Once an economic center of the former East Germany, Leipzig has bloomed culturally in recent years. The growth is illustrated by this site's extensive guide to the city's restaurants, museums, cinemas, theaters, concerts, cabaret shows, tourist attractions, hotels, guided tours, flea markets, and multimedia entities.

FRANCONIA & THE GERMAN DANUBE

Hotel Bayerischer Hof Bayreuth. www.bayerischer-hof.com
This hotel wears three roofs: historic landmark, cozy inn, and home of the annual Richard Wagner festival. The site provides hotel photos and a festival program. You can reserve a room or buy tickets online.

MUNICH

Aktuelle Munchen. www.muenchen.de
It looks like a scaled-down version of its German counterpart, but the English section of this Munich guide covers all the tourist basics: special travel packages, meetings and conventions, museums and theaters, hotels, transportation and festivals. Note to revelers: the official Oktoberfest page is located here.

Munich Airport. www.munich-airport.de
Wondering how to get back to the airport after a long night at the beer garden? This site can help. The Munich airport's online guide directs travelers to and from the terminal, and provides timetables, parking information, a virtual reality airport view, and more.

Munich Complete Guide.homepages.munich.netsurf.de/Nikolaus.Duttler/ munich.htm

A local resident offers insider tips, such as how to get free beer, as well as dining tips, a detailed guide to bars and nightclubs, lodging recommendations, more beer guides, photographs, and links.

Oktoberfest Guides. www.oktoberfest-guides.com

Festive folk from throughout the world gather in Munich for this acclaimed celebration of beer, bratwurst, boisterous oompah bands, and other forms of excess. While promoting particular Oktoberfest tour packages, this site also provides festival news, live Web cams, links to other beer sites, and hotel information with online booking.

Welcome to Munich. www.perob.com/munich

An Englishman now living in Munich shares his view of the German city. You have to pass through a couple of pages of quotes and silly graphics to get to the meat of the site, but once you're there, you'll find information on attractions like the Glockenspiel, a multi-ethnic restaurant guide, a truly extensive beer guide, and a look at cultural quirks such as Munich's rampant graffiti art.

THE BAVARIAN ALPS

Bavarian Alpine Net Guide. www.bavaria.com

This guide to Bavaria covers culture, travel, entertainment, shopping, and business. Visit any of these sections to be led via narration and photos through the region, or, if you know what you want, click on the index icon to go directly to beer, opera, castles, rafting, or whatever strikes your fancy.

Highlights Outside Munich in Upper Bavaria. homepages.munich.netsurf.de/ Nikolaus.Duttler/bavaria.htm

This site offers a low-resolution but nonetheless enticing preview of what you'll find in the mountains outside Munich: beautiful peaks, lakes, and castles, including the famous Neuschwanstein.

Holiday in Allgäu. www.allgaeu-schwaben.com

The Allgäu region of the Bavarian Alps is home to innumerable castles, health spas, resorts, and mountain-hiking tours, all of which are listed and described at this site. This seemingly bottomless pool of Allgäu information also directs visitors to cultural excursions, festivals, museums, transportation, hotels, natural wonders, and cute little villages.

LAKE CONSTANCE (BODENSEE)

Lake Constance/Bodensee Home Page. www.bodensee-info.com

Find out how to arrange a holiday in orchard-filled, spa-speckled Lake Constance. Through this site, you can stay abreast of special travel packages and guided-tour offers, get to know the historic towns in the area, and take a peek at the museums and galleries.

HEIDELBURG, STUTTGART, & THE NECKAR VALLEY

Heidelburg Hotel Directory. www.visit-heidelberg.com

This hotel directory, which offers online booking, doubles as a brief guide to the quaint German city's events, museums, boat trips, and castle.

Stuttgart. www.stuttgart-tourist.de

This perky tourists' guide claims that Stuttgart is always in season and then proves it with a great deal of information about the city's cuisine, exhibitions, festivals, markets, music, theater, museums, and sightseeing tours. Want even more facts? Fill out a form in the hotels section to order brochures.

Stuttgart City Guide. www.stgt.com/stuttgart/homee.htm
For a little Stuttgart appetizer, try this site's "pictorial walkabout," a photo tour of the city's more notable buildings. The guide also lists hotels, restaurants, museums and galleries, night spots, festivals, swimming pools, radio stations, and other assorted tidbits.

Stuttgart Airport. www.stuttgart-airport.de
If you're flying to or from the Stuttgart Airport, check their site before you go. You can find an international flight schedule as well as real-time arrival and departure announcements.

FRANKFURT

Boomtown Frankfurt. www.boomtown-frankfurt.com
Along with a look at Frankfurt's architecture, ranging from glorious historic cathedrals to high-tech skyscrapers, this site provides a full city and travel guide covering weather, lodging, transportation, city tours, museums, shopping, dining, nightlife, festivals, and the Rhine castles on the outskirts of town.

Frankfurt.de. www.frankfurt.de
Each major section (science, history, business, sports, etc.) of this busy guide to the equally busy industrial metropolis is broken down into several subgroups. Under the culture heading, for example, you can find museums and galleries, ballet, theater, literature, music, film, public art, architecture. The tourism section covers essentials such as hotels, sightseeing, and travel packages.

RHINELAND

Central Middle Rhine Valley Castles and Towers. www.rhinecastles.com
Have a look at dozens of towering castle hotels that speckle the Rhineland countryside. You can even make reservations online to stay in one of these grand dwellings. Too much? You can also find information on visiting some of the castle museums and restaurants and on castle-seeing river cruises.

City of Cologne Tourist Office. www.koeln.org
You may know about the enormous Cologne cathedral and its climbable spires, but have you heard of the city-on-the-Rhine's chocolate museum or its thriving art and music centers? Learn about these and other attractions, as well as Cologne's convention centers, online.

Dusseldorf Landeschauptstadt. www.duesseldorf.de/f_tour_e.htm
Take an online promenade through Dusseldorf's fashionable Königsallee district or on the banks of the Rhine. Or you can peek over the gate of the Benrath Palace. This site's photos and descriptive text will also give you a taste of the city's cultural scene, museums, restaurants, and shops. For the practical traveler, a chart with links and a breakdown of amenities helps you sort through hotel recommendations.

BREMEN, LOWER SAXONY, & NORTH HESSE

✪ Expo 2000. www.expo2000.de
Find out what wonders are on tap for the World Exposition 2000 in Hannover, a 5-month-long international extravaganza organized around the exploration of the relationships among humans, nature, and technology. You can preview some of the exhibits, take a peek at the high-tech Expo theme park, and buy tickets online. And don't miss the colorful Expo-for-kids page, starring Twipsy the mascot.

Hannover Online. www.hanover.de
Visitors may go to Hannover for Expo 2000, but they'll stay for the city's rich history and masterful baroque gardens. This site directs Expo-goers and general tourists alike

to attractions, events, city tours, historic buildings, parks, accommodations, restaurants, bars, night clubs, shops, and more.

The Seaports of Bremen and Bremerhaven. **www.bremen-ports.de**

Though geared primarily toward business people involved in shipping and foreign trade, this site offers historical information, statistics, and photographs of the seaports, which bring them to life as tourist attractions.

Welcome to Bremen. **www.bremen-tourism.de**

There's more to see than the sea in Bremen. This site will show you the town's art galleries, specialty museums, fairy tale theater, architecture, and bustling market place. You can also book travel packages and hotel rooms online.

HAMBURG

Hamburg. **www.hamburg.de**

Boasting that Hamburg is the greenest city in Germany, this guide urges visitors to visit parks and nature reserves as well as the museums and theaters listed here. The site also provides an overview of Hamburg's government, economy, harbor traffic, and educational institutions.

Hamburg Tourist Board. **www.hamburg-tourism.de**

Through this site, you can book a room at any of more than 200 Hamburg hotels or get help buying all sorts of theater tickets. You can also find information on guided tours aboard buses or boats. The shopping and dining guides are essentially ads, but the Info section bubbles over with photos and facts about Hamburg's history and culture.

Subway System of Hamburg.

metro.ratp.fr:10001/bin/select/english/germany/hamburg

Type in the names of the nearest Hamburg subway station and the station where you want to go, and this site will spit out a route for you. You can also check the list of station names or the subway map for further guidance.

University of Hamburg. **www.rrz.uni-hamburg.de**

Go immediately to the Time Out in Hamburg section of this site. Most of the cultural-events links here lead to sites in German, but the general information (history, transportation, youth hostels, media, weather, economy, etc.) is in English. So are the vast, photo-filled online sightseeing tour and the slide-show virtual walking tour.

Index

FROMMER'S® COMPLETE TRAVEL GUIDES

FROMMER'S® DOLLAR-A-DAY GUIDES

Australia from $50 a Day
California from $60 a Day
Caribbean from $70 a Day
England from $70 a Day
Europe from $60 a Day
Florida from $60 a Day

Hawaii from $70 a Day
Ireland from $50 a Day
Israel from $45 a Day
Italy from $70 a Day
London from $85 a Day
New York from $80 a Day

New Zealand from $50 a Day
Paris from $85 a Day
San Francisco from $60 a Day
Washington, D.C.,
   from $60 a Day

FROMMER'S® PORTABLE GUIDES

Acapulco, Ixtapa &
   Zihuatanejo
Alaska Cruises & Ports of Call
Bahamas
Baja & Los Cabos
Berlin
California Wine Country
Charleston & Savannah
Chicago

Dublin
Hawaii: The Big Island
Las Vegas
London
Maine Coast
Maui
New Orleans
New York City
Paris

Puerto Vallarta, Manzanillo
   & Guadalajara
San Diego
San Francisco
Sydney
Tampa & St. Petersburg
Venice
Washington, D.C.

FROMMER'S® NATIONAL PARK GUIDES

Family Vacations in the
   National Parks
Grand Canyon

National Parks of the
   American West
Rocky Mountain

Yellowstone & Grand Teton
Yosemite & Sequoia/
   Kings Canyon
Zion & Bryce Canyon

FROMMER'S® GREAT OUTDOOR GUIDES

New England
Northern California

Southern California & Baja
Washington & Oregon

FROMMER'S® MEMORABLE WALKS

Chicago
London

New York
Paris

San Francisco
Washington D.C.

FROMMER'S® IRREVERENT GUIDES

Amsterdam
Boston
Chicago
Las Vegas

London
Los Angeles
Manhattan

New Orleans
Paris
San Francisco

Seattle & Portland
Vancouver
Walt Disney World
Washington, D.C.

FROMMER'S® BEST-LOVED DRIVING TOURS

America
Britain
California

Florida
France
Germany

Ireland
Italy
New England

Scotland
Spain
Western Europe

THE UNOFFICIAL GUIDES®

Bed & Breakfast in
  New England
Bed & Breakfast in
  the Northwest
Beyond Disney
Branson, Missouri
California with Kids
Chicago

Cruises
Disneyland
Florida with Kids
The Great Smoky &
  Blue Ridge
  Mountains
Inside Disney
Las Vegas

London
Miami & the Keys
Mini Las Vegas
Mini-Mickey
New Orleans
New York City
Paris
San Francisco

Skiing in the West
Walt Disney World
Walt Disney World
  for Grown-ups
Walt Disney World
  for Kids
Washington, D.C.

SPECIAL-INTEREST TITLES

Born to Shop: France
Born to Shop: Hong Kong
Born to Shop: Italy
Born to Shop: New York
Born to Shop: Paris
Frommer's Britain's Best Bike Rides
The Civil War Trust's Official Guide
  to the Civil War Discovery Trail
Frommer's Caribbean Hideaways
Frommer's Europe's Greatest Driving Tours
Frommer's Food Lover's Companion to France
Frommer's Food Lover's Companion to Italy
Frommer's Gay & Lesbian Europe
Israel Past & Present
Monks' Guide to California

Monks' Guide to New York City
The Moon
New York City with Kids
Unforgettable Weekends
Outside Magazine's Guide
  to Family Vacations
Places Rated Almanac
Retirement Places Rated
Road Atlas Britain
Road Atlas Europe
Washington, D.C., with Kids
Wonderful Weekends from Boston
Wonderful Weekends from New York City
Wonderful Weekends from San Francisco
Wonderful Weekends from Los Angeles

GET YOUR FREE TRIAL ISSUE!

FRESH. No-punches-pulled. Sometimes in your face. But ALWAYS crammed with hot tips, cool prices, and useful facts. That's every single issue of Arthur Frommer's BUDGET TRAVEL magazine.

Save 37% off the newsstand price! **Call Today!** **1-800-829-9121**

ARTHUR FROMMER'S
Budget Travel
vacations for real people

WHEREVER YOU TRAVEL, *H*ELP IS NEVER FAR AWAY.

From planning your trip to providing travel assistance along the way, American Express® Travel Service Offices are always there to help you do more.

Germany

BERLIN
Reiseland American Express (R)
Bayreuther Strasse 37-38
(49) (30) 2149830

Reiseland American Express (R)
Friedrichstrasse 172
(49) (30) 20174025

COLOGNE
Reiseland American Express (R)
Burgmauer 14
(49) (221) 9259010

DUSSELDORF
Reiseland American Express (R)
Konigsalle 98a
(49) (211) 386910

FRANKFURT
Reiseland American Express (R)
Kaiserstrasse 8
(49) (69) 2105111

HAMBURG
American Express Travel Service
Hamburg Airport, Terminal 4
Flughafenstrasse 1-3
(49) (40) 5005980

Reiseland American Express
Ballindamm 39
(49) (40) 309080

MUNICH
Reiseland American Express (R)
Promenadenplatz 6
(49) (89) 29090145

do more AMERICAN EXPRESS

Travel

www.americanexpress.com/travel

American Express Travel Service Offices are found in central locations throughout Australia.